SOURCES
FOR
AMERICAN STUDIES

SOURCES
FOR
AMERICAN STUDIES

Edited by
Jefferson B. Kellogg
and
Robert H. Walker

CONTRIBUTIONS IN AMERICAN STUDIES, NUMBER 64

GREENWOOD PRESS
WESTPORT, CONNECTICUT • LONDON, ENGLAND

Library of Congress Cataloging in Publication Data
Main entry under title:

Sources for American studies.

(Contributions in American studies, ISSN 0084-9227 ;
no. 64)
Bibliography: p.
Includes indexes.
1. United States—Historiography—Addresses, essays,
lectures.   2. United States—Bibliography—Addresses,
essays, lectures.   3. United States—Study and teaching—
Addresses, essays, lectures.   I. Kellogg, Jefferson B.
II. Walker, Robert Harris, 1924-   III. Series.
E175.S58   1983   973'.072   82-11701
ISBN 0-313-22555-9 (lib. bdg.)

Library of Congress Catalog Card Number: 82-11701
ISBN: 0-313-22555-9
ISSN: 0084-9227

First published in 1983

Greenwood Press
A division of Congressional Information Service, Inc.
88 Post Road West
Westport, Connecticut 06881

Printed in the United States of America

10   9   8   7   6   5   4   3   2   1

to John L. Landgraf
who sponsored the creation of
American Studies International
out of the ashes of the
Fulbright *American Studies Newsletter*

ABOUT THE EDITORS

Jefferson B. Kellogg, who received his Ph.D. in American Studies from George Washington University, has served as editor of *American Studies International*. Currently he is with the Clary Institute in Washington, D.C.

Robert H. Walker is series editor of Greenwood Press's Contributions in American Studies series. He is Professor of American Civilization at George Washington University and has served as editor of *American Quarterly* and *American Studies in the United States*. He is the author of *American Studies Abroad* (Greenwood Press, 1975).

Contents

viii   Contents

Acknowledgments

The compilers of the bibliographies that comprise this volume have our fundamental appreciation: We are particularly grateful for the extra efforts put forth by those scholars who went back to their original essays and updated them with the kind of judgment that would have been very hard to find elsewhere.

We are no less appreciative of those scholars who offered to survey fields covered earlier by authors who were not available for this effort. In fact, the contributions of several of these individuals are more than simply updates of earlier works. They stand independently as comprehensive essays of the activities in their fields during the past decade. In this regard we must mention Dewey Wallace, Jr., Larry Mintz, and Christopher Salter. Bernard Mergen provided an addendum not only to his original work but also to those on American workers and material culture.

Because this volume stems from *American Studies International* (*ASI*), it is important to identify the individuals who have kept this journal functioning. The editors mainly responsible for soliciting and polishing these works have been Jefferson Kellogg (editor of *ASI* for two years and co-editor of this volume) and Wilton Corkern (1979-1982).

Since the publication of *American Studies: Topics and Sources* (*ASTS*), *ASI* has, for a second time, shifted its anchorage in the bay of bureaucracy. Casting off the last line to the boatyard where it was first assembled, the journal moved to the lee of the American

Studies Office of the U.S. Information Agency. In exchanging a connection with the Fulbright program for one more directly concerned with American studies abroad, the journal now has a setting entirely appropriate to its mission of responding to the needs and interests in American studies from outside the United States. In making this administrative transition, we were greatly assisted by Robert Coonrod, Alice Ilchman, and William LaSalle. The presence of Townsend Ludington in this office during 1980-1981 was also happily fortuitous, as was the advent of Dr. Leslie High. We are particularly grateful for the support of Daniel J. Terra, Ambassador-at-Large for Culture.

My commitment to this project arises from the experience of a decade as senior editor for *ASI* and as the compiler of *ASTS.* The subjects and authors of these essays were matters of my own judgment, for better or for worse. Jefferson Kellogg has been a full partner in the design of this book and has done the job of assembling it.

Robert H. Walker

Introduction

This volume lists and places in context some three thousand items dealing with the study of the United States. The items can be approached through an author index that also furnishes complete imprint data, including indication of softbound availability, and through discussions in topical essays.

The essays have appeared in or have been acquired for publication by *American Studies International* (*ASI*). Their authors have been asked to stress works that are both recent and available, preferably in paperbound editions. The subjects have been identified from among those of special interest to scholars who study the United States outside its borders. *ASI* has tried to cover fields that have been sufficiently active to demand informed selection from the large numbers of works appearing in print.

The scope and utility of the present volume doubles when it is used in conjunction with *American Studies: Topics and Sources* (*ASTS*) (Westport, Conn.: Greenwood Press, 1976). This book is, in effect, a second volume to that one. The dividing line between them is the year 1976, with the essays acquired prior to that date having appeared in *ASTS*. The present volume not only extends the coverage begun by the first one, but also furnishes supplements to the essays in *ASTS*, compiled by the original author whenever possible.

With the convenience of the reader in mind, we have divided this volume into two parts. Part I contains new essays, submitted since

1976, followed, when appropriate, by an addendum updating the essay. The essays are arranged alphabetically by topic. Part II consists of materials designed to make current the *ASTS* essays. We have arranged them as they appeared in *ASTS*. The cumulative index includes all titles in both parts of the present volume.

These two books together embrace thirty-seven distinct approaches to American studies with a cumulative bibliography of approximately five thousand entries. All of the entries were written within the last eleven years, and each entry has been made as current as possible. These collections have not followed any preconceived notion of what comprises American studies. Instead, we have responded to expressions of need and interest and have moved directly toward areas showing activity, growth, and sometimes redefinition and controversy. We are proud of the eminence and competence of the authors of these essays. Moreover, we believe that their knowledge and judgment help make this collection not only the most comprehensive but also the most discerning guide to American studies.

One item falls outside the pattern of this collection. Its story began with Saunders Redding's moderate, academic approach to the question of the Afro-American place in American studies. When Amiri Baraka, who followed Redding to the George Washington University campus, was invited to make a statement on this subject, he chose to respond to the earlier piece. The result is not so much an exchange of views as a demonstration of drastically different levels of concern as reflected by these two figures, each so prominent in the literary and academic history of the Afro-American equation. It is also a demonstration—perhaps unparalleled in its dramatic intensity—of the range and potency inherent in this question. Because Baraka's essay depends on Redding's for much of its meaning, we have reprinted the earlier one as well. To assure the proper historical and bibliographic perspective, Jefferson Kellogg has furnished a special introduction.

It is impossible to collect so many thoughtful essays without forming some opinion about the evolution of American studies. If the editors of *ASI* have indeed identified the areas of maximum interest, and if our contributors have selected the works crucial to reflecting these active facets, then we have within these covers a heuristic definition of the new directions in American studies.

We continue to feel that the evidence reveals a twofold role for American studies in the world of teaching and scholarship. The more obvious of these roles is in the broadening of traditional fields of inquiry: a function represented by eleven essays in this collection. They are readily recognizable even though they range from linguistics to foreign policy, from poetry to military studies, from the Supreme Court to architecture. They show how traditional fields have been expanded by the crossing of disciplinary lines. They show a resistance to conventional kinds of specialization. They show an appetite for learning from adjacent areas as well as a wish to contribute beyond a predictable audience. Whether the focus be journalism, music, or economics, the impetus is toward compiling a large view by making the pieces understandable and assimilable.

A smaller group of essays identifies the second role assumed by American studies and continues a demonstration, begun in *ASTS,* of the growth of American studies through cooption and adoption. At first this field was notable for promoting conversation between members of established departments who needed to learn from one another. Many programs were initiated simply by bringing the faculty in American history together with colleagues in American literature and perhaps by adding some from government, religion, art, or philosophy. However, before long the effort to find a common denominator was complicated by a schism in method. So long as the scholars were essentially historians, regardless of whether their subject was fiction or labor unions, there was no outsized obstacle to communication. But once the behavioral scientists joined the movement, difficulties of a more profound nature were presented. Some of us may have thought we had solved this problem when we asked our students to read *Babbitt* with *Middletown* and pointed out how the sociology and the fiction fortified one another. But we had, of course, only scratched a persistent itch that, it now seems, may be chronic, as shown in the essay by Thomas L. Hartshorne. The assembled essays demonstrate that, in a movement now fifty years old, there are still major unsolved problems in those areas where historical and behavioral methods meet head on.

The essays on immigration, folklore, Afro-American studies, and detective fiction illustrate the function of American studies in successively providing at least an introduction to, and sometimes a context for, topics that had been underemphasized in academe. Although by no means alone in this process, American studies programs on many campuses took the lead in sponsoring black studies, woman studies, immigration and minority studies, regional and urban studies, popular culture, and folklore. Some of the innovations came with particular applications, for example, material culture with museums, urban and regional studies with historic preservation. A number of the newer fields bore particular relevance to archives, libraries, historical societies, and offices of policy and planning.

These topics tend to come with their intrinsic methods—some with more than a single method. We noted, in the Introduction to *ASTS,* how these methods grew ineluctably and unselfconsciously out of the materials. Urban studies, our case in point, was shown to emerge as a discipline uniquely compounded from logical responses to the subject matter inevitably involved: from sewerage systems to satiric verse. The examples available in the present collection—folklore, immigration studies—reveal a similar internal integrity arising from their focus. Insomuch as American studies has continued to define itself by accepting various new points of concentration, it has come to resemble nothing so much as an encampment surrounded by a ring of outposts. Each outpost may be comfortably dug in to its own revetments and may even enjoy a secure line of communication with the command post. But what is happening at the center of operations?

The center of American studies is closer to something called cultural history than to anything else. This label has been used most commonly to cover a kind of fusion between social and intellectual history, sociology and cultural anthropology. This is an extremely active area, so much so that in 1980 Philip I. Mitterling was able to assemble a 581-page bibliography stressing works published since 1950 (*U.S. Cultural History: A Guide to Information Sources*, Detroit: Gale). This useful compendium is arranged in eleven sections covering most topics usually associated with history in its most general sense: economic, political, and social thought; historiography; religion; science and medicine. It does not recognize, as primary topics, work in the social sciences or in such fields as minority studies, woman studies, urban studies, or folklore.

How does cultural history define itself during the thirty years covered by this collection? By attrition. The only change noted by Mitterling is the putative escape of social history "which now is attempting to achieve an identity with distinctive content and several methodologies" (p. ix). If this is correct, it means only that social history is acting out the same drama that has engaged American studies almost from the first.

Mitterling should by no means be faulted for not finding a central discipline in cultural history, although his colleagues may be reluctant to recognize the departure of one of their central constituencies. The study of national character may be to cultural history what cultural history is to American studies. If this is so, then the words of Michael McGiffert, quoted approvingly by Thomas Hartshorne in one of the essays that follow, sound an alarm in regard to probing for method; for, as these two scholars agree, "the subject is currently in a theoretical shambles." Is the chaotic state of the study of national character representative of its setting, cultural history? Is cultural history currently lacking the structure and priorities that would offer a comforting sense of order to American studies?

For more than a generation, American studies grew confidently by merely crossing the lines between one kind of history and another. The disjunction between quantification, the culture concept, textual criticism, and other nonhistorical elements was interesting, sometimes irritating, sometimes productive, but rarely crucial. In the last fifteen years, however, American studies has been progressively stretching its functional definition by establishing outposts in oral history and the film, minority studies and the decorative arts. One can see the ring of campfires burning brightly.

If there is no universally accepted idea of order at the center, how does this make American studies different from many other academic programs? Departments are often more an arrangement than a discipline. Thus it is not surprising that few leaders of the American studies movements—in spite of the plethora of workshops on method—ever expected that the study of the United States could be conducted in accordance with a rigid theory or procedure. It may be time to stop sifting through the communiqués for a battle plan that was never sent and seldom intended. So long as American studies sponsors an expanding purview with an open interest in combining likely points of view, it will surely make its contributions to the collection and dissemination of knowledge.

The bibliographic essays reflect this condition. They are the products of American scholars, however, and may reflect only what is happening in one nation. American studies abroad, to judge from the pages of *ASI*, is probably less complicated by diversity and more controlled in its growth. From our foreign colleagues we learn of flourishing activity characterized by a buttressing of the more conventional pillars of American studies: history, literature, and government, with some notable excursions into such more contemporary subjects as film (in France) and popular culture (in Germany). From a modest beginning, American studies in Africa shows considerable new growth. China and Korea contribute increasingly to the internationalization of the subject. The extensive, longstanding programs in India and Japan continue to stress literature, as is natural in countries where the study of America begins with the study of language. There is now a notable addition of first-class publications in history, economics, and foreign policy. For at least a generation in Europe, Canada, and the Antipodes, American studies has been a well-organized international venture. American studies abroad has exhibited such achievement that this collection of essays will surely be the last to reflect a domestic monopoly. Indeed, American studies has been thoroughly internationalized.

PART I

NEW ESSAYS

Redding and Baraka: Two Contrasting Views on Afro-American Studies

JEFFERSON B. KELLOGG

Since 1962, the mandate of this journal has been to present to the international community of Americanists interpretations of American culture and history from Americans and non-Americans alike. The continuous exchange of views between scholars and students of different nations—not only in these pages, but also in conferences, meetings, and personal encounters—has served to broaden the perspective of every member of this community.

So this issue is, in a sense, a departure from the standard format of *ASI* in that it presents the different views of two Americans. We think that our international audience will pardon this transgression, however, for this exchange between Saunders Redding and Imamu Amiri Baraka provides an interesting glimpse of the controversy surrounding the study of black America that has blossomed in the past two decades.

Concern with America's racial situation has been the single most divisive issue throughout the nation's history. And Americans have not suffered this history without benefit of foreign perspective. Tocqueville's prescient thought on the problems Americans could anticipate because of the fundamental inconsistency in the treatment of black Americans is an early example.

Portrait of Frederick Douglass. Ambrotype, 4¹/₄" x 3³/₈". Photographer and date unknown. Negative number 07512. National Portrait Gallery, Smithsonian Institution, Washington, D.C.

Gunnar Myrdal's *An American Dilemma* is a classic example of an "outsider's" ability to probe into the enduring peculiar institutions of mid-20th-century American society. And Werner Sollors' book on Baraka, and Michel Fabre's writing on Richard Wright, are but two recent examples of the continuing contribution of non-Americans to this area of American social history.

Yet many of the works that have appeared as part of this burgeoning field of study represent more than simply a maturing of Afro-American historical scholarship. They also represent a significant change in American self-consciousness. The study of the American past has been radically altered, and perception of the role of black Americans has been fundamentally expanded, by this historiographic revolution. Much of the conflict that has accompanied, and sometimes stimulated, this writing can be appreciated only by looking at debates among Americans.

These two essays stand as provocative documents in modern American racial thought. The conflict of ideas they offer represents different interpretations of the importance of race consciousness in contemporary America. Redding urges, in this essay and in other works, that race should be a negligible factor in judging the merits of scholarship, in evaluating individual performance in any endeavor, and in one's perception of his worth and role in society. He has publicly lamented the burden that race-consciousness places on black Americans by obligating many to sacrifice creative abilities to racial concerns. He has attacked traditional scholarship for ignoring and distorting the truth of the black American past while simultaneously championing the ideal of a truly integrated society.

In contrast, much of Baraka's writing, and certainly his political and civic activity, has emphasized the need of Afro-Americans to foster their cultural, economic, and political independence. This he sees as a prerequisite to achieving self-respect, self-determination, and hence freedom within American society. Of course, Baraka suggests that consciously developing a racial perspective is only part of the continuing struggle of black Americans. To be placed in its proper perspective, race must be seen as an aspect of the imperialist oppression of black Americans throughout the centuries. But this focus on racial independence has certainly been a consistent theme in his developing ideology.

Redding's and Baraka's works reveal different ways of reacting to racial conflict. That's what makes these two essays so valuable. While functioning in very different milieus, these two men have spent much of their lives analyzing the dynamics of racial prejudice. And they offer distinctly different opinions of the appropriate role of race consciousness in American society.

But Redding's essay on "The Black Revolution in American Studies" (which first appeared in the Autumn, 1970 *AS/*) must also be appreciated as a period piece. It was written in the midst of the enormous emotional and intellectual upheaval accompanying the emergence of Afro-American studies on predominately white campuses. It is a period piece in the sense that it voices the fears expressed by many scholars during those tumultuous days regarding the maintenance of academic standards.

As a result of the social unrest accompanying the civil rights agitation of the 1960s, American universities finally had begun to recruit significant numbers of black students. Quite naturally, with the diversification of student populations came demands for the expansion of curricula, and a revision of traditional scholarly views, in the fields of American history, literature, etc. This expanded scope of American scholarship was to open American eyes to the fact that they had long ignored much of their past. Throughout America educational institutions responded, but the nature of this response concerned many scholars who offered caveats to students, faculty, and administrators.

These scholars expressed concern that while these areas of study receive new emphasis there be a free exchange of ideas among all groups. However, the acrimony that accompanied much of the activity on American campuses led to intense black and white hostility and self-imposed racial segregation, violating the spirit of open intellectual exchange. Others expressed concern that political movements centered in small pockets of special interest might appear, and that universities must prevent political concerns from ever dominating academic concerns.

Much of this activity represented more than simply a movement to expand and enhance university curricula. It also fostered group pride and identity and a sense of cultural uniqueness that were essential elements of the entire civil rights movement. But often accompanying these developments were demands that courses be offered exclusively for blacks, and that faculty and administrators be chosen on the basis of race. Arguments for a test of color to determine who might attend and teach courses were intolerable to many;

Mrs. Annie Mason of Jefferson County, Mississippi, showing her grandson the family bible containing part of her family history. Photograph by Roland Freeman, 1977.

the conflict was often intense; and blacks and whites emerged as advocates of both positions.

What really underlay all these concerns was the demand that these new programs be carefully planned and structured and that they be held to the same standards of academic respectability as traditional programs. I'm referring to positions argued by professionals who supported the essential broadening of American historical perspective, but who warned of certain violations that could in the long run impede the progress of black studies. I'm not referring to those who were fundamentally opposed to this healthy expansion of university life—of both its courses of study and its participants; scholars who sent up smokescreens about academic standards and fears of exacerbated racial tension when they really meant to oppose this necessary democratization of American thought.

While Redding's essay was clearly motivated by this concern that black studies earn the same respectability as other academic disciplines, it also reflects his fundamental position on the limits of race consciousness. It is on this issue that Baraka takes such exception. While attacking American scholarship for neglecting and misrepresenting so much of the nation's past, Redding advocates multi-racial cooperation in revising this history. He also envisages this "black revolution in American studies" taking place within the framework of traditional scholarly disciplines. And he argues that if "black studies" encompasses more than the study of the black American past it encompasses too much. Baraka's response is that this position compromises the racial integrity of black Americans and detracts from their struggle for self-determination.

Redding represents the traditional integrationist stance that has characterized most of the black American struggle for equality—a position that has had some of its long-accepted doctrines subjected to vigorous and convincing rebuttal. And Baraka takes this opportunity to challenge this school of thought. But each reader must judge if Redding is guilty of the charges Baraka levels against him: that he is steeped in an anti-black consciousness; that he suggests that the Afro-American people don't exist as a people at all; and that his position on race supports views that contribute to the oppression of black Americans. □

The Black Revolution in American Studies

SAUNDERS REDDING

The concept "black studies," conceived in frustration and bitterness by an articulate and highly emotional minority, is of questionable validity as a scholarly discipline. It encompasses too much. It presumes no less than the universal social, cultural, and literary history of blacks from pre-Islamic times to the present and the biological and anthropological linkage of all black people. It presumes, too, a genetic constant, although the theory of a genetic constant has been repudiated by the best scientific minds for a hundred years. The Black Studies concept is action-oriented, and to the extent that it is so oriented it is anti-intellectual. Represented in a mystique called "Negritude," it embraces a heavy, indeed, overriding emotional component that is referred to as "soul force," which force conditions ways of acting, feeling, and thinking that are distinctly racial and that characterize black people wherever they are and under whatever conditions they exist. All black men, therefore, are brothers both in the genetic and spiritual sense.

The advocates of this way of thinking have no corpus of cognitive knowledge to fall back on. They adduce the works of Marcus Garvey (whose recently discovered "lost papers" they cannot wait to get into), the romantic appeal of the Back-to-Africa movement, the position—which is grossly misunderstood—that Franz Fanon takes in *The Wretched of the Earth*, and various statements put forth by the self-exiled Stokeley Carmichael. Fortunately few of the advocates of this way of thinking are professional academicians; they lack the authority to dilute the demanding intellectual endeavor that a mastery of black studies requires. This is not to say that they totally lack influence. They are of the Black Revolution, leaders and spokesmen for activist groups and political programs. They speak their views from respectable platforms, and they publish them in the Black Muslim newspaper *Mohammed Speaks, Black World* (formerly *Negro Digest*), and *Ramparts.*

Many, and perhaps most, black scholars, who are also of the Revolution, neither condemn nor exculpate the non-academic revolutionaires. They say, truthfully enough, that there are emotional components and biases in all humanistic thought and learning, and, having defined them, the job of the academician is to modify or correct them by disseminating true knowledge. They say that Western learning begins from a bias that can be summarized as "Rah, rah, whites!" and that, proceeding from this, white scholars generally have distorted facts, knowledge, and the truth by excluding blacks from, or by defaming the role of blacks in, the history and culture of the Western world, and particularly the history and culture of America. Black scholars submit that this is likely due to the whites's conscience-stricken realization that the ideals—social, political, and religious: in short, humanitarian—which were and are set forth as the basis for human action and interaction, have been ignored; and the way to ease the abraded conscience is to write American history and to examine American civilization so as to exclude from consideration the victims of this falling away. White scholars have found justification for this exclusion in questionable theories, obsessively rationa-

---

Jay Saunders Redding is a distinguished historian, teacher, and literary critic. He received Ph.B and M.A. degrees from Brown University and has taught at many institutions, including Morehouse College, Southern University, Hampton Institute, George Washington University, and Brown University. He is currently Ernest I. White Professor of American Studies and Humane Letters at Cornell University.

His publications transcend any narrowly defined academic disciplines. He has published numerous articles on literary criticism, particularly on black American writing, and a widely respected anthology titled Cavalcade: Negro American Writing from 1760 to the Present *(1971), which he edited with Arthur P. Davis. His historical works include* They Came in Chains from Africa *(1951),* The Lonesome Road: Biographical History of Black America *(1958), and* The Negro *(1967). And he has published two provocative autobiographical works,* No Day of Triumph *(1942) and* On Being Negro in America *(1951).*

lized by some of the most eminent American minds from Thomas Jefferson to George F. Kenan, and in dubious psychological and social data and "proof" of black people's inherent inferiority.

This way of thinking has produced several interlocking complementary reactions and results, and black scholars and intellectuals have documented them in recent works that no honest student of American civilization should ignore. The scholarly caliber of John Hope Franklin's *From Slavery to Freedom* (now updated), of Benjamin Quarles' *The Negro in the Making of America*, and of Kenneth Clark's *Dark Ghetto* is very high. Less scholarly, but important to an understanding of the reactions and results mentioned above, is Austin, Fenderson, and Nelson's *The Black Man and the Promise of America*. Then there are certain personal books and an official report: *Manchild in the Promised Land*, by Claude Brown; *Soul on Ice*, by Eldridge Cleaver; *The Autobiography of Malcolm X*; and the *Report of the National Advisory Commission on Civil Disorders*.

The results and the reactions that these books explore and document are social. They document the development and the operation of race prejudice. They present evidence of the American whites' calculated avoidance of knowledge and learning about American blacks. They give information about the operation of this willful ignorance in the day-to-day rounds of American life, and about the efforts of blacks as individuals and as communities to accommodate and to moderate the ignorance of whites, which is commonly called "racism."

A second result of the exclusion of black people from a role in the drama of American civilization and a place in American history is—or rather, was; for this is not new—the institution of courses in Negro history and literature in Negro high schools and colleges, where white supervision of curricula is minimal and careless. The tradition of studying Negro history and literature is more than a half century old. It goes back to W. E. B. DuBois, the black social historian, who, believing that the solution to the "Negro problem was a matter of systematic investigation," tried to induce white institutions (notably the University of Pennsylvania and Harvard) to adopt black courses. He did not succeed, but he did inaugurate (in 1904) the Atlanta University Studies program, which focused on Negro material, and which annually published scholarly monographs and papers on the Negro. DuBois inspired Carter G. Woodson, also a Harvard Ph.D., who founded the Association for the Study of Negro Life and History in 1915, set up a company to publish books about blacks, edited and issued the quarterly *Journal of Negro History* (which the Association still issues), and himself wrote the texts—*The Negro in Our History* and *Negro Makers of History*—most widely used down to the Second World War.

A third result of the neglect of the black experience in American studies is the black student revolution—a social as well as an intellectual rebellion against the "irrelevance" of so much that passes for education in American institutions of higher learning. The social phase of the black student revolution, like the instruction in black courses in Negro schools, goes back a long way—a fact which Harry Edwards' book, *Black Students*, an excellent account

Local history class, Hampton Institute, Hampton, Virginia, 1899, by Frances B. Johnston. Established to educate blacks after the Civil War, Hampton admitted a few American Indians. Negative number LC-USZ62-38149. Prints and Photographs, Library of Congress, Washington, D.C.

of contemporary temper and attitudes, fails to report on. It goes back to the 1920s. At Lincoln University, at Hampton Institute, and at Shaw University, private black colleges administered and faculty-staffed principally by whites, students rebelled against the patronizing "missionary" attitudes of their white instructors and against the rigid "etiquette of race" that characterized all their relations with them. White administrators and instructors were said to feel that blacks were not capable of really mastering the more demanding subjects, and that, perhaps excepting the manual arts, the subjects they were taught by the few black teachers—physical education, music, and a "folk variety of Negro history"—were not worth learning anyway. In short, the rebellion was against the inferior black status per se. The students demanded and gradually got more black administrators and teachers, a modification (at Hampton and Shaw) of the social rules that stigmatized them as irresponsible, sexually irrepressible "children," and increased respect as maturing human beings.

Not until the 1950s, when court decisions and steadily mounting pressures at home and abroad challenged the American status quo, and, among other things, made for a substantial increase in the enrollment of black students in predominantly white colleges—not until then did the intellectual phase of the black student revolution begin to acquire definition. Even now, though, the definition is blurred by social factors and an emotional cloud cover and is rendered imprecise by the rhetoric of revolution. "Soul," "black nationalism," "black separatism," and "black power" have been taken to mean what they seem to mean in the formation of black student unions and alliances and in the demand—bitterly ironic and cynical—on predominantly white campuses for autonomous black studies programs to be directed and taught by blacks for black students only. In "The Role of Afro-American Education," one of the essays in *Basic Black: A Look at the Black Presence on Campus*, it is argued that "Black studies must be taught from a black perspective. The spirit of blackness must pervade . . . Black education must be based on both ideological and pedagogical blackness." The fact that one trained and practicing as a scholar can make such an argument is a measure of the extent to which emotionalism blurs, and, if not checked, will dilute the content that black studies must have if it is to attain respectability as a scholarly discipline.

Black studies can attain that respectability. There are both black and white scholars—at Berkeley, Brown, Harvard, Michigan, Texas, and Yale—who believe this and are working toward that end. They seem agreed that "black studies" is a misnomer. They prefer Afro-American studies, a title designating a body of potentially manageable knowledge focusing upon the experience of black people in America, in, specifically, what is now the United States. Afro-American studies is not African studies, which, thanks to British universities and Berkeley, Boston University and predominantly black Howard University, has been deemed academically respectable for a decade. Afro-American studies is not conceived as structurally dependent on other area studies, like Latin American studies, for instance, which is also an independent discipline; or Caribbean studies, which scholars at the University of the West Indies and the University of Puerto Rico are making distinct and independent.

All this is to say that Afro-American studies is basically American studies, an interdisciplinary major that must draw upon relevant knowledge and experience outside the United States. I have suggested elsewhere that a line of historical continuity and development peculiar to what is now the United States has generated a new breed of black man with a new "Americanized" orientation to life, with, demonstrably, a special culture and, one strongly suspects, a different psychological and emotional structure from that of his "brothers" in Africa, in South America, and in the Caribbean. Until scholars conscientiously pursue this line of development, American studies will remain diminished and of questionable validity. Until this development is pursued, Americans will remain poorly equipped to deal with the problems that confront them. An intellectual pursuit—any intellectual pursuit—serves a social function too. That, of course, is what education is all about. And when American students black and white complain about lack of "relevance," they are saying that education in America is not preparing them to serve an important social function, and they are saying this no matter what their definition of importance is.

Although the integration of Afro-American studies with American studies will probably require a new methodology for the measurable attainment of respectable scholarly performance and achievement, much of the material to be integrated is already at hand. Some of it was produced before the intellectual phase of the black student revolution got under way. The scholars who produced it were aiming at a revision of the American past; they were intent on correcting the errors of fact and the faults of interpretation of other American historians. C. Vann Woodward certainly had this in mind when he wrote *Reunion and Reaction, The Strange Career of Jim Crow,* and *The Burden of Southern History.* So did Leon Litwack in preparing *North of Freedom,* and Kenneth Stampp when he wrote *The Peculiar Institution.* Though all of these works, appearing in the late 1950s and early 1960s, draw upon sources that have been neglected by writers of "standard" American history, none of them begins to fill what American blacks feel to be the most urgent need—that is, the recreation of the American blacks' history as separate from (but not independent of) the history of American whites.

There have been efforts along this line, and they continue at a quickened pace. Scholars and intellectuals of both races have turned out more histories of black Americans in the past decade than in the preceding half century. Although Herbert Aptheker's *A Documentary History of the Negro* is good, the editor too often assumes that the collected documents can stand alone and independent of the historical background which produced them. Blaustein and Zangrando do not make this mistake in their more particularized *Civil Rights and the American Negro,* a compendium of legislative acts, court decisions, Executive Orders, and official public policy speeches documenting and illustrating the Negro's struggle for civil rights. The materials in *The Black American,* edited by Leslie H. Fishel, Jr. and Benjamin Quarles, are more discrete; some of them were chosen on the basis of non-historical criteria; but all relate directly or indirectly to the major themes of the book—"the primary role of the Negro in American history and the importance of the Negro's own history in America."

A different class of historical works—many of them first published years ago and now reprinted—were written, as Charles H. Wesley, who co-authored one of them, says, "to create a sense of pride on the one hand and appreciation on the other." In other words, they were written for black Americans. Only rarely do these books avoid the distortions that some of them purposely employ to counterbalance the distortions of white history. Only the very best of them is free of the intellectual and emotional parochialism that characterizes the race chauvinist. The best is Benjamin Brawley's *A Social History of the American Negro,* which is now reprinted after fifty years. Were it updated by a scholar as highly qualified as the original author was, *A Social History* would be all but indispensable. Markedly lesser achievements than Brawley's are Arnold Schuster's *White Power: Black Freedom,* and recent collections of historical writings edited by Dwight Hoover (*Understanding Negro History*), by Ross Baker (*The Afro-American*), by Bracey, Meier, and Rudwick (*Black Nationalism in America*), and by Charles E. Wynes (*The Negro in the South Since 1865.*) Whether or not St. Clair Drake, a very perceptive black social scientist, is right in describing the "ultimate purpose" of historical works written specifically for the black American audience as "defining ourselves for ourselves" and "getting ourselves together—necessary conditions for an intelligent participation in a democratic society," one thing is certain: these works challenge contemporary scholarship in American studies with the facts of black Americans' stolen past and contested future.

Upwards of thirty anthologies of literary writings by blacks have been issued in the last twelve months. Many of these are quickies, collections of contemporary writings published in the hope of riding the wave of the fad for anything black. Others are intended as textbooks in black literature courses, and the selections are representative of the development of Negro writing as art. Their editors establish both a critical and historical context. *On Being Black*, edited by Charles T. Davis and Daniel Walden, has a brilliant critical introduction touching upon the "black aesthetic," and Addison Gayle's anthology, *Black Expression*, has an equally brilliant historical introduction. *Black Voices*, which was edited by Abraham Chapman, and *From the Ashes*, edited by Budd Schulberg, are important because they present work of a whole new crop of black writers heretofore unpublished.

Finally, there are current books that deal with the black American experience from the point of view of traditional scholarly disciplines. Using the methods and tools and providing the insights of psychology, sociology, economics, political science, and cultural anthropology, these books are responsive to the notion of the black American's "difference," and how that difference came to be. The books are "studies," but not all of them deserve the definition. The "black perspective" intrudes, as in Floyd McKissick's *3/5 of a Man*, which Justice William Douglas declares "a must," not because of its scholarly and objective examination of American jurisprudence as it affects the Negro, but because of its "mood . . . which reveals the depth of anguish and anger in the black community." In Greer and Poussaint's *Black Rage*, a study of the psychology of black youth, mood is restricted to the author's introduction. And except for the somewhat sensational title, *The Forty Billion Dollar Negro*, the black perspective is entirely absent from Vivian Henderson's study of the black experience in the American economy.

Taken altogether, the books mentioned in this essay—and dozens not mentioned—are a measure of the deficiencies of most American studies programs; of the extent to which American scholars have been either oblivious to or inexcusably mistaken about black Americans and the materials and substantive issues involving black Americans. These books suggest, too, the dimensions of the educational revolution that must take place in American studies and that, hopefully, is now gathering momentum. Adversaries of the revolution have already surfaced, but they will scarcely prevail against the persistent work of even a small handful of dedicated scholars of both races who are rediscovering old, neglected historical facts, publishing and testing new theories in the social sciences, and devising new instruments of scholarly humanistic endeavor. The adversaries of the revolution in American studies will scarcely prevail, either, against the demands for "relevance" by a great and growing number of students. □

A Reply to Saunders Redding's "The Black Revolution in American Studies"

IMAMU AMIRI BARAKA

Saunders Redding's writing has, in the main, consistently upheld views that this author feels are not only "conservative," but are basically supportive of the oppression of the Afro-American nation and white chauvinism in general. Though, to be sure, Redding, like everyone else, is not perfect, and some-times contradictory fragments ease through which speak of confusion more than consolidated white chauvinism (or Great Nation Chauvinism). The fact that Redding is black means this white chauvinism is even more effective within the circles Redding is adept at spreading it.

His article, "The Black Revolution In American Studies," is classic in this sense. It begins, predictably enough, like the subtle "nigger calling" of one of the Southern Agrarians, babbling . . . &c. "The concept 'black studies' con-ceived in frustration and bitterness by an articulate and highly emotional minority, is of questionable validity as a scholarly discipline. . . ." This little sentence is the core dictum of the racism and national oppression that grew out of the European slave trade; that the Afro-American people do not exist as a people at all, but in some servile non-person relationship to their white masters. The first understanding we must come to in order to oppose this imperialist philosophy is that the Afro-American people in the United States not only exist but are an *oppressed nation.* They have a history, culture, literature, music, art, related to but at the same time distinct from these categories of Anglo-America, though without focus on these Afro-American life dimensions, no real description of the United States as an actual entity can be offered.

Redding says of black studies, "it encompasses too much," that it seeks to go back to "pre-Islamic times" (not very far back really, the 7th century, only the 11th century if one is talking about the beginning of deep penetration into sub-Saharan [Black] Africa). But could one take up American studies without studying the people who came to be Americans, their history and development? Why would anyone want to? The Afro-American people are connected to Africa, as the Euro-American people are connected to Europe. To understand the present, we have to look at history; obviously Redding knows this, when it comes to any other people. The denial of this, concerning Afro-American people, is white chauvinism.

Redding also resents that black studies is "action oriented," and therefore "anti-intellectual." It *is* action-oriented since its appearance in the curricula of American universities came as a result of recent struggle, part of the struggle of the Black Liberation Movement. The inclusion of black studies on these

---

Imamu Amiri Baraka (Leroi Jones) is a prominent figure in a remarkably wide range of fields. He has distinguished himself as a dramatist with such plays as The Baptism, The Toilet, Dutchman, *and* The Slave. *His poetry has appeared in many anthologies and periodicals, and in a personal collection,* The Dead Lecturer: Poems *(1964). In addition, he has edited such works as* Black Fire: An Anthology of Afro-American Writing *(1968) with Larry Neal, and* The Moderns: An Anthology of New Writing in America *(1963).*

But Baraka is probably equally well known for his community activism and his espousal of a black nationalist philosophy. In 1964 he founded the Black Arts Repertory Theater School in Harlem, a precursor to much of the cultural activity that then blossomed in

black communities throughout America. In 1966 he founded Spirit House, another theater group, in Newark, New Jersey. This served as a base for the Black Community Development and Defense Organization, and then the Committee for a Unified Newark, both aggressive community-action organizations that he helped establish. He was later a prime mover of such politically active organizations as the Congress of African People and the national Black Political Convention.

Baraka received his B.A. from Howard University in 1954. He has taught poetry, drama, literature, and creative writing at such institutions as the New School for Social Research, Columbia University, the University of Buffalo, San Francisco State College, and George Washington University.

campuses is only as a result of the attacks Afro-Americans made on the capitalist and racist American system in the 60s. (And already the burgeoisie are trying to cut away even these few gains, e.g., the Baake decision.)

Redding has the classic bourgeois world view that intellectual activity must be the antithesis of action, but as Marx said, any professor can understand the world, the struggle is to change it! Black studies, at its most lucid, seeks to expand the very nature of intellectual activity by including a whole area of human life and endeavor artificially excluded by slavery and racism. It is "anti-intellectual" to say that black studies is of "questionable validity"; why less valid than English or Germanic studies, etc? Except to justify the super-exploitation and oppression of a whole nation of people (who do not exist for the white racist American bourgeoisie, except as laboring automatons).

Redding reacts negatively to the bourgeois nationalist "mystique" called Negritude, and so do I. But we have to make a distinction between resistance to imperialism and colonialism, which black people all over the world have done and still have to do, and the cultural nationalism of one segment of the black petty bourgeoisie that "pimps" its existence off the legitimate revolutionary struggle of the Black Masses! The Negritude of a Senghor is laughable, except we remember the people of Senegal reeling under Senghor's neo-colonialism. We see then that this Negritude does not serve the majority of Senegalese since they are still exploited and oppressed, and revolution still must be made, even against this Wizard of Negritude who is also a wizard of continuing the (indirect) rule of imperialism.

But Redding is so steeped in a defensive anti-black consciousness in trying to be "a scholar," not a black scholar; "a critic," not a black critic; and, one would suppose, "a man," not a black man (all of which are impossible in a racist society), that he has long ago succumbed to the succubus of *compradorism*. Compradorism among the black petty burgeois intellectuals takes one form by denying the particular historical and cultural experience of the Afro-American nation and "integrating" them into America, a process which has never taken place in reality. And this, objectively, is in the service of US imperialism which has always reduced us to 0. The separateness of black life in America was the oné constant that served to show off and develop black life in relief, though it could always be defined by the official ruling class definers as not existing at all.

Redding confuses *Black Nationalism*, which has legitimate reasons for existing (though only its revolutionary form, which is resistance to national oppression, should be upheld), with the fact of the existence of the Afro-American people and their lives in a way different from that of the slave-masters or whites or others in general, though there are similarities between all working-class people and oppressed nationalities, as far as the conditions under which they are forced to live.

Redding also sees racism as merely a *moral lapse*, rather than as a tool of capitalism to superexploit one group of people even more so than the "average" worker in the US. He seems not to understand that racism is a description of one aspect of the social relations under capitalism, and that unless the economic base of this sick oppressive ideology is destroyed, it will continue.

Redding's line reminds one of the official line of the NAACP national leadership which, because its salaries are paid by the absolutely questionable "largesse" of the corporations, thinks that the US can be "integrated." But this denies the real nature of this society which is *based on* the systematic super-exploitation and exclusion of the Afro-American people from slavery forward. Racism is not a lamentable moral lapse or simply, as Redding has it, "the ignorance of whites," it is the basic social organization of this society.

But Redding's confusion is obvious as well. Although he has a basic comprador-like view, he does mention some scattered works by blacks that "document the development and the operation of race prejudice," as if this could partially legitimatize or "make respectable" the demand for black studies. Redding also mentions the exclusion of Afro-Americans from American history and says, "The tradition of studying Negro history and literature is more than a half century old." This sounds like the racist history we were brought up on which would say things like "The first Negro architect," as if blacks throughout the world knew nothing about architecture, before white racists allowed one to get a US architect's license (the Great Pyramids notwithstanding). Redding treats racism as if *it* were legitimate, as if it really is a case of a backward people being allowed to come forward to see the light of civilization, rather than the bloody saga of black resistance to the slave trade, slavery, and national oppression. He also uses DuBois questionably by quoting an early statement of Dubois' that the solution to the "Negro problem was a matter of systematic investigation." Dubois meant, then, that racism could be solved by shedding light on misconceptions and "white ignorance." But Dubois, certainly by the time of *Black Reconstruction* (1935) or even *The Negro* (1915), saw the international nature of imperialism and capitalism as the material base of racism. Redding ignores these later perceptions of Dubois' since, I would imagine, Dubois' evolution from petty bourgeois scholar, to apologist for black capitalism, through Pan-Africanism, until he arrived at his Marxist position, distresses Redding, so he chooses to ignore it.

Redding also does not clearly understand the role of the black students in the struggle for black studies. He charges them, and certain writers, with emotionally blurring "the content that black studies must have if it is to attain respectability as a scholarly discipline." But if it were not for the black students fighting on the campuses for black studies, in reflection of what the black masses were doing in the streets of America, there would be no black studies in the first place! The inclusion of black studies on these campuses came only as a result of student struggle, and if some of the rhetoric which accompanied these struggles was overblown, even metaphysical and idealistic, the revolutionary core of those struggles was correct. Black studies would not yet be on these campuses, nor would it remain, if it had to depend solely on the efforts of Redding-type intellectuals and their pleas for "moral uplift" among the bourgeoisie. Black studies came only as a result of struggle and confrontation, as usual.

Redding wants Afro-American studies to "attain that respectability" and indeed this is probably his cry concerning everything in black life. But it is racism that makes black life *not respectable*, the social organization and

Women welders, New Britain, Connecticut, 1943, by Gordon Parks. Negative number WB-34282 FSA/OWI collection, Prints and Photographs, Library of Congress, Washington, D.C.

ideology of capitalism! Redding thinks that if he says, "Hey, some of this black stuff is actually well done and scholarly," that the powers that be will say, "Oh, yes, now that you mention it there are some real scholars here . . . black studies is hereby respectable!" But this is simply house-servant fantasy which serves as neat propaganda for a corrupt and unwork-able system which cannot be fundamentally changed except through revolutionary means.

Redding's final shot that "Afro-American studies is basically American studies" is the burden of the thinking that lurks throughout his entire essay. Of course Afro-American studies can be seen as part of American studies, but as Bruce Franklin has pointed out (*The Victim as Artist and Criminal*, Oxford) American literature, for instance, as taught in these universities ought really be called Anglo-American or white American literature, or actually white man American literature. It is no more than a reflection of the racist society itself. (And we need more and more independent Afro-American studies programs, not "inclusion" in American studies, which would simply justify the removal of Afro-American studies or its weakening through some fake "integration.") Also, American studies itself is having no picnic breaking through the barrier of English department colonialism that still does not understand that "George Washington and them" won that war in 1776. But this approach of Reddings' eliminates the national character of the Afro-American people and the fact that there is an Afro-American nation in the US with a history and culture of its own. In a revolutionary country, this national development would be supported, documented, and given the presence it needs to reflect upon and improve itself. This national character and a certain amount of autonomy would be encouraged. (Certainly regional political autonomy in those areas where that nationality was concentrated, e.g., in the US, the Black South, the homeland of the Afro-American nation.) And this approach would finally encourage the Afro-American people to make a voluntary union with the overall US multinational state, but such a union, such "integration," can only be based on the control of the American economy and state by the people, and the control of the black nation by the black masses. But in the US today, the world center of capitalism and racism, the cry must continue to go up of SELF DETERMINATION FOR THE AFRO-AMERICAN NATION IN THE BLACK BELT SOUTH/ LIBERATION FOR THE BLACK NATION!!

Redding sees the inclusion of black materials in American studies programs as "the educational revolution that must take place in American studies" and that "the adversaries of the revolution . . . will scarcely prevail," still talking about the integrating of America under imperialism. Sure, American studies will be revolutionized by the progress of the American Revolution itself, but Afro-American studies will also continue to develop as a summation of the lives of the Afro-American people, on one hand, and one catalyst for further struggle to transform those lives, on the other. And in the best of those programs of Afro-American studies will be seen the clear and irreducible motion of the black masses for self-determination and democratic rights. □

Bibliography

General & Key

Chan, Shih. *A Brief History of the United States*. Peking: Foreign Languages, 1976.

DuBois, W.E.B. *Black Reconstruction*. . . . New York: Harcourt Brace, 1935 (reprint, Meridian 1969).

————. *The Negro*, New York: H.Holt, 1915.

Franklin, Bruce. *The Victim As Artist And Criminal*. New York: Oxford, 1978.

Haywood, Harry. *Black Bolshevik*. Chicago: Liberator Press, 1978.

————. *For A Revolutionary Position On The Negro Question*. Chicago: Liberator, 1975.

Lenin, V. I. *Sociology And Statistics*. Collected Works, Moscow: Progress Pub.

Marx, Karl & Engels, F. *The Civil War In The US*. New York: International Publishers, 1961.

McAdoo, B. *Pre-Civil War Black Nationalism*. Report Newark, N.J.: Peoples' War, Box 663, 1977.

RCL, Afro American Comm. *The Black Nation*. Newark: Peoples' War, 1977.

Stalin, J. V. *Foundations of Leninism*. Peking: Foreign Languages Press, 1975. (See especially "The National Question")

————. *Marxism And The National-Colonial Question*. San Francisco: Prol Pub., 1975.

Representative Afro-American Literature (Chronological Order)

Douglass, Frederick. *Narrative of the Life of Frederick Douglass*. (See *The Life and Writings of Frederick Douglass*, ed. Philip Foner, 1950-55, New York: International Publishers.)

Turner, Nat. *The Confessions of Nat Turner*, New York: Thos. Hamilton, 1861.*

Walker, David. *Appeal*. . . . Boston: D. Walker, 1829.*

Garnet, Henry Highland. *An Address To The Slaves*, 1843.*

Brown, William Welles. *Clotel*, (1853) Report New York: Arno, 1961.

DuBois, W.E.B. *The Souls of Black Folk*, Chicago: A.C. McClurg, 1903 (Reprint New York, Fawcett 1961).

————. *Darkwater*. Washington, D.C.: Austin Jenkins, 1920.

Hughes, Langston. "The Artist And The Racial Mountain." *The Nation*. Vol 122, No 31 (June 1926).

————. *Selected Poetry*. New York: Knopf, 1959.

————. *Scotsboro Ltd*. New York: Golden Stair, 1932.

————. *The Big Sea*. New York: Knopf, 1940.

————. *Good Morning, Revolution* (ed. by Faith Berry). Connecticut: L.Hill, 1973.

McKay, Claude. *Selected Poems*. New York: Bookman Associates, 1953.

————. *Home To Harlem*. New York and London: Harpers, 1928.

Wright, Richard. *Uncle Tom's Children*. New York: Harpers, 1938.

————. *Black Boy*. Cleveland: World Publishers, 1945.

————. *American Hunger* (Orig pt of *Blk Boy* suppressed by Publishers) New York Harpers, 1977.

————. *"Blueprint for Negro Literature," Richard Wright Reader*.

---

* Included in *Black Writers of America*. Barksdale & Kinnamon (see below)

Ward, Theodore. "Big White Fog." *Black Theater USA.* Hatch & Shine, New York: Free Press, 1974.

Walker, Margaret. *For My People.* New Haven: Yale, 1942.

————. *Jubilee.* New York: Houghton-Mifflin, 1966.

Baldwin, James. *The Fire Next Time.* New York: Dial, 1963.

————. *Blues For Mr. Charlie.* New York: Dial, 1964.

Jones, LeRoi. *Dutchman.* New York: Wm. Morrow, 1964.

————. *Blues People.* New York: Wm. Morrow, 1962.

Malcolm, X. (w/ Alex Haley). *The Autobiography of Malcom X.* New York: Doubleday, 1964.

Baraka, Amiri. *The Motion Of History.* New York: Wm. Morrow, 1978.

Anthologies And Collections

Locke, Alain. *The New Negro.* New York: Atheneum, 1968 (original edition 1925).

Brown, Sterling. *Negro Caravan.* New York: Arno, 1969 reprint (original edition 1941).

Bontemps, Arna & Hughes, Langston. *Negro Poetry.* New York: Doubleday, 1949.

Baraka, Amiri & Neal, Larry. *Black Fire.* New York: William Morrow, 1969.

Barksdale & Kinnamon. *Black Writers Of America.* New York: Macmillan, 1972.

Miller, Ruth. *Black American Literature.* California: Glencoe/Macmillan, 1971.

Hatch & Shine. *Black Theater U.S.A.* New York: Free Press, 1974.

Explanation of Bibliography

Chan	Objective: political-economic overview of US history, so *real* development of US & Afro-Americans can begin to be understood.
DuBois	*Black Reconstruction.* Indispensable to understanding the development of Afro-Americans in this country.
DuBois	*The Negro.* No real understanding of black studies can be had without a correct historical overview of the Afro-American nationality.
Franklin	Establishes the essentially racist character of academic views of "American Literature" and culture and their relationship to academic views of "Black Studies."
Haywood	*Black Bolshevik* lays out the scientific and historical emergence of the view that there is an Afro-American nation inside the US.
Haywood	*For A Revolutionary Position*, similar to Haywood.
Lenin	Scientific basis for Afro-American Nation thesis.
Marx etc.	In depth analysis of Civil War and effect on blacks and US future.
McAdoo	An analysis of basic ideological tendencies within Afro-American nation historically.

RCL   Treatise on history of Afro-American people.
Stalin   Includes basic scientific analysis of "National Question."
             Marxism & The National Question is a classic work on the rise of
             nations and national oppression.

Representative Afro-American Literature

The works included here are all part of what I feel constitute the "Revolutionary Tradition In Afro-American Literature." (This is in contrast to the "liberal" or conservative or assimilationist or capitulationist trends, which also exist, obviously, in Afro-American literature.)

DOUGLASS & the Slave Narratives are the real beginnings of an Afro-American literature as a *genre*. TURNER, WALKER, GARNET all are part of the pre-civil war revolutionary nationalist tradition which runs parallel and extends beyond the slave narratives.

W.W. BROWN, the beginning of Afro-American Belles Lettres tradition as the genuine ideological reflection of the black masses (as are the works cited above).

DUBOIS is the indispensable historian and man of letters who forms the link between the 19th century and the Harlem Renaissance.

HUGHES, as part of the urban revolutionary nationalist intelligentsia that formed in the early part of the 20th century, is one of the most influential of all Afro-American writers, as well as CLAUDE MCKAY. (Obviously there are many other fine writers out of the Harlem Renaissance, but Hughes and McKay, to this author, are the most important.)

RICHARD WRIGHT was the voice of the 30s and remains the most important fiction writer in Afro-American literature.

WARD is a giant of a dramatist, hidden and obscured by racist America. His "Big White Fog" remains the most striking ideological portrait of an Afro-American family.

MARGARET WALKER has written the classic Afro-American poem, "For My People," and her poetry makes exemplary uses of the oral and folk tradition of Afro-American life.

BALDWIN's works, most often, fit into the tradition I have outlined, and "Blues For Mr. Charlie" was truly an important and prophetic work.

JONES/BARAKA's best works represent an attempt to continue the revolutionary tradition.

MALCOLM X's autobiography, like the slave narratives or "Black Boy" or even "Black Bolshevik," is a classic Afro-American autobiography and crucial for understanding the present period.

Anthologies and Collections

LOCKE's New Negro opened the door to the Harlem Renaissance. BROWN's chronicled further development. BONTEMPS/HUGHES work is a general survey of Afro-American poetry. BARAKA/NEAL's work presents the 60s Black Arts Movement. Both the BARKSDALE/KINNAMON and MILLER works are useful anthologies in studying Afro-American literature. But the Miller work is just adequate, the Barksdale-Kinnamon book is *outstanding*! The HATCH/SHINE anthology is the classic collection of Afro-American drama, a really well done work, with critical introductions to each play.

Selected Secondary Sources

by Jefferson B. Kellogg

Redding's essay and Baraka's appended bibliography only begin to mention important sources for the study of Afro-American history. The following list, while by no means inclusive, suggests some additional titles. I have indicated paperback editions with an asterisk (*).

Aptheker, Herbert, ed. *American Negro Slave Revolts.* New York: International Publishers, 1969.* This study, first published in 1943, documents the widespread and varied acts of rebelliousness that Aptheker says were characteristic of American slaves.
Berlin, Ira. *Slaves Without Masters: The Free Negro in the Antebellum South.* New York: Vintage, 1976.* A comprehensive study of the free Negro, including conditions of life in different areas of the South, community institutions, patterns of work, and the group's vulnerability as the sectional conflict mounted.
Blassingame, John W. *The Slave Community: Plantation Life in the Antebellum South.* New York: Oxford University Press, 1972.* A view of plantation life from the slave's perspective that shows how they established a sense of identity and cultural independence not appreciated in traditional historical scholarship.

Cruse, Harold. *The Crisis of the Negro Intellectual.* New York: Morrow, 1967.*
A critical view of Negro intellectual thought from Garveyites and leaders of
the Harlem Renaissance of the post-World War I era to the Black Power
adovcates of the 1960s.

Drake, St. Clair and Horace R. Cayton. *Black Metropolis.* New York: Harcourt,
Brace and World, 1970.* A classic work of the formation of a black urban
community and its institutions, this study of Chicago first appeared in 1945.

Elkins, Stanley. *Slavery: A Problem in American Institutional and Intellectual
Life,* 3rd edition. Chicago: University of Chicago Press, 1976.* Received
most of its notoriety from the section on slave personality that ascribes to
slaves a subservience against which much recent scholarship has reacted;
includes an essay on the historiography of slavery.

Filler, Louis. *The Crusade Against Slavery, 1830–1860.* New York: Harper and
Row, 1960.* A comprehensive view of the many factions of anti-slavery
agitation in this period.

Franklin, John Hope. *The Free Negro in North Carolina, 1790–1860.* New
York: Norton, 1971.* Originally published in 1943, this work is still one of
the better state studies on the subject.

Fredrickson, George M. *The Black Image in the White Mind: The Debate on
Afro-American Character and Destiny, 1817–1914.* New York: Harper and
Row, 1977.* Examines the changing nature of American race prejudice as
influenced by social, political, and scientific issues in this period.

Gara, Larry. *The Liberty Line: The Legend of the Underground Railroad.*
Lexington: University Press of Kentucky, 1967.* Revises long-standing beliefs of the organization, support, and activity of the underground railroad.

Garfinckel, Herbert. *When Negroes March.* New York: Atheneum, 1969.*
Study of the March on Washington Movement of 1942, a black, direct-
action campaign led by A. Philip Randolph to attack employment discrimination.

Genovese, Eugene. *The Political Economy of Slavery: Studies in Economy
and Society in the Slave South.* New York: Vintage, 1967.* Suggests how
this planter-dominated social and economic system proved ruinous to the
South.

————. *Roll Jordan Roll: The World the Slaves Made.* New York: Vintage,
1976.* Enormous work that reinterprets much previously accepted belief
about American slavery; emphasizes the active role blacks played in establishing their cultural independence and in establishing relationships to
slaveholders.

————. *The World the Slaveholders Made: Two Essays in Interpretation.*
New York: Pantheon, 1969. These essays provide more of the author's
provocative, Marxist interpretations of Southern society.

Gossett, Thomas F. *Race: The History of an Idea in America.* New York:
Schocken, 1965.* A broad survey of the scientific and social influences on
the development of race theories and their application in America.

Greene, Lorenzo J. *The Negro in Colonial New England.* New York: Athe-
neum, 1968.* First published in 1942, this work focuses on slavery in New
England in the period 1620–1776 and suggests many contrasts with the
Southern institution.

Gutman, Herbert G. *The Black Family in Slavery and Freedom, 1750–1925*. New York: Random, 1977.* A thoroughly revised view of the black family, emphasizing its creative and adaptive capacity and its emergence from slavery as a powerful institution in black life.

Harlan, Louis R. *Booker T. Washington: The Making of a Black Leader, 1856–1901*. New York: Oxford University Press, 1975.* Volume I of a biography of this powerful black educator, essayist, and nationally recognized spokesman who preached accommodation to the white South while privately supporting attacks on the American racial system.

Jackson, Luther P. *Free Negro Labor and Property Holding in Virginia, 1830–1860*. New York: Atheneum, 1971.* Originally published in 1942, it endures as an important state study of the free black.

Jordan, Winthrop D. *White Over Black: American Attitudes toward the Negro, 1550–1812*. New York: Norton, 1977.* The classic study of the origin of American racial attitudes that includes enormous detail on religious, scientific, political, and sexual manifestations in American thought.

Lane, Ann J., ed. *The Debate Over Slavery: Stanley Elkins and His Critics*. Urbana: University of Illinois Press, 1971.* Includes several interesting essays that respond to Elkins' controversial thesis on the effect of slavery on slave personality.

Meier, August. *Negro Thought in America, 1880–1915: Racial Ideologies in the Age of Booker T. Washington*. Ann Arbor: University of Michigan Press, 1966.* A work that focuses on Negro community institutions in this period and the contrasting ideologies of Booker T. Washington and W.E.B. DuBois.

Meier, August and Elliott Rudwick. *From Plantation to Ghetto*. 3rd edition. New York: Hill and Wang, 1976.* A general history that concentrates on 19th- and 20th-century black activity; includes an excellent bibliography.

Meier, August and Elliott Rudwick, eds. *The Making of Black America*. New York: Atheneum, 1969.* A two-volume collection of essays in the fields of history, sociology, and political science that deals with black activism from colonial times to the modern civil rights movement.

Mullin, Gerald W. *Flight and Rebellion: Slave Resistance in 18th Century Virginia*. New York: Oxford University Press, 1974.* An analysis of slave rebelliousness as affected by such variables as the degree of cultural assimilation and type of work performed.

Osofsky, Gilbert. *Harlem: The Making of a Ghetto, 1890–1930*. New York: Harper and Row, 1966.* Examines the transformation of New York's Harlem area into America's largest black community.

Osofsky, Gilbert, ed. *Puttin' On Ole Massa*. New York: Harper and Row, 1969.* Contains the slave narratives of Henry Bibb, William Wells Brown, and Solomon Northrup and an essay on the significance of this type of historical resource.

Phillips, Ulrich B. *American Negro Slavery*. Baton Rouge: Louisiana State University, 1967.* Published in 1918, this sympathetic view of slavery argues the innate inferiority of Negroes and the benefit of the system to both races; reaction to Phillips over the past several decades has served as a remarkable stimulus to the serious study of slavery.

Quarles, Benjamin. *Black Abolitionists*. New York: Oxford University Press, 1969.* A study of the role of blacks in publicly attacking slavery; includes a discussion of black political participation and the self-improvement efforts that paralleled this activity.

————. *Frederick Douglass*. New York: Atheneum, 1968.* Written in 1948, this endures as an important work on this intriguing figure who made such an enormous contribution to the understanding of American race history.

Rose, Willie Lee. *Rehearsal for Reconstruction: The Port Royal Experiment*. New York: Oxford University Press, 1976.* A study of the Sea Island Negroes of South Carolina during the Civil War and the efforts of Northerners that anticipated the activities of the Reconstruction era.

Rudwick, Elliott. *Race Riot at East St. Louis, July 2, 1917*. New York: Atheneum, 1972.* Examines the dynamics of this vicious episode, including the competition for jobs between blacks and whites that kindled the conflagration; the effect of the white press; and the complicity of state and local authorities.

————. *W.E.B. DuBois: Propagandist of the Negro Protest*. New York: Atheneum, 1968.* Concentrates on DuBois' role in founding and promoting the N.A.A.C.P., concluding with his controversial exit from the organization in 1934.

Stampp, Kenneth. *The Era of Reconstruction, 1865–1877*. New York: Vintage, 1965.* Dismantles many long-held myths of those years while analyzing the failure of Reconstruction.

Stanton, William. *The Leopard's Spots: Scientific Attitudes toward Race in America, 1815–59*. Chicago: University of Chicago Press, 1966.* Examines the development of the scientific basis of 19th-century race prejudice while focusing on the activity of the American school of anthropology dominated by Samuel Morton, Josiah Nott, and George Gliddon.

Starobin, Robert S. *Industrial Slavery in the Old South*. New York: Oxford University Press, 1971.* The major contribution of this work is that it studies not plantation slavery, but the use of slaves in Southern industry from 1790 to 1861.

Tuttle, William M., Jr. *Race Riot: Chicago in the Red Summer of 1919*. New York: Atheneum, 1970.* Documents race relations in Chicago at the end of World War I, particularly the labor conflict that caused the riot.

Wade, Richard. *Slavery in the Cities: The South, 1820–1860*. New York: Oxford University Press, 1967.* Contrasts urban with rural slavery in terms of institutional life, living arrangements, work habits, and factors that caused its decline prior to the Civil War.

Wharton, Vernon L. *The Negro in Mississippi, 1865–1890*. New York: Harper and Row, 1965.* First published in 1947, this is an important state study of the effect of the new social order on the freed black.

Wood, Peter H. *Black Majority: Negroes in Colonial South Carolina from 1670 through the Stono Rebellion*. New York: Norton, 1975.* Covers the years 1670 to 1740, emphasizing the development of the unique Afro-American culture of the slaves who played an active role in shaping that frontier society.

Architectural History in the United States: A Bibliographical Essay

CARL W. CONDIT

☐The study of American architecture would appear to be flourishing if one measures activity and production in quantitative terms and, to a considerable extent, in qualitative as well. Historiography and aesthetic theory have been long established, the antecedents going back to the many Renaissance treatises on architecture, and if the art has yet to be given its *Poetics*, the principles of its historical study have been well conceptualized and fruitfully applied to the problems of the discipline. The systematic study of architectural history in the United States arose in the late nineteenth century, probably beginning with Russell Sturgis's *European Architecture* (1896), but it was not until World War I that an overdue appreciation of the American tradition first engaged the attention of serious scholars. Fiske Kimball's *Thomas Jefferson, Architect* (1916) is probably the most important of the pioneer works. The absence of general histories during the following years meant that Lewis Mumford's *Sticks and Stones* (1924), a highly individualistic and most unacademic interpretive essay, could seem like a wholly novel book. There is no question that it proved illuminating in its searching evaluations, but after the passage of fifty years the student might raise questions about the validity of the author's viewpoint, or at least about the timing of its launching in the newborn study of architectural development in the United States.

Mumford was strongly critical of the revivalistic architecture of the nineteenth century, especially the Roman and Renaissance manifestations of the *fin de siecle*. As a consequence, *Sticks and Stones* turned out to be the unintended forerunner of a myopia that afflicted much of the study of architectural history until recent years. The dogmas of the Bauhaus became the criteria of judgment, so that the architecture of more than a century was often divided into two bodies labeled bad and good, depending, respectively, on whether there were elements of past styles in formal design or whether such design arose from the blind ignorance of history demanded by the gospel according to Walter Gropius.

Comprehensive historical scholarship of a quality worthy of its subject came in the 1920s with Fiske Kimball's *Domestic Architecture of the American Colonies* (1922) and his *American Architecture* (1928); and although the later volume is now regarded as having been superseded by more recent works, I will raise questions about the validity of this relegation in more detailed discussion of particular books. Architectural history in the United States did not reach the status of a separate university discipline on a par with other areas of history and the humanities until the establishment of the Society of Architectural Historians and its associated journal in 1941. With the end of World War II, meetings, courses, papers, books, awards, and controversies began to multiply, so that the bibliography of the subject now threatens to overwhelm the general history of the visual arts, of which it was always regarded a part.

The numerous works that pour out year by year may be classified into three im-

Carl W. Condit has taught at Northwestern University since 1945, where he is presently Professor of History, Art History and Urban Affairs. He has been a Research Associate at the Smithsonian Institution, and the recipient of the Abbot Payson Usher Prize of the Society for History and Technology, and the History and Heritage Award from the American Society of Civil Engineering. His publications include American Building Art: The Nineteenth Century *(1960);* American Building Art: The Twentieth Century *(1961);* The Chicago School of Architecture *(1964);* American Building: Material and Techniques *(1968);* Chicago 1910–29: Building, Planning and Urban Technology *(1973);* Chicago 1930–1970: Building, Planning and Urban Technology *(1974); and* The Railroad and the City: A Technological and Urbanistic History of Cincinnati *(1977).*

precisely defined categories founded on the knowledge, experience, and standards of their various authors. At the lowest level lies a great multitude of generally expensive, richly illustrated books designed either for the coffee tables of living rooms or the reception desks of architectural offices. They are for the most part pictorial albums, often dignified with subtitles like "pictorial essay" or "pictorial history," and they are superficial, factually poverty stricken as well as inaccurate, and unmarked by analytical or critical insights. They may be quickly dismissed The second category is difficult to classify. It consists of books generally aimed at the practicing architect or planner—monographic in subject and sometimes highly technical in exposition—that usually present particular building types, like factories, or particular structural forms, like concrete shells or steel space frames. They ought properly to engage the attention of the historian, but their authors are usually innocent of historical training and viewpoint. The third group is composed of the genuinely historical works complete with comprehensive texts, adequate numbers of illustrations, properly documented sources in notes or bibliographies, and thoroughly detailed indexes. They vary greatly in quality and scope, but they aim to recover the past that it may inform the present (contrary to the ruling doctrine of the contemporary architectural profession), and the authors do not shrink from producing a text appropriate to the range and complexity of the facts.

The rapidly growing number of books that have been published since the founding of the SAH represent for the most part a high level of achievement, and the annual prizes and honors that have been awarded by official bodies constitute recognition of accomplishments that stand in the front rank of world scholarship. One has only to recall that the respective authors of the definitive work on Victorian architecture in England, the first thoroughgoing account of Imperial Roman architecture through the reign of Hadrian, and the comprehensive studies of much pre-Columbian building in Meso-American—to mention the works of a few scholars who are currently productive—are members of university faculties in the United States. As impressive as contemporary scholarship is, however, it nevertheless exhibits certain unsatisfactory features to one who reflects on the whole body of work.

To begin with, the old dichotomy between the fine and the useful arts, a doctrine advanced largely by German theorists in the last century, continues to mark the academic study of architectural evolution. Most articles and books tend to emphasize matters of style in its traditional sense, stylistic provenance, documents, and formal details, so that the *Journal of the Society of Architectural Historians* holds limited interest for industrial archeologists and historians of technology—that is, for persons concerned with the fabric of building in its material and working character. Since architecture is the most highly technical of the symbolic arts, and since the process of building covers a wide range of creative activities, historians eventually arose who sought to redress this imbalance by examining the structural aspects of the art. The authors of the great source documents in architectural theory, most notably Vitruvius and Palladio, were as much concerned with technique as with form, and both have always been proper subjects of scholarly investigation. But the study of architectural technology, unfortunately, has tended to be as specialized as the traditional formal study.

A more serious weakness of the discipline is the extremely uneven historical treatment of the country's various geographical or political regions and the various kinds of structures that make up our building environment. Indeed, it may be said that the corpus of American architecture to a great extent lies unrecorded and undescribed in any historical account. Chicago is the only city in the nation the architecture, planning, and urban technology of which have been subjected to adequately detailed investigation. New York, on the other hand, ought to be the scandal of the profession. The leading city of the country, the only one which exhibits the entire building development of post-Renaissance urbanism, the site of the only electrified rail terminals in America and the largest of their kind in the world—this supreme concentration of modern structural art has been presented to us in pocket guides and coffee-table books composed of exterior photographs without text, plans, details, or structural characteristics. In the same way, there are no books that treat the total architectural development of Boston, Washington, New Orleans, and San Francisco, to name the cities that most deserve the attention of historians. A beginning has been made in the case of Philadelphia, as I shall note later, but it is not a true historical analysis.

As scandalous as the failure to show proper concern for New York is the absence of a comprehensive work on the architecture of the state capitols. The great majority were built in the middle or late nineteenth century; most were derived in varying degrees from the Capitol in Washington, but they are architectural and structural masterpieces in their own right.* The architecture of rural America, vernacular as well as consciously designed, needs to be examined in an analytical way, not in the simple-minded terms of the state guides. A particular manifestation of rural architecture that has been almost totally neglected is the great body of county court houses in the small towns. They range from the whimsical and the untutored romantic (the one in Wellington, Ohio, for example, was done in the "Ottoman" style) to carefully designed revivalistic works often produced by strongly individualist local talents. At the other end of the scale is the skyscraper, known throughout the world as the distinctive American contribution to modern architecture, but only its Chicago phase has been adequately studied. This particular hiatus exists, of course, because the architecture of New York still awaits its historian. The architectural and engineering design of the American railroad terminal reached a level in the early twentieth century that compelled the attention of European architects, but no study has yet appeared that is concentrated on the stations of the United States. The list of omissions could easily be extended; I have emphasized what seem to be the most glaring cases.

There are reasons for this state of affairs beyond the personal tastes of those who labor in the vineyard. Architecture, for all the attention it has attracted in recent years, is not a popular art, as music, drama, movies, and even ballet are popular arts. Unlike the performing arts, all architecture is static, yet the complex forms cannot be readily grasped by passive visual examination. It is technical and mathematical in its structure, its materials, their interaction, and even in its visible form. Students drawn from the humanities often find the action of vaults and domes incomprehensible, while those with the requisite technological training may be artistically illiterate. The sensitive reader can be taught to grasp readily enough the symbolic role of literary imagery, but architectural symbolism is so recondite as to lead to controversy among the ablest theorists, to say nothing of

* Professor Condit has noted that since the submission of his essay has appeared *Temples of Democracy: The State Capitols of the U.S.A.*, by Henry-Russell Hitchcock and William Seale.

gross confusion among practicing architects and their celebrators. Moreover, most architecture exists in an urban milieu, and its function is intimately bound up with the social, economic, material, and engineering complexities of the city, and with the visual complexities out of which the city dweller tries to form coherent and meaningful images of his surroundings. The sheer magnitude of the modern city, the sheer multiplicity and diversity of modern buildings render the traditional academic specializations increasingly fragmentary and ultimately misleading before the reality of the contemporary urban experience.

I will explore these broad reflections further in terms of individual works. In order to make an extensive and multi-dimensional bibliography manageable, I have divided it into the following categories: general works, that is, those covering the entire domain of American architecture; equivalent works treating structural form, action, and materials; works dealing with particular historical periods; those concerned with geographical regions; monographic treatises and biographies; journals and reference works.

General Works

If anyone may be said to have founded American architectural history and taken a major hand in bringing it to maturity, the choice would very likely be Fiske Kimball, although one may argue that Lewis Mumford played a role in the process with his *Sticks and Stones* of 1924. Kimball's *Thomas Jefferson, Architect* (1916) and *Domestic Architecture of the American Colonies* (1922) constitute the initial steps (both are discussed further under Monographs and Historical Periods, respectively), while his comprehensive *American Architecture* (1928), which superseded the earlier and weaker books by Talbot Hamlin and Thomas E. Tallmadge, laid down the general principles that most architectural historians have followed ever since. His was the traditional art-historical approach, with its emphasis on plan, style, aesthetic form, and ornamental details, and it has been followed through the years, as the articles in the *Journal of the SAH* regularly indicate. One might suppose that Kimball's book would have been superseded by Burchard and Bush-Brown's *The Architecture of America: A Social and Cultural History* (1961), but except for buildings erected since 1928, that is most emphatically not the case. The authors, established scholars in the field, chose to treat American architecture as an aspect of the nation's social and cultural history, and while that treatment is illuminating in its way, the presentation of architecture *per se* is unsatisfactory because of the poverty of concrete detail.

Superior works by virtue of their steady focus on the building arts are the two books by James M. Fitch, *American Building: The Historical Forces That Shaped It* (1966) and *American Building: The Environmental Forces That Shape It* (1972). The first is an admirable interpretive and analytical treatise on the stylistic, structural, intellectual, and social factors that have determined over the years the functional and aesthetic character of architecturally designed buildings. The second volume is unique: it represents the pioneer attempt to treat building as a mediating device, like clothing, between the naked human being and an often hostile nature. The result is virtually a physiological examination of modern building, done in both descriptive and prescriptive terms. Fitch is the most effective writer among architectural historians; he commands a vigorous and literate style that makes all the more prominent the tedious character of most architectural writing.

Vincent Scully's *American Architecture and Urbanism* (1969) suggests by its title the long overdue history of building in relation to its urban milieu. The book is in this respect, however, a disappointment, even though the author carries his starting point back to our native pre-Columbian cultures. Scully is an imaginative historian whose works often reveal insights that escape the more tradition-bound scholar. *American Architecture* is rich in such insights, but the dominant tone is that of a dazzling stylistic performance in the Ruskinian manner that relies excessively on personal interpretation and too little on the details of the working urban fabric. A minor earlier work that aims to relate expensive architecture to great wealth is Wayne Andrews's *Architecture, Ambition and Americans* (1955). It is another interpretive essay claimed by its author to be social history, but it was more accurately labeled by Vincent Scully as "socialite history." All the foregoing works contain bibliographies, bibliographical essays, or bibliographical notes. Scully's essay at the conclusion of *American Architecture* is easily the best.

Structural History

The only books in which the author has attempted a complete and unified account of structural development are those by Carl W. Condit, the two-volume *American Building Art* (1960, 1961) and *American Building: Materials and Techniques* (1968). They are pioneer attempts to treat building forms as part of the history of technology. The first, on the structural techniques of the nineteenth century, is weakened by errors, omissions, and an inadequate bibliography, especially of primary sources. The second, restricted to the twentieth century, is relatively free of errors and includes a comprehensive bibliography. The third represents a condensation, extension, correction, and revision of the earlier two, the chief improvement being the inclusion of an appropriately detailed discussion of colonial building techniques.

Certain works of civil engineering have either been regarded as quasi-architectural in character or have in the twentieth century been treated in part as objects of architectural design. Bridges have always had the status of formal architecture chiefly because of the enormous influence of the Roman tradition, which has extended virtually without break to our own day. The only general treatise that does some justice to the American achievement is David B. Steinman and Sara Ruth Watson's *Bridges and Their Builders* (1957), but in truth the reader will find more on the subject in the appropriate chapters of Condit's volumes. Steinman is particularly good on suspension bridges, having made a special study of the Roeblings, and on works from his own hand, the inordinate number of which were included because Steinman was the Frank Lloyd Wright of bridge engineers by virtue of his pathological egotism. A modest though well-informed interpretive essay concerned with aesthetic rather than structural character is Elizabeth Mock's *The Architecture of Bridges* (1949). Both the Steinman and Mock volumes suffer from the absence of bibliographies, which is unforgivable in the case of the former. A sumptuous volume focused on the American achievement is David Plowden's *Bridges: The Spans of North America* (1974). It is a big, expensive book devoted mainly to presenting the best bridge photography I have seen (mostly Plowden's own work), but this distinction is offset by serious weaknesses. The author is not at home in structural theory and evolution, so that his text is predominantly biographical and marked by a steady flow of errors. He seems not to understand the distinction between simple and continuous trusses, and thus mistakenly identifies the Southern Pacific's Pecos River bridge, the most elegant truss span in the nation, as composed of simple trusses when it is in fact continuous.

Following the establishment of the Tennessee Valley Authority in 1933, the structures of waterway control have been regarded as objects of architectural as well as engineering concern. The architects of the first group of TVA's hydroelectric installations (1933–45) not only raised the design of industrial

Courtesy, Historic American Building Survey

At the time of its completion in 1889, the Chicago Auditorium Building was the largest and most complex building in America. Dankmar Adler and Louis Sullivan designed this monument of 19th-century architecture.

building to its highest aesthetic level, but also introduced the important concept of total design. No single book remotely approaches an adequate treatment of this complex subject. Perhaps John H. Kyle's *The Building of TVA* (1958) is less unsatisfactory than others. It is well illustrated but with much too brief an introductory text. The equivalent book for the Bureau of Reclamation is *Dams and Control Works* (1938), a collection of technical monographs on the chief projects that were written for the trained engineer. There have been several revisions in recent years. The bibliographies in both books are inadequate, and the reader might find the appropriate chapter in Condit's *American Building Art: The*

Twentieth Century a more useful preliminary guide. For the serious student of the history of structural technology who is untrained in its rudiments, a readable, non-mathematical introduction to the relevant theory is Salvadori and Heller's *Structure in Architecture* (1963).

Historical Periods

Since academic historians always tend toward specialization, monographic works and those restricted to well–defined periods and regions far outnumber the more comprehensive variety. On the building arts of the American Indian, Lewis Morgan's *Houses and House–Life of the American Aborigines* (1881) is a classic. The results of his investigations will never be superseded because he was probably the last anthropologist able to observe at first hand the structures and modes of life of the native cultures. The authors of later works have concentrated chiefly on the building arts of Southwestern peoples, and they have produced a number of books of which the fundamental text is very likely George A. Kubler's *The Art and Architecture of Ancient America* (1962).

Colonial building attracted the attention of historians long before the architecture of the Republic was regarded as the proper subject of scholarly concern. Fiske Kimball was the pioneer, and his *Domestic Architecture of the American Colonies and of the Early Republic* (1922) remains in many ways a fundamental text. Talbot Hamlin, a distinguished historian in his own right, called it "a work of profound and accurate scholarship; remarkable both in its scope and its . . . precision." (*Greek Revival Architecture in America,* p. 384.) Harold R. Shurtleff's *The Log Cabin Myth* (1939), in spite of its narrowly focused title, is an original work on the building techniques of the Colonies. To a considerable extent it provided the basis for the structural descriptions of Hugh Morrison's *Early American Architecture from the First Colonial Settlements to the National Period* (1952), a comprehensive treatment which is at present the authoritative work on the first two centuries of American building. It includes extensive bibliographical notes. For the various political, social, and artistic periods that characterize the two centuries of our national history, there is only a single work of distinguished scholarship, a state of affairs for which the entire profession ought to be ashamed. Talbot Hamlin's *Greek Revival Architecture in America* (1944) is a first-rate example of traditional architectural history in its sure grasp of the subject, its thoroughness, its bibliographical material, and its illustrations. Interpretive essays on various phases of American architecture and urbanism in the nineteenth century were contributed by four well-known historians (Fein, Hitchcock, Scully, and Weisman) to *The Rise of an American Architecture* (1970), edited by Edgar Kaufmann, Jr.

When we survey the literature of the late nineteenth and twentieth century we come to another long hiatus in the history of building in the United States. Except for scattered monographs and the extensive literature on Chicago, there is little more than a few guides, catalogues, and pictorial albums on the immensely creative and protean age extending from the Civil War to the triumph of the modern style following the second World War. An early history of the skyscraper that needs to be corrected and updated is Francisco Mujica's *History of the Skyscraper* (1930). A voluminously illustrated survey, rich with quantitative data, of the many buildings and other structures erected under the public works programs of the New Deal is C. W. Short and R. Stanley-Brown's *Public Buildings* (1939). Again, except for regional and monographic works, the rise and spread of the modern style is treated only in two slim catalogues of the Museum of Modern Art, *Built in USA: 1932–1944* (1944) and *Built in USA: Post-War Architecture* (1952). The prime source document on the functional, aesthetic, and social theory of modern architecture is Louis Sullivan's *Kindergarten Chats,* originally written in 1901–02 but available with various shorter writings in an anthology of 1947. Sullivan's theories were also developed in his *Autobiography of an Idea* (1926) and in various articles collected by Maurice English in *The Testament of Stone* (1963).

Regional Works

No geographical segment of American architecture has been more thoroughly documented than that of Chicago and its tributary region. Frank A. Randall's *History of . . . Building Construction in Chicago* (1949), a handbook unique to the discipline of architectural and urban history, surveys the entire structural development of Chicago's core building by building, giving the name of the building, address, architect (if any), engineer (if a separate designer), height, mode of construction, and type of foundation. A general photographic essay on the architecture of the region is Wayne Andrews's *Architecture in Chicago and Mid-America* (1968). Detailed works dealing at length with the city's extraordinary achievement in architecture, planning, and urban technology through the successive phases of its history are the following: Thomas E. Tallmadge, *Architecture in Old Chicago* (1941), covering the period from the founding of the city to 1893; C. W. Condit, *The Chicago School of Architecture* (1964), concentrating on the early development of a modern urban architecture chiefly in the years 1885 to 1910; H. Allen Brooks, *The Prairie School* (1972), an examination primarily of the residential work of the later Chicago movement of which Wright was for a time the central figure; Condit, *Chicago, 1910–70: Building, Planning, and Urban Technology* (2 vols., 1973, 1974), books aimed at presenting the entire technological, designing, and planning basis of modern community existence. Hugh Duncan's *Culture and Democracy* (1965) is a confused and overblown social history derived about equally from George Herbert Mead and Louis Sullivan that describes the interaction of society and architecture in the Middle West during the life of the architect (1856–1924). Nearly half the book is taken directly from Sullivan without benefit of quotation marks.

For the time being the student of New York architecture must content himself with a series of picture-books: another of Wayne Andrews's photographic excursions, *Architecture in New York* (1969); a survey of officially designated landmarks, Alan Burnham's *New York Landmarks* (1963); a similar work compiled by the New York Community Trust, *The Heritage of New York* (1970); Nathan Silver's melancholy survey of vanished glories, *Lost New York* (1967); and Cervin Robinson and Rosemarie Bletter's *Skyscraper Style: Art Deco in New York* (1975), confined to ornamental features and hence a rather thin book on a great architectural development. Ada Louise Huxtable's *The Architecture of New York* (1964) is considerably better than the foregoing for its historical narrative, but the single volume so far issued in a planned series is subtitled *Classic New*

York and is thus confined to colonial and early Republican architecture. The best that can be said for these books is that they identify for the student a few buildings that need to be considered in a serious historical investigation.

Other cities and states have fared better. Rhode Island aroused the interest of leading scholars. Henry-Russell Hitchcock's *Rhode Island Architecture* (1939) was at the time of its preparation the first architectural survey of an entire state, and it remains an excellent example of representative selectivity for three centuries of building. More concentrated, more thorough, and more truly historiographic is Antoinette F. Downing and Vincent Scully's *The Architectural Heritage of Newport, Rhode Island, 1640–1915* (1952). Other pioneers in uncovering the architectural heritage of various regions are Beatrice Ravenel, in *The Architects of Charleston* (1945), and Henry C. Forman, in *The Architecture of the Old South* (1948). Similar works of uneven quality have followed in recent years on the architecture of Philadelphia, Washington (confined mainly to buildings of the nineteenth century), St. Augustine, Detroit, Indianapolis, and the states of Hawaii, Ohio, and Texas (see the bibliography at the end of this essay for individual titles). Of these I would select three for particular comment. George B. Tatum's *Penn's Great Town* (1961) is the best for its dense factual detail, but it offers the reader a series of discrete buildings rather than a continuous history. Albert Manucy's *The Houses of St. Augustine* (1962) is a little prize, a thorough analysis of the structural and formal character of early residential work. W. Hawkins Ferry's *The Buildings of Detroit* (1968) is the most ambitious of the urban studies and a model for cities that are not architecturally in the front rank. In addition to the above there are currently in print 34 separate guides covering the architecture of 24 different cities and states, prepared by many different individuals and organizations, all of which are available from the office of the Society of Architectural Historians.

Monographs

Monographic literature, like that on historical periods and regions, is highly uneven in quality. The concentration of works on Richardson and the leaders of the Chicago movement reveals not only the compelling attraction that the city has exercized, but also the influence of modernistic theories on architectural history and journalism. Long before Chicago was discovered by historians, the Eastern architects engaged the attention of monographers. Mariana Van Rensselaer was the first in the field with her handsomely illustrated volume, *Henry Hobson Richardson and His Works* (1888), which rested on a direct acquaintance with the man and his office. One of the most sumptuous volumes devoted to the designs of a single architectural office is *A Monograph of the Works of McKim, Mead and White, 1879–1915* (1915), a collaborative product of the office staff itself. The reprinting of this work with a long overdue appraisal by Leland Roth (see bibliography) reminds us again of how much the other New York architects need a similar re-examination. We are still waiting for monographs on Cass Gilbert, Carrère and Hastings, George B. Post, and Warren and Wetmore, to name a few New York architects who changed the skyline of America. Earlier figures who helped to shape a national architecture have received more scholarly attention than the New Yorkers: Jefferson, in Fiske Kimball's pioneer study, *Thomas Jefferson, Ar-*

chitect (1916), and Strickland, a great constructive architect of the Greek Revival, in Agnes Gilchrist's *William Strickland, Architect and Engineer* (1950).

The first book to treat any architect of the Chicago movement is Hugh Morrison's *Louis Sullivan, Prophet of Modern Architecture* (1935), which appeared six years before anyone other than the Chicago participants themselves were aware of the city's immense accomplishment. Since Sullivan was profoundly influenced by Richardson, it seemed appropriate, though it was fortuitous, that Henry-Russell Hitchcock's *The Architecture of H. H. Richardson and His Times* (1936) should appear in the following year. And it was the indefatigable Hitchcock again who produced the first American book on Wright, *In the Nature of Materials: The Buildings of Frank Lloyd Wright, 1887–1941* (1942), not quite definitive up to its time but close to it for an entirely original work. Commissions of Wright's Chicago period that escaped Hitchcock may be found in Grant C. Manson's *Frank Lloyd Wright to 1910* (1958), the last work

Courtesy, Historic American Building Survey

The Reliance Building combined the utilitarian, steel-framed construction of the early Chicago "skyscrapers" with the innovative use of a glass and glazed terra cotta exterior. This building was designed by John Root and Daniel Burnham, and completed in 1895.

to be published within the architect's 92-year life. The most convenient anthologies of Wright's numerous writings were both edited by Frederick Gutheim: *Frank Lloyd Wright: Selected Writings, 1894–1940* (1941), and *In the Cause of Architecture: . . . Essays for Architectural Record, 1908–1952* (1976).

John Wellborn Root had long ago been the subject of an idolatrous biography by his sister-in-law, Harriet Monroe, but a comprehensive critical examination of his work came only with Donald Hoffmann's *The Architecture of John Wellborn Root* (1973). Root's partner and the greatest single figure in the history of urban planning in the United States, Daniel Burnham, finally received the biographical and critical treatment he deserved in Thomas Hines's *Burnham of Chicago* (1974), which wholly supersedes Charles Moore's rather simple-minded biography of 1921, except for the letters in the earlier work. Mies van der Rohe, a latter-day Chicagoan by adoption, has been the subject of three monographs (see bibliography), which more than anything else remind us that an adequate study of this influential architect still lies in the future.

Special types of buildings, some of which do not fit the traditional categories of high design, and which in the nineteenth and early twentieth century would not even have been regarded as architecture, have lately become matters of scholarly inquiry. Industrial architecture is a product of the vernacular and utilitarian building of the previous century, and because of the affinities between this tradition and the modern movement, architects, critics, and historians have paid increasing attention to industrial construction. The most thorough work, carefully done in the analytical spirit, is Grant Hildebrand's *Designing for Industry: The Architecture of Albert Kahn* (1974). The book was particularly welcome because Kahn's work formed the greatest single influence on the design of contemporary industrial buildings.

The railroad station belongs to a special category of the structural complex, in which sophisticated architectural design meets equally high levels of civil, mechanical, and electrical engineering. In spite of a brave beginning, the comprehensive work on the American development has yet to appear. Carroll Meeks's *The Railroad Station: An Architectural History* (1956) is a broad survey that covers Europe as well as North America, but as the subtitle indicates, the author is concerned with planning, style, and formal design, little with engineering features. Very nearly the opposite characterization would apply to John Droege's *Passenger Terminals and Trains* (1916), which is as much concerned with operations, track layouts, signal and interlocking systems, coach yards, and maintenance equipment as with the design of station buildings. Both the Meeks and Droege volumes are well illustrated, but only Meeks includes a bibliography. The railroad passenger car is a social institution as well as an architectural and engineering work, and perhaps ought to receive more attention from cultural historians than it has. Two volumes from the same hand, Arthur Dubin's *Some Classic Trains* (1964) and *More Classic Trains* (1974), are pictorial albums with much historical data that may serve as a beginning. They are probably the most lavishly illustrated books ever published, with a total of 2,800 plates in the two volumes.

Periodicals and Reference Works

The only periodical devoted exclusively to articles in the history of architecture is the *Journal of the Society of Architectural Historians,* a distinguished example of the learned press that has been published continuously since 1941. *Technology and Culture,* founded in 1959, has published articles in the history of structural technology, but building history represents only a small fraction of its contents. For primary sources (other than original drawings and the buildings themselves) one must turn to the professional architectural journals, most of which were founded in the late nineteenth century. Among those providing the most extensive coverage of the building scene, the following have suspended publication: *American Architect and Building News, Architectural Forum, Architecture,* and *Pencil Points* (superseded by *Progressive Architecture*). Those that continue today are *Architectural Record* (for long the most authoritative in the field), *Progressive Architecture,* and *Inland Architect.* The last is now a regional journal based in Chicago that is more interpretive and critical than strictly presentational. The leading journals of the construction industry since 1874 have been *Engineering News-Record* and its predecessors, *Engineering News* and *Engineering Record.* The full understanding of their articles requires familiarity with the rudiments of structural theory, but they are virtually the records of a civilization, indispensable to serious historical inquiry into the material and technological basis of social life. A less technical periodical for the construction of large-scale works is *Civil Engineering,* a poor man's version of the formidable *Proceedings of the American Society of Civil Engineers.* Many magazines devoted to inventions in the building and mechanical arts have come and gone since the early nineteenth century; a convenient list of the better known may be found in the bibliography of Condit's *American Building Art: The Nineteenth Century* (pp. 350–351).

The railroad so powerfully shaped the entire range of building up to 1920 that the leading journals of the industry are important for source materials. Those that are no longer published are the *American Railroad Journal* (the oldest in the field, founded in 1832), *Railroad Gazette,* and *Railway Review. Railway Age,* first issued in 1856, is still in existence, though much reduced in content from what it once was.

Reference works in architectural and structural history are few in number, limited in use, and sometimes marked by weaknesses that may mislead as much as guide. The one indispensable tool, valuable above all others, is the voluminous collection of drawings produced, assembled, organized, and preserved by the Historic American Building Survey, founded in 1935 and slowly expanded to cover all the regions of the country. The drawings have been prepared either by professional architects or by trained apprentices working under them, and they are close in quality to the working drawings produced in any architectural office. The chief repository is the Library of Congress, but copies of many are available in the leading architectural libraries. A similar collection of drawings for civil engineering works is now being created by the Historic American Engineering Record. A valuable microfilm record of original Chicago drawings is preserved in the Burnham Library of the Chicago Art Institute, and a large photographic collection has been accumulated over many years by the Avery Library of Columbia University. Other illustrative and written documents may be found in the archives of state and municipal historical societies, as well as the municipal reference libraries of the larger cities.

Among reference books the *Biographical Dictionary of American Architects* (1956), by Henry F. and Elsie R. Withey, is a useful compendium in some places but marked by omissions in others. More thorough in individual articles and more accurate than the Withey volume is the *Biographical Dictionary of American Civil Engineers* (1972), a collaborative work sponsored by the American Society of Civil Engineers. Eugene S. Ferguson's *Bibliography of the History of Technology* (1968) includes a section on civil engineering, and other titles useful to the architectural historian are scattered through the pages. A non-historical though nonetheless valuable reference tool is Caleb Hornbostel's *Materials for Architecture* (1961), an encyclopedic work with abundant empirical detail on physical properties, chemical constituents, appropriate uses, and the like. It was compiled for practicing architects but is valuable for historians concerned with the material and structural basis of building.

The history of American architecture, as I have repeatedly suggested in this essay, contains many gaps; the relevant documents are extensive in quantity and for the most part easily accessible, so that the historian can complain neither of a want of materials nor of scope for his talents.□

BIBLIOGRAPHICAL SUMMARY

General Works
* Andrews, Wayne. *Architecture, Ambition and Americans*. New York: Harper and Brothers, 1955.
* Burchard, John, and Bush-Brown, Albert. *The Architecture of America: A Social and Cultural History*. Boston: Little, Brown and Company, 1961.
* Fitch, James M. *American Building: The Environmental Forces That Shape It*. Boston: Houghton, Mifflin, 1972.
* Fitch, James M. *American Building: The Historical Forces That Shaped It*. Boston: Houghton, Mifflin, 1966.
  Kimball, Fiske. *American Architecture*. Indianapolis: Bobbs Merrill, 1928.
* Mumford, Lewis. *Sticks and Stones*. New York: Horace Liveright, 1924.
* Scully, Vincent. *American Architecture and Urbanism*. New York: Frederick A. Praeger, 1969.

Works on Structural History
Condit, Carl W. *American Building Art: The Nineteenth Century*. New York: Oxford University Press, 1960.
Condit, Carl W. *American Building Art: The Twentieth Century*. New York: Oxford University Press, 1961.
* Condit, Carl W. *American Building: Materials and Techniques*. Chicago: University of Chicago Press, 1968.
Kyle, John H. *The Building of TVA*. Baton Rouge: Louisiana State University Press, 1958.
Mock, Elizabeth B. *The Architecture of Bridges*. New York: Museum of Modern Art, 1949.
Plowden, David. *Bridges: The Spans of North America*. New York: Viking Press, 1974.
Steinman, David B. *The Builders of the Bridge*. New York: Harcourt, Brace and Company, 1945.
Steinman, David B., and Watson, Sara Ruth. *Bridges and Their Builders*. New York: Dover Press, 1957.
Trachtenberg, Alan. *Brooklyn Bridge, Fact and Symbol*. New York: Oxford University Press, 1965.
United States Department of the Interior, Bureau of Reclamation. *Dams and Control Works*. 3rd edition. Washington: Government Printing Office, 1954.

Works on Historical Periods
Burg, David F. *Chicago's White City of 1893*. Lexington: University Press of Kentucky, 1976.

*Hamlin, Talbot. *Greek Revival Architecture in America.* New York: Oxford University Press, 1944.

Hitchcock, Henry-Russell, and Drexler, Arthur, eds. *Built in USA: Post-War Architecture.* New York: Museum of Modern Art, 1952.

Isham, Norman M. *Early American Houses.* Boston: Walpole Society, 1928.

Kaufmann, Edgar, Jr., ed. *The Rise of an American Architecture.* New York: Frederick A. Praeger, 1970.

*Kidney, Walter C. *The Architecture of Choice: Eclecticism in America, 1880–1930.* New York: George Braziller, 1974.

*Kimball, Fiske. *Domestic Architecture of the American Colonies and of the Early Republic.* New York: Charles Scribners' Sons, 1922.

Kubler, George A. *The Art and Architecture of Ancient America.* Baltimore: Penguin Books, 1962.

Mock, Elizabeth, ed. *Built in USA, 1932–1944.* New York: Museum of Modern Art, 1944.

*Morgan, Lewis H. *Houses and House-Life of the American Aborigines.* Chicago: University of Chicago Press, reprint, 1965.

Morrison, Hugh. *Early American Architecture from the First Colonial Settlements to the National Period.* New York: Oxford University Press, 1952.

Mujica, Francisco. *A History of the Skyscraper.* New York: Archeology and Architecture Press, 1930.

Short, C. W., and Stanley-Brown, R. *Public Buildings.* Washington: Government Printing Office, 1939.

Shurtleff, Harold R. *The Log Cabin Myth.* Cambridge: Harvard University Press, 1939.

*Sullivan, Louis. *Kindergarten Chats and Other Writings.* New York: Wittenborn, Schultz, 1947.

Regional Works

*Andrews, Wayne. *Architecture in Chicago and Mid-America.* New York: Athenaeum, 1968.

*Andrews, Wayne. *Architecture in New York.* New York: Harper and Row, 1969.

Ball, Rick A., et al. *Indianapolis Architecture.* Indianapolis: Indiana Architectural Foundation, 1975.

Brooks, H. Allen. *The Prairie School: Frank Lloyd Wright and His Midwest Contemporaries.* Toronto: University of Toronto Press, 1972.

Burnham, Alan, ed. *New York Landmarks.* Middletown: Wesleyan University Press, 1963.

Campen, Richard N. *Ohio: An Architectural Portrait.* Chagrin Falls: West Summit Press, 1973.

Condit, Carl W. *Chicago, 1910–29: Building, Planning, and Urban Technology.* Chicago: University of Chicago Press, 1973.

Condit, Carl W. *Chicago, 1930–70: Building, Planning, and Urban Technology.* Chicago: University of Chicago Press, 1974.

*Condit, Carl W. *The Chicago School of Architecture.* Chicago: University of Chicago Press, 1964.

Downing, Antoinette F., and Scully, Vincent. *The Architectural Heritage of Newport, Rhode Island, 1640–1915.* Cambridge: Harvard University Press, 1952.

Duncan, Hugh. *Culture and Democracy.* Totowa, N.J.: Bedminster Press, 1965.

Ferry, W. Hawkins. *The Buildings of Detroit.* Detroit: Wayne State University Press, 1968.

Forman, Henry C. *The Architecture of the Old South: The Medieval Style.* Cambridge: Harvard University Press, 1948.

Hiroa, Te Rangi (Buck, Peter H.). *Arts and Crafts of Hawaii, II: Houses.* Honolulu: Bishop Museum Press, 1964.

* Hitchcock, Henry-Russell. *Rhode Island Architecture.* Providence: Rhode Island Museum Press, 1939; reprinted Cambridge: MIT Press, 1968.

Huxtable, Ada Louise. *The Architecture of New York: A History and Guide;* vol. I, *Classic New York.* New York: Anchor Books, 1964.

* Koeper, Frederick. *Illinois Architecture.* Chicago: University of Chicago Press, 1968.

Maddex, Diane. *Historic Buildings of Washington, D.C.* Pittsburgh: Ober Park Associates, 1973.

Manucy, Albert. *The Houses of St. Augustine, 1565–1821.* St. Augustine: St. Augustine Historical Society, 1962.

New York Community Trust. *The Heritage of New York.* New York: Fordham University Press, 1970.

Randall, Frank A. *History of the Development of Building Construction in Chicago.* Urbana: University of Illinois Press, 1949.

Ravenel, Beatrice St. Julien. *Architects of Charleston.* Charleston: Carolina Art Association, 1945.

Robinson, Cervin, and Bletter, Rosemarie. *Skyscraper Style: Art Deco in New York.* New York: Oxford University Press, 1975.

Robinson, William D., and Webb, Todd. *Texas Public Buildings of the Nineteenth Century.* Austin: University of Texas Press, 1974.

* Silver, Nathan. *Lost New York.* Boston: Houghton, Mifflin, 1967.

Tallmadge, Thomas E. *Architecture in Old Chicago.* Chicago: University of Chicago Press, 1941.

Tatum, George B. *Penn's Great Town.* Philadelphia: University of Pennsylvania Press, 1961.

Monographs

* Blaser, Werner. *Mies van der Rohe.* New York: Frederick A. Praeger, 1965.

* Bush-Brown, Albert. *Louis Sullivan.* New York: George Braziller, 1960.

Connely, Willard. *Louis Sullivan as He Lived.* New York: Horizon Press, 1960.

Current, Karen and William R. *Greene and Greene: Architects in the Residential Style.* Fort Worth: Amon Carter Museum, 1974.

Droege, John. *Passenger Terminals and Trains.* New York: McGraw-Hill, 1916; reprinted Milwaukee: Kalmbach Publishing Company, 1968.

Dubin, Arthur. *More Classic Trains.* Milwaukee: Kalmbach Publishing Company, 1974.

Dubin, Arthur. *Some Classic Trains.* Milwaukee: Kalmbach Publishing Company, 1964.

English, Maurice, ed. *The Testament of Stone: Themes of Idealism and Indignation from the Writings of Louis Sullivan.* Evanston: Northwestern University Press, 1963.

Gilchrist, Agnes. *William Strickland, Architect and Engineer.* Philadelphia: University of Pennsylvania Press, 1950.

Gutheim, Frederick, ed. *Frank Lloyd Wright: Selected Writings, 1894–1940.* New York: Duell, Sloan and Pearce, 1941.

Gutheim, Frederick, ed. *In the Cause of Architecture: Wright's   Essays for Architectural Record, 1908–1952.* New York: Architectural Record, 1976.

Hamlin, Talbot. *Benjamin Latrobe.* New York: Oxford University Press, 1955.

Hilberseimer, Ludwig. *Mies van der Rohe.* Chicago: Paul Theobald, 1956.

Hildebrand, Grant. *Designing for Industry: The Architecture of Albert Kahn.* Cambridge: MIT Press, 1974.

Hines, Thomas. *Burnham of Chicago.* New York: Oxford University Press, 1974.

* Hitchcock, Henry-Russell. *The Architecture of H. H. Richardson and His Times.* New York: Museum of Modern Art, 1936; revised edition Hamden, Conn.: Archon Books, 1961.

* Hitchcock, Henry-Russell. *In the Nature of Materials: The Buildings of Frank Lloyd Wright, 1887–1941.* New York: Duell, Sloan and Pearce, 1942.

Hoffmann, Donald. *The Architecture of John Wellborn Root.* Baltimore: Johns Hopkins University Press, 1973.

Hoffmann, Donald, ed. *The Meaning of Architecture: Buildings and Writings by John Wellborn Root.* New York: Horizon Press, 1967.

Johnson, Philip C. *Mies van der Rohe.* New York: Museum of Modern Art, 1947.

Kilham, Walter H., Jr. *Raymond Hood, Architect.* New York: Architectural Book Publishing Company, 1973.

Kimball, Fiske. *Thomas Jefferson, Architect.* Cambridge: Riverside Press, 1916.

Manson, Grant C. *Frank Lloyd Wright to 1910: The First Golden Age.* New York: Reinhold Publishing Company, 1958.

Meeks, Carroll L. V. *The Railroad Station: An Architectural History.* New Haven: Yale University Press, 1956.

A Monograph of the Works of McKim, Mead and White, 1887–1915. New York: Architectural Book Publishing Company, 1915; reprinted New York: Benjamin Blom, 1973.

Monroe, Harriet. *John Wellborn Root.* Boston: Houghton, Mifflin, 1896; reprinted Chicago: Prairie School Press, 1966.

* Morrison, Hugh. *Louis Sullivan, Prophet of Modern Architecture.* New York: W. W. Norton, 1935; reprinted New York: Peter Smith, 1952.

Nelson, George. *Industrial Architecture of Albert Kahn, Inc.* New York: Architectural Book Publishing Company, 1939.

O'Gorman, James F. *The Architecture of Frank Furness.* Philadelphia: Philadelphia Museum of Art, 1973.

Paul, Sherman. *Louis Sullivan, An Architect in American Thought.* Englewood Cliffs: Prentice-Hall, 1962.

* Sullivan, Louis H. *The Autobiography of an Idea.* New York: American Institute of Architects, 1926.

* Twombley, Robert C. *Frank Lloyd Wright: An Interpretive Biography.* New York: Harper and Row, 1973.

* van Rensselaer, Mariana Griswold. *Henry Hobson Richardson and His Works.* Boston: Houghton, Mifflin Company, 1888; reprinted New York: Dover Press, 1969.

Journals
American Architect and Building News
American Railroad Journal
Architectural Forum
Architectural Record
Architecture
Civil Engineering
Engineering News
Engineering News-Record
Engineering Record
Inland Architect
Journal of the Society of Architectural Historians
Pencil Points
Progressive Architecture
Railroad Gazette
Railway Age
Railway Review
Technology and Culture

Reference Works

American Society of Civil Engineers, Committee on History and Heritage of American Civil Engineering. *A Biographical Dictionary of American Civil Engineers*. New York: American Society of Civil Engineers, 1972.

Ferguson, Eugene S. *Bibliography of the History of Technology*. Cambridge: MIT Press, 1968.

Hornbostel, Caleb. *Materials for Architecture*. New York: Reinhold Publishing Company, 1961.

United States Department of the Interior, National Park Service. *Historic American Building Survey*. Washington: Historic American Building Survey, 1935 et seq.

Withey, Henry F. and Elsie R. *Biographical Dictionary of American Architects*. Los Angeles: Hennessey and Ingalls, 1956.

*indicates paperback availability

ADDENDUM

Professor Condit submitted these additional comments to his essay.

In mid-1979, Leland Roth's Concise History of American Architecture appeared--a surprisingly thorough and well-illustrated work for its length, and one that clearly supersedes the Burchard and Bush-Brown volume of 1961. In the short compass at his disposal, Roth was compelled to focus on the traditional stylistic approach, but he has given us most of the essentials.

New York architecture continues to be neglected, although a growing body of doctoral dissertations, some finding their way in revised form into the hands of publishers, give promise of an early end to the long drought.

These titles should be added to the bibliography, all under "General Works":

Davidson, Marshall, and G. E. Kidder-Smith. A Pictorial History of Architecture in America. 2 volumes. New York: American Heritage Publishing Company and W. W. Norton and Company, 1976.

Jordy, William H., and William H. Pierson. American Buildings and Their Architects. 4 volumes. Garden City: Doubleday and Company, 1970-72.

Roth, Leland M. A Concise History of American Architecture. New York: Harper and Row, 1979.

American Detective Fiction

ROBIN W. WINKS

Detective fiction, together with its out-riders, the gothic novel and the spy thriller, has long displaced the cowboy novel as the staple of American popular writing. As such, detective fiction is central to most debates concerning the legitimacy of the study of "popular culture," since it combines the traditional scholar's normal form of source material—the printed book—with that which traditional scholars often have disliked most, formula fiction written primarily for sales. While French and German scholars have written a number of substantial works on detective fiction (usually limiting themselves to European, including British, examples of the *genre*),[1] there has been markedly little serious interest in such literature amongst the American or British groves of academe until recently. Now an outpouring of books, especially on American writers, and particularly in the last five years, has helped demonstrate that universities might well take the murder mystery more seriously if they want to find a handy mirror to the nation's paranoia, as well as another point of entree into the study of American aspirations and myth.

To be sure, most teachers will find their courses on detective fiction quickly labeled "trashy lit" by their students, for it still seems necessary to apologize for reading Ross Macdonald when one might read Milton instead. The argument that some simply will not read Milton (which implies that Macdonald is to be taken as a worst case example), or that students may be led on to "higher things" if they are first brought to books through Ian Fleming is, of course, the voice of despair, even the coward's way out. Yet many of us have only ourselves to blame if English departments still doubt the value of Amanda Cross or Robert Parker, for the great bulk of the American scholarship on detective fiction continues to make one of two strategic errors in both conception and execution.

The commonest strategy, and a deadly and wrong one it is, arises from the desire to take the high road by proving that any number of great and respected figures were actually writing detective fiction all along. Thus (and with some reason) Dickens and Conrad are trotted out, ritual references to the Bible, Oedipus, and Voltaire's *Zadig,* are served up, and we are told that T.S. Eliot, William Faulkner, and any number of other high culture figures on occasion went slumming. Bringing the prince to the slum does not render the slum into a palace, however, and one may be permitted to doubt the long-range efficacy of such high mindedness. It is certainly true that the American detective story owes its origins, in form especially, to James Fenimore Cooper's Leatherstocking at least as much as to the more frequently invoked parentage of Edgar Allan Poe. Unlike English detective fiction, which has been nicely (though in important ways misleadingly) summarized as "snobbery with violence," thus invoking the social fabric from which the English environment of crime is woven, American detective fiction is predominantly interested in the lone avenger, the man (and increasingly the woman) who will set right the ills of society when society can no longer set right those ills for itself. The private eye, the Continental Op; the continuum from Leatherstocking through many of Zane Grey's heroes to Sam Spade, Marlowe, Archer, Spenser, *et al,* is obvious and true enough even though obvious. Certainly *Intruder in the Dust* contains a mystery; so does *Benito Cereno,* and *The House of the Seven Gables,* and a good bit more of Twain than *Pudd'nhead Wilson.* All fine writers have introduced us to mysteries, some more overtly so than any of these: Jorge Luis Borges, especially in "Death and the Compass"; Carlos Fuentes in *The Hydra Head,* Hans Erich Nossack in *To the Unknown Hero,* even Dylan Thomas in *The Death of the King's Canary.*[2]

The function of the "even" here is to remind us of our problem. All literature contains a mystery, but this does not mean that all writers are writing mysteries, for the creative act sets the mystery inherent in *Moby Dick* or *Der Zauberberg* or "Swan Lake" apart from the mystery specifically concocted as a vehicle for entertainment and instruction by the Macdonalds, Ross, John D., and Phillip (no relation, as *Time* magazine would say). In taking the high road, some authors have thrown important fresh light on those who inhabit that road by the conventional wisdom of established critics, as Nadya Aisenberg does in *A Common Spring* (1980)[3] with Dickens, Conrad, and Graham Greene.

Edgar Allan Poe (1809-1849). Engraved by Homer Bryan Hall and Sons, New York City, after 1860. Photo courtesy Prints and Photographs Division, Library of Congress, Washington, D.C. Negative number US Z 62-1877.

But very little has been observed along the way about those who are travelling on the low road as it is conventionally conceived. To seek to "validate" Mickey Spillane by showing he is the direct descendant of Cooper is both to patronize Spillane and to fail to see that detective fiction, even as defined within the narrower bounds of formulaic fiction, is worth taking seriously in its own right.

For Zane Grey's cowboy has come down from the mountain, out off the prairie, and has left his mustang behind, to get into his new Mustang and drive the freeways of Los Angeles in pursuit of that same epiphany sought by Shane and found by Gary Cooper in "High Noon." It is this line—that of popular fiction popularly conceived and popularly consumed—that most needs to be pursued. Yet, in such pursuit many writers have shown an equally bad sense of strategy to those on the high road, or have chosen the right strategy (that of the alleged low road) and then executed the strategy deplorably. For one must admit that when one turns to so-called critical works on Agatha Christie or Dorothy Sayers, or in the United States to most books on Ross Macdonald, Ellery Queen, or Dashiell Hammett, one finds them lacking in critical depth. Too often such "studies" become mere summaries of plots, collections of bits of gossip, and source books for playing trivia games (what kind of Scotch does Jonathan Hemlock drink? Laphroaig. What kind of gin does Travis McGee drink? Until his last book, Plymouth. What kind of beer does Spenser drink? Originally Amstel, now Tuborg). It is no wonder that markedly few "serious" critics have explored the murder mystery when they encounter a critical infrastructure of this kind, and though Edmund Wilson was mistaken in answering his question, "Who cares who killed Roger Ackroyd?" with the reply, no one of taste and good judgment, one can understand how he arrived at such a conclusion. Few studies take detective fiction seriously, for itself. Yet it is not necessary to demonstrate the importance of a body of literature, for any literature that helps us to come to terms with our environment is valuable, as therapeutic as reading Freud's *Civilization and its Discontents* is therapeutic, enjoyable, and—holiest of holies—significant.

The comparison with the fiction of the American West, made explicit by John Cawelti in *The Six-Gun Mystique* and *Adventure, Mystery and Romance*,[4] gives rise to another observation: "serious" literary critics who write from within received canons of taste have proved notoriously bad in predicting the "serious" literary interests of subsequent generations. The case of the neglect of Herman Melville is well known, but it is equally instructive to remember Barrett Wendell, professor of literature (amongst other activities) at Harvard, who in 1900 sought to describe the literature that had come out of the American West, finding it the result of a "relaxed inexperience," appealing to the "lower sort of Americans," and likely to "revert to the ancestrally extinct" in relation to the tastes of the East coast. He was prepared to venture the opinion that perhaps four of the writers then representative of the "great confused west" would stand the test of time. They were George Horatio Derby, Charles Farrar Browne (that is, Artemus Ward), David Ross Locke (Petroleum Nasby), and Alfonso Newcomer. True, one must ask the right questions to get useful answers, and when Henry Nash Smith wrote *Virgin Land* half a century later he was asking different questions. As the land

Scene from the 1941 film, "The Maltese Falcon," directed by John Huston and starring Humphrey Bogart, Peter Lorre, Sidney Greenstreet, and Mary Astor. Dashiell Hammett's 1929 novel of the same name is one of the most famous of the "tough-guy" private eye novels.

of beginning again became, in the California novel, the land of the last chance, perceptions altered.

Detective fiction helps one explore changing perceptions of personal integrity. It shows us how to laugh in the midst of frustration, how to take joy from experience, how to tolerate complexity. The writer of good detective fiction—"good" in the sense of being true, interesting, and significant—such as Arthur Lyons or Robert Parker, like the writer of "good" history (in the same sense of "good")[5] must have an icicle in the eye. Through all the phases of the *genre*: the set-piece puzzle of the nineteenth century, the locked room mystery of the 1920s, the Golden Age of the late 20's and 30's when the hard-boiled private eye emerged in the United States and the detective novel of manners was created by Dorothy L. Sayers and Agatha Christie in England, and the development of the procedural crime-and-police novel by Hillary Waugh and Ed McBain in America—all shared a common concern with the way we die now. Some few authors would break the conventions of popular taste for their period—Christie broke every one of Ronald Knox's famous decalogue—while most wrote within the rules of the game as their readers came to expect it. Some, Rex Stout, for example, pressed each book to the edge of the prevailing rules, as when he attacked the FBI just at the point when some few "serious" commentators were doing so as well (in *The Doorbell Rang*).[6] Thus one may, through the *genre*, trace the changing preoccupations, the fears, the sexual mores, of a vast American public. Erle Stanley Gardner allowed no vulgarity to pass the lips of Perry Mason, but as A.A. Fair he did permit Bertha Cool both *damn* and *hell*; today sex, psychology, and privacy as seen by McBain, or Lawrence Block, or Charles McCarry reflect the society as it sees itself ever more clearly.[7]

A particularly noticeable trend is toward the world weary non-hero, betrayed from within by the institution that once nurtured and protected him, who discovers that no prospect pleases, and that all men (and women) are vile. This is more the hallmark of the spy story and the thriller, perhaps, than of detective and mystery novels as normally defined—though there is, at base, less difference between these elements of the *genre* than some overly precious commentators profess to find. Sin, retribution, guilt, dread—all the connotations of Kafka caught up by the mystery novelist—are equally present in thriller fiction, whether it be of espionage, counter-espionage, professional or amateur. George Stade interprets thriller fiction in relation to what cultures, generations, and individuals find "sinister," and he argues that the reader will see to it that thrillers function "as he needs them to function," thus providing an unforced definition of that which we often label "enjoyment."[8] Ralph Harper, on the other hand, in *The World of the Thriller,* sees such fiction in terms of existentialism and the philosophy of Martin Heidegger.[9] Both are correct, and neither contradicts the American Adam.

There is, however, an honest debate about the rôle of spy fiction in relation to detective fiction that has developed, in particular, in the United States. Some students of mystery fiction are offended by the claim made on behalf of some spy fiction that it is particularly realistic because it is framed within very real cold war contexts. Yet surely "realism" is, like romanticism, a convention: within realism, some is "really real" and some is not. Jacques Barzun, in particular, has criticized spy fiction for depicting ubiquity as a child craves it: "Nine is the age of seeking omniscience on a low level."[10] So much for James Bond, Quiller, Colonel Russell, and Matt Helm.

Spy fiction is also charged with glorifying violence, with justifying a State which can give an agent a license to kill and a special number that implies he is not alone in exercising such power, that he is a killing machine. Certainly spy thriller fiction has gone through many of the same changes as more traditional detective fiction, for the days when the hero of a John Buchan or Richard Harding Davis thriller would, because he was a gentleman and the rules of the game required it, risk his life to rescue a villain, are gone; Matt Helm kills whenever (and whomever) the need dictates. Larry McMurtry has observed that the Secret Agent has replaced the high mimetic western, that as the Western novel and motion picture offered "an acceptable orientation to violence" for most Americans, an urban age has spawned an urban figure, "the Secret Agent [as] an undated Gunfighter."[11] Certainly the line from Natty Bumppo to Marlowe was clear enough; so is the line from Cooper's *Spy* to Bond, although more complexly so, as Martin Green notes.:[12]

> ...though one cannot regard Bond as an encouraging sign, one must regard him as a sign. It would be unhelpful to treat him moralistically.[13]

One can say that treated mythically he shows up the [John D.] MacDonald myth as profoundly healthy by comparison. Travis McGee is the hero of a strong, intelligent, many-sided culture, though one obsessed with sexuality and with male chauvinist sexuality, with its attendant nightmares of emasculation and ambiguities of sado-masochism. ... Bond is surely the hero of a corrupt culture, willing to 'believe in' mere brutality of appetitie, unrelated to any cultural idea. Above all, one can say that the MacDonald novels are much more interesting than Ian Fleming's, because they reveal the normative mind of their culture, working at a normal, alternately high and low, pitch of intensity.

In the monthly publication of the paperback edition of MacDonald's *The Green Ripper*[14]—which turns on the efforts by a religious cult rather like the Hare Krishna to train followers for urban guerilla warfare—law enforcement officers in California reported finding substantial arms caches in the mountain retreat of such a group. If detective fiction is a mirror to a culture, then spy fiction is no more a clouded mirror than any other, though it deals more with collectively sordid truths and less with individual cases.

Still, the two strategic errors continue: the high road, the low road, and neither is there before us, for even yet there is no book that compares and contrasts British and American detective fiction in the way Wilbur R. Miller has compared *Cops and Bobbies*;[15] there is no scholarly journal devoted in a rigorous way to the study of the genre;[16] there is no reprint house that has systematically brought back into print those books, two hundred or more, that are needed for a consecutive, sound approach to the history of modern detective fiction.[17] It is said that Americans read more mystery novels than any other kind of book; if so, they appear to have questioned their basic assumptions remarkably little, as the relatively short bibliography that follows will demonstrate. Perhaps we were awaiting Thomas Pynchon's *The Crying of Lot 49,* in which all possibility for a "solution" disappears; on the edge of the irrational, we may at last begin to take seriously this most rationalistic of all American literature.[18] □

NOTES

1. The classic study is *Esthétique du roman policier* (Paris, 1947) by Thomas Narcejac, while Rainer Schönhoar, *Novelle und Kriminalsschema: Ein Strukturmodelldeutscher Erzählkunst zum 1800* (Bad Homburg, 1969) and Horst Conrad, *Die Literarische Angst: Das Schreckliche in Schauerromantik and Detektivgeschichte* (Düsseldorf, 1974), are representative of the German approach.

2. "Death and the Compass" first appeared, in Spanish, in *Ficciones* (Buenos Aires, 1956); Fuentes (New York, 1978); Nossack (New York, 1974); Thomas, with John Davenport (New York, 1977).

3. Subtitled *Crime Novel and Classic* (Bowling Green, 1980).

4. Bowling Green, 1970, and Chicago, 1976; the second book is sub-titled *Formula Stories as Art and Popular Culture.*

5. I have developed this idea at length previously, in *The Historian as Detective* (New York, 1969).

6. (New York, 1965).

7. Representative titles by all authors mentioned in this essay are cited in part II of the bibliography to my *Detective Fiction* (Englewood Cliffs, N.J., 1980).

8. Stade, "I've Been Reading Thrillers," *Columbia Forum* (Spring, 1970), pp. 34-37.

9. (Baltimore, 1974).

10. Barzun, "Meditations on the Literature of Spying," *The American Scholar,* XXXIV (Spring, 1965), 172-73.

11. McMurty, *In a Narrow Grave: Essays on Texas* (New York, 1965), p. 24.

12. *Transatlantic Patterns: Cultural Comparisons of England with America* (New York, 1977), pp. 129-30.

13. Nonetheless, this is how Bond is generally dealt with. See, among several titles, Ann S. Boyd, *The Devil with James Bond!* (Richmond, Va., 1967); Lycurgus M. Starkey, Jr., *James Bond's World of Values* (Nashville, 1966); and Oreste del Buono and Umberto Eco, eds., *The Bond Affair* (London, 1966).

14. (New York, 1980).

15. Subtitled *Police Authority in New York and London, 1830-1870* (Chicago, 1977).

16. The earliest journal into the field was *The Armchair Detective,* now published quarterly in New York by The Mysterious Press; under Allen J. Hubin and Otto Penzler, in the last two to three years it has begun to move from its "fanzine" format and content to a more rigorous position. A new journal, *Clues: Journal of Detection,* with Pat Browne as the editor, began publication in 1980.

17. The Garland Publishing Company has reprinted, in cloth editions, *Fifty Classics of Crime Fiction, 1900-1950* (New York, 1976), with prefaces by Jacques Barzun and Wendell Hertig Taylor. Some might think the selection somewhat Anglophilic, for it contains thirty-six titles (including one Australian) from British authors, fourteen from American, and none from any other source. The Mystery Library (Del Mar, Cal.: Publisher's Inc., 1976-79) has published twelve reprints of classics, together with useful scholarly apparatus; six are by Americans. But the great majority of the American titles most needed for an understanding of the history of American detective fiction are now out of print.

18. This argument is extended in my *Detective Fiction,* cited above.

Selective Bibliography

The amount of casual, journalistic writing about American detective fiction is enormous, since detective authors often become quasi-public figures: Dashiell Hammett (particularly through the autobiography of Lilian Hellman),

Raymond Chandler, Rex Stout, Robert Ludlum, and Ross Macdonald are examples. Often book reviews, especially in the provincial press, are joined with short interview articles. Since 1968 *The Armchair Detective,* initiated primarily by Allen J. Hubin, and published in White Bear Lake, Minn., more recently in Del Mar, Cal., and now by The Mysterious Press in New York City, has printed an annual bibliography of secondary sources which includes much of the ephemeral material and all of the important. One may keep abreast of the new literature through weekly review columns in *The New York Times Book Review,* a monthly column in *The New Republic,* and with irregularity in most commercial journals with regular reviews of fiction and criticism. Second-hand dealers' catalogues are also very helpful. New critical studies, as well as new fiction (and much old), are stocked automatically by four book stores, which will fill orders by mail: Murder Ink., at 271 West 87th Street, New York 10024, the first specialty book store of this type; The Mysterious Bookshop, 129 West 56th Street, New York; Moonstone Book-cellars, Inc., 2145 Pennsylvania Avenue, N.W., Washington, D.C. (which also somewhat heretically handles science fiction); and Scene of the Crime, 13636 Ventura Boulevard, Sherman Oaks, California.

General Bibliographies, Directories, and Encyclopaedias (not limited to America)

Barnes, Melvyn. *Best Detective Fiction.* London: Clive Bingley, 1975. Weak.

Barzun, Jacques, and Taylor, Wendell Hertig. *A Catalogue of Crime.* New York: Harper & Row, 1971; rev. ed., 1974. Highly personal, intelligent, Anglophilic but good on the Americans, and indispensable.

Gaute, J.H.H. and Odell, Robin. *The Murderers' Who's Who.* New York: Methuen, 1979. On factual crime; contains excellent bibliography.

Hagen, Ordean A. *Who Done It? A Guide to Detective, Mystery and Suspense Fiction.* New York: R.R. Bowker, 1969. A librarian's reference tool, with some errors, but superbly organized.

Hubin, Allen J. *The Bibliography of Crime Fiction, 1749-1975.* Del Mar, Cal.: Publisher's Inc., 1979. Lists all mystery, detective, suspense, police, and gothic fiction in book form published in English.

Hubin, Allen J. *Crime Fiction Collection.* Pacific Palisades: International Bookfinders, 1979; privately printed. A superb sale catalogue for Allen Hubin's personal collection of twenty-five thousand volumes, the largest private sale of detective fiction in the United States in recent years.

Keating, H.R.F. ed. *Crime Writers: Reflections on Crime Fiction.* London: BBC, 1978. Generally on British writers, but good on Dashiell Hammett and Patricia Highsmith.

La Cour, Tage, and Mogensen, Harald. *The Murder Book: An Illustrated History of the Detective Story.* New York: McGraw-Hill, 1971. Excellent illustrations and good summary histories.

McCormick, Donald. *Who's Who in Spy Fiction.* New York: Taplinge, 1977. Heavily British but sound on the Americans.

Mystery Wrtiers of America. *Mystery Writer's Handbook.* Cincinnati: Writer's Digest, 1976. Heavily American.

Pate, Janet. *The Book of Sleuths.* Chicago: Contemporary Books, 1977. As interested in film as is publications.

Penzler, Otto; Steinbrunner, Chris; and Lachman, Marvin. *Detectionary.* New York: Overlook Press, 1977. Biographical dictionary of leading characters in detective and mystery fiction.

Penzler, Otto, ed. *The Great Detectives.* Boston: Little, Brown, 1978. Essays, by the creators of famous fictional detectives, on their creations.

Penzler, Otto. *The Privates Lives of Private Eyes and Spies, Crime Fighters, and Other Good Guys.* New York: Grosset & Dunlap, 1979. Good bibliographies and short filmographies.

Radcliffe, Elsa J. *Gothic Novels of the Twentieth Century: An Annotated Bibliography.* Metuchen, N.J.: Scarecrow press, 1979. On occasion gothic fiction crosses over into detective fiction.

Steinbrunner, Chris, and Penzler, Otto, eds. *Encyclopedia of Mystery & Detection.* New York: McGraw-Hill, 1976. The best encyclopedia, with checklists of films and books.

Winn, Dilys, ed. *Murder Ink: The Mystery Reader's Companion.* New York: Workman, 1977. A delightful assortment of miscellaneous knowledge.

Winn, Dilys, *Murderess Ink: The Better Half of the Mystery.* New York: Workman, 1979. Equally miscellaneous, somewhat less amusing.

General Histories (excluding those which do not deal with American authors at all)

Buchloh, Paul G., and Becker, Jens P. *Der Detektivroman.* Darmstadt: Wissenschaftliche Buchgesellschaft, 1973. Good on differences between English and American fiction.

Haycraft, Howard. *Murder for Pleasure: The Life and Times of the Detective Story.* New York: Appleton-Century, 1941. Still the standard history to its date.

Hoveyda, Fereydoun. *Historie du roman policier.* Paris: Les Editions du Pavillon 1965. On eroticism in Jean Cocteau and Mickey Spillane, *et al.*

Murch, A.E. *The Development of the Detective Novel.* New york: Philosophical Library, 1958. Limited to the nineteenth century.

Quayle, Eric. *The Collector's Book of Detective Fiction.* London: Studio Vista, 1972. On the book as object.

Queen, Ellery. *Queen's Quorum.* Boston: Little, Brown, 1951. Includes a history of the short story.

Sayers, Dorothy L., ed. *The Omnibus of Crime.* New York: Payson and Clarke, 1929. Contains the most perceptive history to its date; heavily English.

Symons, Julian. *Bloody Murder: From the Detective Story to the Crime Novel.* London: Faber & Faber, 1972. A sound history of a nearly world-wide basis.

Periodicals

The Armchair Detective. 1968-, in White Bear Lake, Minn., Del Mar, Cal., and New York City.

Clues: Journal of Detection. 1980-, in Bowling Green, Ohio. Not seen.

The Journal of Popular Culture. 19-, in Bowling Green, Ohio. Frequent articles, some excellent and some weak.

The Mystery Monitor. 1976-, in Wheaton, Maryland. Very irregular.

The Mystery Reader's Newsletter. 1969-, in Melrose, Mass. Largely American.

The Not So Private Eye. 1978-, in Parlin, N.J. a fanzine.

The Popular Culture Scholar. 1977-78, lapsed, from Frostburg, Md. Vol. I, no. 1, devoted to detective fiction.

Red Herrings. 287 individually numbered issues to date, from London and variously in England. Bulletin of the Crime Writers' Association, with some material on the United States.

Works of Literary and Critical Analysis: Mystery and Detective Fiction

Allen, Dick, and Chacko, David, eds. *Detective Fiction: Crime and Compromise.* New York: Harcourt, Brace, 1974. An anthology of examples of the *genre* with some of the simpler though more perceptive critical essays.

Aisenberg, Nadya. *A Common Spring: Crime Novel & Classic.* Bowling Green, Ohio: Bowling Green University Popular Press, 1979. Largely British but useful theoretical treatment of relationship of detective fiction to myths and fairy tales.

Ball, John, ed. *The Mystery Story.* Del Mar, Cal.: Publisher's, Inc., 1976. General, non-critical essays, unrigorous and congratulatory.

Byrd, Max. "The Detective Detected: From Sophocles to Ross MacDonald." *The Yale Review,* 64, (1974), 72-83. One of the most intelligent tracings of key themes.

Cawelti, John G. *Adventure, Mystery, and Romance: Formula Stories as Art and Popular Culture.* Chicago: University of Chicago Press, 1976. Intelligently combines detective, mystery, and western popular fiction.

Charney, Hanna. *"This Mortal Coil": The Detective Novel of Manners.* Madison, N.J.: Fairleigh Dickinson University Press, 1980. Sound structuralist inquiry based on Roland Barthes.

Conrad, Horst. *Die Literarische Angst: Das Schreckliche in Schauerromantik und Detektivgeschichte.* Düsseldorf: Bartelsmann 1974. Fine inquiry into the literary function of anxiety, pity, and sex, with an excellent bibliography.

Eames, Hugh. *Sleuths, Inc.* Philadelphia: Lippincott, 1978. Weak on Hammett and Chandler.

Green, Martin. *Transatlantic Patterns: Cultural Comparisons of England with America.* New York: Basic Books, 1977. Uses Sayers and John D. MacDonald.

Grossvogel, David I. *Mystery and Its Fictions: From Oedipus to Agatha Christie.* Baltimore: The Johns Hopkins University Press, 1979. Generally European, though Poe is included.

Harper, Ralph. *The World of the Thriller.* Baltimore: The Johns Hopkins University Press, 1974. An excellent statement on the typonomy of the thriller.

Hartman, Geoffrey H. *The Fate of Reading and Other Essays.* Chicago: University of Chicago Press, 1975. Includes a fine essay on the mystery story, focussing on Ross Macdonald.

Haycraft, Howard, ed. *The Art of the Mystery Story.* New York: Grosset & Dunlap, 1946. A fine collection of superb common sense.

Lambert, Gavin. *The Dangerous Edge.* London: Barrie & Jenkins, 1975. An attempt to account for mystery writers through their early lives; interesting on Chandler and Hitchcock.

Landrum, Larry N; Browne, Pat; and Browne, Ray B., eds. *Dimensions of Detective Fiction.* Bowling Green, Ohio: Popular Press, 1976. Generally disappointing, largely descriptive.

McAleer, John. "The Game's Afoot: Detective Fiction in the Present Day." *Kansas Quarterly,* 10, (1978), 21-38. A good way of being brought up-to-date.

Margolies, Edward. *Which Way Did He Go? The Life and Times of the Private Eye.* New York: Holmes & Meier, 1979. Hammett, Chandler, Macdonald, and Chester Himes.

Mason, Bobbie Ann. *The Girl Sleuth: A Feminist Guide.* Old Westbury, N.Y.: The Feminist Press, 1975. The Bobbsey Twins, Nancy Drew, etc., once over lightly but intelligently.

Nevins, Francis M., Jr., ed. *The Mystery Writer's Art.* Bowling Green, Ohio: Bowling Green University Popular Press, 1970. A mixed bag with some usefull essays.

Pfeiffer, Hans. *Die Mumie in Glassarg: Bemerkungen zur Kriminalliteratur.* Rudolstadt: Greifenverlag, 1960. Good on criminality itself.

Routley, Erik. *The Puritan Pleasures of the Detective Story: From Sherlock Holmes to Van der Valk.* London: Victor Gollancz, 1972. The best attack on the weaknesses in the *genre* since Edmund Wilson, written by someone who knows what he is talking about, as Wilson did not.

Rycroft, Chalres. *Imagination and Reality: Psycho-Analytical Essays, 1951-1961.* London: Hogarth Press: Institute of Psycho-Analysis, 1968. Applies Freudian insights to detective fiction.

Schulz-Buschhaus, Ulrich, ed. *Formen und Idealogien der Kriminalroman.* Frankfurt: Athenaion, 1975. Sound on Socialist Realism.

Todorev, Tzvetan. *The Poetics of Prose.* Ithaca, N.Y.: Cornell University Press, 1977. An intriguing "typology of detective fiction," probably wrong.

Winks, Robin W., ed. *Detective Fiction.* Englewood Cliffs, N.J.: Prentice-Hall, 1980. A volume in the Twentieth Century Views series.

Watson, Colin. *Snobbery with Violence: Crime Stories and Their Audience.* London: Eyre and Spottiswoodie, 1971. Largely British class analysis with some American relevance.

Philosophical

Champigny, Robert. *What Will Have Happened: A Philosophical and Technical Essay on Mystery Stories.* Bloomington, Ind.: Indiana University Press, 1977. Difficult and rewarding.

Portuondo, Jose Antonio. *En torno a la novela detectivesca.* Havana: Páginas, 1946. Avant-garde for its time, this is a brief inquiry into the values of the *genre.*

Individual Authors (Poe is omitted for obvious reasons)

Cain, James M.

Cain, James M. "The Art of Fiction." *The Paris Review,* 73, (1978), 117-38.

Chandler, Raymond.

Bruccoli, Matthew J. *Raymond Chandler: A Checklist.* Kent, Ohio: Kent State University Press, 1968.

Chandler, Raymond. *The Simple Art of Murder.* Boston: Houghton Mifflin, 1950.

Dunham, Philip. *Down These Mean Streets a Man Must Go.* Chapel Hill: University of North Carolina Press, 1963.

Holden, Jonathan. "The Case of Raymond Chandler's Fiction as Romance." *Kansas Quarterly,* 10, (1978), 41-47.

Jameson, Fredric. "On Raymond Chandler," *The Southern Review,* n.s., 6, (1970), 624-50.

MacShane, Frank. *The Life of Raymond Chandler.* New York: E.P.: Dutton, 1976.

Hamilton, Donald.

Erisman, Fred. "Western Motifs in the Thrillers of Donald Hamilton." *Western American Literature,* 10, ( ), 283-92.

Hammett, Dashiell.

Marcus, Steven. "Introduction" to *The Continental Op.* New York: Macmillan, 1975.

Wolfe, Peter. *Beams Falling: The Art of Dashiell Hammett.* Bowling Green, Ohio: Bowling Green State University Press, 1980.

Himes, Chester.

Himes, Chester. *The Quality of Hurt.* Garden City, N.Y.: Doubleday, 1971.

MacDonald, John D.

The JDM Bibliophile. A mimeographed journal from Downey, Cal., begun *c*1963.

The JDM Master Checklist. Downey, Cal.: Moffatt House, 1969.

Campbell, Frank D., Jr. *John D. MacDonald and the Colorful World of Travis McGee.* San Bernardino, Cal.: Borgo Press, 1977.

Macdonald, Ross.

Bruccoli, Matthew J. *Kenneth Millar/Ross Macdonald: A Checklist.* Detroit: Gale Research, 1971.

Hartman, Geoffrey. "The Mystery of Mysteries." *New York Review of Books,* (May 18, 1972), 31-34.

Macdonald, Ross. "Down These Streets a Mean Man Must Go." *Antaeus,* (25/26; 1977), 211-16.

Macdonald, Ross. *On Crime Writing.* Santa Barbara: Capra Press, 1973.

Speir, Jerry. *Ross Macdonald.* New York: Frederick Ungar, 1978.

Wolfe, Peter. *Dreamers Who Live Their Dreams: The World of Ross Macdonald's Novels.* Bowling Green, Ohio: Bowling Green University Popular Press, 1976.

Parker, Robert B.

Geherin, David. *Sons of Sam Spade: The Private-Eye Novel in the 70s.* New York: Frederick Ungar, 1980. With smaller sections on Roger L. Simon and Andrew Bergman.

Post, Melville Davisson.

Norton, Charles. *Melville Davisson Post: Man of Many Mysteries.* Bowling Green, Ohio: Bowling Green State University Popular Press, 1973.

Queen, Ellery.

Nevins, Francis M., Jr. *Royal Bloodline: Ellery Queen, Author and Detective.* Bowling Green, Ohio: Bowling Green University Popular Press, 1974.

Stout, 1974.

The Gazette: The Journal of The Wolfe Pack. From New York, 1979-.

McAleer, John. *Rex Stout: A Biography.* Boston: Little, Brown, 1977.

The above listing omits articles that appear in *The Armchair Detective,* the *Journal of Popular Culture,* and those publications listed above under "Periodicals."

Spy Fiction

Becker, Jens-Peter. *Der englische Spionsgeroman.* Munich: Wilhelm Goldmann, 1973.

Jeffreys-Jones, Rhodri. *American Espionage: From Secret Service to CIA.* New York: Free Press, 1977. Largely a history, but with a good chapter on the spy in American popular culture.

Merry, Bruce. *Anatomy of the Spy Thriller.* Dublin: Gill and Macmillan, 1977. Rather too self-consciously serious but with much that is sound.

Robin W. Winks is Professor of History and Master of Berkeley College at Yale University, where he has taught since 1957. From 1969 to 1971 he served as Cultural Attache to the American Embassy in London, and during the American Bicentennial he was a principal advisor to the Dept. of State, planning a series of five international conferences on American Studies which resulted in several publications, including his own Other Voices, Other Views. *His academic field is the comparative history of race relations, and comparative imperialisms, on which he has published several books.*

Recent Literature in American Economic History

JAMES H. SOLTOW

The purpose of this essay is to review the principal developments in the scholarship of American economic history since the early 1960s. First, a word about the general nature of the subject may be useful. Since economic history is not regarded as a separate discipline in the departmental organization of American universities, its practitioners in this country are usually identified academically as either historians or economists. However, this "dual" discipline does have its own professional organization, the Economic History Association (founded in 1940), and a scholarly forum in the *Journal of Economic History*. In addition, several subdisciplines of economic history have their own organizations or journals—*Business History Review, Agricultural History,* and *Labor History.* (Since labor history was thoroughly explored in a recent issue, this article will not deal with the subject. See James R. Wason, "American Workers and American Studies." *American Studies International,* XII (Winter 1974) 10-36.) Two other journals, *Explorations in Economic History* (formerly *Explorations in Entrepreneurial History*) (1963-) and *Research in Economic History: An Annual Compilation of Research* (1976-) are under the editorial direction of academics although distributed by commercial publishers. In addition, periodicals in general history (including those oriented toward state and local history), economics, and other social sciences often publish articles of interest to economic historians.

During the past decade and a half, the new economic history, emanating from the economics side of the discipline, drew much attention. From the late 1950s, cliometricians (as they became known) argued that systematic application of economic theory and quantitative evidence to test explicitly formulated hypotheses would lend greater precision to the study of historical economic processes. Ralph L. Andreano (ed.), *The New Economic History: Recent Papers on Methodology* (New York: John Wiley & Sons, 1970) includes a selection of essays on methodology produced in the course of the debate between new economic historians and their critics; Robert W. Fogel and Stanley L. Engerman (eds.), *The Reinterpretation of American Economic History* (New York: Harper & Row, 1971) contains a collection of articles illustrating the application of the new economic history to a variety of subjects, most dealing with 19th-century United States history; Lance E. Davis *et al.*, *American Economic Growth: An Economist's History of the United States* (New York: Harper & Row, 1972) develops a new economic history synthesis of the American experience; Lance E. Davis and Douglass C. North, *Institutional Change and American Economic Growth* (Cambridge: Cambridge University Press, 1971) attempts to develop an economic theory of institutional change; Jeffrey G. Williamson, *Late Nineteenth-Century American Development: A General Equilibrium History* (Cambridge: Cambridge University Press, 1974) represents the most ambitious effort to date to write econometric history; and Peter D. McClelland, *Causal Explanation and Model Building in History, Economics, and the New Economic History* (Ithaca: Cornell University Press, 1975), is a recent survey of methods.

Thomas C. Cochran, "Economic History, Old and New," *American Historical Review*, LXXIV (June 1969) 1561-1572, places the methodological controversy over cliometrics in the long-run perspective of the history of the discipline, suggesting that "the difference between old and new economic historians is, in part, a controversy over types of models: the old say that realistic models usually have to be too highly generalized or too complex to allow the assumption of mathematical relationships; the new are primarily interested in applying operative models to economic data." George Rogers Taylor and Lucius F. Ellsworth (eds.), *Approaches to American Economic History* (Charlottesville: University Press of Virginia, 1971) demonstrates the variety of approaches currently employed in the study of economics; here eight leading scholars discuss the relevance of their respective methodologies (both quantitative and non-quantitative) to the analyses of the materials of economic history. The point is clear: a meaningful assessment of the recent output of American economic history must take into account the contributions of scholars employing a variety of methods.

Unfortunately, the most recent comprehensive bibliographical guides to the subject are now almost a decade old: *American Economic History Before 1860*, compiled by George Rogers Taylor (New York: Appleton-Century-Crofts, 1969), and *American Economic History Since 1860*, compiled by Edward C. Kirkland (New York: Appleton-Century Crofts, 1971). Robert W. Lovett, *American Economic and Business History Information Sources* (Detroit: Gale Research Company, 1971) is also useful. Details about ongoing scholarly developments can be traced in the articles and book reviews contained in the journals mentioned earlier. Special mention should be made of a new and expanded edition of an important reference work: U.S. Bureau of the Census, *Historical Statistics of the United States,*

Colonial Times to 1970 (2 vols; Washington, D. C.: Government Printing Office, 1975).

The Seventeenth and Eighteenth Centuries: Economic Development in a Context of Colonialism

A relatively neglected subject in earlier years, research on the economic history of the colonial period carried out since the early 1960s produced a number of important studies whose findings placed the economic experience of the colonies in a new perspective. At the time of independence, Americans lived in a complex and dynamic economy—one which enabled them to produce a high average level of wealth compared to that of contemporary Europe, a generalization amply supported in Alice H. Jones, *American Colonial Wealth: Documents and Methods* (3 vols.; New York: Arno Press, 1977).

Since economic advancement was connected with market-oriented activity, particularly the export of staple commodities, the workings of commerce were crucial, a topic approached in several ways. Jacob M. Price, *France and the Chesapeake: A History of the French Tobacco Monopoly, 1674-1791, and of Its Relationship to the British and American Tobacco Trades* (2 vols.; Ann Arbor: University of Michigan Press, 1973) traces in detail the development and organization of the French market for tobacco and its influence upon economic growth in the Chesapeake colonies, America's major tobacco producers. In another work, "Economic Function and the Growth of American Port Towns in the Eighteenth Century," *Perspectives in American History*, VIII (1974) 123-186, Price emphasizes the importance of the emergence of major provincial business centers—Philadelphia, New York, and Boston—not only as shipping points for their respective hinterlands but also as entrepreneurial decision-making centers. Carville Earle and Ronald Hoffman, "Urban Development in the Eighteenth-Century South," *Perspectives in American History*, X (1976) 7-78, argues that staple flows and their linkage effects were the principal determinants of the distinctive pattern of urban development in the southern colonies, while Aubrey Land, "Economic Behavior in a Planting Society: The Eighteenth-Century Chesapeake," *Journal of Southern History*, XXXIII (November 1967) 469-485, discusses the mercantile, "urban-type" activities of leading planters. John J. McCusker, *Money and Exchange in Europe and America, 1600-1775. A Handbook* (Chapel Hill: University of North Carolina Press, 1977) contains a compilation, with explanation, of rates of exchange between colonial and European currencies. Joseph A. Ernst, *Money and Politics in America, 1755-1775* (Chapel Hill: University of North Carolina Press, 1973) explores the economics and politics of the currency issue in the decades prior to the Revolution, emphasizing the relationship between currency, credit, and trade. James F. Shepherd and Gary M. Walton, *Shipping, Maritime Trade, and Economic Development of Colonial North America* (Cambridge: Cambridge University Press, 1972) presents an analysis of colonial shipping, patterns of foreign trade, and the balance of payments in the late colonial period. Marc Egnal, "The Economic Development of the Thirteen Continental Colonies, 1720 to 1775," *William and Mary Quarterly*, XXXII (1975) 191-222, sets forth a tentative model pointing to some of the likely sources of economic growth in the half century prior to independence. Robert P. Thomas, "A Quantitative Approach to the Study of the Effects of British Imperial Policy upon Colonial Welfare: Some Preliminary Findings," *Journal of Economic History*, XXV (December 1965) 615-638, and Peter D. McClelland, "The Cost to America of British Imperial Policy," *American Economic Review*, LIX (May 1969) 370-381, differ on exact amounts, but both conclude on the basis of their calculations that the economic burden of British mercantilistic regulation upon the American economy was slight. However, Marc Egnal and Joseph A. Ernst, "An Economic Interpretation of the American Revolution," *William and Mary Quarterly*, XXIX (January 1972) 3-32, point to the restrictive effects of British legislation upon the ambitions of colonials for greater economic sovereignty.

Other recent studies have focused on economic development at the regional or community level. Historical geographers made several notable contributions: James T. Lemon, *The Best Poor Man's Country: A Geographical Study of Early Southeastern Pennsylvania* (Baltimore: Johns Hopkins University Press, 1972), an analysis of the interplay of society and land in the settlement of Pennsylvania; Carville V. Earle, *The Evolution of a Tidewater Settlement System: All Hallow's Parish, Maryland, 1650-1783* (Chicago: University of Chicago, Department of Geography, 1975), a study of economic change in one community; and Robert D. Mitchell, *Commercialism and Frontier: Perspectives on the Early Shenandoah Valley* (Charlottesville: University Press of Virginia, 1977), an investigation of the growth of market-oriented activity on an 18th-century frontier area. Sung Bok Kim, *Landlord and Tenant in Colonial New York: Manorial Society, 1664-1775* (Chapel Hill: University of North Carolina Press, 1978) emphasizes the role of large landowners in the Hudson River Valley as developmental agents and the institution of tenancy as an economically useful alternative to land ownership for some prospective settlers. Stephanie G. Wolf, *Urban Village: Population, Community, and Family Structure in Germantown, Pennsylvania, 1683-1800* (Princeton: Princeton University Press, 1976) details the basic patterns of life of common people in the context of the growth of a community strongly oriented to values of the market and individual achievement. Origins and early growth of communities in the New England colonies form the subject of several studies containing information about economic life: Darrett B. Rutman, *Winthrop's Boston: Portrait of a Puritan Town, 1630-1649* (Chapel Hill: University of North Carolina Press, 1965); Rutman, *Husbandmen of Plymouth: Farms and Villages in the Old Colony, 1620-1692* (Boston: Beacon Press, 1967); Rutman, "People in Process: The New Hampshire Towns of the Eighteenth Century," *Journal of Urban History*, I (May 1975) 268-292; Philip J. Greven, Jr., *Four Generations: Population, Land, and Family in Colonial Andover, Massachusetts* (Ithaca: Cornell University Press, 1970); and Kenneth A. Lockridge, *A New England Town: The First Hundred Years* (New York: W. W. Norton, 1970).

Two books about slavery in the colonial period explore social and political as well as economic aspects of this institution: Edmund S. Morgan, *American Slavery, American Freedom: The Ordeal of Colonial Virginia* (New York: W. W. Norton, 1975) and Peter H. Wood, *Black Majority: Negroes in Colonial South Carolina from 1670 through the Stono Rebellion* (New York; Alfred A. Knopf, 1974). Little research has been directed recently to indentured servitude in spite of the large numbers of English and other Europeans who migrated to America in the 17th and

18th centuries as servants under indenture for a term of years. However, several recent articles have begun to shed new light on this component of the unfree labor force: David Galenson, "Immigration and the Colonial Labor System: An Analysis of the Length of Indenture," *Explorations in Economic History,* XIV (October 1977) 360-377; Galenson, "British Servants and the Colonial Indenture System in the Eighteenth Century," *Journal of Southern History,* XLIV (February 1978) 41-66; Galenson, "'Middling People' or 'Common Sort'?: The Social Origins of Some Early Americans Reconsidered," *William and Mary Quarterly,* XXXV (July 1978) 499- 524; Russell R. Menard, "From Servant to Freeholder: Status Mobility and Property Accumulation in Seventeenth-Century Maryland," *William and Mary Quarterly,* XXX (January 1973) 37-64; and Robert O. Heavner, "Indentured Servitude: The Philadelphia Market, 1771-1773," *Journal of Economic History,* XXXVIII (September 1978) 701-713.

As for economic opportunity for members of the free white population, Jackson Turner Main, *The Social Structure of Revolutionary America* (Princeton: Princeton University Press, 1965) emphasizes the large proportion of middle-class property owners as a distinctive feature of colonial society. However, Gary B. Nash, "Urban Wealth and Poverty in Pre-Revolutionary America," *Journal of Interdisciplinary History,* VI (Spring 1976) 545-584, calls attention to the existence of a significant level of poverty in 18th-century America.

The economic effects of the American Revolution—the war and the achievement of political sovereignty—are traced in Curtis P. Nettels, *The Emergence of a National Economy, 1775-1815* (New York: Holt, Rinehart and Winston, 1962). E. James Ferguson, *The Power of the Purse: A History of American Public Finance, 1776-1790* (Chapel Hill: University of North Carolina Press, 1961) discusses the methods by which the newly independent United States financed its military operations against the British army as well as the politics of financial policy-making. Robert A. Gross, *The Minutemen and Their World* (New York: Hill and Wang, 1976) is a case study of the impact of war and independence upon the ordinary people of a New England town. James F. Shepherd and Gary M. Walton, "Economic Change After the American Revolution: Pre- and Post-War Comparisons of Maritime Shipping and Trade," *Explorations in Economic History,* XIII (October 1976) 397-422, analyzes changes in patterns of American foreign trade that took place after the Revolution, while Edward C. Papenfuse, *In Pursuit of Profit: The Annapolis Merchants in the Era of the American Revolution, 1763-1803* (Baltimore: Johns Hopkins University Press, 1975) shows how members of one merchant community adjusted to war and postwar conditions.

The Nineteenth Century: Economic Growth and Development

The emphasis of recent scholarship dealing with 19th-century American economic history can be stated in one word—growth—as scholars sought not only to explain the industrial predominance of the United States by the end of the century but also to formulate more general theories of economic development. Stuart Bruchey, *The Roots of American Economic Growth, 1607-1861* (New York: Harper & Row, 1965) approaches economic growth as an aspect of social change. In *Growth of the Modern American Economy* (New York: Dodd, Mead & Company,

1975), the same author presents a concise summary of the more recent scholarship on 19th-century economic change. Harold G. Vatter, *The Drive to Industrial Maturity: The U. S. Economy, 1860-1914* (Westport, Conn.: Greenwood Press, 1975) also incorporates into his account the results of the latest research.

Until the early 1960s, it was widely assumed that the Civil War (1861 1865) stimulated economic growth and led to industrialization. Reviewing statistical data on growth rates before, during, and after the war—data not readily available to earlier historians—Thomas C. Cochran, "Did the Civil War Retard Industrialization?" *Mississippi Valley Historical Review,* XLVIII (September 1961) 197-210 (reprinted in Thomas C. Cochran, *The Inner Revolution: Essays on the Social Sciences in History* [New York: Harper & Row, 1964]) answers his question in the affirmative, a conclusion also reached in Stanley L. Engerman, "The Economic Impact of the Civil War," *Explorations in Entrepreneurial History,* III (Spring 1966) 176-199. David T. Gilchrist and W. David Lewis (eds.), *Economic Change in the Civil War Era* (Greenville, Del.: Eleutherian Mills—Hagley Foundation, 1965) contains an assessment of the war's qualitative effects on various sectors of the economy, made by leading scholars who found that the conflict appears to have had little significant impact on economic institutional change.

While serious questions were being raised about the role of the Civil War in American industrialization, historians were examining two exciting hypotheses of American economic growth, both of which directed attention to the antebellum period. One of the most widely read books on economic history ever published, W. W. Rostow, *The Stages of Economic Growth: A Non-Communist Manifesto* (Cambridge: Cambridge University Press, 1960) contains a new version of an old device of economic history—stage theory—and defines its crucial stage as the "take-off" period when economic growth becomes the "normal condition" of a society—the years between 1843 and 1860 in the United States. In contrast to Rostow's emphasis on the stimulative effects of railroad building during a brief, crucial set of years, Douglass C. North, *The Economic Growth of the United States, 1790-1860* (Englewood Cliffs, N.J.: Prentice-Hall, 1961) points to cotton as the "engine" of economic growth in the period before the Civil War, as earnings from the export of this staple generated structural changes through the whole economy. Both of these books inspired much discussion and further investigation by other scholars. However, historians could find no empirical evidence to support crucial elements of Rostow's theory, particularly a doubling of the rate of capital formation during the "take-off," and they questioned his analysis of the role of railroads as a leading sector. Studies of inter-sectional trade flows and of food production and consumption in the South failed to uncover evidence for North's contention, built upon hypotheses advanced by earlier economic historians like Guy S. Callender and Louis B. Schmidt, that the Southern market was basic to the growth of commercial agriculture in the Northwest and of manufacturing industry in the Northeast.

If the past decade-and-a-half recorded little progress toward development of a general theory of national economic growth, and indeed a weakening of a widely held explanation, the period witnessed a substantial advance in measuring American economic performance in the 19th century. An important point of reference consisted of the statistical methods and concepts used by the National

The scale and drama of the new heavy industry was captured by W. A. Rogers in this drawing reproduced as an engraving in Harper's Weekly, *March 14, 1891.*

Bureau of Economic Research in studies of 20th-century economic trends, particularly the national income and product framework developed by Simon Kuznets and his colleagues. The series that is perhaps of broadest interest is contained in Robert E. Gallman, "Gross National Product in the United States, 1834-1909," in *Output, Employment, and Productivity in the United States After 1800* (Conference on Research in Income and Wealth, Studies in Income and Wealth, XXV; New York: Columbia University Press, 1966), which concludes that the American GNP grew an average of 48 per cent per decade from the mid-1830s to the end of the century, or 16 per cent per decade in GNP per capita. Paul A. David, "The Growth of Real Product in the United States Before 1840: New Evidence, Controlled Conjectures," *Journal of Economic History,* XXVII (June 1967) 151-197, explores what the author calls a "statistical dark age" in an attempt to measure the rate of economic growth during the five decades before 1840. Data in Richard A. Easterlin, "Interregional Differences in Per Capita Income, Population, and Total Income, 1840-1950," in *Trends in the American Economy in the Nineteenth Century* (Conference on Research in Income and Wealth, Studies in Income and Wealth, XXIV; Princeton: Princeton University Press, 1960) and "Regional Income Trends, 1840-1950" in Seymour E. Harris (ed.), *American Economic History* (New York: McGraw-Hill, 1961) suggest how different regions of the United States participated in national growth. Paul A. David and Peter Solar, "A Bicentenary Contribution to the History of the Cost of Living in America," *Research in Economic History* II (1977) 1-80, contributes a continuous consumer price index as well as an annual series of money wages of "common laborers" since 1774. Stanley Lebergott, *Manpower in Economic Growth: The American Record Since 1800* (New York: McGraw-Hill, 1964) and "Labor Force and Employment, 1800-1960," in *Output, Employment, and Productivity* shows trends in levels of employment and composition of the labor force. Lance E. Davis and John Legler, "The Government in the American Economy, 1815-1902: A Quantitative Study," *Journal of Economic History* XXVI (December 1966) 514-552, presents annual estimates of government revenues and expenditures by region through most of the 19th century.

Dorothy S. Brady, in her "Introduction" to *Output, Employment, and Productivity*, calls attention to the skill, ingenuity, and imagination which authors of statistical accounts such as these bring to their task, but both she and William Parker, in his "Introduction" to *Trends in the American Economy*, caution against misinterpretation of quantitative data. As the latter notes, "the data for the nineteenth century are deficient and the adjustments frequently arbitrary." Moreover, as Parker points out, measurements of economic aggregates, however accurate, can only suggest to historians fruitful approaches by which they may attempt to answer economic history's major question: "By what socio-economic mechanism was this record of economic change produced?"

Business

A major characteristic of the 19th-century American economy was decentralized decision-making by a multitude of entrepreneurs, an observation that suggests the central role played by business and the market in the growth process. While historians have not yet developed a widely accepted set of principles of entrepreneurship, several useful syntheses have appeared. Elisha P. Douglass, *The Coming of Age of American Business* (Chapel Hill: University of North Carolina Press, 1971) supplies an account of the institutional development of business to the end of the nineteenth century, based upon a careful sifting of the monographic literature produced by entrepreneurial and business historians. Herman E. Krooss and Charles Gilbert, *American Business History* (Englewood Cliffs, N. J.: Prentice Hall, 1972) surveys the evolution of the American business system, emphasizing the institutions that developed out of the efforts of businessmen to deal with the problems which they faced. Thomas C. Cochran, *200 Years of American Business* (New York: Basic Books, 1977) gives perspective to the United States experience with meaningful comparisons of the record of American business with that of business in other leading industrial nations; the same author's *Business in American Life: A History* (New York: McGraw-Hill, 1972) discusses the relationships between change in business and change in other areas of society.

Research conducted in the "borderlands" between economic history and the history of law has shown the importance of the creation by government of a legal framework through which the multitude of entrepreneurs of 19th-century America operated. The ways in which lawmaking built, extended, and implemented the market and created new forms of organization are spelled out in detail in the several works of the pioneer of this field, James Willard Hurst: *Law and Economic*

Growth: The Legal History of the Lumber Industry in Wisconsin, 1836-1915 (Cambridge: Harvard University Press, 1964); *Law and Social Process in United States History* (Ann Arbor: University of Michigan Press, 1960); and *The Legitimacy of the Business Corporation in the Law of the United States, 1780-1970* (Charlottesville: University Press of Virginia, 1970). Lawrence M. Friedman, *Contract Law in America: A Social and Economic Case Study* (Madison: University of Wisconsin Press, 1965) discusses the meaning and role of this type of law in the context of the 19th-century market economy. Three articles by Harry N. Scheiber, "Federalism and the American Economic Order, 1789-1910," *Law and Society Review*, X (Fall 1975) 57-118; "The Road to *Munn*: Eminent Domain and the Concept of Public Purpose in the State Courts," *Perspectives in American History*, V (1971) 329-404; and "Property Law, Expropriation, and Resource Allocation by Government: the United States, 1789-1910," *Journal of Economic History*, XXX (March 1973) 232-251, explore significant aspects of public policy which reinforced the decision-making powers of private entrepreneurs in the 19th century.

Transportation and Communication

The transportation revolution has been regarded as a central theme of the history of 19th-century America, but research carried out since the early 1960s has supplied new dimensions of understanding of the role of canals and railroads in economic change. Albert Fishlow, *American Railroads and the Transformation of the Ante-Bellum Economy* (Cambridge: Harvard University Press, 1965) and Robert W. Fogel, *Railroads and American Economic Growth: Essays in Econometric History* (Baltimore: Johns Hopkins University Press, 1964) offer sweeping reassessments of the impact of the railroad on 19th-century economic development, attempting to measure the social savings created by this innovation—the difference between the cost of shipping goods in a given year by rail and the hypothetical cost of shipping the same goods by waterways and roads—as well as analyzing the effects of the railroad on the growth of manufacturing and agriculture.

Continuing research on the developmental role of government in transportation affirmed the findings of studies made in the 1940s and 1950s about the importance of state investment in "internal improvements," especially in the early phases of the transportation revolution. Recent works along this line include: Carter Goodrich, *Government Promotion of American Canals and Railroads, 1800-1890* (New York: Columbia University Press, 1960); Goodrich (ed.), *Canals and Economic Development* (New York: Columbia University Press, 1961); Goodrich, "Internal Improvements Reconsidered," *Journal of Economic History*, XXX (June 1970) 289-311; Harry N. Scheiber, *Ohio Canal Era: A Case Study of Government and the Economy, 1820-1861* (Athens: Ohio University Press, 1969); Stephen Salsbury, *The State, the Investor, and the Railroad: The Boston & Albany, 1825-1867* (Cambridge: Harvard University Press, 1967); Nathan Miller, *The Enterprise of a Free People: Aspects of Economic Development in New York State During the Canal Period, 1792-1838* (Ithaca: Cornell University Press, 1962); Julius Rubin, *Canal or Railroad: Imitation and Innovation in the Response to the Erie Canal in Philadelphia, Baltimore, and Boston* (Philadelphia: American Philosophical Society, 1961); and Robert J. Parks, *Democracy's Railroads: Public Enterprise in*

Westward expansion of the population was materially aided by the development of transcontinental railroads. Engraved after a drawing by A. R. Ward. Reproduced, courtesy of the Smithsonian Institution.

Jacksonian Michigan (Port Washington, N.Y.: Kennikat Press, 1972). At the federal level, Robert W. Fogel, *The Union Pacific Railroad; A Case in Premature Enterprise* (Baltimore: Johns Hopkins University Press, 1960) reappraises the policy of subsidizing the nation's first transcontinental railroad. Stanley L. Engerman, "Some Economic Issues Relating to Railroad Subsidies and the Evaluation of Land Grants," *Journal of Economic History,* XXXII (June 1972) 443-463, discusses implications of the questions raised by this study and others which followed it.

Arthur M. Johnson and Barry E. Supple, *Boston Capitalists and Western Railroads: A Study in the Nineteenth-Century Railroad Investment Process* (Cambridge: Harvard University Press, 1967) examines the developmental role played by private investors in the construction of western railroads in the mid- and late 19th century. Dorothy R. Adler, *British Investment in American Railways, 1834-1899* (edited by Muriel E. Hidy; Charlottesville: University Press of Virginia, 1970) studies the process of external financing of U. S. railroads. Albert Fishlow, "Productivity and Technological Change in the Railroad Sector, 1840-1910," in *Output, Employment, and Productivity,* sets out a quantitative record of the development of this sector. Various aspects of the transportation revolution are discussed in the following works: Erick F. Haites, James Mak, and Gary M. Walton, *Western River Transportation: The Era of Early Internal Development,* 1910-1960 (Baltimore: Johns Hopkins University Press, 1975); Ralph D. Gray, *The National Waterway: A History of the Chesapeake and Delaware Canal, 1769-1965* (Urbana: University of Illinois Press, 1967); James P. Baughman, *Charles Morgan and the Development of Southern Transportation* (Nashville: Vanderbilt University Press, 1968); Oscar O. Winther, *The Transportation Frontier: Trans-Mississippi West, 1865-1890* (New York: Holt, Rinehart and Winston, 1964); Julius Grodinsky, *Transcontinental Railway Strategy, 1869-1893* (Philadelphia: University of Pennsylvania Press, 1962); Richard C. Overton, *Burlington Route: A History of the Burlington Lines* (New York: Knopf, 1965); Charles N. Glaab, *Kansas City and the Railroads* (Madison: State Historical Society of Wisconsin, 1962); Albro Martin, *James J. Hill and the Opening of the Northwest* (New York: Oxford University Press, 1976); and George Rogers Taylor, "The Beginnings of Mass Transportation in Urban American," *Smithsonian Journal of History,* I (Summer, Autumn 1966) 35-50, 31-54.

In addition to a transportation revolution, there occurred in the 19th century a communications revolution, the early phases of which are analyzed in Allan R. Pred, *Urban Growth and the Circulation of Information: The United States System of Cities, 1790-1840* (Cambridge: Harvard University Press, 1973). Changes in marketing, particularly wholesaling, form the subject of Glenn Porter and Harold C. Livesay, *Merchants and Manufacturers: Studies in the Changing Structure of Nineteenth-Century Marketing* (Baltimore: Johns Hopkins University Press, 1971). John G. Clark, *The Grain Trade in the Old Northwest* (Urbana: University of Illinois Press, 1966) discusses the marketing of the principal cash crops of the Old Northwest, while Harold D. Woodman, *King Cotton and His Retainers: Financing and Marketing the Cotton Crop of the South, 1800-1925* (Lexington: University Press of Kentucky, 1968) performs a similar task for the South's major export commodity.

Finance

Economic growth of the kind experienced in 19th-century America involved large demands for capital funds to finance not only a rising level of output of goods and services but also movement into new types of activities and into new regions. Herman E. Krooss and Martin R. Bly, *A History of Financial Intermediaries* (New York: Random House, 1971) is a comprehensive survey of a wide range of financial institutions that developed to bridge the gap between savers and investors. Benjamin J. Klebaner, *Commercial Banking in the United States: A History* (Hinsdale, Ill.: Dryden Press, 1974) is a brief but useful account of the history of commorcial banking. Development of capital markets in the 19th century forms the subject of a series of articles by Lance E. Davis—"Capital Immobilities and Finance Capitalism: A Study of Economic Evolution in the United States, 1820-1920," *Explorations in Entrepreneurial History,* I (Fall 1963) 88-105; "The Investment Market, 1870-1918: The Evolution of a National Market," *Journal of Economic History,* XXV (September 1965) 355-399; and "The New England Textile Mills and the Capital Markets: A Study of Industrial Borrowing, 1840-1860," *ibid.,* XX (March 1960) 1-30. Richard E. Sylla explores the developmental role of banking in "American Banking and Growth in the Nineteenth Century: A Partial View of the Terrain," *Explorations in Economic History,* IX (Winter 1971/72) 197-227; "Federal Policy, Banking Market Structure, and Capital Mobilization in the United States, 1863-1913," *Journal of Economic History,* XXIX (December 1969) 657-686; and "Forgotten Men of Money: Private Bankers in Early U. S. History," *ibid.* XXXVI (March 1976) 173-188. Case studies relating banking policies and practices to regional, state, or local development in the 19th century include: Erling A. Erickson, *Banking in Frontier Iowa, 1836-1865* (Ames: Iowa State University Press, 1971); George D. Green, *Finance and Economic Development in the Old South: Louisiana Banking, 1804-1861* (Stanford: Stanford University Press, 1972); Alice E. Smith, *George Smith's Money: A Scottish Investor in America* (Madison: State Historical Society of Wisconsin, 1966), Alan L. Olmstead, *New York City Mutual Savings Banks, 1819-1861* (Chapel Hill: University of North Carolina Press, 1976), and Donald R. Adams, Jr., *Finance and Enterprise in Early America: A Study of Stephen Girard's Bank, 1812-1831* (Philadelphia: University of Pennsylvania Press, 1978). Important legal aspects of financial history are related in James Willard Hurst, *A Legal History of Money in the United States, 1774-1970* (Lincoln: University of Nebraska Press 1973) and Peter J. Coleman, *Debtors and Creditors in America: Insolvency, Imprisonment for Debt, and Bankruptcy, 1607-1900* (Madison: State Historical Society of Wisconsin, 1974).

The "Bank War" of the 1830s continued to generate scholarly production, with new ground and fresh interpretations of the circumstances surrounding the economic events of the decade provided in Peter Temin, *The Jacksonian Economy* (New York: W. W. Norton, 1969); Jean A. Wilburn, *Biddle's Bank: The Crucial Years* (New York: Columbia University Press, 1967); Robert V. Remini, *Andrew Jackson and the Bank War* (New York: W. W. Norton, 1967); and Marie Elizabeth Sushka, "The Antebellum Money Market and the Economic Impact of the Bank War," *Journal of Economic History*, XXXVI (December 1976) 809-835. Aspects of banking regulation are discussed in Arthur Fraas, "The Second Bank of the United States: An Instrument for an Interregional Monetary Union," *Journal of Economic History*, XXXIV (June 1974) 447-467, and Hugh T. Rockoff, "Varieties of Banking and Regional Economic Development in the United States, 1840-1860," *ibid.* XXXV (March 1975) 160-181. Recent works on federal monetary policies during the Civil War and immediate postwar years include: Bray Hammond, *Sovereignty and an Empty Purse: Banks and Politics in the Civil War* (Princeton: Princeton University Press, 1970); Irwin Unger, *The Greenback Era: A Social and Political History of American Finance, 1865-1879* (Princeton: Princeton University Press, 1964); Walter T. K. Nugent, *The Money Question During Reconstruction* (New York: W. W. Norton, 1967); Nugent, *Money and American Society, 1865-1880* (New York: Free Press, 1968); and Allen Weinstein, *Prelude to Populism: Origins of the Silver Issue, 1867-1878* (New Haven: Yale University Press, 1970).

Edwin J. Perkins, *Financing Anglo-American Trade: The House of Brown, 1800-1880* (Cambridge: Harvard University Press, 1975) uses the experience of a leading firm to trace institutional changes in the financing of international trade in the 19th century. The same author's "Foreign Interest Rates in American Financial Markets: A Revised Series of Dollar-Sterling Exchange Rates, 1835-1900," *Journal of Economic History*, XXXVIII (June 1978) 392-417, offers a new series of dollar-sterling exchange rates that modifies data presented earlier in Lance Davis and J. R. T. Hughes, "A Dollar-Sterling Exchange, 1803-1894," *Economic History Review*, XIII (August 1960) 52-78. Jeffrey G. Williamson, *American Growth and the Balance of Payments, 1820-1913: A Study of the Long Swing* (Chapel Hill: University of North Carolina Press, 1964) presents an analysis of international capital flow as well as exports and imports in relating foreign trade to domestic growth in the 19th century.

Industry

The growth of manufacturing was a highly visible element of 19th-century economic growth as the sector advanced from a minor position in 1800 to account for nearly one-quarter of the nation's output by 1900. For a review of the extensive body of literature dealing with the development and application of technology to industry, the most useful starting point is Paul Uselding, "Studies of Technology in Economic History," Research in Economic History, I Supplement (1977) 159-219. As Uselding notes, much of the recent research in this specialized area of economic history has been stimulated in one way or another by H. J. Habakkuk, American and British Technology in the Nineteenth Century (Cambridge: Cambridge University Press, 1962) and his analysis of the relationship of choice of industrial technique to available relative supplies of labor and capital. However, something of the wide range of approaches employed in the study of technology and its contribution to productivity advance can be seen in the works of several scholars: Nathan Rosenberg, Technology and American Economic Growth (New York: Harper & Row, 1972) and Perspectives in Technology (Cambridge: Cambridge University Press, 1976), advancing a concept of "technological convergence" (among many significant and useful observations and generalizations); Jacob Schmookler, Invention and Economic Growth (Cambridge: Harvard University Press, 1966), relating the activities of inventors to their perception of the profitability of specific lines of invention; and Bruce Sinclair, Philadelphia's Philosopher Mechanics: A History of the Franklin Institute, 1824-1865 (Baltimore: Johns Hopkins University Press, 1974), a study of the institutional aspects of technical research.

Historians pursued a number of lines of investigation of the growth of manufacturing in the 19th century in addition to the technological dimension. Diane Lindstrom, Economic Development in the Philadelphia Region, 1810-1850 (New York: Columbia University Press, 1978) develops an "Eastern demand" model of the early industrialization of Philadelphia, locating the most significant markets for the city's manufactures within the East itself. Peter Temin, Iron and Steel in Nineteenth-Century America: An Economic Inquiry (Cambridge: M.I.T. Press, 1964) contains an analysis of the interaction between supply and demand factors in the growth of this basic industry. Albert W. Niemi, Jr., State and Regional Patterns in American Manufacturing (Westport, Conn.: Greenwood Press, 1974) gives an account of changes in the regional distribution of industrial activity after 1860. Alfred D. Chandler, Jr., "Anthracite Coal and the Beginnings of the Industrial Revolution in the United States," Business History Review, XLVI (Summer 1972) 141-181, relates the availability of cheap energy to the expansion of the factory system in manufacturing, while Vera F. Eliasberg, "Some Aspects of Development in the Coal Mining Industry, 1839-1918," in Output, Employment, and Productivity, provides a measure of total energy consumption in the United States in the 19th century. Dorothy S. Brady, "Relative Prices in the Nineteenth Century," Journal of Economic History, XXIV (June 1964) 145-203, includes an analysis of the introduction and proliferation of a variety of new consumer goods in 19th-century

American pride in industrial development is recorded in this 1876 lithograph by Currier & Ives. Reprinted, courtesy of the Library of Congress.

America. Allan R. Pred, *The Spatial Dynamics of U. S. Urban-Industrial Growth, 1800-1914* (Cambridge: M.I.T. Press, 1966) advances a model of "urban-size growth," explicitly linking industrialization and urbanization in the half century after 1860. Anthony F. C. Wallace, *Rockdale: The Growth of an American Village in the Early Industrial Revolution* (New York: Knopf, 1978) views an industrial community from the vantage point of the anthropologist. Concrete examples of the process of "transfer of capital" and entrepreneurial skills from foreign trade to manufacturing are supplied in Frances W. Gregory, *Nathan Appleton: Merchant and Entrepreneur, 1779-1861* (Charlottesville: University Press of Virginia, 1975) and James B. Hedges, *The Browns of Providence Plantations: The Nineteenth Century* (Providence: Brown University Press, 1968). David T. Gilchrist (ed.), *The Growth of the Seaport Cities, 1790-1825* (Charlottesville: University Press of Virginia, 1967) explores the relationship between maritime commerce and early manufacturing in the setting of the nation's largest business centers. Other works which deal with aspects of 19th-century industrial development include: Paul K. McGouldrick, *New England Textiles in the Nineteenth Century: Profits and Investment* (Cambridge: Harvard University Press, 1968); Norman L. Crockett, *The Woolen Industry of the Midwest* (Lexington: University Press of Kentucky, 1970); Margaret Walsh, *The Manufacturing Frontier: Pioneer Industry in Antebellum Wisconsin, 1830-1860* (Madison: State Historical Society of Wisconsin, 1972); Anita S. Goodstein, *Biography of a Businessman: Henry W. Sage, 1814-1897* (Ithaca: Cornell University Press, 1962); Peter J. Coleman, *The Transformation of Rhode Island,*

1790-1890 (Providence: Brown University Press, 1963); and Carol E. Hoffecker, *Wilmington Delaware: Portrait of an Industrial City, 1830-1910* (Charlottesville: University Press of Virginia, 1914).

Agriculture in the North

Agriculture declined in relative importance as the American economy became industrialized, but throughout the 19th century the sector experienced expansion in manpower, capital, and land employed, and contributed significantly to the nation's growth. John T. Schlebecker, *Whereby We Thrive: A History of American Farming, 1607-1972* (Ames: Iowa State University Press, 1975) serves as a readable brief introduction to the history of agriculture in the United States; but Paul W. Gates, *The Farmers's Age: Agriculture, 1815-1860* (New York: Holt, Rinehart and Winston, 1960) provides a synthesis in greater depth covering a shorter span of years, as does Gilbert C. Fite, *The Farmers' Frontier, 1865-1900* (New York: Holt, Rinehart and Winston, 1966). Clarence H. Danhof, *Change in Agriculture: The Northern United States, 1820-1870* (Cambridge: Harvard University Press, 1969) examines the responses of farmers to the potential of growing markets and new technology.

Allan G. Bogue, *From Prairie to Corn Belt: Farming on the Illinois and Iowa Prairies in the Nineteenth Century* (Chicago: University of Chicago Press, 1963) considers the whole range of problems confronting the operator of a Middle Western farm business from initial settlement to the end of the century. Specialized branches of agribusiness are discussed in Eric E. Lampard, *The Rise of the Dairy Industry in Wisconsin: A Study in Agricultural Change, 1820-1920* (Madison: State Historical Society of Wisconsin, 1963) and in James W. Whitaker, *Feedlot Empire: Beef Cattle Feeding in Illinois and Iowa, 1840-1900* (Ames: Iowa State University Press, 1975). Morton Rothstein, "American in the International Rivalry for the British Wheat Market, 1860-1914," *Mississippi Valley Historical Review,* XLVII (December 1960) 401-418, focuses on innovations in the marketing of agricultural commodities. Donald L. Winters, "Tenancy as an Economic Institution: The Growth and Distribution of Agricultural Tenancy in Iowa, 1850-1900," *Journal of Economic History,* XXXVII (June 1977) 382-408, reappraises the economic prospects of tenant farmers, and David E. Schob, *Hired Hands and Plowboys: Farm Labor in the Midwest, 1815-60* (Urbana: University of Illinois Press, 1975) furnishes new information about farm workers. Anne Mayhew, "A Reappraisal of the Causes of Farm Protest in the United States, 1870-1900," *Journal of Economic History,* XXXII (June 1972) 464-475, examines the response of farmers to the growing commercialization of agriculture in the late 19th century. Essays contained in three recent symposium volumes offer fresh approaches to many specific topics: D. P. Kelsey (ed.), *Farming in the New Nation: Interpreting American Agriculture, 1790-1840* (Washington D.C.: Agricultural History Society, 1972); James W. Whitaker (ed.), *Farming in the Midwest, 1840-1900* (Washington D.C.: Agricultural History Society, 1974); and James H. Shideler (ed.), *Agriculture in the Development of the Far West* (Washington D.C.: Agricultural History Society, 1975).

Recent research has provided new dimensions of understanding about the profitability of frontier land speculation and the economic functions of land speculators. Robert P. Swierenga, "Land Speculation and Its Impact on American

Economic Growth and Welfare: A Historiographical Review," *Western Historical Quarterly,* VIII (July 1977) 283-302, surveys the changing interpretations of American land history. Swierenga's own work, *Pioneers and Profits: Land Speculation on the Iowa Frontier* (Ames: Iowa State University Press, 1968), is based upon analysis of a large sample of transactions, concluding with an emphasis on the developmental role of western land agents. For the evolution of government land disposal policy, Paul W. Gates, *History of Public Land Law Development* (Washington, D.C.: Government Printing Office, 1968) summarizes the provisions of the statutes, and Malcolm J. Rohrbough, *The Land Office Business: The Settlement and Administration of American Public Lands, 1789-1837* (New York: Oxford University Press, 1968) discusses adminstrative structure and policies. William W. Savage, Jr., *The Cherokee Strip Live Stock Association: Federal Regulation and the Cattleman's Last Frontier* (Columbia: University of Missouri Press, 1973) provides a case study of interrelationships among homesteaders, cattlemen, Indians, and the federal government in the maneuvering for control of vast areas of western land in the late 19th century.

Some dimensions of the "agricultural revolution" in America are measured in William N. Parker and Judith L. V. Klien, "Productivity Growth in Grain Production in the United States, 1840-60 and 1900-10," in *Output, Employment, and Productivity;* Robert E. Gallman, "Changes in Total U. S. Agricultural Factor Productivity in the 19th Century," *Agricultural History,* XLVI (January 1972) 191-210, and "The Agricultural Sector and the Pace of Economic Growth: U. S. Experience in the Nineteenth Century," and Richard A. Easterlin, "Farm Production and Income in Old and New Areas at Mid-Century," both in David C. Klingaman and Richard K. Vedder (eds.), *Essays in Nineteenth Century Economic History: The Old Northwest* (Athens: Ohio University Press, 1975). The circumstances surrounding adoption of an important innovation are discussed in Paul A. David, "The Mechanization of Reaping in the Ante-Bellum Midwest," in David, *Technical Choice, Innovation, and Economic Growth* (Cambridge: Cambridge University Press, 1975); Alan L. Olmstead, "The Mechanization of Reaping and Mowing in American Agriculture, 1833-1870," *Journal of Economic History,* XXXV (June 1975) 327-352; and Lewis R. Jones, "The Mechanization of Reaping and Mowing in American Agriculture, 1833-1870: Comment," *ibid.* LXXVII (June 1977) 451-455. Margaret W. Rossiter, *The Emergence of Agricultural Science: Justus Liebig and the Americans, 1840-1880* (New Haven: Yale University Press, 1975) discusses developments in agricultural science, while Roy V. Scott, *The Reluctant Farmer: The Rise of Agricultural Extension to 1914* (Urbana: University of Illinois Press, 1970) deals with the education of farmers in new scientific methods.

The Southern Economy: Slavery and Growth

What distinguished the South from other regions of the United States before the Civil War was the existence of a large slave labor force, employed primarily in the commercial production of staple commodities, principally cotton. Although contemporary observers and historians have long debated questions about slavery, the debate intensified during the past decade and a half, as scholars applied new methodology and fresh points of view to an effort to advance our understanding of the impact of the slave experience on blacks and the influence of the institution of slavery, directly or indirectly, on regional economic progress. As a prime example of the method of the new economic history applied to an old problem of American history, Robert W. Fogel and Stanley L. Enterman, *Time on the Cross: The Economics of American Negro Slavery* and *Time on the Cross: Evidence and Methods* (Boston: Little, Brown, 1974) occupied a central position in a discussion which revolved around the authors' strong argument that slavery was a profitable and efficient labor system in the context of the antebellum Southern economy. Neither their conclusions nor their method went unchallenged, however, with the strongest critique delivered by other practitioners of econometric history, contained in Paul A. David *et al.*, *Reckoning with Slavery: Critical Study in the Quantitative History of American Negro Slavery* (New York: Oxford University Press, 1976). Gavin Wright, *The Political Economy of the Cotton South: Households, Markets, and Wealth in the Nineteenth Century* (New York: W. W. Norton, 1978) puts his study in a broad framework, directing an econometric analysis to an exploration of the impact of slavery and cotton production upon the course of Southern economic development through much of the 19th century. Examples of the large periodical literature generated in the continuing controversy over the profitability of slavery, the viability of the system and the nature of the Southern economy are contained in Hugh G. J. Aitken (ed.), *Did Slavery Pay? Readings in the Economics of Black Slavery in the United States* (Boston: Houghton Mifflin, 1971), including the famous essay by Alfred H. Conrad and John R. Meyer, "The Economics of Slavery in the Antebellum South," which first appeared in 1957. These issues are further explored in William N. Parker (ed.), *The Structure of the Cotton Economy of the Antebellum South* (Washington, D.C.: Agricultural History Society, 1970).

At the same time that economic historians were pursuing their investigations of the economics of slavery, social historians were employing more traditional methods to examine slavery and its relationship to other institutions in Southern society. With a Marxist perspective, Eugene D. Genovese, *Roll, Jordan, Roll: The World the Slaves Made* (New York: Pantheon, 1974) provides a detailed description of slave life, emphasizing the slaveowner's employment of paternalism as a device to make the exploitative system function. Other studies of slavery set in a broad social context, contributing to an understanding of the economic meaning of the "peculiar institution," include: John W. Blassingame, *The Slave Community: Plantation Life in the Antebellum South* (New York: Oxford University Press, 1972) and Leslie H. Owens, *This Species of Property: Slave Life and Culture in the Old South* (New York: Oxford University Press, 1976). Various interpretations are set forth in the selections contained in Allen Weinstein and Frank O. Gatell (eds.), *American Negro Slavery: A Modern Reader* (New York: Oxford University Press, 1968). Essays in Laura Foner and Eugene D. Genovese (eds.), *Slavery in the New World: A Reader in Comparative History* (Englewood Cliffs, N.J.: Prentice-Hall, 1969) place the experience of the Southern United States in international perspective.

Special apsects of the history of slavery and of the state of the antebellum economy are considered in an abundant monographic literature, some examples of which follow. Claudia D. Goldin, *Urban Slavery in the American South, 1820–1860: A Quantitative History* (Chicago: University of Chicago Press, 1976) advances an economic explanation for the decline of slavery in Southern cities as a challenge to the sociological interpretation of Richard C. Wade, *Slavery in the Cities* (New

York: Oxford University Press, 1964). Robert S. Starobin, *Industrial Slavery in the Old South* (New York: Oxford University Press, 1970) examines the employment of slave labor in Southern industries, while Fred Bateman and Thomas Weiss, "Manufacturing in the Antebellum South," *Research in Economic History*, I (1976) 1-44, surveys the industrial condition of the antebellum South. Management of the plantation as a business enterprise is discussed in William K. Scarborough, *The Overseer: Plantation Management in the Old South* (Baton Rouge: Louisiana State University Press, 1966); R. Keith Aufhauser, "Slavery and Scientific Mangement," *Journal of Economic History*, XXX (December 1973) 811-824; and Jacob Metzer, "Rational Management, Modern Business Practices, and Economics of Scale in the Ante-Bellum Southern Plantations," *Explorations in Economic History*, XII (April 1975) 123-150. Production of foodstuffs in relation to the region's food requirements is examined in Sam B. Hilliard, *Hog Meat and Hoe Cake: Food Supply in the Old South, 1840-1860* (Carbondale: Southern Illinois University Press, 1972) as well as in essays by Robert E. Gallman and by Raymond C. Battalio and John Kagel in *The Structure of the Cotton Economy*. Julius Rubin, "The Limits of Agricultural Progress in the Nineteenth-Century South," *Agricultural History*, VLIX (April 1975) 362-373, explores the effects of ecological problems on food production in the South in the 19th century. Ira Berlin, *Slaves Without Masters: The Free Negro in the Antebellum South* (New York: Pantheon, 1974) includes material on the economic life of free blacks.

The picture of slavery and its economic effects is not complete without at least a glance at the postwar situation. Stephen J. Decanio, *Agriculture in the Postbellum South: The Economics of Production and Supply* (Cambridge: M.I.T. Press, 1974) is an econometric study of the adjustments made in agriculture to institutional change. Roger L. Ranson and Richard Sutch, *One Kind of Freedom: The Economic Consequences of Emancipation* (Cambridge: Cambridge University Press, 1977) and Robert Higgs, *Competition and Coercion: Blacks in the American Economy, 1865-1914* (Cambridge: Cambridge University Press, 1977) bring theory and statistics to an anaylsis of changes in the economic status of the black population after emancipation. John W. Blassingame, *Black New Orleans, 1860-1880* (Chicago: University of Chicago Press, 1973) is a social history which includes an account of the economic experience of one community of urban blacks.

The Twentieth Century: The Corporation and the State

The rise of the large business corporation appears in perspective to have been "one of the major changes in history, comparable to the rise of medieval feudalism or of commercial institutions at the close of the middle ages," to quote Thomas C. Cochran, *American Business in the Twentieth Century* (Cambridge: Harvard University Press, 1972), which discusses changes in business since 1900 in the context of the economic, social, and political environment. Corporate bureaucracy and concentration of economic power appeared to many to be a central tendency of the 20th-century American economy, contrasting with the dispersion of decision-making power among small firms in the mid-19th century. It is not surprising that various hypotheses have been advanced to explain the nature of change in the "government of the business system," the institutional pattern through which economic decisions were made. The vast body of literature focusing on the early history of the modern corporation is ably summarized in Glenn Porter, *The Rise of Big Business, 1860-1910* (New York: Thomas Y. Crowell, 1973).

The most comprehensive history of the big business sector in America is Alfred D. Chandler, Jr., *The Visible Hand: The Managerial Revolution in American Business* (Cambridge: Harvard University Press, 1977), which analyzes the emergence of large business units as a response to the technology of high volume production and the growth of mass markets. The historical development of the modern corporation and the constitution of what some observers have termed a "center economy" can be traced in the accounts of several individual industries. Three useful case studies of different kinds of industries, demonstrating the changing relationships of technology, the market, and industrial structure are: Harold F. Williamson *et al.*, *The American Petroleum Industry: The Age of Energy, 1899-1959* (Evanston: Northwestern University Press, 1963); Alfred S. Eichner, *The Emergence of Oligopoly: Sugar Refining as a Case Study* (Baltimore: Johns Hopkins University Press, 1969); Reese V. Jenkins, *Images and Enterprise: Technology and the American Photographic Industry, 1839 to 1925* (Baltimore: Johns Hopkins University Press, 1975). Vincent P. Carosso, *Investment Banking in America: A History* (Cambridge: Harvard University Press, 1970) contains an analysis of changes in the position of the finance capitalist in the business system. Louis Galambos, *Competition and Cooperation: The Emergence of a National Trade Association* (Baltimore: Johns Hopkins University Press, 1966) discusses the attempts of members of the cotton textile industry to meet competitive and other problems through voluntary association. James H. Soltow, *Origins of Small Business: Metal Fabricators and Machinery Makers in New England, 1890-1957* (Philadelphia: American Philosophical Society, 1965) explores the efforts of small firms to develop a "strategy of size" by adaptation to niches in the modern industrial economy.

Another approach to the history of the large corporation is through business and company biography, some recent examples of which include: Joseph Frazier Wall, *Andrew Carnegie* (New York: Oxford University Press, 1970); Harold C. Livesay, *Andrew Carnegie and the Rise of Big Business* (Boston: Little, Brown, 1975); Robert Hessen, *Steel Titan: The Life of Charles N. Schwab* (New York: Oxford University Press, 1975); Alfred D. Chandler, Jr. and Stephen Salsbury, *Pierre S. Dupont and the Making of the Modern Corporation* (New York: Harper and Row, 1971); Henrietta M. Larson, Evelyn H. Knowlton, and Charles S. Popple, *History of Standard Oil (New Jersey): New Horizons, 1927-1950* (New York: Harper and Row, 1971); and Ralph W. Hidy, Frank E. Hill, and Allan Nevins, *Timber and Men: The Weyerhauser Story* (New York: Macmillan, 1963). Works dealing with changes in business functions and management methods include, in addition to a considerable periodical literature: Hugh G. J. Aitken, *Taylorism at Watertown Arsenal: Scientific Management in Action, 1908-1915* (Cambridge: Harvard University Press, 1960); Alan R. Raucher, *Public Relations and Business, 1900-1929* (Baltimore: Johns Hopkins University Press, 1968); Daniel Nelson, *Managers, and Workers: Origins of the New Factory System in the United States,*

1880-1920 (Madison: University of Wisconsin Press, 1975); and Robert Ozanne, *A Century of Labor-Management Relations at McCormick and International Harvester* (Madison: University of Wisconsin Press, 1967).

How various elements in society viewed the large corporation and how business leaders perceived their own role in society provide the themes of several studies. Louis Galambos, *The Public Image of Big Business in America, 1880-1940* (Baltimore: Johns Hopkins University Press, 1975) measures the growing acceptance of business bureaucracy by several segments of the middle class, while James Gilbert, *Designing the Industrial State. The Intellectual Pursuit of Collectivism in America, 1880-1940* (Chicago: Quadrangle Books, 1972) analyzes the views of a group of intellectuals about the large corporation. The subject of Morrell Heald, *The Social Responsibilities of Business: Company and Community, 1900-1969* (Cleveland: Case Western Reserve University, 1970) is the search by business for a social role and rationale appropriate to an age of corporate bureaucracy and economic power held by large units. Herman E. Krooss, *Executive Opinion: What Business Leaders Said and Thought on Economic Issues, 1920s-1960s* (Garden City, N.Y.: Doubleday, 1970) examines the comments and prophesies of business leaders about a variety of public issues.

An expansion of federal government regulation accompanied the rise of the large corporation, much of it accomplished during the Progressive movement of the early 20th century and the New Deal of the 1930s. Traditionally, historians had viewed the economic policy of these administrations as an effort by liberals to restrain the power of the business community and to protect the public interest. From the "New Left" of the 1960s came several works that posed a challenge to this interpretation. Gabriel Kolko, *The Triumph of Conservatism: A Reinterpretation of American History, 1900-1916* (Glencoe: Free Press, 1963) sees the major theme of the Progressive period to be the establishment of "political capitalism," or the use of government by big business leaders to achieve stability in industries which they had monopolized. In *Railroads and Regulation, 1877-1916* (Princeton: Princeton University Press, 1965), Kolko applies the concept of political capitalism to the transportation sector. In a similar vein, James Weinstein, *The Corporate Ideal in the Liberal State, 1900-1918* (Boston: Beacon Press, 1968) perceives the reform measures of this era as a business-directed institutional adjustment to meet the needs of the large corporation. For the 1930s, Paul D. Conkin, *The New Deal* (New York: Thomas Y. Crowell, 1967) emphasizes the creation of a system of security for big business. These works served to demonstrate the shallowness of the older interpretation which had often confused political rhetoric with social change and thus had viewed regulation as a victory of "the people" over "the interests." But the radical approach did not establish a framework for the study of government-business relations in 20th-century America. A new synthesis would have to be built upon the detailed studies of specific situations, emphasizing the complexities of the many facets of the relationships between the private and public sectors in modern society, some elements of which are suggested in works like Robert H. Wiebe, *Businessmen and Reform: a Study of the Progressive Movement* (Cambridge: Harvard University Press, 1962) and Arthur M. Johnson, "Continuity and Change in Government-Business Relations," in John Braeman, Robert H. Bremner, and Everett Walters (eds.), *Change and Continuity in Twentieth-Century America* (New York: Harper and Row, 1966).

Since railroads were the nation's first big businesses and the first to be regulated, it is useful to turn next to the subject of railroad regulation. Thomas K. McCraw, "Regulation in America: A Review Article," *Business History Review,* XLIX (Summer 1975) 159-183, examines in critical fashion the large body of literature dealing with the performance of regulatory commissions. Ari and Olive Hoogenboom, *A History of the ICC: From Panacea to Palliative* (New York: W. W. Norton, 1976) supplies a useful summary account of this important federal commission from its beginnings in 1887 to the 1970s. Recent monographs about various aspects of transportation regulation include: George H. Miller, *Railroads and the Granger Laws* (Madison: University of Wisconsin Press, 1971), which emphasizes the role of local merchants in the movement for state legislation that preceded federal action; Paul W. MacAvoy, *The Economic Effects of Regulation: The Trunk-Line Railroad Cartels and the Interstate Commission Before 1900* (Cambridge: M.I.T. Press, 1965), an attempt to estimate the initial results of federal regulation upon rate-making; Albro Martin, *Enterprise Denied: Origins of the Decline of American Railroads, 1897-1917* (New York: Columbia University Press, 1971), a definition of the "American Railroad Problem" of the early 20th century as unwillingness of the ICC to grant adequate rate increases, thus discouraging the flow of investment funds to the railroad industry; Stanley P. Caine, *The Myth of a Progressive Reform: Railroad Regulation in Wisconsin, 1903-1910* (Madison: State Historical Society of Wisconsin, 1970), an assessment of the role of various interest groups in the establishment of railroad regulation in one state; and Arthur M. Johnson, *Petroleum Pipelines and Public Policy, 1906-1959* (Cambridge: Harvard University Press, 1967), a case study of the impact of regulation of this form of transportation upon the industry it served.

In contrast to the setting of rates which came to characterize the regulation of transportation and other utilities, government policy has emphasized encouragement and enforcement of competition in industry, an approach embodied in antitrust legislation. William Letwin, *Law and Economic Policy in America: The Evolution of the Sherman Antitrust Act* (New York: Random House, 1965) discusses the origins and early applications of the Sherman Act of 1890, the basic statute in this field. Ellis W. Hawley, *The New Deal and the Problem of Monopoly: A Study in Economic Ambivalence* (Princeton: Princeton University Press, 1966) analyzes the conflicts over public policy toward business during the 1930s, when policy changed from encouragement of price-setting by industrialists under the National Recovery Administration to vigorous enforcement of the antitrust laws. Robert F. Himmelberg, *The Origins of the National Recovery Administration: Business, Government, and the Trade Association Issue, 1921-1933* (New York: Fordham University Press, 1976) traces the efforts of trade association politicians through the 1920s and early 1930s to revise the antitrust laws, while Sidney Fine, *The Automobile Under the Blue Eagle: Labor, Management, and the Automobile Manufacturing Code* (Ann Arbor: University of Michigan Press, 1963) emphasizes the labor provisions of the industry's "code of fair practices" established under NRA. Little agreement exists concerning the general issue of concentration of economic power in America. But Alfred D. Chandler, Jr., "The Structure of American Industry in the Twentieth Century: A Historical Overview," *Business History Review,* XLIII (Autumn 1969) 255-298, analyzes the changing levels of concentration among different industries from the early years of the century to the 1960s.

The Depression era witnessed an enlargement of the scope of federal regulatory authority over a number of kinds of business deemed to have a "public interest." The difficulty of defining the "public interest" in business regulation, even during a period when prestige of business leaders stood at a low level, is demonstrated in John Braeman, "The New Deal and the 'Broker State': A Review of the Recent Scholarly Literature," *Business History Review,* XLVI (Winter 1972) 400-429, a discussion of some of the monographs treating business legislation in the 1930s. A case study of the impact of regulation upon one important industry over the long term is contained in Gerald D. Nash, *United States Oil Policy, 1890-1964: Business and Government in Twentieth-Century America* (Pittsburgh: University of Pittsburgh Press, 1968). Less attention has been directed by historians to the overall pattern of business–government relations since World War II, although interest in the role of the corporation in modern society has encouraged economists, political scientists, and others to contribute to a growing body of literature on the subject. One effort to place developments in an historical perspective is Otis L. Graham, Jr., *Toward a Planned Society: From Roosevelt to Nixon* (New York: Oxford University Press, 1976), which emphasizes interaction between government and organized interest groups from the 1930s to the 1970s.

The economic demands of modern warfare led to development of a special relationship between business and the military, which came to be called a "military-industrial complex." Robert D. Cuff, "An Organizational Perspective on the Military-Industrial Complex," *Business History Review,* LII (Summer 1978) 250-267, suggests that the relations between business, government, and defense be approached "as an historical problem in the evolution of organizational forms." His own study of *The War Industries Board: Business-Government Relations During World War I* (Baltimore: Johns Hopkins University Press, 1973) is a detailed account of the first chapter in the history of the "complex." Two articles by Paul A. C. Koistinen are also useful: "The 'Industrial-Military Complex' in Historical Perspective: World War I," *Business History Review,* XLIV (Winter 1967) 387-403, and "The 'Industrial-Military Complex' in Historical Perspective: The Inter-War Years," *Journal of American History,* LVI (March 1970) 819-839. Donald J. Mrozek, "The Truman Administration and the Enlistment of the Aviation Industry in Postwar Defense," *Business History Review,* XLVIII (Spring 1974) 73-94, and Richard A. Aliano, *American Defense Policy from Eisenhower to Kennedy: The Politics of Changing Military Requirements, 1957-1961* (Athens: Ohio University Press, 1975) direct attention to the political forces encouraging the growth of close connections between defense industry and the military in the 1940s and 1950s respectively.

While monetary and fiscal policies did not regulate industry directly, these efforts by government to promote economic stability and growth affected the environment in which business decision-making took place. Milton Friedman and Anna J. Schwartz, *A Monetary History of the United States, 1867-1960* (Princeton: Princeton University Press, 1963) stresses the authors' belief in the importance of the influence of the stock of money on economic conditions, a conclusion which has been challenged and supported in a considerable literature over the last

"Long Stairway in the Mill District," January 1941, by Jack Delano, is part of a massive photo study of Depression America undertaken by the Farm Security Administration to record the country's most serious economic crisis. Photo courtesy of the Library of Congress.

decade and a half. Elmus R. Wicker, *Federal Reserve Monetary Policy, 1917–1933* (New York: Random House, 1966) elaborates the process by which government policy was formulated in this area from World War I to the beginning of the New Deal. Herbert Stein, *The Fiscal Revolution in America* (Chicago: University of Chicago Press, 1969) traces the major steps in this "revolution," symbolized by the contrast between Herbert Hoover's recommendation of a large tax increase in 1931 and John Kennedy's recommendation of a large tax reduction in 1962, both designed to reduce unemployment. Robert Lekachman, *The Age of Keynes* (New York: Random House, 1966) contains a history of the impact of Maynard, Lord Keynes' ideas on economic thought and policy in the United States. Robert A. Gordon, *Economic Instability and Growth: The American Record* (New York: Harper and Row, 1974) is an account of federal economic policy from the end of World War I to the Nixon administration.

Efforts to explain the origins and persistence of the economic catastrophe of the 1930s continue to be made. Peter Temin, *Did Monetary Forces Cause the Great Depression?* (New York: W. W. Norton, 1976) weighs the monetarist and Keynesian models of the Great Depression, arguing that historical data do not support the former interpretation. Robert Sobel, *The Great Bull Market: Wall Street in the 1920s* (New York: W. W. Norton, 1968) relates weaknesses in the institutional structure of investment banking to the crash of the stock market in 1929, while Susan E. Kennedy, *The Banking Crisis of 1933* (Lexington: University Press of Kentucky, 1973) offers an explanation of that traumatic event in the financial life of the nation. Lester V. Chandler's *America's Greatest Depression 1929-1941* (New York: Harper & Row, 1970) is a useful compendium of the principal economic events during the decade, their effects on various groups, and policies devised to deal with the problems that were perceived. Jim Potter, *The American Economy Between the World Wars* (New York: John Wiley, 1974) in a summary account intended for British readers seeks an explanation of the Depression in the United States in the developments of the 1920s.

Recent research on foreign economic policy, an area lying on the academic borderland between economic and diplomatic history, has tended to focus on the role of business influence in policy-making. Writers of the "New Left" view foreign policy, like domestic policy, as the product of a conspiracy of corporate business, in this case to secure new opportunities for trade and investment abroad. Examples of this approach include: William A. Williams, *The Roots of the Modern American Empire* (New York: Random House, 1969); Walter LaFeber, *The New Empire: An Interpretation of American Expansion, 1860-1898* (Ithaca: Cornell University Press, 1963); Carl P. Parrini, *Heir to Empire: United States Economic Diplomacy, 1916-1923* (Pittsburgh: University of Pittsburgh Press, 1969); Lloyd C. Gardner, *Economic Aspects of New Deal Diplomacy* (Madison: University of Wisconsin Press, 1964); and Joyce and Gabriel Kolko, *The Limits of Power: The World and United States Foreign Policy, 1945-1954* (New York: Harper and Row, 1972).

However, the findings of other scholars call into question the existence of a simple relationship between presumed business interests and the realities of American foreign policy. Joan Hoff Wilson, *American Business and Foreign Policy, 1920-1933* (Lexington: University Press of Kentucky, 1971) sees the business community as too fragmented to play a significant role in the formulation of foreign policy in the 1920s, and Charles P. Kindleberger, *The World in Depression, 1929-1939* (Berkeley: University of California Press, 1973) emphasizes the reluctance of American officials to assume leadership of the international economy after World War I. Richard H. Werking, *The Master Architects: Building the United States Foreign Service, 1890-1913* (Lexington: University Press of Kentucky, 1977) shows how State Department officials attempted in the early 20th century to mobilize support from businessmen to push their own plans for an expanded foreign service. Robert B. Zevin, "An Interpretation of American Imperialism," *Journal of Economic History*, XXXII (March 1972) 316-360, suggests that American political leaders often sought to use economic means to attain ideological goals. This last theme is elaborated in Michael J. Hogan, *Informal Entente: The Private Structure of Cooperation in Anglo-American Economic Diplomacy, 1918-1928* (Columbia: University of Missouri Press, 1977), which argues that government officials attempted to use private business to advance objectives defined by the diplomatic establishment after World War I, and in Irvine H. Anderson, Jr., *The Standard-Vacuum Oil Company and United States East Asian Policy, 1933-1941* (Princeton: Princeton University Press, 1975), which stresses the blurred lines of demarcation between diplomatic, military, and corporate responsibility in analyzing the exercise of influence in foreign policy-making.

Even if little basic agreement exists about the reasons for the direction of United States foreign economic policy, we can discern the overall shape of the record of American foreign investment and trade. Mira Wilkins, *The Emergence of Multinational Enterprise: American Business Abroad from the Colonial Era to 1914* and *The Maturing of Multinational Enterprise: American Business Abroad from 1914 to 1970* (Cambridge: Harvard University Press, 1970, 1974) provide a straightforward account of the process of expansion by United States corporations into other parts of the world since the 19th century. Ilse Mintz, *Cyclical Fluctuations in the Exports of the United States Since 1879* (New York: National Bureau of Economic Research, 1967) and Robert Lipsey, *Price and Quantity Trends in the Foreign Trade of the United States* (Princeton: Princeton University Press, 1963) analyze secular and cyclical movements in the nation's international transactions.

Toward A Welfare State

Like other industrial nations, the United States in the 20th century has allocated growing amounts of resources for welfare purposes and has enacted an increasingly elaborate network of legislation to protect the working population. There is no adequate synthesis of the history of welfare legislation, but recent overviews of some of the principal elements and issues are contained in the symposium numbers of *Current History*, June and July 1973: "The Dimensions of Poverty in America" and "American Social Welfare in Perspective." Samuel Mencher, *Poor Law to Poverty Program: Economic Security Policy in Britain and the United States* (Pittsburgh: University of Pittsburgh Press, 1968) and June Axinn and Herman Levin, *Social Welfare: A History of the American Response to Need* (New York: Dodd Mead, 1975) offer interpretive accounts of the history of social welfare. James L. Clayton, "The Fiscal Limits of the Warfare-Welfare State: Defense and Welfare Spending in the United States Since 1900," *Western Political Quarterly*, XXIX (September 1976) 364-383, presents an account of trends in government expenditures in this area, showing the extent to which evolution toward a welfare state served as an engine of growth of the modern public sector. Even more than in other areas of economic history, we must rely on the monographic literature.

Considerable attention has been directed to the study of the origins and early history of the American welfare state—the period before the 1930s, when almost all welfare functions were performed by state and local governments or by the private sector. Roy Lubove, *The Professional Altruist: The Emergence of Social Work as a Career, 1880-1930* (Cambridge: Harvard University Press, 1965) discusses the professionalization of social work. Biographical accounts of two leading social workers are contained in Walter I. Trattner, *Homer Folks: Pioneer in Social Welfare* (New York: Columbia University Press, 1968); and Clarke A. Chambers, *Paul U. Kellogg and the SURVEY: Voices for Social Welfare and Social Justice* (Minneapolis: University of Minnesota Press, 1971). Scott M. Cutlip,

Fund-Raising in the United States: Its Role in America's Philanthropy (New Brunswick: Rutgers University Press, 1965) describes the innovation of the Community Chest concept, by which private charitable organizations extended their appeal for funds to a new "mass market" of small donors. Kenneth L. Kusmer, "The Functions of Organized Charity in the Progressive Era: Chicago as a Case Study," *Journal of American History*, LX (December 1973) 657-678, gives an account of the forces and factors, altruistic and otherwise, that influenced the expansion of private charity in one major city. Roy Lubove, *The Struggle for Social Security, 1900-1935* (Cambridge: Harvard University Press, 1968) and Hace Sorel Tishler, *Self-Reliance and Social Security, 1870-1917* (Port Washington, N.Y.: Kennikat Press 1971) trace the development of controversy over various types of welfare legislation on the state level in the early years of the century. The movement for workmen's compensation, the first type of social insurance enacted in the United States, is examined in Lawrence M. Friedman and Jack Ladinsky, "Social Change and the Law of Industrial Accidents," *Columbia Law Review*, LXVII (January 1967) 50-82; Robert Asher, "Business and Workers' Welfare in the Progressive Era: Workmen's Compensation Reform in Massachusetts, 1880-1911," *Business History Review*, XLIII (Winter 1969) 452-475; and Joseph F. Tripp, "An Instance of Labor and Business Cooperation: Workmen's Compensation in Washington State (1911)," *Labor History*, XVII (Fall 1976) 530-590. Paul T. Ringenbach, *Tramps and Reformers, 1873-1916: the Discovery of Unemployment in New York* (Westport, Conn · Greenwood Press, 1973) deals with early attempts to solve the problem of unemployment. Jeremy P. Felt, *Hostages of Fortune: Child Labor Reform in New York State* (Syracuse: Syracuse University Press, 1965) and Walter I. Trattner, *Crusade for the Children: History of the National Child Labor Committee and Child Labor Reform in America* (Chicago: Quadrangle Books, 1970) trace the efforts to prohibit child labor, and Moses Stambler, "The Effect of Compulsory Education and Child Labor Laws on High School Attendance in New York City, 1898-1917," *History of Education Quarterly*, VIII (Summer 1968) 189-214, discusses the growth of a closely related type of legislation. Lawrence M. Friedman, *Government and Slum Housing: A Century of Frustration* (Chicago: Rand McNally & Company, 1968) explores the development of laws to deal with housing conditions. Blanche D. Coll, *Perspectives in Public Welfare: A History* (Washington, D.C.: U.S. Government Printing Office, 1969) gives a brief factual report of public assistance to the economically dependent through the 1920s. James Leiby, *Charity and Correction in New Jersey: A History of State Welfare Institutions* (New Brunswick: Rutgers University Press, 1967) contains a comprehensive account of a single state's welfare system. Clarke A. Chambers, *Seedtime of Reform: American Social Service and Social Action, 1918-1933* (Minneapolis: University of Minnesota Press, 1963) emphasizes the consolidation during the 1920s of welfare programs established during the Progressive Era.

The breakdown of the old system of private and local government responsibility for welfare during the Great Depression, which led to the entry of the federal government into this field on a large scale for the first time, is described in Albert U. Romasco, *The Poverty of Abundance: Hoover, the Nation, the Depression* (New York: Oxford University Press, 1965); Bonnie R. Fox, "Unemployment Relief in Philadelphia, 1930-1932: A Study of the Depression's Impact on Voluntarism," *Pennsylvania Magazine of History and Biography*, XCIII (January 1969) 86-108;

and Charles M. Kimberly, "The Depression in Maryland: The Failure of Voluntarism," *Maryland Historical Magazine,* LXX (Summer 1975) 189-202. Circumstances surrounding legislative action in various areas of welfare during the period of the New Deal are discussed in the following works: Theron A. Schlabach, *Edwin E. Witte: Cautious Reformer* (Madison: State Historical Society of Wisconsin, 1969), a biography of the man known as the "father of social security"; Arthur J. Altmeyer, *The Formative Years of Social Security* (Madison: University of Wisconsin Press, 1968), an insider's account of enactment of the Social Security Act and its implementation; John A. Garraty, *Unemployment in History: Economic Thought and Public Policy* (New York: Harper & Row, 1978), a broadly based study extending beyond the boundaries of the United States in the 1930s; Daniel Nelson, *Unemployment Insurance: The American Experience, 1915-1935* (Madison: University of Wisconsin Press, 1969), outlining efforts to deal with this problem prior to establishment of a program on a national basis; Winifred Bell, *Aid to Dependent Children* (New York: Columbia University Press, 1965), tracing the origins and development of this federal-state "relief" program; and Daniel S. Hirshfield, *The Lost Reform: The Campaign for Compulsory Health Insurance in the United States from 1932 to 1943* (Cambridge: Harvard University Press, 1970), explaining the failure to establish national health insurance.

The literature, both scholarly and polemical, generated during the "war on poverty" in the 1960s is enormous, and the events too recent to gain much historical perspective. However, Sar A. Levitan and Robert Taggart, *The Promise of Greatness* (Cambridge: Harvard University Press, 1976); Eli Ginzberg and Robert M. Solow (eds.), *The Great Society: Lessons for the Future* (New York: Basic Books, 1974); and Robert H. Haveman (ed.), *A Decade of Federal Antipoverty Programs: Achievements, Failures, and Lessons* (New York: Academic Press, 1977) provide useful summary accounts as well as reasonable appraisals of social policy and social legislation in the 1960s.

Wealth and Population

Only in recent years have historians directed much attention toward the study of wealth and income distribution in the American past. Where little information exists about the income of the population generally, as for the period before 1929, profiles of wealth distribution have served as a proxy for income distribution in making generalizations about the extent of economic equality-inequality in society.

The starting point for reading on this subject must be Peter H. Lindert and Jeffrey G. Williamson, "Three Centuries of American Inequality," *Research in Economic History,* I (1976) 69-123, which furnishes a summary statement of apparent trends in wealth and income distribution since the beginning of American history, based on the existing literature; the essay contains an extensive bibliography, including Williamson's own monographic contributions. The most comprehensive analysis of wealth distribution in mid-19th-century America is Lee Soltow, *Men and Wealth in the United States, 1850-1870* (New Haven: Yale University Press, 1975). The following studies of patterns of wealth distribution in selected populations of early America include useful discussions of methods employed and sources of data used in this type of research: Gloria L. Main, "Inequality in Early America: The Evidence from Probate Records of Massachusetts and Maryland," *Journal of Interdisciplinary History,* VII (Spring 1977) 559-581; Jackson Turner Main, "The Distribution of Property in Colonial Connecticut," in James K. Martin (ed.), *The Human Dimensions of Nation Making: Essays on Colonial and Revolutionary America* (Madison: State Historical Society of Wisconsin, 1976); and James T. Lemon and Gary B. Nash, "The Distribution of Wealth in Eighteenth-Century America: A Century of Change in Chester County, Pennsylvania, 1693 1802," *Journal of Social History,* II (Fall 1968) 1-24. Many more detailed studies of wealth and income over the span of American history will help to determine how accurate are the inequality trends outlined by Lindert and Williamson.

Historical Demography

In spite of the uniqueness of American population growth in the context of world experience, "the dearth of work on population by American economic historians can only be a source of wonder," comments Richard A. Easterlin in "Population Issues in American Economic History: A Survey and Critique," *Research in Economic History,* I Supplement (1977) 131-158. However, Easterlin and others have been working to catch up with European demographic historians. In this essay, Easterlin points to the major issues that have emerged from recent research in fertility, mortality, and immigration in American history, with a review of the relevant literature on each of these questions: (1) possible improvement in life expectancy and mortality, 1800-1880; (2) relationship between a decline in fertility and industrialization-urbanization in the 19th century; and (3) effect of immigration on growth of population and of per capita output. The interested reader would do well to go directly to Easterlin's discussion.

In addition to the work of economic historians reviewed by Easterlin, social historians have made useful contributions to historical demography, of which a few examples may be mentioned. Studies of colonial communities by Greven, Lockridge, and Rutman, cited earlier in this essay in the section on colonial history, deal with aspects of population change. Robert V. Wells, *The Population of the British Colonies in America before 1776: A Survey of Census Data* (Princeton: Princeton University Press, 1975) discusses the usefulness of the scattered census data available for individual colonies in the 17th and 18th centuries. A symposium on "Dislocation and Emigration: The Social Background of American Immigration," *Perspectives in American History,* VII (1973) provides qualitative analyses, for several countries, of the circumstances surrounding the decisions of large numbers of people to undertake trans-Atlantic migration during the 19th century.

Marc Bloch remarked that "the past is, by definition, a datum which nothing in the future will change. But the knowledge of the past is something progressive which is constantly transforming and perfecting itself." It is certain that no other period witnessed as great a transformation of knowledge of the American economic past as did the last fifteen years. Historical research challenged both old assumptions, like the role of the Civil War in American industrialization, and new hypotheses, such as the concept of the "take-off." In spite of—or perhaps in part because of—methodological and ideological differences among scholars who wrote economic history, new methods, new approaches, new insights, and new information all contributed to an expansion of our understanding of economic processes in history, or at least reduced some of the barriers to understanding. The activity of economic historians since the early 1960s led to a redefinition of many important issues, encouraged the application of more precise analysis in research and writing, and opened up some new lines of investigation, even if it appeared that little progress was being made toward creation of a generally accepted overarching theory of economic change that fit the circumstances of the American past. □

James H. Soltow is Professor of History and former Chairman of the department at Michigan State University where he has taught since 1959. He received his Ph.D. in history in 1954 from the University of Pennsylvania and was a Fulbright fellow at the University of Louvain in 1965-66. Among his publications are Origins of Small Business: Metal Fabricators and Machinery Makers in New England, 1890-1957, The Economic Role of Williamsburg, *"American Institutional Studies: Present Knowledge and Past Trends," in the* Journal of Economic History, *and "Entrepreneurial Strategy in Small Industry: Belgian Metal Fabricators," in the* Proceedings of the American Philosophical Society. *He is also a co-author, with Sidney Ratner and Richard Sylla, of* The Evolution of the American Economy: Growth, Welfare, and Decision Making.

ADDENDUM

Professor Soltow has offered a number of additions to his original essay. These appear under the same headings that Soltow used in his August 1978 piece.

Introduction

The Business History Conference (founded in 1954) and the Economic and Business Historical Society (founded in 1975) publish papers presented at their annual meetings under the respective titles of Business and Economic History and Essays in Economic and Business History.

The Seventeenth and Eighteenth Centuries: Economic Development in a Context of Colonialism

The rate of economic growth in colonial America remains something of a puzzle due to the absence of data about total output, but tentative estimates of growth rates in this "statistical dark age" are set forth in George Rogers Taylor, "American Economic Growth Before 1840: An Exploratory Essay," Journal of Economic History, XXIV (December 1964), and Terry L. Anderson, "Economic Growth in Colonial New England: 'Statistical Renaissance,'" Journal of Economic History, XXXIX (March 1979). James F. Shepherd and Gary M. Walton emphasize the role of the colonial export sector in The Economic Rise of Early America (Cambridge: Cambridge University Press, 1979).

Gary M. Walton, as do Thomas and McClelland, concludes that the economic burden of British mercantilist regulation upon the American economy was slight in "The New Economic History and the Burdens of the Navigation Acts," Economic History Review, XXIV (November 1971).

James C. Riley, "Foreign Credit and Fiscal Stability: Dutch Investment in the United States, 1781-1794," Journal of American

History, LXV (December 1978), points to the importance of European capital in establishing the finances of the new nation.

The Nineteenth Century: Economic Growth and Development

Business

Tony A. Freyer, "Negotiable Instruments and the Federal Courts in Antebellum American Business," Business History Review, L (Winter 1976), and Charles W. McCurdy, "American Law and the Marketing Structure of the Large Corporation, 1875-1890," Journal of Economic History, XXXVIII (September 1978), show how decisions of the federal judiciary contributed to the creation of a national market and a national business system in different ways in different periods. Morton J. Horwitz, The Transformation of American Law, 1780-1860 (Cambridge: Harvard University Press, 1977), details changes in private law that encouraged entrepreneurial freedom and stimulated economic growth. A special issue of the Business History Review, LIII (Autumn 1979), focuses on the impact of law on business and economic development in America.

Transportation and Communication

A useful summary of the historiographical controversies generated by the works mentioned in the first paragraph of this section is contained in Patrick O'Brien, The New Economic History of the Railways (New York: St. Martin's Press, 1977). Another book that should be mentioned is John F. Stover, Iron Road to the West: American Railroads in the 1850s (New York: Columbia University Press, 1978). Clyde and Sally Griffen, Natives and Newcomers: The Ordering of Opportunity in Mid-Nineteenth Century Poughkeepsie (Cambridge: Harvard University Press, 1978), and Peter R. Decker, Fortunes and Failures: White-Collar Mobility in Nineteenth-Century San Francisco (Cambridge: Harvard University Press, 1978), contain information about the economic and social characteristics of local businessmen in two rather different nineteenth-century communities. Carole Rifkind, Main Street: The Face of Urban America (New York: Harper and Row, 1977), presents a well-organized pictorial record of changes in the architecture of central business districts across the country.

Finance

Important aspects of banking and finance in nineteenth-century America are discussed in Richard H. Timberlake, Jr., The Origins of Central Banking in the United States (Cambridge: Harvard University Press, 1978), and John A. James, Money and Capital Markets in Postbellum America (Princeton: Princeton University Press, 1978). The development of specialized firms to furnish credit information is described in James D. Norris, R. G. Dun and Company 1841-1900: The Development of Credit Reporting in the Nineteenth Century (Westport, Connecticut: Greenwood Press, 1978), and James H. Madison, "The Evolution of Commercial Credit Reporting Agencies in Nineteenth-Century America," Business History Review, XLVIII (Summer 1974).

Industry

Merrit Roe Smith, Harpers Ferry Armory and the New Technology: The Challenge of Change (Ithaca: Cornell University Press, 1977), is a case study of the institutional aspects of technical research and innovation that should be added to the studies of technological contributions to productivity. Additional works dealing with aspects of nineteenth-century industrial development include Edward P. Duggan, "Machines, Markets, and Labor: The Carriage and Wagon Industry in Late-Nineteenth-Century Cincinnati," Business History Review, LI (Autumn 1977); and Margaret Walsh, "Pork Packing as a Leading Edge of Midwestern Industry, 1835-1875," Agricultural History, 51 (October 1977), and "The Democratization of Fashion: The Emergence of the Women's Dress Pattern Industry," Journal of American History, 66 (September 1979). Glenn Porter, ed., Regional Economic History: The Mid-Atlantic Area Since 1700 (Greenville, Wilmington, Del.: Eleutherian Mills-Hagley Foundation, 1976), includes proceedings of a conference held to develop approaches to the study of economic change in this area. Working Papers from the Regional Economic History Research Center, issued several times each year since 1977 and also edited by Porter, include the findings of current research about the economic history of the Philadelphia and Baltimore areas.

The Southern Economy: Slavery and Growth

Explorations in Economic History, 16 (January 1979), contains papers focused on the issues raised in the Ransom and Sutch book. Another approach, along Marxist lines, is used in Jay Mandle, The Roots of Black Poverty: The Southern Plantation Economy After the Civil War (Durham: Duke University Press, 1978); Jonathan M. Wiener, Social Origins of the New South: Alabama, 1860-1885 (Baton Rouge: Louisiana State University Press, 1978); and Weiner, "Class Structure and Economic Development in the American South, 1865-1955," American Historical Review, 84 (October 1979). Harold D. Woodman, "Sequel to Slavery: The New History Views the Postbellum South," Journal of Southern History, 43 (1977), offers a critical analysis of both of these approaches to the study of the postbellum southern economy and suggests an alternative of his own.

The Twentieth Century: The Corporation and the State

Mansel G. Blackford, Pioneering a Modern Small Business: Wakefield Seafoods and the Alaskan Frontier (Greenwich, Conn.: JAI Press, 1979), is one of the few useful histories of a small firm in the era of large-scale enterprise. Jonathan R. T. Hughes, The Governmental Habit: Economic Controls from Colonial Times to the Present (New York: Basic Books, 1977), places the growth of governmental power in economic decision making in the twentieth century in long-term perspective. Albro Martin, "Uneasy Partners: Government-Business Relations in Twentieth-Century American History," Prologue:

The Journal of the National Archives, 11 (Summer 1979), surveys
changing interpretations of relations between the public and
private sectors since the late nineteenth century. A special issue
on "Corporate Liberalism," Business History Review, LII (Autumn
1978), points to ways in which businessmen sought to accommodate
the growing power of government in the twentieth century.

Railroads were affected not only by regulation, but also by
government policy toward competing forms of transportation, especially public expenditures on roads and highways for automobiles
and trucks. Aspects of this subject are explored in James A.
Dunn, Jr., "The Importance of Being Earmarked: Transport Policy
and Highway Finance in Great Britain and the United States,"
Comparative Studies in Society and History, 20 (January 1978);
Anthony F. Herbst and Joseph S. K. Wu, "Some Evidence of Subsidi-
zation: The U.S. Trucking Industry, 1900-1920," Journal of
Economic History, XXXIII (June 1975); and Mark H. Rose, Interstate:
Express Highway Politics, 1941-1956 (Lawrence, Kansas: Regents
Press of Kansas, 1979).

Burton I. Kaufman, The Oil Cartel Case: A Documentary Study of
Antitrust Activity in the Cold War Era (Westport, Conn.: Greenwood
Press, 1978), is a case history of the effects of foreign policy
considerations on the government's antitrust case against some of
the nation's largest corporations. An additional study of welfare
legislation is Martha Derthick, Policymaking for Social Security
(Washington: Brookings Institution, 1979), which traces the political history of social security from the 1930s to the 1970s.

American Folklore Bibliography

RICHARD M. DORSON

□The best books on American folklore are yet to be written. Not that a great many titles cannot be cited, as one may see in Charles Haywood's giant *A Bibliography of North American Folklore and Folk Song* (1951; reprinted as "2nd revised edition" but actually not corrected, 2 volumes, New York: Dover, 1961), which in its lax inclusion of all kinds of titles and numerous errors of citation reflects the confused state of the field. The first Ph.D. in folklore in the United States was awarded in 1953 and presently only three universities confer doctorates in folklore (Indiana University since 1949, the University of Pennsylvania since 1959, and the University of Texas since 1972). Of these professional folklorists only a handful deal with American folklore through an American studies perspective. The leanings of the first generation of academic folklorists have been toward literature, ethnology, linguistics, and foreign area studies. Still there exists a respectable shelf of titles that can be profitably consulted by Americanists. Folklore is an indispensable component of any American studies program, for it deals directly with the lives and ideas of the average man and woman, of work groups, of minority cultures, ultimately of all segments of American society.

In selecting the titles that follow I emphasize interpretive works which relate folklore to American civilization, and eschew collections of tales or songs or other genres, unless they help establish that relationship in a special way. Such collections must also meet proper scholarly standards of comparative annotation and informant data. Occasionally I mention titles as examples of deficient scholarship, but such a list could be enormously extended, under the head of my neologism "fakelore." Where pertinent, I unblushingly cite my own works.

General studies of American folklore

Constance Rourke was the first to recognize the existence of an indigenous American folklore. Her *American Humor, A Study of the National Character* (1931; *New York: Harcourt Brace Jovanovich, 1971) is well known for its portrayal of the Yankee, backwoodsman, and blackface minstrel as three American folktypes influential on playwrights and authors. But it is her posthumous volume, *The Roots of American Culture* (1942; *New York: Harcourt Brace Jovanovich, 1966) which expands her concept—derived from Herder—of varied folk traditions shaped by the national experience and permeating the culture. "A Note on Folklore" in that book succinctly and prophetically states her thesis: "No other people has created its folklore and tried to assimilate it and turn it to the purposes of the creative imagination and of self-understanding, all within a brief span" (page 243). In that essay she employs folk in a number of compounds, some of her own coining, to underscore the point that the American experience contains a large folklore component, that "probably we are still a folk ... rather than a schooled and civilized people" (page 244). Her terms include folk-oddments, folk-possessions, folk-novels, folk-expression, folk-heroes, folk-tales, folk-talk, folk-movement, folk-play, folk-ways, folk-life, folk-drama, folk-materials, folk-literature, folk-language, folk-origin, and folk-satire. Rourke recognized folk elements in obscure corners of American life, among small-town craftsmen, musicians, painters, religious cultists, actors, and entertainers. Lacking formal training in folk-

Richard M. Dorson has been Professor of History and Folklore at Indiana University since 1957, and since 1963 has served as Director of the University's Folklore Institute. He has been the recipient of fellowships from the American Council of Learned Societies, the Guggenheim Foundation and the Library of Congress, and in 1956–57 was a Fulbright Professor of American studies at the University of Tokyo. He served as editor of the Journal of American Folklore *from 1958–1963, vice-president of the International Society for Folk Narrative Research from 1959–1964, and in 1964 founded the* Journal of the Folklore Institute. *Mr. Dorson has participated in international folklore congresses throughout the world, and is the author of more than twenty books, and 200 articles.*

lore, which was not then available to her in the United States, she approached her subject intuitively and with sure instinct for research materials. Her work was a beginning that has not been properly followed up.

A number of my own writings have attempted to develop "A Theory for American Folklore," the title of an essay first printed in the *Journal of American Folklore* in 1959. It presented the thesis that special circumstances of American history and civilization, such as colonization, slavery, the westward movement, immigration, regionalism, and mass culture, generated distinctive folk traditions. This thesis furnished the framework for my *American Folklore* (Chicago: University of Chicago Press, 1959). The original essay and others expanding on this theory, for example, "Folklore in Relation to American Studies," were reprinted in my *American Folklore and the Historian* (Chicago: University of Chicago Press, 1971). Some of my other articles and papers collected in *Folklore: Selected Essays* (Bloomington: Indiana University Press, 1972), for instance, "History of the Elite and History of the Folk," and in *Folklore and Fakelore* (Cambridge: Harvard University Press, 1976), which contains "Oral History, Oral Literature and the Folklorist," bear on the theory. A new perspective correlating folk expression with mainstream currents in four historical periods is used in my *America in Legend* (New York: Pantheon, 1973, *1974).

Some surveys and symposia will be useful to the student of American folklore. On the introductory level Jan H. Brunvand's *The Study of American Folklore* (New York: Norton, 1968), describes the genres of oral folklore, using American examples. Brunvand has also prepared *Folklore: A Research Guide* (*New York: St. Martin's Press, 1976) presenting guidelines to folklore scholars, bibliographical aids, and a model of a folklore term paper. In *The Study of Folklore* (Englewood Cliffs, N.J.: Prentice Hall, 1965), Alan Dundes collected previously published theoretical articles illustrating approaches to folklore as a discipline. Sixteen professional folklorists contributed original essays on their areas of expertise to *Folklore and Folklife, An Introduction,* edited by Dorson (Chicago: University of Chicago Press, 1972). On the level of original theory, thirteen younger scholars, eight holders of the doctorate in folklore, collaborated to write *Toward New Perspectives in Folklore,* edited by Américo Paredes and Richard Bauman (Austin and London: University of Texas Press for the American Folklore Society, 1972). They emphasized the concept of folklore as performance and communication, and referred to social science models in linguistics, sociology, psychology, and anthropology for fructifying ideas. By contrast, the conference papers published in *American Folk Legend, A Symposium,* edited by Wayland Hand (Berkeley, Los Angeles, London: University of California Press, 1971) develop a specifically American conception of the legend. The essays utilize field data on Pennsylvania Germans, Navaho Indians, Kentucky mountaineers, and city dwellers, and examine psychological, historical, and conceptual implications of legend-making and legend-telling within the American ethos. The conference folklorists agreed that legend was a shifting and elusive form, reflecting varying degrees of belief, and that United States legends differed from their Old World counterparts, which had grown to a large extent from medieval demonology. This volume is of first importance for the Americanist interested in folklore.

One of the contributors to these last two symposia, Alan Dundes, directed his attention to the American scene in five of his twenty *Analytic Essays in Folklore*

(The Hague, Paris: Mouton, 1975). In one perceptive essay he traces the anxieties that Americans project into folk sayings, jokes, and customs which relate to fears of the future.

Historical

Only a few themes in American history have yet gained the attention of folklorists. The Mormons have fared quite well. In *Saints of Sage and Saddle* (Bloomington: Indiana University Press, 1956), Austin and Alta Fife recount in chronological form the legends and songs that grew around Joseph Smith and Brigham Young, the westward trek to Salt Lake City, the Mountain Meadows Massacre, the Three Nephites, profane elder J. Golden Kimball, and other personalities and episodes celebrated in Mormon history. The Fifes have adroitly synthesized their own field materials with documentary testimonials and other historical sources of Mormon spiritual history. Specialized treatments are Hector Lee's *The Three Nephites: the Substance and Significance of the Legend in Folklore* (Albuquerque: University of New Mexico Press, 1949), the first scholarly examination of the white-robed strangers who mysteriously appeared to succour Saints in distress; and Thomas Cheney's *The Golden Legacy* (Layton, Utah: Peregrine Smith, 1973), a report of the anecdote cycle, sans comparative notes, surrounding the ex-cowboy J. Golden Kimball who became a staunch if not properly decorous pillar of the Church of Jesus Christ of Latter-day Saints.

American military history remains a largely untapped subject for the folklorist. In *Uncertain Glory: Folklore and the American Revolution* (Detroit: Folklore Associates, 1971), Tristram P. Coffin attempted several scattershot approaches to his subject: consideration of oral traditions extant at the time of the American Revolution, such as ballads and songs, notably Yankee Doodle; hymns composed by William Billings; propagandistic writings that entered tradition; fiction about spies; and heroes of questionable legendary status, for example Paul Revere and Ben Franklin. Coffin's deliberate blurring of the distinction between folklore and fakelore and his sketchy handling of disparate materials produce a confusing work. A useful source book for future studies of Revolution folklore is George Carey's edition of *A Sailor's Songbag: An American Rebel in an English Prison 1777–1779* (Amherst, Mass.: University of Massachusetts Press, 1976), which presents the song texts, with the editor's glosses and notes, from a manuscript kept by an American prisoner of war in England's Forton Prison. As for the Civil War, B. A. Botkin has assembled one of his customary grab-bag treasuries, this one titled *A Civil War Treasury of Tales, Legends, and Folklore* (New York: Random House, 1960), which may provide some leads to future scholars of Civil War folklore, although the bulk of the contents is literary and journalistic rather than folk. One famous military episode of frontier Indian fighting has received folkloric treatment. Bruce Rosenberg in *Custer and the Epic of Defeat* (University Park, Pa.: Pennsylvania State University Press, 1974) examines the conflicting accounts of Custer's last stand and the speculations that have grown around the event, and then compares the Custer episode with Old World epic poems and romances of heroes who perished with their armies on the battlefield.

Regional

A superior older regional collection that recognizes the various oral genres, annotates the texts richly, and in an astute introduction conveys the flavor of an isolated Appalachian community is *Folklore from the Schoharie Hills, New York* (Ann Arbor: University of Michigan Press, 1937), by Emelyn E. Gardner, a professor from Wayne State University who spent six summers in those hills. Few folklorists have ventured beyond collection to interpretive assessment of a region. Vance Randolph has collected every oral genre from the Ozarks in separate volumes of folktales, folksongs, folk speech, and folk belief, and compiled a splendid annotated bibliography of Ozark folklore, but his valuable body of work remains on the level of text-gathering. Similarly, Leonard Roberts has placed on record excellent specimens of traditional tales from Pine Mountain, Kentucky. In *Up Cutshin and Down Greasy,* expanded as *Sang Branch Settlers* (Austin: Published for the American Folklore Society by the University of Texas Press, 1974), he presented the folkways of one family. Hunting anecdotes, Civil War stories, old wives' recipes, witch tales, as well as Märchen and folksongs fill the repertoire of the folklore-laden Couch family members. For demonstrating the role of the family unit as a channel of transmitting folk materials, and indicating the range of these materials, *Sang Branch Settlers* deserves high marks.

A few regional ethnographies move beyond collecting to attempt portraits of folk culture. An older account of South County, Rhode Island, written as a string of reminiscences by "Shepherd Tom" Hazard under the title *The Jonny-Cake Letters* (1880; reprinted as *The Jonny-Cake Papers,* Boston: printed for the subscribers, 1915), constitutes a unique participant's eye view of a folk region, in contrast to the modern folklorist's self-conscious investigation (see R. M. Dorson, "The Jonny-Cake Papers," *Journal of American Folklore* 58, 1945, pp. 104–112). A five–month field trip to the Upper Peninsula of Michigan to explore the folk narrative traditions of Ojibwa and Potawatomi Indians, occupational groups of miners, lumberjacks, lakesmen, and immigrant groups of Finns, French-Canadians, and Cornishmen, resulted in Dorson's *Bloodstoppers and Bearwalkers* (Cambridge: Harvard University Press, 1952, *1972). Field experiences and encounters with storytellers in the fraternal towns of northern Michigan are included. Comparably, George Carey inquired into the subculture of white-water fishermen living on Maryland's Eastern Shore and set forth in *A Faraway Time and Place* (Washington and New York: Luce, 1971) a spread of local anecdotes, legends, folk names and folk sayings skillfully interwoven into the life of the "proggers." Commendable for bringing together in one volume folk beliefs and personal narratives about death omens and revenants is William Lynwood Montell's *Ghosts Along the Cumberland, Deathlore in the Kentucky Foothills* (Knoxville: University of Tennessee Press, 1975).

Two selections of essays by regional folklorists are available: Louise Pound's *Nebraska Folklore* (Lincoln: University of Nebraska Press, 1959) and *Mody Boatright, Folklorist,* edited by Ernest B. Speck (Austin and London: Published for the Texas Folklore Society by the University of Texas Press, 1973). Pound is particularly good on historical analyses of pseudo-Indian legends. Boatright, long-time professor of English at the University of Texas, writes on oilfield lore and frontier humor of the Southwest. His *Folk Laughter on the American Frontier* (New York: Macmillan, 1949) also drew largely from Texas examples in its studies of oral and written humor of the tall-tale and comic anecdote.

Heroes

Books on American heroes, collective and individual, abound, but only a handful of titles serve our purposes. Such a production as Frank Shay's *Here's Audacity: American Legendary Heroes* (New York: Macaulay, 1930) is pure fakelore although of historical interest as the first publication to bring together in one volume these concocted pseudo-demigods. There is no satisfactory general study of American heroes from the folklore point of view. For specific heroes, Daniel G. Hoffman has written in *Paul Bunyan, Last of the Frontier Demigods* (Philadelphia: University of Pennsylvania Press for Temple University Publications, 1952) the only scholarly work on the ever-growing shelf of Paul Bunyan fakelore volumes. Hoffman documents the slender trickle of oral tradition about the giant lumberjack who received his chief boost from the brochures issued by a lumber company advertising executive. John Henry, the Negro steel-driver on the Big Bend Tunnel in West Virginia in 1862, celebrated in song for defeating a steam drill but dying with his hammer in his hand, has been the subject of two searching biographical inquiries: one by Guy B. Johnson, *John Henry, Tracking Down a Negro Legend* (1929; New York: AMS Press, 1969), and one by Louis W. Chappell, who ob-

Courtesy, Library of Congress

Card games such as faro were popular among those engaged in the taming of the American frontier; Harper's Weekly, *October 3, 1857.*

jected to Johnson's use of some of his pre-publication materials, *John Henry, A Folk-Lore Study* (1933; Port Washington, N.Y.: Kennikat, 1968). Both scholars uncovered only slight evidence for a historical basis to the tradition, and noted that it persists in ballad and work song rather than in prose legend.

John Henry is not a talked-about hero. One folk hero who was much talked about in the 1820s and '30s on the Ohio and Mississippi Rivers as a bragging, brawling roustabout was *Mike Fink, King of Mississippi Keelboatmen*, whose life and exploits Walter Blair and Franklin Meine recounted (1933, Westport, Conn.: Greenwood Press, 1971); subsequently they reprinted the subliterary sources of the legends in *Half Horse Half Alligator* (Chicago: University of Chicago Press, 1956). Some of the Mike Fink stories appeared in the Crockett almanacs published in Nashville and later in Eastern cities from 1835 to 1856, but the chief figure was Davy Crockett, the congressman from Tennessee who soared into national prominence as a frontier yarnspinner and the hero of tall-tale exploits, adventures, and scrapes in the backwoods and foreign lands. Richard M. Dorson selected tales and woodcuts from the almanacs in *Davy Crockett, American Comic Legend* (1939; Westport, Conn.: Greenwood Press, 1977; and New York: Arno Press, 1977). They belong to the vein of journalistic humor of the Old Southwest, several removes from oral folk tradition. A first-rate evocation of a Mexican folk hero of the later Southwest, Gregorio Cortez, remembered in ballad and legend, was produced by Américo Paredes in *"With His Pistol in His Hand": A Border Ballad and Its Hero* (Austin, Texas: University of Texas Press, 1958). Paredes outlines the contemptuous attitudes of Anglos and Texas Rangers toward Mexicans against which Gregorio Cortez fought to bring a sense of dignity and nobility to his people.

An opportunity for an authoritative study and collection of a folk hero from living oral tradition was muffed by Mody Boatright in *Gib Morgan, Minstrel of the Oil Fields* (Texas Folk-Lore Society Publication XX, 1945) when he failed to present literal oral texts or name the informants of the whoppers attributed to oil driller Gib Morgan, who died in 1909, but whose technological tales endured. The fullest analytical and textual study of a tall-tale folk hero is William H. Jansen's "Abraham 'Oregon' Smith: Pioneer, Folk Hero, and Tale-Teller" (Indiana University dissertation, Bloomington, 1949, printed by Arno Press, New York, 1977). "Oregon" Smith, so-called from his whoppers about Oregon in the days of the overland trail, resided in Indiana and Illinois, while *Jones Tracy, Tall-Tale Hero from Mount Desert Island*, lived off the Maine coast, dying in 1939 at the age of 83; C. Richard K. Lunt printed texts of his long bows (*Northeast Folklore X:* 1968; Orono, Maine: The University Press, 1969). A large cycle of marvelous windies from the Rogue River mountain wilderness of southwest Oregon emanated from Hathaway Jones (1870–1937) and were captured, most of them in literary reworkings, by Stephen Dow Beckham in *Tall Tales from Rogue River, The Yarns of Hathaway Jones* (Bloomington and London: Indiana University Press, 1974). An exemplary smaller study and collection, Roger Mitchell's *George Knox, From Man to Legend* (*Northeast Folklore IX, 1969; Orono, Maine: The University Press, 1970), brings to light a Maine lumberjack hero who died in 1892 at the age of thirty, but who lives on in the oral legends about his supernatural feats ascribed to traffic with the devil.

Occupational

The folklore of occupations remains a largely untilled field, even at the collecting level. Collections from sailors, lumberjacks, cowboys, and miners concentrate chiefly on folksongs, while folklorists have only begun to turn their attention to industrial workers. George Korson pioneered in the recording of Pennsylvania anthracite coal miners' songs and legends, in *Coal Dust on the Fiddle* (1943; Hatboro, Pa.: Folklore Associates, 1965); the songs and lore of bituminous coal miners around the country, in *Minstrels of the Mine Patch* (1938; Hatboro, Pa.: Folklore Associates, 1964); and traditions of Pennsylvania Dutch farmer-miners, in *Black Rock* (Baltimore: The Johns Hopkins Press, 1960). Korson, a journalist assigned to cover mining towns, once asked himself the question, "Do miners sing songs?" and his books provide the answer. They present faithfully the song texts dealing with the miners' life and dangers and emotions, but Korson revealed other traditional aspects of the miners' culture in the form of journalistic pieces, rather than in texts recording their personal experiences, oral history, and anecdotal legends. *Black Rock* attempts a fuller historical treatment than the earlier two works.

The most successful interpretive study of occupational folklore—indeed the only one—is Mody Boatright's *Folklore of the Oil Industry* (Dallas: Southern Methodist University Press, 1963). The oil drillers of Texas and Oklahoma did not sing folksongs, and Boatright was obliged to discover and identify the categories of their lore. He cleverly diagnosed them as tale cycles about doodlebugs and other devices for finding oil, lucky and unlucky oil fortune-hunters, daredevil drillers, and boom-town sagas. A superior collection of occupational folksongs, because of the half-dozen clever essays interspersed among the texts, is Fanny Hardy Eckstorm and Mary Winslow Smyth's *Minstrelsy of Maine* (Boston: Houghton Mifflin and Company, 1927). One essay compares ballad-making to the formulaic pattern in sensational journalism, and another traces the transition of a literary ballad composed by John Greenleaf Whittier to a folk ballad collected from a lumberjack-singer. It is regrettable that other field collections, of songs or tales or smaller genres, do not emulate this model and enrich their presentation of texts with accompanying essays relating the folklore to the American scene. A brilliant example of how such a result may be achieved, in a format different from that used by Eckstorm and Smyth, is the edition prepared by Austin and Alta Fife of N. Howard "Jack" Thorp's *Songs of the Cowboys,* originally privately printed in Estancia, New Mexico in 1908. The Fifes reproduced the little booklet in facsimile, but then printed the song texts with extended glosses presenting the bibliographical data about the dispersion of the songs, and cultural data about the references and symbolic meanings of range life in the songs (New York: Clarkson Potter, 1966).

Literature

Constance Rourke first outlined the network of relationships between American folk comedy and American literature in her *American Humor* (1931; *New York: Harcourt Brace Jovanovich, 1971). In the Yankee peddler, the frontier ringtailed roarer, and the blackface minstrel, she perceived indigenous folktypes that major authors, from Mark Twain to Henry James, transmuted into generic characters. Rourke made skilful use of fugitive sources, such as Yankee plays, the Crockett almanacs, and memoirs of itinerant actors, but she never adequately distinguished between folklore and popular culture, and her successors compounded the flaw. The best general study to date is Daniel G. Hoffman's *Form and Fable in American Fiction* (1961; *New York: Norton, 1973), which concentrates on Hawthorne, Melville, Twain, and Faulkner. Hoffman is knowledgeable about folklore scholarship, and discovers such new information as Hawthorne's reading of William Hone's *Every-Day Book,* an 1838 compendium of English customs, celebrations, usages, and folk rituals. To Rourke's thesis he adds the psychoanalytic archetypal patterns of myth formulated by C. G. Jung, and, like other literary critics who have not engaged in fieldwork, he blurs the division between folklore in printed form and folklore in living context, in terms of their effect on the artist. The worst study is by Gene Bluestein, *The Voice of the Folk,* pretentiously subtitled *Folklore and American Literary Theory* (*Amherst: University of Massachusetts Press, 1972). Bluestein writes four chapters without citing a single field collection of American folklore, and shows little awareness or comprehension of his subject matter. He slavishly paraphrases Rourke, and for good measure tosses in Herder, John and Alan Lomax, and Bob Dylan, but his chapters on Emerson and Whitman have little or nothing to do with folklore.

A model study of an individual author has been written by Ronald Baker, *Folklore in the Writings of Rowland E. Robinson* (Bowling Green, Ohio: Bowling Green University Popular Press, 1973). Although tabbed as a minor local colorist writing about Vermont scenes and characters in the 1880s and '90s, Robinson maintained a faithful audience that came to include summer visitors of New York literati. Baker examines the multiple genres of folklore and folklife that Robinson wove into his sketches of storytelling situations and village activities in Danvis in the Green Mountains of Vermont. His work avoids mechanical enumeration of folkloric items, the usual practice of folklore-in-literature critics, and discusses their existence in tradition and Robinson's techniques of incorporating them into his fiction.

Ballad, Folksong, Folk Music

The ballads originating on American soil and responding to American experiences, a corpus distinct from the imported English and Scottish traditional ballads and the Anglo-Irish broadside ballads, were identified, discussed in informative essays, and indexed by G. Malcolm Laws in *Native American Balladry* (rev. ed., Philadelphia: American Folklore Society, 1964). Laws considers these themes in American life most productive for ballad-making: murders by unrequited lovers; hardships and death in the mines, on the river drive, and in the engine cab; feats of outlaws and bad men; action on the range or before the mast. How a lumberjack folk bard composed satirical songs between 1860 and 1885 that passed into tradition in Maine and the Maritimes is a detective story engrossingly told by Edward D. Ives in *Larry Gorman, The Man Who Made the Songs* (*Bloomington: Indiana University Press, 1964).

Where popular music leaves off and folk music begins is a complicated question that Bill C. Malone has handled skilfully in *Country Music, U.S.A.* (Austin and London: Published for the American Folklore Society by the University of Texas Press, 1968). His history of Southern American rural music embraces a variety of musical styles called not only country music but also mountain, western, and bluegrass, and he recognizes how popular singers and instrumentalists adopted traditional songs for recording, radio, and television appearances, and in stage shows such as the Grand Ole Opry. In passing he points to the adoption of "folk music" by urban left-wing intellectuals in the 1930s, a theme developed by R. Serge Denisoff in *Great Day Coming, Folk Music and the American Left* (Urbana: University of Illinois Press, 1971). The contrived folksongs sung by Woody Guthrie, Pete Seeger, Burl Ives, and Bob Dylan never did, as Denisoff indicates, arouse the working class they idealized.

Folklife and Material Culture

In recent years the term folklife has been frequently used to signify the non-oral aspects of traditional culture. Folklife as defined by the group of research papers in *American Folklife*, edited by Don Yoder (Austin and London: University of Texas Press, 1976), covers more than the material culture of pioneer log houses in Indiana, Afro-American coil basketry in South Carolina, and folk boats in French Louisiana. It also covers tensions between Latins and Anglos in the lower Rio Grande Valley, the German-American colonial custom of "shooting in" the New Year, and anecdotes about nineteenth-century tollgates in upstate New York. The title of the book is pretentious for this miscellany, but serves to stake out a claim for regional ethnological studies of pre-industrial, pre-urban cultural forms. Henry Glassie has probed most deeply into folklife theory and empirical studies in two major works, *Pattern in the Material Folk Culture of the Eastern United States* (1968; *Philadelphia: University of Pennsylvania Press, 1971), and *Folk Housing in Middle Virginia: Structural Analysis of Historic Artifacts* (Knoxville: University of Tennessee Press, 1975). In the first book Glassie delineated regional areas with common patterns of traditional house and barn construction. In the second he considered historically the house types in Goochland and Louisa counties and discovered architectural changes corresponding to cultural change. For this inquiry he developed a transformational grammar of traditional house designs. The rich data, supported with photographs and drawings by the author, and the highly sophisticated theoretical explication of the data defy any quick summary. A detailed study of an individual craftsman from a Jungian point of view is Michael O. Jones, *The Hand Made Object and Its Maker* (Berkeley and Los Angeles: University of California Press, 1975).

Oral History

Two doctoral dissertations in folklore that have been published in revised form rely heavily on the new techniques of oral history. Folklorists have engaged in oral interviewing since the beginnings of their discipline, but they have tended to slight historical traditions. Lynwood Montell deliberately concentrated on remembrances of past events and personalities from former residents in the Negro settlement of Coe Ridge in southern Kentucky, a settlement now dispersed. His *The Saga of Coe Ridge* (1970; *New York: Harper and Row, 1972) reconstructs the history of the community from pioneer homesteading times to the final moonshining era of the 1920s, and separates the more factual from the more folkloric elements by the technique of motif analysis. Where Montell did make some complementary use of documentary records, Gladys Marie Fry relied almost exclusively on oral interviews with descendants of slaves for the new historical information she uncovered in *Night Riders in Black Folk History* (Knoxville: University of Tennessee Press, 1975). In the course of her recording sessions on traditions of life

Courtesy, Library of Congress

The Ghost Dance of the Sioux Indians, The Illustrated London News, *January 3, 1891.*

under slavery, Fry kept hearing references to night riders or night doctors who threatened to kill runaway slaves and sell their bodies to medical schools. Fry placed this body of references within a pattern of bogeyman figures terrorizing blacks in ante-bellum and post-bellum times: patterollers, overseers, ghosts, and Ku Klux Klaners.

Urban

Folklorists are beginning to recognize that their province lies as much in the city as in the country. The first symposium addressing itself to this subject, held at Wayne State University in 1968, resulted in a book titled *The Urban Experience and Folk Tradition,* edited by Américo Paredes and Ellen Stekert (Austin, Texas:

Published for the American Folklore Society by the University of Texas Press, 1971). While opening up the subject, the work did little more than suggest possible topics, such as ethnic cultures in the city, the problems of Appalachian women coping with urban medical systems, black riots of the 1960s as performances, and urban hillbilly music. A special study of high merit is Charles Keil's *Urban Blues* (*Chicago: University of Chicago Press, 1966), which follows in close detail the successful efforts of studio technicians and record producers to remold Southern rural Negro blues singers B. B. King and Bobby Bland into cabaret and recording artists for city audiences. Benjamin A. Botkin assembled two of his catch-alls of semi-folklore around city themes, in *Sidewalks of America* (Indianapolis: Bobbs-Merrill, 1954) and *New York City Folklore* (New York: Random House, 1956). Like his other treasuries, these are miscellaneous compilations from diversified sources usually several removes from oral texts, but Botkin's introductions and some of the selections illuminate the neighborhood characters, landmarks, occupations, and activities that contribute to urban traditions. One can find, for example, variant accounts of Mrs. O'Leary's cow kicking the bucket that started the great Chicago fire of 1871, and stories that sprang up in the wake of the San Francisco earthquake of 1906, two spectacular city folk-disasters of our history.

A recent production of refreshing originality, *Urban Folklore from the Paperwork Empire,* has been conceived by folklorist Alan Dundes and businessman Carl Pagter (Austin, Texas: American Folklore Society, 1975). Refuting the sacred premise of folkloristics that oral tradition provides the primary criterion of folkness, the authors present specimens of humorous letters, cartoons, posters, and gag stuff that circulate through typed, dittoed, mimeographed and Xeroxed reproduction. They prove by juxtaposing variant texts that these sub rosa materials change their phrasing and appearance in the same manner as do spoken and sung pieces.

Although admittedly a collectanea, *Mexican Folk Narrative from the Los Angeles Area,* assembled by Elaine K. Miller (Austin and London: Published for the American Folklore Society by the University of Texas Press, 1973) deserves recognition as a scholarly harvest of ethnic urban folklore. Miller finds legends incorporating religious and supernatural beliefs—in virgins and saints, the Devil *(El diablo),* revenants, such as *llorona,* the widely reported wailing woman, and the *duende,* a mischievous goblin—to be far more prevalent than fictional tales, and usually alleged to have occurred in Mexico rather than in California.

Afro-American

A large bibliography could be constructed for Afro-American folklore collections, but there are few major interpretive studies. That a good many theoretical studies of smaller length, in article or essay form, do exist has been conclusively demonstrated by Alan Dundes in his anthology, *Mother Wit from the Laughing Barrel* (*Englewood Cliffs, N.J.: Prentice-Hall, 1973). Here he has recaptured, for example, the probing exchange between black novelist Ralph Ellison and critic

Stanley Edgar Hyman over the uniqueness or universality of the "darky" archetype.

The one full-length interpretive work, unique in being a sophisticated and comprehensive analysis by a historian of American Negro ideas and attitudes as expressed in folklore, is Lawrence W. Levine's *Black Thought and Black Consciousness* (New York: Oxford University Press, 1977). Through religious and secular songs, folktales, anecdotes, humor, hero legends, and folk speech, Levine identifies viewpoints of black Americans, in slavery and freedom. A single minded use of folksongs to reveal eighteenth- and nineteenth-century messages transmitted as double entendres in spirituals, Miles Mark Fisher's *Negro Slave Songs in the United States* (1953; *Secaucus, N.J.: Citadel Press, 1969) stretches the evidence beyond plausibility. "I'm Bound for de Promised Land" need not necessarily signify the intention of the singer to escape from a Southern plantation to a Northern state. Fisher did, however, support his argument with ample references from travel literature, biographies, and memoirs in his attempt to convey the Negro outlook. A clever study of Afro-American folk religion based on tape-recorded data, Bruce Rosenberg's *The Art of the American Folk Preacher* (New York: Oxford University Press, 1970), analyzed Negro oral sermons, delivered without recourse to scripts, as formulaic compositions, according to the hypothesis framed by Milman Parry and Albert Lord.

A few collections that help reveal the wealth of black folk expression and folk belief may be mentioned. A great compendium of raw texts, tape-recorded by an Episcopalian minister, Harry W. Hyatt, who traveled through the Southeast talking with hoodoo doctors and hoodoo victims, is the four–volume work titled *Hoodoo–Conjuration–Witchcraft–Rootwork* (Hannibal, Mo.: Western Publishing Company, 1970–74). The title words are all synonyms for the magical practices that form the central belief system and furnish the key metaphor in Afro-American culture. In *American Negro Folktales* (*Greenwich, Conn.: Fawcett, 1967) Dorson presents 186 oral narratives from his collection of a thousand tales recorded in 1952 and 1953 in Michigan, Arkansas, and Mississippi, with comparative notes and introductory essays challenging the thesis of extensive African origins of Afro-American tales. The formation of an even more indigenous oral expressive tradition in Northern urban ghettos, composed of scatological toasties, dozens, and jokes, was documented by Roger Abrahams in *Deep Down in the Jungle* (1964; *rev. ed. Chicago: Aldine, 1970). Abrahams obtained his sampling from a small group of black teenagers in the Camingerly neighborhood of south Philadelphia. The repertoire of black toasts, the long rhyming story recitations popular in contemporary Afro-American culture, some richly obscene, was brought to light by Bruce Jackson in *Get Your Ass in the Water and Swim Like Me* (Cambridge, Mass.: Harvard University Press, 1974). Jackson recorded most of his toasts from prison inmates.

A number of collections and studies of Afro-American spirituals and blues exist. (See Charles Keil, *Urban Blues,* under "Urban"). Perhaps the most ambitious is John Lovell, Jr.'s *Black Song–The Forge and the Flame* (New York: Macmillan, 1972). Lovell contends that Africa is the cradle of civilization; that the Negro spiritual in the United States derives from African musical tradition; that its poetry and music represent a high artistic expression; and that Negro spirituals have traveled from the United States around the world. The book could have benefited from pruning and editing, to sift the original research from the undigested accumulation of notes and the constant editorializing.

Immigrant–Ethnic

Folkloric investigations of American immigrant groups have been slow in developing. The first full-length study, *South Italian Folkways in Europe and America,* by Phyllis H. Williams (1938; New York: Russell and Russell, 1969) was actually intended as a handbook for social workers dealing with Southern Italian immigrants in New Haven and New York slums. Williams presented first the Old Country beliefs and practices and then the New World retentions and adjustments of magical ideas and saints' day celebrations. The peasant immigrants divided their faith between the *maga* (magician) and the physician. A parallel effort, this time by a professional folklorist, Carla Bianco, compared the desolate village life in Roseto Valfortore in Italy with the booming town life of its offspring, Roseto in Pennsylvania, whose residents worked in slate quarries and blouse mills. *The Two Rosetos* (Bloomington and London: Indiana University Press, 1974) is rich with historical and social context; taped interviews with the American Rosetans; sensitive descriptions of cultural traditions in daily life, such as *malocchio,* belief in the evil eye, and cures by saints and madonnas; and representative texts of tales and songs. Bianco uncovers a peasant myth of America, "real, as a land for work, sweat, and sacrifice; unreal, as a magic universe with infinite possibilities for fabulous strokes of luck . . ." (page 43). Bianco's book presents ethnic folklore with great skill and sophistication, and illustrates cultural change without riding a thesis.

In the only other full-length immigrant-ethnic study to meet professional standards, Jerome R. Mintz investigated the Hasidic community of Brooklyn and published *Legends of the Hasidim* (*Chicago: University of Chicago Press, 1968). Unlike most immigrant groups, this sect of East European Jews strove to isolate itself from all external influences, even of non-Hasidic Jews, but Mintz reveals in his life histories, ethnographic commentary, and miracle-working tales how Americanisms did creep into their orthodoxy. When a *Rebbe* failed to exorcise a *dybbuk* from a child, the young Hasid told the father to take him to a psychiatrist. A limited but careful scrutiny of a group comparable to the Hasidim in their close-knit orthodoxy was undertaken by Willard B. Moore in *Molokan Oral Tradition, Legends and Memorates of an Ethnic Sect* (Berkeley and Los Angeles: University of California Press, 1973: Folklore Studies 28). Moore interviewed members of the Spiritual Christian Molokan community of Los Angeles whose forebears emigrated from Russia in the early years of the twentieth century, and published personal histories, memorates, supernatural legends, and family anecdotes. Most of the narratives deal with religious affairs, such as dangers averted by Molokan prophets, omens, and faith healing, and Moore devotes a chapter to the *sobranie,* the Molokan church that serves as the "forum for interaction." Two amateurish but suggestive semi-compilations are by Rudolf Glanz, *The Jew in Old American Folklore* (New York: Ktav, 1961) and *The Jew in Early American Wit and Graphic Humor* (New York: Ktav, 1973). Glanz has unearthed anecdotes, observations, jokes, and cartoons from nineteenth-century periodicals dealing with the Jewish comic stereotype, which he reprints with connecting glosses.

The Indian

For all the flood of publications on North American Indian tribal cultures, no folklorist has sought to analyze in any depth Native American folklore and mythology in relation to American mainstream culture. In *Bloodstoppers and Bearwalkers* (cf. "Regional") Dorson juxtaposed Ojibwa, Potawatomi, and Sioux oral narratives with those from ethnic and occupational groups in Michigan's Upper Peninsula, and in "Comic Indian Anecdotes" (reprinted in *Folklore and Fakelore;* cf. "General Studies") he examined bi-racial humor in which the Indian emerges as an underdog trickster discomfiting the white man. Of special interest is the psychoanalytical reading of the Winnebago trickster cycle in Paul Radin, *The Trickster, A Study in American Indian Mythology,* with commentaries by Karl Kerenyi and C. G. Jung (New York: Philosophical Library, 1956), but the far-out interpretations of the tales, so overtly phallic as to require little symbolic extension, have little bearing on the American scene. The lacunae in Americanist folklore studies are nowhere more dramatically seen than in the inattention to the first Americans.□

*indicates paperback availability

ADDENDUM

Professor Dorson offered the following comments and titles to update his essay. The headings of this addendum appear in his original contribution.

General Studies of American Folklore

A revised edition of Jan H. Brunvand's The Study of American Folklore appeared in 1978, published by Norton. Brunvand also published Readings in American Folklore (New York: Norton, 1979), a selection of interpretive articles that reveals the paucity of historical analyses. The latest overview of the field is set forth admirably by Barre Toelken in The Dynamics of Folklore, accompanied by an equally judicious Instructor's Manual (Boston: Houghton Mifflin, 1979). Toelken emphasizes the process of folklore transmission rather than the static genres of folk material.

Occupational

In a collection and study with both occupational and regional aspects, I Heard the Old Fisherman Say: Folklore of the Texas Gulf (Austin and London: University of Texas Press, 1978), Patrick B. Mullen examines magical and empirical folk beliefs, buried treasure legends, local character anecdotes, and tall tales of Texas coastal fishermen. He considers the style and functions of specimen texts against the social and cultural milieu of this hazardous occupation.

Ballad, Folksong, Folk Music

Edward D. Ives has produced a biographical study and song collection comparable to his work on Gorman in Joe Scott, the Woodsman-Songster (Urbana: University of Illinois Press, 1978), a work distinguished by its tracking down of elusive evidence and sensible analyses of the song texts. Unlike Gorman the satirist, Scott composed narrative songs with a lyrical element on topical events.

Urban

Urban Folklore from the Paperwork Empire, by Alan Dundes and Carl
Pagter, has been reprinted as Work Hard and You Shall Be Rewarded
(Bloomington: Indiana University Press, 1979).

Afro-American

Recently Daryl Cumber Dance, a self-trained black collector,
assembled a comprehensive tale harvest from Virginia in Shuckin'
and Jivin': Folklore from Contemporary Black Americans (Bloomington: Indiana University Press, 1978), rich in bawdy and racist
jokes. The contents thoroughly disprove the case for African
origins of Afro-American oral narratives in current circulation.

The material culture of Afro-Americans, long neglected in favor of
their exuberant oral expression, is beginning to receive attention,
as in John M. Vlach's illustrated catalog of a museum exhibit he
assembled, The Afro-American Tradition in Decorative Arts (Cleveland Museum of Art, 1978). Separate chapters deal with basketry,
musical, wood carving, quilting, pottery, boatbuilding, black-
smithing, architecture, and graveyard decoration. Vlach perceives
strong African influences in coiled grass baskets, drums, cane
fifes, and banjoes. Modified influences appear in quilting patterns, wooden walking sticks, the shotgun house, and the single-log
canoe.

A major bibliographical aid, Afro-American Folk Cultures, An
Annotated Bibliography of Materials from North, Central and South
America and the West Indies (2 vols.; Philadelphia: Institute for
the Study of Human Issues, 1978), has recently been completed by
John F. Szwed and Roger Abrahams, who contend that Afro-American
folk cultures do exist as isolable entities in the New World.
Entries are arranged alphabetically by author and annotated with
useful content summaries.

Themes in the History of American Foreign Policy

ALEXANDER DeCONDE

☐ Foreign policy as a distinct subject received slight attention in the early historical literature of the United States. Before the Civil War pioneering studies such as those by Theodore Lyman, Jr., *The Diplomacy of the United States* (Boston: Wells and Lilly, 1826) and William H. Trescot, *The Diplomacy of the Revolution: An Historical Study* (New York: D. Appleton, 1852) and *The Diplomatic History of the Administrations of Washington and Adams, 1789–1801* (Boston: Little, Brown, 1857), recounted the development of foreign policy as revealed in official documents. These histories focused on an elite of decisionmakers and gave a one-sided defense rather than an analysis of policy. Not until the end of the nineteenth century, when historical scholarship in the United States was establishing itself as an academic discipline, did American diplomatic history begin taking form as a discrete subject.

The Spanish-American War, along with the international recognition accorded the United States as a world power, stimulated among Americans an unprecedented interest in world affairs. So historians of foreign relations took up the study of rivalries among nations, mainly political and military conflict, from the perspective of the American makers of policy. Other historians, particularly Frederick Jackson Turner, an expert in the diplomacy of the Federalist era as well as of the frontier, and his disciples concentrated more on the domestic than on the international aspects of foreign relations. They studied the domestic pressures that shaped American foreign policy and assessed its effect on internal politics.

United States intervention in the First World War intensified the awareness of academic historians of their country's stake in the politics of Europe and Asia. Diplomatic history of all kinds, but especially that of Europe, gained in popularity.

In the 1920's the domestic battle over the League of Nations, the Washington Conference on naval disarmament, and other issues of worldwide significance kept active this scholarly interest in foreign relations. Yet few scholars specialized in American diplomatic history. Those who wrote on the subject often did so because American foreign policy touched their own fields of specialization European, British Empire, Asian, or Latin-American history. Nonetheless, a few specialists in the history of American foreign policy began appearing, as did a small but impressive literature on the subject. Pervasive themes in that literature were those of conflict and of America's diplomatic successes in a world dominated by power politics.

Several scholars of the twenties, but especially Samuel F. Bemis, stressed multi-archival research. This trend accelerated in the thirties. Washington, D.C., where access to government records was more readily available to scholars than in other capitals, became a center for the study of recent diplomacy. Textbooks in American diplomatic history reflected this multi-archival approach and growth in the field. Bemis published a distinguished text that synthesized the literature of American diplomatic history with a thoroughness that surpassed its predecessors. The book's approach was international but its theme was strongly nationalistic. Several years later Thomas A. Bailey broke new ground with a remarkably readable text grounded on the thesis that public opinion shaped foreign policy in the United States. He, too, wrote within a nationalist context. Later textbooks, several of excellent quality, softened the nationalistic approach.

The early monographic literature also stressed nationalism, and virtually ignored the colonial period. Finally Max Savelle, in *The Origins of American Diplo-*

Alexander DeConde is Professor of History at the University of California, Santa Barbara, where he has taught since 1961, having served as Chairman of the Department from 1963–67. He received his Ph.D. from Stanford University in 1949, and he has taught at Duke University and the University of Michigan. He has been the recipient of Guggenheim and Fulbright Awards, has served as President of the Society for Historians of American Foreign Relations, and has been a member of the Executive Board of the Organization of American Historians. In addition to his numerous articles and reviews, Professor DeConde is the author of The American Secretary of State: An Interpretation *(1962),* A History of American Foreign Policy *(1963, 2nd ed., 1971), and* Half-Bitter, Half-Sweet: An Excursion into Italian-American History *(1972), among others. He is currently the Editor-in-Chief of the forthcoming* Dictionary of the History of American Foreign Policy *macy: The International History of Angloamerica, 1492-1763* (New York: Macmillan, 1967), brought together in one book the results of years of research. He covers in detail the international involvements of England's North American colonies, and stresses a theme of international history. His is the basic work on the pre-independence background of American, or colonial, relations with foreign powers. In *Benjamin Franklin and American Foreign Policy** (Chicago: University of Chicago Press, 1954) Gerald Stourzh also probes pre-revolutionary foreign relations, but within a narrower context. Within a theme of realism he concentrates on Franklin's ideas relating to foreign policy. Combining diplomatic and intellectual history, Stourzh depicts Franklin as a hard-headed realist who believed in his people's destiny to expand.

Felix Gilbert, *To the Farewell Address: Ideas of Early American Foreign Policy** (Princeton: Princeton University Press, 1961), also analyzes colonial assumptions concerning international affairs. He maintains that American attitudes toward foreign policy derived from English ideas and he stresses continuity in those attitudes from the colonial period into the early national era.

For the American Revolution the standard work is still Bemis' *The Diplomacy of the American Revolution** (New York: D. Appleton-Century, 1935). Within a nationalistic context it advances the thesis that Americans did well in their diplomacy because they were able to profit from the distresses of European powers. For the international politics of independence the fullest treatment based on multi-archival research is Richard B. Morris, *The Peacemakers: The Great Powers and American Independence** (New York: Harper and Row, 1965). Although it differs in emphasis, like Bemis' book it depicts American diplomacy as righteous and that of America's protagonists as unscrupulous. On the diplomacy of the French alliance in the revolution a basic book is William C. Stinchcombe, *The American Revolution and the French Alliance* (Syracuse: University of Syracuse Press, 1969), which covers, besides diplomacy, the effect of the French alliance on American politics during the revolution. The still useful Edward S. Corwin, *French Policy and the American Alliance of 1778* (Princeton: Princeton University Press, 1916), approached the subject from the perspective of European diplomacy.

Most of the literature on foreign policy in the Federalist era concentrates on relations with England and France. A detailed account that follows the theme of Europe's distresses contributing to America's successes is Arthur B. Darling, *Our Rising Empire, 1763-1803* (New Haven: Yale University Press, 1940). Paul Varg, *Foreign Policies of the Founding Fathers* (East Lansing: Michigan State University Press, 1963) and Richard W. Van Alstyne, *Genesis of American Nationalism* (Waltham, Mass., Blaisdell Pub. Co., 1970), interpret American policymaking as an expression of early nationalism. The most recent survey of the diplomacy of the period that synthesizes the interpretive literature is Lawrence S. Kaplan, *Colonies into Nation: American Diplomacy 1763-1801* (New York: Macmillan, 1972).

In *Jay's Treaty: A Study in Commerce and Diplomacy** (New York: Macmillan, 1923), Bemis sees the treaty as an instrument of peace, while Jerald A. Combs, in *The Jay Treaty: Political Battleground of the Founding Fathers* (Berkeley: University of California Press, 1970), appraises it in terms of "realism," arguing that both Federalists and Republicans thought and acted with an awareness of balancing foreign policy with the power available to carry it out. Bradford Perkins, *The First Rapprochement: England and the United States, 1795–1805* (Phil.: University of Pennsylvania Press, 1955), elaborates the theme that capable diplomacy, particularly by the British, and a unique community of interests made possible the first Anglo-American understanding. Charles R. Ritcheson, *Aftermath of Revolution: British Policy toward the United States, 1783–1795* (Dallas: Southern Methodist University Press, 1969), also interprets England's position favorably.

Several books on relations with France maintain that careful statesmanship by Talleyrand and other French diplomatists as well as by Americans such as John Adams overcame heated American nationalism to keep the Quasi-War from expanding into a full-scale conflict. The ambitions and enmities of Alexander Hamilton, Thomas Jefferson, John Adams, and others, according to these studies, also helped determine if there would be continuing war or peace. These themes are in Alexander DeConde, *Entangling Alliance: Politics and Diplomacy under George Washington* (Durham, N.C.: Duke University Press, 1958) and *The Quasi-War: The Politics and Diplomacy of the Undeclared War with France, 1797–1801* (New York: Scribner's 1966) and Albert H. Bowman, *The Struggle for Neutrality: Franco-American Diplomacy During the Federalist Era* (Knoxville: University of Tennessee Press, 1974), which is strongly pro-Jeffersonian. Variations on these themes can be found in biographical studies such as Lawrence S. Kaplan, *Jefferson and France: An Essay on Politics and Political Ideas* (New Haven: Yale University Press, 1967); Marvin Zahniser, *Charles Cotesworth Pinckney: Founding Father* (Chapel Hill: University of North Carolina Press, 1967); Gerard H. Clarfield, *Timothy Pickering and American Diplomacy, 1795–1800* (Columbia: University of Missouri Press, 1969); and Peter P. Hill, *William Vans Murray Federalist Diplomat: The Shaping of Peace with France, 1797–1801* (Syracuse: Syracuse University Press, 1971).

Three scholarly monographs are basic for the study of relations with Spain in this period. Samuel F. Bemis, *Pinckney's Treaty: A Study of America's Advantage from Europe's Distress, 1783–1800* (Baltimore: The Johns Hopkins Press, 1926), advances the thesis of the subtitle. Arthur P. Whitaker, in *The Spanish-American Frontier: 1783–1795: The Westward Movement and the Spanish Retreat in the Mississippi Valley** (Boston: Houghton Mifflin, 1927), and *The Mississippi Question: A Study in Trade, Politics, and Diplomacy* (New York: D. Appleton-Century, 1934), focuses on the frontier and the clash with Spaniards there. He asserts that these western border developments were most influential in forming American policy toward Spain.

Several of these books also deal with Jeffersonian policy. The basic account for the outstanding achievement of that policy, the purchase of Louisiana, is in Henry Adams, *History of the United States of America during the Administrations of Jefferson and Madison* (9 vols., New York: Scribner's, 1889–1909), which by supporting the thesis of fortuitous diplomacy gives Jefferson little credit for gaining the heart of the North American continent. Elijah Wilson Lyon, *Louisiana in French Diplomacy, 1759–1804** (Norman: University of Oklahoma Press, 1934), also expounds a theme of fortuitous circumstances but explains the purchase from the perspective of French colonial and foreign policy.

The War of 1812 has attracted more scholarly investigation and speculation than has the Louisiana Purchase. In his *History,* Henry Adams advances the thesis that conflict over maritime rights brought on this second war between the United States and Britain. Julius W. Pratt in *Expansionists of 1812* (New York: Macmillan, 1925) maintains that the agitation of war hawks in Congress and the lust of western expansionists led to war. Later scholarship adds details and variations to these approaches but generally supports the thesis that maritime grievances formed the basic cause for war. The important works here are Alfred L. Burt, *The United States, Great Britain, and British North America: From the Revo-*

Courtesy, Prints and Photographs Division, Library of Congress

"The Louisiana Purchase. Messrs. Monroe and Livingstone completing Negotiations with Tallyrand, April 30, 1803." Reproduced by C. H. Nichols from a painting by H. E. Whorf.

lution to the Establishment of Peace After the War (New Haven: Yale University Press, 1940); Bradford Perkins, *Prologue to War: England and the United States, 1805–1812** (Berkeley: University of California Press, 1961), which also emphasizes America's concern over national honor as a cause, and is now the best-balanced work on the subject; Reginald Horsman, *The Causes of the War of 1812* (Philadelphia: University of Pennsylvania Press, 1962); and Roger H. Brown, *The Republic in Peril: 1812* (New York: Columbia University Press, 1964), which insists that Republican party unity, rather than sectional considerations, based on the assumption that republican government would be endangered without a response to England's maritime violations, triggered war.

Pratt's expansionist thesis touches on a theme, that of continental empire, that runs through much of nineteenth-century diplomatic history. In *The Rising American Empire** (New York: Oxford University Press, 1960) Richard W. Van Alstyne subjects this theme to a sweeping critical analysis. Samuel F. Bemis' *John Quincy Adams and the Foundations of American Foreign Policy* (New York: Knopf, 1949) is the most thorough and scholarly treatment of expansion into Florida and across the continent by treaty. It also covers the shaping of the Monroe Doctrine. Most studies of the doctrine maintain that the danger from Europe to the newly independent Latin American countries was more imagined than real. Even if the European powers had decided upon intervention, the British fleet, not the Monroe Doctrine, deterred them. The fullest treatment of this thesis is in Dexter Perkins, *The Monroe Doctrine, 1823–1826* (Cambridge: Harvard University Press, 1927). Variations on this theme can be found in Arthur P. Whitaker, *The United States and the Independence of Latin America, 1800–1830* (Baltimore: Johns Hopkins Press, 1941); George Dangerfield, *The Era of Good Feelings** (New York: Harcourt, Brace, 1952); and Bradford Perkins, *Castlereagh and Adams: England and the United States, 1812–1823* (Berkeley: University of California Press, 1964). Ernest R. May's *The Making of the Monroe Doctrine* (Cambridge: Harvard University Press, 1975) reinterprets the genesis of the doctrine and argues that domestic political considerations, not European dangers, dictated Monroe's concept.

The most intensive works on continental expansionism deal with the events of the 1840's under the concept of Manifest Destiny. Historians differ over the meaning, significance, and even existence of the phenomenon. Since Manifest Destiny, however interpreted, encompasses the acquisition of territory by conquest, critics view it as nothing more than aggression gilded by pious sentiment, or merely an American form of imperialism. Albert K. Weinberg, *Manifest Destiny: A Study of Nationalist Expansionism in American History* (Baltimore: Johns Hopkins Press, 1935), scrutinizes the intellectual inconsistencies and rhetoric associated with the concept. Justin H. Smith, *The War with Mexico* (2 vols., New York: Macmillan, 1919), defends expansion within the scope of Manifest Destiny and places major responsibility for war on Mexico. Norman A. Graebner, *Empire on the Pacific: A Study of American Continental Expansion* (New York: Ronald Press, 1955), denies the existence of Manifest Destiny as a calculated movement into Oregon and California. He argues that Eastern merchants interested in trade in the Pacific area "determined the course of empire."

Frederick Merk, on the other hand, insists that Manifest Destiny existed as a nationalist phenomenon throughout the land. He differentiates between "mission" and aggressive expansion, or Manifest Destiny. He also argues that politicians as an excuse for imperialism used the idea that Texas' involvements with European powers threatened the security of the United States. Expansion, they insisted, was necessary as a means for defending the nation. Merk's interpretations are in *Manifest Destiny and Mission in American History: A Reinterpretation** (New York: Knopf, 1963); *The Monroe Doctrine and American Expansion, 1843–1849** (New York: Knopf, 1966); *Fruits of Propaganda in the*

Tyler Administration (Cambridge: Harvard University Press, 1971); and *Slavery and the Annexation of Texas* (New York: Knopf, 1972). The fullest treatment of expansionism in the 1840's based on multiarchival research is David M. Pletcher, *The Diplomacy of Annexation: Texas, Oregon, and the Mexican War* (Columbia: University of Missouri Press, 1973). Unlike Smith, he criticizes President James K. Polk, and places American policy within a broad international setting.

Conventional students of foreign policy hold that Manifest Destiny died with the coming of the Civil War. Dissenters argue that it remained alive during that war, which among other things determined who within American society would dominate further expansion. But the historiography of the Civil War diplomacy has usually hinged on relations with England which set the pattern for the policies of the other major powers toward the conflict. Britain's intervention could have assured the success of Southern secession. The following studies explain why Britain did not intervene: Ephraim D. Adams, *Great Britain and the American Civil War* (2 vols., London: Longmans, Green, 1925); Frank L. Owsley, *King Cotton Diplomacy: Foreign Relations of the Confederate States of America* (2nd ed., rev. by Harriet C. Owsley, Chicago: University of Chicago Press, 1959), whose pro-Southern attitude is balanced by Jay Monaghan, *Diplomat in Carpet Slippers: Abraham Lincoln Deals with Foreign Affairs* (Indianapolis: Bobbs-Merrill, 1945), which gives the Union position and depicts it as dominated by Lincoln; Stuart L. Bernath, *Squall Across the Atlantic: American Civil War Prize Cases and Diplomacy* (Berkeley: University of California Press, 1970); Frank J. Merli, *Great Britain and the Confederate Navy, 1861–1865* (Bloomington: Indiana University Press, 1970); Mary L. Ellison, *Support for Secession: Lancashire and the American Civil War* (Chicago: University of Chicago Press, 1972), which revises the theory that English textile workers supported the Union cause even at the cost of famine; Brian Jenkins, *Britain and the War for the Union* (Montreal: McGill-Queens University Press, 1974), which takes the story to 1862 and analyzes the Canadian relationship in detail; and David P. Crook, *The North, the South, and the Powers, 1861–1865* (New York: Wiley, 1974), the most well-rounded scholarly account.

Recent scholarship clarifies the hitherto neglected relationship to France. The most thorough scholarly study, Lynn M. Case and Warren F. Spencer, *The United States and France: Civil War Diplomacy* (Phil.: University of Pennsylvania Press, 1970), confirms the traditional view that France's policy toward the conflict followed the British pattern. Alfred J. Hanna and Kathryn A. Hanna, *Napoleon III and Mexico: American Triumph over Monarchy* (Chapel Hill: University of North Carolina Press, 1971), nationalistically depicts the French intervention in Mexico, from the American point of view, as sinister.

Most historians have portrayed the post-Civil War period and the Gilded Age as a time when foreign policy stood still, or moved only in response to more important domestic developments. Ernest N. Paolino, *The Foundations of American Empire: William Henry Seward and U.S. Foreign Policy* (Ithaca: Cornell University Press, 1973), dissents from this view. He places the origins of American imperialism in the 1860's. David M. Pletcher, *The Awkward Years: American Foreign Relations under Garfield and Arthur* (Columbia: University of Missouri

Press, 1962), and Milton Plesur, *America's Outward Thrust: Approaches to Foreign Affairs, 1865–1890* (DeKalb: Northern Illinois University Press, 1971), also stress continuity between continental expansion and overseas imperialism. Paul Kennedy, *The Samoan Tangle: A Study in Anglo-German-American Relations, 1878–1900* (New York: Barnes & Noble, 1974) places such expansion in a context of world-wide imperialism.

One school concerned with such expansionism takes as its model Charles A. Beard's economic interpretation as advanced in the 1920's. Beard maintained that American businessmen, interested in foreign markets, sponsored overseas imperialism or the New Manifest Destiny. Julius W. Pratt, in the *Expansionists of 1898: The Acquisition of Hawaii and the Spanish Islands* (Baltimore: Johns Hopkins Press, 1936), refuted Beard's thesis as it applied to the coming of the Spanish American War, but some historians consistently clung to the Beard idea. Two prominent works that follow this hypothesis are William A. Williams, *Roots' of the Modern American Empire: A Study of the Growth and Shaping of Social Consciousness in a Marketplace Society** (New York: Random House, 1969), and Walter F. LaFeber, *The New Empire: An Interpretation of American Expansion, 1860–1898** (Ithaca: Cornell University Press, 1963). Williams maintains that American agrarians produced a marketplace mentality used as a model by commercial interests in overseas expansion. Both scholars depict expansionist business interests as guiding foreign policy. They and other economic determinists contend that war came in 1898 because in the 1880's and 1890's the United States suffered severe depressions. The domestic economy could not absorb industrial overproduction, so the ruling establishment searched for markets abroad where it could dump surpluses.

Other historians interpreted the New Manifest Destiny as a fresh departure, even as an aberration. Regardless of the differences over these interpretations, recent scholarship regards 1898 as a point of fundamental change in the direction of the nation's foreign policy. The United States assumed new responsibilities that influenced its position in world affairs for much of the twentieth century. Scholars such as Ernest R. May in *Imperial Democracy: The Emergence of America as a Great Power** (New York: Harcourt, Brace & World, 1961) and in *American Imperialism: A Speculative Essay* (New York: Atheneum, 1968) and David F. Healy, *U.S. Expansionism: The Imperialist Urge in the 1890's* (Madison: University of Wisconsin Press, 1972), explore imperialism in such terms and within the context of an elitist, policy-shaping establishment. This change in national direction, as Charles S. Campbell, *Anglo-American Understanding, 1898–1903* (Baltimore: Johns Hopkins Press, 1957) and Bradford Perkins, *The Great Rapprochement: England and the United States, 1895–1914* (New York: Atheneum, 1968) explain, was accompanied by a rapprochement with Great Britain of far-reaching significance.

Since the New Manifest Destiny provoked noteworthy dissent, Robert L. Beisner, *Twelve Against Empire: The Anti-Imperialists, 1898–1900* (New York: McGraw-Hill, 1968) and E. Berkeley Tompkins, *Anti-Imperialism in the United States: The Great Debate, 1890–1920** (Philadelphia: University of Pennsylvania Press, 1970) examined the ideas and tactics of the anti-imperialists. They portray the anti-imperialists not as pure idealists, but as men who sought power as realistically as their opponents. A still provocative, well-written critical analysis of American imperialism at work is Walter Millis, *The Martial Spirit: A Study of Our War with Spain* (New York: Houghton Mifflin, 1931).

Students of relations with Asian countries also explored the imperialist theme. The conventional wisdom praises the United States for having been friendlier and less imperialistic toward China than were other great powers. It claims that the open door policy saved China from partition by European imperialists. Other more critical scholarship sees American policy as hitch-hiking imperialism wherein the United States benefited from the use of force by others. It views the open door policy as being based on myth and as not saving China from anything. Some economically oriented scholars place it within a pattern of economic expansion called "open door imperialism." Within the extensive literature on the open door policy and dollar diplomacy these books are noteworthy: Tyler Dennett, *Americans in Eastern Asia: A Critical Study of the Policy of the United States with Reference to China, Japan, and Korea in the 19th Century,* (New York: Macmillan, 1922); Charles S. Campbell, *Special Business Interests and the Open Door Policy* (New Haven: Yale University Press, 1951); Charles Vevier, *The United States and*

Courtesy, Prints and Photographs Division, Library of Congress

"Curiosity of the Japanese at Witnessing the Girl Working One of Wheeler and Wilson's Sewing Machines in Willard's Hotel Laundry, Washington, D.C." A wood engraving in Frank Leslie's Illustrated Magazine, *1860.*

China, 1906–1913: A Study of Finance and Diplomacy (New Brunswick: Rutgers University Press, 1955); Thomas J. McCormick, *China Market: America's Quest for Informal Empire, 1893–1901* (Chicago: Quadrangle, 1967); Paul A. Varg, *The Making of a Myth: The United States and China, 1897–1912* (East Lansing: Michigan State University Press, 1968); Marilyn B. Young, *The Rhetoric of Empire. American China Policy, 1895–1901* (Cambridge: Harvard University Press, 1968); Jerry Israel, *Progressivism and the Open Door: America and China, 1905–1921* (Pittsburgh: University of Pittsburgh Press, 1971); and Michael Hunt, *Frontier Defense and the Open Door: Manchuria in Chinese-American Relations, 1895–1911* (New Haven: Yale University Press, 1973).

Students of relations with Japan often stress conflict of national interests and frequently link the conflict to the American obsession with the open door idea as well as to Japanese expansionism. On these themes a still useful older study is Thomas A. Bailey, *Theodore Roosevelt and the Japanese-American Crises: An Account of the International Complications Arising from the Race Problem on the Pacific Coast* (Stanford: Stanford University Press, 1934). Other important analyses based on more recent scholarship are Howard K. Beale, *Theodore Roosevelt and the Rise of America to World Power* (Baltimore: Johns Hopkins Press, 1956), which covers much more than relations with Japan; Raymond A. Esthus, *Theodore Roosevelt and Japan* (Seattle: University of Washington Press, 1966), Charles E. Neu, *An Uncertain Friendship. Theodore Roosevelt and Japan, 1906–1909* (Cambridge: Harvard University Press, 1967); Eugene P. Trani, *The Treaty of Portsmouth: An Adventure in American Diplomacy* (Lexington: University of Kentucky Press, 1969); and Akira Iriye, *Pacific Estrangement: Japanese and American Expansion, 1897–1911* (Cambridge: Harvard University Press, 1972).

Revisionism, or the challenging of established interpretations, is as evident in the literature of Asian-American relations as it is elsewhere in historical writing, but the first major revisionist clash in American diplomacy involving professionally trained historians occurred in the 1920's and 1930's over the causes of American intervention in the First World War. The conventional interpretation held that Germany's unrestricted use of the submarine forced war on the United States. Revisionists attacked this "submarine school" view saying that intervention had been a mistake, or even the result of an Anglo-American conspiracy. Charles Seymour, *American Diplomacy during the World War* (Baltimore: Johns Hopkins Press, 1934) and *American Neutrality: 1914–1917* (New Haven: Yale University Press, 1935) presents the submarine thesis, and Ernest R. May, *The World War and American Isolation* (Cambridge: Harvard University Press, 1959) gives the best-balanced account in defense of Woodrow Wilson's policies and the submarine school. The most readable and popular revisionist book is Walter Millis, *Road to War, 1914–1917* (Boston: Houghton Mifflin, 1935), and the most heavily documented revisionist account is Charles C.Tansill, *America Goes to War* (Boston: Little, Brown, 1938), while Patrick Devlin, *Too Proud to Fight: Woodrow Wilson's Neutrality* (New York: Oxford University Press, 1975), places responsibility for taking the nation to war on the president himself.

Two important volumes emphasize capitalist ideology as being a determinant of American policy. Arno J. Mayer, *Political Origins of the New Diplomacy, 1917–1918** (New Haven: Yale University Press, 1959) and *Politics and Diplo-*

macy: Containment and Counterrevolution at Versailles, 1918–1919 (New York: Vintage Books, 1967), depicts the United States as the main pillar of the capitalist world. Norman Gordon Levin, Jr., *Woodrow Wilson and World Politics: America's Response to War and Revolution** (New York: Oxford University Press, 1968) argues that Wilson brought the United States into Europe's war to preserve capitalism and that Wilsonian ideology set the pattern for twentieth-century American foreign policy. On the peacemaking itself two books by Thomas A. Bailey, *Woodrow Wilson and the Lost Peace** (New York: Macmillan, 1944) and *Woodrow Wilson and the Great Betrayal* (New York: Macmillan, 1945), blame the president for the failure of the United States to support the League of Nations. Ralph Stone, *The Irreconcilables: The Fight Against the League of Nations* (Lexington: University of Kentucky Press, 1970), chronicles the opposition to Wilson's peace program and maintains that historians have exaggerated the power of irreconcilable Senate opponents.

Those who have studied the relationship with Russia in this period agree on at least one thing: that it was bad. This theme runs through Thomas A. Bailey, *America Faces Russia: Russian-American Relations from Early Times to Our Day* (Ithaca: Cornell University Press, 1950). William A. Williams, *American-Russian Relations, 1781–1947* (New York: Rhinehart, 1952), chastises American policymakers for hostility toward the Soviets. George F. Kennan, *Soviet-American Relations, 1917–1920* (2 vols., Princeton: Princeton University Press, 1956, 1958), places responsibility for the hostility upon Soviet leaders, essentially their hatred of Western capitalism. Betty M. Unterberger, *America's Siberian Expedition, 1918–1920: A Study in National Policy* (Durham: Duke University Press, 1956), analyzes the American intervention in Siberia and concludes that it sought to restrain Japanese imperialism and not just to strangle communism.

The obsessive concern of policymakers with bolshevism continued through the 1920's into the 1930's, but the theme of greatest interest to historians of these decades is the confrontation of isolationists and internationalists. Scholars differ over the nature of isolationism and the depth of its influence, but most accept it as a force of considerable emotional and political impact that long influenced the shaping of American foreign policy. In the thirties and forties the concept of collective security became more important. The fullest treatments of isolationism are Selig Adler, *The Isolationist Impulse: Its Twentieth Century Reaction** (New York: Abelard-Schuman, 1957) and Manfred Jonas, *Isolationism in America, 1935–1941* (Ithaca: Cornell University Press, 1966). Important books that deal with aspects of isolationism and internationalism are: Walter Johnson, *The Battle Against Isolation* (Chicago: University of Chicago Press, 1944); Wayne S. Cole, *America First: The Battle Against Intervention, 1940–1941* (Madison: University of Wisconsin Press, 1953); *Senator Gerald P. Nye and American Foreign Relations* (Minneapolis: University of Minnesota Press, 1962); *Charles A. Lindbergh and the Battle Against American Intervention in World War II* (New York: Harcourt, Brace, Jovanovich, 1974); and Geoffrey S. Smith, *To A Nation: American Countersubversives, the New Deal, and the Coming of World War II* (New York: Basic Books, 1973). For collective security the most thorough analysis is Roland N. Stromberg, *Collective Security and American Foreign Policy: From the League of Nations to NATO* (New York: Praeger, 1963). Analyses of both concepts are in Alexander DeConde, ed., *Isolation and Security: Idea and Interests in Twentieth Century American Foreign Policy* (Durham: Duke University Press, 1957).

Other important books in the literature of this period touch on economic policy, armaments, and the peace movement. Carl P. Parrini, *Heir to Empire: United States Economic Diplomacy, 1916–1923* (Pittsburgh: University of Pittsburgh Press, 1969), maintains that Republican successors continued Wilson's program of world leadership based on an open-door global economy. Joan Hoff Wilson, *American Business and Foreign Policy, 1920–1933** (Lexington: University of Kentucky Press, 1971), points out that contrary to established views, the business community did give Republican administrations unified support. Robert H. Ferrell, *American Diplomacy in the Great Depression: Hoover-Stimson Foreign Policy, 1929–1933* (New Haven: Yale University Press, 1957), maintains that the Great Depression so overwhelmed Republican makers of policy that they found themselves unable to deal effectively with international crises. L. Ethan Ellis, *Republican Foreign Policy, 1921–1933* (New Brunswick: Rutgers University Press, 1968), also underscores the seriousness of the depression but suggests that Republican leaders were not devoid of accomplishment.

Studies of the peace movement explore the domestic sources of foreign policy within a theme of immediate failure but of long-range influence for peace advocates. They were continuously aware that international politics could affect vital domestic issues and *vice versa*. Important peace monographs are C. Roland Marchand, *The American Peace Movement and Social Reform, 1898–1918* (Princeton: Princeton University Press, 1972); Robert H. Ferrell, *Peace in Their Time: The Origins of the Kellogg-Briand Pact* (New Haven: Yale University Press, 1952); Charles Chatfield, *For Peace and Justice: Pacifism in America, 1914–1941* (Knoxville: University of Tennessee Press, 1971); and Lawrence S. Wittner, *Rebels Against War: The American Peace Movement, 1941–1960** (New York: Columbia University Press, 1969).

A considerable literature focuses on Asian policy in these years. Although outmoded by later scholarship, Alfred W. Griswold, *The Far Eastern Policy of the United States** (New York: Harcourt, Brace, 1938), is important because it was the first study that gave interpretive coherence to the policies of the thirties. Its theme of the continuity of the special American friendship for China influenced scholars for decades. Dorothy Borg, *American Policy and the Chinese Revolution, 1925–1928* (New York: Macmillan, 1947), offers the most thorough analysis available of the American responses to Chinese nationalism. In *The United States and the Far Eastern Crisis of 1933–1938: From the Manchurian Incident through the Initial Stage of the Undeclared Sino-Japanese War* (Cambridge: Harvard University Press, 1964), she argues against a widely held view that Franklin D. Roosevelt and Cordell Hull were addicted to the open-door concept. At least until 1938, she asserts, they were flexible and strove to improve relations with Japan. Other writers view Japan's invasion of Manchuria in 1931 as the first attack against the collective security structure of the 1920's and hence as the real beginning of the Second World War. Variations on this theme are in William L. Neumann, *America Encounters Japan: From Perry to MacArthur** (Baltimore: Johns Hopkins Press, 1963); Armin Rappaport, *Henry L. Stimson and Japan,*

1931–1933 (Chicago: University of Chicago Press, 1963); and Christopher Thorne, *The Limits of Foreign Policy: The West, the League and the Far Eastern Crisis of 1931–1933* (London: Hamilton, 1972).

Akira Iriye, in *After Imperialism: The Search for a New Order in the Far East, 1921–1931* (Cambridge: Harvard University Press, 1965) and *Across the Pacific: An Inner History of American-East Asian Relations** (New York: Harcourt, Brace & World, 1967), offers a cross-cultural approach to the study of foreign policy. He analyzes the policies and the behavior of Americans, Russians, and Chinese, as well as the Japanese, toward each other. He also suggests that in the 1920's and 1930's the United States attempted, but ultimately failed, to establish a new political order in East Asia based on cooperation between the major powers.

Historians of foreign policy have not probed relations with Latin America as deeply as they have policy toward Asian countries. Nonetheless, within the broader twentieth-century experience of the United States with Latin America, scholars explored the themes of big brother imperialism beginning with Theodore Roosevelt, dollar diplomacy, missionary diplomacy, Caribbean interventions under various guises, and the nature of the good neighbor policy. Although outdated and dubious in its ethnocentric defense of United States policies, Samuel F. Bemis, *The Latin American Policy of United States: An Historical Interpretation* (New York: Harcourt, Brace, 1943), retains value because it is still the major scholarly monograph that attempts the full sweep of the relationship with Latin America with other than a textbook coherence. Other useful surveys that cover a special aspect of that relationship, and also from a nationalist perspective, are Dexter Perkins, *A History of the Monroe Doctrine* (2nd ed., Boston: Little, Brown, 1955) and Wilfrid H. Callcott, *The Western Hemisphere: Its Influence on United States Policies to the End of World War II* (Austin: University of Texas Press, 1968).

In *The United States and Cuba, 1898–1902: Generals, Politicians, and the Search for Policy* (Madison: University of Wisconsin Press, 1963) David F. Healy asserts that in Cuba the United States established an informal protectorate and controlled the country through the manipulation of trade and investments. He also argues that American policymakers later used this technique of informal imperialism throughout the Caribbean. Dana G. Munroe, in *Intervention and Dollar Diplomacy in the Caribbean, 1900–1921* (Princeton: Princeton University Press, 1964) and *The United States and the Caribbean Republic, 1921–1933* (Princeton: Princeton University Press, 1974), interprets American actions favorably. The United States, he believes, intervened to maintain stability so as to ensure its own security. Historians are divided in their assessments of Woodrow Wilson's Latin American policy, but recent scholarship is generally critical. Some scholars see that policy as well-intentioned but misguided missionary diplomacy; others considered it arrogant and ignoble. Useful analyses reflecting these themes are Kenneth J. Grieb, *The United States and Huerta* (Lincoln: University of Nebraska Press, 1969); P. Edward Haley, *Revolution and Intervention: The Diplomacy of Taft and Wilson with Mexico, 1910–1917* (Cambridge: Massachusetts Institute of Technology Press, 1970); and Joseph S. Tulchin, *The Aftermath of War: World War I and U.S. Policy Toward Latin America* (New York: New York University Press, 1971).

Interpretations of the good neighbor policy suggest that it began in the administration of Herbert Hoover, that it reflected a continuity in policy from Wilson to Franklin D. Roosevelt, and that it started from scratch in Roosevelt's administration. Most historians do agree that the policy did not survive the Roosevelt years. Variations on the good neighbor theme are in Alexander DeConde, *Herbert Hoover's Latin American Policy* (Stanford: Stanford University Press, 1951); Donald M. Dozer, *Are We Good Neighbors?: Three Decades of Inter-American Relations, 1930–1960* (Gainesville: University of Florida Press, 1959); Bryce Wood, *The Making of the Good Neighbor Policy* (New York: Columbia University Press, 1961); David Green, *The Containment of Latin America: A History of the Myths and Realities of the Good Neighbor Policy* (Chicago: Quadrangle Books, 1971); and Dick Steward, *Trade and Hemisphere: The Good Neighbor Policy and Reciprocal Trade* (Columbia: University of Missouri Press, 1976).

Scholars have carefully examined most aspects of foreign policy under Franklin D. Roosevelt, but much of the literature concentrates on the themes of isolation, neutrality, and intervention in the Second World War. Conventional scholarship maintains that Roosevelt was always an internationalist but could not lead the country into commitments of collective security any faster than the prevailing isolationist sentiment of the American people would permit. Some historians insist that in the early 1930's, at least, Roosevelt was an isolationist. What was for years the standard interpretation also praised intervention in the war as necessary for America's security. It maintained that the Axis powers, through aggressions, forced the United States into the war. The most cogent expression of this theme is in William L. Langer and S. Everett Gleason, *The Challenge to Isolation, 1937–1940* (New York: Harper, 1952) and *The Undeclared War, 1940–1941* (New York: Harper, 1953), volumes written under the sponsorship of the Council on Foreign Relations. Other books that play on this theme are Basil Rauch, *Roosevelt: From Munich to Pearl Harbor: A Study in the Creation of a Foreign Policy* (New York: Creative Age Press, 1950); Herbert Feis, *The Road to Pearl Harbor: The Coming of the War between the United States and Japan** (Princeton: Princeton University Press, 1950); Donald F. Drummond, *The Passing of American Neutrality, 1937–1941* (Ann Arbor: University of Michigan Press, 1955); Robert A. Divine, *The Illusion of Neutrality* (Chicago: University of Chicago Press, 1962); *The Reluctant Belligerent: American Entry into World War II** (New York: Wiley, 1965); *Roosevelt and World War II** (Baltimore: Johns Hopkins Press, 1969); and Gloria J. Barron, *Leadership in Crisis: FDR and the Path to Intervention* (Port Washington, N.Y.: Kennikat Press, 1973).

Revisionists denounced those who defended the policies of the Roosevelt administration as propagators of "official" history and condemned even the more scholarly writers favorable to this interpretation as "court historians." These revisionists expressed an animosity toward Roosevelt and his advisers; they contended that the causes of intervention lay in the attitude of these officials. Charles A. Beard set the pattern for the anti-Roosevelt revisionism. In *American Foreign Policy in the Making, 1932–1940: A Study in Responsibilities* (New Haven: Yale University Press, 1946) and *President Roosevelt and the Coming of* the War, 1941: A Study in Appearances and Realities (New Haven: Yale University Press, 1948), he argued that Roosevelt deceived the American people by professing a desire for peace while plotting to bring the country into the war. He accused Roosevelt of provoking the Japanese into attacking Pearl Harbor so as to hasten intervention. Beard also maintained that Roosevelt's expansion of presidential power in foreign relations endangered constitutional government. Other revisionist accounts that go along with the Beard themes are George E. Morgenstern, *Pearl Harbor: The Story of the Secret War* (New York: Devin-Adair, 1947); Charles C. Tansill, *Back Door to War: The Roosevelt Foreign Policy,*

Courtesy, Prints and Photographs Division, Library of Congress

"Laocoon," a pen and ink drawing by Clifford K. Berryman, September 26, 1938.

1933–1941 (Chicago: H. Regnery Co., 1952); and Robert A. Theobald, *The Final Secret of Pearl Harbor: The Washington Contribution to the Japanese Attack* (New York: Devin-Adair, 1954). Three important mildly revisionist studies are Richard N. Current, *Secretary Stimson: A Study in Statecraft* (New Brunswick: Rutgers University Press, 1954); Paul W. Schroeder, *The Axis Alliance and Japanese-American Relations, 1941* (Ithaca: Cornell University Press, 1958); and Lloyd C. Gardner, *Economic Aspects of New Deal Diplomacy* (Madison: University of Wisconsin Press, 1964). Other significant books on this subject are James V. Compton, *The Swastika and the Eagle: Hitler, the United States, and* the Origins of World War II (Boston: Houghton Mifflin, 1967); Arnold A. Offner, American Appeasement: United States Foreign Policy and Germany, 1933-1938* (Cambridge: Harvard Univ. Press, 1969); Waldo H. Heinrichs, Jr., American Ambassador: Joseph C. Grew and the Development of the United States Diplomatic Tradition (Boston: Little, Brown, 1966); Mark L. Chadwin, The Hawks of World War II (Chapel Hill: University of North Carolina Press, 1968); and Roberta Wohlstetter, Pearl Harbor: Warning and Decision* (Stanford: Stanford University Press, 1962).

The literature on wartime diplomacy reflects a number of themes, but especially prominent are those on planning for victory and for the postwar world. Anne Armstrong, Unconditional Surrender: The Impact of the Casablanca Policy Upon World War II (New Brunswick: Rutgers University Press, 1961), condemns unconditional surrender as unnecessarily prolonging the war whereas Raymond G. O'Connor, Diplomacy for Victory: FDR and Unconditional Surrender* (New York: Norton, 1971), defends that policy. Students of the decisions at Yalta generally view them as part of normal compromises in diplomacy, as a reflection of the realities of coalition warfare, as appeasement of the Soviets, or as realistic adjustments to a new balance of power. Diane S. Clemens, Yalta (New York: Oxford University Press, 1970), accepts the readjustment concept but contends that the Soviets probably conceded more than did the United States. Robert A. Divine, Second Chance: The Triumph of Internationalism in America during World War II (New York: Atheneum, 1967), maintains that during the war Americans had a second chance to support collective security through the formation of the United Nations and this time they carried through their commitment to the collective concept.

Concern over the results of Yalta diplomacy became enmeshed in academic controversy over whether idealism or realism motivated American policymaking. The most influential book on the history of American foreign policy during the postwar decades was composed of a series of lectures given by George F. Kennan, American Diplomacy, 1900-1950* (Chicago: University of Chicago Press, 1951), that attacked traditional moralism in American policy and urged a policy anchored in principles of realism.

Also in the fifties prominent scholars followed a theme of "consensus history" wherein they minimized conflict in policymaking. By stressing success they in effect supported the establishment's version of the past. At the end of the decade and in the early 1960's young historians who adopted a radical or New Left approach to American diplomatic history attacked the consensus philosophy. They argued, as had Beard, that American foreign policy developed out of conflicting interests and that it had been and was motivated by an economically based expansionist ideology.

The writings of William A. Williams, notably The Tragedy of American Diplomacy* (Cleveland: World Pub. Co., 1959; rev. ed., 1962) and The Contours of American History (Cleveland: World Pub. Co., 1961), elaborated on the Beard themes and became a model for much of the New Left writings on foreign policy. Williams and others often associated with the department of history of the University of Wisconsin advanced the open-door theory of American diplomatic history. It maintained that American policymakers sought to compensate for chronic problems of overproduction and depression at home by penetrating foreign markets through an open door for their capitalist enterprises. They built an informal empire based on trade rather than colonies, and used the open-door approach to bring global predominance to the United States. New Leftists argue that this economic expansionism, wedded to an older concept of mission, led to repeated efforts by policymaking elitists to remake the world in America's image.

New Left theory has aroused the greatest controversy in its assessment of American policy in the cold war. The conventional interpretation of the cold war blames the Soviets for starting the confrontation, and defends American leaders as acting logically in response to communist aggression by trying to contain it. Since this view comes often from the writings and memoirs of those who helped shape cold-war philosophy, or from historians who wrote in the interest of policy, radicals attack this interpretation as an echo of official policy. New Leftists insist that the United States, using its power ruthlessly, sought to restructure the world for the profit of American capitalists and was intransigent in dealing with the Soviet Union. The United States, they say, is at least as responsible as the Soviet Union, and probably more so, for launching and persisting in the cold war.

Noteworthy among the many books that support the conventional analysis are William H. McNeil, *America, Britain, and Russia: Their Cooperation and Conflict, 1941–1946* (London: Oxford University Press, 1953); Herbert Feis, *Churchill, Roosevelt, Stalin: The War They Waged and the Peace They Sought** (Princeton: Princeton University Press, 1957); *Between War and Peace: The Potsdam Conference** (Princeton: Princeton University Press, 1960); *Japan Subdued: The Atomic Bomb and the End of the War in the Pacific* (Princeton: Princeton University Press, 1961) revised as *The Atomic Bomb and the End of World War II** (Princeton: Princeton University Press, rev. ed., 1966); *Contest Over Japan* (New York: Norton, 1967); and *From Trust to Terror: The Onset of the Cold War, 1945–1950* (New York: Norton, 1970); John L. Gaddis, *The United States and the Origins of the Cold War, 1941–1947* (New York: Columbia University Press, 1972), which accepts some revisionists views; George C. Herring, Jr., *Aid to Russia, 1941–1946: Strategy, Diplomacy, the Origins of the Cold War* (New York: Columbia University Press, 1973); and Lisle A. Rose, *Dubious Victory: The United States and the End of World War II* (Kent, Ohio: Kent State University Press, 1973).

Important books that fit within the New Left pattern, or are close to it, are Thomas G. Paterson, *Soviet-American Confrontation: Postwar Reconstruction and the Origins of the Cold War** (Baltimore: Johns Hopkins Press, 1975); Gabriel Kolko, *The Politics of War: The World and United States Foreign Policy, 1943–1945** (New York: Random House, 1968); Joyce and Gabriel Kolko, *The Limits of Power: The World and United States Foreign Policy, 1945–1954* (New York: Harper and Row, 1972); Lloyd C. Gardner, *Architects of Illusion: Men and Ideas in American Foreign Policy, 1941–1949* (Chicago: Quadrangle Books, 1970); Walter LaFeber, *America, Russia, and the Cold War, 1945–1966** (New York: Wiley, 1967); and Denna F. Fleming, *The Cold War and Its Origins, 1917–1960* (2 vols., Garden City: Doubleday, 1961).

In dealing with the origins of the cold war, conventional scholars usually stress continuity between Roosevelt's and Harry S. Truman's policies. On this important and controversial question of atomic diplomacy these historians argue that the necessity to save lives in a bloody invasion of Japan's islands and to end the war quickly persuaded Truman to use atomic bombs. Revisionists deplore the atomic slaughter of human beings as cruel and unnecessary. Gar Alperovitz, in *Atomic Diplomacy: Hiroshima and Potsdam: The Use of the Atomic Bomb and the American Confrontation with Soviet Power* (New York: Simon & Schuster, 1965), insists that the establishment leaders decided to drop the bombs on Japan to intimidate the Soviets. In a more thoroughly researched book, *A World Destroyed: The Atomic Bomb and the Grand Alliance* (New York: Knopf, 1975), Martin F. Sherwin in part supports the revisionist thesis, but says that intimidation of the Soviets was not the main reason for dropping the bomb. He also sees Roosevelt rather than Truman as setting the policy of using atomic diplomacy to limit Soviet ambitions in the postwar world.

Although New Leftists attracted a large following, they did not persuade the more orthodox scholars to change their approach to the history of American foreign policy. Nonetheless, the radical historians held up to renewed scrutiny foreign policy decisions that deserved the critical study they had previously escaped. This dissenting scholarship exposed weaknesses in conventional histories which accepted government policies at face value.

For a few years relations with Asia did not fall within America's cold war strategy. The most important aspect of those relations was the disintegration of Nationalist China and the triumph of Chinese communism. American policymakers supported Chiang Kai-shek hoping that he would build a stable China friendly to the United States and strong enough to replace Japan as the major power in Asia. Most scholars consider this policy one of the noteworthy failures of the postwar era. Variations on this theme are in Akira Iriye, *The Cold War in Asia: A Historical Introduction** (Englewood Cliffs, N.J.: Prentice-Hall, 1974); Paul A. Varg, *The Closing of the Door: Sino-American Relations, 1936–1946* (East Lansing: Michigan State University Press; 1973); Barbara W. Tuchman, *Stilwell and the American Experience in China, 1911–1945* (New York: Macmillan, 1970); Tang Tsou, *America's Failure in China, 1941–1950** (Chicago: University of Chicago Press, 1963); and Herbert Feis, *The China Tangle: The American Effort in China from Pearl Harbor to the Marshall Mission** (Princeton: Princeton University Press, 1953).

Popular as well as scholarly wisdom links the failure in China to American difficulties in Korea. It maintains that American policymakers, not understanding the realities of Asian politics, placed Korea within the pattern of cold-war theory and ignored the yearning of her people for unification. This misunderstanding, along with Soviet miscalculations, the argument goes, triggered war. Assuming mistakenly that the United States would not fight, the Soviets supported the North Korean communist program of unifying the peninsula by conquest. Dissenting views place the cause for war in local conditions and in the larger context of relations with China and Japan.

Most scholars hold to the interpretation that President Harry S. Truman and his advisers decided upon intervention in the Korean War on the basis of the Munich analogy. American leaders believed that British and French abandonment of

Czechoslovakia to Adolf Hitler in Munich in 1938 demonstrated that appeasement merely rewarded aggression. Truman's policymakers assumed that if they did nothing the North Koreans would not be appeased for long. So to avoid future aggressions, as in Hitler's case, the United States had to fight. Another analysis contends that domestic political considerations, essentially the Republican charge that Truman was "soft" on communism, forced firmness and hence intervention in Korea. These interpretations can be found in Leland M. Goodrich, *Korea: A Study of U.S. Policy in the United Nations* (New York: Council on Foreign Relations, 1956); Glenn D. Paige, *The Korean Decision: June 24–30, 1950* (New York: Free Press, 1968); Richard H. Rovere and Arthur M. Schlesinger, Jr., *The MacArthur Controversy and American Foreign Policy* (New York: Farrar, Straus and Giroux, rev. ed., 1965); John W. Spanier, *The Truman-MacArthur Controversy and the Korean War* (Cambridge: Harvard University Press, 1959); Ronald J. Caridi, *The Korean War and American Politics: The Republican Party as a Case Study* (Philadelphia: University of Pennsylvania Press, 1968); and Robert R. Simmons, *The Strained Alliance: Peking, P'yongyang, Moscow and the Politics of the Korean Civil War* (New York: Free Press, 1975).

Many Americans now view the era of Dwight D. Eisenhower as one of peace and stability. Scholars of liberal persuasion, however, deplore his policies, particularly as inspired and carried out by Secretary of State John Foster Dulles, as so reckless as to bring the nation to the brink of nuclear war, as reviving isolationism, or as institutionalizing the cold war. A one-sided bitter indictment is Herman Finer, *Dulles over Suez: The Theory and Practice of His Diplomacy* (Chicago: Quadrangle, 1964). More balanced in their criticism are Townsend Hoopes, *The Devil and John Foster Dulles* (Boston: Little, Brown, 1973), and Alexander L. George and Richard Smoke, *Deterrence in American Foreign Policy: Theory and Practice* (New York: Columbia University Press, 1974).

John F. Kennedy accepted and continued the Eisenhower-Dulles commitment to a policy of globalism. Friendly intellectuals who wrote accounts of his presidency portray him as a courageous wielder of power. Dissenters picture him as an inflexible cold-war warrior responsible for dangerous confrontations with the Soviet Union as over the status of Berlin and missiles in Cuba. Noteworthy defenders are Roger L. Hilsman, *To Move A Nation: The Politics of Foreign Policy in the Administration of John F. Kennedy* (New York: Dell Pub. Co., 1967) and Graham T. Allison, *Essence of Decision: Explaining the Cuban Missile Crisis** (Boston: Little, Brown, 1971). Critical is Richard J. Walton, *Cold War and Counterrevolution: The Foreign Policy of John F. Kennedy* (New York: Viking, 1972).

Among scholars, except for those who were part of the policymaking establishment, Lyndon B. Johnson's foreign policies have few defenders. Critics are harshest in their assessments of his intervention in the Dominican Republic and his escalation of the war in Vietnam. Jerome Slater, *Intervention and Negotiation: The United States and the Dominican Revolution* (New York: Harper & Row, 1970), defends Johnson's action. Walt W. Rostow, *The Diffusion of Power: An Essay in Recent History* (New York: Macmillan, 1972), not only defends Johnson but also cold-war policy as a whole. Critical are Theodore Draper, *The Dominican Revolt: A Case Study in American Policy* (New York: Commentary, 1968); Abraham F. Lowenthal, *The Dominican Intervention* (Cambridge: Harvard University Press, 1972); Arthur M. Schlesinger, Jr., *The Bitter Heritage: Vietnam and American Diplomacy, 1941–1966** (Boston: Houghton Mifflin, 1966); George McT. Kahin and John W. Lewis, *The United States in Vietnam* (rev. ed., New York: Dial Press, 1969); Townsend Hoopes, *The Limits of Intervention: An Inside Account of How the Johnson Policy of Escalation in Vietnam was Reversed* (New York: D. McKay Co., 1969); Chester L. Cooper, *The Last Crusade: America in Vietnam* (New York: Dodd, Mead, 1970); and David Halberstam, *The Best and the Brightest* (New York: Random House, 1972). Richard J. Barnet, *Roots of War: The Men and Institutions behind U.S. Foreign Policy** (New York: Atheneum, 1972) argues that the United States fought presidential wars for more than a generation because war had become more than a response to other nation's actions; it had become institutionalized in the American domestic structure. Peter A. Poole, *The United States and Indo-China from FDR to Nixon** (Hinsdale, Ill.: Dryden Press, 1973), follows a variation on this theme, and Russell H. Fifield, *Americans in Southeast Asia: The Roots of Commitment* (New York: Crowell, 1973), places policy in a broad regional setting and is mildly critical of American policy.

While most of the writing in the history of American foreign policy surveyed here focuses on conflict and crises, there is a considerable literature on the peaceful interaction of peoples and nations, on cross-cultural history, on economic cooperation across national boundaries, on immigration history, peace history, and other areas that have influenced foreign policy. Examples of cross-cultural history are Robert S. Schwantes, *Japanese and Americans: A Century of Cultural Relations* (New York: Harper, 1955); James A. Field, *America and the Mediterranean World, 1776–1882* (Princeton: Princeton University Press, 1969); and Alexander DeConde, *Half-Bitter, Half-Sweet: An Excursion into Italian-American History* (New York: Scribner's 1971). Mira Wilkins, in *The Emergence of Multinational Enterprise: American Business Abroad from the Colonial Era to 1914* (Cambridge: Harvard University Press, 1970) and *The Maturing of Multinational Enterprise: American Business Abroad from 1914–1970* (Cambridge: Harvard University Press, 1974), analyzes economic factors beyond the conflict theme. The most important broad study in peace history and pacifism is Peter Brock, *Pacifism in the United States: From the Colonial Era to the First World War* (Princeton: Princeton University Press, 1968).

Students of American foreign policy most often deal with the themes of power and conflict, and with the motivations of ruling elites, but they no longer do so exclusively. In recent years they more and more have concerned themselves with social problems that nurtured animosities across frontiers. They have recognized the importance of public opinion, nationalism, racism, ethnicity, religion, and various intangibles in confrontations between societies, as well as the significance of elitist makers of foreign policy. The historian of American foreign policy is now often a synthesizer of materials from diplomatic, political, economic, intellectual, cultural, psychological, and the social sources. He is an interpreter of the past on an international scale and not just the chronicler of the negotiations and deeds of those at the top. □

EPILOGUE

by Alexander DeConde*

In the five years since the completion of the original essay,
scholars have published nearly two-hundred volumes that focus on
some aspect of the history of American foreign relations. Most
historians, as well as political scientists, concerned with foreign
relations concentrated on twentieth-century topics. Although Cold
War revisionism still attracted attention, it no longer aroused the
deep emotions, at least outwardly, that it had in the early 1970s.
New Left history lost the prominence it had briefly enjoyed, and
those historians who favored an economic, or capitalist, interpretation of America's foreign policy now appeared less controversial
than in the past. Some of their views, such as criticisms of
containment and globalism, gained considerable acceptance among
diplomatic historians, while other aspects of their theory still
stimulate controversy.

Foreign scholars appear to have been influenced to a considerable
extent by New Left historiography, particularly by its theoretical
approach to the origins and motivations of American imperialism.
See, for example, Alberto Aquarone, Le origini dell'imperialismo
americano: Da McKinley a Taft (1897-1913) (Bologna: il Mulino,
1973). Perhaps the most noticeable new trend in recent historiography is the increasing number of monographs and articles on the
history of America's foreign relations being written by foreign
scholars. Akira Iriye, under the auspices of the University of
Chicago, has even launched a series of books on American foreign
policy prepared by foreign historians from the perspective of their

*Richard Speed assisted in the research for this epilogue.

own countries. As before, various syntheses, in series and in textbooks, continued to be published. Noteworthy in this respect is Alexander DeConde, ed., The Encyclopedia of American Foreign Policy (3 vols., New York: Scribner's, 1978), composed of ninety-five essays by some ninety scholars that "explore concepts, themes, large ideas, theories, doctrines, and distinctive policies." It offers various ideological perspectives in selected topics covering much of the history of American foreign policy, from its beginning through the Vietnam War.

Although scholars in recent years have not devoted as much attention to the origins of American foreign relations as they have to other periods, three monographs on the American Revolution offer insights to early diplomacy from foreign perspectives. In The French Navy and American Independence: A Study of Arms and Diplomacy, 1774-1787 (Princeton: Princeton University Press, 1975), Jonathan R. Dull examines French policy from the viewpoint of military and diplomatic requirements. While French intervention in the war of the revolution helped achieve independence for the United States, Dull concludes, it failed to achieve the objective of weakening Great Britain and therefore did not serve the interest of the French state. Horst Dippel, Germany and the American Revolution, 1770-1800: A Sociohistorical Investigation of Late Eighteenth Century Political Thinking, trans. Bernard A. Uhlendorf (Chapel Hill: University of North Carolina Press, 1977), ranges well beyond traditional diplomatic history into ideas and perceptions. He confirms old views that the American Revolution had an impact on European thinkers, especially in France, but adds new thoughts as to its influence on Germans.

Nikolai N. Bolkhovitinov, The Beginnings of Russian-American Relations, 1775-1815, trans. Elena Levin (Cambridge, Mass.: Harvard University Press, 1975), also ventures into an area historians previously have not explored in depth. It analyzes social, cultural, and scientific relations as well as the usual diplomatic ties, and offers fresh data on the attitude of Russian intellectuals toward the American Revolution. Celebrations during the bicentennial of the American Revolution produced a number of symposia by American and foreign scholars. An example of the fine work emanating from this activity is Lawrence S. Kaplan, ed., The American Revolution and "A Candid World" (Kent, Ohio: Kent State University Press, 1977). In this symposium, historians attempted to explain what the American leaders hoped Europe's statesmen would contribute to the revolutionary effort, and to what extent these desires were satisfied.

Several new studies of diplomacy in the early National period explore the objectives and motivations of territorial expansionists. In a fresh synthesis, *This Affair of Louisiana (New York: Scribner's, 1976), Alexander DeConde analyzes the diplomacy and politics of the Louisiana purchase within the theme of conscious Jeffersonian expansionism. He suggests that the acquisition emerged logically out of an established Anglo-American imperial tradition. James Leitch Wright, Jr., in Britain and the American

Frontier, 1783-1815 (Athens, Ga.: University of Georgia Press, 1975), concentrates on conflict rather than rapprochement, as have some other scholars, and maintains that Britain sought to block American westward expansion even at the risk of war. Burton Spivak, Jefferson's English Crisis: Commerce, Embargo, and the Republican Revolution (Charlottesville: University of Virginia Press, 1979), ties together Jefferson's ideas on foreign policy, economics, and republicanism, giving special attention to the policy of economic coercion and the embargo of 1807. Howard Jones, To the Webster-Ashburton Treaty: A Study in Anglo-American Diplomacy, 1783-1843 (Chapel Hill: University of North Carolina Press, 1977), in contrast, focuses on the diplomacy of compromise, demonstrating that Daniel Webster and Lord Ashburton considered negotiations, and ultimately the treaty, an alternative to war.

In a broad synthesis, United States Foreign Relations, 1820-1860 (East Lansing: Michigan State University Press, 1979), Paul Varg analyzes three themes--expansion, anti-European isolationism, and commerce--and believes that within the goals set by its practitioners, foreign policy was a success. Gene M. Brack's monograph, Mexico Views Manifest Destiny, 1821-1846: An Essay on the Origins of the Mexican War (Albuquerque: University of New Mexico Press, 1975), is less concerned with the politics of Washington, D.C. He follows the trend of viewing American policy from the adversary's perspective as well as Washington's, and depicts Mexican leaders as fearing American imperialism and seeking to avoid war. His thesis concludes that an aroused Mexican public opinion forced government leaders to resist American demands and hence doomed   ⁻ Mexico to fight a war it could not win. Donald S. Spencer, in Louis Kossuth and Young America: Study of Sectionalism and Foreign Policy, 1848-1852 (Columbia: University of Missouri Press, 1977), on the other hand, concerns himself mainly with American domestic politics. He explains more about the Young America movement than have others, but reaffirms the views of past scholars that by mid-century, Northerners and Southerners viewed virtually all public questions from antagonistic positions.

Several new volumes deal with special aspects of diplomacy during the Civil War. In general, they provide more detail or additional insight on their subjects, but do not modify established interpretations on the larger issues. See, for example, Richard I. Lester, Confederate Finance and Purchasing in Great Britain (Charlottesville: University of Virginia Press, 1975), which focuses on Anglo-Confederate commercial relations and argues that Confederate agents in England helped prolong the war through their purchases of military supplies; Norman B. Ferris, Desperate Diplomacy: William H. Seward's Foreign Policy, 1861 (Knoxville: University of Tennessee Press, 1976), and The Trent Affair: A Diplomatic Crisis (Knoxville: University of Tennessee Press, 1977). Adrian Cook, The Alabama Claims: American Politics and Anglo-American Relations, 1865-1872 (Ithaca, N.Y.: Cornell University Press, 1975), probes an important aspect of postwar Anglo-American diplomacy and maintains that the expectations of the American public concerning treaty negotiations were so high that they made the efforts of diplomats

to achieve an equitable settlement almost impossible. Contrary to
the views of Anglo-American liberals, Cook says, the Washington
treaty did not prove itself an important precedent for arbitration
of international disputes. Thomas D. Schoonover, in Dollars over
Dominion: The Triumph of Liberalism in Mexican-United States
Relations, 1861-1867 (Baton Rouge: Louisiana State University Press,
1978), also writes within a context of liberalism. Commitment to
vague liberal ideals by American and Mexican leaders in this
period, the thesis goes, led to diplomatic cooperation between the
two and to United States economic penetration in Mexico.

In a sweeping synthesis, *The Transformation of American Foreign
Relations: 1865-1900 (New York: Harper, 1976), Charles S. Campbell
covers all the major issues of the diplomacy of an increasingly
powerful democracy in the last half of the nineteenth century and
analyzes the latest scholarly interpretations. He attempts, in
particular, to explain overseas expansionism. Two new studies that
vary in their interpretations probe the last manifestation of
continental expansionism. See Ronald J. Jensen, The Alaska
Purchase and Russian-American Relations (Seattle: University of
Washington Press, 1975), and Howard I. Kushner, Conflict on the
Northwest Coast: American-Russian Rivalry in the Pacific Northwest, 1791-1867 (Westport, Conn.: Greenwood Press, 1975). A book
that touches on a previously tangential aspect of late-nineteenth-
century imperialism, at least as far as the United States was
concerned, is Thomas J. Noer, Briton, Boer, and Yankee: The United
States and South Africa, 1870-1914 (Kent, Ohio: Kent State
University Press, 1978). It stresses that American attitudes
toward Anglo-Saxon mission, racism, and economic expansion motivated support for British control of South Africa.

A small volume that deals with a technical military problem also
sheds additional light on a controversial aspect of the coming of
the Spanish-American War. Hyman G. Rickover, How the Battleship
Maine Was Destroyed (Washington: Dept. of the Navy, 1976), argues
convincingly that an internal explosion sank the ship and that the
Spaniards were not responsible. Richard B. Welch, Jr., Response
to Imperialism: The United States and the Philippine-American
War, 1899-1902 (Chapel Hill: University of North Carolina Press,
1978), now offers the fullest treatment of the darker side of the
new manifest destiny. He concludes that the war accentuated racial
antagonisms, not only in the Philippines but also in the United
States. Göran Rystad, Ambiguous Imperialism: American Foreign
Policy and Domestic Politics at the Turn of the Century (Lund,
Sweden: Esselte Studium, 1975), is another foreign appraisal of
American imperialism influenced by New Left revisionism. Organized
efforts to maintain peace in these years receive thorough attention
in Calvin D. Davis, The United States and the Second Hague Peace
Conference: American Diplomacy and International Organization,
1889-1914 (Durham, N.C.: Duke University Press, 1976), and David
S. Patterson, Toward a Warless World: The Travail of the American
Peace Movement, 1887-1914 (Bloomington: Indiana University Press,
1976). For later aspects of the peace movement, see Ernest C.
Bolt, Ballots before Bullets: The War Referendum Approach to Peace

in America, 1914-1941 (Charlottesville: University of Virginia
Press, 1977), and Charles DeBenedetti, Origins of the Modern
American Peace Movement, 1915-1929 (Millwood, N.Y.: KTO Press,
1978).

Several new volumes assess the relationship with China. Robert A.
Hart, *The Eccentric Tradition: American Diplomacy in the Far East
(New York: Scribner's, 1976), offers a broad synthesis, whereas
Delber L. McKee, Chinese Exclusion versus the Open Door Policy,
1900-1906: Clashes over China Policy in the Roosevelt Era
(Detroit: Wayne State University Press, 1976), covers a narrower
problem, essentially the interaction of ethnic animosity with
foreign policy. He demonstrates the importance of racism as an
element in American policy toward China. A brief monograph,
Jeffrey Dorwart, The Pigtail War: American Involvement in the
Sino-Japanese War of 1894-95 (Amherst, Mass.: University of Massa--
chusetts Press, 1975), gives the fullest account of the American
concern over this Asian conflict.

The major development in Caribbean policy during this period, the
diplomacy of the Panama Canal, receives attention from three
studies. David G. McCullough, The Path Between the Seas: The
Creation of the Panama Canal, 1870-1914 (New York: Simon and
Schuster, 1977), offers no new interpretation but gives the reader
a well-written synthesis. Walter La Feber, *The Panama Canal:
The Crisis in Historical Perspective (New York: Oxford, 1978), and
Paul B. Ryan, *The Panama Canal Controversy: U.S. Diplomacy and
Defense Interests (Stanford, Calif.: Hoover Institution Press,
1977), analyze the problems created by the issue of the canal in
American diplomacy and domestic politics, giving particular atten-
tion to the controversy over sovereignty in the canal zone that
lead to the treaties with Panama approved in 1978. La Feber
criticizes American policy from the beginning, while Ryan defends
it. Another aspect of Latin American policy is covered in David
F. Healy, Gunboat Diplomacy in the Wilson Era: The U.S. Navy in
Haiti, 1915-1916 (Madison: University of Wisconsin Press, 1976).
Healy presents the intervention in and occupation of Haiti as a
case study illustrating multiple facets of Woodrow Wilson's
Caribbean policy.

The diplomacy of World War I has not encouraged recent monographic
efforts covering the whole story, but scholars have produced a
number of studies of important episodes. In The Lusitania
Disaster: An Episode in Modern Warfare and Diplomacy (New York:
Free Press, 1975), Thomas A. Bailey and Paul B. Ryan present the
fullest and most detailed account of the sinking that shook up
American neutrality. They conclude, contrary to revisionist
sentiment, that the British neither armed nor used the ship as bait
to involve the United States in war. Patrick Devlin, Too Proud to
Fight: Woodrow Wilson's Neutrality (New York: Oxford University
Press, 1974), analyzes the American decision for war and concludes
that it came from Wilson himself. It was essentially a presidential decision. Arthur Walworth, America's Moment: 1918--
American Diplomacy and the End of World War I (New York: Norton,

1977), concentrates on the months that preceded the Paris Peace
Conference of 1919, advancing the thesis that the informal discussions of Allied leaders at this time foreshadowed themes that
would appear at the conference and affect it tragically.   Keith
L. Nelson, Victors Divided: America and the Allies in Germany,
1918-1923 (Berkeley: University of California Press, 1975), deals
with the American occupation of the Rhineland as a compromise
vital to the success of the Paris peace conference.   See also
Edward B. Parsons, Wilsonian Diplomacy: Allied-American Rivalries
in War and Peace (St. Louis: Forum Press, 1978), which focuses on
Wilson's "anti-Allied antipathy."

Postwar economic foreign policy continues to attract scholarly
attention. Michael J. Hogan, Informal Entente: The Private
Structure of Cooperation in Anglo-American Diplomacy, 1918-1928
(Columbia: University of Missouri Press, 1977), argues that the
United States sought international economic cooperation through
private business fostered by the government.   In a study that
blends diplomatic, economic, and business history, The End of
French Predominance in Europe: The Financial Crisis of 1924 and
the Adoption of the Dawes Plan (Chapel Hill: University of North
Carolina Press, 1976), Stephen A. Schuker views the London economic conference of 1925 and the economic reconstruction that
followed as a turning point in European postwar international
politics. Melvyn P. Leffler, The Elusive Quest: America's Pursuit
of European Stability and French Security, 1919-1933 (Chapel Hill:
University of North Carolina Press, 1979), pursues a similar theme
but concentrates on the foreign policy attitudes of Republican
administrations in the United States. Frederick C. Adams,
Economic Diplomacy: The Export-Import Bank and American Foreign
Policy, 1934-1939 (Columbia: University of Missouri Press, 1976),
examines foreign economic policy in the years immediately
following. He advances the thesis that Franklin D. Roosevelt's
administration used the bank to advance New Deal objectives at
home and to influence developments abroad. Irvine H. Anderson,
Jr., The Standard Vacuum Oil Company and United States East Asian
Policy, 1933-1941 (Princeton: Princeton University Press, 1975),
examines the relationship between oil men and diplomats and documents their cooperation in matters of policy.

Scholars are now probing naval policy during the 1920s and 1930s,
not only from the archives of several countries, but also from
comparative political perspectives. Roger Dingman, Power in the
Pacific: The Origins of Naval Arms Limitation, 1914-1922 (Chicago:
University of Chicago Press, 1976), for example, approaches arms
limitation through "the politics of national defense" within each
country involved as well as through traditional diplomacy. Thus,
internal political considerations as well as international
developments helped shape agreement on the limiting of navies.
James R. Leutze, Bargaining for Supremacy: Anglo-American Naval
Collaboration, 1937-1941 (Chapel Hill: University of North Carolina
Press, 1977), focuses on elements of conflict rather than the
"popularly held concept of cooperation." He argues that as war
approached, the British accepted the concept of United States

supremacy and subordinated naval rivalry to the political objective of gaining American support.

The foreign policy of Franklin D. Roosevelt continues to fascinate scholars. Four recent books in particular subject it to careful scrutiny. Robert Dallek, Franklin D. Roosevelt and American Foreign Policy, 1932-1945 (New York: Oxford, 1979), gives the fullest coverage, touching on all important aspects of foreign affairs while Roosevelt held office. In carefully balanced assessments, Dallek depicts Roosevelt as his own decision maker in foreign policy; as a superb political leader; and as one who in the Spring of 1941 believed the United States would go to war and who dissembled in order to win national support for his policies. Thomas A. Bailey and Paul B. Ryan, Hitler vs. Roosevelt: The Undeclared Naval War (New York: Free Press, 1979), examine closely one aspect of Roosevelt's policy--relations with Germany that led to fighting at sea and then all-out war--and, like Dallek, view it favorably. They conclude that neither side desired a land war with the other and that Roosevelt did not seek to bring the nation into war by stealth. More strongly than either Dallek or Bailey and Ryan, William E. Kinsella, Jr., *Leadership in Isolation: F. D. R. and the Origins of the Second World War (Cambridge, Mass.: Schenkman, 1978), asserts that Roosevelt recognized the "inevitability of war with . . . Germany, Japan, and Italy" before his contemporaries and shaped foreign policy accordingly. Joseph P. Lash, Roosevelt and Churchill, 1939-1941: The Partnership that Saved the West (New York: Norton, 1976), concludes that in the Autumn of 1941, Roosevelt tried to provoke war with Germany and was right in trying to do so.

Martin V. Melosi, The Shadow of Pearl Harbor: Political Controversy over the Surprise Attack, 1941-1946 (College Station: Texas A&M Press, 1977), examines the question of who was responsible for the naval disaster and how Roosevelt handled it politically. Melosi points out that the administration unwittingly created scapegoats, gave the impression of a cover-up, and as a result kept political controversy alive for years. George Q. Flynn, Roosevelt and Romanism: Catholics and American Diplomacy, 1937-1945 (Westport, Conn.: Greenwood, 1976), attempts to penetrate the hazy area of religion's influence on foreign policy. Flynn contends that as a result of foreign policy and war, Roosevelt played a major role in nationalizing the Catholic Church in the United States. Irwin F. Gellman, Good Neighbor Diplomacy: United States Policies in Latin America, 1933-1945 (Baltimore: Johns Hopkins, 1979), reexplores another aspect of Roosevelt's diplomacy and reaffirms the traditional view, asserting that the Good Neighbor policy bore his distinctive marks and did not, as revisionists have suggested, flow out of policies initiated in previous administrations.

Several important books dissect Roosevelt's wartime diplomacy in Asia and America's partnership with Great Britain. Michael Schaller, The U.S. Crusade in China, 1938-1945 (New York: Columbia

University Press, 1979), argues that the Roosevelt leadership
viewed China's social revolution unrealistically, backed the wrong
side, and initiated a quarter of a century of Sino-American hostility. Christopher Thorne, *Allies of a Kind: The United States,
Britain and the War Against Japan, 1941-1945 (London: Hamish
Hamilton, 1979), plays out in considerable detail the old theme
that the Anglo American partnership, "a fusion of national identi-
ties," was a remarkable achievement in Asia as well as in Europe,
and that it was based on a common Anglo-Saxon culture. William R.
Louis, Imperialism at Bay: The United States and the Decolonization of the British Empire, 1941-1945 (New York: Oxford, 1978),
stresses discord rather than harmony between the allies. He documents the deep differences between Roosevelt and Winston Churchill
over colonialism and what should be the postwar fate of European
empires.

Roosevelt's wartime attitude toward Josef Stalin and Russia lies
near the center of much of the Cold War literature. Perhaps the
most noteworthy book in recent Cold War historiography is Daniel
Yergin, Shattered Peace: The Origins of the Cold War and the
National Security State (Boston: Houghton Mifflin, 1977). Yergin
contends that the Cold War transformed American life, keeping
Americans organized for perpetual confrontation with a foreign foe,
even for a "hot war." Their leaders created what he terms the
"national security state." In Yergin's thesis, this posture of
permanent military readiness derived from "anti-communism and a new
doctrine of national security." Ralph Levering looked into Cold
War origins through a study of public attitudes. In American
Opinion and the Russian Alliance, 1939-1945 (Chapel Hill: University
of North Carolina Press, 1976), he concludes that the most important element in shaping people's views on foreign policy is the
interpretation or slant given events by opinion makers, especially
the president. "National leadership," in other words, had "enormous power" in forming Cold War attitudes toward Russia.

Yonosuke Nagai and Akira Iriye, eds., The Origins of the Cold War
in Asia (New York: Columbia University Press, 1977), present seven-
teen separate essays that delineate the views of Japanese and
American scholars on Cold War issues in Asia. Lisle A. Rose,
Roots of Tragedy: The United States and the Struggle for Asia
(Westport, Conn.: Greenwood, 1976), explains how containment and
Cold War policy shifted to include Asia as well as Europe as a
result of the Korean War. Lewis M. Purifoy, *Harry Truman's China
Policy: McCarthyism and the Diplomacy of Hysteria, 1947-1951 (New
York: New Viewpoints, 1976), insists that an anti-communist frenzy
brought on, unnecessarily, the Cold War confrontation with the
communist regime in China.

Cold War scholarship has devoted much less attention to Latin
America than to Asia. An exception is a book of case studies by
Cole Blasier, *The Hovering Giant: U.S. Responses to Revolutionary
Change in Latin America (Pittsburgh: University of Pittsburgh Press,
1976), which places Latin American policy within a global context.
Specifically, Blasier explores the reaction of the United States to

Latin seizures of its citizens' properties. Herbert S. Dinerstein, The Making of a Missile Crisis: October 1962 (Baltimore: Johns Hopkins, 1976), analyzes the greatest Soviet-American confrontation of the era and how it brought the Cold War to Latin America. He views the confrontation as emanating from the misperceptions John F. Kennedy and Nikita S. Khrushchev had of each other, and hence as needless.

Among the various books on the nuclear arms race that have appeared recently, Robert A. Divine, Blowing on the Wind: The Nuclear Test Ban Debate, 1954-1960 (New York: Oxford, 1973), is noteworthy. In appraising the response of Americans and their leaders to the danger of fallout from nuclear tests, Divine concludes that testing cannot be divorced from the larger issue of arms limitation.

As is to be expected, those concerned with the Vietnam War have produced a considerable literature. Much of it, however, is made up of special pleading, of journalistic impressions, or of works that lack a structure built on archival sources. Nonetheless, scholars have written a number of perceptive studies. In the fullest, though not most detailed, survey of the war yet, George C. Herring, *America's Longest War: The United States and Vietnam, 1950-1975 (New York: Wiley, 1979), draws on limited official sources and the secondary literature. Herring's thesis places the war within the context of Harry Truman's containment policy extended to Asia. Robert L. Gallucci, *Neither Peace nor Honor: The Politics of American Military Policy in Viet-Nam (Baltimore: Johns Hopkins, 1975), assumes that American policy was wrong and explains why. Herbert Y. Schandler, The Unmaking of a President: Lyndon Johnson and Vietnam (Princeton: Princeton University Press, 1977), views American involvement as part of a failure in the decision-making process, and hence Johnson's failure. Guenter Lewy, *America in Vietnam (New York: Oxford, 1978), analyzes military operations thoroughly and, on the other hand, offers one of the few defenses of American policy during that war by one not in an offi- cial position. Gareth Porter, A Peace Denied: The United States, Vietnam, and the Paris Agreements (Bloomington: Indiana University Press, 1975), and Allan E. Goodman, The Lost Peace: America's Search for a Negotiated Settlement of the Vietnam War (Stanford: Stanford University Press, 1978), give balanced accounts of the peace negotiations and of the agreements that terminated the con- flict. Porter stresses that the United States persistently rejected, until the end, any kind of settlement that would allow Vietnamese revolutionaries political power. Goodman follows the same theme but gives broader coverage by analyzing all the efforts for peace.

In France's Vietnam Policy: A Study of French-American Relations (Westport, Conn.: Greenwood, 1978), Marianna P. Sullivan assesses a side effect of the war, the hostility it accentuated in relations with France. A skillful journalistic analysis of the Vietnam War in its later years, and of other aspects of American policy, is Tad Szulc, The Illusion of Peace: Foreign Policy in the Nixon Years (New York: Viking, 1978). Szulc characterizes American policy in

these years as governed by "an extraordinary immorality."   A
British journalist, William Shawcross, in an influential and controversial study, Sideshow: Kissinger, Nixon and the Destruction
of Cambodia (New York: Simon and Schuster, 1979), also condemns
American policy in Southeast Asia.

Until recently, scholars have given much less attention to American
relations with the peoples and nations of the Middle East than with
those of the Far East.   Thomas A. Bryson, American Diplomatic
Relations with the Middle East, 1784-1975: A Survey (Metuchen,
New Jersey: Scarecrow, 1977), is the first book to cover relations
from the beginning.   Robert W. Stookey, *America and the Arab
States: An Uneasy Encounter (New York: Wiley, 1975), is also broad,
but focuses on recent American policy, which it criticizes as
promoting distrust and antagonism among Arabs.   One reason for
this Arab ill will, Stookey says, is American support of Israel.
Philip A. Baram, The Department of State in the Middle East, 1919-
1945 (Philadelphia: University of Pennsylvania Press, 1978), on the
other hand, criticizes the State Department elite for being anti-
Zionist and pro-Arab.   He demonstrates that American interest in
the Middle East is not a recent development.   For more data on
American policy toward Israel, see Kenneth R. Bain, The March to
Zion: United States Policy and the Founding of Israel (College
Station: Texas A&M Press, 1979).

American concerns in the Middle East are wrapped up in ethnic
issues and the need for oil.   These concerns fit within the trend,
now quite evident, of broadening the content of American diplomatic
history to encompass far more than the usual negotiations over
political issues.   A good example of this expanded content is
Morrell Heald and Lawrence S. Kaplan, Culture and Diplomacy: The
American Experience (Westport, Conn.: Greenwood, 1977).   Through
a number of case studies, this book illustrates the influence of
private institutions and individuals in the shaping of foreign
policy.   It advances the thesis that the cultural setting is not
merely background for the making of policy; it is a "vital cog."
Alfred E. Eckes, Jr., A Search for Solvency: Bretton Woods and
the International Monetary System, 1941-1971 (Austin: University of
Texas Press, 1975), combines diplomacy with economics.   He explains
how an elite of economists and other intellectuals who shared a
common theoretical perspective assessed global problems.   Similarly,
Warren I. Cohen, The China Connection: Roger S. Greene, Thomas W.
Lamont, George E. Sokolsky and American-East Asian Relations (New
York: Columbia University Press, 1978), explores the influence of
selected private individuals, as leaders of opinion, on the forming
of foreign policy.

As before, themes, rather than straightforward narrative, continue
to be a major concern to most scholars engaged in the study of
American diplomatic history.

Time's American Adventures: American Historians and Their Writing Since 1776

WILLIAM H. GOETZMANN

Appropriately enough, virtually the entire two hundred year span of America's national existence falls within a period in which men and women characteristically oriented and interpreted their experiences historically. The Revolution itself might be described as a product of historical thinking. Lawyers talked about the evolution of the British Empire. Latter day Puritan ministers projected the Revolution as the millennium their typologies had predicted. Colonial observers in Britain wrote of the inevitable decline in society in Gibbonesque fashion. Tom Paine saw the break with England as the climactic moment of freedom towards which all history had been aiming.

This chapter originally appeared as William H. Goetzmann, "Time's American Adventures: American Historians and Their Writing Since 1776," *Social Science Quarterly*, Vol. 57, No. 1, June 1976, pp. 3-48. Reprinted by permission of the University of Texas Press.

And Thomas Jefferson justified independence by means of an analogue with the historic migration of the Anglo Saxon peoples out of the forests of Germany into Britain, then to America.

By the same token in 1976, despite valiant Bicentennial efforts and striking commercial successes, history no longer seemed central to American thought or even to that of western Europe. Recently, the trans-Atlantic historian, J. H. Plumb (1970), has written its epitaph. History has been replaced by new journalism, structuralism, psychology, systems analysis and the urgent felt need for contemporary problem-solving. In the anxious modern world the task that the historian performs appears to many to have little "work value"—either in predictive terms or in the area of moral imperatives. Policy makers steeped in history are said to be "preparing for the last war." And has it become true that "those who neglect the past are not necessarily condemned to repeat it?" Certainly time itself has become so relative and multiplicitous that the historian, who once saw his role as that of its keeper, stands, in the words of Henry Adams, "sorely perplexed." Why all this is so now, and why it was not apparently so for almost two hundred years, form the underlying questions of this essay which briefly surveys American historical writing and its role in the culture since 1776. This essay seeks generally to ask what have American historians been doing for two hundred years and how and why, and finally to look at the ways in which contemporary historians are facing up to reports of the death in their family of knowledge. In short, I hope, insofar as historians really have had anything to do with it, to trace time's American adventures.

Time is, of course, the essence but not the only subject matter of history. Traditionally the historian has been concerned with telling a story—the story of human ideas and behavior as it unfolded through time past. This has meant that the historian has had to be concerned with the discovery and relationship of facts or events out of which he creates the mosaic of his story. In turn this has raised important questions of validation especially as history moved from myth-making and the edifying moral tale to pretensions of scientific accuracy. Since the seventeenth century, any serious historian has had to submit his facts to his peers for verification as well as present a story whose interior logic is in some sense convincing to his audience. There can be neither fantasizing nor "history of the absurd." This has meant that, by and large, history itself has become dependent on science and thus rightly deserves to be numbered among the social sciences, though it appears to lack some of the attributes of a true science. Predictability is one of these. Yet there is a sense in which the historian predicts—not about the future but about the past. Characteristically the historian works not only inductively from archives, printed materials and even objects, but he also develops an hypothesis about the past which he seeks to verify. Sometimes this can be done with precision through the location of incontrovertible documentary evidence attesting to an event. On other occasions he is working with trends, situations and complex personalities where the evidence can never be more than persuasive and colored by the historian's own point of view or interpretation.

History, particularly in America, has gone through an evolution from the conviction that absolute truth is scientifically attainable to an awareness of the relative position of the historian as interpreter. Much of this theory has been borrowed from European thinkers such as Von Ranke, Croce, and Collingwood. The most recent original contribution has been made, however, by the American, Morse Peckham. Peckham (1970: 202–225) has argued essentially that there is no past at all. The historian lives only in the present and his story or research is merely a set of signals alerting his reader to the existence of surviving pieces of evidence out of which, if one chooses, one can fashion a story; and if the reader follows the author's directions in his intellectual Easter egg hunt, that story is likely to be a convincing if not satisfying story that provides insight into human behavior at the present time. History can say nothing about the past. It can only speak to the present because the existing present materials are all we have. Peckham's position inevitably leads to the conclusion that history is not science at all but a mode of social inquiry sparked by present day concerns and at the same time an interesting means of self-expression—interesting because of its mimetic qualities. It forms a kind of *trompe l'oeil* landscape with figures in it, but it can never be the real thing because that is past and gone forever. In short, for Peckham history is a form of art but a very special form dependent upon verifiable directional signals as to the existence of physical evidence that will make the art more convincing to the scientifically conditioned mind.

Perhaps this interpretation is extreme, but it puts the historian's current situation rather clearly. On the one hand he is engaged in a scientific enterprise and thus subservient to the canons and criteria of science. He cannot go back to myth-making or even to the currently chic "advocacy history" if it is false to the tests of verification. On the other hand, it is clearly subject to interpretation, configuration, insights, even the idiosyncratic language and means of presentation commanded by the historian, to the point where it becomes an art form and probably demands an underlying philosophy, or at least a logic, as well. Perhaps it is this very tension—so overt in the writing of history—that makes it *sui generis* as a discipline. Very likely it is this dual lens capacity, this binocular approach to human behavior, that gives to history its peculiarly human and hence compelling power as a means of organizing and judging one's experience.

Though it rests upon scientific principles, and often borrows scientific models, history, unlike science and most social sciences, does not deal in abstractions. Along with the phenomenon of change through time, its essence lies in the concrete, the specific and the artistically convincing. It presents a satisfactorily verified world into which one can enter and lose himself. In some ways it is the dramatization of the scientific mind in action. Indeed one recent commentator (Winks, 1968), perhaps thinking of Hercule Poirot or Sherlock Holmes, has seen the historian as a kind of hero-detective. Clearly, then, history is tragedy as well as trends, and it can be farce with the historian in some subtle way always the hero. But the practice of history in America did not spring full-blown with self-awareness. Appropriately enough it evolved—historially.

The New World and History

The full bibliographical story of the development of American historiography is much too extensive to recount here and can be found in numerous book-length works.[1] It is important to note that from the beginning—even in the colonial period of American history—Americans were self-conscious about their role in history. Puritan writers saw themselves and their people as participants in a great cosmic drama that had been unfolding since the days of Adam. American history was cosmic history and it was part of a typology carried over from Medieval tradition. The Franciscans at the outset of the Age of Discovery, inspired by the twelfth century mystic, Joachim of Fiore, saw the discovery of the New World as the beginning of the last phase of converting the world's heathen, after which would come the Christian millennium and the reconstitution of paradise.

Columbus himself was profoundly influenced by Joachim and the discoverer's *Letters From the New World* (1493) clearly indicated that he thought he had discovered the terrestrial paradise of Adam and Eve somewhere in northern South America. He was also confident that he had discovered the fabled King Solomon's Mines whose riches would help rebuild the temple at Jerusalem, and that certainly within 150 years all mankind would be converted to Christianity. Thus, in a certain sense, Columbus himself assumed the role of historian and prophet and laid down the basic framework, however mystical, for the progressive historial tradition that has so dominated American writing. In his wake followed numerous Spanish historians, the most significant of whom was Geromino de Mendieta, whose *Historia Eclesiastica Indiana* (1571) recounted the conquest of the New World strictly in terms of a Christian typology of progress, relating each step in the Conquest to incidents in the Bible. Mendieta even went so far as to portray Cortez as Moses smashing the heathen idols and the 12 Franciscans that he imported into Mexico as the reincarnations of the 12 Apostles (Phalen, 1956). Only Bartolome de las Casas in his numerous polemics on behalf of the Indians saw anything but progress resulting from the Spanish Conquest. His *Very Brief Account of the Destruction of the Indies* (1553), recounting the atrocities committed by the Spaniards against the Indians, was a critical, controversial work, eagerly translated by Protestant opponents of Spain. As such it forms the beginning of the "Black Legend" of Catholic and Spanish cultural inferiority in the New World.[2] It is also the spiritual ancestor of such contemporary Indian advocacy histories as Vine Deloria's *Custer Died For Your Sins* (1969) and Dee Brown's *Bury My Heart at Wounded Knee* (1971).

Biblical typology or cosmic drama as a framework for history was Medieval and Catholic or Hebraic in origin, but it was quickly adopted by Protestant theologians and historians. The Protestant version, however, closely followed the steps of the Seven Vials of Wrath in the Book of Revelation, celebrating the purity of the early Christian Church, seeing a decline into "Babylonian Captivity" with the ascent of the Popes and the beginning of a coming millennium with the advent of the Reformation. Perhaps the most famous inspiration for Protestant historians was John Foxe's *Acts and Monuments* (1554), better known as *Foxe's Book of Martyrs*. Foxe recounted the tribulations of latter-day martyrs from John Huss onward, but his book, so full of trials and tribulations and physical horrors in which he took an unseemly relish, was in the end optimistic, even millennial. He saw England under Calvinism as the starting point for world redemption. The importance of the ancient works is, of course, that they established the fundamental myth or rhythm of American history which, until very recently, has been the story of inevitable triumph over adversity and progress toward a millennium in a world allowed by divine providence to start over again. No matter what its ideological or technical characteristics, American historiography has been a literature of Manifest Destiny. History, if not God, has been on our side. As the years went by history and God became synonymous.

No more than a cursory glance at very early American historiography reveals the theme of inevitable conquest over adversity and ultimate triumph. William Bradford's *Plymouth Plantation* (written 1630–1650, published 1855), Cotton Mather's *Magnalia Christi Americana* (1702), Edward Johnson's *Wonder Working Providence of Zion's Savior in New England* (1654) and the fragmentary survivals of Jonathan Edwards' projected historical work all ring the changes on this theme as does Captain John Smith's *The Generall Historie of Virginia, New-England and the Summer Isles* (1624). Bradford's work recounted in swelling prose the triumphs of the Pilgrims as they crossed the stormy ocean, endured the howling wilderness and prevailed over adversity to see a land of peace and plenty arise. Mather, the American Plutarch, wrote of "the Wonders of the Christian Religion, flying from the deprivations of Europe, to the American Strand . . . ." In so doing he celebrated the Christian triumphs of New England's larger-than-life founding fathers, some of whom were also his venerated ancestors. Johnson and Smith wrote the first significant versions of American frontier history with attendant epic overtones—the one celebrating the inland march of New England's Puritans, the other the difficult but promising conquest of Virginia's damp and bloody ground. Edwards with persuasive intensity interpreted all human history as culminating in the actual second coming of Christ to New England (Tuveson, 1968: 55–57, 100–101).

By and large, buttressed by centuries of Christian confidence and at the same time wishing to promote the New World and their own mighty deeds, early American historians wrote in the epic vein of Hakluyt or promotional pamphlet literature such as *Joyeful Newes Out of the Newe Found World*. From the beginning "boosterism" has been innate in the American historical imagination. There is, of course, abundant evidence of darkness and depression in the sermons and closet notes of the early historians, as there certainly would be of later ones, but history, as Peter Gay (1968: 122 and passim) has observed, is public. It is also a vision in some sense of the long run of mankind and few historians have been willing, until recent times, to concede that humanity will not "endure and prevail." Mythologically perhaps it confronts the certainty of individual death with assurances of immortality for mankind.

Historians, the Revolution, and the Enlightenment

If history was eschatology for the early colonial writers, it underwent some refinement during the era of the American Revolution. Four significant histories of that event, or at least closely related to it, appeared by 1805. Among the most important was that of Governor Thomas Hutchinson of Massachusetts. A much-hated Tory political figure, Hutchinson produced a three volume *History of the Colony of Massachusetts Bay* (1764–1828) that carried the story of its turbulent times down to 1774, the eve of the Revolution. Hutchinson had many scores to settle, including an animus against the Puritans for their persecution of his ancestor Anne Hutchinson, but he wrote with a detachment that might even have commanded the notice of David Hume.

The most widely read historians of the Revolution, however, were two men and a woman. William Gordon, a friend of John Adams, removed himself to England so that he could write objectively about the war. Unfortunately neither the English nor the Americans liked his book, *The History of the Rise, Progress And Establishment of the Independence of the United States of America . . .* (1788). David Ramsay, a South Carolinian, was much more successful with his *The History of the American Revolution* (1789), and some present day historians take pleasure in it despite the fact that, like Gordon's work, it was largely plagiarized from the *Annual Register,* a London-published running account of the recent war (Kraus, 1953: 62–73). The most ambitious history of the Revolution was Mercy Otis Warren's three volume *History of the . . . American Revolution . . .* published in 1805. Mistress Warren was a friend of Abigail Adams and derived a great deal of information from John Adams and other founding fathers. Her history, though highly patriotic, placed the war in the world context of the British Empire and then related it to the entire course of human history, thus making it a piece of patriotic typology (Kraus, 1953: 78–80). All four historians, however, the Tory Hutchinson, the copyists Gordon and Ramsay and the bluestocking Mercy Warren, attempted, or at least professed to have attempted, critical research in the sources. They strove in their own ways to achieve an objectivity that bespoke the impact of the Scientific Revolution on historiography. Still it would be many years before the American Revolution was properly served by historians.

The impact of the Enlightenment upon American historical writing is perhaps best illustrated by two other works not directly aimed at a Revolutionary War audience. The first, Thomas Jefferson's *Notes on Virginia* (1787), is an answer to aspersions cast on America by the Frenchmen Count Buffon and Abbé Raynal. Assuming the role of both geographer and historian, Jefferson fitted Virginia into a rationalistic Enlightenment version of the Great Chain of Being. He began with Virginia's geography—its boundaries, soil, topography, landscape, vegetation, climate, etc.—then worked his way up nature's ladder to the Indian, the Negro and finally the history of the white settlers' quest for free political institutions. Along the way Jefferson wrestled sincerely with the question of the Negro and the Indian, deciding regretfully

Mercy Otis Warren (Mrs. James Warren). Oil on canvas, painted about 1763 by John Singleton Copley (1738–1815). Bequest of Winslow Warren. Photograph courtesy Museum of Fine Arts, Boston, Massachusetts.

that nature, according to the present evidence, had made them inferior to the white man. But, in general, nature and nature's creatures in America were in no way inferior to anything in Europe. On the contrary, by the canons of environmental determinism so prevalent in Enlightenment thinking, the unspoiled quality of nature in America had produced superior creatures and purer, better institutions. As history, Jefferson's *Notes on Virginia* occupied an uncertain position. Jefferson himself believed in a kind of continuous present in which no creature ever became extinct and yet he was forced continually into the past in his treatise on American space (Boorstin, 1948: 41–53). He also thought in terms of generations which, though not as sacred as were the Puritan ancestors, nonetheless made the world as he found it beyond the limits of Monticello.

The other interesting work of the period, *A Brief Retrospect of the Eighteenth Century* (1803), was written in two volumes by Samuel Miller, a Presbyterian clergyman in New York City. Miller's work was encyclopedic but it had a point. He attempted to show that all of the achievements of the Scientific Revolution and the Enlightenment were not threats to orthodox religion in America but rather demonstrated the beneficence of God. Miller, a product of Scottish Enlightenment thought, attempted to show that God, in enlightening man, was distinctly on his side and never more so than in America. For Miller, religion had no quarrel with science. He demonstrated this in the *Brief Retrospect,* the first intellectual history by an American. In so doing he charted the course that a powerful stream of American Protestant thought was to take for much of the nineteenth century (Hovenkamp, 1976).

Despite the impressive European Enlightenment works of Hume, Gibbon, Voltaire, Montesquieu and Condorcet, history as such hardly flourished in America during the Revolutionary Era and the early years of the Republic. On the other hand, history was not scorned. At one level it flourished in the patriotic mythmaking of Mercy Otis Warren and the indefatigable efforts of the huckster biographer, Parson Mason Weems (1800), who made Washington a god who "could not tell a lie" (see also Wecter, 1941). On another level it was revered as a precious resource. No one was consulted by the founding fathers as much as Montesquieu. His *Sprit of the Laws* was a bible. In addition the men who were fashioning America ransacked the past—the works of Tacitus and Livy, Herodotus and Thucydides, even Molesworth's tragic history of the late Danish Republic—to find guidance in their own endeavors (Bailyn, 1967: 22–54). They made the Roman Republic a model and this extended even into a reverence for Virgil, Cicero, and the architecture of Vitruvius. To the founding fathers history was a "usable past" or, in Voltaire's terms, "philosophy teaching by example," since men down through the ages were basically the same, part of a universal species whose true nature as individuals John Locke had so well understood. History reflected universal principles that remained unchanged or at most went in endless cycles paralleling Newtonian planetary motion (Persons, 1954). That was why the past was really usable and why busy men, building a nation, felt no urgent need to write new history except as propaganda. The age old histories along with the Bible contained all the truth that was necessary.

History, Patriotism, and the Early Republic

Although Enlightenment views of history persisted through the Revolutionary Era, in countless ways Americans began to develop a new consciousness of time and a new sense of the impingement of history. In part this arose in response to local needs, if not pride. But in a more profound sense it arose out of larger developments in Western civilization itself. The decades following the Revolution saw the publication of numerous state histories and the formation of local historical societies. During the confusing formative period as the Republic came into being, state or colony histories became important devices for identifying the cultural or political unit to which one properly owed allegiance, be it Connecticut, Pennsylvania, New York, South Carolina—or the confederation of states soon to be called the United States. In the jostling among the new states for political power it seemed necessary to record clearly each colony's respective contribution to the successful revolution. Chronicles and compilations though most of them were, state histories served a social and political need. This was true even in the emerging frontier West. In 1784 John Filson of Cincinnati published a little book that was to have emotional impact far beyond what even he could have imagined. The book was entitled *Discovery, Settlement, and Present State of Kentucke,* and it had as an appendix a brief biography of Daniel Boone who became America's second (after Washington) great hero and the archetype of a continuing national myth. From Filson's Boone came Cooper's Leatherstocking and a whole sense of the romantic atavism of the frontier experience that was to culminate in Frederick Jackson Turner's historical vision of the frontier in American history and a thousand western epics in print and now on film.

The rising interest in native or local history began to create a literary market in America which in turn had a strange effect upon would-be men of letters in the early Republic. Washington Irving, for example, first gained fame in collaborating with James Kirke Paulding on a burlesque history, *Diedrich Knickerbocker's History of New York* (1809) which lampooned the quaint ways of the old Dutch aristocracy. Then Irving, lamenting the lack of history in America, went to Europe. He became famous as a writer of tales virtually all of which, like *Rip Van Winkle,* involved time and history. Then he turned directly to the writing of history with his studies of the Alhambra, of the conquest of Granada, of Columbus, and at last with his American histories of John Jacob Astor's fur-hunting Astorians of the Rocky Mountains and *The Adventures of Captain Bonneville U.S.A.* (1837). The grandest historical subject of all, the Spanish conquest of the New World, he gave to a friend, William Hickling Prescott. Irving, early America's most famous writer, in a sense had to go to Europe to discover American history. The same largely applied to James Fenimore Cooper, who, in exile and trying to steep himself in ruined castles and decadent Venetian grandeur, nonetheless felt irresistibly pulled back to the adventures of Leatherstocking, Uncas and old tales of Puritan and New York settlement. Not even the writing of *A History of the Navy of the United States of America* (1839) could wipe these visions of

Washington Irving. Oil on canvas, undated, by Daniel Huntington (1816–1906). Photograph courtesy National Portrait Gallery, Smithsonian Institution, Washington, D.C. Negative number 07322.

societal evolution away. Cooper as novelist, however, was fortunate. When he wrote the genre was in vogue. But slightly before his time, histories and chronicles were the only way narrative could be brought before a public heretofore nurtured on sermons, tracts, political pamphlets, and moral uplift writing of the most directly relevant nature. Almost overnight, however, in the years after the War of 1812 the American past in any form became a vogue. Epic poems, novels, plays, histories, and even document-collecting became fashionable. Jared Sparks began collecting the crucial diplomatic correspondence of the American Revolution partially to recover or preserve the past and partially to fuel an emerging sense of nationalism.

Romanticism and History

The renewed interest in time that began to overtake Americans was also the result of an earlier awakening to such matters in Europe. The critical eye of Enlightenment scholarship had been engaged in scrutinzing the past for outmoded "superstitions" for nearly half a century with the astonishing result that a new sense of history was reborn. As early as 1762, J. G. Winckelmann had unearthed the ruins of Herculaneum and Pompeii, while in the same year James Stuart and Nicholas Revett published their works on the architecture of the ancient world. A pagan vogue for the minute examination of the ancient world culminated in one sense in Edward Gibbon's great history, *The Decline and Fall of the Roman Empire* (1776–88), in another sense with Napoleon's Egyptian campaign and the discovery of the Rosetta Stone, key to Egyptian history, and in still another sense with the rise of German "higher" critical studies of the Bible and its authenticity, capped by David Friedrich Strauss' important *Das Leben Jesu* (1826).

In the sciences, time was fast becoming the dominant paradigm. Abraham Gottlob Werner and James Hutton argued over the aqueous or volcanic origins of the earth; William Smith in England and Thomas Say in America discovered the fossil dating method which enabled geologists to reconstruct a temporal sequence of ancient geological horizons; German *Natur-philosophers* became fascinated with the embryonic development of plants and their relationship to the history of species ("ontogeny recapitulates phylogeny"); Erasmus Darwin published his evolutionary *Zoonomia* while his grandson set out on the *Beagle* to trace the origin of species, and Charles Lyell made geology a branch of history with his doctrine of uniformitarianism. In Europe at least, the static world of Newton had become the changing, dynamic world of time and history.

In 1818, following in the footsteps of Washington Irving, a contingent of Boston scholars including George Ticknor, Edward Everett, and George Bancroft departed for Europe and Germany in particular. Others followed, including Theodore Parker, William Hickling Prescott, and Francis Parkman. Out of these European experiences arose not only the American Romantic Movement but a fascination with one of Romanticism's central themes— history. Romantic America produced four notable historians: John Lothrop

Motley, William Hickling Prescott, Francis Parkman, and George Bancroft (Levin, 1959). They were all New Englanders and had been exposed to heavy doses of European Romanticism. All four were concerned with the evolution of civilizations and their works were grand epics and pageants.

Motley wrote on the rise of the Dutch Republic using acid portraiture and epic battle scenes to juxtapose the virtuous Protestant Dutch against the villainous Spaniards. William Hickling Prescott, virtually blinded in a college accident, took the development of the Spanish Empire as his subject. In 1838 he published *The History of the Reign of Ferdinand and Isabella the Catholic* in three volumes. His greatest works, however, were *The Conquest of Mexico* (1843) and *The Conquest of Peru* (1847). In these volumes he recounted the exciting story of conquest and commanded huge reading audiences in the United States. But, at the same time, his subject was civilization. The Spaniards he portrayed, not entirely without justification, as proto-Puritans whose will, self-discipline, and efficiency contrasted with the pagan, sybaritic tendency of the Aztecs and the Incas. In grand operatic tableaux Prescott presented Cortez confronting Montezuma in gorgeous splendor, or before a cast of thousands with Cortez hurling the Aztec sacrificial idols from the Teocalli with seeming impunity. Such scenes clearly indicated that one civilization was replacing another. The time of the Aztecs had come.

Parkman, after scouting the West for himself in 1846, published *The Oregon Trail* which instantly made him famous and also ruined his health. As a result of his trip west, Parkman's eyes could never tolerate light. He could not see except dimly. His nerves permitted only short periods of concentration during a day, and his body was wracked with pain. Yet he too insisted on taking on the role of the historian. Working through most of the nineteenth century in absolutely heroic fashion, Parkman (1869–92) produced his monumental multi-volume history of the war between France and Britain for North America. Parkman was another master of narrative, preferring to conceal his message in descriptions of forests and lakes, portraits of towering archetypal figures like LaSalle or Montcalm and Wolfe, or in heroic action, though in his final volumes (esp. Parkman, 1887) he did make an attempt at writing social history.

Motley, Prescott, and Parkman will perhaps forever be known as masterful Romantic narrators—men of letters who just happened to write history in extremely dramatic and lucid fashion. And yet they were much more. Each was an extensive and careful researcher, utilizing sources from archives all over Europe and the Americas in critical fashion. In this sense they were as "scientific" as any historians since their time. They also ever so subtly espoused the scientific currents of the day. They eschewed superhuman causes for complex events. Each saw man and society in evolution, with Parkman even raising the question of atavism which did not become fashionable until the late nineteenth century. However, like the Romantics, Motley, Prescott, and Parkman preferred to conceal the stage machinery of scholarship and to proceed with their stories by means of symbols, images, and significant, highly charged (even melodramatic) actions. They were historians of uncommon men and uncommon events. Perhaps their elitist Boston backgrounds dictated their interests and subtle techniques.

William Hickling Prescott. Lithograph, 1850, by Francis D'Avignon, after a daguerreotype by Mathew Brady. Photograph courtesy National Portrait Gallery, Smithsonian Institution, Washington, D.C. Negative number 07888.

George Bancroft, on the other hand, was a democrat—both philosophically and as a practicing politician (Levin, 1959: 5–6; Nye, 1944). Thoroughly familiar with the cultural revolutions of nineteenth-century Europe and thankful for the free, levelling spirit of Jacksonian America, Bancroft detected a common spirit in the people that equipped each individual for democratic leadership. Consequently his ten-volume *History of the United States* was partisan—democratic and transcendental in spirit—"the best history of the United States from the Jacksonian point of view" declared Leopold von Ranke, and the "longest Fourth of July oration in American history" declared others. Bancroft's history, not always scrupulously researched, hardly pretended to be scientific. Rather, it was the outward or symbolic expression of the innate democratic spirit that Bancroft believed characterized the American people.[3] In this sense it was the long narrative counterpart to an essay by Emerson or Thoreau.

If democracy was Bancroft's theme, self-identity in a so-called democratic society was the theme of a now forgotten but important historian of mid nineteenth-century America, William Wells Brown. The first black novelist to publish in the United States, Brown was a fugitive slave from Lexington, Kentucky who escaped to freedom in 1847. Best known as the author of *Clotel, or the President's Daughter* ... (1853), a novel about Thomas Jefferson's mulatto daughter, Brown, as a result of a tour of Europe, turned to history. In 1855 he published *St. Domingo: Its Revolution and Its Patriots*, then in 1863, *The Black Man: His Antecedents, His Genius, and His Achievements*. In 1874 he completed *The Rising Sun, or the Antecedents and the Advancement of the Colored Race*, his most extensive work. Brown's work is significant because it represented the way in which a minority, cast off from its traditions in the process of enslavement and transportation to America, sought in history to rediscover the roots of an identity. *The Black Man*, for example, was a compilation of 57 biographies of famous black historical figures including Benamin Banneker, Nat Turner, Toussaint L'Ouverture, Crispus Attucks, Alexander Dumas, Denmark Vesey, and Frederick Douglass. Other black historians of the day added Hannibal and Hamilcar to their list in a world search for identity in an alien land.

The same technique of identity through history was employed by another group seeking liberation in American society at about the same time—women. Lydia Maria Child published *History of the Condition of Women in Various Ages and Nations* (2 vols., 1835) which saw the United States as the place where woman's dreams throughout the ages could potentially be fulfilled. Elizabeth Ellet celebrated the "creative spirited" woman in three works: *The Women of the American Revolution* (2 vols., 1848), *Pioneer Women of the West* (1852) and *Women Artists in All Ages and Countries* (1859).[4] In the books of these now all but forgotten writers whose works have previously seemed out of the "mainstream" of American historiography, can be seen one of history's clearest utilities. Like George Bancroft, both blacks and intellectual women were also attempting to use the past to define America and chart its future possibilities for the groups they represented.

History Professionalized

While Americans at mid-century were writing epics in search of identity, European scholarship was growing progressively more scientific, philological and critical. In Germany the historical seminar developed along with the monograph and the Ph.D. Just as in Biblical studies, the accent in German historical seminars was upon origins of ideas, customs, institutions. This of course paralleled not only developments in science but it also echoed the German search for identity which began with Herder but which was accelerated during the era of Napoleonic occupation. In the 1860s young Americans trained in German seminars began to return to America, imbued with the scientific spirit of inquiry and the "germ" theory of history which traced the institutions of freedom back to the tribes in Teutonic forests at the dawn of civilization. A group of these scholars led by Herbert Baxter Adams created the first American history seminar at the new Johns Hopkins University founded in 1876 entirely on the German model. The history seminar at Hopkins became justly famous as the cradle of such eminent American historians as Frederick Jackson Turner and Woodrow Wilson.

At the suggestion of Hopkins President Daniel Coit Gilman, Herbert Baxter Adams also took the lead in organizing the American Historical Association at Saratoga Springs, New York in 1881 (Goetzmann, 1968). The creation of the American Historical Association reflected the increasing professionalization of the learned professions in America. The National Academy of Science was organized in 1863. The American Social Science Association was founded in 1865; in 1876 the American Chemical Society; and in 1883, the Modern Language Association. There were many others during the period and they all reflected an increasing organization and rationalization of American life from business and labor to transportation networks. They also reflected a desire to create conscious standards and principles to which all serious professionals could adhere.

Inevitably all this cast a shadow on the amateur historian like Parkman or Bancroft who created his own standards and principles. It relegated these historians to the status of crude but heroic pioneers; at age 83 Bancroft was invited to serve as president of the American Historical Association more out of sentiment and symbolism than in admiration for his work. Nonetheless a professional organization was necessary for historians in the United States because, thanks to the Land Grant College Act of 1862, universities were springing up all across the country and along with them departments of history that had to be staffed with competent, certified professionals. The American Historical Association and the network of professors it helped to develop saw to that and so rode on the crest of a long-term academic wave that lasted until the 1930s. The American Historical Association also sponsored the publication of reports, collections of source materials edited in model fashion, an *American Historical Review,* a Committee of Seven to establish guidelines for instruction in the public schools, and an annual meeting that rotated between Washington, New York and Chicago (Goetzmann, 1968).

Meanwhile the writing of "amateur" or non-academic history went on. James Schouler (1880–99) and Herman von Holst (1876–92) wrote widely applauded abolitionist histories of the Civil War. Their work was topped by the excellent eight volume treatise on the same subject by retired industrialist James Ford Rhodes (1893–1906). Senator Albert J. Beveridge (1916–19) wrote a monumental life of John Marshall; J. G. Nicolay and John Hay (1890) wrote a comparable life of Lincoln; and Theodore Roosevelt wrote histories and biographies about practically everything and everybody, but the most important of his works was *The Winning of the West* (2 vols., 1889). His friend General Hiram M. Chittenden meanwhile wrote a definitive *History of the American Fur Trade of the Far West* (2 vols., 1902), while the novelist Edward Eggleston pioneered in social history with his *The Transit of European Civilization to North America* (1901). The New Yorker John Bach McMaster did Eggleston one better with his massive eight volume *History of the People of the United States* (1883–1913). McMaster, however, began as an amateur and ended as a professional. He taught for 37 years at the University of Pennsylvania and became a pillar of the American Historical Association (Goldman, 1945).

Out in California the antiquarian Hubert Howe Bancroft (1890) turned thoroughly professional, establishing in effect a history factory where under his supervision and under his name a team of researchers and writers turned out some 40 volumes on the history of California, every state and territory in the American West, the north Mexican states and the native races of the western hemisphere. Eastern reviewers were only with difficulty persuaded to notice them but they made an immense impact on western readers and California's search for identity. They represented the largest undertaking in "booster history" that America had yet seen (Caughey, 1945).

Though the whole vast range and variety of "amateur," "literary" histories continued to command large public audiences throughout the nineteenth century, by 1895 more than half of the academic historians had been trained in Germany in what came to be called "scientific history" (Higham, 1965: 92). Ironically enough, the men who made their living by writing books that sold were dubbed by the new academicians "amateurs" while the professoriat whose main task was teaching students and reproducing their own kind considered themselves "professionals." This split in historical ranks persists to the present time, much to the confusion of the general public. What the professoriat had achieved, however, was a whole new market for their printed works—a captive audience of students and historical societies, such as the Wisconsin State Historical Society, which they controlled. This was appealing to publishers in a day of ever-increasing business organization because it enabled them by counting student enrollments to forecast the market for certain types of books—notably texts—with much greater accuracy. It marked the beginning of a new era of mass-think and standard curricula in the public schools, junior colleges, state colleges, and many universities. If scientific theory became, as Higham (1965: 92) states, a "new orthodoxy" in theory, it was much more devastatingly so in the marketplace of hard practical economics.

The Varieties of Scientific History

Theoretically scientific history appears to have been a trifurcated effort. As it first came out of German seminars, it focused on methodology. The historian was not to seek out the grand synthesis. He was not to chart the shape of time, nor was he to express any form of idealistic philosophy in his work. History may or may not have artistic symmetry—that was not the historian's concern. Rather his task was to locate sources—original documents—determine their validity and then their relationship to one another from as objective a point of view as possible. His task was to get the facts and these facts themselves, in a true inductive fashion, would automatically suggest a pattern, however limited. Such studies produced the monograph, severely restricted in scope, more conscious of limits than implications. They also produced the scientific paper or article as a major vehicle of communication for the historian, and professional journals, largely subsidized ventures, which have proliferated in history from that day to this.

The stance of the historian was strictly objective. Unlike the romantic historian, he did not enter into the events themselves, but perforce stood aloof above men and movements in the past. So strong was this impulse to depersonalize history that focus on individuals gave way to the study of institutions—a concept borrowed from the emerging disciplines of economics and sociology. In what Gillispie (1960) has called in another context the cutting "edge of objectivity" the scientific historian was not concerned with why events happened but rather how they related to one another as a system. He focused on the "who, what, where, when and how" with as much critical precision, and sometimes pedantry, as he could muster. In short the scientific historian envied the physical scientist his laboratory, and in the seminar he created his own.

Perhaps the oustanding effort at scientific history in the sense outlined above was Justin Winsor's *Narrative and Critical History of the United States* (1884–89), a multivolume collaborative work consisting of a series of very erudite but disjointed essays loosely following the chronology of American history. In each essay or component of the work, the footnotes far overshadowed the running narrative and proved to be infinitely more interesting and lasting. Winsor's work remains a mine of fascinating undigested information. This bothered Winsor not a bit, for, as Higham (1965: 95) points out, he "confessed with positive pride that he had made history 'a thing of shreds and patches.' "

Less inclined to disjointed folly, Henry Adams established a seminar at Harvard in 1870 and undertook to teach Medieval history in the German method. As he (Adams, 1931: 302–303) put it, "He frankly acted on the rule that a teacher, who knew nothing of his subject, should not pretend to teach his scholars what he did not know, but should join them in trying to find the best way of learning it. The rather pretentious name of historical method was sometimes given to this process of instruction, but the name smacked of German pedagogy . . . ." He added, however, "as pedagogy, nothing could be more triumphant. The boys worked like rabbits, and dug holes all over the field of archaic society." Somewhat later, seeking a scientific base line for American history, Adams embarked on his *History of the United States During the Administrations of Jefferson and Madison* (1889–91). Definitely limited in scope, the study nonetheless ran to nine volumes, and despite copious and extended use of documentary quotation and seemingly Olympian detachment the work proved to be a justification of the Adams family more than a balanced history of the period. Although the *History* was brilliantly written in places, Adam's own judgment of the work proved to be correct. It was a failure.

In a very real sense strict scientific history failed because the historian looking in from the outside failed to understand science. He truly believed for a time that science was pure induction, that the facts themselves suggested order, and that any phenomenon was worth studying. The function of hypothesis was not clear to the pioneer scientific historian. In fact he would have regarded it as a "philosophical" intrusion into the process of inquiry which was certain to destroy the desired objectivity. It would have taken him right back to the puerile Romantics.

The best scientific history was produced by men who did intrude with hypothesis. The prime example of this was, of course, the work of Frederick Jackson Turner (see Billington, 1973: chs. 4 and 5; Hofstadter, 1968: esp. 47–164). A man thoroughly trained in the exacting methods of the Hopkins seminar, Turner reacted strongly against the germ theory of history. His own dissertation researches in local Wisconsin history convinced him that environment, the crude exigencies of the wilderness and the frontier experience were the formative influences upon American behavior. Armed with all the apparatus from other social scientific disciplines—maps, census statistics, economic data, etc.—Turner tested this hypothesis to his satisfaction. The result was his address at the annual meeting of the American Historical Association in Chicago in 1893, "The Significance of the Frontier In American History" in which he proclaimed his hypothesis as hypothesis (see Turner, 1920). With Turner scientific history in America had come of age. Scientific research had produced a question of epic, even poetic grandeur that challenged the tradition, focused upon the American rather than the European scene, made local materials relevant for students, opened out onto numerous problems and questions that remain unsolved even today, and suggested a unique shape to the American character. Legions of historians have made careers answering questions that Turner raised in this one dramatic, suggestive address (see Billington, 1966).

Later Turner, becoming ever steeped in the skills of ancillary disciplines, advanced a second hypothesis. American history down to the Civil War could be interpreted primarily in terms of the dynamic interplay among geographic sections or regions of the country. This formed the thesis of his only real book, *Rise of the New West* (1906). His geographical hypothesis in this instance far more complex and subtle than the frontier hypothesis, has not been superseded. Several generations have carried it forward, including Turner's own contemporaries, Ulrich B. Phillips, a southern historian, and Charles Beard, also known for his economic interpretation of history. In a later period the Texas historian, Walter Prescott Webb, expanding on his own rural experience, refined the concept even further with his environmental study, *The Great Plains* (1931). The persistence of regional historical societies attests to the interest in the Turnerean geographic approach down to the present.

While Turner was developing his frontier hypothesis, still another school of scientific historians emerged with an equally intriguing hypothesis. In the 1890s Charles M. Andrews and Herbert Levi Osgood both revolted against the germ theory of history but in a way quite different from Turner. For Andrews, a Hopkins product, and Osgood, a Columbia Ph.D., the remote past in Teutonic forests had little relevance to what they had observed of Atlantic Coast civilization in the colonial era. Andrews' micro-study of a Connecticut River town suggested nothing of German customs or ancestry. Thus, along with Osgood, he concluded that historians should study the more immediate past and in particular he urged the mining of the resources of the British Public Records Office. Osgood himself moved to London to be in a position to do so. By 1907 he had published three volumes, entitled *The American Colonies in the Seventeenth Century* that launched what came to be known as the "imperial school" of American history. In the same year Osgood's student, George Louis Beer, added a volume entitled, *British Colonial Policy, 1754–1764.* This was the first of four volumes which treated British colonial policy since 1578 as a system. According to Beer the proper perspective on American history was through British eyes. Andrews, ever the perfectionist, published his work last of all, four volumes entitled, *The Colonial Period of American History* (1934–38). His work was far more comprehensive than those of Osgood and Beer in that he insisted that the whole New World system be included. For Andrews, Canada and the Caribbean colonies were interrelated with those of North America and crucial to British policy. So complete had been the researches of Osgood, Beer and Andrews, however, that rather than opening up new questions as Turner had done, they appeared to have supplied the last word (Higham, 1965: 162–165).

Still another aspect of scientific history derived from Charles Darwin and Herbert Spencer. As we have seen, modern history itself began with a sense of evolution and time quarried out of the continuous present theories of the Enlightenment. Nonetheless Darwin's theory of evolution provided a poten- tial scientific buttress for evolutionary belief arrived at by other, less scientific means. Spencer's writings gave an overt direction to evolutionary develop- ment as mankind progressed inevitably to ever higher stages of civilization until it reached the stage of perfect equilibrium with the environment which Spencer called "equilibration." If nothing else Spencer's popular historical and sociological writings allowed scientific historians to feel that their researches were cumulative and that in their own field progress was inevitable (see Hofstadter, 1944: 31–50; Peel, 1971).

The problem with the Darwinian-progressive model was that few if any serious American historians followed it. As an intellectual concept it had to be dealt with, but only John Fiske, the Harvard popularizer, and perhaps Captain Alfred Thayer Mahan, the naval historian who believed in survival of the fittest, could be seen directly paralleling Spencer's progressive outline (Hofstadter, 1944: 13–15, 19–22, 183–184). Indeed the most important disciple of Spencer was the founder of modern American anthropology, Lewis Henry Morgan. His *Ancient Society,* published in 1877, assumed that all men were the same everywhere but only in different stages of development that rose from "savagery" to "barbarism" to "civilization" according to technological attainments. Virtually the only significant group of historians who paralleled Spencer's progressive line were the Marxists who found Morgan's work intriguing and who espoused the same kind of deterministic view of history though starting from Hegel's dialectics (Herreshoff, 1967).

The two most prominent American historians to address themselves to the teleology of Spencerian evolutionary history and the implications of Darwin were Brooks and Henry Adams. Brooks Adams (1896) amalgamated Spencer, Morgan and Marx along with the laws of thermodynamics. Eschewing the teleology of Spencer and Marx, Brooks Adams in *The Law of Civilization and Decay* (1896) saw a cyclical or pulsating rhythm to history which was essentially directionless. He saw history as a movement according to laws. Human society in movement oscillates "between barbarism and civilization or what amounts to the same thing, from a condition of physical dispersion to one of concentration." He classified societies according to the amount of measurable energy they possessed. Then Adams combined energy with mass (i.e. population) to determine the "velocity" of a civilization. Velocity in turn governed centralization or concentration of energy and resources and this was governed by the institutions of fear—religion, the military and the artistic establishment, soon to be replaced by the capitalist who promoted greed. Greed in turn promoted economic competition which, governed by the non-producing capitalist consumer, led to waste, decay, degradation and the replacement by another civilization, and so on endlessly through time. In *America's Economic Supremacy* (1900) Adams actually measured the rise of American supremacy and the corresponding degradation of Britain in tons of pig iron and pints of beer consumed per capita respectively.

Henry Adams, it is clear, never believed in a science of history.[5] His Harvard seminar experience with its cynicism (see p. 18) demonstrated this. Thus when, despite the fact that he detested pedantry and never attended the annual meetings of the American Historical Association, he was elected its president in 1894, he decided to send the members a letter calling their attention to the implications of science for their craft. "We cannot help asking ourselves" he wrote, "what would happen if some new Darwin were to demonstrate the laws of historical evolution" (B. Adams, 1919). Having implied that he was on the track of such a law he set sail for the South Seas on a pleasure cruise (Samuels, 1964). The best of what he had to say to Darwinistic historians was contained in "The Rule of Phase Applied to History" (1909) and "A Letter to American Teachers of History" (1910). In the former he posited a law of acceleration in history, building upon the Yale physical chemist Josiah Willard Gibbs' phase rule. Adams divided history into four phases delimited by the inverse square rule—the religious phase ending in 1600, the mechanical phase ending in 1900, the electrical phase the duration of which was the square root of 300 or 17½ years, and the ethereal phase, the square root of 17½ or four years, making human history terminate at about 1921. At that point all human history would end—especially as the historian Adams, who expected to be dead by then, would know it.

Thus using physical science as a model, Adams reduced scientific history to absurdity. In the "Letter to American Teachers of History," Adams further demonstrated the futility of scientific history. On the one hand, he observed that Darwinistic biology implied planetary progress; on the other, the law of entropy dictated that the universe was running down. The best that could be hoped for was equilibrium and equilibrium meant stasis or death—according to biologists quoted by Adams. In a way so clever and subtle that it seems to have escaped most historians, Adams proclaimed the utter irrelevancy of science to history. He himself turned from the dynamo to the Virgin and to worshipping the beauty that he found so serenely present in the cathedrals of Medieval France.

Progressive History

Still, history could not or would not be quits with science and the philosophies emerging from it. The period from 1890 to 1915, sometimes called the Progressive Era, was also the great age of the Progressive historian who took his cue from the rapid flowering of American Pragmatism (see Hofstadter, 1968; White, 1949). Pragmatism, whose chief prophets were C. S. Peirce, William James, and John Dewey, began with the espousal of the "chance universe" implied by the chance mutations described by Darwin in *On the Origin of Species.* If the world was a world of chance, then there were no absolutely predictable scientific laws and human behavior was especially contingent. In a probabilistic universe the most problematic thing was man himself. Thus it behooved the historian who wished to be in step with the new science to avoid the long run prophetic teleologies of Spencer and concentrate upon short run problems bringing history to bear on their solution.

By the 1890s the country abounded in such problems. Monopolies and trusts dominated America. Railroads and grain elevator operators exploited the farmer and consumer alike. Banking rested in the hip pocket of J. P. Morgan. Even food was adulterated. On top of that depressions wracked the decade while muckrakers raked the underside of American life in popular journals. To many of these causes the professional historians responded. Their German training impressed them with the strong civil role that the professoriat enjoyed in Germany and they sought a similar role in an America that needed them (Higham, 1965: 11). In Wisconsin, for example, Turner, Charles R. Van Hise, R. T. Ely and J. Allen Smith among others served as consultants to Governor Robert La Follette in one of the country's earliest "brain trusts" (Billington, 1973: chs. 11 and 12). There historian, economist, and political scientist worked together to help solve some of the urgent problems of what rapidly became a very Progressive state. Involvement in political reform made the scholar's work relevant. In the historian's case it called forth a sense of the "usable past," as pure a pragmatic concept as any philosopher was able to imagine. Men like John R. Commons, Turner's friend, concerned with labor strife, turned to labor history in an effort to get to the bottom of the trouble (Higham, 1968: 175). Others turned to sectional analysis with regard to agricultural problems, marketing problems and freight rate differentials. Turner's theory of sections was especially useful here. Working with LaFollette in Wisconsin became a kind of Camelot to Turner, and when LaFollette left for Washington and the dairymen-vocationalists took over the running of the University, Camelot was sadly over and Turner left for Harvard.

In the East, E. R. A. Seligman and James Harvey Robinson went beyond pragmatism to Marxism in the attempted solution to social problems (Higham, 1965: 179). They both became convinced that any real answer to society's dilemmas must begin with a careful class analysis. The classic in this genre was supplied by Charles A. Beard with his *Economic Interpretation of the Constitution* (1913). Beard, with a rigidly cultivated scientific objectivity, analysed the "class affiliations" of the Constitution-makers and purportedly by induction came to the conclusion that each was motivated by greed, short-term motives, and was a prisoner of his class. Beard thus epitomized the "amoral moralist" who knew how to use the past.[6] His classic study could be applied to any legislature, any public deliberative body. It was a searchlight in the darkness as powerful as that of any muckraker, and because it was a history it was presumably more accurate and most lasting.

Beard became famous but there were other men employing similar techniques. Equally important in his time was the institutional economist Thorstein Veblen whose *Theory of the Leisure Class* (1899) was only the first of his many institutional analyses of the evils of American culture. This book traced the history of a leisure class who lived off the labors of others and demonstrated their power and superiority by consuming the world's goods as conspicuously if not as absurdly as possible. Veblen as writer invariably projected an ironic sense of comedy that was not to be duplicated until the days of Charlie Chaplin.

Out in Washington state a young literary historian, Vernon L. Parrington, who had once been the University of Oklahoma football coach, influenced by J. Allen Smith, began work on a masterpiece in the Progressive tradition that brought to light an American intellectual history. *Main Currents in American Thought* (Vols. I and II) finally came out in 1927 but it was the product of the earlier Progressive Era. In *Main Currents,* Parrington took a frankly political stand on behalf of Jeffersonian democracy and then applied a class test to the writers and intellectuals that America had produced. Rarely if ever did Parrington find a writer "deserting his class." If he did he was a real culture hero. Generally, however, Parrington's was a Manichean version of American thought, designed to show that ideas, even literary creations, were class-determined and aligned in polar opposites. *Main Currents* was a monumental synthesis in the interests of reform (see Hofstadter, 1968: 349–434).

Hofstadter (1968: xvii) has aptly written of the Progressive historians, "if pragmatism . . . provided American liberalism with its philosophical nerve, Progressive historiography gave it memory and myth." He added that the Progressive historians "attempted to find a usable past related to the broadest needs of a nation fully launched upon its own industrialization, and to make history an active instrument of self-recognition and self-improvement." The failure of the Progressive historians stemmed from two things—their lack of a sense of the complexities of human behavior and their inveterate belief that if men could see society's wrongs they would right them. In this they harked back to the days of the Puritans whom they despised. The Progressive historians in their blind faith created a liberal hagiography for an audience more interested in expediency than morality.

Modernism and History

At about the same time as the rise of Progressive historiography many of the same figures, most notably James Harvey Robinson and Harry Elmer Barnes, were involved in The New History Movement (Higham, 1965: 111–120). The New History was at base economic and sociological, but it involved the historian deeply with all of the emerging social science disciplines to the point where history itself began to lose its identity. This was symptomatic of a time that prefigured "the death of history." While historians had been building university departments and becoming thoroughly professional, other breakthroughs in knowledge had occurred that threatened to move history out of its central role as organizer of human experience. Anthropology under Franz Boas came of age, providing alternative contemporary models for human conduct. Sociology became extremely relevant to current social problems as did economics. Science was amazed by Albert Einstein's relativity theory which altered man's concept of time itself. And Freudian psychology, beyond discovering another landscape of the mind, made everyman his own case historian. Literature was altered forever by research in Frazer's *Golden Bough* and other comparative mythologies as well as by the discovery of the stream of consciousness. In art, exotic anthropological models, such as primitive statues and African masks, provided new forms with great implications.

More important, with the shattering of time, traditional spatial perspectives were also altered, and cubism made the simultaneous experiencing of space possible. This was dramatically demonstrated in the Armory Show of 1913, the same year Beard's book on the Constitution appeared and John B. Watson announced the doctrine of behaviorism in psychology. All of this added up to a great western European cultural revolution now called "Modernism" which was a response to the crisis generated by the confrontation of a deepseated tradition by new breakthroughs in knowledge and insight into human conduct.

As a result of Modernism, history lost its nerve as well as its subject matter in the fragmentation of time and consciousness. True, the Great War and the corrupt decade of the 1920s, not to mention the depression of the 1930s, were blows to the optimistic Progressives—blows to historians in particular who felt helpless and impractical. Their straightforward probings of human nature had failed to move men toward the good, the true, and the beautiful. But the deeper cause for the collapse of history was a basically changed reality with which they were not yet equipped to deal. The 1920s saw carryovers from the Progressive Era such as Parrington's great work, and Charles and Mary Beard's *The Rise of American Civilization* (1927), but for the most part historians turned to iconoclasm as in James Truslow Adams' *The Founding of New England* (1921), diatribes on behalf of isolation such as those by Beard (1936a; 1936b; 1939; 1940; 1946), Harry Elmer Barnes (1930; 1973), and C. Hartley Grattan (1929; 1936; 1939), a return to colorful narrative in search of a lost tradition as in the work of Van Wyck Brooks (1944–52), Samuel Eliot Morison,[7] and Carl Sandburg (1926–39), or more searching expressions of despair echoed by Charles Beard and Carl Becker.

Becker delivered perhaps the most sweeping expression of the new relativism in his famous address, "Everyman His Own Historian" while Beard echoed the William James of "The Will to Believe" in 1871 in his "Written History an Act of Faith" (1934). Some notable historians abandoned ship as did Allan Nevins and his followers in 1939 when they founded the Society of American Historians dedicated to the proposition that history should be written to be read, not guarded as the private preserve of the professor and his captive student audience. The Society took as its hero Francis Parkman (Higham, 1965: 80–82).

And yet, though in disarray, if not despair, with history ranking very low in the priorities of new funding agencies such as the Social Science Research Council (Higham, 1965: 118), some historians persisted and laid the foundations for a post-World War II resurgence of history in a new identity. Morison, Kenneth Murdock, and Perry Miller at Harvard began to resurrect the Puritans. The former, especially in *The Builders of the Bay Colony* (1930), *The Puritan Pronaos* (1936) and *Three Centuries of Harvard* (1936), uncovered the lost humanity of the Puritan world. James G. Randall (1937), Charles Ramsdell (1937: 3ff), Howard K. Beale (1946), Avery O. Craven (1939, 1942), Allan Nevins (1947, 1950), and the young David Potter (1942) opened up the whole question of the Civil War, again making use of advances in psychology and a new sense of the contingency of human events. Diplomatic history flourished, especially under Samuel Flagg Bemis (e.g., 1923, 1926, 1935, 1943), who not only took the diplomacy of the American Revolution for his own special province in a spate of excellent books but also brought Latin America into the American diplomatic history ken. Beyond this he launched an impressive series in *American Secretaries of State and their Diplomacy* and later wrote definitive works on the foundations of American foreign policy (see Bemis, 1940). Able scholars such as Dexter Perkins (1941, 1955), Julius Pratt (1925, 1936), Justin Smith (1911, 1919), Isaac J. Cox (1918), Arthur B. Darling (1940), Charles Seymour (1921), and A. P. Whitaker (1934), along with Bemis, created virtually a whole new field of history. Concerned by the experience of the Great War, they translated this concern into understanding international relations for future reference.

Intellectual history, too, came of age in two extraordinary books that far surpassed the work of Parrington. Merle Curti of Wisconsin published *The Growth of American Thought* (1943) which he called "a social history of American thought." His subject was the growth of "knowledge, values, and the institutions of intellectual life." Never quite able to break away from the Progressive's affinity for institutions, Curti concentrated on the latter and largely avoided the dissection of philosophical ideas, but he performed a mighty service in describing the broad institutional base out of which arose American ideas. Ralph Henry Gabriel, who, along with Stanley T. Williams, an English professor at Yale, was one of the pioneers of the interdisciplinary American Studies Movement, wrote an even more subtle history of American ideas—*The Course of American Democratic Thought* (1940). Gabriel, much interested in religious ideas, sought for universal moral principles that ran through American life. These could serve to fortify the country against the demoralization of the depression and the menace of totalitarian Fascism and Communism which threatened to be the wave of the future when Gabriel published his book in the dark days of 1940.

Like the Progressives before him, Gabriel still searched for a "usable past." He did so, however, in a sophisticated fashion benefitting from the pre-war atmosphere at Yale created by Thurman Arnold, Bronislaw Malinowski, and Jerome Frank. Using the anthropological culture concept as his matrix, Gabriel traced the adventures of three ideas through the history of American thought—natural law, individualism, and the mission of America. Selective rather than encyclopedic, Gabriel analyzed symbolic and important figures in some depth. The ideas of these figures provided insight into the course of American democratic thought which was seen by Gabriel as an American state religion, not dictated but freely chosen and critically evaluated by the people. With Gabriel's quiet masterpeice, American historians had begun to know how to use and to relate to the new social sciences that threatened to overwhelm them. In 1951, largely under the auspices of historians and students of literature, the American Studies Association was formed, not to advance provincialism, but to continue the kind of cultural analysis that Gabriel and others of his generation had begun—in the days when history had almost, but not quite, lost its nerve.

The Post-War Search for Tradition

Victory over the forces of totalitarianism in World War II seemed to inspire a new sense of confidence in American historians. In the postwar years, buttressed by the prosperity in colleges crowded with returning veterans and then eventually the wartime "baby boom," academic historians and the public alike took a new interest in searching for and celebrating the American tradition. This was reflected in the proliferation and enlargement of departments of history and the spawning of numerous American Studies Programs, most notably at Yale, the University of Pennsylvania, and Minnesota. It was also reflected in the launching of many large projects for the definitive publication of the papers of America's famous men beginning with the Jefferson and Franklin projects at Princeton and Yale respectively.

After Truman, outgoing presidents routinely established "presidential libraries" and massive public and private funding supported historical restorations such as Colonial Williamsburg and Mystic Seaport. The war itself produced at least one epic historical production, Admiral Samuel Eliot Morison's multi-volume *History of the United States Naval Operations in World War II* (1947–62), in the long run perhaps Morison's most impressive work. But then Morison, like the other historians of his time, fell to work celebrating the American tradition. His chief interest was the epic story of the European discovery of America which he described definitively in at least three volumes and a revision of his biography of Columbus. Morison also celebrated the feats of famous American sailors in biographies of John Paul Jones and Matthew Calbraith Perry.

At the same time in Richmond, Virginia, newspaper editor Douglas Southall Freeman worked steadily and successfully away at three impressive multi-volume projects—biographies of Virginia's heroes, Robert E. Lee and George Washington, and a detailed study of Lee's "lieutenants." Free-lance historian Bruce Catton helped launch a new, beautifully illustrated historical journal aimed at the public and called, significantly enough, *American Heritage.* This journal grew out of an earlier publication of the same name launched by the Society of American Historians who were dedicated to good popular history writing. It was a tremendous success. Catton himself reached large audiences with his multi-volume history of the northern side of the American Civil War, beginning with his impressive *Stillness at Appomatox* (1953; see also Catton, 1951, 1952).

Allan Nevins turned his formidable talents to the writing of volumes of American business history which, though as objective as he could make them, still tended to glorify American business. His history of the Standard Oil Company incorporated in two works, *John D. Rockefeller: The Heroic Age of American Enterprise* (1940) and *Study in Power: John D. Rockefeller, Industrialist and Philanthropist* (1953), sparked criticism from Progressive historians Ralph Hidy and Chester McArthur Destler. Likewise, Nevins' multi-volume history of the Ford Motor Company engaged him in debate with Matthew Josephson who was best known for his pre-war attacks on the American establishment, *The Robber Barons* (1935) and *The Politicos* (1938).

Critical voices were rare in post-war America, however. Rather the best work was still involved in charting the course of what Arthur Schlesinger Jr. (1949) called "the vital center." Schlesinger himself burst on the scene with a precocious work greatly influenced by Charles Beard, *The Age of Jackson* (1945). An immensely exciting work, *The Age of Jackson* was a Liberal, economically-oriented reassessment of Jackson that portrayed him as a public hero defending the people against the special interests. In a sense it read the New Deal into mid-nineteenth century America. This placed Schlesinger, a political activist, squarely in the Progressive historian tradition, and his masterful multi-volume history of *The Age of Roosevelt* (3 vols. 1957, '59, '60) was a major work of what Lionel Trilling was calling in a more general context "the liberal imagination." Countless historians worked this vein in post-war America. Among the best and brightest of them were Louis

Hartz of Harvard, Eric Goldman of Princeton, and Richard Hofstadter of Columbia.

Hartz, author of *The Liberal Tradition in America* (1955), saw no other American tradition than Liberalism, though he sometimes had to torture his definition of the word to make his point. The absence of feudal institutions in America, Hartz argued, ignoring slavery, enabled America to begin as a liberal nation and to continue in this political tradition throughout its history. Goldman, in his important book, *Rendezvous With Destiny* (1952), realized that liberal advance did not go unimpeded, but he pointed with some pride to a native reform tradition that always somehow seemed to get Americans back on the right track. Goldman's sentiments were echoed by Daniel Aaron in *Men of Good Hope* (1951) and later in *Writers on the Left* (1961).

The late 1940s and the 1950s were dominated by historians writing studies of the American reform tradition. Of all these Richard Hofstadter's work was perhaps the most impressive. His *The American Political Tradition* (1948) was a set of sometimes critical portraits that recharted the American mainstream in a way that identified "the vital center." His *The Age of Reform* (1955), carrying that story from Populism through the New Deal, was a landmark in American historiography. It not only suggested the extent to which Populist demands had been incorporated into legislation without the farmers even knowing that they had won, but it also introduced a new concept into American historiography, "the status revolution." Learning from literary criticism as well as sociology and anthropology, Hofstadter avoided a simplistic Beardian economic interpretation of political events and concentrated on the effects of belief and status competition. This dramatized a whole new school of historiography—the "symbol and myth school."

Mind Over Matters: The Symbol and Myth School

Hofstadter did not invent the method. Indeed Ralph Henry Gabriel had included in his pre-war book, *The Course of American Democratic Thought,* an important chapter on "Pre-Sumter Symbols of Nationalism." In addition the Texan pioneer of American Studies, Henry Nash Smith, had published in 1950 his important, *Virgin Land: The American West as Symbol and Myth.* Smith's book, by far the most successful to date in the genre, involved the use of literary analysis applied to a whole range of historical documents from political addresses to newspaper articles and dime novels. Smith succeeded in demonstrating that, more often than not, belief, more than reality, motivated actions in settling the American frontier. Specifically he pointed to the image of the West as a garden which impelled settlers to move with great expectations into the harsh, unpromising arid lands of the West described by John Wesley Powell (1878) in the nineteenth century and Walter P. Webb (1931) in the twentieth. Smith's book had two further aspects of significance. It underscored the idea that there did exist a common American myth or set of beliefs and therefore fitted into what was coming to be known as "the consensus school of American historiography." And, in adopting a literary method which avoided narrative and chronology, mixed genres, explored in belief a new reality, and strikingly juxtaposed figures and concepts, Smith produced a "modernist," experimental piece of American history.

Both Hofstadter and Smith have had many imitators. Such books as Marvin Meyers' *The Jacksonian Persuasion* (1957), Leo Marx's *The Machine in the Garden* (1964) and John William Ward's *Andrew Jackson, Symbol for an Age* (1953) suggest the range of their influence. For more than two decades the "symbol and myth" approach was a mainstay of the interdisciplinary-minded, anthropologically-oriented American studies scholar. Only in the mid-seventies did it come under fire from scholars who saw it as a false short cut to extensive and serious analysis of culture. Its critics argue that, in a sense, the symbol and myth approach erroneously substitutes a part of reality for the whole. Synechdoche is its besetting sin (see Kuklick, 1972: 1435–1450).

History: Consensus and/or Paradox

Perhaps the major figure to emerge from the "consensus school" of historians was Daniel Boorstin of Chicago. Drawing his insights on America from his experience abroad, Boorstin saw America as an inventive, pragmatic nation that had survived because it avoided enslavement to any doctrinaire ideology except perhaps a mildly liberal Lockeanism. He made this point clearly in *The Genius of American Politics* (1953) and somewhat less overtly in *The Lost World of Thomas Jefferson* (1948). These works were overshadowed, however, by his monumental paean to pragmatic American consensus, *The Americans*. In these volumes, *The Colonial Experience* (1958), *The National Experience* (1965), and *The Democratic Experience* (1973), Boorstin concentrated on common men and common practical experience. He celebrated the "go-getters," "the boosters," the social inventors who managed to push America along by creating an endless series of satisfying community experiences that kept pace with advancing technology. Throughout the three volumes Boorstin rang the changes on Locke's theory of man and society in a state of nature. No one since the Founding Fathers had taken Locke quite so seriously and with such broad application. But beyond the fundamental influence of Locke, Boorstin saw no role for philosophies or ideologies in the meaningful experiences of Americans. He has, of course, been criticized for this and for essentially leaving confrontation as well as tragedy and irony out of the American story (Diggins, 1971: 153–180). Yet such was his ingenuity, so startling were his insights and imagination where concerned with commonplace America, that in some sense he has seemed the Ralph Waldo Emerson of American historiography.

A virtually unclassifiable historian of the post-war generation was David Potter of Yale. Burdened with editing *The Yale Review*, Potter wrote little, but his book, *People of Plenty* (1954), made an impact on American thought almost comparable to that of Frederick Jackson Turner, whom he resembled in many ways. *People of Plenty* cast a shadow over the Progressive interpretation of the American experience that so dominated post-war America.

Steeping himself in the social sciences, Potter offered his book as an example of interdisciplinary methodology, but also as a reinterpretation of the American past. It was not the frontier or Teutonic germs that had shaped America, but the fact of abundance. Americans, declared Potter, were literally people of plenty and this fact shaped all of our institutions and customs from the Madison Avenue marketplace to child-rearing habits. Abundance, wrote Potter, made democracy possible. The implications of his book were wide-ranging. In an era when Americans thought to export democracy to the world, Potter's work suggested that economic problems had better be solved first. Beyond this, with Turnerian end-of-the-frontier echoes, Potter's work raised the question as to what might happen to America when abundance ceased to be the prevailing condition. With Potter's work, the sunny optimism of Progressive historiography should rightly have come to an end.

Meanwhile in the 1950s and early 1960s other currents of thought and other visions were beginning to invade American historical thinking. A new despair had begun to arise in the midst of academic prosperity. In part this was generated by social scientists like Daniel Bell in *The End of Ideology* (1960), David Riesman in *The Lonely Crowd* (1950), and C. Wright Mills' slashing Marxist attacks in works like *The Power Elite* (1956). A certain kind of tragic vision had been introduced by the theologian-historian Reinhold Niebuhr whose most powerful books were *The Irony of American History* (1952), *The Children of Light and The Children of Darkness* (1944) and *Moral Man and Immoral Society* (1932). In the 1950s too, and echoing Niebuhr, European existentialism came to dominate many American intellectuals.

The pathos of paradox and situation, the essential contradictions of American life began to loom larger. Out of this climate two schools emerged. The first, in many ways, took its cue from Henry Adams and saw Americans not as people of plenty but as people of paradox. The clearest statement of this theme was made by R. W. B. Lewis in *The American Adam* (1955), which became a seminal book for many. Even earlier in placing American foreign policy in historical context, the political scientist Gabriel Almond, in *The American People and Foreign Policy* (1950), had seen the American character split between a shrewd Uncle Sam and a generous Statue of Liberty. The theme of paradox has been a powerful one in American historiography and refuses to die. Its most recent articulation has been Michael Kammen's imaginative *People of Paradox* (1972).

Existential History: Regions, Roots and Races

The great high point of existential historiography, however, was the monumental work of Perry Miller. Beginning as one of those pre-war historians who sought to locate and re-establish the American tradition, Miller first examined the Puritans. *Orthodoxy in Massachusetts* (1933) defined the particular political situation of New England's Non-separating Congregationalists and resurrected the Puritans as human beings. His magisterial *New England Mind* (2 vols. 1939, 1953), however, limned the whole landscape of Puritan thought in all its subtle intricacies, creating a world as fascinating if not fantastic as that being created at the same time by the Southern novelist William Faulkner. Miller's work, however, was divided into two volumes. The first, *The Seventeenth Century,* portrayed the emergence and development of Puritan thought. The second volume, *From Colony to Province,* charted the decline of Puritanism with a sense of tragic grandeur. Due to Miller, the intellectual history of colonial New England became virtually an industry within the historical profession. It would be impossible to trace accurately Miller's vast influence and unprofitable to list all of his disciples, but among the most prominent have been Alan Heimert in *Religion and the American Mind: From the Great Awakening to the Revolution* (1966); Edmund Morgan whose works include *The Puritan Dilemma* (1958), *The Visible Saints* (1963), *Roger Williams, The Church and The State* (1967) and a recent work on Virginia, *American Slavery, American Freedom, The Ordeal of Colonial Virginia* (1976); Darrett Rutman with *Winthrop's Boston* (1965) and Robert Middlekauff with *The Mathers: Three Generations of Puritan Intellectuals 1596–1728* (1971).

Miller's work has also evoked a reaction from a whole generation of post-Miller historians of New England. In the main they object to Miller's theme of declension but they also argue that the declension theme emerged because Miller focused so intently upon intellectuals and theology, *per se* (Dunn, 1972; 661–679). Taking their cue from the economic approach of Miller's successor, Bernard Bailyn, especially his *New England Merchants in the Seventeenth Century* (1955), and the work of Lucien Febre, Fernand Braudel and the French *Les Annales* school, a new generation of New England historians has seen continuity and the persistence of Puritan institutions and life styles well into the nineteenth century. The most notable of the post-Miller scholars have concentrated on family history, genealogy, and town studies where one of Miller's disciples, Edmund Morgan, was a pioneer with *The Puritan Family* (1944). Other works in this vein include Michael Zuckerman's *Peaceable Kingdoms* (1970) and Kenneth Lockridge's *A New England Town: The First Hundred Years* (1970). Paul Boyer and Stephen Nissenbaum have even used post-Millerian techniques of social history to unravel definitively the mystery of the Salem Witchcraft Trials in *Salem Possessed* (1974).

Existential history did not begin and end in New England, however. Contemplating the situation of the defeated South, Wilbur J. Cash, a North Carolina newspaperman, wrote *The Mind of the South* in 1941. An indictment of the South, Cash's book at the same time was essentially a story of cultural tragedy. This theme was picked up by C. Vann Woodward, notably in *The Origins of the New South* (1951), *Tom Watson, Agrarian Rebel* (1938) and *The Burden of Southern History* (1960). Woodward with great sympathy saw the South as the only section of the United States that had experienced defeat and cultural occupation, which in turn gave Southerners a special perspective on American history. This held true for Woodward as a Southerner especially. He could see that the defeat of the South had two causes: Northern economic supremacy coupled with Southern complicity in greed, and the South's policy of institutionalized racism.

Woodward, however, did more than brood about the situation. In 1955, during the integration crises, he wrote *The Strange Career of Jim Crow,* which indicated that segregation in transportation facilities was not an ancient Southern custom, not rooted in the folkways and mores, but a comparatively recent development. The book strongly suggested that there was no validity to the Southern argument that federal laws could not legislate custom away—especially in the case of transportation facilities—because of the comparatively recent adoption of segregated transportation facilities. Woodward, who wielded great influence as spokesman for the enlightened South, combined the Progressive historian's desire to find a usable past with the existentialist sense of the irony and tragedy of history itself.

Southern historians, however, could look in turn at the story of the Negro and see further irony and tragedy in history. The first great voice to articulate this situation in modern fashion was the Marxist historian, W. E. B. DuBois, whose *The Souls of Black Folk* (1903) saw the Negro caught between a dominant white culture and his own black identity in a country to which he preferred, if allowed, to pledge allegiance. Surprisingly, it was not the black historians who picked up on DuBois's theme but white historians of black culture. Black historians tended to be progressive and optimistic and at times militant in their outlook rather than tragic and existential. Saunders Redding (1958, 1967), Benjamin Quarles (1948, 1953, 1961, 1962, 1969), Henry Bullock (1967), Daniel Thompson (1910, 1963), Earle Thorpe (1961, 1967, 1969, 1971), John Hope Franklin (1943, 1947, 1961, 1963, 1968), and John Blassingame (1972, 1973), to name the most prominent of recent black historians, all have seemed Progressive in their recounting of the black experience.

White historians, on the other hand, have seemed closer to DuBois or the black novelist, Ralph Ellison, whose *Invisible Man* (1952) was the great American existential novel of the 1950s. Kenneth Stampp in his *The Peculiar Institution* (1956) tried to rewrite Ulrich Phillips' pioneer work but saw nothing ironic in thinking of the Negro as a "white man in a black skin." Stanley Elkins in *Slavery* (1959) likened the black slave's experience to life in Nazi concentration camps and, drawing heavily upon T. W. Adorno's *Authoritarian Personality* (1950), pictured the black as being "Samboized" by the ordeal. In slavery not only the Negro's African culture disappeared but his ego was pulverized and re-shaped again. For Elkins the tragedy was that in ante-bellum America, unlike Latin America with its Church, there were no institutions to exercise moral suasion over white tormentors. Critics of Elkins have believed that he painted too glowing a picture of Latin American institutions and that he carried the concentration camp analogy too far. Black reactors to Elkin's work found the "Sambo" portrait insulting and counter-productive to their search for a black identity.

Perhaps the best, most searching historical account of the origins and rise of racism in America has been Winthrop Jordan's *White Over Black* (1968). The most interesting, sympathetic, yet not patronizing description of ante-bellum black culture has been Eugene Genovese's *Roll Jordan Roll* (1974). David Brion Davis at Yale has attacked the problem of American slavery from a world perspective in his two volumes to date, *The Problem of Slavery in*

Western Culture (1966) and *The Problem of Slavery in the Age of Revolution, 1770–1823* (1975) while Carl Degler at Stanford has attempted a comparison of slavery between the cultures in the hemisphere in *Neither Black nor White: Slavery and Race Relations in Brazil and the United States* (1971). George Fredrickson in *The Black Image in the White Mind* (1971) and Thomas Gossett in *Race: The History of an Idea in America* (1965) have also added significantly to the rapidly growing literature on the subject (see Stanton, 1960).

The greatest controversy has been generated by Robert Fogel and Stanley Engerman's *Time on the Cross* (1974), a cliometric study of the slave and slave conditions in the South. Employing massive research teams and computers, Fogel and Engerman used statistics and intricate sampling formulae to prove that slavery was profitable and hence, not likely to die out; that slaves did have a culture of their own and a family life; that the slave was relatively better off than the northern worker of the same period; and that slaves were upwardly mobile. At first Fogel and Engerman's work was enthusiastically received and the profession stood in ignorance and awe of their new research technique as well as their findings (Woodward, 1974). But soon rebuttal (David, *et al.*, 1975; Gutman, 1975) followed as historians questioned their research, sampling techniques, and conclusions. A dramatic, heavily-attended symposium (Walton, ed., 1975) took place at Rochester, New York in 1974, which ended in the denunciation of their work though not its conclusive refutation. History had intersected with present politics (Haskell, 1975: 33–39).

A Saga Re-examined: The New Western History

While numerous historians have been scrutinizing the South from modern perspectives still another set of scholars has begun to reassess the role of the West in the life of the nation. This group forms what might loosely be termed the "post-Turner school." For many western historians a dialogue with Turner and his ardent disciple, Ray Allen Billington, continues to be the main focus of their work. In 1954 Stanley Elkins and Eric McKitrick reopened the Turner question with their collection *A Meaning for Turner's Frontier* in which they included an essay comparing the frontier situation with that of a World War II instantly-created town. They found in the town's experience many analogies to Turner's description of the frontier which, to them, made his thesis plausible. Other defenses of Turner were supplied by Billington in *America's Frontier Heritage* (1966) and Merle Curti's (1959) computerized study of Trempealeau County in Wisconsin.

The arch foe of the Turner thesis was George Wilson Pierson of Yale whose essays critical of Turner, written over many years, finally resulted in a substitute hypothesis—the theme of mobility. This he incorporated into *The Moving American* (1972).

Meanwhile several other approaches to the western experience suggested themselves to post-Turnerians. One, generated by Earl Pomeroy in *The*

Territories and the United States (1947) focused upon the political ties between the West and the East using territorial politics as the immediate subject matter. Building upon Pomeroy's theme, Howard R. Lamar wrote *Dakota Territory* (1956) and *The Far Southwest* (1966), both of which argued for the political determination of cultural units. This flew directly in the face of the environmental determinism of Turner and Walter Webb. In *The Far Southwest,* for instance, Lamar analysed a region that was geographically homogeneous but yet formed the setting for four quite different cultural patterns in Utah, Arizona, Colorado, and New Mexico. These cultural patterns were determined, Lamar argued, by the kinds of economic and political systems brought *to* the region, not *generated out* of the region. The role of the federal government in developing or impeding the development of the West has also formed the subject for books by William Turrentine Jackson (1952), Robert Utley (1963, 1967, 1974), Richard Bartlett (1962), and William Goetzmann (1959).

In Goetzmann's work, which was strongly influenced by the American studies movement, a transcendance of economic and political determinants was attempted in a larger vision of the impact of American culture on the West. His two books, *Army Exploration in the American West* (1959) and *Exploration and Empire: The Explorer and the Scientist in the Winning o:' the American West* (1966) examined the role of art, photography, science, belief, myth, and the military as well as politics and economics in forming an overall view of the West in the American mind. Goetzmann argued that explorers, scientists, and artists who went West were "programmed" to interpret what they saw in terms largely fashioned in Eastern cultural centers. The early impressions thus formed largely governed the later course of Western development in a self-fulfilling prophecy. Goetzmann thus combined aspects of the symbol and myth school with detailed institutional history as well as a broadened view of the history of science in his attempted revision of Western history.

Four notable recent works following similar lines are: Roderick Nash, *Wilderness in the American Mind* (1967), G. Edward White, *The Eastern Establishment and the Western Experience* (1968), Kevin Starr, *Americans and the California Dream* (1973) and Richard Slotkin's *The Frontier Myth of Regeneration Through Violence* (1973). A variation on the role of belief in fashioning Western behavior is presented by Michael Lesy in his striking *Wisconsin Death Trip* (1973) which uses photography as its primary medium supplemented by newspaper accounts and state insane asylum records to present a view of Jackson County, Wisconsin far different from and much bleaker than that revealed in Curti's study of Trempealeau County. Lesy's book essentially added the dimension of psycho-history to Western history.

Still other Western historians studied the rise of cities and towns. Richard Wade's *The Urban Frontier* (1959) cogently argued that key cities supplied the values and habits of large areas in the West. Robert Dykstra refined this view in his perceptive study *The Cattle Towns* (1968). Gerald Nash in his *The American West in the Twentieth Century* (1973) saw the West as entirely dominated by towns and cities in an "oasis" culture, while Reyner Banham in

Los Angeles, a City of Four Ecologies (1971) discussed the rise of the sprawling western metropolis and its ever-expanding sphere of influence in terms of the interplay between urban and natural landscapes.

Concurrently with ongoing studies of white settlements, another group of historians has been studying the Indian and American Indian policy. The works of F. P. Prucha (1962), Robert Utley (1963, 1967, 1974), and Wilbur Jacobs (1950, 1966, 1972) are noteworthy in this field as are Alvin Josephy's *The Patriot Chiefs* (1961) and *The Indian Heritage of America* (1968). Peter Farb in *Mankind's Rise to Civilization* (1968), has offered the interesting idea that Indians perished before the white man's onslaughts because their culture was too advanced and too refined and hence too inflexible. Other more popular works on the Indian which come under the heading of "advocacy history" are Vine Deloria's *Custer Died For Your Sins* (1969), Dee Brown's *Bury My Heart At Wounded Knee* (1971) and Leslie Fiedler's *The Return of the Vanishing American* (1968). Perhaps the most fruitful new approach to Indian history is that of Richard Metcalf (1974). By showing how white sources can be combined with anthropological information to reconstruct Indian political history Metcalf has opened up a new field for Western historians. In many ways all of these recent works suggest that the field of Western history is rapidly attaining a high degree of sophistication and complexity and that the West is now "old" and "jaded" enough perhaps to offer itself as a subject for tragedy and as an example to other developmentally emerging sections of the world.

Radical History

Like virtually everything else in America, history did not pass serenely through the decade of the 1960s. Indeed it learned much from it. Concerned about the war in Vietnam and America's global policies, a new school of radical diplomatic historians emerged, led by William Appleman Williams (1959, 1967), Walter Lefeber (1963, 1967), and Barton J. Bernstein (1966, 1968). Intersecting with their work and distinctly Leninist in its outlook was the work of Gabriel Kolko, especially *The Politics of War: The World and United States Foreign Policy* (1968). The outlook embodied in many of these works was perhaps unwittingly echoed or keyed by Senator J. William Fulbright's widely disseminated, *The Arrogance of Power* (1966), which contrasted sharply with Walt Whitman Rostow's *The Diffusion of Power* (1972). In this period old-fashioned multi-archival diplomatic history seemed to be rapidly giving way to histories, justifications, and interpretations of American policy that somehow reflected a prevalent post-war view that what America did or planned to do was all that mattered.

Domestic policy also formed the backdrop and *raison d'être* for the new radical historians who called for a new approach to and reassessment of the American past. The most prominent of the radical historians were Eugene Genovese in *The Political Economy of Slavery* (1967), Herbert Aptheker, perennially interested in slave revolts, Staughton Lynd in *Intellectual Origins of American Radicalism* (1968) and *Class Conflict, Slavery and the United*

States Constitution (1967), Christopher Lasch in *The New American Radicalism* (1965) and David Herreshoff, *American Disciples of Marx* (1967).

The consistent point driven home relentlessly by the radical historians was the need to examine American history not with an eye to consensus but to confrontation. They assailed consensus historians as myth-makers who willingly or not glorified America and averted their eyes from its contradictions, crimes and absurdities. Moreover, they accused traditional historians of being "elitist" in that they focused on prominent men and unusual events rather than studying the common man and woman. Jessie Lemisch (1968) sounded this note most clearly when he called for history to be written "from the bottom up." And as a final corollary the radical historians insisted that the historian not pretend to be neutral. Fairness, they characteristically asserted, demanded that history be value-oriented, that the historian use his work to right the wrongs of the past and present. Thus the radical historians appeared to be living in and for the present. The writing of history was not "science" but self-expression—a present-oriented species of activism that formed one very logical consequence of Morse Peckham's view of history.

1976: History Alive and Well

If Peckham was right and history can be only the reflection of present sentiments using vestiges of the past as a kind of language, then Clio's—or Time's—American adventures as recounted in this essay represent not a reconstruction of what actually happened but rather a Bicentennial view of the importance or function of past historiography today. Moreover it is clear that J. H. Plumb's announcement of "the death of history" is premature. Since, as this essay demonstrates, the writing of history grows out of a concern for present events at all times; since it is a form of self-expression about those current events using special, very powerful convincing devices, it would appear that the present, with its multiplicity of causes, concerns, and problems, is perhaps demanding more history and more *kinds* of history than at any previous time.

In a recent essay calling for a re-charting of the mainstream of American experience Robert Sklar (1975) seemed to suggest that indeed there was no mainstream but rather that there were many streams and rivulets which have marked the course of American experience. "Herstory" or woman's history has assumed a commanding importance as has the history of the blacks, the Mexican-Americans, the Oriental-Americans, and the First Americans. All forms of ethnic history and minority history necessitating studies in ethnology, have risen to central importance. And now that the extended family and the nuclear family have all but vanished, they are commanding great attention from the historian. So too has the history of children and the inarticulate assumed a new importance in a society that is census and welfare conscious (Calhoun, 1973; Coles, 1963, 1967, 1970, 1971a, 1971b, 1972). This has led in very recent times to the rapid advance of cliometrics or computer based research borrowed from opinion poll sampling techniques. History seems to be moving away from the idiosyncratic and the particular to the general and the study of the masses who, in the words of Braudel, "move very slowly."

A concern for the masses and the inarticulate has also led to a heightened interest on the part of historians in the evidence of material culture. Historical archeology is a fast-rising vogue that goes beyond mere antiquarian interest. A fascination with material culture has led in turn to architectural history and ecological history, and a new importance attaches to the history of science and its effect on culture. Here the most influential book has been Thomas Kuhn's *The Structure of Scientific Revolutions* (1962, rev. 1970). And surely the most intriguing of the behavioral sciences for the historian is psychology. A new school of psycho-history (see Crunden, 1973) with its own journal, *The Journal of Psychohistory,* has appeared within the last decade. Drawing sustenance from the theories of people as widely diverse as Sigmund Freud, Carl Jung, Harry S. Sullivan, J. B. Watson, Geza Roheim, and Erik Erikson, psychohistory nonetheless still appears to have two major defects. It is only as convincing as the psychological theory upon which it rests, and available in-depth information is far too scanty to be very persuasive to the discerning reader. It will hardly do to assert, as has one recent historian (Rogin, 1975), that, because Andrew Jackson's mother left him ashore to work on a Revolutionary War prison ship and subsequently died, all of Jackson's actions can be explained by an acute case of "mother deprivation."

Nor will the current rage for Marxist theory among a determined band of historians be broadly convincing despite *detente.* Even less promising, though perhaps revealing of the time, is a cross-fertilization between Marxism and psycho-theory that has begun to appear in some books (Rogin, 1975: 86). Clearly some historians (see White, 1973) at the present time appear to be impatient with complexity and longing for models or abstractions—a "metahistory" that will make the task of understanding mass man or woman much simpler. They are at one with Henry Adams in those confusing days before the Great War when, "sorely perplexed" and disoriented by science and changing times, he called for "the aid of another Newton."

And yet with all its confusions and complexities, reflective of the present time, history appears to possess greater power in the popular mind than historians think it has. In a very real sense, since the days when Thomas Jefferson wrote "posterity shall judge," virtually every American figure has somehow felt himself accountable to the historians of a future generation. Recent presidents have been acutely conscious of their possible places in history—even to the extent of disastrously recording their every moment by means of recording machines and their human counterparts, (e.g., Goldman, 1969; Schlesinger, 1965; Sorensen, 1963, 1965, 1969). Thus, in the minds of our public figures, history, as in the days of ancient Rome, becomes a popular tribunal. A court beyond the last resort, posterity, no matter what the ontological basis of history may come to be, will inexorably judge.□

Footnotes

[1] The best overall treatment of American historiography is Higham (1965). The present author is much indebted to this work. Other studies include Kraus (1953), Wish (1962), Cunliffe and Winks (1969), Skotheim (1966, 1969), Duberman (1969), Van Tassel (1960), Wish (1960), Loewenberg (1972), Handlin, *et al.* (1954), Basler, *et al.* (1960).

[2] See Hanke (1959: 74–96). Page 77 reproduces a page from the English translation of Las Casas' book, dated 1583.

[3] For a characteristic expression of his philosophy, see Bancroft (1954).

[4] The best treatment of these writers is Conrad (1976).

[5] Jordy (1952) gives Adams the label "scientific historian" but then demonstrates that Adams did not believe in scientific history.

[6] See White (1949: 27–31, 32–46). White (1949: 76–93), however, applies the term to Veblen.

[7] Morison (1942) is a good example. After the war Morison also sailed across the Atlantic in a replica of Columbus's ship.

References

Adams, B. *The Law of Civilization and Decay.* New York: Macmillan, 1896, 1910.

———, ed. *The Degradation of the Democratic Dogma.* New York: Macmillan, 1919.

Adams, H. *The Education of Henry Adams.* New York: Modern Library, 1931: 302–303. Orig. ed. privately printed, 1907; first public printing, 1918.

Bailyn, B. *The Ideological Origins of the American Revolution.* Cambridge, Mass.: Harvard University Press, 1967.

Bancroft, G. "The Office of the People in Art, Government and Religion," in J. L. Blau, ed., *Social Theories of Jacksonian Democracy.* New York: Liberal Arts Press, 1954: 263–273.

Bancroft, H. H. *Literary Industries.* San Francisco: H. H. Bancroft Co., 1890.

Barnes, H. E. *World Politics in Modern Civilization.* New York: Alfred A. Knopf, 1930.

———. *The Chickens of the Interventionist Liberals Have Come Home to Roost: The Bitter Fruits of Globalony.* New York: Revisionist Press, 1973.

Bartlett, R. *Great Surveys of the American West.* Norman, Okla.: University of Oklahoma Press, 1962.

Basler, R. B., D. H. Mugridge, and B. McCrum. *A Guide to the Study of the United States of America.* Washington, D.C.: U. S. Government Printing Office, 1960.

Beale, H. K. "Causes of the Civil War," *Social Science Research Council Bulletin No. 54,* 1946.

Beard, C. *The Devil Theory of War: An Inquiry into the Nature of History and the Possibility of Keeping out of War.* New York: Vanguard, 1936a.

———. *The Discussion of Human Affairs.* New York: Macmillan, 1936b.

——. *Giddy Minds and Foreign Quarrels: An Estimate of American Foreign Policy.* New York: Macmillan, 1939.

——. *The Old Deal and the New.* New York: Macmillan, 1940.

——. *American Foreign Policy in the Making, 1932–1940: A Study in Responsibilities.* New Haven: Yale University Press, 1946.

Bemis, S. F. *Jay's Treaty.* New York: Macmillan, 1923.

——. *Pinckney's Treaty.* Baltimore: Johns Hopkins Press, 1926.

——. *The Diplomacy of the American Revolution.* New York: Appleton-Century, 1935.

——. *John Quincy Adams and the Foundations of American Foreign Policy.* New York: Alfred A. Knopf, 1940.

——. *Latin American Policy of the United States.* New York: Harcourt Brace, 1943.

Bernstein, B. J., ed. *The Truman Administration.* New York: Harper and Row, 1966.

——, ed. *Towards a New Past: Dissenting Essays in American History.* New York: Pantheon, 1968.

—— and A. J. Matusow, eds. *Twentieth Century America.* New York: Harcourt, Brace, Jovanovich, 1972.

Beveridge, A. J. *Life of John Marshall.* 4 Vols. Boston: Houghton Mifflin, 1916–19.

Billington, R. A. *America's Frontier Heritage.* New York: Holt, Rinehart and Winston, 1966.

——. *Frederick Jackson Turner, Historian, Scholar, Teacher.* New York: Oxford University Press (esp. chs. 4 and 5), 1973.

Blassingame, J. *The Slave Community: Plantation Life in the Antebellum South.* New York: Oxford University Press, 1972.

——. *Black New Orleans 1860–1880.* Chicago: University of Chicago Press, 1973.

Boorstin, D. *The Lost World of Thomas Jefferson.* Boston: Henry Holt, 1948.

Brooks, V. *Makers and Finders.* 5 Vols. New York: E. P. Dutton, 1944–52.

Bullock, H. A. *A History of Negro Education in the South from 1619 to the Present.* Cambridge, Mass.: Harvard University Press, 1967.

Calhoun, D. *The Intelligence of a People.* Princeton, N. J.: Princeton University Press, 1973.

Caughey, J. W. *Hubert Howe Bancroft: Historian of Western America.* Berkeley: University of California Press, 1945.

Catton, B. *Mr. Lincoln's Army.* Garden City, N. Y.: Doubleday, 1951.

——. *Glory Road.* Garden City, N. Y.: Doubleday, 1952.

——. *Stillness at Appomatox.* Garden City, N. Y.: Doubleday, 1953.

Coles, R. *The Desegregation of the Southern Schools.* Boston: Atlantic Monthly Press, 1963.

——. *Children of Crisis.* Boston: Atlantic Monthly Press, 1967.

——. *Uprooted Children.* Pittsburgh: University of Pittsburgh Press, 1970.

——. *The Middle Americans.* Boston: Atlantic Monthly Press, 1971a.

——. *Migrants, Sharecroppers, Mountaineers.* Boston: Atlantic Monthly Press, 1971b.

——. *Farewell to the South.* Boston: Atlantic Monthly Press, 1972.

Columbus, C. *Letters from the New World.* Barcelona: Pedro Posa, 1493.

Conrad, S. P. *Perish the Thought: The Intellectual Woman in Romantic America.* New York: Oxford University Press, 1976.

Cox, I. J. *The West Florida Controversy, 1798–1913.* Baltimore: Johns Hopkins University Press, 1918.

Craven, A. O. *The Repressible Conflict.* Baton Rouge, La.: Louisiana State University Press, 1939.

——. *The Coming of the Civil War.* New York: Charles Scribner's Sons, 1942.

Crunden, R. M. "Freud, Erikson, and the Historian: A Bibliographic Survey. *Canadian Review of American Studies* 4 (Spring 1973): 48–63.

Cunliffe, M. and R. Winks. *Pastmasters.* New York: Harper and Row, 1969.

Curti, M. *The Making of an American Community: A Case Study of Democracy in a Frontier Community.* Stanford: Stanford University Press, 1959.

Darling, A. B. *Our Rising Empire, 1763–1803.* New Haven: Yale University Press, 1940.

David, P. A., H. G. Gutman, R. Dutch, P. Temin, G. Wright. *Reckoning with Slavery: Critical Essays in the Quantitative History of American Negro Slavery.* New York: Oxford University Press, 1975. Introduction by K. Stampp.

Diggins, J. P. "The Perils of Naturalism: Some Reflections on Daniel J. Boorstin's Approach to American History." *American Quarterly* 23 (May 1971): 153–180.

Duberman, M. *The Uncompleted Past.* New York: Random House, 1969.

Dunn, R. "The Social History of Early New England." *American Quarterly* 24 (December 1972): 661–679.

Franklin, J. H. *The Free Negro in North Carolina 1790–1860.* Chapel Hill, N. C.: University of North Carolina Press, 1943.

——. *From Slavery to Freedom: A History of American Negroes.* New York: Alfred A. Knopf, 1947.

——. *Reconstruction: After the Civil War.* Chicago: University of Chicago Press, 1961.

——. *The Emancipation Proclamation.* Garden City, N. Y.: Doubleday, 1963.

——. *Color and Race.* Boston: Houghton Mifflin, 1968.

Gay, P. *A Loss of Mastery: Puritan Historians in Colonial America,* New York: Alfred A. Knopf, 1968.

Gillespie, C. C. *The Edge of Objectivity: An Essay on the History of Scientific Ideas.* Princeton, N.J.: Princeton University Press, 1960.

Goetzmann, W. H. *Army Exploration in the American West, 1803–1863.* New Haven: Yale University Press, 1959.

——. "Foreword," *General Index to the Papers and Annual Reports of the American Historical Association.* Washington, D. C.: Carrollton Press, 1968.

Goldman, E. F. *John Bach McMaster: American Historian.* Philadelphia: University of Pennsylvania Press, 1945.

——. *The Tragedy of Lyndon Johnson.* New York: Alfred A. Knopf, 1969.

Grattan, C. H. *Why We Fought.* New York: Vanguard, 1929.

——. *Preface to Chaos: War in the Making.* New York: Dodge, 1936.

——. *The Deadly Parallel.* New York: Stackpole, 1939.

Gutman, H. G. *Slavery and the Numbers Game: A Critique of "Time on the Cross."* Urbana: University of Illinois Press, 1975.

Handlin, O., A. M. Schlesinger, S. E. Morison, F. Merk, A. M. Schlesinger, Jr., P. H. Buck. *Harvard Guide to American History.* Cambridge, Mass.: Belknap Press, 1954. O. Handlin, ed., 2nd edition, 1967; F. Friedel, ed., 3rd edition, 1974.

Hanke, L. *Aristotle and the American Indian.* Bloomington, Ind.: University of Indiana Press, 1959.

Haskell, T. L. "The True and Tragical History of Time on the Cross." *New York Review of Books* (October 2, 1975): 33–39. Review of David, *et al.* (1975), Gutman (1975), and Walton (1975).

Herreshoff, D. *American Disciples of Marx.* Detroit: Wayne State University Press, 1967.

Higham, J. "The Historical Profession," "Theory," "American History." in J. Higham, L. Krieger, and F. Gilbert, *History.* Englewood Cliffs, N. J.: Prentice-Hall, 1965.

Hofstadter, R. *Social Darwinism in American Thought.* Boston: Beacon Press, 1944.

——. *The Progressive Historians, Turner, Parrington, Beard.* New York: Alfred A. Knopf, 1968.

Hovenkamp, H. "Science and Religion in America: 1800–1860," unpublished PhD dissertation. University of Texas at Austin, 1976.

Jackson, W. T. *Wagon Roads West.* Berkeley: University of California Press, 1952.

Jacobs, W. *Diplomacy and Indian Gifts.* Stanford: Stanford University Press, 1950.

——. *Wilderness Politics and Indian Gifts.* Lincoln, Neb.: University of Nebraska Press, 1966.

——. *Dispossessing the American Indian.* New York: Scribners, 1972.

Jordy, W. *Henry Adams, Scientific Historian.* New Haven: Yale University Press, 1952.

Kraus, M. *The Writing of American History.* Norman, Okla.: University of Oklahoma Press, 1953.

Kuklick, B. "Myth and Symbol in American Studies." *American Quarterly* 24 (October 1972): 1435–1450.

LeFeber, W. *The New Empire: An Interpretation of American Expansion, 1860–1898.* Ithaca: Cornell University Press, 1963.

——. *America, Russia and the Cold War, 1945–1966.* New York: Wiley, 1967.

Lemisch, J. "The American Revolution Seen From the Bottom Up," in B. J. Bernstein, ed., *Toward a New Past: Dissenting Essays in American History.* New York: Pantheon, 1968: 3–29.

Levin, D. *History as Romantic Art.* Stanford: Stanford University Press, 1959.

Loewenberg, B. J. *American History in American Thought: Christopher Columbus to Henry Adams.* New York: Simon and Schuster, 1972.

Metcalf, R. "Who Should Rule at Home: Native American Politics and Indian-White Relations." *Journal of American History* 61 (December 1974): 651–665.

Morison, S. E. *Admiral of the Ocean Sea.* 2 Vols. Boston: Little, Brown, 1942.

Nevins, A. *Ordeal of the Union.* 2 Vols. New York: Charles Scribner's Sons, 1947.

——. *The Emergence of Lincoln.* 2 Vols. New York: Charles Scribner's Sons, 1950.

Nicolay, J. G. and J. Hay. *Abraham Lincoln: A History.* 10 Vols. New York: Century, 1890.

Nye, R. *George Bancroft, Brahmin Rebel.* New York: Alfred A. Knopf, 1944.

Parkman, F. *France and England in North America.* Boston: Houghton Mifflin, 1869–1892.

——. *The Old Regime in Canada.* Boston: Houghton Mifflin, 1887.

Peckham, M. "Aestheticism to Modernism: Fulfillment or Revolution?" in *The Triumph of Romanticism.* Columbia, S. C.: University of South Carolina Press, 1970.

Peel, J. D. Y. *Herbert Spencer: The Evolution of a Sociologist.* New York: Basic Books, 1971.

Perkins, D. *Hands Off: A History of the Monroe Doctrine.* Boston: Little, Brown, 1941.

——. *The American Approach to Foreign Policy.* Cambridge, Mass.: Harvard University Press, 1955.

Persons, S. "The Cyclical Theory of History in Eighteenth Century America." *American Quarterly* 6 (Summer 1954): 147–163.

Phalen, J. *The Millenial Kingdom of the Franciscans in the New World: A Study of the Writings of Gerónimo de Mendieta 1525–1604.* Berkeley: University of California Press, 1956.

Plumb, J. H. *The Death of the Past.* Boston: Houghton Mifflin, 1970.

Potter, D. *Lincoln and his Party in the Secession Crisis.* New Haven: Yale University Press, 1942.

Powell, J. W. *Report upon the Lands of the Arid Regions of the United States.* Washington, D. C.: U. S. Government Printing Office, 1878.

Pratt, J. *Expansionists of 1812.* New York: Macmillan, 1925.

——. *Expansionists of 1898.* Baltimore: Johns Hopkins University Press, 1936.

Prucha, F. P. *American Indian Policy in the Formative Years.* Cambridge, Mass.: Belknap Press, 1962.

Quarles, B. *Frederick Douglass.* Washington, D. C.: Associated Publishers, 1948.

——. *The Negro in the Civil War.* Boston: Little, Brown, 1953.

——. *The Negro in the American Revolution.* Chapel Hill, N. C.: University of North Carolina Press, 1961.

——. *Lincoln and the Negro.* New York: Oxford University Press, 1962.

——. *Black Abolitionists.* New York: Oxford University Press, 1969.

Ramsdell, C. W. "Changing Interpretations of the Civil War." *Journal of Southern History* 3 (Feb.–Nov., 1937): 3ff.

Randall, J. G. *Civil War and Reconstruction.* Boston: D. C. Heath, 1937.

Redding, J. S. *The Lonesome Road: The Story of the Negro's Part in America.* New York: Doubleday, 1958.

——. *The Negro.* Washington, D. C.: Potomac Books, 1967.

Rhodes, J. F. *History of the United States from the Compromise of 1850.* 7 Vols. New York: Macmillan, 1893–1906.

Rogin, M. P. *Fathers and Children: Andrew Jackson and the Subjugation of the American Indian.* New York: Alfred A. Knopf, 1975.

Samuels, E. *Henry Adams.* 3 Vols. Cambridge, Mass: Belknap Press, 1947, 1958, 1964.

Sandburg, C. *Abraham Lincoln.* 6 Vols. New York: Harcourt, Brace, 1926–1939.

Schlesinger, A. M., Jr. *The Vital Center.* Boston: Houghton Mifflin, 1949.

——. *A Thousand Days: John F. Kennedy in the White House.* Boston: Houghton Mifflin, 1965.

Schouler, J. *History of the United States under the Constitution.* 6 Vols. New York: Dodd, Mead, 1880–1899.

Seymour, C. *Woodrow Wilson and the World War: A Chronicle of Our Own Times.* New York: Yale University Press, 1921.

Sklar, R. "The Problem of an American Studies 'Philosophy': A Bibliography of New Directions." *American Quarterly* 27 (August 1975): 245–262.

Skotheim, R. *American Intellectual Histories and Historians.* Princeton, N. J.: Princeton University Press, 1966.

——, ed. *The Historian and the Climate of Opinion.* Reading, Mass.: Addison Wesley, 1969.

Smith, J. H. *The Annexation of Texas.* New York: Baker and Taylor, 1911.

——. *The War with Mexico.* New York: Macmillan, 1919.

Sorensen, T. C. *Decision-Making in the White House.* New York: Columbia University Press, 1963.

——. *Kennedy.* New York: Harper and Row, 1965.

——. *The Kennedy Legacy.* New York: Macmillan, 1969.

Stanton, W. *The Leopard's Spots: Scientific Attitudes towards Race in America, 1815–59.* Chicago: University of Chicago Press, 1960.

Thompson, D. H. *The Highlanders of the South.* New York: Eaton and Mains, 1910.

——. *The Negro Leadership Class.* Englewood Cliffs, N. J.: Prentice-Hall, 1963.

Thorpe, E. E. *The Mind of the Negro: An Intellectual History of Afro-Americans.* Baton Rouge: Ortlieb Press, 1961.

——. *Eros and Freedom in Southern Life and Thought.* Durham, N. C.: Seeman Printery, 1967.

——. *The Central Theme of Black History.* Durham, N. C.: Seeman Printery, 1969.

——. *Black Historians: A Critique.* New York: Morrow, 1971.

——. *The Old South: A Psychohistory.* Durham, N. C.: Seeman Printery, 1972.

Turner, F. J. *The Frontier in American History.* New York: Henry Holt, 1920.

Tuveson, E. L. *Redeemer Nation.* Chicago: University of Chicago Press, 1968.

Utley, R. M. *The Last Days of the Sioux Nation.* New Haven: Yale University Press, 1963.

——. *Frontiersmen in Blue: The U. S. Army and the Indians 1848–1905.* New York: Macmillan, 1967.

———. *Frontier Regulars: The United States Army and the Indian 1866–1891.* New York: Macmillan, 1974.

Van Tassel, D. D. *Recording America's Past.* Chicago: University of Chicago Press, 1960.

Von Holst, H. *The Constitutional and Political History of the United States.* 8 Vols. Chicago: Callaghan, 1876–1892.

Walton, G. M., ed. "A Symposium on Time on the Cross." *Explorations in Economic History* 12 (Fall 1975): 333–457.

Webb, W. P. *The Great Plains.* New York: Ginn and Co., 1931.

Wecter, D. *The Hero in America: A Chronicle of Hero Worship.* New York: Charles Scribner's Sons, 1941.

Weems, M. *A History of the Life and Death, Virtues and Exploits of General George Washington with Curious Anecdotes equally honorable to himself and exemplary to his young Country Men.* Philadelphia: M. Carey, 1800. Reprint edition, ed. M. Cunliffe. Cambridge: Harvard, 1962.

Whitaker, A. P. *The Mississippi Question, 1795–1803: A Study in Trade, Politics, and Diplomacy.* New York: Appleton-Century, 1934.

White, H. *Metahistory: The Historical Imagination in Nineteenth Century Europe.* Baltimore: Johns Hopkins University, 1973.

White, M. *Social Thought in America: The Revolt Against Formalism.* New York: Beacon Press, 1949.

Williams, W. A. *The Tragedy of American Diplomacy.* Cleveland: World, 1959.

———. *The Roots of the Modern American Empire.* New York: Random House, 1967.

Winks, R., ed. *The Historian as Detective: Essays on Evidence.* New York: Harper and Row, 1968.

Wish, H. *The American Historian.* New York: Oxford University Press, 1960.

———, ed. *American Historians.* New York: Oxford University Press, 1962.

Woodward, C. V. "Review of R. Fogel and S. Engerman, *Time on the Cross,*" *New York Review of Books* 21 (May 2, 1974).

William H. Geotzmann is Stiles Professor of American Studies and Professor of History at the University of Texas at Austin. His fields are intellectual and cultural history and the history of science in America. His books include Army Exploration in the American West, 1803–63 *and* Exploration and Empire: The Role of the Explorer and the Scientist in the Exploration and Development of the American West, 1800–1900, *winner of the 1967 Pulitzer Prize in History. Professor Goetzmann is currently a fellow at the Center for Advanced Study in the Behavioral Sciences at Stanford University, California.*

The Resurgence of American Immigration History

RUDOLPH J. VECOLI

A decade ago in a paper entitled "Ethnicity: A Neglected Dimension of American History," I argued that historians had by and large ignored the multi-cultural character of the American people.[1] I went on to suggest that this myopia was the consequence of an assimilationist ideology which had shaped the perspectives and careers of several generations of scholars. Ten years later we are inundated by a virtual flood of books, articles, and dissertations dealing with the roles of race, nationality, and religion in American history. Conferences, learned papers, and courses on ethnic themes proliferate at an amazing rate. How does one account for this dramatic turnabout?

While it is beyond the scope of this essay to explore fully the causes of this change, allow me to suggest that the new pluralistic outlook of the historical profession is reflective of a basic reorientation which has taken place in the larger society. Briefly, the turmoil which convulsed American society in the 1960s shattered the Melting Pot ideology. Following the thrust of the Black Power movement, a chorus of ethnic groups renounced Anglo-conformity and celebrated their distinctive heritages. In politics, in the arts, in everyday life, a heightened ethnic consciousness permeated the society. The seventies, as Michael Novak observed, was to be the decade of the ethnics.[2] Bemused by this unexpected phenomenon, historians and social scientists launched a many-sided inquiry into the nature and origins of ethnic pluralism in the United States. Despite the groundbreaking work of Marcus Lee Hansen, Theodore Blegen, and Oscar Handlin,[3] the field of immigration history had been marginal to the interests of most historians. The current concern with ethnic diversity has placed it at the very center of scholarly research and discussion. Questions regarding immigration engage the minds of historians of the family, labor, and the city, as well as specialists in ethnic history. Who were the immigrants? Why did they emigrate? How did they respond to America? In what ways and at what rates did they assimilate? What did they retain of Old World cultures? How and why did they create ethnic communities? How have they and their children affected American culture, society, and politics? Old questions, but now being asked with renewed vigor and addressed with new research methodologies.

Historical scholarship rests upon an infrastructure of research facilities and resources. Two decades ago these were largely nonexistent for the study of immigration history. Thanks to the stimulus of the "new pluralism," that has now changed. The National Endowment for the Humanities, the Ethnic Heritage Studies Program of the U.S. Office of Education, the National Historical Publications and Records Commission, private foundations, and ethnic communities

Rudolph J. Vecoli is Professor of History and Director of the Immigration History Research Center at the University of Minnesota. He holds a B.A. from the University of Connecticut, an M.A. from the University of Pennsylvania, and his Ph.D. from the University of Wisconsin. He has served as Visiting Professor at Uppsala University in Sweden, and Senior Fulbright-Hays Research Scholar in Italy. He is the author of The People of New Jersey *and of numerous articles dealing with the history of American ethnic groups and immigration, particularly the Italian Americans. He serves on the editorial boards of* Ethnicity, Italian Americana, International Migration Review, *and* Studi Emigrazione *(Rome). He is a member of the board of directors of the American Italian Historical Association and the Immigration History Society.*

have all provided generous funding for building collections, preparing reference tools, and sponsoring research. Before reviewing the scholarship of recent years, it might be helpful to describe the infrastructure which has made it possible. The following components will be discussed: Research Centers and Collections; Microform and Reprint Editions; Reference Tools; and Historical Societies and Publications.

Research Centers and Collections

Immigration has long been a topic of controversy in the United States. A vast literature, partly polemical, partly scholarly, deals with "the immigrant as problem." Such writings, with some exceptions, were based on English language sources and from an Anglo-American point-of-view. The "new immigration history" is concerned with the *interior history* of the ethnic communities. Seeking to write their history "from the inside out," as it were, the student requires primary sources which record the experiences of the immigrants in their own words. Letters, diaries, organizational records, newspapers, church archives, and *belle lettres;* all immigrant groups generated such documentation in abundance. However, these materials were long neglected by the nation's archives and libraries.[4] While a few major institutions like the New York Public Library and the Library of Congress acquired ethnic publications as a matter of course, there was no systematic effort to gather and preserve such sources. As a consequence much of value has been lost. Fortunately ethnic communities assumed the task of historical preservation themselves. The excellent collections of the American Jewish Archives, the Polish Museum of America, and the Norwegian American Historical Associations are fruits of this foresight.[5] In the past decade a broad spectrum of institutions across the country have begun actively to collect ethnic records. State historical societies, city and county libraries, universities, and research institutes are busily searching the attics and basements of ethnic America. Outstanding examples of such efforts are the Immigration Sources Project of the Bentley Historical Library, University of Michigan; the Ethnic Studies Program of the Pennsylvania Historical and Museum Commission; and the Slavic American Collection of the Lovejoy Library, Southern Illinois University at Edwardsville.[6]

A recent development has been the emergence of research centers devoted exclusively to the study of migration and ethnicity. Such centers not only develop archival and library resources, they also seek to promote scholarly work through seminars, conferences, and publications. The Immigration History Research Center, University of Minnesota, was established in 1965 with the objective of documenting and studying immigration from Eastern, Central, and Southern Europe and the Middle East. Several years later, the Center for

Migration Studies, Staten Island, New York, was founded with a primary emphasis upon Italian immigration and the role of the Roman Catholic Church *vis-a-vis* the phenomenon of migration. The Balch Institute of Philadelphia, a privately endowed institution dedicated to the cultivation of ethnic, racial, and minority group history, came into being in 1971. Meanwhile the Asian American Studies Center at the University of California-Los Angeles was developing a collection and publishing materials on immigration from the Far East. The Research Institute on Immigration and Ethnic Studies of the Smithsonian Institution (1973) seeks to facilitate and disseminate research on immigration into the United States, especially since the Immigration Act of 1965.[7] In addition there are numerous smaller centers which focus upon single ethnic groups such as the Basque Studies Center, University of Nevada, Reno; the Slovenian Research Center, Kent State University, Ohio; and the Finnish-American Historical Archives, Suomi College, Hancock, Michigan. Although these research institutions vary considerably in scope, resources, and activities, they all actively promote immigration and ethnic studies. Other specialized libraries too numerous to mention collect ethnic materials although their primary interest may be labor, business, or religious history.[8] Responding to these widespread initiatives, the Society of American Archivists has established a Committee on Ethnic Archives to help coordinate and guide collecting in this area.

Microfilm and Reprint Editions

The heightened interest in immigration history has inspired the large-scale publication of both scholarly literature and source materials in microform and reprint editions. The full forty-one volumes of the U.S. Immigration Commission Reports (Washington, D.C., 1911), for example, have been reissued in both hard copy and microfilm.[9] Several thousand volumes pertaining to immigration have been reprinted by Arno Press, R and E Research Associates, and other reprint houses.[10] Arno has also published special reprint collections on Asian Americans, Irish Americans, Italian Americans, American Jews, and Scandinavian Americans. These reprint collections tend to be rather indiscriminate miscellanies of works of scholarship, immigrant writings, novels, and ephemera. Previously unpublished doctoral dissertations and master's theses are included. Many of these student papers are also available in microfilm or xerox copies from Xerox University Microfilms. Micropublishers have reproduced manuscript collections, pamphlet libraries, organizational archives, and periodical and newspaper files pertaining to the immigrant experience.[11] In addition, many microfilming projects such as those of the Immigration History Research Center have been funded by grants from the National Historical Publications and Records Commission and the National Endowment for the Humanities. The microfilming of the ethnic press has been an especially high priority for reasons of preservation as well as dissemination. The Ethnic Records Microform Project, administered by the Center for Research Libraries of Chicago, has concentrated on the photocopying of foreign language newspapers.[12] Availability of particular titles can be determined by consulting *Newspapers in Microform* published by the Library of Congress (LC), while current microfilming projects are reported in the *Newspaper and Gazette Report,* office of the Newspaper Microfilming Coordinator, Serial Division, LC. Through these reprint and microfilm editions, scholars anywhere now have ready access to long out-of-print works as well as to unique source materials.

Reference Tools

The immigration historian today is confronted with an *embarras de richesses.* Fortunately the bibliographers have been hard at work and imposed some order upon this avalanche of publications. Several recent bibliographies have taken on the formidable task of providing general guides to the literature on immigration and ethnicity. Wayne C. Miller, *et al.*, eds., *A Comprehensive Bibliography for the Study of American Minorities* (2 vols., New York: New York University Press, 1976) is indeed the most comprehensive; two other excellent works are: John D. Buenker and Nicholas C. Burkel, *Immigration and Ethnicity. A Guide to Information Sources* (Detroit: Gale Research Co., 1977) and Lois Buttlar and Lubomry R. Wynar, *Building Ethnic Collections: An Annotated Guide for School Media Centers and Public Libraries* (Littleton, Colo.: Libraries Unlimited, 1977). Each of these provides annotated citations to the English language literature for several score ethnic groups. Further recently published reference works useful to the student of immigration history are: Lubomry R. Wynar, *Encyclopedic Directory of Ethnic Organizations in the United States* (Littleton, Colo.: Libraries Unlimited, 1975) and (with Ann T. Wynar) *Encyclopedic Directory of Ethnic Newspapers and Periodicals in the United States* (2nd. ed., Littleton, Colo.: Libraries Unlimited, 1976); and Paul Wasserman and Jean Morgan, *Ethnic Information Sources of the United States* (Detroit: Gale Research Co., 1976). In addition, numerous bibliographies have been prepared for particular ethnic groups. Examples are: William Wong Lum and Paul M. Ong, comps., *Theses and Dissertations on Asians in the United States* (Asian American Research Project, University of California, Davis, 1974) with two supplements; Adam S. Eterovich, *A Guide and Bibliography to Research on Yugoslavs in the United States and Canada* (San Francisco: R and E Research Associates, 1975); Joseph W. Zurawski, *Polish American History and Culture: A Classified Bibliography* (Chicago: Polish Museum of Chicago, 1975); Don Heinrich Tolzmann, *German Americana: A Bibliography* (Metuchen, N.J.: Scarecrow, 1975); Francesco Cordasco, *Italian Americans: A Guide to Information*

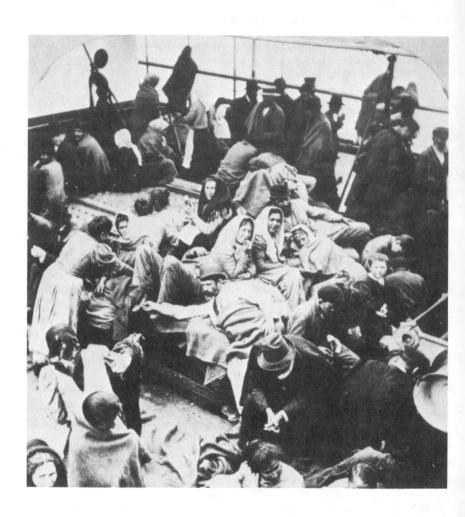

Immigrants arriving aboard ship, probably at Ellis Island, New York, copyright 1902. Photo by William Rau, Prints and Photographs Division, Library of Congress.

Sources (Detroit: Gale Research Co., 1978); and Michael Cutsumbis, *A Bibliographical Guide to Materials on Greeks in the United States, 1890–1968* (New York: Center for Migration Studies, 1970). Other bibliographies focus upon a geographical area: John E. Bodnar, comp., *Ethnic History in Pennsylvania: A Selected Bibliography* (Harrisburg, Pa.: Pennsylvania Historical and Museum Commission, 1974); and Lubomry R. Wynar, *et al.*, *Ethnic Groups in Ohio with Special Emphasis on Cleveland: An Annotated Bibliographical Guide* (Cleveland: Ethnic Heritage Studies, Cleveland State University, 1975).

Current publications in immigration and ethnic history can best be followed through *America: History and Life* (American Bibliographical Center-Clio Press, Santa Barbara, Cal.) which contains article abstracts, an index to book reviews, and a bibliography of books, articles, and dissertations. An Annual Index with subject headings for "immigration" and related topics facilitates access. Journal articles are indexed and abstracted in the annual *Ethnic Studies Bibliography* (Pittsburgh: University Center for International Studies, University of Pittsburgh, Vol. 1, 1975–) and in the quarterly *International Migration Review* (Staten Island, N.Y.: Center for Migration Studies, Vol. 1, 1966–).

While bibliographical aids are many, guides to original source materials in immigration history are as yet few. Of course, the vast records of the federal government, such as the Immigration and Naturalization Service files and the Department of State diplomatic and consular correspondence, to mention only two relevant record groups, are well catalogued and often available on microfilm.[13] However, the documentation of the ethnic groups themselves is widely scattered in libraries and archives across the country and not readily retrievable. The lack of union lists of newspapers, catalogues of library holdings, and guides to archives constitutes a major obstacle to research. Such reference tools, however, are beginning to appear. For example, Yuji Ichioka, *et al.*, *A Buried Past: An Annotated Bibliography of the Japanese American Research Project Collection* (Berkeley and Los Angeles: University of California Press, 1974) is an excellent guide to Japanese language sources, while Esther Jerabek, *Czechs and Slovaks in North America: A Bibliography* (New York: Czechoslovak Society of Arts and Sciences in America, 1976) is an invaluable compilation of over 7,600 items, for the most part in Czech and Slovak. Jan Wepsiec, *Polish American Serial Publications 1842–1966: An Annotated Bibliography* (Chicago, 1968) is a model guide which needs to be emulated for other ethnic groups. The Immigration History Research Center has initiated an "Ethnic Bibliography Series" of which two have been published: Joseph Szeplaki, comp. and ed., *Hungarians in the United States and Canada: A Bibliography* (St. Paul, Mn.: Immigration History Research Center, University of Minnesota, 1977); and Robert P. Gakovich and Milan M. Radovich, comps., *Serbs in the United States and Canada: A Comprehensive Bibliography* (St. Paul, Mn.: Immigration History Research Center, University of Minnesota, 1976). Useful is Stanley B. Kimball, ed., *Slavic-American Imprints: A Classified Catalog* (Edwardsville, Ill.: Lovejoy Library, Southern Illinois University, 1972). Other guides report on sources for particular geographic areas: Robert E. Wilson and Frank A. Zabrosky, comps., *Resources on the Ethnic and the Immigrant in the Pittsburgh Area: A Preliminary Guide* (Pittsburgh, 1976); and Joseph G. Svoboda and David G. Dunning, comps., *Preliminary Guide to Ethnic Source Materials in Great Plains Repositories* (Lincoln, Neb.: University Libraries and Center for Great Plain Studies, University of Nebraska, 1978).

Historical Societies and Publications

The Immigration History Society, founded in 1965, is a professional association of scholars. Its current membership of over 500 drawn from various disciplines and countries reflects the healthy state of the field. The Society sponsors sessions at learned society meetings, seeks to advance the study of immigration history, and publishes a semi-annual newsletter.[14] In addition to reports on current publications, conferences, and research in progress, the newsletter features historiographical essays. Moreover, the "rediscovery of ethnicity" has revitalized the older immigrant historical societies and encouraged the formation of new ones. The Scotch-Irish Society formed in 1889 was the earliest of these, but the Norwegian American Historical Association (1925) has served as a model of scholarly research and publication.[15] The Chinese Historical Society of America, the American Hungarian Studies Foundation, the American Italian Historical Association, the Polish American Historical Association, the Swedish Pioneer Historical Society, the Slovak Studies Association, and the American Historical Society of Germans from Russia are some of the ethnically based organizations which are currently active in the field of immigration history. The societies maintain libraries and archives, host conferences, publish journals and books, and recognize scholarly achievement.[16]

Writings in immigration history appear in a broad spectrum of publications. Depending upon their emphasis such articles may be published in thematic journals such as *Labor History,* in state or regional history journals, or in ethnic historical society journals. Recourse must be had to the indexes cited above to follow this widely dispersed literature. There is no journal of immigration history as such, but three recently established journals publish occasional articles in American immigration history. All three are interdisciplinary and global in scope. The *International Migration Review* (Vol. I, 1966–) tends to stress contemporary issues of migratioin policy and migrant adjustment.[17] *The Journal of Ethnic Studies* (Vol. I, 1973–) publishes a mix of sociological, historical, and literary studies with an emphasis upon racial minorities. *Ethnicity* (Vol. I, 1974–) has a strong orientation toward contemporary issues of group life.[18] A recently established journal, *MELUS* (Vol. 5, 1978–) is devoted to the history and criticism of the multi-ethnic literature of the United States.[19] Immigration historians are currently debating the need for a journal devoted exclusively to their specialty.

Recent Scholarship

Given the outpouring of books and articles on immigration history in recent years, we can at best sample the literature in this brief review.[20] For writings prior to 1972, the reader is referred to the comprehensive historiographical essays in William H. Cartwright and Richard L. Watson, Jr., eds., *The Reinterpretation of American History and Culture* (Washington, D.C.: National Council for the Social Studies, 1973).[21]

First, one must observe that no major synthesis has appeared in recent years of the character of Marcus Lee Hansen's *The Immigrant in American History* or Oscar Handlin's *The Uprooted.*[22] The essays in John Higham's *Send These to Me: Jews and Other Immigrants in Urban America* (New York: Atheneum, 1975) offer a suggestive theoretical and comparative perspective, while American immigration is placed in a global context in Franklin D. Scott, *The Peopling of America: Perspectives on Immigration* (Washington, D.C.: American Historical Association, AHA Pamphlets 241, 1972). Recent texts incorporating current scholarship are: Philip Taylor, *The Distant Magnet: European Emigration to the U.S.A.* (New York: Harper & Row, 1972), especially good on the causes and commerce of the trans-Atlantic migrations, and Maxine Seller, *To Seek America: A History of Ethnic Life in the United States* (Jerome S. Ozer, 1977), which emphasizes the persistence of ethnic cultures.

On the causes of the mass migrations, the conceptual framework developed by Brinley Thomas and Frank Thistlethwaite has greatly influenced subsequent research.[23] Much of this work has been carried on in the countries of emigration. The "Sweden and America After 1860" project at the University of Uppsala has produced a series of dissertations and studies over a ten-year period dealing with various aspects of the Swedish exodus. The results of this project are summarized in Harald Runblom and Hans Norman, *From Sweden to America* (Minneapolis: University of Minnesota Press, 1976). The Uppsala project inspired analogous research in neighboring countries: Kristian Hvidt, *Flight to America: The Social Background of 300,000 Danish Emigrants* (New York: Academic Press, 1975) and Reino Kero, *Migration from Finland to North America in the Years between the United States Civil War and the First World War* (Turku,

Finland: Migration Studies C 1, Institute for Migration, 1974).[24] The
"push" factors in various countries are explored in essays edited by
Donald Fleming and Bernard Bailyn, *Dislocation and Emigration: The
Social Background of American Immigration* (Cambridge, Mass.:
Perspectives in American History, VII, 1973), while Charlotte Erickson,
ed., *Emigration from Europe 1815–1914: Select Documents* (London:
Adam & Charles Black, 1976) provides supporting materials. On the
Atlantic crossing, Maldwyn Allen Jones, *Destination America: 1815–
1914* (New York: Holt, Rinehart & Winston, 1976) is a vivid pictorial
and textual record.

The contemporary search for "roots" among Americans has inspired a good deal of writing which seeks to interpret the experience
of particular immigrant groups. Certain works of an evocative quality
have attracted a broad readership: Richard Gambino, *Blood of My
Blood: The Dilemma of the Italian-Americans* (Garden City, N.Y.:

*Immigrants at Ellis Island, New York, about 1910. Photo by George Bain, Prints and Photographs
Division, Library of Congress.*

Doubleday & Co., 1974); Andrew M. Greeley, *The Most Distressful Nation: The Taming of the American Irish* (Chicago: Quadrangle Books, 1972); and Irving Howe, *World of Our Fathers* (on East European Jews in America) (New York: Simon and Schuster, 1976). Other, more traditional scholarly histories of ethnic groups include: Henry L. Feingold, *Zion in America: The Jewish Experience from Colonial Times to the Present* (New York: Twayne, 1974); Lawrence J. McCaffrey, *The Irish Diaspora in America* (Bloomington: Indiana University Press, 1976); Gerald F. De Jong, *The Dutch in America* (Boston: Twayne, 1975); George J. Prpic, *The South Slav Immigration in America* (Boston: Twayne, 1978) and La Vern Rippley, *The German-Americans* (Boston: Twayne, 1976).

Reflective of the rising ethnic consciousness is the attention which historians have paid to immigrant groups hitherto largely neglected. Examples are: William A. Douglas and Jon Bilbao, *Amerikanuak: Basques in the New World* (Reno: University of Nevada Press, 1975); and H. Brett Melendy, *Asians in America: Filipinos, Koreans, and East Indians* (Boston: Twayne, 1977). The following collective works report on studies in progress: Norris Hundley, ed., *The Asian American: The Historical Experience* (Santa Barbara, Cal.: Clio Books, 1976); Michael G. Karni, *et al.*, *The Finnish Experience in the Western Great Lakes Region: New Perspectives* (Turku, Finland: Migration Studies C 3, Institute for Migration, 1975); Hilary Conroy and T. Scott Miyakawa, eds., *East Across the Pacific: Historical and Sociological Studies of Japanese Immigration and Assimilation* (Santa Barbara, Cal.: Clio Press, 1972); S.M. Tomasi, ed., *Perspectives in Italian Immigration and Ethnicity* (New York: Center for Migration Studies, 1977); and Sidney Heitman, ed., *Germans from Russia in Colorado* (Ann Arbor, Mich.: University Microfilms International, 1978).

Several documentary volumes have also appeared in recent years: Charlotte Erickson, *Invisible Immigrants: The Adaptation of English and Scottish Immigrants in Nineteenth-Century America* (Coral Gables, Fla.: University of Miami, 1972), an extraordinary collection of family letters with a valuable commentary; Victor G. and Brett de Bary Nee, *Longtime Californ': A Documentary Study of an American Chinatown* (New York: Pantheon, 1972), a vivid rendering of the Chinese immigrant experience through oral memoirs; and H. Arnold Barton, ed., *Letters from the Promised Land: Swedes in America, 1840–1914* (Minneapolis: University of Minnesota Press, 1975), a wide-ranging assortment of documents.

The Bicentennial celebration stimulated many publications devoted to exploring the ethnic diversity of particular states and regions. Certain parts of the country such as the Great Plains rediscovered their immigrant roots.[25] Among the resulting volumes are: Helen Z. Papanikolas, ed., *The Peoples of Utah* (Salt Lake City: Utah State Historical Society, 1976); Galen Bulen, *et al.*, *Broken Hoops and Plains People: A Catalogue of Ethnic Resources in the Hu-*

manities: Nebraska and Surrounding Areas (Lincoln, Neb.: Nebraska Curriculum Development Center, 1976); Gordon O. Hendrickson, ed., Peopling the High Plains: Wyoming's European Heritage (Cheyenne, Wyo.: Wyoming State Archives and Historical Department, 1977); James A. Halseth and Bruce A. Glasrud, eds., The Northwest Mosaic: Minority Conflicts in Pacific Northwest History (Boulder, Col.: Pruett, 1977); and Barbara Cunningham, ed., The New Jersey Ethnic Experience (Union City, N.J.: Wm. H. Wise & Co., 1977).

In recent years American historians have sought to apply theories of modernization to an understanding of American social history. Immigration viewed as a passage from traditionalism to modernity has particularly lent itself to such interpretations. The monographic literature, therefore, has increasingly addressed itself to the processes of adjustment whereby immigrant peasants accommodated themselves to an industrial, urban social order. Was the impact of migration totally disruptive of their pre-modern cultures and social relationships? Was their ethnic heritage an asset or liability in the struggle for survival and advancement? What was the nature of their ethnic communities and how did they affect the place of the immigrant in the larger society? In grappling with these questions, historians have employed new methodologies which facilitate the study of the lives of common people.[26] Cliometrics, the application of the computer to the analysis of statistical data, has permitted the reconstruction of certain behavior of individuals or groups over time. A second innovation has been the rediscovery of oral history. Through the use of recorders, the memories of immigrants have been tapped and taped.[27] Most important, however, has been the growing mastery by students of immigrant languages and cultures which enables them to utilize the abundant sources which document the interior history of the ethnic communities. In all these ways, the allegedly "inarticulate" immigrants now speak to us in eloquent voices.

Although the trend is toward a joining of methodologies, one can distinguish between those works which emphasize quantitative analysis and those which emphasize ethnocultural analysis. In the first category are most of the social mobility studies. Since the publication of Stephan Thernstrom's Poverty and Progress,[28] questions of geographical and occupational mobility have absorbed the attention of many historians. Through the meticulous compilation and analysis of statistical data they have sought to measure changes in occupation, residence, educational achievement, property ownership, and other indices of social status. Increasingly they have attempted comparative studies of social mobility among various immigrant groups. To what degree was America the "Land of Opportunity" for each of them? Thernstrom's The Other Bostonians: Poverty and Progress in the American Metropolis, 1880–1970 (Cambridge, Mass.: Harvard University Press, 1973) is a prime example of the genre. Other works in this vein include: Howard P. Chudacoff,

Mobile Americans: Residential and Social Mobility in Omaha, 1880–1920 (New York: Oxford University Press, 1972); Howard M. Gitelman, *Workingmen of Waltham: Mobility in American Urban Industrial Development 1850–1890* (Baltimore: The Johns Hopkins University Press, 1974); Thomas Kessner, *The Golden Door: Italian and Jewish Immigrant Mobility in New York City* (New York: Oxford University Press, 1977); Dean R. Esslinger, *Immigrants and the City: Ethnicity and Mobility in a Nineteenth Century Midwestern Community* (Port Washington, N.Y.: Kennikat, 1975); Clyde and Salley Griffen, *Natives and Newcomers: The Ordering of Opportunity in Mid-Nineteenth Century Poughkeepsie* (Cambridge, Mass.: Harvard University Press, 1977); and Michael P. Weber, *Social Change in an Industrial Town: Patterns of Progress in Warren Pennsylvania, from Civil War to World War I* (University Park, Pa.: Pennsylvania State University Press, 1975).

Reflecting the current vogue of urban history, all of these studies focus on cities. One of the few monographs which deals with social mobility in a rural setting is Gordon W. Kirk, Jr., *The Promise of American Life: Social Mobility in a Nineteenth-Century Immigrant Community, Holland, Michigan 1847–1894* (Philadelphia: The American Philosophical Society, 1978).[29] Although the quantitative approach has surfaced hidden dimensions of the social structure, the ideological bias underlying this approach has been perceptively identified by James A. Henretta, "The Study of Social Mobility: Ideological Assumptions and Conceptual Bias," *Labor History,* XVIII (Spring 1977), 165–178.

Henretta's maxim that "the point of departure for the study of any cultural group must be its own values and aspirations" may serve as the *motif* for the ethnocultural approach to immigration history. While often utilizing statistical evidence, these works are distinguished by extensive research in ethnic sources and sensitivity to cultural influences. The typical monograph deals with the experience of one or perhaps several immigrant groups within a particular city. Their distinctive accommodation to the urban, industrial environment, including their forms of mobility, is interpreted as being shaped in large part by their particular cultural patterns. Such works usually devote considerable attention to the Old World backgrounds, institutions, and internal politics of the ethnic communities. Among the noteworthy titles in this category are: Josef Barton, *Peasants and Strangers: Italians, Romanians and Slovaks in an American City* (Cambridge, Mass.: Harvard University Press, 1975); John Bodnar, *Immigration and Industrialization: Ethnicity in an American Mill Town, 1870–1940* (Pittsburgh: University of Pittsburgh Press, 1977); Virginia Yans-McLaughlin, *Family and Community: Italian Immigrants in Buffalo, 1880–1930* (Ithaca, N.Y.: Cornell University Press, 1977); John W. Briggs, *An Italian Passage: Immigrants to Three American Cities, 1890–1930* (New Haven, Conn.: Yale University

Immigrant arriving at New York City. Photo copyrighted 1900 by R. F. Turnbull, Prints and Photographs Division, Library of Congress.

Press, 1978); John Modell, *The Economics and Politics of Racial Adjustment: The Japanese of Los Angeles, 1900–1942* (Urbana, Ill.: University of Illinois Press, 1977); Kathleen Neils Conzen, *Immigrant Milwaukee, 1836–1860: Accommodation and Community in a Frontier City* (Cambridge, Mass.: Harvard University Press, 1976); Jo Ellen McNergney Vinyard, *The Irish on the Urban Frontier: Detroit, 1850–1880* (New York: Arno, 1976); James P. Walsh, ed., *The San Francisco*

Irish 1850–1976 (San Francisco: The Irish Literary & Historical Society, 1978); Dennis Clark, *The Irish in Philadelphia: Ten Generations of Urban Experience* (Philadelphia: Temple University Press, 1974); and Caroline Golab, *Immigrant Destinations* (Philadelphia: Temple University Press, 1977), on Polish immigrants in Philadelphia.

Several collections of essays also deal with immigrant adjustment to modern America: Allen F. Davis and Mark H. Haller, eds., *The Peoples of Philadelphia: A History of Ethnic Groups and Lower Class Life, 1790–1940* (Philadelphia: Temple University Press, 1973); Melvin G. Holli and Peter d'A. Jones, eds., *The Ethnic Frontier: Essays in the History of Group Survival in Chicago and the Midwest* (Grand Rapids, Mich.: Wm. B. Eerdmans, 1977); Richard L. Ehrlich, ed., *Immigrants in Industrial America 1850–1920* (Charlottesville: University of Virginia, 1977) and John Higham, ed., *Ethnic Leadership in America* (Baltimore, Md.: The Johns Hopkins University Press, 1978).

Modernization theories have been applied in a provocative manner to the encounter of agricultural immigrants with the American industrial system. Herbert Gutman, "Work, Culture and Society in Industrializing America, 1815–1919," *American Historical Review,* LXXVIII (June 1973), 531–88, argued that several generations of rural newcomers brought their pre-industrial work habits and attitudes into American factories with subsequent periods of conflict and violence. On the other hand, Gerald Rosenblum, *Immigrant Workers: Their Impact on American Labor Radicalism* (New York: Basic Books, 1973) attributed the lack of a militant working class to a basic conservatism of Eastern and Southern Europeans. Correctives to the Rosenblum thesis can be found in: Edwin Fenton, *Immigrants and Unions: A Case Study: Italians and American Labor, 1870–1920* (New York: Arno, 1975); Rudolph J. Vecoli, "Italian American Workers, 1880–1920: Padrone Slaves or Primitive Rebels?" in Tomasi, ed., *Perspectives in Italian Immigration and Ethnicity,* 25–49; and Michael M. Passi, *et al., For the Common Good: Finnish Immigrants and the Radical Response to Industrial America* (Superior, Wis.: Tyomies Society, 1977). Also relevant to these issues is John E. Bodnar's *Immigration and Industrialization* and his article, "Immigration and Modernization: The Case of Slavic Peasants in Industrial America," *Journal of Social History,* X (Fall 1976), 44–71.

The ethnocultural approach has also had a profound influence upon the writing of American political history. The former dominance of an economic interpretation of political behavior has given way to a new emphasis upon the role of ethnoreligious attachments and cultural issues in American politics. Following the lead of Lee Benson and Samuel P. Hays,[30] historians have applied quantitative techniques to establish the social bases of partisanship. Through the analysis of demographic and voting data, such studies have demonstrated a strong correlation between political affiliation and ethnic identification.

Among the many recent works of the "New Political History," one may cite: Samuel T. McSeveney, *The Politics of Depression: Political Behavior in the Northwest, 1893–1896* (New York: Oxford University Press, 1972); Richard J. Jensen, *The Winning of the Midwest: Social and Political Conflict, 1888–1896* (Chicago: University of Chicago Press, 1971); William A. Gudelunas, Jr. and William G. Shade, *Before the Molly Maguires: The Emergence of the Ethno-Religious Factor in the Politics of the Lower Anthracite Region, 1844–1872* (New York: Arno, 1976); Douglas V. Shaw, *The Making of an Immigrant City: Ethnic and Cultural Conflict in Jersey City, New Jersey, 1850–1877* (New York: Arno, 1976); Thomas M. Henderson, *Tammany Hall and the New Immigrants* (New York: Arno, 1976); Edward R. Kantowicz, *Polish-American Politics in Chicago, 1888–1940* (Chicago: University of Chicago Press, 1975); Ronald H. Bayor, *Neighbors in Conflict: The Irish, Germans, Jews and Italians of New York City, 1929–1941* (Baltimore, Md.: Johns Hopkins University Press, 1978); Ronald P. Formisano, *The Birth of Mass Political Parties: Michigan, 1827–1681* (Princeton University Press, 1971); and Frederick C. Luebke, *Bonds of Loyalty: German-Americans and World War I* (DeKalb, Ill.: Northern Illinois University Press, 1974).

Thanks largely to the influence of Joshua Fishman's pioneering work, *Language Loyalty in America,*[31] recent writings in immigration history have tended to emphasize the persistence of ethnic cultures. Rather than the traditional assumption that assimilation was rapid and inevitable, scholars now place more stress on the immigrants' resistance to absorption, their efforts at linguistic and cultural maintenance, and the ensuing interethnic conflicts. These are the themes not only of many of the community and political studies cited above, but also of works in religious history. Particularly since the publication of Harold J. Abramson's *Ethnic Diversity in Catholic America* (New York: John Wiley & Sons, 1973), there has been considerable attention paid to immigrant groups of the Roman Catholic faith. A number of monographs have explored the intricate relationship between religion and ethnicity as a source of both solidarity and conflict within the immigrant communities: Jay P. Dolan, *The Immigrant Church: New York's Irish and German Catholics, 1815–1865* (Baltimore, Md.: Johns Hopkins University, 1975); Silvano M. Tomasi, *Piety and Power: The Role of the Italian Parishes in the New York Metropolitan Area 1880–1930* (Staten Island, N.Y.: Center for Migration Studies, 1975); Victor Greene, *For God and Country: The Rise of Polish and Lithuanian Ethnic Consciousness in America, 1861–1910* (Madison, Wis.: Wisconsin Historical Society, 1975); and Richard M. Linkh, *American Catholicism and European Immigrants 1900–1924* (Staten Island, N.Y.: Center for Migration Studies, 1975). In addition, two volumes of collected essays dealing largely with Roman Catholic immigrants are Randall Miller and Thomas Marzik, eds., *Immigrants and Religion in Urban America* (Philadelphia: Temple University Press, 1977) and Keith Dyrud, *et al., The Other Catholics* (New York: Arno Press, 1978).

Other studies which investigate particular manifestations of ethnic consciousness are: Odd Sverre Lovoll, *A Folk Epic: The Bygdelag in America* (Boston: Twayne, 1975), a study of Norwegian American organizations based upon regional attachments; Dorothy Burton Skardal, *The Divided Heart: Scandinavian Immigrant Experiences through Literary Sources* (Lincoln, Neb.: University of Nebraska Press, 1974); Rose Basile Green, *The Italian American Novel: A Document of the Interaction of Two Cultures* (Rutherford, N.J.: Fairleigh Dickinson University Press, 1974); and Melvin I. Urofsky, *American Zionism from Herzl to the Holocaust* (Garden City, N.Y.: Anchor Press, 1975).

Conclusion

Even this cursory inventory suggests the extent and variety of recent writings in immigration history. It is clear that a pluralistic perspective has transformed the basic paradigm of American historiography. Ethnicity has been generally accepted as a pervasive attribute which affected all areas of American life. While traditional histories of immigrant groups are being written, the new departure is that students of politics, labor, or whatever, now incorporate the ethnic factor in their studies. This is a fundamental break with the historical scholarship of the past, and presages a rewriting of the history of the United States which will be multi-ethnic, multi-racial, and multi-lingual in its interpretation of the American experience (or better yet, *experiences*).

It has been impossible in this essay to do more than hint at the important research which is being carried on in the countries of emigration. By its very nature international migration entails the interaction of the cultures and economies of two societies. As such, it is as important an historical phenomenon for the countries of origin as it is for the countries of destination. During the past decade much significant work has been accomplished in those countries which parallels the resurgence of immigration scholarship in the United States. A mutual interest in the migrations has stimulated considerable cooperation among American historians and their colleagues overseas. The potential for such international collaboration has only been scratched. This subject deserves extended discussion in its own right, but that is for another time.□

Footnotes

[1]In *The State of American History,* ed. Herbert J. Bass (Quadrangle, 1970), 70–88.

[2]Michael Novak, *The Rise of the Unmeltable Ethnics* (New York: Macmillan, 1971). On the revival of ethnicity see also: William Greenbaum, "America in Search of a New Ideal: An Essay on the Rise of Pluralism," *Harvard Educational Review,* XLIV (August 1974), 411–40; Nathan Glazer and Daniel P. Moynihan, eds., *Ethnicity Theory and Experience* (Cambridge, Mass.: Harvard University Press, 1975); Andrew M. Greeley, *Ethnicity in the United States: A Preliminary Reconnaissance* (New York: John Wiley & Sons, 1974).

[3]One could add the names of George M. Stephenson and Carl Wittke. The work of this generation of immigration historians is described and evaluated in Rudolph J. Vecoli, "European Americans: From Immigrants to Ethnics," in *The Reinterpretation of American History and Culture,* ed. William H. Cartwright and Richard L. Watson, Jr. (Washington, D.C.: National Council for the Social Studies, 1973), 81–112.

[4]On this issue see Rudolph J. Vecoli, "The Immigration Studies Collection of the University of Minnesota," *The American Archivist,* XXXII (April 1969), 139–45; Robert M. Warner and Francis X. Blouin, Jr., "Documenting the Great Migrations and a Century of Ethnicity in America," *The American Archivist,* XXXIX (July 1976), 319–28; Nicholas V. Montalto, "The Challenge of Preservation in a Pluralistic Society: A Report on the Immigration History Research Center, University of Minnesota," *The American Archivist,* XLI (October 1978).

[5]Addresses of these institutions are: American Jewish Archives, 2101 Clifton Avenue, Cincinnati, Ohio 45220; Polish Museum of America, 984 North Milwaukee Avenue, Chicago, Ill. 60622; Norwegian-American Historical Association, St. Olaf College, Northfield, Minn. 55067.

[6]Warner and Blouin, "Documenting the Great Migrations"; see listings in John D. Buenker and Nicholas C. Burckel, *Immigration and Ethnicity. A Guide to Information Sources* (Detroit: Gale Research Co., 1977), 227–39.

[7]Addresses of these institutions are: Immigration History Research Center, University of Minnesota, 826 Berry Street, St. Paul, Minn. 55114; Center for Migration Studies, 209 Flagg Place, Staten Island, N.Y. 10304; Balch Institute, 18 S. 7th Street, Philadelphia, Pa. 19106; Asian American Studies Center, 322 Campbell Hall, University of California-Los Angeles, Calif. 90024; Research Institute on Immigration and Ethnic Studies, Smithsonian Institute, 955 L'Enfant Plaza, S.W., Washington, D.C. 20560. See also Mr. Vecoli's article on the Immigration History Research Center in "Research and Publication," page 87–88 of this issue.

[8]Examples are the Walter P. Reuther Library, Wayne State University, Detroit, Michigan 48202; the Center for the Study of American Catholicism, University of Notre Dame, Notre Dame, Ind. 46556; the

Archives of Industrial Society, University of Pittsburgh, Pittsburgh, Pa. 15213.

⁹The reprint edition is by Arno Press; the microfilm edition is by Northern Micrographics, La Crosse, Wisconsin 54601.

¹⁰Arno Press Catalogue, *Ethnic Studies 1978* (Three Park Avenue, New York, N.Y. 10016); R and E Research Associates, Inc., *Ethnic Minorities in America* (4843 Mission Street, San Francisco, Calif. 94112).

¹¹Bibliographies of dissertations on a wide variety of subjects, including "Minorities: Racial, Religious, and Ethnic," are available upon request from University Microfilms International, 300 North Zeeb Road, Ann Arbor, Michigan 48106. For annual guides to materials available on microform see *National Register of Microform Masters* (Washington: Library of Congress, 1965–   ), and *Guide to Microforms in Print* (Westport, Conn.: Microform Review, Inc., 1961–   ). Relevant oral history and documentary collections are available on microform from Microfilming Corporation of America, 21 Harristown Road, Glen Rock, N.J. 07452.

¹²Edward V. Kolyszko, "Preserving Ethnic Records on Microfilm: The Ethnic Records Microform Project," *Microform Review,* II (October 1973); and "Preserving the Polish Heritage in America: The Polish Microfilm Project," *Polish American Studies,* XXXII (1975), 59–63. On the microfilm projects of the Immigration History Research Center see also "Carpatho-Ruthenian Heritage to be Preserved," *Spectrum,* I (September 1975).

¹³U.S. National Archives and Records Services, *Guide to the National Archives of the United States* (Washington, D.C.: U.S. Government Printing Office, 1974); for document series available on microfilm see NARS, *National Archives Microfilm Publications* (Washington, D.C.: U.S. Government Printing Office, 1974). See also Joseph B. Howerton, "The Resources of the National Archives for Ethnic Research," *The Immigration History Newsletter,* V (November 1973), 1–8, and Michael N. Cutsumbis, "The National Archives and Immigration Research," *The International Migration Review,* IV (Spring 1970), 90–99.

¹⁴Immigration History Society, Carlton C. Qualey, Editor-treasurer, c/o Minnesota Historical Society, 690 Cedar Street, St. Paul, Minn. 55101. Membership dues are $3.00 per year.

¹⁵John C. Appel, "Immigrant Historical Societies in the United States, 1880–1950," (unpublished doctoral dissertation, University of Pennsylvania, 1950); Odd S. Lovoll and Kenneth O. Bjork, *The Norwegian American Historical Association 1925–1975* (Northfield, Minn., 1975).

¹⁶Most, but not all, ethnic historical societies are listed in Donna McDonald, comp. and ed., *Directory Historical Societies and Agen-*

cies in the United States and Canada, Tenth Edition, 1975–76. (Nashville, Tenn.: American Association for State and Local History, 1975).

[17]*International Migration Review,* 209 Flagg Place, Staten Island, N.Y. 10304. A cumulative index has been published (Volumes 1 to 10, Spring 1964 to Winter 1976); this includes the forerunner to the *IMR,* the *International Migration Digest,* published from 1964 to 1966.

[18]*The Journal of Ethnic Studies,* Western Washington University, Bellingham, Washington 98225; *Ethnicity,* Academic Press, Inc., 111 Fifth Ave., New York, N.Y. 10003. *Ethnicity* is edited at the Center for the Study of American Pluralism, National Opinion Research Center, 6030 South Ellis Ave., Chicago, Ill. 60637.

[19]*MELUS,* Department of English, University of Southern California, Los Angeles, California 90007. This is the journal of the Society for the Study of the Multi-Ethnic Literature of the United States; volumes 1–4 appeared in the form of the *MELUS Newsletter.*

[20]For the purpose of this essay, only writings dealing with immigration of the post-colonial period and from outside the Western Hemisphere will be discussed. Publications in other than the English language and in the social sciences will not be included. Articles and unpublished dissertations, for the most part, will not be reviewed. Space constraints impose those admittedly arbitrary limits. Professor A. William Hoglund of the University of Connecticut has compiled a comprehensive listing of all dissertations relating to immigration which is to be published in the near future.

[21]See the essays by Rudolph J. Vecoli, "European Americans: From Immigrants to Ethnics," 81–112, and Roger Daniels, "The Asian American Experience," 139–48. See also the historiographical review by Daniels, "American Historians and East Asian Immigrants," in Norris Hundley, Jr., ed., *The Asian American: The Historical Experience* (Santa Barbara, Calif.: Clio Books, 1976), 1–25.

[22]*The Immigrant in American History* (first ed. 1940; New York: Harper Torchbook, 1964); *The Uprooted* (first ed. 1951; second ed., Boston: Atlantic Monthly Press Book, 1973).

[23]Brinley Thomas, *Migration and Economic Growth: A Study of Great Britain and the Atlantic Economy* (Cambridge, England: University Press, 1954); Frank Thistlethwaite, "Migration from Europe Overseas in the Nineteenth and Twentieth Centuries," XIe Congrès International des Sciences Historiques, Stockholm, 1960, *Rapports, V: Histoire Contemporaine* (Göteberg-Stockholm-Uppsala: Almquist & Wiksell, 1960), 32–60.

[24]For a critical review of this literature see: Ingrid Semmingsen, "Nordic Research into Emigration," *Scandinavian Journal of History,* III (1978), 107–129.

[25]For a retrospective view of the literature see Frederick C. Luebke,

"Ethnic Group Settlement on the Great Plains," *The Western Histori-cal Quarterly,* VIII (October 1977), 405–430.

[26]For discussions of research techniques, reports, and reviews see the *Historical Methods Newsletter* published quarterly by the Univer-sity Center for International Studies and the Department of History, University of Pittsburgh, Pittsburgh, PA 15260.

[27]An example of this work is June Namias, *First Generation: Oral Histories of Twentieth-Century American Immigrants* (Boston: Beacon Press, 1978).

[28]*Progress and Poverty: Social Mobility in a Nineteenth Century City* (Cambridge, Mass.: Harvard University Press, 1964).

[29]The first of this kind of study, however, was set in a Wisconsin frontier county: Merle Curti, *The Making of an American Community; a Case Study of Democracy in a Frontier County* (Stanford, Calif.: Stanford University Press, 1959).

[30]Lee Benson, *The Concept of Jacksonian Democracy: New York as a Test Case* (Princeton: Princeton University Press, 1961); Samuel P. Hays, "The Social Analysis of American Political History, 1880–1920," *Political Science Quarterly,* LXXX (September 1965), 373–94. For critical reviews of writings in ethnocultural political history see: Samuel T. McSeveney, "Ethnic Groups, Ethnic Conflicts, and Recent Quantitative Research in American Political History," *International Migration Review,* VII (Spring, 1973), 14–33; and Paul Kleppner, "Immigrant Groups and Partisan Politics," *The Immigration History Newsletter,* X (May 1978), 1–5. For an ambitious effort to reinterpret the entire span of American political history from an ethnocultural perspective see: Robert Kelley, "Ideology and Political Culture from Jefferson to Nixon," *The American Historical Review,* LXXXII (June 1977), 531–582.

[31]Fishman, *et al., Language Loyalty in the United States: The Maintenance and Perpetuation of Non-English Mother Tongues by American Ethnic and Religious Groups* (Janua Linguarum, Series Maior, 21; The Hague: Mouton, 1966). Another work which has influenced subsequent research in immigration studies is Milton Gordon, *Assimilation in American Life: The Role of Race, Religion and National Origins* (New York: Oxford University Press, 1964).

The History of American Journalism: A Bibliographical Essay

JOSEPH P. McKERNS

☐ The profession of journalism is often called "history in a hurry", which may or may not be an appropriate description, but American newspapers, magazines, radio, television, photography and documentary film have provided historians with a wealth of documentation on the day-to-day history of the United States. American journalism history is a microcosm of American history because within any period of the nation's development its media of communication reflect the hopes and fears, the dominant ideas and ideals of the American public and its government. The social historian, the political historian, the intellectual historian, the historian of race relations, and the student of American life will find in the pages of the daily and periodical press and through the sight and sound of broadcasting and motion pictures a fairly accurate mirror-image of society in the United States.

It is with this in mind that the following seeks to present the major contributions to the study of American journalism history. This essay does not exhaust the literature of the field but it does contain those works which the author believes best represent it. Also, in reading the essay one may detect a lack of discussion on certain subjects, e.g., the role of women and minorities in the media. This is not done by design. Instead, as in the other disciplines of American history, these areas, with only a few exceptions, have not received the attention of scholars until recently.

The author directs those seeking a more comprehensive list of works on American journalism to two excellent bibliographies: Warren C. Price, *The Literature of Journalism: An Annotated Bibliography* (Minneapolis: University of Minnesota Press, 1959) and Warren C. Price and Calder M. Pickett, *An Annotated Journalism Bibliography, 1958–1968* (Minneapolis: University of Minnesota Press, 1970).

The Foundations of American Journalism

American journalism did not spring from the soil of the New World, instead its roots are found in the European, especially English, journalism that preceded it. It can be said that the American press shares a common heritage with the press of the Western World, but it is to England and to the development of journalism there that scholars have turned to observe the strongest roots of the American press. The evolution of the Anglo-American sense of the importance of journalism in the dissemination of political ideas is masterfully documented in Frederick S. Siebert, *Freedom of the Press in England, 1476–1776* (Urbana: University of Illinois Press, 1952). Supplementary to this is Frederick S. Siebert, Theodore Peterson and Wilbur Schramm, *Four Theories of the Press* (Urbana: University of Illinois Press, 1956) which discusses the effects of the Protestant Reformation, and rationalist and humanist philosophy on the relationship of the press to the crumbling authoritarian government of England in the 16th and 17th centuries. The role of the press in the emergence of a more libertarian government in England and in the American colonies in the late 17th and the 18th century is also examined.

One important facet of the struggle for press freedom in England during this period is meticulously researched in Cyprian Blagden, *The Stationers' Company* (Cambridge: Harvard University Press, 1960). The first English newspaper, the *Oxford* (or London) *Gazette* was not begun until 1665, but it was preceded by several "almost" newspapers. The first of these was the corantos, beginning in the 1620's which were printed at irregular intervals and usually covered a single topic. They were followed in the 1640's by reports of domestic events which were printed daily and called *Diurnall Occurrences*. Joseph Frank, *The Beginnings of the English Newspaper* (Cambridge: Harvard University Press, 1961) provides a highly readable description of the development of English journalism for this period up to the Restoration.

Although the first printing press was brought to the American colonies in 1638 and set up at Cambridge, the first newspaper, *Publick Occurrences Both Foreign and Domestick*, was not begun until 1690 in Boston and was quickly suppressed after one issue by the government. The first "permanent" American newspaper, the *Boston News-Letter* was not founded until 1704. Colonial printing presses were kept busy turning out copies of bibles, sermons, textbooks, laws and tracts, and American newspapers developed slowly at first. It was not until colonial disaffection with the Crown began to grow that newspapers were founded and published to any great extent. One work on the period through the American Revolution that has withstood the test of time since it was first issued in 1810 is Isaiah Thomas, *The History of Printing in America* (Bibliography and Reference Series, No 62, New York: Burt Franklin. Reprint of the 1874 edition). Thomas, the founder and first president of the American Antiquarian Society, has provided a storehouse of data on newspapers as well as magazines, books and printing in general. Thomas was a journalistic leader in the American Revolution and his accomplishments are examined in Annie R. Marble, *From 'Prentice to Patron: The Life Story of Isaiah Thomas* (New York: Appleton-Century-Crofts, 1935). Studies of two other printers help to define the role played by them in the colonies: Richard F. Hixson, *Issac Collins: A Quaker Printer in 18th Century America* (New

Brunswick: Rutgers University Press, 1968) and Ward L. Miner, *William Goddard, Newspaperman* (Durham: Duke University Press, 1962). Goddard published newspapers in Rhode Island, Pennsylvania, and Maryland colonies and was very dependent upon the assistance of his mother, Sarah, and his sister, Mary Katherine, in putting out the papers. These two women are indicative of several women who played important roles on early newspapers.

Many American newspapers were begun not for the dissemination of political ideas and information, but for the dissemination of commercial news to the mercantile and business community. This information often appeared in the form of advertising which was then, and still is, the lifeblood of American journalism. The relationship between advertising and journalism in a capitalistic press system is described by Frank Presbrey, *The History and Development of Advertising* (Garden City: Doubleday, 1929) and James P. Wood, *The Story of Advertising* (New York: Ronald Press, 1958). Printers were often pressed for money because many ads went unpaid for and subscribers were tardy with their payments. Mary Ann Yodelis, *Who Paid the Piper? Publishing Economics in Boston, 1763-1775* (Journalism Monographs, No. 38, Minneapolis: Association for Education in Journalism, February 1975) offers an excellent case study of this problem. In addition to political and commercial needs, newspapers also provided for literary and other cultural needs. A study of one newspaper, Hennig Cohen, *The South Carolina Gazette, 1732–1775* (Columbia: University of South Carolina Press, 1953) meshes its history with a study of 18th century society and culture in that state.

The trial and acquittal in 1735 of John Peter Zenger, printer of the *New York Weekly Journal,* on charges of seditious libel has been heralded as a landmark in the concept of a press free to criticize government, a concept which came to fruition in the First Amendment. Journalism historians have lionized Zenger's courage in attacking New York's Royal Governor, William Cosby, in his newspaper, but until Henry Noble MacCracken, *Prologue to Independence: The Trials of James Alexander, 1715–1756* (New York: James H. Heineman, 1964) the role of Alexander as a major influence on the newspaper and in the Anti-Cosby party had been largely ignored. Leonard W. Levy, *Legacy of Suppression* (Cambridge: The Belknap Press of the Harvard University Press, 1960) offers a scholarly counterargument to the significance of the Zenger trial by demonstrating that the current interpretation of the meaning of the First Amendment as a license to criticize authority, did not begin to crystalize until after the Anti-Federalist reaction to the Alien and Sedition Acts of 1798 and the election of Thomas Jefferson to the presidency in 1800.

The interpretation of American journalism history is, and has been, dominated by the Progressive paradigm of American history and as a result the study of the press's role in conflict situations, particularly political conflict, permeates the literature. Arthur M. Schlesinger Sr., *Prelude to Independence: The Newspaper War on Britain, 1764–1776* (New York: Knopf, 1958) is a detailed study of the press's role in promoting the Revolution. Likewise, Donald H. Stewart, *The Opposition Press of the Federalist Period* (Albany: The State University of New York Press, 1969) examines the use of the press by opposing political factions in order to further their interests in the young nation. It is the standard reference for the period. Lewis Leary, *That Rascal Freneau: A Study in Literary Failure* (New Bruns-wick: Rutgers University Press, 1941) studies the role played by Philip Freneau, editor of the *National Gazette,* who was the principal newspaper spokesman for Thomas Jefferson at the time of his ideological clash with Alexander Hamilton and the Federalists. This era in American history in which the nation was divided between Federalist and Anti-Federalist sentiment has been called the "Dark Ages" of American journalism by Frank Luther Mott because of the vituperative-ness of the political newspapers of the time. This interpretation is challenged by William E. Ames, *A History of the National Intelligencer* (Chapel Hill: University of North Carolina Press, 1972). The newspaper was founded in 1800 in Wash-ington, D.C. as a more moderate supporter of Thomas Jefferson. Ames focuses upon the history of that newspaper until its expiration in the 1860's as a means to study the political journalism of the time. In so doing he proposes that Mott's "Dark Ages" must now be dealt with as conceivably the most important age in all of American journalism history. A study of another publication which parallels the *National Intelligencer* both in significance and in time is Norval Neil Luxon, *Niles' Weekly Register: News Magazine of the Nineteenth Century* (Baton Rouge: Louisiana State University Press, 1947)

Sectionalism and Civil War
The demise of the Federalist party was hastened by the outcry against the Alien and Sedition Acts of 1798 and within two decades the nation would be enjoying an "Era of Good Feelings" under the administration of James Monroe. It was a time when the party of Thomas Jefferson would dominate national politics with little or no opposition. But this peace would be broken in the 1820s as con-

Joseph P. McKerns is Assistant Profes-sor in the School of Journalism at Southern Illinois University. Previously he was Director of the Communications Re-search Center of the College of Communications and Assistant Pro-fessor of Journalism at the University of Tennessee, Knoxville. For several years he was a reporter, editor and photog-rapher for newspapers and magazines in the East and Midwest. He has taught journalism at the University of Maryland, where he was also Assistant Dean of the College of Journalism, at the University of Minnesota, and at St. Bonaventure Uni-versity. He received an A.B. in Commu-nication Arts and American Studies at the University of Nortre Dame, an M.A. in Journalism from the Ohio State University, and a Ph.D. in Mass Communications at the University of Minnesota. McKearns has published articles on communications history, ethics, and law.

troversies over slavery, commerce and economics became intertwined and began to divide the nation. Out of the tangled controversies new political factions would arise to replace the party of Jefferson and the dormant Federalist party. The nation's press responded by aligning itself with the Whigs or the Democrats, or with factions within each party. It is during this decade that correspondents from newspapers outside of the nation's capital were sent to Washington to report on the activities of the federal government. The story of the growth of the Washington press corps from this early time to the 1970s is told in F. B. Marbut, *News from the Capital: The Story of Washington Reporting* (Carbondale: Southern Illinois University Press, 1971). Men dominated the press corps, but several women also rose to prominence in reporting news of the national government as is described in Maurine Hoffman Beasley, *The First Women Washington Correspondents* (GW Washington Studies, No. 4, Washington, D.C.: George Washington University, January, 1976). A peculiar relationship has developed between the president and the press since the time of George Washington. The White House press corps is supposed to report objectively on the actions of the president, but often the reporters' objectivity is compromised when they are used to send up trial balloons or are manipulated in order to protect or enhance the public image of the chief executive. The best source on the evolution of presidential press relations is James E. Pollard, *The Presidents and the Press* (New York: Macmillan, 1947).

In the 1820s while white men were speaking for or against slavery in the capital the first newspaper published by blacks in the United States, *Freedom's Journal,* was founded in New York in 1827. Its editors declared "Too long have others spoken for us." This marked the first in a long line of brave but short-lived newspapers owned by blacks which espoused the abolition of slavery. A good summary of this topic is offered by Carter R. Bryan, *Negro Journalism in America Before Emancipation* (Journalism Monographs, No.12, Minneapolis: Association for Education in Journalism, September, 1969). Probably the best known black newspaper before Emancipation was Frederick Douglass' *North Star* which he began in Rochester, N.Y. in 1847. Details on both the man and the newspaper are found in Arna Bontemps, *Free at Last: The Life of Frederick Douglass* (New York: Dodd, Mead, 1971). The efforts of William Lloyd Garrison and others to gain public support for the end of slavery saw public opinion begin to turn in their favor following the murder of Elijah P. Lovejoy, an abolitionist editor, in 1837. John Gill, *Tide Without Turning: Elijah P. Lovejoy and Freedom of the Press* (Boston: Beacon Press, 1958) examines this turning point.

Regional press characteristics began to be more clearly defined after 1820. Politically, the press of the South became increasingly Democratic in tone, but there were some exceptions. Robert Neal Elliot Jr., *The Raleigh Register, 1799–1863* (Chapel Hill: University of North Carolina Press, 1955) studies one of these exceptions, a North Carolina newspaper which was founded as a Jeffersonian weekly but was transformed into a Whig supporter. Bertram Holland Flanders, *Early Georgia Magazines* (Athens: University of Georgia Press, 1944) is a valuable study of literary periodicals published in Georgia between 1802 and 1865 which suggests the pattern of magazine development in other states of the Deep South.

Newspapers in the newer states of the Midwest and West often acted as "boosters" of the virtues of their home town and home state. The editors of these newspapers became civic leaders and allied themselves and their papers with the local business community and its interests. This aspect is examined in three fine studies: George S. Hage, *Newspapers on the Minnesota Frontier, 1849–1860* (St. Paul: Minnesota Historical Society, 1967); William H. Lyon, *The Pioneer Editor in Missouri, 1808–1860* (Columbia: University of Missouri Press, 1965) and Archer H. Shaw, *The Plain Dealer* (New York: Knopf, 1942). The latter concerns an important Cleveland, Ohio, newspaper.

In the years between 1833 and 1851 the American newspaper began to assume characteristics closer to those associated with present day newspapers. Until 1833 the press was not a "mass" medium, i.e., it did not seek to appeal to large, diverse groups of people. The predominantly political and mercantile tone of the press appealed instead to a relatively small, homogeneous sector of the society. The newspaper audience mostly consisted of the propertied class and professionals in the community. Newspaper content was aimed at readers who were active in politics or business, and not at the semi-skilled worker or craftsman with only a passing interest in the two. Also, most newspapers in 1833 cost about six cents an issue—payable on a monthly, quarterly, semi-annual or annual basis—a price too high for many to afford. The circulation of daily papers in New York and other cities seldom exceeded 4,000 and was usually far less than that. When Andrew Jackson, the "common man," the man of the people, was elected

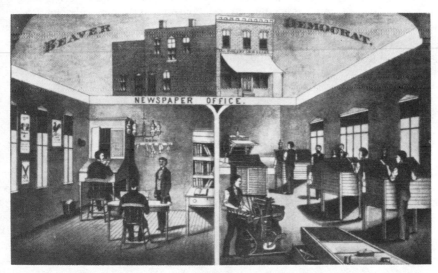

Photo courtesy Prints and Photographs Division, Library of Congress.

Advertisement, lithograph, from Beaver Co., Pa., Atlas, *1876.*

to the presidency in 1828 the nature of American society changed and with it that of the newspaper. In 1833 in New York a printer named Benjamin Day started a newspaper, the *New York Sun,* which revolutionized American journalism. Day sold his newspaper for one cent—payable daily—a price many could afford. The content was bright and lively, i.e., what journalists today call feature articles and human interest stories. The *Sun* seemed to treat political news and business news as if they didn't exist. Within six months it was selling 8,000 copies a day, a total nearly twice that of any competitor. New Yorkers who had seldom or never bought a newspaper before began to buy Day's paper and soon its circulation was in tens of thousands. But Day's success was surpassed by James Gordon Bennett, a Scottish immigrant, who founded the *New York Herald* in 1835. Bennett's formula for success could be called "sex, scandal and murder," but this is an oversimplification. Bennett was the first editor to seek out the news instead of waiting for it to come to him. He assigned reporters to cover the courts, the police precincts, Wall Street, New York society, religion, sports, politics and the theater. He hired sloops, trains, coaches, express riders and used carrier pigeons in order to get news from distant places quicker than anyone else. The *Herald's* success was noted by others and its imitators were legion. From then on a newspaper's significance would not be marked solely by its political influence. Circulation size and the amount of advertising lineage became just as important. Bennett's achievements are detailed by Oliver Carlson, *The Man Who Made the News: A Biography of James Gordon Bennett* (New York: Duell, Sloan & Pearce, 1942).

In 1841 the *Sun* and the *Herald* were joined by a third important "Penny Press" newspaper, Horace Greeley's *New York Tribune.* The *Tribune* was not an imitator of the others, but it still was able to count its circulation in the tens of thousands. Greeley, who along with Joseph Pulitzer and William Randolph Hearst is probably the best known and most written about American journalist, made his paper a leader of editorial and public opinion. It seemed as though no humane cause was too insignificant for the *Tribune's* pages according to Glydon G. Van Deusen, *Horace Greeley: Nineteenth Century Crusader* (Philadelphia: University of Pennsylvania Press, 1953).

If American journalism seemed to be out of balance because of the sensationalism of Bennett's *Herald* and the editorial shrillness and partisanship of Greeley's *Tribune,* the balance was restored by a fourth penny newspaper, the *New York Times* founded by Henry Raymond and George Jones in 1851. The *Times* prided itself upon the objectivity and lack of emotion in its reportage and editorial opinion, according to Elmer Davis, *History of the New York Times, 1851–1921* (New York: New York Times Co., 1921). Although the most famous penny newspapers were located in New York, other cities such as Baltimore, had noteworthy ones too. Consult Gerald W. Johnson, F. R. Kent, H. L. Mencken and Hamilton Owens, *The Sunpapers of Baltimore* (New York: Knopf, 1937).

While the penny newspapers won the largest circulations during the period before the Civil War, many American newspapers continued to fulfill their more traditional role as political commentators. The *New York Evening Post,* edited by William Cullen Bryant, was one of these. Social critics and satirists who used the regular newspaper column as a vehicle for personal commentary joined the voices of the newspapers' editorial "we" as the nation approached the outbreak of war. On these aspects consult Charles H. Brown, *William Cullen Bryant* (New York: Scribner's, 1971) and John M. Harrison, *The Man Who Made Nasby: David Ross Locke* (Chapel Hill: University of North Carolina Press, 1960).

In the years before the Civil War improvements in newspaper printing technology allowed publishers to achieve high circulation and increase revenue while maintaining relatively low costs. The development of photography and the invention of the telegraph also had advantageous effects on journalism. Although photographs could not be reproduced in newspapers and magazines until late in the 19th century, they were often used as models for woodcuts used to illustrate news stories. The development of photography as a medium of communication is told in Beaumont Newhall, *The History of Photography from 1839 to the Present Day*, 2nd ed. rev. (New York: The Museum of Modern Art, 1964); Helmut and Alison Gernsheim, *The History of Photography from the Camera Obscura to the Beginning of the Modern Era* (London: Thames and Hudson, 1969) and Peter Pollack, *The Picture History of Photography*, 2nd. ed. rev. (New York: Abrams, 1969).

The telegraph had a more immediate impact on the press. Its use by daily newspapers in particular made previous long-distance news gathering practices obsolete. The use of the telegraph led to the organization of the first significant cooperative newsgathering agency in America, The New York Associated Press, in 1848. For a well-written account of its beginnings consult Oliver Gramling, *AP: The Story of News* (New York: Farrar and Rinehart, 1940). To many military historians, the American Civil War is the first modern war. Likewise, many journalism historians who have studied the news coverage of it see it as the beginning of modern war correspondence. The use of the telegraph by correspondents in the field permitted them to file reports of battles and other war news with their newspapers in a matter of hours instead of days or weeks. But this more rapid transmission of information caused security problems for civil and military authorities and as a result news stories were often censored. Also, the high cost of telegraphed messages forced reporters to trim their writing style, thus bringing it more in line with the newswriting style of today. Two books by J. Cutler Andrews, *The North Reports the Civil War* (Pittsburgh: University of Pittsburgh Press, 1955) and *The South Reports the Civil War* (Princeton: Princeton University Press, 1970) are the most complete, dispassionate and documented sources on the period. Emmet Crozier, *Yankee Reporters: 1861–1865* (New York: Oxford University Press, 1956) and Louis M. Starr, *Bohemian Brigade: Civil War Newsmen in Action* (New York: Knopf, 1954) are noteworthy for their examination of news censorship. A scholarly treatment of Abraham Lincoln's press relations is offered by Robert S. Harper, *Lincoln and the Press* (New York: McGraw-Hill, 1951).

The Civil War was a key event in the transition of the United States from a rural-agrarian based society to an urban-industrial based society. The contrast between the two is highlighted by Albert Lowther Demaree, *The American Agricultural Press, 1819–1860* (New York: Columbia University Press, 1941) and David E. Forsyth, *The Business Press in America, 1750–1865* (Philadelphia: Chilton Books, 1964).

The Press in the Age of Enterprise

The years from the 1830's through the Reconstruction period are noted for their personal journalism, i.e., the personality of the leading newspaper editors of the time seemed to be embodied in their papers. The names of Bennett, Greeley, Raymond and Bryant were synonomous with that of their publications. Between 1869 and 1878 these men died and with them, at least to some journalism historians, personal journalism also died. Following the death of Greeley the *Tribune* passed into the hands of the Reid family and underwent a transformation from liberal to conservative Republicanism. This change is noted in Bingham Duncan, *Whitelaw Reid: Journalist, Politician, Diplomat* (Athens: University of Georgia Press, 1975). While the *New York Tribune* remained as the GOP's voice in the East, the *Chicago Tribune* became the Republican leader in the Midwest. Phillip Kineley, *The Chicago Tribune: Its First Hundred Years*, Vol. I, 1847–1865; Vol. II, 1865–1880; Vol. III, 1880–1900 (Chicago: The Chicago Tribune Co., 1943, 1945, 1946), a company sponsored effort, is a detailed but partisan and incomplete source on the newspaper. For a brief interval in the early 1870's the *Tribune* was edited by a liberal Republican, Horace White. This atypical interlude is described in Joseph Logsdon, *Horace White: Nineteenth Century Liberal*, (Contributions in American History, No. 10, Westport: Greenwood, 1971).

Political cartoons rose to significance in the years following the Civil War and became an effective means of political and social commentary. Morton Keller, *The Art and Politics of Thomas Nast* (New York: Oxford University Press, 1968) is a valuable study of the most famous political cartoonist in American history. Stephen Hess and Milton Kaplan, *The Ungentlemanly Art: A History of American Political Cartoons* (New York: Macmillan, 1968) goes beyond the obvious names, such as Nast, and provides interesting insights into many other cartoonists.

Following Reconstruction new journalistic voices were raised in the South in an effort to reconcile the bitterness of the war years. Among those Southern editors and publishers who attained national as well as regional respect for their editorial opinions three stand out: Henry Watterson of the *Louisville Courier-Journal;* Henry W. Grady of the *Atlanta Constitution* and Josephus Daniels of the *Raleigh News and Observer.* Daniels would become Woodrow Wilson's Secretary of the Navy. Excellent studies of these men are offered by Joseph Frazier Wall, *Henry Watterson: Reconstructed Rebel* (New York: Oxford University Press, 1956); Raymond B. Nixon, *Henry W. Grady: Spokesman of the New South* (New York: Knopf, 1943) and Joseph L. Morrison, *Josephus Daniels: The Small-d Democrat* (Chapel Hill: University of North Carolina Press, 1966).

The quest for black identity began with the first black newspaper in 1827 and reached heights during the latter part of the 19th century. Selections on the role of black newspapers in this quest are collected in Martin Dann, ed., *The Black Press (1827–1890)* (New York: G. P. Putnam's Sons, 1971). The quest continued on into the 20th century and one of its regional leaders was William Monroe Trotter. Trotter, who was graduated *magna cum laude* from Harvard University in 1895, began a newspaper in 1901 which battled for racial equality and integration. Stephen R. Fox, *The Guardian of Boston: William Monroe Trotter* (New York: Atheneum, 1970) movingly describes Trotter's life.

In the final three decades before the turn of the century, New York City was a microcosm of the social ills of the country. By 1900, 80 percent of the city's population was either foreign born or first generation naturalized Americans; most were non-Protestant, poor and uneducated. Several newspapers in the city failed to take note of their changed audience and continued to espouse editorial opinions based upon ideas popular with the dominant, native American Protestants. Two such newspapers were the *New York World*, before its purchase by Joseph Pulitzer, and the *Brooklyn Eagle*. George T. McJimsey, *Genteel Partisan: Manton Marble, 1834–1917* (Ames: Iowa State University Press, 1971) examines the *World's* editor who advocated Spencerian social ideas. Raymond A. Schroth, *The Eagle and Brooklyn* (Westport: Greenwood, 1974) describes a newspaper out of touch with its community, because as Brooklyn became predominantly Jewish and Italian, the *Eagle* held on to its Protestant point of view.

Other newspapers did note the changes in society and its resultant ills, and out of this came a different kind of newspaper which employed sensational reporting techniques and editorial crusades in conjunction with a concern for honesty, integrity and the betterment of people, especially the underprivileged. The giant of

Photo courtesy Prints and Photographs Division, Library of Congress.

Lithograph, Vim, June 29, 1898.

this "New Journalism" era was Joseph Pulitzer, himself an immigrant. Julian S. Rammelkamp, *Pulitzer's Post-Dispatch, 1878–1883* (Princeton: University of Princeton Press, 1966) examines Pulitzer's early efforts in St. Louis where he supported middle class values and opposed dishonest government. His principal competitor was the *Globe-Democrat*, an outstanding paper, as described in Charles C. Clayton, *Little Mack: Joseph B. McCullagh of the St. Louis Globe-Democrat* (Carbondale: Southern Illinois University Press, 1969) which has been overshadowed by the more famous Pulitzer newspaper.

The sensational news coverage of the penny press newspapers of New York had disappeared by the 1870's, but when Pulitzer purchased the *World* in 1883 he re-introduced sensationalism into New York journalism. Pulitzer used these techniques not only to increase readership, but to attract attention to the plight of the immigrant working class living in the city's tenement districts. George Juergens, *Joseph Pulitzer and the New York World* (Princeton: Princeton University Press, 1966) shows how Pulitzer contributed innovations and refinements on the traditional journalistic form, thus defining the New Journalism. W. A. Swanberg, *Pulitzer* (New York: Scribner's, 1967) is as equally revealing of his personality as it is of his journalistic accomplishments.

Outside of New York others contributed their own variations on Pulitzer's journalistic style. Edward W. Scripps thought of his chain of newspapers as "classrooms for the working class." A valuable collection of Scripps' writings that is interwoven with excellent research is Oliver Knight, ed., *I Protest: Selected Disquisitions of E. W. Scripps* (Madison: University of Wisconsin Press, 1966). In Kansas City in the 1880's, the *Star* crusaded for civic improvement and honest politics as described in Icie F. Johnson, *William Rochhill Nelson and the Kansas City Star* (Kansas City: Burton, 1935). The same goals were pursued in Dallas, Texas by the *News* according to Ernest Sharpe, *G. B. Dealey of the Dallas News* (New York: Henry Holt, 1955). Will C. Conrad, Kathleen F. Wilson and Dale Wilson, *The Milwaukee Journal: The First Eighty Years* (Madison: University of Wisconsin Press, 1964) tells how the newspaper and the city grew together.

Unfortunately, many publishers and editors were blind to the humanitarian objectives of Pulitzer's sensationalism and saw only his rapidly growing circulation figures. Pulitzer's success was attributed solely to the appeal of sensationalism and imitators copied it. The "Yellow Journalism" of the 1890's was the New Journalism without its social consciousness and foremost among its practitioners was William Randolph Hearst, a man whose journalistic career spanned nearly seven decades. W. A. Swanberg, *Citizen Hearst* (New York: Scribner's, 1961) paints Hearst as "the great American enigma" and is an admirable attempt to understand the mind of a man who wanted to be president. John Tebbel, *The Life and Good Times of William Randolph Hearst* (New York: Dutton, 1952) provides a sound documentation of the Hearst publishing empire.

Sadly, Joseph Pulitzer became a parody of himself as he permitted his *World* to sink to the depths of Yellow Journalism in its news coverage of the Spanish-American War because of competition from Hearst's *New York Journal*. Charles H. Brown, *The Correspondents' War* (New York: Scribner's, 1967) is a major contribution to the literature on the war.

In the midst of the no-holds-barred circulation battle between the *World* and the *Journal*, Adolph S. Ochs purchased the *New York Times*. The *Times* in 1896 was a shadow of its former self. Following the death of its founder, Raymond, in 1896, the paper had steadily declined until its circulation dropped to less than 9,000. The *World's*, the *Journal's* and the *Herald's* circulations were in the hundreds of thousands. Ochs revived the *Times* and reclaimed its prestige by offering New Yorkers an alternative to the shrill, sensational, yellow journals. Gerald W. Johnson, *An Honorable Titan: A Biographical Study of Adolph S. Ochs* (New York: Harper & Bros., 1946) and Meyer Berger, *The Story of the New York Times, 1851–1951* (New York: Simon & Schuster, 1951) are well researched studies of this important period in the famous newspaper's proud history.

During the Spanish-American War newspaper circulation would pass the one million mark for the first time, but few papers were read outside of their immediate circulation area. Magazines became the first "national" medium of communication in the United States. Frank Luther Mott's monumental, Pulitzer Prize winning study of magazines is the most authoritative on the subject. In *A History of American Magazines, 1741–1850* (New York: Macmillan, 1930); *A History of American Magazines*, Vol. II, *1850–1865;* Vol. III, *1865–1885;* Vol. IV, *1885–1905;* Vol. V, *Sketches of 21 Magazines, 1905–1930* (Cambridge: Harvard University Press, 1938, 1938, 1957, 1968) Mott relates the development of magazines to the social and economic impulses of the times. Among the most successful and most significant magazines, between 1900 and 1917 were *McClure's, Cosmopolitan, Munsey's, Collier's* and the *Saturday Evening Post*. These "Muckrakers" gained a nation-wide audience with exposes of corrupt government, monopolistic trusts, race relations and deteriorating cities. C. C. Reiger, *The Era of the Muckrakers* (Chapel Hill: University of North Carolina Press, 1932) is an exhaustive study of crusading magazines and their writers. Louis Filler, *Crusaders for American Liberalism* (New York: Harcourt, Brace, 1939) examines the link between muckraking and the Progressive movement. Among the best studies of individual muckrakers are Peter Lyon, *Success Story: The Life and Times of S. S. McClure* (New York: Scribner's, 1963); Mary E. Tomkins, *Ida M. Tarbell* (New York: Twayne, 1974) and Justin Kaplan, *Lincoln Steffens* (New York: Simon & Schuster, 1974). Louise Ware, *Jacob A. Riis* (New York: Appleton-Century-Crofts, 1938) discusses the muckraking of the great American documentary photographer.

Individual characteristics distinguishing one newspaper from another began to disappear early in the 20th century as increasing numbers of papers began to rely on wire services and syndicates for news from distant places. In order to service clients at both ends of the political spectrum, these suppliers of news adopted a straightforward, objective style of reporting. Gradually, in part because of their influence, newspapers became more like one another. Victor Rosewater, *History of Cooperative News Gathering in the United States* (New York: Appleton-Century-Crofts, 1930), Joe Alex Morris, *Deadline Every Minute: The Story of the United Press* (Garden City: Doubleday, 1957) and Elmo Scott Watson, *A History of Newspaper Syndicates in the United States, 1865-1935* (Chicago: Publishers' Auxiliary, 1936) are good references.

Journalism and the Electronic Age

When Joseph Pulitzer died in 1911 his will forbade the sale of his *New York World*. After 1900 the newspaper had regained, through its liberal crusades and high professional standards, the prestige it lost earlier as a result of the excesses of its Spanish-American War coverage but by 1930 it was losing nearly two million dollars per year. Pulitzer's heirs went to court to break the will. Their request was granted and in 1931 the evening *World* was sold to the Scripps-Howard organization and merged with the *Telegram*. The morning *World*, to many journalists a symbol of the best in American journalism, was killed. The Pulitzer tradition was carried on by the family's *St. Louis Post-Dispatch* which was brilliantly lead by Oliver Kirby Bovard, its editor during the Depression. Bovard was trained on Pulitzer's *World* until 1910 and James W. Markham, *Bovard of the Post-Dispatch* (Baton Rouge: Louisiana State University Press, 1954) makes a strong, authoritative argument that if Bovard was placed in charge of the New York paper it might have survived.

In its final years the *World* had an excellent staff of writers and editors including Walter Lippmann, editor of the editorial page, and Heywood Brown, its combatively liberal political columnist. After 1931 Lippmann became a political columnist for the *New York Herald Tribune*. Lippmann had one of the sharpest intellects in American journalism, and his career of more than 50 years is perhaps the most interesting of all journalistic careers. John Luskin, *Lippmann, Liberty and the Press* (University: University of Alabama Press, 1972) does an admirable job of summarizing Lippmann's complex life, his youthful flirtation with Socialism, his years with the *New Republic* and the *World* and his long association with the politically conservative *Herald Tribune*. Hari N. Dam, *The Intellectual Odyssey of Walter Lippmann* (New York: Gordon, 1973) contributes much to the understanding of the evolution of what the author calls Lippmann's "protean thought." Heywood Broun stayed on with the new *World-Telegram* and continued his liberal commentary on American life. Dale Kramer, *Heywood Broun: A Biographical Portrait* (New York: Current Books—A. A. Wynn, 1949) offers the best work on Broun although the definitive study of him has yet to be written. Broun, a supporter of labor, was among the principal organizers of the American Newspaper Guild in 1933, an attempt to improve the working conditions of reporters. Daniel J. Leab, *A Union of Individuals: The Formation of the American Newspaper Guild, 1933-1936* (New York: Columbia University Press, 1970) documents its early years as a "militant labor union."

Personal journalism had a revival in the 20th century as certain editors and publishers, and a few writers, injected their personalities into their publications. The most outstanding of these was William Allen White, owner-editor of the *Emporia* (Kansas) *Gazette* and a principal voice of Midwestern Republicanism and small town America between 1900 and 1944. White's *The Autobiography of William Allen White* (New York: Macmillan, 1946) is among the best of its genre and a classic statement on journalism. John D. McKee, *William Allen White: Maverick on Main Street* (Westport: Greenwood, 1975) is the most recent and best study on him. John D. Stark, *Damned Upcountryman: William Watts Ball, A Study in American Conservatism* (Durham: Duke University Press, 1969) is a

Schumm photo: seven-year old newsboy, Columbus Circle, New York City, 1910.

good period study of a white supremacist editor who was influential in local politics in the South. Carl Bode, *Mencken* (Carbondale: Southern Illinois University Press, 1969) is the most authoritative study of H. L. Mencken, a genius of 20th Century American letters and journalism. Marion K. Sanders, *Dorothy Thompson: A Legend in Her Time* (Boston: Houghton Mifflin, 1973) is an outstanding examination of a significant individual. Gaeton Fonzi, *Annenberg: A Biography of Power* (New York: Weybright & Talley, 1970) is a perceptive study of the personality of the head of one of the nation's largest communications empires. Jerome Edwards, *The Foreign Policy of Col. McCormack's Tribune, 1929–1941* (Reno: University of Nevada Press, 1971) is a scholarly work on Robert R. McCormack and his power-base, the *Chicago Tribune*, which he considered as *the* Fourth Estate.

The entrance of radio into the news business after 1920, and that of television after the Second World War, in competition with the print media, would force the latter to redefine its relationship to the news. Erik Barnouw, *A Tower in Babel: A History of Broadcasting in the United States to 1933; The Golden Web: A History of Broadcasting in the United States, 1933–1953; The Image Empire: A History of Broadcasting in the United States from 1953* (New York: Oxford University Press, 1966, 1968, 1970) provides the most comprehensive and detailed history of broadcasting and all its aspects, i.e., news, entertainment, regulation and economics. Erik Barnouw, *Tube of Plenty: The Evolution of American Television* (New

York: Oxford University Press, 1975) is a condensed and updated version of the three aforementioned volumes. Gleason L. Archer, *History of Radio to 1926* (New York: American Historical Society, 1938) is also valuable particularly because the author was able to talk with many of the pioneers of early radio. Sydney W. Head, *Broadcasting in America: A Survey of Television and Radio*, 3rd ed. (Boston: Houghton Mifflin, 1975) is a comprehensive treatment of broadcasting history, technology, economics, regulation and societal effects although it is less detailed than Barnouw's work. Walter B. Emery, *Broadcasting and Government* (East Lansing: Michigan State University Press, 1961) is an excellent study of the sensitive relationship between broadcasters and the federal government. As a legal text it is outdated, but its value lies in the historical perspective it achieves.

Before television added sight to radio's sound, the motion picture newsreel gave the American public the chance to see the news as well as read and hear about it. Raymond Field, *The American Newsreel, 1911–1967* (Norman: University of Oklahoma Press, 1972) is the best source on it. The role of government in providing news and information to the public has always been clouded by charges of propaganda. Richard Dyer MacCann, *The People's Films: A Political History of U.S. Government Motion Pictures* (New York: Hastings House, 1973) is the most authoritative on the subject.

The yellow journalism of the 1890's and tabloid journalism of the 1920's and the 1930's stigmatized the press as a profit motivated purveyor of cheap thrills and vicarious experiences. To its many critics it seemed as though the press was using the freedom from regulation it enjoyed under the First Amendment to make money instead of using it to fulfill its vital role as an independent source of information in a democracy. The Commission on Freedom of the Press, chaired by Robert M. Hutchins, issued a report in 1947, *A Free and Responsible Press* (Chicago: University of Chicago Press, 1947) which urged the press to be "socially responsible," i.e., to use its freedom to report news that is vital to a decision-making electorate. J. Edward Gerald, *The Social Responsibility of the Press* (Minneapolis: University of Minnesota Press, 1963) is a profound statement of the need for a professionally responsible press. One of the duties of a socially responsible press is to convey to society an understanding of its problems. Theodore M. Brown, *Margaret Bourke-White: Photojournalist* (Ithaca: Andrew Dickinson Museum of Art, 1972) provides fresh insights into the communicative power of photography by focusing on the work of an outstanding social critic of the 1930's. A. William Bluem, *Documentary in American Television* (New York: Hastings House, 1965) is a thoughtful and thorough examination of television as an instrument for the achievement of social progress.

The establishment American press had seldom provided responsible coverage of the problems of minority groups until the Civil Rights movement of the 1960's forced attention on them. Likewise, journalism historians had seldom given serious attention to the contributions of black journalists until the last decade. Among the most recent and best works on this much neglected subject are Roland E. Wolseley, *The Black Press U.S.A.* (Ames: Iowa State University Press, 1971); Andrew Buni, *Robert L. Vann of the Pittsburgh Courier: Politics and Black*

Journalism (Pittsburgh: University of Pittsburgh Press, 1974); John D. Stevens, *From the Back of the Foxhole: Black Correspondents in World War II* (Journalism Monographs, No. 27, Minneapolis: Association for Education in Journalism, February, 1973).

Magazines continued to prosper in the 20th century as individual circulations numbered in the millions. One of the most prosperous was the *Saturday Evening Post* which became a fixture in millions of American homes. John Tebbel, *George Horace Lorimer and the Saturday Evening Post* (Garden City: Doubleday, 1948) is the best book on Lorimer who edited the magazine between 1899–1937. After World War II many of the large circulation magazines began to experience financial difficulties. The large circulations which had brought prosperity to many proved to be their undoing. Production costs soared and advertising rates were increased in order to bring in more revenue. But after 1950, magazines, the first national medium, were in competition with television, the newest national medium, and magazines lost advertisers to television which offered larger audiences at a lower unit cost. The demise of the *Post* is indicative of other magazines of its kind and its problems are best told in Otto Friedrich, *Decline and Fall* (New York: Harper & Row, 1970). An encyclopedic study of magazines since 1895 is provided by Theodore Peterson, *Magazines in the Twentieth Century*, 2nd. ed. (Urbana: University of Illinois Press, 1964). Also useful for information on this period are James L. C. Ford, *Magazines for Millions* (Carbondale: Southern Illinois University Press, 1969) and John Tebbel, *The American Magazine: A Compact History* (New York: Hawthorne, 1969).

One of the most significant developments in magazine publishing in the 20th century was the appearance of the weekly news magazine of which *Time* was the first in 1923. *Time* and its imitators, most notably *Newsweek*, offered their readers a condensation of the week's important news, plus regular coverage of the arts, science, law, and lifestyles. But it was not what *Time* reported that made it unique, rather it was its style of reporting that set it apart from more traditional magazines. *Time*, under the guidance of its owner, Henry R. Luce, developed its own personality and language, e.g. calling its writers **Timen** and Time-Life publications **Lucepress**. Robert T. Elson, *Time Inc.: The Intimate History of a Publishing Enterprise, 1923–1941* and Robert T. Elson, *The World of Time Inc.: An Intimate History of a Publishing Enterprise, 1941–1960* (New York: Atheneum, 1968, 1973) is an authorized, but objective, study. W. A. Swanberg *Luce and His Empire* (New York: Scribner's, 1972) is an interesting though at times simplistic, study of Luce's power and his misuse of it.

The decades since the end of the Second World War have been difficult ones for the news media. In particular, major newspapers and television network news departments have been severely criticized for their supposed political biases. To liberals, the news media appeared at times to be monolithically conservative, while conservatives have accused the media of being monolithically liberal. James Aronson, *The Press and the Cold War* (Indianapolis: Bobbs-Merrill, 1970) offers a strong argument that the press has played a major role in promoting fear of Communism during the Cold War, which Aronson dates to the Bolshevik Revolution. The CBS Network has long been considered the leader in television journalism. Its coverage of the nation's social and political ills has brought it acclaim, but it also led to CBS being identified with the Eastern liberal establishment during the Nixon presidency. Alexander Kendrick, *Prime Time: The Life of Edward R. Murrow* (Boston: Little Brown, 1969) is the definitive study of the man who is probably the most responsible for CBS's highly regarded reputation. But it is also an indictment of commercial television and the ratings system which, the author says, shuns controversial programming. A similar theme is found in a book by Murrow's colleague, Fred W. Friendly, *Due to Circumstances Beyond Our Control* (New York: Random House, 1967). William Small, *To Kill a Messenger* (New York: Hastings House, 1970) is a detailed account of CBS news coverage of the social and political upheaval of the 1960's and of the criticism of the network that it generated.

The Vietnam War and the crisis of credibility and divisiveness it caused in the nation also affected American journalism. Gay Talese, *The Kingdom and the Power* (New York: World, 1969) describes the internal struggle over editorial policy at the *New York Times* during the 1960's and is the best recent history of that newspaper. News coverage of the war also re-introduced the controversy over the line separating objective, dispassionate reporting from patriotism. Joseph J. Mathews, *Reporting the Wars* (Minneapolis: University of Minnesota Press, 1957) and Phillip Knightley, *The First Casualty* (New York: Harcourt, Brace & Jovanovich, 1975) are the best sources for the history of war correspondence. The anti-Vietnam War protest, and the related Counterculture movement, generated its own journalism in the 1960's because its adherents believed the establishment news media was failing to provide full coverage of anti-establishment positions. Robert J. Glessing, *The Underground Press in America* (Bloomington: Indiana University Press, 1970) and Laurence Leamer, *The Paper Revolutionaries: The Rise of the Underground Press* (New York: Simon & Schuster, 1972) are perceptive studies on the subject. Finally, after years of controversy and accusations of journalistic conspiracy and bias, the clash between government and the press peaked during the news media's coverage of Watergate. William E. Porter, *Assault on the Media: The Nixon Years* (Ann Arbor: University of Michigan Press, 1976) is a penetrating, well documented study of this period which should remain as a standard reference for some time to come.

Themes in American Journalism History
The interpretation of American journalism history has been dominated by the Progressive interpretation of American history and its principal advocates, Frederick Jackson Turner, Charles A. Beard and Vernon Louis Parrington. This interpretation has placed the development of journalism within the context of the Progressives' belief in the unilinear march of progress and liberalism. The heroes of journalism have been crusading editors such as Horace Greeley and Joseph Pulitzer who battled the dark forces of conservatism, repression and reactionary social ideas. Studies of great men in journalism dominate much of the literature. Willard G. Bleyer, *Main Currents in the History of American Journalism* (Boston:

Houghton Mifflin, 1927) concentrates on the contributions of individuals in de-fining the meaning of journalism history in a manner similar to Parrington's *Main Currents in American Thought*. Alfred M. Lee, *The Daily Newspaper in America* (New York: Macmillan, 1937); Frank Luther Mott, *American Journalism*, 3rd. ed. (New York: Macmillan, 1962) and Edwin Emery, *The Press and America* 3rd. ed. (Englewood Cliffs: Prentice-Hall, 1972) document the development of journalism in the United States as the nation passes through the context of Turner's frontier thesis into the context of Beard's urban-industrial frontier. The time has come for a radically different interpretation of journalism history grounded in the context of a paradigm other than that of the Progressive interpretation. Journalism history, like the history of the United States, is a mosaic and the Progressive interpreta-tion has supplied only a part of the total picture. The rest of it is incomplete.□

EPILOGUE

by Joseph P. McKerns

The dominance of the Progressive interpretation of American journalism history waned in the 1970s as historians turned to the work
of scholars in social, cultural, and intellectual history and the
social sciences in search of new conceptualizations. This period
of scholarly vitality and creativity, which should continue through
the 1980s, was initiated by James W. Carey's provocative essay,
"The Problem of Journalism History," Journalism History, 1 (Spring
1974). Carey's essay drew a wide response from journalism historians who published their ideas on new directions in journalism
historiography.

Several excellent essays were published in a special issue of
Journalism History, 2 (Summer 1975), devoted to "Seeking New Paths
in Research." Subsequent historiographical essays of note are
Hazel Garcia, "'What a Buzzel Is This. . .About Kentuck?' New
Approaches and an Application," Journalism History, 3 (Spring
1976); Joseph P. McKerns, "The Limits of Progressive Journalism
History," Journalism History, 4 (Autumn 1977); and Jean Ward,
"Interdisciplinary Research and the Journalism Historian," Jour-
nalism History, 5 (Spring 1978).

The quarterly Journalism History is a valuable scholarly journal,
the only one of its kind in the field. Since its first issue in
1974 it has published research articles, historiographical essays,
and bibliographies of high quality. Its scope of interest includes
all of the mass media, from print to film to video, throughout
American and world history. Each issue contains book reviews and
abstracts of research published in other journals. It regularly

devotes an entire issue to articles on a single subject; e.g., the Autumn 1975 issue on the mass media in the 1920s and the Summer 1978 issue on "Studies in Ethics." Other special issues are noted below. Its editor from the beginning has been Professor Tom Reilly of the Department of Journalism at California State University-Northridge.

In addition to developing new conceptualizations, journalism historians have turned their attention to such subjects as women, blacks, and other minorities in journalism history--subjects that received little attention in the past. Two special issues on women in American journalism were published by Journalism History (Winter 1974-75, and Winter 1976-77). In addition to informative articles on individual women journalists, each issue contains valuable bibliographies on women in all areas of mass communication. A three-part series by Anne Mather, "A History of Feminist Periodicals," Journalism History, 1 (Autumn 1974), 1 (Winter 1974-75), and 2 (Spring 1975), is also noteworthy. Two important books that share the theme that women have been significant participants in journalism history, and have often had to battle strong male opposition to their participation, are Marion Marzolf, Up From the Footnote: A History of Women Journalists (New York: Hastings House, 1977), and Maurine Beasley and Sheila Silver, Women in Media: A Documentary Source Book (Washington, D.C.: Women's Institute for Freedom of the Press, 1977). The neglected role of the woman printer is examined in Richard I. Demeter, Primer, Presses, and Composing Sticks: Women Printers of the Colonial Period (Hicksville, N.Y.: Exposition Press, 1979).

The role of minorities in journalism history has been the subject of two Journalism History special issues: "The Black Press," 4 (Winter 1977-78), and "Spanish Language Media," 4 (Summer 1977). Both issues also include comprehensive bibliographies. A thoughtful examination of the reaction of black journalists to World War II is found in Lee Finkle, Forum for Protest: The Black Press During World War II (Cranbury, N.J.: Fairleigh Dickinson University Press, 1975).

The biography remains a staple of journalism history and among the best scholarly studies of the past few years are two on women. Paula Blanchard, *Margaret Fuller: From Transcendentalism to Revolution (New York: Delacorte, 1978), examines the brilliant nineteenth-century intellectual, editor, and foreign correspondent and literary critic of the New York Tribune. Robert Peel, *Mary Baker Eddy: The Years of Authority (New York: Holt, Rinehart and Winston, 1977), tells of the founding of the Christian Science Monitor, one of the world's great newspapers.

Fresh and informative biographies of two major journalists are William M. Armstrong, E. L. Godkin: A Biography (Albany: State University of New York Press, 1978), on the much-written-about editor of the Nation and the New York Post; Charles A. Fecher, Mencken: A Study of His Thought (New York: Alfred A. Knopf, 1978);

and W. H. A. Williams, H. L. Mencken (Boston: Twayne Publishers, 1977). Also of note is John Milton Cooper, Jr., Walter Hines Page: The Southerner as American, 1855-1918 (Chapel Hill: University of North Carolina Press, 1977), the first biography on Page since the 1920s. A biography that also describes the building of a major media empire is George Mills, Harvey Ingham and Gardner Cowles, Sr.: Things Don't Just Happen, edited by Joan Bunke (Ames: Iowa State University Press, 1977).

The publication of two journalists' correspondence gives insights into, and details on, nineteenth-century journalism: William Cullen Bryant II and Thomas G. Voss, eds., The Letters of William Cullen Bryant, Vol. II, 1836-49 (New York: Fordham University Press, 1977), and George E. Fortenberry, Stanton Gardner and Robert H. Woodward, eds., The Correspondence of Harold Frederic, Vol. I (Fort Worth: Texas Christian University Press, 1977). Frederic was the London correspondent of the New York Times in the 1880s and early 1890s. Paul M. Zall, ed., *Comical Spirit of Seventy-Six: The Humor of Francis Hopkinson (San Marino, Calif.: The Huntington Library, 1976), discusses Hopkinson's role as national jester, like Will Rogers or Art Buchwald in later times. This study uses his writings to illuminate the use of humor in newspaper propaganda from the Revolution to the Constitutional Convention. Who Was Who in Journalism, 1925-1928 (Detroit: Gale Research Co., 1978), includes over 4,000 biographies of men and women journalists plus other information on the news media of the time.

Although a great deal has been written about Edward R. Murrow, R. Franklin Smith's biography, *Edward R. Murrow--The War Years (Kalamazoo, Mich.: New Issues Press, 1978), offers a unique study based on extensive quotations obtained in primary research with twenty-nine of Murrow's wartime colleagues. A contemporary of Murrow's, Walter Winchell, is also the subject of a well-written biography: Herman Klurfeld, Winchell: His Life and Times (New York: Praeger, 1976). These two men and other influential, pioneer broadcast journalists of the 1930s and 1940s are examined in two perceptive and readable books: Irving Fang, Those Radio Commentators (Ames: Iowa State University Press, 1977), and David H. Culbert, News for Everyman: Radio and Foreign Affairs in Thirties America (Westport, Conn.: Greenwood Press, 1976).

In the past, New York journalism dominated the attention of journalism historians. However, in recent years several excellent studies of regional and frontier journalism have appeared. Thomas H. Heuterman, Movable Type: Biography of Legh R. Freeman (Ames: Iowa State University Press, 1979), contributes to our understanding of the growth of journalism in the West through the life of an editor who published newspapers on sixteen sites after the Civil War. Another view of frontier journalism is found in Monte Burr McLaws, Spokesman for the Kingdom: Early Mormon Journalism and the Deseret News, 1830-1898 (Provo: Brigham Young University Press, 1977). Equally noteworthy are Herndon J. Evans, The Newspaper Press in Kentucky (Lexington: University Press of Kentucky, 1977);

Alan Robert Miller, The History of Current Maine Newspapers
(Lisbon Falls, Maine: Eastland Press, 1978); and Wesley Norton,
Religious Newspapers in the Old Northwest to 1861: A History,
Bibliography and Record of Opinion (Athens: Ohio University Press,
1977).

Two studies on magazines offer a detailed look at journalism at
both ends of the political spectrum: Martin F. Doudna, Concern
About the Planet: The Reporter Magazine and American Liberalism,
1949-1968 (Westport, Conn.: Greenwood Press, 1977), and Samuel A.
Schreiner, Jr., The Condensed World of Reader's Digest (New York:
Stein and Day, 1977). For most of its first 100 years, the
Washington Post was an average newspaper at best. Its history from
1877 through the stormy years of Watergate is recorded in Chalmers
M. Roberts, The Washington Post: The First 100 Years (Boston:
Houghton-Mifflin Co., 1977). A more provocative and controversial
examination of the growth and influence of the Post and other major
media institutions, including Time, the Los Angeles Times, and
CBS, is David Halberstam, *The Powers That Be (New York: Alfred A.
Knopf, 1979).

Three books that explore the relationship, often strained or
manipulative, between the press and the government are: Culver H.
Smith, The Press, Politics, and Patronage: The American Govern-
ment's Use of Newspapers, 1789-1875 (Athens: The University of
Georgia Press, 1977), which is valuable mostly for its discussion
of the Jacksonian Era; Allan M. Winkler, The Politics of Propa-
ganda: The Office of War Information, 1942-45 (New Haven: Yale
University Press, 1978), a well-documented study; and Dorothy
Garfield, Unmailable: Congress and the Post Office (Athens: The
University of Georgia Press, 1977). The formative period of
English and American journalism is the subject of a collection of
papers in Donovan H. Bond and W. Reynolds McLeod, eds., *Newslet-
ters to Newspapers: Eighteenth-Century Journalism (Morgantown,
W. Va.: The School of Journalism, West Virginia University, 1977).

One of the social causes that the American press has frequently
championed is the organizing activity of the labor movement. It
is ironic, therefore, that too often within its own industry the
press has acted like the industrialists it has often opposed.
William E. Ames and Roger A. Simpson, Unionism or Hearst, the
Seattle Post-Intelligencer Strike of 1936 (Seattle: Pacific
Northwest Labor History Association, 1978), thoughtfully examines
a facet of the labor history of journalism. A unique, pioneering
form of journalism that used dramatic reenactment of history and
current events, an off-stage narrator, and actual newsreel footage
to explain social and political issues of the day is the subject
of Raymond Fielding's The March of Time, 1935-1951 (New York:
Oxford University Press, 1978). Two books which illuminate other
facets of the visual communication of ideas and opinion are Thomas
C. Blaisdell, Peter Selz and University of California Seminar,
The American Presidency in Political Cartoons, 1776-1976 (Berkeley:
University Art Museum, 1976), and Lewis L. Gould and Richard

Greffe, Photojournalist: The Career of Jimmy Hare (Austin:
University of Texas Press, 1977). Hare was among those photogra-
phers active in the early days of pictorial journalism, and he
worked primarily with Collier's and Frank Leslie's Illustrated
Newspaper from the 1880s through World War I.

Edwin Emery's comprehensive history of American journalism, The
Press and America: An Interpretative History of the Mass Media,
4th ed., (Englewood Cliffs, N.J.: Prentice-Hall, 1978), remains
the standard reference and classroom text in the field. Emery's
son, Michael, co-authored the fourth edition, and the two collaborated on a noteworthy historiographical essay, "Images of America
in Its Twentieth Century Media," published in Revue Francaise
D'Etudes Américaines N'6 (October 1978). Michael Schudson,
Discovering the News: A Social History of the News (New York:
Basic Books, 1978), theorizes that the developing and changing
system of news values parallels the developing and changing values
of American culture. Hanno Hardt, *Social Theories of the Press:
Early German and American Perspectives (Beverly Hills, Calif.: Sage
Publications, 1979), argues that the development of a critical-
intellectual tradition in the study of communication must begin
with an understanding of its history and that the intellectual
history of the field will yield theoretical insights into the
relationship between the media and the advancement of society.
George N. Gordon, *The Communication Revolution: A History of Mass
Media in the United States (New York: Hastings House, 1977),
attempts a comprehensive, thematic approach, but lacks a conceptual
center.

Two books that go beyond the "treasury of great reporting" approach
to journalism history are Lawrence W. Lichty and Malachi C.
Topping, *American Broadcasting: A Source Book on the History of
Radio and Television (New York: Hastings House, 1975), and Calder
M. Pickett, *Voices of the Past: Key Documents in the History of
American Journalism (Columbus, Ohio: Grid Inc., 1977). Pickett's
collection of documents is especially well chosen and covers the
full expanse of American journalism history. In addition to news
reports, Pickett includes editorials, essays, advertisements,
speeches, transcripts, and songs that, along with Pickett's analytical interludes, bring to life the rich and diverse spirit of
American journalism.

American English: A Bibliographic Essay

RAVEN I. McDAVID, JR.

Since colonial times, observers have commented on the differences between American English as they found it and the standard speech (or other varieties) of the United Kingdom. These comments range from the petty gripes of travelers to serious and extensive investigations. Hardly a day goes by without some new observation or, more often, a rephrasing of an old one. Comments on American English may appear anywhere. As an index of American culture, the topic interests linguists, anthropologists, sociologists, folklorists, historians, criminologists, as well as students of literature and the general laity.

Sorting out this material is a formidable task. Despite his omnivorous reading and many contacts with other students of the language, even the indefatigable H. L. Mencken had to rely on commercial clipping services; at that, he missed some items and could provide critical perspective on only a handful. This essay, too, does not pretend to be exhaustive; it reflects the experience and interests of the writer. Nevertheless, it should help an interested layman find his way, while reminding him that no filing system, however efficient, can substitute for close observation and informed judgment.

Bibliographies

Essentially, every student of American English must be his own bibliographer. The only recent attempt at a comprehensive bibliography is Brenni*; it were best ignored (see *Journal of English and Germanic Philology* LXIV, 574–8). Kennedy is comprehensive and indispensable, but it has not been updated (the briefer Kennedy and Sands treats English language and literature; its 1972 updating ignores the early work of 1927). Furthermore, it treats the entire history and geographical spread of English. Allen *Linguistics* (1967, 1977), indispensable for the graduate student, are limited in size; they go beyond American English in several directions, notably general linguistics.

The reference guides to periodical literature are undependable. Each covers a limited number of publications, in a restricted field of general or scholarly interest; an article on American English which might be of general interest—or of particular interest to education, humanities, or social sciences—may be ignored by all indexes. One often does not know which reference guide to consult unless he knows the journal an article appeared in; and in such instances it is easier to go directly to the journal, which usually publishes a cumulative index at regular intervals. *Dissertation Abstracts* does not have as effective cross-referencing as it might have; in compensation, the abstracts are more likely than mere titles to give the reader an idea of the importance of a given work. Copies are easily obtained; and even those institutions which microfilm their own dissertations make their work known to the editors of *DA.*

Bibliographical supplements to scholarly publications are often spotty. That to *Publications of the Modern Language Association (PMLA)* now has little on language; that to *General Linguistics* is likely to slight matters of intense lay concern like lexicography and usage. For many years (1925–69) *American Speech* published a bibliography in each issue; this feature lapsed during the malaise of the journal in the 1960s, and has not been resumed. Of special merit is Avis *Bibliography,* though limited to Canadian English. Bahr and Avis-Kinloch provide later and fuller coverage.

---

* *All works referred to in this essay are cited fully in the Bibliography but they are not necessarily in the section corresponding to their mention in the text.*

Among general works with extensive formal bibliographies are Baugh *History,* Baugh and Cable, Krapp *English Language,* Mencken *Language* 1919–1923. Later versions of Mencken—1936–1963—have no formal bibliographies but extensive bibliographical information in the footnotes. The brief McDavid "English Language" excluded dialectology, lexicography, and non-English dialects, but useful bibliographical information on those topics is found in the contributions of Avis, Cassidy, Haugen, Read and others to the same volume (Sebeok); similar information is found in the various contributions to Marckwardt.

No general dictionary published in the United States since Webster 1909 has offered a bibliography. Research dictionaries— the *Oxford English Dictionary* (1933), the *Dictionary of American English* (*DAE,* 1938–44), the *Dictionary of Americanisms* (*DA,* 1951), the *Dictionary of Canadianisms* (1967)—have bibliographies; however, such bibliographies are concerned with the sources of citations, which are rarely works on the language itself.

Works on special topics often have bibliographies, but their extent and emphasis depend on the interest and energy—often the ideology—of the authors. For instance, the *Handbook of the Linguistic Geography of New England* (Kurath *et al.* 1939, 2d ed. 1973) contains a general bibliography of the field; the *Linguistic Atlas of the Upper Midwest* (Allen) lists only works concerned with the immediate region. Symposia, *e.g.* R. McDavid-Duckert *Lexicography,* sometimes have bibliographies (Gates), the quality and comprehensiveness depending on the editors. For individual scholars, bibliographies are

---

Raven I. McDavid, Jr. is Professor Emeritus of English at the University of Chicago where he has taught since 1957. He received his B.A. from Furman University in 1931, and his M.A. and Ph.D. from Duke University in 1933 and 1935. In 1972 he was awarded a Litt. D. from Duke, and in 1965 he was a Fulbright professor at Johannes Gutenberg Universität in Mainz, Germany. This spring he is teaching at Louisiana State University, Baton Rouge. Professor McDavid has published widely in the field of linguistics, has been editor of the Linguistic Atlas of the Middle and South Atlantic States since 1975, and is an active member of a number of professional organizations, including the American Dialect Society which he served as president in 1967–8. In 1969 he received the David Russell Award for Distinguished Research from the National Council of Teachers of English. The research for this study was made possible by the Newberry Library, Chicago.

often appended to portraits (R. McDavid "Kurath"), obituaries (Hill "Marckwardt"), Festschriften (L. Davis *Studies,* Scholler-Reidy), or volumes of selected essays, such as those edited by Anwar Dil in the Stanford-Pakistan series, *e.g.,* Haugen *Ecology,* R. McDavid *Varieties.*

Serials

The most important periodical is *American Speech,* founded in 1925 at the instigation of Mencken and with the endorsement of most of the prominent scholars in the field, *e.g.,* Louise Pound of Nebraska, A. G. Kennedy of Stanford, Albert C. Baugh of Pennsylvania. Pound, the original editor, was succeeded in 1933 by Cabell Greet of Columbia, and after an interlude the editorship devolved upon John Algeo of Georgia, a dynamic figure in the study of modern English. A general magazine dealing with American English and its affiliates, it has attracted a wide range of contributors from timid beginners to such giants as Leonard Bloomfield, Otto Jespersen, and Edgar Sturtevant, among linguists, and among literary scholars Walter Blair and Howard Mumford Jones. It is now the principal publication of the American Dialect Society.

Related to *American Speech* are two other journals issued by the American Dialect Society, which was founded in 1889, charged with preparing an American dialect dictionary analogous to that for the British Isles (Wright 1898–1905). *Dialect Notes* (1889–1939) was the first publication specifically concerned with American English. Although the Society in that period was never large and was afflicted more than most organizations with financial and editorial problems—only six volumes appeared during the life of *DN*—the journal indicates a wide range of interest in North American English. Reorganized in 1942, the Society in 1944 began a new series, *Publications of the American Dialect Society.* Since from the beginning *PADS* had tended to become a monograph series, this function was officially recognized when the Society assumed responsibility for *American Speech;* from a semi-annual publication *PADS* has become a supplement.

Orbis, founded in 1952 by Sever Pop at the Louvain Center for General Dialectology, regularly publishes articles on American dialects. The *Journal of English Linguistics,* published since 1967 by Western Washington University in Bellingham, has a wide concern with American English as well as with other varieties of the language; most of its publications are of general interest. The *Canadian Journal of Linguistics* (1954–) emphasizes things Canadian, but its articles on English are of interest to readers in the United States since the international boundary is even more permeable in language than in other aspects of culture. The even more frankly local *RLS* (*Regional Language Studies—Newfoundland;* 1968–) also has significant articles; for instance, Aldus 1969 (Anglo-Irish dialects—a bibliography, *RLS* 2) is important to everyone concerned with the origins of New World English.

With the recent proliferation of information, scholars today generally have a narrower range of interest than their predecessors. Few students of classical or Romance linguistics now are as interested in American English as were Sturtevant, Charles S. Grandgent, and more recently Robert A. Hall, Jr. The Modern Language Association, ironically, is chiefly concerned with literature, and the Linguistic Society of America moves increasingly to theoretical concerns (the newer LACUS—Linguistic Association of Canada and the United States—not to be confused with the Canadian Linguistic Association—occasionally offers something of general interest). Rarely today does one find American English discussed in the *American Journal of Philology,* in *PMLA,* or in *Language.* Most of the new journals dealing with language follow Chomsky and Lees in rejecting the "dull cataloguer of data" for more elegant theoretical concerns.

General Works

The basic work for the study of American English is H. L. Mencken, *The American Language.* The original edition (1919) of a philological work by an iconoclastic social critic was received with incredulity by many professional scholars. With the author still under suspicion because of his skepticism toward a war to "make the world safe for democracy," the work was sometimes looked on as another bit of pro-German propaganda. In fact, Mencken had been interested in American English since boyhood, had commented on the subject as early as 1898, and had begun work on the manuscript in 1915; federal censorship merely provided him with time to concentrate by taking him away from editorial writing. When the first edition sold out immediately, public demand led to a second edition in 1921, a third in 1923. A drastically revised fourth edition (1936) offered a new thesis, the ascendency of American over British; its organization was followed in the

Critic H. L. Mencken, photographed on his 75th birthday, September 12, 1955. Prints and Photographs Division, Library of Congress.

massive supplements of 1945 and 1948 and in the 1963 abridgment by R. McDavid (all four of the last are still in print). *The*

American Language has influenced all subsequent investigations of the national idiom. Such diverse scholars as Haugen, Kurath, R. McDavid, and Allen Walker Read have acknowledged their indebtedness; they and their colleagues kept Mencken informed of their research so that the bibliographical footnotes in the Supplements rival the text in bulk.

Although Mencken was not the first writer to discuss American English at length, most of his predecessors are less accessible. Tucker *American English* is a tamer contemporary of Mencken. Reprinted earlier works include Pickering; Bartlett *Dictionary* 1848, 1859; Schele de Vere; Farmer; and Thornton.

More formal than Mencken and reflected in *The American Language* from the third edition (Mencken acknowledges access to the manuscript) is George Philip Krapp, *The English Language in America,* especially good in the discussion of early pronunciation, notably for New England. Although some of its conclusions are dated—new evidence has been provided by dialect research on both sides of the Atlantic, by the historical dictionaries, and by such studies as Dobson—it remains a monumental work, deservedly reprinted.

Of recent studies, the best is Forgue, a lively work by a Mencken scholar who has distressed the professional guardians of French linguistic chastity. Written for a European audience, it necessarily explains things Americans take for granted, and, therefore, provides the American reader with fresh perspectives. A decade later than Mencken 1963 and free of the structure of previous editions, it is the most up to date treatment of American English, though the fact that it is in French has kept it from being known in the United States as widely as it deserves.

Also in the Menckenian tradition is Pyles—literate, witty, astringent, without footnotes, designed for the general reader but regrettably out of print. Still available is Marckwardt *American English,* designed for both the general reader and the beginning student. It derives from the course assignments which Marckwardt and Thomas A. Knott developed at the University of Michigan in the 1930s—the first influential course in American English, though George Hempl had previously offered such a course at Michigan at the turn of the century. Laird, like Pyles, is a popular treatment by a serious scholar, with a minimum of apparatus. Less successful is Dohan, a dilute extract of Mencken without the Menckenian skepticism toward new linguistic revelations. Flexner is frankly designed to entertain a popular audience. Dillard *All American English* and *American Talk* reflect hostility toward the methods of historical linguistics in general and of linguistic geography in particular. As a practitioner of those disciplines, I am disqualified from further comment. For Canadian English, McConnell *Voice* is a remarkable combination of scholarship and popularization, suitable for any audience from junior high school to past-doctoral seminar.

Anthologies

American publishers have issued numerous collections of essays on linguistic topics, designed as the subject matter for a course or as a supplement to the course textbook. Since American colleges are the principal market, these collections naturally emphasize American English. Oriented towards a general introduction to linguistics—with strong sections on usage, lexicography, and dialectology—is Allen *Readings,* one of the most successful. Emphasizing American English as a symbol of American culture is Babcock. Somewhere in between are Bailey and Robinson, and Shores; other collections are listed at the end of this essay.

Dictionaries

Although Dryden, Swift, and their contemporaries called for a lexicographer to fix the language forever, beyond the power of capricious change to alter, the English worry about such matters far less than they used to. As far as their usage is concerned, dictionaries are useful tools but not objects for veneration; standards proceed from the usage of the cultivated and are not externally imposed. But in the United States, where a community rarely has a hereditary elite, linguistic etiquet is often learned from external models, such as grammars and dictionaries. Noah Webster epitomizes that search for an external standard independent of British models, through his "blue back speller" (1783) and his dictionaries of 1806, 1828, and 1841. Subsequently his name has lent an aura of authority to the publications of G & C Merriam, notably their large dictionaries (inept publicity brought upon the Merriam 1961 many undeserved accusations of debasing the language).

The "International" series of Merriam dictionaries has had no effective competition since World War I. From the 1860s, Merriam has concentrated on the production of dictionaries and related works. To this end it has maintained a permanent editorial cadre and steadily developed its file of citations to over eleven million. No competitor has been willing to spend as much in research and development; as a result, such competitors have usually faded after a successful edition or two. The *Century Dictionary,* the nearest American analog to the *Oxford,* lapsed after an unsuccessful 1909 supplement, though its materials have been incorporated in several later works. The nineteenth-century dictionaries of Joseph Worcester went unrevised after his death; the Funk and Wagnalls *Standard* and *New Standard* were creditable competitors of Merriam 1890 and 1909, but there has been no successor. The *Webster's New World (WNWD)* (1952) and the *Random House (RHD),* both advertised as encyclopedic, were "collegiate" dictionaries with non-lexicographical material added; so, essentially, is the *American Heritage (AHD),* merchandised on the strength of a so-called "usage panel" (largely of *belletristes*) and of undisguised hostility to the Merriam *Third New International* (see Creswell). No American publisher can pretend to have produced a serious competitor to the *Third New International;* if one should appear it would soon be dwarfed by the impending *Fourth.*

More highly competitive is the so-called "collegiate" field—the prototype being the Merriam *Webster's Collegiate,* abridgments of the *Internationals.* Originally designed as handy reference works for undergraduates, with about 90,000 entries (against the 450,000 or so of the *Internationals*), they have a ready market among laymen who wish something handy and moderately priced. From the 1929 Depression through World War II, Merriam dominated this field, thanks to the decline of the competition (Funk and Wagnalls, Winston; the *Macmillan Modern Dictionary* of 1938 appeared at an inauspicious time and never caught on). Since 1945 several new competitors have appeared under various (and sometimes changing) corporate auspices: *American College Dictionary (ACD), WNWD College Edition, RHD College Edition, AHD,* matched by various printings of Merriam's *New Collegiate, Seventh New Collegiate,* and *New Collegiate,* eighth edition. There are differences in detail: Merriam and World arrange the meanings of a word in historical order, the others in estimated order of relative frequency; pronunciation keys vary slightly; all publishers except Merriam favor a single alphabet, with proper names interspersed among the commonalty. But at bottom they are very much alike, edited with care but avoiding novelty; intangibles, rather than absolute quality, are likely to influence one's choice. The judgment of Dykema is still valid: none is perfect but none is to be despised. Of the same general quality, but of smaller dimensions, are the "desk" dictionaries, originally designed for secretaries in business offices. Perhaps the best of these is the *Thorndike-Barnhart Desk Dictionary,* edited by Clarence Barnhart, a student and friend of Leonard Bloomfield and original editor of the *ACD.* As an editor of dictionaries for specific markets (such as the 1963 work that accompanied the *World Book Encyclopedia*) he is comparable in energy and versatility to Noah Webster. Other successful desk dictionaries have been produced by Doubleday and Scribner.

Although one thinks chiefly of general dictionaries like Merriam's when discussing American lexicography, there are some notable American research dictionaries in the tradition of the *Oxford.* The *Dictionary of American English (DAE)* was inaugurated by Sir William Craigie, one of the last editors of the *Oxford,* on realizing that such a dictionary was necessary to provide an adequate record of the language. The *DAE* treats both innovations and survivals in New World English; its successor, the *Dictionary of Americanisms (DA)* of Mitford M. Mathews, includes only innovations. Analogous historical works are W. S. Avis's *Dictionary of Canadianisms* and George

Story's *Dictionary of Newfoundland English* (in progress). One should also mention F. G. Cassidy and Robert LePage, *Dictionary of Jamaican English,* which sheds light on the present-day speech of the American South, and especially on the relationships between the speech of American blacks and the creolized English of the West Indies. The forthcoming *Dictionary of American Regional English*

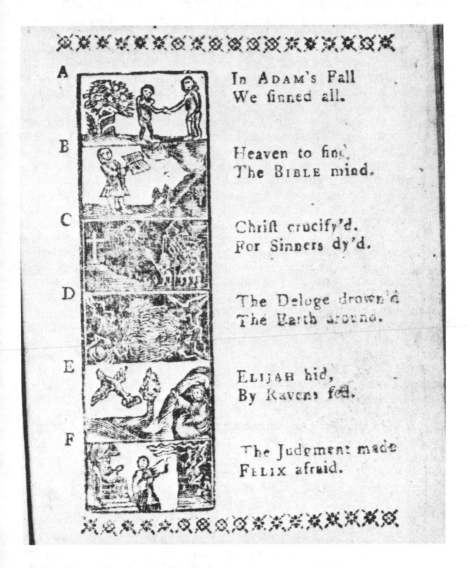

The New England Primer, *Improved edition of 1773, the book from which generations of young Americans learned to read. Printed in Boston by T. and J. Fleet, at the* Bible & Heart *in Cornhill.*

(Cassidy) and the *Historical Dictionary of American Slang* (Lighter) will be discussed later. One of many interesting topical dictionaries is the *Dictionary of American Political Words and Phrases* (Sperber and Trittschuh).

With dictionaries important artifacts in American culture—their importance in America far exceeds it in Britain; and there is no British analog to the profitable "collegiate" dictionaries in America—and with the making and selling of dictionaries a profitable and highly competitive business, criticism of dictionaries and their makers can be severe. No past editor has been immune to such criticisms (Laughlin), which reached all-time intensity in the appraisal of the Merriam *Third.* In all fairness, this misappraisal was brought about by the Merriam Company itself, through a poorly conceived publicity release which stressed the lexical novelties, the unconventional sources of citations—athletes, stage comedians, airline flight tables—and the alleged abdication of authority in favor of general usage. It mattered little to the critics of the *Third* that Samuel Johnson had accepted the rule of usage in the 1755 preface to his dictionary or that the Sanskrit grammarians had enunciated this principle twelve centuries before Johnson. To the American journalist or literary critic it is still unthinkable that a dictionary might recognize the unprintable *ain't* as sometimes used in the speech of the educated. At all events, the *Third* began to receive widespread condemnation within a day after the distribution of the publicity release and three weeks before the official date of publication. The attacks on the *Third* led to editorial timidity among Merriam's competitors; the *American Heritage,* in particular, did its best to take a contrary stance though its actual editorial policies differed little (Creswell).

From criticism of the *Third,* ultimately, came a reexamination of the lexicographical tradition in English through various means: case books for undergraduate research (the best is Sledd and Ebbitt); dissertations (Laughlin, Creswell); symposia (R. McDavid-Duckert, Weinbrot). Also came the founding of two centers in lexicography— one at Indiana State University for the history of the craft, the other at the University of Western Ontario for lexicographical resources, chiefly collections of citations which might be examined by makers of future dictionaries—and the founding of a Dictionary Society of North America. Recent overviews with full bibliographies are Barnhart and McMillan.

Americanisms

Chapter II of Mencken 1936–1963 presents a historical survey of the various definitions of the term *Americanism,* beginning with Witherspoon. No two observers agree exactly: Mathews specifies that a word or meaning must be attested by written or printed sources to have entered the language in what is now the United States. With

Canadianisms, Avis is less rigid; it accepts not only words and meanings that first entered English in what is now Canada, but also those that are associated with Canadian history and culture. Thus it includes *chowder,* almost certainly taken into English from Canadian French but first attested in print in New England.

Accurate classification of Americanisms—as indeed of Canadianisms, Australianisms, South Africanisms, and the like— requires similar careful study of Briticisms: linguistic forms that, though part of the original stock of English, did not journey overseas, or that have originated in England since the diaspora of English and have become identified with the British Isles. So long as English could be presumed the property of the homeland, it was difficult to identify these features or even to promote the study of them. But with England now contributing less than a fourth of the total of native speakers of English—even disregarding the millions who have as a native language an indigenous variety of English in Asia or Africa— such a proprietary attitude is outmoded. Regrettably, students of Briticisms are rare; the most dedicated is the protean Allen Walker Read, whose work when published (it was begun in the 1930s) is sure to be a landmark in the historical study of English.

Most studies of Americanisms involve the lexicon: words and meanings, the kinds of features most easily identified by the laity. Yet certain phonological features seem to be of North American origin, though they are limited in their regional distribution:

> 1) The upgliding diphthong in *bird*: New York City and the Lower South, in New York City often coalescing with the /oi/ of *Boyd.*
> 2) The monophthongization of /oi/, so that *oil* may become homonymous with *all:* parts of the inland South.
> 3) The loss of the contrast between *cot* and *caught:* northeastern New England, western Pennsylvania, most of Canada, parts of the Rocky Mountains and Pacific Coast.
> 4) Striking variation in the vowels /ai/ and /au/, according to what follows, with centralized beginnings before voiceless consonants, *knife/knives, house/houses:* Canada, eastern Virginia, the South Carolina coastal plain.

Some grammatical features, too, seem to qualify as Americanisms: though *dove* /dov/ as the past tense of *dive* may occur in some variety of British regional speech (there is no firm evidence that it does), in North America it is widely found in cultivated usage and is spreading among the younger and better educated. However, discussions of Americanisms concentrate on the vocabulary as more easily attested in print.

Nevertheless, such discussions are more balanced than those of early travelers, who tended to notice such exotic features as American Indian loans, frontier tall talk, and urban slang. These aspects of American usage still titillate those who deplore the decline of the language (like the critics of the Merriam *Third*) or who bemoan American corruption of French linguistic chastity (like Étiemble). Still, the citation files of dictionaries disclose the same creativity in more decorous fields such as medicine: *anesthesia* (1846), *appendicitis* (1886), *appendectomy* (1903), *geriatrics* (1909).

Mathews is by far the best treatment of Americanisms: as a consultant he also indicated Americanisms in the 1971 revision of *WNWD* College Edition. Mathews *Words* 1966, 1976 (the latter for schools) are more popular treatments, which by their selectivity call attention to apparently novel features, much like earlier works. Of these earlier works, as we have seen, many have been reprinted. Examples of earlier attitudes are found in Mathews 1931.

Pronunciation

The pronunciation of Americans has attracted almost as much attention from strangers as has their vocabulary. To the first generations of travelers, the mixture of dialects and languages—especially in such centers as New York, Philadelphia, and Charleston—and the lack of identifiable local "accents" drew much more attention than any regional or local peculiarities. But by 1800 it was clear that the educated American was not speaking like the educated Briton, and that his speech could identify his region. By the 1920s there was a sizeable body of writing on the subject (Kurath "American Pronunciation", which includes a discography—an inventory of recordings of American speech). The best-known work in the field, Kenyon, is still in print in its last revised (tenth) edition. More recent are Thomas *Introduction* 1946, 1958, and Bronstein. Kurath-R. McDavid provides a basic structural overview of cultured American English, based on field phonetics of high quality. Kurath *Phonology* extends this to include British Received Pronunciation and the analysis to establish historical affiliations. For a contrasting approach see Trager-Smith or Hill, its exegesis. On intonation the most detailed treatment is still Pike.

Early European travelers frequently commented on the singular freedom of American English from dialects; indeed, by European standards, there are minimal regional differences. On the other hand, every regional variety of educated American English and the corresponding variety of folk speech are closer to each other than British Received Pronunciation and the Cockney of London. Moreover, there is no single variety of American cultivated speech that enjoys the kind of preeminence enjoyed by Received Pronunciation, the upper-class French of Paris, or educated Muscovite Russian. At one time cultivated Bostonian was favored as a model, perhaps because it somewhat resembled RP in an age when Americans still felt a sense of inferiority when confronted by British mores; but just as often the

Boston accent was rejected as pretentious and affected. More recently the speech of the Great Lakes Basin has been favored as a model by elocutionists and by such public performers as radio and television announcers. Under such titles as *General American, Consensus English* and *Network English* it has been set up as an ideal for the less affluent to emulate on their way up the social ladder. However, many communities old and new—Philadelphia and Charleston, New Orleans and St. Louis, Salt Lake City and San Francisco—see no reason to reject their own traditions of excellence, which concede superiority to no other center. At least for the forseeable future, America is like pre-Periclean Hellas, with a multivalent standard.

The representation of American pronunciation in dictionaries varies considerably. As late as the *New Collegiate,* Merriam showed a bias toward RP and eastern New England. The attempt of the *Third* to do justice to the facts by recognizing the extensive variety of American cultivated usage—and at the same time to simplify and modernize its pronunciation key—was frequently cited by hostile critics as another example of abdicating standards rather than as an attempt to be more accurate. Other dictionaries, perhaps under greater influence from radio and television, use as a model the speech of the Great Lakes Basin. The introductions to the last two generations of dictionaries usually point out that educated American speech comes in many phonological packages and advise their readers to follow familiar models of cultivated usage when those models conflict with their dictionary. The order in which alternate pronunciations are listed in a general dictionary has nothing to do with social preference; at most the order indicates what the editors feel is the relative frequency of the alternates in educated use. Any pronunciation listed in a general dictionary without a caveat can be assumed to be acceptable in educated speech. Regrettably, the sanity of dictionary editors is not matched by equal sanity among laymen, teachers, or the editors of newspaper columns on usage.

The only dictionary of American pronunciation is Kenyon-Knott. Although both editors were aware of the variety in American cultivated speech—both had done synchronic and diachronic studies—it was published too early to use the massive evidence from the regional surveys; there has been no revision, though the publisher (Merriam) has provided some updating. Unlike its opposite number in England, the dictionary edited first by Daniel Jones and later by Jones's student A. C. Gimson, it has never been widely used. In contrast to the situation in Europe, American teachers are not trained in the International Phonetic Alphabet. Linguistic geographers use a finely graded variety of IPA developed by Kurath (the *New England Atlas* was the first major survey anywhere to use an alphabet based on IPA); for teaching English as a second language it is customary to use a phonemic transcription, such as that presented in Trager-Smith. A more theoretically oriented discussion is in Wang.

The Study of Regional Dialects

As the United States became settled and local and regional varieties of English became established and received comment, interest grew in making systematic study of these varieties. The first motivation was antiquarian: the American Dialect Society (1889) was organized with the specific charge to produce a dialect dictionary on the model of Wright, which was proceeding under the aegis of the English Dialect Society. Although the aim was not realized at the time, interest in regional varieties of American English remained strong, and in 1929—following linguistic atlases in Germany, France, Italy, and elsewhere—the American Council of Learned Societies endorsed a Linguistic Atlas of the United States and Canada. Originally planned as a single survey of two nations under the direction of Hans Kurath, it has developed into a series of autonomous but interconnected regional investigations. Of these, two have been published: New England (Kurath *et al.* 1939–43, reprinted 1972) and the Upper Midwest (Allen 1973–76). Five others, with field work completed, are being edited, with parts already in the hands of their publishers: the Middle and South Atlantic States (Kurath, R. McDavid, O'Cain, *et al.* 1979–), the North-Central States (Marckwardt, R. and V. McDavid, Payne *et al.*, 1976–), California and Nevada (D. Reed, Metcalf, *et al.*, in progress), Oklahoma (Van Riper *et al.*, in progress), the Gulf States (Pederson *et al.* 1972–). For other regions, work is less advanced though considerable interviewing has been done. The most widely known summary of these projects is R. McDavid 1958; progress reports appear in *PADS* through 1968, since then in the *Newsletter* of the ADS. C. Reed *Dialects* 1967, 1977 is a more extensive treatment, Shuy *Discovering Dialects* a good introduction.

The presentation of data varies from region to region. The *New England Atlas* was published in cartographic form, like the French and Italian atlases, with a *Handbook* (Kurath *et al.* 1939, 2d ed. 1973). Allen 1973–6 indicates the types of individual responses, but does not publish the full phonetic data. The *Atlas of the Middle and South Atlantic States* presents the phonetic data in list form analogous to Orton 1962–71. For the North-Central States, full phonetic data, unedited, is available in microfilm and Xerox copies of the field records; similar publication is planned for California-Nevada and Oklahoma. The Gulf States records will be published in microfiche; ultimately a complete lexicon of the materials will be edited.

Regional surveys also are interpreted in summary volumes. For the Atlantic Seaboard (New England and the Middle and South Atlantic States) there are three partial summaries: Kurath *Word Geography* (vocabulary), Atwood *Survey* (verb forms), Kurath-R. McDavid *Pronunciation;* for the vocabulary of California and Nevada there is Bright. The three volumes of Allen *Atlas* are somewhere between summaries and full publication. Summary volumes and handbooks are planned for the other regional surveys. Two important publications based on evidence other than that gathered by *Atlas* techniques are Atwood *Texas* and G. Wood; the latter is the largest-scale project for which data has been gathered solely by postal check lists, a technique introduced into American linguistic geography by A. Davis. Such check lists were also used in gathering supplementary data for the Upper Midwest and the California-Nevada surveys.

The handbook for each regional survey, published or pending, will include a bibliography of regional speech. Such bibliographies are inevitably selective; the preliminary bibliography for the North-Central States (R. McDavid-Pritchett) lists some 600 titles. A very full bibliography for the Southern states, with the region generously interpreted, is McMillan; Pederson, for the same region, is briefer but useful.

Several anthologies are devoted to essays on American dialects. Allen-Underwood and Williamson-Burke are excellent general anthologies, useful for university classes; Shores-Hines is restricted to papers presented to a continuing regional section of ADS. R. McDavid *Dialects* reflect his experience with the various regional surveys over three decades; Kurath *Studies*, representing a far longer career, is a group of short new essays distilling his experience and his theoretical perspective.

While the various regional atlases have been proceeding autonomously at different paces, the original objective of the ADS is in process of being realized though in a manner not envisaged at the outset. Wentworth, a useful stopgap, relied largely on published lists and the editor's personal reading and observations. On a far larger scale, the *Dictionary of American Regional English* (*DARE;* Cassidy, in press) will be one of the most important works of American linguistic scholarship. Unlike Wright, there was a rather detailed assessment beforehand of the relationships of the regional varieties; in this way Cassidy builds directly on the regional atlases. Like Wright, Cassidy combines field data with a reading program; the field work—1002 records in all fifty states—adapts the atlas methodology, emphasizing the vocabulary more, pronunciation less. The reading program utilizes regional novels, diaries, local newspapers, and the like; all data is put into computer storage to facilitate editing.

The best study of regional and local speech from past documents is Eliason 1958.

Social Dialects

The European surveys could assume a basic opposition between a uniform standard language and a variety of local dialects and concentrate on local folk speech; even Wright thought in those terms. The situation in the United States is different: no single prestigious variety but a diversity of regional standards, each related to the folk and common speech of its region. Consequently the American regional surveys have recorded not only the folk speech of the least educated but the cultivated speech of each region (taking cultivated informants not only from regional centers but from smaller communities of greater stability), and in almost every community interviewing a speaker of an intermediate type—in some places this informant being closer to the folk, in others closer to the cultivated. With three types of informants it is possible to sketch social differences in speech and suggest the direction of change at the time of the field work—something no previous survey had attempted though Jaberg had shown how surveys of folk speech might reveal social forces. The *Atlas* interviews provided the evidence for a study of New York (Frank), were utilized for another (Hubbell), and have provided a frame for several others—*e.g.,* Howren, Pederson "Chicago", Udell, Billiard, O'Cain, Uskup, Hopkins, M. Miller, and Sanders.

However, no one associated with the *Atlas* project has ever asserted that its materials could provide a full picture of the social variations in the speech of any community, let alone in all America. For this reason, Kurath and his associates have urged intensive follow-up studies in every region. As Kurath "Investigation" put it, the ideal development of sociolinguistic research would have been to start with simple communities in the heart of dialect areas, and add one variable at a time until the large metropolitan areas were reached. In linguistic geography it is necessary to choose informants from the longest settled and most stable elements of the population; the discipline originated as a branch of historical linguistics, testing the regularity of sound change and offering explanations for apparent exceptions. The methods of linguistic geography would exclude the recent arrivals in the community, whose speech by its very difference from local models might be of greatest concern to such community agencies as the local schools. With the expansion of metropolitan centers, the newcomers in northern and western cities were largely blacks, Spanish Americans, and Southern poor whites—properly ignored in the surveys of the Middle Atlantic States and the Great Lakes Basin, but conspicuously present in the current population. Kurath's scheme would have dealt with these groups but would have insisted on developing the methodology beforehand.

However, conditions would not permit this leisurely development. In the social crises of the 1960s a new type of dialect investigation, with emphasis on the practical problems of the schools, was needed for the urban areas. This type of investigation should examine the speech of these new arrivals and assay it against the backgrounds of the stable populations investigated by the traditional regional surveys; the background would include not only the host communities but the sources of the new population when evidence was available.

The best-known studies of the new type have been conducted in metropolitan environments, chiefly New York and Detroit: Labov *Social Stratification;* Shuy, Wolfram and Riley; and Wolfram *Detroit Negro Speech.* An investigation in a relatively unurbanized area is Wolfram and Christian. Implications are found in the two collections of Labov *Language* and *Patterns.*

Because the most conspicuous urban social group are the Americans of African descent, at whose social disabilities the civil rights movement of the 1960s was primarily directed, their speech has prompted a great deal of discussion, not always characterized by scholarly objectivity. Out of this discussion several issues have emerged: Is there a typologically distinct "Black English"? How is the speech of American blacks related to the languages of Africa and to the creolized English of the West Indies? How is it related to other varieties of American and British English, including the speech of the transported whites (especially the Irish) who were settled in the West Indies before British West Indian sugar culture followed the Dutch model and relied for labor on blacks enslaved in Africa? Several bibliographies of the subject have appeared, of which Brasch-Brasch is the most comprehensive (for its limitations see Algeo). The most widely known book on the subject is Dillard *Black English,* to a large extent a polemic; Dillard *Lexicon* restates the argument. Professional reviews of it are few, *e.g.,* D'Eloia, Wolfram *Language.* Laymen, who constitute most of the reviewers, tend to emphasize the piety of the argument as an expiation of white guilt.

Other studies are less spectacular. Turner is the most serious work on the speech of American blacks in a classic creolizing situation; it deals with rural isolated populations. Williamson describes adult black speech in a southern city; Dunlap compares the usage of black and white elementary students in another city. Historical evidence and dialects of English in areas where African influence is improbable—western England, Ireland, Newfoundland (*e.g.,* Paddock)—suggest caution in extrapolating from the example of the population studied by Turner. Curtin shows that the black population of the North American mainland derived from far smaller slave importations than that of the West Indies. There are only hints (*e.g.,* Forgue) that the urban "creolization" may be of recent origin, stemming from the progressive decline of informal black-white contacts since Emancipation; that such informal contacts were always less frequent in the North than in the South is perhaps part of the picture of the distinctive "Black English" which has been sketched chiefly by speakers of suburban white inland northern English. The *Linguistic Reporter* (1959–) keeps the profession abreast of current activities in social dialect work. The Center for Applied Linguistics provides useful bibliographical services.

The study of non-English dialects in the United States (French in Canada, as an official language, has as long a history as North

American English, though its European ties were far weaker from 1763 to the 1960s) is associated particularly with Einar Haugen. German dialects have been studied, *inter alia* by Reed and Seifert, Gilbert (for bibliography, see Viereck "Dialects" 1967, 1968); Slovak by Meyerstein; Greek by Macris "Loanwords"; Portuguese by Pap; Finnish by Larmouth; Yiddish by Weinreich et al. *Field* 1954, 1964, 1965, Fishman *Yiddish,* Herzog *Yiddish,* and L. Davis "Vowels." Spanish, with rural communities in Texas and the further Southwest and colonies of various national origins (Cuban, Mexican, Peruvian, Puerto Rican) in almost every large American city, has attracted an enormous interest; see Ornstein. For broader implications see Weinreich *Languages* and Fishman *Language Loyalty,* as well as Haugen's works. Fishman *Readings* is a useful anthology on sociolinguistics, not restricted to North America.

Literary Dialect

Since Chaucer's *Reeve's Tale,* which used forms of Northern Middle English for comic effect, literary artists have attempted to convey the flavor of dialects of English different from their own—sometimes casually, sometimes seriously and systematically. Whether it is possible to delineate as many subvarieties as Mark Twain asserted he did in *Huckleberry Finn* (he was probably having fun with his readers), there have been analyses of some very successful representations: Ives for Joel Chandler Harris; Downer for Lowell's *Biglow Papers;* Foster for the Conjure Woman stories of Charles W. Chesnutt; Rulon for *Huckleberry Finn.* As accurate knowledge of regional and social dialects becomes available, it is possible to make surer judgments on the accuracy with which a dialect is represented. We now often have information on both the folk speech of the characters described and the cultivated speech of the author through which the folk speech is perceived. For example, middle westerners tend to interpret Harris's *Brer Rabbit* as *Brair* not *Bruh* as the author pronounced it. With this kind of knowledge available, it is unlikely that writers today would commit some of the grotesqueries of eye-dialect that were perpetrated in the nineteenth century. Linguists and students of literature generally agree that the reader does not expect absolutely faithful preproduction of dialect, even if it were possible, only the hint of authenticity.

Spelling

The Simplified Spelling Movement seems to have run its course. Even the Chicago *Tribune,* for long the flagship of the reformers, has struck its colors, just as Merriam earlier jettisoned most of Noah Webster's innovations, like *cag* and *aker* for *keg* and *acre.* The serious

"The First Step," engraving from Harper's New Monthly, *September, 1873.*

study of spelling now emphasizes the systematic relationships that can be discovered between the sounds of English and their graphic representations. Such study may have various theoretical and practical ends, among the last being the teaching of reading and spelling in the schools. The most detailed study of such correspondences is Hanna *et al.*; a somewhat briefer analysis of the same school is Venezky *Linguistics and Spelling.* Among works advocating the teaching of reading through spelling patterns are R. Hall and Fries *Linguistics and Reading.* Bloomfield and Barnhart, probably the most imaginative pedagogical work derived from these principles, is a development of the experimental materials Bloomfield designed in the 1930s but never published in his lifetime. By now, almost every American publisher concerned with the early grades has its own set of materials following these principles. A summary of these developments is found in Ives and Ives.

All works of this kind emphasize that English spelling is not simple chaos but that it can be mastered as a series of patterns, many of them of very high frequency. From a theoretical point of view, Chomsky-Halle makes an eloquent case for the adequacy of English spelling as a reflection of the sound system, pointing to such regular morphophonemic alternations as *century/centurion, history/ historian.* However, if we may discuss melancholy practicalities, the efficacy of the system is not reflected in the writing that students produce in the classroom. Mastery of English spelling still demands pedestrian and systematic drill, though the new knowledge can make such drill more rational and effective than it has been in the past.

Grammar

The term *grammar* has two meanings which are often confused. To the scholar the grammar of a language is simply a description of the way the language operates; to the public, however, it is the study of linguistic etiquet, the kinds of differences within a speech community that set off preferred from stigmatized language behavior—what linguists call *usage.*

The study of grammar goes back to two ancient traditions which did not interact: India and classical Hellas. The first, represented by Paṇini (*c.* 400 BC) was concerned with the accurate interpretation of the sacred Vedic texts; the second, represented by Dionysius Thrax (200 BC) and others, was the expression of Greek philosophical curiosity about the universe.

With the Romans, grammar—the grammar of Greek—becomes a practical secular tool for teaching a prestigious language (Greek) to speakers of another language—in this first instance, Latin. Later, with the ascendancy of Rome and the subsequent rise of Christianity, Latin became the prestigious language for Western Europe, the language of law, religion, and learning. It was acquired by speakers of vernacular languages, with Latin grammar—not too different from the grammar of Greek, on which the Latin texts were based—as the basis of teaching. Later, when standard varieties of the vernacular arose and were taught to those who used nonstandard varieties, the terminology of Latin grammar was adapted to the vernacular situation, in spite of differences in language structure: in the vernaculars, inflection (change in the forms of words to signify grammatical relationships) was far less important than in Latin, Greek, or Sanskrit. But because there was no other grammatical model in use in the classroom, Latin grammar became the basis of the grammars of the vernacular, including the "traditional" English grammar of the American schools.

The rise of descriptive linguistics in the nineteenth century—strongly concerned both with comparative Indo-European and with the strikingly different native languages of Asia, Africa, and the Americas—led to a new tradition of examining the grammar of each language in terms of its own patterns and not in terms of the classical tongues. Until World War II, this descriptive grammar was mostly a research tool for field studies in unfamiliar languages (v. Bloomfield), with notable exceptions in the work of Henry Sweet and Otto Jespersen. It did not attract public attention in the United States until military necessity led to the recruiting of descriptive linguists to develop an Intensive Language Program for the armed forces and to the application of descriptive techniques not only to such unfamiliar tongues as Burmese and Malay but to French, German, Russian, and other languages of Europe. The success of descriptive linguistics in this program and in related programs for teaching English to speakers of other languages, led to its adaptation to the teaching of English grammar in the schools; Trager-Smith, Fries *Structure,* Francis *Structure,* Hill represent the theoretical statements from which the teaching materials were derived.

As the dominant theoretical approach to grammatical analysis, the descriptivist—or structuralist—gave way in the 1960s to the generative approach with which the name of Noam Chomsky is particularly associated in its transformationalist manifestation. Where the structuralists were concerned with the analysis of language phenomena into primary components, the generativists were concerned with the production of grammatical utterances from underlying deep structures by a series of derivational rules. Chomsky's dialectical skill enabled him and his followers to convince many teachers that his approach was more germane than that of the structuralists to the needs of the schools so that generative grammar grew in prestige even more rapidly than structuralism had grown. Because it lends itself easily to theoretical speculation—one of Chomsky's most eloquent disciples decried the typical linguist of the earlier school as a "dull cataloguer of data" (Lees)—there have arisen many schools among the generativists, and there has been not a little comment from other linguists (*e.g.* Labov *Patterns*) that this fine concern with theory represents a sterile withdrawal from the real world in which language is used.

Other theoretical approaches have risen to compete with the structuralist and the transformational generativist: the stratificationalist of Sidney Lamb and Michael Halliday *System and Function* and *Exploration,* and the tagmemic of Kenneth Pike *Language* and *Selected Writings.* Because of Pike's wide field experience as a student of language—he has probably worked with more languages than any other linguist—and his active part in the composition program at Michigan (Pike "Contribution"), tagmemics may be more effective than any other grammatical model in the teaching of writing. In the meantime, we must remember that though the study of grammar—whatever be the model—can be an exciting intellectual exercise, there is no evidence that this study *per se* has any influence on the quality of what a student actually writes. A good overview of competing analyses is Francis "Approaches."

Usage

When the American layman talks about grammar—and complains that the greatest failure of the public schools has been in the teaching of grammar—he is not speaking of grammar as a description of the language, but of the ways in which standard English differs from other varieties; in short, he is speaking of usage. The emphasis of such lay discussion is not descriptive of how people actually use the language but prescriptive of how it is conceived people ought to use it.

Prescription is not bad in itself; it is the basis of all education. Language teachers, whether of a foreign language or of a new (usually more prestigious) variety of their own language, have to be prescriptive, especially in times of widening educational and economic opportunities. Thus the rise of the middle classes in the Renaissance prospered the publication of grammars of the vernaculars. But as in treating illness, the diagnoses on which a linguistic prescription may be based are not all of the same validity. Since the vernaculars of Europe developed their own standard varieties, the teaching of usage has been based only in part on observation of the facts, in great measure on tradition, on analogizing from classical Latin, and on personal prejudice.

The shaky underpinnings of linguistic prescriptivism are revealed in nations of highly diverse cultural traditions. In France, the Académie theoretically has the authority to legislate on language matters, though its judgments often are not rendered till time has made the question moot—and then may be ignored. In England there was an unsuccessful movement toward an academy, for which Johnson's *Dictionary* became a sort of surrogate (Allen "Samuel

Johnson"); in practice the Received Standard of London enjoys a common-law recognition of its preeminence. In both England and France there is often failure of the educated—more often of the would-be educated—to understand the nature of linguistic prestige. The failure is even more general in the United States, where no single local variety is esteemed above all others, but where the pressures of cultural assimilation and social mobility and psychic insecurity create a demand for universal linguistic standards, however fictitious. In response to these pressures, teaching usage—"good" or "correct" English—became a matter of listing "common errors" and attempting to eradicate them. Part of the task was assumed by the usage notes in dictionaries, part by the school grammars, part by various usage manuals—guides for the perplexed and insecure (Mencken abridged). Only a few of these manuals (*e.g.,* J. Lesslie Hall, Krapp *Guide;* Fowler *Dictionary,* Fowler-Gowers revised ed.) were derived from serious observation of the language; even these were often misled by personal crotchets. No American work, however highly touted, has achieved the kind of preeminence which Fowler and Fowler-Gowers have attained in the Commonwealth, and to some extent even in the United States.

In the 1930s several studies went behind the dictates of authority toward actual usage: Leonard, Marckwardt-Walcott, Fries *Grammar.* The last established a pattern for objective studies. The status of linguistic forms is determined by the social position of who uses them, not the reverse; to establish the social position of a speaker or writer, one employs such non-linguistic criteria as education, occupation, family background, and associations. Fries demonstrated that by objective criteria there are relatively few grammatical differences between "standard English" and "vulgar English"; the important differences between these varieties are matters of fluency, facility, and versatility, reflecting different experiences with the language, notably in reading and writing.

What Fries *Grammar* did was to provide a specific kind of evidence in keeping with the judgment of Johnson's 1755 preface: that opinion is powerless against usage, and that no book can substitute for informed and sensitive observation. But most of those who have subsequently written on usage (Evans-Evans is an exception) have continued in the older tradition, feeling that the public is incapable of transcending simplistic judgments on right and wrong.

The older viewpoint surfaced vigorously in 1961. Publicity for the Merriam *Third* announced an "abdication of authority" (Merriam's slogan had been "the supreme authority") in favor of the supremacy of usage, which the second *New International* had recognized in 1934. The editors curtailed the number of cautionary labels (jettisoning the misconstrued *colloq.*), and generally conveyed the atmosphere of a word or meaning by an illustrative citation; in various other ways they attempted to recognize the ways Americans actually use the language. But the criticism of the *Third* suggested that many dictionary users, or at least dictionary critics, were less concerned with principles than with minor details. That *finalize,* for instance, had been attested in standard English since the 1920s meant less to these critics than that the word was tainted by association with advertising. Reflecting this current of reaction are such works as Baker, Bernstein, Follett *et al.* Far less attention has been given such more objective works as Copperud and Crisp (a reprise of Leonard). Latest on the market, though already past its zenith, is Morris-Morris, which like the *American Heritage Dictionary,* also edited by Mr. Morris, has been marketed on the strength of a "usage panel," whose qualifications are less their knowledge of the language than their facility and wit in expressing strong reactionary opinions. It has even been suggested that Morris-Morris is a burlesque, or at least a *reductio ad absurdum,* of the whole tradition of usage manuals.

While one group of critics deplore the relaxation of standards by linguists, lexicographers, and English teachers, another group deny that any standard should be taught, arguing that teaching a standard—sometimes even the teaching of reading and writing—is the repressive instrument of a corrupt society. A resolution arguing "Students' Right to Their Own Language" was passed in 1974 by the College Conference on Composition and Communication, an organization within the National Council of Teachers of English. Over the last decade the NCTE itself—which had sponsored the studies of Leonard, Marckwardt-Walcott, and Fries—has shied away from a relatively mild statement on usage and the teaching of standard English prepared for its Commission on the English Language. Bombarded from both left and right, those who would make objective appraisals of usage and of attitudes toward usage have had hard going.

There are few overviews of the problem. Copperud *Usage,* a useful work, contents itself with summarizing the attitudes in other publications. The best broad-gauge treatment of the problem is Creswell. Beginning with the 318 judgments of the usage panel for the *American Heritage,* it examines successively the usage notes in the *AHD,* treatments in nine other dictionaries, and ten usage guides. The dictionaries range from the second *New International* (1934) to *Webster's New World,* second college edition (1971); the usage guides from Krapp *Guide* to Ebbitt's fifth edition of Perrin's *Writer's Guide and Index to English.* Omitted for various reasons are Marckwardt-Walcott, Fries *Grammar,* Copperud, and the British-oriented Fowler and Fowler-Gowers; Fowler-Nicholson, directed at an American audience, is included. Morris-Morris was too late for inclusion.

Creswell reveals an amusing inconsistency among those who write on usage, both in the items with which they are concerned and in attitudes toward particular items. Very few of the "controversial"-items are uniformly condemned (*ain't* stands almost alone); items condemned by some may be ignored by others. Since the teaching of usage is likely to remain an important task in the schools, Creswell recommends the accumulation of very large bodies of evidence amenable to computer sorting, the model being Kučera-Francis. The idea of a massive body of evidence to be tapped at will is appealing (v. Mencken 1963:413–414); a gesture has been made in that direction by the University of Western Ontario, with the blessing of the lexicography committee of the Modern Language Association. But there are obstacles: scholars lack the funds to make independent collections on a large scale, and established publishers of dictionaries wish to protect their heavy investments in citation-files.

Independent surveys of usage face other problems: since they are forced to build their own organizations and often rely on voluntary workers for collecting their data, they can take relatively small samples. Scargill *et al.* suggests the diversity of Canadian usage, with some interesting deviations from what schoolbooks prescribe; for instance, *genuine* with the vowel of *wine* in the final syllable is not only predominant but is spreading among the younger and better educated. But the number of items included is small; and though the number of respondents is large, their distribution among the provinces is not proportionate to the English-speaking population.

Serious students of language have always recognized that usage is not a simple matter of right and wrong but of decorum—the fitness of a particular linguistic form for the situation in which it is used—but this recognition has not always extended uniformly to teachers, textbook writers, and lexicographers. Since the appearance of the Merriam *Third,* and the spate of adverse criticism it evoked from those believing in a simple dichotomy between good and evil in language, there have been several attempts to describe the complexity of the problem. One of the most influential is Joos *Clocks,* which puts it in a series of parables; Joos "Homeostasis" restates the thesis in more conventional scholarly language, but both remind the reader that usage is a matter of a number of interlocking dimensions. Similar statements are found in Allen *Readings* (2nd ed.) and R. McDavid 1967. Card, R. McDavid, and V. McDavid (in MacLeish) suggest an adaptation of this multidimensional analysis to the practical needs of lexicographers. None of these classifications is definitive or can be in a changing language; nor can the status of a given linguistic form be assumed immutable.

Names

In onomastics even more than in dialectology, Americans have lagged behind their European colleagues. Much serious work was accomplished, notably by Robert Ramsay and his students at the University of Missouri (Mencken 1963:663), but until recently the field was dominted by amateurs with a stronger feeling for color and romance than for solid historical and linguistic data. The United States Board on Geographical Names, founded in 1890, concentrated on decisions as to which of various competing local designations should be accepted as official. With World War II its duties and expertise grew, and it has made increasing use of linguists and historians. The recent directors, such as professional geographers Meredith P. Burrill and Donald Orth, have brought high standards to the office.

Laymen, including foreign observers, have long been interested in the variety of names used in America—family names, given names, place and topographical names, and names of miscellaneous artifacts (including the Anglicization of names from other languages). Chapter 10 of Mencken (1936, 1948, 1963) is one of the most extensively documented studies. George R. Stewart (1945, 1959, 1971) are lively and sound introductions to placename study. For personal names Elsdon C. Smith has analogous studies. In 1952 the founding of the American Name Society, an action in which Smith was the driving force, signaled that the study of names in the United States had achieved the same professional dignity that it had long enjoyed in Europe. *Names,* the journal of the ANS, was soon followed by local and regional publications, of which *Names in South Carolina* (1954–), founded by Claude Neuffer, is the oldest.

The bibliography of place names—Canadian as well as United States—has been summarized in Sealock and Seely 1948, 1967, with frequent supplements in *Names.* Local studies range wide in intended audience and in comprehensiveness, from Neuffer-Neuffer, an admirable discussion of South Carolina place names for students in elementary schools, to Orth, an awesomely detailed though thoroughly readable treatise on Alaska. In collaboration with the Interior Department, the ANS is now conducting a systematic study of place names in the United States; under the direction of Byrd Granger of Arizona and now of Fred Tarpley of East Texas University, it has made great progress but is still far from complete.

Slang and Argot

American slang—under which are popularly subsumed various kinds of informal usage, from frontier tall talk to the specialized argots of criminal subcultures (for the problem of definition, see Dumas and Lighter)—has attracted attention since colonial times. Even more than the discussions of dialect and proper names, those of slang have tended to be casual, anecdotal, incidental, sensational, and uncritical. Serious treatment has been handicapped by the transiency and volatility of slang: although some forms such as *gams* (legs) and *bamboozle* (to cheat), have remained slang for centuries, far more have either disappeared from use like *phiz* (face) or have been absorbed in the standard language like *mob*. And since the greatest vitality of slang is found in oral communication, good printed citations are harder to come upon than for other varieties of the language. The bibliography is tremendous (*v.* the notes to Ch. 11 of Mencken 1936, 1948, 1963); many interesting items appear in out-of-the-way publications. Conversely, the various types of popular entertainment—moving pictures, radio, television—can rapidly disseminate a new phrase and wear it out as rapidly. These problems are recognized in the editing of Jonathan Lighter's *Historical Dictionary of American Slang* (in progress); a pilot project, Lighter, deals in depth with one large group in one short period, the American Expeditionary Force in France 1917–18. Meanwhile, the most impressive dictionary of slang is still Farmer and Henley. Of more recent works the best is Wentworth-Flexner, twice revised by Flexner.

It is difficult to distinguish slang from argot; in fact, *slang* was originally used to describe the in-group language of the criminal subcultures. The distinction now most commonly made is that *slang* is a generally disseminated, modish, informal type of language, while *argot*—again informal—is restricted to an inner group of those who practice a particular activity. The shop talk of arts and crafts, licit or otherwise, is of the same order; perhaps that of the confidence man is a little harder to master because success in his field is a little harder to come by than, say, in literary criticism. But in every instance, mastery of the argot sets the participant in the subculture off from the outsider; as Maurer has often said, one may become a drug addict without mastering the argot, but only addicts have mastered it.

The argots of greatest interest are those of the criminal professions; their most successful student is David W. Maurer who insists that these argots be studied in the context of their subculture. His archives are magnificent; they are continually being enlarged by his wide range of contacts among the criminal professions and among such legitimate groups as physicians and law enforcement officers (he was a consultant for the Kinsey study of American sexuality). His ambition to prepare a dictionary of American criminal argot may not be fulfilled—his activities have been restricted by recent illness—but his work will make such a dictionary possible. In addition to some hundreds of articles and reviews, he has produced books on the confidence racket, on racing, on pickpockets, on narcotics and narcotic addiction (with Vogel) and on moonshining. Especially useful is his updating of Ch. 11 (American Slang) in Mencken and his revision of the bibliographical notes.

While Maurer's dictionary remains in the files, a competent, handy work is Goldin, Lipsius, and O'Leary. Kantrowitz-Kantrowitz, restricted to a segment of prison vocabulary—the various designations used by inmates in one of the hostels provided by the state of Illinois—is an admirable example of the kinds of results that can be obtained by following sound research methods in a difficult situation.

This sketch has necessarily omitted many works and authors of interest; however, it provides an outline of the field—of aspects of the study of American English—and mentions most of the important students. Following up its leads, through the works accessible in university libraries should keep the most inquisitive student busy for some time.□

Bibliography

Bibliographies
Aldus, Judith B. *Anglo-Irish Dialects: A Bibliography.* Regional Language Studies II, 1967.
Allen, Harold B. *Linguistics and English Linguistics.* New York: Appleton-Century-Crofts, 1966.
———. 2d ed.; Arlington Heights, Ill.: AHM Publishers, 1976.
———. "English as a Second Language," in Sebeok, *Trends,* 295–320.
American Speech, 1925–69.
Avis, Walter S. *A Bibliography of Writings on Canadian English 1957–1965.* Toronto: W. Gage, 1965.
———. "The English Language in Canada," in Sebeok, *Trends,* 40–74.
———, and A. M. Kinloch. *Writings on Canadian English 1792–1975.* Toronto: Fitzhenry and Whiteside, 1978.
Bahr, Dieter. *A Bibliography of Writings on Canadian English 1857–1976.* Heidelberg: Winter.
Barnhart, Clarence L. "American Lexicography, 1945–1973." *American Speech* LIII, 83–141.
Baugh, Albert C. *History of the English Language.* New York and London: Appleton-Century-Co., Inc., 1934.
———. 2d ed. New York and London: Appleton-Century-Crofts, 1957.
——— and Thomas Cable, 3d ed. Englewood Cliffs, New Jersey: Prentice-Hall, 1978.
Brasch, Ila W. and Walter M. *A Comprehensive Annotated Bibliography of American Black English.* Baton Rouge: LSU Press, 1974.
Brenni, Vito J. *American English: A Bibliography.* Philadelphia: University of Pennsylvania Press, 1963.
Cassidy, Frederic G. "Dialect Studies, Regional and Social," in Sebeok, *Trends,* 75–100.
Davis, Lawrence M., ed. *Studies in Linguistics in Honor of Raven I. McDavid, Jr.* University, Alabama: University of Alabama Press, 1972.
Francis, W. Nelson. "Approaches to Grammar," in Sebeok, *Trends,* 122–144.
Gates, J. Edward. "A Bibliography on General and English Lexicography," in R. McDavid-Duckert, *Lexicography,* 320–337.
General Linguistics 1955–
Haugen, Einar. "Bilingualism in the Americas; A Bibliography and Research Guide." *PADS* 26, 1956.

————. *The Ecology of Language.* Anwar S. Dil (ed.) Stanford, California: Stanford University Press, 1972.

————. "Bilingualism, Language Contact and Immigrant Languages in the United States," in Sebeok, *Trends,* 505–91.

Hill, Archibald A. "Albert Henry Marckwardt." *Language,* LII, 667–81.

Ives, Sumner A. and Josephine P. "Linguistics and Reading," in Marckwardt, *Linguistics,* 243–63.

————. "Linguistics and the Teaching of Reading and Spelling," in Sebeok, *Trends,* 228–49.

Kennedy, Arthur G. *A Bibliography of Writings on the English Language from the Beginning of Printing to the End of 1922.* Cambridge and New Haven: Harvard U. Press, Yale U. Press, 1927: reprinted New York: Hafner, 1961.

———— and Donald B. Sands. *A Concise Bibliography for Students of English.* 5th ed. Stanford, California: Stanford University Press, 1972.

Kurath, Hans. "A Bibliography of American Pronunciation 1888–1928." *Language,* V, 1929, 155–62. (Includes discography)

McDavid, Raven I., Jr. "Hans Kurath." *Orbis,* IX, 1960, 597–612.

————. "The English Language in the United States," in Sebeok, *Trends,* 5–39.

————. *Varieties of American English.* Anwar S. Dil (ed.). (With a bibliography by William Kretzschmar). Stanford, California: Stanford University Press, 1979.

———— and Glenda Pritchett. *A Bibliography of the Speech of the North-Central States.* Chicago: Linguistic Atlas of the North-Central States, 1976.

McMillan, James B. *Annotated Bibliography of Southern American English.* Coral Gables, Florida: University of Miami Press, 1971.

————. "American Lexicology, 1956–1973." *American Speech,* LIII, 141–163.

Pederson, Lee A. *An Annotated Bibliography of Southern Speech.* Southeastern Education Laboratory. Monograph 1. Atlanta: Southeastern Education Laboratory, 1968.

Publications of the Modern Language Association (PMLA) 1886– .

Read, Allen Walker. "Approaches to Lexicography and Semantics," in Sebeok, *Trends,* 145–205.

Scholler, Harald and John Reidy, "Publications of Hans Kurath," (pp. 268–71, in *Lexicography and Dialect Geography: Festgabe für Hans Kurath Zeitschrift für Dialektologie und Linguistik,* Heft, 9). Wiesbaden: Franz Steiner Verlag, 1973.

Sealock, Richard B. and Pauline A. Seely. *A Bibliography of Place Name Literature, United States, Canada, Alaska and Newfoundland.* Chicago: American Library Association, 1948. 2nd ed. 1967.

Smith, Elsdon C. *Personal Names: A Bibliography.* New York: New York Public Library, 1952.

Venezky, Richard L. "Linguistics and Spelling," in Marckwardt, *Linguistics*, 264–74.

Viereck, Wolfgang. "German Dialects Spoken in the United States and Canada and Problems of German-English Contact, Particularly in North America: A Bibliography." *Orbis*, XVI, 1967, 549–68.

———. (Supplement to Viereck 1967), *Orbis*, XVII, 1968.

Wang, William S.Y. "Approaches to Phonology," in Sebeok, *Trends*, 101–21.

Serials

American Journal of Philology 1880–

American Speech (AS) 1925–

Canadian Journal of Linguistics (CJL) 1954–

Dialect Notes (DN) 1889–1939. 6 vols.

Dissertation Abstracts 1938–

General Linguistics (GL) 1955–

International Journal of American Linguistics (IJAL) 1935–

Journal of English Linguistics (JEngL) 1967–

Journal of English and Germanic Philology (JEGP) 1902–

Language 1925–

LACUS Forum (Linguistic Association of Canada and the United States) 1974–

Linguistic Reporter 1959–

Names 1952–

Names in South Carolina 1954–

Orbis 1952–

Publications of the American Dialect Society (PADS) 1944–

Publications of the Modern Language Association (PMLA) 1886–

RLS (Regional Language Studies—Newfoundland) 1968–

General Works

Dillard, Joey L. *All-American English.* New York: Random House, 1975.

———. *American Talk.* New York: Random House, 1976.

Dohan, Mabel. *Our Own Words.* New York: Alfred A. Knopf, 1974.

Flexner, Stuart B. *I Hear America Talking.* New York: Van Nostrand-Reinhold, 1976.

Forgue, Guy J. *La Langue des Américains.* Paris: Aubier-Montaigne, 1972.

Krapp, George Philip. *The English Language in America.* New York: Century Company for the Modern Language Association of America, 1925.

———. 2d ed. New York: Ungar, 1960.

Laird, Charlton. *Language in America.* Englewood Cliffs, N.J.: Prentice-Hall, 1971.

McConnell, Ruth E. *Our Own Voice: Canadian English and How It is Studied.* Toronto: Gage, 1979.

Marckwardt, Albert H. *American English.* New York: Oxford Press, 1958.
Mencken, Henry Louis. *The American Language.* New York: Knopf, 1919.
————. 2d ed. 1921.
————. 3d ed. 1923.
————. 4th ed. 1936.
————. Supplement one. 1945.
————. Supplement two. 1948.
————. One volume abridged ed.: The fourth edition and the two supplements, abridged, with new material, by Raven I. McDavid, Jr., with the assistance of David W. Mauer, 1963.
Orkin, Mark M. *Speaking Canadian English.* Toronto: General Publishing, 1970.
Pyles, Thomas. *Words and Ways in American English.* New York: Random House, 1952.
Scargill, M.H. *A Short History of Canadian English.* Vancouver, B.C.: Sono Press, 1977.
Tucker, Gilbert M. *American English.* New York: Knopf, 1921.

Anthologies
Allen, Harold B. *Readings in Applied English Linguistics.* New York: Appleton-Century-Crofts, 1958.
————. 2d ed. 1964.
————. and Michael Linn. 3d ed. in progress.
————. and Gary Underwood. *Readings in American Dialectology.* New York: Appleton-Century-Crofts, 1971.
————. Enola Borgh, and Verna L. Newsome. *Focusing on Language: A Reader.* New York: Crowell, 1973.
Babcock, C. Merton. *The Ordeal of American English.* Boston: Houghton, Mifflin, and Co., 1961.
Bailey, Richard W. and Jay L. Robinson. *Varieties of Present-Day English. New York: Macmillan, 1972.*
Chambers, J. K. *Canadian English: Origins and Structures.* Toronto and London: Methune, 1975.
Clark, Virginia P., Paul A. Eschholz, and Alfred P. Rosa. *Language: Introductory Readings.* New York: St. Martin's, 1972.
Davis, Lawrence M. *Studies in Linguistics in Honor of Raven I. McDavid, Jr.* University, Alabama: University of Alabama Press, 1972.
Escholz, Paul A., Alfred F. Rosa, and Virginia Clark. *Language Awareness.* New York: St. Martin's, 1974.
Fishman, Joshua A. *Readings in the Sociology of Language.* The Hague: Mouton, 1968.
Gates, J. Edward. *Papers in Lexicography in Honor of Warren P. Cordell.* Terre Haute, Indiana, 1969.
Gilbert, Glenn. *The German Language in America: A Symposium.* Austin: University of Texas Press, 1971.

Hungerford, Harold, Jay Robinson and James Sledd. *English Linguistics: An Introductory Reader.* Glenview, Illinois: Scott, Foresman, 1970.

Kerr, Elizabeth and Ralph M. Aderman. *Aspects of American English.* New York: Harcourt, Brace and World, 1963.

———. 2d ed. New York: Harcourt Brace Jovanovich, 1971.

McDavid, Raven I., Jr. and Audrey R. Duckert. *Lexicography in English.* Transactions of the New York Academy of Sciences 211, 1973.

MacLeish, Andrew. *Studies for Harold B. Allen.* Minneapolis: University of Minnesota Press, 1979.

Marckwardt, Albert H. *Linguistics in School Programs. National Society for the Study of Education, Yearbook 69, Part II.* Chicago: University of Chicago Press, 1970.

Mathews, Mitford M. *The Beginnings of American English.* Chicago: University of Chicago Press, 1931. Reprinted 1963.

Scargill, M. H., and P. G. Penna *Looking at Language: Essays in Introductory Linguistics.* Toronto: Gage, 1966.

Scholler, Harald and John Reidy. *Lexicography and Dialect Geography: Festgabe fur Hans Kurath Zeitschrift für Dialektologie und Linguistik,* Heft 9. Wiesbaden: Franz Steiner Verlag, 1973.

Sebeok, Thomas R., Albert H. Marckwardt, *et al. Current Trends in Linguistics 10: Linguistics in North America.* The Hague: Mouton, 1973.

Shores, David L. *Contemporary English: Change and Variation.* Philadelphia: Lippincott, 1972.

——— and Carole P. Hines. *Papers in Language Variation: SAMLA-ADS Collection.* University, Alabama: University of Alabama Press, 1977.

Weinbrot, Howard. *New Aspects of Lexicography.* Carbondale, Illinois: Southern Illinois Press, 1972.

Sledd, James H. and Wilma Ebbitt. *Dictionaries and* That *Dictionary.* Chicago: Scott, Foresman, 1962.

Weireich, Uriel, *et al. The Field of Yiddish.* Publications of the Linguistic Circle of New York, III, 1954.

———. 2d collection. The Hague: Mouton, 1965.

———. 3d collection. The Hague: Mouton, 1969.

Williamson, Juanita and Virginia Burke. *A Various Language.* New York: Holt, Rinehart, and Winston, 1971.

General Dictionaries

American College Dictionary *(ACD).* Clarence Barnhardt (ed.) New York: Random House, 1947.

American Heritage Dictionary (AHD). William Morris (ed.) New York: American Heritage, 1969.

Barnhardt, Clarence, *Thorndike-Barnhart Desk Dictionary.* New York: Doubleday, 1951.

———. *World Book Encyclopedia Dictionary.* Chicago: Field Enterprises, 1963.

Century Dictionary. William Dwight Whitney (ed.). New York: The Century Company, 1889–91.
———. *Cyclopedia of Names.* 1894.
———. *Atlas.* 1897.
———. *New Volumes.* 2 vols. 1909.
Doubleday Dictionary. Sidney Landau and Ronald Bogus (eds.). New York: Doubleday, 1975.
Funk and Wagnalls Standard Dictionary of the English Language. Francis A. Vizetelly (ed.). New York and London: Funk and Wagnalls, 1909.
———. *New Standard Dictionary.* Vizetelly, (ed.), 1913.
———. *Standard College Dictionary.* 1963.
Johnson, Samuel. *A Dictionary of the English Language.* London: W. Strahan, 1755.
Macmillan's Modern Dictionary. New York: Macmillan, 1938.
Random House Dictionary. Jess Stein (ed.). New York: Random House, 1966.
———. College Edition, 1968.
Scribner-Bantam English Dictionary. Edwin B. Williams (ed.) New York: Scribner's, 1977.
Webster, Noah. *A Compendious Dictionary of the English Language.* Hartford: Hudson and Goodwin, 1806; New Haven: Increase Cook & Co., 1970, reprinted with an introduction by Philip B. Gove, Bounty Books.
———. *American Dictionary of the English Language.* (2 vols.). New York: S. Converse, 1826. Reprinted Johnson Reprint Co., 1968.
———. 2d ed. 1841.
———. Rev. ed., Chauncey Goodrich. Springfield: G & C Merriam Co., 1847.
———. Royal Quarto ed., revised, 1864.
Webster's International Dictionary. (WID). 1890.
Webster's New International Dictionary (WNID). 1909.
———. 2d ed. 1934.
Webster's *Third New International Dictionary.* 1961.
Webster's Collegiate Dictionary. 1916.
———. 5th ed. 1936.
Webster's New Collegiate Dictionary. 1949.
Webster's Seventh New Collegiate Dictionary. 1963.
Webster's New Collegiate Dictionary. 8th ed. 1973.
Webster's New World Dictionary. Cleveland and New York: World Publishing Company, 1952.
———. College Edition, 1953.
———. 2d College Ed., 1971.

Historical Dictionaries
Cassidy, Frederic G. and Robert LePage. *Dictionary of Jamaican English.* 1967.
Dictionary of Americanisms (DA). Mitford M. Mathews (ed.). Chicago: University of Chicago Press, 1951.

Dictionary of American English (DAE). Sir William Craigie and James R. Hulbert, (eds.). Chicago: University of Chicago Press, 1938–44.

Dictionary of Canadianisms. Walter S. Avis, et al., (eds.). Toronto: W. Gage, 1967.

Lighter, Jonathan. Historical Dictionary of American Slang. (In progress).

Mathews, Mitford M. Americanisms. Chicago: University of Chicago Press, 1966.

Oxford English Dictionary. Sir James A.H. Murray, et al. (eds.). Oxford: The University Press, 1884–1928.

————. Supplement and bibliography, 1933.

————. Second Supplement. 4 vols. R.W. Burchfield (ed.). 1972.

Read, Allen Walker. The English of England: A Historical Dictionary of Briticisms. (In progress).

Story, George. Dictionary of Newfoundland English. (In progress).

Thornton, Richard. An American Glossary. (2 vols.). Philadelphia and London: Francis and Gregory, 1912.

————. (Vol. 3). Published in installments in Dialect Notes, Vol. VI, 1931–9.

Special Dictionaries

Bartlett, John Russell. Dictionary of Americanisms: A Glossary of Words and Phrases Usually Regarded as Peculiar to the United States. New York: Bartlett and Welford, 1848. Reprinted Regency, 1976.

————. 2d ed. Boston: Little, Brown and Company, 1959.

————. 4th ed. Reprinted Johnson Reprint 1977.

Cassidy, Frederic G. Dictionary of American Regional English. (In progress. To be published by the Belknap Press of Harvard University.)

Farmer, John S. and William Ernest Henley. Dictionary of Slang and Its Analogues, Past and Present. (7 vols.) London: 1890–1904. (Frequently reprinted.)

Goldin, Hyman, Frank O'Leary, and Morris Lipsius. Dictionary of American Underworld Lingo. New York: Twayne, 1950.

Jones, Daniel. An English Pronouncing Dictionary. London: J.M. Dent, 1917.

Kenyon, John S. and Thomas A. Knott. A Pronouncing Dictionary of American English. Springfield, Mass.: G & C Merriam Co., 1944.

Lighter, Jonathan. "The Slang of the American Expeditionary Forces in Europe 1917–19: An Historical Glossary." American Speech, XLVII, 5–142.

Neuffer, Claude H. and Irene, The Name Game: From Oyster Point to Keowee. Columbia, S.C.: The Sandlapper Store, 1977.

Orth, Donald J. Dictionary of Alaska Place Names. U.S. Geological Survey: Professional Paper 567. Washington, D.C.: U.S. Government Printing Office, 1967.

Smith, Elsdon C. *Dictionary of American Family Names.* New York: Harper, 1956.

————. *New Dictionary of American Family Names.* New York and Evanston: Harper and Row, 1972.

Sperber, Hans and Travis Trittschuh. *Dictionary of American Political Words and Phrases.* Detroit: Wayne State Press, 1962.

Stewart, George R. *American Place-Names: A Concise and Selected Dictionary for the Continental United States of America.* New York: Oxford Press, 1970.

Wentworth, Harold. *American Dialect Dictionary.* New York: Crowell, 1944.

————,and Stuart Berg Flexner. *Dictionary of American Slang.* New York: Crowell.

————. 2d ed. 1967.

————. 3d ed. 1975.

Wright, Joseph. *English Dialect Dictionary.* (6 vols.). Oxford: The University Press, 1898–1905.

Pronunciation

Bronstein, Arthur. *The Pronunciation of American English.* Englewood Cliffs, New Jersey: Prentice-Hall, 1960.

Dobson, E.J. *English Pronunciation 1500–1700.* Oxford: The Clarendon Press, 1957.

Kenyon, John S. *American Pronunciation.* Ann Arbor: George Wahr, 1924.

————. 10th ed. 1954.

Kurath, Hans. *A Phonology and Prosody of Modern English.* Heidelberg: Carl Winter; Ann Arbor; University of Michigan Press, 1964.

Pike, Kenneth L. *The Intonation of American English.* Ann Arbor: University of Michigan Press, 1945.

Thomas, Charles K. *Introduction to the Phonetics of American English.* New York: Ronald, 1946.

————. 2d ed. 1958.

Regional Dialects

Allen, Harold B. *Linguistic Atlas of the Upper Midwest.* (3 vols.). Minneapolis: University of Minnesota Press, 1973–6.

Atwood, E. Bagby. *A Survey of Verb Forms in the Eastern United States.* Ann Arbor: University of Michigan Press, 1953.

————. *The Regional Vocabulary of Texas.* Austin, Texas: University of Texas Press, 1962.

Avis, Walter S. "The English Language in Canada," in Sebeok, *Trends,* 40–74.

Bright, Elizabeth. *A Word Geography of California and Nevada.* Berkeley and Los Angeles: University of California Press, 1971.

Cassidy, Frederic. "Dialect Studies, Regional and Social," in Sebeok, *Trends,* 75–100.

Davis, Alva L. "A Word Atlas of the Great Lakes Region." Diss. (microfilm). University of Michigan, 1949.

Eliason, Norman A. *Tarheel Talk.* Chapel Hill: University of North Carolina Press, 1958.

Jaberg, Karl. *Aspects géographiques de langage.* Paris: E. Droz, 1936.

Kurath, Hans. *A Word Geography of the Eastern United States.* Ann Arbor: University of Michigan Press, 1949.

———. *Studies in Area Linguistics.* Bloomington, Indiana: Indiana University Press, 1972.

——— and Raven I. McDavid, Jr. *The Pronunciation of English in the Atlantic States.* Ann Arbor: University of Michigan Press, 1961.

———. Raven I. McDavid, Jr., Raymond K. O'Cain, *et al. Linguistic Atlas of the Middle and South Atlantic States.* Chicago: University of Chicago Press, 1979.

———. *et al. Handbook of the Linguistic Geography of New England.* Providence, R.I.: American Council of Learned Societies, 1939.

———. 2d ed., with a map inventory and complete word index by Audrey R. Duckert. New York: AMS, 1973.

———. *Linguistic Atlas of New England.* (3 vols. bound as 6). Providence: American Council of Learned Societies, 1939–43. Reprinted, 3 vols. New York: AMS, 1972.

McDavid, Raven I., Jr. "American English Dialects." Ch. 9 in Francis, *Structure,* 480–593.

———. *Dialects in Culture.* University, Alabama: University of Alabama Press, 1979.

———. *Varieties of American English.* Anwar S. Dil (ed.). Stanford: Stanford University Press, 1979.

McDavid, Virginia. "Verb Forms in the North-Central States and Upper Midwest." Diss. (microfilm). University of Minnesota, 1956.

Marckwardt, Albert H., Raven I. McDavid, Jr., Virginia McDavid, Richard C. Payne, *et al.* "Linguistic Atlas of the North-Central States." (Basic Materials [unedited field records] published as Chicago MSS in cultural anthropology series XXXVIII, nos. 200–208, 1976–78.

Orton, Harold, *et al. Survey of English Dialects.* Introduction, 4 vols. (each in 3 parts). Leeds: E.J. Arnold, 1962–71.

Pederson, Lee A., *et al. Linguistic Atlas of the Gulf States.* In progress.

Reed, Carroll A. *Dialects of American English.* Cleveland: World Publishing Company, 1967.

———. 2d ed. Amherst, Massachusetts: University of Massachusetts Press, 1977.

Reed, David W., Allan Metcalf, *et al. Linguistic Atlas of California and Nevada.* In progress.

Sanders, Willease. "Selected Grammatical Features of the Speech of Blacks in Columbia, S.C." Diss. (microfilm) University of South Carolina, 1978.

Shuy, Roger W. *Discovering American Dialects.* Champaign, Illinois: National Council of Teachers of English, 1967.
Van Riper, William Robert, *et al. Linguistic Atlas of Oklahoma.* In progress.
Wood, Gordon. *Vocabulary Change.* Carbondale, Illinois: Southern Illinois Press, 1971.

Social Dialects

Algeo, John. "A Black English Bibliography." (Review of Brasch & Brasch, 1972). *American Speech,* XLIX, 1974, 142–6.
Billiard, Charles. "The Speech of Fort Wayne, Indiana." Diss. (Microfilm), Purdue University, 1969.
D'Eloia, Sarah G. "Issues in the Analysis of Nonstandard Negro English: A Review of J.L. Dillard's *Black English.*" JEngL, VII, 1973, 87–106.
Dillard, Joey L. *Black English.* New York: Random House, 1972.
———. *The Lexicon of Black English.* New York: Seabury, 1977.
Dunlap, Howard G. "Social Aspects of a Verb Form: Native Atlanta Fifth-Grade Speech—the Present Tense of Be." *PADS,* 1974, 61–62.
Frank, Yakira. "The Speech of New York City." Diss. (Microfilm), University of Michigan, 1948.
Herndobler, Robin. "The Speech of Chicago's East Side: A White Working-Class Community." Diss. (Microfilm), University of Chicago, 1977.
Hopkins, John. "The White Middle-Class Speech of Savannah, Georgia." Diss. (Microfilm), University of South Carolina, 1975.
Howren, Robert R. "The Speech of Louisville, Kentucky." Diss., (Microfilm), Indiana University, 1958.
Hubbell, Allan F. *The Pronunciation of English in New York City: Consonants and Vowels.* New York: King's Crown, 1950.
Kurath, Hans. "The Investigation of Urban Speech." *PADS,* XLIX, 1968, 1–7.
Labov, William. *The Social Stratification of English in New York City.* Washington, D.C.: Center for Applied Linguistics, 1966.
———. *Language in the Inner City.* Philadelphia: University of Pennsylvania Press, 1972.
———. *Sociolinguistic Patterns.* Philadelphia: University of Pennsylvania Press, 1972.
McDavid, Raven I., Jr. "Historical, Regional and Social Variation." *JEngL,* I, 24–40.
Miller, Michael I. "Inflectional Morphology in Augusta, Georgia: A Sociolinguistic Description." Diss. (Microfilm), University of Chicago, 1978.
O'Cain, Raymond K. "A Social Dialect Study of Charleston, South Carolina." Diss. (Microfilm), University of Chicago, 1972.
Paddock, Harold. "A Dialect Survey of Carbonear, Newfoundland." MA thesis (typescript), Memorial University of Newfoundland, 1966.

Pederson, Lee A. "The Pronunciation of English in Chicago: Conso-
    nants and Vowels." *PADS,* XLIV, 1965. 44.
Sanders, Willease. "Selected Grammatical Features of the Speech of
    Blacks in Columbia, S.C." Diss. (microfilm) University of South
    Carolina, 1978.
Shuy, Roger W., Walter a. Wolfram, and William K. Riley. *Field
    Techniques in an Urban Language Study.* Washington, D.C.:
    Center for Applied Linguistics, 1968.
Turner, Lorenzo D. *Africanisms in the Gullah Dialect.* Chicago: Uni-
    versity of Chicago Press, 1949. Reprint New York: Arno Press,
    1969; Ann Arbor: University of Michigan Press, 1974.
Udell, Gerald R. "The Speech of Akron, Ohio." Diss. (Microfilm),
    University of Chicago, 1966.
Uskup, Frances L. "The Speech of Chicago Elites." Diss. (Microfilm),
    Illinois Institute of Technology, 1964.
Williamson, Juanita V. "A Phonological and Morphological Study of
    the Speech of the Negro of Memphis, Tennessee." *PADS,* L,
    1968.
Wolfram, Walter A. *A Sociolinguistic Description of Detroit Negro
    Speech.* Washington, D.C.: Center for Applied Linguistics, 1969.
————. (Review of Dillard 1972). *Language,* XLIX, 1973, 670–79.
———— and Donna Christian. *Appalachian Speech.* Arlington, Virginia:
    Center for Applied Linguistics, 1976.

Non-English Dialects and Bilingualism

Allen, Harold B. "English as a Second Language," in Sebeok, *Trends,*
    295–320.
Davis, Lawrence M. "The Phonology of Yiddish-American Speech."
    Diss. (Microfilm), University of Chicago, 1967.
————. "The Stressed Vowels of Yiddish-American Speech." *PADS,*
    XLVIII, 1967.
Fishman, Joshua A. *Yiddish in America.* Indiana University Research
    Center in Anthropology, Folklore and Linguistics, Publication 36.
    IJAL, XXXI, No. 1, Part II, 1965.
————. *Language Loyalty in the United States.* The Hague: Mouton,
    1966.
Gilbert, Glenn. *Linguistic Atlas of Texas German.* Austin, Texas:
    University of Texas Press, 1972.
Haugen, Einar. "The Analysis of Linguistic Borrowing." *Language,*
    XXVI, 1950, 210–231.
————. *The Norwegian Language in America.* 2 vols. Philadelphia:
    University of Pennsylvania Press, 1953.
————. Reprinted, 1 vol., Indiana University Press, 1969.
————. *The Ecology of Language.* Anwar S. Dil (ed.). Stanford,
    California: Stanford University Press, 1972.
————. "Bilingualism, Language Contact and Immigrant Languages
    in the United States," in Sebeok, *Trends,* 505–91.
Herzog, Marvin I. *The Yiddish Language in Northern Poland.* Indiana

University Research Center in Anthropology, Folklore, and Linguistics, Publication 37. *IJAL,* XXXI, No. 2, Part III, 1965.

Larmouth, Donald W. "Grammatical Interference in American Finnish." Diss. (Microfilm), University of Chicago, 1972.

Macris, James. "English Loanwords in New York City Greek." Diss. (Microfilm), Columbia University, 1955.

——. "Changes in the Lexicon of New York City Greek." *American Speech,* XXXII, 1967, 102–109.

Meyerstein, Goldie Piroch. "Selected Problems of Bilingualism Among Immigrant Slovaks." Diss. (Microfilm), University of Michigan, 1957.

——. "Bilingualism Among American Slovaks." *PADS,* XLVI, 1960, 1–19.

Ornstein, Jacob. *Three Essays on Linguistic Diversity in the Spanish-Speaking World.* The Hague: Mouton, 1976.

Pap, Leo. Portuguese-American Speech: *An Outline of Speech Conditions Among Portuguese Immigrants in New England and Elsewhere in the United States.* New York: King's Crown, 1949.

Reed, Carroll A. and Lester G. Seifert. *A Linguistic Atlas of Pennsylvania German.* Marburg/Lahn, 1954.

Sawyer, Janet B. "A Dialect Study of San Antonio, Texas: A Bilingual Community." Diss. (Microfilm), University of Texas, 1957.

——. "Social Aspects of Bilingualism in San Antonio, Texas." *PADS,* XLI, 1964, 7–15.

Weinreich, Uriel. *Languages in Contact.* Publications of the Linguistic Circle of New York #1, 1953.

——. *et al. Language and Culture Atlas of Ashkenazic Jewry.* In progress.

Literary Dialect

Downer, James W. "The Dialect of the *Biglow Papers.*" Diss. (Microfilm), University of Michigan, 1958.

Foster, Charles William. "Phonology of the Conjure Tales of Charles W. Chesnutt." *PADS,* LV, 1971.

Ives, Sumner. "A Theory of Literary Dialect." *Tulane Studies in English,* II, 1950, 137–82.

——. "The Phonology of the Uncle Remus Stories." *PADS,* XXII, 1954.

——. "Dialect Differences in the Stories of Joel Chandler Harris." *American Literature,* XXVII, 1955, 58–96.

Rulon, Curt. "Geographical Distribution of the Dialect Areas in *The Adventures of Huckleberry Finn.*" *Mark Twain Journal,* XIV, 1966, 9–12.

Reading and Spelling

Bloomfield, Leonard and Clarence Barnhart. *Let's Read.* Detroit: Wayne State University Press, 1961.

——. Bronxville: Clarence L. Barnhart, Inc., 1963.

Chomsky, Noam and Morris Halle. *The Sound Pattern of English.* New York and Evanston: Harper and Row, 1968.

Fries, Charles C. *Linguistics and Reading.* New York: Holt, Rinehart and Winston, 1962.

Hall, Robert A., Jr. *Sound and Spelling in English.* Philadelphia: Chilton Books, 1961.

Hanna, P.R., *et al. Phoneme-Grapheme Correspondences as Cues to Spelling Improvement.* Washington, D.C.: U.S. Government Printing Office, 1966.

Ives, Sumner A. and Josephine P. "Linguistics and Reading," in Marckwardt, *Linguistics,* 243–63.

————. "Linguistics and the Teaching of Reading and Spelling," in Sebeok, *Trends,* 228–49.

Venezky, Richard L. *Linguistics and Spelling.* Madison, Wisconsin: Wisconsin Research and Development Center for Cognitive Learning, 1969.

————. "Linguistics and Spelling," in Marckwardt, *Linguistics,* 264–74.

————. *The Structure of English Orthography.* The Hague: Mouton, 1970.

Webster, Noah. *American Spelling Book.* 1783, Reprinted: Beatty, 1974.

Grammar

Bloomfield, Leonard. *Language.* New York: Holt, 1933.

Chomsky, Noam. *Syntactic Structures.* The Hague: Mouton, 1957.

————. *Aspects of the Theory of Syntax.* Cambridge, Massachusetts: MIT Press, 1965.

Francis, W. Nelson. *The Structure of American English.* New York: Ronald, 1958.

————. "Approaches to Grammar," in Sebeok, *Trends,* 122–44.

Fries, Charles C. *The Structure of English.* New York: Harcourt, Brace and Company, 1952.

Halliday, Michael A.K. *System and Function in Language,* Gunther Kress (ed.). Oxford: The University Press, 1976.

————. *Explorations in the Functions of Language.* Amsterdam: Elsevier, 1977.

————. Angus McIntosh, and Peter Strevens. *The Linguistic Sciences and Language Teaching.* London: Longman's, 1964.

Hill, Archibald A. *Introduction to Linguistic Structures: From Sound to Sentence in English.* New York: Harcourt, Brace and Company, 1958.

Jespersen, Otto. *A Modern English Grammar on Historical Principles.* (7 vols.). Heidelberg: C. Winter, 1909–19. Reprinted London: Allen & Unwin, 1954.

Lamb, Sidney. *An Outline of Stratificational Grammar.* Washington, D.C.: Georgetown University Press, 1966.

Lees, Robert B. (Review of Chomsky 1957). *Language,* XXX, 1957, 375–408.

Pike, Kenneth L. "A Linguistic Contribution to Composition." *College Composition and Communication,* XV, 1964, 82–88.

———. *Language in Relation to a Unified Theory of the Structure of Human Behavior.* The Hague: Mouton, 1967.

———. *Selected Writings.* Ruth M. Brend (ed.). The Hague: Mouton, 1970.

Sweet, Henry. *New English Grammar.* (2 vols.). Oxford: The University Press, 1891–98.

Trager, George L. and Henry Lee Smith, Jr. *An Outline of English Structure.* Studies in Linguistics: Occasional Papers 3. Norman, Oklahoma: The Battenburg Press, 1951.

Usage

Allen, Harold B. "Samuel Johnson and the Authoritarian Tradition." Diss. (Microfilm), University of Michigan, 1942.

———. "Introduction, Part IV, Linguistics and Usage," in Allen, *Readings,* (2d ed.), 291–4.

Baker, Sheridan. *The Complete Stylist.* New York: Thomas Y. Crowell, 1966.

Bernstein, Theodore. *Watch Your Language.* Manhassett, New York: Channel Press, 1958.

———. *The Careful Writer.* New York: Atheneum, 1965.

———. *Miss Thistlebottom's Hobgoblins.* New York: Farrar, Straus and Giroux, 1971.

Bryant, Margaret. *Current American Usage.* New York: Funk & Wagnalls, 1962.

Evans, Bergen and Cornelia. *A Dictionary of Contemporary American Usage.* New York: Random House, 1957.

Card, William, Raven I. McDavid, Jr., and Virginia McDavid. "A Systemic Set of Usage Labels for a Dictionary," in MacLeish, *Studies.*

Copperud, Roy H. *A Dictionary of Usage and Style.* New York: Hawthorn Books, 1964.

———. *American Usage: The Consensus.* New York: Van Nostrand, 1970.

Creswell, Thomas J. "Usage in Dictionaries and Dictionaries of Usage." *PADS,* LXIII, 1975, 63–4.

Crisp, Raymond M. "Changes in Attitudes Toward English Usage." Diss. (Microfilm), University of Illinois, 1971.

Étiemble, Rene. *Parlez-vous Franglais?* Paris: Gallimard, 1964.

Fowler, Henry W. *A Dictionary of Modern English Usage.* London: Oxford Press, 1926.

———. (2d ed.), Revised by Sir Ernest Gowers. London: Oxford Press, 1965.

Fries, Charles C. *American English Grammar.* New York: D. Appleton-Century, 1940.

Hall, J. Lesslie. *English Usage: Studies in the History and Uses of English Words and Phrases.* Chicago: Scott, Foresman, 1917. Reprinted Gordon Press.

Joos, Martin. *The Five Clocks.* Publications of the Indiana University Research Center in Anthropology, Folklore and Linguistics, Publication 22. *IJAL,* XXVIII, 1962, No. 2, Part 5. Reprint Harcourt, Brace and Company, 1967.

———. "Homeostasis in English Usage." *College Composition and Communication,* XII, October 1962, 18–22.

Krapp, George Philip. *A Comprehensive Guide to Good English.* Chicago: Rand, McNally, 1927.

Laughlin, Rosemary. "The American With His Dictionary." Diss. (Microfilm), University of Chicago, 1968.

Leonard, Sterling A. *Current English Usage.* English Monograph No. 1, National Council of Teachers of English. Chicago: NCTE, 1932.

McDavid, Raven I, Jr. "Historical, Regional, and Social Variation." *Journal of English Linguistics* I, 1967, 24–40.

Marckwardt, Albert H. and Fred G. Walcott. *Facts About Current English Usage.* English Monograph No. 7, NCTE. New York: D. Appleton-Century Co., Inc., 1938.

Morris, William and Mary. *Harper Dictionary of Contemporary American Usage.* New York and Evanston: Harper and Row, 1975.

Nicholson, Margaret. *A Dictionary of American English Usage.* (Based on H.W. Fowler, *A Dictionary of Modern English Usage.*) New York: Oxford University Press, 1957.

Perrin, Porter. *Writer's Guide and Index to English.* Revised by Wilma R. Ebbitt. Glenview, Illinois: Scott, Foresman, 1972.

Scargill, M.H., *et al. Modern Canadian English Usage.* Toronto: McClelland and Stuart, 1974.

Witherspoon, John. "The Druid 5–7." (Essays on American Usage.) *Pennsylvania Journal and Weekly Advertiser,* Philadelphia, May 9–30, 1781. Reprinted in Mathews 1931, 14–30.

Slang and Argot

Kantrowitz, Nathan and Joanne. *Stateville Names.* Waukesha, Wisconsin: Maledicta, 1979.

Maurer, David W. *The Big Con.* Indianapolis: Bobbs-Merrill, 1941.

———. (2d ed.) New York: New American Library (Signet Books), 1962.

———. "The Argot of the Race Track." *PADS,* XVI, 1951.

———. "Whiz Mob." *PADS,* XXIV, 1955, 1–199; XXXI, 1959, 14–30. Reprinted New Haven: College and University Press, 1964.

———. *The American Confidence Man.* Springfield, Illinois: Charles C. Thomas, 1974.

―――. *Kentucky Moonshine.* Lexington, Kentucky: University Press of Kentucky, 1976.
――― and Victor H. Vogel. *Narcotics and Narcotic Addiction.* Springfield, Illinois: Charles C. Thomas, 1954.
―――. 2d ed. 1962.
―――. 3d ed. 1967.
―――. 4th ed. 1973.

Miscellaneous

Curtin, Philip D. *The Atlantic Slave Trade: A Census.* Madison: University of Wisconsin Press, 1969.
Dykema, Karl J. (review of) "Webster's New World Dictionary, College Edition." *American Speech,* XXIX, 1954, 59–65.
Farmer, John S. *Americanisms Old and New.* London: T. Poulter and Sons, 1889. Reprinted Detroit: Gale, 1976.
Kučera, Henry and W. Nelson Francis. *Computational Analysis of Present Day American English.* Providence, R.I.: Brown University Press, 1966.
McDavid, Raven I., Jr. "The English Language in the United States," in Sebeok, *Trends,* 5–39.
Mathews, Mitford M. *American Words.* Cleveland: Collins-World, 1976.
Pickering, John. *Vocabulary, or Collection of Words and Phrases Which Have Been Supposed to be Peculiar to the United States of America.* 1817. Reprinted New York: Burt Franklin, 1972.
Read, Allan Walker. "Approaches to Lexicography and Semantics," in Sebeok, *Trends,* 145–205.
Schele de Vere, Maximilian. *Americanisms: The English of the New World.* New York: Scribner, 1871. Reprinted, Johnson Reprint.
Smith, Elsdon C. *American Surnames.* Philadelphia: Chilton Book Co., 1969.
Stewart, George R. *Names on the Land.* New York: Random House, 1945.
―――. (2d ed.) Boston: Houghton Mifflin, 1958.

ADDENDUM

Professor McDavid submitted the following additions to his original essay.

Dictionaries

Brewer, Annie M. Dictionaries, Encyclopedias and Other Word-Related Books 1966-1974. Detroit: Gale, 1975.

Linguistic Atlases

That of the Middle and South Atlantic states is slower in appearing than we would like. But the first fascicles will be out shortly.

Names

Fred Tarpley, ed. Place Names USA. A collection of essays in support of the national survey, one for each state and the District of Columbia.

Non-English Dialects and Bilingualism

Metcalf, Allan. Chicano English. Arlington: Center for Applied Linguistics, 1979.

General Works

An important work, tentatively entitled First Person Singular: The Making of Linguistics, edited by Raymond K. O'Cain and Boyd Davis, is in press with E. Karl Koerner of Ottawa University. It is to appear presumably in his series Historiographica Linguistica.

American Military Studies

MARTIN K. GORDON

Introduction

☐ Writings in the general field of American military studies have become so extensive that it is impossible to capture more than the highlights of the subject within the span of a single essay. This article, therefore, will discuss primarily key reference works, historiographic trends, and some organizations and studies in the field.

Three specialized basic reference books are John Quick, *Dictionary of Weapons & Military Terms* (New York: McGraw-Hill Book Company, 1973) which is just what the title says it is, a basic English language dictionary of key terms used over the centuries in the armies of Europe and the United States; the *Acronyms and Initialisms Dictionary* (Detroit: Gale Research Co., 1973, 4th ed.) which is a guide to alphabetic designations, acronyms, and similar condensed appellations used, especially by the military, in the United States; and Vincent J. Esposito, ed., *The West Point Atlas of American Wars* (New York: Praeger Publishers, 1959, 2 vols.) which contains detailed maps and brief operational summaries of every military action in which United States forces have been involved between 1689 (the War of the Grand Alliance/King William's War) and 1953 (the Korean War).

Historiography

To the student of American culture taken as a whole, the debate over the usefulness, scope, and nature of American military history is almost as worthy of study as American military studies itself. As John Shy wrote about the United States Army, "More than military professionals in other societies, American career officers have always felt a special need to justify their very existence." "The American Military Experience: History and Learning," *Journal of Interdisciplinary History* 1 (Winter 1971): 205–228, reprinted in his *A People Numerous and Armed: Reflections on the Military Struggle for American Independence* (New York: Oxford Univ. Press, 1976, p. 225–254). This insight might apply equally to those American historians who study the military rather than some other aspect of American culture.

Walter Millis began the discussion in the foreword to his *Arms and Men: A Study of American Military History* (New York; Mentor Paperback, 1958). He wrote that although Americans had taken a new and broader interest in military history after the Second World War, it paralleled "the contemporary transformation in the whole character of war itself. The advent of the nuclear arsenals has at least seemed to render most of the military history of the Second War as outdated and inapplicable as the history of the War with Mexico." He asked if military history could "shed any illumination upon the extraordinarily difficult, the seemingly insoluble, military problems which confront the nation today?" His *Arms and Men* was an attempt to answer that question. He succeeded brilliantly. As the first significant study of the entire American military establishment (Army, Navy, Air Force, Marine Corps) in its political and cultural context, Millis produced a study still worth reading for its insights into the environment in which American military (taken in the broad sense) leaders have worked. It is also one of the first major military histories to be written by a civilian historian.

W. Frank Craven, *Why Military History?* (Colorado Springs, CO: U. S. Air Force Academy, The Harmon Memorial Lectures in Military History, No. One, 1959) took up Millis' questioning of the usefulness of military history in the nuclear age. Craven accepted one of Millis' key premises: military history is or should be useful in some more tangible manner than are general academic contributions to knowledge. Craven then argued that *Arms and Men* was the best rejoinder to Millis' concern, saying, "I do not agree with all of its conclusions, but I consider the work nevertheless to be an admirable example of the modern approach to military history, an approach that emphasizes the interrelationship of war and society, an approach that reflects the current difficulty we find in defining any military problem as a purely military problem."

Martin K. Gordon is a civilian military historian with the Historical Division, Office of Chief of Engineers, Department of the Army. He was previously with the History and Museums Division, Headquarters, U. S. Marine Corps. A holder of the Ph.D. from George Washington University, he also has graduated from the Universities of Notre Dame and Wisconsin. He has published articles on various aspects of the American militia and on Patrick Magruder, Librarian of Congress at the time the British burned the Library in 1814. A former curator of the Milwaukee County Historical Society, Mr. Gordon is a member of several of the organizations discussed in his article. Although he acknowledges the assistance of the historians and librarians in the Division with various aspects of his article, the views expressed therein are strictly his own and in no way represent the U. S. Marine Corps or any other government agency.

Meanwhile, C. Vann Woodward, "The Age of Reinterpretation," *American Historical Review* 66 (October 1960): 1–19, reprinted Washington, DC: Service Center for Teachers of History of the American Historical Association, Pub. No. 35, 1961 argued that this generation of historians must take advantage of new opportunities for research to interpret the old order to the new. New explosives and new means of delivery made a new military history more important because national leaders had been trained in outmoded interpretations, the values and precepts of the age of firearms could not be carried into the nuclear ago, and the political collapse of Europe in the world opened new research opportunities. Again the need for major changes in military history were called for while Woodward explained what the "free security" provided to the United States by the British Royal Navy between 1815 and the 20th century had meant to the development of the American character.

Millis elaborated on his earlier remarks in *Military History* (Washington: Service Center . . . Pub. No. 39, 1961). After reviewing the history of military history, he defined and typed it, then ascribed three functions to it. They were: to train professional military men, to educate governments and to inform peoples in the military requirements of the times. He then argued that military history had lost those functions. It was irrelevant to modern war and it must become more civilian and broader in scope to survive. Military history has made both of those changes in the years since Millis first made these observations.

A 1967 symposium, "Contemporary History and War," *Military Affairs* 32 (Spring 1968): 1–19 devoted to a dialogue between academic and official historians on the topic of the Army's plans for writing the history of its operations during the War in Vietnam broke free of the ghost of Millis' concern for useful relevant military history. Charles B. MacDonald, an Army historian, discussed the Army's plans and pointed out that the 1947 unification of the armed forces meant that service-level history could no longer deal with strategic concerns as it had in World War II. The scope of service history would have to be more operational as the role of the individual services declined in the over-all conduct of modern American military operations. John Shy, a commentator, argued that the Vietnam War should be studied as an essentially political war. He urged official historians to go beyond a no longer applicable traditional approach, to a holistic study of the Army and its ecology. He thought the operational history of the official historians would describe only a small part of what the Army actually did in Vietnam. Another participant, Leonard Krieger, while pointing out the conventional nature of official history, did admit to its being a good source of materials for academic historians.

Allan R. Millett, "American Military History: Over the Top," (Herbert J. Bass, ed., *The State of American History*, Chicago: Quadrangle Books, 1970, p. 157–182) attempted to stop the professional discussions about Millis' 1958 concern for the usefulness of military history. He pointed out, "Scholarly activity since World War II has elevated military history to full intellectual status." He felt the major task of military historians was "to rewrite American military history from a civilian viewpoint, to counter the military claim that professional interests are the only criteria for studying our military past." In other words, it was time to abandon the military's definition of military history as "lessons" of command and strategy. Millett was concerned with the relationship between military history and other university-level academic specialties. After a useful historiographic survey of recent writings in major aspects of military history, he called for two reforms for military historians: that they expose themselves "to research in military affairs in other disciplines and the methodologies they use, and that we stop apologizing for our interest in military history as if it were a boyish enthusiasm we had never outgrown." Thus, he felt there was no need to find a special usefulness to justify the study of military history and that growth might come through interdisciplinary work.

Peter Paret, "The History of War," *Daedalus: The Historian and the World of the Twentieth Century* 100 (Spring 1971): 376–396, ignoring Millett's work, returned to a consideration of the problems posed by Millis in 1961. Paret placed American military history in its European context and even pointed out that military historians of other nationalities have also felt that their work should be utilitarian. American military historians work in disciplinary isolation, but he also felt, that the isolation was two way. He correctly added that few United States historians studying topics with a military dimension study that dimension or perspective in their work. At a time of change in most categories of research and teaching in history, Paret was struck by the separation of the history of military institutions and of war from those trends.

The two way isolation of military history from the mainstream of American historic thought that Paret noted can be seen in Bernard Mergen, "Surveying Journals of American Studies" published in volume 12, number 3 of this magazine in 1974. Mergen surveyed 100 journals which "contribute to an understanding of American life" from a variety of perspectives. Not one military-oriented journal made that list. Paret might accept this. However, he did urge that more attention be paid to the interdisciplinary thrust which some newer journals in the field were adopting as a possible solution to this isolation and lack of usefulness.

John Shy, "The American Military Experience," (previously cited) attempted to answer some of these concerns. He posed a technique, borrowed from the social sciences, to answer the question of the value of military history in the nuclear age. He asked if the international behavior of a nation could be understood in terms of its national peculiarities. In other words, applying learning theory, can one explain American governmental or popular behavior in issues involving war and the military in terms of learned responses, an engrained pattern, which operates beneath the level of full consciousness?

In another 1971 essay, "The Military Conflict Considered as a Revolutionary War," reprinted in the same anthology, Shy demonstrated another possible solution to the problem posed by Millis and Woodward. He did not directly discuss the debate but provided a new insight into the military history of the American Revolution. By placing it in the perspective of revolutionary warfare, he offered a definition of the war that was independent of the debate: "the concept of the Revolutionary War, not as an instrument of policy or a sequence of military operations, but as a social process of political education that can be explored and should be analyzed."

In the same year that Shy used new methods and definitions to demonstrate not only new interpretations of the military history of the American Revolution but also the scholarly vitality of military history, Theodore Ropp published "Forty Years of the Military Institute, 1933–1972," *Military Affairs* 35 (October 1971): 89–91. He summarized the history of the American Military Institute, (Dept. of History, Kansas State University, Manhattan, KS 66506) which through publishing *Military Affairs* and its joint sessions at professional meetings with other historical organizations, is an important group of academic and government military historians. Ropp discussed changes in outlooks within the profession and noted Millis' 1961 article as a still valid analysis of the uncertainties which have come into the professional literature since World War II.

A pair of articles in the October 1972 *Military Affairs* (vol. 36) illustrate recent trends and arguments within the context of this debate. Peter Karsten (p. 88–92) in "Demilitarizing Military History: Servants of Power or Agents of Understanding?" urged official historians to use the social sciences to ask more questions than they were doing and attacked official historians, the "servants of power" for not asking important questions. Paul J. Scheips, an experienced official historian, replied in "Military History and Peace Research," (p. 92–96). He agreed with the need for interdisciplinary work and summarized the new and growing field of peace research and offered several suggestions for new research including a study of those who use cold war jargon. Scheips had earlier in "Quincy Wright, 1890–1970," *Military Affairs* 35 (April 1971): 49 summarized the life and work of one of the early pioneers in the field of peace research.

The impact of peace studies on American teaching was summarized in Richard Martin, "Scores of Colleges Add Majors in 'Peace and Conflict Studies'; The Range: Quarrels to War," *Wall Street Journal* March 5, 1974.

Photo, courtesy James Dacey

Russell F. Weigley, *The End of Militarism (Colorado Springs, CO: U. S. Air Force Academy, The Harmon Memorial Lectures in Military History No. 15, 1973, reprinted in *The Military and Society: Proceedings of the Fifth Military History Symposium, Colorado Springs: U. S. Air Force Academy, 1972, available from the Goverment Printing Office (GPO), Washington, DC 20402, no. 088-070-00367-8 for $I.90), observed that the study of traditional militarism was of no help in studying the role of the modern military in society. He drew a distinction between militarism and the "military way" and developed in a more contemporary framework Alfred Vagts' concepts of the new civilian militarism (Vagts, *A History of Militarism: Civilian and Military, Revised Edition, New York: Free Press Paperback, Macmillan Co., 1959). Several essays in The Military and Society discuss the changing nature of military studies in the context of the relationship between the military and society, the theme of the 1972 symposium. Information on available Harmon Lectures (17 in number to date) and on the biennial symposia (6 in number to date) is available from the Department of History at the Air Force Academy.

Theodore Ropp, "War: From Colonies to Vietnam," (William H. Cartwright & Richard L. Watson, Jr., eds., The Reinterpretation of American History, Washington, DC: National Council for the Social Studies, 1973, p. 207–226) wrote a survey of current works in the field of American military history, broadly defined to include such areas as naval history and history of technology. Those areas are only recently being given the attention they deserve and Ropp's essay outlined recent work and gave suggestions for further research.

Edward N. Saveth, "A Decade of American Historiography, The 1960's," p. 17–34 in the same volume, contributed a background context to part of this debate in his discussion of the concern in the American historical profession over the usefulness of their work in that decade. He noted especially a leading military historian, Louis Morton, who in 1970 wondered if historians should play a direct role in the formulation of national policies, "The Historian and the Policy Process," History Teacher 4 (November 1970): 23–29. Reinterpretation, although written primarily for high school teachers, also contains useful bibliographic surveys by Jack P. Greene on the American Revolution and Robert F. Durden on the Civil War and Reconstruction.

This debate, begun by Millis at the end of the 1950s, had an effect on official historians. Ronald Spector, an Army historian, in "Getting Down to the Nitty-Gritty: Military History, Official History and the American Experience in Vietnam," Military Affairs 38 (February 1974): 11–12 explained the role of official history against the critiques of the peace historians and pointed out his belief that, "military history is neither a guidebook for generals and strategists nor a blueprint for peace researchers: but a way of understanding our experience as a nation." He pointed out that Allan Millett, an academic historian, had said the same thing four years earlier. Benis M. Frank, a Marine Corps historian, wrote along similar themes in discussing the scope of the government's oral history programs, distinguishing between official, academic, and popular military history in "Afterthought," (Oral History Review: 1974, New York: Oral History Association, 1974, p. 93–96).

This discussion continued with a professed lack of interest on the part of the civilian historians now dominant in the field in the concern over the usefulness of military history. Along with John Shy's and others' works in interdisciplinary military studies, Dennis E. Showalter, "A Modest Plea for Drums and Trumpets," *Military Affairs* 39 (April 1975): 71-74 reminded those interested in military studies that operational history, the history of the deeds of armed forces, was the essence of the subject. He felt that most modern military historians avoided operations out of a desire to make military history respectable; to disassociate themselves from war-gamers, amateurs, hobbyists, and popular writers; to avoid romanticizing war; to avoid favoring the status quo; and, to emphasize the context of war.

Allan Millett's 1975 essay also demonstrated the continued swing away from concern over the usefulness of military history. The discussion over the academic respectability of the discipline remained however along with questions about the lack of an historiographic tradition in that speciality. (*"American Military History: Struggling Through the Wire," paper presented at the International Commission on Military History, Washington, DC, August, 1975. Papers presented at this meeting will be published later this year by Military Affairs/Aerospace Historian Press.) Although the quantity and quality of writings about military history were steadily improving, Millett no longer thought "that the speciality is making any significant impact on the general writing or teaching of American history," which was his preference in objectives. He pointed out that American military historians seemed to prefer to debate the didactic value of their subject rather than engage in any meaningful historiographic work. He defined "drum and bugle" military history as including the books about battles, campaigns, weapons and equipage, and military men (singularly and collectively) which were beneath the dignity of academic historians. Millett, an academic historian, divided the problem into three categories: the intellectual and institutional milieu that shaped the writing of American military history; the writings on America's wars; and, the historiography of American military institutions.

Another paper presented at the same symposium by B. Franklin Cooling, "Technology and the Frontiers of Military History," called for new efforts to understand the relationship between the history of technology and military history. His paper was reprinted in part in *Military Affairs* 39 (December 1975): 206-207. Cooling called for greater use of museums and greater international cooperation to study that interaction. He saw, "The need for greater amalgamation of antiquarians (amateurs and collectors), with archivists, curators, librarians, and professional academic-writer-historians in the field of military-technological history." Cooling, unlike Millett, wanted to work with those outside the academic community towards reaching new understandings of the interplay of traditional military history and its neglected technological underpinnings.

In the same issue of *Military Affairs*, p. 181-190, Clark Reynolds, "American Strategic History and Doctrines: A Reconsideration," redefined military history as "the study of organized conflict in human relations" or "strategic history" which had a new meaning in the 1970s and was no longer adrift as Millis had lamented in 1961. Reynolds held that the combining of different sources with the use of a

Photo, courtesy James Dacey

sweeping overview of history that would not regard war as episodic but as part of a continuum would yield general reconsideration of any country's military doctrines.

Thus, several new directions in American military studies can be seen emerging. First is a multidisciplinary thrust towards understanding the military in various national social contexts. Spearheaded by sociologists and political scientists, the Inter-University Seminar on Armed Forces & Society publishes *Armed Forces and Society: An Interdisciplinary Journal on Military Institutions, Civil-Military Relations, Arms Control and Peacekeeping, and Conflict Management* (Social Sciences Bldg., Box 46, 1126 East 59th St., Chicago, IL 60637). More specifically sociological is the *Journal of Political & Military Sociology* (Dept. of Sociology, Northern Illinois University, DeKalb, IL 60115, semiannual). *The Journal of Conflict Resolution* (Sage Publications) also international in scope, founded in 1956, antedates the other two magazines, both founded in the last five years.

ABC-Clio, Inc., Riviera Campus, 2040 A. P. S., Box 4397, Santa Barbara, CA 93103, is a press which publishes extensive bibliographies in the field of war and peace studies. Sage Publications, 275 S. Beverly Drive, Beverly Hills, CA 90212, and 44 Hatton Garden, London, EC1N 8ER, publishes extensively in the sociological-oriented field of the armed forces and society. Sage published Kurt Lang's *Military Institutions and Sociology of War: A Review of the Literature with Annotated Bibliography* (1972) which studied the literature of this viewpoint. A recent volume in the Sage Series on Armed Forces and Society is Hamilton I. Mc-

Cubbin, Barbara B. Dahl, and Edna J. Hunter, eds., *Families in the Military System* (1976).

A second new direction is that of increased cooperation among all those interested in American military studies. The American Military Institute was mentioned earlier. An early off-shoot was the Company of Military Historians (287 Thayer St., Providence, RI 02906). The Company publishes the *Military Collector & Historian*, which is devoted to uniforms, military art, equipage and weapons, and, in general, the military material culture of the armed forces. Warren W. Hassler, Jr., "Allies or Enemies: The Antiquarian and Historian," *Military Collector & Historian* 25 (Spring 1973): 22–23 outlined, from the point of view of the collector, the relationship between antiquarians and historians and how their work should be of mutual benefit. A third national military history organization is the Council on Abandoned Military Posts (CAMP), (P. O. Box 171, Arlington, VA 22210), publishers of *Periodical*, a quarterly magazine. CAMP is devoted to the archaeological and historical study of historic military posts and their preservation. CAMP's monthly newsletter, *Heliogram*, carries book reviews and reports on current developments in subjects of interest to its members. There is some overlap in membership between all these organizations, but their programs and publications still tend to work separately.

Perhaps another solution to these debates lay in a path that American Studies has outlined in other subject areas. That is why this article has the title it has. The members and authors in the Company and CAMP have contributed to understanding American military culture. Paret and Millett in their essays have outlined intellectual approaches that ignore this concept whereas Ropp accepts the importance of some popular histories in his essay and Cooling outlines new paths of cooperation. That which Cooling describes in his essay could be named military material culture. The "studies" approach, as distinct from the historical approach that Millett calls for, could ask questions that the military historians, disturbed first by the nuclear revolution in warfare and next by the general questionings of the 1960s, would deem, and perhaps properly so, not part of their competency. This concept also has implications for the related fields of military popular culture and military folklore, areas in which work needs to be done.

A third new direction is that of an approach to American military history as a continuous process. Reynolds, cited earlier, applied this approach to the maritime aspects of America's military past. Russell F. Weigley in two books has gone beyond episodic battle history to study the "American" nature of military thought defined in its narrow army/ground warfare sense. *Towards an American Army: Military Thought from Washington to Marshall* (New York: Columbia Univ. Press, 1962) is an early examination of the continuing debate among Americans and especially among regular Army officers over what should American military policy be? Weigley followed that with *The American Way of War: A History of United States Military Strategy and Policy* (New York: Macmillan, 1973, Macmillan Wars of the United States series). He argued that there was a characteristically American way of war in which the object of military strategy had come to mean total destruction of the enemy. While other contemporary historians argued that with nuclear balance of the Korean War era and later, the United States in its military actions was returning to its earlier traditional pattern of limited wars.

While Weigley and Reynolds were concerned with intellectual patterns, Marcus

Cunliffe, *Soldiers and Civilians: The Martial Spirit in America, 1775–1865* (Boston: Little, Brown, 1968) attempted to capture popular attitudes about the military and its place in society. Providing a large amount of material as well as some interpretation, Cunliffe saw professional military, non-professional military, and anti-militarist views emerge in the century he studied. Another book that looked beyond episodic development to study the Army in a broader context is C. Robert Kemble, *The Image of the Army Officer in America: Background for Current Views* (Westport, CT: Greenwood Press, 1973, Contributions in Military History No. 5). Kemble used primarily literary sources to discuss cultural stereotypes of the Army officer and demonstrated, that with the possible exception of the Vietnam War years, that image was more likely to change in peace than in wartime.

These studies, as does most of American military history, concentrated on the Army. This cultural bias towards the study of ground forces in a major maritime country is itself of interest. *Arms and Men* cited earlier dealt with all of the services, however. *Command & Commanders in Modern Military History: Proceedings of the Second Military History Symposium* (Colorado Springs, CO: U. S. Air Force Academy, 1968, available from GPO, no. 0874-0003 for $1.50) studied various aspects of American, British, and German sea, ground, and air command in World Wars I and II.

One study which places the Navy in the context of the society of its time is Harold D. Langley, *Social Reform in the United States Navy, 1798–1862* (Urbana: Univ. of Illinois Press, 1967). *The American Neptune: A Quarterly Journal of Maritime History,* published by the Peabody Museum of Salem Massachusetts, is a leading journal in its field. The recent publication, Robert Seager, II, and Doris D. Maguire, eds., *Letters and Papers of Alfred Thayer Mahan* (Annapolis: U. S. Naval Institute Press, 1975, 3 vols.) might also help to redress this imbalance.

Photo courtesy Prints and Photographs Division, Library of Congress.

Spanish-American war dead ready for burial, Arlington National Cemetery, Washington, D.C., 1898.

During and after the Vietnam War, military historians began to see continuities in America's approach to limited wars. Besides John Shy's essays, another example of this approach is in S. A. Swartzrauber, *"River Patrol Relearned," (*Naval Review, 1970* Annapolis: U. S. Navel Institute Press, 1970, p. 120–157) which discussed the Navy's need to relearn how to fight riverine warfare from the point of view of a professional Navy officer concerned with current problems. Swartzrauber should be compared with George E. Buker, *Swamp Sailors: Riverine Warfare in the Everglades, 1835–1842* which discussed the development of the doctrine of riverine warfare during the Second Seminole War.

This long summary of the historiography of American military history has barely scratched the surface of the debates over these themes. For example, there are articles on these topics in practically every volume of *Essays in Some Dimensions of Military History* (Carlisle Barracks, PA, 17013: Military History Research Collection, 1972- annual, 4 vols. to date, free from the Collection). The *Essays* reprint selected lectures on American and foreign military history given each year at the Army War College.

This historiography is important for two reasons, first, because of the three aspects of this subject, popular, academic, and official or governmental, which touch on many areas of American culture. Secondly, the methods and problems of those who write in this area might also in themselves say something about American culture in its military aspects.

Also, many of the articles and books cited above are rich in bibliographic insights into developments in military history. In addition to the monographs, the Millett, Ropp, Saveth, Karsten, Schieps, Showalter, Cooling, and Reynolds articles all have full bibliographic footnotes.

Bibliography

Robin Higham, *A Guide to the Sources of United States Military History* (Hamden, CT: Archon Books, 1975) is an excellent current starting source for work in the field. It is a chronologically organized introduction to military, naval, and air history from the European beginnings of the United States to 1974. It includes bibliographic, biographic, historical, and documentary sections in each essay, as well as suggestions for further research. In an interesting example of the broadening scope of military studies, it concludes with a chapter on "Museums as Historical Resources" by Philip K. Lundeberg of the Smithsonian Institution.

Recently, *Military Affairs* and its sister, more specialized magazine *Aerospace Historian* have begun a new publishing program based at Eisenhower Hall, Kansas State University, Manhattan, KS 66506. A recent publication, edited by Robin Higham and Carol Brandt, is *The United States Army in Peacetime: Essays in Honor of the Bicentennial* which explores a recent interest by historians in the armed forces' contributions to the nation in peacetime in such areas as exploration, the national parks, public health, and foreign affairs. A list of publications is available from the publisher.

Later this year, as mentioned in connection with the Millett (1975) and Cooling papers, this press will publish the 1975 ACTA of the International Commission on Military History. That anthology will also include articles on sources for the study of military history in the National Archives and in the Library of Congress and an essay on naval history resources in the United States.

Another bibliographic series is published for free distribution by the library, United States Military Academy, West Point, NY 10996. Alan C. Aimone, *Bibliography of Military History, and his *Official Records of the American Civil War: A Researcher's Guide, and Marie T. Capps and Theodore G. Stroup, *The Library Map Collection: Period of the American Revolution, 1753–1800 are of general value.

Library Publications, Kansas State University Library, Manhattan, KS 66506 has published several important bibliographies. Among them are Arthur D. Larson, *Civil-Military Relations and Militarism: A Classified Bibliography Covering the United States and Other Nations of the World (1971); John Greenwood, *American Defence Policy Since 1945: A Preliminary Bibliography (1973); and, of interest because of the lack of coverage elsewhere of these materials, Allen R. Millett and B. Franklin Cooling, *Doctoral Dissertations in Military Affairs (1972) updated in the April 1973 Military Affairs and thereafter in the February issue. This bibliography covers all known dissertations in English in its field.

Sample specialized bibliographies are Brooke Nihart, "Popular Military History," (Marine Corps Gazette, July 1975, p. 16–18), and George Siehl, "Cloak, Dust Jacket, and Dagger," (Library Journal October 15, 1972: 3277–3283). This bibliography on intelligence operations has been updated by several articles in Military Affairs.

The Macmillan Company's Wars of the United States Series is misnamed in as much as service histories and volumes on other topics of military interest are included within it. This series attempts to combine current research with documentation that serves as guides to the sources for each topic.

New materials have come out in the field of western studies. The Arthur H. Clark Co., 1264 S. Central Avenue, Glendale, CA 91204, publishes the Frontier Military Series, 1800–1900 which reprints rare primary and secondary accounts of the military history of the west. Presidial Press, Box 5248, Austin, TX 78763 has published, John H. Jenkins, ed., the Papers of the Texas Revolution, 1835–1836 (1976, 10 vols.). The same press also publishes the journal Military History of Texas and the Southwest. By Valor & Arms, P.O. Box 2243, Fort Collins, CO 80522, is another new magazine which reprints documents and early scholarly studies as well as popular history and art about the post-Civil War American West.

Government Programs

Almost all of the service historical programs have published bibliographies and most have published guides to sources for further research. These programs are not equipped to conduct more than modest amounts of research by mail but all are willing to help a scholar traveling in the United States if the scholar will visit the offices of the program in person. In the case of those programs which maintain oral history collections, a personal visit is essential because those depositories, as part of their programs, do not circulate or copy their tapes and transcripts.

The Army's program is divided into two parts. The already mentioned field activity, the U. S. Military History Research Collection, Carlisle Barracks, holds numerous manuscript and published source materials. In addition to the *Essays,* the Collection publishes bibliographies on various aspects of military history based on their holdings. The most recent volume is Roy S. Barnard, *Oral History.* Information on this series can be obtained from the Director at the address given earlier.

The Chief of Military History, Center of Military History, Room 6A-015, Forrestal (North) Building, 1000 Independence Avenue, SW, Washington, DC 20314, distributes a free catalog of the Center's publications. A recent publication, Norman M. Cary, Jr., *Guide to U. S. Army Museums and Historic Sites* (1975, available from GPO no. 088-920-00561-4 for $3.00) is broader than the title indicates. It covers museums and historic sites in the United States with a military history orientation and hence is of interest to students of technology and historic sites.

The Office of Air Force History has published Mary Ann Cresswell and Carl Berger, comps., *United States Air Force History: An Annotated Bibliography* (1971, available from GPO no. 0870-0307 for .50) and Lawrence J. Paszek, comp., *United States Air Force History: A Guide to Documentary Sources* (1973, available from GPO no. 0870-0322 for $1.80). Researchers can contact the program at the Albert F. Simpson Historical Research Center (3825-HOA), Maxwell Air Force Base, Alabama 36112.

The Director of Naval History, Naval Historical Center, Washington Navy Yard, Washington, DC 20374, distributes, besides a free list of available publications, *United States Naval History: A Bibliography, Sixth Edition* (1972). Dean C. Allard and Betty Bern, *U. S. Naval History Sources in the Washington Area and Suggested Research Subjects* (1970, available from GPO, no number given, for $1.00) is an essential starting point for the researcher in naval history.

The Director of Marine Corps History and Museums, Headquarters, U. S. Marine Corps (CODE HD), Washington, DC 20380 distributes free catalogues of the Division's publications as well as bibliographies and guides to sources. Jack B. Hilliard and Harold A. Bivins, comps., *An Annotated Reading List of United States Marine Corps History* (1971), Benis M. Frank, *Marine Corps Oral History Catalog* (1975), and Charles A. Wood, *Marine Corps Personal Papers Collection Catalog* (1974), are good references for the researcher interested in this field.

Truman R. Strobridge, U. S. Coast Guard Historian, Public Affairs Division, U. S. Coast Guard Headquarters (G-APA/83), 400 7th Street, SW, Washington, DC 20590, has available for free distribution *An Annotated Bibliography of the Coast Guard* and *The U. S. Life Saving Service: An Annotated Bibliography.*

Research By Mail

While none of these government programs will do extensive research by mail, all of them can advise on the sources available for study within their areas of expertise and some will sell microfilm copies of source material held by them. Some programs can assist in declassifying records of recent eras that might be wanted by a particular researcher. All of them can advise on obtaining their publications if there are problems in ordering them from the Government Printing Office.

The National Archives' catalog, *National Archives Microfilm Publications* (Washington, DC 20408: National Archives and Records Service, 1974, available free) contains lists of what is available on microfilm from the National Archives. The National Archives has sponsored a series of conferences which analyze its holdings in its relation to a particular war, era, or theme. Lists of the National Archives Conference Series can be obtained from the publishers, Ohio University Press, Administrative Annex, Athens, OH 45710, and, more recently, Howard University Press, 2935 Upton St., NW, Washington, DC 20059.

The Library of Congress Manuscript Division distributes a list, "Manuscript Collections on Microfilm" which lists materials available from that division. The Library Photoduplication Service also has an extensive microfilm publication program that ranges from the complete printed records of the "Alabama Claims Commission, 1882–85," to "Statements of Japanese Officials on World War II." Inquiries about that series should be addressed to Dept. C, Photoduplication Service. Both offices are at the Library of Congress, Washington , DC 20540.

To conclude on an optimistic note, advice for scholars wishing to publish in American journals can be found in the previously cited *The Military and Society: Proceedings of the Fifth Military History Symposium,* p. 104–111, "The Writing and Publishing of Military History."□

UPDATE

by Martin K. Gordon

Reference Works

In the four years since the publication of "American Military Studies," a number of reference works for the student of the American military have appeared. The first two, however, cover more than just the United States, and are of basic value for any study of the modern military. Dale E. Floyd, The World Bibliography of Armed Land Conflict from Waterloo to World War I: Wars, Campaigns, Battles, Revolutions, Revolts, Coups d'Etat, Insurrections, Riots, Armed Confrontations, 2 volumes (London: George Prior Publishers, 1979 and Wilmington, Delaware: Michael Glazier, Inc., 1979), covers all parts of the world and includes even more categories than its subtitle indicates. Volume 1, for example, includes sections on military photography and military professionalism. The user should be aware that the books and articles referenced are under the most specific heading possible. For example, a book on European military museums will be entered under Europe and not under military museums. The second basic international reference book is Thomas Parrish, ed., The Simon and Schuster Encyclopedia of World War II (New York: Simon and Schuster, 1978). It contains 4,000 entries and is useful for fast research on current explanations of World War II events and terms.

Webster's American Military Biographies (Springfield, Massachussetts: G & C Merriam Company, 1978), contains 1,033 biographies written for this book. Who Was Who in American History--The Military (Chicago: Marquis Who's Who, Inc., 1975), is a compilation of biographies of military figures that have appeared in the various editions of Marquis' Who's Who.

Historiography

The American Military Institute, the leading professional organization for military historians, celebrated its fortieth anniversary with a commemorative issue of its journal, Military Affairs.
That issue, Volume 41, Number 2 (April 1977), contains several
articles on the history of the study of the military in America.
It includes articles on American military history and journalism
and essays on "European Military History in America: The State of
the Art," and "The Universities and the Teaching of Military
Subjects on Third World Areas." While that issue furnishes essays
and references for retrospective study, the next issue contains
Jack C. Lane's "American Military Past: The Need for New
Approaches," 41 (October 1977). Lane argues that more attention
should be devoted to the harmony and agreement of trends in
society and developments in the military establishment, and less
to studies of conflicts and tensions. He also argues that more
attention should be paid to local, rather than national, sentiments and politics as a fruitful source of new interpretations of
American civil-military relations. His footnotes are starting
places for mastering the literature of those possibilities for
interpretive work. Military Affairs and the American Military
Institute can be reached at Eisenhower Hall, Kansas State University, Manhattan, Kansas 66506.

Ronald F. Lee, *The Origin and Evolution of the National Military
Park Idea (Washington, D.C.: National Park Service, 1973), is an
account of the shift in preservationist sentiment from local and
private interests to the federal government as the proper source
for preserving battlefields and other military sites of historic
interest. It is available from the Chief Historian, National
Park Service, Department of the Interior, Washington, D.C. 20240.
Available from the Office of Communications of the National Park
Service is their catalog, *Sales Publications, which lists all
their guides to the military park sites in the United States.
William S. Coker, ed., *The Military Presence on the Gulf Coast
(Pensacola, Florida: Gulf Coast History and Humanities Conference,
John C. Pace Library, University of West Florida, 1978), includes
essays on the French, British, Spanish, and American military and
naval services along the Gulf Coast of Florida.

The U.S. Air Force Academy Military History Symposia continued to
study new themes. *The American Military on the Frontier:
Proceedings of the Seventh Military History Symposium (Colorado
Springs, Colorado: U.S. Air Force Academy, 1978, available from
the Government Printing Office, Washington, D.C., order no.
008-070-00423-2), includes sections on the influence of the military on the frontier and that of the frontier on the military, as
well as a section, "Military Life on the Frontier," which studies
the role of enlisted men and of women. *Air Power and Warfare:

Proceedings of the Eighth Military History Symposium, published in
1979 and also available from the GPO, contains a number of essays
on the development of air power in the twentieth century that will
help to redress the tendency of military historians to concentrate
on the study of ground forces.

The faculty at the United States Naval Academy has edited two
anthologies that should stimulate further research into the United
States' history as a maritime power. Kenneth J. Hagan, ed., In
Peace and War: Interpretations of American Naval History, 1775-
1978 (Westport,Connecticut: Greenwood Press, 1978), is as much
concerned with the formulation of naval policy, the Navy's internal history, and its role as an instrument of diplomacy as with
the wars it has fought. Robert W. Love, Jr., ed., Changing
Interpretations and New Sources in Naval History (New York:
Garland Publishing Inc., 1980), contains papers from the 1977
naval history symposium at the U.S. Naval Academy. The papers
cover European and Japanese naval topics while presenting new
concepts in American naval history.

Meanwhile, *A Guide to the Study and Use of Military History
(Washington, D.C.: Center of Military History, 1979, available
from the GPO, order no. 008-029-00105), was not designed to break
new ground, but to serve as a reference work on the history and
nature of official military history and a guide to current U.S.
Army military history, art, and museum programs. It contains
sections on current methodologies and bibliographies and a section
that summarizes military history in other parts of the Department
of Defense, outside the United States, and in the academic world.

The history and role of black Americans in the armed forces
continues to be of great interest. Morris MacGregor and Bernard
Nalty, eds., Blacks in the United States Armed Forces: Basic
Documents (Wilmington, Delaware: Scholarly Resources, Inc., 1977),
provides thirteen volumes of facsimile reproductions of documents
that reach from the Colonial period through the middle 1960s. A
study that supports Jack Lane's argument for the importance of
understanding military history at the local level is Lowell D.
Black, *The Negro Volunteer Militia Units of the Ohio National
Guard, 1870-1954: The Struggle for Military Recognition and
Equality in the State of Ohio (Manhattan, Kansas: Military
Affairs/Aerospace Historian Publishing, Eisenhower Hall, Kansas
State University, 1976), which is an interpretive study that is
also a published doctoral dissertation.

The literature on the role of women in the modern military
establishment is so voluminous that it is beyond the scope of
this essay. But an excellent example of the historical work being
carried out on the role of women is Patricia Stallard, Glittering
Misery: The Dependents of the Indian Fighting Army (San Rafael,
California: Presidio Press, 1978). Weldon B. Durham, "'Big Brother' and the 'Seven Sisters': Camp Life Reforms in World War
I," Military Affairs, 42 (April 1978), studies the impact of

social reform movements on Army camp life.

As can be seen from this summary, studies of the military, naval, and air establishments continued the trend, discussed in my first essay, of concentrating on non-combat aspects. But new publications demonstrate that American military studies cannot be simplistically characterized as moving only in one direction.

Four books on the Civil War illustrate this point. The first three focus on the popular culture of the war, while the fourth shows the importance of examining the Army and the Navy together in combat. William Frassanito examines Civil War photographs as historical documents and studies contemporaneous maps and battle accounts. He then researches the battlefields as they are today, and photographs the sites portrayed in the Civil War era photographs. He uses this comparison of photograph and document to develop new accounts and to correct misperceptions about events during the battle. His two books to date are Gettysburg: A Journey in Time (New York: Charles Scribners Sons, 1975), and Antietam: The Photographic Legacy of America's Bloodiest Day (New York: Charles Scribners Sons, 1978). Thomas L. Connelly, *The Marble Man: Robert E. Lee and His Image in American Society (Baton Rouge: Louisiana State University Press, 1978), shows how Lee became an American symbol and how that image has been manipulated by ensuing generations. The book has aroused controversies about the role of Lee during the Civil War and after his death. Rowena Reed, Combined Operations in the Civil War (Annapolis, Maryland: U.S. Naval Institute Press, 1978), provides the first full account of combined Army-Navy amphibious operations. She shows how, by the end of the war, amphibious warfare had become an instrument for projecting force into the enemy's heartland.

Another aspect of the interplay of the American military and its environment is Willard B. Robinson, American Forts: Architectural Form and Function (Urbana: University of Illinois Press, 1977). Willard's thesis is that a clearly defined function produced beauty of form. Thus, because they developed from precise strategic principles, some of America's forts are among the nation's most functional and beautiful pre-twentieth-century structures. Stanley South, Palmetto Parapets (1974), and Kenneth E. Lewis, Camden: A Frontier Town (1976), both examine early fortifications in the context of their inhabitants. These archeological and anthropological studies examine material objects as they were used. They were published by the Institute of Archeology and Anthropology, University of South Carolina, Columbia, South Carolina.

The Brookings Institution in Washington, D.C., working from the perspective of the social sciences, has published several studies that investigate such issues as the appropriate composition of the armed forces, how they should be used, and how they have been used since World War II as an instrument of political will. A catalog of their publications is available.

The differences between popular military history and the scholarly and official approaches were highlighted by the controversy over William Manchester, *American Caesar: Douglas MacArthur, 1880-1964 (New York: Dell Publishing, 1979). That biography has been heavily criticized by John E. Wiltz, "William Manchester's American Caesar: Some Observations," Military Affairs 43 (October 1979), and Forrest Pogue, "The Military in a Democracy: A Review of American Caesar," International Security 3 (Spring 1979).

Film and Propaganda

The mutual cultural influences of military organizations and civilian society have been examined increasingly in recent years. Lawrence H. Suid, *Guts and Glory: Great American War Movies (Reading, Massachusetts: Addison-Wesley, 1978), explores the relationship between the Pentagon public relations staff and the Hollywood film industry. Although there are numerous minor errors in the book, it stands as the first serious effort to examine the mechanics of how a film maker obtains cooperation and support from the armed forces. Other accounts focus on in-depth studies of the World War II era. Gregory D. Black and Clayton R. Koppes, "OWI Goes to the Movies: The Bureau of Intelligence's Criticism of Hollywood, 1942-43," Prologue: The Journal of the National Archives 6 (Spring 1974), and Richard W. Steele, "The Greatest Gangster Movie Ever Filmed: Prelude to War," Prologue, 11 (Winter 1979), both supplement Suid by analyzing the relationships of a civilian agency and of the Army with Hollywood film makers. A history of the Office of War Information is Allan M. Winkler, The Politics of Propaganda: The Office of War Information, 1942-1945 (New Haven: Yale University Press, 1978). A comparative study is Leila J. Rupp, Mobilizing Women for War: German and American Propaganda, 1939-1945 (Princeton: Princeton University Press, 1978).

New Aspects

With the passage of time and the declassification of documents, new aspects of the American military can now be studied. The records of the Joint Chiefs of Staff (JCS) at the beginning of the Cold War are now available. University Publications of America, Inc., in Washington, D.C., has published several series of JCS documents on microfilm. Michael Glazier, Inc., has published a recently declassified three-volume history of the JCS written by their official historians, The History of the Joint Chiefs of Staff: The Joint Chiefs of Staff and National Policy. A secondary account that provides background information is Michael S. Sherry, Preparing for the Next War: American Plans for Postwar Defense, 1941-45 (New Haven: Yale University Press, 1977). A JCS historian has used some of these materials in Walter S. Poole, "From Conciliation to Containment: The Joint Chiefs of Staff and the Coming of the Cold War, 1945-1946," Military Affairs, 42 (February 1978).

Both primary materials and secondary histories are being published on the history of American military and naval intelligence. University Publications of America and Michael Glazier, Inc., have published series of documents relating to MAGIC. (The term MAGIC is used to refer either to any intercepted Japanese message or to the entire program devoted to breaking the Japanese codes.) The two published series of sources are not identical. A potential customer should write for catalogs before placing any orders with those firms. The Department of Defense has published a five-volume set, The "Magic" Background of Pearl Harbor (Washington, D.C.: GPO, 1978, order no. 008-000-00233-9).

W. J. Holmes, Double-Edged Secrets: U.S. Naval Intelligence Operations in the Pacific During World War II is an autobiographical account by a participant in those operations. Jeffery M. Dorwart, The Office of Naval Intelligence: The Birth of America's First Intelligence Agency is an examination of both official and personal records that document the beginnings of the United States' first intelligence agency. Both books were published in 1979 by the U.S. Naval Institute Press, Annapolis, Maryland. Joseph E. Persico, *Piercing the Reich: The Penetration of Nazi Germany by American Secret Agents During World War II (New York: Ballantine Books, 1979), also uses recently available sources to open aspects of World War II to further interpretation. David Kahn, "World War II History: The Biggest Hole," Military Affairs, 39 (April 1975), outlines research opportunities about intelligence in World War II.

Update

"American Military Studies" reported on a series of papers given at the International Commission on Military History meeting in Washington, D.C., in August 1975. Those papers have since been published in International Commission on Military History, *Acta No. 2, Washington, D.C. (Manhattan, Kansas: Military Affairs/ Aerospace Historian Publishing, 1977). *Essays in Some Dimensions of Military History, published for free distribution by the U.S. Army Military History Institute at Carlisle Barracks, Pennsylvania, reached five volumes before the series ended. A selection from that series has been published in Russell F. Weigley, ed., New Dimensions in Military History: An Anthology (San Rafael, California: Presidio Press, 1975).

Robin Higham, ed., A Guide to the Sources of United States Military History has been updated and new chapters have been added. The second edition of that essential bibliographic tool will be published within the next few years.

Government Programs

The literature on the United States' involvement in warfare in
Southeast Asia is beyond the extent of this essay, but each of the
military services' historical programs (Army, Navy, Air Force,
Marine Corps) have published either official or intermediate
histories of their involvement in that conflict. The Historian,
Office of the Secretary of Defense, contracted with the Rand
Corporation, an Air Force-oriented think tank, for a series of
interviews with prominent Vietnamese refugees who arrived in the
United States in 1975. That study has been reprinted as Stephen
T. Hosmer, Konrad Kellen, and Brian M. Jenkins, The Fall of South
Vietnam: Statements by Vietnamese Military and Civilian Leaders
(New York: Crane-Russak Co., 1980). Those interviews furnish
unusual insights into the relationship of the Republic of South
Vietnam and the United States. Each service historical program
has a catalog of their publications that includes their studies on
the war in Southeast Asia; they can be obtained by writing the
respective offices.

*Publications of the U.S. Army Center of Military History can be
obtained from The Center of Military History, ATTN: DAMH-HSP,
Rm. 4136, Pulaski Building, 20 Massachusetts Ave., N.W.,
Washington, D.C. 20314. The U.S. Army Military History Institute,
Carlisle Barracks, Pennsylvania 17013, continues to publish its
bibliography series. For example, number 14 is *Colonial America
and the War for Independence (1976), and number 17 is *The United
States Army and the Indian Wars in the Trans-Mississippi West,
1860-1898 (1978). Availability and distribution of that series
is inconsistent and the Institute should be written directly for
information on how to obtain their publications. *Marine Corps
Historical Publications in Print can be obtained from the
Commandant of the Marine Corps, CODE HD, Headquarters, U.S. Marine
Corps, Washington, D.C. 20380. *Historical Program and List of
Historical Works of the United States Air Force can be obtained
from the Chief, Office of Air Force History, Bldg. 5681, Bolling
Air Force Base, Washington, D.C. 20332. *Naval Historical Publi-
cations in Print is available from the Naval Historical Center,
Department of the Navy, Washington, D.C. 20374.

A military history office that has become active in recent years
is the Historical Division, Office of Chief of Engineers, DAEN-
ASH, Washington, D.C. 20314. That program, the historical program
of the Army Corps of Engineers, has published documentary works
such as Frank N. Schubert, ed., *March to South Pass: Lieutenant
William B. Franklin's Journal of the Kearney Expedition of 1845
(Washington: GPO, 1979, order no. 008-022-00134-4), which is a
journal of an Army Engineer in the American West. Albert E.
Cowdrey, *A City for the Nation: The Army Engineers and the
Building of Washington, D.C. (Washington: GPO, 1979, order no.
008-022-0013-8), is an account of the role of the Corps of
Engineers in the development of the nation's capital city. Alfred
M. Beck, ed., *Engineer Memoirs: Interviews with Lieutenant

General Frederick J. Clarke (Washington: Historical Division,
Office of Chief of Engineers, 1980), is a transcript of oral
history interviews with a former Chief of Engineers who at one
point in his career was the Engineer-Commissioner member of the
Board of Commissioners that administered the affairs of the
District of Columbia. The last two works combined with Martin K.
Gordon, "Congress and the District of Columbia: The Military
Impact on Federal Control," Capitol Studies, 6 (Fall 1978), supply
a survey history of the military establishment at the seat of
government of a stable country. (Capitol Studies is published by
the U.S. Capitol Historical Society, 200 Maryland Ave., N.E.,
Washington, D.C. 20315.)

Conclusion

American military studies continues to be an active field, with
emphases both on new areas, such as women, enlisted personnel,
and the popular culture of the Civil War, and on traditional areas
for which new sources have opened, such as World War II intelligence and the role of the Joint Chiefs of Staff during and
immediately after that war. The relationship between the American
military and the civilian world in which it operates continues to
be explored, but the significant trends have not changed since my
original essay.

Sources for the Study
of American Music

H. WILEY HITCHCOCK

☐ Nothing like this article could have been written a quarter-century ago. The past twenty-five years or so have seen a quantum leap in American-music studies—in quantity, depth, breadth, and excellence. In part this reflects a general quickening of interest in the American musical past; in part an acceptance of the validity of all kinds of music—an acceptance encouraged by the availability on long-playing records of even the most esoteric and exotic musics; and in part a more liberal view of what historical musicology, especially in a fluid, diverse, and democratic society like that of the United States, can or should concern itself with. The earliest spokesman for this new view was Charles Seeger. In 1950 Seeger issued a call to arms: he asserted bluntly that "the majority of musicologists are not primarily interested in music, but in the literature of European fine-art music, its grammar and syntax"; he pointed out that fine-art music is but one of four main traditional idioms in world culture—primitive, folk, popular, and fine-art—and argued that in a dynamic culture like that of the United States, the fine-art idiom may well be the weakest or at any rate the least universal or representative of the culture.

Seeger challenged us to write about the history of *music* rather than *a* music, i.e., the history of musical culture in the large rather than the history of a single musical idiom. His challenge has been taken up, consciously or not, by many in the past decades, including not only musicologists and other musicians who have written on American music, but also scholars in other fields who for the first time have come to realize that there is no reason to imagine that American music lies mysteriously outside of American culture, or indeed outside Western culture as a whole.

This shift of orientation is evident in the succession of books that have been accepted as "standard" American histories of music—not of American music exclusively but of Western music in general. The first of these in English even to mention American music was Paul Henry Lang's *Music in Western Civilization* (New York: W. W. Norton, 1941), a 1100-page book in which American music is accorded some 17 pages. The next standard American survey of music history to be published was Donald Jay Grout's *History of Western Music* (New York: W. W. Norton, 1960), which treats American music about as summarily as does Lang. However, in the eleven-volume Prentice-Hall History of Music Series, which began to appear in 1964, one entire volume deals with American music [it happens to be my own *Music in the United States: A Historical Introduction* (2nd rev. ed., Englewood Cliffs, New Jersey: Prentice-Hall, 1974)] , and in two others—Bruno Nettl's *Folk and Traditional Music of the Western Continents* (2nd rev. ed., 1973) and Eric Salzman's *Twentieth-Century Music: An Introduction* (2nd rev. ed., 1974)—American music is amply discussed. Finally, the very title of Edith Borroff's *Music in Europe and the United States* (Englewood Cliffs, New Jersey: Prentice-Hall, 1971) suggests the new legitimacy and status of American music in the context of the musical historiography of Western civilization as a whole.

In histories of American music per se, a similar shift of viewpoint has been apparent. The first attempt at a history of American music was by an Alsatian immigrant, Frederic Louis Ritter, who came to America at the age of twenty-seven, wrote a *History of Music* in the 1870s out of his lectures at Vassar College (it does not mention American music), and then in 1883 published *Music in America*. Ritter's book concerned itself exclusively with what I call the "cultivated tradition" of American music—essentially our fine-art music—and

H. Wiley Hitchcock is Professor of Music and Director of the Institute for Studies in American Music at Brooklyn College of the City University of New York. He has also taught at the University of Michigan, New York University, and Hunter College. He has been the recipient of Guggenheim and Fulbright Senior Research Fellowships to Italy and France, has been President of the Music Library Association, and has served on the editorial boards of the Journal of the American Musicological Society and American Quarterly. Professor Hitchcock is President of the Charles Ives Society and area editor of the forthcoming 6th edition of Grove's Dictionary of Music and Musicians, as well as Editor of the Prentice-Hall History of Music Series and of the Earlier American Music reprint series.

measured it critically by the standards of European fine-art music. Ritter went so far as to claim that "the people's song . . . is not to be found among the American people," thus relieving himself of any responsibility for discussing the "vernacular tradition" of American music (essentially the many kinds of folk and popular music). Louis Elson's *History of American Music* (1904) shared Ritter's orientation.

Oscar G. T. Sonneck, who organized the Music Division of the Library of Congress and published a number of superb specialized monographs on American music (which I shall cite in due course), complained in a lecture of 1916 titled "The History of Music in America" that American music historians had been too narrowly restrictive in their viewpoint. "Our books," said Sonneck, "deal more with the history of music and musicians *in America* than with the history of *American* musical life." He did not, however, develop this idea into a full-scale history, nor was his complaint acted upon by the next historian of American music, John Tasker Howard.

Howard's *Our American Music* (New York: Crowell, 1931) was far more extensive than any earlier survey, and within the next fifteen years, sensitive to the newly awakened interest of Americans in their past that was characteristic of the 1930s and '40s, he revised it twice (1939, 1946). Nevertheless, he did not change his basic viewpoint, which was governed by European fine-art music ideals and which saw American music as having engaged in a long, arduous struggle to rise to European levels of musical excellence.

The next history of American music, and the first to adopt the multilateral, multilevel approach urged by Charles Seeger, was *America's Music* (New York: McGraw Hill, 1955), by Gilbert Chase. Chase proudly pointed out that "in this book, some fifteen chapters [of thirty-one] deal, in whole or in part, with various phases of American folk, primitive, and popular music." He clearly attempted to redress the balance between concern for the tradition of fine-art music based on European models—virtually the only tradition dealt with by earlier writers of American-music history—and the other three traditions, and he went so far as to say that in his opinion "important" American music *was* important only to the degree that it was "different from European music." Insisting on this point, which, against the background of earlier American-music histories, was revolutionary, Chase acted like any good revolutionary: he denied any virtues in the old régime. He devalued American fine-art music (at least of the nineteenth and early twentieth centuries) to the point of bankruptcy, suggesting that a single popular song by Stephen Foster was worth any number of concertos by Edward MacDowell. In short, he shifted the criteria of significance for American music by about 180 degrees.

My own *Music in the United States* attempts to steer a middle course. On the one hand, it does not denigrate or devalue those American composers of the nineteenth century (especially) who, seeking to found a tradition of fine-art music, could only begin by borrowing from Europe—attitudes and ideals, notions of style and structure. Almost by definition, their music is poorer in artistic content than its European models; however, it was an important segment of our musical culture, and as a historian I accepted it as such. On the other hand, and certainly influenced by Seeger and Chase, I attempted to view American music "in the round, believing that pop songs as well as art songs, player-pianos as well as piano players, rock as well as revival hymns, are important parts of the American musical experience."

This kind of acceptance, without a priori judgments of significance based primarily on aesthetic assessment, of all the kinds of music America has made, used, sung, and played, seems now to prevail. As a result, specialized studies in American music are flourishing as never before. Although there exists no general comprehensive index to such studies, whether of book or article length, two bibliographical guides, both of them published by the Institute for Studies in American Music at Brooklyn College of the City University of New York, should be mentioned at the outset. One is Richard Jackson's *United States Music: Sources of Bibliography and Collective Biography* (1973), an intelligently, shrewdly, and often wittily annotated list of some 100 basic sources. The other is Rita H. Mead's *Dissertations in American Music: A Classified Bibliography* (1974), which lists no fewer than 1226 doctoral essays that either deal exclusively with American music or touch on it in some way, including not only dissertations written in departments of music but in others such as sociology, anthropology, theater history, education (excluding, however, dissertations without historical interest, i.e., "tests and measurements" studies), American studies, and the like; references are given for abstracts in *Dissertation Abstracts.* Further bibliographical leads to specialized studies in American music are to be found in Howard's *Our American Music* (4th rev. ed., 1954), Chase's *America's Music* (2nd rev. ed., 1966; 3rd ed. in preparation), and my *Music in the United States.*

The pioneer scholar in specialized studies in early American music, to this day hardly matched in meticulous thoroughness and exhaustive detail, was Oscar Sonneck. His most extensive works were *Early Concert-Life in America: 1731– 1800* (Leipzing: Breitkopf & Hartel, 1907; reprinted New York: Adler, 1949), *Early Opera in America* (1915; reprinted New York: B. Blom, 1963), and a monumental *Bibliography of Early Secular American Music: 18th Century* (1905; rev. ed. by W. T. Upton, 1945; rev. ed. reprinted New York: Da Capo Press, 1964). Sonneck was also the first important biographer of American composers through his double monograph, *Francis Hopkinson, the First American Poet-Composer;* and *James Lyon, Patriot, Preacher, Psalmodist* (1905; reprinted New York: Da Capo Press, 1974). Sonneck's bibliography has been extended to 1825 by Richard Wolfe in his masterly three-volume *Secular Music in America 1801–1825* (New York Public Library, 1964). Two scholars who have emulated Sonneck both in their concentration on early American music and their happy combination of solid scholarship and graceful writing are Irving Lowens, whose articles have been gathered into a book, *Music and Musicians in Early America* (New York: W. W. Norton, 1964), and Richard Crawford, who has produced very rich critical biographies of two eighteenth-century New England composers and compilers of music for the "singing schools," *Andrew Law, American Psalmodist* (Evanston, Illinois: Northwestern University Press, 1963) and *William Billings of Boston: Eighteenth-Century Composer* (Princeton, New Jersey: Princeton University Press, 1975; co-authored with David McKay). Yet another scholar who may be likened to Sonneck as an indefatigable documentary historian is Robert Stevenson, whose *Protestant Church Music in America* (New York: W. W. Norton, 1970) is immensely rich in bibliographical detail.

In many ways the early to mid-nineteenth century is the *terra incognita* of American music. The main reason for this is that American musical culture expanded and became infinitely more diversified, as did the nation itself; there are whole areas still unstudied in any systematic or historically meaningful way, and much of the art music, along with the airy trifles that may best be called "household music," lies dusty and unperformed today, hence effectively unknown, unstudied, and unrelated (by writers) to American culture. Some of the most illuminating writing on music and musical life comes from the period itself. Examples include the kaleidoscopic journal of the virtuoso pianist Louis Moreau Gottschalk, edited by Jeanne Behrend as *Notes of a Pianist* (New York: A. Knopf,

Courtesy, Prints and Photographs Division, Library of Congress

Photograph by Frances B. Johnston, Detroit, 1903.

1964); *Chronicles of Stephen Foster's Family,* edited by E. F. Morneweck (Pittsburgh, Pennsylvania: University of Pittsburgh Press, 1944); and Lowell Mason's *Musical Letters from Abroad* (1854; reprinted New York: Da Capo Press, 1967), of which an *American Quarterly* reviewer wrote, "No serious student of nineteenth-century American priggery can afford to ignore them."

A major contribution to the socio-cultural history of the American lyric theater is Robert C. Toll's *Blacking Up: The Minstrel Show in Nineteenth-Century America* (New York: Oxford University Press, 1974). A complementary study, concentrating on the music itself, is Hans Nathan's *Dan Emmett and the Rise of Early Negro Minstrelsy* (Norman, Oklahoma: University of Oklahoma Press, 1962). Along with Emmett, Stephen Foster was the major mid-nineteenth-century composer for the minstrel shows (and for hearth and home); his life is chronicled in J. T. Howard's *Stephen Foster, America's Troubadour* (1934; rev. ed. 1953; reprinted New York: Peter Smith, 1962), and his music's extraordinary hold on the American consciousness is explored in a book now in press, William Austin's *Susanna, Jeanie, and the Old Folks at Home* (New York: Macmillan).

Broad-gauge surveys of American music between the Civil War and World War I are lacking. One book that reveals some major changes in taste during the period—and, in fact, before and after it—although from only a single vantage point (that of the New York Philharmonic orchestra), is Howard Shanet's history, *Philharmonic* (New York: Doubleday, 1974). This country's first virtuoso conductor, a major tastemaker in our concert life, drew a self-portrait in *Theodore Thomas: A Musical Autobiography* (1905; reprinted, New York: Da Capo Press, 1964). Thomas' counterpart in popular music was the bandmaster Sousa; he published an autobiographical account, *Marching Along* (1928; reprinted, New York: Vienna House, 1974), and his long career is detailed in Paul E. Bierley's *John Philip Sousa, American Phenomenon* (New York: Appleton, 1973). The most extraordinary and significant composer of the period was Charles Ives. Besides his own *Memos* (New York: W. W. Norton, 1972)—written, as their editor John Kirkpatrick puts it, "to answer questions from people curious about his music"—and *Essays Before a Sonata and Other Writings,* edited by Howard Boatwright (New York: W. W. Norton, 1962), two other books on Ives are especially noteworthy: one contains the posthumous recollections of family, friends, acquaintances, and fellow-musicians as gathered in *Charles Ives Remembered: An Oral History,* by Vivian Perlis (New Haven, Connecticut: Yale University Press, 1974); and the other, on Ives and American culture, by the historian (not musicologist) Frank R. Rossiter, is in press (New York: Liveright).

Sources for the study of American folk music—or rather "musics," for there are many different folk traditions—are numerous but very uneven. The most comprehensive bibliographical guide is Charles Haywood's two-volume *Bibliography of North American Folklore and Folksong* (2nd rev. ed., New York: Dover, 1961).

The "shape-note" tradition of Southern folk hymnody is treated extensively in a series of books by George Pullen Jackson, beginning with the seminal *White Spirituals in the Southern Uplands* (1933; reprinted, New York: Dover, 1965).

Indian music was the lifelong preoccupation of Frances Densmore, most of whose many books have been reprinted by Da Capo Press. Bruno Nettl surveys the variety of tribal musics in *North American Indian Styles* (Austin, Texas: University of Texas Press, 1954).

Eileen Southern's *The Music of Black Americans* (New York: W. W. Norton, 1971) is so far the most scholarly and comprehensive survey—perhaps stronger, however, on black art music than folk music. Antebellum slave music has proved, understandably, quite resistant to studies in depth. Nevertheless, Dena S. Epstein has published two documentary articles of great value: "African Music in British and French America," *Musical Quarterly,* LIX (1973), 61–91; and "Slave Music in the United States before 1860," *Notes,* XX (1963), 195–212, 377–90, both of which are the basis of a book in progress. Less documentary but still thoughtful is Harold Courlander's *Negro Folk Music U.S.A.* (New York: Columbia University Press, 1963).

The literature on the various black musics that met and mingled to form early jazz is enormous but, again, very uneven. Let me cite here only those that are particularly well documented and that lead out to other sources. On country blues: Samuel B. Charter's *The Country Blues* (New York: Rinehart, 1959). On ragtime: Rudi Blesh and Harriet Janis's *They All Played Ragtime* (4th rev. ed., New York: Oak Publications, 1971). On urban blues: Charles Keil's *Urban Blues* (Chicago, Illinois: University of Chicago Press, 1966). On black gospel music: Tony Heilbut's *The Gospel Sound* (New York: Simon and Schuster, 1971).

Finally, on jazz itself: still valuable as the most objective and well-documented history of the genre is *The Story of Jazz* (New York: Oxford University Press, 1956; Mentor paperback), by Marshall Stearns, although as a style-critical study (at least of jazz to about 1930) Gunther Schuller's *Early Jazz: Its Roots and Early Development* (New York: Oxford University Press, 1968) is superior. (Schuller is at work on a companion volume concerning later jazz.)

Apart from the most recent general histories of American music mentioned near the beginning of this article, studies of twentieth-century American music that attempt to relate it to more general cultural and societal developments are few in number. Eric Salzman, in *Twentieth-Century Music* (cited earlier), does a particularly good job of discussing American music in the context of Western music in general. He has also published a perceptive analysis of the American musical mood of 1924–46 as revealed in the journal *Modern Music*, in his article "Modern Music in Retrospect," *Perspectives of New Music*, II/2 (Spring–Summer 1964), 14–20. Leonard B. Meyer cunningly relates avant-garde American music after World War II to developments in other arts in *Music, the Arts, and Ideas* (Chicago, Illinois: University of Chicago Press, 1967). Two journals that explicitly attempt to explore such interrelationships are *The Arts in Society* and *Popular Music and Society*. For the most part, however, a sense of what twentieth-century American music is all about (in a non-technical way) is best got from certain composers' writings about themselves and others. Virgil Thomson's *The State of Music* (1939; 2nd ed., New York: Vintage Books, 1962) is concerned with both the aesthetic and economic ways and means of the American composer. Aaron Copland's *Music and Imagination* (Cambridge, Massachusetts: Harvard University Press, 1952) and Roger Sessions' *Questions About Music* (Cambridge, Massachusetts: Harvard University Press, 1970), both based on Charles Eliot Norton lecture series at Harvard, are illuminating distillations of the musical credos of the two composers. John Cage's essays and lectures, exquisitely and precisely written, are unparalleled sources on the experimental music of chance and indeterminacy; they are gathered in two books, *Silence* (Middletown, Connecticut: Wesleyan University Press, 1961) and *A Year From Monday* (Middletown, Connecticut: Wesleyan University Press, 1968).

Finally, in the hope of suggesting to readers a bibliographical tool that will help in locating future studies in American music, *RILM Abstracts* should be mentioned. This is the quarterly journal of the International Repertory of Musical Literature; it includes abstracts, indexed by computer, of all significant literature on music that has appeared since 1 January 1967—including, of course, literature on American music. □

* indicates paperback availability.

EPILOGUE

by H. Wiley Hitchcock

My original essay went to press just before the U.S. Bicentennial
year of 1976. Predictably, that year saw a flurry of activity in
American-music publications, including books and articles, musical
editions of significance, historically oriented phonorecording
series of various dimensions, long-range research projects, and
even video productions. Some foretold a "boom and bust" cycle,
predicting gloomily that the Bicentennial skyrocket would soon
fizzle. But such has not been the case. My claim in 1975 that
"studies in American music are flourishing as never before" can be
reiterated--and underlined--now, in 1980. Thus, although the
Bicentennial atmosphere was especially salubrious for American-
music scholarship, there seems to have been no slackening of
energy or achievement in these past four years. (As I drafted
this paragraph, I was interrupted with an invitation to join the
editorial board of a new journal, American Music, to appear under
the auspices of the Sonneck Society. The Society was organized in
1975 for "research dealing with all aspects of American music and
music in America" and was named for the Oscar Sonneck whom I
described in my earlier ASI article as "the pioneer scholar in
specialized studies in early American music.")

Perhaps the most helpful way of organizing this epilogue to my
1975 essay would be to bring up to date each of the principal
sections of the former, which dealt successively with general
histories of American music; specialized studies in the various
chronological eras of American-music history; folk music, popular
music, and jazz; and bibliographical tools.

No new significant general histories of American music have appeared since 1975. We still await the third edition of Gilbert Chase's seminal America's Music (announced initially as a "Bicentennial edition" to be published by the University of Illinois Press). And we look forward to a history-in-progress by Charles Hamm (for W. W. Norton and Co.) that will be keyed to the 100-disc "Recorded Anthology of American Music" funded by The Rockefeller Foundation, produced in 1976-78 by New World Records, and distributed free to more than 7,000 college and university music departments and other facilities throughout the world (and sold virtually at cost to other educational institutions and individuals.)

Significant sources for the study of early American music have appeared. One sign of the increasing attention to this nation's music by the musicological establishment is the commitment of the American Musicological Society, as co-publisher with the Colonial Society of Massachusetts, to The Complete Works of William Billings (distributed by the University Press of Virginia). Volume II of the hymns and anthems of this doughty Colonial Bostonian composer was issued in 1977; Volume I is soon to be published, to be followed by two more. As the first "collected works" of any American composer, this project is a milestone. Billings has also been well served bibliographically by Hans Nathan in William Billings: Data and Documents (Detroit: Information Coordinators, Inc., 1976; for the College Music Society). Three other important contributions to our knowledge of Revolutionary War and Federal-era music are Gillian Anderson's monumental collection of lyrics and tunes, Freedom's Voice in Poetry and Song (2 vols.; Wilmington: Scholarly Resources, Inc., 1977); Irving Lowens's Bibliography of Songsters Printed in America Before 1821 (Charlottesville: University of Virginia Press, 1977; for the American Antiquarian Society) ("songster" is defined by the author as "a collection of three or more secular poems intended to be sung"--a once-popular genre of publication); and Raoul Camus's definitive survey of The Military Music of the American Revolution (Chapel Hill: University of North Carolina Press, 1976).

Reaching back still further than these works is the valuable little study by Richard G. Appel, *The Music of the Bay Psalm Book: 9th Edition (1698) (Brooklyn: Institute for Studies in American Music, 1975), which includes facsimiles and transcriptions of the first music to be printed in English-speaking North America. And reaching forward to the Civil War is the bibliodiscography, *American Music Before 1865 in Print and on Records (same publisher, 1976), with a preface by myself; the book was voted by Library Journal as one of the outstanding reference books of the year.

The nineteenth century remains (as in 1975) the least thoroughly and masterfully explored in American music. Two books have helped to fill the gap. One I mentioned as forthcoming in my earlier article: Wiliam Austin's Susanna, Jeanie, and The Old Folks at Home (New York: Macmillan, 1975)--obviously on Stephen Foster, and a fascinating multi-dimensional study exploring the hold that Foster's songs have had on the American consciousness from his time to ours. The other is Daniel W. Patterson's sovereign study, and anthology of music, The Shaker Spiritual (Princeton University Press, 1979), dealing with the music and movement-- "dance," one is tempted to say--of that quirky and fervent sect of "shaking Quakers."

Charles Ives (1874-1954) has continued as a deservedly focal point of attention on the part of American scholars, rooted as he was in nineteenth-century culture but prefiguring so many of the radical musical developments of the twentieth. When I wrote in 1975, Vivian Perlis's *Charles Ives Remembered (New Haven: Yale University Press, 1974), had not yet won the coveted Kinkeldey Prize of the American Musicological Society as the best musicological book of its year (nor the asterisk here, indicating its availability as a paperback); and Frank Rossiter's psycho-cultural study of Ives was still in press, to be published as Charles Ives and His America (New York: Liveright/W. W. Norton). Nor had my own *Ives (London: Oxford University Press, 1977), yet appeared; it is a study not of the man but of his music. Since 1974, the Charles Ives Society, under grants from the American Academy and Institute of Arts and Letters, has continued quietly but effectively with a long-range program of editing (and re-editing) Ives's music along scholarly-critical lines. (Copyright problems preclude a conventional matched set of "collected works," but Society-supported and -approved editions published commercially carry a telltale imprimatur from the Society.) A major international congress on Ives convened in October 1974, his centennial year--the Charles Ives Centennial Festival-Conference, the first such convention ever to center on an American composer. As a result of this congress a variegated book of "papers and panels" appeared, An Ives Celebration, edited by Vivian Perlis and myself (Urbana: University of Illinois Press, 1977).

With Ives, we turn the corner into the twentieth century. All too few significant studies have appeared in the last few years. Composers' writings, about themselves and others, continue to be the most insightful and revealing. Among them I would cite especially The Writings of Elliott Carter (Bloomington: Indiana University Press, 1977), and John Cage's Empty Words: Writings '73-'78 (Middletown: Wesleyan University Press, 1979). Ranging more broadly, and a book that might have been titled "Contemporary Music in American Culture Over Two Decades," is the brilliant collection of critical writings, *Richard Franko Goldman: Selected Essays and Reviews, 1948-1968 (Brooklyn: Institute for Studies in American Music, 1980). Goldman's telescopic range of perspective is counterbalanced by the microscopic investigation of *The New Worlds of Edgar Varese (same publisher, 1979), with essays by experts Elliott Carter, Robert P. Morgan, and Chou Wen-chung.

I cited in 1975 articles by Dena Epstein on the music of slavery; she revised these and added much new material based on twenty-five years of research in a spectacularly pathbreaking documentary history, Sinful Tunes and Spirituals: Black Folk Music to the Civil War (Urbana: University of Illinois Press, 1977). Equally solid, scholarly, well written, and illuminating is Charles Hamm's Yesterdays: Popular Song in America (New York: W. W. Norton, 1979), a panoramic survey from Anglo-American stage songs of the Colonial period to the rock-and-roll of yesterday. More unconventional in scholarly style--even offbeat in its profusion of authors and graphics--but still a gold mine of accurate information in a field strewn with glittering but distorted nuggets of misinformation is *The Rolling Stone Illustrated History of Rock and Roll, edited by Jim Miller (New York: Rolling Stone Press/ Random House, 1976). Frank Tirro's Jazz: A History (New York: W. W. Norton, 1977), attempts to be comprehensive but has been variously received by critics; it is keyed to the excellent recorded anthology selected and annotated by Martin Williams, The Smithsonian Collection of Classic Jazz (Washington: Smithsonian Institution, 1973). Since I have just cited phonorecords--and what better "sources for the study of American music"?--let me mention also another anthology, Folk Music in America (Washington: Library of Congress, 1976), a fifteen-record series. (And New World Records' "Recorded Anthology of American Music," noted earlier, includes a generous representation not only of art music but of folk music, pop music, dance music, and jazz.)

In conclusion, I should like to point out some open-ended, ongoing series of American-music publications that continue to add to the significant sources for study, and some important new and forth-coming bibliographical tools.

Da Capo Press of New York initiated almost a decade ago, under my direction, a series of reprints of musical scores long out of print, "Earlier American Music," which now stands at some twenty volumes. ("Da capo" is the musicians' term for "repeat, from the beginning.) Typical of the variety of music included are the volumes scheduled for publication in 1980: a set of twenty-two Minstrel-Show Songs by Stephen Foster; two cycles of Songs to Poems by Arlo Bates by George W. Chadwick; The Stoughton Musical Society's Centennial Collection of Sacred Music (1878); and Jeremiah Ingalls's Christian Harmony (1805). Similar to this series, but with the music newly edited and including extensive scholarly-critical introductions, are the volumes of "Recent Researches in American Music," also under my editorial direction, published by A-R Editions, Inc., of Madison, Wisconsin. "RRAM" has included Anthology of Early American Keyboard Music, 1787-1830 (Vols. I-II); the Colonial ballad opera (1767) The Disappointment (Vols. III-IV); The Philadelphia Sonatas (Vol. V) for harpsichord or pianoforte by Philadelphia's leading Federal-era musician, Alexander Reinagle; and another ballad opera, of 1783, The Poor Soldier (Vol. VI), by John O'Keeffe and William Shield.

Mentioned earlier was Hans Nathan's William Billings: Data and Documents. This is Number 2 in the College Music Society's series, "Bibliographies in American Music" (Detroit: Information Coordinators, Inc.). Other volumes in print are Charles Schwartz's George Gershwin: A Selective Bibliography and Discography (No. 1); Donna K. Anderson's Charles T. Griffes: An Annotated Biblio-Discography (No. 3); and H. Earle Johnson's First Performances in America to 1900 (No. 4). Complementing these bibliographies is another massive one, with over 5,000 entries: Women in American Music: A Bibliography of Music and Literature (Westport: Greenwood Press, 1979), compiled by Adrienne Fried Block and Carol Neuls-Bates. Less narrowly specialized but extremely well annotated and, overall, one of the most useful recent sources for American-music study, is David Horn's The Literature of American Music . . . a fully annotated bibliography (Metuchen: The Scarecrow Press, 1977).

Not by chance do I close this essay by citing Mr. Horn's book. He is British, a librarian at Exeter University. It is suggestive to realize that American-music studies are not only in healthy estate in this country, in the hands of American scholars; studies by foreign scholars are of increasing incidence and importance. American music has assumed international significance.

Recent Interpretations
of the American Character

THOMAS L. HARTSHORNE

☐ It is a commonplace that Americans are more concerned with their national identity and spend more time trying to explain themselves to themselves than people of other nations. Not surprisingly, this persistent concern tends to intensify in periods of crisis. It was to be expected, then, that the tumult of the 1960s would result in a massive outpouring of books attempting to describe what was happening in and to the United States and why. In this profusion of print, however, the number of books explicitly devoted to the study of the American character was small compared to the number of such studies made during the 1950s. Why? For one thing, the upheavals of the decade revealed a degree of diversity and social cleavage which made the concept of national character appear less plausible and less valuable as a descriptive and analytical tool. Further, the crises that the United States faced were largely internal, and Americans historically have demonstrated an increased interest in the national character only during external crises, when the nation was thought to be in some sort of confrontation or competition with another nation; purely internal crises have not stimulated the same degree of interest. The Cold War, for example, made Americans think about their national character more than usual; the Depression did not. Finally, there has occurred a significant decline of confidence in the validity of the conceptual apparatus of the national character study. As Michael McGiffert has noted, the subject is currently in a theoretical shambles; there is little certainty as to how it might be profitably approached, and there are increasingly nagging questions as to whether "national character" is a meaningful subject for serious investigation and even whether it exists at all.

Consequently, in compiling the following selection, I have not confined myself to books which use the phrase "American character" to describe their subject. Instead, I have employed a working definition which is widely inclusive and theoretically imprecise, but which has the advantage of being consistent with definitions adopted by previous writers on the subject (who also tended to be vague about just what it was that they were doing). In the following list, therefore, one will find books consisting of large-scale generalizations about the United States purporting to describe social structure, the value system, ways of life, systems of belief, fundamental world views, typical personalities, behavioral patterns, and so on, singly or in combination. The list excludes problems of theory as well as all those writings which attempt to describe the American character as it is supposed to have existed at some point in the past. Readers interested in these subjects should consult the admirable compilations of writings assembled by Michael McGiffert and published in *American Quarterly* in 1963 (Volume XV, Summer Supplement, Number 2, Part 2) and 1969 (Volume XXI, Summer Supplement, Number 2, Part 2). The following selection may be considered as a supplement to and an update of McGiffert's list. "Recent" is to be understood as meaning "since 1960."

The striking thing about most of these recent books is the extent to which they restate, with minor variations, ideas elaborated by previous writers. The influence of the Frontier Thesis on George W. Pierson's *The Moving American* (New York: Knopf, 1973) is obvious. Pierson repeats Turner's description of the American character, although he maintains that geographic mobility rather than the frontier was the formative influence. Richard Engler's *The Challenge of Diversity* (New York: Harper and Row, 1964) is another variant on the frontier theme stressing the significance of the experience of constantly meeting new situations and

Thomas L. Hartshorne is Associate Professor of History at Cleveland State University in Cleveland, Ohio, where he teaches courses in American social and intellectual history as well as courses in recent U. S. history. Professor Hartshorne is the author of The Distorted Image: Changing Conceptions of the American Character Since Turner, *which was published in 1968. He is currently conducting research on the cultural history of the United States since 1945.*

challenges in the shaping of the American character. *The Adjusted American: Normal Neuroses in the Individual and Society* by Snell Putney and Gail Putney (New York: Harper and Row, 1964) recalls the work of people like Karen Horney and Erich Fromm in discussing the neurotic anxieties Americans suffer as a consequence of status insecurities produced by living in a competitive, mobile society. Helene Zahler offers a comparable description of the American character in *The American Paradox* (New York: Dutton, 1964), but does not couch her analysis in psychiatric terms. Murray Levin also focuses on status insecurity to explain recurrent outbreaks of political hysteria to which Americans are prone in his work, *Political Hysteria in America: The Democratic Capacity for Repression* (New York: Basic Books, 1971), which recalls the analysis offered by Richard Hofstadter and the other contributors to *The New American Right.*

Most of the time the parallels between contemporary and past works are not as apparent, but there is unmistakably a persistent concern with certain problems and themes. For example, the essays in John A. Hague, ed., *American Character and Culture: Some Twentieth Century Perspectives* (DeLand, Florida: Everett Edwards Press, 1964) and Roger L. Shinn, ed., *The Search for Identity: Essays on the American Character* (New York: Harper and Row, 1964) say little that is distinctively new (except for David Potter's essay, "American Women and the American Character," in the former volume). Instead, one finds several essays oriented around the much-discussed conformity-diversity polarity in the American character. Others emphasize optimism as a significant American trait and assert that it would be well for Americans to lose some of their innocence and become more aware of tragedy and evil. This theme was especially popular in the American character literature of the late 1940s and early 1950s. Reinhold Niebuhr and Alan Heimert express a similar point of view in *A Nation So Conceived: Reflections on the History of America From Its Early Vision to Its Present Power* (New York: Scribners, 1963). Rory McCormick also argues that one of the most substantial obstacles Americans face in their efforts to improve the quality of life in the United States is their innocence, especially their refusal to face unpleasant facts about themselves, in *Americans Against Man* (New York: Corpus Books, 1970). A highly original and interesting exploration of the role of diversity in American history is Robert Wiebe's *The Segmented Society: An Introduction to the Meaning of America* (New York: Oxford University Press, 1975). Recent books emphasizing such previously and widely described traits as a passion for individual freedom, a drive to achieve, and a belief in equality are John Morton Blum, *The Promise of America: An Historical Inquiry* (Boston: Houghton, Mifflin, 1966); Seymour Martin Lipset, *The First New Nation: The United States in Historical and Comparative Perspective* (New York: Basic Books, 1963); Don Martindale, *American Social Structure* (New York: Appleton, Century, Crofts, 1960); and Hans J. Morgenthau, *The Purpose of American Politics* (New York: Knopf, 1960).

Also consistent with the past history of writings on the American character is the existence of a large number of books by foreign authors. A representative selection includes Alan Ashbolt, *An American Experience* (New York: P. S. Eriksson, 1967); D. W. Brogan, *America in the Modern World* (New Brunswick, New Jersey: Rutgers University Press, 1960); Alexander Campbell, *The Trouble With Americans* (New York: Praeger, 1971); J. P. Clark, *America, Their Amer-*

ica (New York: Africana Publishing, 1969); Susan Cooper, *Behind the Golden Curtain: A View of the U. S. A.* (New York: Scribners, 1966); Hans Habe, *The Wounded Land: Journey Through a Divided America* (New York: Coward-Mc-Cann, 1964); Robert Hargreaves, *Superpower: A Portrait of America in the 1970s* (New York: St. Martins Press, 1973); Ronald Segal, *The Americans: A Conflict of Creed and Reality* (New York: Viking Press, 1969); and Herbert von Borch, *The Unfinished Society* (New York: Hawthorn Books, 1962). These writers express widely divergent points of view, but again it is easy to detect the presence of standard themes: prejudice and violence (Clark, Habe, Segal), provincialism (Cooper), the divergence between the American ideal and the American reality (Ashbolt, Campbell), and the necessity for Americans to come to terms with the problems of history, to which they have hitherto felt themselves to be immune (Brogan, Hargreaves, von Borch). The above writers are all, to a varying degree, critical of the United States. Two foreign commentators who are not are Raymond L. Bruckberger in *Image of America* (New York: Viking Press, 1959) and Jean-Francois Revel in *Without Marx or Jesus: The New American Revolution Has Begun* (New York: Doubleday, 1971). Both see in the United States the best hope for a revolutionary revival which will significantly expand the scope of individual freedom throughout the world.

Of course not all the works on the American character simply repeated what previous authors had said. The events of the 1960s did have an impact. In general, for instance, those books published early in the decade were, for obvious reasons, more optimistic and less critical than those published during the dark and bitter later years. The most obvious manifestation of the change in mood was the growing preoccupation with violence. Many past writers had noted a predisposition to violence in the American character, but had done so only perfunctorily and had treated this trait as insignificant and incidental. William Carlos Williams' *In the American Grain* (New York: A. and C. Boni, 1925) and D. H. Lawrence's *Studies in Classic American Literature* (London: M. Secker, 1924) are unusual in dwelling on the dark undercurrent of violence in the American psyche. In the late 1960s, however, many writers insisted that violence was an unmistakable and significant feature of American history and the American character, and offered arguments to support Rap Brown's remark that "Violence is as American as cherry pie." The most comprehensive work here is Hugh Davis Graham and Ted Robert Gurr, eds., *The History of Violence in America, Historical and Comparative Perspectives: A Report Submitted to the National Commission on the Causes and Prevention of Violence* (New York: Praeger, 1969). Other discussions of the subject are David Abrahamsen, *Our Violent Society* (New York: Funk and Wagnalls, 1970); Ovid Demaris, *America the Violent* (Cowles Book Co., 1970); Hugh Davis Graham et al., eds., *Violence: The Crisis of American Confidence* (Baltimore, Maryland: The Johns Hopkins University Press, 1971); Richard Hofstadter and Michael Wallace, eds., *American Violence: A Documentary History* (New York: Knopf, 1970); Alphonso Pinkney, *The American Way of Violence* (New York: Random House, 1972); Thomas Rose, ed., *Violence in America: A Historical and Contemporary Reader* (New York: Random House, 1969); and Arthur Schlesinger, Jr., *Violence: America in the Sixties* (New York: New American Library, 1968). It is indicative that Henry Steele Commager in *Meet the U. S. A. (New York: Institute for International Education, 1970), a general survey of American life and institutions written for foreign students, devotes one whole chapter out of a set devoted to such topics as the political system, the economy, and religion in America, to "Law and Lawlessness." The general verdict returned by these writers is that the United States has had a violent history, that Americans were and are a violent people—perhaps not the most violent in the world, but certainly more violent than the inhabitants of the other Western democracies—and that Americans have an enormous capacity to overlook their own violent behavior and to delude themselves into believing that they are a peaceful people. Among the conditions offered to explain this violent disposition are the frontier experience, racial and ethnic animosities, a revolutionary tradition which sanctions violence and helps to create a pervasive distrust of authority, and rapid industrialization and urbanization, which uproots people and tends to weaken the social fabric by weakening interpersonal ties.

The most popular theme in the recent literature on the American character, though, has been the idea that Americans are becoming increasingly imprisoned in a socio-economic system dominated by large bureaucracies, mass production technology, a narrowly utilitarian rationality, and a cheap and meretricious mass culture, all tending collectively to diminish or destroy the possibilities for the full development of individual potentials and for real human contact. Such analyses are often highly reminiscent of the criticisms of conformity made during the 1950s, except the disease was now usually called "alienation." There were many variations among writers who adopted this position.The range of the political spectrum was wide, from the radical perspective of Herbert Marcuse in *One-Dimensional Man: Studies in the Ideology of Advanced Industrial Society (Boston: Beacon Press, 1964) to the conservative stance of George Roche in The Bewildered Society (New Rochelle, New York: Arlington House, 1972) with intermediate points in the works of left-tending liberals like Richard Goodwin, *The American Condition (Garden City, New York: Doubleday, 1974) and Sidney J. Slomich, The American Nightmare (New York: Macmillan, 1971). The primary area of focus varied from Fred J. Cook's examination of the decay of personal ethical standards among the affluent and powerful in America in The Corrupted Land: The Social Morality of Modern America (New York: Macmillan, 1966) to Walter Kerr's rueful look at Americans' lost capacity for joy in The Decline of Pleasure (New York: Simon and Schuster, 1962), while Vance Packard in *A Nation of Strangers (New York: McKay, 1972) and Alvin Toffler in *Future Shock (New York: Random House, 1970) both deplored the potentially dangerous emotional effects of rapid rates of mobility and change. Toffler argues that it is possible to minimize such effects through imaginative planning for the future and implies that Americans might retain control over their destinies and see to it that "change" continues to mean "progress." On the other hand, Judith Mara Gutman in Is America Used Up? (New York: Grossman-Publishers, 1973) and Andrew Hacker in *The End of the American Era (New York: Atheneum, 1971) both see a draining away of the self-confidence, idealistic commitment, and sense of adventure in the American people and conclude that America is indeed used up and that the American era has indeed ended. Jules Henry, while indignant about the undesirable effects of America's "pecuniary culture" in *Cul-

ture Against Man (New York: Random House, 1963), is more hopeful, implying that improvement may be possible through a return to the values and methods of the past, especially in education. Finally, in *Beyond Conformity* (New York: Free Press of Glencoe, 1961), Winston White maintains that the characteristic anger and despair of the critics of American society is completely misdirected, for what is really happening in the United States is not standardization and the submergence of the individual into an undifferentiated mass, but rather a massive structural differentiation resulting in a vastly increased scope of free choice for individuals.

Of course, White's book was published early in the decade. Later, views like his were distinctly out of fashion among writers on the American character. For

"The Stride of a Century," a lithograph published in 1876 by Currier and Ives.

most of them the effects of mass production technology, bureaucracy, and corporate dominance were unfortunate, not to say disastrous. But some saw prospects for a reformation, especially among the young who, it was believed, had the instinctive wisdom to recognize and reject the stultifying and dehumanizing forces in modern life and to cultivate a new way of living, a new set of values, and a new way of looking at the world. At the beginning of the decade, Paul Goodman in *Growing Up Absurd: Problems of Youth in the Organized System* (New York: Random House, 1960) had pointed out that the young were having trouble adjusting to modern conditions of life because they knew instinctively that the society as it was constituted was not worth adjusting to. Later writers who celebrated the young's rejection of the values and mores of an over-organized society and found reason for hope in their revolt and in the emergence of what came to be called the counter-culture were Robert Hunter, *The Storming of the Mind (Garden City, New York: Doubleday, 1972); Kevin Kelly, Youth, Humanism, and Technology (New York: Basic Books, 1972); Henry Malcolm, Generation of Narcissus (Boston: Little, Brown, 1971); Charles Reich, *The Greening of America (New York: Random House, 1970); Theodore Roszak *The Making of a Counter-Culture: Reflections on the Technocratic Society and Its Youthful Opposition (Garden City, New York: Doubleday, 1969); Philip Slater, *The Pursuit of Loneliness: American Culture at the Breaking Point (Boston: Beacon Press, 1970); Tad Szulc, Innocents at Home: America in the 1970s (New York: Viking Press, 1974); and William Irwin Thompson, *At the Edge of History (New York: Harper and Row, 1971). Similar criticisms of American society are offered by Michael Novak in The Rise of the Unmeltable Ethnics: Politics and Culture in the 1970s (New York: Macmillan, 1972) and Peter Schrag in *The Decline of the Wasp (New York: Simon and Schuster, 1971), but they place their hopes for the salvation of American society from the baneful influence of up-tight, antiseptic, neurotic middle-class white Anglo Saxon Protestants not in the young but in the various ethnic groups of the United States.

Some writers diverged from this position. Arnold Beichman in *Nine Lies About America (New York: Library Press, 1972) maintained that the accusations being directed against American society, culture, and character were not only wrong, but radically, irrevocably, and dangerously wrong. And, just as he had during the 1950s, Daniel Boorstin offered some unique and fascinating notions about the American character. In *The Image, or What Happened to the American Dream (New York: Atheneum, 1962) he described and deplored the basic lack of contact with reality manifested in America's mass culture. In *The Americans: The Democratic Experience (New York: Random House, 1973) he presented a highly unorthodox examination of recent American history to show how contemporary America had come to be dominated by such forces as technology, commerce, mass production, and the consumption ethic. In both of these works his description and analysis of American culture and how it grew was quite consistent with the works previously mentioned. But in The Decline of Radicalism: Reflections on America Today (New York: Random House, 1969) he revealed his basic conservatism by applying to contemporary conditions some of the ideas about America which he had previously developed. Specifically, he insisted that a sense of community did exist in the United States, as it had always existed, and that if it was in danger, the danger came from the contemporary radicals who were preaching so much about it. One is inevitably reminded of his previous warnings about the dangers of attempting to formulate an explicit verbal definition of the American ideology, warnings expressed in *The Genius of American Politics (Chicago, Illinois: University of Chicago Press, 1953).

It seems to me that recent books on the American character have exhibited the same general features as their predecessors. Underlying a surface concern with contemporary conditions—violence is the most conspicuous example—one finds a focus on themes that have been standard in the literature: materialism, conformity, anxiety, and the discrepancy between creed and performance. Further, one finds that the same social and historical factors are pointed out as the formative influences: the Puritan heritage, the immigrant experience, the frontier, a high degree of social and geographic mobility, and—most conspicuous and significant of all—industrialism and mass production technology. To be sure, one does find differences of emphasis in the more recent works. It is highly unusual, for example, to find so many writers preaching the virtues of mysticism, whether spontaneous or chemically induced, as a corrective to the pseudo-rationality of modern society. Nevertheless, the underlying concern with the effects of industrialization, while perhaps more stridently expressed in recent works, is hardly new; indeed, it has existed since the Industrial Revolution came to the United States. Americans have never been wholly comfortable with the machine and its effects, and their discomfort has been quite apparent in the books on the American character written since 1960.□

* indicates paperback availability.

The Renascence of Classical American Philosophy

JOHN J. McDERMOTT

I believe that philosophy in America will be lost between chew-
ing a historic cud long since reduced to woody fiber, or an apolo-
getics for lost causes (lost to natural science), or a scholastic,
schematic formalism, unless it can somehow bring to consciousness America's own needs and its own implicit principle of successful action.[1]

Descriptive terms such as German philosophy, French philosophy and
American philosophy carry with them some intrinsic difficulties. Some commentators object to this national adjectival approach to philosophy as necessarily
narrowing or even jingoistic. From their perspective, philosophy has universal
significance and should not be identified with the cultural life of a single people,
region or historical period. On behalf of this position, it must be agreed that efforts
to confine philosophy to the interests and language of a single cultural tradition
are inevitably procrustean and even counter to the long-standing mission of philosophical inquiry, to seek the truth however and wherever that journey takes us.
Consequently, no philosophical position is to be ruled out of consideration simply

because its origins are antique or it proceeds trom a tradition and a language different from the one native to the philosopher in question.

The above strictures are to be taken as a caveat to those who believe that philosophic inquiry can be restricted by historical, linguistic or even naturalistic confines. This is a method which is at best reductionistic and at worst propagandistic. These strictures, however, do not preclude the significance of the historical and cultural contextuality which attends all philosophical activity. The history of philosophy over and again attests to the presence of an historical matrix from which the philosophers formulate their version of the world, a version as culturally idiosyncratic as it is profound. Can one conceive of Plato and Aristotle as other than Greek philosophers; of Anselm as other than a medieval monk; of Descartes as other than a protege of the new mathematics and science of the seventeenth century; of Hegel as other than a realization of German *Systemphilosophie?* The point here is not that these philosophers are reduced to their cultural contexts, or even that their respective contexts are able to account for the distinctive quality of their work. Rather, our intention is to indicate that the great philosophers proceed from their inherited linguistic, cultural and historical settings in a way that enables them to feed off those settings and yet transcend them. It is both a paradox and a truism that those thinkers who attempt to ignore their inherited setting and thereby issue "universal" truths, *ab ovo,* inevitably find their work to be of significance to very few. To the contrary, with regard to creative and seminal philosophers, their own cultural setting accounts for the origin of their work. It does not, however, account for its extensive influence. That influence is due rather to their ability to understand and transform their situation in a way which has distinctive meaning for world culture. In that vein, for example, Aristotle, Augustine, Leibniz and Marx take their place alongside Lao Tzu, Buddha and Jesus as pro-

John J. McDermott has been Chairman of the Department of Philosophy and Humanities at Texas A. and M. University since 1977, and is currently the President of the Society for the Advancement of American Philosophy. He previously taught at Queens College of the City University of New York and at St. Francis College. In addition to numerous scholarly articles he has published The Writings of William James *(1967, 1977),* The Writings of Josiah Royce *(1969),* The Philosophy of John Dewey *(1973), and* The Culture of Experience: Philosophical Essays in the American Grain *(1976).*

found articulators of their own experience as well as harbingers of the possible experiences of others in distant cultures.

The above comments are a backdrop to an examination of the thorny question of the relationship between American philosophy and philosophy in America. A full-scale analysis of this relationship would require nothing less than a focused survey of the history of American culture, a project far outdistancing the scope of the present essay. Nonetheless, some clarifying remarks are in order. The prepossessing character of America on the world scene tends to cloud from view the fact that for more than one and one-half centuries America was a colony of England. Furthermore, given geographical range, America most often followed the cultural proprieties of Spain and France as well as those of England. In short, with regard to the affairs of high culture, the arts, literature and philosophy, American achievements were thought to be second hand. Whatever may have been the actual aesthetic achievements of American vernacular culture during the Colonial period, the fact remains that American self-consciousness as to the worth of its cultural activities was dependent on evaluation from abroad.

The first public salvo against this cultural self-denigration was the prophetic utterance of Emerson in his "Preface" to his essay on "Nature":

> Our age is retrospective. It builds the sepulchres of the fathers. It writes biographies, histories, and criticism. The foregoing generations beheld God and nature face to face; we, through their eyes. Why should not we also enjoy an original relation to the universe? Why should not we have a poetry and philosophy of insight and not of tradition, and a religion by revelation to us, and not the history of theirs? Embosomed for a season in nature, whose floods of life stream around and through us, and invite us, by the powers they supply, to action proportioned to nature, why should we grope among the dry bones of the past, or put the living generation into masquerade out of its faded wardrobe? The sun shines to-day also. There is more wool and flax in the fields. There are new lands, new men, new thoughts. Let us demand our own works and laws and worship.[2]

Partially in response to the call of Emerson and others of his time, and partially in response to the explosive implications of the publication of Darwin's *The Origin of Species*, American thought in the last decades of the nineteenth century took the direction of originality. Led by Chauncey Wright (1830–1875) and the young Charles Sanders Peirce (1834–1914), the distinctive interests and persuasions of American philosophy began to develop. If previous centuries had shown America to be derivative (an arguable contention), the last four decades of the nineteenth century revealed American intellectual and philosophical thought to be both original and substantial in influence. Indeed, no less than "Charles Darwin is reported to have observed that there were enough brilliant minds at the American Cambridge in the 1860's to furnish all the universities of England."[3] In quick succession, each with a distinctive flair and contribution, American philosophy of that period was graced with the appearance of William James (1842–1910), Josiah

Royce (1855-1916), John Dewey (1859-1952), George Herbert Mead (1863-1931) and George Santayana (1863-1952). Accompanied by other, less well-known thinkers, as, for example, G. H. Howison (1834-1916), W. T. Harris (1835-1909) and Thomas Davidson (1840-1900), this period came to be known as the Golden Age of American philosophy, or, more modestly, as the Classical Age. Whatever nomenclature one wishes to append to this period, there is no doubt as to its unusual importance in the history of American culture, nor, above all, to its singular importance in the history of American philosophy.

This is not to say, of course, that significant philosophers and philosophical developments did not take place after the Classical period. A "second generation" of important philosophers was led by C. I. Lewis (1883-1964), Brand Blanshard (1892-   ) and the coming in 1924 of Alfred North Whitehead (1861-1947) to Harvard University.[4]

Appropriately, it was Harvard University that extended the invitation to Whitehead, for although John Dewey was an extremely notable exception, the entire Classical period, from Peirce to Whitehead, was dominated by Harvard University, either on behalf of its teachers or on behalf of its graduate students of philosophy, many of whom became the premier teachers of the succeeding generation.[5] This contention is not in any way to be taken as a denigration of the important philosophical work found at the University of Chicago at the turn of the century or the subsequent significance of the Columbia University development of pragmatic and historical naturalism which flourished in the second, third and fourth decades of this century—traditions largely due to the influence of John Dewey. Rather, it is simply a matter of fact that Harvard had the edge.

After the second world war, the philosophical situation in America took on a very different cast. The political upheaval in Continental Europe caused many outstanding philosophers to emigrate to the United States. During the decade of the 1930s, America received Herbert Feigl, Herbert Marcuse, Rudolph Carnap, Carl Hempel, Hans Reichenbach and Alfred Tarski, among others. Further, as is well known, the war forced Bertrand Russell to stay in America from 1938 until 1944. As a result of these events, the positivism of the Vienna Circle, sophisticated Hegelian-Marxism of the Frankfurt School and the Russellian approach to philosophy all had a foothold on the American scene. After the second world war, these influences were joined by the flood of writings from France and Germany on behalf of Phenomenology and Existentialism. Many American students once again returned to England for their philosophical education and brought back the early messages of logical empiricism, ordinary language, philosophy and linguistic analysis—varieties of what came to be known subsequently by the generic term, analytic philosophy.

From 1950 until 1965, the student of philosophy in America, a term now used advisedly, was confronted with a bewildering array of philosophical materials from Europe. Although the emphasis differed, as dependent on the individual university and graduate program in question, American philosophy students at that time were reading Wittgenstein, Ayer, Austin, Kierkegaard, Nietzsche, Camus, Sartre, Husserl, Heidegger, Marcel or Merleau-Ponty. The more professionally oriented graduate schools were characterized more by the technical accompaniment of logic than by that of languages. Increasingly, argumentation superseded interpretation as the proper mode of philosophical discourse, whether found verbally or as written in the learned journals. Whatever else one wants to say about this development of philosophy in America after the war, it remains incontrovertible that interest in Classical American philosophy had all but disappeared from the academic philosophical scene.

From one point of view, the comparative neglect of Classical American philosophy after the second world war is baffling. Surely, no other major western culture would so completely abandon its own philosophical tradition. Can one think of French philosophy without constant, even if critical, recourse to Descartes? Or *mutatis mutandis* can one similarly think of German philosophy in relation to Kant or British philosophy in relation to Hume? As a general response, the answer would be no! Yet, from another point of view, the neglect is understandable, even if lamentable. America, again by tradition, has prided itself on being ever open to novelty, be it ideas or things. Less praiseworthy, but also endemic to American culture, has been its susceptibility to the belief that native culture is inferior to that spawned elsewhere. This proceeds from a complex historical dialectic between a peculiar American version of the oriental doctrine of "face" and a long-standing sense of cultural inferiority, the latter healed apparently only by periodically imported European wisdom. As with other comments made above, these contentions also deserve extensive commentary, but they too would take us beyond the mandate of the present essay.

Lest the reader doubt the neglected status of Classical American philosophy in the 1960s, I offer some autobiographical comments. When the present writer set out in 1965 to prepare a comprehensive edition of the works of William James, the publication scene was revealing. I found multiple paperback editions of the popular writings of James in print: *The Varieties of Religious Experience, Pragmatism* and *The Will to Believe and Other Essays in Popular Philosophy.* They were casually "introduced," if introduced at all, and poorly printed. James's major philosophical writings, such as *Essays in Radical Empiricism* and *A Pluralistic Universe,* were out of print and difficult to obtain. In response to this situation, I published *The Writings of William James* (New York, 1967, 1968; Chicago, 1977) which included among its eight hundred and ten pages of James's philosophy a complete text of *Pragmatism* and a complete text of Ralph Barton Perry's 1943 edition of *Essays in Radical Empiricism* and *A Pluralistic Universe.* Appended to this volume was an updated and corrected version of Ralph Barton Perry's "Annotated Bibliography of the Writings of William James" (pp. 811–858). The response to this volume was revealing. A consensus revealed surprise at the range of James's interests, fascination with the comparative contemporaneity of his thought, and, significantly, an acknowledgment of his technical philosophical virtuosity. Soon after this publication of the *Writings of William James,* other editions appeared; some claimed James for phenomenology (Bruce Wilshire, *William James: The Essential Writings,* New York, 1971) and others pointed to his catholicity of interests, philosophical as well as literary (Andrew J. Reck, ed., *Introduction to William James,* Bloomington, 1967; John K. Roth, ed., *The Moral Equivalent of War and Other Essays,* New York, 1971; Gay Wilson Allen, ed., *A William James Reader,* Boston, 1971).

A similar situation was extant when I began preparation of a comprehensive edition of the writings of Josiah Royce. Virtually all of his works were out of print and the few to escape that fate were published without introduction and without scholarly apparatus. Royce was still regarded by many as a throwback to the German idealists. He was thought to be a derivative thinker and there was little acknowledgment of the extensive development in his thought or of the range of his interests. In 1968, prodded by the editorial wisdom of Morris Philipson, The University of Chicago Press set out to present the works of Royce in a comprehensive format. The first volume was an edition of Royce's book *The Problem of Christianity* published originally in 1913. The Chicago edition of this work has a perceptive and detailed introduction by John E. Smith. In 1969, the Chicago series was continued by the publication of *The Basic Writings of Josiah Royce,* two volumes, edited by John J. McDermott. Included in these volumes was "An Annotated Bibliography of the Published Works of Josiah

Courtesy, Library of Congress

John Dewey (1859–1952) is remembered not only for his extensive writing in American philosophy but also for his theories and efforts for educational reform and his trenchant social commentary.

Royce" by Ignas Skrupskelis. As with the earlier mentioned response to the James volume, so too here did the reviewers stress their surprise at the variety of Royce's writings, especially with regard to his work in social history and religion. The fourth volume of this series was published in 1974, entitled *The Letters of Josiah Royce,* edited by John Clendenning. The fifth and final volume, a biography of Royce by Clendenning, is now in preparation. At this writing, the Chicago series is the most substantial version of Royce now in print and there are no present plans, unfortunately, for a collected and critical edition of his writings. This is especially to be regretted because the Royce Archives at Harvard University contain a considerable amount of unpublished papers, notably on logic, which merit wider public attention.

In the late 1960s, John Dewey's writings were better represented than those of James or Royce. The standard comprehensive edition was that of Joseph Ratner, *Intelligence in the Modern World* (New York, 1939), but it had the defect of presenting all excerpted materials and followed themes designated as significant by the editor, rather than by Dewey himself. In 1960, Richard Bernstein edited a helpful collection of Dewey's essays, *On Experience, Nature and*

Freedom (Indianapolis, 1960). All but one of these essays, however, were confined to Dewey's work after 1930. Another coherent collection of Dewey's writings was to be found in *John Dewey on Education*, edited by Reginald Archambault (New York, 1964). At this time, most of Dewey's original books were still in print, even if only in paperback editions. An attempt to provide a minimally comprehensive edition of Dewey's writings can be found in *The Philosophy of John Dewey*, two volumes, edited by John J. McDermott (New York, 1973).

The upshot of these developments with regard to the works of James, Royce and Dewey is that an effort was made to provide competent and comprehensive editions of their works and to overcome the haphazard and casual presentations of their major writings. These efforts, at least in the case of Dewey and James, acted as a creative backdrop to a major breakthrough on the American philosophical scene. For the first time, national funding was provided for a collected, critical edition of the writings of philosophers. The first venture, largely supported by The National Endowment for the Humanities, was that devoted to the works of John Dewey. Originated by The Center for Dewey Studies of Southern Illinois University at Carbondale, and partially supported by a grant from The John Dewey Foundation and from Mr. Corliss Lamont, the entire project is edited by Jo Ann Boydston. At this time, the full scope of the project is not yet confirmed but upwards of fifty volumes are projected. The first five volumes are published and gathered under the appellation of "The Early Works, 1882–1898." They include Dewey's "Early Essays," his writings on Leibniz, psychology, ethics and his periodic and episodic pieces during that period. The next group of volumes are referred to as "The Middle Works, 1899–1924." Of the fifteen volumes projected for this period, four have been published, containing Dewey's classic writings on education, his many journal articles and book reviews of that time, and his important work of 1903, *Studies in Logical Theory*. "The Later Period, 1925–1952," is projected as having twenty-five volumes. To this will be added an index and other important editorial information. Some ten volumes of correspondence await confirmation as to actual publication. Of the volumes published thus far, it can be said that they are characterized by helpful introductions, accurately emended texts and impeccable editorial supervision by Ms. Boydston. When this massive project is completed, even serious students of Dewey will be awed anew at his prodigious output, his learning, and above all his extraordinary ability to sustain intellectual quality over such an extensive span of time and work.

Between the publication of "The Early Works" of John Dewey and the initial volumes of "The Middle Works," the National Endowment for the Humanities funded a second proposal for a collected, critical edition of the writings of a major Classical American philosopher, William James. Sponsored by The American Council of Learned Societies, this edition, inclusive of unpublished writings, is projected to be sixteen volumes. The general editor is Frederick Burkhardt and the textual editor is Fredson Bowers. The publisher is Harvard University Press. The introductions to these James volumes are much more extensive than those found in the Dewey edition, and take as their task to provide the genesis of the text, its major contentions and an analysis of the critical response to the text over the years of its existence. The James edition has not been published in chronological order, although when finished it can be read that way. The first volume, published in 1975, was *Pragmatism*, with an introduction by H. Standish Thayer. Succeeding volumes published are: *The Meaning of Truth* (1975), with an introduction by Thayer; *Essays in Radical Empiricism* (1976), with an introduction by John J. McDermott; *A Pluralistic Universe* (1977), with an introduction by Richard J. Bernstein. Volumes now in press include *Some Problems in Philosophy, The Will to Believe,* and *Essays in Philosophy.* As with the Dewey volumes, this edition of James establishes an exact text, inclusive of James's emendations, subsequent to the first printing. In the James volumes, an added feature is the work of Ignas Skrupskelis, who has traced every reference or allusion made by James to its original source. The result is a veritable map to the panoply of persons and issues which laced the Euro-American intellectual scene of the late nineteenth and early twentieth century.

The collected, critical editions of James and Dewey, when completed, will provide the student of American philosophy with a vast amount of philosophical and cultural material from which to assess their significance as thinkers. Provided also will be a rich context for the understanding of almost a century of vibrant philosophical activity. Although not as technically proficient or nearly as complete, the Chicago series of Royce volumes adds a still further enriching context for understanding that period in American and European cultural history.

I turn now to the last three thinkers of the Classical period, C.S. Peirce, George Santayana and George H. Mead. The story of Peirce's inability to publish most of his writings during his lifetime is now a depressing biographical chapter in any history of American philosophy. After his death, in 1914, many boxes of his papers were sold to Harvard University where they languished for years, uncatalogued and unsung. Due to the efforts of two young philosophers then at Harvard University, Charles Hartshorne and Paul Weiss, six volumes of these papers were published between 1931 and 1935.[6] In 1958, this series was brought to a completion by the publication of volumes VII and VIII, under the editorial supervision of Arthur W. Burks. Before and during this time, several smaller anthologies of Peirce's writings were published: *Chance, Love and Logic,* ed., Morris R. Cohen, 1923; *The Philosophy of Peirce,* ed., Justus Buchler, 1940; *Charles S. Peirce, Essays in the Philosophy of Science,* ed., Vincent Tomas, 1957; *Charles S. Peirce, Values in a Universe of Chance,* ed., Philip P. Wiener, 1958. A much later collection of *The Essential Writings* of Peirce was edited by Edward C. Moore in 1972.

The collected papers of Peirce, however, did not exhaust the treasure trove of his writings. This was made clear with the publication of Richard Robin's *Annotated Catalogue of the Papers of C. S. Peirce* in 1967. Robin's catalogue made clear that the *Collected Papers,* although a magnificent endeavor in its time, fell short in scope and in editorial organization. It came, then, as very welcome news last year when the National Endowment for the Humanities announced its funding support of the publication of a collected and critical edition of the works of Charles S. Peirce. This edition is to be prepared chronologically and will be under the supervision of the distinguished Peirce scholar, Max H. Fisch. When completed and joined with the edition of Peirce's mathematical writings, edited by Carolyn Eisele, we shall have extant virtually all of Peirce's work, arranged and edited in the best tradition of scholarship.

With regard to the work of George Santayana, a similar program is underway. Santayana's writings have been periodically reprinted in paperback editions and two volumes have been devoted to his unpublished writings: *Santayana—Animal*

Faith and Spiritual Life, ed., John Lachs, 1967, and *Physical Order and Moral Liberty,* eds., John Lachs and Shirley Lachs, 1969. Other collections of Santayana's essays have appeared and it can be said that a high proportion of his works are available in one form or another. Yet, as with the other Classical American philosophers, his reputation has suffered from the unavailability of a comprehensive edition of his writings. Preliminary investigations for a collected and critical edition have been made under the editorial supervision of Herman J. Saatkamp, Jr., and the National Endowment for the Humanities has responded with a grant to sustain further preparation of this project.

The last thinker under direct consideration is that of George H. Mead. A colleague of John Dewey for ten years at the University of Chicago, Mead remained there after Dewey's departure. A profound teacher, he published comparatively little in his lifetime. After his death, many of Mead's manuscripts and lectures were published: *The Philosophy of the Present,* 1932; *Mind, Self and Society,* 1934; *Movements of Thought in the Nineteenth Century,* 1936; and *The Philosophy of the Act,* 1938. These volumes are still in print and have been supplemented by the publication of Andrew J. Reck's edition of most of Mead's previously published essays under the title of *Selected Writings,* 1964. A bibliography of Mead's writings, including details about his unpublished work, can be found in David Miller's authoritative study, *George Herbert Mead—Self, Language and the World,* 1973. Miller is now preparing an edition of some of the unpublished papers of Mead.

In addition to the extraordinary developments in the area of scholarly editions of the writings of the American Classical philosophers, the last ten years has also witnessed the publication of important works in the area of secondary literature. The two standard works in the history of American philosophy have been by Herbert Schneider, 1946, and by Joseph Blau, 1952. In 1977, there appeared an impressive two-volume study published by G. P. Putnam's entitled *A History of Philosophy in America.* Written by Elizabeth Flower and Murray Murphey, it is thorough and philosophically sophisticated. Its range is from the Puritans to C. I. Lewis and will soon take its place as the standard history of American philosophy despite its title, which announces "Philosophy in America."

In the last decade, two important biographies have been published. The first by Gay Wilson Allen on *William James,* 1967, and the second, *The Life and Mind of John Dewey,* 1973, by George Dykhuizen. As mentioned earlier, a biography of Royce is in progress and so too are biographies of Peirce and Whitehead underway, the first by Max Fisch and the second by Victor Lowe. Of note also in this regard is the recent publication of *The Poems of John Dewey,* edited by Jo Ann Boydson, 1977. As with all of Ms. Boydston's editing, this volume is a model of scholarship and her introduction provides a lucid account of the circumstances surrounding Dewey's writing of poetry and an accompanying perspective on an aspect of Dewey's life heretofore little known.

Commentaries on the American philosophers have also increased both in quantity and quality. As a further testament to the renascence of American philosophy, in 1974 The Society for the Advancement of American Philosophy was founded. Now in its fifth year, the Society has over four hundred active members and meets four times a year. The Executive Committee of the Society is presently examining the feasibility of a journal devoted to themes in American philosophy. This renewal of interest, coupled with the publication of collected, critical editions of the Classic American philosophers, should considerably enhance the quality of work in American philosophy. Assuming that the "Editions" are published as planned, the year 1990 should bring us over one hundred volumes of superbly edited works in American philosophy.

Now aside from the sheer aesthetic and editorial importance of these events, what significance accrues for the study of philosophy in the widest sense of that term? First, it gives to those who are teaching and writing philosophy in America a local touchstone from which to understand essential dimensions of contemporary philosophy. The work of present-day philosophers as diverse as W. V. O. Quine, Nelson Goodman, Wilfred Sellars and J. H. Randall, Jr. is inseparable from the influences of the earlier Classical American period.

Second, European philosophers are used to working from a tradition which is characterized not only by brilliance but by girth. In the past, American philosophy was represented by isolated works, leaving the enormous scope of each major thinker hidden from view. The publication of the respective collected works will present an imposing and coherent body of materials from which to proceed. In short, the tradition of Classical American philosophy will take its public place among the other great and warranted philosophical traditions of the past. This will give a new generation, whatever its geographical location, an opportunity to evaluate the continuing worth of American philosophy.

Finally, quite aside from the importance of the renewed availability of the works of the American philosophers, we stress here the intrinsic importance of the works themselves. The American philosophers address themselves, at one time or another, to virtually every significant philosophical theme, most often in a language which is accessible and rich. Their disputes, insights and failings constitute one of the truly creative philosophical clusterings in the history of philosophy. Their work is seminal for our work, and the general admonition of Santayana is still to the point: those of us who forget the past will be condemned to relive it. Such a reliving would be done in ignorance, which is certainly an unforgivable condition for philosophers.□

NOTES

[1] John Dewey, "The Need for a Recovery of Philosophy," in John J. McDermott, ed., *The Philosophy of John Dewey* (New York: G. P. Putnam's Sons, 1973) I, p. 96.

[2] Ralph Waldo Emerson, "Nature," *Works* (Boston: Houghton, Mifflin and Company, 1903) I, p. 3.

[3] cf. Philip P. Wiener, *Evolution and the Founders of Pragmatism* (Cambridge: Harvard University Press, 1949) p.v. For a further detailed consideration of this period, cf. Ralph Barton Perry, *The Thought and Character of William James*, 2 Vols. (Boston: Little, Brown and Company, 1935).

[4] For a discussion of the major American philosophers after the Classical period cf. Andrew J. Reck, *Recent American Philosophy* (New York: Pantheon Books, 1964) and *The New American Philosophers* (Baton Rouge: Louisiana State University Press, 1968).

[5]For a brilliant, provocative and contentious evaluation of the central importance of the Harvard philosophy department during this period, cf. Bruce Kuklick, *The Rise of American Philosophy–Cambridge, Massachusetts, 1860–1930* (New Haven: Yale University Press, 1977).

[6]The fascinating story of how this Peirce project came to be is retold in later interviews given by Hartshorne and Weiss. See "Recollections of Editing the Peirce Papers," *Transactions of the Charles S. Peirce Society*, 6 (1970), pp. 149–188.

SELECTED SECONDARY SOURCES

This bibliographical appendix will provide the reader with some knowledge of recent activity in the field of American philosophy. The books listed here are an addition to those mentioned in the course of the discussion above.

Allen, Gay Wilson, *William James* (New York: The Viking Press, 1967). Based on the Harvard collection of James's family papers, this is now the standard biography.

Ames, Van Meter, *Zen and American Thought* (Honolulu: University of Hawaii Press, 1962). Ames writes provocative chapters on the important American literary and philosophical thinkers, each from a Zen perspective.

Ayer, A. J. *The Origins of Pragmatism* (San Francisco: Freeman, Cooper and Company, 1968). The concentration here is on the central themes of the philosophy of Peirce and James.

Boler, John F., *Charles Peirce and Scholastic Realism* (Seattle: University of Washington Press, 1963). A careful analysis of the influence of Duns Scotus on the philosophy of Peirce.

Cahn, Steven M., ed., *New Studies in the Philosophy of John Dewey* (Hanover: The University Press of New England, 1977). A collection of essays which focuses alternately on Dewey's social philosophy, metaphysics, aesthetics, epistemology, ethics and philosophy of education.

Conkin, Paul K., *Puritans and Pragmatists* (New York: Dodd, Mead and Company, 1968). This book is extremely informative as to the lives and times of the major figures in American intellectual history.

Corti, Walter Robert, *The Philosophy of George Herbert Mead* (Hamburg: Felix Meiner Verlag, 1973). A collection of essays by European and American scholars on the range of Mead's thought. It includes a bibliography of Mead's writings.

Corti, Walter Robert, *The Philosophy of William James* (Hamburg: Felix Meiner Verlag, 1976). A collection of essays devoted to the life and thought of William James. A helpful bibliography of secondary sources is included.

Cotton, J. Harry, *Royce on the Human Self* (Cambridge: Harvard University Press, 1954). Regarded as a classic in Royce scholarship, this book is a systematic study of the importance of self in relation to Royce's total philosophical work.

Dykhuizen, George, *The Life and Mind of John Dewey* (Carbondale: Southern Illinois University Press, 1973). The first detailed biography of John Dewey. It provides the personal and professional context necessary to understand Dewey's writings.

Eames, S. Morris, *Pragmatic Naturalism* (Carbondale: Southern Illinois University Press, 1977). A pragmatic philosophical approach to the problems of nature, knowledge, values and education.

Easton, Loyd D., *Hegel's First American Followers* (Athens: Ohio University Press, 1966). A presentation of the thought of four early German-American Hegelians, accompanied by a translation of several of their essential writings.

Flower, Elizabeth and Murray Murphey, *A History of Philosophy in America*, 2 Vols. (New York: G. P. Putnam's Sons, 1977). These volumes are comprehensive and extremely competent, in both style of presentation and philosophical content. They are sure to become the standard historical reference work in American philosophy.

Fuss, Peter, *The Moral Philosophy of Josiah Royce* (Cambridge: Harvard University Press, 1965). A monograph devoted to the development of Royce's ethical theory in relation to his epistemology and theory of community.

Goetzmann, William H., *The American Hegelians* (New York: Alfred A. Knopf, 1973). A valuable anthology of the writings of the American Hegelians with an appended annotated bibliography.

Goudge, Thomas A., *The Thought of C. S. Peirce* (New York: Dover Publications, Inc., 1969). Originally published in 1950, this is still a well-regarded general treatment of Peirce's work.

Howie, John and Buford, Thomas O., eds., *Contemporary Studies in Philosophical Idealism* (Cape Cod, Massachusetts: Claude Stark & Co., 1975). Vigorous restatements of the American idealist tradition.

Kuklick, Bruce, *Josiah Royce* (Indianapolis and New York: The Bobbs-Merrill Company, Inc., 1972). This is an intellectual biography of Royce, with a unique focus on his work in logic and methodology.

McDermott, John J., *The Culture of Experience–Philosophical Essays in the American Grain* (New York: New York University Press, 1976). This book is concerned with the significance of the writings of James and Dewey for an analysis and critique of contemporary culture.

Merrill, Kenneth R. and Robert W. Shahan, eds., *American Philosophy–From Edwards to Quine* (Norman: University of Oklahoma Press, 1977). An overview of American philosophy, including essays on the Transcendentalists, Royce and Santayana.

Miller, David L., *George Herbert Mead* (Austin: University of Texas Press, 1973). An excellent, comprehensive study of the thought of Mead.

Mills, C. Wright, *Sociology and Pragmatism* (New York: Paine-Whitman Publishers, 1964). An attempt to provide an analysis of the social and political context which gave rise to pragmatism.

Moore, Edward C., *American Pragmatism: Peirce, James and Dewey* (New York: Columbia University Press, 1961). Interpretive essays which are concerned with ethics, religion, epistemology and metaphysics.

Morganbesser, Sidney, ed., *Dewey and His Critics* (New York: The Journal of Philosophy, Inc., 1977). A collection of essays by John Dewey and polemical rejoinders by his peers. All of them are reprinted from the *Journal of Philosophy*.

Morris, Charles, *The Pragmatic Movement in American Philosophy* (New York: George Braziller, 1970). The focus here is on semiotic, axiology, methodology and cosmology, in the thought of James, Peirce, Dewey and Mead.

Munson, Thomas N., *The Essential Wisdom of George Santayana* (New York: Columbia University Press, 1962). A synoptic view of Santayana's thought gathered around the theme of his notion of "essence."

Murphy, Murray, *The Development of Peirce's Philosophy* (Cambridge: Harvard University Press, 1961). A controversial interpretation of Peirce, which holds that Peirce never attained any systematic version of his own thought.

Novak, Michael, *American Philosophy and the Future* (New York: Charles Scribner's Sons, 1968). Original interpretations of the American philosophers, often with contemporary culture themes in mind.

Potter, Vincent G. S. J., *Charles S. Peirce on Norms and Ideals* (Worcester, Massachusetts: The University of Massachusetts Press, 1967). This book is devoted to the importance of the categories in Peirce's doctrine of the normative sciences.

Rosenthal, Sandra B., *The Pragmatic A Priori* (St. Louis: Warren H. Green, Inc., 1976). An examination of the epistemology of C. I. Lewis.

Rucker, Darnell, *The Chicago Pragmatists* (Minneapolis: University of Minnesota Press, 1969). The story of the imaginative work in the social sciences as found at the University of Chicago from 1895 until 1930.

Scheffler, Israel, *Four Pragmatists* (New York: Humanities Press, 1974). Although other topics are considered, this is fundamentally an epistemological critique of the philosophy of James, Peirce, Mead and Dewey.

Seigfried, Charlene, *From Chaos to Context* (Athens: Ohio University Press, 1978). A trenchant and detailed study of James's notion of pure experience.

Singer, Beth J., *The Rational Society* (Cleveland: The Press of Case Western Reserve University, 1970). An examination of Santayana's social and political philosophy.

Thayer, H. S., *Meaning and Action* (Indianapolis, and New York: The Bobbs-Merril Company, Inc., 1968). A thorough and critical history of pragmatism, including an analysis of the European influences.

White, Morton, *Pragmatism and the American Mind* (New York: Oxford University Press, 1973). A collection of White's essays on the American philosophers and on the philosophical dimensions in American intellecual history.

White, Morton, *Science and Sentiment in America* (New York: Oxford University Press, 1972). An interpretative and often critical history of American philosophy from the seventeenth century forward.

Wild, John, *The Radical Empiricism of William James* (Garden City, New York: Doubleday & Company, Inc., 1969). A version of James's thought which finds it anticipatory and continuous with European phenomenology and existentialism.

Wilshire, Bruce, *William James and Phenomenology: A Study of "The Principles of Psychology"* (Bloomington: Indiana University Press, 1968). A study of James's *Principles of Psychology* from the perspective of Husserlian Phenomenology.

ADDENDUM

by John J. McDermott

Since the publication of my original essay in American Studies International in the Spring of 1978, several developments are worth noting. Further, a number of bibliographical items must be added to the original list of "Selected Secondary Sources."

The major developments relate to the various collected critical editions of the writings of William James, Charles Sanders Peirce, and John Dewey. Since 1978, the editors of the Works of William James, published by Harvard University Press, have added three volumes to the original four. Volume five is Essays in Philosophy, with an introduction by John J. McDermott; volume six is The Will to Believe, with an introduction by Edward H. Madden; and volume seven is Some Problems of Philosophy, with an introduction by Peter Hare. In press and due to be published within the next year are The Principles of Psychology and Essays in Morality and Religion. The remainder of James's writings, including several volumes on his unpublished work, are now in editorial preparation. The entire series will comprise sixteen volumes.

With regard to the ongoing critical edition of the works of John Dewey, published by Southern Illinois University Press, we now have volumes five through eight of "The Middle Works." This middle period of Dewey's writings goes from 1899 until 1924. Volumes nine and ten are presently in press and the last five volumes are in preparation. It should be noted that because of its intrinsic interest, Dewey's classic work in metaphysics, Experience and Nature (1925), will be published earlier than its chronological schedule, perhaps within the next year.

Considerable progress has been made on the <u>Writings of Charles S. Peirce: A Chronological Edition</u>. It is projected as twenty volumes of text, each with a historical introduction and an index, plus supplementary volumes containing comprehensive indexes, a bibliography, and a new catalog of the Peirce Papers in a single chronological order. The publisher will be Indiana University Press. Volume I (1857-1866) is due this year, and volumes II, III and IV are in an advanced stage of preparation.

The George Santayana edition is now underway. Projected at twenty volumes, the first one, <u>Persons and Places</u>, is due in 1981. The Philosophical Documentation Center is going to publish <u>George Santayana: A Bibliographical Checklist, 1880-1980</u>, as edited by Herman Saatkamp and John Jones.

I repeat here my remark in the first edition of this essay: "The publication of the respective collected works will present an imposing and coherent body of materials from which to proceed. In short, the tradition of Classical American philosophy will take its public place among the other great and warranted philosophical traditions of the past." It is a pleasure to announce that in the intervening two years this work has proceeded rapidly and with sustained high quality.

Selected Secondary Sources

*Clebsch, William. <u>American Religious Thought</u> (Chicago: The University of Chicago Press, 1973). A provocative and insightful treatment of the thought of Jonathan Edwards, R. W. Emerson, and especially William James.

Coughlan, Neil. <u>Young John Dewey: An Essay in American Intellectual History</u> (Chicago: The University of Chicago Press, 1973). An interpretation of Dewey's personal values during his formative years.

Damico, Alfonso, J. <u>Individuality and Community: The Social and Political Thought of John Dewey</u> (Gainesville: University Presses of Florida, 1978). This book seeks to show the importance of Dewey's philosophical thought for his social and political judgments.

Deledalle, Gérard. <u>Théorie et Pratique du Signe</u> (Paris: Payot, 1979). Beginning with a discussion of Saussure, this work is an analysis of Peirce's semiotic.

Deledalle, Gérard. <u>L'Idée D'Expérience dans la Philosophie de John Dewey</u> (Paris: Presses Universitaires de France, 1967). A chronological history of Dewey's notion of experience from 1904 until 1952.

Deledalle, Gérard. Histoire de la Philosophe Américaine (Paris: Presses Universitaires de France, 1954). An overview from Europe's leading interpreter of American philosophy.

Gouinlock, James. The Moral Writings of John Dewey (New York: Hafner Press, 1976). A helpful and well-selected compilation of Dewey's writings on moral philosophy and social ethics.

"Psychological Studies of the James Family." The Psychohistory Review VII, 1-2 (Summer-Fall, 1979). Essays on Henry James, Sr., Mary Robertson James, William James, and Henry James, Jr.

Robinson, Daniel. Royce and Hocking: American Idealists (Boston: The Christopher Publishing House, 1968). A comparative study, which contains some interesting correspondence of both Royce and Hocking to their contemporaries.

Smith, John. Purpose and Thought: The Meaning of Pragmatism (New Haven: Yale University Press, 1978). An original and thorough analysis of pragmatist epistemology.

*Zeltner, Philip. John Dewey's Aesthetic Philosophy (Amsterdam: B. R. Gruner, 1975). The focus here is on Dewey's notion of experience as aesthetic.

Contemporary American Poetry at the Crossroads

WILLIAM CLAIRE

American poetry of the period since the World War is unquestionably brilliant, dynamic, and new in the sense that it yields fresh images of contemporary places, persons and activities. It stirs the reader into an intense awareness of what it means to be alive in the middle of the twentieth century.

Stephen Stephanchev, in 1965[1]

Perhaps what we come down to is the plainest of all simplicities, yet one of the hardest to get by heart: there is not much poetry very far from talk—not much of anything worth saying that cannot be said in the first place.

Michael Heffernan, in 1979[2]

After several vibrant and influential decades, modern American poetry has a decidedly *fin de siècle* quality to it. Despite considerable attainment and individual attempts to extend poetic language, little on the horizon suggests dramatic changes in any collective sense through the 1980s. While there are unusual public manifestations of popularity, there are few if any commanding influences among senior living American poets, and while there is steady achievement among many at the middle and mature stages of their careers, no one can lay claim to the laurels that bedecked a host of significant poets in past years.

The deaths of Allen Tate and Robert Lowell, both of whose influence had diminished in recent years, are late examples of the sad litany of departures from the contemporary scene. A mere listing, while staggering in its diversity, is a necessary adjunct to any consideration of American poetry now. Aiken, Auden, Berryman, Bishop, Bogan, Cummings, Eliot, Frost, Merton, O'Hara, Plath, Jarrell, Moore, Olson, Pound, Ransom, Roethke, Rukeyser, Sandburg, Stevens, Van Doren, James Wright, and Louis Zukofsky are among those whose death in the past two decades has taken influential voices with disciples and readers from the scene.

For many American poets, those deaths represent a legacy and challenge as well as an enormous gap. It is unclear who among the current poets will

William Claire was the founding editor and publisher of Voyages, *a national literary magazine published from Washington, 1967–1973. His poems have appeared in* American Scholar, Carleton Miscellany, Chelsea, The Nation, The New York Times, *and many other journals and anthologies. His essays on contemporary writers have appeared in* Antioch Review, New Republic, American Scholar, *and other publications. He is the author of five books and chapbooks, including* Publishing in the West: Alan Swallow, *which won a "Best Title Award for 1975" from the* Library Journal. *A book he edited and introduced,* Essays of Mark Van Doren, 1924–1972, *will appear in Summer, 1980. Born in Northampton, Massachusetts, he was educated at Columbia College, Columbia University, and Georgetown University. He is currently Director of the Washington Office of the State University of New York. He is a member of P.E.N., the Poetry Society of America, and the Cosmos Club. He was recently selected by the Academy of American Poets to introduce the first Katherine Garrison Chapin Memorial Lecture at the Guggenheim Museum, and was one of the poets invited to the White House celebration of American poets in 1980. Photo by Rollie McKenna.*

be able to carry the baton. What is clear is that there are several strong poets content to explore their private linguistic developments apart from public response. With the possible exception of Robert Penn Warren,[3] who continues to amaze younger poets with his productivity, no American poet now or in the near future appears likely to become a figure capable of widespread attention beyond the ever growing confines of the poetry circuit.

Accomplished poets such as Howard Nemerov, John Logan (who has yet to have his collected poems published), Galway Kinnell, Adrienne Rich, and John Ashbery remain likely candidates for continued distinction. Allen Ginsberg, Lawrence Ferlinghetti and Gary Snyder remain capable of attracting followers, but no truly dominant or heroic figures exist in the Eliot, Pound, or Frost traditions. American poetry, lacking a center, has become increasingly democratized and decentralized. There are no specific critics or schools of absolute influence, like the "New Critics" of the World War II era, no *must* literary journals and no particularly significant regional groupings despite strong loyalties in the Pacific Northwest, in New York City, and some parts of the South: even these are diminishing. In a quarter-century span, American poetry evolved from a passionate conviction of a few to the concern of many. Nonetheless, the situation now is a far cry from the 1960s when American poetry replaced British poetry among Anglo-influences and became an international cultural phenomenon of some magnitude.

Paradoxically, for the first time in American history, poetry is enjoying a definite upsurge in interest in all parts of the country. While its audiences do not match the popular and performing arts, and while poetry is by no means celebrated in high public places, poets find themselves no longer regarded as outsiders in the wider cultural context.[4] Several poetry readings are held weekly in major cities and in many smaller communities. There has been a marked interest in creative writing programs in the schools, and public appearances by poets are not uncommon in many of the 3,000–plus universities, colleges, and community colleges sprinkled over the 50 states.

An additional paradox: simultaneously with this plateau of public acceptance, the large commercial publishing houses have become a kind of censor in their lack of interest in new poets. As more and more of these firms become divisions of conglomerates, not even lip service is paid to new poets knocking on the Kafka-like doors. Gone forever, it seems, are those gentleman or lady editors who assigned, if in excruciatingly modest terms, a few places for poets. *Ergo,* the chance of any new poets making a splash on the national literary waters remains problematical.

The drying-up of major New York, Chicago, or Boston publishing houses as a source of new poetry has led to an increase in the number of small university presses that are publishing poetry. The small press movement, which grew out of an interest in fine printing on the west coast, is now national. Although there are cries of despair, many well known poets are content to have books brought out by smaller presses. Additionally, some 1,000 literary or small magazines are currently being published in the United States. In short, American poetry is not centered anywhere, but it is happening everywhere.

*Self portrait by American poet Edward Estlin Cummings ("e e cummings"), 1894–1962. Oil on canvas, 20" x 15",
1958. Negative number 079171. National Portrait Gallery, Smithsonian Institution, Washington, D. C. A good paperback biography of Cummings is Charles Norman, E. E. Cummings, the Magic Maker (Indianapolis: Bobbs-Merril,
1972). A slender autobiographical volume by Cummings, also in paper, is i: six non lectures (Cambridge, Mass.:
Harvard University Press, 1953).*

Nor do the leading American poets necessarily live in the great urban centers. Among senior poets, Robert Penn Warren, Archibald MacLeish, Richard Wilbur, and Richard Eberhart live in disparate parts of rural New England; James Dickey in Columbia, South Carolina; and Robert Bly on a farm in Minnesota. Poets like James Merrill, and W.S. Merwin, both significant influences, tend to spend as much time out of the US as in; John Logan and Robert Creeley live in Buffalo, New York; Howard Nemerov in St. Louis; and so on.

While poets and their followers have a way of keeping in touch, the decentralization and physical diaspora[5] of poets and the lack of leading figures are in dramatic contrast to the easy and rather precise groupings of the 1950s and '60s.

This was the era of the war of anthologies, when poets were considered either academics or experimental beatniks. While simplistic, these distinctions literally forced poets to take sides. Except in rare instances today, usually based on new ethnic and sexual distinctions, poetry resists pat categories. While there are groupings of woman, black, Hispanic, gay, native American, and other poets, the age particularly lacks major national anthologies of the kind that 20 years ago were hotly debated in every academic English department and in "the supernatural darkness of cold water flats" as characterized in Allen Ginsberg's powerful poem, "Howl."

Not a single poet appeared in both the famous now dated Hall, Pack, Simpson *New Poets of England and America* (1957) and Donald M. Allen's *The New American Poetry* (1960). In the absence of leading anthologies, both retain some influence. If some of the differences still remain, they are rarely talked about today. The orthodoxies have faded on both sides except by the most mediocre practitioners of both. And one recent anthology, *The New Naked Poetry: Recent Contemporary Poetry In Open Forms* (1976), edited by Berg and Mezey, has as the majority of its choices, poets who are full-time academics.

If any of the earlier groupings tend to gather together now, it is those whose spiritual grandfathers were Ezra Pound or William Carlos Williams; the Black Mountain School adherents of whom Robert Duncan and Robert Creeley are now its senior citizens; the San Francisco Renaissance of which Kenneth Rexroth and Lawrence Ferlinghetti are still its most famous products (although Rexroth, with his lyric poems and his wide learning and interest in Orientalia, is difficult to categorize); the Beat Generation of whom Allen Ginsberg remains the greatest hero; and the New York poets, most of whom first met at Harvard and who were deeply influenced by the late Frank O'Hara, Kenneth Koch, and John Ashbery. Each of these groupings has followers today, but it is no longer a matter of passionate conviction. Other influential poets who have undergone stylistic changes in recent years have adherents; namely, Amiri Bakara (formerly LeRoi Jones), who once edited the important magazine *Yugen;* Gary Snyder, who writes from the Sierra Nevadas or the Orient; and Denise Levertov, born in England, but a voice highly regarded in the US for many years and a poet with a particular interest in young writers.

Many other American poets have sustained solid reputations. James

Dickey, whose output seems to have diminished considerably since the publication of his novel, *Deliverance,* has written poems such as "The Heaven of Animals" and "The Sheep Child" which have a permanent place in the anthologies of the latter half of this century. Louis Simpson, born in Jamaica, West Indies, who once characterized, "American Poetry" in a widely quoted poem:

> Whatever it is, it must have
> A stomach that can digest
> Rubber, coal, uranium, moons, poems.
>
> Like the shark, it contains a shoe.
> It must swim for miles through the desert
> Uttering cries that are almost human.[6]

Adrienne Rich is the strongest of those poets who have explored feminist themes. David Wagoner, who also edits *Poetry Northwest;* Charles Simic, born in Yugoslavia, and one of the younger poets to have a following; Maxine Kumin; W.D. Snodgrass; Richard Hugo; and principally, William Stafford, David Ignatow and A.R. Ammons have disciples.

William Stafford, born in 1914, is an interesting case study. An unknown quantity until age 50 and the author of the 1963 National Book Award winning *Traveling Through The Dark,* he symbolizes the modern poetry movement in America. While he lives in virtual isolation in Lake Oswego, Oregon, he has become a quintessential journey-man poet by visiting colleges all over the country. In an unassuming, gentle way, he has established an impeccable reputation among peers, younger poets, and the public. Generous with his time and contributions to obscure literary magazines and presses, he represents the modern spirit in American poetry at its best.

All of the poets mentioned above, and at least three dozen others who cannot be noted, are writing a personal poetry that is autobiographical in the best sense, reflecting as they do upon inner life in relation to the externals of living. Poets are sharing their privacy through the intimate details of poetry though no longer in the heavy confessional mode of Lowell, Anne Sexton, or Plath. These poets are continually affirming, often in strikingly clear language, what it means to be human and writing poetry now.

> Look. no one ever promised for sure
> that we would sing. We have decided
> to moan. In a strange dance that
> we do not understand till we do it, we
> have to carry.

Thus, William Stafford begins a poem titled simply, "An Introduction To Some Poems,"[7] which characterizes the determination of many modern poets, inheritors of an illustrious tradition, to carry on. A. Poulin, Jr., poet-editor of one of the currently circulating anthologies, *Contemporary American Poetry,* refers to the earlier tradition and its relationship to modern poets. "Today's poets," he says, "have succeeded in making poetry often radically personal" and respond to experience "in a visceral rather than intellectual fashion." While "T.S. Eliot and his followers described the human condition," today's poets "people that waste land, mostly with themselves. They have described the deterioration and sterility of the individual self and, having done so, have fabricated a cumulative metaphor for our own age."[8]

The cumulative metaphor is the accumulation of voices unafraid to speak. In a marvelous nine line poem, David Wagoner concludes, in "The Poets Agree To Be Quiet By The Swamp,"[9]

> Therefore the poets may keep quiet.
> But the corners of their mouths grin past their hands.
> They stick their elbows out into the evening
> Stoop, and begin the ancient croaking.

If American poets never abandoned the landscape as dramatically as did abstract expressionist painters of the 1950's, many have adopted a stance that may be in tune once again with the Whitman explorations a century ago, if lacking his idealism and vision. Even that most complicated of American poets, and perhaps a true visionary, John Ashbery, in his recent *Self Portrait In A Convex Mirror*,[10] voices his belief that communication might come

> Now and in the future, in cool yards,
> In quiet small houses in the country,
> Our country, in fenced areas, in cool shady streets.

According to David Kalstone, "Whitman's invitation to loaf and invite their souls can't have had many responses more mysterious, peculiar, searching and beautiful than Ashbery's recent poems."[11] Both the interior landscape and the personal aspects of the lives of five poets are examined in Kalstone's *Five Temperaments,* an excellent guide to the work of Lowell, Bishop, Merrill, Rich, and Ashbery. His book, and a recent issue of *Antaeus* on "Poetry and Poetics" would give interested readers insights into contemporary verse. They would discover not only how difficult it is to generalize about the contemporary scene but that generality itself is the enemy of many poets.

Because so much of the territory has been staked out before them, the process of writing poetry comes down to what David Ignatow once described as ". . . to be alone, to eat and sleep alone, to adventure alone: cry of the human."[12] A very astute critic (with the exception of less than a dozen people, American poetry lacks major criticism), Ralph Mills Jr., titled his recent book *Cry of the Human.* He examines Galway Kinnell, Philip Levine, and Ignatow, among others, and believes that new American poets may have a closer bond with their seniors such as Stanley Kunitz, Muriel Rukeyser, and Karl Shapiro; those who began in the 1930s and who had to seek their own voices, "searching them out through the arduous process of trying on and discarding models, guides and influences from the poetic tradition and from modernist writers alike, without the benefit of any shared aesthetic principle or revolutionary artistic purpose."[13]

The lack of shared aesthetic principles represents a difficult challenge to younger poets, those aged 20 to 30, who are in danger of being caught up in the new popularity and in political careerism—the search for grants—that is pervasive. The temptations are real and were virtually unknown fifteen years

Portrait of Walt Whitman, 1819–1896, the father of modern American poetry, taken in 1872 by photographer G. Frank E. Pearsall, active 1871–1896. Accession number 76.95, National Portrait Gallery, Smithsonian Institution, Washington, D. C. The standard biography of Whitman is Gay Wilson Allen, The Solitary Singer, a Critical Biography of Walt Whitman *(New York: Macmillan, 1955). A good paperback edition of Whitman's work, with an American studies introduction, is John Kouwvenhoven, ed.,* Leaves of Grass and Selected Prose by Walt Whitman *(New York: Modern Library, 1950).*

ago. Almost all of the poets mentioned previously have learned from their predecessors and some, like Ignatow, have earned their spurs through a lifetime of conscious application to their craft. A former businessman, like Stafford born in 1914, Ignatow is another exception to the rule and one who is just becoming known. He would dispute the Whitman tradition in terms of its optimism. Although a descendant of the urban poetics of Williams, he speaks in a direct voice of the difficulties of modern life with stark reality. He is to urban life what Stafford is to the vast spaces of the west, and it is curious that these two poets, both virtually ignored until their 50s, are very much at the center of influence among younger poets.

There are some guides to the younger generation of poets. Over ten years ago, *Tri Quarterly*, a first-rate publication from Northwestern University, included poets such as Louise Glück, Dennis Schmitz, and Marvin Bell in an issue, *Under 30: Fiction, Poetry and Criticism of the New American Writers*, and many of their choices have held up. William Heyen, in his splendid *American Poets in 1976* (1976), included such poets as Linda Pastan, Dave Smith, and Paul Zimmer and asked them to speak about their work in the same manner as John Ciardi's *Mid-Century American Poets* (1950), published a full generation ago. What resulted was some 29 poets (of all ages) writing about the sources of their inspiration and including more than 150 poems. The volume is an excellent guide to the current state of poetry in America, what Heyen calls "our diversity of interest, our understanding of ourselves and our worlds."[14]

Another guide to the youngest generation of poets is Daniel Halpern's *The American Poetry Anthology* (1975), a selection of 76 poets from some 250 considered who were born after 1934. These are poets whom Halpern said were descendants of "a poetic line" that had been "polished by the elegant hand of Wilbur, expanded by the generous hand of Ginsberg, sliced and pared by Creeley, and had its syntax shaken soundly by Merwin in his influential collections *The Moving Target* and *The Lice*."[15] Halpern, whose own journal, *Antaeus,* is published in Tangier, London, and New York, demonstrates, by his selections, one of the major influences on younger poets today, the widespread translations of foreign works. Whereas in the 1950s and '60s a few poets like St. John Perse, Lorca, and Borges were read avidly here, newer translations have had an almost overpowering effect. Subtle imitations have cropped up in the language of younger poets based on their readings of Neruda of Chile, Vallejo of Peru, the French of Char, Ponge, and Desnos, and others like Yehuda Amichai of Israel, Andrei Vozneshensky of Russia, and those from many other continents. It is too early to tell whether the influence will be a good one, but there is definitely a new international flavor to American verse that has had a salutary impact on a wider cultural understanding.

Meanwhile, American poets continue to speak in authentic voices and with autobiographical overtones. The confessional era of Lowell, Sexton, and Plath has been muted considerably to what Paul Fussell calls a "natural alliance between technique and theme."[16] A.R. Ammons, who teaches at Cornell University was, like William Stafford, overlooked for many years, but has become an important voice in recent years and, like Stafford, has received the National Book Award and other prizes for his work. In his widely anthologized poem, "Corson's Inlet,"[17] a voice comes through in a "rhythm that sounds like that of well-written prose." It gives him an opportunity to say:

> I allow myself eddies of meaning

as he ambles down a New Jersey shoreline "with its roundly unplanned contours." in order to "understand at once both a valuable intellectual and emotional range of possibiiities and a verse form that can render them suggestively." The poet continues:

> I have reached no conclusions, have erected
>   no boundaries.

In another important Ammons poem, "Gravelly Run,"[18] he concludes:

> no use to make any philosophies here:
>   I see no
> god in the holly, hear no song from
> the snowbroken weeds; Hegel is not the winter
> yellow in the pines: the sunlight has never
> heard of trees: surrendered self among
>   unwelcome forms: stranger,
> hoist your burdens, get on down the road.

If any conclusions can be reached about American poetry today, they can be found in the poems of William Stafford and A.R. Ammons, in the new surrealism of the younger generation, and in the carefully selected details of autobiography of many others. Yet for all of the individual attainment, American poetry today is in a holding pattern, not dissimilar to the early part of the century before modernism took hold and revolutionized and restructured both idiom and taste.

In many respects, everything that can happen in a century of poetry has happened in the period from 1915-1980. There are disagreements about the current strength of American poetry and doubts as to where it is going. Michael Heffernan, in *The American Poetry Review,* a newspaper format published bi-monthly from Philadelphia which is widely read in poetry circles, says "ours is a resourcefully minor poetry at present, a poetry of echoes and silences, of conditioned responses and exquisite gestures."[19] And Richard Pevear has worried about the "sudden, massive increase in the teaching of verse composition" while voicing additional concerns for an "institutionalized poetry-network that has sprung up over the past two decades" by which he means the constant search for grants and imitation of the previous masters of poetry. He also deals with the influence of foreign poets by stating that many American poets are writing in an English that "sounds like a rather loose translation of some probably interesting original."[20]

While it is unlikely that giants like Wallace Stevens or William Carlos Williams are waiting in the wings, it is too soon to sound the death knell for the balance of this century. Clearly the stage is set for new presentations, for poets to capture the meaning and moment of their times. If the projected voices remain off-stage, the props are in place. Daniel Hoffman, a former consultant in poetry at the Library of Congress, said recently . . . "At this moment, we are the contemporaries of five or six generations of poets. There are probably more poets of considerable talent writing today than at any given moment in the past." But, he added, "we're also at a crossroads. We've lost the great ones—Stevens, Eliot, Auden, Lowell. The giants have all gone but those who are left are writing in many modes and styles, opening up new kinds of experience."[21]   □

Notes

1. The quotation is taken from the opening statement of Stephen Stepanchev, in his *American Poetry Since 1945,* New York: Harper & Row, 1965.

2. Quotation from Michael Heffernan in the *American Poetry Review* 8 (January-February 1979):1 in a review titled "Practicing The Scales of Science."

3. A strong case for Robert Penn Warren's status as the leading American poet was made by Dave Smith in an article titled "He Prayeth Best Who Loveth Best." in *American Poetry Review* 8:1.

4. The White House, under the patronage of the First Family, honored American poets, on January 3, 1980. It was the first time in U.S. history that a gathering of this kind was held, specifically for poets, in the White House.

5. In the invaluable *Directory of American Poets* 1975 Edition, published by Poets & Writer, Inc. New York City, the 1,500 contemporary poets listed come from over 45 states, as well as territories of the U.S. A 1980–81 edition has just been released, and includes fiction writers.

6. Simpson poem, quoted in A. Poulin, Jr., *Contemporary American Poetry* (Boston: Houghton-Mifflin, 1975).

7. Stafford poem, an extract, quoted in Poulin.

8. Poulin, from an introduction titled "Contemporary American Poetry: The Radical Tradition," *Contemporary American Poetry,* pp. 459–473.

9. David Wagoner, in *Collected Poems,* 1956–1976 (Bloomington: Indiana University Press, 1976).

10. John Ashbery, in *Self Portrait In A Convex Mirror,* an extract (New York: Viking Press, 1975).

11. David Kalstone, *Five Temperaments* (New York: Oxford University Press, 1977).

12. Quoted in Ralph Mills, Jr., *Contemporary American Poetry; Cry of the Human* (Urbana: University of Illinois, 1975).

13. Mills, *Contemporary American Poetry.*

14. William Heyen, *American Poets in 1976* (Indianapolis: Bobbs-Merrill, 1976), "Introduction."

15. Daniel Halpern, *The American Poetry Anthology* (New York: Avon, 1975), "Introduction."

16. Paul Fussell in the special issue of *Antaeus,* No. 30–31, "Poetry and Poetics" edited by Daniel Halpern.

17. Ibid.

18. The extracts from Ammons' "Gravelly Run" are quoted in A.R. Ammons *Corsons' Inlet* (Ithaca: Cornell University Press, 1965).

19. Heffernan's comments appeared in a review of four volumes of poetry by younger poets in *The American Poetry Review* 8:1.

20. Richard Pevear, in *The Hudson Review* (Autumn, 1977), pp. 457–458.

21. Daniel Hoffman was one of several former consultants in poetry invited back to Washington for a reunion in 1978. He and others were interviewed by Ruth Dean, in *The Washington Star,* on March 6, 1978.

Journals

Among the most important journals publishing poetry in the United States are:

Antaeus. Daniel Halpern, ed. 1 West 30 St., New York, New York 10001.

Carleton Miscellany. Carleton College, Northfield, Minnesota 55057.

The Hudson Review. F. Morgan, ed. 65 East 55th St., New York, New York 10022.

The Massachusetts Review. Memorial Hall, University of Massachusetts, Amherst, Massachusetts 01002.

New York Quarterly. William Packard, ed. P.O. Box 2415 Grand Central Station, New York, New York 10017.

The Paris Review. 541 East 72 St., New York, New York 10021.

Partisan Review. I Richardson St., Rutgers University, New Brunswick, New Jersey 08903.

Poetry (Chicago). John Frederick Nims, ed. 1228 North Dearborn Parkway, Chicago, Illinois 60610.

Prairie Schooner. Bernice Slote, ed. 201 Andrews Hall, University of Nebraska, Lincoln, Nebraska 68588.

Sewanee Review. George Core, ed. University of the South, Sewanee, Tennessee 37375.

The Smith. Harry Smith, ed. 5 Beekman Street, New York, New York 10038.

South Carolina Review. Clemson University, Clemson, South Carolina 29631.

Virginia Quarterly Review. One West Range, Charlottesville, Virginia 22903.

Besides the above literary or "little" magazines, there are many wider circulating publications noted for their poetry. Among them are:

The Atlantic. Peter Davison, ed. 8 Arlington St., Boston, Massachusetts 02116.

The Nation. 333 Sixth Avenue, New York, New York 10014.

The New Republic. 1220 19th St. N.W., Washington, D.C. 20036.

The New Yorker. Howard Moss, Poetry Editor, 25 West 43 St., New York, New York 10036.

Anthologies

The most important anthologies include:

Allen, Donald M., ed. *The New American Poetry,* (New York: Grove, 1960).

Carroll, Paul. *The Poem in its Skin,* (Chicago: Follet. 1968) (also includes valuable commentaries).

Heyen, William., ed. *American Poets in 1976,* (Indianapolis: Bobbs-Merrill Co. 1975).

Halpern, Daniel., ed. *The American Poetry Anthology.* (New York: Avon, 1965).

Hall, D., Pack, R. & Simpson, L., eds. *New Poets of England and America.* (New York: New American Library, Meridian Books, 1962).

Poulin, A. Jr., ed. *Contemporary American Poetry.* Second Edition. (Boston: Houghton-Mifflin, 1975. (A third edition is due in 1980, with additional poets).

Stanford, Ann., ed. *The Women Poets in English.* (New York: McGraw-Hill, 1977).

Strand, Mark., ed. *The Contemporary American Poets.* (Cleveland: World, 1969).

Representative American Poets, 1979–1980

The following poets represent influential voices of American poetry at this time:

A.R. Ammons, John Ashbery, Imamu Amiri Baraka, Robert Bly, Gwendolyn Brooks, Robert Creeley, J.V. Cunningham, James Dickey, Robert Duncan, Allen Ginsberg, Richard Eberhart, Louise Glück, Anthony Hecht, Daniel Hoffman, Richard Hugo, Lawrence Ferlinghetti, David Ignatow, Donald Justice, Kenneth Koch, Galway Kinnell, Maxine Kumin, Stanley Kunitz, Philip Levine, Denise Levertov, John Logan, Archibald MacLeish, James Merrill, William Meredith, W.S. Merwin, Howard Nemerov, Kenneth Rexroth, Adrienne Rich, Karl Shapiro, Charles Simic, Louis Simpson, William Jay Smith, W.D. Snodgrass, Garry Snyder, William Stafford, Mark Strand, Ann Stanford, May Swenson, David Wagoner, Robert Penn Warren, Reed Whittemore, and Richard Wilbur.

Critical Studies

The most valuable critical studies of recent years include:

Dickey, James. *Babel to Byzantium: Poets and Poetry Now.* (New York: Farrar, Straus & Giroux, 1968).

Howard, Richard. *Alone with America.* (New York, Atheneum, 1969).

Hungerford, Edward B., ed. *Poets in Progress: Critical Prefaces to Thirteen Modern American Poets.* (Evanston: Northwestern University Press, 1967).

Jarrell, Randall. *Poetry and the Age.* (New York: Knopf. 1965).

Kalstone, David. *Five Temperaments.* (New York: Oxford, 1977).

Kherdian, David. *Six San Francisco Poets.* (Fresno: The Giligian Press. 1969).

Mazzaro, Jerome, ed. *Modern American Poetry.* (New York: David McKay Co. 1970).

Mills, Ralph J., Jr. *Cry of the Human.* (Urbana: University of Illinois Press, 1974).

Nemerov, Howard, ed. *Poets on Poetry.* (New York: Basic Books, 1961).

————. *Reflexions on Poetry and Poetics.* (New Brunswick: Rutgers University Press, 1972).

Ostroff, Anthony, ed. *The Contemporary Poet as Artist and Critic.* (Boston: Little, Brown and Co. 1964).

Parkinson, Thomas, ed. *A Casebook on the Beat,* (New York: Crowell, 1961).

Pierce, Roy Harvey. *The Continuity of American Poetry,* (Princeton: Princeton University Press, 1961).

Poulin, A., Jr., ed. *Making in All Its Forms,* (New York: Dutton, 1974).

Rexroth, Kenneth. *American Poetry in the Twentieth Century,* (New York: The Seabury Press, 1973).

Rosenthal, M.L. *The New Poets: American and British Poetry Since World War II,* (New York: Oxford University Press, 1962).

Stepanchev, Stephen. *American Poetry Since 1945,* (New York: Harper & Row, 1965).

Writers at Work: The Paris Review Interviews, (New York: The Viking Press. Second Series, 1965; Third Series, 1967; Fourth Series, 1974).

The Supreme Court of the United States: A Bibliographical Essay

ARTHUR S. MILLER

□One of the most studied but least understood of American governmental institutions is the Supreme Court of the United States. Thousands of articles and hundreds of books and monographs have been written about it. In the main, though not entirely, these studies discuss what the Court does—its decisions—rather than the High Bench as an institution. Those decisions are law, much of which is constitutional law. That law cannot realistically be separated from the 101 men who since 1789 have sat upon the Court. The Supreme Court is what it does; and what it does is to issue on the order of 150 decisions "on the merits" each year, while summarily denying review in the approximately 4000 other cases that are annually filed. The decisions on the merits have a definite, albeit immeasurable, impact upon American society. (The decisions of the Court are published in bound volumes by the Government Printing Office, Washington, D.C. There are approximately 430 at this time.)

This essay is directed toward the law as announced by the Court, insofar as it relates to American society, and to the Court's institutional position: its history, the Justices as individuals, and the interrelations of law and politics in the Court's operations. With some exceptions, only books are mentioned; references to the massive periodical literature, mostly on law rather than the Court as a segment of American government, may be found in the *Index to Legal Periodicals, Social Sciences Index, Readers Guide to Periodical Literature,* and the *New York Times*

Index. As with any other governmental institution, the Supreme Court is fair game for commentary, often slashing and critical, from anyone who has both the capacity to write and an available medium for publication.

Despite the immense literature on the Court, several lacunae exist in knowledge about its operations. (These will be mentioned below.) The main source of information about the Court is what the Justices choose to tell us, principally in their opinions, but at times in off-bench statements and in the collected papers that some leave behind. There are several reasons for the failures of scholarship. First, the Supreme Court is in its internal operations one of the most secretive of all governmental organizations. Walter F. Murphy's *Elements of Judicial Strategy** (Chicago: University of Chicago Press, 1964) is a pioneering attempt to probe the Court's internal mysteries. On the lack of information about the Court and its operations, see Arthur S. Miller and D. S. Sastri, "Secrecy and the Supreme Court: On the Need for Piercing the Red Velour Curtain," 22 *Buffalo Law Review* 799 (1973). Some of the better, albeit incomplete, accounts of the Court may be found in biographies of the Justices; leading examples are listed below.

Another reason for the failure of scholarship is the inability of those who live far from Washington, D.C., where the Supreme Court sits, to be able routinely to observe it at close hand. These scholars, accordingly, have only the opinions of the Justices as a data base. The third reason overlaps with the second: the symbolic role of the Court, which many think ought to be shrouded in mystery in order to retain its power and prestige. See, however, William Ray Forrester, "Are We

Arthur S. Miller has been Professor of Law at George Washington University since 1961. He has also taught at Emory University, and lectured at many universities and institutions in America and abroad. His consulting activities include work for the Senate Select Committee on Presidential Campaign Activities (1973–74), for which he was Chief Consultant; the Senate Subcommittee on Separation of Powers (1970–74); and the Commission on Congress and the Control of American Foreign Policy (1974). In addition to numerous articles, his publications include Racial Discrimination and Private Education: A Legal Analysis (1957); The Supreme Court and American Capitalism (1968); The Supreme Court and the Living Constitution (1969); The Modern Corporate State: Private Governments and the American Constitution (1976); Presidential Power (1977); and The Supreme Court: Myth and Reality (1978).

Ready for Truth in Judging?," 63 *American Bar Association Journal* 1212 (1977), arguing, as do Miller and Sastri (above), for more public knowledge about the Court and its operations.

A final, and again overlapping, factor contributes to the failure of scholarship—the fact that many who write about the American judicial system proceed on the assumption that it adheres to an idealistic model of the judiciary often attributed to Blackstone. That assumption is criticized in Judith Shklar, *Legalism* (Cambridge, Mass.: Harvard University Press, 1964), and Arthur S. Miller, *The Supreme Court: Myth and Reality* (Westport, Conn.: Greenwood Press, 1978). [For a somewhat comparable analysis of the British courts, pioneering in its scope, see J. A. G. Griffith, *The Politics of the Judiciary* * (Manchester: Manchester University Press; London: Fontana Paperback, 1977).] That focus of scholarly activity contributes in large part to an inability to perceive, and thus to study, all parts of the Supreme Court's activities.

Legal periodicals in the United States number in the hundreds. Many publish articles about the Supreme Court; however, these articles are mainly about its decisions (the law). Some of the more important constitutional decisions are parsed with an intensity similar to that of the medieval scholastics who pored over Aristotle and wrote learned exegeses on what he said, rather than observing contemporary political phenomena. So it is with those who write about the Court for the law journals; the opinions of the Justices are dissected in long, heavily footnoted, and often badly-written expositions. These authors tediously examine all of the nuances of language that the Justices use, hoping to find in that superficial analysis a Rosetta Stone to greater knowledge about the Court. Such writings are often exercises in futility. Even so, some of them are valuable. Perhaps the best appears in the *Harvard Law Review,* which each November publishes an analysis of the Court's activities during the previous term (which runs from October of one year through June of the following year). Included are statistics of the Court's work during that term. Another example is *The Supreme Court Review,* published annually by the University of Chicago Press in a hardbound volume. Included each year are several essays, all by professionals, most of which discuss specific decisions; others, however, take a broader view. [An analysis of American legal periodicals and their shortcomings may be found in Arthur S. Miller, "The Law Journals," *Change; The Magazine of Higher Learning,* Vol. 5, No. 10 (Winter, 1973–74).]

HISTORY AND THE SUPREME COURT

No up-to-date history of the Supreme Court exists. Now in the process of being written, however, is a multi-volume study commissioned under the terms of the will of Justice Oliver Wendell Holmes. Three volumes have been published: Julius Goebel, *Antecedents and Beginnings to 1801;* Charles Fairman, *Reconstruction and Reunion, 1864–88;* and Carl B. Swisher, *The Taney Period, 1836–64* (all three volumes are published by Macmillan Co. in New York). This series, when completed (eight additional volumes have been commissioned), should be the definitive history of the Court—although, again, the studies thus far published tend to be orthodox examinations of judicial doctrine rather than inquiries into the High Bench as an on-going governmental institution. There is little inquiry into the

Court's impact on society—on, that is, the attitudes and behavior patterns of the American people.

Older interpretations, now out of date but still useful for the period they cover, are Charles Warren, *The Supreme Court in United States History* (Boston: Little, Brown, revised ed., 1935) (traces the Court's history to 1918); and Homer C. Hockett, *The Constitutional History of the United States* (New York: Macmillan, 1939). For those who want a brief, yet complete account of the Court's history, Carl B. Swisher, *American Constitutional Development* (Boston: Houghton, Mifflin, revised ed., 1954) is well done. For a much shorter yet insightful exposition see Robert McCloskey, *The American Supreme Court** (Chicago: University of Chicago Press, 1960). Others worth consulting include: Alfred Kelly and Winfred Harbison, *The American Constitution—Its Origin and Development* (New York: Norton & Co., 5th ed., 1976); Alpheus Thomas Mason, *The Supreme Court from Taft to Warren** (Baton Rouge: Louisiana State University Press, revised ed., 1968); Wallace Mendelson, *Capitalism, Democracy and the Supreme Court* (New York: Appelton-Century-Crofts, 1960); and Robert H. Jackson, *The Struggle for Judicial Supremacy* (New York: Alfred A. Knopf, 1941).

THE JUSTICES AS INDIVIDUALS

Of the men who have sat upon the Supreme Court, many are completely unknown today; their exploits, such as they were, are unheralded and unsung. They were, in brief, mediocre lawyers who were placed on the bench because their philosophies coincided with those of Presidents, and served their undistinguished careers with little public and no historical notice. Not so, however, for the giants of Supreme Court history; several dozen books have been written about them. Of these, two are particularly noteworthy for their revelations about the internal operations of the Court: Alpheus Thomas Mason, *Harlan Fiske Stone: Pillar of the Law* (New York: Viking Press, 1956) and J. Woodford Howard, *Mr. Justice Murphy: A Political Biography* (Princeton: Princeton University Press, 1968). Mason's biography of Chief Justice Stone merits special attention, for it was criticized by several reviewers for telling too much about the internal operations of the Court. The Murphy biography is somewhat less revealing, but nonetheless still rewarding reading for those who wish to learn about the High Bench in the critical period of the 1940s.

Whether the Court should be treated so deferentially without probing its internal mysteries, as those who criticized Professor Mason asserted, is a matter of some dispute. But there is little discussion in the literature. The best defense of the orthodox position of keeping such matters secret is Paul Mishkin, "The High Court, the Great Writ, and the Due Process of Time and Law," 79 *Harvard Law Review* 56 (1965). The contrary view is expressed in Arthur S. Miller and Alan W. Scheflin, "The Power of the Supreme Court in the Age of the Positive State: A Preliminary Excursus," 1967 *Duke Law Journal* 273, 522. Now being written is a "muckraking" expose of the Court and the way the Justices operate, by Bob Woodward and Scott Armstrong, reporters for the *Washington Post* (to be published in 1978).

Most biographies of the Justices tend to be uncritical encomia, written with a rather breathless style of awe and reverence. Nonetheless, some are rewarding reading. Among them are Gerald T. Dunne, *Hugo Black and the Judicial Revolution* (New York: Simon and Schuster, 1977); Alpheus Thomas Mason, *Brandeis: A Free Man's Life* (New York: Viking Press, 1946); William O. Douglas, *Go East, Young Man** (New York: Random House, 1974) (autobiography of the Justice who served longest on the Court); Robert Shogan, *A Question of Judgment: The Fortas Case and the Struggle for the Supreme Court* (Indianapolis, Indiana: Bobbs-Merrill & Co., 1972); Carl B. Swisher, *Stephen J. Field, Craftsman of the Law** (Washington, D.C.: Brookings Institution, 1930; Phoenix paperback, 1969); Philip B . Kurland, *Mr. Justice Frankfurter and the Constitution* (Chicago: University of Chicago Press, 1971); Max Lerner, *The Mind and Faith of Justice Holmes* (Boston: Little, Brown & Co., 1943); L. Baker, *John Marshall: A Life in Law* (New York: Macmillan, 1974); and Gerald T. Dunne, *Justice Joseph Story and the Rise of the Supreme Court* (New York: Simon and Schuster, 1971).

Appointment of Supreme Court Justices is by the President, but each must be confirmed by the Senate (by majority vote). First-rate accounts of the process may be found in Henry J. Abraham, *Justices and Presidents: A Political History of Appointments to the Supreme Court** (New York: Oxford University Press, 1974) and H. W. Chase, *Federal Judges: The Appointing Process* (Minneapolis: University of Minnesota Press, 1973). It is fair to say that those selected reflect the value preferences of the Presidents, as tempered by the need for Senate approval.

LAW, POLITICS, AND THE SUPREME COURT

Orthodox thinking about the Supreme Court still maintains that the Court is a "legal" rather than a "political" institution. But that pretense has long been under attack. There is a growing realization, to the point of well-nigh unanimous acknowledgment, that the Justices do in fact make policy—legislate however much some instances of judicial legislation may be deplored. The orthodoxy denies the legitimacy under the Constitution of judicial law-making. American law students, furthermore, still study the Court and its decisions as they do any other court of law. Teaching materials in the law schools by and large are reproductions of Supreme Court decisions, larded with some commentary—which often is an exposition of other decisions. For one of the better coursebooks used in law schools, see Gerald Gunther, *Cases and Materials on Constitutional Law* (Mineola, New York: Foundation Press, 9th ed., 1975). The most comprehensive treatment of the law of the Constitution may be found in Lester S. Jayson et al., *The Constitution of the United States of America, Analysis and Interpretation* (Washington, D.C.: Government Printing Office, 1973; supplemented biennially with pocket parts). See also Laurence Tribe, *American Constitutional Law* (Mineola, New York: Foundation Press, 1978).

One must consult texts, often but not always written by political scientists rather than lawyers, to be able to learn about the Supreme Court's law-making proclivities, set against those of other governmental agencies. Perhaps the leading such treatment is Martin Shapiro, *Law and Politics in the Supreme Court* (New York: Free Press, 1964). Shapiro's views are critically analyzed in Jan Deutsch, "Neutrality, Legitimacy, and the Supreme Court: Some Intersections Between Law and Political Science," 20 *Stanford Law Review* 169 (1968). A more general, and comparative, view of the propensity of judges to make law is Henry J. Abraham, *The Judicial Process: An Introductory Analysis of the Courts of the United States, England, and France** (New York: Oxford University Press, 3rd edition, 1975). Victor Rosenblum, *Law as a Political Instrument* (New York: Doubleday & Co., 1955) is a useful brief introduction. See also C. Herman Pritchett and Alan F. Westin, editors, *The Third Branch of Government: Eight Cases in Constitutional Politics* (New York: Harcourt, Brace & World, Inc., 1963). Say the editors: Those "who are limited solely to the edited opinions of Supreme Court Justices and expert commentary on those opinions will not be able to obtain a clear image of [the] modern court and its role in the American political process."

Since at least 1803, the Court has been under attack for its assertion of a power to rule on the validity of the actions of other governmental officials, state and federal. Two such assaults, proceeding from widely divergent viewpoints, are of particular interest. Louis Boudin, *Government by Judiciary* (New York: Godwin & Co., 1932, two volumes) develops in a thorough and scholarly way the manner in which the Justices at one period struck down socio-economic legislation. During the time of roughly 1885 to 1937, they operated as "the first authoritative faculty of political economy in the world's history," as economist John R. Commons put it in his *Legal Foundations of Capitalism* (New York: Macmillan, 1924; *Madison, Wisconsin: University of Wisconsin Press paperback, 1959). Boudin's was an attack from the American liberal-left on a conservative Court. To his book

Courtesy, Library of Congress

This drawing of the Supreme Court in session, by Carl J. Becker, appeared in *Harper's Weekly*, January 28, 1888.

should be compared Raoul Berger, *Government by Judiciary; The Transformation of the Fourteenth Amendment* (Cambridge, Mass.: Harvard University Press, 1977). Berger bitterly criticizes the Justices for not following what he considers to be the only valid theory of constitutional interpretation—that of ascertaining the intentions of the Members of Congress who drafted the Fourteenth Amendment, and following it rigorously. That theory is refuted in Arthur S. Miller, "An Inquiry into the Relevance of the Intentions of the Founding Fathers," 27 *Arkansas Law Review* 583 (1973). Berger's book is a right-wing assault on the Court for being too "liberal" in the area of civil rights and liberties.

Perhaps the most influential single essay along similar lines is Herbert Wechsler, "Toward Neutral Principles of Constitutional Law," 75 *Harvard Law Review* 1 (1959), reprinted in Herbert Wechsler, *Principles, Politics and Fundamental Law* (Cambridge, Mass.: Harvard University Press, 1961). Refutation of that position may be found in Arthur S. Miller, *The Supreme Court: Myth and Reality* (Westport, Conn.: Greenwood Press, 1978), and in Eugene V. Rostow, *The Sovereign Prerogative: The Supreme Court and the Quest for Law* (New Haven, Conn.: Yale University Press, 1962). See also Charles Black, *The People and the Court: Judicial Review in a Democracy* (New York: Macmillan, 1960).

The late Professor Alexander Bickel of the Yale Law School was one of the more influential commentators on the Court and its activities. His several books all merit attention, particularly *The Least Dangerous Branch: The Supreme Court at the Bar of Politics* (Indianapolis, Indiana: Bobbs-Merrill, 1963) and *The Supreme Court and the Idea of Progress* (New York: Harper & Row, 1970). Two rather more critical analyses are Charles S. Hyneman, *The Supreme Court on Trial* (New York: Atherton Press, 1963) and Philip B. Kurland, *Politics, the Constitution, and the Warren Court* (Chicago: University of Chicago Press, 1970). A balanced account, written by a political scientist whose early death meant the loss of one of the better minds, is Robert G. McCloskey, *The Modern Supreme Court* (Cambridge, Mass.: Harvard University Press, 1972). Also useful is Richard Y. Funston, *Constitutional Counterrevolution? The Warren Court and the Burger Court: Judicial Policy Making in Modern America* (New York: Schenkman Publishing Co., Inc., 1977).

That the Supreme Court has been under fire, at times quite heavy, does not mean that it does not have its defenders. These defenses, as with the attacks, tend to vary with the personal predilections of the author; they are, in sum, of a distinct ideological bent. One of the more notable recent attacks on the Court, which is simultaneously a stout statement of approval of the Court under Chief Justice Earl Warren (1953–1969), is Leonard Levy, *Against the Law: The Nixon Court and Criminal Justice* (New York: Harper & Row, 1974). Professor Levy also edited a valuable collection of essays, *Judicial Review and the Supreme Court: Selected Essays* (New York: Harper & Row, 1967).

Perhaps the most thoughtful and balanced analysis of the Court's law-making is Louis Lusky, *By What Right? A Commentary on the Supreme Court's Power to Revise the Constitution* (Charlottesville, Va.: Michie Co., 1975). In the same vein, although rather troubled in his defense of the Court, are two books by Archibald Cox: *The Role of the Supreme Court in American Government* (New York: Oxford University Press, 1976) and *The Warren Court: Constitutional Decision as an*

Instrument of Reform* (Cambridge, Mass.: Harvard University Press, 1968). For treatment by a judicious political scientist of the manner in which the Justices view their modern role, see Henry J. Abraham, *Freedom and the Court: Civil Rights and Liberties in the United States** (New York: Oxford University Press, 3rd edition, 1977). Professor Abraham's book is a study of the reconciliations a polity that calls itself democratic must make between the persistent demands for individual freedom and the rights of the community. In the same vein is John P. Roche, *Courts and Rights: The American Judiciary in Action** (New York: Random House, 2nd edition, 1966). And for a trenchant, hard-hitting essay in defense of his constitutional decisions, see Hugo L. Black, *A Constitutional Faith* (New York: Alfred A. Knopf, 1968) and "The Bill of Rights," 35 *New York University Law Review* 866 (1960). On the other hand, one of the best-known of American judges, Learned Hand, wrote in *The Bill of Rights* (Cambridge, Mass.: Harvard University Press, 1958; New York: Atheneum, 1964), a penetrating evaluation of the Court's work built around his belief in "judicial self-restraint."

The American people have never been quite willing fully to accept the fact of judicial law-making. But it is a fact and will continue to be a fact as long as the Court exists. Two particularly good law-journal essays on the question are Robert A. Dahl, "Decision-Making in a Democracy: The Supreme Court as a National Policy-Maker," 6 *Journal of Public Law* 279 (1957) and Judge J. Skelly Wright, "The Role of the Supreme Court in a Democratic Society—Judicial Activism or Restraint?," 54 *Cornell Law Review* 1 (1968). And see Louis Kohlmeier, *God Save This Honorable Court* (New York: Scribners, 1973).

Since all concede that the Supreme Court makes formal law, the question that is immediately presented is: What difference does it make in the mental attitudes and behavior patterns of the American people when the Court issues a decree? There can be no question that some behavior patterns, particularly of some public officials, are altered; but how much, when, and in what circumstances was little studied in the past. "It would be difficult to think of another scholarly profession which speaks as little of the consequences of its acts . . . and as much about the circumstances of its own behavior," said Dean Edward Levi in "The Nature of Judicial Reasoning," 32 *University of Chicago Law Review* 395 (1965). The need for studying the consequences of judicial decisions is adumbrated in Arthur S. Miller, "On the Need for 'Impact Analysis' of Supreme Court Decisions," 53 *Georgetown Law Journal* 374 (1965).

In the past two decades, a growing number of studies probe various aspects of judicial law-making and its impact on the social order, but it is fair to say that none has as yet presented a comprehensive theory accepted by all. See, however, Theodore Becker and M. M. Feeley, editors, *The Impact of Supreme Court Decisions** (New York: Oxford University Press, 2nd edition, 1973); Kenneth Dolbeare and P. E. Hammond, *The School Prayer Decisions: From Court Policy to Local Practice* (Chicago: University of Chicago Press, 1971); R. M. Johnson, *The Dynamics of Compliance: Supreme Court Decision-Making from A New Perspective* (Evanston, Illinois: Northwestern University Press, 1968); Stephen Wasby, *The Impact of the United States Supreme Court* (Homewood, Illinois: Dorsey Press, 1970); and David R. Manwaring et al., *The Supreme Court as Policy-Maker: Three Studies on the Impact of Judicial Decisions* (Carbondale, Illinois: Public Affairs Research Bureau of Southern Illinois University, 1968). See also Alan F. Westin,

*Anatomy of a Constitutional Law Case** (New York: Macmillan, 1958), setting forth in great detail all aspects of the famous "Steel Seizure Case" of 1952.

Little scholarly attention has been accorded the inputs to the adversary process, which the Supreme Court adheres to, other than to restate past precedents and similar matter. Informing the judicial mind, however, "is one of the most complicated questions," said Justice Felix Frankfurter during oral argument in Brown v. Board of Education, 347 U.S. 483 (1954). The entire oral argument in that famous case is reproduced in Leon Friedman, *Argument* (New York: Chelsea House, 1969). A study of the general problem is Arthur S. Miller and Jerome A. Barron, "The Supreme Court, the Adversary System, and the Flow of Information to the Justices: A Preliminary Inquiry," 61 *Virginia Law Review* 1187 (1975). See also, Anthony Lewis, *Gideon's Trumpet** (New York: Random House, 1964), setting forth the manner in which the case of Gideon v. Wainwright, 372 U.S. 335 (1963) was argued. And see Justice William J. Brennan, "Working at Justice," in Alan F. Westin, editor, *An Autobiography of the Supreme Court* (New York: Macmillan, 1963); Alexander Bickel, *The Unpublished Opinions of Mr. Justice Brandeis* (Cambridge, Mass.: Harvard University Press, 1957; *Chicago: University of Chicago Press, 1967); Dean Alfange, "The Relevance of Legislative Facts in the Constitutional Law," 114 *University of Pennsylvania Law Review*

637 (1966); Paul Rosen, *The Supreme Court and Social Science* (Urbana, Illinois: University of Illinois Press, 1972); Kenneth Karst, "Legislative Facts in Constitutional Law," 1960 *Supreme Court Review* 75; and Learned Hand, "Sources of Tolerance," 79 *University of Pennsylvania Law Review* 1 (1930).

Two other intellectual activities merit mention. The first is the application—the updating—of the Constitution to times of emergency. In this connection, see Clinton Rossiter, *Constitutional Dictatorship: Crisis Government in the Modern Democracies* (Princeton, New Jersey: Princeton University Press, 1948); and the updated book by the same author, *The Supreme Court and the Commander in Chief**

Courtesy, Library of Congress

A "chorus of grief-stricken conservatives" react to the appointment of Louis Brandeis to the Supreme Court. Drawn by Nelson Greene, *Puck,* February 19, 1916.

354   Sources for American Studies

(Ithaca, New York: Cornell University Press, 1976, expanded edition with an introductory note and additional text by Richard P. Longaker). See also Paul L. Murphy, *The Constitution in Crisis Time, 1918–1969** (New York: Harper & Row, 1972); Edward S. Corwin, *Total War and the Constitution* (New York: Alfred A. Knopf, 1947); and Arthur S. Miller, *Presidential Power* (St. Paul, Minnesota: West Publishing Co., 1977).

A second trend is the application of game theory and Guttman scaling to Supreme Court decisions. See, for illustrative examples, Glendon Schubert, *Quantitative Analysis of Judicial Behavior* (Glencoe, Illinois: The Free Press, 1959) and *Judicial Behavior: A Reader in Theory and Research* (New York: Rand McNally & Co., 1964), and also by the same author, "Policy Without Law," 14 *Stanford Law Review* 284 (1962). There are other examples of the genre, but it is fair to say that this type of political behavioralism is dying out—principally because it is a form of scholarly astrology. It merely substitutes a pseudo-scientific alchemy for the more traditional linguistic analyses. The matter is mentioned only because of its faddish nature. See, however, Sheldon Goldman and Thomas P. Jahnige, *The Federal Courts as a Political System** (New York: Harper & Row, 2nd edition, 1976) for an analysis of how the federal judicial system works within the larger context of American politics.

Finally, some theoretical studies of the jurisprudence of the Supreme Court are quite valuable, each in a different way. Notable examples include Fred Cahill, *Judicial Legislation: A Study in American Legal Theory* (New York: Ronald, 1952); Edmond Cahn, editor, *Supreme Court and Supreme Law** (Bloomington, Indiana: Indiana University Press, 1954); Wolfgang Friedmann, *Law in a Changing Society* (Harmondsworth, England: Penguin Books, second edition, 1972); Theodore L. Becker, *Political Behavioralism and Modern Jurisprudence* (New York: Rand McNally & Co., 1964); Karl Llewellyn, *Jurisprudence: Realism in Theory and Practice* (Chicago: University of Chicago Press, 1962); Wilfred Rumble, *American Legal Realism: Skepticism, Reform, and the Judicial Process* (Ithaca, New York: Cornell University Press, 1968); Julius Stone, *Social Dimensions of Law and Justice* (Stanford, California: Stanford University Press, 1966); and Morris Raphael Cohen, *Reason and Law* (New York: Free Press, 1950).

Oddly, no up-to-date bibliography of the Supreme Court exists. Most of the books and articles cited in this article, however, contain extensive footnotes and, at times, bibliographical data. Of special note in that regard is Henry J. Abraham, *The Judicial Process: An Introductory Analysis of the Courts of the United States, England and France** (New York: Oxford University Press, 3rd edition, 1975). See also Fannie J. Klein, *The Administration of Justice in the Courts* (Dobbs Ferry, New York: Oceana Publications, 1976, two volumes) and Dorothy Tompkins, *The Supreme Court of the United States: A Bibliography* (Berkeley, California: Bureau of Public Administration, University of California, 1959).□

indicates paperback availability

SUPPLEMENT

by Arthur S. Miller

Scholarly and popular interest in the Supreme Court of the United States has hit an all-time high. In late 1979, publication of Bob Woodward and Scott Armstrong, The Brethren: Inside the Supreme Court (New York: Simon and Schuster, 1979), catapulted the justices into nationwide attention. The volume is the most revealing account of a sitting Court ever published. It is not, however, a scholarly book; the authors are "investigative" reporters for the Washington Post who managed to pierce the facade of secrecy of the High Bench. Because some, perhaps many, of their facts are perhaps not facts at all but mere speculation, the book is controversial. An insightful review is Anthony Lewis, "Supreme Court Confidential," The New York Review of Books, Feb. 7, 1980, p. 3.

Of much more value is the Congressional Quarterly's Guide to the U.S. Supreme Court (Washington: Congressional Quarterly, Inc., 1979). In 1022 large, double-columned pages, the editor, Elder Witt, has produced a highly valuable book, not only for the layman but for students of the Court. It is an invaluable reference book, one that is sure to be of more lasting significance than The Brethren.

A number of specialized books and articles merit attention. Lucius J. and Twiley W. Barker, Civil Liberties and the Constitution: Cases and Commentaries (third ed., Englewood Cliffs, New Jersey: Prentice-Hall, 1978), is a useful compilation of a fast-growing area of constitutional law and the Supreme Court's importance in its development. Robert Stern and Eugene Gressman, Supreme Court Practice (fourth ed., Washington: Bureau of National Affairs, 1978), is for the lawyer-specialist; it is indispensable for those who practice before the Court. Herman Pritchett, The American Constitution (third ed., New York: McGraw-Hill Book Co., 1977), is for the undergraduate student but quite valuable as an introduction to the work of the Supreme Court. Gerhard Casper and Richard A. Posner, *The Workload of the Supreme Court (Chicago: American Bar Foundation, 1976), deals with an important current controversy--whether the annual caseload of the justices (about 4000 filed each year) places too onerous a burden on the nine men.

Older studies, left out of the previous essay because of space limitations, that are of value include Paul A. Freund, *The Supreme Court of the United States: Its Business, Purposes, and Performances (Cleveland: World Publishing Co, 1961); and Charles G. Haines, The American Doctrine of Judicial Supremacy (second ed., Berkeley: University of California Press, 1932). The Freund volume is a Meridian Books paperback.

Discussions of the Supreme Court's role in effecting social and legal change in the United States may be found in Gary J. Jacobsohn, Pragmatism, Statesmanship, and the Supreme Court (Ithaca: Cornell University Press, 1977); and in Arthur S. Miller, Social Change and Fundamental Law: America's Evolving Constitution (Westport, Conn.: Greenwood Press, 1979). Owen M. Fiss, The Civil Rights Injunction (Bloomington: Indiana University Press, 1978), is a brief but important analysis of the growing propensity of federal courts to impose affirmative constitutional duties on government. An important analogous study is Robert Cover & Owen M. Fiss, The Structure of Procedure (Mineola, New York: Foundation Press, Inc., 1979). For a statistical record of the first hundred men to serve on the Supreme Court, giving full biographical data plus a rating of their judicial records, see Albert P. Blaustein and Roy Mersky, The First One Hundred Justices: Statistical Studies on the Supreme Court of the United States (Hamden, Conn.: The Shoe String Press, Inc., 1978). Only Justice John Paul Stevens, the 101st member of the Court, is not in the compilation.

Lon L. Fuller, "The Forms and Limits of Adjudication," 92 Harvard Law Review 353 (1978), is an essay that has had considerable influence for twenty years in manuscript form. It deals with litigation as a form of social ordering. Other important essays include Martin Shapiro, "The Supreme Court: From Warren to Burger," in Anthony King, ed., *The New American Political System (Washington: American Enterprise Institute, 1978); Owen M. Fiss, "The Forms of Justice," 93 Harvard Law Review 1 (1979); Chester James Antieau, "The Jurisprudence of Interests as a Method of Constitutional Adjudication," 27 Case Western Reserve Law Review 825 (1977); and three by John Hart Ely: "Toward a Representation-Reinforcing Mode of Judicial Review," Maryland Law Review 451 (1978); "Constitutional Interpretivism: Its Allure and Impossibility," 53 Indiana Law Journal 399 (1978); and "On Discovering Fundamental Values," 92 Harvard Law Review 5 (1978).

M. Judd Harmon, ed., Essays on the Constitution of the United States (Port Washington, New York, 1978), has several valuable essays on the Supreme Court, including Henry J. Abraham, "The Supreme Court in the Evolving Political Process"; Martin Shapiro, "The Constitution and Economic Rights"; C. Herman Pritchett, "Judicial Supremacy from Marshall to Burger"; and Walter F. Murphy, "The Art of Constitutional Interpretation: A Preliminary Showing." A symposium in Volume 6, No. 4 of the Hastings Constitutional Law Quarterly (1979) contains several essays criticizing Raoul Berger's Government by Judiciary: The Transformation of the Fourteenth Amendment (Cambridge, Mass.: Harvard University Press, 1977), as well as Berger's reply thereto. And in Stephen Halpern & Charles Lamb, eds., Supreme Court Activism and Restraint, the Columbia University Press will publish in 1981 a number of essays analyzing the controversy of "judicial activism."

The following books, all published by Greenwood Press, are useful additions: Howard Ball, Judicial Craftsmanship or Fiat? Direct Overturn by the United States Supreme Court (1977); John Brigham, Constitutional Language: An Interpretation of Judicial Decision (1978); Thomas B. Marvell, Appellate Courts and Lawyers: Information Gathering in the Adversary System (1978); and John E. Semonche, Charting the Future: The Supreme Court Responds to a Changing Society 1890-1920 (1978). Professor Ely's articles, mentioned above, are included in Democracy and Distrust: A Theory of Judicial Review (Cambridge, Mass.: Harvard University Press, 1980). In Stephen J. Wasby, *The Supreme Court in the Federal Judicial System (New York: Holt, Rinehart and Wilson, 1978), a behavioral scientist analyzes the Court systemically. John R. Schmidhauser, Judges and Justices: The Federal Appellate Judiciary (Boston: Little, Brown and Co., Inc., 1979), analyzes federal courts, including the Supreme Court, using a "conceptual framework ...adapted from Max Weber's theory positing the close relationship of independent, professional judiciaries and market capitalism."

Theodore J. Lowi, *The End of Liberalism: The Second Republic of the United States (second ed., New York: W.W. Norton, 1979), is a provocative discussion of the shortcomings of "interest-group liberalism" and a call for "juridical democracy" led by the Supreme Court. Finally, Arthur S. Miller, "Constitutional Law: Crisis Government Becomes the Norm," 39 Ohio State Law Journal 736 (1978), forecasts the development of constitutional law and the role of the Supreme Court in American government.

Each of the essays and books mentioned above have either bibliographies or extensive footnotes, or both. Many articles are published about the Supreme Court in law journals and political science reviews. Most are tedious exegeses of Supreme Court opinions, with the author splitting hairs with the opinion of the Justices--often concluding that a decision was correct but for the wrong reasons.

The debate about the Court and its position in the American constitutional order shows no sign of diminishing. But the writers,

speaking generally, are discussing an organ of government that does
not now, did not in the past, and will not in the future have
nearly so much political power as the writers assume. The twentieth
century, and surely the twenty-first, belongs to the executive--
in the United States and elsewhere. A useful study for purposes
of seeing the American presidency in perspective with the Supreme
Court and Congress is Richard M. Pious, *The American Presidency
(New York: Basic Books, 1979). To understand the Court one must
understand the political process. Lowi's book, cited above, and
that by Pious are indispensable in that venture.

PART II

UPDATING AMERICAN STUDIES: TOPICS AND SOURCES

Recent Publications on American Religious History: A Bibliographical Essay and Review

DEWEY D. WALLACE, JR.

Henry F. May wrote in 1964, "For the study and understanding of American culture, the recovery of American religious history may well be the most important achievement of the last thirty years."[1] Allowing some margin for exaggeration in this remark, it was nonetheless true that in the 1950s and 1960s studies in American religious history reached a new maturity and were generally recognized as supplying a crucial dimension to the historical study of American society and culture. One of the principal features of this maturity was the recognition that American religious history could no longer be treated mainly as the history of different religious denominations in isolation from the whole culture (though denominational histories old and new continue to be useful for reference), but that the religiosity both of the particular

* This essay updates Sydney E. Ahlstrom's "Bibliography of American Religious History," *ASI* 11 (Autumn 1972).

denominations and of the American people apart from their more traditional religious bodies, was deeply interwoven with all the other threads of American life and history.

May also wrote in 1964 that "the recovery of American religious history has restored a knowledge of the mode, even the language, in which most Americans, during most of American history, did their thinking about human nature and destiny."[2] In the 1970s, that point does not seem to need arguing any longer, as an explosion of studies in American religious history testifies. Thus, if the preceding period saw a maturing in the study of American religious history and the recognition of religion's interconnection with other strands of the American experience, the last decade has produced an abundance of studies which assume that interconnection and probe it with increasing methodological sophistication.

Various methodologies are currently employed in the investigation of American religion, including the statistical and quantitative, the anthropological, the use of the phenomenological tools of the History of Religions, and more philosophical or theological approaches. But if any general tendency in method is discoverable, it has probably been away from that kind of intellectual and cultural history which was so important in launching the mature study of American religion (and which was perhaps best exemplified in the work of Perry Miller) and toward a more social-scientific approach. This methodological approach has been accompanied by a shift of focus from the ideas of leaders and theologians to the ideals and patterns of behavior of ordinary people, including those groups often slighted by an earlier historiography—women, blacks and other ethnic minorities, and members of less mainstream religious bodies.

In 1972 a comprehensive "Bibliography of American Religious History," prepared by Sydney E. Ahlstrom, appeared in the eleventh volume of *American Studies: An International Newsletter* (No. 1, Autumn), pp. 3-16, and was reprinted in Robert Harris Walker, ed., *American Studies: Topics and Sources* (Westport, Conn.: Greenwood Press, 1976), pp. 10-21. The books included in that earlier bibliography need not be mentioned again, and thus this bibliographical essay can be limited to a selection of studies of American religion written during the 1970s. Only where needed to fill gaps in the earlier bibliography, or to explain a trend by referring to earlier titles, have books published prior to 1970 been included. Articles in journals have been omitted, and source materials have been cited sparingly, mostly in edited collections; a list of the many recent facsimile reprints of colonial and nineteenth-century source materials in American religion would require a much larger scope.

Reference Works

Reference works useful in the study of American religion continue to appear. Nelson R. Burr's two-volume *A Critical Bibliography of Religion in America* (Princeton: Princeton Univ. Press, 1961), has been followed recently by Ernest R. Sandeen and Frederick Hale, *American Religion and Philosophy: A Guide to Informational Sources,* Vol. 5 in the American Studies Information

Guide Series (Detroit: Gale Research Co., 1978). Hale and Sandeen have provided judicious and succinct descriptions of the items included. Edwin Scott Gaustad's *Historical Atlas of Religion in America* has been revised (New York: Harper & Row, 1976), with significant new maps and charts, and is accompanied with two large fold-out color maps which are admirable for grasping the geography of American religion. An extremely useful new reference tool is Henry Warner Bowden, *Dictionary of American Religious Biography* (Westport, Conn.: Greenwood Press, 1977), which in 572 pages covers 425 names generally conceded to be significant in American religious history. Two appendices, listing his subjects by denomination and place of birth, provide quick glimpses of his data.

Also useful as reference works are handbooks surveying the many different American religious groups. Two new works of this sort have appeared to be set alongside a new edition of an old one. The old one is Frank S. Mead, *Handbook of Denominations* (Nashville: Abingdon Press, 1975), now in its sixth edition, which lists a number of American religious bodies alphabetically, with some classification by type, and provides basic factual information, including statistics on members and clergy. The changes made through its various editions have not been very ambitious and it is therefore inadequate for many newer religious groups. Recent efforts of a similar type have been far more ambitious. The nearly fifteen hundred pages of Arthur Carl Piepkorn, *Profiles in Belief, The Religious Bodies of the United States and Canada,* 4 vols. (New York: Harper & Row, 1977-1979), arranged for publication after Piepkorn's death by John H. Tietjen, use a very traditional typology of theological and ecclesiastical family to outline some of the history, but mostly the beliefs, of the major American Christian churches. Traditionally theological in its approach, it is nonetheless done with considerable learning and precision, but the more unusual cults are neglected. Full bibliographies are included. Quite different is the case with J. Gordon Melton, *The Encyclopedia of American Religions,* 2 vols. (Wilmington, N.C.: Consortium Books, 1978), which is not an alphabetical encyclopedia at all, but a much more thorough attempt to provide a complete typology of American religious bodies than is Piepkorn's. Including some 1200 groups, it provides nearly inaccessible information about small and barely recognized groups, including fifteen different "Flying Saucer Groups" and nineteen examples of "Neo-Paganism." It is thus an indispensable source for such things, but its treatment of the major religious groups breaks no new ground and falls short of Piepkorn's. An extensive index enhances its usefulness.

Surveys and Denominational Histories

The beginning of the decade saw the publication of Sydney E. Ahlstrom's masterful survey, *A Religious History of the American People** (New Haven: Yale University Press, 1972). By all odds this is the best survey, its usefulness enhanced by an excellent bibliography, but it has nonetheless been criticized, perhaps not altogether fairly, for mainly following the lines of earlier surveys rather than breaking new ground with a fresh approach. Ahlstrom's work did not end the production of such surveys, however, as Robert T. Handy's *A History of the Churches in the United States and Canada* (New York: Oxford Univ. Press, 1976; *1979), testifies. Jelling a lifetime of teaching about American religion into a perceptive treatment of the whole story, this work gains perspective from the inclusion of Canada, whose religious history parallels and intersects that of its southern neighbor at many points. This work raises the possibility of illuminating American religious history by a comparative approach to the study of religion in the various places which began as outposts of European colonialism.

A listing of more thematic surveys might properly begin with another book which profits from the combined treatment of religion in the United States and Canada, E.R. Norman, *The Conscience of the State in North America* (Cambridge: Univ. Press, 1968). This thin book focuses on church-state issues and argues that the pattern of the state's relationship to the churches in the United States was far more similar to British ways, as comparison with Canada shows, than commonly thought. Two rather small thematic surveys have appeared during the past decade in the Chicago History of American Religion series, *Dissent in American Religion,* * by Edwin Scott Gaustad (Chicago: Univ. of Chicago Press, 1973), and *American Religious Thought: A History,* * by William A. Clebsch (Chicago: Univ. of Chicago Press, 1973). Granted the acknowledged importance of dissidence in American religious history, Gaustad illuminates the story of American religion by attention to certain individuals and groups notorious for the difficulties they caused others. Clebsch's book concentrates on three major religious thinkers, Edwards, Emerson, and William James, each of whom, according to the author, sought "to divert American spirituality from its natural spillover into moralism by translating the religious impulse into being at home in the universe."

Russell E. Richey, ed., *Denominationalism* (Nashville: Abingdon, 1977), is a collection of essays around that important theme in American religion. A larger effort at thematic history is Cushing Strout, *The New Heavens and New Earth: Political Religion in America* (New York: Harper & Row, 1974; *1975), which proceeds as a dialogue carried on by the author with Tocqueville's comments about American religion. In the process, interesting points are made about the intertwining of religion and politics in America. More topical than thematic as surveys are two treatments of church and state relations in America: Elwyn A. Smith, *Religious Liberty in the United States: The Development of Church-State Thought Since the Revolutionary Era* * (Philadelphia: Fortress Press, 1972), and Richard F. Moran, *The Supreme Court and Religion* (New York: Free Press, 1972), a brief, objective history of that controverted subject. A number of excellent articles, drawn from various journals and collections, and many with strong thematic character, appear in John M. Mulder and John F. Wilson, eds., *Religion in American History: Interpretive Essays* * (Englewood Cliffs, N. J.: Prentice-Hall, 1978). *God's New Israel: Religious Interpretations of American Destiny,* * edited by Conrad Cherry (Englewood Cliffs, N. J.: Prentice-Hall, 1971), weaves sources and commentary around the theme of the subtitle.

Several volumes in a series intended for the general reader provide surveys of particular periods. Dewey D. Wallace, Jr., *The Pilgrims** (Wilmington, N. C.: Consortium Books, 1977), using the term "pilgrims" in a broad sense, covers both British background and the story of religion in the settlement of the colonies, focusing on the transformation of traditional patterns by a new situation. Martin E. Marty, *Religion, Awakening and Revolution** (Consortium Books, 1977), treats the latter part of the colonial period, especially the revolutionary era, as a "hinge" period in the formation of much that is distinctive in American religious attitudes. The first half of the nineteenth century in America is surveyed rather briefly by Louis B. Weeks, *A New Christian Nation** (Consortium Books, 1977), and the later part of the century more fully by Myron J. Fogde, *The Church Goes West** (Consortium, 1977). Also to be included among surveys of periods is Paul A. Carter, *The Spiritual Crisis of the Gilded Age* (De Kalb: Northern Illinois Univ. Press, 1971), which contains fascinating chapters on such matters as the religious dilemma created by evolution and anxiety over a future life.

Surveys of particular traditions and denominations continue to be produced and to take their places alongside older, standard works. Robert T. Handy, *A Christian America, Protestant Hopes and Historical Realities** (New York: Oxford Univ. Press, 1971), is an interpretive essay portraying the thwarting of Protestant expectations rather than a survey of Protestantism. Also strongly thematic, but more detailed as a survey, is Martin E. Marty, *Righteous Empire: The Protestant Experience in America** (New York: Dial Press, 1970). Among new additions to the shelves filled with traditional denominational histories are Thomas T. McAvoy, *History of the Catholic Church in the United States* (South Bend: Notre Dame Univ. Press, 1969); E. Clifford Nelson, *Lutheranism in North America 1914-1970* (Minneapolis: Augsburg, 1972); Frederick A. Norwood, *The Story of American Methodism* (Nashville: Abingdon, 1974); Robert A. Baker, *The Southern Baptist Convention and Its People,* 1607-1972 (Nashville: Broadman Press, 1974); Henry L. Feingold, *Zion in America: The Jewish Experience from Colonial Times to the Present** (New York: Twayne Publishers, 1974); and two continuations, the second volume on the Disciples of Christ by David Edwin Harrell, Jr., *The Social Sources of Division in the Disciples of Christ, 1865-1900* (Atlanta: Publishing Systems Inc., 1973), and the completion of Ernest Trice Thompson's *Presbyterians in the South* with second and third volumes (Richmond: John Knox, 1973). Books on some of the smaller American denominations will appear in later sections.

Puritanism and Its English Background

As useful as general surveys and denominational histories are, their scope is severely limited by their method. The most important elements in the study of American religion do not follow denominational lines, but are powerful impulses that work their way into the very stuff of American life, cutting across all distinctions of denomination. Thus most of the topics in the remainder of this essay represent impulses or movements which transcend the boundaries of particular groups. The most important and seminal studies in American religious history are those that identify some significance for American history and culture in the intersection of a particular religious impulse with some place, time, or group within the American experience.

Puritanism was such an impulse, and one which was important in the launching of several of the colonies of British North America. Keith Thomas' large work on *Religion and The Decline of Magic** (New York: Scribner's, 1971), is a monumental exploration of many different facets of English popular religion that makes many important points about both the continuing survival of folk religion in Protestant lands and the impact of the Reformation upon traditional notions of the sacred. Patrick Collinson, *The Elizabethan Puritan Movement* (Berkeley: Univ. of Calif. Press, 1967), is a definitive analysis of that subject, if any book can ever be so described. B. R. White, *The English Separatist Tradition: From the Marian Martyrs to the Pilgrim Fathers* (London: Oxford Univ. Press, 1971), is an incisive work by a noted student of the English Separatists and Baptists that has become the standard treatment. If Collinson's work has any flaw, it is its inattention to theology and intellectual history, but several recent works have made important contributions of that sort: John S. Coolidge, *The Pauline Renaissance in England: Puritanism and the Bible* (Oxford: Clarendon Press, 1970), which analyzes insightfully the way in which Puritans were saturated in, and thought by means of, a biblical, particularly Pauline, idiom; and J. Sears McGee, *The Godly Man in Stuart England: Anglicans, Puritans, and the Two Tables, 1620-1670* (New Haven: Yale University Press, 1976), which makes considerable advance over older studies in the effort to define and distinguish Puritan and Anglican.

English Protestant eschatology is surveyed in Paul Christianson, *Reformers and Babylon: English Apocalyptic Visions from the Reformation to the Eve of the Civil War* (Toronto: Univ. of Toronto Press, 1978). Dealing with the English background of American Puritanism, but also carrying the story to the colonial experience, is E. Brooks Holifield, *The Covenant Sealed: The Development of Puritan Sacramental Theology in Old and New England, 1570-1720* (New Haven: Yale Univ. Press, 1974). Holifield's conclusion that "Puritan sacramental reflection was guided more by perennial Reformed assumptions than by cultural and social experience" calls in question many interpretations of New England religion which seek to derive religious changes primarily from some idiosyncratic local transition. Holifield's approach, which dips back into the continental Reformation as well as into English religious history to show that colonial developments could be aspects of theological changes in the larger Christian world, is likely to prove fruitful in explaining a number of other religious issues of colonial New England.

The important studies by Perry Miller included in Ahlstrom's earlier bibliography greatly revived interest in American Puritanism. But as has been noted frequently in the last decade,[3] the more recent direction in the study of American Puritanism has been away from the monolithic "Puritan mind" of Miller toward a more pluralistic understanding of colonial New England. A single work that describes the whole Puritan experience in New England, and synthesizes the latest scholarship without pushing any interpretive thesis, is

Francis J. Bremer, *The Puritan Experiment** (New York: St. Martin's Press, 1976). For the newcomer to Puritan studies, this is, as it aims to be, an excellent starting point. Bremer has also collaborated with Alden T. Vaughan in editing a collection of articles drawn from journals, *Puritan New England: Essays on Religion, Society, and Culture** (New York: St. Martin's Press, 1977).

General attempts to interpret the American Puritan phenomenon continue. Darrett B. Rutman, *American Puritanism: Faith and Practice** (Philadelphia: J. B. Lippincott, 1970), denying that any general "Puritan mind" existed, seeks to limit the meaning of the term "Puritanism" to the ideology and activities of a group of the clergy. Such an approach, however, ignores one of the principal thrusts of Collinson's study of the English Puritans—that Puritanism was often a pressure from the laity to which the clergy only haltingly responded. Another conclusion of Rutman's is that Puritanism in America served to reinforce traditional social mores, a conclusion that differs markedly from what is usually said of Puritanism in England—that it was often destructive of custom and tradition. For example, David Little's *Religion, Order, and Law: A Study in Pre-Revolutionary England** (New York: Harper & Row, 1969), argues convincingly that Puritanism was a revolutionary force in disrupting a traditional society. Of course Puritanism could function differently on different sides of the Atlantic, but any general thesis about it should operate at a level of sufficient generality to include as wide a range of possibilities as the Puritan phenomenon actually seems to incorporate. Larzer Ziff, *Puritanism in America: New Culture in a New World** (New York: Viking Press, 1973), views Puritanism as a movement that developed as a means of coping with growing social disorder. As a result, his highly suggestive discussion of events in Puritan New England tends to reductionism.

Stephen Foster, on the other hand, in his *Their Solitary Way: the Puritan Social Ethic in the First Century of Settlement in New England* (New Haven: Yale University Press, 1971), shows a stronger sense of the symbiotic relationship between ideals of order and revolutionary change within Puritan life and thought and contains balanced discussions of the relationship of Puritanism to capitalism and democracy. James W. Jones, *The Shattered Synthesis: New England Puritanism Before the Great Awakening* (New Haven: Yale Univ. press, 1973), basically follows along lines set out by Perry Miller, attempting to bring greater precision to that interpreter's theme that "preparation" was a chink in the Calvinist wall which led to the gradual emergence of a more anthropocentric outlook. Jones's book would have been stronger had it paid more attention to theological developments outside of New England. A literary approach to the Puritan phenomenon, particularly through an examination of Puritan imagination and rhetoric, characterizes a very rich but sometimes difficult work by Sacvan Bercovitch, *The Puritan Origins of the American Self** (New Haven: Yale Univ. Press, 1975), which is concerned with that in subsequent American life to which the distinctive New England rhetoric pointed. Also interested in Puritan rhetoric is *Power and the Pulpit in Puritan New England* (Princeton: Princeton Univ. Press, 1975), by Emory Elliott, a psychological analysis of the "myths and metaphors" of Puritan sermons. Elliott tries to explain some of the transitions through which New England Puritan thought passed, particularly the emergence of the theme of assurance.

More specialized studies dealing with Puritanism and New England religion abounded in the 1970s. David D. Hall, *The Faithful Shepherd: A History of the New England Ministry in the Seventeenth Century* (Chapel Hill: Univ. of North Carolina Press, 1972), has a wider focus than the title indicates. Like many of those treatments of New England Puritanism already noted, it grounds its subject in European background and then retells the story of important episodes of New England religious history from its particular perspective. William T. Youngs, Jr., *God's Messengers: Religious Leadership in Colonial New England, 1700-1750* (Baltimore: Johns Hopkins Univ. Press, 1976), can be considered a continuation of Hall's story, but with a more precise look at the clergy as such, with more attention to the details of everyday religion, and with some recourse to quantitative methods. Since his conclusion deals with the transformation of clerical ideals and behavior wrought by the Great Awakening, this book should also be considered an important addition to the literature concerning that colonial religious upheaval.

The Puritan ideal also involved the state, and Puritan political thought is analyzed in T.H. Breen, *The Character of the Good Ruler: Puritan Political Ideas in New England, 1630-1730* (New Haven: Yale Univ. Press, 1970). Other aspects of the Puritan viewpoint are examined in David E. Stannard, *The Puritan Way of Death: A Study in Religion, Culture, and Social Change* (New York: Oxford Univ. Press, 1977), and Winton U. Solberg, *Redeem the Time: The Puritan Sabbath in Early America* (Cambridge: Harvard Univ. Press, 1977). Stannard, informed by a growing recent literature on the cultural meaning of death and funeral customs, perceptively traces changing attitudes towards death in Puritan society; Solberg provides the full history of Puritan sabbatarianism that has long been a desideratum.

The relationship of Puritan to aboriginal Indian has in the last decade been a matter of spirited controversy. Alden T. Vaughan, *New England Frontier: Puritans and Indians, 1620-1675** (Boston: Little, Brown & Co., 1965), argued that the Puritans deserve a more favorable judgment for their treatment of the Indian than usually accorded them, begetting a flurry of rebuttal and support. That seminal book has been reissued (New York: Norton, 1979*), with a new introduction that discusses the reactions following its first publication and that includes some modifications in the original thesis, making it a balanced discussion of the whole matter. This new introduction is also an excellent guide to the recent literature on the topic. In addition to the Indian, the wilderness itself presented a new experience for the Puritan settlers. This interaction of consciousness and geography is probed in Peter N. Carroll, *Puritanism and the Wilderness: The Intellectual Significance of the New England Frontier, 1629-1700* (New York: Columbia Univ. Press, 1969).

Much new light has been cast on witchcraft at Salem, a traumatic episode in the consciousness of New England. Two new studies of European witchcraft provide indispensable background. E. William Monter, *Witchcraft in France and Switzerland: The Borderlands During the Reformation* (Ithaca:

Cornell Univ. Press, 1976), is especially relevant because of its treatment of witchcraft in Calvinist Geneva—a place he finds that was relatively free of witchcraft panics, had a low rate of convictions compared to accusations, and experienced an early decline of executions for witchcraft. A. D. J. MacFarlane, *Witchcraft in Tudor and Stuart England** (New York: Harper & Row, 1970), employs methods drawn from anthropology as well as statistical data to describe the dynamics of local witchcraft practices and prosecutions in the villages and towns of Essex. Chadwick Hansen, *Witchcraft at Salem* (New York: George Braziller, 1969), broke new ground in empathetically recreating the reality of witchcraft for a society which believed in it. Hansen's rehabilitation of Cotton Mather's reputation in relation to the Salem episode is noteworthy. But other authors have employed different methods in the effort of explanation, most notably Paul Boyer and Stephen Nissenbaum, *Salem Possessed: The Social Origins of Witchcraft** (Cambridge: Harvard Univ. Press, 1974), who, instead of concerning themselves with witchcraft generally, sought to answer the question of why accusations of witchcraft appeared in Salem village when they did. Through examining patterns of village life, property ownership, and social interaction, they conclude that very particular local conditions were responsible.

Boyer and Nissenbaum's study of witchcraft is illuminating because it is based on an analysis of local materials. The same kind of attention to local situations has made Robert G. Pope, *The Half-Way Covenant: Church Membership in Puritan New England* (Princeton: Princeton Univ. Press, 1969), an exceedingly important study. Pope uses local data to revise previous notions about religious decline and the impact of the half-way convenant in the Puritan churches. Also local in approach, Paul R. Lucas, *Valley of Discord: Church and Society Along the Connecticut River, 1636-1725* (Hanover, N.H.: Univ. Press of New England), portrays Puritan religion in Connecticut society. He emphasizes the "bewildering array of contradictory beliefs and practices" found there, a further assault on the image of a monolithic Puritanism. But Lucas's account of Puritanism minimizes the extent to which the variety he cites reflected changes in the outlook of English-speaking Protestants as a whole.

Biographical studies dealing with important Puritan religious leaders have been numerous. Frank Shuffelton, *Thomas Hooker, 1586-1647* (Princeton: Princeton Univ. Press), provides treatment of the thought of that important minister among the first settlers. Roger Williams continues to attract biographers and analysts, as John Garrett, *Roger Williams: Witness Beyond Christendom* (New York: MacMillan, 1970), and W. Clark Gilpin, *The Millenarian Piety of Roger Williams* (Chicago: Univ. of Chicago Press, 1979), show. B.R. Burg, *Richard Mather of Dorchester* (Lexington: Univ. Press of Kentucky, 1976), places that Massachusetts founder in the context both of his particular parish and the wider concerns of the colony. Robert Middlekauf, *The Mathers: Three Generations of Puritan Intellectuals, 1596-1728* (London: Oxford Univ. Press, 1971, *1976), is a brilliant account of the intellectual development which transpired in the minds of an important dynasty of preachers. His work includes an especially informative analysis of the piety of the last of them, Cotton Mather, who is also a subject for David Levin in *Cotton Mather: The Young Life of the Lord's Remembrancer, 1663-1703* (Cambridge Univ. Press, 1978). Samuel Willard, a leading theologian among second generation New Englanders, has been the subject of two new studies: Seymour Van Dyken, *Samuel Willard, 1640-1707: Preacher of Orthodoxy in an Era of Change* (Grand Rapids: Eerdmans, 1972), an exposition of his theological ideas within a biography, and Ernest B. Lowrie, *The Shape of the Puritan Mind: The Thought of Samuel Willard* (New Haven: Yale Univ. Press, 1974).

Among source materials on New England Puritanism of use to the general investigator are Phyllis M. Jones and Nicholas R. Jones, eds., *Salvation in New England: Selections from the Sermons of the First Preachers* (Austin: Univ. of Texas, 1977), including sermons by Davenport, Hooker, Cotton, Shepard, and Bulkeley; and one facsimile reprint of a writing unusually rich in what it discloses about Puritanism, John Norton, *Abel Being Dead, Yet Speaketh (1658): A Biography of John Cotton* (Delmar, N.Y.: Scholars' Facsimiles & Reprints, 1978), introduction by Edward J. Gallagher.

Other Colonial Traditions

The impulse behind the formation of the Quakers, a movement important not only in colonial Pennsylvania but also in Rhode Island, New Jersey and the Carolinas, has in the last generation been regarded as an aspect of the wider Puritan impulse. Melvin B. Endy, Jr., *William Penn and Early Quakerism* (Princeton: Princeton Univ. Press, 1973), however, stresses the "Enlightenment" implications of Quaker spiritualism and its incipient rationalism, particularly in the case of Penn himself, thus distancing him from the Puritan center. In this connection the picture of Puritan radicalism portrayed in Christopher Hill, *The World Turned Upside Down: Radical Ideas During The English Revolution* (New York: Viking Press, 1972), must also be taken into consideration, with its image of a more generalized radical, and even incipiently rationalist, movement growing up on the edges of Puritanism. J. William Frost, *The Quaker Family in Colonial America** (New York: St. Martin's Press, 1973), is broader than its title indicates. This work includes chapters on Quaker theology and piety which are among the most informative written on those matters, at least for American Quakerism, as well as discussions of everyday life and attitudes in the Quaker community. Accounts of the development of the Friends in Pennsylvania can be found in Edwin B. Bronner, *William Penn's "Holy Experiment": The Founding of Pennsylvania 1681-1701* (New York: Temple Univ. Publications, 1962), and Richard Bauman, *For the Reputation of Truth: Politics, Religion, and Conflict among the Pennsylvania Quakers, 1750-1800* (Baltimore: Johns Hopkins Press, 1971), which describes the Friends' loss of political control in their colony and their reaction to the American Revolution. The Baptists were another group who were separatists from the main Puritan body, and their doings have been carefully detailed in the monumental volumes of William G. McLoughlin, *New England Dissent, 1630-1833: The Baptists and the Separation of Church and State*, 2 vols., (Cambridge: Harvard Univ. Press, 1971).

Henry Ward Beecher (1813–1887), nineteenth century clergyman and revivalist. Engraving, 1870, by John Chester Buttre, after a photograph by Augustus Morand and William Momberger. Photograph courtesy National Portrait Gallery, Smithsonian Institution, Washington, D.C. Negative number 79.86.

Religion in the settlement of some of the other colonies ought not to be neglected, though many fewer studies in this area have recently appeared. John Tracy Ellis, *Catholics in Colonial America* (Baltimore: Helicon Press, 1965), remains standard for its subject; Charles Edwards O'Neill, *Church and State in French Colonial Louisiana: Policy and Politics to 1732* (New Haven: Yale Univ. Press, 1966), addresses a neglected story; George L. Smith, *Religion and Trade in New Netherland* (Ithaca: Cornell Univ. Press, 1973), provides some introduction to Dutch Calvinism and society in the Netherlands at the time of colonization, with the thesis that commercial preoccupations had a way of crowding out other concerns among the Dutch; and Jacob R. Marcus, *The Colonial American Jew, 1492-1776,* 3 vols. (Detroit: Wayne State Univ. Press, 1970), gives a thoroughly detailed account of its subject. The story of James Blair, who as commissary for the Bishop of London sought to bring some order to Anglicanism in Virginia, is recounted in Parke Rouse, Jr., *James Blair of Virginia* (Chapel Hill: Univ. of North Carolina Press, 1971).

Much of the story of religion in the settlement of the American colonies consists of efforts to recreate in the new world patterns which had been developed long before and which had long served as a kind of framework for old world experience. But new world conditions eroded those patterns, and before much of the eighteenth century had elapsed, it was clear that new patterns of religious response would be needed in a new land. Three events which were the bearers of powerful cultural impulses with profoundly religious elements served as catalysts in the formation of more distinctively American religious ways: the Great Awakening, the American Revolution with its attendant forming of a new nation, and the coming of the Enlightenment to the new land. The writings on eighteenth-century American religion are arranged most helpfully under these three headings.

The Great Awakening

Consideration of the Great Awakening in the historical scholarship of the 1970s dawned with Richard Hofstader's assertion, in his posthumously published *America at 1750: A Social Portrait** (New York: Knopf, 1971), that the Great Awakening was "the first major intercolonial crisis of the mind and spirit," and was even more fundamental than the colonial wars in creating "a popular intercolonial movement" and in defining a "dominant religious style" that gave American life a distinctive spiritual quality. The story of the Awakening in its various geographical phases has been well told in three older books by Maxson, Gewehr, and Gaustad, all listed in Ahlstrom's earlier bibliography. Two new collections of source materials can now be added to the literature on the Awakening: Richard L. Bushman, ed., *The Great Awakening: Documents on the Revival of Religion, 1740-1745* (New York: Athenaeum, 1970), and Douglas Sloan, ed., *The Great Awakening and American Education: A Documentary History* (New York: Teachers College Press, 1973). A number of articles in F. Ernest Stoeffler, ed., *Continental Pietism and Early*

*American Christianity** (Grand Rapids: Eerdmans, 1976), deal with influences other than British and discuss evangelicalism in the colonies among the denominations of German background. James Tanis, *Dutch Calvinistic Pietism in the Middle Colonies: A Study in the Life and Theology of Theodorus Jacobus Frelinghuysen* (The Hague, Netherlands: Martinus Nijhoff, 1967), broke new ground in pinning down the Dutch antecedents of evangelical religion in the colonies. George W. Pilcher, *Samuel Davies: Apostle of Dissent in Colonial Virginia* (Knoxville: Univ. of Tennessee Press, 1971), portrays a leader of the southern Awakening.

Interest in Jonathan Edwards has long been important in the study of the Great Awakening, but there has been an ebb in the production of books about him. Perry Miller's treatment of Edwards, for all its brilliance, now seems a bit too eisegetical, while a less imaginative treatment, like that of Conrad Cherry, *The Theology of Jonathan Edwards: A Reappraisal** (New York: Doubleday, 1966), probably comes closer to the heart of Edwards' own concerns. The important new contribution to the study of Edwards, however, is to be found in three additional volumes in the Yale University Press edition of his works. Published in 1970, 1972, and 1977 respectively, they include the same kind of substantial introductions that characterized the first volumes: *Original Sin*, edited by Clyde A. Holbrook; *The Great Awakening*, edited by C.C. Goen; and *Apocalyptic Writings*, edited by Stephen J. Stein. The junior Jonathan Edwards is the subject of a recently published biography, Robert L. Ferm, *A Colonial Pastor: Jonathan Edwards the Younger, 1745-1801* (Grand Rapids: Eerdmans, 1976).

Missions, humanitarianism, and the foundation of colleges have conventionally been cited among the more tangible consequences of the Great Awakening. The last of these effects is explored in Howard Miller, *The Revolutionary College: American Presbyterian Higher Education 1707-1837* (New York: New York Univ. Press, 1976).

Another consequence of evangelical religion is confronted in Phillip Greven, *The Protestant Temperament: Patterns of Child-Rearing, Religious Experience, and the Self in Early America* (New York: Knopf, 1977). Sifting through a large body of material about childhood in colonial America, Greven describes as authoritarian and repressive an evangelical style of child-rearing which he contrasts with the acceptance of greater assertiveness in children characteristic of the "genteel." In spite of much fascinating material, Greven's thesis suffers from a lack of clear definition for his groups and a certain circularity of argument.

Religion and the American Revolution

The Great Awakening is no longer conventionally interpreted as a conservative force in American life, but as one of the impelling forces behind the American Revolution. Richard L. Bushman, in *From Puritan to Yankee: Character and the Social Order in Connecticut, 1690-1765* (Cambridge: Harvard Univ. Press, 1967; *Norton, 1970), argues, for example, that the anti-revivalist party inhabited a world "organized around traditional concepts of the social order," whereas evangelicals had become habituated to the defiance of the standing order. Evangelical millennialism could also spur change, as James West Davidson documents in *The Logic of Millennial Thought: Eighteenth-Century New England* (New Haven: Yale Univ. Press, 1977). Davidson traces the roots of millenialism in earlier English and colonial thinking and shows how millennialism received further impetus through the Awakening and bore fruit as it was diffused through revolutionary ideology. Another treatment of the millennialism of this period appears in Nathan O. Hatch, *The Sacred Cause of Liberty: Republican Thought and the Millennium in Revolutionary New England* (New Haven: Yale Univ. Press, 1977), which stresses the later consequences of millennial thinking.

Religion interwove with the coming of the American Revolution in ways other than those connected with the Great Awakening. The older book by Carl Bridenbaugh, *Mitre and Sceptre** (New York: Oxford Univ. Press, 1962), established the important role of the controversy between Anglicans and colonial Dissenters over a colonial episcopate in the alienation of the colonists from the mother country. Michael Walzer, *The Revolution of the Saints* (Cambridge: Harvard Univ. Press, 1965; *Athenaeum, 1968), documented the revolutionary character of Calvinism, and though he does not deal with colonial Puritanism, his book is relevant here. Bernard Bailyn, *The Ideological Origins of the American Revolution** (Cambridge: Harvard Univ. Press, 1967), while not focusing mainly on religious causes for the revolution, certainly showed the relationship of even secular revolutionary theory with the Dissenting posterity of the English Puritans. In Page Smith, ed., *Religious Origins of the American Revolution** (Missoula, Montana: Scholars Press, 1976), documents are interwoven with argument in order to maintain the closest possible connection between religion and revolution. The Puritan election sermon has been commonly cited as an institutional means by which potentially revolutionary political ideals were kept before the attention of the populace, and A. W. Plumstead, ed., *The Wall and the Garden: Selected Massachusetts Election Sermons 1670-1775* (Minneapolis: Univ. of Minnesota Press, 1968), has gathered a number of these into a single volume.

Recent studies of colonial Anglicanism have tended to center on the period of the Revolution. In *Bishops by Ballot: an Eighteenth-Century Ecclesiastical Revolution* (New York: Oxford Univ. Press, 1978), by Frederick V. Mills, Sr., the struggle over a colonial episcopate is examined as an inner Anglican issue with an outcome that had far-reaching consequences within that denomination. Thomas E. Buckley, S.J., *Church and State in Revolutionary Virginia, 1776-1787* (Charlottesville: Univ. Press of Virginia, 1977), gives a detailed examination of the controversy over the separation of church and state, concluding that this struggle became a model for thinking about church and state relations elsewhere in the United States. He emphasizes that the evangelical movement in Virginia was important in bringing about separation and in giving rise to ideas about a nation both "Christian" and yet without an established church. Recent biographies of leaders of colonial Anglicanism during this period include Joseph Ellis, *The New England Mind in Transition: Samuel Johnson of Connecticut, 1696-1772* (New Haven: Yale Univ. Press,

1973), and Bruce E. Steiner, *Samuel Seabury 1729-1796* (Ohio Univ. Press, 1971).

The Enlightenment

The Great Awakening is usually contrasted with the Enlightenment as a countervailing force in colonial experience. But a masterful new treatment of *The Enlightenment in America,* * by Henry F. May (New York: Oxford Univ. Press, 1976), takes a much more complex view of the interrelationship of these impulses in American life. Noting that at the beginning of the eighteenth century British Protestants generally thought of enlightenment, progress, and Protestant religion as forces moving together, he suggests that the evangelical Awakening advanced definitions of these forces as being opposed to each other, while a moderate form of Enlightenment rationalism and a moderate evangelicalism eventually came to terms with each other, allowing religion and reason to walk hand in hand again as the "Didactic Enlightenment." This last term names one of the four major phases of the Enlightenment which May describes, and in the description of each of them he avoids treating ideas apart from those who held them, always firmly planting ideas in the soil of the persons, groups and institutions to which they were related. This is the strongest aspect of his book. Moreover, for May the Enlightenment was not something that merely had an impact on religion, but was itself a religious movement.

Evangelical America

Protestantism in nineteenth-century America was powerfully shaped by the evangelical impulse, so that even alternative currents can be defined by their relationship to that impulse. This evangelical Protestantism was a dominant factor in the cultural life of the whole nation in that century. The evangelical religious approach, rooted in the Puritan past and formed by the Great Awakening, absorbed certain elements of the American Enlightenment and then, in the early nineteenth century, flowered in the renascent revivalism of the Second Great Awakening, in that coalition of evangelical denominations which can be dubbed a kind of "Evangelical United Front", in the ideal of a "Christian America," and in the multifarious missionary and reform efforts and societies of the "Benevolent Empire."

The evangelical revival in the South in its earliest phase is the subject of John B. Boles, *The Great Revival, 1787-1805: The Origins of the Southern Evangelical Mind* (Lexington: Univ. Press of Kentucky, 1972). Boles gives a more pluralistic interpretation of its origin than those who trace it chiefly to the great Kentucky revival of 1800. He interprets the southern revival as a "revitalization movement" growing out of social anxieties and concludes that it created a distinctively southern kind of evangelicalism. Dickson D. Bruce, Jr., *And They All Sang Hallelujah: Plain-Folk Camp-Meeting Religion, 1800-1845* (Knoxville: Univ. of Tennessee Press, 1974), by means of an anthropological approach, attempts to provide an account of the religious symbols of southern popular religion and their function in the lives of those who held them. But most important of all the studies of southern evangelicalism is Donald G. Mathews, *Religion in the Old South** (Chicago: Univ. of Chicago Press, 1977). Mathews turns back to the eighteenth century in order to bring perspective to the whole sweep of southern evangelicalism and shows how its earlier revolutionary impact was gradually compromised both as it became more middle class and as the host society became more intractable about its "peculiar institution." The special dilemmas of southern evangelicalism are vividly portrayed, and the evangelicalism of the slaves is included as an integral part of the story. By a very subtly nuanced analysis, Mathews lays to rest many hackneyed views about southern religion.

Charles Roy Keller's older work on *The Second Great Awakening in Connecticut* (New Haven: Yale Univ. Press, 1942), remains a standard account of the beginnings of the New England revival. Stephen E. Berk, *Calvinism versus Democracy: Timothy Dwight and the Origins of American Evangelical Orthodoxy* (Hamden, Conn.: Archon Books, 1974), analyzes the impact of Dwight as a leader of the Second Awakening, concluding that Dwight was important in leading New England orthodoxy "toward a practical evangelical activism." Lyman Beecher succeeded Dwight in the leadership of northern evangelicalism and is the subject of a sympathetic popular biography by Stuart A. Henry, *Unvanquished Puritan* (Grand Rapids: Eerdmans, 1973), as well as the initial character considered in a fascinatingly written and richly suggestive new account, Marie Caskey, *Chariot of Fire: Religion and the Beecher Family* (New Haven: Yale Univ. Press, 1978). Caskey, after outlining the main tendencies of Lyman's thought, shows how that legacy was modified or rejected by his numerous and creative progeny. This book discloses much about the character of evangelical Protestantism in nineteenth-century America.

The local impact of the Second Awakening has attracted some scholars. An example is a new treatment of revivalism and evangelicalism in a particular locale important in the revivalist Finney's career, Paul E. Johnson, *A Shopkeeper's Millennium: Society and Revivals in Rochester, New York, 1815-1837** (New York: Hill and Wang, 1978). Deftly interweaving the story of religion with the story of the growth of a city, Johnson traces the significance for working-class persons of their adoption of evangelical religion. Using the Durkheimian point of view that religion is the glue of society, Johnson nonetheless avoids the more conspiratorial views of religion as social control which characterized some earlier studies. Less successful as an analysis of the impact of evangelical religion on an urban situation is Marion L. Bell, *Crusade in the City: Revivalism in Nineteenth-Century Philadelphia* (Lewisburg: Bucknell Univ. Press, 1977), which stresses the conservatism of evangelicalism in that city.

Other important books investigate broad aspects of northern evangelicalism. Donald M. Scott, *From Office to Profession: the New England Ministry 1750-1850* (Philadelphia: Univ. of Pa. Press, 1978), picks up the story of ministers in New England where Young's book left them and convincingly traces the transformation of the ministry from its status as a near public office

oriented to the life of the whole community to a profession offering specialized service to a "self-selected clientele." The revivals and reforms of these
clergy are interpreted as efforts to shore up traditional values in a changing
society that in the process transformed the religious tradition, begetting
new conceptions of Christian citizenship and social responsibility. William
Gribben, in *The Churches Militant: The War of 1812 and American Religion*
(New Haven: Yale Univ. Press, 1973), studied the reactions of the religious
community to that event, which he saw giving further impetus for an evangelical America: "America's symbiotic union of religion and politics not only
developed into crusading nationalism but also provided the rationale for
fervid, and continuing, reform." George M. Marsden, *The Evangelical Mind
and the New School Presbyterian Experience: A Case Study of Thought and
Theology in Nineteenth-Century America* (New Haven: Yale Univ. Press,
1970), building upon the assumption that New School Presbyterians "embodied the characteristics that virtually all observers agree were typical of the
mainstream of American Protestantism," found in this group a characteristic
blend of revivalism, reformism, Christian nationalism, and millenialism.

Marsden's book, like Berk's on Dwight and Caskey's on the Beechers, emphasizes the liberalizing modifications in the inherited Calvinism made by the
evangelicals, especially in relation to the vexed question of the freedom of the
will. Several books explore that and other theological matters important in
evangelical Protestantism. Sidney Earl Mead's *Nathaniel William Taylor,
1786-1858: A Connecticut Liberal* (Chicago: Univ. of Chicago Press, 1942),
remains the indispensable work on that significant modifier of an older Calvinism. With a wider sweep than evangelicalism alone, E. Brooks Holifield,
*The Gentlemen Theologians: American Theology in Southern Culture,
1795-1860* (Durham: Duke Univ. Press, 1978), is a valuable new study. Jerry
Wayne Brown, *The Rise of Biblical Criticism in America, 1800-1870: The New
England Scholars* (Middletown, Conn.: Wesleyan Univ. Press, 1969), studies
the impact of the new German biblical scholarship upon American Protestants. Two recent books explore the relationship of Protestantism and science: Theodore Dwight Bozeman, *Protestants in an Age of Science: The
Baconian Ideal and Antebellum American Religious Thought* (Chapel Hill:
Univ. of North Carolina Press, 1977), which shows how important science was
to conservative Presbyterians in a pre-Darwinian age, as they used science
"doxologically" in the praise of the Creator and drew upon its methodology
for their theology; and Herbert Hovenkamp, *Science and Religion in America,
1800-1860* (Philadelphia: Univ. of Pennsylvania Press, 1978), which provides
a more synoptic treatment of the subject.

For many evangelicals, the ultimate outcome of their efforts was envi-
sioned as a transformed nation, even a transformed world. Hence the importance to them of missions and reforms. John A. Andrew, III, *Rebuilding the
Christian Commonwealth: New England Congregationalists & Foreign Missions, 1800-1830* (Lexington: Univ. Press of Kentucky, 1976), connects the
formation of mission societies to social forces in New England life and portrays the transplanting of New England ideals to new climes. Robert F. Berkhofer, Jr., *Salvation and the Savage: An Analysis of Protestant Missions and*

American Indian Response, 1787-1862 (Lexington: Univ. Press of Kentucky, 1965; *Athenaeum, 1972), looks at home missions, but is not always well informed about the religious groups involved. Carroll Smith-Rosenberg, *Religion and the Rise of the American City: The New York City Mission Movement, 1812-1870* (Ithaca: Cornell Univ. Press, 1971), finds concern for the problems of the city and urgency about its Christianization rooted in the Second Awakening and shows how interest in the souls of the poor could develop into concern for their economic conditon.

The great reform cause that drained off so much energy from other reforms by mid-century was antislavery, and a close relationship between that movement and evangelicalism has long been acknowledged by historians of American religion. Various ramifications of that interconnection appear in Bertram Wyatt-Brown, *Lewis Tappan and the Evangelical War Against Slavery* (Cleveland: The Press of Case Western Reserve Univ., 1969), and Lewis Perry, *Radical Abolitionism: Anarchy and the Government of God in Antislavery Thought* (Ithaca: Cornell Univ. Press, 1973). James H. Moorhead, *American Apocalypse: Yankee Protestants and the Civil War* (New Haven: Yale Univ. Press, 1978), considers the ways in which the war took on millennial overtones for northern evangelicals. The involvement of one denomination in the aftermath of the war is examined in Ralph E. Morrow, *Northern Methodism and Reconstruction* (East Lansing: Michigan State Univ. Press, 1956).

Religion Among American Blacks

While considering the importance of abolition and civil war for the shaping of white Protestantism, the blacks who were presumably the objects of Yankee Christian concern must not be overlooked. And in keeping with a new awareness about the history and culture of Afro-Americans, many books dealing with religion among both slaves and free blacks have appeared. Lester B. Scherer, *Slavery and the Churches in Early America, 1619-1819* (Grand Rapids: Eerdmans, 1975), recounts the ways in which the churches interacted with the institution of slavery. *In His Image, But...Racism in Southern Religion, 1780-1910,* by H. Shelton Smith (Durham: Duke Univ. Press, 1972), portrays the attitudes of southern religionists to blacks both under bondage and after emancipation. David M. Reimers, *White Protestantism and the Negro* (New York: Oxford Univ. Press, 1965), is basically the story of how the major denominations regarded and related to blacks among their numbers, bringing the tale into the twentieth century. Two other studies give a more detailed picture of two denominations: Andrew E. Murray, *Presbyterians and the Negro—A History* (Philadelphia: Presbyterian Hist. Soc., 1966), and Harry V. Richardson, *Dark Salvation: The Story of Methodism as It Developed Among Blacks in America* (Garden City: Doubleday, 1976).

The religious life of American blacks has been the chief focus of other studies, both more general and more particular in scope. Donald G. Mathews, *Religion in the Old South,* already cited, has a discussion of black evangelicalism; that is also the subject of another book, *Black Religion and American Evangelicalism: White Protestants, Plantation Missions, and the Flowering of*

Negro Christianity, 1787-1865 (Metuchen, N.J.: The Scarecrow Press, 1975), by Milton C. Sernett. Religion among antebellum southern blacks is the subject of an important book by Albert J. Raboteau, *Slave Religion: The "Invisible Institution" in the Antebellum South** (New York: Oxford Univ. Press, 1978), which threads its way through a whole host of controversial matters, coming to judicious conclusions concerning the tortured questions of African survivals, the relation of religion to passivity, and the extent of black transformation of the Christianity of whites. Carol V.R. George, *Segregated Sabbaths: Richard Allen and the Rise of Independent Black Churches, 1760-1840** (New York: Oxford Univ. Press, 1973), provides an entry into the study of religion among the free blacks of the North. Information on other groups is available in Joseph R. Washington, Jr., *Black Sects and Cults: The Power Axis in an Ethnic Ethic** (Garden City, N.Y.: Doubleday, 1973).

Protestantism After the Civil War

Henry Ward Beecher, the scion of a family renowned in evangelical annals, came into prominence on the American religious scene as an ardent supporter of black freedom and union during the Civil War. An enlightening chapter on his "reputation" appears in Carter, *The Spiritual Crisis of the Gilded Age,* already cited, and William G. McLoughlin has written an interesting essay on *The Meaning of Henry Ward Beecher* (New York: Knopf, 1970). A more substantial contribution is Clifford E. Clark, Jr., *Henry Ward Beecher: Spokesman for a Middle-Class America* (Urbana: Univ. of Illinois Press, 1978), which views Beecher as having "articulated the attitudes and values of a new urban middle class."

The evangelicalism which the Beechers had so typified was by the last decades of the nineteenth century experiencing divisions which not only concerned the nature of Christian activity in the world but also the very definition of the Christian message. Thus the major impulses within Protestantism in the latter part of the nineteenth century and the beginning of the twentieth century represented a division within the evangelical movement between the Social Gospel and liberal theology on one hand and Fundamentalism and the Holiness and Pentecostal movements on the other.

The "new theology," as liberal Protestantism was frequently called in the latter nineteenth century, was not without its roots in earlier evangelicalism, particularly in the emphasis upon religious experience and the playing down of dogma characteristic of the evangelicals in their revolt against an older Calvinism. Something of the link between earlier evangelicalism and the later liberal theology can be seen in Horace Bushnell, long regarded as one of the pioneers of liberalism. His major programmatic essays, in which he laid down the lines of a new theological method, can be examined in a fine edition of some of his writings, H. Shelton Smith, ed., *Horace Bushnell* (New York: Oxford Univ. Press, 1965). The most important new contribution to the study of Protestant liberalism is William R. Hutchison, *The Modernist Impulse in American Protestantism* (Cambridge: Harvard Univ. Press, 1976), in which a relatively larger role in shaping the "new theology" is given to earlier Unitarian developments than was the case in treatments of the subject during the 1960s. But Hutchison acknowledges the evangelical background as well. His book provides excellent definition of the topic as well as a chronology of the movement and also gives attention to its relation to general culture. An analysis and appreciation of some of the main tendencies and thinkers (including philosophers as well as theologians) who carried the movement down to more recent times is Randolph Crump Miller, *The American Spirit in Theology* (Philadelphia: United Church Press, 1974). Though not limited to Protestants, *Church History in the Age of Science: Historiographical Patterns in the United States, 1876-1918,* by Henry Warner Bowden (Chapel Hill: Univ. of North Carolina Press, 1971), recounts the impact of the new liberal and scientific history on American religion.

Social liberalism among American Protestants did not perfectly correlate with theological liberalism, but there was a great deal of overlap. The problems of mass immigration, rapid urbanization, and industrialism coupled with conflicts between labor and capital confronted American Protestantism with serious challenges. Part of the reaction of one major Protestant group is documented in Lawrence B. Davis, *Immigrants, Baptists, and the Protestant Mind in America* (Urbana: Univ. of Illinois Press, 1973). An older historiography tended to see the liberal theology as a novel Protestant movement of response to new currents; the Social Gospel movement in American Protestantism has been regarded similarly. It is significant, then, that Henry F. May, author of an important treatment of *The Protestant Churches in Industrial America* (New York: Harper & Row, 1949), has provided a new introduction to his 1967 paperback reissue in which he acknowledges that he earlier minimized the connections between antebellum evangelical reform and the later Social Gospel, while still maintaining that the approach of later nineteenth-century Protestantism to social problems was significantly different from that of earlier evangelicalism. Among recent studies of different aspects of Protestant social religion are Peter J. Frederick, *Knights of the Golden Rule: The Intellectual as Christian Social Reformer in the 1890's* (Lexington: Univ. of Kentucky Press, 1976); Nathan I. Huggins, *Protestants Against Poverty: Boston's Charities, 1870-1890* (Westport, Conn.: Greenwood, 1971); and Alvin W. Skardon, *Church Leader in the Cities: William Augustus Muhlenberg* (Philadelphia: Univ. of Penn. Press, 1971). Robert T. Handy, ed., *The Social Gospel in America, 1870-1920* (New York: Oxford Univ. Press, 1966), is an excellent collection of writings selected from three social gospel leaders, Rauschenbusch, Gladden and Ely. A more varied anthology is Ronald C. White, Jr. and C. Howard Hopkins, eds., *The Social Gospel: Religion and Reform in Changing America* (Philadelphia: Temple Univ. Press, 1976).

"Fundamentalism" names a movement of conservative Protestant reaction to the "new theology" and the Social Gospel, but it too had roots in earlier Protestant developments. The search for such roots in earlier Protestant orthodoxies has been an obvious enough course, but Marsden's book, already cited, has noted rather surprisingly that many of the elements of later Fundamentalism seem prefigured in earlier "New School" evangelicalism. James F. Findlay's biography of *Dwight L. Moody: American Evangelist, 1837-1899*

(Chicago: Univ. Of Chicago Press, 1969), depicts, among other things, the revivalistic impulse increasingly veering towards that constellation of ideas and attitudes which are denominated as Fundamentalist. The classic study of Fundamentalism in recent times, however, is Ernest R. Sandeen, *The Roots of Fundamentalism: British and American Millenarianism 1800-1930* (Chicago: Univ. of Chicago Press, 1970; *Baker Book House, 1978), which regards the Fundamentalist movement as being at its core a combination of Orthodox Calvinist biblicism and Darbyite or Plymouth Brethren eschatology and dispensationalism. He corrects earlier stereotypes of Fundamentalism by regarding it as an urban and northern movement, and minimizes aspects of the movement that appealed to earlier students, such as the opposition to evolution. Timothy Weber, *Living in the Shadow of the Second Coming: American Premillennialism, 1875-1925* (New York: Oxford Univ. Press, 1979), provides further investigation of Fundamentalist eschatology. Ewing Jorstad, *The Politics of Doomsday: Fundamentalists of the Far Right* (Nashville: Abingdon Press, 1970), explores the "radical right" politics of some Fundamentalists, which he sees, as does Weber, as related to their premillennial eschatology. The biographical sketches in C. Allyn Russell, *Voices of American Fundamentalism* (Philadelphia: Westminster Press, 1976), restore perspective to the subject by making the reader aware that the Fundamentalist movement included a broad range of leaders.

Not simply to be classed as Fundamentalists, and yet sharing with them a fear of liberal tendencies in American Protestantism and a commitment to old-fashioned revivalism, are the Holiness and Pentecostal groups. The Holiness impulse was an attempt to preserve and even revive an earlier Wesleyan evangelicalism. *Perfectionist Persuasion: The Holiness Movement and American Methodism, 1867-1936* (Metuchen, N.J.: Scarecrow Press, 1974), by Charles Edwin Jones, is a useful account. There have been many modern studies of the Pentecostal movement, mostly sparked by the recent "charismatic revival," a new outburst of the Pentecostal religiosity of glossolalia and faith healing. Robert Mapes Anderson, *Vision of the Disinherited: The Making of American Pentecostalism* (New York: Oxford Univ. Press, 1979), not only provides an extensive bibliography of this subject, but also skillfully wends his way through many different aspects of the story of American Pentecostalism, though sometimes with excessive psychosocial reductionism. David Edwin Harrell, Jr., *All Things Are Possible: The Healing and Charismatic Revivals in Modern America* (Bloomington: Univ. of Indiana Press, 1975), focuses on more recent leaders and developments.

Unitarianism

Early in the nineteenth century, New England Unitarianism rejected central elements of evangelicalism and incorporated more of the motifs of the Enlightenment than did its rival. Yet to study the Unitarian impulse through Daniel Walker Howe, *The Unitarian Conscience: Harvard Moral Philosophy, 1805-1861* (Cambridge: Harvard Univ. Press, 1970), is likely to impress the reader with the broad range of things which Unitarians shared with at least the more moderate evangelicals in the first Unitarian generations. A popular life of the principal Unitarian patriarch is Jack Mendelsohn, *Channing: The Reluctant Radical* (Boston: Little, Brown & Co., 1971); a later Unitarian leader is studied in J. Wade Caruthers, *Octavius Brooks Frothingham: Gentle Radical* (The Univ. of Alabama Press, 1977). A brief introduction to a group now merged with the Unitarians is provided by Ernest Cassara, ed., *Universalism in America: A Documentary History* (Boston: Beacon Press, 1971).

New Religious Groups

The United States has been unusually fertile in the production of new sect groups. But it is a mistake to see the welter of these groups as a formless chaos; rather, they fall into certain basic configurations that can be regarded as the eccentric and extreme offshoots of impulses prominent in mainstream Protestantism. Thus Protestantism, especially in America, and especially on the frontier, had a strong restorationist impulse, an urge to recreate original apostolic Christianity in its pristine form. That impulse was the basic factor in the emergence of various groups that took the simple name of "Christian," but it also bore fruit in Mormonism, with its claim to the discovery of further evidence about the true character of pure Christianity. *The Mormon Experience: A History of the Latter-day Saints* (New York: Knopf, 1979), by Leonard J. Arrington and Davis Bitton, is an interesting and analytical account by two Mormon historians who recognize the interconnection of the movement with the restorationist impulse. Mark P. Leone, *Roots of Modern Mormonism* (Cambridge: Harvard Univ. Press, 1979), is an anthropologist's study of the Mormon community.

The Mormons, as they sought to build their new society first at Nauvoo and then in Utah, combined the Utopian impulse with restorationism. But in some other groups important in nineteenth-century America, such Utopianism and communalism was the paramount feature from the beginning. Henri Desroche studies such a group in *The American Shakers: From Neo-Christianity to Presocialism* (Amherst: Univ. of Mass. Press, 1971). Two recent books investigate John Humphrey Noyes and his community: Maren Lockwood Carden, *Oneida: Utopian Community to Modern Corporation** (New York: Harper & Row, 1971), and Robert David Thomas, *The Man Who Would Be Perfect: John Humphrey Noyes and the Utopian Impulse* (Philadelphia: Univ. of Penn. Press, 1977).

Alongside restorationism and Utopianism, millennialism may be regarded as a basic impulse of American Protestantism, and it too has been fruitful in producing sect groups. The student of American religious history can study many different sides of this impulse through the essays in Edwin S. Gaustad, ed., *The Rise of Adventism* (New York: Harper and Row, 1974). Health reform and the founding of the Seventh-Day Adventists was the subject of Ronald L. Number's biography, *Prophetess of Health: A Study of Ellen G. White* (New York: Harper & Row, 1976). Another millennialist group, much further from the Protestant mainstream in its principal ideas, is studied in James A. Beckford, *The Trumpet of Prophecy: A Sociological Study of Jehovah's Witnesses* (New York: Wiley & Sons, 1975).

American evangelicalism believed that in the conversion experience there was a real entry of God's Spirit into the life of the believer. The Quakers represented a rather unorthodox twist in this notion; much more so did various groups which began to proclaim a new age of the spirit or a new spiritual religion which would replace traditional Christianity. These groups, if carried to the present, include the Eastern mystical sects in the United States, on which the recent literature is extensive, though some books have attempted a more synoptic approach. Among these are two by Robert S. Ellwood, Jr., *Religious and Spiritual Groups in Modern America* * (Englewood Cliffs, N.J.: Prentice-Hall, 1973), in which the author attempts to set such American groups in the long stream of what he identifies as the "Alternative Reality Tradition," a pantheistic spiritualism stretching back to antiquity; and *Alternative Altars: Unconventional and Eastern Spirituality in America* (Chicago: Univ. of Chicago Press, 1979), which is more interested in connecting such groups to American cultural history. New England transcendentalism has long been identified as related to such things, and it is studied, as a religious movement, in Catherine Albanese, *Corresponding Motion: Transcendental Religion and the New America* (Philadelphia: Temple Univ. Press, 1977).

Transcendentalist and spiritualist interests led very naturally into a concern with mental healing, which was being experimented with in various ways all through the nineteenth century in America. This is treated in a psychohistorical and Freudian way in Gail Thain Parker, *Mind Cure in New England: From the Civil War to World War I* (Hanover, New Hampshire: Univ. Press of New England, 1973). Mary Baker Eddy, the foundress of Christian Science, is a major figure in Parker's book, and she and her movement are discussed by a historian who is himself a Christian Scientist in Stephen Gottschalk, *The Emergence of Christian Science in American Religious Life* (Berkeley: Univ. of Calif. Press, 1973). This informative book, however, is not always deft in its handling of general background material about American religious history. Many other small religious groups, and many persons not identified with such groups at all, have nevertheless been touched with the spiritualizing and mental healing impulses of what is generally termed "New Thought" or the "Metaphysical" movement, and share much with the outlook of Christian Science, though usually without the precision of doctrine characteristic of the latter. A good introduction to many of these groups and to the general spirit which they represent can be found in J. Stillson Judah, *The History and Philosophy of the Metaphysical Movements in America* (Philadelphia: Westminster Press, 1967).

The spiritual outlook of these groups has always had, whether recognized or not, a certain kinship with importations of Eastern religion into America. Such imports can be studied in several popular treatments, including John Charles Cooper, *Religion in the Age of Aquarius* * (Philadelphia: Westminster Press, 1971); Jacob Needleman, *The New Religions* * (Garden City, N.Y.:

Doubleday, 1970); and Marvin H. Harper, *Gurus, Swamis and Avatars: Spiritual Masters and Their American Disciples* (Philadelphia: Westminster Press, 1971). A study of a particular group is James V. Downton, Jr., *Sacred Journeys: The Conversion of Young Americans to Divine Light Mission* (New York: Columbia Univ. Press, 1979). Dealing both with recent Buddhist groups in America as well as Buddhism among Japanese-American immigrants are Charles S. Prebish, *American Buddhism** (North Scituate, Mass.: Duxbury Press, 1979), and Emma McCloy Layman, *Buddhism in America* (Chicago: Nelson and Hall, 1976). A social scientific approach to data about many different religious groups outside the American religious mainstream can be found in the varied essays brought together in Irving I. Zaretsky and Mark P. Leone, editors, *Religious Movements in Contemporary America* (Princeton: Princeton Univ. Press, 1974).

Roman Catholicism in America

Roman Catholicism in the United States was the largest and clearest case of a religious body appearing outside the mainstream of evangelical Protestantism. To evangelical Protestants it was an alien intrusion into *their* Christian America. Both Protestants and Roman Catholics tended to focus on that which kept them apart in the first years of their contact with one another in the new land. Hence the importance of Jay P. Dolan, *Catholic Revivalism: The American Experience, 1830-1900** (Notre Dame, Ind.: Univ. of Notre Dame Press, 1978), which recounts the story of certain Catholic developments which are surprisingly akin to Protestant revivalism, even concluding that Catholic revivalism in America fostered the same kind of generic religious experience called "evangelical" as did the Protestant. Dolan also shows some very distinct differences between Catholic and Protestant piety, but his effort to portray Roman Catholic piety rather than institutional developments is an important new direction for the study of that religious group in America. Essays on different aspects of American Catholicism can be found in Philip Gleason, ed., *Catholicism in America** (New York: Harper & Row, 1970).

Two types of books predominate among recent studies of American Roman Catholicism. One type consists of studies of American Catholics as a part of the history of the urban immigration of the later nineteenth century; the other type consists of books about Catholicism on the contemporary American scene, often with special reference to the problems of renewal, making this sometimes an intra-Catholic, controversial literature. Among studies relating Catholicism to immigration are Silvano M. Tomasi, *Piety and Power: The Role of Italian Parishes in the New York Metropolitan Area, 1880-1930* (New York: Center for Migration Studies, 1975); Jay P. Dolan, *The Immigrant Church: New York's Irish and German Catholics, 1815-1865** (Baltimore: Johns Hopkins Univ. Press, 1975); Richard M. Linkh, *American Catholicism and European Immigrants, 1900-1924* (New York: Center for Migration Studies, 1975); Harold J. Abramson, *Ethnic Diversity in Catholic America* (New York: John Wiley & Sons, 1973); and Donna Merwick, *Boston Priests, 1848-1910: A Study* *of Social and Intellectual Change* (Cambridge: Harvard Univ. Press, 1973), which argues that "Yankee" Catholics controlled Boston Catholicism to a surprisingly late date.

Treatments of contemporary Catholicism include such portraits of the American Catholic built upon social scientific data as William T. Liu and Nathaniel J. Pallone, editors, *Catholics/U.S.A.: Perspectives on Social Change* (New York: Wiley & Sons, 1970), containing papers on many different aspects of Catholic life; and Andrew M. Greeley, *The American Catholic: A Social Portrait** (New York: Basic Books, 1977), which makes a number of revisionist points about the wealth, education, and religious orientation of American Roman Catholics. Forceful as presentations of opinion as well as analyses of the contemporary Catholic church are John Cogley, *Catholic America** (Garden City, N.J.: Doubleday, 1973), with some background historical material, and David J. O'Brien, *The Renewal of American Catholicism* (New York: Oxford Univ. Press, 1972; *Paulist Press). Episodes of interchurch exchange are recounted in Lerond Curry, *Protestant-Catholic Relations in America, World War I Through Vatican II* (Lexington: Univ. Press of Kentucky, 1972).

Judaism in America

Judaism, like Catholicism, grew rapidly in America through nineteenth-century immigration, particularly in the latter part of the century. And, appropriately, immigration and adaptation to American ways have been prominent themes in the literature about American Jews. Thomas Kessner, *The Golden Door: Italian and Jewish Immigrant Mobility in New York City 1880-1915* (New York: Oxford, 1977), compares Jewish immigrants with one group of Roman Catholic immigrants, arguing that certain factors operative among Jews resulted in their more rapid achievement of success in America, though religion as such is somewhat slighted in his analysis. A particularly important book about Jewish adaptation in America is Leon A. Jick, *The Americanization of the Synagogue, 1820-1870* (Hanover, N.H.: Univ. Press of New England, 1976), which minimizes the influence of German Jewish programmatic Reform and interprets the changing religious usages of American Jews, at least for the period covered, as the consequence of pragmatic adaptation to American ways by the laity. The adaptation of Jews to life in America is also the subject of Irving Howe's massive but popular volume, *World of Our Fathers: The Journey of the East European Jews to America and the Life They Found and Made** (New York: Simon and Schuster, 1976).

Some might argue that, at least so far as the preservation of Judaism is concerned, the formation of Ethical Culture represented an over-adaptation; that movement can be studied in a recent monograph on its founder, *From Reform Judaism to Ethical Culture: The Religious Evolution of Felix Adler,* by Benny Kraut (Cincinnati: Hebrew Union College Press, 1979). A valuable study of a group who resisted what they regarded as excessive over-adaptation is Marshall Sklare, *Conservative Judaism: An American Religious Movement** (New York: Schocken Books, 1972), a revised edition of an earlier work. That American Jews had other interests besides adaptation to their new American home is attested to by Naomi W. Cohen, *American Jews and the Zionist Idea* (New York: KTAV, 1975).

Many other aspects of Judaism in America besides that of the adaptation of immigrants to a new land are explored in several useful symposia and general treatments. Joseph L. Blau, *Judaism in America: From Curiosity to Third Faith** (Chicago: Univ. of Chicago Press, 1976), supplements a brief historical sketch with a fuller discussion of some of the main issues important for understanding contemporary American Judaism. Marshall Sklare, *America's Jews** (New York: Random House, 1971), provides an overview of American Judaism from a sociological perspective, with data concerning Jewish family life, education, intermarriage, and other similar matters. Two volumes edited by Jacob Neusner on *Understanding American Judaism: Toward the Description of a Modern Religion* (New York: KTAV, 1975), draw together essays and articles on *The Rabbi and the Synagogue* (Vol. I) and *Sectors of American Judaism: Reform, Orthodoxy, Conservatism, and Reconstruction* (Vol. II). More miscellaneous in its contents is Bernard Martin, ed., *Movements and Issues in American Judaism: An Analysis and Sourcebook of Developments Since 1945* (Westport, Conn.: Greenwood, 1978).[4]

Recent Religious Developments

The literature dealing with more recent developments in American religion can also be related to certain important impulses in American religious life, but such impulses are more difficult to pinpoint when the advantage of extended hindsight is absent. Originally published in 1952, Herbert Wallace Schneider's essay on *Religion in Twentieth Century America* has been reissued in a revised edition (New York: Atheneum, 1964*); in spite of its age, it contains many fine insights. The essays brought together in William G. McLoughlin and Robert N. Bellah, editors, *Religion in America** (Boston: Beacon, 1968), deal with very contemporary interests and supplement Schenider's book. Martin E. Marty, *A Nation of Behavers* (Chicago: Univ. of Chicago Press, 1976), supplies a new behavioral typology for the "mapping" of the current American religious scene. *Religion in America, 1950 to the Present,* by Jackson W. Carroll, Douglas W. Johnson, and Martin E. Marty (New York: Harper & Row, 1979), uses maps and statistical tables to identify trends and patterns. A more regional approach to the current scene is Samuel S. Hill, Jr. et al., *Religion and the Solid South** (Nashville: Abingdon, 1972).

A few more particular impulses important in the contemporary scene can be investigated in such recent books as Samuel McCrea Cavert, *The American Churches in the Ecumenical Movement: 1900-1968* (New York: Association Press, 1968) and *Church Cooperation and Unity in America: A Historical Review, 1900-1970* (New York: Association Press, 1970); Edward E. Thornton, *Professional Education for Ministry: A History of Clinical Pastoral Education* (Nashville: Abingdon Press, 1970), a book which is programmatic as well as historical; Harold E. Quinley, *The Prophetic Clergy: Social Activism Among Protestant Ministers* (New York: Wiley & Sons, 1974); and Michael H. Ducey,

William Ashley "Billy" Sunday (1862–1935), flamboyant evangelist of the early twentieth century. Lithograph by George Bellows, 1923. Photograph courtesy National Portrait Gallery, Smithsonian Institution, Washington, D.C. Negative number 74.69.

Sunday Morning: Aspects of Urban Ritual (New York: Free Press, 1977), the latter two sociological in approach.

Most of the interpretive essays dealing with the current religious scene in the United States have been concerned with what is by now the somewhat tortured question of civil religion: Is there a religious tradition and general piety separate from that of the particular denominations that can be identified as the civil religion that is also the real functional religion of Americans? That has been the question, and one breakthrough in the more recent literature has been the attempt to gain greater historical perspective on the question. Catherine L. Albanese, *Sons of the Fathers: The Civil Religion of the American Revolution* (Philadelphia: Temple Univ. Press, 1976), has employed the methods of comparative religions to understand the ways in which events and persons of the American Revolutionary era became symbols of national religion. Her chapter on the religious valorization of George Washington by his countrymen is especially persuasive. The general discussion about civil religion in America can be traced in two books by one of the earlier participants in the discussion, Sidney Mead: *The Nation With the Soul of A Church* (New York: Harper & Row, 1975), and *The Old Religion in the Brave New World* (Berkeley: Univ. of Calif. Press, 1977). Another regular participant in the discussion, Robert N. Bellah, *The Broken Covenant: American Civil Religion in Time of Trial** (New York: Seabury, 1975), takes a less positive view of civil religion than he did earlier. John F. Wilson's fresh approach, *Public Religion in American Culture* (Philadelphia: Temple Univ. Press, 1979), suggests the very problematic and complex nature of the whole discussion. The essays in Russell E. Richey and Donald G. Jones, *American Civil Religion** (New York: Harper & Row, 1974), provide a good orientation to the whole subject.

Notes

* Indicates paperback edition.

1. Henry F. May, "The Recovery of American Religious History," *The American Historical Review*, LXX (October, 1964), p. 79.

2. Ibid.

3. For example, Michael McGiffert, "American Puritan Studies in the 1960's," *William and Mary Quarterly*, XXVII (June, 1970), pp. 36-67.

4. Professor David A. Altshuler, my colleague at The George Washington University, kindly proferred many helpful suggestions in the preparation of the paragraphs on American Jewish bibliography.

Dewey D. Wallace, Jr. has been Professor of Religion at The George Washington University since 1974, teaching courses in the history of Religion in the United States. He received the Ph.D. degree from Princeton University where he was a Rockefeller Doctoral Fellow in Religion. He is the author of The Pilgrims *(1977), a treatment of religion in early Colonial America,* Puritans and Predestination *(forthcoming in early 1982 from the University of North Carolina Press), and articles on Puritanism and English Protestantism which have appeared in* Church History, The Harvard Theological Review, *the* Archiv für Reformationsgeschichte, *and elsewhere.*

Autobiography in American Culture: Looking Back at the Seventies

ALBERT E. STONE

From the viewpoint of 1980, there seems no reason to repudiate the observation I made originally in 1972 and revised in 1975: autobiography is a flourishing national pastime and one of the livelier fields of current American studies. The phenomenon of Alex Haley's *Roots,* both as "faction" and a smash hit on television, is one sign of popular interest and cultural significance. If for many readers *Roots* falls well short of *The Autobiography of Malcolm X,* there are other recent works whose imaginative power to verify another's experience have been recognized almost overnight. The instant classic is a favorite Madison Avenue artifact, of course, but it seems that Lillian Hellman's *Pentimento,* Theodore Rosengarten's *All God's Dangers: The Life of Nate Shaw,* and Maxine Hong Kingston's *The Woman Warrior* genuinely merit the praise and critical acclaim they have received. The American tradition of personal narrative that today's writers and collabora-

* This essay is an update of Stone's "Autobiography in American Culture," *ASI* 11 (Winter 1972).

tors inherit from Franklin and Douglass, Thoreau and Whitman, Adams and Stein, Black Elk and Malcolm X shows little sign of decay.

Despite proclamations of the end of autobiography, no such catastrophe has yet hit our bookstores or publishing houses. Neither fiction (with its cannibalistic sub-genres of surfiction and the non-fictional novel), nor documentary and personal journalism, nor the visual media, nor the public and private nightmares of history itself have succeeded in closing down the autobiographical enterprise. Indeed, the reverse seems closer to the truth: autobiography fattens on these competing forces and allied forms of personal expression. Alfred Kazin embraces them all when he observes, "the experience of being so much a 'self'—constantly explaining oneself and telling one's story—is as traditional in the greatest American writing as it is in a barroom."[1]

Counterpointing the popular and scholarly implications of this national habit led in many directions in the mid- and late-1970s. Because autobiography is a capacious category of storytelling, it has a way of slipping through scholars' nets. On the one hand, autobiographies lend themselves, either singly or in selected groups, to a variety of ideological interpretations and vocabularies. This impingement is perhaps most clearly seen in the politicized areas of social experience addressed in such university programs as Women's Studies, Afro-American Studies, and Native American Studies. Stephen Butterfield's polemical *Black Autobiography in America* is a case in point.[2] But the sometimes narrower devotees of literary criticism, history, psychology, sociology, religion, and philosophy peruse autobiographies through their own special spectacles, too. An excellent bibliographical survey of this complex interaction is Robert F. Sayre's "The Proper Study—Autobiographies in American Studies."[3] Another, even more theoretical critique is James Olney's "Autobiography and the Cultural Movement," the introduction to his recent rich anthology, *Autobiography: Essays Theoretical and Critical.*[4]

Whereas Sayre succinctly and shrewdly traces the autobiographical impulse through American literary and cultural history, Olney brings together an international symposium. He opens with Gusdorf's epochal essay of 1956 (here translated for the first time), includes a fine selection of seminal statements by Starobinski, Spender, Cox, Howarth, Renza and others, and adds several very provocative pieces written for this occasion.[5] For Americanists, the most stimulating of these new interpretations are Barrett John Mandel's "Full of Life Now," Sayre's "Autobiography and the Making of America," and Elizabeth Bruss's "Eye For I: Making and Unmaking Autobiography in Film."[6] Indeed, Mandel's discussion of autobiography and fiction and the necessary, cocreative role of the reader is the most sensible I have read on these central problems. Bruss is equally fresh and precise in juxtaposing linguistic and film images as vehicles of personal recreation within a culture increasingly dominated by impersonal technologies. Though she foresees the end of traditional written autobiography as movies and television turn all of us into viewers, button-pushers, and screen images, Bruss's very argument celebrates the unique power of words to satisfy deep desires people have to share identity-creating experience.

Samuel L. Clemens (Mark Twain), 1835–1910, and Helen A. Keller, 1880–1968, two prominent American auto-biographers, are pictured together in this photograph by Isabel V. Lyon, taken about 1908. Photograph courtesy National Portrait Gallery, Smithsonian Institution, Washington, D.C. Negative number 79.166.

Both in his introduction and in an earlier essay, "Autos * Bios * Graphein: The Study of Autobiographical Literature,"[7] Olney notes how attention in much of this recent criticism has shifted from *bios* (life as the past acts and thoughts available for recreation), to *autos* (the "I" who remembers, imagines, is self-conscious), and especially towards *graphein* (strategies of self-composition). Four recent books on the American autobiographical tradition illustrate varieties of emphasis and balance among these interlocking autobiographical elements.

The most graphical, ahistorical, and non-psychological is Mutlu Konuk Blasing's *The Art of Life: Studies in American Autobiographical Literature*.[8] "We conceive of ourselves in the image of fiction," she boldly asserts. This preoccupation with the autobiographer as creative artist leads to a mixture of familiar and strange bedfellows: Thoreau, Whitman, and Adams—conventional choices—and James's Prefaces to the New York Edition (not *A Small Boy and Others* or even *The American Scene*), Williams's *Paterson*, and the *Collected Poems* of Frank O'Hara. (I am reminded of some of Olney's choices of texts in *Metaphors of Self*.[9]) Blasing's preference is always for words over actions, form over expressed motive. For her, therefore, autobiographical consciousness can only be the turning back of time by the imagination. She shows little sympathy for the backward *and* forward motions of memory and consciousness responding to pressures from a surviving historical record—what the historian does—or the possibly equally systematic reflections of a self reimagining itself moving through the life cycle and a series of historical moments—what the analyst and analysand create together. These are Eriksonian possibilities for autobiography once voiced in "Gandhi's Autobiography: The Leader as a Child," and later recapitulated in *Life History and the Historical Moment*.[10]

A second work also stressing *graphein* and *autos* over *bios* is Robert B. Stepto's *From Behind the Veil: A Study of Afro-American Narrative*.[11] In a spare style which contrasts strikingly with Butterfield's political rhetoric, Stepto traces a traditional pattern in black narratives of the self. He begins with the "call" issued by early writers—the ex-slave narrators, Washington, and Du Bois—to recount the ascent from slavery to articulate selfhood and one's reimmersion in the black experience. This leads to "responses" by twentieth-century writers, chiefly J.W. Johnson, Wright, and Ellison. Literary and rhetorical categories and the guiding presence of a "pregeneric myth" govern the focus of this severely selective history. Because nuances of ideology and private psychology must be subordinated to the collective myth and its forms, little room remains for hybrid but influential or culturally significant texts like *Cane, The Autobiography of Malcolm X*, or *Blueschild Baby*. Nonetheless, his distinction between personal history and autobiography— between self-authentication and self-identification—is carefully argued. In particular, Stepto's anatomy works well on the slave narratives. His discussion is a model of clarity and should be set alongside the historical treatments of C.W. Nichols, John Blassingame, and W.W. Nichols and other literary treatments like David Minter's.[12]

Autobiography is a mode of prophecy and communal myth for others besides Afro-Americans, and this strain in cultural history is traced by

G. Thomas Couser in *American Autobiography: The Prophetic Mode.*[13] Because he believes this to be *the* predominant mode and motive in our tradition, Couser includes a broader range of illustrative texts than either Blasing or Stepto. In fact, the didactic impulse to conflate personal history and community values is discovered just about everywhere: in the Puritans and Franklin, of course, but also in nearly all later celebrants of the self from Thoreau, Whitman, and Louis Sullivan to Malcolm X, Mailer, and Pirsig. Though his strategy is comparative, Couser finds in each text that prophetic vision that bends *bios* away from verifiable, particular, self-defining actions into mythic narrative. *Autos* hence becomes the writer's self-image in terms of others' expectations and assumptions. Thus as prophetic document, *The Education of Henry Adams* is not read as a place where its author reveals the absence of Marian Hooper Adams, nor are Adams's present-day readers distinguished from the special audience Adams addressed in the privately published book of 1907 or the hypothetical readers named in its preface. Autobiographical audiences always include both "the self and others," Phyllis Greenacre believes.[14] Couser simplifies this insight just as he also simplifies the Biblical varieties of prophecy on which his thesis stands. His approach in important respects recapitulates the argument of W.C. Spengemann and L.R. Lundquist's 1965 essay, "Autobiography and the American Myth."[15]

In some respects, Thomas Cooley's *Educated Lives: The Rise of Modern American Autobiography*[16] balances more adroitly than Blasing, Stepto, or Couser the conflicting claims Olney sees between history, self, and writing. Like Blasing and Stepto, Cooley selects his texts carefully to make his thesis. By concentrating upon Adams, Twain, Howells, and James as exemplars of the turn-of-the-century switch from autobiographies of "cultivation" to stories of "education," Cooley highlights *autos* as the central issue in a history of consciousness. William James, Wilhelm Dilthey, and Erik Erikson lend support to this modern concept of the individual as one who develops through distinct stages of growth in shifting adaptations to environment.

The self in the pages of *The Education, The Autobiography, A Boy's Town,* and *A Small Boy and Others* is indeed cumulative, distinctive, situational. In earlier autobiographies like those of Franklin and Thoreau, by contrast, personal identity is more clearly a matter of universal human qualities and innate capacities to be unfolded. Psychological realism, therefore, links these prophetic four to later autobiographers like Stein, as it also makes connections to many forms of fiction in the twentieth century. Unfortunately, Cooley's stimulating discussion of general pattern and individual variant is conducted in chapters even briefer than Stepto's. In advancing his thesis in terms of a generation of experimental intellectuals and artists, Cooley (as cultural historian) might have been even more original had he ranged *sideways* as well as *forward*. Besides discussing Steffens, Stein, and Sherwood Anderson as successors, he might also have examined additional writers like Jane Addams, Alexander Berkman, Andrew Carnegie, or Booker T. Washington. This might have allowed us to see more precisely what historical and social circumstances attended this cultural shift in autobiographical consciousness and what possibly were its racial, sexual, or occupational boundaries.

Taken together, then, these four intelligent studies of American autobiography advance knowledge of autobiography as history less than they illuminate questions of rhetoric, literature, and psychology. They reflect the privileged position literature still holds in American culture studies. Given this emphasis on autobiography as literary act, it should come as no surprise that historians and social scientists in the 1970s failed to explore autobiography as carefully or imaginatively as literary critics. Irving Louis Horowitz notes this neglect in "Autobiography as Presentation of Self for Social Immortality," one of several essays in a special issue of *New Literary History* devoted to "self-confrontation and social vision."[17]

There is, for example, no "American historian" whose comprehensive knowledge of autobiography matches that of Karl J. Weintraub. Nor, as far as I know, is there yet any comprehensive study of biography and autobiography as historical documents. Yet as John Blassingame, Sayre, and others assert, autobiography is a matchless repository and complex historical document. Autobiographers almost always conceive of themselves as living history as their own fate, which is Kazin's argument in "The Self as History: Reflections on Autobiography." Meditating on the autobiographical self "as a creature of history and history as a human creation," Kazin explores personal narrative in what is for him a significantly new perspective. For years, literary critics have invoked his earlier essay, "Autobiography as Narrative," to support the belief that modern autobiographers essentially compose fictions, not verifiable histories.[18] Yet in that previous piece Kazin puzzled over the autobiographical impulse which leads a Hemingway to write both *A Moveable Feast* and *The Sun Also Rises.* That difference, he now asserts, is historical consciousness, the vision that places the person (but not necessarily the private psyche) at the center of social, temporal experience. Only as the cultural critic recognizes the various implications and manifestations of living and reliving a common past in a unique way does autobiography's full significance as cultural document become available. So far, our best guide to this task is the work of the European historian Weintraub, behind whom looms the immense presence of Dilthey.[19]

As Kazin and others frequently note, women, blacks, and other oppressed individuals often reflect a keener historical consciousness than do white males, for whom history is likely to be at once more comforting, mysterious, and threatening. Therefore it is understandable that personal history flourishes among members of groups who have newly stepped on the stage of public history—or are now perceived by readers and publishers to have done so. For such writers, the impulse to fantasize a personal past is often checked by a sense of social realities pressing to be protested against. As Roger Rosenblatt observes, "no black American author has ever felt the need to invent a nightmare to make his point."[20]

Discussion of black autobiography in the past half-dozen years has been particularly vigorous and varied in perspective. Not only are there now four full-length books in print (by Barton, Smith, Butterfield, and Stepto), plus Russell Brignano's bibliography, but the black tradition in autobiography has become the subject of university courses, several symposia, and special issues in journals.[21] The Summer, 1975, number of *Kansas Quarterly* is notable for bringing together autobiographical reminiscences of Gordon Parks and critical essays by Mary W. Burger, George E. Kent, and Elizabeth Schultz.[22] The imaginative and ideological power of works like *Up From Slavery* and *The Autobiography of Malcolm X* has been explored in several fruitful ways: *thematically* in Rosenblatt's "Black Autobiography: Life as the Death Weapon"; *comparatively* in Stephen Whitfield's "Three Masters of Impression Management: Benjamin Franklin, Booker T. Washington, and Malcolm X as Autobiographers"; and in *individually* focussed essays like Paul John Eakin's excellent "Malcolm X and the Limits of Autobiography" and James Cox's "Autobiography and Washington."[23]

For some reason, the 1970s saw less comprehensive and less exciting work on women's life stories than on black autobiographies. There is as yet neither a full-length study of American women's autobiographies nor an adequate bibliographical guide to this large literature. Several provocative general speculations have been made by Patricia Meyer Spacks, whose *The Female Imagination* includes a vigorous critique of Mary McCarthy, Lillian Hellman, and Anais Nin.[24] Suzanne Juhasz and Mary Mason have also written general statements about what is distinctively feminine in the autobiographies of women from both Europe and America.[25] Lillian Schlissel has examined frontier women's diaries.[26] The diary form itself, as either the anteroom to autobiography or a special form thereof, is examined in Robert Fothergill's *Private Chronicles.*[27] In much of this literature the unique place of Anais Nin, that matchless diarist and undogmatic feminist, is now acknowledged. Indeed, the canonical place of the *Diary* seems as clear for women's studies as that of *The Autobiography of Malcolm X* in modern black autobiography and the autobiographies of Michel Leiris for theorists and comparatists. Two recent books by Nin herself—*A Woman Speaks* and *In Favor of the Sensitive Man, and Other Essays*—contain eloquent defenses of her lifelong dedication to the inward voyage of exploration, of which the *Diary* is the multivolumed yet unified result.[28] Robert Zaller's *A Casebook on Anais Nin* reprints many perceptive pieces; an especially sensitive one on *Diary-I* is by Tristine Rainer.[29] Nevertheless, this whole rich field of cultural criticism, stimulated recently by the autobiographies of so many women like Abigail McCarthy and Margaret Mead, Mae West and Shirley MacLaine, Maya Angelou and Nikki Giovanni, Maxine Hong Kingston and Sylvia Plath, lies open to further cultivation by historians, bibliographers, psychoanalysts, and literary critics.

American Indian autobiography, though a much sparser field than women's lives, and one patrolled until quite recently by anthropologists, has emerged in the past few years as a discrete literary and historical subject. Lynn W. O'Brien's *Plains Indian Autobiographies* marks a beginning, in one geographical area at least, as a survey.[30] William F. Smith's "American Indian Autobiographies" is a very helpful description and literary evaluation of a number of works in this literature, stretching from Charles Eastman's *Indian Boyhood* (1902) to *Lame Deer: Seeker of Visions* (1972).[31] If for most Wasichu readers the special place in this tradition of *Black Elk Speaks* seems assured, additional grounds for believing so can be found in two perceptive pieces which explore Neihardt's role in the collaboration: Sally McClusky's "Black Elk Speaks—And So Does John Neihardt," and Carol T. Holly's "*Black Elk Speaks* and the Making of Indian Autobiography."[32]

Neihardt's signal achievement gives literary form and historical significance to Black Elk's early life, while allowing the white reader to experience Black Elk at the center of his world by virtue of his vision. No purely temporal or social definition of identity could have done justice to the Sioux holy man's autobiographical performance—any more than it can for the reader of other American spiritual autobiographers like Woolman, Thoreau, Merton, or Annie Dillard. How to incorporate into cultural analysis this transcendent essence of personality and the timeless dimension of human experience is a challenge accepted by several scholars in recent years. Despite different approaches and assumptions, these explorations of autobiographical works all address Dillard's existential question, "what do we think of nothingness, those sickening reaches of time in either direction?"[33] Before sentience, beneath consciousness, and after death are zones which language has trouble penetrating. No simple Jamesian, Freudian, or Jungian categories have yet succeeded in clarifying the nuances of self and soul suggested when Thoreau casts his fishing line upward into the clouds, Anais Nin drums on her belly, or Shirley MacLaine lies warmly under a single blanket in the frigid darkness of Bhutan. The soul demands equal time from the self in these narratives as in many others; the unconscious has its say at least as clearly in personal history as in poetry and fiction. Yet these mysterious depths of human experience are inseparable from culture and language.

This enigma has been examined recently in several fascinating essays, including Mandel's "Full of Life Now," Burton Pike's "Time in Autobiography," Janet Varner Gunn's "Autobiography and the Narrative Experience of Temporality as Depth," and John Sturrock in "The New Model Autobiographer."[34] Both ends of the life cycle—childhood and approaching death—open onto timelessness and the unconscious. I have used psychoanalytic insights of Phyllis Greenacre and the ecological imagination of Edith Cobb to explore childhood and creativity as visionary experience in Louis Sullivan's *The Autobiography of an Idea*.[35] Liliane Arensberg focuses attention upon a different childish preoccupation in her essay on death in *I Know Why the Caged Bird Sings*.[36] In fact, Arensberg's essay, as does Couser's broader one on "The Shape of Death in American Autobiography,"[37] illustrates the continuing need for close scrutinies of particular lives and texts in order to put flesh on the bare bones of abstract arguments like Rosenblatt's in "Black Autobiography: Life as the Death Weapon."

Indeed, one fact to be learned from this whole rich and multifaceted literature on American autobiography—which this brief survey has by no means exhausted[38]—is the necessity of systematically shifting focus from text to context to conceptual framework and, I would argue, back to text again. After all, autobiography is a cultural artifact celebrating individual consciousness and experience. It is valid and important chiefly to the cultural critic interested in how people, events, things, relationships, ideas, and emotions have become meaningful to a single mind as it uses language to pattern the past. As cultural critics, therefore, the task is precisely the same as the one Ronald Grele ascribes to oral history: "Our aim is to bring to conscious articulation the ideological problematic of the author, to reveal the cultural context in which information is being conveyed, and to transform an individual story into a cultural narrative, and so to understand more fully what happened in the past."[39] But the oral historian with the tape recorder, like the anthropologist on a reservation, has the storyteller in his grip; he or she looks in from the outside, with a sheaf of questions in hand. From within autobiography, however, comes the perennial voice of the self—Anais Nin's in this case: "There is not one big, cosmic meaning for all," she cries, "there is only the meaning we each give to our life, an individual meaning, an individual plot, like an individual novel, a book for each person. To seek a total unity is wrong."[40] How to balance Grele and Nin, and to see autobiography in its cultural usefulness as a participant/observer art and science (and thus allied methodologically to anthropology and psychoanalysis as well as to literary criticism and history), is the challenge of the 1980s that autobiography presents to American studies.   □

Notes

1. "The Self as History: Reflections on Autobiography," in *Telling Lives, the Biographer's Art,* Marc Pachter, ed. (Washington, D.C.: New Republic Books, National Portrait Gallery, 1979), 76.

2. *Black Autobiography in America* (Amherst: University of Massachusetts Press, 1974).

3. "The Proper Study—Autobiographies in American Studies," *American Quarterly* 29 (Bibliographical Issue, 1977), 241–62.

4. James Olney, ed., *Autobiography: Essays Theoretical and Critical* (Princeton: Princeton University Press, 1980). Hereinafter, Olney.

5. Jean Starobinski, "The Style of Autobiography," reprinted from *Literary Style: A Symposium,* Seymour Chatman, ed. (New York: Oxford University Press, 1971), 285–94; Stephen Spender, "Confessions and Autobiography," reprinted from *The Making of a Poem* (New York: W. W. Norton, 1962), 63–72; James M. Cox, "Recovering Literature's Lost Ground Through Autobiography," reprinted from *The Southern Review* 14 (October, 1978), 633–52; William L. Howarth, "Some Principles of Autobiography," reprinted from *New Literary History* 5 (Winter, 1974), 363–81; Louis A. Renza, "The Veto of the Imagination: A Theory of Autobiography," reprinted from *New Literary History* 9 (Autumn, 1977), 1–26.

6. Mandel, "Full of Life Now," in Olney, 49–72; Sayre, "Autobiography and the Making of America," in Olney, 146–68; Bruss, "Eye for I: Making and Unmaking Autobiography in Film," in Olney, 296–320.

7. "Autos*Bios*Graphein: The Study of Autobiographical Literature," *South Atlantic Quarterly* 77 (Winter, 1978), 113–23.

8. *The Art of Life: Studies in American Autobiographical Literature* (Austin: University of Texas Press, 1977).

9. *Metaphors of Self: The Meaning of Autobiography* (Princeton: Princeton University Press, 1972).

10. Erik Erikson, "Gandhi's Autobiography: The Leader as a Child," *American Scholar* 35 (Autumn, 1966), 632–46; *Life History and the Historical Moment: Diverse Presentations* (New York: W. W. Norton, 1975), 113–68.

11. *From Behind the Veil: A Study of Afro-American Narrative* (Urbana: University of Illinois Press, 1979).

12. C. W. Nichols, *Many Thousand Gone: The Ex-Slaves' Account of their Bondage and Freedom* (Bloomington: Indiana University Press, 1969); Blassingame, *The Slave Community: Plantation Life in the Antebellum South* (New York: Oxford University Press, 1972), 227–35; "Black Autobiographies as History and Literature," *Black Scholar* 5 (December, 1973–January, 1974), 2–9; W. W. Nichols, "Slave Narratives: Dismissed Evidence in the Writing of Southern History," *Phylon* 32 (Winter, 1971), 403–409; Minter, "Conceptions of Self in Black Slave Narratives," *American Transcendental Quarterly* 24 (1974), 62–68.

13. Couser, *American Autobiography: The Prophetic Mode* (Amherst: University of Massachusetts Press, 1979).

14. Greenacre, "The Childhood of the Artist: Libidinal Phase Development and Giftedness," *Emotional Growth: Psychoanalytic Studies of the Gifted and a Great Variety of Other Individuals* (New York: International Universities Press, 1971), Vol. II, 481.

15. "Autobiography and the American Myth," *American Quarterly* 17 (Fall, 1965), 501–519.

16. *Educated Lives: the Rise of Modern Autobiography in America* (Columbus: Ohio State University, 1976).

17. "Autobiography as Presentation of Self for Social Immortality," *New Literary History* 9 (Autumn, 1977), 173–79.

18. Kazin, "The Self as History," pp. 76–77; "Autobiography as Narrative," *Michigan Quarterly Review* 3 (Fall, 1964), 210–16.

19. Karl J. Weintraub, "Autobiography and Historical Consciousness," *Critical Inquiry* 1 (June, 1975), pp. 821–48; *The Value of the Individual: Self and Circumstance in Autobiography* (Chicago: University of Chicago Press, 1978); Wilhelm Dilthey, *Pattern and Meaning in History* (New York: Harper and Row, 1960).

20. "Black Autobiography: Life as the Death Weapon," in Olney, 171.

21. Rebecca C. Barton, *Witnesses for Freedom: Negro Americans in Autobiography* (Oakdale, N.Y.: Dowling College Press, 1976); Sidonie Smith, *Where I'm Bound: Patterns of Slavery and Freedom in Black American Autobiography* (Westport, Conn.: Greenwood Press, 1974); Russell Brignano, *Black Americans in Autobiography: An Annotated Bibliography of Autobiographies and Autobiographical Books Written since the Civil War* (Durham, N.C.: Duke University Press, 1974).

22. Burger, "I, Too, Sing America: The Black Autobiographer's Response to Life in the Midwest and Mid-Plains," *Kansas Quarterly* 7 (Summer, 1975), 43–57; Kent, "Maya Angelou's *I Know Why the Caged Bird Sings* and Black

Autobiographical Tradition," *ibid.,* 72–78; Schultz, "To Be Black and Blue: The Blues Genre in Black American Autobiography," *ibid.,* 81–96.

23. "Three Masters of Impression Management: Benjamin Franklin, Booker T. Washington, and Malcolm X as Autobiographers," *South Atlantic Quarterly* 77 (Autumn, 1978), 399–417; Eakin, "Malcolm X and the Limits of Autobiography," *Criticism* 18 (Summer, 1976), 230–242 (reprinted in Olney, pp. 181–93); Cox, "Autobiography and Washington," *Sewanee Review* 85 (April June, 1977), 235–61.

24. Spacks, *The Female Imagination* (New York: Avon Books, 1976), 232–41, 381–84, 390–93. See also Spacks, "Reflecting Women," *Yale Review* 63 (October, 1973), 26–42; "Women's Stories, Women's Selves," *Hudson Review* 30 (Spring, 1977), 29–46.

25. Juhasz, "Some Deep Old Desk and Capacious Hold-All: Form and Women's Autobiography," *College English* 39 (February, 1978), 663–68; Mason, "The Other Voice: Autobiographies of Women Writers," in Olney, 207–35.

26. "Women's Diaries on the Western Frontier," *American Studies* 18 (Spring, 1977), 87–100.

27. Fothergill, *Private Chronicles: A Study of English Diaries* (London: Oxford University Press, 1974).

28. Nin, *A Woman Speaks: The Lectures, Seminars, and Interviews of Anais Nin,* Evelyn J. Hinz, ed. (Chicago: Swallow Press, 1975); *In Favor of the Sensitive Man, and Other Essays* (New York: Harcourt Brace and Jovanovitch, 1976).

29. Rainer, "Anais Nin's *Diary I:* The Birth of the Young Woman as an Artist," in *A Casebook on Anais Nin,* Robert Zaller, ed. (New York: New American Library, 1974), 161–68.

30. *Plains Indian Autobiographies* (Boise: Boise State College, 1973).

31. "American Indian Autobiographies," *American Indian Quarterly* 2 (Autumn, 1975), 237–45.

32. McCluskey, *"Black Elk Speaks* —And So Does John Neihardt," *Western American Literature* 6 (Winter, 1972), 231–42; Holly, *"Black Elk Speaks* and the Making of Indian Autobiography," *Genre* 12 (Spring, 1979), 117–36.

33. Dillard, *Pilgrim at Tinker Creek* (New York: Harper's, 1974), 7.

34. Pike, "Time in Autobiography," *Comparative Literature* 28 (Fall, 1976), 326–42; Gunn, "Autobiography and the Narrative Experience of Temporality as Depth," *Soundings* 60 (Summer, 1977), 194–209; Sturrock, "The New Model Autobiographer," *New Literary History* 9 (Autumn, 1977), 51–63.

35. Albert E. Stone, "Autobiography and the Childhood of the American Artist: The Example of Louis Sullivan," in *American Character and Culture in a Changing World,* J. A. Hague, ed. (Westport, Conn.: Greenwood Press, 1979), 293–322.

36. "Death as Metaphor of Self in *I Know Why the Caged Bird Sings," College Language Association Journal* 20 (December, 1976), 273–91.

37. "The Shape of Death in American Autobiography," *Hudson Review* 31 (Spring, 1978), 53–66.

38. A sampling of other current criticism of American autobiography is: Timothy D. Adams, "The Contemporary American Mock-Autobiography,"

Clio 8 (Spring, 1979), 417–28; Lynn Z. Bloom, "Gertrude in Alice in Everybody: Innovation and Point of View in Gertrude Stein's Autobiography," *Twentieth-Century Literature* 24 (Spring, 1978), 81–93; Michael G. Cooke, "Do You Remember Laura?, or The Limits of Autobiography," *Iowa Review* 9 (Spring, 1978), 58–72; Paul John Eakin, "Alfred Kazin's Bridge to America," *South Atlantic Quarterly* 77 (Winter, 1978), 81–93; Roger J. Porter, "Unspeakable Practices, Writable Acts: Franklin's *Autobiography*," *Hudson Review* 32 (Summer, 1979), 224–38; Patricia Meyer Spacks, "Stages of Self: Notes on Autobiography and the Life Cycle," *Boston University Journal* 25, No. 2 (1977), 7–17; Albert E. Stone, "Cato's Mirror: The Face of Violence in American Autobiography," in *Prospects: An Annual of American Cultural Studies,* Vol. III. Jack Salzman, ed. (New York: Burt Franklin, 1977), 331–69; Mas'ud Zavarzadeh, *The Mythopoeic Reality: The Postwar American Nonfictional Novel* (Urbana: University of Illinois Press, 1976).

39. "Movement Without Aim: Methodological and Theoretical Problems in Oral History," in *Envelopes of Sound: Six Practitioners Discuss the Method, Theory, and Practice of Oral History and Oral Testimony* (Chicago: Precedent Pub., 1975), 142.

40. *Diary of Anais Nin,* Vol. I. (New York: Harcourt Brace and Jovanovich, 1966), vii.

Albert E. Stone *is Professor of English and Chairman of the American Studies Program at the University of Iowa. Previously he taught at Yale (where he received his BA and PhD degrees in American Studies) and at Emory. During 1968-69, he was Fulbright lecturer at Charles University, Prague. He is the author of* The Innocent Eye: Childhood in Mark Twain's Imagination *(1961) and* Autobiographical Occasions and Original Acts: Studies in Modern American Autobiography *(forthcoming, 1982). He has also edited Crèvecoeur's* Letters From An American Farmer & Sketches of XVIII-Century America *(for the Penguin American Library, 1981), and* The American Autobiography: A Collection of Critical Essays *(1981). Recent lecture tours and seminars have taken him to India (1976), Tunisia (1980), France and Switzerland (1981). Currently he is on the Advisory Board of Editors for* Research in English and American Literature *(West Germany).*

"Interpreting Nineteenth-Century American Literature": A Supplement

ARLIN TURNER

Scholarly writing and publishing on nineteenth-century American literature continued in an increasing stream through the 1970s, and it is pleasant to note that major historical and critical works and important bibliographical, textual, and other aids to research are scheduled for future publication.

Among the significant historical and interpretative works on inclusive subjects that have appeared during this decade are the following: Daniel Aaron, *The Unwritten War: American Writers and the Civil War* (New York: Alfred A. Knopf, 1973); Walter Blair and Hamlin Hill, *America's Humor, From Poor Richard to Doonesbury* (New York: Oxford University Press, 1978); Paul F. Boller, Jr., *American Transcendentalism, 1830–1860; An Intellectual Inquiry* (New York: G. P. Putnam's Sons, 1975); Bernard I. Duffey, *Poetry in America: Expression and Its Values in the Times of Bryant, Whitman, and Pound* (Durham, North Carolina: Duke University Press, 1978); Edward Halsey Foster, *The Civilized Wilderness: Backgrounds of American Romantic Literature* (New York: Macmillan, 1975); Harold Kaplan, *Democratic Humanism and*

Henry James (1843–1916). Photograph by Alice Boughton (1865/6–1943), 19.6 × 16.3 cm., 1906. National Portrait Gallery, Smithsonian Institution, Washington, D. C.

American Literature (Chicago: University of Chicago Press, 1972); Russel B. Nye, *Society and Culture in America: 1830–1860* (New York: Harper and Row, 1974); Robert D. Richardson, Jr., *Myth and Literature in the American Renaissance* (Bloomington, Indiana: Indiana University Press, 1978); Henry Nash Smith, *Democracy and the Novel: Popular Resistance to Classic American Writers* (New York: Oxford University Press, 1978); Janis P. Stout, *Sodoms in Eden: The City in American Fiction before 1860* (Westport, Connecticut: Greenwood, 1976); Eric Sundquist, *Home As Found: Authority and Genealogy in Nineteenth-Century American Literature* (Baltimore, Maryland: Johns Hopkins University Press, 1979); Cecelia Tichi, *New World, New Earth: Environmental Reform in American Literature from the Puritans through Whitman* (New Haven, Connecticut: Yale University Press, 1979).

The following works are more restricted in scope: Clive Bush, *The Dream of Reason: American Consciousness and Cultural Achievement from Independence to the Civil War* (New York: St. Martin's Press, 1978); Thomas Cooley, *Educated Lives: The Rise of Modern Autobiography in America* (Columbus, Ohio: Ohio State University Press, 1976); David M. Fine, *The City, the Immigrant, and American Fiction, 1880–1920* (Metuchen, New Jersey: Scarecrow Press, 1977); Rudolf Glanz, *The Jew in Early American Wit and Humor* (New York: Ktav, 1972); Bruce Granger, *American Essay Serials from Franklin to Irving* (Knoxville, Tennessee: University of Tennessee Press, 1978); Susan Kuhlmann, *Knave, Fool, and Genius: The Confidence Man As He Appears in Nineteenth-Century Fiction* (Chapel Hill, North Carolina: University of North Carolina Press, 1973); Lucinda H. Mackethan, *The Dream of Arcady: Place and Time in Southern Literature* (Baton Rouge, Louisiana: Louisiana State University Press, 1979); Roy R. Male, *Enter, Mysterious Stranger: American Cloistral Fiction* (Norman, Oklahoma: University of Oklahoma Press, 1979); Moritz Busch, *Travels between the Hudson and the Mississippi, 1851–1852* (Lexington, Kentucky: University Press of Kentucky, 1971); Marjorie Pryse, *The Mark and the Knowledge: Social Stigma in Classical American Fiction* (Columbus, Ohio; Ohio State University Press, 1979); Kenneth M. Roemer, *The Obsolete Necessity: America in Utopian Writings, 1888–1900* (Kent, Ohio: Kent State University Press, 1976); Anne Rowe, *The Enchanted Country: Northern Writers in the South, 1865–1910* (Baton Rouge, Louisiana: Louisiana State University Press, 1978); William J. Scheick, *The Half Blood: A Cultural Symbol in Nineteenth-Century American Fiction* (Lexington, Kentucky: University Press of Kentucky, 1979); Michael Slater, *Dickens on America and Americans* (Austin, Texas: University of Texas Press, 1978); Kevin Starr, *Americans and the California Dream: 1850–1915* (New York: Oxford University Press, 1973); Taylor Stoehr, *Nay-Saying in Concord: Emerson, Alcott, and Thoreau* (Hamden, Connecticut: Archon, 1979); Peter F. Walker, *Moral Choices: Memory, Desire, and Imagination in Nineteenth-Century American Abolition* (Baton Rouge, Louisiana: Louisiana State University Press, 1978); Jean F. Yellin, *The Intricate Knot: Black Figures in American Literature* (New York: New York University Press, 1972).

In keeping with the principle that every generation interprets its literary past by its own lights, contributions of minorities have received increased scholarly and critical attention in recent years. The most significant writings by blacks, Latin Americans, and American Indians belong to the twentieth century rather than the nineteenth century, but slave narratives first published during the abolition era have been republished and discussed, and several Negro authors have been reprinted and evaluated anew. Most prominent among them is Charles W. Chesnutt, on whom J. Noel Heermance has published a book with the subtitle, *America's First Great Black Novelist* (Hamden, Connecticut: Shoe String Press, 1974). Sylvia Render has collected a volume of short fiction by Chesnutt (Washington, D. C.: Howard University Press, 1974); Curtis W. Ellison and E. W. Metcalf, Jr., have published a reference guide to Chesnutt (Boston: G. K. Hall, 1977). For another Negro author of the nineteenth century, Jay Martin and Gossie H. Hudson have edited *The Paul Laurence Dunbar Reader* (New York: Dodd, Mead, 1975); Peter Revell has published a volume in the Twayne United States Authors Series (Boston: G. K. Hall, 1979); and E. W. Metcalf, Jr., has compiled a bibliography (Metuchen, New Jersey: Scarecrow Press, 1975). *The Booker T. Washington Papers*, edited by Louis R. Harlan, which in 1979 reached *Volume VIII, 1904–6* (Urbana: University of Illinois Press), will be, when complete, one of the major collections of personal papers in print. Accounts of Indian captivity during the past century have been reprinted in a multi-volume collection (New York: Garland Publishing). It may be expected that the literature produced by other racial and national minorities within the country (Oriental, German, Italian, Irish, etc.) will receive comparable study in the future.

The subject of women and American literature of the nineteenth century has been treated at length and from various angles, reflecting the widespread public interest in the place of women in modern society. Nina Baym's book, *Woman's Fiction: A Guide to Novels by and about Women in America, 1820–1870* (Ithaca, New York: Cornell University Press, 1978), should be mentioned, along with Judith Fetterley's *The Resisting Reader: A Feminist Approach to American Fiction* (Bloomington: Indiana University Press, 1978), and two books on women in the writings of Henry James by Mary Doyle Springer and Edward Wagenknecht (see page 18 below). Other books that can be added to this list are the following: Susan Phinney Conrad, *Perish the Thought: Intellectual Women in Romantic America, 1830–1860* (New York: Oxford University Press, 1976); John Eakin, *The New England Girl: Cultural Ideals in Hawthorne, Stowe, Howells and James* (Athens, Georgia: University of Georgia Press, 1976); *American Women Writers*, Volume I, "a critical reference guide," edited by Lina Mainiero (New York: Frederick Unger, 1979, to be concluded in two additional volumes); Barbra Ekman, *The End of a Legend: Ellen Glasgow's History of Southern Women* (Uppsala, Sweden: Almquist & Wiksell, 1976); Thomas Buchanan Read, *The Female Poets of America* (Detroit, Michigan: Gale Research, 1978, reprinted from the 1857 edition); Mary T. Tardy, *The Living Female Writers of the South* (Detroit, Michigan: Gale Research, 1978, reprinted from the 1872 edition). Kate Chopin is prominent among nineteenth-century women authors being reprinted and discussed. Per Seyersted, author of her biography (Baton Rouge, Louisiana: Louisiana State University Press, 1969), and editor of the two-volume edition

Harriet Beecher Stowe (1811–1896). Oil on canvas by Alanson Fisher (1807–1884), 86.4 × 68 cm., 1853. National Portrait Gallery, Smithsonian Institution, Washington, D. C.

of her complete works (Baton Rouge, Louisiana: Louisiana State University Press, 1970), edited for the reprint series of the Feminist Press (Old Westbury, New York, 1974), Chopin's *The Awakening* in a volume with several of her stories. The Arno Press (New York) publishes a reprint series of "Rediscovered Fiction by American Women."

The Georgia Review of Winter, 1979, bearing the label "Focus on Women," includes twenty-four poets and fiction writers, all women; seven literary essays, five of them by women about women, two by men about women; an illustrated article on a woman folk artist; and ten book reviews, every one but two of which has a woman as writer or subject, or both. Any other editor who makes the attempt, whatever his purpose may be, will find this near approach to totality difficult to surpass.

The Twayne United States Authors Series (TUSAS) adds volumes regularly, furnishing succinct accounts of the lives and writings of the well over 300 authors thus far included. The series meets the special need of providing more information on many of our lesser authors than is readily available elsewhere. Some of the pamphlets in the Western Writers Series serve the same purpose.

Two composite biographical works are the *Dictionary of Literary Biography: Volume One, The American Renaissance in New England*, edited by Joel Myerson (Detroit, Michigan: Gale Research, 1978), and *Southern Writers: A Biographical Dictionary*, edited by Louis D. Rubin, Jr., and others (Baton Rouge, Louisiana: Louisiana State University Press, 1979). A useful supplementary volume is the *Encyclopedia of Southern History*, edited by Robert W. Twyman and David C. Roller (Baton Rouge, Louisiana: Louisiana State University Press, 1979).

The journal *American Literature* has reached its fiftieth year. The index to those fifty years now being compiled (to supplement and supersede the two earlier index volumes) will serve as a valuable guide to scholarship in American literature in that period. A similar purpose is served by Lewis Leary's compilations, *Articles on American Literature Appearing in Current Periodicals*, with entries beginning in 1900, of which the third volume, covering the years 1968–1975, came out in 1979 (Durham, North Carolina: Duke University Press). The *Mississippi Quarterly* publishes an annual bibliography compiled by a committee of the Society for the Study of Southern Literature. A conflation of those lists for the years 1968–1975, compiled by Jerry T. Williams, has been published (Boston: G. K. Hall, 1978). A comparably useful work is Matthew J. Bruccoli and C. E. Frazer Clark, Jr., eds., *First Printings of American Authors*, four volumes (Detroit: Gale Research, 1978).

The scholar working in American literature is blessed with an increasing number of bibliographies, including many single-author bibliographies, as is evident in the lists at the end of this essay. The University of Pittsburgh Press publishes a Series in Bibliography. G. K. Hall has accumulated an extensive list of bibliographical works, including *An Annotated Bibliography of American Literary Periodicals, 1741–1850* (by Jayne K. Kribbs, 1977), and annotated bibiographies of individual writers. The same company has published reference guides to *British and American Utopian Literature, 1516–1975* (by

Lyman Tower Sargent, 1979), and reference guides to separate authors. Similarly valuable works are Clayton L. Eichelberger, ed., *A Guide to Critical Reviews of United States Fiction, 1870–1910*, Volume II (Metuchen, New Jersey: Scarecrow Press, 1974), and O. B. Emerson and Marion C. Michael, compilers, *Southern Literary Culture: A Bibiliography of Masters' and Doctors' Theses* (University, Albama: University of Alabama Press, 1979).

The Center for Editions of American Authors, sponsored by the American Literature Section and its parent organization, the Modern Language Association, made a large contribution to scholarship in American literature. It presented convincing arguments for the preparation of correct and dependable texts for literary works; it established principles and procedures for producing optimum texts; it supported and supervised the production of approved texts of selected authors; and it outlined methods for making the texts available for wide distribution while protecting the accuracy of the texts in future reprintings. When the program of the CEAA was brought to a close, the Modern Language Association created the Center for Scholarly Editions as an agency for inspecting and approving editions of authors in various languages. The National Endowment for the Humanities has announced its intention to supervise the preparation of texts under grants from its funds. Whether or not the CSE or the NEH will be effective in assuring the quality of texts, there can be no doubt that literary texts prepared in the future will benefit from the influence of the CEAA.

The list below summarizes the present status of the main textual editions of American literary works (published or approved for publication):

CHARLES BROCKDEN BROWN (Kent, Ohio: Kent State University Press)
Wieland and "Memoirs of Carwin"
Arthur Mervin
JAMES FENIMORE COOPER (Albany, New York: State University Press of New York)
Gleanings in Europe: Switzerland
The Pioneers
The Pathfinder
Letters and Journals, six volumes (Cambridge, Massachusetts: Harvard University Press)
STEPHEN CRANE (Charlottesville, Virginia: University Press of Virginia)
Complete
JOHN W. DE FOREST (Carbondale, Illinois: Southern Illinois University Press)
Witching Times
RALPH WALDO EMERSON (Cambridge, Massachusetts: Harvard University Press)
Journals and Notebooks, 14 volumes
Nature, Addresses, and Lectures
Essays; First Series
Early Lectures, 3 volumes
HAROLD FREDERIC (Fort Worth, Texas: Texas Christian University Press)
Correspondence

NATHANIEL HAWTHORNE (Columbus, Ohio: Ohio State University Press)
Complete, except for *The English Notebooks*, a volume of miscellanies, and the letters, all of which are scheduled for 1980 or 1981

W. D. HOWELLS (Bloomington, Indiana: Indiana University Press)
Twenty-three volumes of fiction, criticism, and autobiography

WASHINGTON IRVING (Madison, Wisconsin: University of Wisconsin Press and Boston: G. K. Hall, Twayne)
Nineteen volumes, including fiction, sketches, biography, history, journals, letters, and miscellanies

WILLIAM JAMES (Cambridge, Massachusetts: Harvard University Press)
Seven volumes

JAMES RUSSELL LOWELL (DeKalb, Illinois: Northern Illinois University Press)
The Biglow Papers (Series I)

HERMAN MELVILLE (Evanston, Illinois: Northwestern University Press and the Newberry Library)
Eight novels

EDGAR ALLAN POE (Cambridge, Massachusetts: Harvard University Press)
Poems
Tales and Sketches, two volumes

WILLIAM GILMORE SIMMS (Columbia, South Carolina: University of South Carolina Press)
Four volumes

HENRY DAIVD THOREAU (Princeton, New Jersey: Princeton University Press)
Five volumes

MARK TWAIN (Berkeley, California: University: University of California Press)
From the Mark Twain Papers: Nearly complete; thirteen volumes of literary manuscripts, notebooks, and letters
Previously published works (with the University of Iowa):
Ten volumes

WALT WHITMAN (New York: New York University Press)
Seventeen volumes

With support from the National Endowment for the Humanities and the Ford Foundation, a non-profit corporation has been formed under the name Literary Classics of the United States, the purpose of which is to make American literary works available in hard-cover, durable, and moderately priced volumes of 1200 to 1500 pages. The intention is to arrange for the use of texts that meet authoritative standards when they exist, and to make sure that good texts are used in other instances. The president of the corporation is Daniel Aaron; the vice president is Richard Poirier; the headquarters address is One Lincoln Plaza, New York, New York 10023. The plan is to bring out within a year the first volume for each of ten or a dozen authors. The authors and the editors selected thus far are as follows:

Authors	Editors
Henry Adams	Ernest Samuels
Stephen Crane	J. C. Levenson
Ralph Waldo Emerson	Joel Porte
Nathaniel Hawthorne	Arlin Turner
William Dean Howells	Edwin H. Cady
Washington Irving	James W. Tuttleton
Henry James	Loon Edol
Thomas Jefferson	Merrill D. Peterson
Herman Melville	G. Thomas Tanselle
Francis Parkman	David Levin
Edgar Allan Poe	G. R. Thompson
Harriet Beecher Stowe	Kathryn Kish Sklar
Mark Twain	James Cox
Walt Whitman	Justin Kaplan

Scholarly publishing in the 1970s gave space to the authors who usually receive the most attention, Poe, Henry James, Hawthorne, and Mark Twain prominent among them. Other nineteenth-century writers who gained prominence during the decade were likely to be those who were critical of governmental and social affairs in their time. The interest in the writings of Thoreau and Melville, for example, may have owed something to similar elements in recent public attitudes; but the interests of scholars were broad enough to include authors in all genres and with various outlooks, as will be indicated in the following list of representative works.

HENRY ADAMS—Ferman Bishop, *Henry Adams*, TUSAS (Boston: G. K. Hall, 1979); Earl N. Harbert, *The Force So Much Closer Home: Henry Adams and the Adams Family* (New York: New York University Press, 1977); Earl N. Harbert, *Henry Adams: A Reference Guide* (Boston: G. K. Hall, 1978).

LOUISA MAY ALCOTT—Martha Saxton, *Louisa May: A Modern Biography of Louisa May Alcott* (Boston: Houghton Mifflin, 1977); Madeleine B. Stern, *Behind a Mask: The Unknown Thrillers of Louisa May Alcott* (New York: Morrow, 1975).

GEORGE BANCROFT—Robert H. Canary, *George Bancroft*, TUSAS (Boston: G. K. Hall, 1974).

DAVID BELASCO—Lise-Lone Marker, *David Belasco: Naturalism in the American Theatre* (Princeton, New Jersey: Princeton University Press, 1975).

ALICE BROWN—Dorothea Walker, *Alice Brown*, TUSAS (Boston: G. K. Hall, 1974).

ORESTES BROWNSON—Hugh Marshall, *Orestes Brownson and the American Republic: An Historical Perspective* (Washington, D. C.: Catholic University Press, 1971).

WILLIAM CULLEN BRYANT—William Cullen Bryant II and Thomas G. Voss, eds., *The Letters of William Cullen Bryant, I, 1809–1836* (New York: Fordham University Press, 1975); Judith Turner Phair, *William Cullen Bryant and His Critics, 1808–1872: A Bibliography* (Troy, New York: Whitston, 1974).

JOHN BURROUGHS—Perry D. Westbrook, *John Burroughs*, TUSAS (Boston: G. K. Hall, 1974).

GEORGE W. CABLE—Arlin Turner, ed., *Critical Essays on George W. Cable* (Boston: G. K. Hall, 1980).

ELLERY CHANNING—Robert N. Hudspeth, *Ellery Channing*, TUSAS (Boston: G. K. Hall, 1973).

CHARLES W. CHESNUTT—(See page 8 above.)

THOMAS HOLLY CHIVERS—Charles M. Lombard, *Thomas Holly Chivers*, TUSAS (Boston: G. K. Hall, 1979).

KATE CHOPIN—(See page 8 above.) Marlene Springer, *Kate Chopin and Edith Wharton: A Reference Guide* (Boston: G. K. Hall, 1976).

SAMUEL LANGHORNE CLEMENS—Paul Fatout, ed., *Mark Twain Speaks for Himself* (West Lafayette, Indiana: Purdue University Press, 1978); Robert L. Gale, *Plots and Characters in the Works of Mark Twain* (Hamden, Connecticut: Archon, 1973); William M. Gibson, *The Art of Mark Twain* (New York: Oxford University Press, 1976); Hamlin Hill, *Mark Twain: God's Fool* (New York: Harper and Row, 1973); Sholom J. Kahn, *Mark Twain's Mysterious Stranger: A Study of the Manuscript Texts* (Columbia, Missouri: University of Missouri Press, 1978); David B. Kesterson, *Critics on Mark Twain* (Coral Gables, Florida: University of Miami Press, 1973); Arthur G. Pettit, *Mark Twain and the South* (Lexington, Kentucky: University of Kentucky Press, 1974); Thomas Asa Tenney, *Mark Twain: A Reference Guide* (Boston: G. K. Hall, 1978); George Sanderlin, *Mark Twain: As Others Saw Him* (New York: Coward, McCann, 1978); Dennis Welland, *Mark Twain in England* (Atlantic Highlands, New Jersey: Humanities Press, 1978).

JAMES FENIMORE COOPER—John Decker and John P. McWilliams, *James Fenimore Cooper*, Critical Heritage Series (London: Routledge and Kegan Paul, 1974); John P. McWilliams, Jr., *Political Justice in a Republic: James Fenimore Cooper's America* (Berkeley, California: University of California Press, 1973); Blake Nevius, *Cooper's Landscapes: An Essay on the Picturesque Vision* (Berkeley, California: University of California Press, 1976); H. Daniel Peck, *A World by Itself: The Pastoral Moment in Cooper's Fiction* (New Haven, Connecticut: Yale University Press, 1977); Stephen Railton, *Fenimore Cooper: A Study of His Life and Imagination* (Princeton, New Jersey: Princeton University Press, 1978); Warren S. Walker, *Plots and Char-*

acters in the Fiction of James Fenimore Cooper (Hamden, Connecticut: Shoe String Press, 1978).

STEPHEN CRANE—Andrew T. Crosland, compiler, *A Concordance to the Complete Poetry of Stephen Crane* (Detroit, Michigan: Gale Research, 1975); Robert W. Stallman, *Stephen Crane: A Critical Bibliography* (Ames, Iowa: Iowa State University Press, 1972).

EMILY DICKINSON—Sharon Cameron, *Lyric Time: Dickinson and the Limits of Genre* (Baltimore, Maryland: Johns Hopkins University Press, 1979); Paul J. Ferlazzo, *Emily Dickinson*, TUSAS (Boston: G. K. Hall, 1976); Karl Keller, *The Only Kangaroo Among the Beauty: Emily Dickinson and America* (Baltimore, Maryland: Johns Hopkins University Press, 1980); Inder Nath Kher, *The Landscape of Absence: Emily Dickinson's Poetry* (New Haven, Connecticut: Yale University Press, 1974); Brita Lindberg-Seyersted, *Emily Dickinson's Punctuation* (Oslo, Norway: University of Oslo, 1976); Rebecca Patterson (edited by Margaret H. Freeman), *Emily Dickinson's Imagery* (Amherst, Massachusetts: University of Massachusetts Press, 1980); Richard B. Sewall, *The Life of Emily Dickinson* (New York: Farrar, Straus, and Giroux, two volumes, 1974); Robert Weisbuch, *Emily Dickinson's Poetry* (Chicago: University of Chicago Press, 1975).

PAUL LAURENCE DUNBAR—(See page 8 above.)

RALPH WALDO EMERSON—Gay W. Allen, a biography to be published late in 1980 (New York: Viking Press); Jeanetta Boswell, *Ralph Waldo Emerson and the Critics: A Checklist of Criticism, 1900–1977* (Metuchen, New Jersey: Scarecrow Press, 1979); Joel Porte, *Representative Man: Ralph Waldo Emerson in His Time* (New York: Oxford University Press, 1979); David Porter, *Emerson and Literary Change* (Cambridge, Massachusetts: Harvard University Press, 1978); Hyatt H. Waggoner, *Emerson as Poet* (Princeton, New Jersey: Princeton University Press, 1974).

HAROLD FREDERIC—(See page 11 above.)

HENRY BLAKE FULLER—Loring Silet, *Henry Blake Fuller and Hamlin Garland: A Reference Guide* (Boston: G. K. Hall, 1977).

MARGARET FULLER—Margaret Vanderhaar Allen, *The Achievement of Margaret Fuller* (University Park, Pennsylvania: Pennsylvania State University Press, 1979); Joel Myerson, *Critical Essays on Margaret Fuller* (Boston: G. K. Hall, 1980); Ellen Wilson, *Margaret Fuller, Bluestocking, Romantic, Revolutionary* (New York: Farrar, Straus, and Giroux, 1977).

HAMLIN GARLAND—Jackson Bryer and others, *Hamlin Garland and the Critics: An Annotated Bibliography* (Troy, New York: Whitston, 1973); Robert

Gish, *Hamlin Garland: The Far West* (Boise, Idaho: Boise State University, 1976); See HENRY BLAKE FULLER above.

ELLEN GLASGOW—(See page 8 above.)

JOEL CHANDLER HARRIS—R. Bruce Bickley and others, *Joel Chandler Harris: A Reference Guide* (Boston: G. K. Hall, 1978).

EDWARD EVERETT HALE—John R. Adams, *Edward Everett Hale*, TUSAS (Boston: G. K. Hall, 1977).

NATHANIEL HAWTHORNE—Arne Axelson, *The Links in the Chain: Isolation and Independence in Nathaniel Hawthorne's Fictional Characters* (Stockholm, Sweden: Almquist & Wiksell, 1974); Nina Baym, *The Shape of Hawthorne's Career* (Itahca, New York: Cornell University Press, 1976); Richard H. Broadhead, *Hawthorne, Melville, and the Novel* (Chicago: University of Chicago Press, 1976); John R. Byers, Jr., and James J. Owen, *A Concordance to the Five Novels of Nathaniel Hawthorne*, 2 volumes (New York: Garland Publishing, 1979); C. E. Frazer Clark, Jr., *Nathaniel Hawthorne: A Descriptive Bibiography* (Pittsburgh, Pennsylvania: University of Pittsburgh Press, 1978); J. Donald Crowley, *Hawthorne: A Collection of Criticism* (New York: McGraw-Hill, 1974); Rita Gollin, *Nathaniel Hawthorne and the Truth of Dreams* (Baton Rouge, Louisiana: Louisiana State University Press, 1979); Raymona Hull, a book on Hawthorne and his family in Europe (Pittsburgh, Pennsylvania: University of Pittsburgh Press, in press); James O. Mays, a book on Hawthorne as consul, in preparation; James Mellow, a book on Hawthorne and his wife, in preparation; Edwin H. Miller, a biography of Hawthorne, in preparation; Barbara Mouffe, ed., *Hawthorne's Lost Notebook: 1835–1841* (University Park, Pennyslvania: Pennsylvania State University Press, 1978); Taylor Stoehr, *Hawthorne's Mad Scientists: Pseudoscience and Social Science in Nineteenth-Century Life and Letters* (Hamden, Connecticut: Shoe String Press, 1978); Arlin Turner, *Nathaniel Hawthorne: A Biography* (New York: Oxford University Press, 1980); Alfred Weber, *Die Entwicklung der Rahmenerzählungen Nathaniel Hawthornes: "The Story Teller" and andere frühe Werke* (Berlin, Germany: Schmidt, 1972).

PAUL HAMILTON HAYNE—Jack Debellis, *Sidney Lanier, Henry Timrod, and Paul Hamilton Hayne: A Reference Guide* (Boston: G. K. Hall, 1978).

THOMAS WENTWORTH HIGGINSON—James Tuttleton, *Thomas Wentworth Higginson*, TUSAS (Boston: G. K. Hall, 1978).

RICHARD HOVEY—William R. Linneman, *Richard Hovey*, TUSAS (Boston: G. K. Hall, 1976).

JULIA WARD HOWE—Deborah Pickman Clifford, *Mine Eyes Have Seen the Glory: A Biography of Julia Ward Howe* (Boston: Little Brown, 1979).

WILLIAM DEAN HOWELLS—George Arms and others, *Selected Letters of W. D. Howells* (Boston: Twayne, Volume I, 1852–1872, and Volume II, 1873–1881, 1980; six volumes in all are to be published); Vito J. Brenni, *William Dean Howells: A Bibliography* (Metuchen, New Jersey: Scarecrow Press, 1973); Edwin H. Cady, ed., *W. D. Howells As Critic* (London: Routledge & Kegan Paul, 1973); George C. Carrington and Ildiko de Papp Carrington, *Plots and Characters in the Fiction of William Dean Howells* (Hamden, Connecticut: Shoe String Press, 1976); Clayton L. Eichelberger, *Published Comment on William Dean Howells through 1920: A Research Bibliography* (Boston: G. K. Hall, 1976).

WASHINGTON IRVING—Wayne R. Kime, *Pierre M. Irving and Washington Irving: A Collaboration in Life and Letters* (Waterloo, Ontario: Wilfrid Laurier University Press, 1977); Andrew B. Myers, ed., *A Century of Commentary on the Works of Washington Irving, 1860–1974* (Tarrytown, New York: Sleepy Hollow Restorations, 1976); Martin Roth, *Comedy and America: The Lost World of Washington Irving* (Port Washington, New York: Kennikat, 1976); Haskell Springer, *Washington Irving: A Reference Guide* (Boston: G. K. Hall, 1976).

HELEN HUNT JACKSON—Evelyn I. Banning, *Helen Hunt Jackson* (New York: Vanguard, 1973).

HENRY JAMES—Charles R. Anderson, *Person, Place and Thing in Henry James's Novels* (Durham, North Carolina: Duke University Press, 1977); Leon Edel, ed., *The Letters of Henry James, Vol. I, 1843–75*, 1974; *Vol. II, 1875–83*, 1975 (Cambridge, Massachusetts: Harvard University Press); Philip Grover, *Henry James and the French Novel: A Study in Inspiration* (New York: Barnes and Noble, 1973); Robert Emmet Long, *The Great Succession: Henry James and the Legacy of Hawthorne* (Pittsburgh, Pennsylvania: University of Pittsburgh Press, 1979); Kristin Pruitt McColgan, *Henry James (1917–1959): A Reference Guide* (Boston: G. K. Hall, 1979); Harry T. Moore, *Henry James* (New York: Viking; London: Thames and Hudson, 1974); Elsa Nettels, *James and Conrad* (Athens, Georgia: University of Georgia Press, 1977); Sergio Perosa, *Henry James and the Experimental Novel* (Charlottesville, Virginia: University Press of Virginia, 1978); Beatrice Ricks, *Henry James: A Bibliography of Secondary Works* (Metuchen, New Jersey: Scarecrow Press, 1975); Daniel J. Schneider, *The Crystal Cage: Adventures of the Imagination in the Fiction of Henry James* (Lawrence, Kansas: Regents Press of Kansas, 1978); Dorothy McInnis Scura, *Henry James (1860–1874): A Reference Guide* (Boston: G. K. Hall, 1979); Mary Doyle Springer, *A Rhetoric of Literary Character: Some Women of Henry James* (Chicago: University of Chicago Press, 1979); William T. Stafford, *A Name, Title, and Place Index to the Critical Writings of Henry James* (Englewood, Colorado: Microcard Editions, 1975); Edward Wagenknecht, *Eve and Henry James: Portraits of Women and Girls in His Fiction* (Norman, Oklahoma: University of Oklahoma Press, 1978).

WILLIAM JAMES—Charlene Haddock Seigfried, *Chaos and Context: A Study in William James* (Athens, Ohio: Ohio University Press, 1978); Ignas K. Skrupskelis, *William James: A Reference Guide* (Boston: G. K. Hall, 1977).

THOMAS JEFFERSON—William K. Bottorff, *Thomas Jefferson*, TUSAS (Boston: G. K. Hall, 1979).

SARAH ORNE JEWETT—Gwen L. Nagel and James Nagel, *Sarah Orne Jewett: A Reference Guide* (Boston: G. K. Hall, 1977).

RICHARD MALCOLM JOHNSTON—Bert Hitchcock, *Richard Malcolm Johnston*, TUSAS (Boston: G. K. Hall, 1978).

GRACE KING—Robert Bush, ed., *Grace King of New Orleans: A Selection of Her Writings* (Baton Rouge, Louisiana: Louisiana State University Press, 1973).

SIDNEY LANIER—(See PAUL HAMILTON HAYNE above.)

HENRY DEMAREST LLOYD—E. Jay Jernigan, *Henry Demarest Lloyd*, TUSAS (Boston: G. K. Hall, 1976).

GEORGE CABOT LODGE—John W. Crowley, *George Cabot Lodge*, TUSAS (Boston: G. K. Hall, 1976).

HENRY WADSWORTH LONGFELLOW—Andrew Hillen, ed., *The Letters of Henry Wadsworth Longfellow* (Cambridge, Massachusetts: Harvard University Press, III: 1844–1856, IV: 1857–1865, 1972).

JAMES RUSSELL LOWELL—Thomas Wortham, ed., *The Biglow Papers (First Series): A Critical Edition* (DeKalb, Illinois: Northern Illinois University Press, 1977).

CATHERINE McDOWELL (SHERWOOD BONNER)—William L. Frank, *Sherwood Bonner*, TUSAS (Boston: G. K. Hall, 1976).

CORNELIUS MATHEWS—Allen F. Stein, *Cornelius Mathews*, TUSAS (Boston: G. K. Hall, 1974).

HERMAN MELVILLE—R. Bruce Bickley, Jr., *The Method of Melville's Short Fiction* (Durham, North Carolina: Duke University Press, 1975); Watson G. Branch, ed., *Melville: The Critical Heritage* (London: Routledge & Kegan Paul, 1974); See Broadhead, NATHANIEL HAWTHORNE above; William B. Dillingham, *Melville's Short Fiction, 1853–1856* (Athens, Georgia: University of Georgia Press, 1977); Marvin Fisher, *Going Under: Melville's Short Fiction and the American 1850's* (Baton Rouge, Louisiana: Louisiana State University

Press, 1977); Michael T. Gilmore, *Twentieth Century Interpretations of Moby-Dick: A Collection of Critical Essays* (Englewood Cliffs, New Jersey: Prentice-Hall, 1977); Edward S. Grejda, *The Common Continent of Men: Racial Equality in the Writings of Herman Melville* (Port Washington, New York: Kennikat, 1974); Edwin H. Miller, *Melville* (New York: Braziller, 1975); Merton M. Sealts, *The Early Lives of Melville: Nineteenth Century Biographical Sketches and Their Authors* (Madison, Wisconsin: University of Wisconsin Press, 1975); Rowland A. Sherrill, *The Prophetic Melville: Experience, Transcendence, and Tragedy* (Athens, Georgia: University of Georgia Press, 1979); William H. Shurr, *The Mystery of Iniquity: Melville as Poet, 1857–1891* (Lexington, Kentucky: University Press of Kentucky, 1972).

FRANK NORRIS—Jesse E. Crisler and Joseph R. McElrath, Jr., *Frank Norris: A Reference Guide* (Boston: G. K. Hall, 1974); Don Graham, *The Fiction of Frank Norris: An Aesthetic Context* (Columbia, Missouri: University of Missouri Press, 1978).

BILL NYE—David B. Kesterson, *Bill Nye: The Western Writings* (Boise, Idaho: Boise State University, 1976).

WILLIAM DOUGLAS O'CONNOR—Jerome Loving, *Walt Whitman's Companion: William Douglas O'Connor* (College Station, Texas: Texas A & M University Press, 1977).

EDGAR ALLAN POE—Carl L. Anderson, *Poe in Northlight: The Scandinavian Response to His Life and Work* (Durham, North Carolina: Duke University Press, 1973); J. Lasley Dameron and Irby B. Cauthen, Jr., *Edgar Allan Poe: A Bibliography of Criticism, 1827–1867* (Charlottesville, Virginia: University Press of Virginia, 1974); Joan D. Grossman, *Edgar Allan Poe in Russia: A Study in Legend and Literary Influence* (Atlantic Highlands, N. J.: Humanities Press, 1973); David Halliburton, *Edgar Allan Poe: A Phenomenological View* (Princeton, New Jersey: Princeton University Press, 1973); Stuart Levine and Susan Levine, *The Short Fiction of Edgar Allan Poe* (Indianapolis, Indiana: Bobbs-Merrill, 1976); Wolf Mankowitz, *The Extraordinary Mr. Poe: A Biography of Edgar Allan Poe* (London: Weidenfeld and Nicholson, 1978); John Carl Miller, *Building Poe Biography* (Baton Rouge, Louisiana: Louisiana State University Press, 1977); John Carl Miller, *Poe's Helen Remembers* (Charlottesville, Virginia: University Press of Virginia, 1979); Julian Symons, *The Tell-Tale Heart: The Life and Works of Edgar Allan Poe* (New York: Harper and Row, 1978); G. R. Thompson, *Poe's Fiction: Romantic Irony in the Gothic Tales* (Madison, Wisconsin: University of Wisconsin Press, 1973).

WILLIAM HICKLING PRESCOTT—Donald G. Darnell, *William Hickling Prescott*, TUSAS (Boston: G. K. Hall, 1975).

FREDERIC REMINGTON—Fred Erisman, *Frederic Remington* (Boise, Idaho: Boise State University, 1975).

CATHERINE MARIA SEDGWICK—Edward H. Foster, *Catherine Maria Sedgwick*, TUSAS (Boston: G. K. Hall, 1974).

WILLIAM GILMORE SIMMS—Jon L. Wakelyn, *The Politics of a Literary Man: William Gilmore Simms* (Westport, Connecticut: Greenwood, 1973).

SEBA SMITH—Milton and Patricia Rickels, *Seba Smith*, TUSAS (Boston: G. K. Hall, 1977).

EDMUND CLARENCE STEDMAN—Robert J. Sholnick, *Edmund Clarence Stedman*, TUSAS (Boston: G. K. Hall, 1977).

HARRIET BEECHER STOWE—Elizabeth Ammons, ed., *Critical Essays on Harriet Beecher Stowe* (Boston: G. K. Hall, 1980); Thomas F. Gossett has a book on Harriet Beecher Stowe in press; E. Bruce Kirkham, *The Building of Uncle Tom's Cabin* (Knoxville, Tennessee: University of Tennessee Press, 1977); Jean Ashton, *Harriet Beecher Stowe: A Reference Guide* (Boston: G. K. Hall, 1977).

BAYARD TAYLOR—Paul C. Wermuth, *Bayard Taylor,* TUSAS (G. K. Hall, 1973).

HENRY DAVID THOREAU—Richard Lebeaux, *Young Man Thoreau* (Amherst, Massachusetts: University of Massachusetts Press, 1977); Michael Meyer, *Several More Lives to Live: Thoreau's Political Reputation in America* (Westport, Connecticut: Greenwood, 1977); James McIntosh, *Thoreau as Romantic Naturalist: His Shifting Stance Toward Nature* (Ithaca, New York: Cornell University Press, 1974); Joseph J. Moldenhauer, Jr., ed., *Illustrated Maine Woods: With Illustrations from the Gleason Collection* (Princeton, New Jersey: Princeton University Press, 1974); James Thorpe, *Thoreau's Walden* (San Marino, California: Huntington Library, 1977).

HENRY TIMROD—(See PAUL HAMILTON HAYNE above.)

LESTER FRANK WARD—Clifford H. Scott, *Lester Frank Ward,* TUSAS (Boston: G. K. Hall, 1976).

BOOKER T. WASHINGTON—(See page 8 above.)

BARRETT WENDELL—Robert Self, *Barrett Wendell*, TUSAS (Boston: G. K. Hall, 1975).

EDITH WHARTON—Marlene Springer, *Kate Chopin and Edith Wharton: A Reference Guide* (Boston: G. K. Hall, 1976).

GEORGE WASHINGTON WHITMAN—Jerome M. Loving, ed., *Civil War Letters of George Washington Whitman* (Durham, North Carolina: Duke University Press, 1975).

WALT WHITMAN—Gay W. Allen, *The New Walt Whitman Handbook* (New York: New York University Press, 1975); Gloria A. Francis and Artem Lozynsky, compilers, *Whitman at Auction: 1899–1972* (Detroit, Michigan: Gale Research, 1978); Arthur Goldon, od., *Walt Whitman: A Collection of Criticism* (New York: McGraw-Hill, 1974); Edwin H. Miller, ed., *The Collected Writings of Walt Whitman: The Correspondence: Volume VI: A Supplement with a Composite Index* (New York: New York University Press, 1977); Floyd Stovall, *The Foreground of Leaves of Grass* (Charlottesville, Virginia: University Press of Virginia, 1974); Mark Van Doren, ed., *The Viking Portable Walt Whitman* (revision, chronology, bibliographical checklist by Gay W. Allen; New York: Viking, 1974); William White, *The Collected Writings of Walt Whitman: Daybooks and Notebooks,* 3 vols. (New York: New York University Press, 1978).

JOHN GREENLEAF WHITTIER—Albert J. Von Frank, *Whittier: A Comprehensive Annotated Bibliography* (New York, Garland, 1975).

Recent Views of the American Landscape: A Geographic Perspective

CHRISTOPHER L. SALTER

In the past six years, landscape analysis and new views of the American environment have produced an interesting, if not volumi- nous, literature. Deriving in part from the student-led Earth Day of April 1970 and its aftermath of desultory environmental efforts, a more analytic school of landscape observers has emerged. The associated considerations of the built environment reflect in part the environmental concerns of the activists of the late 1960s and early 1970s because it was during that time that millions of Americans first realized the malleability of the physical environ- ment. And such perception was the essential first step to more scholarly commentaries on the analysis and appreciation of the American landscape.

Because of the catholic nature of the writers who have professed interest in this humanization of the American earth, the associated literature ranges from works in urban planning to advertising trade journals. For the purposes of this short update, however, we will consider primarily the views of geographers that have appeared in journals and books.

Yi-fu Tuan of the University of Minnesota brought focus to this heightened interest in landscape with his*Topophilia: A Study of Environmental Perception, Attitudes, and Values (New York: Prentice- Hall, 1974). In this benchmark work, Tuan demonstrated the debt that geographers owe to psychologists, urban planners, anthropolo- gists, historians and sociologists, to cite just a few of the professional literatures he draws from in this commentary on human attachment to place. In a significant thrust, Tuan directed the bulk of his book toward analysis of urban space. Such a concentration is in line with the expanded American participation in the planning process, the bulk of which is appropriately directed toward the city and its artificial environment. This civic energy is being tapped by municipal and professional populations alike as citizens show new interest in the design and impact of residential developments, transportation networks, and urban renewal projects. Tuan carries his analysis of the city right up to the present moment with the publication of his most recent book, Landscapes of Fear (New York: Pantheon, 1980), in which the city again is given intensive treatment.

Professor Tuan has added considerable dimension to the American study of environments by numerous professional articles as well as an additional book. *Space and Place: The Perspective of Experience (Minneapolis: University of Minnesota Press, 1979), and his seminal "Ambiguity in Attitudes Toward Environment," Annals of the Association of American Geographers (December 1973), provide additional philosophical guidelines for the analysis of the human setting, as well as rich bibliographic examples of the diversity of sources that can yield information on the study of the human sense of place. As Tuan points out in his 1973 article, the mixed feelings people have toward place require looking at "the problem of perception, attitudes, value, judgment and behavior that are the quintessentially human horizons of our own field." Tuan has been the most prolific of the geographers who have given wit and energy to these lines of inquiry.

Another major book that has appeared since Professor Dunbar's initial essay is John Fraser Hart's *The Look of the Land (New York: Prentice-Hall, 1975). This volume is one of a series on "Foundations in Cultural Geography," and Hart's work is primarily concerned with the patterns, structures, and culture of the American rural landscape. In this work he crafts a well-written folk cultural geography of the United States that offers a solid relationship between cultural systems and their associated cultural landscapes. This book, particularly in conjunction with the other titles in this series, provides an important resource for students of the American scene.

One of the most significant themes to derive from the intensified interest in landscape in the last six years is the concern with historic preservation. Carol J. Galbreath in "Small Town Preservation--A Systematic View," Historic Preservation (April-June 1975), demonstrates how the preservation of a landscape can have economic as well as cultural significance. She points out that the act of trying to marshal community and economic forces for the purpose of preservation stimulates local civic leadership and, consequently, a sense of community: "Powers may or may not be concentrated in a few hands, but the power structure can be clearer than in big cities . . . In some towns, factions regroup, if not unite, using historic preservation as a common denominator." This use of landscape as a factor in social cohesion is one of the nearly universal phenomena related to the growing awareness of, and interest in, the human design of the American landscape.

Geographer Peirce Lewis of the Pennsylvania State University outlined elements of this same allure of the American small town in his brilliant "Small Town in Pennsylvania," Annals, AAG (June 1972). Lewis has produced two particularly important additions to the landscape literature. In "Common Houses, Cultural Spoor," Landscape, Vol. 19 (1975), he provides a richly illustrated essay on house types as a significant tool for the analysis of cultural diffusion and persistence. In "The Unprecedented City" in The American Land, Alexix Doster III, ed. (Washington: The Smithsonian Institution, 1979), Lewis utilizes tools of landscape analysis to call attention to the positive and attractive elements of the American city that are frequently overshadowed by the common litany of evils of American urban space.

Lewis turned his attention to a large urban settlement in his volume on New Orleans, *New Orleans: The Makings of an Urban Landscape (Cambridge, Mass.: Ballinger, 1976). This rich book is one of a series by geographers on major American cities, but the Lewis volume does the most effective job of relating the landscape dimension to the fabric of the city. Some would argue that New Orleans itself provides an author with a special advantage, but one of the axioms that guides Lewis--as well as other authors cited in this essay--is the conviction that the ordinary landscape is rich in symbols and signals, making it unnecessary for the student of the American landscape to seek only the exotic and highly touted locales that evoke interest by mere mention of their names.

This theme of the intrinsic value and significance in mundane landscapes is the philosophic foundation of a volume edited by Donald Meinig of Syracuse University. In *The Interpretation of Ordinary Landscapes (New York: Oxford University Press, 1979), he emphasizes the potential for intelligent inference of the cultural meaning generated by everyday landscapes. Meinig, who established himself as a thoughtful practitioner of landscape analysis in his "Environmental Appreciation: Localities as a Humane Art," Western Humanities Review (Winter 1971), was the primary organizer of the Syracuse Conference on Landscape Analysis in 1975. This volume is the outcome of that session and brings together Tuan, Lewis, Meinig, David Sopher, David Lowenthal, J. B. Jackson and Marwyn Samuels. Meinig points out in his introduction that the landscape "is, first of all, the unity we see, the impression of our senses rather than the logic of the sciences." He explains that the concept of landscape is similar, but not identical, to nature, scenery, environment, places, region, area or geography. This ambiguity is accepted and used to promote the personal, speculative interpretation of varied vistas of the cultural landscape. Such a theme is elaborated in Meinig's own essay, "The Beholding Eye."

Lewis, Meinig, and Tuan offer general methodologies for the process of landscape analysis while Samuels, Lowenthal, and Jackson grapple with the problems inherent in discovering and understanding the specific "authors" of humanized landscapes. Samuels gives full attention to this question of authorship, while Lowenthal points out that the very process of attaching singular value to a setting initiates cultural activities that are bound to provoke change in that landscape. Sopher deals in depth with the landscape of home and establishes a provocative framework for cross-cultural analysis of landscape features and associated attitudes. In an article on the British geographer W. G. Hoskins, Meinig chronicles the development of the intellectual curiosity that can and should be brought to the consideration of common features in the humanized environment.

Perhaps the most stimulating book on the analysis of everyday features of the American city is the volume Close-up: How to Read the American City (New York: Praeger, 1973). This book was written by Grady Clay, editor of Landscape Architecture, and although he is not a geographer by profession, his keen eye for landscape and its cultural features makes him, to use Professor Dunbar's term, a crypto-geographer par excellence. In Close-up, Clay fashions a new vocabulary and perspective for the exploration of American urban environments, providing the reader with a provocative tool for understanding the intentions as well as the results of the shaping of city space. Clay has been able to support this interest in his work with his journal, and students of the American landscape would benefit from perusing that journal's back issues.

An additional approach to the analysis of city space is offered in *San Francisco's Chinatown: How Chinese a Town? by C. L. Salter (Palo Alto: R and E Research Associates, 1978). By analyzing the elements of spatial and functional morphology in Chinatown, Salter attempts to show how city space can be patterned after not only indigenous design, but foreign models as well. In an earlier article, "The Convenience of Environmental Ignorance," The Professional Geographer (August 1977), Salter outlined the high cost of inadequately understanding what the genetic factors were in the creation of urban space and the American landscape. An additional article of considerable interest that focused upon one of the common features of the American city was "Urban Graffiti as Territorial Markers" by David Ley and Roman Cybriwsky in the Annals of the AAG (December 1974).

The journal Landscape, founded in 1951 by J. B. Jackson, has long been a creative outlet for commentaries on the American land. In the late 1960s and early 1970s, however, with new owners and new management, the journal experienced a difficult time of adjustment. In the last five years, the continued financial and philosophical support of Blair Boyd and the arrival of Bonnie Loyd as managing editor have allowed Landscape to reemerge as a dominant professional outlet for good and significant writing. Selecting five articles from this period of rebirth will illustrate the scope and nature of this journal's contribution.

In "How Does a Garden Grow? Primary Succession in New Tract
Developments" by Helen Worthen, Vol. 19, 3 (May 1975), there is a
discussion of the complexity of a gardener's decision in the
unsettled lands of new tract developments. Worthen's study is a
captivating chronicle of the social, philosophical, and territorial
aspects of the gardened landscape in suburbia. As one of the
gardeners she interviewed stated, "I saw Hawaii Five-O on TV and
I thought, 'That's what I want. . .' We may be a California family
now, but I hope to be a Hawaiian family someday."

Dennis Dingemans authored an article entitled "The Urbanization of
Suburbia: The Renaissance of the Row House," Vol. 20, 1 (October
1975), which represents the citizen and scholar's interest in the
landscapes of renewal. The sequence has two facets as Dingemans
outlines it: the return to central city, with its associated use
of landscape as therapy in the do-it-yourself renewal process; and
the proliferation of the common-wall townhouse as an architectural
style, especially in California and Florida. He shows that this
latter development has occurred partially in response to new environmental goals of community green space and a wish for reduced
maintenance schedules for the individual homeowner. This process
of neighborhood revitalization has been given good additional
coverage in lucid articles by James Borchert ("Alley Landscapes of
Washington"), and Lydia Burton and David Morley ("Neighborhood
Survival in Toronto"), both in the Fall 1979 issue of Landscape,
Vol. 23, 1.

"Towards Landscape Sensibility" by S. Robert Aiken, in Vol. 20, 3
(Spring 1976), draws together many strands of the attitudes toward
landscape. Writing of themes of environment, landscape, place, and
personal perspectives, Aiken asserts that "landscape is process,
not product; a moving picture, not photography." This moving
picture that Aiken presents to the reader takes its script from
literature, philosophy, travel journals, and theology, as well as
more orthodox geographic sources. Its eclectic nature is enhanced
by an extensive bibliography.

Two additional selections from Landscape that deal with vital
themes in the analysis of the American scene are Richard Francaviglia, "Main St. USA: The Creation of a Popular Image," Vol. 21,
3 (Spring-Summer 1977), and Christopher Winters, "The Social
Identity of Evolving Neighborhoods," Vol. 23 (1979). In the
former, Francaviglia uses his study of Disneyland to pinpoint the
landscape elements that have been replicated in Midwestern towns
pursuing revitalization and new shopping malls attempting to
replicate turn-of-the-century "Main St." simplicity and intimacy.
He continues this study in "Main St. Revisited" in Places Vol. 1
(1974). (This journal experienced its birth and demise within the
period covered by this update. Reviewing its pages would provide
a student of landscape with a number of interesting articles
brought to print by editor Donald Ballas.)

Christopher Winters continues to develop the landscape-as-therapy
perspective in his analysis of the important social components of
the neighborhood rejuvenation process. Examples are drawn from
both American coasts, and catalysts include working-class people in
search of community, artists in quest of inexpensive loft space,
and young professionals and plain folk searching for affordable
housing. These themes are further developed in a detailed article
by Roman Cybriwsky in "Social Aspects of Neighborhood Change,"
Annals of the AAG (March 1978). The issue of neighborhood destruction caused by this process of importing a new home-owner class is
also addressed.

These articles and books, then, with their varied concern for
environmental attitudes, historic preservation, neighborhood
renewal, patterns of the countryside, and appreciation of the good
and the bad of the American city, give some indication of the
nature of contemporary geographic views of the American landscape.
Just as the vistas are varied and representative of highly disparate histories of development, so too are the commentaries made
by the observers included above. That variety is stimulating in
the fare it provides the reader, and the overall vitality of
literature on the landscape is reassuring to any student of our
national scene. If we truly begin to understand what it is we
have created in our shaping of the built environment, we will be
able to set ourselves to the task of better designing the landscapes still to come.

The American Presidents, 1789-1981

KENNETH DAVISON

Between 1973 and 1981 appeared a number of collections of primary source material plus important new biographical works and monographs relating to many of America's thirty-eight presidents. The most seminal of these new publications for an understanding of the American presidency are cited below. In addition, a few items omitted from my 1973 bibliographical essay are included.

George Washington (1789-1797)

Washington, George. The Diaries of George Washington. Edited by Donald Jackson and Dorothy Twohig. 6 vols. Charlottesville: University Press of Virginia, 1976-1980. The most recent edition covering the years 1748-1799.
_____. George Washington: A Biography in His Own Words. Edited by Ralph K. Andrist with an introduction by Donald Jackson. New York: Newsweek, distributed by Harper & Row, 1973.
Emery, Noemie. Washington: A Biography. New York: Putnam, 1976.
*Flexner, James Thomas. Washington: The Indispensable Man. New York: New American Library, 1979. A one-volume edition abridged from Flexner's four-volume work published 1965-1972.
Jones, Robert Francis. George Washington. World Leaders Series, No. 80. Boston: Twayne Publishers, 1979.
Ketchum, Richard M. The World of George Washington. New York: American Heritage Publishing Co., 1974.
*McDonald, Forrest. The Presidency of George Washington. New York:

Norton, 1975. A volume in the American Presidency series.
*Marshall, John. George Washington. 5 vols. Edited by Marcus
    Cunliffe and Arthur M. Schlesinger, Jr. New York: Chelsea
    House, 1980.
Thistlethwaite, Mark. The Image of George Washington: Studies in
    Mid-Nineteenth-Century History Painting. New York: Garland
    Publishing Co., 1979.
*Wall, Charles C. George Washington, Citizen-Soldier. Charlottes-
    ville: University Press of Virginia, 1980.

John Adams (1797-1801)

Adams, John. John Adams: A Biography in His Own Words. Edited
    by James Bishop Peabody. With an introduction by L.H. Butter-
    field. New York: Newsweek, 1973.
Brown, Ralph A. The Presidency of John Adams. Lawrence:
    University Press of Kansas, 1975. Written for the general
    reader and based upon secondary rather than primary materials.
East, Robert Abraham. John Adams. World Leaders Series, No. 78.
    Boston: Twayne Publishers, 1979.
*Shaw, Peter. The Character of John Adams. New York: Norton,
    1977.
Shepherd, Jack. The Adams Chronicles: Four Generations of
    Greatness. Introduction by Daniel Boorstin. Boston: Little,
    Brown, 1975. Prepared in conjunction with the production of
    a television series of the same name.

Thomas Jefferson (1801-1809)

*Jefferson, Thomas. The Portable Thomas Jefferson. Edited and
    with an introduction by Merrill D. Peterson. New York:
    Penguin, 1977.
_____ . Thomas Jefferson: A Biography in His Own Words.
    2 vols. New York: Newsweek, distributed by Harper & Row,
    1974.
_____ . Selected Writings. Edited by Harvey C. Mansfield, Jr.
    Illinois: AHM Publishing Corp., 1979.
_____ . Thomas Jefferson Papers. Washington: Library of
    Congress, 1974. 65 reels. 35 mm.
Bottorff, William K. Thomas Jefferson. United States Authors
    Series No. 327. Boston: Twayne Publishers, 1979.
Brodie, Fawn M. Thomas Jefferson: an Intimate History. New York:
    Norton, 1974.
Johnstone, Robert M., Jr. Jefferson and the Presidency: Leader-
    ship in the Young Republic. Ithaca: Cornell University Press,
    1978.
McDonald Forrest. The Presidency of Thomas Jefferson. Lawrence:
    University of Kansas, 1976.
*Malone, Dumas. Jefferson and His Time. 5 vols. Boston: Little,
    Brown, 1948-1974. Definitive treatment by a master historian.
    Volumes four and five cover the presidential years. Extensive
    bibliographies in each volume.

Smith, Page. Jefferson: A Revealing Biography. New York: American Heritage Publishing Co., distribution by McGraw-Hill, 1976

James Madison (1809-1817)

Madison, James. James Madison: A Biography in His Own Words. Edited by Merrill D. Peterson, with an introduction by Robert A. Rutland. New York: Newsweek, distributed by Harper & Row, 1974.
_____. The Papers of James Madison. Thirteen volumes to date. Edited by Robert A. Rutland and Charles F. Holeson. Charlottes-ville: University Press of Virginia, 1962. Covers the years from March, 1751 to March, 1791.
Moore, Virginia. The Madisons: A Biography. New York: McGraw-Hill, 1979.
Schultz, Harold Seessel. James Madison. Rulers and Statesmen of the World Series, No. 13. New York: Twayne Publishers, 1970.

James Monroe (1817-1825)

*Dangerfield, George. The Awakening of American Nationalism: 1815-1818. New York: Harper & Row, 1965.

John Quincy Adams (1825-1829)

Shepherd, Jack. Cannibals of the Heart: A Personal History of Louisa Catherine and John Quincy. New York: McGraw, 1980.

Andrew Jackson (1829-1837)

Jackson, Andrew. The Papers of Andrew Jackson. Vol. I, 1770-1803, edited by Sam B. Smith and Harriet C. Owsley. Knoxville: University of Tennessee Press, 1980.
*Curtis, James C. Andrew Jackson and the Search for Vindication. Edited by Oscar Handlin. Boston: Little, Brown, 1976. A critical but balanced biography.
Davis, Burke. Old Hickory: A Life of Andrew Jackson. New York: Dial Press, 1977. Popular treatment for the general audience. About half of the volume is devoted to the presidential years.
Latner, Richard B. The Presidency of Andrew Jackson: White House Politics 1829-1837. Athens: University of Georgia Press, 1979.
Remini, Robert V. Andrew Jackson and the Course of American Empire, 1769-1821. New York: Harper & Row, 1977. The first volume of a new biography by the scholar called the "foremost Jacksonian scholar of our time." Brings together the best of recent scholarship by Remini and others.

_____. The Revolutionary Age of Andrew Jackson. New York: Harper & Row, 1976. A very lively recreation of the issues and personalities prominent in the Age of Jackson

*Rogin, Michael Paul. Fathers and Children: Andrew Jackson and the Subjugation of the American Indians. New York: Random, 1976.

*Russo, David J. The Major Political Issues of the Jacksonian Period and the Development of Party Loyalty in Congress 1830-1840. Transactions Series. Vol. 62, Pt. 5. Philadelphia: American Philosophical Society, 1972.

Sellers, Charles Grier, comp. Andrew Jackson, A Profile. New York: Hill and Wang, 1971. A collection of essays by eleven authorities on the career of Jackson.

Martin Van Buren (1837-1841)

*Remini, Robert V. Martin Van Buren and the Making of the Democratic Party. New York: W.W. Norton, 1970.

William Henry Harrison (1841)

Goebel, Dorothy Burne. William Henry Harrison: A Political Biography. Philadelphia: Porcupine Press, 1974. Reprint of 1926 edition based upon the author's thesis at Columbia University.

John Tyler (1841-1845)

Tyler, Lyon Gardiner. The Letters and Times of the Tylers. New York: Da Capo Press, 1970. 3 vols. Reprint of the 1884-1886 edition. The most valuable published source of materials on John Tyler.

Chidsey, Donald B. And Tyler Too. New York: Elsevier/Nelson Books, 1978. Reprint of 1963 edition.

Merk, Frederick and Merk, Lois. Fruits of Propaganda in the Tyler Administration. Cambridge: Harvard University Press, 1971.

Morgan Robert J. A Whig Embattled: The Presidency Under John Tyler. Reprint of 1954 edition. Hamden, CT.: Shoe String Press, Inc., 1974.

James K. Polk (1845-1849)

Polk, James K. Correspondence of James K. Polk. Edited by Herbert Weaver and Wayne Cutler. Nashville: Vanderbilt University Press, 1969- Five volumes published from 1969 to 1979 covering the period 1817-1841.

Schroeder, John H. Mr. Polk's War: American Opposition and Dissent, 1846-1848. Madison: University of Wisconsin Press, 1973.

428   Sources for American Studies

Zachary Taylor (1849-1850)

Hamilton, Holman. The Three Kentucky Presidents: Lincoln, Taylor,
    Davis. Lexington: University Press of Kentucky, 1978. A
    bicentennial contribution by a well-known authority.
Rayback, Joseph G. Free Soil: The Election of 1848. Lexington:
    The University Press of Kentucky, 1970.

Millard Fillmore (1850-1853)

Fillmore, Millard. Millard Fillmore Papers. Edited by Frank H.
    Severance. New York: Kraus Reprint Co., 1970. 2 vols.
    Originally published by the Buffalo Historical Society in
    1907.
Barre, W.L. The Life and Public Services of Millard Fillmore.
    New York: B. Franklin, 1971. Reprint of 1856 edition.
Dix, Dorothea Lynde. The Lady and the President: The Letters
    of Dorothea Dix and Millard Fillmore. Edited by Charles M.
    Snyder. Lexington: University Press of Kentucky, 1975.
Scarry, Robert J. Millard Fillmore, 13th President. Moravia,
    New York: Robert J. Scarry, 1970. Later edition of
    Millard Fillmore, the Man and the Cabin.

Franklin Pierce (1853-1857)

Bell, Carl I. They Knew Franklin Pierce. Springfield, Vermont:
    April Hill, 1980.
Hawthorne, Nathaniel. The Life of Franklin Pierce. New York:
    Garrett Press, 1970. Reprint of the 1852 edition. A
    campaign biography by Pierce's college classmate at Bowdoin.

James Buchanan (1857-1861)

Auchampaugh, Philip C. James Buchanan and His Cabinet on the
    Eve of the Secession. Reprint of 1926 edition. Boston: J.S.
    Canner and Co., 1965.
Smith, Elbert B. The Presidency of James Buchanan. Lawrence:
    University Press of Kansas, 1975.

Abraham Lincoln (1861-1865)

Anderson, David D. Abraham Lincoln. U.S. Authors Series,
    No. 153. New York: Twayne Publishers, 1970.
Basler, Roy Prentice. A Touchstone for Greatness: Essays,
    Addresses, and Occasional Pieces About Abraham Lincoln.
    Westport, Conn.: Greenwood Press, 1973.
Brogan, Denis W. Abraham Lincoln. Revised edition. Duckworth
    England Publishers, 1980. Biblio. Dist.
Davis, Cullom, et. al. eds. The Public and the Private Lincoln:
    Contemporary Prospectives. Carbondale: Southern Illinois
    University Press, 1979.

Dell, Christopher. Lincoln and the War Democrats: The Grand
    Erosion of Conservative Tradition. Rutherford, N.J.: Fairleigh
    Dickinson University Press, 1975.
Findley, Paul A. Lincoln: The Crucible of Congress. New York:
    Crown Publishers, Inc. 1979.
Forgie, George B. Patricide in the House Divided: A Psychological
    Interpretation of Lincoln and His Age. New York. Norton,
    1979.
Handlin, Oscar and Handlin, Lillian. Abraham Lincoln and the Union.
    Library of American Biography. Boston: Little, Brown and Co.,
    1980.
Lattimer, John K. Lincoln and Kennedy: Medical and Ballistic
    Comparisons of Their Assassinations. New York: Harcourt,
    Brace, Jovanovich, 1980.
Lincoln-Lore: Lincoln in the Popular Mind. Edited by Ray B.
    Browne. Bowling Green, Ohio: Popular Press, 1974.
Mellon, James. The Face of Lincoln. New York: Viking Press,
    Inc., 1980.
Mitgang, Herbert. Abraham Lincoln, A Press Portrait: His Life
    and Times from the Original Newspaper Documents of the Union,
    Confederacy, and Europe. Chicago: Quadrangle Books, 1971.
Nichols, David A. Lincoln and the Indians: Civil War Policy
    and Politics. Columbia: University of Missouri Press, 1978.
Oates, Stephen B. Our Fiery Trial: Abraham Lincoln, John Brown
    and the Civil War Era. Amherst: University of Mass. Press,
    1979.
*   . With Malice Toward None: The Life of Abraham Lincoln.
    New York: New American Library, 1978.

Andrew Johnson (1865-1869)

Johnson, Andrew. Papers of Andrew Johnson. Edited by LeRoy Graf
    and Ralph W. Haskins. Five vols. to date (1822-1862).
    Knoxville: University of Tennessee Press, 1967-
*Benedict, Michael Les. The Impeachment and Trial of Andrew
    Johnson. First edition. New York: Norton, 1973.
Brabson, Fay Warrington. Andrew Johnson: A Life in Pursuit
    of the Right Course, 1808-1875; the Seventeenth President of
    the United States. Durham, N.C.: Seeman Printery, 1972.
Castel, Albert. The Presidency of Andrew Johnson. The American
    Presidency Series. Lawrence: Regents Press of Kansas, 1979.
Mantell, Martin E. Johnson, Grant, and the Politics of Re-
    construction. New York: Columbia University Press, 1973.
Nash, Howard Pervear. Andrew Johnson: Congress and Reconstruction.
    Rutherford, N.J.: Fairleigh Dickinson University Press, 1972.
*Sefton, James E. Andrew Johnson and the Uses of Constitutional
    Power. Library of American Biography. Boston: Little, Brown
    and Co., 1980.
Smith, Gene. High Crimes and Misdemeanors: The Impeachment and
    Trial of Andrew Johnson. New York: Morrow, 1977.
Trefousse, Hans Louis. Impeachment of a President: Andrew
    Johnson, the Blacks and Reconstruction. Knoxville: University
    of Tennessee Press, 1975.

Ulysses S. Grant (1869-1877)

Grant, Ulysses S. The Papers of Ulysses S. Grant. Edited by
    John V. Simon. 8 vols. to date (1837-1863). Carbondale:
    Southern Illinois University Press, 1967-
Carpenter, John Alcott. Ulysses S. Grant. Rulers and Statesmen
    of the World Series, No. 14. New York: Twayne Publishers,
    1970.
Goldhurst, Richard. Many Are the Hearts: The Agony and the
    Triumph of Ulysses S. Grant. New York: Reader's Digest Press,
    1975.
McFeely, William S. Grant: A Biography. New York: W.W. Norton
    and Co., Inc., 1981.

Rutherford B. Hayes (1877-1881)

Hayes Historical Journal. Fremont, Ohio: Hayes Historical Society,
    1976. A semi-annual publication featuring the life and times
    of Hayes. Well illustrated.
Pabst, Anna Catherine Smith. The Birthplace of R.B. Hayes,
    Delaware, Ohio. (s.l.:s.m., 1972).

James A. Garfield (1881)

Garfield, James A. The Diary of James A. Garfield. Edited by
    Frederick D. and Harry J. Brown. 3 vols. to date (1848-1887).
    East Lansing: Michigan State University Press, 1967-
Bates, Richard O. The Gentleman from Ohio: A Biography of
    James A. Garfield. Durham, N.C.: Moore Publishing Co., 1973.
Doenecke, Justus D. The Presidencies of James A. Garfield and
    Chester A. Arthur. American Presidency Series. Lawrence:
    Regents Press of Kansas, 1981.
Leech, Margaret, and Brown,Harry J. The Garfield Orbit.
    New York: Harper & Row, 1978.
Peskin, Allan. Garfield. Kent, Ohio: Kent State University
    Press, 1978.
*Rosenberg, Charles E. The Trial of the Assassin Guiteau:
    Psychiatry and Law in the Gilded Age. Chicago: University
    of Chicago Press, 1976.
Taylor, John M. Garfield of Ohio, the Available Man. New York:
    Norton, 1970

Chester A. Arthur (1881-1885)

Doenecke, Justus D. The Presidencies of James A. Garfield and
    Chester A. Arthur. American Presidency Series. Lawrence:
    Regents Press of Kansas, 1981.
Reeves, Thomas C. Gentleman Boss: The Life of Chester Alan
    Arthur. New York: Alfred A. Knopf, 1975. The first full-
    scale biography, based upon intensive research and new

manuscript finds. Substantially revises older assumptions about Arthur and his era.

Grover Cleveland (1885-1889; 1893-1897)

No new studies.

Benjamin Harrison (1889-1893)

No new studies.

William McKinley (1897-1901)

Gould, Lewis L. The Presidency of William McKinley. The American Presidency Series. Lawrence: Regents Press of Kansas, 1980.

Theodore Roosevelt (1901-1909)

Alfonso, Oscar M. Theodore Roosevelt and the Phillipines, 1897-1909. New York: Oriole Editions, 1973.
Burton, David H. Theodore Roosevelt. World Leaders Series, No. 17. New York: Twayne Publishers, 1972.
*_____. Theodore Roosevelt and His English Correspondents: A Special Relationship of Friends. Transactions Ser.: Vol. 63 Pt. 2. Philadelphia: American Philosophical Society, 1973.
_____. Theodore Roosevelt: Confident Imperialist. Philadelphia: University of Pennsylvania Press, 1969.
Dyer, Thomas G. Theodore Roosevelt and the Idea of Race. Baton Rouge: Louisiana State University Press, 1980.
Egloff, Franklin R. Theodore Roosevelt: An American Portrait. New York: Vantage Press, 1980.
Gable, John A. The Bull Moose Years: Theodore Roosevelt and the Progressive Party. Port Washington, N.Y.: Kennikat Press, 1978.
Gardner, Joseph L. Departing Glory: Theodore Roosevelt as ex-President. New York: Scribner, 1973.
McKee, Delber L. Chinese Exclusion Versus the Open Door Policy, 1900-1906: Clashes over China Policy in the Roosevelt Era. Detroit: Wayne State University Press, 1977.
Marks, Frederick W. Velvet on Iron: The Diplomacy of Theodore Roosevelt. Lincoln: University of Nebraska Press, 1979.
*Morris, Edmund. The Rise of Theodore Roosevelt. New York: Ballantine, 1980.
Norton, Aloysius A. Theodore Roosevelt. United States Authors Series, No. 371. Boston: Twayne Publishers, 1980.
Theodore Roosevelt Association. Theodore Roosevelt Association Journal. Oyster Bay, N.Y.: Theodore Roosevelt Association, 1975-

William Howard Taft (1909-1913)

Anderson, Donald F. William Howard Taft: A Conservative's
    Conception of the Presidency. Ithaca, New York: Cornell
    University Press, 1973.
Coletta, Paolo E. The Presidency of William Howard Taft.
    Kansas: University Press, 1973.
Minger, Ralph. E. William Howard Taft and United States Foreign
    Policy: The Apprenticeship Years 1900-1908. Champaign:
    University of Illinois Press, 1975.
Scholes, Walter and Scholes, Marie F. Foreign Policies of the
    Taft Administration. Columbia: University of Missouri Press,
    1970.

Woodrow Wilson (1913-1921)

Hoover, Herbert. The Hoover-Wilson Wartime Correspondence.
    Edited and with commentaries by Francis William O'Brien.
    Ames, Ia.: Iowa State University Press, 1974.
_____. Two Peacemakers in Paris: the Hoover-Wilson Post-
    Armistice Letters, 1918-1920. Edited by Francis William
    O'Brien. College Station: Texas A & M University Press,
    1978.
Wilson, Woodrow. The Papers of Woodrow Wilson. Edited by
    Arthur S. Link, et. al. 35 vols. to date (1856-1916). Princeton:
    Princeton University Press, 1966-
Anderson, David B. Woodrow Wilson. World Leaders Series, No. 76,
    Boston: Twayne Publishers, 1978.
Canfield, Leon H. Presidency of Woodrow Wilson. Cranbury, N.J.:
    Fairleigh Dickinson University Press.
Devlin, Patrick. Too Proud to Fight: Woodrow Wilson's Neutrality.
    New York: Oxford University Press, 1975.
*Gilderhus, Mark T. Diplomacy and Revolution: U.S.-Mexico
    Relations Under Wilson and Carranza. Tucson: University
    of Arizona Press, 1977.
*Huthmacher, J. Joseph and Susman, Warren, eds. Wilson's Diplomacy:
    An International Symposium. Cambridge, MA.: Schenkman
    Publishing Co., 1973.
Mulder, John M. Woodrow Wilson: The Years of Preparation.
    Princeton, N.J.: Princeton University Press, 1977.
Parsons, Edward B. Wilsonian Diplomacy: Allied-American Rivalries
    in War and Peace. St. Louis: Forum Press, 1978.
Pisney, Raymond F., ed. Virginians Remember Woodrow Wilson.
    Mouseion Press, 1978.
_____. Woodrow Wilson: Idealism and Reality. Verona, Va.:
    McClure Press, 1977.
_____. Woodrow Wilson in Retrospect. Verona, Va.: McClure
    Press, 1978. A publication of the Woodrow Wilson Birthplace
    Foundation including addresses sponsored by the organization
    from 1940 to 1959 and some of the papers presented during the
    Centennial of Wilson's birth in Staunton, Virginia.
Safford, Jeffrey J. Wilsonian Maritime Diplomacy, 1913-1921.
    New Brunswick, N.J.: Rutgers University Press, 1978.

Walworth, Arthur Clarence. America's Moment, 1918: American
  Diplomacy at the End of World War I. New York: Norton, 1977.

Warren G. Harding (1921-1923)

Grieb, Kenneth J. The Latin American Policy of Warren G. Harding.
  Fort Worth: Texas Christian University Press, 1976.
Trani, Eugene P. and Wilson, David L. The Presidency of Warren G.
  Harding. Lawrence: Regents Press, 1977.

Calvin Coolidge (1923-1929)

Coolidge, Calvin. The Talkative President: The Off-the Record
  Press Conferences of Calvin Coolidge. Edited by Robert H.
  Ferrell and Howard H. Quint. New York: Garland Publisher, 1979.

Herbert Hoover (1929-1933)

Hoover, Herbert Clark. The Hoover-Wilson Wartime Correspondence.
  Edited and with commentaries by Francis William O'Brien.
  Ames, Iowa: Iowa State University Press, 1974.
_____. Two Peacemakers in Paris: the Hoover-Wilson Post-
  Armistice Letters, 1918-1920. Edited by Francis William
  O'Brien. College Station: Texas A & M University Press, 1978.
United States. Herbert Hoover: Proclamation and Executive Orders,
  March 4, 1929 to March 4, 1933. 2 vols. Washington: Govern-
  ment Printing Office, 1974.
_____. Public Papers of the Presidents of the United States,
  Herbert Hoover, 1929-1933. 4 vols. Washington: Government
  Printing Office, 1974-1977. The first volume of several to
  follow containing most of the public messages and statements
  of President Hoover released by the White House during 1929.
  Those not printed are listed in Appendix A along with the
  texts of public statements made by Hoover from his nomination
  to his inauguration.
Best, Gary Dean. The Politics of American Individualism:
  Herbert Hoover in Transition, 1918-1921. Westport, Conn.:
  Greenwood Press, 1975
Burner, David. Herbert Hoover: the Public Life. Westminster,
  Md: Alfred A. Knopf, Inc., 1978.
Curry, Earl R. Hoover's Dominican Diplomacy and the Origins
  of the Good Neighbor Policy. Modern American History Series:
  Vol. 5. New York: Garland Publishing, Inc. 1979.
Eckley, Wilton. Herbert Hoover. United States Authors Series,
  No. 385. Boston: Twayne Publishers, 1980.
Fausold, Martin L. and Mazuzan, George T., eds. The Hoover
  Presidency: A Reappraisal. Albany: State University of
  New York Press, 1974. Ten essays offering a major reevaluation
  of the Hoover era. Fausold is writing a new study of the
  Hoover Presidency. Nine persuasive essays, plus an introductory
  chapter and bibliographical note, based on a conference held

April 27-28, 1973 at State University College, Geneseo, New York.

Hoover Presidential Library Association. _Herbert Hoover, the Un-_
common Man. West Branch, Iowa: Hoover Presidential Library
Association, 1974.

Lisio, Donald J. _The President and Protest: Hoover, Conspiracy_
and the Bonus Riot. Columbia: University of Missouri Press,
1974.

McLean, Hulda H. _Genealogy of the Herbert Hoover Family._ Stanford,
Cal.: Hoover Institution Press, 1967.
_____. _Genealogy of the Herbert Hoover Family: Errata and_
Addenda. Stanford, Calif.: Hoover Institution, 1976.

Robinson, Edgar E. and Bornet, Vaughn D. _Herbert Hoover:_
President of the United States. Stanford, Calif.: Hoover
Institution Press , 1975.

*Romasco, Albert U. _Poverty of Abundance: Hoover, the Nation,_
the Depression. New York: Oxford University Press, 1968.

Schwarz, Jordan A. _The Interregnum of Despair: Hoover, Congress,_
and the Depression. Champaign: University of Illinois Press,
1970.

Tracey, Kathleen, compiled by. _Herbert Hoover: A Bibliography of_
His Writings and Addresses. Stanford, Calif.: Hoover Institution Press, 1977.

*Wilson, Joan Hoff. _Herbert Hoover: Forgotten Progressive._
Boston: Little, Brown, 1975. An excellent brief interpretive
biography based upon considerable research in the Hoover
Papers by one of the leading young scholars of the Hoover
period. Contains a good bibliographical essay on the Hoover
sources and secondary literature, including a valuable list
of papers read at professional meetings and dissertations on
Hoover.

Franklin Delano Roosevelt (1933-1945)

Center for Cassette Studies. _Index to the Complete Recorded_
Speeches of Franklin Delano Roosevelt: 278 Speeches dating
from 1920 to 1945. North Hollywood, Calif.: 1974.

Roosevelt, Franklin Delano. _Complete Presidential Press_
Conferences of Franklin D. Roosevelt. New York: Da Capo Press,
1972.

Roosevelt and Churchill: Their Secret Wartime Correspondence.
Edited by Francis L. Lowenheim _et al._ New York: Saturday
Review Press, 1975. Includes most of the vital personal
correspondence between the two leaders from 1939 to 1945.

Bailey, Thomas Andrew. _Hitler vs. Roosevelt: The Undeclared_
Naval War. New York: Free Press, 1979.

Beschloss, Michael R. _Kennedy and Roosevelt: The Uneasy_
Alliance. New York: W.W. Norton and Co., Inc., 1980.

*Bishop, James Alonzo. _FDR's Last Year: April 1944 - April 1945._
London: Hart-Davis MacGibbon, 1975.

Dallek, Robert. _Franklin D. Roosevelt and American Foreign_
Policy, 1932-1945. New York: Oxford University Press, 1979.

Davis, Kenneth S. _FDR: The Beckoning of Destiny, 1882-1928:_
A History. New York: Putnam, 1972. Places Roosevelt against

the background and happenings of almost half a century and shows
how the man and his career were shaped and influenced by the
world in which he lived.
_____. Invincible Summer: An Intimate Portrait of the
Roosevelts, Based on the Recollections of Marion Dickerman.
New York: Atheneum, 1974.
Dorsett, Lyle W. Franklin D. Roosevelt and the City Bosses.
Port Washington, N.Y.: Kennikat Press, 1977.
Frisch, Morton J. Franklin D. Roosevelt: The Contribution of the
New Deal to American Political Thought and Practice. New York:
Twayne Publishers, 1975.
*Kinsella, William E. Leadership in Isolation: FDR and the
Origins of the Second World War. Cambridge, Mass.: Schenkman,
1980.
Lash, Joseph P. Roosevelt and Churchill, 1939-1941: The Partner-
ship that Saved the West. New York: Norton, 1976.
Lawson, Don. FDR's New Deal. 1st ed. New York: Crowell, 1979.
Lippman, Theo. The Squire of Warm Springs: F.D.R. in Georgia,
1924-1945. Chicago: Playboy Press, 1977.
Roosevelt, Elliott. A Rendezvous with Destiny: The Roosevelts
of the White House. New York: Putnam, 1975.
_____. An Untold Story: The Roosevelts of Hyde Park. New
York: Putnam Sons, 1973.
_____. Mother R.: Eleanor Roosevelt's Untold Story. New York:
Putnam, 1977.
Roosevelt, James. My Parents: A Differing View. Chicago:
Playboy Press, 1976.
Rosen, Elliot A. Hoover, Roosevelt, and the Brain Trust: From
Depression to New Deal. New York: Columbia University Press,
1977.
Tugwell, Rexford Guy. In Search of Roosevelt. Cambridge: Harvard
University Press, 1972.
_____. Roosevelt's Revolution: The First Year, a Personal
Perspective. New York: Macmillan, 1977.
Venkataramani, M.S. The Sunny Side of F.D.R. Athens: Ohio
University Press, 1973.
White, Graham J. FDR and the Press. Chicago: University of
Chicago Press, 1979.

Harry S. Truman (1945-1953)

Cochran, Bert. Harry Truman and the Crisis Presidency. New York:
Funk and Wagnalls, 1973. Critical of Truman.
*Donovan, Robert J. Conflict and Crisis. The Presidency of Harry
S. Truman, 1945-1948. New York: W.W. Norton and Company,
1979. The best and fullest account of Truman's first term.
Gosnell, Harold F. Truman's Crises: A Political Biography of
Harry S. Truman. Westport, Conn.: Greenwood Press, 1980.
A basic scholarly study of Truman's entire career. Makes use
of manuscript sources, social science analysis, and the new
monographs on the postwar period. Gosnell takes a middle
position on Truman, between the liberal interpretations of
the fifties and sixties and the revisionist criticisms of the
seventies.

*Hamby, Alonzo L. Beyond the New Deal: Harry S. Truman and American
    Liberalism. New York: Columbia University Press, 1973. The
    most complete scholarly account of the Truman Administration to
    date.
Haynes, Richard F. The Awesome Power: Harry S. Truman as
    Commander in Chief. Baton Rouge: Louisiana State University
    Press, 1973.
Heller, Francis H., ed. The Truman White House: The Administration
    of the Presidency, 1945-1953. Lawrence: Regents Press of
    Kansas, 1980. Edited for the Harry S. Truman Literary Institute
    for National and International Affairs. See pp. 237-239 for a
    list of primary sources on the Truman White House. Includes
    other bibliographical references and an index.
Kirkendall, Richard S., ed. The Truman Period as a Research Field.
    Columbia: University of Missouri Press, 1967; and The Truman
    Period as a Research Field: A Reappraisal, 1972. Columbia:
    University of Missouri Press, 1974. Four essays touching upon
    aspects of domestic politics. The second edition contains
    new essays, commentaries by the authors of the first edition,
    and an updated comprehensive bibliography.
McCoy, Donald R. and Richard T. Ruetten. Quest and Response:
    Minority Rights and the Truman Administration. Lawrence:
    University Press of Kansas, 1973. The best study of civil rights
    and minority problems under Truman.
*Miller, Merle. Plain Speaking: An Oral Biography of Harry S.
    Truman. New York: Berkley Publishing Corp., 1980. A record
    of conversations with the former president in the early 1960's.
    Originally intended for a television series, but issued in
    book form instead.
Snetsinger, John. Truman, the Jewish Vote, and the Creation of
    Israel. Stanford: Hoover Institution Press, 1974.
Thomson, David S. A Pictorial Biography: HST. Text by David
    S. Thomson. New York: Grosset & Dunlap, 1973.
Walton, Richard J. Henry Wallace, Harry Truman, and the Cold
    War. New York: Viking, 1976. A study of the 1948 campaign
    and the Wallace-Truman debate over the origins and intentions
    of the Cold War.
Yarnell, Allen. Democrats and Progressives: The 1948 Presidential
    Election as a Test of Postwar Liberalism. Berkeley: University
    of California Press, 1974. Argues that the Wallace Progressives
    made it easier for Truman to take tough stands on foreign policy
    issues, thus aiding the Democrats in their 1948 victory.

Dwight David Eisenhower (1953-1961)

Eisenhower, Dwight D. Letters to Mamie. Garden City, N.Y.:
    Doubleday, 1978. Edited with commentary by John S.D. Eisenhower.
Ambrose, Stephen E. Ike: Abilene to Berlin; the Life of Dwight
    D. Eisenhower from his Childhood in Abilene, Kansas, Through his
    Command of the Allied Forces in Europe in World War II. New
    York: Harper & Row, 1973.
*Alexander, Charles C. Holding the Line: The Eisenhower Era, 1952-
    1961. Bloomington: Indiana University Press, 1975.

Caute, David. The Great Fear: The Anti-Communist Purge Under
    Truman and Eisenhower. London: Secker and Warburg, 1978.
Killian, James Rhyne, Jr. Sputnik, Scientists, and Eisenhower:
    A Memoir of the First Special Assistant to the President for
    Science and Technology. Cambridge: MIT Press, 1977.
Kinnard, Douglas. President Eisenhower and Strategy Management:
    A Study in Defense of Politics. Lexington: University Press
    of Kentucky, 1977.
Lyon, Peter. Eisenhower: Portrait of the Hero. Boston: Little,
    Brown, 1974. A full biography which attempts to study the man
    from boyhood to retirement.
Reichard, Gary W. The Reaffirmation of Republicanism: Eisenhower
    and the Eighty-Third Congress. Knoxville: University of
    Tennessee Press, 1975.
Richardson, Elmo R. The Presidency of Dwight D. Eisenhower.
    American Presidency Series. Lawrence: Regents Press of
    Kansas, 1979.
Sixsmith, Eric Keir Gilborne. Eisenhower as Military Commander.
    New York: Stein and Day, 1973.

John F. Kennedy (1961-1963)

Kennedy, John Fitzgerald. The Kennedy Presidential Press
    Conference. Introd. by David Halberstam. New York: E.M.
    Coleman Enterprises, 1978.
Bradlee, Benjamin. Conversations with Kennedy. New York: W.W.
    Norton, 1975. Based on private notes kept by Kennedy's
    neighbor and Washington Post editor.
*Brauer, Carl M. John F. Kennedy and the Second Reconstruction.
    New York: Columbia University Press, 1979.
Freed, Donald and Lane, Mark. Executive Action: Assassination of
    a Head of State. New York: Dell Pub. Co., 1973.
Gromyko, Anatolii Andreevich. Through Russian Eyes: President
    Kennedy's 1036 Days. Washington: International Library, 1973.
    Professor Gromyko, son of Soviet Foreign Minister Andrei
    Gromyko, heads the Foreign Policy Section in the USA Institute
    of the USSR Academy of Sciences and is considered one of
    Russia's leading "Americanists."
Heath, Jim F. Decade of Disillusionment: The Kennedy-Johnson
    Years. Bloomington: Indiana University Press, 1975. The first
    balanced survey of the period. Portrays Kennedy as a cautious
    leader despite his bold rhetoric.
Longford, Frank Pakenham, 7th Earl of. Kennedy. London:
    Weidenfeld and Nicolson, 1976.
Lord, Donald C. John F. Kennedy: The Politics of Confrontation
    and Conciliation. Woodbury, N.Y.: Barron's, 1977.
*Miroff, Bruce. Pragmatic Illusions: The Presidential Politics of
    John F. Kennedy. New York: Longman McKay, 1976.
*Paper, Lewis J. John F. Kennedy: The Promise and the Performance.
    New York: Da Capo, 1980.
Parmet, Herbert S. Jack: The Struggles of John F. Kennedy.
    New York: The Dial Press, 1980.

Schwab, Peter and Shneidman, J. Lee. John F. Kennedy. Boston:
    Twayne Publishers, 1974.
Toscano, Vincent L. Since Dallas: Images of John F. Kennedy in
    Popular and Scholarly Literature, 1963-1973. San Francisco:
    R & E Research Associates, 1978.

Lyndon Baines Johnson (1963-1969)

Califano, Joseph. A Presidential Nation. New York: W. W. Norton
    & Co., 1975. A key Johnson aide describes the LBJ White House
    with emphasis on domestic operations.
*Kearns, Doris. Lyndon Johnson and the American Dream. New York:
    New American Library, 1977.
Schandler, Herbert Y. The Unmaking of a President: Lyndon
    Johnson and Vietnam. Princeton, N.J.: Princeton University
    Press, 1977.
Valenti, Jack. A Very Human President. New York: Norton, 1976.

Richard M. Nixon (1969-1973)

Nixon, Richard M. The Memoirs of Richard Nixon. New York: Grosset
    & Dunlap, 1978.
_____. The Real War. New York: Warner Books, 1980.
Arnold, William A. Back When It All Began: The Early Nixon Years:
    Being Some Reminiscences of President Nixon's Early Political
    Career by His First Administrative Assistant and Press Secretary.
    New York: Vantage Press, 1975.
Atkins, Ollie. The White House Years: Triumph and Tragedy.
    Chicago: Playboy Press, 1977.
*Burke, Vincent J. Nixon's Good Deed: Welfare Reform. New York:
    Columbia University Press, 1974.
Cavan, Sherri. Twentieth Century Gothic: America's Nixon. San
    Francisco: Wigan Pier Press, 1979.
*Frost, David. I Gave Them A Sword: Behind the Scenes of the Nixon
    Interviews. New York: Ballantine, 1978.
Jones, Alan M., Jr., ed. U.S. Foreign Policy in a Changing World:
    The Nixon Administration, 1969-1973. New York: David McKay,
    1973.
Kissinger Henry. White House Years. Boston: Little, Brown and
    Company, 1979.
Morrison, Rodney J. Expectations and Inflation: Nixon, Politics
    and Economics. Lexington, Mass.: Lexington Books, 1973.
    Includes bibliographic references.
*Porter, William Earl. Assault on the Media: The Nixon Years.
    Ann Arbor: University of Michigan Press, 1976.
Price, Raymond. With Nixon. New York: Viking Press, 1977.
*Rather, Dan and Gates, Gary Paul. The Palace Guard. New York:
    Warner, 1975.
Safire, William L. Before the Fall: An Inside View of the Pre-
    Watergate White House. Garden City, N.Y.: Doubleday, 1975.
Schoenebaum, Eleanora W. Profiles of an Era: The Nixon/Ford Years.
    New York: Facts on File, Inc., 1979.

Szulc, Tad. The Illusion of Peace: Foreign Policy in the Nixon
    Years. New York: Viking Press, 1978.

(Publications Relating to "Watergate")

Ball, Howard. No Pledge of Privacy: The Watergate Tapes Litigation.
    Port Washington, N.Y.: Kennikat Press, 1977.
Boyan, A. Stephen. Constitutional Aspects of Watergate: Documents
    & Materials. 5 vols. Dobbs Ferry, N.Y.: Oceana Publications,
    1976.
*Drew, Elizabeth. Washington Journal: The Events of 1973-1974.
    New York: Vintage Books, 1976.
The End of a Presidency. By the staff of the New York Times. New
    York: Holt, Rinehart and Winston, 1974.
*Evans, Les and Myers, Allen. Watergate and the Myth of American
    Democracy. New York: Path Press, 1974.
The Fall of a President. By the staff of the Washington Post. New
    York: Delacorte Press, 1974.
*Halpern, Paul J., ed. Why Watergate? Palisades Calif.: Palisades
    Press, 1975.
Jaworski, Leon. The Right and the Power: The Prosecution of
    Watergate. New York: Reader's Digest Press, distributed
    by Crowell, 1976.
*Sorensen, Theodore C. Watchmen in the Night: Presidential
    Accountability After Watergate. Cambridge, Mass.: The
    MIT Press, 1975.
United States Congress. House of Representatives Committee on
    the Judiciary. Impeachment of Richard M. Nixon, President
    of the United States: The Final Report of the Committee on
    the Judiciary. House of Representatives, Peter W. Rodino, Jr.
    chairman, with an introd. by R. W. Apple, Jr. New York:
    Viking Press, 1975.
White, Theodore Harold. Breach of Faith: The Fall of Richard
    Nixon. 1st ed. New York: Atheneum, 1975.
Woodward, Bob and Bernstein, Carl. The Final Days. New York:
    Simon and Schuster, 1976.

Gerald R. Ford (1974-1977)

Collins, Paul. Gerald R. Ford: A Man in Perspective: As
    Portrayed in the Gerald R. Ford Mural by Paul Collins. Photo-
    graphy by John R. Fulton, Jr. and Candace Brown; text by Tom
    LaBelle; design by Candace Brown; pref. by Fred Myers; poetry
    by W. Randolph Brown. Grand Rapids: Eerdmans, 1976.
Congressional Quarterly, Inc. President Ford: The Man and His
    Record. Washington: Congressional Quarterly, Inc., 1974.
    A convenient overview of the President's political career
    and legislative record to August 1974 when he assumed the
    leadership of the nation.
Casserly, John J. The Ford White House: The Diary of a Speech-
    writer. Boulder: Colorado Associated University Press, 1977.
A Discussion with Gerald R. Ford: The American Presidency: held
    on March 25, 1977 at the American Enterprise Institute for

Public Policy Research, Washington, D.C. Washington: The
Institute, 1977.

Hersey, John Richard. The President. 1st ed. New York: Knopf,
1975.

*Kraus, Sidney, ed. The Great Debates: Carter vs. Ford, 1976.
Bloomington: Indiana University Press, 1979.

Mollenhoff, Clark R. The Man Who Pardoned Nixon. New York: St.
Martin's Press, 1976.

Reeves, Richard. A Ford, Not a Lincoln. New York: Harcourt Brace
Jovanovich, 1975. A journalistic account of Ford's first hundred
days in the White House.

Sidey, Hugh. Portrait of a President. New York: Harper & Row,
1975. A pictorial biography of the first few months of the
Ford Administration.

ter Horst, J.F. Gerald Ford and the Future of the Presidency.
New York: The Third Press, 1974. A brief biography based upon
the author's twenty-five year friendship with the President.
Included is a discussion of the first thirty days of the Ford
Administration, the Nixon pardon, and the events surrounding
the author's resignation as Ford's first Press Secretary.

United States. 95th Congress, 1st session, 1977. Tributes to
Honorable Gerald R. Ford, President of the United States, to
commemorate him for his years of service to the nation, February
1, 1977: delivered in the House of Representatives of the
United States. Washington: U.S. Govt. Print. Off., 1977.

James Earl Carter (1977-1981)

Carter, Jimmy. A Government as Good as its People. New York:
Simon and Schuster, 1977. A collection of Carter's campaign
speeches, interviews, and informal statements covering the
years 1971 to 1977.

*_____. Why Not the Best? Nashville: Broadman Press, 1977.

*Baker, James Thomas. A Southern Baptist in the White House.
Philadelphia: Westminster Press, 1977.

*Bitzer, Lloyd and Theodore Rueter. Carter vs. Ford: The Counterfeit
Debates of 1976. Madison: The University of Wisconsin Press,
1980.

Carter, Hugh. Cousin Beedie and Cousin Hot: My Life with
the Carter Family of Plains, Georgia. Englewood Cliffs, N.J.:
Prentice-Hall, Inc., 1978.

Collins, Tom. The Search for Jimmy Carter. Waco, Tex.: Word
Books, 1976.

*Congressional Quarterly, Inc. President Carter. Washington: Con-
gressional Quarterly, Inc., 1977. Contains in-depth political
and biographical profiles of President Carter, Vice President
Mondale, and each Cabinet appointee, and a summary of the 1976
presidential election campaign.

de Mause, Lloyd, and Ebel, Henry, eds. Jimmy Carter and American
Fantasy: Psychohistorical Explorations. New York: Two
Continents, 1977. Five essays which probe the psychology of
Carter's leadership.

Fink, Gary M. Prelude to the Presidency: The Political Character and Legislative Leadership Style of Governor Jimmy Carter. Westport, Conn.: Greenwood Press, 1980. The first in-depth examination of Carter's four years as Governor of Georgia. Includes a dozen vignettes of Carter political advisers and intimates.

Glad, Betty. Jimmy Carter: From Plains to the White House. New York: W. W. Norton & Co., 1980.

Ilefley, James and Marti. The Church that Produced a President. New York: Wyden Books, 1977. Examines the spiritual roots of Jimmy Carter.

Jennings, Genelle. Into the Jaws of Politics: The Charge of the Peanut Brigade. Huntsville, Ala.: Strode Publishers, 1979.

*Kucharsky, David. The Man from Plains: The Mind and Spirit of Jimmy Carter. New York: Harper & Row, 1977. Analyzes the impact of Jimmy Carter's fundamentalism on his political beliefs and action.

Mazlish, Bruce and Diamond Edwin. Jimmy Carter: A Character Portrait. New York: Simon and Schuster, 1979.

Miller, William Lee. Yankee from Georgia: The Emergence of Jimmy Carter. New York: Time Books, 1978.

Neyland, James. The Carter Family Scrapbook: An Intimate Close-up of America's First Family. New York: Grosset & Dunlap, 1977.

The Presidential Campaign, 1976. Compiled under the direction of the Committee on House Administration, U.S. House of Representatives. Washington: U.S. Government Printing Office, 1978. 2 vols. A documentary collection covering the period from Carter's announcement of his candidacy to his immediate post-victory statements and exchanges with President Ford.

Sarkesian, Sam C., ed. Defense and the Presidency: Carter's First Years. Boulder: Westview Press, 1979.

Schram, Martin. Running for President: A Journal of the Carter Campaign. New York: Pocket Books, 1976.

Shoup, Lawrence H. The Carter Presidency and Beyond: Power and Politics in the 1980s. Palo Alto, Calif.: Ramports Press, 1980. A case study of Jimmy Carter's political roots, presidency, and 1980 election prospects.

Stroud, Kandy. How Jimmy Won: The Victory Campaign from Plains to the White House. New York: Morrow, 1977.

Walker, Barbara J. The Picture Life of Jimmy Carter. New York: Watts, 1977.

*Witcover, Jules. Marathon: The Pursuit of the Presidency, 1972-1976. New York: New American Library, 1978. A detailed account of the 1976 campaign for the presidency by a veteran Washington correspondent.

*Wooten, James T. Dasher: The Roots and the Rising of Jimmy Carter. New York: Warner Books, 1979. A journalist's book based upon interviews with the Carter family and his experience as Atlanta Bureau Chief and White House correspondent.

Postscript to "Revolution in American Education: A Bibliographical Essay"

JOHN A. HAGUE

The original article called attention to a number of works that argued that the public school system should be radically revised or destroyed. Since 1975 a number of writers have questioned whether educational institutions can be expected to reform the society of which they are a part. Samuel Bowles and Herbert Gintis, *Schooling in Capitalist America: Educational Reform and the Contradictions of Economic Life (New York: Basic Books, 1976), show some of the ways in which schools reflect economic forces, and L. Steven Zwerling in Second Best: The Crisis of the Community College (New York: McGraw Hill, 1976), suggests that community colleges frequently retard mobility and preserve the status quo. Similar concerns are voiced by Christopher J. Hurn in The Limits and Possibilities of Schooling: An Introduction to the Sociology of Education (Boston: Allyn and Bacon, 1978), and by Richard H. De Lone in Small Futures: Inequality, Children, and the Failure of Liberal Reform (New York: Harcourt Brace Jovanovich, 1978), a report of the Carnegie Council on Children.

As one might expect, a number of works have defended the role of the public school in American society. Among these are The Revisionists Revised: A Critique of the Radical Attack on the Schools by Diane Ravitch (New York: Basic Books, 1978), and *The Enduring Effects of Education by Herbert Hyman, Charles R. Wright, and John Shelton Reed (Chicago: University of Chicago Press, 1975).

The majority of writers, while recognizing serious failures within the educational system, nevertheless believe that schools can be much better than they are. For example, Kenneth Keniston in *All

Our Children: The American Family Under Pressure (New York: Harcourt Brace Jovanovich, 1978), agrees that "one of the crucial roles of schools as they actually work in America is not to equalize but to sort and classify children for roles in a stratified world." Nevertheless, he also insists that "it is perfectly reasonable to expect schools to contribute to the goal of equal opportunity instead of perpetuating the status of birth." Michael Schiro has written Curriculum for Better Schools: The Great Ideological Debate (Englewood Cliffs, N.J.: Educational Technology Publications, 1978), and Jonathan P. Sher has taken a hard and careful look at rural schools, *Education in Rural America: A Reassessment of Conventional Wisdom (Boulder, Colorado: Westview Press, 1977). Both works combine critical and hopeful appraisals. In a somewhat similar vein, Mary Lou Zoglin wrote Power and Politics in the Community College (Palm Springs, Calif.: ETC Publications, 1976), and Jerome Karabel and A. H. Halsey have co-authored *Power and Ideology in Education (New York: Oxford University Press, 1977). Three other volumes in this tradition are Teaching Styles and Pupil Progress by Neville Bennett with Joyce Jordan, George Long, and Barbara Wade, foreword by Jerome Bruner (Cambridge: Harvard University Press, 1976); Human Characteristics and School Learning by Benjamin S. Bloom (New York: McGraw Hill, 1976); and Accent on Learning by K. Patricia Cross (San Francisco: Josey-Bass, 1976).

A number of works have focused on the results (or lack of results) in the ongoing effort to integrate American schools. Among the most prominent are Equal Educational Opportunity for Blacks in U.S. Higher Education, Institute for the Study of Educational Policy (Washington: Howard University Press, 1976); School Desegregation by Harold B. Gerard and Norman Miller (New York: Plenum Press, 1975); The Invisible Children: School Integration in American Society by Ray C. Rist (Cambridge: Harvard University Press, 1978); and Minority Education and Caste: The American System in Cross Cultural Perspective by John U. Ogbu (New York: Academic Press, 1978). All of these books remind us of the many and subtle ways in which schools resist profound change.

The literature of recent years points to a number of special interest areas that affect educational practices and institutions. Titles previously cited call attention to the vastly increased populations enrolled in community colleges. A book by Wayne Dennis and Margaret Daniels, The Intellectually Gifted--An Overview (New York: Grune and Stratton, 1976), and a report to the Carnegie Council on Children by John Gliedman and William Roth, Handicapped Children in America (New York: Academic Press, 1978), remind us that both gifted and handicapped children require special attention. The Graying of the Campus (New York: Educational Facilities Laboratories, 1978), points to demographic changes that highlight the importance of continuing education, and *Coming to Our Senses: The Significance of the Arts for American Education (a special project panel, David Rockefeller, Jr., chairman; New York: McGraw Hill, 1977), notes a neglected area in the curriculum.

In the area of higher education, the past five years has been a
time of soul-searching analyses. Some of the most impressive books
were those sponsored by the Carnegie Council on Policy Studies in
Higher Education. A trilogy of works on curriculum deserves
special mention: Curriculum: A History of the American Under-
graduate Course of Study, by Frederick Rudolph (San Francisco:
Jossey-Bass, 1977); Missions of the College Curriculum: A Contem-
porary Review with Suggestions by the Carnegie Foundation for the
Advancement of Teaching (San Francisco: Jossey-Bass, 1978); and
Arthur Levine's Handbook on Undergraduate Curriculum (San Francisco:
Jossey-Bass, 1978). Other monographs sponsored by the Carnegie
Council on Policy Studies include Presidents Confront Reality:
From Edifice Complex to University Without Walls (San Francisco:
Jossey-Bass, 1977), and Fair Practices in Higher Education: Rights
and Responsibilities of Students and Their Colleges in a Period of
Intensified Competition for Enrollments (San Francisco: Jossey-
Bass, 1979). One additional report of the Council on Policy
Studies, Investment in Learning: The Individual and Social Value
of American Higher Education, was written by Howard R. Bowen with
the collaboration of Peter Clecak. *The Perpetual Dream--Reform
and Experiment in the American College, edited by David Riesman
and Gerald Grant (Chicago: University of Chicago Press, 1979),
raises basic questions about the "is and ought" of the campus
community.

A number of college presidents have given us personal accounts of
challenges and opportunities in higher education. Nathan Pusey
gives us the most descriptive title, American Higher Education,
1945-1970, A Personal Report (Cambridge, Massachusetts: Harvard
University Press, 1978). Theodore R. Gross labels his book The
Reality and Promise of Open Education (New York: Anchor Press,
1979), and Gail Thain Parker's book bears the title The Writing on
the Wall (New York: Simon and Schuster, 1979).

As one examines the materials educators publish to describe their
enterprises, one learns quickly that education is very much in the
mainstream of American culture. Here and there one still finds
voices pleading for radical alternatives. *Education by Choice:
The Case for Family Control, by John E. Coons and Stephen D. Sugarman (Berkeley: University of California Press, 1979), is one
example. Most writers, however, are committed to making the system
work. To that effort they bring a rapidly growing technology and
a growing knowledge of curricula, pedagogy, and administrative
structures. They also bring an awareness of the magnitude of the
problems they confront. Teachers, in short, are like engineers,
city planners, doctors, and a host of other professionals. Their
techniques and training have improved, but they are not sure
whether this will enable them to educate more effectively or
whether it merely gives them new insights into "the Myth of
Sisyphus."

American Workers and American Studies Since 1974

BERNARD MERGEN

The opportunity to update Dr. Wason's fine essay is doubly welcome; first, because so much good new scholarship has been published since 1974, and second, because his original contribution to American Studies International was so wide ranging that it provides a strong base upon which to build my own survey. Dr. Wason took a broad view of labor history, including in his bibliography works on economics, immigration, and race, as well as the narrower institutional studies of labor organizations. What I intend to do is to follow his original organization, adding new titles and a few older but still useful works, then add three new sections that I feel are in harmony with his purpose--one on women, one on occupational folklife, and one on the visual aspects of the history of American workers.

One of the most useful research tools in labor history is the three-volume index to Trade Union Publications: The Official Journals, Convention Proceedings, and Constitutions of International Unions and Federations 1850-1941, edited by Lloyd G. Reynolds and Charles C. Killingsworth (Baltimore: The Johns Hopkins Press, 1944-1946). The first volume of this fine work contains brief histories of the major craft and industrial unions founded before 1940; the other two volumes contain the indexes. A complement to Reynolds and Killingsworth is B. Naas and C. Sakr, American Labor Union Periodicals: A Guide to Their Location (Ithaca, N.Y.: Cornell University Press, 1956). A third related research guide is Walter Goldwater's Radical Periodicals in America, 1890-1950 (New Haven, Conn.: Yale University Press, 1964.)

A large number of reprints and microfilms of labor documents have
appeared in the past few years. Arno Press in New York has
reprinted The Annual Reports of the National Labor Relations Board,
1936-1965 in 10 volumes, and Leon Stein and Philip Taft selected
105 books on labor for another Arno reprint series. The Microfilming Corporation of America in Glen Rock, New Jersey, has an
ongoing series of American Labor Unions' Constitutions and Proceedings. The same company has also filmed the Powderly and Hayes
Knights of Labor Papers and the Papers of the Southern Tenant
Farmer's Union. Greenwood Press in Westport, Connecticut, has
microforms of the State Labor Reports to 1900 of some thirteen
states.

Robert Dubin's Handbook of Work, Organization, and Society (Chicago:
Rand McNally, 1976), contains several excellent essays with exten-
sive bibliographies on such topics as "The Language of Work" and
"Work and Leisure." A Biographical Dictionary of American Labor
Leaders, edited by Gary M. Fink and Milton Cantor (Westport, Conn.:
Greenwood Press, 1974), is a useful update of the earlier Who's
Who in American Labor.

Among new periodicals, Labor Studies Journal, George Meany Center
for Labor Studies, Silver Spring, Maryland 20903, and International
Labor and Working Class History, History Department, Yale University, New Haven, Connecticut 06520, are the most useful, containing
essays, reviews, and news of meetings and current research. An
older, indispensable journal is the Labor Law Reporter, Commerce
Clearing House, Washington, D.C.

American Theories of the Labor Movement

One of the most influential new books arguing a thesis is Harry
Braverman's *Labor and Monopoly Capital (N.Y.: Monthly Review
Press, 1974). Braverman's theory is that by redefining the word
"skill," managers have made it appear that automation and complex
technology have reduced the size of the working class. On the
contrary, Braverman argues, the "working class" is defined by its
relationship to those who design the machines and the products made
by them. These engineers and managers are the "capitalists" who
control the workers by constantly decreasing the level of skill
needed to do a job. Braverman's thesis should be compared to that
of Robert Blauner in *Alienation and Freedom: The Factory Worker
and His Industry (Chicago: University of Chicago Press, 1964), who
found that some workers in a highly automated chemical plant
"regained" a sense of control over their complex technological
environment.

Daniel Rodgers, *The Work Ethic in Industrial America, 1850-1920
(Chicago: University of Chicago Press, 1978), and James B. Gilbert,
Work Without Salvation: America's Intellectuals and Industrial
Alienation, 1880-1910 (Baltimore: The Johns Hopkins University
Press, 1977), offer similar theories of the effect of industriali-
zation on the concept of work. Both show that as work became
increasingly mechanized and routinized, the concept of work was

redefined by apologists for capitalism into an activity which had extrinsic rewards and which could be mitigated by leisure-time pursuits. The result of these changes was that by about 1920, workers were left without personal satisfaction in their labor, but were still tormented by the accusation of idleness if they were unemployed. The focus of Rodgers and Gilbert on the history of ideas is not typical of historians of the working class, but they have obviously benefited from the work of E. P. Thompson and David Montgomery.

Labor in an Age of Revolution, 1764-1819

Two recent studies of American workers in the 18th and early 19th centuries deserve attention. Philip S. Foner's Labor and The American Revolution (Westport, Conn.: Greenwood Press, 1976), is a general survey focusing on urban workers. Daniel H. Calhoun's *Intelligence of a People (Princeton, N.J.: Princeton University Press, 1973), is a brilliant exploration of the concept of intelligence and its relation to American education. His chapter on shipbuilding in the United States as contrasted with Britain will be of interest to students of American labor history.

"Workies" and Utopias, 1819-1840

Excellent research on the period of early industrial development has been done in the past few years. The outstanding new book on this era is Anthony F. C. Wallace, *Rockdale (N.Y.: Knopf, 1978). This careful study of a cluster of textile mill villages on Chester Creek near Philadelphia covers the years 1825 to 1865 in great detail. Wallace, an anthropologist, provides information on the owners, workers, and their families; on technology and business organization; and on the freethinkers and evangelical ministers who battled for the minds of both capitalists and operatives. Another study of early textile manufacturing is Thomas Dublin's Women at Work: The Transformation of Work and Community in Lowell, Massachusetts, 1826-1860 (N.Y.: Columbia University Press, 1979). Two studies of urban workers contribute much to our understanding of social change: Bruce Laurie, Working People of Philadelphia, 1800-1850 (Philadelphia: Temple University Press, 1980), and Susan E. Hirsch, Roots of the American Working Class: The Industrialization of Crafts in Newark, 1800-1860 (Philadelphia: University of Pennsylvania Press, 1978).

Marcus Cunliffe, Chattel Slavery and Wage Slavery: The Anglo American Context, 1830-1860 (Athens: University of Georgia, 1980), offers an interesting analysis of the debate over the relative harshness of slavery and capitalism. One abolitionist, Charles Edward Lester, became convinced that the "Lords of the Lash" were preferable to the "Lords of the Loom." Britain, as Cunliffe points out, became a negative reference group used to justify slavery. In the Northern states, the distinction between chattel and wage slavery was often not as important as the distinctions between laborer, journeyman, and clerk. Richard P. Horwitz explores the

meanings of these and related terms in <u>Anthropology Toward History:</u>
<u>Culture and Work in a 19th-Century Maine Town</u> (Middletown, Conn.:
Wesleyan University Press, 1978).

Industrialization and American Labor, 1840-1873

Great strides have been made toward explaining the impact of
industrialization on workers. Alan Dawley, *<u>Class and Community:</u>
<u>The Industrial Revolution in Lynn</u> (Cambridge: Harvard University
Press, 1976); Howard Gitelman, <u>Workingmen of Waltham: Mobility in</u>
<u>American Urban Industrial Development, 1850-1890</u> (Baltimore: The
Johns Hopkins University Press, 1977); and Daniel Walkowitz,
<u>Worker City, Company Town: Iron and Cotton Workers Protest in</u>
<u>Troy and Cohoes, N.Y., 1855-1884</u> (Urbana: University of Illinois
Press, 1978), are three of the best books written in the tradition
of Herbert Gutman. David Montgomery continues to pursue his
research on the impact of mechanization and bureaucratization on
labor. His earlier essays have been collected and published as
<u>Workers' Control in America: Studies in the History of Work,</u>
<u>Technology, and Labor Struggles</u> (Cambridge: Cambridge University
Press, 1979).

Years of Depressed Growth and Violence, 1873-1899

The best of the new books on this period is John T. Cumbler,
<u>Working-Class Community in Industrial America: Work, Leisure, and</u>
<u>Struggle in Two Industrial Cities, 1880-1930</u> (Westport, Conn.:
Greenwood Press, 1979). It examines shoemaking in Lynn, Massachusetts, picking up where Dawley leaves off, and textile manufacturing in Fall River, Massachusetts. A much needed Western
perspective is provided by Richard Lingenfelter's <u>The Hardrock</u>
<u>Miners: A History of the Mining Labor Movement in the American</u>
<u>West, 1863-1893</u> (Berkeley: University of California Press, 1974).
Stuart Brandes offers a brief look at <u>American Welfare Capitalism,</u>
<u>1880-1940</u> (Chicago: University of Chicago Press, 1976), while
Harold C. Livesay provides a short study of <u>Samuel Gompers and</u>
<u>Organized Labor in America</u> (Boston: Little, Brown, 1978). Robert
Babcock provides some comparative perspective in <u>Gompers in Canada:</u>
<u>A Study in American Continentalism Before the First World War</u>
(Toronto: University of Toronto Press, 1974).

After sixty years of study, labor historians are finally recognizing the need to understand the internal governing structure of
the national unions that compose the AFL. Warren Van Tine has
contributed his <u>The Making of the Labor Bureaucrat: Union Leader-</u>
<u>ship in the United States, 1870-1920</u> (Amherst: University of
Massachusetts Press, 1974), toward that understanding.

Progress and Reaction, 1900-1914

Our knowledge of this brief but significant period has been
enriched by the work of William Graebner, <u>Coal Mining Safety in the</u>
<u>Progressive Period</u> (Lexington: University Press of Kentucky, 1976);

Jurgen Kocka, *White-Collar Workers in America, 1890-1940: A
Socio-Political History in International Perspective (Beverly
Hills: Sage, 1979); and Tamara Hareven, *Amoskeague: Life and
Work in an American Factory (N.Y.: Pantheon, 1978). Professor
Hareven's study extends to the early 1930s, describing through
oral histories the conditions in a large New Hampshire textile
mill.

War, "Normalcy," and Depression, 1914-1932

The essays of David Brody have been collected in.*Workers in
Industrial America: Essays on the 20th-Century Struggle (N.Y.:
Oxford University Press, 1980), providing a convenient introduc-
tion to a wide range of topics in recent labor history. James
Green, *The World of the Worker: Labor in Twentieth Century
America (N.Y.: Hill & Wang, 1980), is also a good starting place.
Sally M. Miller's Victor Berger and the Promise of Constructive
Socialism, 1910-1920 (Westport, Conn.: Greenwood Press, 1973), is
a limited but useful supplement to the studies of socialism by
Shannon, Weinstein, and Harrington.

A neglected aspect of labor history, the struggle of black workers
for recognition by both organized labor and employers, is taken up
by Jervis Anderson in his biography of *A. Philip Randolph (N.Y.:
Harcourt, Brace, 1973), and by William H. Harris in Keeping the
Faith: A. Philip Randolph, Milton P. Webster, and the Brotherhood
of Sleeping Car Porters, 1925-1937 (Urbana: University of Illinois
Press, 1978). A good anthology of essays on immigrant Jewish
workers is Ezra Mendelsohn, editor, YIVO Annual of Jewish Social
Science, Volume XVI, Essays on the American Jewish Labor Movement
(N.Y.: YIVO Institute for Jewish Research, 1976).

Industrial Unionism: Labor and the New Deal, 1933-1939

The great leaders of the CIO are receiving scholarly attention.
Melvyn Dubofsky and Warren Van Tine provide the best biography of
John L. Lewis (Chicago: Quadrangle, 1977); Walter Reuther and his
family are presented by his brother Victor in *The Brothers
Reuther (Boston: Houghton Mifflin, 1976); Charles Larrowe's Harry
Bridges: The Rise and Fall of Radical Labor in the United States
(Westport, Conn.: Lawrence Hill & Co., 1972), is not adequate to
its subject, but fills a gap temporarily; Nell Irvin Painter's
The Narrative of Hosea Hudson: His Life as a Negro Communist in
the South (Cambridge: Harvard University Press, 1979), illuminates
the complexity of radical protest in the United States in this
period.

Individual and local unions have received scholarly attention in
recent books by Thomas R. Brooks, Communications Workers of
America: The Study of a Union (N.Y.: Mason/Charter, 1977); John
G. Kruchko, *The Birth of a Union Local: The History of UAW Local
674, Norwood, Ohio, 1933-1940 (Ithaca: New York State School of
Industrial and Labor Relations, Cornell University, 1972); Peter

Friedlander, The Emergence of a UAW Local, 1946-1939: A Study in Class and Culture (Pittsburgh: University of Pittsburgh Press, 1975); and Robert Zieger, *Madison's Battery Workers, 1934-1952: A History of Federal Labor Union 19587 (Ithaca: New York State School of Industrial and Labor Relations, Cornell University, 1977). Zieger's book is especially noteworthy because it is the only study of a federal labor union--that is, a local directly affiliated with the AFL--and it is very well researched and written.

Several participants in the labor movement of the 1930s have written autobiographies. Among them are: Wyndham Mortimer of the auto workers, Organize! My Life as a Union Man (Boston: Beacon Press, 1971); H. L. Mitchell of the Southern Tenant Farmers, Mean Things Happening in This Land (Montgomery, Alabama: STFU Association, 1979); Len De Caux, editor of the CIO News in the late 1930s, Labor Radical: From the Wobblies to the CIO (Boston: Beacon Press, 1970); and James Matles of the United Electrical Workers, Them and Us (Boston: Beacon Press, 1974).

James Gross, The Making of the National Labor Relations Board: A Study in Economics, Politics, and the Law, Volume I, 1933-1937 (Albany: State University of New York Press, 1974), is a good beginning for a much needed study of the NLRB. For an interesting study of the philosophy of the NLRB in recent years, see Julius Getman, Stephen Goddberg, and Jeanne Herman, Union Representation Elections: Law and Reality (N.Y.: Russell Sage Foundation, 1976).

Labor Against Fascism and Communism, 1940-1955

One might add labor's struggles with gangsterism to Dr. Wason's list of "isms" in this period. Vernon Jensen describes some of this conflict in Strife on the Waterfront: The Port of New York Since 1945 (Ithaca: Cornell University Press, 1974). Political struggles are described in Roger Keeran, The Communist Party and the Auto Workers Union (Bloomington: Indiana University Press, 1980), and James C. Foster, The Union Politic: The CIO Political Action Committee (Columbia: University of Missouri Press, 1975).

Dry Rot and Ferment: Labor, 1956-1973

Joseph Goulden's Meany (N.Y.: Atheneum, 1972), and Joseph Carter's Labor Lobbyist: The Autobiography of John W. Edelman (N.Y.: Bobbs-Merrill, 1974), are good surveys of the AFL-CIO under George Meany. Jimmy Hoffa, Dave Beck, and the teamsters have been given popular treatment by Stephen Brill, *The Teamsters (N.Y.: Simon and Schuster, 1978); Farrell Dobbs, *Teamster Power (N.Y.: Monad Press, 1973); Dan Moldea, *The Hoffa Wars (N.Y.: Ace Books, 1979); John McCallum, Dave Beck (Mercer Island, Washington: Writing Works, Inc., 1978); and James R. Hoffa, Hoffa: The Real Story (N.Y.: Stein and Day, 1972).

With the election of Lane Kirkland as president of the AFL-CIO in November of 1979, and Meany's death a few months later, an era in American labor history came to an end. Although organized labor is facing many problems in 1980, recent successful organizing drives by the steelworkers in Newport News, Virginia; the merger of the Retail Clerks and the Amalgamated Meatcutters and Butcher Workmen into a new 1.2 million member union called the United Food and Commercial Workers International Union; and the militancy displayed by women workers who now compose forty-two percent of the American labor force are hopeful signs.

Women and Labor

Barbara Mayer Wertheimer's *We Were There: The Story of Working Women in America (N.Y.: Pantheon, 1977), is the first attempt to provide a comprehensive view of women in the labor movement. Leslie Woodcock Tentler, Wage-Earning Women: Industrial Work and Family Life in the United States, 1900-1930 (N.Y.: Oxford, 1979); David Katzman, Seven Days a Week: Women and Domestic Service in Industrializing America (N.Y.: Oxford, 1978); and Chester W. Gregory, Women in Defense Work During World War II (N.Y.: Exposition Press, 1974), cover three important periods of industrial development. Judith O'Sullivan and Rosemary Gallick's Workers and Allies: Female Participation in the American Trade Union Movement 1824-1976 (Washington, D.C.: Smithsonian Institution, 1975), contains useful brief biographies of women labor leaders and organizers. Their book was written to accompany a traveling exhibit developed by the Smithsonian Institution Traveling Exhibition Service. A recent important contribution to the history of women workers is Susan Estabrook Kennedy, If All We Did Was to Weep at Home: A History of White Working-Class Women in America (Bloomington: Indiana University Press, 1980).

Occupational Folklife and Work Cultures

Although a few pioneer folklorists such as Benjamin Botkin, George Korson, and Mody Boatright were interested in the songs and tales of industrial workers, the development of the field of occupational folklife is a recent phenomenon, owing much to the work of Archie Green, whose Only a Miner: Studies in Recorded Coal-Mining Songs (Urbana: University of Illinois Press, 1971), is a contribution to the history of labor, music, and popular culture. By examining the processes by which oral traditions are transmitted in isolated communities, and how this oral material is adapted by commercial entertainers, Green has abolished forever the old, simple distinctions between folk and elite, work and leisure. Another study of music, this time the songs sung by union members in protest against working conditions, is Philip Foner's American Labor Songs of the Nineteenth Century (Urbana: University of Illinois Press, 1975). Foner's collection is accompanied by a small phonograph record containing some of the songs. There are also several long-playing records of work and labor songs available from the Folk Music Division of the Library of Congress.

The field of occupational folklife was given prominence and definition by the Smithsonian Institution in a series of summer folk
festivals in the 1970s. Papers by some of the scholarly participants in these festivals have been published by The California
Folklore Society as Working Americans: Contemporary Approaches to
Occupational Folklife (Los Angeles: California Folklore Society,
1978), edited by Robert H. Byington. The essays by Robert
McCarl, Rober Abrahams, Robert Byington, Jack Santino, and Archie
Green give a good introduction to theoretical and methodological
considerations. W. Kornblum's The Urban Folk Study: Blue-Collar
Community (Chicago: University of Chicago Press, 1974), is a
sociological rather than folkloristic approach and might be
compared with Ely Chinoy's Automobile Workers and the American
Dream (Garden City, N.Y.: Doubleday, 1955), or Bennett Berger's
*Working Class Suburb: A Study of Automobile Workers in Suburbia
(Berkeley: University of California Press, 1960).

Anthropologists too have studied American workers. Three recent
publications in Holt, Rinehart and Winston's "Case Studies in
Cultural Anthropology" series are useful: William Pilcher, The
Portland Longshoremen (1972); Frederick Gamst, *The Hoghead: An
Industrial Ethnology of the Locomotive Engineer (1980); and William
Friedland and Dorothy Nelkin, Migrant Agricultural Workers in
America's Northeast (1971).

Historians are also looking at broad cultural and folkloric
elements in the working class. The essays by Gary Kulik, Alan
Dawley, Paul Faler and others in American Workingclass Culture:
Explorations in American Labor and Social History (Westport, Conn.:
Greenwood Press, 1979), edited by Milton Cantor, point toward new
directions in social history. Bernard Mergen's "Blacksmiths and
Welders: Identity and Phenomenal Change," Industrial and Labor
Relations Review, 25 (April 1972), and "Work and Play in an
Occupational Subculture: American Shipyard Workers, 1917-1977,"
in *Play: Anthropological Perspectives (West Point, N.Y.: Leisure
Press, 1978), edited by Michael Salter, are attempts to understand
the interaction of technological, cultural, and institutional
factors as they affect worker behavior.

Visual Aspects of American Labor

It was Donald Drew Egbert's *Socialism and American Art (Princeton:
Princeton University Press, 1967), that first directed my attention
to the uses of art and architecture in studying American labor.
The potential is great, and the few illustrated histories only
scratch the surface. The best of the picture books is M. B.
Schnapper, *American Labor: A Pictorial History (Washington, D.C.:
Public Affairs Press, 1972). Additional visual material appears
in William Cahn, A Pictorial History of American Labor (N.Y.: Crown
Publishers, 1973), and The American Worker (Washington, D.C.:
Government Printing Office, 1976), edited by the Department of
Labor for the Bicentennial celebration. There are a number of
excellent documentary films on the labor movement; most of them are

conveniently catalogued in <u>American Labor Films</u> (N.Y.: Film Library Information Council, 1979).

Four useful articles suggest some of the opportunities for future research in the area of labor and material culture: John H. Keiser, "The Union Miners Cemetery at Mt. Olive, Illinois: A Spirit-Thread of Labor History," <u>Journal of the Illinois State Historical Society</u>, 62 (Autumn 1969); Linda Nochlin, "The Paterson Strike Pageant of 1913," <u>Art in America</u>, 62 (May-June 1974); Lois Dinnerstein, "The Iron Worker and King Solomon: Some Images of Labor in American Art," <u>Arts</u>, 54 (September 1979); and John W. Bennett, "Using Union Memorabilia as a Teaching Aid," <u>Labor Studies Journal</u>, 3 (Fall 1978).

The history of American labor will continue to hold the interest of American studies scholars because of the great potential for interdisciplinary research and because work is still central to the operation of the cultural system. Post-industrial and future-shock theories to the contrary, most Americans, like most men and women throughout the world, are concerned with making a living in some way. Any light we can cast on this process, and any contribution we can offer toward making it more tolerable, will undoubtedly be appreciated.

"The Underdeveloped Discipline": A Summary Perspective

DANA F. WHITE

The State of Contemporary Urban History

Although the field of urban history might still be termed underdeveloped, it could hardly be described as under-studied. For
much like the movement that identifies itself as American studies,
this subdiscipline seems inherently self-conscious and self-
analytical. Historiographical and methodological essays appear,
mushroom, and are cloned, depending upon one's perspective, at a
gratifying, overwhelming, or alarming rate. A few have been
noteworthy.

Peter G. Goheen's "Interpreting the American City: Some Historical
Perspectives," Geographical Review, 64 (July 1974), in reviewing
the historiography of the subdiscipline, underlines "the need for
reformulation of research questions in order to present a coherent
concept of the city" so that we shall be able, for the first time,
"to write cities into the national history." For historical
geographers, Goheen suggests "three themes that reflect the scales
at which the geographer can focus his investigation": "the characteristics of the small communities that comprise the social and
residential environment of the city; the symbolic and functional
meaning of the city as a corporate entity; and the urban center as
an influence in the life of the nation." Similarly, "Urban History," by John B. Sharpless and Sam Bass Warner, Jr., American
Behavioral Scientist, 21 (November/December 1977), recommends a
cross-disciplinary perspective, suggesting that geography and
economics "have the most useful concepts for an urban history"
worthy of the name. At this point, Sharpless and Warner propose,
"it is possible to summarize most of the work of American urban

historians as being a series of urban related studies which built
on established interests in social and economic reform and its
concerns for the contrasts among the social circumstances of rich
and poor, whites, blacks, and immigrants." An "enormous body of
historical information" has been collected; "Yet we remain on the
edge of a social-scientific utilization of these data." With
signal caution, Sharpless and Warner predict that "American historians may now be in a position to begin the study of urban
history."

In "American Urban History as an Example of Recent Historiography,"
History and Theory, 18 (1979), Michael Frisch evidences considerably more satisfaction with what has been achieved and a good deal
more optimism about what promises to get done. However, the
author of the masterful *Town into City: Springfield, Massachusetts, and the Meaning of Community, 1840-1880 (Cambridge: Harvard,
1972), certainly one of the best community studies, approaches his
analysis of the field from a perspective considerably different
from those in the articles discussed above. Frisch's historiographical foray is less concerned with the self-contained world of
urban history--questioning as it does, for example, "whether or
not it is a valid sub-discipline"--than it is with the larger
disciplinary universe of the "New Social History." Viewed within
this wider disciplinary context, both the record and the progress
of urban history seem more substantial. What is more, Frisch's
frame of reference is consciously and refreshingly comparative,
since it relates American scholarship to European (mainly Marxist)
analysis. James Henretta's "Social History as Lived and Written,"
American Historical Review, 84 (December 1979), which may be read
as a companion piece to Frisch's--internal evidence suggests a
mutually helpful dialogue between the two authors--also adopts
the comparative framework. Henretta contrasts what he calls the
"inbred pragmatic American approach to historical reality," which
has led "cognitive anthropologists and phenomenologically inclined
historians to comprehend the consciousness of individuals and
social groups" as their major achievement, to the more intellec-
tualized or idealized histories of the French Annalistes and mostly
British Marxists. In one of two "Comments" regarding Henretta's
essay in the "AHR Forum," American Historical Review, 84 (December
1979), Robert F. Berkhofer, Jr. judges this piece as evidence of
"the ascendancy of a new paradigm in American historiography to
replace the older, so-called consensus interpretation of the
American past." "The synthesis of all of United States history
according to the social interpretation is very near," Berkhofer
asserts, "and so Henretta's article offers a rationale for an
approach already predominant in the profession rather than a plea
for seeking to establish itself." It also offers, as does Frisch's
essay, a larger context for assessing the state of urban history--
one that comprehends advances in the New Social History, the
contributions of the Annalistes, and the advances in Marxian
analysis. For this, students, researchers, and critics of the
subdiscipline--if, indeed, it qualifies as such--must be grateful.

Grateful, but not sanguine! As James E. Cronin reported in "The
Problem with Urban History: Reflections on a Recent Meeting,"
Urbanism Past & Present, No. 9 (Winter 1979-80), concerning the
September 28-29, 1979 conference on the Dynamics of Modern
Industrial Cities held at the University of Connecticut--which
"was intended, as its major organizer Bruce Stave put it, 'to
redirect the field' for the 1980s"--"the latent sense of disappointment (among the participants) was very real . . . we all felt
it." That the "rather exalted set of aims, which the conference
organizers set for themselves . . . guaranteed that their efforts
would fall short" comes as no surprise to Cronin, in that "it
would seem impossible to 'redirect' anything without a clear sense
of where one wishes to go." Projecting beyond the Storrs
conference, Cronin concludes that "If one reads at all broadly in
the literature of urban history, one finds persistent echoes of
self-doubt, a sense of drift and bewilderment about the past,
present, and future of the field." Missing from the field, Cronin
suggests, is a coherent and governing conceptual focus (such as
Marxism) and, consequently, "a good deal of the unease with which
some of our leading urban historians contemplate their own present
and future stems from their semi-conscious recognition that
Marxian analysis (or, if one wishes to call it differently, a
political-economic approach) is the looming frontier in urban
analysis." Whether "a political-economic approach"--as set forth
in David Harvey's influential (and dense) *Social Justice and the
City (Baltimore: Johns Hopkins, 1973)--constitutes the "looming
frontier in urban analysis" remains to be seen; that the relationship between academic urban history and, as Cronin terms it, "some
notion of applied urban history" (emphasis mine) is central to the
"persistent echoes of self-doubt . . . sense of drift and bewilderment about the past, present, and future of the field" seems
beyond question. Simply put, urban history has failed to meet
the expectations of many who entered the field over the past two
decades.

Many of us, as the subtitle of the original essay phrased it,
looked for "Interdisciplinary Directions in American Urban
History." Many of us, to return to the first scholarly work
referred to in the initial text of this article, looked for
history to develop as the coequal to "the long-established fields
(e.g., urban sociology and political science) and . . . the
relatively new ones (urban economics and geography)" as they were
described in the Social Science Research Council survey of *The
Study of Urbanization, edited by Philip M. Hauser and Leo F.
Schnore (New York: Wiley, 1965). It never happened. Quite the
contrary, for my judgment then, a full decade ago, would require
only a change of tense to describe the situation now: "the
saddest tale of all was told of history!" What is more, with
planned cutbacks in graduate programs, anticipated declines in
research funds, and potential reductions in the publication of
journals, monographs, and texts, the future of academic urban
history would appear to be--again, depending upon one's
perspective--modest to grim. It is to applied urban history,
then, that we must look for the promise of the future.

That promise will be found in new and innovative approaches, as
well as in established but unexplored places. One of the latter,
for example, is the American Association for State and Local
History, 1400 Eighth Avenue South, Nashville, Tennessee 37203,
which listed in its Fall 1979 catalog 38 books under its own
imprint, the 51-volume Bicentennial series "The States and the
Nation" (published by W. W. Norton & Company), and over 100 "AASLH
Technical Leaflets"--all "Books and technical information for,"
a cover blurb explains, "Historical societies and museums, Public
historians, Historic preservationists, Genealogists and researchers,
Archives and special libraries, Museum Studies, Art and antique
collectors." The January 1980 issue of the Association's History
News included articles on "Social History Hits the Streets:
Williamsburg Characters Come to Life," "Social History in Shoe
City: Workers of Lynn, Massachusetts," and "Joseph Duffey on
Social History: An Interview" with the Chairman of the National
Endowment for the Humanities. In addition, for its standard
centerfold offering it contained Technical Leaflet #123, an eight-
page, how-to-do-it piece and bibliography on "Using Oral History
for a Family History Project." In a decidedly "bearish market"
for history, the AASLH has been openly "bullish." In a crisis
situation, marked by a worsening job crunch, which influenced
thirteen major professional bodies--including the American
Historical Association, the Organization of American Historians,
the Southern Historical Association, the Organization of American
Historians, the Southern Historical Association, the Association
for the Study of Afro-American Life and History, and the American
Studies Association--to band together and form the National
Coordinating Committee for the Promotion of History, the AASLH
has gone its own way, and with notable success.

A less radical departure, paradoxically, will be found in public
history, one of those "new and innovative approaches" alluded to
above. The Public Historian, published on a quarterly basis by
the Graduate Program in Public Historical Studies at the University
of California at Santa Barbara since Fall 1978, at this writing is
in the process of becoming the official voice of the field, now
that it is affiliated with the National Council on Public History.
Although it bears the subtitle "A Journal of Public History," this
quarterly, based upon a review of its first four numbers, has been
more academic than applied. What I suggested after a reading of
early issues of the Journal of Urban History in the last supplement to "The Underdeveloped Discipline" (American Studies: Topics
and Sources, 1976), applies even more so to The Public Historian:
it should "resist the temptation of proving itself 'respectable'
according to the standards set by other historical journals, and
prove itself the leader and innovator in the field." It should be
concerned less with the academic, more with the applied.

A number of other approaches that relate either directly or
indirectly to applied urban history have been mapped out in recent
years. The Public Works Historical Society, 1313 E. 60th Street,
Chicago, Illinois 60637, publishes a monthly Newsletter, has
prepared a massive and valuable History of Public Works in the

United States, 1776-1976 (1976), and issues regularly a series of
pamphlet-sized "Essays in Public Works History." The essays have
appeared with such urban-oriented titles as Chicago's Quest for
Pure Water by James C. O'Donnell (#1); Pragmatic Environmentalist:
Sanitary Engineer George E. Waring, Jr. by Martin V. Melosi (#4);
Transportation Innovation and Changing Spatial Patterns in Pittsburgh, 1850-1934 by Joel A. Tarr (#6); and Fresno's Water Rivalry:
Competition for a Scarce Resource, 1887-1970 (#8). On a less
ambitious, but still valuable, basis, The Planning History Group
issues the Planning History Bulletin, Centre for Urban and Regional
Studies, University of Birmingham, P.O. Box 363, Birmingham B15
2TT, England; American Urban Guides, Box 186, Washington, D.C.
20044, has introduced American Urban Guidenotes: The Newsletter of
Guidebooks, which appeals especially to peripatetic urbanists; and
the Historian's Office of the U.S. Department of Energy, Office of
the Secretary, 7G-033 Forrestal Building, Washington, D.C. 20545,
distributes Energy History Report, a recent number of which
reflected upon the relationships of business history and urban
history to this new field (#5, May 1980).

In oral history, one of the most vital areas of contemporary
American scholarship, much is being done that relates to the urban
scene. The Oral History Association, Baylor University, Box 228,
Waco, Texas 76703, publishes the Oral History Association Newsletter and the Oral History Review, an annual of such exceptionally
high quality that it should serve as a model for other professional
journals locked into a quarterly schedule of publication. A new
entry in the field, the International Journal of Oral History,
promises to add a multinational dimension to the field and,
potentially, a special awareness concerning urban history, since
its able editor was trained in that specialty.

Those of us who identify first as urbanists, then as academics,
must beware of over-ambition, of setting unrealistic goals, of
coming on, as a participant at a recent conference quipped, as
"street-fighting historians." "Make no little plans," Daniel
Burnham exhorted; "but beware," Frederick Gutheim added, "of grand
designs!" Charles E. Lindblom and David K. Cohen have probed the
limits of *Usable Knowledge: Social Science and Social Problem
Solving (New Haven: Yale, 1979). It should be required reading
for all entrants into the field of applied urban history or, for
that matter, any of the policy sciences.

New Sources and Research Efforts

For teachers of urban history, the selection of surveys and
anthologies continues to grow. The second edition of *A History
of Urban America (New York: Macmillan, 1976), by Charles N. Glaab
and A. Theodore Brown, not only expands considerably on the first,
but also adds sizable new chapters on the recent past. Another
major overview is provided in *Urban America: From Downtown to
No Town (Boston: Houghton Mifflin, 1979), by David R. Goldfield.
and Blaine A. Brownell, which concentrates upon "space--specific-
ally, spatial relationships within and between cities" as "the

thread that ties together the elements of this book." It thereby provides a fresh and potentially valuable format for introducing students to the physical environment of both the historical and contemporary city. A number of period surveys have been made available recently to supplement these more inclusive texts. Prisoners of Progress: American Industrial Cities 1850-1920 (New York: Macmillan, 1976), by Maury Klein and Harvey A. Kantor, is an angry indictment of the impact of urbanization--one that should ensure heated, if not always illuminating, classroom debate. William H. Wilson's *Coming of Age: Urban America, 1915-1945 (New York: Wiley, 1974), is a narrative account, at once innovative and traditional, of a complex period in the development of the metropolitan framework. And Zane L. Miller's *The Urbanization of Modern America: A Brief History (New York: Harcourt Brace Jovanovich, 1973), is a concise and amply illustrated text that might be used either as a summary volume following more specialized monographic studies or as the token urban history assignment in an American history survey course.

Other, more miscellaneous books for classroom use are also readily available. Henry F. Bedford's *Trouble Downtown: The Local Context of Twentieth-Century America (New York: Harcourt Brace Jovanovich, 1978), adopts the tone of the investigative reporter in examining such significant localized "metaphors" as "'Not Enough Pay': Lawrence, 1912"; "The Booze Business: Chicago in the 1920s"; "Detroit in Depression and War: The 1930s and 1940s"; "Peaceful Souls and Tired Feet: Montgomery, 1955"; and "The Fuse Blows: Watts, 1965." Bedford's direct and personalized narrative format, his skillful use of illustrations, and his forthright recognition of regional variations--"Texans, after all, differ from Pennsylvanians"--combine to create a book with unusual classroom potential. *Cities in Transition: Social Changes and Institutional Responses in Urban Development (New York: New Viewpoints, 1979), by Peter R. Gluck and Richard J. Meister, seeks "to examine from a historical and analytical perspective the way in which governance institutions responded to the challenges associated with rapid urban development." This aim is pursued in a series of crisp chapters which examine politics in a historical framework, producing, thereby, a focus more generally urban studies than history, but a challenging one, nonetheless.

Carole Rifkind's *Main Street: The Face of Urban America (New York: Harper & Row, 1977), may be categorized as photo-history, but must also be recognized as an unusually imaginative representation. It is organized, for example, into four parts--"Origins," "Structure," "Experience," and "Change"--containing such subtitles as "Wilderness," "Grid," "Trail" and "Depot" (under the first), and "Growth," "Renewal," and "Preservation" (under the last). Main Street, in sum, is an imaginative delight. Tamara K. Hareven and Stephan Thernstrom are series editors of the "Documentary History of American Cities" (New York: New Viewpoints), which has been in production since 1976. The volume on *Detroit, edited by Melvin G. Holli (1976), is representative of the high quality

of the series. Whether the focus upon urban biography
is broad enough to attract a sufficient readership for a more
regular publication schedule remains to be seen. Lastly, *An
Urban World (Boston: Little Brown, 1974), edited by Charles Tilly,
may best be described as an urban studies text in a historical
framework. As is true of all of Tilly's work, it is of remarkably
high caliber.

Urbanism Past & Present, Department of History, University of
Wisconsin, Milwaukee, P.O. Box 413, Milwaukee, Wisconsin 53201,
the successor publication to the Urban History Group Newsletter,
has appeared biannually since its inaugural number for Winter
1975-76. It is without question the best guide to what is happening in urban studies from a multidisciplinary perspective,
including geography, economics, policy studies and, of course,
history. A typical issue of Urbanism Past & Present will feature
three or four articles, one or more notes on research and methods,
and a section devoted to news items about conferences and projects, as well as a detailed bibliography of books and articles
listed on a regional basis. Supplementary sources for gaining
an overview of directions within the field will be found in
Reviews in American History, the Journal of Social History, and
the Journal of Interdisciplinary History.

Preparing for this essay, I found the most serious attention being
given to the Annalistes, the British Marxists--particularly E. P.
Thompson, anthropologist Anthony F. C. Wallace, and Herbert G.
Gutman. So intense is the scrutiny of the works and the messages
of these movers and shakers that it sometimes seemed that the New
Social History was in the process of becoming the New Intellectual
History. Still, although there are discernible unities in the
field, as the survey to follow will demonstrate, research in
American urban history continues to evidence a multiplicity of
approaches and topics.

The New Urban History: Quantitative Explorations by American
Historians (Princeton: Princeton University, 1974), edited by
Leo F. Schnore, is a superb introduction to some of the best
recent work in the field; what is more, it is the subject of some
thoughtful speculation about the "possibilities and limitations
of current urban history" by Sharpless and Warner (1977). The
"possibilities" are demonstrated in Peter R. Decker's Fortunes
and Failures: White-Collar Mobility in Nineteenth-Century San
Francisco (Cambridge: Harvard, 1978), which combines collective
biography, social geography, and the reconstitution of urban form
in a brilliant and readable synthesis. Somewhat narrower in
focus, but evidencing similar narrative power and sense of control,
is Alan Dawley's *Class and Community: The Industrial Revolution
in Lynn (Cambridge: Harvard, 1976), certainly one of the strongest
of the mobility studies. The subject of the exercise of power in
American cities has been approached from several different angles.
David C. Hammack, in "Elite Perceptions of Power in Cities of the
United States, 1880-1900: The Evidence of James Bryce, Moisei
Ostrogorski, and their American Informants," Journal of Urban

History, 4 (August 1978), and in "Problems in the Historical Study of Power in the Cities and Towns of the United States, 1800-1960," American Historical Review, 83 (April 1978), has provided highly sophisticated analyses of social-scientific debates over the meaning and exercise of power within a historical context. Alan D. Anderson, in The Origin and Resolution of an Urban Crisis: Baltimore, 1890-1930 (Baltimore: Johns Hopkins, 1977), has examined the interweaving of administrative decision making with technolo- gical-economic change, all within the framework of a single municipal system. J. Rogers Hollingsworth and Ellen Jane Hollings- worth, in their Dimensions in Urban History: Historical and Social Science Perspectives on Middle-Size American Cities (Madison: University of Wisconsin, 1979), have offered, through a sequence of related case studies, what they suggest is "a modest contribu- tion to a more sociological-historical approach to cities," a description far too self-effacing for this innovative approach to public policy and political culture.

Notable studies in the culture of cities, aspects of urban life less amenable to quantification or systematization, continue to enrich the offerings in our subdiscipline. Helen Lefkowitz Horowitz's Culture & the City: Cultural Philanthropy in Chicago from the 1880s to 1917 (Lexington: University of Kentucky, 1976), to adopt a bit of social-science jargon, details the infrastructure of Chicago's upper-class network as that "set" attempted to maintain some sense of social control or hegemony through the agency of "civicism," as it was called then--civic education or socialization, as we might term it today. Paul E. Johnson's *A Shopkeeper's Millennium: Society and Revivals in Rochester, New York, 1815-1837 (New York: Hill and Wang, 1978), provides an even sharper picture of urban reform by focusing carefully upon the political economy of one municipality in the early throes of urban- ization and, in the process, enlarging upon the distinctive form of American family capitalism in this transition period. Paul Boyer's ambitious Urban Masses and Moral Order in America, 1820-1920 (Cambridge: Harvard, 1978), represents the macrocosm to Paul John- son's microcosm in its intent to encompass the entirety of urban uplift in one thick monograph--an effort that at times proves overambitious but one that is, for the most part, very rewarding and challenging. And this is but a sampling of recent offerings in the field. Still, it represents a careful selection of the most significant works, in terms of both approach and subject matter. In order to complete this review of recent work in the field, however, there remains the task of singling out the actual product- ions and the anticipated achievements of a handful of urban historians.

Two very productive and important scholars who merit special note are Allan R. Pred and Michael B. Katz. Pred's distinctive approach to the analysis of urban systems may be seen best in his Urban Growth and the Circulation of Information: The United States System of Cities, 1790-1840 (Cambridge: Harvard, 1973). Katz's unique handling of quantitative material will be found in *The

People of Hamilton, Canada West: Family and Class in a Mid-Nineteenth City (Cambridge: Harvard, 1975). The important publications of Pred and Katz have been reviewed extensively.

The work in progress of two other practitioners in the field has been the subject of much discussion and speculation. James Borchert's study of alley dwellings in the District of Columbia has been under way for the past decade. His dissertation and several articles, the most accessible being "Alley Landscapes of Washington," Landscape, 23 (1979), are available; his recently published book, Alley Life in Washington: Family, Community, Religion and Folklife in the City, 1850-1970 (Urbana: University of Illinois, 1980), should certainly establish his reputation for interdisciplinary scholarship. Theodore Hershberg's standing has depended more upon his organizational and entrepreneurial skills than upon publications in print. Since his announcement to the profession concerning "The Organization of Historical Research," American Historical Association Newsletter, 12, No. 7 (October 1974), his potential impact on the field has been much discussed. Through his creation, the Philadelphia Social History Project, Hershberg has, as Michael Frisch has commented, "sought to build a data bank of unprecedented reach and proportion: a machine-readable storehouse of quantitative information about all the people, not just a sample, who lived in Philadelphia between 1850 and 1880,together with data on the streets, businesses, and institutions of the city." A number of articles have emanated from the Project, many of them published in the Historical Methods Newsletter; a further collection, edited by Hershberg, is scheduled for publication in Toward a New Urban History: Work, Space, and Group Experience in Nineteenth-Century Philadelphia (New York: Oxford, forthcoming). Without question, the Project has been controversial. Critics carp about a "boondoggle" and advocates enthuse about a research utopia. At this point, however, it seems premature to judge its ultimate value. Still, at the very least, it has provided many of us an almost Burnhamesque vision of what might be. Theodore Hershberg, his harshest critics would be forced to agree, has made "no little plans."

Urban design has not been a central focus of this essay; still, one recent effort in this direction merits special attention. The American City: From the Civil War to the New Deal (Cambridge: MIT, 1979 ; translated from the Italian by Barbara Luigia La Penta), consists of four lengthy sections, one by each of the major authors: Mario Manieri-Elia's "Toward an 'Imperial City': Daniel H. Burnham and the City Beautiful Movement"; Francesco Dal Co's "From Parks to the Region: Progressive Ideology and the Reform of the American City"; Giorgio Ciucci's "The City in Agrarian Ideology and Frank Lloyd Wright: Origins and Development of Broadacres"; and Manfredo Tafuri's "The Disenchanted Mountain: The Skyscraper and the City." This volume marks, let us hope, a watershed in American urban history. It represents a collaborative effort by Americanists not based in the United States to traverse territory not already staked out and overworked by scholars already

on the scene. Such fresh perspectives are welcome, should be
encouraged, and are bound to enlighten. The work of one other
scholar in a related area--urban form, the two-dimensional aspect
of the environment--also merits attention. John W. Reps, whose
work was discussed in the first version of this essay, continues
his series that might well be subtitled "the mapping of urban
America" with Tidewater Towns: City Planning in Colonial Virginia
and Maryland (Charlottesville: University of Virginia, 1972), and
Cities of the American West: A History of Frontier Urban Planning
(Princeton: Princeton University, 1979). These later volumes
reflect the strengths and weaknesses already noted in his earlier
work: on the one hand, a genius for unearthing and organizing
historical maps and city views; on the other, an inclination to
concentrate almost entirely upon visual evidence and to ignore its
political, social, and economic context. When applied to only one
city, as in his Monumental Washington: The Planning and Development of the Capital Center (Princeton: Princeton University, 1967),
the basic flaws in Reps's methodology stand out sharply and almost
painfully. The weight of his production impresses more than does
its depth.

Methodology is the forte of two outstanding analyses of African
Americans in cities. David M. Katzman's *Before the Ghetto: Black
Detroit in the Nineteenth Century (Urbana: University of Illinois,
1973), meets John Blassingame's challenge to reject the false
categorization of "enduring ghettoes" in favor of the true situation of "enduring communities." In the process of challenging
earlier "ghetto" and "ethnic" models, however, Katzman has attempted to resurrect and recast--unsuccessfully, in my judgment--
W. Lloyd Warner's particular version of the concept of "caste."
What is more, he seems to have accepted, without due caution, some
of E. Franklin Frazier's harsher observations of the *Black
Bourgeoise: The Rise of a New Middle Class (New York: Free Press,
1957), and ignored the context in which that book was written, its
audience, and the biases of its author. All this said, Katzman's
is a major achievement; indeed, Before the Ghetto marks a new and
important direction in African American historiography. Kenneth
L. Kusmer's *A Ghetto Takes Shape: Black Cleveland, 1870-1930
(Urbana: University of Illinois, 1976), is even better. Not only
is it a skillful community study, it is also a valuable survey of
basic and recent scholarship in the field. Finally, John W.
Blassingame's *Black New Orleans 1860-1880 (Chicago: University of
Chicago, 1973), while lacking the methodological sophistication so
evident in the Katzman and Kusmer volumes, is a straightforward
narrative history of the building of that community. It is a
fascinating and, as might be expected, very well-written monograph
that lends itself well to classroom use.

The Geography of the Field

It may be argued that the historiography of blacks in cities tells
us less about the world of Afro-American urbanites than about the
universe of urban historians. In his description of "the demography of the profession," Robert F. Berkhofer, Jr. points out that

"The largest age cohort in the profession today grew to intellectual and professional maturity during the foreign and domestic
controversies of the 1960s. For many of these scholars the social
interpretation of history represents, therefore, a repudiation of
the moral and ideological presuppositions of consensus history
(of the 1950s) as well as its conceptual bases." An even more
literal "geography of the profession" would place it neatly in a
sector bordered to the south by Philadelphia, to the north by
Boston, to the west by fringe communities along the shores of the
Great Lakes, and to the east by those nations (mainly European)
which fed their peoples to New York City. It is to New York and
such cities as Boston, Chicago, and Philadelphia that immigrants
flocked--from Europe, then the American South, and now Latin
America. It is to these cities that urban historians look for
their subject matter, approaches, and, ultimately, employment.
Thus, returning once again to the question of the historiography
of blacks in cities, more has been written on African Americans in
New York and Chicago than in Atlanta and New Orleans, although the
American South has been until recent years, and seems now in the
process of becoming once again, the heartland of black America.
In a very real sense, then, American urban history has been North-
eastern and, to a lesser extent, Midwestern. An academic imperialism has been at work: the metropolis is all; the colonies count
only as backdrop to its development and change.

In no region of the nation is this academic imperialism more
manifest than in the American South. While its plantation life
and culture have been a favorite subject of "scholar carpetbag-
gers," so designated by C. Vann Woodward, its towns and cities have
received little historical attention. Indeed, it has only been
within the past five years that the modern South, as opposed to
the plantation South, has attracted much popular or scholarly
notice--except, of course, as the initial staging ground for the
Civil Rights movement. In recent years, especially since the
publication of Kirkpatrick Sale's paranoid diatribe about the
*Power Shift: The Rise of the Southern Rim and Its Challenge to
the Eastern Establishment (New York: Vintage, 1975), the American
South--as defined either by the Bureau of the Census or according
to membership in the Confederate States of America--has been viewed
as in the larger context of the so-called "sunbelt." Carl Abbott
has examined the genesis of "The American Sunbelt: Idea and
Region" in the Journal of the West (July 1979); and David C. Perry
and Alfred J. Watkins have edited an interesting volume of original
articles on *The Rise of the Sunbelt Cities, Volume 14 in "Urban
Affairs Annual Reviews" (Beverly Hills: Sage, 1977), the first
four of which are essentially historical.

The best introduction to the urban South per se is *The City in
Southern History: The Growth of Urban Civilization in the South
(Port Washington, N.Y.: Kennikat, 1977), edited by Blaine A.
Brownell and David R. Goldfield, which should be supplemented by
those classic anthologies on The Urban South (Chapel Hill: Uni-
versity of North Carolina, 1954), edited by Rupert B. Vance and

Nicholas J. Demerath, and on Culture in the South (Chapel Hill:
University of North Carolina, 1935), edited by W. T. Couch. Two
analytical essays that merit attention are Anne Firor Scott's "The
Study of Southern Urbanization," Urban Affairs Quarterly, 1 (March
1966), which is particularly valuable for its coverage of antebellum
cities; and Leonard P. Curry's "Urbanization and Urbanism in the
Old South: A Comparative View," Journal of Southern History, 40
(February 1974), which argues "that southern cities were more
peculiarly urban than peculiarly southern." Strongly influenced
by Richard C. Wade's hypothesis in *Slavery in the Cities: The
South 1820-1860 (New York: Oxford Press, 1964), that the urbanization process was so powerful as to threaten the continuation of
the institution of slavery--an interpretation demolished by Robert
S. Starobin in *Industrial Slavery in the Old South (New York:
Oxford, 1970), and by Claudia Dale Goldin in Urban Slavery in the
American South 1820-1860: A Quantitative History (Chicago:
University of Chicago, 1976)--Curry emphasizes similarities, North
and South, and overlooks divergences. It is not his evidence that
is necessarily faulty, it must be added, for his is a careful
analysis; it is the framework in which it is presented, a literal
acceptance of Arthur M. Schlesinger's "urban manifesto" of 1940
(criticized in the first version of the present essay) which
attempted to replace "one unmanageable and, for all practical
purposes, indefinable general causal force with still another, by
substituting 'city' for 'frontier.'" Unfortunately, this perspective has been widespread among urban historians who have written
about the South. Too few have read, or seem to have grasped
fully, William Diamond's warnings "On the Dangers of an Urban
Interpretation of History."

The history of a single southern city may serve to test the
hypothesis that southern cities were more peculiarly urban than
peculiarly southern. Atlanta, Georgia--as were Boston and Chicago,
two cities examined in earlier editions of this essay--has been
the subject of much and varied study. A Comparative Atlas of
America's Great Cities: Twenty Metropolitan Regions, by Ronald
Abler and John S. Adams (Minneapolis: Association of American
Geographers and University of Minnesota Press, 1976), is a magnificent production and a superb comparative overview of the metro-
polises covered. *Metropolis in Georgia: Atlanta's Rise as a
Major Transaction Center (Cambridge, Mass.: Ballinger, 1976), by
Truman A. Hartshorn and others, is a useful companion volume to
the series of pamphlet-sized monographs that supplements the
Association of American Geographers' "Comparative Metropolitan
Analysis Project." In "How Atlanta Grew: Cool Heads, Hot Air,
and Hard Work," first published in 1978 and since reprinted in
Andrew Marshall Hamer, editor, *Urban Atlanta: Redefining the
Role of the City (Atlanta: Georgia State University, 1980), I
proposed, together with Timothy J. Crimmins, a four-part periodi-
zation of the city's history based upon the systematic and
organized promotion of its boosters. We wrote the footnotes to
this article to provide a beginning bibliography of Atlanta
history through 1976. In "Urban Structure, Atlanta," Journal of
Urban History, 2 (February 1976), Crimmins and I offered our own

Burnhamesque plans for a history of the city, along the lines of "urban structuring" presented in the first version of this essay. Three of the four essays in "Part Two: New South" of Olmsted South: Old South Critic/New South Planner (Westport, Connecticut: Greenwood Press, 1979), which I edited with Victor A. Kramer, treat suburban development, park expansion, and parkway planning as aspects of the structuring of turn-of-the-century Atlanta. In Automobile Age Atlanta: The Making of a Southern Metropolis 1900-1935 (Athens: University of Georgia, 1979), Howard L. Preston, who wrote the chapter on parks and parkways in Olmsted South, utilized creatively the concept of "automobility" to explain city building over time. And, in "Applying Urban History to City Planning: A Case Study in Atlanta," The Public Historian, 1 (Summer 1979), Stephen W. Grable probed skillfully for the potential contributions that urban history might make to the planning of a present-day "new town in town."

These studies demonstrate that Atlanta was, in fact, "peculiarly southern": that it was new, since it achieved significant urban status only after the American Civil War; that it was New South, as it responded to regional and national trends and demands in becoming a transfer point and transaction center; and that, most important of all, it was biracial, not multi-ethnic according to what has been promoted as the American norm.

The debate over the distinctiveness of a peculiarly southern identity endures. It was articulated in its classic modern statement in Ulrich B. Phillips's "The Central Theme in Southern History," American Historical Review, 34 (October 1928), and carried on into such recent interpretations as the social-scientific analysis of John Shelton Reed's *The Enduring South: Subcultural Persistence in Mass Society (Chapel Hill: University of North Carolina, 1975), and the historiographic account of Carl N. Degler's Place Over Time: The Continuity of Southern Distinctiveness (Baton Rouge: Louisiana State University, 1977). In this short focus, the debate will not be resolved. Nevertheless, two recent projects demonstrate Atlanta's peculiarly southern past. "Living Atlanta," a fifty-part radio documentary series that covers the period from 1917 to 1946, is promoted as "an oral history from World War I thru World War II." It is this and more: its fifty half-hour shows are based on over 350 hours of taped interviews with more than 200 residents of the city who lived through the era. Its "peculiarly urban" shows include "Public Education," "Working on the Railroads," "Professional Women," and "The Great Depression"; its "peculiarly southern" shows number "The Etiquette of Race Relations," "Atlanta's Black Colleges," "Sweet Auburn Avenue--Center of Black Life," and "The Black Move to Atlanta's West Side"--subjects not confined to some limited "minority group," but to the "other Atlanta."

The city's biracial makeup, consequently, is the central theme of this locally produced public-radio documentary series. (Information on how to acquire cassettes of shows can be addressed to "Living Atlanta," WRFG, P.O. Box 5332, Atlanta, Georgia 30307.)

In a similar fashion, <u>Atlanta Women: From Myth to Modern Times</u>
(Atlanta: Atlanta Historical Society, 1980; P.O. Box 12423,
Atlanta, Georgia 30355), the catalog produced by Darlene R. Roth
and Louise E. Shaw for a year-long exhibition, takes as its central
theme not feminism, but the work and activities of women on "both
sides of town"--again, the inevitable biracial emphasis. Atlanta's
biracial character is significant today, and it has permeated its
history. Black Atlanta, unlike New York's Harlem or Chicago's
"Black Metropolis," has never been a "minority community" in the
strictest sense of that term. Thus, a roster of its Afro-American
citizens would include W. E. B. Du Bois, E. Franklin Frazier,
James Weldon Johnson, Walter White, Henry O. Flipper, Ira De A.
Reid, Jesse O. Thomas, Julian Bond, and Martin Luther King, Jr.--
all of whom have left some record of black Atlanta. A list of
white writers of such caliber would be much shorter.

A listing of writings on Atlanta that have appeared since the
compilation of the bibliographic notes to "How Atlanta Grew" must
impress, if only for its range and length. The city's two major
businesses have been the subject of competent studies in the
scholarly <u>Delta: The History of an Airline</u> (Athens: University of
Georgia, 1979), by W. David Lewis and Wesley Phillips Newton, and
in the popular <u>Coca-Cola: An Illustrated History</u> (Garden City,
N.Y.: Doubleday, 1978), by Pat Watters. What appears to be
Atlanta's major industry to visitors and residents alike, the
construction of major buildings, is the subject of <u>Beaux Arts to
Bauhaus and Beyond: An Architect's Perspective</u> (New York: Watson-
Guptill Publications, 1976), by the retired Director of the
Department of Architecture at Georgia Tech University, Harold
Bush-Brown, as well as of <u>The Architect as Developer</u> (New York:
McGraw-Hill, 1976), by the region's most influential and contro-
versial builder, John Portman, with Jonathan Barnett. Another
autobiographical account of city building in Atlanta is that of
former Commissioner of Budget and Planning Leon S. Eplan in
"Atlanta: Planning, Budgeting, and Neighborhoods," in Anthony
James Catanese and W. Paul Farmer, editors, <u>Personality, Politics,
and Planning: How City Planners Work</u> (Beverly Hills: Sage, 1978).
Autobiographical in the more traditional--and powerful--sense is
Rosemary Daniell's <u>Fatal Flowers: On Sin, Sex, and Suicide in the
Deep South</u> (New York: Holt, Rinehart and Winston, 1980), and Pat
Watters's interviews with and musings on <u>The Angry Middle-Aged Man</u>
(New York: Grossman, 1976).

Personal experiences of another order are found in recent novels
set in the city. Bronte Woodward's <u>Meet Me at the Melba</u> (New York:
Delacorte Press, 1977), evokes everyday life in Atlanta during the
1920s and 1930s with wit, power, and a high degree of accuracy.
Richard Kluger's <u>Members of the Tribe</u> (Garden City, N.Y.: Doubleday, 1977), shifts the venue of the tragic Leo Frank Case and,
through this historical and artistic fakery, inadvertently highlights the differences between the Old South city of Savannah, to
which he moves the action, and the New South city of Atlanta,
where the lynching actually occurred. As Steven Hertzberg has

demonstrated in his able Strangers Within the Gate City: The
Jews of Atlanta, 1845-1915 (Philadelphia: Jewish Publication
Society of America, 1978), a more complex order than the fictional
one predominated.   Elizabeth Forbush's *Savage Sundown (Los
Angeles: Pinnacle Books, 1980), presents a fictionalized account
of the violent expulsion of black Georgians from nearby Forsyth
County in 1912 and its repercussions on Atlanta. As expected,
another kind of historical novel, this one of the very recent
past, made its appearance shortly after the arrival of James Earl
Carter to the White House. Two examples of this literary version
of "Jimmy stuff" are Milton Machlin's *Atlanta (New York: Avon,
1979), which traces the rise of a down-home-born-again-small-town
politico against the backdrop of an Atlanta transformed by the
Civil Rights Movement; and Norman Keifetz's Welcome Sundays (New
York: Putnam, 1979), which follows a similar, but artistically
more interesting, hero, this time a football coach, through the
development of a world championship team. Both are entertainments, but each, in its own fashion, has a good touch of Atlanta
in it.

The following are novels set in the self-proclaimed "Capitol of
the New South" that have a contemporary, rather than historical,
flavor. *Marvin & Tige (New York: St. Martin's Press, 1977), a
remarkable first novel by Frankcina Glass, examines the relationship between a young black street kid and a middle-aged white
corporate drop-out in a plot that is humorous, touching, inter-
racial, and big-city. The Salt Eaters (New York: Random House,
1980), by Toni Cade Bambara, is black "black humor," set in "a
city somewhere in the South called Claybourne," portions whereof
and characters within conjuring up Atlanta scenes and people.
Sharky's Machine (New York: Delacorte Press, 1978), by William
Diehl, which might well be subtitled "A Novel of Intrigue, Violence, and Lust," fits neatly the Newsweek category of "schlock-
buster" and might be best understood as the libidinous side of
Atlanta's urge to become "The New International City." Finally,
The House Next Door (New York: Simon and Schuster, 1978), an
Atlanta Amityville Horror by Anne Rivers Siddons, weds architec-
ture with demonology--fittingly enough in the modern American
city that has most bedeviled architectural critics.

Margaret Mitchell's Gone With the Wind (New York: Macmillan,
1936), as is true of the film based on the novel, continues to
be written about and argued over; however, its value as a
historical novel now seems settled. As Floyd C. Watkins has
dissected it in his In Time and Place: Some Origins of American
Fiction (Athens: University of Georgia, 1977), this so-called
"epic" is "narrowly patriotic, prudish, melodramatic, and
sentimental." "Gone With the Wind as Vulgar Literature," his
chapter title and theme, sums up the book neatly: "Much of the
novel is bad, false to the facts of rural and southern life particularly, false to history, and worst of all, false to human
nature." On the other hand, where Mitchell was false, two far
superior writers were true: W. E. B. Du Bois in that remarkable

volume of 1903, *The Souls of Black Folk (New York: Fawcett, 1961);
and Flannery O'Connor in such short stories as "A Good Man Is Hard
to Find," "The Displaced Person," and "The Artificial Nigger."

A scattering of other novels, both before and after Gone With the
Wind, may also be identified for their Atlanta setting. Ca Ira
(New York: United States Publishing Company, 1874), by William
Dugas Trammell, is a dystopian phantasy about Reconstruction
Atlanta. The Fox in the Attic (New York: Macmillan, 1930), by
Harry Lee, resembles much of the youth-comes-of-age realism of
its period. The Southerners (New York: Appleton-Century-Crofts,
1953), by Edna Lee, is a fulsome and enjoyable costume drama of
the turn-of-the-century city. Several of Joel Chandler Harris's
early "Uncle Remus" stories were set in Atlanta, such as "Uncle
Remus and the Savannah Darkey," "As to Education," "Some Advice
to a Colored Brother," and "Uncle Remus on an Electric Car";
thus, this famous voice from the plantation was first heard on a
city's streets. Finally, as Raymond Chandler fathered Philip
Marlowe for Los Angeles and Dashiell Hammett sired Sam Spade for
San Francisco, Ralph Dennis begat Jim Hardman for Atlanta in a
series of twelve novels in the hard-boiled detective school.
The Charleston Knife's Back in Town (New York: Popular Library,
1974), and *The Buy Back Blues (New York: Popular Library, 1977),
are especially evocative of HOTlanta life. And, the series is
"peculiarly southern": "down these mean streets a man must go,"
but unlike Philip Marlowe, Jim Hardman is not alone, for Dennis's
ex-cop hero is accompanied by an ex-football star named Hump
Evans who is, of course, black. In "peculiarly southern" Atlanta,
even the gumshoeing is biracial!

In a thoughtful and provocative review essay, Don Karl Rowney
asks, "What is Urban History?" Journal of Interdisciplinary
History, 0 (Autumn 1977). "Is it possible to formulate a general
statement about what urban history is on reading" the books under
review, he asks? "Clearly, the answer is no. There is so little
that they share in common: no common method, no common objective,
no common generalization about cities, urbanism, or urbanization."
Seldom, Rowney continues, "do we learn very much about the city as
a dependent variable--that is, the city as a result of change in
the society of which it is a part. . . . More often than not the
city is an intervening variable. That is, the city is a rather
vaguely conceived factor that affects the development of certain
types of social relations and, above all, forms a convenient
focus and limit for the researches of historians. In itself,
however, it does not appear to be something we know very much--
or are finding out very much--about." In the end, Rowney concludes: "There are only urban histories and urban historians"--
an evaluation that fairly well sums up the foregoing survey of
the field. And yet there were--are?--all the early hopes, plans,
and dreams for our subdiscipline. Whether they will survive
remains to be seen. In the meantime, concerning our "no little
plans," we might take some consolation in paraphrasing Jake
Barnes's concluding judgment in The Sun Also Rises: "Wasn't it
pretty to think so!"

The Environmental Decade in Literature

MONICA PRONIN AND
JUDITH D. SCHWARZMEIER

The celebration of Earth Day 1980 will mark the end of the first
Environmental Decade - a remarkably short time span in which humankind was faced with eco-disasters so serious as to force a widespread realization of the interdependence of people and the
environment. This sudden "discovery" fostered a major revolution
in sociopolitical attitudes toward the environment - attitudes
reflected at the global, national, and local levels of society.
One measure of the extent to which the movement influenced all
sectors and all societies was the outpouring of environmental
literature throughout this Decade.

The evolution of the environmental movement may easily be traced
from the shelves of the well-stocked library. Although international in scope, this literature received perhaps the greatest
contributions from the English-speaking world. A brief overview
of the key English-language sources and reference systems in the
environmental field follows.

The Awakening

The shifts in historical thought that led to the environmental
revolution we are now witnessing were evident as far back as

Reprinted from Library Journal, May 1, 1980. Published by R.R.
Bowker Co. (A Xerox Company). Copyright 1980 by Xerox Corporation.

the turn of the 19th Century in the writings of Malthus. However,
these shifts began to receive widespread notice only early in
this century, following tbe writings of such naturalists as
John Muir, Gifford Pinchot, and George Perkins Marsh. Aldo
Leopold's Sand County Almanac, published in 1948 (Oxford Univ.
Pr.), became a cornerstone for modern ecological thought. Other
warnings of pending environmental doom were sounded in Fairfield
Osborn's Our Plundered Planet (Little, 1948), Harrison Brown's
The Challenge of Man's Future (Viking, 1954), and - so vividly
that many listened for the first time - Rachel Carson's Silent
Spring (Houghton, 1962). By the 1960's nearly everyone had read
or at least heard of The Quiet Crisis by Stewart Udall (Avon,
1964) and The Population Bomb by Paul Erlich (Ballantine, 1968).
Garrett Hardin's thought-provoking essay "Tragedy of the Commons"
(Science, December 13, 1968) put into stark perspective the
ecological dilemma facing humankind.   These and other writings
helped to turn "ecology" and "environment" into household words
and generated sufficient concern to wring a major response from
the American political machinery - passage of the landmark
National Environmental Policy Act in 1969.

The Decade

The first Earth Day, held on April 22, 1970, officially heralded
the beginning of the Decade and bestowed national recognition
on the environmental movement. It also marked the beginning of
a floodtide of environmental literature. Among the books
appearing early in the Decade were several excellent and thorough
analyses of the ecological predicament: Environment: A Challenge
to Modern Society by Lynton K. Caldwell (Natural History Pr., 1970);
The Environmental Handbook, edited by Garrett De Bell (Ballantine/
Friends of the Earth, 1970); The Closing Circle by Barry Commoner
(Knopf, 1971); The Club of Rome's report Limits to Growth by
Donella H. Meadows, et al.(Universe Bks., 1972); and Only One
Earth by Barbara Ward and Rene Dubos (Norton, 1972). The United
Nations Conference on the Human Environment, held in Stockholm
during June 1972, gave nations their first significant chance to
exchange ideas and address problems as an international community.
Most nations issued national "state of the environment" reports,
which are still available from EIC - The Environment   Information
Center, Inc. In addition, many other documents were generated in
preparation for, during, and after the conference; Caldwell's
In Defense of Earth (Indiana Univ. Pr., 1972) was one of the
major works.

Another mountain of information, much of it highly technical,
became available in periodicals, some of which owed their existence
to the environmental movement. This resource base was often the
first to report on significant environmental happenings. General
but thorough articles on all environmental fields appeared in such
periodicals as Environment, Ambio, Environmental Action, and
Conservation Foundation Letter. Other journals provided a narrower

focus on specialized topics: Journal of the Air Pollution Control Association, Journal of the Water Pollution Control Federation, Bulletin of Environmental Contamination & Toxicology, Journal of Environmental Health, Family Planning Perspectives, Marine Pollution Bulletin, Resource Recovery & Conservation, Journal of Soil & Water Conservation, Environmental Science and Technology, and Environmental Law. Not to be overlooked were the nonenvironmental periodicals that began devoting more and more space to environmental topics. The New York Times, Chemical Engineering Science, Oil & Gas Journal, and Business Week were only a handful out of thousands.

A wealth of invaluable environmental information was also found in the innumerable special reports and conference proceedings generated by every type of organization imaginable: federal, regional, state and local government agencies throughout the worlds, international organizations, research institutes and laboratories, universities, trade and professional associations, citizen groups, and privately owned corporations. Many of these organizations were staffed with experts, and some were prolific publishers of environmental literature. Especially significant had been materials from the U.S. Environmental Protection Agency, General Accounting Office, Congressional Research Service, Office of Technology Assessment, and departments of Agriculture, Commerce, Energy, Health, Education, and Welfare, Interior and Transportation; State of Illinois Institute of Natural Resources; Environment Canada; United Nations and Organization for Economic Cooperation and Development; Worldwatch Institute and Resources for the Future; Universities of Pennsylvania and Illinois; American Chemical Society and the engineering societies; Friends of the Earth, Sierra Club, and Scientists' Institute for Public Information; and Government Institutes, Inc. Perhaps the single most valuable and comprehensive special report issued is the Council on Environmental Quality's annual review of the state of the U.S. environment, Environmental Quality (GPO).

Population and Food Resources

The environmental movement could claim some of the credit for the dramatic drop in population growth in the U.S. and several other nations. This slow detonation of the global population bomb and consequent forestalling of an epidemic food shortage were evident in the literature as the dire warnings of the early 1970's gave way to less panicky essays several years later. Among the significant works of the Decade were Population, Resources, and the Environment by Paul and Anne Erlich (Freeman, 1970); The Commission on Population Growth and the American Future, Final Report (GPO, 1972), an eight-volume series containing papers by noted authorities; documents emanating from the UN World Food Conference in Rome in 1974; Losing Ground by Erik Eckholm (Norton, 1976); and, recently, The Twenty-Ninth Day by Lester Brown (Norton, 1978).

Land Use

Concern about urban land use, an old issue, was well reviewed in
these classics: The City in History by Lewis Mumford (Harcourt
Brace & World, 1961) and The Death and Life of Great American
Cities by Jane Jacobs (Random, 1961). The environmental movement,
however, increased awareness of the need for planning, growth
controls, and environmentally acceptable land management techniques.
The Urban Land Institute, a leader in the field and a prolific
publisher of information on this subject, printed a substantial
series, Management and Control of Growth: Issues, Techniques,
Problems, Trends (3 vols., 1975). Also from ULI came other treatments of urban land use issues, including Large-Scale Development:
Benefits, Constraints, and State and Local Policy Incentives
(1977). Other significant publications on land use were: Super-
highways - Superhoax by Helen Leavitt (Doubleday, 1970); Design
with Nature by Ian McHarg (Natural History Pr., 1971); The Use
of Land: a Citizen's Policy Guide to Urban Growth by a task force
headed by William Reilley and sponsored by the Rockefeller Brothers
Fund (Crowell, 1973); the three-volume Promised Lands series from
INFORM, Subdivisions in Deserts and Mountains by Leslie Allen,
et al. (Vol. 1, 1976), Subdivisions in Florida's Wetlands by Leslie
Allen, et al. (Vol. 2, 1977), and Subdivisions and the Law by
Patricia Simko, et al. (Vol. 3, 1978); Environmental Analysis for
Land Use and Site Planning by William Marsh (McGraw, 1978); and
Earthscape: a Manual of Environmental Planning by John Simonds
(McGraw, 1978).

Protection of natural areas could be counted as one of the Decade's
most heated controversies, yet also as one of its major accomplishments. Additions to the National Park System, Wilderness Areas,
Wild and Scenic Rivers System, and other natural areas had come
about partly as a result of increased public concern and user pre-
sures - a characteristic expression of interest in the environmental
movement. An early philosophical treatment of this interest was
Wilderness and the American Mind by Roderick Nash (Yale Univ.
Pr., 1967). Time-Life published two notable series, The American
Wilderness (1972-75) and The World's Wild Places (1973-78),
describing in words and pictures areas that remain untouched
because of preservation efforts. Perhaps the most heated wilderness
debate of the Decade, still in fact sizzling on the burner, centered
on the future of the publicly owned Alaska lands; John McPhee's
very readable Coming into the Country (Farrar, 1977) probed this
issue from various perspectives. Preservation of wetlands, another
controversial topic, was examined in CEQ's report Our Nation's
Wetlands (GPO, 1978).

Agricultural land issues also became prominent during the 1970's.
Wendell Berry's The Unsettling of America: Culture and Agriculture
(Sierra Club, 1977) challenged orthodox assumptions about
traditional farming techniques that damage the environment.

Energy

Throughout the Decade, the energy issue, spurred on by the 1973
Arab oil embargo and later petroleum shortages, assumed ever in-
creasing importance. Several comprehensive assessments of the
energy situation appeared: A Time To Choose, the Energy Policy
Project of the Ford Foundation (Ballinger, 1974); Nuclear Power
Issues and Choices, a Nuclear Energy Policy Study Group report
sponsored by the Ford Foundation (Ballinger, 1977); Soft Energy
Paths by Amory Lovins (Ballinger, 1977); The Politics of Energy
by Barry Commoner (Knopf, 1979); The Good News About Energy, a
CEQ report (GPO, 1979); and Energy Future, the report of the
Energy Project at the Harvard Business School (Random, 1979).

As the energy issue ballooned, so did several associated environmental issues, including pollution from coal production and usage,
nuclear radiation, and oil spills. Worries about the radiation
dangers of nuclear power plants were punctuated at the end of the
Decade by the failure of Pennsylvania's Three Mile Island nuclear
reactor - the most serious U.S. nuclear accident ever. President
Carter established a special study commission, whose findings,
published in the Report of the President's Commission on the
Accident at Three Mile Island (GPO, 1979), could have far-reaching implications for the nuclear industry. Earlier studies by
the Nuclear Regulatory Commission of the risks associated with
nuclear power - WASH 1400 in 1975 (the so-called Rasmussen Report)
and the later Risk Assessment Review Group Report in 1978
(NUREG/CR-0400) - reflected the mounting concern over radiation,
the unseen enemy.

Oil spills were another spinoff concern of the energy issue.
Jeffrey Potter analyzed several, including the Torrey Canyon and
Santa Barbara incidents, in Disaster by Oil: Oil Spills, Why They
Happen, What They Do, How We Can End Them (Macmillan, 1973).

Economics

While much of the opposition to environmental goals focused on
economic arguments, namely the near-term, high monetary costs of
achieving a clean environment, many thought-provoking discussions
of the interrelationships between economics and the environment
pointed out other less obvious social costs that must be considered
in environmental decision-making. The essays of such well known
authorities as Kenneth E. Boulding, Nicholas Georgescu-Roegen,
and Preston Cloud were gathered together in Steady State Economy,
edited by Herman Daly (Freeman, 1973). Other economic analyses
of note included Environmental Quality Analysis: Theory and
Method in the Social Sciences, edited by Allen V. Kneese and
Blair T. Bower (Johns Hopkins Univ. Pr., 1972); Public Economics
and the Quality of Life, edited by Lowdon Wingo and Alan Evans
(Johns Hopkins, 1977); and Environmental Improvement through
Economic Incentives by Frederick Anderson, et al. (Johns Hopkins,

1978). The Russian response (or non-response) to industrial growth
at the environment's expense was perhaps best documented in Marshall
Goldman's The Spoils of Progress: Environmental Pollution in the
Soviet Union (MIT Pr., 1972).

Air Pollution

The Clean Air Act, passed in 1970, proved to be difficult to
implement, but represented another positive achievement during the
Decade; despite growth in industries and transportation, controls
had prevented air pollution from becoming much worse. The air
pollution problem was reviewed in Vanishing Air, the Ralph Nader
study group report on air pollution (Grossman, 1970), Air Pollution
by A.C. Stern (5 vols., Academic, 1976), and Air Pollution and
Human Health by Lester Lave and Eugene Seskin (Johns Hopkins,
1978).

Water Resources and Pollution

Another major effort by environmentalists resulted in the passage
of the Federal Water Pollution Control Act of 1972 and the Safe
Drinking Water Act of 1974, and in implementation of many successful regional and local water cleanup programs. Early recognition
of water pollution problems was found in Death of the Sweet Waters
by Donald E. Carr (Norton, 1966) and The Frail Ocean by Wesley
Marx (Coward, 1967).

Included among other chronicles of water pollution and water
resources were: The Water Lords by James Fallows (Grossman, 1971);
Environmental Quality and Water Development, edited by Charles Goldman (Freeman, 1973); Supership by Noel Mostert (Knopf, 1974);
Water Pollution Control: Assessing the Impacts and Costs of
Environmental Standards by Ralph Luken and Edward Pechan (Praeger,
1977); Drinking Water and Health (National Academy of Sciences,
1977); and documents from the UN Water Conference, held in Mar
del Plata, Argentina (1977).

Toxic Substances

Eco-disasters involving human exposure to toxic chemicals were
well publicized. Remember dioxins in Seveso, Italy, PBB's on
Michigan dairy farms, kepone in the James River, and a host of
chemicals in the Love Canal section of Niagara Falls, New York?
Such incidents provided the leverage needed to achieve controls
on toxic substances, among them the 1972 ban on most uses of DDT,
passage of the Occupational Safety and Health Act of 1970, the
Federal Insecticide, Fungicide, and Rodenticide Act of 1972,
and the Toxic Substances Control Act of 1977. The pesticide issue
was one that surfaced realtively early, as noted by Pesticides and
the Living Landscape by Robert L. Rudd (Univ. of Wisconsin Pr.,

1964); A. W. A. Brown addressed the issue more recently in Ecology of Pesticides (Wiley, 1978). Other familiar titles on toxics issues were The Withering Rain: America's Herbicidal Folly by Thomas White-side (Dutton, 1971), Since Silent Spring by Frank Graham, Jr. (Fawcett, 1977), The Politics of Cancer by Samuel S. Epstein (Sierra Club, 1978), and Pendulum and the Toxic Cloud by Thomas Whiteside (Yale Univ. Pr., 1979).

Noise Pollution

Before the environmental movement gained momentum, most people just accepted noise pollution as part of their environment. The SST and occupational noise exposure issues helped to publicize the problem and encouraged passage of the Noise Control Act of 1972. Perhaps the best analysis of the problem was Robert Alex Baron's The Tyranny of Noise (St. Martin's, 1970).

Terrestrial Resources

Wise use of forests and minerals, an ever-present concern of the environmental movement, was documented in One-Third of the Nation's Land, a report of the Public Land Law Review Commission (GPO, 1970), Forests for Whom and for What? by Marion Clawson (Johns Hopkins, 1975), and Earthbound: Minerals, Energy, and Man's Future by Charles F. Park and Margaret C. Freeman (Freeman, 1975).

Wildlife

Wildlife protection, a popularized topic in the environmental literature, made headway during the Decade in the passage of the Marine Mammals Protection Act of 1972 and the Endangered Species Acts of 1973, as well as in international efforts to protect endangered species. An early warning of wildlife extinction was sounded in Slaughter the Animals, Poison the Earth by Jack Olson (S & S., 1971). Wildlife and America, a collection of papers edited by Howard P. Brokaw (GPO, 1978), provided a balanced look at the issues.

The End of the Decade

Toward the close of the 1970's many excellent, stimulating treat-ments of environmental problems appeared in print. In contrast to the early doomsday accounts, those offered optimistic alternatives for the future. A few are listed: Small is Beautiful by E.F. Schumacher (Harper, 1976); Ecology and the Politics of Scarcity by William Ophuls (Freeman, 1977); The Human Future Revisited by Harrison Brown (Norton, 1978); Footprints on the Planet by Robert Cahn (Universe Bks., 1978); Reconciling Man with the Environment by Eric Ashby (Stanford Univ. Pr., 1978); and Muddling toward

Frugality by Warren Johnson (Sierra Club, 1978).

With the appearance of Alvin Toffler's vision of a new society, The Third Wave (Morrow, 1980), literature has already begun to penetrate the second Environmental Decade.

Environment Update: A Review of Environmental Literature and Developments in 1979

GEORGE H. SIEHL

The closing months of the "environmental decade," initiated with the signing of the National Environmental Policy Act by President Nixon in January 1970, showed the environmental movement in a position far different from that in which it began. The decade saw environmental concerns broadly supported and pushed to successful legislative and administrative conclusions, but by the end of the decade economic and national security concerns appeared to be in the ascendancy.

The near future for the environmental movement may be a time of struggle to maintain the gains which were made in the 1970's. Certainly all of the easy advances have been made. Americans, in an era of greater economic confidence, could adopt the air of noblesse oblige and make some sacrifices which would benefit the environment. Now that the domestic supply of fuel and mineral resources is finally perceived as finite, concern with economic self-interest is likely to overshadow broader, socially directed attitudes. Increasingly, economic arguments will flourish at the expense of aesthetic ones in determining how resources are developed or allocated.

Developments in 1979 offer some indications of this new direction. In June, for instance, then Energy Secretary James Schlesinger withdrew from an interagency task force which was to report on how use of coal could be increased. Schlesinger's solution, which he submitted to the President, was to amend the Clean Air act to allow for burning of coal under a system of intermittent controls. This would allow burning of coal emitting sulfur dioxide on days when the conditions were likely to limit spread of pollutants, as opposed to building scrubbers in exhaust stacks to continually remove all pollutants, a costly approach.

President Carter's proposal for establishment of the Energy Security Corporation and the Energy Mobilization Board as a means of speeding up the development of domestic energy sources was another example. This proposal, in the words of Robert Cahn writing in the September issue of Audubon, meant that "the President turned, in the eyes of environmental leaders, from staunch friend to potential enemy."

The Sierra Club's timely and topical newsletter, National News Report, took note of the changing public mood concerning the environment as expressed in the November 1979 elections. The post-election issue noted: "Election day 1979, with record low voter turnouts even for an off year, brought little but disappointing news to environmentalists. Ranging from bottle bills to growth control, environmental issues were outspent, outsmarted, and out-voted." The term "outdated" also may have been in the minds of some who voted against the measures or who failed to vote.

In Congress the picture was similar, with no broad new environmental initiatives enacted, although, as has been noted before in these "Environment Updates," the first session of each Congress usually sees new proposals enacted. The process of organizing the Congress and holding hearings, along with approving annual appropriations bills, takes up much of the time of the first session.

One action of the Congress which saw resource develpment take precedence over protection was the approval of completion of the Tellico Dam in the TVA system in Tennessee. Completion of the project had been delayed because of discovery several years ago of an endangered species of fish, the snail darter. As noted last year, the Congress created a special authority to review such cases. The panel reviewed the situation and found in favor of the snail darter. Congress, however, chose to overrule the finding and specifically authorized completion of the Tellico Dam. The fish are to be moved to another location, where it is hoped they will be able to survive.

Such case-by-case reversals, accommodations here and there, and modifications of standards and regulations would appear to be the expected course of events moving into the 1980's. There is little likelihood, however, that the entire array of environmental protection measures will be eliminated. Rather, the pendulum action of public policy issues will move back and forth, with each cycle reducing the distance between the extremes until a centrist range of basic agreement is reached.

This year's selection of environmental literature is, for the most part, a serious minded lot, touching again and again upon the economic aspects of resource management.

Historic Preservation

Perhaps one of the most optimistic outlooks to result from the meetings between preservation and economics is to be found in the area of historic preservation, particularly of buildings.

Lost Toronto (Oxford), by William Dendy, illustrates and describes nearly 100 structures that have been demolished or radically altered in Toronto, Canada. The book makes clear that one of the most pleasant cities in North America has lost much through the removal of the elements of the built environment which Dendy recalls.

Public and private concern is now insuring that more of this richness is preserved. Economics as well as aesthetics is contributing to the saving of old buildings. New Profits from Old Buildings (McGraw-Hill), by Raynor Warner and others, reviews 71 varied preservation projects undertaken by companies. Adaptive reuse can result in cost savings of 30 to 40 percent over new construction, according to the authors, and provide time and tax savings as well.

Another McGraw-Hill title, Laurence Reiner's How to Recycle Buildings, provides a detailed guide to returning buildings to use on a profit-making basis. He notes the social and tax revenue benefits to cities of such an endeavor, stating that local governments will probably soon come to encourage entrepreneurs in these recycling projects. Community groups which wish to encourage revitalization of their areas will find this book a useful guide in approaching business groups which might be encouraged to participate in an urban improvement project which is not necessarily tied to some federal program.

Small Seaports: Revitalization through Conserving Heritage Resources (Conservation Foundation, Washington, D.C.), by John Clark and others, reviews the possibilities for restoring the economic life of older coastal communities.

Offshore, a noneconomic but nonetheless interesting historic preservation effort, is recounted in Edward Miller's U.S.S. Monitor (Leeward Pubs., Annapolis, Md.). The story of the search for the sunken Civil War ironclad is as compelling as the history of her construction and operation against the Confederate Navy. After her resting place was discovered off Cape Hatteras, the area was designated as the first Marine Sanctuary by the Secretary of Commerce in 1975; marine archeology activities have continued there.

An extensive guide to marine accidents has been compiled by Keith Huntress and published by Iowa State University Press as Checklist of Narratives of Shipwrecks & Disasters at Sea to 1860. The 426 citations of items published prior to 1860 may not lead to the location of any downed vessels, but they do provide insight to a time when environmental conditions could directly mean life and death.

Resources and Economics

The harsh school of experience is educating us in the once obscure subject of resource economics. Rising costs of home heating and cooking and gasoline prices, which seem to climb as rapidly as those of gold and silver, have made us concerned participants in the resource allocation process. Events in Iran have helped to make clear that the United States is more dependent than ever upon foreign energy sources.

Sharing Global Resources (McGraw-Hill), by Ruth and Uzi Arad and others, examines supply and pricing of natural resources, along with the efforts of developing nations to secure control over the commodities which they possess. A management scheme which would allow for the sharing of oceanic resources among the nations of the world is offered.

Scarcity and Growth Reconsidered (Johns Hopkins), edited by V. Kerry Smith, contains detailed analyses of the extent, adequacy, and availability of various resources around the world. The work shows that there are competing theories and offers proposals for research to help clarify the situation.

The use of the National Forest Policy Act as a means of resolving resource utilization conflicts such as those involving clearcutting, wilderness protection, and other sensitive management questions related to national forests is examined in National Forest Policy: from Conflict to Consensus (Conservation Foundation). Written by William Shands, Perry Hagenstein, and Marissa Roche, this is one of a series of Issue Reports being published by the Washington, D.C.-based Conservation Foundation.

Not all resources come with easily identified market values. Unpriced Values (Wiley-Interscience), by John Sinden and Albert Worrell, offers a comprehensive presentation of ways of placing comparable values on such considerations as human health, wilderness preservation, outdoor recreation, and scenic beauty. The ability to develop such means of comparison with consumptive resource uses will become increasingly useful in the coming decade.

An example of how the economic impact of environmental or other governmental controls can be measured is contained in a study published by the Urban Land Institute in Washington, D.C. as its Research Report #28. The Cost of Delay Due to Governmental

Regulation in the Houston Housing Market estimates that "home buyers may be paying from $3200 to $5400 per lot for the costs of increased government regulation over the last ten years" under the worst conditions. Otherwise, the increased costs may range from $2300 to over $4100. Consumers are likely to question the benefits they are receiving from government for increased expenditures of this size. It is in cases such as this that means of quantifying the "unpriced values" must be available.

Donald Worster's Dust Bowl: the Southern Plains in the 1930's (Oxford) recounts graphically the social and economic losses that followed the abuse of our agricultural land resource during the drought conditions of the time. The vagaries of climate are such that the dust bowl set of circumstances might be repeated; this detailed chronicle makes one shudder at the project.

State Natural Resource Economics, a study by Elise Chapman for the Council of State Governments (Lexington, Kentucky), examines the broad costs and benefits of state efforts to encourage resource development. Fisheries, timber, grain and coal are the four cases explored. The study states three challenges, which are to increase the use of the natural resource base, mediate the conflicts arising from such expanded use, and integrate resource policies with other community development objectives.

In Managing Ocean Resources: a Primer (Westview), editor Robert Friedheim has clearly shown the varied and complex kinds of information which are necessary to protect and utilize the resources of the sea. The book includes legal, political, scientific, and economic elements which now prevail or which need to be developed in order to secure the fullest benefits available from the ocean.

We are probably inclined to believe that resource management has become terribly complex only since the advent of the environmental movement, or perhaps a bit earlier. Wrong! Charles R. Young sets the date back to 1066 and the Norman conquest of England in The Royal Forests of Medieval England (Univ. of Pennsylvania). This detailed history shows a combination of legal, economic and social problems which is the equal of a forest resource management problem today. Young reveals that the royal forests were an issue of conflict between king and barons and was an issue in the Magna Carta crisis in 1215. This sounds somewhat familiar in terms of the current so-called "Sagebrush Rebellion," which finds some Western states seeking transfer of federal lands to state jurisdiction.

Land Use

Our most fundamental resource is the land. The choices as to how it is to be used are usually the choices in which the individual citizen has the greatest voice. This opportunity to help decide

may come in the form of participation in a zoning hearing, supporting bond proposals for land preservation, or voting for candidates
on the basis of their support for or opposition to community growth
or development. Even more fundamentally, the decision of the
individual property owner as to what he does with his land may
lead to far-ranging changes in patterns of land use.

The map is an important element in reaching many land use decisions.
Maps are also intriguing in their own right. Maps for America.
Cartographic Products of the U.S. Geological Survey and Others
(GPO), by Morris Thompson, captures - and adds to - the fascination
of maps as sources of information and as works of art. The book
describes how maps are created and what they contain in terms of
symbols, lines, and colors. 'T also contains portions of scores of
maps ranging from suburban streets to the moon. A super reference
source.

Robert Healy and John Rosenberg have prepared a second edition of
their Land Use and the States (Johns Hopkins), trying to keep
current with the fast changing situation by revisiting the states
of Vermont, California, Florida, and North Carolina. As Congress
rejected federal land use legislation in 1974, the responsibility
for initiating comprehensive programs has fallen upon the states,
and they have been active in this area, in some cases. This book
helps to keep a general audience informed of that activity.

The problems and concerns with growth are not confined to urban
areas. The Urban Land Institute's Growth and Change in Rural
America finds that now,and for the foreseeable future, nonmetro
areas are subject to steady and sometimes rapid growth. Between
1970 and 1976 there was a net in-migration of 2.3 million people
to such areas. The authors, Glenn Fuguitt, Paul Voss, and J.C.
Doherty, examine the causes for this change in the historical
pattern of net outflow from nonurban areas and discuss the
possible consequences. The suggestions offered for coping with
growth could make this a very useful publication for outlying
cities in the 25,000 to 50,000 population range.

Big cities are more likely to make use of another ULI publication,
Joint Development: Making the Real Estate-Transit Connection.
This is a casebook based upon the experience of Philadelphia,
Washington, Montreal, Boston, and Toronto in coordinating high
density land uses with rapid transit stations. Although meshing
public policy and private development is often difficult, the
study finds that benefits have gone to both the public and
private sectors.

Those interested in obtaining or defeating a change in zoning may
wish to consult Winning at Zoning (McGraw-Hill). Written by Dudley
Hinds, Neil Carn, and Nicholas Ordway, the book explains the what
and why of zoning and provides guidelines on how to go about
being successful in zoning disputes, whichever side you may be
on. Success at times comes through compromise, a technique which
the authors also elaborate upon.

A useful informative guide from the Heritage Conservation and
Recreation Service of the U.S. Department of the Interior is
Land Conservation and Preservation Techniques (GPO). Among the
approaches described in detail are those involving tax incentives,
gift and purchase arrangements, historic structure rehabilitation
and others. Conservationists might find this publication worth
reviewing with friendly tax lawyers, estate planners, and realtors
because owners of appropriate property may find it nearly as
advantageous to utilize one of the programs described as to sell
their property.

The task of administering federal land holdings is often made
difficult because of conflicts with adjoining landowners. William
Shands describes some of the problems which arise and offers
suggestions for solutions or pertinent research in Federal Resource Lands and Their Neighbors (Conservation Foundation).

Ann L. Strong, in Land Banking: European Reality, American
Prospect (Johns Hopkins) recounts the programs of Sweden, the
Netherlands, and France to buy and stockpile land for future use.
With regard to the adoption of this system in the United States,
she examines the major issues involved, feeling that such a program may be the best hope for resolving urban development problems,
but that "does not mean that it waits on our horizon, trouble free."

Environmental Programs

One major reason for the development of environmental programs to
control pollution damage was that resource utilization programs
treated air and water as free sites for the disposal of wastes.
There were other contributors to the pollution problem, of course,
and other environmental values were being sacrificed. Decisions
by consumers and by government threatened open space, wilderness,
and wildlife, for instance. It was the need to accommodate
continued economic and public activity with efforts to maintain
the habitability and pleasantness of the natural world that led
to the development of the environmental processes and programs
which prevail in America today.

Examining the question of whether the government could bring its
various agencies in line with the new environmental ethic, Daniel
Mazmanian and Jeanne Nienaber have focused upon the Corps of Engineers in Can Organizations Change? (Brookings Institution,
Washington, D.C.). Through massive public works projects which
it planned, constructed and managed, the Corps was in a position
to significantly affect economic activity - and environmental
attributes. The authors feel that the Corps of Engineers has
become more accessible and responsive to citizen input in the past
decade and, in so doing, has accepted environmentalists as one
of the publics which they serve.

Timothy O'Riordan and Ralph d'Arge in Progress in Resource
Management and Environmental Planning, Vol. 1 (Wiley) present a

detailed review of environmental management, focusing upon advances
in methodology, changes in thinking on approaches to environmental
management, and the implications of new policy developments. Geared
to a professional audience, this volume includes articles on
population, pollution control in the United Kingdom, and sociological factors such as the perception of environmental quality.

Environmental Impact Analysis Handbook (McGraw-Hill), edited by
John Rau and David Wooten, is a detailed guide for those who need
to undertake an environmental analysis in the field. Individual
chapters describe how to assess socioeconomic, air quality, noise,
energy, water quality, and vegetation and wildlife impacts.
Corporate and research libraries may find this volume pertinent.

The Allen Kneese and Blair Bower report on the leftovers from
industrial and technological processes addresses a central issue.
Their Environmental Quality & Residuals Management (Johns Hopkins)
includes a case study examining the situation regarding airborne,
waterborne, and solid wastes in the Lower Delaware Valley, one
objective of which was to estimate the costs of controlling the
emission of residuals.

A detailed analysis on one controversial environmental issue is
F.L. McEwen and G.R. Stephenson's The Use and Significance of
Pesticides in the Environment (Wiley-Interscience). The authors
note their attempt to indicate grounds for concern in areas
where factual information is lacking, but cite the wide range
of views which prevails between the farmer and the birdwatcher
as to the relative values of a bushel of grain and a songbird.
Their intent is to present a balanced view of the problem and to
encourage further thoughtful research.

Costs and benefits of environmental programs are examined in two
final titles. Who Pays for Clean Water: the Distribution of Water
Pollution Control Costs (Westview), by Elizabeth Lake and others,
compares the economic effects upon various socioeconomic sub-
groups of two means of paying for water pollution control. The
two methods are through tax expenditures or through industry
passing on the costs of cleanup in the form of higher prices to
consumers.

Economists will discover the payoff of our expensive environmental
outlays through reading Myrick Freeman's The Benefits of Environmental Improvement (Johns Hopkins), but lay readers without a
knowledge of microeconomic theory will have to wait for the movie.

Natural History

General readers, come back. From the abstruse world of economic
analysis we move to the domain of things that wiggle, hop, run,
fly, or flower. The widespread interest in the natural world has
been one of the reasons it was easy to generate support for conservation and environmental protection programs. The continued

presence of a bountiful array of living things remains one of the chief benefits (although perhaps not economically quantifiable) of environmental efforts.

Janet Marsh's Nature Diary (Morrow) offers a delightful introduction to the topic, containing both her attractive watercolor illustration of the flora and fauna of the English countryside and her notes of field observations throughout a year.

Closer to home, Kenneth Chambers' A Country-Lover's Guide to Wildlife (Johns Hopkins) contains descriptions and illustrations of mammals, amphibians, and reptiles of the Northeast. Chambers also includes vignettes of his experiences afield, a feature which gives the book a charm lacking in some field guides. Wayne Trimm's black-and-white drawings and color illustrations are useful supplements to the species descriptions.

An excellent regional guide is Stephen Whitney's A Sierra Club Naturalist's Guide to the Sierra Nevada (Sierra Club). The book not only describes many of the plant and animal species to be found in the area but, more interestingly for the home reader, describes the four life-zones found in the Sierra Nevada, explaining the significance of elevation, geography, geology, weather, and other natural determinants of what is to be found where. Contains numerous black-and-white drawings and eight pages of color illustrations of wildflowers.

The grizzly bear once ranged across large areas of the mountain West, and some of the most exciting episodes of the journals of Lewis and Clark describe their encounters with these great animals. Frank C. Craighead, in Track of the Grizzly (Sierra Club), describes the years of field research which he and his brother John conducted on this now disappearing species in the vicinity of Yellowstone National Park. The stories of the trapping, tagging, and subsequent years of following the grizzlies are highly readable, but the important conservation message is brought home in the chapter on "Bureaucracy and the Bear," which describes how the Craighead brothers were forced out of their research program because of political considerations. Recommended.

Not only wild species are nearing the end of the lonely road to extinction. Lawrence Alderson traces the vanishing breeds of domestic animals in the United Kingdom in The Chance to Survive (Stephen Greene Pr.). Not only sentiment should stand in the way of allowing more of these species to slip into extinction, the author writes, for their genetic makeup is a valuable resource. These animals can be productive in environments unsuited to more abundant breeds and could thus be used to meet food requirements of people in these areas. They can also serve in producing new hybrid animals which might be used in now unproductive regions.

Outdoor Recreation

One benefit of maintaining a wholesome environment is that it is
not only fit to play in, but it invites one to do so. The
concern shown by the conservation organizations with keeping the
natural environment productive of fish and game and suitable for
camping and hiking largely provided the base upon which the more
recent, and broader, environmental movement was built.

One of the conservation organizations which first comes to mind
in such a context is the Sierra Club. Ann Gilliam has edited a
collection of writing from the Club's Bulletin in Voices for the
Earth (Sierra Club). While the collection reflects the wide range
of interests of the Club - overpopulation, energy and pollution -
it also contains a thread of articles devoted to the recreational
use of the out-of-doors.

A detailed guide to a recent recreational form is Raymond Bridge's
Bike Touring (Sierra Club). Much information on the construction
and maintenance of a touring bike is contained, along with
suggestions on suitable camping gear and how to plan a bike tour.

For those who prefer getting away from it all on foot, the
Sierra Club offers another reference, Starting Small in the
Wilderness: the Sierra Club Outdoors Guide for Families by Marlyn
Doan. This practical, portable source should be consulted at
home, but can easily be taken along on a backcountry trip.

Environmentalists are sometimes so busy telling others how to take
care of the world that they neglect to take care of the backcountry
portions they use. Laura and Guy Waterman discuss this irony in
Backwoods Ethics: Environmental Concerns for Hikers and Campers
(Stephen Greene Pr., dist.). The Watermans describe the nature and
extent of the problems, then offer detailed suggestions on how to
build a sense of stewardship among outdoor recreationists.
Although drawing heavily upon their New England hiking and rock-
climbing experience, their message has universal applicability.

On Mountains: Thinking about Terrain (McGraw-Hill Paperbacks), by
John Jerome, might well be included above in the natural history
grouping because of the fine discussion of the making and breaking
of mountains. However, his inclusion of the sociology of
mountain dwelling peoples, and especially his section on "mountain
playgrounds," is sufficient reason for including it here. The
latter section is on skiing, and it is the best short piece on the
sport I have read. It is witty, insightful, and evocative. Buy
this book, and throw away all but the skiing chapter - and you'll
still have a bargain. Don't discard a page, though: the whole
book is beautiful.

To serve the 14 million downhill and 6 million cross country skiers
in the United States, there is an invaluable guide to ski areas,
Robert G. Enzel's The White Book of Ski Areas (Rand McNally, dist.).
This reference work provides over 100 pieces of information about

each of some 700 U.S. ski areas and 225 Canadian resorts. Energy shortages and, in 1979-80, snow shortages make detailed information on what facilities are available (such as snow-making capability) more important than ever to the family planning a ski trip. The White Book provides the information without the distraction of the public relations content of many ski area brochures and advertisements.

"Recent Trends in the Study of Popular Culture": Since 1971

LAWRENCE E. MINTZ

The most important trends in the study of popular culture over the past decade are the incredible growth of activity in the field; the impressive and invaluable growth of resources supporting that activity; and the development and implementation of complex, sophisticated theoretical and methodological perspectives which approach popular culture as a "dense," profound social and cultural process rather than as a simple expression or artifact. Taken together, these phenomena have eliminated any lingering doubts concerning the legitimacy of popular culture studies as a serious, respectable, necessary, and important field of inquiry. Indeed, one might claim that the problem facing the popular culture studies in the 1980s is not how to justify this activity as worthwhile, but how to avoid being intimidated by its richness. The "Pop-Eyed Professors" whom Thomas Meehan (later of "Annie" fame, to add irony to insult) caricatured so ignorantly in a 1975 N.Y. Times Magazine feature now find themselves at the very center of any mature investigation of contemporary culture and society.

It has become clichéd to speak of the information "explosion," or to point out that data and sources grow geometrically in the modern intellectual world; but for popular culture studies, the truth of the cliché is itself magnified by the multiple definitions of the field. Popular culture studies are multidisciplinary--involving the activity of literary critics, historians, art critics, psychologists, anthropologists, sociologists, linguists, political and social analysts, and just about any other variety of scholar in the humanities and social sciences, including interdisciplinary endeavors such as American studies and the rapidly expanding area

of communications. It is also multigeneric--including studies of
popular books, fiction and non-fiction, from best sellers to
popular genres such as science fiction, detective fiction, varieties of romances, from The Joy of Cooking to The Joy of Sex;
popular music in all of its many manifestations; the graphic arts
(comic strips, cartoons, posters, t-shirts); newspaper and
magazine journalism, film, broadcasting media, stage entertainments;
and in some broader definitions, sports, circuses, parades,
festivals, fast foods, pinball machines, roller coasters, and all
other forms of popular recreations, leisure activities, and lifestyles. Popular culture is also approached from many different
perspectives and thematic concerns. Blacks, women, ethnics, the
elderly, gays, farmers, bankers, moral majoritarians, educators,
consumers, and other identifiable groups have a legitimate concern
for the thematic handling of their interests and the influences of
popular culture on their group and their group's image. All of
these disciplines, genres, thematic perspectives, interest groups,
and areas produce information concerning popular culture. The
person who sets out to "keep up with the field" is either very
naive, very arrogant, or the owner of a very powerful computer!

Fortunately, however, the systems which help us organize, store,
retrieve, and use information are growing at a rate commensurate
with the "explosion" of knowledge. My colleague Gene Wise has
written that the "information overload" has enormous negative
potential, stifling creative thinking and understanding by drowning
it in a consuming process of accumulating data and becoming
"informed"--"Some Elementary Axioms for an American Culture
Studies," Prospects, 4 (1979). (All references in the text are
cited in full in the bibliography at the end of this essay.) But
the old model of the scholar as "expert" whose knowledge of a
field is complete and stored in his head is giving way to a new
model of the researcher who knows where and how to get information
and how to employ new intellectual systems to understand and to
use the information. The computer, once we are trained to use it
and have easier access to it, will make a tremendous difference.
But of equal importance is the "network" of experts and scholars
and the coordination of their efforts. Archives, collections,
bibliographies, handbooks, professional conferences, journals,
newsletters, and other organizational activities have emerged
during the past decade, making the proliferation of data and
studies a positive and exciting, rather than depressing, phenomenon.

Since the purpose of this essay is to survey recent trends in the
study of popular culture, rather than to provide a definitive
guide to scholarship in the field, the following description of
resources is highly selective and general and intended as an
introduction. It should lead one readily to the much more specific,
particular sources, and it will imply that there is some sort of
loose, informal coordination that amounts to a vaguely defined
"field" which we may call popular culture studies, however independent and remote its components might seem at times.

Much of the credit for this sense of coordination, and for the emergence of the term "popular culture" as the organizing rubric, must be given to Ray Browne and his activities at Bowling Green State University, Bowling Green, Ohio. Beginning in 1967 with the Journal of Popular Culture, Browne has been godfather to a Center for the Study of Popular Culture, with a library and archives; the Popular Culture Association, with its annual convention and regional affiliates; the Popular Press, which publishes many useful books; degree granting programs in popular culture and related studies; numerous journals and newsletters; and dozens of young scholars who have used his success, advice, and encouragement to launch their own careers. Browne recently formed an American Culture Association and a Journal of American Culture, whose relationship to the popular culture activities is still uncertain (and contested), but which clearly expands the opportunities for popular culture studies "a la Bowling Green." Some scholars have criticized the Browne-sponsored activities, noting a democratic "looseness" that tolerates, perhaps even encourages, superficial scholarship. However, despite the problems of quality control (and one can see improvement in all areas), there is enough first-rate work and more than enough positive promoting of activity to justify citing the growth of the Bowling Green operation as one of the most important developments in the field.

A very valuable research tool is the Handbook of Popular Culture, edited by M. Thomas Inge. Two volumes of this three-volume series have appeared (volume three is in press), providing bibliographic essays which survey study opportunities for such fields as anima-tion, automobiles, advertising, best-sellers, illustration, children's literature, comic art, detective fiction, popular music, sports, film, romantic fiction, science fiction, television, and more. Missing, unfortunately, is an essay on theory and method (apparently cancelled from volume three), but, as we shall see below, there are other resources which fill the gap. Eleanor Blum's superb Basic Books in Mass Media has been updated in 1980, covering, as suggested by its subtitle, "General Communications, Book Publishing, Broadcasting, Editorial Journalism, Film, Maga-zines, and Advertising." Nancy Allen has assumed Blum's role of providing a quarterly update, mimeographed and available free of charge from the College of Communications of the University of Illinois. The Aspen Handbook on the Media, edited by William L. Rivers, Wallace Thompson, and Michael Nyhan, lists university courses, research programs, professional groups, libraries and collections, and periodicals and books pertinent to the study of popular culture. These handbooks lead one to the more specific bibliographies, handbooks, and checklists which supplement the general listings. Also of general interest is a recent survey of university courses in the popular culture area, Currents of Warm Life: Popular Culture in American Higher Education, edited by Mark Gordon and Jack Nachbar, that updates and greatly expands two previous Popular Press studies of curricula.

Among the important bibliographic starting points, one should note
Browne's Abstracts of Popular Culture, which tracks relevant work
in the popular magazines; a special issue of American Quarterly,
32:3 (1980), edited by Mike Marsden, that contains important
essays; a very good, often overlooked, special issue of College
English, 38:8 (April 1977); the "Popular Entertainments" issue of
The Drama Review, 18:1 (March 1974); and a number of special issues
of the Journal of Popular Culture which have been devoted to
surveying the field from various perspectives, most notably theory
and method, IX:2 (Fall 1975); sociology, XI:2 (Fall 1977); and
history, XI:1 (Summer, 1977).

One of the bright aspects of pre-1970s popular culture studies was
the existence of many excellent anthologies and general books on
the subject. The growth of the field makes the production of
such volumes more difficult, perhaps even questionable, but a few
good ones have appeared. C. W. E. Bigsby has edited two books,
Approaches to Popular Culture, which offers useful theory and
method surveys, and Superculture: American Popular Culture and
Europe, offering the valuable but rare international perspective.
Ray Browne's Popular Culture and Expanding Consciousness is one
of his better efforts, and his most recent one, Rituals and Ceremonies in Popular Culture, is even finer. Henry Russell Huebel's
Things in the Driver Seat broadens the definition successfully,
and Thomas Kando, Leisure and Popular Culture in Transition,
provides a good sociological overview.

Other welcome contributions include George Lewis, Side-Saddle on
the Golden Calf: Social Structures and Popular Culture in America;
Dennis Alan Mann, The Arts in a Democratic Society; Myron Matlaw,
American Popular Entertainment; Jack Nachbar, Deborah Weiser, and
John Wright, eds., The Popular Culture Reader; Harold Schecter and
Jonna Gormley Semeiks, Patterns in Popular Culture: A Sourcebook
for Writers; David Manning White and John Pendleton, eds., Popular
Culture: Mirror of American Life; and Bernard Rosenberg and David
Manning White, eds., Mass Culture Revisited. Russel B. Nye's 1970
volume, The Unembarrased Muse, is the only real historical overview
of American popular culture; consequently, it is a book that one
cannot be without, but it needs to be revised. Two single-author
texts, among the hundreds of them, deserve separate mention:
Michael Real's Mass-Mediated Culture and Edward Whetmore's
Mediamerica.

A great deal, though by no means all, of the work done in popular
culture studies through the 1960s was theoretically and methodologically primitive. The worst offenders were the English professors and other humanists who, "born again" by the spirit of
relevance and the democratic currents in the university during
the era, turned from their studies of elite art forms to a
descriptive and appreciative interest in popular culture. Papers
presented to the convention of the Popular Culture Association
and published in the early issues of JPC were devoted to summaries,
recapitulations, surface thematic analysis, pseudo-historical

evaluation, and an embarrassing expression of naive, uncritical
enthusiasm. Aficionados of film, jazz, detective fiction--and,
among the younger scholars, of rock, pornography, and the less
respectable fare--came out of the closet to confess their extra-
curricular passions. And, because they had to justify moving their
pastime into the classroom, they created some strange arguments for
academic credibility for popular culture studies--perhaps the best
one was that popular culture should be studied because "it is
there."

On a higher plane, scholars like John Cawelti, Leslie Fiedler,
Abraham Kaplan, David Madden, and others engaged in the aesthetic
debate: How did popular culture differ from "high" culture? Was
it good, bad, neutral? What are the aesthetic bases for classification? This argument became allied to the social-critical
critique, going back to the thirties, forties, and fifties, of
the effects of "mass culture" on a democratic society (see the
essays in the first and last sections of Rosenberg and White,
Mass Culture, for examples). While the "highbrow-lowbrow-middlebrow"
classification derby has all but disappeared, the "popular culture
is destroying our minds" argument lingers on, notably in the
plethora of books which make the case against television, including
Michael Arlen, The View from Highway 1: Essays on Television;
Jerry Mander, Four Arguments for the Elimination of Television;
Gene Klavan, Turn That Damned Thing Off; Ruth K. Goldsen, The Show
and Tell Machine; Tony Schwartz, The Responsive Chord; Marie Winn,
The Plug-In Drug, and many others.

Theoretical arguments advanced during the late 1960s and the 1970s
have challenged and effectively shaken the legitimacy of these
casual approaches, particularly of the tendency to see the obvious,
overt themes of a work of art as directly "reflecting" or "influencing" opinion, values, attitudes, dispositions, or "zeitgeist."
But despite the many reasons why this practice is questionable, it
is still prevalent. Bruce Lohoff noted, in 1972, that the field--
at least as represented by the Journal of Popular Culture--was
thoroughly dominated by the above-mentioned English professors,
and recent reassessments of Lohoff's observations by Marsden, and
by Gordon and Nachbar, both cited above, reaffirm that, though
there is an increasingly important input from communications and
from the social sciences, textual explication is still dominant.
It should be noted that while this approach is "unscientific" and
logically problematic (for one thing, it is often tautological,
reading the culture from its art, and vice versa for the same
theme), at its best it is intriguing, persuasive, and stimulating.
(See Robert Sklar on film, Movie-Made America, and on television,
Prime-Time America; Greil Marcus, Mystery Train, and Charles
Gillett, The Sound of the City, on popular music, among others.)

But in the past decade a new and exciting collection of tools and
techniques have emerged, and if none of them have provided a
definitive, single "key" which unlocks the meaning of popular
culture, taken together they do amount to a new generation of

inquiry that is vastly more sophisticated, challenging, and potentially useful. Again, it is not within the scope of this essay to
provide a definitive account; indeed, a good discussion of any one
of the theoretical perspectives or methods that follow and their
applications to popular culture studies would be a separate chapter.

To begin with, the new popular culture studies demand a more complex
reading of the texts and artifacts. It is forbidden to assume that
a statement or description necessarily "means" what the critic
thinks it might, and more importantly, that it is necessarily an
index to the thinking or feeling of the creator, distributor, or
consumer. Indeed, that we must list three types of involved
individuals is crucial. Popular culture is not a thing or entity;
it is a process involving those who bring it into being, those who
are responsible for its being available, and those who use it.
Using it is a terribly profound and elusive issue that suggests
motives and functions that are not inherent in the object itself.
If I go to a movie on a date, my "consumption" of the film already
has dimensions that are not discernible from the film--just as
making the film may have motives and functions, such as profit,
that cannot be deduced, at least readily, from the images on the
screen. So we need to explore ways of getting beneath the surface
of the text to find meanings in context and process.

One such area of inquiry stays, for the most part, with the text or
artifact, but rather than "reading" it literally, it seeks to find
encoded meaning in its structure, language, genre, formula,
convention, signs, images, symbols, and so forth. These inquiries--
which are by no means comfortably lumped together, but differ
radically and are often constructed to refute each other!--suggest
that the meaning of the popular culture experience involves the
expectations and needs of the audience, and that its appeal rests
upon familiar recreations of sight, sound, and psychologically
located disposition or understanding. The mind reacts to these
stimuli and creates the meaning. What is useful to the interpreter
(or the collector or organizer) are not the variations or specific,
unique expressions in the individual text, but the recurring
patterns, the common elements in a form or type of expression.

These patterns are often, though not always, linguistic or
structural. In a 1974 keynote address and JPC article, Hayden
White suggested that structuralism, as practiced by Levi-Strauss,
Barthes, and others, would provide the key to our eventual understanding of popular culture. In 1980, at least, it is safe to say
that structuralism has not delivered upon that promise. There have
been a few successful attempts, but for the most part the theory
is far more evident than any persuasive examples of its application.
Other allied or similar approaches, including Jan Radway's
stimulating application of phenomenology, "Phenomenology, Linguistics, and Popular Culture," Journal of Popular Culture, XII
(Summer 1978), and several interesting psychoanalytic attempts,
have been tried. While all of them are theoretically an improvement
(because they do acknowledge the complex reality of the process),

they have not provided the kind of "proof" or scientific grounding that they demanded when they repudiated the first generation work.

John Cawelti's important work, begun with The Six-Gun Mystique and developed brilliantly in Adventure, Mystery, Romance, argues persuasively that there is more to be learned from an examination of the rules which govern genre--formula and convention--than from the variations of individual producers and works. Cawelti's approach works best, of course, where these genres, formulas, and conventions are most pronounced and influential--such as in the western, the hard-boiled detective novel, the romance, and, as shown by the work of Horace Newcomb, TV: The Most Popular Art, the t.v. dramas--but it does work. And it suggests through its success that the other approaches to the text as recreating and fulfilling expectations will work, too.

A better way of dealing with the text or artifact itself is that of content analysis (again, there are many different varieties), which "reads" themes somewhat literally, but seeks to avoid subjective impressions and inappropriate emphasis on particular sources by expanding the data base. This is accomplished by counting, in a large sample of works of a given type, recurring phenomena such as how many professionals on soap operas are minorities, or evil, or sexy, or whatever. This data can then be arranged statistically and interpreted. Bradley Greenberg's Life On Television: Content Analysis of U.S. TV Drama provides a good example of this technique and its applications.

Moving from the handling of text to the consideration of context and process, another important development in popular culture studies is the application of theories in the sociology of knowledge and of demographic research that asks who is using what artifacts, and how is that use consistent with other aspects of the lives of the users. Herbert Gans's important book, Popular Culture and High Culture, suggests that we abandon a value-oriented classification system in favor of finding "taste cultures" which are defined, in part, by preferences in popular culture. Gans's actual sample groups, organized by income, age, and ethnic/ racial status, are a beginning in this process, but they are too broad and they are wedded potentially to the old good/bad designations. His approach can be taken further, for example, by looking at how the field of popular music breaks down into dozens of distinct styles (punk, hard rock, progressive country, soul, top-40's, new wave, etc.), and how each style appeals to a particular "taste culture," encoding values and self-identifications in the expressions of art. A wonderful example of this kind of examination is Dick Hebdige's book, Subculture: The Meaning of Style, which uses British youth and popular music as the case study. Demographic data is now available that allows the scholar to pinpoint rather precisely the consuming group for a particular product, so that generalizations about the significance of trends in television, film, magazine readership, music, and other popular culture areas can be more accurate and more meaningful.

Along with the demographic data, cognitive and communications theories are being advanced to explore how art plays a role in acculturating members to a particular group by articulating, distilling, and exemplifying values and norms. Work in this arena is speculative--indeed, as much so as the earlier impressionistic studies of text--but it moves beyond citing statements as primary evidence of influence or reflection in favor of a more complex, circular process of cultural reinforcement. Michael Real's Mass-Mediated Culture is a fine example of this thinking, as are the writings of John Caughey, "Artificial Social Relations," American Quarterly, XXX:1 (Spring 1978) (who has an important extension in progress); Gary Alan Fine, "Popular Culture and Social Interaction: Production, Consumption, and Usage," Journal of Popular Culture, XI:2 (Fall 1977); Robert Jewett and John Lawrence, The American Monomyth; James Monaco, ed., Media Culture: Television, Radio, Books, Magazines, Newspapers, Movies; Edgar Morin, L'Esprit du Temps; Roger Rollin, "Against Evaluation: The Role of the Critic of Popular Culture," Journal of Popular Culture, IX:2 (Fall 1975), and "The Freud Connection: Psychoanalytic Approaches to Popular Culture Audience Response" (unpublished paper); Marcello Truzzi, Sociology and Everyday Life; Pershing Vartanian, "Popular Culture Studies: A Problem in Socio-Cultural Dynamics," Journal of Popular Culture, XI:1 (Summer 1977), and numerous others. In the fledgling field of communications, the work is already so enormous that even citing highlights and trends is intimidating. Indeed, as the bibliographic references and handbooks reveal, the output in communications theory and research is probably as large as the total output of all the other approaches combined, and in many ways it is accurate in considering itself to be a separate, if parallel, field. Communications research shares the trend outlined thus far of closer, more complex examination of process and context as well as text.

Closely related to this trend is the work of the Marxist and neo-Marxist critics who are searching for a sounder understanding of the role of popular culture in expressing ideology, expanding and maintaining hegemony, and influencing public sentiment. Among the many scholars contributing useful work in this area are Robert Cirino, Don't Blame the People and We're Being More Than Entertained; Todd Gitlin, The Whole World is Watching; Herbert Marcuse, One-Dimensional Man; Herbert Schiller, Communications and Cultural Domination; and Raymond Williams, Communications, "Communications as Cultural Science," Journal of Communications, 24:3 (Summer 1974), and The Long Revolution. Their approach is in turn related to those who call for a closer look at the production and distribution processes of popular culture. It is amazing how often we forget that popular culture is essentially an industry, and that commercial, technological, and professional considerations (including the personalities and relationships of the producers) play a crucial role in determining what gets produced and to what we have access. Richard A. Peterson's edition of essays, The Production of Culture, is indispensable, required reading, and the work of Paul DiMaggio, "Market Structure, the Creative Process, and Popular Culture: Toward an Organizational Reinterpretation of Mass

Culture Theory," Journal of Popular Culture, XI:2 (Fall 1977); Ben
Stein, The View from Sunset Boulevard; Gaye Tuchman, Making News:
A Study in the Construction of Reality; and the chroniclers of
specific industries such as popular music (Steve Chapple and Reebee
Garofalo, Rock 'N' Roll is Here to Pay), film (Tino Balio, ed.,
The American Film Industry), and many others remind us of the folly
of ignoring this dimension.

Finally, we must cite the anthropological approaches to popular
culture as ritual as important manifestations of cultural life.
Ray Browne, Rituals and Ceremonies in Popular Culture; Victor
Turner, Dramas, Fields, and Metaphors: Symbolic Action in Human
Society and The Ritual Process: Structure and Anti-Structure;
Mary Douglas, Natural Symbols and Implicit Meanings: Essays in
Anthropology, and others have emphasized the broader view of popular
culture as process, as a complex, deeply seated reality of which
the actual artistic product is but the tip of the iceberg.

The new methodologies and theoretical directions share a common
starting point: they reject description, appreciation, and simple,
superficial analysis and they assert that popular culture must be
approached as a complex social and cultural phenomenon--as one
which must be treated as a process involving the production, distribution, and use of that product which is the text or artifact.
The bibliography which follows includes a reference of research
guides and aids, some additional theoretical and methodological
citations, and a number of recent studies in the various disciplines, genres, themes, and perspectives which characterize popular
culture studies in the 1980s.

Selected Bibliography

Abbs, Peter. Reclamations: Essays on Culture, Mass Culture, and
     the Curriculum. London: Heinemann Educational Books, 1980.

Adler, Richard and Douglas Cater, eds. Television as a Cultural
     Force. N.Y.: Praeger, 1976.

_____. Television as a Social Force.
     N.Y.: Praeger, 1975.

Allen, Nancy, ed. "New Books in the Communications Library"
     (quarterly), U. of Illinois, College of Communications, 1979
     and continuing.

*Arens, W. and Susan P. Montague, eds. The American Dimension:
     Cultural Myths and Social Realities. Port Washington, N.Y.:
     Alfred, 1976.

Arlen, Michael J. Thirty Seconds (advertising). N.Y.: Farrar,
     Straus, Giroux, 1980.

_____. The View From Highway 1: Essays on Tele-
    vision. N.Y.: Farrar, Straus, Giroux, 1976.

Arpad, Joseph J. "Immediate Experience and the Historical Method,"
    Journal of Popular Culture, XI:1 (Summer 1977), 140-154.

Astre, Georges-Albert and Claude-Jean Betrand, eds. "Mass Media et
    Idéologie Aux Etats-Unis," (special issue), Review Francaise
    d'Etudes Americaines, 6 (October 1978).

*Balio, Tino, ed. The American Film Industry. Madison: U. of
    Wisconsin, 1976.

*Barnouw, Erik. Tube of Plenty: The Evolution of American Televi-
    sion. N.Y.: Oxford, 1977.

Barthes, Roland. Mythologies. N.Y.: Hill and Wang, 1972.

Berger, Arthur Asa. The Comic-Stripped American. N.Y.: Walker, 1973.

*Berger, Peter and Thomas Luckmann. The Social Construction of
    Reality: A Treatise in the Sociology of Knowledge. Garden
    City, N.Y.: Doubleday, 1967.

*Bettelheim, Bruno. The Uses of Enchantment: The Meaning and
    Importance of Fairy Tales. N.Y.: Vintage, 1977.

Bigsby, C. W. E., ed. Approaches to Popular Culture. Bowling Green:
    Popular Press, 1977.

*_____, ed. Superculture: American Popular Culture and
    Europe. Bowling Green: Bowling Green Press, 1975.

Bird, Fredrick. "The Contemporary Ritual Milieu," in Ray Browne,
    ed., Rituals and Ceremonies in Popular Culture. Bowling Green:
    Popular Press, 1980, 19-35.

Bleich, David. Subjective Criticism. Baltimore: Johns Hopkins, 1978.

Blum, Eleanor, ed. Basic Books in the Mass Media. 2nd edition.
    Urbana: U. of Illinois, 1980.

Bogart, Leo. The Age of Television: A Study of Viewing Habits
    and the Impact of Television on American Life. N.Y.: Ungar,
    1972.

Bouissac, Paul. Circus and Culture: A Semiotic Approach.
    Bloomington: Indiana U., 1976.

Browne, Ray B., ed. "Focus on International Popular Culture"
    (special issue), Journal of Popular Culture, 13:1 (Summer
    1979).

_____, and Marshall Fishwick, eds. <u>Icons</u>
  <u>of America</u>. Bowling Green: Popular Press, 1977.

_____, ed. <u>Popular Culture and the Expanding</u>
  <u>Consciousness</u>. N.Y.: John Wiley, 1973.

_____, Sam Grogg, Jr. and Larry Landrum, eds.
  "Theories and Methodologies in Popular Culture," (special
  issue), <u>Journal of Popular Culture</u>, IX:2 (Fall 1975).

Burns, Elizabeth and Tom Burns, eds. <u>Sociology of Literature and</u>
  <u>Drama</u>. Baltimore: Penguin, 1973.

*Cantor, Muriel G. <u>Prime Time Television: Content and Control</u>.
  Beverly Hills: Sage, 1980.

_____. <u>The Hollywood TV Producer: His Work and His</u>
  <u>Audience</u>. N.Y.: Basic Books, 1972.

Caughey, John. "Artificial Social Relations," <u>American Quarterly</u>,
  XXX:1 (Spring 1978), 70-89.

*Cawelti, John. <u>Adventure, Mystery, and Romance: Formula Stories</u>
  <u>as Art and Popular Culture</u>. Chicago: U. of Chicago, 1977.

*_____. <u>The Six-Gun Mystique</u>. Bowling Green: Popular Press,
  1973.

Chaney, David. <u>Fictions and Ceremonies: Representations of</u>
  <u>Popular Experience</u>. N.Y.: St. Martins, 1979.

*Chapple, Steve and Reebee Garofalo. <u>Rock 'N' Roll is Here to Pay:</u>
  <u>The History and Politics of the Music Industry</u>. Chicago:
  Nelson-Hall, 1978.

Christgau, Robert. <u>Any Old Way You Choose It: Rock and Other Pop</u>
  <u>Music, 1967-1973</u>. Baltimore: Penguin, 1973.

*Cirino, Robert. <u>Don't Blame the People: How the News Media Use</u>
  <u>Bias, Distortion, and Censorship to Manipulate Public Opinion</u>.
  N.Y.: Vintage, 1971.

_____. <u>We're Being More Than Entertained</u>. Honolulu:
  Lighthouse, 1977.

Cohn, William and Susan Tamke, eds. "History and Popular Culture,"
  (special issue), <u>Journal of Popular Culture</u>, XI:1 (Summer
  1977).

*Comstock, George A. <u>Television in America</u>. Beverly Hills: Sage,
  1980.

*Cripps, Thomas. Slow Fade to Black: The Negro in American Films, 1900-1942. N.Y.: Oxford, 1977.

Davison, Peter, Rolf Meyersohn, and Edward Shils, eds. Literary Taste, Culture and Mass Communication. 14 volumes. Teaneck, N.J.: Somerset House, 1978.

Denisoff, Serge. Solid Gold: The Popular Record Industry. New Brunswick, N.J.: Transaction Books, 1975.

DiMaggio, Paul. "Market Structure, the Creative Process, and Popular Culture: Toward an Organizational Interpretation of Mass Culture Theory," Journal of Popular Culture, XI:2 (Fall 1977), 436-52.

*Douglas, Ann. The Feminization of American Culture. N.Y.: Avon, 1978.

*Douglas, Mary. Implicit Meanings: Essays in Anthropology. London: Routledge and Kegan, 1978.

_____. Natural Symbols. Middlesex, England: Penguin, 1973.

Drake, Carlos, ed. "Folklore," (special issue), Journal of Popular Culture, VI:4 (Spring 1973).

Duncan, Hugh Dalziel. Communication and Social Order. N.Y.: Oxford, 1962.

Dunlop, Donald. "Popular Culture and Methodology," Journal of Popular Culture, IX:2 (Fall 1975), 375-83.

Eagleton, Terry. "Ideology, Fiction, Narrative," Social Text, I (Summer 1979).

Eco, Umberto. The Role of the Reader: Explorations in the Semiotics of Texts. Bloomington, Indiana: Indiana U., 1979.

Fine, Gary Alan. "Popular Culture and Social Interaction: Production, Consumption, and Usage," Journal of Popular Culture, XI:2 (Fall 1977), 453-66.

_____, ed. "Sociology: In Depth," (special issue), Journal of Popular Culture, XI:2 (Fall 1977).

*Fiske, John and John Hartley. Reading Television. N.Y.: Methuen, 1979.

Frith, Simon. The Sociology of Rock. London: Constable, 1976.

*Gans, Herbert. Popular Culture and High Culture: an Analysis and Evaluation of Taste. N.Y.: Basic Books, 1974.

*Geist, Christopher and Ray B. Browne, eds. Popular Abstracts.
    Bowling Green: Popular Press, 1978.

Gerbner, George, Larry Gross, et als. Trends in Network Television
    Drama and Viewer Concept of Social Reality, 1967-1976.
    Philadelphia: Annenberg School, 1977.

Gillespie, David F. "Sociology of Popular Culture: The Other Side
    of a Definition," Journal of Popular Culture, VI (1972),
    292-300.

Gillett, Charles. The Sound of the City: The Rise of Rock and
    Roll. N.Y.: Outerbridge and Dienstfrey, 1970.

.Gitlin, Todd. The Whole World is Watching: Mass Media in the
    Making and Unmaking of The New Left. Berkeley: U. of Cali-
    fornia, 1980.

*Goldsen, Ross K. The Show and Tell Machine. N.Y.: Delta, 1978.

Goodlad, J. S. A Sociology of Popular Drama. Totowa, N.J.: Rowman
    and Littlefield, 1972.

^Gordon, Mark and Jack Nachbar. Currents of Warm Life: Popular
    Culture in American Higher Education. Bowling Green:
    Popular Press, 1980.

Gordon, Thomas F. and Mary Ellen Verna. Mass Communications Effects
    and Processes: A Comprehensive Bibliography, 1950-1975.
    Beverly Hills: Sage, 1978.

Gowans, Alan. The Unchanging Arts: New Forms for the Traditional
    Functions of Art In Society. N.Y.: Lippincott, 1971.

*Greenberg, Bradley S. Life on Television. Norwood, N.J.: Ablex,
    1980.

*Guttmann, Allen. From Ritual to Record: The Nature of Modern
    Sports. N.Y.: Columbia U., 1978.

Hall, John. The Sociology of Literature. London: Longman, 1979.

*Hammel, William. The Popular Arts in America, 2nd edition. N.Y.:
    Harcourt, Brace, Jovanovich, 1977.

*Hawkes, Terence. Structuralism and Semiotics. Berkeley: Univer-
    sity of California, 1977.

*Hebdige, Dick. Subculture: The Meaning of Style. N.Y.: Methuen,
    1979.

Hellman, Mary. Popular Culture: Source Book. Del Mar: Publisher's
    Inc., 1977.

Hirsch, Paul M. "Social Science Approaches to Popular Culture: A
    Review and Critique," Journal of Popular Culture, XI:2 (Fall
    1977), 401-13.

*Holland, Norman N. The Dynamics of Literary Response. N.Y.:
    Norton, 1975.

*Huebel, Harry Russell, ed. Things in the Driver's Seat: Readings
    in Popular Culture. Chicago: Rand McNally, 1972.

Inge, M. Thomas, ed. Handbook of Popular Culture. Three volumes.
    Westport, Connecticut: Greenwood Press, 1978, 1980, 1981
    (volume three in press).

Jewett, Robert and John Shelton Lawrence. The American Monomyth.
    Garden City, N.Y.: Doubleday, 1977.

Johnson, Nicholas. How to Talk Back to Your Television Set.
    Boston: Little, Brown, 1970.

Kando, Thomas M. Leisure and Popular Culture in Transition. St.
    Louis: C. V. Mosby, 1975, 1980 revised ed.

_____. "Popular Culture and its Sociology," Journal of
    Popular Culture, IX:2 (Fall 1975), 438-455.

Kelly, R. Gordon. "Literature and the Historian," American
    Quarterly, 26 (May 1974), 141-59.

Kirby, E. T. "The Shamanistic Origins of Popular Entertainments,"
    The Drama Review, 18:1 (March 1974), 5-15.

Kirby, Michael ed. "Popular Entertainments" (special issue),
    The Drama Review, 18:1 (March 1974).

Klavan, Gene. Turn That Damned Thing Off. Indianapolis: Bobbs-
    Merrill, 1972.

Kuklick, Bruce. "Myth and Symbol in American Studies," American
    Quarterly, 24 (Fall 1972), 435-50.

*Lancy, D. F. and B. A. Tindall, eds. The Anthropological Study of
    Play. Cornwell, N.Y.: Leisure Press, 1976.

Landrum, Larry. "Proteus at Bay: Methodology and Popular Culture,"
    Journal of Popular Culture, IV:2 (Fall 1975), 497-508.

Lazare, Donald, ed. "Mass Culture, Political Consciousness, and
    English Studies," (special issue), College English, 38:8
    (April 1977).

*Lewis, George H., ed. Side-Saddle on the Golden Calf: Social Structures and Popular Culture in America. Pacific Palisades: Goodyear, 1972.

Lohoff, Bruce A. "Popular Culture: The Journal and the State of the Study," Journal of Popular Culture, 6 (1972), 453-362.

Mander, Jerry. Four Arguments for the Elimination of Television. N.Y.: Morrow Quill, 1978.

Mann, Dennis Alan ed. The Arts in a Democratic Society. Bowling Green: Popular Press, 1976.

_____. "Ritual in Architecture: The Celebration of Life," in Browne, Rituals and Ceremonies in Popular Culture, (1980).

*Marcus, Greil. Mystery Train: Images of America in Rock 'N' Roll Music. N.Y.: Dutton, 1976.

*Marcuse, Herbert. One-Dimensional Man. Boston: Beacon, 1964.

Marsden, Michael, ed. "The Channels of American Culture: Mass Media and American Studies," (special issue), American Quarterly, 32:3 (1980).

Matlaw, Myron, ed. American Popular Entertainment. Westport, Connecticut: Greenwood Press, 1977.

*Mellers, Wilfred. Music in a New Found Land. N.Y.: Stonehill, 1975.

Melly, George. Revolt into Style: The Pop Arts. Garden City, N.Y.: Anchor, 1971.

Mertz, Robert J. and Michael Marsden. "American Culture Studies: A Discipline in Search of Itself," Journal of Popular Culture, IX:2 (Fall 1975), 461-70.

Mintz, Lawrence E. and M. Thomas Inge, eds. American Humor: an Interdisciplinary Newsletter. Two issues yearly, volumes 1-3 in hardbound edition, N.Y.: AMS Press, 1978.

Monaco, James, ed. Celebrity: Who Gets it, How They Use it, Why it Works. N.Y.: Delta, 1978.

*_____, ed. Media Culture: Television, Radio, Books, Magazines, Newspapers, Movies. N.Y.: Dell, 1978.

Morin, Edgar. L'Esprit du Temps. Two volumes (originally 1962, 1975). Paris: Bernard Grasset, 1975.

_____. "Studies in Mass Communication,"
     Performance 3, I:3 (July-August 1972), 116-130.

*Nachbar, Jack, Deborah Weiser, and John Wright, eds. The Popular
     Culture Reader. Bowling Green: Popular Press, 1978.

*Newcomb, Horace, ed. Television: The Critical View, 2nd edition.
     N.Y.: Oxford, 1979.

_____. TV: The Most Popular Art. Garden City,
     N.Y.: Anchor, 1974.

*Nye, Russel B. The Unembarrassed Muse. N.Y.: Dial, 1970.

Peterson, Richard A. The Production of Culture. Beverly Hills:
     Sage, 1976.

_____. "Where the Two Cultures Meet: Popular
     Culture," Journal of Popular Culture, XI:2 (Fall 1977),
     385-400.

Pool, Ithiel de Sola et als, eds. Handbook of Communications.
     Chicago: Rand McNally, 1973.

Radway, Janice A. "Phenomenology, Linguistics, and Popular
     Culture," Journal of Popular Culture, XII (Summer 1978),
     88-89.

Real, Michael. Mass-Mediated Culture. Englewood Cliffs, N.J.:
     Prentice Hall, 1977.

_____. "Media Theory: Contributions to an Understanding
     of American Mass Communications," American Quarterly, 32:3
     (1980), 238-58.

Rivers, William L., Wallace Thompson, and Michael J. Nyhan, eds.
     Aspen Handbook on the Media. N.Y.: Praeger, 1979.

Rollin, Roger B. "Against Evaluation: The Role of the Critic of
     Popular Culture," Journal of Popular Culture, IX:2 (Fall
     1975), 355-65.

_____. "The Freud Connection: Psychoanalytic Approaches
     to Popular Culture Audience Response," unpublished paper
     presented to the Popular Culture Association, 1980.

Rosenberg, Bernard and David Manning White, eds. Mass Culture
     Revisited. N.Y.: Van Nostrand, 1971.

Salzman, Jack, ed. Prospects (an annual journal of American
     Studies). N.Y.: Burt Franklin, 1974 and yearly.

Sapir, David and Christopher Crocker. The Social Use of Metaphor.
    Philadelphia: U. of Pennsylvania, 1977.

Schecter, Harold, ed. "Focus on Myth and American Popular Art,"
    (special issue), Journal of American Culture, 2:2.

*_____. The New Gods: Psyche and Symbol in Popular
    Art. Bowling Green: Popular Press, 1980.

*_____, and Jonna Gormley Semeiks, eds. Patterns in
    Popular Culture: A Sourcebook for Writers. N.Y.: Harper and
    Row, 1980.

*Schiller, Herbert I. Communications and Cultural Domination.
    White Plains, N.Y.: Pantheon, 1978.

*_____. The Mind Managers. Boston: Beacon, 1973.

*Scholes, Robert. Structuralism in Literature. New Haven: Yale U.,
    1974.

Schwartz, Tony. The Responsive Cord. Garden City, N.Y.: Anchor,
    1974.

*Sklar, Robert. Movie-Made America: A Cultural History of the
    American Movies. N.Y.: Random House, 1976.

_____. "Popular Culture Smokes Dope," American Quarterly,
    27 (August 1975).

_____. Prime-Time America: Life On and Behind the
    Television Screen. N.Y.: Oxford, 1980.

*Spradley, James P. and David McCurdy, eds. Conformity and Conflict:
    Readings in Cultural Anthropology. Boston: Little, Brown,
    4th ed., 1980.

*_____, and Michael A. Rynkiewich. The Nacirema:
    Readings on American Culture. Boston: Little, Brown, 1975.

*Stein, Benjamin. The View From Sunset Boulevard. N.Y.: Doubleday,
    1980.

Sterling, Christopher H. and Timothy Haight, eds. The Mass Media:
    Aspen Guide to Communication Industry Trends. N.Y.: Praeger,
    1978.

Toll, Robert C. On With the Show: The First Century of Show
    Business in America. N.Y.: Oxford, 1976.

*Towsen, John H. Clowns. N.Y.: Dutton, 1978.

Trimmer, Joseph F., ed. "A New Continent of Categories: Popular
     Culture in America," (special issue), Indiana Social Studies
     Quarterly, XXVI:3 (Winter 1973-4).

*Truzzi, Marcello. Sociology and Everyday Life. Englewood Cliffs,
     N.J.: Prentice Hall, 1968.

*Tuchman, Gaye, Arlene Kaplan Daniels, and James Benet, eds.
     Hearth and Home: Images of Women in the Mass Media. N.Y.:
     Oxford, 1978.

*_____. Making News: A Study in the Construction of
     Reality. N.Y.: Free Press, 1978.

*Turner, Victor. Dramas, Fields, and Metaphors: Symbolic Action
     in Human Society. Ithaca, N.Y.: Cornell U., 1975.

*_____. The Ritual Process: Structure and Anti-Structure.
     Ithaca: Cornell U., 1977 (reprint of 1969 ed.).

_____. "Frame, Flow and Reflection: Ritual and Drama as
     Public Liminality," in Michel Benamou and Charles Caramello,
     eds. Performance in Postmodern Culture. Madison: Coda Press,
     1977.

U.S. Civil Rights Commission. Window Dressing on the Set.
     Washington: Government Printing Office, 1977. Updated
     edition, 1979.

Vartanian, Pershing. "Popular Culture Studies: A Problem in
     Socio-Cultural Dynamics," Journal of Popular Culture, XI:1
     (Summer 1977).

*Venturi, Robert, Densise Scott Brown, and Steven Izenour.
     Learning From Las Vegas. Cambridge: MIT Press, 1972, 1977.

Weibel, Kathryn. Mirror, Mirror: Images of Women Reflected in
     Popular Culture. N.Y.: Anchor, 1977.

Wertheim, Arthur F. Radio Comedy. N.Y.: Oxford, 1979.

*Whetmore, Edward J. Mediamerica: Form, Content, and Consequences
     of Mass Communication. Belmont: Wadsworth, 1979.

White, David Manning and John Pendleton, eds. Popular Culture:
     Mirror of American Life. Del Mar: Publishers, Inc., 1977.

White, Hayden. "Structuralism and Popular Culture," Journal of
     Popular Culture, VII (Spring 1974), 759-75.

Williams, Raymond. Communications. London: Penguin, 1976.

_____. "Communications as Cultural Science,"
Journal of Communications, 24:3 (Summer 1974).

_____. The Long Revolution. N.Y.: Columbia U., 1961.

Wilmeth, Don B. "American Popular Entertainment: A Historical
Perspective," Choice, 14 (October 1977), 987-1004.

*Winn, Marie. The Plug-In Drug. N.Y.: Bantam, 1978.

Wise, Gene. "'Paradigm Dramas' in American Studies: A Cultural
and Institutional History of the Movement," American
Quarterly, XXXI:3 (1979).

_____. "Some Elementary Axioms for an American Culture
Studies," Prospects, 4 (1979), 517-47.

*Wood, Michael. America In the Movies; or 'Santa Maria, It Had
Slipped My Mind.' N.Y.: Dell, 1976.

Wright, David E. and Robert Snow. "Consumption as Ritual in the
High Technology Society," in Browne, ed. Ritual and Ceremony
in Popular Culture, 1980.

Supplement to "American Things: A Neglected Material Culture"

BERNARD MERGEN

It is safe to say that the material aspects of American culture are no longer neglected. Several American studies programs now have regular courses that introduce students to objects and artifacts as data for the analysis of American history. Some universities have affiliations with museums that allow students to work with curators on the preservation, research, and interpretation of collections. Many museums are developing new exhibits based on interdisciplinary research that reflect current trends in American studies. These exhibits often are accompanied by publications that can be used in teaching about material culture in the classroom. Among the outstanding examples are Claudia B. Kidwell and Margaret C. Christman, Suiting Everyone: The Democratization of Clothing in America (Washington, D.C.: Smithsonian Institution, 1974); Peter C. Marzio, ed., *A Nation of Nations (N.Y.: Harper & Row, 1976); Joshua C. Taylor, *America as Art (Washington, D.C.: Smithsonian Institution, 1976; republished by Harper & Row, 1979); Patricia Hills, Turn-of-the-Century America (N.Y.: Whitney Museum, 1977); and Perry Duis, *Chicago: Creating New Traditions (Chicago: Chicago Historical Society, 1976).

In addition to the new developments in museum exhibiting, four traditional fields of scholarship have contributed to the definition of material culture studies. As Dr. Skramstad's earlier essay indicated, art and architectural history have provided models for the study of all kinds of material artifacts. From the pioneering work of Lewis Mumford, to James Belasco's Americans on the Road: From Autocamp to Motel, 1910-1945 (Cambridge, Mass.: Massachusetts Institute of Technology Press, 1979), and Jeffrey

Meikle's Twentieth Century Limited: Industrial Design in America,
1925-1939 (Philadelphia: Temple University Press, 1979), critics of
architectural and industrial design have stimulated their readers
to reconsider the   built environment.

The study of technology and technological history has provided a
second model. In this area, the work of Ruth Schwartz Cowan, "The
'Industrial Revolution' in the Home: Household Technology and
Social Change in the Twentieth Century," Technology and Culture, 17
(January 1976); Robert E. Snow and David E. Wright, "Coney Island:
A Case Study in Popular Culture and Technical Change," Journal of
Popular Culture, 9 (Spring 1976); and May N. Stone, "The Plumbing
Paradox: American Attitudes toward Late Nineteenth-Century Domes-
tic Sanitary Arrangements," Winterthur Portfolio, 14 (Autumn 1979),
deserve special mention.

A third source of ideas and methods for the study of material
culture may be found in anthropology and archaeology. James Deetz,
*In Small Things Forgotten: The Archeology of Early American Life
(Garden City, N.Y.: Doubleday Anchor Books, 1977), is the foremost
example of an archaeologist working with American historial materials to provide new insights into early American culture.
Historical archaeology has contributed to the history of American
slavery, as John Otto's essay, "Artifacts and Status Differences,"
in Research Strategies in Historical Archaeology, edited by Stanley
South (N.Y.: Academic Press, 1977), makes clear. Miles Richardson's The Human Mirror: Material and Spatial Images of Man (Baton
Rouge: Louisiana State University Press, 1974), contains several
excellent essays on theory and methods of analyzing objects in
their cultural contexts.

The fourth field that has contributed significantly to material
culture studies is popular culture. The three-volume Handbook of
American Popular Culture, edited by M. Thomas Inge (Westport,
Conn.: Greenwood Press, 1979, 1980, 1981), contains bibliographical
essays on topics such as comic art, advertising, circus and outdoor
entertainment, and games and toys that are replete with references
to books and articles using objects to study their particular
subject. Another useful contribution in the area of mass-produced
objects is Robert Atwan, Donald McQuade, and John W. Wright,
*Edsels, Luckies, & Frigidaires: Advertising the American Way
(N.Y.: Dell Publishing Company, 1979).

As a new, formal field of material culture studies emerges from
these older disciplines, we can anticipate attempts to define the
field. Many of the publications of the American Association for
State and Local History, such as Robert A. Weinstein and Larry
Booth's Collection, Use, and Care of Historical Photographs
(Nashville, Tennessee: AASLH, 1976), and Rudy J. Favretti and Joy
P. Favretti's *Landscapes and Gardens for Historic Buildings:
Reproducing and Recreating Authentic Settings (Nashville: AASLH,
1978), are extremely useful introductions to the practical problems
that material objects create. They discuss such issues as the

collection, storage, and interpretation of objects for the public. Thomas J. Schlereth attempts to provide an overview of the developments in the emerging field in his useful essay, "Material Culture Studies in America: Notes Toward a Historical Perspective," in Material History Bulletin, 8 (1979).

A philosophical approach is taken by Paul J. Nagy in "Thoughts and Things: Pragmatism, Material Culture, and the Celebration of Ordinary Experience," The Southern Quarterly, 15 (January 1977). Stephan Bann shows how objects take on different meanings in different exhibit contexts in a stimulating essay, "Historical Text and Historical Object: The Poetics of the Musee de Cluny," in History and Theory, 17 (October 1978). Three brilliant examples of how to do material culture analysis are provided by Kenneth Ames, "Meaning in Artifacts: Hall Furnishings in Victorian America," Journal of Interdisciplinary History, 9 (Summer 1978); Clifford Clark, "Domestic Architecture as an Index to Social History: The Romantic Revival and the Cult of Domesticity in America," Journal of Interdisciplinary History, 7 (Summer 1976); and Roger L. Welsch, "Front Door, Back Door," Natural History, 88 (June-July 1979). An excellent anthology of essays, *Material Culture and the Study of American Life has been edited by Ian M. G. Quimby (N.Y.: Norton, 1978).

A Revision of "History, Anthropology, and the American Indian"

WILCOMB. E. WASHBURN

The attempt to provide a good general history of the American Indian has been made by Wilcomb E. Washburn in his *The Indian in America (New York: Harper and Row, 1975), and by George Pierre Castile, North American Indians: An Introduction to the Chichimeca (New York: McGraw-Hill, 1979). Washburn's volume, in the New American Nation Series, attempts to organize the vast panorama of Indian history in a roughly chronological fashion, but distinguishes three periods of Indian-white interaction: when the Indian was independent, when he existed on a plane of equal power with the white man, and after he had become dependent. In addition to the chronological exposition of Indian-white interaction, a series of chapters attempts to pull together some of the unities of Indian character and culture. Castile, a young anthropologist, presents a breezy but sophisticated account of the Indian from 20,000 years before the present to the latest street demonstrations of Indian radicals. The author avoids some of the "metaphysical wrangles of anthropological theory" and skillfully illustrates many of his points about Indian social structure and the like with examples of non-Indian history.

Another general account with even broader coverage is contained in Gary B. Nash, *Red, White, and Black: The Peoples of Early America (Englewood Cliffs, N.J.: Prentice-Hall, 1974), in which the author attempts to tell the story of how blacks and Indians interacted with European settlers throughout the Colonial period. Nash tries to see Indians and blacks in terms of their own perceptions and interests, rather than in terms of those of their white conquerors. To some extent he succeeds, although all historians who try to write from the point of view of Indians and

blacks are necessarily constrained to see those points of view
through the record left by white observers. A brief summary of
Indian history, that by William T. Hagan, first published in
Chicago's History of American Civilization series in 1961, has
been revised and reissued in 1979. Vine Deloria retains his
reputation as the most famous Indian spokesman, adding to his
previously published work God is Red (New York: Grosset & Dunlop,
1973), and The Metaphysics of Modern Existence (New York: Harper
and Row, 1979); the latter is his interpretation of his reading of
non-Indian philosophers.

Francis P. Prucha is still a leading exponent of government policy
toward the Indian. His American Indian Policy in Crisis: Chris-
tian Reformers and the Indian, 1865-1900 (Norman: University of
Oklahoma Press, 1976), Americanizing the American Indians:
Writings by the 'Friends of the Indian' 1880-1900 (Cambridge,
Mass.: Harvard, 1973), and his edition of D. S. Otis's The Dawes
Act and the Allotment of Indian Lands (Norman: University of
Oklahoma Press, 1973), deal with the disastrous policy of the last
half of the nineteenth century when the Indian tribal structure
was nearly destroyed and the Indian land base reduced. The
importance of the "friends of the Indian" in bringing about that
result is also emphasized in Wilcomb E. Washburn, The Assault on
Indian Tribalism: The General Allotment Law (Dawes Act) of 1887
(Philadelphia: Lippincott, 1975). Another new work is Prucha's
The Churches and the Indian Schools, 1888-1912 (Lincoln: University of Nebraska Press, 1979).

Other books on government policy toward the Indian that have
filled important gaps are Robert A. Trennert, Jr., Alternative to
Extinction: Federal Indian Policy and the Beginnings of the
Reservation System, 1846-51 (Philadelphia: Temple University Press,
1975); Ronald N. Satz, *American Indian Policy in the Jacksonian
Era (Lincoln: University of Nebraska Press, 1975); and Edmund
Jefferson Danziger, Jr., Indians and Bureaucrats: Administering
the Reservation Policy During the Civil War (Urbana: University
of Illinois Press, 1974). Government policy of a more recent
vintage has been ably dealt with by Kenneth R. Philp, *John
Collier's Crusade for Indian Reform, 1920-1954 (Tucson: University of Arizona Press, 1977). A book mentioned in the earlier
article as being prepared for publication was Bernard W. Sheehan,
*Seeds of Extinction: Jefferson Philanthropy and the American
Indian (New York: Norton, 1974).

Alden Vaughan's favorable view of the Puritans in their relationship with the Indians in his New England Frontier, cited in the
earlier article, was challenged directly and massively by Francis
Jennings, whose *The Invasion of America: Indians, Colonialism,
and the Cant of Conquest (New York: Norton, 1976), was a slashing
attack on the honor and honesty of the pious progenitors of New
England. Jennings' book seemingly swept the field with its
thesis, which echoed a sentiment prevalent in America as it
wrestled with its Vietnam experience.

Tribal histories continue to pour from the presses with undimi-
nished vigor. Two books dealing with the same tribe illustrate
the process. James A. Clifton's The Prairie People: Continuity
and Change in Potawatomi Indian Culture, 1665-1965 (Lawrence:
Regents Press of Kansas, 1977), is a massive account of how the
Potawatomi--particularly the Prairie Band of Potawatomi, today
located near Topeka, Kansas--have adapted to the various challen
ges confronting them. Using the massive historical evidence that
remains and applying an anthropological perspective to this
material, Clifton demonstrates more clearly than anyone before him
how Potawatomi culture and life, particularly patterns of leadership, have been affected by the forced changes that the tribe has
experienced. R. David Edmunds's The Potawatomis: Keepers of the
Fire (Norman: University of Oklahoma Press, 1978), won the Parkman
Prize of the Society of American Historians for its smooth chronological account of the men and events that affected the tribe
until their removal from the Great Lakes area in the 1830s.
Edmund's historical account is little influenced by anthropological insights.

The student of tribal histories should consult the Newberry
Library's Center for the History of the American Indian series of
tribal and regional bibliographies, of which eighteen have been
published as of the time of this writing. These brief, handy
bibliographies, written by leading experts in the field, are
published by the Indiana University Press for the Newberry Library.

In the history of ideas, perhaps the most provocative book to
emerge in the period was Robert Berkhofer, *The White Man's
Indian: Images of the American Indian from Columbus to the
Present (New York: Random, 1979). Berkhofer spends several
hundred pages pointing out how the white man misconstrued and
misconceived the nature and character of the Indian, but concludes
that the Indian ultimately conformed to the white man's flawed
image! A more massive attempt to deal with the image of the
Indian in England in the sixteenth and seventeenth centuries is
H. C. Porter's The Inconstant Savage: England and the North
American Indian, 1500-1660 (London: Duckworth, 1979). However,
this effort by a Cambridge scholar is flawed by the tedious and
uncritical character of many of the glossies on those writers--
including Shakespeare and Sir Thomas More--who reflected a
knowledge of explorers' accounts of the American Indian.

Perhaps the most important book concerned with the idea of the
Indian published since the earlier article is Richard Slotkin,
Regeneration Through Violence: The Mythology of the American
Frontier, 1600-1860 (Middletown: Wesleyan University Press, 1973).
Slotkin's study deals particularly with Indian captivity narra-
tives and the light they throw on the white American's perception
of his own character and destiny. The reader seeking to delve
deeper into American captivity narratives may wish to consult the
Narratives of North American Captivities, 311 titles in 111
volumes selected and arranged by Wilcomb E. Washburn (New York:

Garland Publishing, Inc.). The collection, published throughout the 1970s, is expected to be complete in 1980.

One of the most exciting and novel interpretations of the Indian's relationship to his environment is Calvin Martin, Keepers of the Game: Indian-Animal Relationships and the Fur Trade (Berkeley: University of California Press, 1978). The book is a forerunner to Martin's proposed study of the disease factors in American history, a little studied subject of immense importance. For the student who wants to get an overview of the role of archeologists in uncovering the Indian past, Gordon R. Willey and Jeremy A. Sabloff, A History of American Archeology (San Francisco: W. H. Freeman, 1974, with new revised edition scheduled for publication in 1980), is recommended.

"Communal History in America": An Addendum

ROBERT S. FOGARTY

In the few years since the publication of "Communal History in America" there has been a steady flow of books and articles about utopianism. A new journal, Alternative Futures, edited by Alexandra Aldridge and Meritt Abrash, now serves as a critical clearinghouse for new research, for reviews, and for bibliographic notes. It is an interdisciplinary journal that publishes articles on utopian literature and thought, communal history and social experiments, utopian/dystopian science fiction, and non-technical futures research.

With the publication of Alternative Futures we have a necessary step in the definition of a field of inquiry variously called futures or utopian studies, but it is with the publication of a major synthetic work such as Utopian Thought in the Western World, by Frank E. and Fritzie Manuel (Cambridge, Mass.: Harvard University Press, 1979), that we can see the range of possibilities subsumed under the title utopian. The Manuels have long been interested in the intellectual sources of utopian thought; their latest massive volume begins with More and ends with Marx. The scope of their work is impressive, but equally impressive is a slim volume by John F. C. Harrison, The Second Coming: Popular Millenarianism 1780-1850 (New Brunswick, N.J.: Rutgers University Press, 1979), which traces the prophetic tradition in England and examines the popular and folk religions generated by Richard Brothers and Joanne Southcott in Britain and by the Shakers and Mormons in America.

Comparative studies in utopian history are bound to increase as scholars look beyond local history to understand the philosophical

and religious sources of experimental communities such as the
Swedish colony at Bishop Hill, Illinois or the Fourierist inspired
phalanxes. For example, Christopher Johnson's Utopian Communities
in France: Cabet and the Icarians, 1839-1851 (Ithaca, N.Y.:
Cornell University Press, 1974), is an indispensable study for
anyone interested in understanding the American offshoots of that
movement. And the most significant study of American communal
groups in recent years employs a comparative framework. Laurence
Veysey's *The Communal Experience (Chicago: University of Chicago
Press, 1978), chronicles the twin impulses of mysticism and
anarchism in the Vedanta ashrams and at the Ferrer Colony at
Stelton, New Jersey.

Although the international and comparative dimensions will play a
prominent part in future research, there are still many areas of
American utopian history to be explored. Charles LeWarne's
examination of communal and cooperative groups in the Pacific
Northwest, *Utopias on Puget Sound, 1885-1915 (Seattle: University
of Washington Press, 1978), is a detailed study of anarchist and
socialist colonies founded at the turn of the century. Dolores
Hayden's brilliant *Seven American Utopias (Cambridge, Mass.:
M.I.T. Press, 1976), looks at communal architecture and the
building processes communities used to give expression to their
cooperative ideals. Hayden's work broke new ground, and additional
work on the use of space by communards is sure to follow.

One would have thought that little more could be written about the
Shakers, but June Sprigg has captured their sensibility and their
practical feel for objects in her beautiful *By Shaker Hands (New
York: Knopf, 1975). And John Ott has given us a brief history of
one community in his guidebook, Hancock Shaker Village (Pittsfield,
Mass.: Shaker Community, 1976). Further work on the Shakers was
aided by the publication of the two-volume annotated bibliography,
Shaker Literature, by Mary L. Richmond (Hanover, N.H.: University
Press of New England, 1976). Greenwood Press has just published
my own Dictionary of American Communal and Utopian History which
contains sketches of 150 utopians, histories of 50 colonies, and
a checklist of communal settlements from 1776 to 1919. Such
studies necessarily draw on older works, but increasingly there is
a body of contemporary scholarship that is revisionist in tone and
temper.

Three such revisionist works have been published since the last
bibliographic essay. Robert Thomas's psycho-history of Oneida's
John Humphrey Noyes, The Man Who Would Be Perfect (Philadelphia:
University of Pennsylvania Press, 1977), casts Noyes within the
context of his family and his youthful struggles. Klaus Wust's
The Saint Adventurers of the Virginia Frontier (Edinburg, Va.:
Shenandoah History Publishers, 1977), throws new light on the
controversies between Conrad Beissel and the Eckerlin brothers
over control at Ephrata, while Kenneth Roemer's The Obsolete
Necessity (Kent, Ohio: Kent State University Press, 1976), is a
new look at utopian fiction of the Bellamy generation and suggests

that these writers feared the social upheavals of their age and tried to escape it through utopian fantasy. Roemer uncovered a whole host of novels from the late nineteenth century and Lyman Tower Sargent's bibliography of British and American utopian fiction materials suggests that scholars have only begun to explore the tip of the iceberg we now call science fiction. Research on literary fantasies is growing and we are just beginning to see some isolated studies of contemporary communal groups, such as Hugh Gardner's *The Children of Prosperity (New York: St. Martin's Press, 1978), a useful study of thirteen rural communes founded in the 1960s.

The events at Jonestown, the demise of Synanon, and the rise of the Unification Church are all still open subjects. Much has been written about communal history in the last few years, and if current scholarly interest continues at the same pace additional revisions to this bibliography will be in order.

Regional Studies on the Chicago Model: Since 1975

THOMAS J. SCHLERETH

In the five-year period since the publication of the previous essay, so much excellent scholarship on Chicago's cultural history has surfaced that a brief sequel is appropriate. As in the preceding article, I have confined my review of recent literature to research dealing with topics from the 1870s to the 1920s, the period in which the most convincing case can be made for studying Chicago as a striking microcosm of the nation's political, economic, literary, social, cultural, and artistic development.[1] I have argued the validity of this thesis in an article, "America, 1871-1919: A View of Chicago," American Studies, 17 (Fall 1976). My insistence in that essay, as in this one, on a cross-disciplinary perspective to the study of Chicago received support from Perry Duis's survey, Chicago: Creating New Traditions, a profusely illustrated exhibition catalog written to accompany the Chicago Historical Society's Bicentennial exhibit of the same name.[2] Duis and I agree that the principal areas of Chicago's cultural history spanning the years between the Great Fire and the Great War are: politics and reform; industrial, transportation and merchandising activity; literary realism; and innovations in architecture and city planning.

Neighborhoods and ethnicity have always been critical ingredients in Chicago's political history. Following the national trend among urban historians who are examining the city in microcosm, recent research on Chicago has focused particularly on several south- and west-side neighborhoods. Glen Holt and Dominic Pacyga have provided us with the best introductory overview, *Chicago: A Historical Guide To The Neighborhoods: The Loop and the South Side, (Chicago: Chicago Historical Society, 1979), that analyzes fourteen communities using the 1909 edition of the Rand-McNally New Standard Map of Chicago as a base map.[3] The primer also includes a perceptive use of historical photography (Holt was the historian who researched the photography used in the Meyer and Wade volume, Chicago: Growth of a Metropolis, cited in the previous essay) and detailed economic and social statistics. One interesting use that can be made of the Holt/Pacyga volume is to have students compare it to Albert Hunter's Symbolic Communities: The Persistence and Change of Chicago's Local Communities (Chicago: University of Chicago Press, 1974), a work that reexamines most of the neighborhoods originally defined by Edward L. Burchand, District Fact Book For Seventy-five Chicago Local Communities (1935) and others of the Chicago School of Urban Sociology. In a general fashion, Hunter attempts to identify those things that have remained constant in the Chicago neighborhoods and those that have changed, such as the trend towards racial rather than ethnic segregation.

While the detailed, interpretive studies of many individual Chicago neighborhoods are still lodged largely in the primary sources, as suggested in Frank Jewell's section on "Neighborhoods" in the Annotated Bibliography of Chicago History (Chicago: Chicago Historical Society, 1979), portents of a "new" local history have already appeared. Two of south-side Chicago's famous neighborhoods--Prairie Avenue and Hyde Park--have been examined with painstaking research. Victor Dyer has compiled a model bibliographical guide to the city's most fashionable millionaire's row of the 1880s, and Jean Block has attempted to read the communal history of Hyde Park from 1856 to 1910 through its extant housing stock.[4] Recent research into the city's west-side communities runs the gamut of the economic and social status prevalent in the nineteenth-century city. Seminar participants interested in social mobility and ethnic and racial identity could read, in concert, sociologist Richard Sennett's Families Against The City: Middle Class Homes of Industrial Chicago, 1872-1890[5], and compare it to Ira Berkow's oral history of Jewish immigrant life around an open-air market, Maxwell Street: Survival in a Bazaar (New York: Doubleday, 1979); and labor historian William Adelman's on-site explorations of the working-class ghettos in the Pilsen area and the police and labor violence in the Haymarket.[6]

A future area of local history study into which enterprising students might venture is the study of the processes of suburbanization. This complex phenomenon has not been studied on a community-by-community level since the initial research by the Park-Burgess school in the 1920s. One tentative model worthy of further testing has been proposed by Barbara M. Posadas, "A Home In the Country: Suburbanization in Jefferson Township, 1870-1889," Chicago History, 7 (Fall 1978).[7]

As in most American cities, ethnicity was often a component in Chicago's suburbanization process. The flight of the south-side Irish still farther south and west is a migration still to be chronicled and interpreted. At present, most students of Chicago ethnicity continue to study their subjects in situ. For similar classroom analysis, we now have several excellent documentary collections of social scientific data, an anthology of first-rate essays on most of the major ethnic communities, and a handful of new monographic studies on what might be called "the Catholic ethnics."

The City of Chicago's Department of Development and Planning provides two documentary sourcebooks, each of which can be adapted to an assortment of exercises introducing students to basic concepts in quantitative history, particularly demography. The People of Chicago: Who We Are and Who We Have Been: Census Data on Foreign Stock and Race, 1837-1970, is basically a census-by-census analysis of the city's population by country of origin with a helpful "Mother Tongue Addendum." The detailed footnotes, offering the necessary qualifications that must be made about the demographic data, are, in themselves, a valuable teaching tool. If The People of Chicago's principal value is in its statistical data, then the major value of Historic City: The Settlement of Chicago is its cartographic materials. Using a series of fold-out, color-coded maps that accompany the paperback, one can chart the internal migrations of twenty-one ethnic populations in 1870, 1900 and 1920. Imposed on a 1970 street pattern of Chicago, the maps also show changes in built-up areas, shorelines, railroad networks, and rivers and harbors. [8]

In *The Ethnic Frontier: Essays in the History of Group Survival in Chicago and the Midwest (Grand Rapids, Michigan: Wm. B. Eerdmans, 1977), Melvin G. Holli and Peter d'A. Jones have assembled the best current scholarly introduction to a wide range of issues dealing with Chicago ethnicity: the role of ethnic leaders, ethnicity and housing, and the inner dynamics of specific ethnic communities. Two of the anthology's authors, Edward R. Kantowicz and Edward H. Mazur, have also done new monographic studies on the city's Poles and Jews, respectively.[9] Inasmuch as many of Chicago's "meltable" and "unmeltable" ethnics were Catholics, a recent study by James M. Sanders, The Education of an Urban Minority: Catholics in Chicago, 1833-1965 (New York: Oxford University Press, 1977), fills a significant gap in the story.[10]

Barbara C. Schaaf and Charles Fanning provide equally valuable works on one of the city's most highly visible of Catholic sub-cultures, the Chicago Irish.[11] Both Schaaf and Fanning propose an interpretation of Irish urban ward politics in the nineteenth century, deploying the Dunne/Dooley persona as primary evidence. Political scientist Michael McCarthy, "On Bosses, Reformers and Urban Growth: Some Suggestions For A Political Typology of American Cities," Journal of Urban History, 4 (1977), pp. 29-38, offers other explanations, using comparative data from Chicago and New York. McCarthy argues that some cities have had political machines outside the political boundaries of the city. When the middle class becomes overwhelmingly suburban, as he believes it did in Chicago (e.g., another instance of a research hypothesis on suburbs waiting to be validated or disproved), then the nucleus for a reform movement is missing and bossism and machine politics prevail.

In the past five years, however, students of Chicago politics have been less interested in bosses than in reformers. Two new emphases emerge from the recent literature: women as urban reformers and slum clearance as urban reform. John P. Rousmaniere's short summary essay, "Cultural Hybrid in the Slums: The College Woman and the Settlement House, 1889-1894," College Settlement Association, 22 (1970), pp. 45-66, is the place to begin, followed by new studies by Kenneth L. Kusmer, Kristin S. McGrath, and Thomas Philpott.[12] With Philpott's careful cross-disciplinary analyses of both the reformers' social and political philosophy and the physical structures they built to implement that policy of social control, we have an excellent model on which to conduct similar studies of the urban built environment. Guy Szuberla has also demonstrated this approach in his argument that settlement house architecture such as the Hull House of Irving and Allen Pond reflected a strong desire to "Americanize" the immigrant.[13] A parallel theme echoes through Devereux Bowly's The Poorhouse: Subsidized Housing in Chicago, 1895-1976 (Carbondale, Illinois: Southern Illinois University, 1978).

Another mainstay of cross-disciplinary research, particularly in the field of American studies, has been the exploration of the reciprocal interrelationship between history and literature. In the context of specific courses on Chicago, this has meant using Chicago authors and their works as perspectives on the city's cultural history, and when studying the creative corpus of Chicago writers, examining the historical milieu in which their literary achievement took place.[14] Recent research continues to validate the approach when using the fiction, poetry, and prose writing of the 1871-1919 era. Although no new major syntheses have appeared to displace the major literary interpretations of the period (e.g., Duffey, Kramer, Duncan), four short articles on the city's social novels by Ann Douglas, Charles Fanning, Anthony Grosch, and Carl Smith should be added to any bibliography on Chicago fiction.[15]

Also of value is a new bibliography of fiction about Illinois describing works by author, title, subject, and place name. Prepared by Thomas L. Kilpatrick and Patsy-Rose Hoshiko, Illinois! Illinois! An Annotated Bibliography of Fiction (Metuchen, N.J.: The Scarecrow Press, 1979), contains over 1200 annotated entries on novels dealing with Chicago. On the important interrelationship between Chicago journalism, literature, and social reform, we now have John Erickson's dissertation, "Newspapers and Social Values: Chicago Journalism, 1890-1910" (University of Illinois at Urbana, 1973). On the interconnection between the first of Chicago's and the nation's little literary magazines and the intellectual history of fin-de-siecle America, we can learn from Wendy L. Clauson Schlereth's history of ideas contained in her dissertation, "The Chapbook: A Journal of American Intellectual Life, 1894-1898" (University of Iowa, 1980). Finally, in the past five years important reassessments of four major participants in the so-called

"Chicago Renaissance" have been published. Jonathan Yardley has done the now standard biography of Ring Lardner while Robert Conrow has updated information about fellow newspaperman/poet Eugene Field.[16] In Henry B. Fuller of Chicago, The Ordeal of A Genteel Realist in Ungenteel America, Bernard Bowron establishes the literary and historical context for this much misunderstood novelist, editorialist, and member of Poetry magazine which, in turn, has been given a thoroughly researched, in-depth study by Ellen Williams in her analysis of Harriet Monroe and the Poetry Renaissance: The First Ten Years of Poetry, 1912-1922.[17] Williams notes how Monroe, through family connections and personal tenacity, gained access to the city board rooms and corporate offices. Seeking to combine philanthropy and poetry, young Harriet convinced a hundred fellow Chicagoans (mostly businessmen) to subscribe fifty dollars a year for five years to support her magazine. A Philadelphia paper sneered at Chicago for using "the proceeds of pork for the promotion of poetry," but this mode of cultural underwriting was more the rule than the exception during the 1871-1919 era when most of the city's major cultural institutions were founded.

The individuals who were "movers and shakers" in both worlds—business and art—have received some attention in the past decade. Perhaps the best overview, strictly in terms of business history, is a careful statistical and demographic study by Jocelyn Maynard Ghent and Frederic Cople Jaher of 1186 members of the Chicago business elite, two thirds of whom made their own fortunes in manufacturing, meatpacking, and merchandising.[18] An important area of Chicago business history that I almost totally neglected in my initial review of the literature was merchandising, particularly mail-order selling. I now use reprint catalogs from Sears, Roebuck and Montgomery Ward in my Chicago course and I have suggested the range of American studies teaching techniques that can be developed from these rich, versatile primary sources that once were the arbiters of taste, culture, and life-style of much of rural and small-town America.[19] Although the Montgomery Ward firm lacks a substantial historical treatment, there is a detailed study of Sears, Roebuck by Boris Emmet and John Jeuck, Catalogues and Counters: A History of Sears, Roebuck & Company (Chicago: University of Chicago Press, 1950).

Lawrence P. Bachman's perceptive reassessment of Julius Rosenwald (probably the most astute Sears executive, 1862-1922) illustrates, however, that the current interpretive trend in the historical study of Chicago businessmen emphasizes less their corporate acumen than the purpose, scope, and impact of their cultural philanthropy.[20] I have explored this intriguing problem in American cultural history through the career of a single Chicagoan, Charles Hutchinson, then through one cultural activity (music) over a single generation. Helen Lefkowitz Horowitz has surveyed the entire generation from the 1880s to 1917 in several arenas of cultural life.[21] Several of the Chicago institutions analyzed by Horowitz, The Newberry Library, the Fine Arts Building, and the Art Institute, have been studied.[22] In its centennial year, the

Art Institute received both internal and external reevaluation.[23] There is now an excellent interpretive digest of "The Chicago Little Theatre, 1912-1917," by Homer N. Abegglen, in The Old Northwest, 3 (June 1977), as well as a bit of pioneering spade work by James S. Newell (unpublished Ph.D. dissertation, Wayne State University, 1973) on "The Development and Growth of the Kenneth Sawyer Goodman Memorial Theatre and School of Drama, Chicago, Illinois, 1925-1971."

Chicago is currently home for fifty-eight colleges and universities, many of which have their origins in the nineteenth century. Inasmuch as educational history can be an excellent entry point into the history of ideas, the University of Chicago serves as an intellectual history laboratory for the exploration of American research and scholarly publishing in sociology[24], law[25], education[26], religion[27], political science[28], physics[29], and history.[30] Also available is an anthology of selections from the papers of the university's first eight chief executives,[31] and a photographic interpretation of the university's architectural environment.[32]

Architecture in Chicago, which the British Architectural Review recently called "the New World's most architectural city," continues to be a source of enormous historical interest to scholars, preservationists, and building buffs of every sort. The AR devoted its entire October 1977 issue to both a historical ("How Chicago Happened") and a contemporary ("Change of Heart in Process City") appraisal of the city's built environment. A particularly valuable exercise that teachers can initiate that dissects the streetscape as a historical landscape is the perceptive block-by-block analysis these British architects give to "Halsted Street: A Journal Through Average Chicago." William T. Brown's *Architecture Evolving: An Illinois Sage (Chicago: Tech'em Inc., 1976), offers similar teaching strategies using the Chicago context. Brown's primer was especially prepared for "those who are not conversant with sophisticated architectural issues but who wish to gain an introduction to a new body of knowledge and who may or may not live daily among the architectural monuments." The book, which covers the three basic Chicago architectural schools--Commercial, Prairie, and Miesan--is intended, in Brown's estimate, "as much for those in the rural suburbs as for those in the metropolis."

In the first and last of the three major Chicago architectural movements--Commercial and Miesan or, as they are sometimes labelled, Chicago School I (1880-1920) and Chicago School III (1938-)--the majority of recent research has been on the modern era. With the exception of a brief essay by Jack Tager that explores the interrelationship of business entrepreneurs, real estate speculators, and architectural firms[33], and two delightful, nostalgic picture books of "lost Chicago" assembled by David Lowe[34], the major historiographical focus--Nory Miller called it "a war of ideas"-- has been by the modernists about the modernists.

The "war" Miller refers to is a "battle of the books": two books, to be exact, that grew out of two major architectural exhibitions mounted in 1977. One is by Miesan Oswald W. Grube, 100 Years of

Architecture in Chicago, another by revisionist Stuart E. Cohen, labelled Chicago Architects.[35] While the nuances of this major split in Chicago architectural historiography are too numerous and complicated to narrate here, the basic positions of the two exhibitions can be summarized by noting where they opened in Chicago.[36] The functionalist, rationalist, technologically minded 100 Years of Architecture was housed in Chicago's Museum of Contemporary Art; the Chicago Architects' paean to the eclectic, the romantic, and the historic appeared in the city's art moderne Time and Life Building.

Grube and associates survey the triumph of a rational aesthetic, particularly as revealed in the evolution of the Chicago skyscraper. This aesthetic insists that the logical facade of a building should be a visual expression of how it is held up and the logical plan of a building should be uninterrupted, generic space. That is to say, Chicago, and hence modern, architecture should be viewed primarily as an expression of modern technology. 100 Years also claims to delineate this historical development over a century, thereby showing the "continuity of structure and form" between two architectural schools: 1871 to 1893, and 1938 to the present.

Stuart Cohen, on the other hand, is primarily interested in rescuing from oblivion the "city's unknown and forgotten architecture." Thus Chicago Architects is a useful review of those Midwestern builders (George Frederick Keck, Andrew Rebori, Emery Stanford Hall, Howard Van Doren Shaw) who are mentioned only briefly by historical surveyors. Moreover, Cohen's appreciation of those whom John Entgenza has called "the minor poets" (men such as Hugh Garden, Irving Pond, Dwight Perkins, Henry Ives Cobb) is a definite contribution to our historical knowledge and a fine example of detailed archival research.

Within this framework, Cohen's sixteen-page essay (the remainder of the book contains superb illustrations) sets out to document that work of Chicago architects "which is most unknown today because it represents a diversity of formal, spatial, symbolic and technological ideas which cannot be discussed as the work of a school." Rather, it is, claims Cohen, "the architecture of a private experience, mostly houses, schools, and churches, rather than large corporate or government commissions." Although Cohen insists that his argument "does not relate either in ideology or chronological sequence to the cleansed history of Chicago architecture," he certainly deploys the structural-functional tradition as his polemical foil. These two paperbacks are useful battle reports in Chicago's escalating architectural cold war; as such they can be pitted against each other in the classroom, dramatizing for students the fact that architectural history is not always the tranquil, noncontroversial discipline that its critics sometimes claim.

Of course, one Chicago architect about whom there has always been abundant controversy is Frank Lloyd Wright; understandably, materials continue to pour forth from a cadre of investigators who probe the master's writings and buildings. For studying

Wright's Chicago years there is now a paperback reprint of Grant
Manson's *Frank Lloyd Wright to 1910 (New York: Van Nostrand
Reinhold, 1958); Robert C. Twombly has rewritten and expanded his
earlier biography, Frank Lloyd Wright: An Interpretive Biography
(New York: Harper & Row, 1973), and issued it under a new title,
Frank Lloyd Wright: His Life and His Architecture (New York: John
Wiley & Sons, 1979); and a detailed Plan for Restoration and
Adaptive Use of the Frank Lloyd Wright Home and Studio (Chicago:
University of Chicago Press, 1979). The Plan, in addition to being
a significant contribution to the study of the early years of the
Prairie School, is an exceptional example of the painstaking tech-
niques of restoration archaeology. It reveals the exceedingly
complex series of changes (most made by Wright himself) in the
fabric of the house and studio between 1889 and 1957.

With regard to Wright and the Prairie School, the following works
make the teacher-scholar's task a bit easier. William Allin
Storrer traveled over 78,000 miles in search of Wright's total
oeuvre and now, in a newly revised second edition, thinks he has
finally compiled it.[37] On a more local level, Paul E. Sprague has
prepared a new Guide to Frank Lloyd Wright and Prairie School
Architecture in Oak Park (Oak Park, Ill.: Landmarks Commission,
1976), while Thomas A. Heinz edits the Frank Lloyd Wright Newsletter from Oak Park. Robert L. Sweeney's Frank Lloyd Wright: An
Annotated Bibliography (Los Angeles: Hennessey & Ingalls, 1978),
now supercedes Kenneth Starosciak's compendium mentioned in the
previous essay.

If one wishes to teach Chicago architectural development through
arch individualists like Wright, there is a parallel approach that
uses archetypal buildings. Recent scholarship on single structures
includes: John Vinci on Sullivan's Stock Exchange Trading Room,
James O'Gorman on H. H. Richardson's warehouse for Marshall Field,
and Harry Price on Sullivan's Auditorium Building.[38] Another
superb source of background information, in addition to elevation
drawings, floor plans, and photographs, are the brochures prepared
by the Commission on Chicago Historical and Architectural Landmarks
on individual Chicago sites, structures, and districts.[39] The
Commission has also taken the lead in pointing out a direction in
urban architectural history that I would predict will dominate the
energies of many researchers in the 1980s: nineteenth- and
twentieth-century vernacular housing. Chapter Two, "Chicago Houses
and Styles," of a new Commission publication by Linda Legner is a
fine introductory field-guide to simple row houses and storefronts,
ordinary greystones and Beaux-Arts apartments, unpretentious
bungalows, and ballon-frames.[40]

Such ubiquitous, prefabricated housing stock, erected block-by-
block by real estate developers and contractors, now makes up the
bulk of Chicago's seventy-five neighborhoods. To begin any
comprehensive analysis of this extensive laboratory of urban
material culture, I urge students to read a short essay by J. B.
Jackson, the dean of American landscape historians;[41] followed by
Irving Cutler's fine geographical work, Chicago: Metropolis of the

Mid-Continent; and then Brian Berry's social, economic, and demographic portrait, Chicago: Transformation of an Urban System.[42]

Planners, of course, develop urban systems. In turn, planners and
their plans are important indices to urban history. Daniel Burnham's comprehensive 1909 Plan for the city of Chicago continues to
attract the most attention from scholars. In the definitive
biography of Burnham, Thomas S. Hines assesses Burnham the planner
(finding him a perfect example of David Noble's "paradox of progressive thought"), while Cynthia Field concentrates primarily on
Burnham's Plan.[43] Others have explored the relation of Chicago
businessmen and the Plan; of Burnham and Fredrick Law Olmsted, the
other nationally known planner working in Chicago (e.g., Riverside
and Jackson Park); and of the deficiencies of the Plan, particularly its short-sightedness concerning the future impact of the
automobile.[44] In addition to the historians of city planning,
geographers and social historians have also begun interpreting the
significance of the placement, type, and size of parks, a key
hallmark of the Burnham Plan.[45]

As part of a seventieth anniversary of the publication of the Plan,
The Art Institute of Chicago (where, in the Burnham Library, the
bulk of the manuscript, graphic, and documentary data on the Plan
is housed) published an excellent exhibition catalog, The Plan of
Chicago, 1909-1979, edited by John Zukowsky (Chicago: The Art
Institute of Chicago, 1979). This work contains, in addition to
two interpretive essays, a valuable checklist of the Plan's
drawings. In conjunction with the Plan exhibition, a symposium
on "The Plan of Chicago: Its Past and Future" took place in the
Spring of 1980, the results of which are published in the special
issue (April 1980) of the Inland Architect.

Burnham openly acknowledged his debt to the 1893 plan of the
World's Columbian Exposition, for which he served as Director of
Works. Hence studying the Chicago World Fairs is a final teaching
technique to be employed in an interdisciplinary course in American
urban studies. With the monographs by David Burg and R. Reid
Badger,[46] and new articles by other researchers,[47] we have almost
total coverage of the 1893 extravaganza. The "Century of Progress,"
while on a scale similar to the Columbian Exposition, has, however,
generated far fewer publications. The best of the lot are articles:
a general introduction by Cathy and Richard Cahan, an account of
discrimination against blacks and the resulting protest, and a
brief assessment of the 1933 Fair's art moderne architecture.[48]

In the past half decade, Chicago studies of the 1871-1919 period
continued to exhibit many of the characteristics of that particular
historical era--rapid growth, exuberant vitality, and genuine diversity. Contemporary research, teaching, and writing about
Chicago during this period has broadened our understanding of how
the numerous innovations and reforms in social and communal life,
literature, and architecture that were pioneered in Chicago had an
impact and a significance that went far beyond the city's limits.
Recent scholarship, in my judgment, thus upholds a thesis that

Frank Lloyd Wright argued in 1918 when he referred to Chicago as "the national capital of the essentially American spirit." For a sixty-year interlude in the city's history, this was certainly true; in the latter half of the nineteenth century and the first quarter of the twentieth century, Chicago's role in the transformation of America from a rural, agrarian society to an urban, technological society was unparalleled.

Notes

[1]While the majority of the titles that I have included in this supplement carry a publication date between 1975-1980, I have added a few earlier studies that were not mentioned in my 1975 essay.

[2](Chicago: Chicago Historical Society, 1976). Duis, along with Glen Holt, writes an illustrated feature column, "Chicago As It Was," in the monthly Chicago Magazine that often includes general articles on topics in the 1871-1919 period.

[3]In addition to the Loop, Holt and Pacyga analyze the Stockyards and the Central Manufacturing District, plus the neighborhoods of Douglas, Oakland, Kenwood, Hyde Park, Grand Boulevard, Washington Park, Armour Square, Bridgeport, Back-of-the-Yards, Canaryville, McKinley-Park, Brighton Park, and Gage Park.

[4]Victor Dyer, Prairie Avenue: An Annotated Bibliography (Chicago: Chicago Architectural Foundation, 1977); Jean F. Block, Hyde Park Houses: An Informal History, 1856-1910 (Chicago: University of Chicago Press, 1979).

[5](Cambridge, Mass.: Harvard University Press, 1970); for the impact of an event such as the Haymarket Riot of 1886 on a neighboring community (Union Park), use Sennett's article, "Genteel Backlash, Chicago-1886," Transaction, 7 (1970), pp. 41-50.

[6]William Adelman, *Haymarket Revisited (Chicago: Illinois Labor History Society, 1976) and his Pilsen and Chicago's West Side (forthcoming, 1980). Just as the Chicago Pullman Strike of 1894, with its wealth of documentation and secondary literature, can be studied as a crucial case study in urban violence and labor relations, so too can the Haymarket crisis be employed in an urban history course. Here two excellent new sources should be included: Herman Kogan's short study of "William Perkins Black: Haymarket Lawyer," Chicago History, 5 (1976), pp. 85-94, and Carolyn Asbaugh's biography, *Lucy Parsons: American Revolutionary (Chicago: Charles H. Kerr, 1976). Inasmuch as the police were a controversial component of all these urban disturbances, Mark Haller's "Historical Roots of Police Behavior: Chicago, 1890-1925," Law and Society Review, 10 (1976), pp. 303-323, provides helpful background. His research deserves to be extended backward into the 1870s.

[7]For Posada's complete methodology, see her dissertation, "Community Structures of Chicago's Northwest Side: The Transition from Rural to Urban, 1830-1889" (unpublished Ph.D. dissertation, Northwestern University, 1976); also consult James E. Clark, "The Impact of Transportation Technology on Suburbanization in the Chicago Region, 1830-1920" (unpublished Ph.D. dissertation, Northwestern University, 1977).

[8]For additional suggestions for cartographic exercises using Chicago as the geographical focus, see my "Past Cityscapes: Uses of Cartography in Urban History," in Artifacts and the American Past: Techniques For the Historian (Nashville: American Association for State and Local History, forthcoming in 1980).

[9]*Polish-American Politics in Chicago (Chicago: University of Chicago Press, 1975); "Minyans For A Prairie City: The Politics of Chicago Jewry, 1850-1940" (unpublished Ph.D. dissertation, University of Chicago, 1974); Charles H. Shanabruch, Toward An American Catholic Identity: The Chicago Experience (Notre Dame, Indiana: University of Notre Dame Press, 1980).

[10]David Hogan provides another perspective in his assessment of "Education and the Making of the Chicago Working Class, 1880-1930," History of Education Quarterly, 18 (Fall 1978), pp. 227-270.

[11]On the Chicago Irish see the prolific work of Charles Fanning: Finley Peter Dunne and Mr. Dooley: The Chicago Years (Lexington, Ky.: University of Kentucky Press, 1979); Mr. Dooley and the Chicago Irish: An Anthology (New York: Arno Press, 1976); "Varieties of Irish-America: The New Home, Chicago," in Blanche Touhill, ed., Varieties of Ireland, Varieties of Irish-America (St. Louis: University of Missouri at St. Louis, 1976); "Mr. Dooley's Bridgeport Chronicle," Chicago History, 1 (Spring 1972), pp. 47-57. Also consult Barbara C. Schaaf, Mr. Dooley's Chicago (Garden City, N.Y.: Anchor Press, 1977).

[12]Kenneth L. Kusmer, "The Functions of Organized Charity in the Progressive Era: Chicago As a Case Study," Journal of American History, 60 (December 1973), pp. 657-678; Kristin S. McGrath, "American Values and the Slums: A Chicago Case Study" (unpublished Ph.D. dissertation, University of Minnesota, 1977); Thomas Philpott, The Slum and the Ghetto Neighborhood--Deterioration and Middle Class Reform: Chicago, 1880-1930 (New York: Oxford University Press, 1978).

[13]Guy Szuberla, "Three Chicago Settlements: Their Architectural Form and Social Meaning," Journal of the Illinois State Historical Society, 70 (May 1977), pp. 114-129.

[14]For instances of other American studies scholars using Chicago literary works in this fashion, consult the various course syllabi on "Chicago Studies/Regional Studies" filed with the Regional American Studies Information Clearinghouse, The American University, Program in American Studies, Washington, D.C.

[15]Ann Douglas, "Studs Lonigan and the Failure of History in Mass Society: A Study in Claustrophobia," American Quarterly, 29 (Winter 1977), pp. 487-505; Charles Fanning, "James T. Farrell and Washington Park: The Novel and Social History, Chicago History, 8 (Summer 1979), pp. 80-91; Anthony Grosch, "Social Issues in Early Chicago Novels," Chicago History, 4 (Summer 1975), pp. 68-77; Carl Smith, "Fearsome Fiction and The Windy City: or, Chicago on the Dime Novel," Chicago History, 7 (Spring 1978), pp. 2-11.

[16]Jonathan Yardley, Ring: A Biography of Ring Lardner (New York: Random House, 1977); Robert Conrow, Field Days: The Life, Times and Reputation of Eugene Field (New York: Scribners, 1974).

[17](Westport, Conn.: Greenwood Press, 1974); (Urbana, Ill.: University of Illinois Press, 1977).

[18]"The Chicago Business Elite: 1830-1930, A Collective Biography," Business History Review, 50 (Autumn 1976), pp. 288-328.

[19]Thomas J. Schlereth, "Mail Order Catalogues as Resources in Material Culture Studies," Prospects: An Annual of American Cultural Studies (forthcoming, 1980).

[20]Lawrence P. Bachmann, "Julius Rosenwald," American Jewish Historical Quarterly, 66 (1976), pp. 89-105.

[21]Thomas J. Schlereth, "Big Money and High Culture: The Commercial Club of Chicago and Charles L. Hutchinson," Great Lakes Review: A Journal of Midwest Culture, 3 (Summer 1976), pp. 15-27; Thomas J. Schlereth, "A 'Robin's Egg Renaissance': Chicago Culture, 1893-1933," Chicago History, 8 (Fall 1979), pp. 144-154; Helen Lefkowitz Horowitz, Culture and the City: Cultural Philanthropy in Chicago from the 1880s to 1917 (Lexington, Ky.: University of Kentucky Press, 1976).

[22]Paul Finkelman, "Class and Culture In Late Nineteenth-Century Chicago: The Founding of The Newberry Library," American Studies, 16 (1975), pp. 5-22; Perry Duis, "'Where is Athens Now?' The Fine Arts Building, 1898-1918," Chicago History, Pt. I, 6 (Summer 1977), pp. 66-78 and Part II, 7 (Spring 1978), pp. 40-53; Donald F. Tingley, "The 'Robin's Egg Renaissance:' Chicago and the Arts, 1910-1920," Journal of the Illinois State Historical Society, 63 (Spring 1970), pp. 30-35.

[23]See, for example, essays by Helen Horowitz, Erne and Florence Frueh, and Peter Marzio in the special issue of Chicago History, 8 (Spring 1979) devoted to the Institute, along with Vera Lenchner Zolberg, "The Art Institute of Chicago: The Sociology of a Cultural Organization," (unpublished Ph.D. dissertation, University of Chicago, 1974).

[24]James T. Carey, *Sociology and Public Affairs: The Chicago School (Beverly Hills, Calif.: Sage Publications, 1975); Fred H.

Matthews, Quest For An American Sociology: Robert E. Park and the
Chicago School (Montreal: McGill-Queens University Press, 1977);
Winifred Rauschenbush, Robert E. Park: Biography of a Sociologist
(Durham: Duke University Press, 1979); and Steven J. Diner, A City
and Its Universities: Public Policy in Chicago, 1892-1919 (Chapel
Hill, N.C.: University of North Carolina Press, 1980).

[25]Frank L. Ellsworth, Law on the Midway: The Founding of the
University of Chicago Law School (Chicago: University of Chicago
Press, 1977).

[26]Katherine Mayhew, The Dewey School: The Laboratory School
of The University of Chicago, 1896-1903 (New York: Columbia University Press, 1966). A figure that predates Dewey both in progressive education concepts and work in Chicago is Colonel Francis
W. Parker: The Children's Crusade, the topic of a well-researched
life by Jack K. Campbell (New York: Columbia University Press,
1967).

[27]Francis Schussler Fiorenza, "American Culture and Modernism:
Shailer Mathew's Interpretation of American Christianity," in
America in Theological Perspective, edited by Thomas M. McFadden
(New York: Seabury Press, 1976), pp. 163-186.

[28]Barry D. Karl, Charles E. Merriam and the Study of Politics
(Chicago: University of Chicago Press, 1974).

[29]Dorothy M. Livingston, The Master of Light: A Biography of
Albert A. Michelson (New York: Scribners, 1973).

[30]Perry Duis, "Bessie Louise Pierce: Symbol and Scholar,"
Chicago History, 5 (Fall 1976), pp. 130-140.

[31]The Idea of the University of Chicago: Selections from the
Papers of the First Eight Executives of the University of Chicago
from 1891 to 1975, edited by D. J. R. Bruckner and William Michael
Murphy (Chicago: University of Chicago Press, 1976).

[32]Dreams In Stone: The University of Chicago, edited by
D. J. R. Bruckner and Irene Macauley (Chicago: University of
Chicago Press, 1976); Harold F. Williamson and Payson S. Wild have
collaborated to do a detailed institutional history, *Northwestern
University: A History, 1850-1975 (Evanston, Illinois: Northwestern
University, 1976), that also uses some historical photography.,

[33]Jack Tager, "Partners in Design: Chicago Architects, Entrepreneurs, and the Evolution of Urban Commercial Architecture,"
South Atlantic Quarterly, 76 (Spring 1977), pp. 204-218. Two
dissertations exploring the dissemination of architectural theory
and practice among architects and clients are Robert Prestiano,
"The Inland Architect: A Study of The Contents, Influence, and
Significance of Chicago's Major Late-Nineteenth Century Architectural Periodical" (unpublished Ph.D. dissertation, Northwestern

University, 1973), and Eileen M. Nichols, "A Developmental Study of Drawings Published in the American Architect and in Inland Architect" (unpublished Ph.D. dissertation, University of Minnesota, 1978).

[34]David Lowe, ^Lost Chicago (Boston: Houghton Mifflin, 1975), and *Chicago Interiors: Views of A Splendid World (Chicago: Contemporary Books, 1979).

[35]Oswald Grube, Peter Pran and Franz Schulze, 100 Years of Architecture in Chicago: Continuity of Structure and Form (Chicago: J. Philip O'Hara, 1976); Stuart E. Cohen, Chicago Architects: Documenting the Exhibition of the Same Name Organized by Laurence Booth, Stuart E. Cohen, Stanley Tigerman, and Benjamin Weese (Chicago: The Swallow Press, 1976).

[36]For a more thorough discussion of the debate, see my review essay on both books in The Old Northwest: A Journal of Regional Life and Letters, 3 (September 1977), pp. 319-323; and Nory Miller's appraisal, "Man of Ideas: Chicago's Battle of Architecture," Inland Architect (March 1976), pp. 8-14.

[37]William Allin Storrer, The Architecture of Frank Lloyd Wright: A Complete Catalog, Second Edition (Cambridge, Mass.: MIT Press, 1978).

[38]John Vinci, *The Stock Exchange Trading Room (Chicago: The Art Institute of Chicago, 1977); James O'Gorman, "The Marshall Field Wholesale Store: Materials Toward a Monograph," Journal of the Society of Architectural Historians, 37 (October 1978), pp. 175-194; Harry Price, The Auditorium Building: Its History and Architectural Significance (Chicago: Roosevelt University, 1976).

[39]For additional information, write Commission on Chicago Historical and Architectural Landmarks, Room 800, 320 North Clark Street, Chicago, Illinois 60610.

[40]City House: A Guide To Renovating Older Chicago-Area Houses, compiled by Linda Legner (Chicago: Commission on Chicago Historical and Architectural Landmarks, 1979).

[41]J. B. Jackson, "Chicago" in American Space: 1865-1876: The Centennial Years (New York: W. W. Norton, 1972), pp. 72-86; also valuable in this context is Richard W. Shepro, "The Reconstruction of Chicago After the Great Fire of 1871 (unpublished B.A. thesis, Harvard University, 1974).

[42]Irving Cutler, Chicago: Metropolis of Mid-Continent, Second Edition (Dubuque, Iowa: Kendall/Hunt Publishing Company, 1976); *Chicago: Transformations of an Urban System, edited by Brian J. L. Berry (Cambridge, Mass.: Ballinger Publishing Company, 1976).

[43]Thomas Hines, Burnham of Chicago: Architect and Planner (New York: Oxford University Press, 1974); Cynthia Field, "The City Planning of D. H. Burnham" (unpublished Ph.D. dissertation, Columbia University, 1974).

[44]Michael P. McCarthy, "Chicago Businessmen and the Plan," Journal of the Illinois State Historical Society, 63 (Autumn 1970), pp. 228-256; Carl Condit, Chicago: 1930-1970: Building, Planning, and Urban Technology (Chicago: University of Chicago Press, 1974); Michael Simpson, "Two Traditions of American Planning: Olmsted and Burnham," Town Planning Review, 47 (April 1976); Paul F. Barrett, "Mass Transit, the Automobile, and Public Policy in Chicago, 1900-1930" (unpublished Ph.D. dissertation, University of Illinois at Chicago Circle, 1976); James E. Clark, "The Impact of Transportation Technology on Suburbanization in the Chicago Region, 1830-1920" (unpublished Ph.D. dissertation, Northwestern University, 1977).

[45]Galen Cranz, "Changing Roles of Urban Parks: From Pleasure Garden to Open Space," Landscape, 22 (Summer 1978), pp. 9-18; Leonard K. Eaton, Landscape Artist in America: The Life and Work of Jens Jensen (Chicago: University of Chicago Press, 1964); Michael P. McCarthy, "Politics and the Parks: Chicago Businessmen and the Recreation Movement," Journal of the Illinois Historical Society, 65 (1972), pp. 158-172.

[46]David Burg, *Chicago's White City (Lexington, Ky.: University of Kentucky Press, 1974); R. Reid Badger, *The Great American Fair: The World's Columbian Exposition and American Culture (Chicago: Nelson-Hall, 1979).

[47]Also see William D. Andrews, "Women and The Fairs of 1876 and 1893," Hayes Historical Journal, 1 (Spring 1977), pp. 173-184; Margaretta Darnall, "From the Chicago Fair to Walter Gropius: Changing Ideals in American Architecture" (unpublished Ph.D. dissertation, Cornell University, 1975); Elizabeth Brown, "American Paintings and Sculpture in the Fine Arts Building of the World's Columbian Exposition" (unpublished Ph.D. dissertation, University of Kansas, 1976).

[48]Cathy and Richard Cahan, "The Lost City of the Depression," Chicago History, 5 (Winter 1976-77), pp. 233-242; Lenox R. Lohr, Fair Management, the Story of a Century of Progress Exposition (Chicago, 1952); August Meier and Elliott M. Rudwick, "Negro Protest at the Chicago World's Fair, 1933-34," Journal of The Illinois State Historical Society, 59 (Summer 1966), pp. 161-171; F. T. Rihlstedt, "Formal and Structural Innovations in American Exposition Architecture: 1901-1939" (unpublished Ph.D. dissertation, Northwestern University, 1973).

"Women's Studies in the United States": New Sources

JOANNA SCHNEIDER ZANGRANDO

The invitation to update my essay, "Women's Studies in the United
States: Approaching Reality," confirms the importance of Women's
Studies research and publication to the enrichment of all scholarly
investigation. That Women's Studies scholarship continues to re-
shape the study and teaching of American culture and to inform
methodologies and interpretations within and across academic disciplines is evident in the publications and other activities, 1975
to the present, cited in this essay.

Women's historians, for example, have expanded the canon of traditional history to include the variety and complexity of women's
experiences as essential to any investigation and understanding of
the past. Women's history researchers have been focusing on such
issues as women and work, sex roles and sexuality, feminism and
feminist consciousness, women and public policy, social relations
between the sexes and among women, the domestic sphere and familial
relations, women and social movements. Increasingly, scholars have
found it imperative to analyze, within these larger areas, the
importance of age, class, race, ethnicity, urban/rural location,
marital status, sexual preference, and life cycle changes.

The inclusion of women as active participants in American culture
demands the consideration of private as well as public experiences
and relationships, but with the recognition that the focus must be
on women themselves and must be from their perspective. That
approach is absolutely crucial to any Women's Studies course or
publication. For example, "family history" is not identical to
women's history. The study of the family, in its many and varied
forms, is a women's history concern when the investigation centers

on women's actual experiences within, and perceptions of, the family unit. In her provocative discussion of "Feminism and Family Revivalism," Chrysalis, No. 8 (Summer 1979), 57-65, Sandi Cooper sets the current scholarly investigation of the family in its social context and analyzes why "research on the family has moved from a cottage industry to mass production" at the same time concern with the family has become a "national obsession." Cooper underscores the essential need, for Women's Studies scholars, of a "feminist perspective" in research on the family.

Academic programs and courses have kept pace with research and publication since 1975. Women's Studies programs numbered over 300 throughout the United States in 1980. In addition, colleges and universities where formally declared programs do not exist offered hundreds and hundreds of Women's Studies courses. (Women's Studies Newsletter, VIII, No. 1 (Winter 1980), 19-26.) At the same time, in part because these courses and programs have been the most recent additions to the curriculum, economic retrenchment threatens their healthy existence in institutions of higher education. The energy of those who administer and teach in Women's Studies pro- grams is threatened, too, again in part because of the newness of the field, by requests to explain and to justify the entire enter- prise.

The National Women's Studies Association was founded in 1977 as a formal communications network for the large number of teachers, researchers, and students in various disciplines that are involved in Women's Studies. The Women's Studies Newsletter, published since 1972, is the official publication of the NWSA. (The Feminist Press, Box 334, Old Westbury, New York. For information about NWSA write to Elaine Reuben, NWSA, University of Maryland, College Park, Maryland 20742.) Among its most important functions, NWSA has sponsored two annual, national Women's Studies conferences designed to attract multi-disciplinary and cross-cultural papers and dialogue. A number of other conferences since 1975 attest to the importance of Women's Studies scholarship. "Women's History" was the topic of the 16th Annual Conference of the National Archives and Records Service, April 22-23, 1976, in Washington, D.C. On November 12-13, 1979, the National Council of Negro Women sponsored "Black Women: An Historical Perspective," announced as the first national scholarly research conference on black women. And in 1978, the Berkshire Conference on the History of Women, at Mount Holyoke College, was second in size only to the American Historical Association annual meeting.[1]

As the decade of the 1980s begins, Women's Studies researchers, students, and teachers have a solid foundation of information, much of it made available since 1975, upon which to draw and to build. Since this is an update of my previous essay, I will maintain similar categories of resources: documentary collections, theme- oriented and general histories, bibliographies, autobiographies and biographies, contemporary feminist writings, literature, behavioral and social science studies, specialized studies, government publi- cations, anthologies, and non-print media. Among specific additional categories are women and the arts and women and work. The number of publications concerned with bibliographic works, literature, specialized studies, the arts, work, and women's friendship and reform-oriented networks has increased, while histories, biographies and autobiographies, contemporary feminism works, and document books appear to have diminished in publication numbers since 1975.

Journals

One of the best ways to keep current with the expanding body of literature is to consult the many fine journals devoted to Women's Studies either exclusively or with some frequency, including special subject issues. Radical America, Monthly Labor Review, and the American Quarterly are some of the journals that publish Women's Studies articles on a regular basis. Examples of special issue publications include Southern Exposure, No. 4 (Winter 1977) on "Women," and Current History (May 1976) on "American Women."

Many of the journals are interdisciplinary and cross-cultural in scope, and they publish the most recent research and ongoing dialogue about research on women's experiences. The following journals, listed alphabetically, are the most informative and basic to Women's Studies research and teaching: Chrysalis, A Magazine of Women's Culture (1727 North Spring Street, Los Angeles, California 90012); Conditions (P.O. Box 56, Van Brunt Station, Brooklyn, New York 11215); Feminist Studies (417 Riverside Drive, New York, New York 10025); Frontiers: A Journal of Women's Studies (University of Colorado, Boulder, Colorado 80309); Heresies: A Feminist Publication on Art and Politics (P.O. Box 766, Canal Street Station, New York, New York 10013); National NOW Times (425 13th Street N.W., Suite 1048, Washington, D.C. 20004); Quest: A Feminist Quarterly (P.O. Box 8843, Washington, D.C. 2003); Signs: Journal of Women in Culture and Society (University of Chicago Press, Chicago, Illinois 60637); Spokeswoman: A Crossroads of Communication for Women (3000 Graham Ct., Falls Church, Virginia); WEAL Washington Report (Women's Equity Action League, 538 National Press Building, Washington, D.C. 2004); Women and Literature (formerly a quarterly, new annual format; Holmes & Meier Publishers, Inc., 30 Irving Place, New York, New York 10003); Women's Studies (c/o Gordon & Breach, Science Publishers, One Park Avenue, New York, New York 10016); and Women's Studies Newsletter (Box 334, Old Westbury, New York 11568). In addition to these excellent journals, another side of publishing in Women's Studies is gained from Linda Palumbo's two-part essay on women's publishing houses, "Feminist Publishing Catalog," in Chrysalis, No. 8 (Summer 1979), 105-120; No. 9 (Fall 1979), 81-94.[2]

Documentary Collections

Two excellent documents collections, particularly useful in interdisciplinary courses on women, have been published since 1975. Documents of working-class women from a variety of first-person accounts, as well as published statistical sources, are contained in Rosalyn Baxandall, Linda Gordon, and Susan Reverby, eds., *America's Working Women: A Documentary History, 1600 to the Present (New York: Vintage, 1976). The introduction to the collection sets the authors' perspective on work and class, and the headnotes to each section place individual selections in understandable context. An excellent example of primary documents on women's experiences throughout the female life cycle, and from the perspective of women, is Gerda Lerner's *The Female Experience: An American Documentary (Indianapolis: Bobbs-Merrill Co., 1977). Again, the introduction to the entire collection and to each of the life cycle divisions makes this book a sophisticated, excellent source book for introductory as well as advanced Women's Studies courses.

General Histories

For courses in women's history, a number of recently published books would be useful. There are two publications dealing with the eighteenth century: Linda Kerber's Daughters of Columbia: American Women in the Era of the American Revolution (Iowa City: University of Iowa Press, 1975), and Mary Beth Norton's *Liberty's Daughters: The Revolutionary Experience of American Women, 1750-1800 (New York: Little, Brown & Co., 1980). In *Woman's Proper Place: A History of Changing Ideals and Practices, 1870 to the Present (New York: Basic Books, 1978), Sheila M. Rothman traces the change in attitudes and in participation of women in the domestic sphere and beyond, and the continuation of societal views of women primarily in the roles of wives and mothers. Rothman discusses the diversity within the woman's movement, class divisions among women, and the part women have played in various social policy areas since the late nineteenth century.

Bibliographies

A number of bibliographic guides to published and non-published materials have enhanced greatly the accessibility of Women's Studies information. New Feminist Scholarship: A Guide to Bibliographies (Old Westbury, N.Y.: The Feminist Press, 1979), edited by Jane Williamson, is a comprehensive guide with thirty subject headings that is useful in many disciplines. In her review essay, "Bibliographies for Research on Women," Signs, 3, No. 2 (Winter 1977), 436-450, Patricia K. Ballou lists bibliographies by specific discipline. The American Quarterly's bibliography issue in 1976 included "Women's Studies/American Studies, 1970-1975," XXIX, No. 3, 263-279, compiled by Donna Gerstenberger and Carolyn Allen. For women's history, one of the most ambitious efforts of historians, archivists, and manuscript librarians has resulted in Women's History Sources: A Guide to Archives and Manuscript Collections in the United States (New York: R. R. Bowker, 1978), edited by Andrea Hinding. This guide contains descriptions of over 18,000 collections of primary sources concerning women's history in the United States, from the Colonial era to the present, and lists over 1,500 respositories.

Other useful history guides include: The Common Women Collective,
Women in U.S. History: An Annotated Bibliography (5 Upland Road,
Cambridge, Massachusetts 02140, 1976); Nupur Chaudhuri, comp.,
Bibliography of Women's History, 1976, 1979 (Conference Group on
Women's History, 1979); Janet L. Sims, comp., The Progress of Afro-
American Women: A Selected Bibliography and Resource Guide (West-
port, Connecticut. Greenwood Press, 1980); and Barbara Sicherman's
review essay in Signs, 1, No. 2 (Winter 1975), 461-485. Among the
most useful bibliographic guides concerning women and the arts are:
Nina Baym, *Woman's Fiction: A Guide to Novels By and About
Women in America, 1820-1870 (Ithaca: Cornell University Press,
1979); Donna G. Bachmann and Sherry Piland, eds., Women Artists:
An Historical, Contemporary and Feminist Bibliography (Metuchen,
N.J.: Scarecrow Press, 1978); Judith A. Hoffberg, "The Women
Artists' Books: A Select Bibliography," Chrysalis, No. 5, 85-87;
Gloria Feman Orenstein, "Review Essay: Art History," Signs, 1,
No. 2 (Winter 1975), 505-525; Diane H. Russell, "Review Essay:
Art History," Signs, 5, No. 3 (Spring 1980), 468-481. One final
guide of particular usefulness is Work and Family Issues: A
Bibliography of Economic and Related Social Science Research,
edited by Hilda Kahne and Judith Hybels, and published in 1979
by the Wellesley College Center for Research on Women.

Biographies and Autobiographies

The three-volume biographical dictionary, Notable American Women,
edited by Edward and Janet James and published in 1971, has become
an indispensable aid to teachers and students of Women's Studies.
So, too, will the supplement, Notable American Women: The Modern
Period, 1950-1975, edited by Barbara Sicherman and Carol Green,
and scheduled for fall 1980 publication by Harvard University
Press. Combined, these volumes should serve as the first resources consulted by anyone seeking biographical information on women
in the United States. Several full-length biographies on literary
figures are welcome additions to information on creative women:
Eileen Aird, Sylvia Plath: Her Life and Work (New York: Harper &
Row, 1975); Robert Hemenway, *Zora Neale Hurston: A Literary
Biography (Urbana, Illinois: University of Illinois Press, 1977);
and Cynthia Griffin Wolff, *A Feast of Words: The Triumph of Edith
Wharton (New York: Oxford University Press, 1977).

Three biographies capture the energy and commitment of well-known
American women: Lois W. Banner's well-written, informative
*Elizabeth Cady Standon: A Radical for Women's Rights (New York:
Little, Brown & Co., 1979); Bell Gale Chevigny's new interpretation
of one of the leading intellectual and literary figures of the
first half of the nineteenth century, *The Woman and the Myth:
Margaret Fuller's Life and Writings (Old Westbury, N.Y.: The
Feminist Press, 1977); and Inez Haynes Irwin's The Story of Alice
Paul and the National Women's Party (Fairfax, Virginia: Denlinger's
Publishers, 1977, reprint). An interesting biography of a woman
not so well known is Carolyn Ashbaugh's *Lucy Parsons: American
Revolutionary (Chicago: Charles H. Kerr Publishing, 1976).
Finally, two collective biographies are informative additions to

Women's Studies scholarship: Dorothy Sterling presents portraits
of three black women activists in *Black Foremothers: Three Lives
(Old Westbury, N.Y.: The Feminist Press, 1979); and Judith Nies
describes the activist commitments of some fairly well-known
women in *Seven Women: Portraits from the American Radical Tradition (New York: Penguin, 1980).

Elizabeth Blackwell's 1895 autobiography, *Opening the Medical
Profession to Women, has been reprinted (New York: Schocken, 1977);
it is a good first-person account of the obstacles faced by
professional women in the second half of the nineteenth century.
Another reprinted edition about professional women, in this case
in relation to feminism in the 1920s, is *These Modern Women:
Autobiographical Essays from the Twenties, edited by Elaine
Showalter from a Nation series on seventeen women in 1926-1927
(Old Westbury, N.Y.: The Feminist Press, 1978). A good source of
autobiographical information is provided by oral histories such
as those published in the special "Women's Oral History" issue of
Frontiers, II, No. 2 (Summer 1977).

Contemporary Feminist Writings

The initial thrust of feminist Women's Studies scholarship contained a good deal of discussion about the history of feminism,
the impact of feminist ideology on contemporary institutions, and
the implications of feminist-informed scholarship on the academic
and publishing professions. Some of this concern continues, often
with specific focus on a particular institution such as the
family: Barbara Easton, "Feminism and the Contemporary Family,"
Socialist Review, 8 (May-June 1978), 11-36; Rayna Rapp, Ellen
Ross, and Renate Bridenthal, "Examining Family History," Feminist
Studies, 5, No. 1 (Spring 1979), 174-200; Sandi Cooper, "Feminism
and Family Revivalism," Chrysalis, No. 9 (Summer 1978), 57-65.
Adrienne Rich examines the relationships among feminism, feminist
education, and racism in *On Lies, Secrets and Silence (New York:
W. W. Norton, 1979). "Politics and Culture in Women's History:
A Symposium" appeared in the spring 1980 issue of Feminist Studies,
6, No. 1, 26-64, and served as a forum for a critical exchange of
views on the nature of ongoing women's history research.

Five recognized scholars discussed the relationship of women's
history to feminism and to "women's culture," primarily in response
to Ellen DuBois' feminist critique of women's history scholarship.
To DuBois, a tendency of women's historians to focus on "women's
culture" separate from, not in relation to, feminism should not be
encouraged. In her disagreement with DuBois' contention that
women's historians should focus on the political aspect of
feminism, Carroll Smith-Rosenberg argues that the analysis of the
interactions of women with each other is a crucial concern to
women's history researchers. To Smith-Rosenberg, "the pressing
questions about feminism center on its relation to the female
world," which she defines as "identification as women," and not as
seeing women as actors/reactors in a male-dominated and defined
political arena. The exchange among the symposium participants

will inform women's history research in the immediate future.[3]

Literature

The relationship between feminism and literary criticism is the
subject of two recent works certain to influence researchers and
teachers in a variety of ways. Judith Fetterley has devoted a book-
length study to a feminist reading of literature, The Resisting
Reader: A Feminist Approach to American Fiction (Bloomington,
Indiana: Indiana University Press, 1978), and Annette Kolodny pursues,
with a good deal of wit, the full implications of feminist criticism
in "Dancing Through the Minefield: Some Observations on the Theory,
Practice, and Politics of a Feminist Literary Criticism," Feminist
Studies, 6, No. 1 (Spring 1980), 1-25. The portrayal of women in
American fiction is the topic of Judith Fryer's informative book,
*The Faces of Eve: Women in the Nineteenth-Century American Novel
(New York: Oxford University Press, 1976). In a series of articles,
Charlotte Goodman has analyzed specific types of women, in specific
circumstances, in American fiction: "Images of American Rural Women
in the Novel," Michigan Papers in Women's Studies, I (June 1975);
"Widening Perspectives, Narrowing Possibilities: The Trapped Woman
in Edith Summers Kelly's Weeds," Regionalism and Female Imagination
(Spring 1977); and "Women and Madness in the Fiction of Joyce Carol
Oates," Women and Literature, V (Fall 1978).

The nature and strengths of relationships among women, especially
between mother and daughter, is portrayed with refreshing, straightforward prose in Maureen Brady's novel, Give Me Your Good Ear,
published by one of the new feminist presses, Spinster's Ink,
located in Argyle, New York (1978). The work of black women is
included in two fine collections: Mary Helen Washington, ed.,
*Black-Eyed Susans: Classic Stories By and About Black Women
(Garden City, N.Y.: Doubleday, 1975); and Alice Walker, ed., Mary
Helen Washington, Intro., I Love Myself When I Am Laughing. . . And
Then Again When I Am Looking Mean and Impressive: A Zora Neale
Hurston Reader (Old Westbury, N.Y.: The Feminist Press, 1980).
Cynthia Griffen Wolff has edited a collection of short stories by
Chopin, Wharton, Jewett and Cather, *Classic American Women Writers
(New York: Harper and Row, 1979).[4] One of the best anthologies,
comprehensive and diverse, and particularly appropriate for intro-
ductory Women's Studies courses, is *By Women: An Anthology of
Literature, edited by Marcia McClintock Folsom and Linda Kirschner
(Boston: Houghton Mifflin, 1976).

Several recent publications are useful additions to information
about women poets. Two special issues of Women's Studies are
devoted to women poets and their poetry from the colonial era to
the present, 5, No. 2 (1977), and 7, Nos. 1 and 2 (1980). Also
beginning with the colonial period is Emily Stipes Watts, *The
Poetry of American Women from 1632 to 1945 (Austin: University of
Texas Press, 1977). Newer developments in poetry by women is the
subject of a collection by Suzanne Juhasz, ed., *Naked and Fiery
Forms: Modern American Poetry by Women, A New Tradition (New York:

Harper and Row, 1976). New publications about specific poets
include: J. Lee Greene, Time's Unfading Garden: Anne Spencer's
Life and Poetry (Baton Rouge: Louisiana State University Press,
1977); Adrienne Rich, *The Dream of a Common Language: Poems
1974-1977 (New York: W. W. Norton & Co., Inc., 1978); and Judith
McDaniel, *Reconstituting the World: The Poetry and Vision of
Adrienne Rich (Argyle, N.Y.: Spinster's Ink, 1979).

Behavioral and Social Science Studies

Most interdisciplinary Women's Studies courses include components
from the behavioral and social sciences, often in the form of
assigned textbooks. Among such texts appropriate for introductory
courses are: Women Today: A Multidisciplinary Approach to Women's
Studies, edited by Catherine Berheide, M. Baker, L. Gugin, F.
Greckel, M. Lipetz and M. Segal (Monterey, California: Brooks/Cole,
1980); Juanita H. Williams, *Psychology of Women: Selected
Readings (N.Y.: W. W. Norton & Co., 1979); *Women and Sex Roles:
A Social Psychological Perspective, edited by Irene H. Frieze,
Jacquelynne E. Parsons, Paula B. Johnson, Diane N. Ruble, and Gail
L. Zellman (N.Y.: W. W. Norton & Co., 1978); and Barbara S.
Deckard, *Women's Movement: Political, Socioeconomic and Psycho-
logical Issues (N.Y.: Harper & Row, 1979). Current research and
theory concerning the psychology of women is the subject of a
journal, first published in the fall of 1976, entitled Psychology
of Women Quarterly. A comprehensive review essay on this topic is
"Psychology and Women" by Mary Brown Parlee, Signs, 5, No. 1
(Autumn 1979), 121-133. A similarly good overview of women in
sociology is "Towards a Women's Perspective in Sociology: Directions and Prospects," by Catherine Berheide and Marcia Segal, S.
McNall, ed., Theoretical Perspectives in Sociology (N.Y.: St.
Martins Press, 1979).

Specialized Studies

Publications in the category of "specialized studies" have
continued to increase in number since 1975. Prominent among the
concerns of historians has been the analysis of woman's "place" or
"sphere" in the nineteenth century. In The Feminization of
American Culture (N.Y.: Alfred A. Knopf, 1977), Ann Douglas
describes the creation of sentimental, popular culture by women,
especially writers in league with the Protestant clergy. Nancy
Cott centers on women's experiences and the boundaries of their
culture in the transition period between the eighteenth and nineteenth centuries in her informative book, *The Bonds of Womanhood:
"Woman's Sphere" in New England, 1780-1835 (New Haven: Yale
University Press, 1977). And Barbara Ehrenreich and Deirdre
English have collected views of, and prescriptions for, the "ideal"
female in *For Her Own Good: 150 Years of the Experts' Advice to
Women (Garden City, N.Y.: Anchor Books, 1978).

Approaching the sphere of women from another perspective--that of
the women themselves and their positive, mutually reinforcing
female friendship networks--Carroll Smith-Rosenberg has helped to

shift the focus of Women's Studies research away from societal
expectations and restrictions to the world women created for themselves. Perhaps the most instructive of her articles in this
regard is "The Female World of Love and Ritual: Relations between
Women in Nineteenth-Century America," Signs, 1, No. 1 (Autumn
1975), 1-29. Mary P. Ryan discusses the positive influence of
female support networks in "The Power of Women's Networks: A Case
Study of Female Moral Reform in Antebellum America," Feminist
Studies, 5, No. 1 (Spring 1979), 66-85. Blanche Wiesen Cook
echoes the importance of women's networks in her study of the late-
nineteenth, early-twentieth centuries, "Female Support Networks
and Political Activism: Lillian Wald, Crystal Eastman, and Emma
Goldman," Chrysalis, 3 (Autumn 1977), 43-61. In Cook's analysis,
women made deliberate choices to engage in support networks based
on female friendship to gain emotional and physical sustenance and
as an alternative to marriage and motherhood. They chose instead
a public-service, politically active life.[5]

The engagement of women in organized reform movements continues to
be a favored topic of research, and several excellent monographs
are the result of this interest. Blanche Glassman Hersh has
examined the lives of fifty-one women reformers who began their
activism as opponents of slavery and moved on to embrace woman's
rights in The Slavery of Sex: Feminist-Abolitionists in America
(Urbana, Illinois: University of Illinois Press, 1978). In her
fresh analysis of the connections between antislavery and woman's
rights activism, Ellen DuBois places emphasis on the development
by women of an independent woman's rights movement as reformers
with whom they worked hardened their opposition against the cause
of woman's rights. DuBois stresses the importance of the woman's
rights movement as being the first independent reform movement
in which women engaged on their own behalf, and claims that their
"discontent with their position was as much cause as effect of
their involvement with the anti-slavery movement"; *Feminism and
Suffrage: The Emergence of an Independent Women's Movement in
America, 1848-1869 (Ithaca: Cornell University Press, 1978).[6]

The first-person accounts of woman's rights advocates of a later
period are captured in Sherna Gluck, ed., *From Parlor to Prison:
Five American Suffragists Talk About Their Lives (N.Y.: Random
House, 1976). The experiences of three political activists, based
on oral interviews with them, is the subject of *Moving the
Mountain: Women Working for Social Change, by Ellen Cantarow,
with Susan Gushee O'Malley and Sharon Hartman Strom (Old Wesbury,
N.Y.: The Feminist Press, 1980). Another book based in large part
on oral interviews as primary sources is Sara Evans' timely study
of the origins of the contemporary feminist movement in the civil
rights movement of the 1960s as well as in the New Left of the same
time period. In *Personal Politics: The Roots of Women's Liberation in the Civil Rights Movement and the New Left (N.Y.: Knopf,
1979), Evans convincingly argues that their participation in the
Student Non-violent Coordinating Committee and in Students for a
Democratic Society provided the catalyst, as well as the skills,
for women to create their own movement for liberation. Mary Aichin

Rothschild treats this same theme in fine detail in "White Women Volunteers in the Freedom Summer: Their Life and Work in a Movement for Social Change," Feminist Studies, 5, No. 3 (Fall 1979), 466-494. Although much of contemporary research centers on the evolution of women working for their emancipation, some attention is focused on their participation in reforms for others. Jacquelyn Dowd Hall's Revolt Against Chivalry: Jessie Daniel Ames and the Women's Campaign Against Lynching (N.Y. Columbia University Press, 1979), is a good book-length example of this aspect of women's active political involvement.[7]

Concern that women have control over their bodies--reproductive freedom and freedom from physical assault--is not restricted to the recent revival of feminism, as many historians have demonstrated.[8] The history of birth control as a political struggle, and the role of women as active participants in the fight to make birth control information available on demand, is the topic of Linda Gordon's *Woman's Body, Woman's Right (N.Y.: Penguin Books, 1975). Gordon is particularly successful in placing the birth control movement in its political context, and in showing the intersections of private and public morality and of social change and public policy. The role that the medical profession played in this movement is described by James Reed in From Private Vice to Public Virtue: The Birth Control Movement and American Society Since 1830 (N.Y.: Basic Books, 1978). Abortion, another important aspect of reproductive freedom and another in which the medical profession played an active, and self-interested, role, is the subject of James C. Mohr's *Abortion in America: The Origins and Evolution of National Policy, 1800-1900 (N.Y.: Oxford University Press, 1978). Finally, in a comprehensive review essay, Barbara Hayler traces the history of abortion as a social and political phenomenon in which the overriding issue has been that of denying control over reproduction to women by the legal and psychological maneuvers of anti-abortion forces; "Abortion," Signs, 5, No. 2 (Winter 1979), 307-323.[9]

The use of the law as a means of discriminating against women is the subject of two recent publications. Albie Sachs and Joan Hoff Wilson have traced the history of women's attempts to gain equal status before the law, and within the legal profession, in Sexism and the Law: Male Beliefs and Legal Bias in Britain and the United States (N.Y.: The Free Press, 1978). In The Chains of Protection: The Judicial Response to Women's Labor Legislation (Westport, Connecticut: Greenwood Press, 1978), Judith A. Baer, in a case-by-case study, analyzes the judicial responses to labor legislation regarding women, from the Muller case (1908) up to the equal pay and employment acts of the mid-1960s. Baer describes how protective labor legislation actually discriminated against industrial working women and how this discrimination was upheld by the courts.

The experiences of women moving to and settling in frontier areas has been the subject of several recent books and articles. Among the most informative are Julie Roy Jeffrey, *Frontier Women: The

Trans-Mississippi West, 1840-1880 (N.Y.: Hill and Wang, 1979);
John M. Faragher, *Women and Men on the Overland Trail (New Haven:
Yale University Press, 1979); Glenda Riley, Women on the American
Frontier (St. Louis: Forum Press, 1977); Christiane Fischer, ed.,
Let Them Speak for Themselves: Women in the American West, 1849-
1900 (Hamden, Connecticut: Anchor Books, 1977); Lillian Schlissel,
"Women's Diaries on the Western Frontier," American Studies, XVIII,
No. I (Spring 1977), 87-100; Christine Stansell, "Women on the
Great Plains, 1865-1890," Women's Studies, Vol. 4 (Summer 1976),
87-98; and John Faragher and Christine Stansell, "Women and Their
Families on the Overland Trail, 1842-1867," Feminist Studies, 2,
Nos. 2 and 3 (1975), 150-166. Women within a family context is
the subject of other studies, including Carl N. Degler, At Odds:
Women and the Family in America, From the Revolution to the
Present (N.Y.: Oxford University Press, 1980); Virginia Yans-
McLaughlin, Family and Community: Italian Immigrants in Buffalo,
1880-1930 (Ithaca: Cornell University Press, 1977); and Linda
Kerber, "The Republican Mother: Women and the Enlightenment--An
American Perspective," American Quarterly, XXVIII, No. 2 (Summer
1976), 187-205. For a fresh analysis of the experience of mother-
hood, Adrienne Rich's Of Woman Born: Motherhood as Experience and
Institution (N.Y.: W. W. Norton & Co., 1977), is essential.

Sharon Harley and Rosalyn Terborg-Penn have edited a valuable
collection on the experiences of black women in the United States,
The Afro-American Woman: Struggles and Images (Port Washington,
N.Y.: Kennikat Press, 1978); and "A Response to Inequality: Black
Women, Racism, and Sexism," Signs, 3, No. 2 (Winter 1977), 339-
361, by Diane K. Lewis, is another welcome addition to this
subject.

The role and participation of women in organized religion has
received a good deal of recent study. A special issue of the
American Quarterly, edited by Janet Wilson James, was devoted to
the issue "Women and Religion," XXX, No. 5 (Winter 1978). This
is an essential volume for anyone interested in the topic of
women and religion. More specific studies include Anne Boylan,
"Evangelical Womanhood in the Nineteenth Century: The Role of
Women in Sunday Schools," Feminist Studies, 4, No. 3 (October
1978), 62-80; Janice Klein, "Ann Lee and Mary Baker Eddy: The
Parenting of New Religions," Journal of Psychohistory, Vol. 6
(Winter 1979), 361-375; and Amanda Porterfield, Feminine Spirituality in America: From Sarah Edwards to Martha Graham (Philadelphia: Temple University Press, 1980).

Women and educational institutions is another area of focus for
Women's Studies scholars. Charlotte Williams Conable has examined
the admission of women to Cornell University in an exemplary case
study, *Women at Cornell: The Myth of Equal Education (Ithaca:
Cornell University Press, 1977). The impact of education on women
is the subject of Ellen Condliffe Lagemann's Generation of Women:
Education in the Lives of Progressive Reformers (Cambridge:
Harvard University Press, 1979). The educated woman and views

toward her is analyzed by Susan Conrad in Perish the Thought:
Intellectual Women in Romantic America, 1830-1860 (N.Y.: Oxford
University Press, 1976). Roberta Frankfort's focus is on the
conflict between a career within the home, or outside of it, for
college-educated women at the turn of the century in Collegiate
Women: Domesticity and Career in Turn-Of-The-Century America
(N.Y.: New York University Press, 1978). And the home-and-family
uses to which formal education could be directed is the subject of
Eileen Boris' "Social Reproduction and the Schools: Educational
Housekeeping," Signs, 4, No. 4 (Summer 1979), 814-820. "Women's
Influence on Education" is the subject of the Spring 1979 issue of
History of Education, 19, No. 1, and Patricia Albjerg Graham's
"Expansion and Exclusion: A History of Women in American Higher
Education" is an excellent survey of patterns of development for
women in higher education in the United States, Signs, 3, No. 4
(Summer 1978), 759-773.

A final topic in the "specialized studies" category remains: the
relation of women to war. Leila J. Rupp, in a comparative study
of Germany and the United States during World War II, Mobilizing
Women for War: German and American Propaganda, 1939-1945
(Princeton: Princeton University Press, 1978), examines the ways
in which the propaganda machinery of each country induced women
to join the war production labor force. The approach in both
countries was to play upon the stereotypical emotions of self-
sacrifice and patriotic service expected of women. Carol R.
Berkin and Clara M. Lovett, in *Women, War, and Revolution (N.Y.:
Holmes & Meier, 1980), analyze the role of women in wars and
revolutions in the United States, as well as in Russia, Mexico,
China, Cuba and France. The views of Crystal Eastman, an activist
in the cause of feminism and labor reform, are unequivocal in
opposition to war as is evident in *Crystal Eastman on Women and
Revolution (N.Y.: Oxford University Press, 1978), edited by
Blanche Wiesen Cook.[10]

Government Publications

The federal government continues to publish information of a
statistical nature concerning the status of women in the United
States in such areas as employment, marital status, family member-
ship, and education. Involvement of women in International
Women's Year activities has resulted in the publication of two
useful reference works: Report of the National Commission on the
Observance of International Women's Year, ". . . To Form a More
Perfect Union. . .": Justice for American Women (Washington, D.C.:
U.S. Government Printing Office, 1976), and National Commission on
the Observance of International Women's Year, The Spirit of
Houston: The First National Women's Conference (Washington, D.C.:
Government Printing Office, 1978).

Anthologies

A number of excellent anthologies, published since 1975, are very
useful texts for Women's Studies courses. *Liberating Women's
History: Theoretical and Critical Essays, edited by Berenice A.
Carroll (Urbana, Illinois: University of Illinois Press, 1976),
is a superb, diverse collection of essays on historiography and
case studies that focus on theoretical questions concerning the
study of women's experiences. It contains such important essays
as Hilda Smith's "Feminism and the Methodology of Women's History,"
as well as such classics as Gerda Lerner's "New Approaches to the
Study of Women in American History." Nancy F. Cott and Elizabeth
H. Pleck, eds., have compiled a number of excellent essays that
embody the most recent research on the social history of American
women, with emphasis on feminism, family, and work, in A Heritage
Of Her Own: Toward a New Social History of American Women (N.Y.:
Simon & Schuster, A Touchstone Book, 1979). In *Women of America:
A History, Carol Ruth Berkin and Mary Beth Norton, eds., have
included interpretive essays on women's status, education, religious and work experiences, feminism, and relation to war, plus
documents for each chapter (Boston: Houghton Mifflin Company,
1979). An anthology particularly suited to interdisciplinary
Women's Studies courses is Jo Freeman's edited collection, *Women:
A Feminist Perspective (Palo Alto, California: Mayfield Publ.,
1979 ed.).[11]

Non-Print Sources

Susan Dye Lee's review essay, "Audiovisual Teaching Materials,"
Signs, 2, No. 3 (Spring 1977), 651-663, suggests the variety of
non-print resources available for Women's Studies courses. Two
excellent films on working-class American women, based on the
recollections of the women involved and using documentary film
footage, are "Union Maids" and "With Babies and Banners: Story
of the Women's Emergency Brigade." Both films center on the
efforts to form industrial unions and to gain union recognition
from management. "Union Maids" focuses on three militant women
organizers in Chicago in the 1930s who confronted opposition to
CIO organizing attempts from without the industrial labor movement and the issues of race and feminism from within. The subject
of "With Babies and Banners" is the formation of the Women's
Emergency Brigade and its involvement in the 1937 General Motors
sitdown strike in Flint, Michigan. The technical quality of this
film--especially the use of archival film footage--is excellent.
(For rentals and sales write New Day Films, P.O. Box 315, Franklin
Lakes, New Jersey 07417). Another fine film is "Antonia: A
Portrait of a Woman," about the musical career of symphony conductor Antonia Brico. (Available from Phoenix Films, Inc., 470 Park
Avenue South, New York, New York 10016). Women's Studies teachers
have used popular, commercial films in their analysis of societal
views of women in a number of ways, as suggested in the following
articles: Andrea Walsh, "Films of Suspicion and Distrust: Under-
currents of Female Consciousness in the 1940s," Film & History,
VIII, No. 1 (February 1978), 1-8; Leslie Fishbein, "Women on the

Fringe: A Film Series," Film & History, VIII, No. 3 (September 1978), 49-58; and June Sochen, "Mildred Pierce and Women in Film," American Quarterly, XXX, No. 1 (Spring 1978), 3-20.

Women and the Arts

A number of well-publicized exhibitions have announced the "discovery," or recovery from general oblivion, of women artists. And their history and works have been captured, too, in several welcome publications: Ann Sutherland Harris and Linda Nochlin, *Women Artists: 1550-1950 (N.Y.: Knopf, 1977); Elsa Honig Fine, Lola B. Gellman, and Judy Loeb, eds., Women's Studies and the Arts (N.Y.: Women's Caucus for Art, 1978); Anthea Callen, *Women Artists of the Arts and Crafts Movement, 1870-1914 (N.Y.: Pantheon Books, 1979); Eleanor Munro, Originals: American Women Artists (N.Y.: Simon & Schuster, 1979); Karen Petersen and J. J. Wilson, Women Artists: Recognition and Reappraisal from the Early Middle Ages to the Twentieth Century (N.Y.: New York University Press, 1976); and an anthology of works by women artists, *In Her Own Image: Women Working in the Arts, edited by Elaine Hedges and Ingrid Wendt (Old Westbury, N.Y.: The Feminist Press, 1980).

A special issue of Women's Studies was devoted to the topic "Women Artists on Women Artists," 6, No. 1 (1978); and news, reviews of art shows, and work by women artists and interviews with them is published in Women Artists News (Box 3304, Grand Central Station, New York, New York 10017). One of the most creative women artists at this time, and one whose art self-consciously incorporates her feminist perspective, is Judy Chicago, author of *Through the Flower: My Struggle as a Woman Artist (Garden City, N.Y.: Double-day Anchor Books, 1977).

Chicago's monumental tribute to women is the exhibition "The Dinner Party," "a symbolic history of women's achievements." For those unable to view the exhibition first-hand, two other sources are available: *The Dinner Party (N.Y.: Doubleday & Co., 1979), and a film, made over a four-year period in which over 400 researchers and artists created "The Dinner Party," entitled "Right Out of History: The Making of Judy Chicago's Dinner Party" (Phoenix Films, Inc., 470 Park Avenue South, New York, New York 10016). Infor-mation on another area of creativity in which women have partici-pated is provided in Christine Ammer's Unsung: A History of Women in American Music (Westport, Connecticut: Greenwood Press, 1980). Ammer includes the history of women in American music for two centuries as conductors, composers, and instrumentalists.

Women and Work

Women's Studies scholars in all of the disciplines during the past decade give every indication of continuing to study women within the context of work: unpaid labor within the home, blue- and white-collar work, entry into the professions, and obstacles to full participation in the paid labor force. The always prevalent pattern of job segregation for women is analyzed in two fine

articles: Alice Kessler-Harris, "Stratifying by Sex: Understanding the History of Working Women," in Richard C. Edwards, et al.,
eds., Labor Market Segmentation (Lexington, Massachusetts: C. D.
Heath & Co., 1975), and Heidi Hartmann, "Capitalism, Patriarchy,
and Job Segregation by Sex," Signs, 1, No, 3, Pt. 2 (Spring 1976),
137-169. Elizabeth M. Almquist provides a sociologist's analysis
of the work force in "Women in the Labor Force," Signs, 2, No. 4
(Summer 1977), 843-855. Two general histories of working-class
women are useful: Susan Estabrook Kennedy's If All We Did Was to
Weep at Home: A History of White Working Class Women in America
(Bloomington, Indiana: Indiana University Press, 1979), and
Barbara Wertheimer's *We Were There: The Story of Working Women in
America (N.Y.: Praeger, 1975).

Working-class women's involvement in work activities and their
local community concerns is the topic of Nancy Seifer's book,
*Nobody Speaks For Me! Self-Portraits of American Working Class
Women (N.Y.: Simon & Schuster, 1976). Louise Kapp Howe has
captured the feelings of beauticians, sales workers, waitresses,
office workers, and homemakers by first-hand observations and
conversations with representatives of these jobs in *Pink Collar
Workers: Inside the World of Women's Work (N.Y.: Avon Books,
1978). The views of working-class women from the nineteenth
century are presented in their words--in poems, songs, essays,
political tracts--in Philip Foner's edition of New England factory
workers' writings, The Factory Girls (Urbana, Illinois: University
of Illinois Press, 1977). One of the best studies of the New
England factory operatives is Thomas Dublin's well-researched and
sensitively written Women at Work: The Transformation of Work and
Community in Lowell, Massachusetts, 1826-1869 (N.Y.: Columbia
University Press, 1979). Dublin is particularly cognizant of the
importance of community to the female operatives who worked and
lived together so intimately in Lowell.

A unique perspective on the types of employment available to
immigrant, working-class women and girls is provided in the edited
collection of letters written by a Jewish, immigrant, working-class
woman between 1910 and 1922. Ruth Rosen and Sue Davidson edited
*The Maimie Papers (Old Westbury, N.Y.: The Feminist Press, 1977),
Maimie Pinzer's (pseudonym) letters to Fanny Howe. Howe, a member
of a prominent Boston family, was concerned with moral reform of
women such as Maimie who, for a brief period, resorted to prosti-
tution in order to survive. Her letters describe the continuous
job search of working-class women and the class-based hierarchy of
various available jobs.[12]

Considerations of class and ethnicity inform the essays in Class,
Sex, and the Woman Worker (Westport, Connecticut: Greenwood Press,
1977), edited by Milton Cantor and Bruce Laurie. The Fall 1975
issue of Feminist Studies 3, Nos. 1 and 2, 92-140, contains three
excellent articles about the relationship of feminism and unionism
at the turn of the century: Alice Kessler-Harris, "Where Are the
Organized Women Workers?"; Nancy Schrom Dye, "Feminism or Unionism?

The New York Women's Trade Union League and the Labor Movement";
and Robin Miller Jacoby, "The Women's Trade Union League and
American Feminism." Jobs in which unionization was not a consideration until the most recent years include clerical and domestic
work. Jean Tepperman describes, from first-person accounts, the
grievances of clerical workers in *Not Servants, Not Machines:
Office Workers Speak Out (Boston: Beacon Press, 1976); and David
Katzman captures the drudgery and the transformation of domestic
service from 1870 to 1920 in Seven Days a Week: Women and Domestic
Service in Industrializing America (N.Y.: Oxford University Press,
1978).

The entry and participation of women in the professions is the
subject of a number of recent works. These include Susan Torre,
ed., Women in American Architecture: A Historic and Contemporary
Perspective (N.Y.: Whitney Library of Design, 1977); Mary Roth
Walsh, *"Doctors Wanted: No Women Need Apply": Sexual Barriers in
the Medical Profession, 1835-1975 (New Haven: Yale University
Press, 1977); Judy Barrett Litoff, American Midwives 1860 to the
Present (Westport, Connecticut: Greenwood Press, 1978); Dee
Garrison, Apostles of Culture: The Public Librarian and American
Society, 1876-1920 (N.Y.: Macmillan Co., 1979); and Barbara J.
Harris, Beyond Her Sphere: Women and the Professions in American
History (Westport, Connecticut: Greenwood Press, 1978), a general
history of women with some attention devoted to women in a few
selected professions.[13] Sally Gregory Kohlstedt has filled a void
of information about women in the science professions with her
informative article, "In from the Periphery: American Women in
Science, 1830-1880," Signs, 4, No. 1 (Autumn 1978), 81-96.
Rosabeth Moss Kanter has described the position of women in the
corporate world in *Men and Women of the Corporation (N.Y.: Basic
Books, 1977), and the career of a woman who established her own
business is related by Sarah Stage in Female Complaints: Lydia
Pinkham and the Business of Women's Medicine (N.Y.: W. W. Norton
& Co., 1979).

Brief biographies of their educational and work experiences are
related by a variety of women in *Working It Out: 23 Women
Writers, Artists, Scientists and Scholars Talk About Their Lives
and Work, edited by Sara Ruddick and Pamela Daniels (N.Y.: Pantheon,
1978). The difficult process of working through the educational
system and then trying to enter into careers, while balancing home
and family responsibilities, seems an enormous task as related by
these contemporary women. Problems of another sort are the subject
of Catherine MacKinnon's *Sexual Harassment of Working Women: A
Case of Sex Discrimination (New Haven: Yale University Press, 1979),
a well-researched, timely, and informative treatment of a subject
only recently taken seriously.[14] The entire Summer 1979 issue of
Feminist Studies, 5, No. 2, is devoted to occupational hazards and
health and protection concerns of working women.

The work that women do within the home has been examined from a
variety of perspectives in recent years. Sociological analysis has

yielded *Women and Household Labor, by Sarah Berk, ed. (Beverly
Hills, California: Sage Publications, 1980); Richard and Sarah
Berk, *Labor and Leisure at Home (Beverly Hills, California: Sage
Publications, 1979); and Catherine Berheide, Sarah and Richard
Berk, "Household Work in the Suburbs: The Job and Its Partici-
pants," Pacific Sociological Review, 19 (October 1976), 491-518.
Building on her earlier analysis of the time women spend on house-
work, Joanne Vanek has examined the impact of technology on work
in the home in "Household Technology and Social Status: Rising
Living Standards and Status and Residence Differences in Housework,"
Technology and Culture, 19 (June 1978), 361-375.[15] Ruth Schwartz
Cowan has studied the uses to which the products of industrial
technology have been put in the home and the "messages" advertisers
of those products relay to their intended audience, the American
housewife. Two of her articles are "Two Washes in the Morning and
a'Bridge Party at Night: The American Housewife between the Wars,"
Women's Studies, 3 (1976), 147-172, and "The 'Industrial Revolution' in the Home: Household Technology and Social Change in the
20th Century," Technology and Culture, 17 (1976), 1-23.

Dolores Hayden, professor of architecture, has examined the
attempts to change the design of the household to the benefit of
women who have traditionally been consigned there, or as a deliberate, direct assault on traditional roles within the home.
"Redesigning the Domestic Workplace," Chrysalis, 1 (1977), 19-29,
and "Two Utopian Feminists and Their Campaigns for Kitchenless
Houses," Signs, 4, No. 2 (Winter 1978), 274-290, are two of
Hayden's articles on this theme of changing physical space within
the home as one means of emancipating women. In 1978, the Rockefeller Foundation funded a small conference designed to allow
participants to analyze the relationship between women's work and
family concerns, to question "how changing social, economic,
cultural, and demographic conditions were involved with women's
labor force participation and family organization." Three of the
papers given at this conference appear in Signs 4, No. 4 (Summer
1979), 607-686: Sheila B. Kamerman, "Work and Family in Industrialized Societies"; Richard A. Cloward and Frances Fox Piven,
"Hidden Protest: The Channeling of Female Innovation and Resistance"; and Walter R. Allen, "Family Roles, Occupational Statuses,
and Achievement Orientations among Black Women in the United
States."[16] Other publications on the topic of work and family
include Martha Norby Fraundord, "The Labor Force Participation of
Turn-of-the-Century Married Women," Journal of Economic History,
39 (June 1979), 35-56; Leslie Woodcock Tentler, Wage-Earning
Women: Industrial Work and Family Life in the United States, 1900-
1930 (N.Y.: Oxford University Press, 1980); and Winifred Bolin,
"The Economies of Middle-Income Family Life: Working Women During
the Great Depression," Journal of American History, 65, No. 1
(June 1978), 60-74.[17]

It is evident indeed that scholarship in Women's Studies, since
1975, has continued to contribute in valuable ways to knowledge
about women's lives and, importantly, to intellectual inquiry
in every discipline. That women have had distinctive experiences,

not always of their own choosing, should come as no surprise to students of American culture. The essential function of the recent scholarship cited in this essay is to put those experiences into perspectives that derive meaning from the past and lend validity to our comprehensions of present realities and of future possibilities.

NOTES

[1] Hilda Smith, Coordinating Committee for Women in the Historical Profession: The First Decade, p. 16. This brief history of the CCWHP was published in 1979 to commemorate the tenth anniversary of the caucus group for women in the historical profession concerned with enhancing the professional status of women in the profession, and promoting women's history as an academic field of study.

[2] See "Women: A Special Issue," Journalism History, 1, No. 4 (Winter 1974-1975).

[3] An earlier statement on this topic is Carroll Smith-Rosenberg's "The New Woman and the New History," Feminist Studies, 3, Nos. 1 and 2 (Fall 1975), 185-198.

[4] Elizabeth Hardwick has selected and written introductions to eighteen works of fiction by American women, Rediscovered Fiction by American Women: A Personal Selection, published by Arno Press. Herland: A Lost Feminist Utopian Novel, by Charlotte Perkins Gilman, serialized in 1915, has been published as a novel for the first time (N.Y.: Pantheon Books, 1979).

[5] D'Ann Campbell, "Women's Life in Utopia: The Shaker Experiment, Sexual Equality Reappraised, 1810-1860," The New England Quarterly, 51, No. 1 (March 1978), 23-38; Lee Chambers-Schiller, "The Single Woman Reformer: Conflict Between Family and Vocation, 1830-1860," Frontiers, 3, No. 3 (Fall 1978), 41-48.

[6] See also Barbara Berg, The Remembered Gate: Origins of American Feminism--The Woman and the City, 1800-1860 (N.Y.: Oxford University Press, 1978).

[7] Women were active in the prohibition movement. David Kyvig describes in "Women Against Prohibition," American Quarterly, XXVIII, No. 4 (Fall 1976), 465-482, some who were not. For other reform activities of women see: Karen J. Blair, The Clubwoman as Feminist: True Womanhood Redefined, 1868-1914 (N.Y.: Holmes & Meier Publishers, Inc., 1980); Margaret S. Marsh, "The Anarchist-Feminist Response to the 'Woman Question' in Late Nineteenth Century America," American Quarterly, XXX, No. 4 (Fall 1978), 533-547; and the special issue of Signs on "Women and the American City," 5, No. 3 (Spring 1980 Supplement).

[8]Susan Brownmiller has traced the history of violence against women in Against Our Will: Men, Women and Rape (N.Y.: Simon and Schuster, 1975).

[9]See also Regina M. Morantz, "Making Women Modern: Middle Class Women and Health Reform in 19th-century America," Journal of Social History, 10 (Summer 1977), 490-507, and Graham J. Barker-Benfield, The Horrors of the Half-Known Life: Male Attitudes Toward Women and Sexuality in 19th-Century America (N.Y.: Harper and Row, 1976).

[10]Susan Hartmann, "Prescriptions for Penelope: Literature on Women's Obligations to Returning World War II Veterans," Women's Studies, 5, No. 3 (1978), 223-239; and Marc Miller, "Working Women and World War II," The New England Quarterly, 53, No. 1 (March 1980), 42-61, indicate other relationships between women and war.

[11]Other useful anthologies include Gerda Lerner, The Majority Finds Its Past: Placing Women in History (N.Y.: Oxford University Press, 1979); Barbara Welter, Dimity Convictions: The American Woman in the Nineteenth Century (Athens, Ohio: Ohio University Press, 1976); Mabel Deutrich and Virginia Purdy, eds., Clio Was a Woman: Studies in the History of American Women (Washington, D.C.: Howard University Press, 1980); and Mary Kelly, ed., Woman's Being, Woman's Place: Female Identity and Vocation in American History (Boston, G. K. Hall & Co., 1979).

[12]Considerations of class and hierarchy within occupations are treated in Susan Porter Benson, "The Clerking Sisterhood: Rationalization and the Work Culture of Saleswomen in American Department Stores, 1890-1960," Radical America, 12, No. 2 (March-April, 1978), 41-55; and Barbara Klaczynska, "Why Women Work: A Comparison of Various Groups in Philadelphia, 1910-1930," Labor History, 17 (1976), 73-87. The ethnic dimension of women's work is described by Carol Groneman, "Working-Class Immigrant Women in Mid-Nineteenth Century New York: The Irish Woman's Experiences," Journal of Urban History, 4, No. 3 (May 1978), 225-73.

[13]See also Richard M. Bernard and Maris A. Vinovskis, "The Female School Teacher in Ante-Bellum Massachusetts," Journal of Social History, 10, No. 3 (March 1977), 332-345.

[14]Another informative book on this topic is Lin Farley's Sexual Shakedown: The Sexual Harassment of Women on the Job (N.Y.: McGraw-Hill, 1978).

[15]Susan J. Kleinberg discusses the relationship between technology and class in "Technology and Women's Work: The Lives of Working Class Women in Pittsburgh, 1870-1900," Labor History, 17 (1976), 58-72.

[16]The Allen paper is indicative of current research on the racial component of the work women do; so, too, is Phyllis A. Wallace, et al., <u>Black Women in the Labor Force</u> (Cambridge, Massachusetts: Massachusetts Institute of Technology Press, 1980).

[17]Other sources on women and work that are useful include Nancy Hoffman and Florence Howe, eds., <u>Women Working: An Anthology of Stories and Poems</u> (Old Westbury, N.Y.: The Feminist Press, 1979); and W. Elliot Brownlee and Mary M. Brownlee, <u>Women in the American Economy: A Documentary History, 1675 to 1929</u> (New Haven: Yale University Press, 1976).

Locating Research Materials: Recent Trends

JOHN C. BRODERICK

The 1970s have been characterized by increased activity in the organization and description of original source material, partly as a result of increased financial support by the United States Government. The National Endowment for the Humanities, through its research materials program, has underwritten the preparation of a number of catalogs, guides, finding aids, etc. In 1975 the National Historical Publications Commission became the National Historical Publications and Records Commission. The change in emphasis made possible the consideration of proposals to edit and publish general guides to state, regional, repository, and subject collections. The NHPRC itself also began to assemble data for a possible national guide to resources.

The guides to manuscript material in the Henry E. Huntington Library are examples of the useful products of such support. Two were published in 1979; two more are expected in 1981, all supported by NEH grants. The 1979 publications were the Guide to American Historical Manuscripts in the Huntington Library and the Guide to Library Manuscripts in the Huntington Library. (The forthcoming guides are devoted to British historical manuscripts and to medieval manuscripts.) The fields of strength in American historical manuscripts at the Huntington, as disclosed by the new guide, remain fairly constant: papers of notable figures from early U.S. history, the Civil War, the westward movement, and California history. The case is altered with respect to literary materials, however. In 1975 the Huntington broadened its scope by acquiring large literary archives of both Conrad Aiken and Wallace Stevens, making it a rival in the field of twentieth-century poetry to such institutions as Yale, the New York Public

Library, the University of Texas, and the University of Chicago.

Among other guides recently published, the following are representative: George P. Hammond, ed., A Guide to the Manuscript Collec-
.tions of the Bancroft Library, Vol. 2, Mexican and Central
American Manuscripts (Berkeley and Los Angeles, 1972); The
Beinecke Rare Book and Manuscript Library: A Guide to Its Collections (New Haven, 1974); and Sam P. Williams, comp., Guide to
the Research Collections of the New York Public Library (Chicago:
American Library Association, 1975).

In addition to guides to individual repositories and collections,
there has been a healthy increase in guides to individual
materials on special subjects, such as Andrea Hinding, and Rosemary Richardson, Archival and Manuscript Resources for the Study
of Women's History: A Beginning (Minneapolis, 1972), and Richard
C. Davis, North American Forest History: A Guide to Archives and
Manuscripts in the United States and Canada (Santa Barbara: ABC-
Clio, 1977).

The task of locating American literary manuscripts in general was
made somewhat easier by the publication of the second edition of
American Literary Manuscripts: A Checklist of Holdings, edited by
J. Albert Robbins (Athens, Ga.: University of Georgia Press, 1977).
The second edition is an improvement upon the first in its more
extensive coverage (about 2,800 authors), its more accurate and
more up-to-date information, and because of the inclusion of about
100 references to published descriptions of particular collections
and a bibliographical listing of more general guides. Nevertheless, this remains a reference tool to be used with care,
especially by the researcher who mistakenly assumes that its
compilers have exhausted the resources of particular repositories.
For a more extensive discussion of its strengths and weaknesses,
see Review, Vol. 1 (1979), pp. 259-300.

In 1978 the National Historical Publications and Records Commission, which had sponsored the Hamer Guide, published its Directory
of Archives and Manuscript Repositories in the United States. The
Directory includes entries for more than 2,500 repositories in
the United States, including Puerto Rico, the Canal Zone, the
Virgin Islands, and the Mariana Islands. Each entry includes
basic information such as name, address, and telephone number;
hours of service; availability of copying facilities; volume of
holdings; a capsule characterization of the holdings and special
areas of collecting interest; and selected bibliographical references. In addition to printed materials and manuscripts, the
Directory contains information on photographs, sound recordings,
architectural drawings, etc. There is a general index, as well as
special lists of repositories by type. Because of the recent date
of this publication, its bibliographical references are among the
most current available.

One of the most urgent issues of the 1970s regarding the preservation and use of original source materials involved questions of
the ownership and disposition of papers of U.S. Government officials, including the president. Stimulated by political
differences and disclosures of irregularities in the donation of
Richard M. Nixon's vice-presidential papers to the National
Archives, the resulting public discussion led to the creation of
a National Study Commission on Records and Documents of Federal
Officials. The Commission was established by Congress in December
1974. It issued its report in April 1977. During the life of the
Commission, a number of meetings, conferences, and symposia were
held, some sponsored by the Commission, some sponsored by
interested professional groups, all concerned with the subject
under deliberation by the Commission. (See, for example, Alonzo
L. Hamby and Edward Weldon, eds., Access to the Papers of Recent
Public Figures: The New Harmony Conference (Bloomington, 1977).)

The immediate outcome of the Commission's report was the enactment
of the "Presidential Records Act of 1978" (P.L. 95-591). That
act, to take effect January 1981, applied only to presidential
records and effectively asserted public ownership of documentary
materials produced or received by the president and his staff as
part of the constitutional, statutory, or other official duties of
the president. The law did recognize the existence of "personal
records" not subject to public ownership, but by definition
narrowed the scope of such personal records. The Presidential
Records Act of 1978 and the years of controversy that preceded it
seem destined to affect, perhaps profoundly, the creation and use
of basic research materials for twentieth-century history. At
this writing, it is too early to say how.

Meanwhile, there is strong and growing interest in less traditional documentary materials for the study of American life.
Through the cooperation of the American Film Institute and the
Library of Congress, an ambitious program to preserve and catalog
American films has been initiated. Two volumes have been
published, covering films of the 1920s and of the 1960s. In a
related field, Vanderbilt University in 1968 began to tape
national television news broadcasts, to index their contents, to
publish the indexes, and to make available for scholarly use
reproductions of segments of one or more broadcasts. Finally, in
1976 Congress authorized the establishment in the Library of
Congress of an American Television and Radio Archive. In one
sense, this action merely formalized developments within the
Library active for a generation, but the formal establishment of
such a program will accelerate such developments.

The 1970s were also marked by the establishment and growth of
various library networks, by means of which subscribers secure
access to catalog and other information in a computer data base.
Such information is made available "online" through computer
terminals in participating libraries. The staple of such data
bases has been catalog information identifying monographs, chiefly
those cataloged through the MARC (machine-readable cataloging)

program of the Library of Congress, but information from other sources has become an increasing part of several data bases. The largest, that of OCLC, Inc., began to include citations to manuscript holdings in 1976. By early 1980, the number of manuscript records in the system was far less than one percent of the total number of records. Nevertheless, the likelihood is that there will be a growing proportion of manuscript records in that system and perhaps eventually a larger proportion in less "general-purpose" systems than OCLC, Inc. The NHPRC, for example, envisions a possible national system for archives and records, to which many of the state and regional surveys will contribute descriptive information. Which is to say that the future will be somewhat like the past, but not entirely.

"Surveying Journals of American Studies": Since 1974

BERNARD MERGEN

The rapid increase in the number of scholarly journals in various
fields of American studies that began in the early 1970s has
continued apace. This brief supplement to the original survey will
not attempt to list all of the new and worthy journals; rather, I
will take this opportunity to make some additions of both older
and newer publications. The titles included here should be
considered basic to any library serving students of the United
States. I have refrained this time from listing subscription
prices because inflation is causing rapid increases. And, it is
always best to inquire about special rates for institutions,
students, retired persons, and other special categories.

There are two new additions in the field of American studies as a
distinct academic discipline. The Journal of American Culture, a
quarterly published by the Popular Culture Center, Bowling Green
State University, Bowling Green, Ohio 43403, is edited by Ray
Browne and Russel Nye. It is a large (ca. 200 pages an issue),
well-designed journal that usually devotes most of each issue to
a special topic. One recent topic, "American Food and Foodways,"
contained excellent essays and bibliographies by historians,
anthropologists, and folklorists. The other new American studies
journal is Prospectus: An Annual of American Cultural Studies,
published by Burt Franklin and Company, Inc., 235 East 44th Street,
New York, N.Y. 11550. This book-sized publication covers a wide
variety of topics in American literature, history, popular culture,
and the arts. It is usually well illustrated and contains essays
on the visual arts and material culture.

American Poetry Review, a bi-monthly, tabloid-sized journal of
poetry, criticism, and interviews, is one I missed in my original
article. It has contained the work of most of the major poets of
the 1970s and has introduced many new poets. Its critical essays
are well written and seem to represent several diverse schools of
poetry. It is relatively inexpensive, with special classroom rates
available. Write: Department S, Temple University Center City,
1616 Walnut Street, Room 405, Philadelphia, Pennsylvania 19103.

Social Science History is a new journal specializing in interdisciplinary historical research with an emphasis on comparative
methods. Each issue contains two or three essays, research notes,
reviews, and news of the Social Science History Association. It
is a quarterly, available from the Center for Political Studies,
Box 1248, University of Michigan, Ann Arbor, Michigan 48106.
Institutional subscriptions should be sent to UCIS Publications,
University Center for International Studies, G-6 Mervis Hall,
University of Pittsburgh, Pittsburgh, Pennsylvania 15260. Another
new journal is The Public Historian, a quarterly from the Graduate
Program in Public Historical Studies, Department of History,
University of California at Santa Barbara, Santa Barbara,
California 93106. This publication serves the growing number of
professional historians who are working outside universities, in
museums, archives, and especially in local, state, and federal
agencies. The goal of the editors is to provide a forum for the
discussion of the problems of historians who are dealing with the
general public. It also publishes articles based on research in
new areas of history, such as the history of government agencies.

Two older journals that also provide reviews and news of interest
to historians working in museums and high schools and for historical societies are History News and History Teacher. History
News, a monthly publication of the American Association of State
and Local History, 1400 Eighth Avenue South, Nashville, Tennessee
37203, has recently expanded to a larger, magazine format. It is
an attractive, well-illustrated journal of about 56 pages an issue.
Each issue also has an insert, a "Technical Leaflet," with information on exhibiting, museum management, oral history, and similar
matters. Because of its frequency, it is an excellent source of
information about government programs and employment in the museum
field. History Teacher, a quarterly of the Society for History
Education, Department of History, California State University at
Long Beach, Long Beach, California 90840, is the only academic
journal I know that regularly reviews audiovisual material for
historians. Its articles on innovative teaching techniques are
extremely useful at all levels of instruction.

In 1978, Eugene Genovese began editing a new quarterly, Marxist
Perspectives, The Cliomar Corporation/MP, 420 West End Avenue,
New York, N.Y. 10024. This large (ca.170 pages) journal combines
poetry and Marxist critiques in anthropology, art history, political economy, and history with a substantial amount of advertising, demonstrating again that radical thought and capitalist

economics may yield profit for both partners. Since I omitted them
the first time, I wish to call attention to three journals that,
if representing a more conservative philosophy than Genovese's,
are more widely read and influential and should, therefore, be
included in every library. American Political Science Review, a
quarterly, is published by the American Political Science Association, 1527 New Hampshire Avenue N.W., Washington, D.C. 20036. Its
articles and reviews cover the mainstream of scholarship in political science. Foreign Affairs is published five times yearly and
presents the views of State Department officers and the representatives of various foreign governments. It is available from P.O.
Box 2315, Boulder, Colorado 80322. The quarterly Daedalus,
American Academy of Arts and Sciences, 165 Allandale Street,
Jamaica Plains Station, Boston, Massachusetts 02130, should also
be read because it seems to be influential among policy makers.
Each issue is devoted to a single theme and its contributors are
usually persons who have published widely on the topic.

I am very happy to report that my obituary on Landscape was
premature. Published three times a year and available from P.O.
Box 7107, Berkeley, California 94707, this publication has been
revived and looks as good as ever. Its essays on a variety of
environmental and architectural subjects are well written and well
illustrated. The most promising new publication in the area of
material culture is the redesigned Winterthur Portfolio: A Journal
of American Material Culture. Now a quarterly under the editorship
of Ian M. G. Quimby, it is available from the University of Chicago
Press, 11030 South Langley Avenue, Chicago, Illinois 60628. It is
a handsome 8-1/2" x 11" publication with excellent illustrations.
Advertised as "an interdisciplinary journal committed to fostering
knowledge of the American past by publishing articles on the arts
in America and the historical context within which they were
developed," Winterthur Portfolio truly reflects the important new
spirit of cooperation between museum curators and academic
historians. Historical Archaeology, a quarterly available from
the American Anthropological Association, 1703 New Hampshire
Avenue N.W., Washington, D.C. 20009, is another valuable source
of information on material artifacts. Material History Bulletin/
Bulletin d'histoire de la culture matérielle, National Museum of
Man, Ottawa, Canada, contains articles on the uses of material
artifacts and good exhibit reviews.

The developing interest in local and regional studies will surely
lead to the creation of new journals. Until then, students
interested in regionalism should subscribe to the various state
historical journals. Two periodicals that may serve as models for
future regional journals are Southern Exposure and Appalachian
Journal: A Regional Studies Review. Southern Exposure is a
quarterly available from P.O. Box 230, Chapel Hill, North Carolina.
It is an interesting mix of historical and contemporary studies of
southern labor, civil rights, religion, and arts and crafts.
Appalachian Journal, published by Appalachian State University,
Boone, North Carolina 28608, is also a quarterly with diverse

interests. A recent special issue edited by David Whisnant on Appalachian culture explored the relationships among Appalachian folk cultures, local elites, federal relief programs, and the mass media.

Women's studies is well served by Signs: Journal of Women in Culture and Society. Interdisciplinary and cross-cultural, its essays, book reviews, and news notes are clearly written and well edited. Signs is available from The University of Chicago Press, 5801 Ellis Avenue, Chicago, Illinois 60637. A journal entitled Women's Studies is published three times a year by Gordon and Breach Science Publishers Ltd., 42 William IV Street, London WC2, England. This journal attempts to cover the fields of literature, history, art, sociology, law, political science, economics, anthropology, and science from a women's perspective. It also contains poetry, short fiction, and film and book reviews.

Finally, I want to add three titles which represent a crucial but often neglected area of American studies--science. Although there are specialized historical journals for the study of some sciences and technology, none that I know attempt to place all science in the context of cultural history, nor deal with the impact of science in our daily lives. Because science is so important, no student of American life can afford to ignore it. The best means for keeping up with new developments in science is to read Science, Scientific American, and Natural History. Science is the weekly publication of the American Association for the Advancement of Science, 1515 Massachusetts Avenue N.W., Washington, D.C. 20005. In addition to highly technical articles, it contains readable essays on public policy relating to science, news of science in the federal government, and excellent book reviews in several fields, including anthropology and the history of science. Scientific American, established in 1845, contains a column on science 50 and 100 years ago, a "Science and the Citizen" section on recent developments of general interest, and well-illustrated articles on energy, military technology, genetics, physics, astronomy, chemistry, and archaeology. It is a monthly, available from P.O. Box 5919, New York, N.Y. 10017. Natural History is the least technical of the three and focuses on anthropology, zoology, botany, and the environment. American material culture and history are also frequently the subject of special columns. A subscription to this attractive monthly magazine includes a membership in the American Museum of Natural History in New York City. Write: Natural History, P.O. Box 5000, Des Moines, Iowa 50348 for subscription rates.

General Bibliography and
Author Index

The following pages constitute an author index and bibliography of the books and articles cited in the preceding essays. Every effort has been made to furnish the most recent edition of these works; paperback editions are indicated by an asterisk(*).

Aaron, Daniel. Men of Good Hope. New York: Oxford University Press, 1961. 168

* _____. The Unwritten War: American Writers and the Civil War. New York: Oxford University Press, 1975. 401

* _____. Writers of the Left. New York: Oxford University Press, 1977. 168

Abbott, Carl. "The American Sunbelt: Idea and Region." Journal of the West, (July 1979). 464

Abbs, Peter. Reclamations: Essays on Culture, Mass Culture, and the Curriculum. London: Heinemann Educational Books, 1980. 497

Abegglen, Homer N. "The Chicago Little Theatre, 1912-1917." The Old Northwest, 3(June 1977). 523

Abler, Ronald and John S. Adams. A Comparative Atlas of America's Great Cities: Twenty Metropolitan Regions. Minneapolis: University of Minnesota Press, 1976. 465

*Abraham, Henry J. Freedom and the Court: Civil Rights and Liberties in the United States. New York: Oxford University Press, 1977. 352

* _____. The Judicial Process: An Introductory Analysis of the Courts of the United States, England and France. New York: Oxford University Press, 1980. 350, 354
_____. Justices and Presidents: A Political History of Appointments to the Supreme Court. New York: Oxford University Press, 1974. 349

_____. "The Supreme Court in the Evolving Political Process." M. Judd Harmon, ed. Essays on the Constitution of the United States. Port Washington, New York., 1978. 357

*Abrahams, Roger. Deep Down in the Jungle. Chicago: Aldine, 1970. 107

Abrahamsen, David. Our Violent Society. New York: Funk and Wagnalls, 1970. 310

Abramson, Harold J. Ethnic Diversity in Catholic America. New York: Wiley, 1973. 200, 384

Adams, Donald R., Jr. Finance and Enterprise in Early America: A Study of Stephen Girard's Bank, 1812-1831. Philadelphia: University of Pennsylvania Press, 1978. 73

Adams, Brooks. America's Economic Supremacy. 1947; New York: Arno.

_____. The Law of Civilization and Decay. New York: Macmillan, 1910. 161, 178

_____, ed. The Degradation of the Democratic Dogma. New York: Macmillan, 1919. 178

Adams, Ephraim, D. Great Britain and the American Civil War. 2 vols., London: Longmans, Green, 1925. 118

Adams, Frederick C. Economic Diplomacy: The Export Import Bank and American Foreign Policy, 1934-1939. Columbia: University of Missouri Press, 1976. 137

*Adams, Henry. The Education of Henry Adams. 1918; New York: Houghton-Mifflin, 1973. 178, 393

_____. History of the United States During the Administrations of Jefferson
and Madison. Abridged. Ernest Samuels, ed. Chicago: University of Chicago
Press, 1967. 115, 116, 159

Adams, James Truslow. The Founding of New England. Boston: Atlantic, 1921. 165

Adams, John R. Edward Everett Hale. Boston: Twayne, 1977. 412

Adams, Timothy D. "The Contemporary American Mock-Autobiography." CLIO, 8
(Spring 1979). 399

*Adelman, William. Haymarket Revisited. Chicago: Illinois Labor History
Society, 1976. 527

*_____. Pilsen and the West Side. Chicago: Illinois Labor History Society, 1982. 5

Adler, Dorothy, R. British Investment in American Railways, 1834-1899.
Charlottesville: University Press of Virginia, 1970. 71

Adler, Richard and Douglas Cater, eds.   Television as a Cultural Force.
New York: Praeger, 1976. 497

_____. Television as a Social Force. New York: Praeger, 1975. 497

*Adler, Selig. The Isolationist Impulse: Its Twentieth Century Reaction.
New York: Abelard-Schuman, 1957. 122

*Adorno, T.W. The Authoritarian Personality. New York: Norton, 1982. 172

Ahlstrom, Sydney E. "Bibliography of American Religious History." American
Studies: An International Newsletter, 1 (Autum 1972). 361

*_____. A Religious History of the American People. Garden City: Doubleday,
1975. 363

Aiken, S. Robert. "Towards Landscape Sensibility." Landscape, 20, 3 (Spring 1976). 42

*Aimone, Alan C. Bibliography of Military History. West Point, New York: U.S.
Military Academy. 284

_____. Official Records of the American Civil War: A Researcher's Guide.
West Point, New York: U.S. Military Academy. 284

Aird, Eileen. Sylvia Plath: Her Life and Work. New York: Harper & Row, 1975. 537

*Aisenberg, Nadya. A Common Spring: Crime Novel & Classic. Bowling Green,
Ohio: Bowling Green University Popular Press, 1980. 49, 58

Aitken, Hugh, G.J. Taylorism at Watertown Arsenal: Scientific Management
in Action, 1908-1915. Cambridge: Harvard University Press, 1960. 80

Aitken, Hugh, G.J., ed. Did Slavery Pay? Reading in the Economics of Black
Slavery in the United States. Boston: Houghton - Mifflin, 1971. 78

Albanese, Catherine L. Corresponding Motion: Transcendental Religion and the
New America. Philadelphia: Temple University Press, 1977. 383

_____. Sons of the Fathers: The Civil Religion of the American Revolution.
Philadelphia: Temple University Press, 1976. 387

Alderson, Lawrence. The Chance to Survive. Brattleboro: Greene, 1979. 486

Aldus, Judith, B. Anglo-Irish Dialects: A Bibliography. Regional Language
Studies II, 1967. 256

*Alexander, Charles C. Holding the Line: The Eisenhower Era, 1952-1961.
Bloomington: Indiana University Press, 1975. 436

Alfange, Dean. "The Relevance of Legislative Facts in the Constitutional
Law." 114 University of Pennsylvania Law Review 637 (1966). 353

Alfonso, Oscar, M. Theodore Roosevelt and the Phillipines, 1897-1909.
New York: Oriole Editions, 1973. 431

Algeo, John. "A Black English Bibliography." American Speech, XLIX (1974). 265

*Aliano, Richard A. American Defense Policy from Eisenhower to Kennedy:
The Politics of Changing Military Requirements, 1957-1961. Athens:
Ohio University Press, 1978. 83

*Allard, Dean C. and Betty Bern. U.S. Naval History Sources in the Washington
Area and Suggested Research Subjects. Washington: G.P.O., 1970. 285

*Allen, Dick, and David Chacko, eds. Detective Fiction: Crime and Compromise.
New York: Harcourt, Brace, 1974. 58

Allen, Gay Wilson. The New Walt Whitman Handbook. New York: New York University
Press, 1975. 416

_____. The Solitary Singer: A Critical Biography of Walt Whitman. New York:
New York University Press, 1967. 338

_____. Waldo Emerson: A Biography. New York: Viking Press, 1981.

_____. William James. New York: The Viking Press, 1967. 323, 325

_____, ed. A William James Reader. Boston: 1971. 319

*Allen, Donald M., ed. New American Poetry. New York: Grove, 1960. 335, 343

Allen, Harold B. "English as a Second Language." Seabok. Trends. 256, 266

_____. "Introduction, Part IV, Linguistics and Usage." Allen. Readings. 1964. 269

_____. Linguistics and English Linguistics. Arlington Heights: AHM, 1976. 256

_____. Linguistic Atlas of the Upper Midwest. (3 vols.) Minneapolis:
University of Minnesota Press, 1973-6. 263

_____. Readings in Applied English Linguistics. New York: Appleton Century
Crofts, 1964. 259

_____. "Samuel Johnson and the Authoritarian Tradition." Dissertation,
University of Michigan, 1942. 269

_____, Enola Borgh, and Verna L. Newsome. Focusing on Language: A Reader.
New York: Crowell, 1973. 259

_____ and Gary Underwood. Readings in American Dialectology. New York:
Appleton-Century-Crofts, 1971. 259

Allen, Margaret V. The Achievement of Margaret Fuller. University Park,
Pennsylvania: Pennsylvania State University Press, 1979. 411

Allen Walter R. "Family Roles, Occupational Statuses, and Achievement
Orientations Among Black Women in the United States." Signs, 4 (Summer, 1979). 549

*Allison, Graham, T. Essence of Decision: Explaining the Cuban Missile Crisis.
    Boston: Little Brown, 1971. 130

Almond, Gabriel. The American People and Foreign Policy. Westport: Greenwood,
    1977. 170

Almquist, Elizabeth, M. "Women in the Labor Force." Signs, 2 (Summer 1977). 547

Alperovitz, Gar. Atomic Diplomacy: Hiroshima and Potsdam: The Use of the
    Atomic Bomb and the American Confrontation with Soviet Power. New York:
    Simon & Shuster, 1965. 129

*Altmeyer, Arthur J. The Formative Years of Social Security. Madison:
    University of Wisconsin Press, 1968. 88

Ambrose, Stephen E. Ike: Abilene to Berlin; the Life of Dwight D. Eisenhower
    from his Childhoood in Abilene, Kansas, through his Command of the Allied
    Forces in Europe in World War II. New York: Harper & Row, 1973. 436

American Society of Civil Engineers. A Biographical Dictionary of American
    Civil Engineers. New York: American Society of Civil Engineers, 1972. 41, 46

Ames, Kenneth. "Meaning in Artifacts: Hall Furnishings in Victoria America."
    Journal of Interdisciplinary History, 9 (Summer 1978). 510

Ames, Van Meter. Zen and American Thought. Honolulu: University of Hawaii Press,
    1962. 325

Ames, William E. A History of the National Intelligence. Chapel Hill:
    University of North Carolina Press, 1972. 209

_____ and Roger A. Simpson. Unionism or Hearst, The Seattle Post-Intelligence's
    Strike of 1936. Seattle: Pacific Northwest Labor History Association, 1978. 227

Ammer, Christine. Unsung: A History of Women in American Music. Westport,
    Connecticut: Greenwood Press, 1980. 546

Ammons, A. R. Corson's Inlet. Ithaca: Cornell University Press, 1965. 342

Ammons, Elizabeth ed. Critical Essays on Harriet Beecher Stowe. Boston:
    G.K. Hall, 1980. 416

Anderson, Alan D. The Origin and Resolution of an Urban Crisis: Baltimore,
    1890-1930. Baltimore: Johns Hopkins, 1977. 461

Anderson, Carl. L. Poe in Northlight: the Scandinavian Response to His Life
    and Work. Durham, North Carolina: Duke University Press, 1973. 415

Anderson, Charles, R. Person, Place and Thing in Henry James' Novels.
    Durham, North Carolina: Duke University Press, 1977. 413

Anderson,David, B. Woodrow Wilson. Boston: Twayne Publishers, 1978. 432

Anderson, David D. Abraham Lincoln. U.S. Authors Series No. 153. New York:
    Twayne Publishers, 1970. 428

Anderson, Donald F. William Howard Taft: A Conservative's Conception of the Presidency. Ithaca, New York: Cornell University Press, 1973. 432

Anderson, Donna K. The Works of Charles T. Griffes. Detroit: Information Coordinators, 1977. 306

*Anderson, Frederick, et. al. Environmental Improvement through Economic Incentives. Baltimore: Johns Hopkins University Press, 1978. 474

Anderson, Gillian. Freedom's Voice in Poetry and Song, 2 vols. Wilmington: Scholarly Resources, Inc., 1977. 303

Anderson, Irvine. H., Jr. The Standard-Vacuum Oil Company and United States East Asian Policy, 1933-1941. Princeton: Princeton University Press, 1975. 86, 137

*Anderson, Jervis. A Philip Randolph. New York: Harcourt, Brace, 1973. 449

Anderson, Robert Mapes. Vision of the Disinherited: The Making of American Pentecostalism. New York: Oxford University Press, 1979. 381

Anderson, Terry L. "Economic Growth in Colonial New England: Statistical Renaissance." Journal of Economic History, XXXIX (March 1979). 91

Andreano, Ralph L. ed. The New Economic History: Recent Papers on Methodology. New York: Wiley, 1970. 63

Andrew, John A., III. Rebuilding the Christian Commonwealth. Lexington: University Press of Kentucky, 1976. 377

Andrews, Charles M. The Colonial Period of American History, 4 vols. New Haven: Yale University Press, 1934, 1936, 1937, 1938. 160

Andrews, Cutler J. The North Reports The Civil War. Pittsburgh: University of Pittsburgh Press, 1955. 213

_____. The South Reports the Civil War. Princeton: Princeton University Press, 1970. 213

*Andrews, Wayne. Architecture, Ambition and Americans. New York: Free Press, 1979. 34, 42

*_____. Architecture in Chicago and Mid-America. New York: Harper and Row, 1973. 37, 43

*_____. Architecture in New York. New York: Harper and Row, 1973. 37, 43

Andrews, William D. "Women and the Fairs of 1876 and 1893." Hayes Historical Journal, 1 (Spring 1977). 532

Andrist, Ralph, K. ed. George Washington: A Biography in His Own Words. New York: Newsweek, distributed by Harper and Row, 1973. 424

Antieau, Chester James. "The Jurisprudence of Interests as a Method of Constitutional Adjudication." 27 Case Western Reserve Law Review 825 (1977). 356

*Aptheker, Herbert, ed. American Negro Slave Revolts. New York: International Publishers, 1969. 25

Aptheker, Herbert. A Documentary History of the Negro People in the United States, 3 vols. New York: Citadel Press. 13

Appel, John C. "Immigrant Historical Societies in the United States, 1880–1950." Unpublished Dissertation. University of Pennsylvania, 1950. 203

*Appel Richard G. The Music of the Bay Psalm Book: 9th Edition (1698). Brooklyn: Institute for Studies in American Music, 1975. 303

Aquarone, Alberto. Le Origini dell'Imperialismo Americano: Da McKinley a Taft (1897–1913). Bologna: il Mulino, 1973. 132

*Arad, Ruth and Uzi. Sharing Global Resources. New York: McGraw Hill, 1979. 481

*Archambault, Reginald, ed. John Dewey on Education. Chicago: University of Chicago Press, 1974. 321

Archer, Gleason L. History of Radio 1926. New York: American Historical Society 1938; Arno. 220

*Arens, W. and Susan P. Montague, eds. The American Dimension: Cultural Myths and Social Realities. Port Washington, New York: Alfred, 1976. 497

Arensberg, Liliane. "Death as Metaphor of Self in I Know Why the Caged Bird Sings." College Language Association Journal, 20 (December 1976). 396, 399

Arlen, Michael J.   Thirty Seconds. New York: Farrar, Straus, Giroux, 1980. 497

_____. The View from Highway 1: Essays on Television. New York: Farrar, Straus, Giroux, 1976. 493, 498

Arms, George, ed. Selected Letters of W. D. Howells. Boston: Twayne, 1981. 413

Armstrong, Anne. Unconditional Surrender: The Impact of the Casablanca Policy Upon World War II. New Brunswick: Rutgers University Press, 1961. 127

Armstrong, William M. E.L. Godkin: A Biography. Albany: State University of New York Press, 1978. 225

Arnold, William A. Back When It all Began: The Early Nixon Years: Being Some Reminiscences of President Nixon's Early Political Career by His First Administrative Assistant and Press Secretary. New York: Vantage Press, 1975. 438

Aronson, James. The Press and the Cold War. Indianapolis: Bobbs-Merrill, 1970. 221

Arpad, Joseph, J. "Immediate Experience and the Historical Method." Journal Popular Culture, XI, 1 (Summer, 1977). 498

*Arrington, Leonard J. and Davis Bitton. The Mormon Experience: A History of the Latter-day Saints. New York: Random, 1980. 382

*Asbaugh, Carolyn. Lucy Parsons: American Revolutionary. Chicago: Charles H. Kerr, 1976. 527, 537

*Ashbery, John. Self Portrait in a Convex Mirror. New York: Penguin, 1976. 341

Ashbolt, Alan. An American Experience. New York: P.S. Erikson, 1967. 309

*Ashby, Eric. Reconciling Man with the Environment. Stanford: Stanford
University Press, 1978. 476

Asher, Robert. "Business and Workers' Welfare in the Progressive Era: Workmen's Compensation Reform in Massachusetts, 1880-1911." Business History
Review, XLIII (Winter 1969). 87

Ashton, Jean W. Harriet Beecher Stowe: A Reference Guide. Boston: G.K. Hall,
1977. 416

Astre, Georges - Albert and Calude-Jean Betrand, eds. "Mass Media et
Ideologie Aux Etats - Unis." Review Francaise d'Etudes Americaines, 6
(October 1978). 498

Atkins, Ollie. The White House Years: Triumph and Tragedy. Chicago:
Playboy Press, 1977. 438

*Atwan Robert, Donald McQuade, and John W. Wright. Edsels, Luckies, and
Frigidaires: Advertising the American Way. New York: Dell Publishing
Company, 1979. 509

Atwood, E. Bagby. The Regional Vocabulary of Texas. Austin, Texas: University
Press, 1962. 263

_____. A Survey of Verb Forms in the Eastern United States. Ann Arbor:
University of Michigan Press, 1953. 263

Auchampaugh, Philip, C. James Buchanan and His Cabinet on the Eve of the
Secession. Boston: J.S. Canner and Co., 1965. 428

Aufhauser, R. Keith. "Slavery and Scientific Management." Journal of
Economic History, XXX (December 1973). 79

Austin, Lettie J., Lewis H. Fenderson and Sophia D. Nelson. The Black Man
and the Promise of America. Glenview: Scott, Foresman, 1970.

Austin, William. Susanna, Jeanie, and the Old Folks at Home. New York:
Macmillan, 1975. 300, 304

Avis, Walter S. A Bibliography of Writings on Canadian English 1957-1965.
Toronto: W. Gage, 1965. 256

_____. "The English Language in Canada." Sebeok. Trends. 256, 263

_____ and A. M. Kinloch. Writings on Canadian English 1792-1975.
Toronto: Fitzhenry and Whiteside, 1978. 256

Axelson, Arne. The Links in the Chain: Isolation and Independence in
Nathaniel Hawthorne's Fictional Characters. Stockholm, Sweden:
Almquist and Wiksell, 1974. 412

*Axinn, June and Herman Levin. Social Welfare: A History of the American Response to Need. New York: Harper and Row, 1975. 86

Ayer, A.J. The Origins of Pragmatism. San Francisco: Freeman, Cooper and Company, 1968. 325

Babcock, C. Merton. The Ordeal of American English. Boston: Houghton, Mifflin and Company, 1961. 259

Babcock, Robert. Gompers in Canada: A Study in American Continentalism Before the First World War. Toronto: University of Toronto Press, 1974. 448

Bachmann, Donna, G. and Sherry Piland, eds. Women Artists: An Historical, Contemporary and Feminist Bibliography. Metuchen, N.J.: Scarecrow Press, 1978. 537

Bachman, Lawrence P. "Julius Rosenwald." American Jewish Historical Quarterly, 66 (1976). 529

*Badger, R. Reid. The Great American Fair: The World's Columbian Exposition and American Culture. Chicago: Nelson-Hall, 1979. 532

Baer, Judith A. The Chains of Protection: The Judicial Response to Women's Labor Legislation. Westport: Greenwood Press, 1978. 542

Bahr, Dieter. A Bibliography of Writings on Canadian English, 1857-1976. Heidelberg: Winter. 256

Bailey, Richard W. and Jay L. Robinson. Varieties of Present-Day English. New York: Macmillan, 1972. 259

Bailey, Thomas A. America Faces Russia: Russian-American Relations from Early Times to Our Day. Ithaca: Cornell University Press, 1950. 122

_____. Hitler vs. Roosevelt: The Undeclared Naval War. New York: Free Press, 1979. 138, 434

_____. Theodore Roosevelt and the Japanese-American Crises: An Account of the International Complications Arising from the Race Problem on the Pacific Coast. Stanford: Stanford University Press, 1934. 121

_____. Woodrow Wilson and the Great Betrayal. New York: Macmillan, 1945. 122

*_____. Woodrow Wilson and the Lost Peace. New York: Macmillan, 1944. 122

_____ and Paul B. Ryan. The Lusitania Disaster: An Episode in Modern Warfare and Diplomacy. New York: Free Press, 1975. 136

*Bailyn, Bernard. The Ideological Origins of the American Revolution. Cambridge: Harvard University Press, 1967. 178, 374

_____. New England Merchants in the Seventeenth Century. Cambridge: Harvard University Press, 1979. 171

Bain, Kenneth R. The March to Zion: United States Policy and the Founding of Israel. College Station: Texas A and M Press, 1979. 141

*Baker, James Thomas. A Southern Baptist in the White House. Philadelphia: Westminster Press, 1977. 440

Baker, L. John Marshall: A Life in Law. New York: Macmillan, 1974. 349

Baker, Ronald. Folklore in the Writings of Rowland E. Robinson. Bowling Green, Ohio: Bowling Green University Popular Press, 1973. 103

Baker, Ross, ed. The Afro-American. New York: Van Nostrand Reinhold, 1970. 13

Baker, Sheridan. The Complete Stylist. New York: Crowell, 1966. 269

*Baldwin, James. Blues for Mr. Charlie. New York: Dell, 1964.

*_____. The Fire Next Time. New York: Dell. 1970. 22

*Balio, Tino, ed. The American Film Industry. Madison: University of Wisconsin, 1976.
    497, 498

Ball, Howard. Judicial Craftmanship or Fiat? Director Overturn by the United
    States Supreme Court. Westport, Connecticut: Greenwood Press, 1977. 357

Ball, John, ed. The Mystery Story. Del Mar, California: Publisher's, Inc., 1976. 58

Ball, Rick A., et al. Indianapolis Architecture. Indianapolis: Indiana
    Architectural Foundation, 1975. 43

Baker, Robert A. The Southern Baptist Convention and its People, 1607-1972.
    Nashville: Broadman Press, 1974. 365

Ball, Howard. No Pledge of Privacy: The Watergate Tapes Litigation. Port
    Washington, New York: Kennikat Press, 1977. 439

Ballou, Patricia K. "Bibliographies for Research on Women." Signs, 3 (Winter 1977). 536

Bambara, Toni Cade. The Salt Eaters. New York: Random House, 1980. 468

Bancroft, George. History of the United States, 10 vols. Boston: Little, Brown,
    1981-75. 155

Bancroft, George. "The Office of the People in Art, Government and Religion."
    J.L. Blau, ed. Social Theories of Jacksonian Democracy. New York: Liberal
    Arts Press, 1954. 178

Bancroft, Hubert H. Literary Industries. 1888; San Francisco: H.H. Bancroft
    Company, 1967. 178

*Banham, Reyner. Los Angeles, A City of Four Ecologies. New York: Penguin, 1973. 175

Bann, Stephan. "Historical Text and Historical Object: the Poetics of the
    Musee de Cluny." History and Theory, 17 (October 1978). 510

*Banner, Lois, W. Elizabeth Cady Stanton: A Radical for Women's Rights. New
    York: Little, Brown, 1980. 537

Banning, Evelyn I. Helen Hunt Jackson. New York: Vanguard, 1973. 413

*Baraka, Amiri. The Motion of History and Other Plays. New York: Morrow, 1978. 22

*_____ and Roy Neal, eds. Black Fire: An Anthology of Afro-American
    Writing. New York: Morrow, 1968. 22

Baram, Philip A. The Department of State in the Middle East, 1919-1945.
   Philadelphia: University of Pennsylvania Press, 1978. 141

Barker, Lucius J. and Twiley W. Civil Liberties and the Constitution: Cases
   and Commentaries. Englewood Cliffs, New Jersey: Prentice-Hall, 1978. 355

Barker-Benfield, Graham J. The Horrors of the Half-Known Life. New York:
   Harper and Row, 1976. 551

Barksdale, Richard and Keneth Kinnamon. Black Writers of America: A Comprehensive
   Anthology. New York: Macmillan, 1972. 22

*Barnard, Roy S. Oral History. U. S. Military History Research Collection,
   Carlisle Barracks. 285

Barnes, Harry E. The Chickens of the Interventionist Liberals Have Come Home
   to Roost: The Bitter Fruits of Globalony. New York: Revisionist Press, 1973. 178

_____ _____. World Politics in Modern Civilization. New York: Alfred A.
   Knopf, 1930. 178

Barnes, Melvyn, P. Best Detective Fiction. London: Clive Bingley, 1975. 56

^Barnet, Richard J. Roots of War: The Men and Institutions behind U.S.
   Foreign Policy. New York: Atheneum, 1972. 131

Barnhart, Clarence L. "American Lexicography, 1945-1973." American Speech LIII. 256

Barnouw, Erik. The Golden Web: A History of Broadcasting in the U.S., 1933-1953.
   New York: Oxford University Press, 1968. 219

_____. The Image Empire: A History of Broadcasting in the United States
   from 1953. New York: Oxford University Press, 1970. 219

_____. A Tower in Babel: A History of Broadcasting in the United States
   to 1933. New York: Oxford University Press, 1966. 219

*_____. Tube of Plenty: The Evolution of American Television. New York:
   Oxford University Press, 1977. 219, 498

Baron, Robert Alex. The Tyranny of Noise. New York: St. Martin's, 1970. 476

Barre, W.L. The Life and Public Services of Millard Fillmore. New York:
   B. Franklin, 1971. 428

Barrett, Paul F. "Mass Transit, the Automobile and Public Policy in Chicago,
   1900-1390." Unpublished dissertation. University of Illinois at Chicago
   Circle, 1976. 532

Barron, Gloria J. Leadership in Crisis: FDR and the Path to Intervention.
   Port Washington, New York: Kennikat Press, 1973. 125

Barthes, Roland. Mythologies. New York: Hill and Wang, 1972. 498

*Bartlett, Richard A. Great Surveys of the American West. Norman, Oklahoma:
   University of Oklahoma Press, 1980. 178

Barton, Arnold H. Letters from the Promised Land: Swedes in America, 1840-1914. Minneapolis: University of Minnesota Press, 1975. 195

Barton, Josef. Peasants and Strangers: Italians, Romanians and Slovaks in an American City. Cambridge, Massachusetts: Harvard University Press, 1975. 197

*Barton, Rebecca C. Witnesses for Freedom: Negro Americans in Autobiography. Oakdale: Dowling, 1976. 398

Barzun, Jacques. "Meditations on the Literature of Spying." The American Scholar, XXXIV (Spring 1965). 55

_____ and Wendell Hertig Taylor. A Catalogue of Crime. New York: Harper and Row, 1974. 56

Basler, R.B., D.H. Mugridge, and B. McCrum. A Guide to the Study of the United States of America. Washington, D.C.: U.S. Government Printing Office, 1960. 178

Basler, Roy Prentice. A Touchstone for Greatness: Essays, Addresses, and Occasional Pieces About Abraham Lincoln. Westport, Connecticut: Greenwood Press, 1973. 428

Bateman, Fred and Thomas Weiss. "Manufacturing in the Antebellum South." Research in Economic History, I (1976). 79

Bates, Richard O. The Gentleman from Ohio: A Biography of James A. Garfield. Durham, North Carolina: Moore Publishing Company, 1973. 430

Baugh, Albert C. History of the English Language. Englewood Cliffs: Prentice-Hall, 1978. 256

Baughman, James, P. Charles Morgan and the Development of Southern Transportation. Nashville: Vanderbilt University Press, 1968. 72

Bauman, Richard. For the Reputation of Truth: Politics, Religion, and Conflict Among the Pennsylvania Quakers, 1750-1800. Baltimore, Maryland: Johns Hopkins University Press, 1971. 370

Baxandall, Rosalyn, Linda Gordon, and Susan Reverby, eds. America's Working Women: A Documentary History, 1600 to the Present. New York: Random, 1976. 536

Baym, Nina. The Shape of Hawthorne's Career. Ithaca, New York: Cornell University Press, 1976. 412

*_____. Woman's Fiction: A Guide to Novels By and About Women in America, 1820-1870. Ithaca: Cornell University Press, 1980. 404, 537

*Bayor, Ronald H. Neighbors in Conflict: The Irish, Germans, Jews and Italians of New York City, 1929-1941. Baltimore, Maryland: Johns Hopkins University Press, 1980. 200

Beale, Howard K. "Causes of the Civil War." Social Science Research Council Bulletin No. 54 (1946). 178

_____. Theodore Roosevelt and the Rise of America to World Power. Baltimore, Maryland: Johns Hopkins Press, 1956. 121

Beard, Charles A. American Foreign Policy in the Making, 1932-1940: A Study in Responsibilities. 1946; New York: Shoestring, 1968. 125, 179

_____ . The Devil Theory of War: An Inquiry into the Nature of History and the Possibility of Keeping out of War. 1936; Westport: Greenwood, 1968. 178

_____. The Discussion of Human Affairs. New York: Macmillan, 1936. 178

* _____.. Economic Interpretation of the Constitution. 1913; New York: Free Press, 1965. 163

_____ . Giddy Minds and Foreign Quarrels: An Estimate of American Foreign Policy. New York: Macmillan, 1936. 179

_____. The Old Deal and the New. New York: Macmillan, 1940. 179

_____ . President Roosevelt and the Coming of the War, 1941: A Study in Appearances and Realities. New Haven: Yale University Press, 1948. 126

_____ and Mary. The Rise of American Civilization. New York: Macmillan, 1927. 165

Beasley, Maurine Hoffman. The First Women Washington Correspondents. George Washington Studies, No. 4. Washington, D.C.: George Washington University, (January, 1976.) 210

_____ and Sheila Silver. Women in Media: A Documentary Source Book. Washington, D.C.: Women's Institute for Freedom of the Press, 1977. 225

*Beck, Alfred M., ed. Engineer Memoirs: Interviews with Lieutenant General J. Clarke. Washington, D.C.: Historical Division, Office of Chief of Engineers, 1980. 294

Becker, Jens-Peter. Der englische Spionsgeroman. Munich: Wilhenlm Goldmann, 1973. 61

Becker, Theodore L. Political Behavioralism and Modern Jurisprudence. New York: Rand McNally and Company, 1964. 354

* _____ and M.M. Feeley. The Impact of Supreme Court Decisions. New York: Oxford University Press, second edition, 1973. 352

Beckford, James A. The Trumpet of Prophecy: A Sociological Study of Jehova's Witnesses. New York: Wiley, 1975. 383

Beckham, Stephen Dow, ed. Tall Tales from Rogue River; The Yarns of Hathaway Jones. Bloomington: Indiana University Press, 1974. 101

Bedford, Henry F. Trouble Downtown: The Local Context of Twentieth-Century America. New York: Harcourt Brace Jovanovich, 1978. 459

Beer, George Louis. British Colonial Policy. New York: Macmillan, 1907. 160

Behrend, Jeanne, ed. Notes of a Pianist. New York: Knopf, 1964. 299

Beichman, Arnold. Nine Lies About America. New York: Library Press, 1972. 313

Beisner, Robert L. Twelve Against Empire: The Anti-Imperialists, 1898-1900.
New York: McGraw-Hill, 1968. 119

Belasco, James. Americans on the Road: From Auto-camp to Motel, 1910-1945.
Cambridge, Massachusetts: MIT Press, 1979. 508

Bell, Carl I. They Knew Franklin Pierce. Springfield, Vermont: April Hill, 1980. 428

Bell, Daniel. The End of Ideology. Glenco: Free Press, 1960. 170

Bell, Marion L. Crusade in the City: Revivalism in Nineteenth-Century Philadelphia.
Lewisburg: Bucknell University Press, 1977. 376

Bell, Winifred. Aid to Dependent Children. New York: Columbia University
Press, 1965. 88

*Bellah, Robert N. The Broken Covenant: American Civil Religion in Time of
Trial. New York: Seabury, 1975.

Bemis, Samuel F. The Diplomacy of the American Revolution. 1935; New York:
Peter Smith, 1957. 114, 179

* _____. In Jay's Treaty: A Study in Commerce and Diplomacy, 1763-
1801. New York: Macmillan, 1972. 114

_____. Jay's Treaty. 1923; Westport: Greenwood, 1975. 179

* _____. John Quincy Adams and the Foundations of American Foreign
Policy. 1940; New York: Norton, 1973. 117, 179

_____. Latin American Policy of the United States. New York: Harcourt
Brace, 1943. 124, 179

_____. Pinckney's Treaty. 1926; Westport: Greenwood, 1973. 115, 179

_____, ed. American Secretaries of State and their Diplomacy,
10 vols. 1928; Totowa: Cooper Square. 165

*Benedict, Michael Les. The Impeachment and Trial of Andrew Johnson. New
York: Norton, 1973. 429

Bennett, John W. "Using Union Memorabilia as a Teaching Aid." Labor Studies
Journal, 3 (Fall 1978). 453

Bennett, Neville, Joyce Jordan, George Long, and Barbara Wade. Teaching
Styles and Pupil Progress. Cambridge: Harvard University Press, 1976. 443

*Benson, Lee. The Concept of Jacksonian Democracy: New York as a Test Case.
Princeton University Press, 1961. 205

Benson, Susan Porter. "The Clerking Sisterhood: Rationalization and the Work Culture of Saleswomen in American Department Stores, 1890-1960." Radical America, 12 (March-April 1978). 551

*Bercovitch, Sacvan. The Puritan Origins of the American Self. New Haven: Yale University Press, 1975. 367

Berg, Barbara. The Remembered Gate: Origins of American Feminism. New York: Oxford, 1978. 550

*Berg, Stephen and Robert Mezey, eds. The New Naked Poetry: Recent Contemporary Poetry in Open Forms. Indianapolis: Bobbs-Merrill, 1976. 335

Berger, Arthur Asa. The Comic-Stripped American. New York: Walker, 1973. 498

*Berger, Bennett. Working Class Suburb: A Study of Automobile Workers in Suburbia. Berkeley: University of California Press, 1960. 452

Berger, Meyer. The Story of the New York Times, 1851-1951. New York: Simon and Schuster, 1951; Arno. 217

*Berger, Peter and Thomas Luckmann. The Social Construction of Reality: A Treatise in the Sociology of Knowledge. Garden City, New York: Doubleday, 1967. 498

Berger, Raoul. Government by Judiciary: The Transformation of the Fourteenth Amendment. Cambridge: Harvard University Press, 1977. 351, 357

Berheide, Catherine M., et al. "Towards a Women's Perspective in Sociology: Directions and Prospects." Theoretical Perspectives in Sociology. New York: St. Martin's Press, 1979. 540

_____, et. al., eds. Women Today: A Multidisciplinary Approach to Women's Studies. Monterey, California: Brooks/Cole, 1980. 540

_____, Sarah Berk and Richard Berk. "Household Work in the Suburbs: The Job and Its Particpants." Pacific Sociological Review, 19 (October 1976). 549

*Berk, Richard and Sarah. Labor and Leisure at Home. Beverly Hills, California: Sage Publications, 1979. 549

*Berk, Sarah, ed. Women and Household Labor. Beverly Hills, California: Sage Publications, 1980. 549

Berk, Stephen E. Calvinism versus Democracy: Timothy Dwight and the Origins of American Evangelical Orthodoxy. Hamden: Anchor Books, 1974. 376

Berkhofer, Robert F., Jr. "Comment." American Historical Review, 84 (December 1979). 455

*_____. Salvation and the Savage. New York: Atheneum, 1972. 378

*Berkhofer, Robert F., Jr. The White Man's Indian: Images of the American Indian from Columbus to the Present. New York: Random, 1979. 513

*Berkin, Carol Ruth and Mary Beth Norton, eds. Women of America. A History. Boston: Houghton Mifflin Company, 1979. 545

* _____ and Clara M. Lovett. Women, War, and Revolution. New York: Holmes & Meier, 1980. 544

Berkow, Ira. Maxwell Street: Survival in a Bazaar. New York: Doubleday, 1979. 519

*Berlin, Ira. Slaves Without Masters: The Free Negro in the Antebellum South. New York: Vintage, 1976. 25, 79

Bernath, Stuart L. Squall Across the Atlantic: American Civil War Prize Cases and Diplomacy. Berkeley: University of California Press, 1970. 118

Bernhard, Richard M. and Maris A. Vinouskis. "The Female School Teacher in Ante-Bellum Massachusetts." Journal of Social History, 10 (March 1977). 551

Bernstein, Barton J., ed. The Truman Administration. New York: Harper and Row, 1966. 179

*_____ , ed. Towards a New Past: Dissenting Essays in American History. New York: Random, 1969. 179

*_____ and A.J. Matuson, eds. Twentieth Century America. New York: Harcourt, Brace, Javanovich, 1972. 179

Bernstein, Theodore. The Careful Writer. New York: Atheneum, 1965. 269

_____. Miss Thistlebottom's Hobgoblins. New York: Farrar, Straus and Giroux, 1971. 269

_____. Watch Your Language. Manhasset: Channel Press, 1958. 269

Berry, Brian J., ed. Chicago: Transformation of an Urban System. Cambridge: Ballinger, 1976. 526, 531

*Berry, Wendell. The Unsettling of America. New York: Avon, 1978. 473

Berstein, Richard, ed. On Experience, Nature and Freedom. Indianapolis, 1960. 321

Beschloss, Michael R. Kennedy and Roosevelt: The Uneasy Alliance. New York: W.W. Norton and Company, Inc., 1980. 434

Best, Gary Dean. The Politics of American Individualism: Herbert Hoover in Transition, 1918-1921. Westport, Connecticut: Greenwood Press, 1975. 433

Bettelheim, Bruno. The Uses of Enchantment: The Meaning and Importance of Fairy Tales. New York: Vintage, 1977. 498

Beveridge, Albert J. Life of John Marshall. 4 vols. Boston: Houghton Mifflin, 1916-19. 179

Bianco, Carla. The Two Rosetos. Bloomington: Indiana University Press, 1974. 108

*Bickel, Alexander. The Least Dangerous Branch: The Supreme Court at the Bar of Politics. Indianapolis, Indiana: Bobbs-Merrill, 1963. 351

_____. The Supreme Court and the Idea of Progress. New York: Harper & Row, 1970. 351

*_____. The Unpublished Opinions of Mr. Justice Brandeis. Chicago: University of Chicago Press, 1967. 353

Bickley, R. Bruce et. al., eds. Joel Chandler Harris: A Reference Guide. Boston: G.K. Hall, 1978. 412

Bickley, R. Bruce Jr. The Method of Melville's Short Fiction. Durham, North Carolina: Duke University Press, 1975. 414

Bierley, Paul E. John Philip Sousa: American Phenomenon. New York: Appleton, 1973. 300

Bigsby, C.W.E., ed. Approaches to Popular Culture. Bowling Green: Popular Press, 1977. 492, 498

*_____. Superculture: American Popular Culture and Europe. Bowling Green: Bowling Green Press, 1975. 492, 498

Billiard, Charles. "The Speech of Fort Wayne, Indiana." Dissertation. Purdue University, 1969. 265

*Billington, Ray A. America's Frontier Heritage. Albuquerque: University of New Mexico Press, 1974. 173, 179

_____. Frederick Jackson Turner, Historian, Scholar, Teacher. New York: Oxford University Press, 1973. 179

Bird, Fredrick. "The Contemporary Ritual Milieu." Ray Browne, ed., Rituals and Ceremonies in Popular Culture. Bowling Green: Popular Press, 1980. 498

Bishop, Ferman. Henry Adams. Boston: G.K. Hall, 1979. 409

*Bishop, James Alfonso. FDR's Last Year: April 1944–April 1945. London: Hart-Davis MacGibbon, 1975. 434

Bitzer, Lloyd and Theodore Rueter. Carter vs. Ford: The Counterfeit Debates of 1976. Madison: The University of Wisconsin Press, 1980. 440

Black, Charles. The People and the Court: Judicial Review in a Democracy. New York: Macmillan, 1960. 351

Black, Gregory D. and Clayton R. Koppes. "OWI Goes to the Movies: The Bureau of Intelligence's Criticism of Hollywood, 1942-43." Prologue: The Journal of the National Archives, 6 (Spring 1974). 291

Black, Hugo L. "The Bill of Rights." 35 New York University Law Review 866 (1960). 352

_____. A Constitutional Faith. New York: Alfred A. Knopf, 1968. 352

*Black, Lowell D. The Negro Volunteer Militia Units of the Ohio National Guard, 1870-1954. Manhattan, Kansas: Kansas State University, 1976. 229

Blackford, Mansel G. Pioneering a Modern Small Business: Wakefield Seafoods and the Alaskan Frontier. Greenwich, Connecticut: Jai Press, 1979. 93

*Blackwell, Elizabeth. Opening the Medical Profession to Women. New York: Schocken, 1977. 538

Blagden, Cyprian. The Stationers' Company: A History, 1903-1959. Stanford: Stanford University Press, 1960. 207

Blair, Karen J. The Clubwoman as Feminist. New York: Holmes and Meier, 1980. 550

*Blair, Walter and Franklin Meine. Half Horse Half Alligator. 1956; Lincoln: University of Nebraska Press, 1981. 101

_____. Mike Fink, King of Mississippi Keelboatmen. 1933; Westport: Greenwood Press, 1971. 101

*Blair, Walter and Hamlin Hill. America's Humor: From Poor Richard to Doonesbury. New York: Oxford University Press, 1980. 401

Blaisdell, Thomas C. and Peter Selz. The American Presidency in Political Cartoons, 1776-1976. Berkeley: University Art Museum, 1976.

*Blanchard, Paula. Margaret Fuller: From Transcendentalism to Revolution. New York: Dell, 1979. 225

*Blaser, Werner. Mies van der Rohe. Cambridge: Birkhauser, 1981. 44

Blasier, Cole. The Hovering Giant: U.S. Responses to Revolutionary Change in Latin America. Pittsburgh: University of Pittsburgh Press, 1976. 139

Blasing, Mutlu Konuk. The Art of Life: Studies in Autobiographical Literature. Austin: University of Texas Press, 1977. 392, 398

Blassingame, John W. "Black Autobiographies as History and Literature." Black Scholar, 5 (December 1973-January 1974). 398

_____. Black New Orleans, 1860-1880. Chicago: University of Chicago Press, 1976. 79, 179, 463

_____. The Slave Community: Plantation Life in the Antebellum South. New York: Oxford University Press, 1977. 25, 78, 179, 398

*Blau, Joseph L. Judaism in America: From Curiosity to Third Faith. Chicago: University of Chicago Press, 1978. 386

*Blauner, Robert. Alienation and Freedom: The Factory Worker and His Industry. Chicago: University of Chicago Press, 1964. 446

*Blaustein, Albert P. and Roy Mersky. The First One Hundred Justices: Statistical Studies on the Supreme Court of the United States. Hamden, Connecticut: The Shoe String Press, Inc., 1978. 356

Blaustein, Robert and Robert Zangrando. Civil Rights and the American Negro. New York: Trident Press, 1968. 13

Bleich, David. Subjective Criticism. Baltimore: Johns Hopkins, 1978. 498

*Blesh, Rudi and Harriet Janis. They All Played Ragtime. New York: Oak Publications, 1971. 301

Bleyer, Willard G. Main Currents in the History of American Journalism. Boston: Houghton Mifflin, 1927; Da Capo. 222

Block, Jean F. Hyde Park Houses: An Informal History, 1856-1910. Chicago: University of Chicago Press, 1979. 527

Bloom, Benjamin S. Human Characteristics and School Learning. New York: McGraw Hill, 1976. 443

Bloom, Lynn Z. "Gertrude in Alice in Everybody: Innovation and Point of View in Gertrude Stein's Autobiography." Twentieth-Century Literature, 24 (Spring 1978). 400

Bloomfield, Leonard. Language. New York: Holt, 1933. 268

_____ and Clarence Barnhart. Let's Read. Detroit: Wayne State University Press, 1961. 267

Bluem, William A. Documentary in American Television. New York: Hastings House, 1965. 220

*Bluestein, Gene. The Voice of the Folk: Folklore and American Literary Theory. Amherst: University of Massachusetts Press, 1972. 103

Blum, Eleanor, ed. Basic Books in the Mass Media. Urbana: University of Illinois, 1980. 491, 498

Blum, John Morton. The Promise of America: An Historical Inquiry. Boston: Houghton Mifflin, 1966. 309

Block, Adrienne Fried and Carol Neuls-Bates. Women in American Music: A Bibliography of Music and Literature. Westport: Greenwood Press, 1979. 306

Blyn, Martin R. and Herman E. Krooss. History of Financial Institutions. Philadelphia: Philadelphia Book Company, 1971.

Boatright, Mody C. Folk Laughter on the American Frontier. New York: Macmillan, 1949. 100

_____. Folklore of the Oil Industry. Dallas: Southern Methodist University Press, 1980. 102

_____. Gib Morgan: Minstrel of the Oil Fields. 1945; Dallas: Southern Methodist University Press, 1965. 101

*Bode, Carl. Mencken. Carbondale: Southern Illinois University Press, 1973. 219

Bodnar, John. Immigration and Industrialization: Ethnicity in an American Mill Town, 1870-1940. Pittsburgh: University of Pittsburgh Press, 1977. 197, 199

_____. "Immigration and Modernization: The Case of Slavic Peasants in Industrial America." Journal of Social History, X (Fall 1976). 199

_____, comp. Ethnic History in Pennsylvania: A Selected Bibliography. Harrisburg, Pennsylvania: Pennsylvania Historical and Museum Commission, 1974. 191

Bogart, Leo. The Age of Television: A Study of Viewing Habits and the Impact of Television on American Life. New York: Ungar, 1972. 498

Bogue, Allan G. From Prairie to Corn Belt: Farming on the Illinois and Iowa Prairies in the Nineteenth Century. Chicago: University of Chicago Press, 1963. 76

Boler, John F. Charles Pierce and Scholastic Realism. Seattle: University of Washington Press, 1963. 325

Boles, John B. The Great Revival, 1787-1805. Lexington: University Press of Kentucky, 1972. 375

Bolkhovitinov, Nikolai N. The Beginnings of Russian-American Relations, 1775-1815. Cambridge: Harvard University Press, 1975. 133

Bolin, Winifred. "The Economics of Middle-Income Family Life: Working Women During the Great Depression." Journal of American History, 65 (June 1978). 549

Boller, Paul F., Jr. American Transcendentalism, 1830-1860; An Intellectual Inquiry. New York: G.P. Putnam's Sons, 1975. 401

Bolt, Ernest C. Ballots before Bullets: The War Referendum Approach.to Peace in America - 1914-1941. Charlottesville: University of Virginia Press, 1977. 136

*Bond, Donovan H. and W. Reynolds McLeod, eds. Newsletters to Newspapers: Eighteenth Century Journalism. Morgantown: West Virginia University, 1977. 227

*Bontemps, Arna. Free at Last: The Life of Frederick Douglas. New York: Dodd, Mead, 1971. 210

*Boorstin, Daniel. The Americans: The Democratic Experience. New York: Random House, 1974. 169, 313

*_____. The Colonial Experience. New York: Random House, 1958. 169

*_____. The Decline of Radicalism: Reflections on America Today. New York: Random House, 1969. 313

*_____. The Genius of American Politics. Chicago: University of Chicago Press, 1958. 169, 313

*_____. The Image, or What Happened to the American Dream. New York: Atheneum, 1962. 313

*_____. The Lost World of Thomas Jefferson. Chicago: University of Chicago Press, 1981. 169, 179

*_____. The National Experience. New York: Random House, 1957. 169

Borch, Herbert von. The Unfinished Society. New York: Hawthorne Books, 1962. 310

Borchert, James. "Alley Landscapes of Washington." Landscape, 23 (1979). 422, 462

_____. Alley Life in Washington: Family, Community, Religion and Folklife in the City, 1850-1970. Urbana: University of Illinois, 1980. 462

Boris, Eileen. "Social Reproduction and the Schools: Educational Housekeeping." Signs, 4 (Summer 1979). 544

Boswell, Jeanetta. Ralph Waldo Emerson and the Critics: A Checklist of Criticism, 1900-1977. Metuchen, New Jersey: Scarecrow Press, 1979. 411

Borg, Dorothy. American Policy and the Chinese Revolution, 1925-1928. New York: Macmillan, 1947. 123

_____. The United States and the Far Eastern Crisis of 1933-1938: From the Manchurian Incident Through the Initial Stage of the Undeclared Sino-Japanese War. Cambridge: Harvard University Press, 1964.

Borges, Jose Luis. "Death and the Compass." Ficciones. New York: Grove Press, 1962. 49

Borroff, Edith. Music in Europe and the United States. Englewood Cliffs: Prentice-Hall, 1971. 206

Botkin, Benjamin A. New York City Folklore. 1956; Westport: Greenwood Press, 1976. 106

_____. Sidewalks of America. 1954, Westport: Greenwood Press, 1976. 106

_____, ed. A Civil War Treasury of Tales, Legends, and Folklore. New York: Random House, 1966. 98

Bottorff, William K. Thomas Jefferson. Boston: G.K. Hall, 1979. 414, 425

Boudin, Louis. Government by Judiciary. New York: Godwin & Company, 1932, two volumes. 350

Bouissac, Paul. Circus and Culture: A Semiotic Approach. Bloomington: Indiana University Press, 1976. 498

Bowden, Henry Warner. Church History in the Age of Science. Chapel Hill: University of North Carolina Press, 1971. 363 , 380

_____. Dictionary of American Religious Biography. Westport: Greeenwood Press, 1977.

Bowen, Howard R. and Peter Clecak. Investment in Learning: The Individual and Social Value of American Higher Education. San Francisco: Jossey-Bass, 1982. 444

*Bowles, Samuel and Herbert Gintis. Schooling in Capitalist America: Educational Reform and the Contradictions of Economic Life. New York: Basic Books, 1976. 442

Bowly, Devereaux. The Poorhouse: Subsidized Housing in Chicago, 1895-1976. Carbondale: Southern Illinois University, 1978. 521

Bowman, Albert H. The Struggle for Neutrality: Franco-American Diplomacy During the Federalist Era. Knoxville: University of Tennessee Press, 1974. 115

Bowron, Bernard. Henry B. Fuller of Chicago: The Ordeal of a Genteel Realist in Ungenteel America. Westport: Greenwood, 1974. 522

Boyan, A. Stephen. Constitutional Aspects of Watergate: Documents and Materials, 5 volumes. Dobbs Ferry, New York: Oceana Publications. 439

Boyd, Ann S. The Devil with James Bond! Westport: Greenwood, 1975. 55

Boydson, Jo Ann, ed. The Poems of John Dewey. Carbondale: Southern Illinois Press, 1977. 323

Boyer, Paul. Urban Masses and Moral Order in America, 1820-1920. Cambridge: Harvard University Press, 1978. 461

*_____ and Stephen Nissenbaum. Salem Possessed: The Social Origins of Witchcraft. Cambridge: Harvard University Press, 1974. 171, 369

Boylan, Anne. "Evangelical Womanhood in the Nineteenth Century: The Role of Women in Sunday Schools." Feminist Studies, 4 (October 1978). 543

Bozeman, Theodore Dwight. Protestants in an Age of Science. Chapel Hill: University of North Carolina Press, 1977. 377

Brabson, Fay Warrington. Andrew Johnson: A Life in Pursuit of the Right Course, 1808-1875; the Seventeenth President of the United States. Durham, North Carolina: Seeman Printery, 1972. 429

*Bracey, John, August Meier and Elliott Rudwick, eds. Black Nationalism in America. Indianapolis: Bobbs-Merrill, 1970. 13

Brack, Gene M. Mexico Views Manifest Destiny, 1821-1846: An Essay on the Origins of the Mexican War. Albuquerque: University of New Mexico Press, 1975. 134

Bradford, William. Plymouth Plantation. Boston: Wright and Potter, 1898. 146

Bradlee, Benjamin. Conversations with Kennedy. New York: W.W. Norton, 1975. 437

Brady, Dorothy S. "Introduction." Output, Employment and Productivity in the United States after 1800. New York: Columbia University Press, 1966.

_____. "Relative Prices in the Nineteenth Century." Journal of Economic History, XXIV (June 1964). 74

Brady, Maureen. Give Me Your Good Ear. Argyle: Spinster's Ink, 1978. 539

Braeman, John. "The New Deal and the 'Broker State': A Review of the Recent Scholarly Literature." Business History Review, XLVI (Winter 1972). 83

_____, Robert H. Bremner, and Everett Walters, eds. Change and Continuity in Twentieth-Century America. New York: Harper and Row, 1966. 81

Branch, Watson G., ed. Melville: The Critical Heritage. London: Routledge and Kegan, 1974. 414

Brande, Stuart. American Welfare Capitalism, 1880-1940. Chicago: University of Chicago Press, 1976. 448

Brasch, Ila W. and Walter M. A Comprehensive Annotated Bibliography of American Black English. Baton Rouge: LSU Press, 1974. 256

*Brauer, Carl M. John F. Kennedy and the Second Reconstruction. New York: Columbia University Press, 1979. 437

*Braverman, Harry. Labor and Monopoly Capital. New York: Monthly Review Press, 1974. 446

Brawley, Benjamin G. A Social History of the American Negro. 1921; New York: AMS Press, 1971. 13

*Breen, T.H. The Character of the Good Ruler: Puritan Political Ideas in New England, 1630-1730. New York: Morton, 1974. 368

*Bremer, Francis J. The Puritan Experiment. New York: St. Martin's Press, 1976. 367

Brennan, William J. "Working at Justice." In Allan F. Westin, ed. An Autobiography of the Supreme Court. New York: Macmillan, 1963. 353

Brenni, Vito J. American English: A Bibliography. Philadelphia: University of Pennsylvania Press, 1963. 256

_____. William Dean Howells: A Bibliography. Metuchen, New Jersey: Scarecrow Press, 1973. 413

Brewer, Annie M., ed. Dictionaries, Encyclopedias, and Other Word-Related Books, 1966-1974. Detroit: Gale, 1975. 272

*Bridenbaugh, Carl. Mitre and Sceptre. New York: Oxford University Press, 1962. 374

*Bridge, Raymond. Bike Touring. San Francisco: Sierra, 1979. 487

Briggs, John W. An Italian Passage: Immigrants to three American Cities, 1890-1930. New Haven, Connecticut: Yale University Press, 1978. 197

Brigham, John. Constitutional Language: An Interpretation of Judicial Decision. Westport, Connecticut: Greenwood Press, 1978. 357

Bright, Elizabeth. A Word Geography of California and Nevada. Berkely: University of California Press, 1971. 263

Brignano, Russell. Black Americans in Autobiography. Durham: Duke University Press, 1974. 398

*Brill, Stephen. The Teamsters. New York: Simon and Schuster, 1978. 450

Brinley, Thomas. Migration and Economic Growth: A Study of Great Britain and the Atlantic Economy. Cambridge, England: University Press, 1954.

Broadhead, Richard H. Hawthorne, Melville, and the Novel. Chicago: University of Chicago Press, 1976. 412

Brock, Peter. Pacifism in the United States: From the Colonial Era to the First World War. Princeton: Princeton University Press, 1968. 131

Brodie, Fawn M. Thomas Jefferson: An Intimate History. New York: Norton, 1974. 425

*Brody, David. Workers in Industrial America: Essays on the 20th-Century Struggle. New York: Oxford University Press, 1980. 449

Brogan, Denis W. Abraham Lincoln. Duckworth: England Publishers, 1980. 428

_____. America in the Modern World. 1960; Westport: Greenwood Press, 1980. 309

Brokaw, Howard P., ed. Wildlife and America. Washington, D.C.: G.P.O., 1978. 476

Bronner, Edwin B. William Penn's "Holy Experiemnt": the Founding of Pennsylvania, 1681-1701. 1963; Westport: Greenwood Press, 1978. 370

Bronstein, Arthur. The Pronunciation of American English. Englewood Cliffs, New Jersey: Prentice-Hall, 1960. 263

*Brooks, H. Allen. The Prairie School: Frank Lloyd Wright and His Midwest Contemporaries. New York: Norton, 1976. 37, 43

Brooks, Thomas R. Communications Workers of America: The Study of a Union. New York: Mason/Charter, 1977. 449

Brooks, Van Wyck. Makers and Finders. 5 volumes. New York: E. P. Dutton, 1944-52. 179

Brown, A.W.A. Ecology of Pesticides. New York: Wiley, 1978. 476

Brown, Charles B. Arthur Mervyn, or Memoirs of the Year 1793. Kent, Ohio: Kent State University Press, 1980. 407

*_____. Wieland and "Memoirs of Carwin." Kent, Ohio: Kent State University Press, 1978. 407

Brown, Charles H. The Correspondents' War. New York: Scribner's, 1967. 216

_____. William Cullen Bryant. New York: Scribner's 1971. 213

*Brown, Claude. Manchild in the Promised Land.New York: New American Library, 1971. 10

*Brown, Dee. Bury My Heart at Wounded Knee. New York: Bantom, 1972. 145, 175

Brown, Elizabeth. "American Paintings and Sculpture in the Fine Arts Building of the World's Columbia Exposition." Unpublished dissertation. University of Kansas, 1976. 532

Brown, Frederick D. and Harry J. The Diary of James A. Garfield. 3 volumes. East Lansing: Michigan State University Press, 1967.

Brown, Harrison. The Challenge of Man's Future. New York: Viking, 1954. 471

_____. The Human Future Revisited. New York: Norton, 1978. 476

Brown, Jerry Wayne. The Rise of Biblical Criticism in America, 1800-1870. Middletown: Wesleyan University Press, 1969.

*Brown, Lester. The Twenty-Ninth Day. New York: Norton, 1978. 472

Brown, Ralph A. The Presidency of John Adams. Lawrence: University Press of Kansas, 1975. 425

Brown, Roger H. The Republic in Peril: 1812. New York: Columbia University Press, 1964. 116

*Brown, Sterling, et. al. Negro Caravan. New York: Arno, 1969. 22

Brown, Theodore M. Margaret Bourke-White: Photo Journalist. Ithaca: Andrew Dickinson Museum of Art, 1972. 220

*Brown, William T. Architecture Evolving: An Illinois Saga. Chicago: Tech'em Inc., 1976. 523

*Brown, William Wells. The Black Man: His Antecedents, His Genius, and His Achievements. 1863; Coral Gables: Mnemosyne. 155

*_____. Clotel, or the President's Daughter. 1853; New York: Macmillan, 1970. 21, 155

Brown, William Wells. The Rising Sun, or the Antecedents and the Advancement of the Colored Race. 1874; New York: Johnson Reprints, 1970. 155

_____. St. Domingo. Its Revolution and its Patriots. 1855; Philadelphia: Historic Publications, 1969.

Browne, Ray B., ed. "Focus on International Popular Culture." Journal of Popular Culture, 13, 1 (Summer 1979). 498

_____. Lincoln-Lore: Lincoln in the Popular Mind. Bowling Green, Ohio: Popular Press, 1974. 428

_____. Popular Culture and the Expanding Consciousness. New York: John Wiley, 1973. 492, 499

*_____. Rituals and Ceremonies in Popular Culture. Bowling Green: Popular Press, 1981. 492, 497

_____ and Marshall Fishwick, eds. Icons of America. Bowling Green: Popular Press, 1977. 499

Browne, Ray B., Sam Grogg, Jr., and Larry Landrum, eds. "Theories and Methodologies in Popular Culture." Journal of Popular Culture, 9, 2 (Fall 1975). 499

*Brownell, Blaine A. and David R. Goldfield, eds. The City in Southern History: The Growth of Urban Civilization in the South. Port Washington, New York: Kennikat, 1977. 464

Brownlee, W. Elliot and Mary M. Women in the American Economy. New Haven: Yale University Press, 1976. 552

Brownmiller, Susan. Against Our Will: Men, Women and Rape. New York: Simon and Schuster, 1975. 551

Bruccoli, Matthew J. Kenneth Millar/Ross Macdonald: A Checklist. Detroit: Gale Research, 1971. 60

_____. Raymond Chandler: A Checklist. Kent, Ohio: Kent State University Press, 1968. 60

_____ and C.E. Frazer Clark, Jr., eds. First Printing of American Authors, 4 volumes. Detroit: Gale Research, 1978. 406

*Bruce, Dickson D., Jr. And They All Sang Hallelujah: Plain-Folk Camp-Meeting Religion, 1800-1845. Knoxville: University of Tennesse Press, 1974. 375

Bruckberger, Raymond L. Image of America. New York: Viking Press, 1959. 310

Bruckner, D.J.R. and Irene Macauley. Dreams in Stone: The University of Chicago. Univerisity of Chicago Press, 1976. 530

Bruckner, D.J.R. and William Michael Murphy, ed. The Idea of the University of Chicago. Chicago: University of Chicago Press, 1976. 530

Bruss, Elizabeth. "Eye for I: Making and Unmaking Autobiography in Film." James Olney, ed. Autobiography. Princeton: Princeton University Press, 1980. 390, 397

*Bruchey, Stuart. Growth of the Modern American Economy. New York: Harper and Row, 1975. 66

*_____. The Roots of American Economic Growth, 1607-1861. New York: Harper and Row, 1968. 66

*Brunvand, Jan H. Folklore: A Handbook for Study and Research. New York: St. Martin's Press, 1976. 97

*_____. Readings in American Folklore. New York: Norton, 1979. 110

_____. The Study of American Folklore. New York: Norton, 1978. 97, 110

Bryan, Carter R. Negro Journalism in America Before Emancipation. Minneapolis: Association for Education in Journalism, September, 1969. 210

Bryant, Margaret. Current American Usage. New York: Funk and Wagnalls, 1962. 269

Bryant, William Cullen,II and Thomas G. Voss, eds. The Letters of William Cullen Bryant, Vol. II, 1836-49. New York: Fordham, 1977. 226, 419

Bryer, Jackson, et. al. Hamlin Garland and the Critics: An Annotated Bibliography. Troy, New York: Whitston, 1973. 411

Bryson, Thomas A. American Diplomatic Relations with the Middle East, 1784-1795: A Survey. Metuchen, New Jersey: Scarecrow, 1977. 141

Buchler, Justus, ed. The Philosophy of Peirce: Selected Writings. AMS Press, 1940. 322

Buchloh, Paul G. and Jens P. Becker. Der Detektivroman. Darmstadt:Wissenschaftlicle Buchgesellschaft, 1973. 57

Buckley, Thomas E., S.J. Church and State in Revolutionary Virginia, 1776-1787. Charlottesville: University Press of Virginia, 1977. 374

Buenker, John D. and Nicholas C. Burckel. Immigration and Ethnicity: A Guide to Information Sources. Detroit: Gale Research Co., 1977. 189, 202

Buker, George E. Swamp Sailors: Riverine Warfare in the Everglades, 1835-1842. Gainesville: University Presses of Florida, 1975. 283

Bulen, Galen, et. al. Broken Hoops and Plains People: A Catalogue of Ethnic Resources in the Humanities: Nebraska and Surrounding Areas. Lincoln, Nebraska: Nebraska Curriculum Development Center, 1976. 196

Bullock, Henry A. A History of Negro Education in the South from 1619 to the Present. Cambridge: Harvard University Press, 1967. 179

Buni, Andrew. Robert L. Vann of the Pittsburgh Courier: Politics and Black Journalism. Pittsburgh: University of Pittsburgh Press, 1974. 220

Bunke, Joan, ed. Harven Ingham and Gardner Cowles, Sr.: Things Don't Just Happen. Ames: Iowa State University Press, 1977.

*Burchard, John and Bush-Brown, Albert. The Architecture of America: A Social and Cultural History. Boston: Little, Brown, 1961. 33, 42

Bureau of Reclamation. Dams and Control Works. Washington: Government Printing Office, 1954.

Burg, B.R. Richard Mather of Dorchester. Lexington: University Press of Kentucky, 1976. 369

*Burg, David F. Chicago's White City of 1893. Lexington: University Press of Kentucky, 1976. 42, 532

Burger, Mary W. "I, Too, Sing America: The Black Autobiographer's Response to Life in the Midwest." Kansas Quarterly, 7 (Summer 1975). 398

*Burke, Vicent J. Nixon's Good Deed: Welfare Reform. New York: Columbia University Press, 1974. 438

Burkhardt, Frederick, et al., eds. Pragmatism: A New Name for Some Old Ways of Thinking. Cambridge: Harvard University Press, 1976. 321

Burner, David. Herbert Hoover: The Public Life. Westminster, Maryland: Alfred A. Knopf, Inc., 1978. 433

*Burnham, Alan, ed. New York Landmarks. New York: Columbia University Press, 1963. 37, 43

Burns, Elizabeth and Tom Burns, eds. Sociology of Literature and Drama. Baltimore: Penguin, 1973. 499

Burr, Nelson R. A Critical Bibliography of Religion in America. Princeton: Princeton University Press, 1961. 362

Burt, Alfred, L. The United States, Great Britain, and British North America: From the Revolution to the Establishment of Peace After the War. New Haven: Yale University Press, 1940. 116

Burton, David H. Theodore Roosevelt. New York: Twayne Publishers, 1972. 431

* _____. Theodore Roosevelt and His English Correspondents: A Special Relationship of Friends. Philadelphia: American Philosophical Society, 1973. 431

_____. Theodore Roosevelt: Confident Imperialist. Philadelphia: University of Pennsylvania Press, 1969. 431

Burton, Lydia and David Morley. "Neighborhood Survival in Toronto." Landscape, 23, 1 (Fall 1979). 422

Busch, Moritz. Travels between the Hudson and the Mississippi, 1851-1852. Lexington, Kentucky: University Press of Kentucky, 1971. 403

Bush, Clive. The Dream of Reason: American Consciousness and Cultural Achievement from Independence to the Civil War. New York: St. Martin's Press, 1978. 403

Bush, Robert, ed. Grace King of New Orleans: A Selection of Her Writings. Baton Rouge, Louisiana: Louisiana State University Press, 1973. 414

*Bush-Brown, Albert. Louis Sullivan. New York: Braziller, 1960. 44

Bush-Brown, Harold. Beaux Arts to Bauhaus and Beyond: An Architect's Perspective. New York: Watson-Guptill Publications, 1976. 467

*Bushman, Richard L. From Puritan to Yankee: Character and the Social Order in Connecticut, 1690-1765. New York: Norton, 1970. 373

_____. ed. The Great Awakening: Documents on the Revival of Religion, 1740-1745. Chapel Hill: University of North Carolina Press, 1970. 372

*Butterfield, Stephen. Black Autobiography in America. Amherst: University of Massachusetts Press, 1974. 390, 397

Buttlar, Lois and Lubomry R. Wynar. Building Ethic Collections: An Annotated Guide for School Media Centers and Public Libraries. Littleton, Colorado: Libraries Unlimited, 1977. 189

Buono, Oreste del and Umberto Eco, eds. The Bond Affair. London: Macdonald and Co., 1966. 55

Byers, John R. and J. Owen James. A Concordance to the Five Novels of Nathaniel Hawthorne, 2 vols. New York: Garland Publishing, 1979. 412

Byington, Robert H., ed. Working Americans: Contemporary Approaches to Occupational Folklife. Los Angeles: California Folklore Society, 1978. 452

Byrd, Max. "The Detective Detected: From Sophocles to Ross MacDonald." The Yale Review, 64 (1974). 58

Cady, Edwin, II, ed. W.D. Howells As Critic. London: Routledge and Kegan, 1973. 413

Cage, John. Empty Words: Writings '73-'78. Middletown; Wesleyan University Press, 1979. 304

Cahan, Cathy and Richard. "The Lost City of the Depression." Chicago History, 5 (Winter 1976-1977). 532

Cahill, Fred. Judicial Legislation: A Study in American Legal Theory. New York: Ronald, 1952. 354

*Cahn, Edmond, ed. Supreme Court and Supreme Law. 1954; New York: Simon and Schuster, 1971. 354

*Cahn, Robert. Footprints on the Planet. Englewood, N.J.: Universe Books, 1979. 476

Cahn, Steven M., ed. New Studies in the Philosophy of John Dewey. Hanover: University Press of New England, 1977. 325

Cahn, William. A Pictorial History of American Labor. New York: Crown Publishers, 1973. 452

Cain, James M. "The Art of Fiction." The Paris Review, 73 (1978). 60

Caine, Stanley P. The Myth of Progressive Reform: Railroad Regulation in Wisconsin, 1903-1910. Madison: State Historical Society of Wisconsin, 1970. 82

Caldwell, Lynton K. Environment: A Challenge to Modern Society. Garden City: Natural History Press, 1970. 471

_____. In Defense of Earth. Bloomington: Indiana University Press, 1972. 471

*Calhoun, Daniel H. The Intelligence of a People. Princeton, N.J. Princeton University Press, 1973. 179, 447

Califano, Joseph. A Presidential Nation. New York: W.W. Norton & Co., 1975. 438

Callcott, Wilfrid, H. The Western Hemisphere: Its Influence on United States Policies to the End of World War II. Austin: University of Texas Press, 1968. 124

*Callen, Anthea. Women Artists of the Arts and Crafts Movement, 1870-1914. New York: Pantheon Books, 1979. 546

Cameron, Sharon. Lyric Time: Dickinson and the Limits of Genre. Baltimore, Maryland: Johns Hopkins University Press, 1979. 411

Campbell, D'Ann. "Women's Life in Utopia: The Shaker Experiment." The New England Quarterly, 51 (March 1978). 556

Campbell, Jack K. Colonel Francis W. Parker: The Children's Crusade. New York: Columbia University Press, 1967. 530

Campbell, Alexander. The Trouble with Americans. New York: Praeger, 1971. 309

Campbell, Charles S. Anglo-American Understanding, 1898-1903. Baltimore: Johns Hopkins Press, 1957. 119

_____. Special Business Interests and the Open Door Policy. New Haven: Yale University Press, 1951.

*_____. The Transformation of American Foreign Relations: 1865-1900. New York: Harper, 1976. 135

*Campbell, Frank D., Jr. John D. MacDonald and the Colorful World of Travis McGee. San Bernardino, California: Borgo Press, 1977. 60

Campen, Richard N. Ohio: An Architectural Portrait. Chagrin Falls: West Summit Press, 1973. 43

Camus, Raoul. The Military Music of the American Revolution. Chapel Hill: University of North Carolina Press, 1976. 303

Canary, Robert H. George Bancroft. Boston: G.R. Hall, 1974. 404

Canfield, Leon H. Presidency of Woodrow Wilson. Cranbury, New Jersey: Fairleigh Dickinson University Press. 432

*Cantarow Ellen, et. al. Moving the Mountain: Women Working for Social Change. Old Westbury, N.Y: The Feminist Press, 1980. 541

Cantor, Milton, ed. American Working Class Culture: Explorations in American Labor and Social History. Westport, Conn: Greenwood Press, 1979. 452

Cantor, Milton and Bruce Laurie, eds. Class, Sex, and the Woman Worker. Westport, Connecticut: Greenwood Press, 1977. 547

*Cantor, Muriel, G. Prime Time Television: Content and Control. Beverly Hills: Sage, 1980. 499

Cantor, Muriel G. The Hollywood TV Producer: His Work and His Audience. New York: Basic Books, 1972. 499

*Capps, Marie T. and Theodore G. Stroup. The Library Map Collection: Period of the American Revolution, 1753-1800. West Point, New York: U.S. Military Academy. 284

Card, William, et. al. "A Systemic Set of Usage Labels for a Dictionary." MacLeish. Studies. 1979. 269

*Carden, Maren Lockwood. Oneida: Utopian Community to Modern Corporation New York: Harper and Row, 1971. 382

Carey, George A. A Faraway Time and Place. New York: Arno, 1977. 99

Carey, George A. ed. A Sailor's Songbag: An American Rebel in an English Prison 1777-1779. Amherst, Massachusetts: University of Massachusetts Press, 1976. 98

*Carey, James T. Sociology and Public Affairs: The Chicago School. Beverly Hills: Sage, 1975. 529

Carey, James W.   "The Problem of Journalism History," Journalism History,
    (Spring 1974). 224

Caridi, Ronald J. The Korean War and American Politics: The Republican Party
    as a Case Study. Philadelphia: University of Pennsylvania Press, 1968. 130

Carlson, Oliver. The Man Who Made the News: A Biography of James Gordon
    Bennett. New York: Duell, Sloan & Pearce, 1942. 212

Carnegie Council on Policy Studies. Fair Practices in Higher Education: Rights
    and Responsibilities of Students and their Colleges in a Period of Intensified
    Competition for Enrollments. San Francisco: Jossey-Bass, 1979. 444

Carnegie Foundation for the Advancement of Teaching. Missions of the College
    Curriculum: A Contemporary Review with Suggestions. San Francisco:
    Jossey – Bass, 1978. 444

Carnegie Council on Policy Studies. Presidents Confront Reality: From Edifice
    Complex to University Without Walks. San Francisco: Jossey-Bass, 1977. 444

Carosso, Vincent P. Investment Banking in America: A History.   Cambridge:
    Harvard University Press, 1970. 80

Carpenter, John Alcott. Ulysses S. Grant. New York: Twayne Publishers, 1970. 430

Carr, Donald E. Death of the Sweet Waters. New York: Norton, 1966 · 475

Carrington, George C., and Ildika Carrington. Plots and Characters in the
    Fiction of William Dean Howells. Hamden, Connecticut: Shoe String Press,
    1976. 413

*Carroll, Berenice A., ed. Liberating Women's History: Theoretical and Critical
    Essays. Urbana, Illinois: University of Illinois Press, 1976. 545

Carroll, Jackson W., et. al. Religion in America: 1950 to the Present.
    New York: Harper and Row, 1979. 386

Carroll, Paul. The Poem in its Skin. Chicago: Follett, 1968. 343

Carroll, Peter N. Puritanism and the Wilderness. New York: Columbia University
    Press, 1969. 368

Carson, Rachel. Silent Spring. New York: Houghton, 1962. 471

Carter, Elliott. The Writings of Elliott Carter. Bloomington: Indiana
    University Press, 1977. 304.

Carter, Hugh. Cousin Beedie and Cousin Hot: My Life with the Carter Family
    of Plains, Georgia. Englewood Cliffs, New Jersey: Prentice Hall, Inc., 1978. 440

Carter, Jimmy. A Government as Good as its People. New York: Simon and Schuster,
    1977. 440

*_____. Why not the Best? Nashville: Broadman Press, 1977.

Carter, Joseph. Labor Lobbyist: The Autobiography of John W. Edelman.
    New York: Bobbs-Merrill, 1974. 450

Carter, Paul. The Spiritual Crisis of the Gilded Age. DeKalb: Northern
    Illinois University Press, 1971. 365

Cartwright, William H. and Richard L. Watson, Jr., eds. The Reinterpretation of American History and Culture. Washington, D.C.: National Council for the Social Studies, 1973. 193, 278

Caruthers, J. Wade. Octavius Brooks Frothingham: Gentle Radical. University: Alabama Press, 1977. 382

*Cary, Norman M.,Jr. Guide to U.S. Army Museums and Historic Sites. G.P.O. Washington, D.C. 1975. 285

Casas, Bartolome de las. Very Brief Account of the Destruction of the Indies. Herma Briffault, Trans. 1553; New York: Seabury, 1974. 145

Case, Lynn, M. and Warren F. Spencer. The United States and France: Civil War Diplomacy. Philadelphia: University of Pennsylvania Press, 1970. 118

Caskey, Marie. Chariot of Fire: Religion and the Beecher Family. New Haven: Yale University Press, 1978. 376

*Cash Wilbur J. The Mind of the South. New York: Random, 1960. 171

*Casper, Gerhard and Richard A. Posner. The Workload of the Supreme Court. Chicago: American Bar Foundation, 1976. 356

Cassara, Ernest, ed. Universalism in America: A Documentary History. Boston: Beacon Press, 1971. 382

Casserly, John J. The Ford White House: The Diary of a Speechwriter. Boulder: Colorado Associated University Press, 1977. 439

Cassidy, Frederic. "Dialect Studies, Regional and Social." Sebeok. Trends. 256, 264

Castel, Albert. The Presidency of Andrew Johnson. Lawrence: Regents Press of Kansas, 1979. 429

Castile, George Pierre. North American Indians: An Introduction to the Chichimeca. New York: McGraw-Hill, 1979.

Catton, Bruce. Mr. Lincoln's Army. Garden City, N.Y.: Doubleday, 1951. 179

_____. Glory Road. Garden City, New York: Doubleday, 1952. 179

_____. Stillness at Appomatox. New York: Doubleday, 1953. 167, 179

Caughey, John."Artificial Social Relations." American Quarterly, XXX, 1 (Spring 1978). 496, 499

_____. Hubert Howe Bancroft: Historian of Western America. 1946; New York: Russell, 1970. 179

Caute, David. The Great Fear: The Anti-Communist Purge Under Truman and Eisenhower. London: Secker and Warburg, 1978. 437

Cavan, Sherri. Twentieth Century Gothic: America's Nixon. San Francisco: Wigan Pier Press, 1979. 438

Calvert, Samuel McCrea. The American Churches in the Ecumenical Movement: 1900-1968. New York: Association Press, 1968.

_____. Church Cooperation and Unity in America. New York: Association Press, 1970.

*Cawelti, John G. Adventure, Mystery, and Romance: Formula Stories as Art and Popular Culture. Chicago: University of Chicago Press, 1977. 58, 495, 499

*_____. The Six-Gun Mystique. Bowling Green: Popular Press, 1973. 51, 495, 499

Center for Cassette Studies. Index to the Complete Recorded Speeches of Franklin Delano Roosevelt: 278 Speeches dating from 1920 to 1945. North Hollywood, California, 1974. 434

*Center for Military History. A Guide to the Study and Use of Military History. Washington, D.C.: Center for Military History, 1979.

Chadwin, Mark L. The Hawks of World War II. Chapel Hill: University of North Carolina Press, 1968. 127

Chambers, Clarke A. Paul V. Kellogg and the SURVEY: Voices for Social Welfare and Social Justice, Minneapolis: University of Minnesota Press, 1971. 86

_____. Seedtime of Reform: American Social Service and Social Action, 1918-1933. 1963; Westport, Connecticut: Greenwood Press, 1980. 87

Chambers, J.K. Canadian English: Origins and Structures. Toronto and London: Methune, 1975. 259

Chambers, Kenneth. A Country-Lover's Guide to Wildlife. Baltimore: Johns Hopkins, 1979. 486

Chambers-Schiller, Lee. "The Single Woman Reformer." Frontiers, 3 (Fall 1978). 550

Champigny, Robert. What Will Have Happened: A Philosophical and Technical Essay on Mystery Stories. Bloomington, Indiana: Indiana University Press, 1977. 59

Chan, Shih. A Brief History of the United States. Peking: Foreign Languages Press, 1976. 20

Chandler, Alfred, D. Jr. "Anthracite Coal and the Beginning of the Industrial Revolution in the United States." Business History Review, XLVI (Summer 1972). 74

_____. "The Structure of American Industry in the Twentieth Century: A Historical Overview." Business History Review, XLIII (Autumn 1969). 82

*_____. The Visible Hand: The Managerial Revolution in American Business. Cambridge: Harvard University Press, 1977. 80

_____ and Stephen Salsbury. Pierre S. Dupont and the Making of the Modern Corporation. New York: Harper and Row, 1971. 80

*Chandler, Lester V. America's Greatest Depression, 1929-1941. New York: Harper & Row,1970. 85

*Chandler Raymond. The Simple Art of Murder. New York: Ballantine, 1977. 60

Chaney, David. Fictions and Ceremonies: Representations of Popular Experience. New York: ST. Martins, 1979. 499

*Chapman, Abraham, ed. Black Voices: An Anthology of Afro-American Literature. New York: New American Library, 1968.

Chapman, Elise. State Natural Resource Economics. Lexington: Council of State Governments, 1979. 482

Chappell,Louis W. John Henry: A Folk-Lore Study. 1933; Port Washington: Kennikat, 1968. 101

*Chapple, Steve and Reebee Garofalo. Rock 'N' Roll is Here to Pay: The History and Politics of the Music Industry. Chicago: Nelson-Hall, 1978. 497, 499

Charney, Hanna. "This Mortal Coil":The Detective Novel of Manners. Madison, New Jersey: Fairleigh Dickinson University Press, 1981. 58

Charter, Samuel B. The Country Blues. New York: Rinehart, 1959. 301

Chase, Gilbert. America's Music from the Pilgrims to the Present. Westport: Greenwood Press, 1981. 297, 298, 303

Chase, H.W. Federal Judges: The Appointing Process. Minneapolis: University of Minnesota Press, 1973. 349

Chatfield, Charles. For Peace and Justice. Pacifism in America, 1914-1941. Knoxville: University of Tennessee Press, 1971. 123

Chaudhuri, Nupur, comp. Bibliography of Women's History, 1976-1979. Conference Group on Women's History, 1979. 537

*Cheney, Thomas E. The Golden Legacy. Layton, Utah: Peregrine Smith, 1973. 98

*Cherry, Conrad. God's New Israel: Religious Interpretations of American Destiny, Englewood Cliffs: Prentice-Hall, 1971. 364

_____. The Theology of Jonathan Edwards: A Reappraisal. New York: Doubleday, 1966. 373

*Chevigny, Bell Gale. The Woman and the Myth: Margaret Fuller's Life and Writings. Old Westbury, New York: The Feminist Press, 1977. 537

*Chicago, Judy. The Dinner Party. New York: Doubleday, & Company, 1979. 546

*_____. Through the Flower: My Struggle as a Woman Artist. Garden City,
    New York: Doubleday Anchor Books, 1977. 546

Chidsey, Donald B. And Tyler Too. New York: Elsevier/Nelson Books, 1978.

Child, Lydia Maria. History of the Condition of Women in Various Ages and
    Nations. 1835; New York: Gordon.

Chinoy, Ely. Automobile Workers and the American Dream.   Garden City, New
    York: Doubleday 1955. 452

Chittenden, Hiram M. The American F r Trade of the Far West, 3 vols.
    1902; Stanford: Academic Reprints, 1954. 157

Christgau, Robert. Any Old Way You Choose It: Rock and Other Pop Music,
    1967-1973. Baltimore: Penguin, 1973. 499

Christianson, Paul K. Reformers and Babylon. Toronto: University of Toronto.

Chudacoff, Howard P. Residential and Social Mobility in Omaha, 1880-1920.
    New York: Oxford University Press, 1972. 197

Ciardi, John. Mid-Century American Poets. New York: Twayne, 1950. 339

*Cirino, Robert. Don't Blame the People: How the News Media Use Bias,
    Distortion, and Censorship to Manipulate Public Opinion. New York:
    Vintage, 1971. 496, 499
_____. We're Being More Than Entertained. Honolulu: Lighthouse, 1977. 496, 499

*City University of New York. The New Words of Edgar Varese. Brooklyn:
    Institute for Studies in American Music, 1979,

Clarfield, Gerard H. Timothy Pickering and American Diplomacy, 1795-1800.
    Columbia: University of Missouri Press, 1969. 115

Clark, C.E. Frazer, Jr. Nathaniel Hawthorne: A Descriptive Bibliography.
    Pittsburgh, Pennsylvania: University of Pittsburgh Press, 1978. 412

Clark, Clifford. "Domestic Architecture as an Index to Social History:
    The Romantic Revival and the Cult of Domesticity in America." Journal
    of Interdisciplinary History, 7 (Summer 1976). 510

Clark, Clifford E., Jr. Henry Ward Beecher: Spokesman for a Middle-Class
    America. Urbana: University of Illinois Press, 1978. 379

Clark, Dennis. The Irish in Philadelphia: Ten Generations of Urban Experience.
    Philadelphia: Temple University Press, 1974. 199

Clark, James E. "The Impact of Transportation Technology on Suburbanization
    in the Chicago Region, 1830-1920." Unpublished Dissertation. Northwestern
    University, 1977. 528, 532

*Clark, John et. al. Small Seaports: Revitalization through Conserving Heritage
    Resources.   Washington, D.C.: Conservation Foundation, 1979. 480

Clark, John C. The Grain Trade in the Old Northwest. 1966; Westport: Greenwood, Press, 1980. 72

Clark, John P. America, Their America. New York: Africana Publishing, 1969. 309, 310

*Clark, Kenneth B. Dark Ghetto. New York: Harper and Row, 1975. 10

Clark, Virginia P.,Paul A. Escholz and Alfred P. Rosa. Language: Introductory Readings. New York: St. Martin's 1972. 259

Chomsky, Noam and Morris Halle. The Sound Pattern of English. New York: Harper and Row, 1968. 268

Chomsky, Noam. Syntactic Structures. The Hague: Mouton, 1957. 268

_____ . Aspects of the Theory of Syntax. Cambridge: MIT Press, 1965. 268

Clauson, Wendy L. "The Chapbook: A Journal of American Intellectual Life, 1894-1898." Unpublished Dissertation. University of Iowa, 1980.

*Clawson, Marion. Forests for Whom and for What? Baltimore: Johns Hopkins University Press, 1975. 476

Clay, Grady. Close-up: How to Read the American City. New York: Praeger, 1973. 421

Clayton, Charles C. Little Mack: Joseph B. McCullagh of the St. Louis Globe Democrat. Carbondale: Southern Illinois University Press, 1969. 216

Clayton, James L. "The Fiscal Limits of the Warfare-Welfare State: Defense and Welfare Spending in the United States Since 1900." Western Political Quarterly, XXIX (September 1976). 86

*Cleaver, Eldridge. Soul on Ice. New York: Dell, 1968. 10

*Clebsch, William A. American Religious Thought: A History. Chicago: University of Chicago Press, 1975. 329, 364

Clemens,Diane, S. Yalta. New York: Oxford University Press, 1970. 127

Clendenning, John, ed. The Letters of Josiah Royce. Chicago: University of Chicago Press, 1970. 320

Clifford, Deborah. Mine Eyes Have Seen the Glory: A Biography of Julia Ward Howe. Boston: Little Brown, 1979. 412

Clifton, James A. The Prairie People: Continuity and Change in Potawatomi Indian Culture, 1665-1965. Lawrence: Regents Press of Kansas, 1977. 513

Cloward, Richard A. and Frances Fox Piven. "Hidden Protest: The Channeling of Female Innovation and Resistance." Signs, 4 (Summer 1979). 549

Cochran, Bert. Harry Truman and the Crisis Presidency. New York: Funk and Wagnalls, 1973. 435

Cochran, Thomas C. American Business in the Twentieth Century. Cambridge: Harvard University Press, 1973. 79

*_____. Business in American Life: A History. New York: McGraw-Hill, 1972. 69

_____. "Did the Civil War Retard Industrialization?" Mississippi Valley Historical Review, XLVIII (September 1961). 67

_____. "Economic History, Old and New." American Historical Review, LXXIV (June 1969). 63

_____. The Inner Revolution: Essays on the Social Sciences in History. New York: Harper & Row, 1964. 67

*_____. Two Hundred Years of American Business. New York: Dell, 1978. 69

Coffin, Tristram P. Uncertain Glory: Folklore and the American Revolution. Detroit: Folklore Associates, 1971. 98

*Cogley, John. Catholic America. Garden City: Doubleday, 1974. 385

Cohen, Hennig. The South Carolina Gazette, 1732-1775. Columbia: University of South Carolina Press, 1953. 208

Cohen, Morris. Reason and Law. New York: Free Press, 1950. 354

_____, ed. Chance, Love and Logic. 1923. 322

Cohen, Naomi W. American Jews and the Zionist Idea. New York: KTAV, 1975. 386

Cohen, Stuart E. Chicago Architects. Chicago: The Swallow Press, 1976. 524, 531

Cohen, Warren I. The China Connection: Roger S. Greene, Thomas W. Lamont, George E. Sokolsky and American East Asian Relations. New York: Columbia University Press, 1978. 141

Cohn, William and Susan Tamke, eds. "History and Popular Culture." Journal of Popular Culture XI, 1 (Summer 1977). 499

*Coker, William S. ed. The Military Presence on the Gulf Coast. Pensacola, Florida: University of West Florida, 1978. 288

Cole, Wayne S. America First: The Battle Against Intervention, 1940-1941. Madison: University of Wisconsin Press, 1953. 122

_____. Charles A. Lindbergh and the Battle Against American Intervention in World War II. New York: Harcourt, Brace, Jovanovich, 1974. 122

_____. Senator Gerald P. Nye and American Foreign Relations. Minneapolis: University of Minnesota Press, 1962. 122

Coleman, Peter J. Debtors and Creditors in America: Insolvency, Imprisonment for Debt, and Bankruptcy, 1607-1900. Madison: State Historical Society of Wisconsin, 1974. 73

_____. The Transformation of Rhode Island, 1790-1890. Providence: Brown University Press, 1963. 76

Coles, Robert. The Desegregation of the Southern Schools. Boston: Atlantic Monthly Press, 1963. 179

_____. Children of Crisis. Boston: Atlantic Monthly Press, 1967. 179

_____. Uprooted Children. Pittsburgh: University of Pittsburgh Press, 1970. 179

_____. The Middle Americans. Boston: Atlantic Monthly Press, 1971. 179

_____. Migrants, Sharecroppers, Mountaineers. Boston: Atlantic Monthly Press, 1977. 179

_____. Farewell To the South. Boston: Atlantic Monthly Press, 1972. 180

Coletta, Paolo E. The Presidency of William Howard Taft. Kansas: University Press, 1973. 432

Coll, Blanche, D. Perspectives in Public Welfare: A History. Washington, D.C.: U.S. Government Printing Office, 1969. 87

Collinson, Patrick. The Elizabethan Puritan Movement. Berkeley: University of California Press, 1967. 366

Collins, Paul. Gerald R. Ford: A Man in Perspective: As Portrayed in the Gerald R. Ford Mural by Paul Collins. Grand Rapids: Eerdmans, 1976. 439

Collins, Tom. The Search for Jimmy Carter. Waco, Texas: Word Books, 1976. 440

Columbus, Christopher. Letters from the New World. Barcelona: Pedro Posa, 1493. 145, 18

Combs, Jerald A. The Jay Treaty: Political Battleground of the Founding Fathers. Berkeley: University of California Press, 1970. 114

Commager, Henry Steele. Meet the U.S.A. New York: Institute for International Education, 1970. 311

Common Women Collective. Women in U.S. History: An Annotated Bibliography. Cambridge, Massachusetts, 1976. 537

*Commoner, Barry. The Closing Circle. New York: Bantom, 1972. 471

_____. The Politics of Energy. New York: Knopf, 1979. 474

*Commons, John R. Legal Foundations of Capitalism. 1924; Madison: University of Wisconsin, 1969. 350

Compton, James V. The Swastika and the Eagle: Hitler, the United States, and the Origins of World War II. Boston: Houghton Mifflin, 1967. 127

*Comstock, George A. Television in America. Beverly Hills: Sage, 1980. 499

*Conable, Charlotte Williams. Women at Cornell: The Myth of Equal Education. Ithaca: Cornell University Press, 1977. 543

Condit, Carl W. American Building Art: The Nineteenth Century. New York: Oxford University Press, 1960. 34, 41

_____. American Building Art: The Twentieth Century. New York: Oxford Univ. Press, 1961. 35, 42

*_____. American Building: Materials and Techniques: Chicago: University of Chicago Press, 1968. 34

_____. Chicago, 1910-29: Building, Planning, and Urban Technology. Chicago: University of Chicago Press, 1976. 43

_____. Chicago, 1930-70: Building, Planning and Urban Technology. Chicago: University of Chicago Press, 1974. 37, 43, 532

*_____. The Chicago School of Architecture. Chicago: University of Chicago Press, 1973. 37, 43

Congressional Quarterly. Guide to the U.S. Supreme Court. Washington, D.C.: Congressional Quarterly, Inc.,1979. 355

*_____. President Carter. Washington: Congressional Quarterly, Inc, 1977. 440

_____. President Ford: The Man and His Record. Washington: Congressional Quarterly, Inc. 1974. 439

*Conkin, Paul D. The New Deal. Harlan Davidson, 1975. 81

*_____. Puritans and Pragmatists. Bloomington: Indiana University Press, 1976. 325

*Connelly, Thomas L. The Marble Man: Robert E. Lee and His Image in American Society. Baton Rouge: Louisiana State University Press, 1978. 290

Connely, Willard. Louis Sullivan as He Lived. New York: Horizon Press, 1960. 44

Conrad, Horst. Die Literavische Angst: Das Schreckliche in Schuerromantik. und Detektivgeschichte. Dusseldorf: Bartelsmann, 1974. 54, 58

*Conrad,Susan P. Perish the Thought: Intellectual Women in Romantic America, 1830-1860. New York: Citadel, 1978. 180, 404, 544

Conrad, Will, C., Kathleen F. Wilson and Dale Wilson. The Milwaukee Journal: The First Eighty Years. Madison: University of Wisconsin Press, 1964. 216

Conrow, Robert. Field Days: The Life, Times and Reputation of Eugene Field. New York: Scribners, 1974. 529

Conroy, Hilary and T. Scott Miyakawa, eds. East Across the Pacific: Historical and Sociological Studies of Japanese Immigration and Assimilation. Santa Barbara: Clio Press, 1972. 195

Conzen,Kathleen Neils. Immigrant Milwaukee, 1836-1860: Accommodation and Community in a Frontier City. Cambridge, Mass.: Harvard University Press, 1976. 198

Cook, Adrian. The Alabama Claims: American Politics and Anglo-American Relations, 1865-1872. Ithaca: Cornell University Press, 1975. 134

Cook, Blance Wiesen."Female Support Networks and Political Activism." Chrysalis, 3 (Autumn 1977). 541

*_____. ed. Crystal Eastman on Women and Revolution. New York: Oxford University Press, 1978.

Cook, Fred, J. The Corrupted Land: The Social Morality of Modern America.
New York: Macmillan, 1966. 311

Cooke, Michael G. "Do You Remember Laura? or the Limits of Autobiography."
Iowa Review, 9 (Spring 1978). 400

Cooley, Thomas, Educated Lives: The Rise of Modern Autobiography in America.
Columbus, Ohio: Ohio State University Press, 1976. 393, 398, 403

Coolidge, John S. The Pauline Renaissance in England: Puritanism and the Bible.
Oxford: Clarendon Press, 1970.

Cooling, Franklin B. "Technology and the Frontiers of Military History." Military
Affairs, Vol. 39 (December, 1975.) 279

*Coons, John E. and Stephen D. Sugarman. Education by Choice: The Case for Family
Control. Berkeley: University of California Press, 1979. 444

Cooper, Chester L. The Last Crusade: America in Vietnam. New York: Dodd, Mead,
1970. 131

*Cooper, James Fenimore. Gleanings in Europe: Switzerland. Albany: State University
Press of New York, 1980. 407.

_____. A History of the Navy of the United States of America. 1839; New York:
Irvington. 150

_____. Letters and Journals, 6 vols. Cambridge: Harvard University Press, 1968. 407

*_____. The Pathfinder. Lawrence: Regents Press, 1973. 407.

*_____. The Pioneers. Albany: State University of New York Press, 1980. 407

Cooper, James Fennimore. A History of the Navy of the United States of America.
1839; New York: Irvington. 150

Cooper, John Charles. Religion in the Age of Aquarius. Philadelphia:
Westminster Press, 1971. 383

Cooper, John Milton, Jr. Walter Hines Page: The Southerner as American, 1855-1918.
Chapel Hill: University of North Carolina Pres, 1977. 226

Cooper Sandi. "Feminism and Family Revivalism." Chrysalis, 9 (Summer 1978). 534, 538

Cooper, Susan. Behind the Golden Curtain: A View of the U.S.A. New York:
Scribners, 1966. 310

*Copland, Aaron. Music and Imagination. Cambridge: Harvard University Press, 1952. 301

Copperud, Roy H. American Usage: The Consensus. New York: Van Nostrand, 1970. 269

_____. A Dictionary of Usage and Style. New York: Hawthorn, 1964. 269

Cordasco, Franceso. Italian Americans: A Guide to Information Sources. Detroit:
Gale Research Co., 1978. 191

*Corti, Walter Robert. The Philosophy of George Herbert Mead. New York: Adler,
1977. 325

_____. The Philosophy of William James. New York: Adler, 1977. 325

Corwin, Edward S. French Policy and the American Alliance of 1778. Princeton:
University Press, 1916. 114

_____. Total War and the Constitution. New York: Alfred A. Knopf, 1947. 354

*Cott, Nancy. The Bonds of Womanhood:"Woman's Sphere" in New England, 1780-1835.
New Haven: Yale University Press, 1977.

_____ and Elizabeth H Pleck, eds. A Heritage of Her Own: Toward a New Social History of American Women. New York: Simon & Schuster, 1979. 545

Cotton, J. Harry. Royce on the Human Self. Cambridge: Harvard University Press, 1954. 325

Couch, William T. Culture in the South. 1934; Westport: Greenwood Press. 465

Coughlan, Neil. Young John Dewey: An Essay in American Intellectual History. Chicago: The University of Chicago Press, 1973. 329

*Courlander, Harold. Negro Folk Music U.S.A. New York: Columbia University Press, 1963. 300

Couser. G. Thomas. American Autobiography: The Prophetic Mode. Amherst: University of Massachusetts Press, 1979. 393. 398

_____. "The Shape of Death in American Autobiography." Hudson Review, 31 (Spring 1978). 396, 399

Cover, Robert and Owen M. Fiss. The Structure of Procedure. Mineola, New York: Foundation Press, Inc., 1979. 356

Cowan, Ruth Schwartz. "The 'Industrial Revolution' in the Home: Household Technology and Social Change in the Twentieth Century." Technology and Culture, 17 (January, 1976). 509, 549

_____. "Two Washes in the Morning and a Bridge Party at Night: The American Housewife between the Wars." Women's Studies, 3 (1976). 549

*Cowdrey, Albert E. A City for the Nation: The Army Engineers and the Building of Washington, D.C. Washington, D.C.: G.P.O., 1979. 293

*Cox, Archibald. The Role of the Supreme Court in American Government. New York: Oxford University Press, 1976. 351

_____. The Warren Court: Constitutional Decision as an Instrument of Reform. Cambridge, Mass.: Harvard University Press, 1968. 352

Cox, Isaac J. The West Florida Controversy, 1798-1913. Baltimore: Johns Hopkins University Press, 1918. 180

Cox, James. "Autobiography and Washington." Sewanee Review, 85 (April-June 1977). 395, 399

_____. "Recovering Literature's Lost Ground Through Autobiography." The Southern Review, 14 (October, 1978). 397

Craighhead, Frank C. Track of the Grizzly. San Francisco: Sierra, 1979. 486

Cranz, Galen. "Changing Roles of Urban Parks: From Pleasure Garden to Open Space." Landscape, 22 (Summer 1978). 532

Craven, Avery O. The Repressible Conflict. Baton Rouge, La: Louisiana State University Press, 1939. 180

* _____. The Coming of the Civil War. 1942; Chicago: University of Chicago Press, 1966. 180

*Craven, Frank W. Why Military History? Colorado Springs: U.S. Air Force Academy, The Harmon Memorial Lectures in Military History No. One, 1959. 274

Crawford, Richard. Andrew Law, American Psalmodist. 1963; New York: Da Capo, 1981. 29

Creswell, Thomas J. "Usage in Dictionaries and Dictionaries of Usage." PADS, LXIII (1975). 269

*Cresswell, Mary Ann and Carl Berger, comps. United States Air Force History: An Annotated Bibliography. Washington, D.C.: G.P.O. 1971. 285

*Cripps, Thomas. Slow Fade to Black: The Negro in American Films, 1900-1942. New York: Oxford, 1977. 500

Crisler, Jesse E. and Joseph R. McElrath, Jr. Frank Norris: A Reference Guide. Boston: G.K. Hall, 1974. 415

Crisp, Raymond M. "Changes in Attitudes Toward English Usage." Dissertation. University of Illinois, 1971. 269

Crockett, Norman, L. The Woolen Industry of the Midwest. Lexington: University Press of Kentucky, 1970.   75

Cronin, James E. "The Problem with Urban History: Reflections on a Recent Meeting." Urbanism Past & Present, No. 9 (Winter 1979-80). 456

Crook, David, P. The North, the South, and the Powers, 1861-1865. New York: Wiley, 197
118

Crosland, Andrew T. A Concordance to the Complete Poetry of Stephen Crane. Detroit, Michigan: Gale Research, 1975. 411

Cross, Patricia K. Accent on Learning. San Francisco: Josey-Bass,1976. 443

Crowley, J. Donald. Hawthorne: A Collection of Criticism. New York: McGraw-Hill, 1974.

Crowley, John W. George Cabot Lodge. Boston: G.K. Hall, 1976. 414

Crozier, Emmet. Yankee Reporters: 1861-1865. New York: Oxford University Press, 1956; Greenwood, 1974. 213

Crunden, R.M. "Freud, Erikson, and the Historian: A Bibliographic Survey." Canadian Review of American Studies,4 (Spring 1973). 180

*Cruse, Harold. The Crisis of the Negro Intellectual. New York: Morrow, 1967. 26

Cuff, Robert D. "An Organization Perspective on the Military-Industrial Complex." Business History Review, LII (Summer 1978). 83

_____. The War Industries Board: Business-Government Relations During World War I. Baltimore: Johns Hopkins University Press, 1973. 83

Culbert, David H. News from Everyman: Radio and Foreign Affairs in Thirties America. Westport, Conn.: Greenwood Press, 1976. 226

Cumbler, John T. Working-Class Community in Industrial America: Work, Leisure, and Struggle in Two Industrial Cities, 1880-1930. Westport, Connecticut: Greenwood Press, 1979. 448

Cunliffe, Marcus. Chattel Slavery and Wage Slavery: The Anglo American Context, 1830-1860. Athens: University of Georgia, 1980. 447

_____. Soldiers and Civilians: The Martial Spirit in America, 1775–1865. Boston: Little, Brown, 1968. 282

_____ and Robin W. Winks. Pastmasters. New York: Harper and Row, 1969. 180

*_____ and Arthur M. Schlesinger, eds. George Washington, 5 vols. New York: Chelsea House, 1980.

Cunningham, Barbara, ed. The New Jersey Ethnic Experience. Union City, New Jersey: William H. Wise & Company, 1977. 196

*Current, Karen. Greene and Greene: Architects in the Residential Style. Debbs Ferry: Morgan, 1974. 44

Current, Richard N. Secretary Stimson: A Study in Statecraft. New Brunswick: Rutgers University Press, 1954. 126

Curry, Earl R. Hoover's Dominican Diplomacy and the Origins of the Good Neighbor Policy. New York: Garland Publishing, Inc. 1979. 433

Curry, Leonard P. "Urbanization and Urbanism in the Old South: A Comparative View." Journal of Southern History, 40 (February 1974). 465

Curry, Lerond. Protestant– Catholic Relations in America: World War I through Vatican II. Lexington: University Press of Kentucky, 1972. 385

*Curti, Merle E. The Growth of American Thought. 1943; New Brunswick: Transaction, 1981. 166

_____. The Making of An American Community: A Case Study of Democracy in a Frontier Country. Stanford: Stanford University Press, 1959. 180, 205

Curtin, Philip D. The Atlantic Slave Trade: A Census. Madison:University of Wisconsin, 1969. 271

*Curtis, James C. Andrew Jackson and the Search for Vindication. Boston: Little, Brown, 1976. 426

Cutler, Irving. Chicago: Metropolis of the Mid–Continent. Dubuque: Kendall/ Hunt, 1976. 525, 531

Cutlip, Scott, M. Fund Raising in the United States: Role in America's Philanthropy. New Brunswick: Rutgers University Press, 1965. 87

Cutsumbis, Michael N. A Bibliographical Guide to Materials on Greeks in the United States, 1890–1968. New York: Center for Migration Studies, 1970. 191

_____. "The National Archives and Immigration Research." The International Migration Review, IV (Spring 1970). 203

Cybriwsky, Roman. "Social Aspects of Neighborhood Change." Annals. (March 1978). 423

Dahl, Robert, A. "Decision-Making in a Democracy: The Supreme Court as a National Policy-Maker". 6 Journal of Public Law 279 (1957), 352

Dallek, Robert. Franklin D. Roosevelt and American Foreign Policy, 1932-1945. New York: Oxford University Press, 1979. 138, 434

*Daly, Herman E, ed. Essays Toward a Steady State Economy. San Francisco: Freeman, 1980. 474

Dam, Hari N. The Intellectual Odyssey of Walter Lippmann. New York: Gordon, 1973. 218

Dameron, J. Lasley and Irby B. Cauthen, Jr. Edgar Allan Poe: A Bibliography of Criticism, 1827-1867. Charlottesville: University Press of Virginia, 1974. 415

Damico, Alfonso, J. Individuality and Community: The Social and Political Thought of John Dewey. Gainesville: University Presses of Florida, 1978. 329

*Dance, Daryl Cumber. Schuckin' and Jivin': Folklore from Contemporary Black Americans. Bloomington: Indiana University Press, 1981. 111

Dangerfield, George. The Awakening of American Nationalism: 1815-1818. New York: Harper and Row, 1965. 426

*_____. The Era of Good Feelings. New York: Harcourt, Brace, 1952. 117

Danhof, Clarence, H. Change in Agriculture: The Northern United States, 1820-1870. Cambridge: Harvard University Press, 1969. 76

Daniell, Rosemary. Fatal Flowers: On Sin, Sex, and Suicide in the Deep South. New York: Holt, Rinehart and Winston, 1980. 467

Daniels, Roger. "American Historians and East Asian Immigrants." Nora Hundley, Jr.,ed. The Asian American: The Historical Experience. Santa Barbara: Clio. 1976. 204

_____. "The Asian American Experience." William H. Cartwright and Richard L. Watson, eds. The Reinterpretation of American History and Culture. Washington D.C.: National Council for the Social Stidies. 1973. 204

Dann, Martin, ed. The Black Press, (1827-1890). New York: G.P. Putnam's Sons, 1971. 215

Danziger, Edmond Jefferson, Jr. Indians and Bureaucrats: Administering the Reservation Policy During the Civil War.Urbana: University of Illinois Press, 1974. 512

Darling, Arthur B. Our Rising Empire, 1763-1803.1940; New York: Shoestring, 1972. 114, 180

Darnall, Margaretta. "From the Chicago Fair to Walter Gropius: Changing Ideals in American Architecture." Unpublished dissertation. Cornell University, 1975. 532

Darnell, Donald G. William Hickling Prescott. Boston: G.K. Hall, 1975. 415

*Darwin, Charles. The Origin of Species. New York: Macmillan, 1962. 162, 317

David, Paul A. "The Growth of Real Product in the United States before
    1940: New Evidence, Controlled Conjectures." Journal of Economic
    History, XXVII (June 1967). 68

_____."The Mechanization of Reaping in the Ante-bellum Midwest."
    Technical Choice, Innovation and Economic Growth.Cambridge:
    Cambridge University Press, 1975. 77

*_____, et al. Reckoning with Slavery: Critical Study in the Quantitative
    History of American Negro Slavery. New York: Oxford University Press,
    1976. 78, 180

_____ and Peter Solar. "A Bicentenary Contribution to the History of
    the Cost of Living in America." Research in Economic History, II (1977). 69

Davidson, James West. The Logic of Millenial Thought: Eighteenth Century
    New England. New Haven: Yale University Press, 1977. 374

_____,Marshall and G.E.Kidder-Smith. A Pictorial History of Architecture
    in America, 2 volumes. New York: Norton, 1976. 47

Davison, Peter, Rolf Meyersohn and Edward Shils.eds. Literary Taste, Culture
    and Mass Communications, 14 volumes. Teaneck, New Jersey: Somerset House,
    1979. 500

*Davis, Allen F. and Mark H. Haller, eds. The Peoples of Philadelphia:
    A History of Ethnic Groups and Lower Class Life, 1790-1940.Philadelphia:
    Temple University Press, 1973. 199

Davis, Alva L. "A Word Atlas of the Great Lakes Region." Dissertation.
    University of Michigan, 1949. 264

Davis, Burke. Old Hickory: A Life of Andrew Jackson. New York: Dial Press, 1977. 426

Davis, Calvin D. The United States and the Second Hague Peace Conference:
    American Diplomacy and the International Organization 1889-1914.
    Durham, North Carolina: Duke University Press, 1976. 135

Davis, Charles T. and Daniel Walden, eds. On Being Black. Greenwhich: Fawcett, 1970. 14

Davis, Cullon, et. al., eds. The Public and the Private Lincoln: Contemporary
    Perspectives. Carbondale: Southern Illinois University Press, 1979. 428

*Davis, David Brion. The Problem of Slavery in the Age of Revolution.
    Ithaca: Cornell University Press, 1976. 173

*_____. The Problem of Slavery in Western Culture. Ithaca: Cornell
    University Press, 1966. 172

Davis, Elmer. History of the New York Times, 1851-1921. New York: New York
    Times Co; 1921; Scholarly, 1971. 212

Davis, Kenneth, S. FDR: The Beckoning of Destiny, 1882-1928: A History.
    New York: Putnam, 1972. 434

_____. Invincible Summer: An Intimate Portrait of the Roosevelts, Based on the Recollections of Marion Dickerman. New York: Atheneum, 1974. 435

Davis, Lance E. "Capital Immobilities and Finance Capitalism: A Study of Economic Evolution in the United States, 1820-1920." Explorations in Entrepreneurial History, I (Fall 1963). 72

_____. "The Investment Market, 1870-1918: The Evolution of a National Market." Journal Economic History, XXV (September 1965). 72

_____. "The New England Textile Mills and the Capital Markets: A Study of Industrial Borrowing,1840-1860." Journal of Economic History, XX (March 1 1960). 72

_____, et. al. American Economic Growth: An Economist's History of the United States. New York: Harper & Row, 1972. 63

_____ and Douglas C. North. Institutional Change and American Economic Growth. Cambridge: Cambridge University Press, 1971. 63

_____ and J.R.T. Hughes. " A Dollar-Sterling Exchange, 1803-1894." Economic History Review. XIII (August 1960). 73

_____ and John Legler. "The Government in the American Economy, 1815-1902: A Quantitative Study." Journal of Economic History, XXVI (December 1966). 69

Davis, Lawrence B. Immigrants, Baptists and the Protestant Mind in America. Urbana: University of Illinois Press, 1973. 380

Davis, Lawrence, M. "The Phonology of Yiddish-American Speech." Dissertation. University of Chicago, 1967. 266

_____."The Stressed Vowels of Yiddish-American Speech." PADS, XLVIII (1967). 266

_____ ed. Studies in Linguistics in Honor of Raven I McDavid, Jr. University, Alabama: University of Alabama Press, 1972. 256, 259

*Dawley, Alan. Class and Community: The Industrial Revolution in Lynn. Cambridge: Harvard, 1979. 448, 460

de Bary Nee, Victor G. and Britt. Longtime Californ: A Documentary Study of an American Chinatown. New York: Pantheon, 1972. 195

*De Bell, Garrett, ed. The New Environmental Handbook. San Francisco: Friends of the Earth, 1980. 471

Debellis, Jack. Sidney Lanier, Henry Timrod, and Paul Hamilton Hayne: A Reference Guide. Boston: G.K. Hall 1978. 412

DeBenedetti, Charles. Origins of the Modern American Peace Movement, 1915-1929. Millwood, New York: KTO Press, 1978. 136

Decanio, Stephen, J. <u>Agriculture in the Postbellum South: The Economics of Production and Supply</u>. Cambridge: M.I.T. Press, 1974. 79

De Caux, Len. <u>Labor Radical: From the Wobblies to the CIO</u>. Boston: Beacon Press, 1970.450

*Deckard, Barbara S. <u>Women's Movement: Political, Socioeconomic and Psychological Issues</u>. New York: Harper & Row, 1979. 540

Decker, John and John P. McWilliams. <u>James Fenimore Cooper</u>. London: Routledge and Kegan, 1974. 410

Decker, Peter R. <u>Fortunes and Failures: White-Collar Mobility in Nineteenth-Century San Francisco</u>. Cambridge: Harvard University Press, 1978. 92, 460

*De Conde, Alexander. <u>This Affair of Louisiana.</u> Baton Rouge: Louisiana State University Press, 1979. 133

De Conde, Alexander, ed. <u>The Encyclopedia of American Foreign Policy</u>. 3 vols. New York: Scribner's 1978. 133

De Conde, Alexander. <u>Entangling Alliance: Politics and Diplomacy under George Washington</u>. Durham, North Carolina: Duke University Press, 1958. 115

_____. <u>Half-Bitter, Half-Sweet: An Excursion into Italian-American History</u>. New York: Scribner's 1971. 131

_____. <u>Herbert Hoover's Latin American Policy</u>. Stanford: Stanford University Press, 1951. 125

_____. <u>The Quasi-War: The Politics and Diplomacy of the Undeclared War with France, 1797-1801</u>. New York: Scribner's, 1966. 115

_____, ed. <u>Isolation and Security: Idea and Interest in Twentieth Century American Foreign Policy</u>. Durham: Duke University Press, 1957, 123

*Deetz, James. <u>In Small Things Forgotten: The Archeology of Early American Life</u>. Garden City, New York: Doubleday Anchor Books, 1977. 509

Degler, Carl N. <u>At Odds: Women and the Family in America, From the Revolution to the Present</u>. New York: Oxford University Press, 1980. 543

*_____. <u>Neither Black nor White: Slavery and Race Relations in Brazil and the United States</u>. New York: Macmillan, 1971. 173

_____. <u>Place Over Time: The Continuity of Southern Distinctiveness</u>. Baton Rouge: Louisiana State University, 1977. 466

De Jong, Gerald F. <u>The Dutch in America</u>. Boston: Twayne, 1975. 195

Deledalle, Gérard. <u>Histoire de la Philosophe Américaine</u>. Paris: Presses Universitaires de France, 1954. 330

_____. <u>L'Idée D'Expérience dans la Philosophie de John Dewey</u>. Paris: Presses Universitaires de France, 1967. 329

_____. Theorie et Pratique du Sigine. Paris: Payot, 1979. 329

Dell, Christopher. Lincoln and the War Democrats: The Grand Erosion of Conservative Tradition. Rutherford, New Jersey: Fairleigh Dickinson University Press, 1975. 42ᶜ

D'Eloia, Sarah G. "Issues in the Analysis of Nonstandard Negro English: A Review of J.L. Dillard's Black English." Journal of English, VII (1973). 265

De Lone, Richard H. Small Futures: Inequality, Children, and the Failure of Liberal Reform. New York: Harcourt Brace Jovanovich, 1978. 442

Deloria, Vine. God is Red. New York: Grosset & Dunlop, 1973. 512

_____. The Metaphysics of Modern Existence. New York: Harper & Row, 1979. 512

*_____. Custer Died for Your Sins. New York: Avon, 1970. 145, 175

Demaree, Albert Lowther. The American Agricultural Press, 1819-1860. New York: Columbia University Press, 1941; Porcupine. 214

Demaris, Ovid. America the Violent. Cowles Book Co., 1970. 310

Demeter, Richard, I. Primer, Presses, and Composing Sticks: Women Printers of the Colonial Period. Hicksville, New York: Exposition Press, 1979. 225

Dendy, William. Lost Toronto. New York: Oxford University Press, 1979. 480

Denisoff, R. Serge. Great Day Coming, Folk Music and the American Left. Urbana: University of Illinois Press, 1971. 104

_____. Solid Gold: The Popular Record Industry. New Brunswick, New Jersey: Transaction Books, 1975. 500

Dennett, Tyler. Americans in Eastern Asia: A Critical Study of the Policy of the United States with Reference to China, Japan and Korea in the 19th Century. New York: Macmillan, 1922. 120

*Dennis, Ralph. The Buy Back Blues. New York: Popular Library, 1977. 469

_____. The Charleston Knife's Back in Town. New York: Popular Library, 1974. ⁄

Dennis, Wayne and Margaret Daniels. The Intellectually Gifted--An Overview. New York: Grune and Stratton, 1976. 443

Department of Defense. The "Magic" Background of Pearl Harbor, 5 vols. Washington, D.C.: G.P.O., 1978.

Department of the Interior. Land Conservation and Preservation Techniques. Washington, D.C.: G.P.O., 1979.

Department of Labor. The American Worker. Washington, D.C.: G.P.O., 1976. 452

*Derthick, Martha. Policymaking for Social Security. Washington, D.C.: Brookings Institution, 1979. 94

Desroche, Henri. The American Shakers: From Neo-Christianity to Presocialism. Amherst: University of Massachusetts Press, 1971. 382

Deutrich, Mabel and Virginia Purdy, eds. Clio was a Woman. Washington, D.C.: Howard University Press, 1980. 551

Deutsch, Jan. "Neutrality, Legitimacy, and the Supreme Court: Some Intersections Between Law and Political Science." 20 Stanford Law Review, 169 (1968). 349

Devlin, Patrick. Too Proud to Fight: Woodrow Wilson's Neutrality. New York: Oxford University Press, 1975. 121, 136, 432

Dewey, John. The Early Works of John Dewey, 1882-1898. 5 vols. Jo Ann Boydston, ed. MLA-CEAA. 321

*_____. Experience and Nature (1929). New York: Dover. 328

_____. The Middle Works of John Dewey, 1899-1924, 8 vols. Jo Ann Boydston, ed. MLA-CEAA. 321

_____. "The Need for a Recovery of Philosophy." John J. McDermott, ed. The Philosophy of John Dewey. New York: G.P. Putnam's Sons, 1973. 324

*Dickey, James. Babel to Byzantium: Poets and Poetry Now. New York: Ecco, 1981. 343

Diehl, William. Sharky's Machine. New York: Delacorte Press, 1978. 468

Diggins, J.P. "The Perils of Naturalism: Some Reflections on Daniel J. Boorstin's Approach to American History." American Quarterly, 23 (May 1971). 180

*Dillard, Annie. Pilgrim at Tinker Creek. New York: Bantam, 1975. 399

Dillard, Joey L. All American English. New York: Random House, 1975. 258

_____. Black English. New York: Random House, 1972. 265

_____. The Lexicon of Black English. New York: Seabury, 1977. 265

Dillingham, William D. Melville's Short Fiction, 1853-1856. Athens, Georgia: University of Georgia Press, 1977.

Dilthey, Wilhelm. Pattern and Meaning in History. New York: Harper and Row, 1960. 398

DiMaggio, Paul. "Market Structure, the Creative Process, and Popular Culture: Toward an Organizational Reinterpretation of Mass Culture Theory." Journal of Popular Culture, XI, 2 (Fall 1977). 496, 500

Diner, Stephen, J. A City and Its Universities: Public Policy in Chicago, 1892-1919. Chapel Hill: University of North Carolina Press, 1980. 530

Dinerstein, Herbert S. The Making of a Missile Crisis: October, 1962. Baltimore: Johns Hopkins, 1976. 140

Dinnerstein, Lois. "The Iron Worker and King Solomon: Some Images of Labor in American Art." Arts, 54 (September 1979). 453

Dingemans, Dennis. "The Urbanization of Suburbia: The Renaissance of the Row House." Landscape, 20, 1 (October 1975). 422

Dingman, Roger. Power in the Pacific: The Origins of Naval Arms Limitation, 1914-1922. Chicago: University of Chicago Press, 1976.   137

Dippel, Horst. Germany and the American Revolution, 1770-1800: A Sociohistorical Investigation of Late Eighteenth Century Political Thinking. Chapel Hill: University of North Carolina Press, 1977.   133

Divine, Robert A. Blowing on the Wind: The Nuclear Test Ban Debate, 1954-1960. New York: Oxford, 1973.   140

_____. The Illusion of Neutrality. Chicago: University of Chicago Press, 1962.   12

*_____. The Reluctant Belligerent: American Entry into World War II. New York: Wiley, 1965.   125

_____. Roosevelt and World War II. Baltimore: Johns Hopkins Press, 1969.   125

_____.   Second Chance: The Triumph of Internationalism in America during World War II. New York: Atheneum, 1967.   127

*Doan, Marlyn. Starting Small in the Wilderness. San Francisco: Sierra, 1979.   487

Dobbs, Farrell. Teamster Power. New York: Monad Press, 1973.   450

Dobson, E.J. English Pronunciation 1500-1700. Oxford: The Clarendon Press, 1957.   263

Doenecke, Justus D. The Presidencies of James A. Garfield and Chester A. Arthur. Lawrence: Regents Press of Kansas, 1981.   430

Dohan, Mabel. Our Own Words. New York: Alfred A. Knopf, 1974.   258

*Dolan, Jay P. Catholic Revivalism: The American Experience, 1830-1900. Notre Dame: Notre Dame Press, 1978.   384

_____. The Immigrant Church: New York's Irish and German Catholics, 1815-1865. Baltimore: Johns Hopkins University Press, 1975.   200, 384

Dolbeare, Kenneth and P.E. Hammond. The School Prayer Decisions: From Court Policy to Local Practice. Chicago: University of Chicago Press, 1971.   352

*Donovan, Robert J. Conflict and Crisis: The Presidency of Harry S. Truman, 1945-1948. New York: W. W. Norton and Company, 1979.   435

Doren, Mark Van, ed. The Viking Portable Walt Whitman. New York: Viking, 1974.

Dorsett, Lyle, W. Franklin D. Roosevelt and the City Bosses. Port Washington, New York: Kennikat Press, 1977.   435

*Dorson, Richard M. America in Legend. New York: Pantheon, 1974.   97

_____. American Folklore. Chicago: University of Chicago Press, 1959.   97

*_____. American Folklore and the Historian. Chicago: University of Chicago Press, 1971.   97

_____. American Negro Folktales. Greenwich, Connecticut: Fawcett, 1967.   107

_____. Bloodstoppers and Bearwalkers. Cambridge: Harvard University Press, 1972. 99, 109

_____. Folklore and Fakelore Cambridge: Harvard University Press, 1976. 97, 109

_____. "The Jonny-Cake Papers." Journal of American Folklore, 58 (1945). 99

_____, ed. Davy Crockett, American Comic Legend. 1939; Westport, Connecticut: Greenwood Press, 1977. 101

_____. Folklore and Folklife: An Introduction. Chicago: University of Chicago Press, 1972. 97

_____. Folklore: Selected Essays. Bloomington: Indiana University Press, 1972. 97

Dorwart, Jeffrey M. The Office of Naval Intelligence: The Birth of America's First Intelligence Agency. Annapolis: U.S. Naval Institute Press, 1979. 292

_____. The Pigtail War: American Involvement in the Sino-Japanese War of 1894-95. Amherst: University of Massachusetts Press, 1975. 136

Doudna, Martin F. Concern About the Planet: The Reporter Magazine and American Liberalism, 1949-1968. Wesport, Connecticut: Greenwood Press, 1977. 227

*Douglas, Ann. The Feminization of American Culture. New York: Avon, 1978. 500, 540

_____. "Studs Lonigan and the Failure of History in Mass Society: A Study in Claustrophobia." American Quarterly, 29 (Winter 1977). 529

*Douglas, Mary. Implicit Meanings: Essays in Anthropology. London: Routledge and Regan, 1978. 497, 500

_____. Natural Symbols. Middlesex, England: Penguin, 1973.

Douglas, William A. and Jon Bilbao. Amerikanuak: Basques in the New World. Reno: University of Nevada Press, 1975. 195

*Douglas, William O. Go East, Young Man. New York: Dell, 1975. 349

Douglass, Elisha P. The Coming of Age of American Business. Chapel Hill: University of North Carolina Press, 1971. 69

*Douglass, Frederick. Narrative of the Life of Frederick Douglass. New York: New American Library, 1968. 21

Dowly, Devereux. The Poorhouse: Subsidized Housing in Chicago, 1895-1976. Carbondale, Illinois: Southern Illinois University, 1978.

Downer, James W. "The Dialect of Biglow Papers." Dissertation. University of Michigan, 1958. 267

Downing, Antoinette F. and Vincent Scully. The Architectural Heritage of Newport, Rhode Island, 1640-1915. Cambridge: Harvard University Press, 1952. 38, 43

Downton, James V., Jr. Sacred Journeys: The Conversion of Young Americans to Divine Light Mission. New York: Columbia University Press, 1979. 384

Dozer, Donald M. Are We Good Neighbors?: Three Decades of Inter-American Relations, 1930-1960. 125

Drake, Carlos, ed. "Folklore." Journal of Popular Culture, VI, 4 (Spring 1973). 500

*Drake, St. Clair and Horace R. Cayton. Black Metropolis. New York: Harcourt, Brace and World, 1970. 26

Draper, Theodore. The Dominican Revolt: A Case Study in American Policy. New York: Commentary, 1968. 120

*Drew, Elizabeth. Washington Journal: The Events of 1973-1974. New York: Vintage Books, 1976. 439

Droege, John. Passenger Terminals and Trains. 1916; Milwaukee: Kalmbach, 1968. 40, 44

Drummond, Donald F. The Passing of American Neutrality, 1937-1941. Ann Arbor: University of Michigan Press, 1955. 125

Duberman, Martin. The Uncompleted Past. New York: Random House, 1969. 180

Dubin, Arthur D. More Classic Trains. Milwaukee: Kalmbach, 1974. 40

_____. Some Classic Trains. Milwaukee: Kalmbach, 1964. 40

Dubin, Robert. Handbook of Work, Organization, and Society. Chicago: Rand McNally, 1976. 446

Dublin, Thomas. Women at Work: The Transformation of Work and Community in Lowell, Massachusetts, 1826-1860. New Jersey: Columbia University Press, 1979. 447, 547

*Du Bois, Ellen. Feminism and Suffrage: The Emergence of an Independent Women's Movement in America, 1848-1869. Ithaca: Cornell University Press, 1978. 541

*Du Bois, W.E.B. Black Reconstruction in America, 1860-1880. 1935; New York: Atheneum, 1969. 18, 121

_____. Darkwater: Voices from Within the Veil. 1920; New York: Schocken, 1969. 21

The Negro. 1915; Millwood: Kraus Reprints, 1975. 18, 21

* _____. The Souls of Black Folk. 1903; New York: New American Library, 1969. 21, 172, 469

Dubofsky, Melvyn and Waren Van Tine. John L. Lewis. Chicago: Quadrangle, 1977. 449

Ducey, Michael H. Sunday Morning: Aspects of Urban Ritual. New York: Free Press, 1977.

Duffey, Bernard. Poetry in America: Expression and Its Values in the Times of Bryant, Whitman and Pound. Durham, North Carolina: Duke University Press, 1978. 401

Duggan, Edward P. "Machines, Markets, and Labor: The Carriage and Wagon Industry in Late-Nineteenth Century Cincinnati." Business History Review, LI (Autumn 1977).

Duis, Perry. "Bessie Louise Pierce: Symbol and Scholar." Chicago History, 5 (Fall 1976). 530

* _____. Chicago: Creating New Traditions. Chicago: Chicago Historical Society, 1976. 508, 518

_____. "'Where is Athens Now?' The Fine Arts Building, 1898-1918." Chicago History, Pt. I, 6 (Summer 1977); Pt. II, 7 (Spring 1978). 529

Dull, Jonathan R. The French Navy and American Independence: A Study of Arms and Diplomacy, 1774-1787. Princeton: Princeton University Press, 1975. 133

Duncan, Bingham. Whitelaw Reid: Journalist, Politician, Diplomat. Athens: University of Georgia Press, 1975. 214

Duncan, Hugh. Culture and Democracy. Totowa, New Jersey: Bedminster Press, 1965. 37, 44

Duncan, Hugh Dalziel. Communication and Social Order. New York: Oxford, 1962. 500

Dundes, Alan. Analytic Essays in Folklore. The Hague, Paris: Mouton, 1975. 97

_____. The Study of Folklore. Englewood Cliffs, New Jersey: Prentice Hall, 1965. 97

_____, ed. Mother Wit From the Laughing Barrel. New York: Garland, 1981. 106

*Dundes, Alan and Carl Pagter. Work Hard and You Shall Be Rewarded: Urban Folklore From the Paperwork Empire. Bloomington: Indiana University Press, 1979. 106, 111

Dunham, Philip. Down These Mean Streets a Man Must Go. Chapel Hill: University of North Carolina Press, 1963. 60

Dunlap, Howard G. "Social Aspects of a Verb Form: Native Atlanta Fifth Grade Speech - The Present Tense of Be." PADS (1974). 265

Dunlop, Donald. "Popular Culture and Methodology." Journal of Popular Culture, XI, 2 (Fall 1975). 500

Dunn, James A., Jr. "The Importance of Being Earmarked: Transport Policy and Highway Finance in Great Britain and the United States." Comparative Studies in Society and History, 20 (January 1978). 94

Dunn, R. "The Social History of Early New England." American Quarterly, 24 (December 1972). 180

Dunne, Gerald T. Hugo Black and the Judicial Revolution. New York: Simon and Schuster, 1977. 349

_____. Justice Joseph Story and the Rise of the Supreme Court. New York: Simon and Schuster, 1971. 349

Durham, Weldon B. "'Big Brother' and the 'Seven Sisters': Camp Life Reforms in World War I." Military Affairs, 42 (April 1978). 289

Dye, Nancy Schrom. "Feminism or Unionism? The New York Women's Trade Union League and the Labor Movement." Feminist Studies, 3 (Fall 1975). 548

Dyer, Thomas G. Theodore Roosevelt and the Idea of Race. Baton Rouge: Louisiana State University Press, 1980. 431

Dyer, Victor. Prairie Avenue: An Annotated Bibliography. Chicago: Chicago Architectural Foundation, 1977. 527

Dykema, Karl J. "Webster's New World Dictionary, College Edition." _American Speech,_ XXIX (1954). 271

*Dykhuizen, George. _The Life and Mind of John Dewey_. Carbondale: Southern Illinois University Press, 1978. 325

Dykstra, Robert. _Cattle Towns_. New York: Atheneum, 1970. 174

Dyrud, Keith, et. al. _The Other Catholics_. New York: Arno Press, 1978.   201

Eakin, John, The New England Girl: Cultural Ideals in Hawthorne, Stowe, Howells and James. Athens, Georgia: University of Georgia Press, 1976. 404

Eakin, Paul John. "Alfred Kazin's Bridge to America," South Atlantic Quarterly, 77 (Winter 1978). 400

_____. "Malcolm X and the Limits of Autobiography," Criticism, 18 (Summer 1976). 395, 399

Eames, Hugh. Sleuths, Inc. Philadelphia: Lippincott, 1978. 58

*Eames, S. Morris. Pragmatic Naturalism: An Introduction. Carbondale: Southern Illinois University Press, 1977. 326

Earle, Carville V. The Evolution of a Tidewater Settlement System: All Hallow's Parish, Maryland, 1650-1783. Chicago: University of Chicago, 1975. 65

Earle, Carville and Ronald Hoffman. "Urban Development in the Eighteenth-Century South." Perspectives in America History, X (1976). 64

East, Robert Abraham. John Adams. World Leaders Series, No. 78. Boston: Twayne Publishers, 1979. 425

Easterlin, Richard A. "Interregional Differences in Per Capita Income, Population and Total Income, 1840-1950."Trends in the American Economy. Princeton: Princeton University Press, 1960. 68

_____. "Farm Production and Income in Old and New Areas at Mid-Century." In David C. Klingaman and Richard K. Vedder, eds. Essays in Nineteenth Century Economic History. Athens: Ohio University Press, 1975. 77

_____."Population Issues in American Economic History: A Survey and Critique." Research in Economic History, I (Supplement 1977). 89

*Eastman, Crystal. Crystal Eastman on Women and Revolution. New York: Oxford University Press, 1978. 544

Easton, Barbara. "Feminism and the Contemporary Family." Socialist Review,8 (May-June 1978). 528

Easton, LLoyd. Hegel's First American Followers: The Ohio Hegelians. Athens: Ohio University Press, 1966. 326

Eagleton, Terry. "Ideology, Fiction, Narrative." Social Text, I (Summer 1979). 500

Eaton , Leonard K. Landscape Artist in America: The Life and Work of Jens Jensen. Chicago: University of Chicago Press, 1964. 532

Eckes,Alfred E., Jr. A Search for Solvency:Bretton Woods and the International Monetary System, 1941-1971. Austin: University of Texas Press, 1975. 141

*Eckholm, Erik P. Losing Ground: Evironmental Stress and World Food Prospects. New York: Norton, 1976. 472

Eckley, Wilton. Herbert Hoover. Boston: Twayne Publishers, 1980. 433

Eckstorm, Fanny Hardy and Mary Winslow Smyth. Minstrelsy of Maine. Boston: Houghton Mifflin and Company , 1927. 102

Eco, Umberto. The Role of the Reader: Explorations in the Semiotics of Texts. Bloomington, Indiana: Indiana University, 1979. 500

Edel, Leon, ed. The Letters of Henry James, 3 volumes. Cambridge: Harvard University Press, 1974, 1975, 1980. 413

Edmunds, R. David. The Potawatomis: Keepers of the Fire. Norman: University of Oklahoma Press, 1978. 513

Edwards, Harry. Black Students. New York: Free Press, 1970. 10

Edwards, Jerome. The Foreign Policy of Col. McCormack's Tribune, 1927-1941. Reno: University of Nevada Press, 1971. 219

*Egbert, Donald Drew. Socialism and American Art. Princeton: Princeton University Press, 1967. 452

Eggleston, Edward. The Transit of European Civilization to North America. 1901; Boston: Beacon Press, 1959. 157

Egloff, Franklin, R. Theodore Roosevelt: An American Portrait. New York: Vantage Press, 1980. 431

Egnal, Marc. "The Economic Development of the Thirteen Continental Colonies, 1720 to 1775." William and Mary Quarterly, XXXII (1975). 64

_____ and Joseph A. Ernst. "An Economic Interpretation of the American Revolution." William and Mary Quarterly, XXIX (January 1972). 65

*Ehrenreich, Barbara and Deirdre English. For Her Own Good: 150 Years of the Experts' Advice to Women. Garden City, New York: Anchor Books 1978. 540

*Ehrlich, Paul. The Population Bomb. New York: Ballantine, 1976. 471

_____ and Anne. Population, Resources and the Environment. San Francisco: Freeman, 1970. 472

Ehrlich, Richard L., ed. Immigrants in Industrial America 1850-1920. Charlottesville: University of Virginia, 1977.

Eichelberger, Clayton L., ed. A Guide to Critical Reviews of United States Fiction, 1870-1910, Volume II. Metuchen, New Jersey: Scarecrow Press, 1974. 407

_____. ed. Published Comment on William Dean Howells Through 1920: A Research Bibliography. Boston: G.K. Hall, 1976. 413

Eichner, Alfred S. The Emergence of Oligopoly: Sugar Refining as a Case Study. 1969; Westport: Greenwood Press, 1978. 80

Eisenhower, Dwight, D. Letters to Mamie Garden City: New York: Doubleday, 1978. 436

Ekman, Barbara. The End of a Legend: Ellen Glasgow's History of Southern Women. Uppsala, Sweden: Almquist and Wiksell, 1976. 404

Eliasberg, Vera F. "Some Aspects of Development in the Coal Mining Industry, 1839-1918." Output, Employment and Productivity. New York: Columbia University Press, 1966. 74

Eliason, Norman A. Tarheel Talk. Chapel Hill: University of North Carolina Press, 1958. 264

*Elkins, Stanley. Slavery: A Problem in American Institutional and Intellectual Life. Chicago: University of Chicago Press, 1976. 26, 172

Ellet, Elizabeth F. Pioneer Woman of the West. 1852; West Newfield: Longwood, 1979. 155

_____. Women Artists in all Ages and Countries . New York: Harper Brothers, 1859. 155

_____. The Women of the American Revolution, 3 volumes. 1848; New York: Haskell House, 1969. 155

Elliot, Emory. Power and the Pulpit in Puritan New England. Princeton: Princeton University Press, 1975. 367

Elliot, Neal, Jr. The Raleigh Register, 1799-1863. Chapel Hill: University of North Carolina Press, 1955. 210

Ellis, Ethan L. Republican Foreign Policy, 1921-1933. New Brunswick: Rutgers University Press, 1968. 123

Ellis, John Tracy. Catholics in Colonial America. Baltimore: Helicon Press, 1965. 372

Ellis, Joseph. The New England Mind in Transition: Samuel Johnson of Connecticut, 1696-1772. New Haven: Yale University Press, 1973. 374

Ellison, Curtis W. and E.W. Metcalf, Jr. Charles W. Chesnutt. Boston: G.K. Hall, 1977.

Ellison, Mary, L. Support for Secession: Lancashire and the American Civil War. Chicago: University of Chicago Press, 1972. 118

*Ellison, Ralph. Invisible Man. New York: Random, 1972. 172

Elson, Robert T. The World of Time Inc.: An Intimate History of a Publishing Enterprise, 1941-1960. New York: Atheneum, 1973. 221

Ellsworth, Frank L. Law on the Midway: The Founding of the University of Chicago Law School Chicago: University of Chicago Press, 1977. 530

*Ellwood, Robert S., Jr. Alternative Altars: Unconventional and Eastern Spirituality in America. Chicago: University of Chicago Press, 1981. 383

*_____. Religious and Spiritual Groups in Modern America. Englewood Cliffs: Prentice-Hall, 1973. 383

Elson, Louis. History of American Music. 1904; New York: Ben Franklin, 1971. 297

Ely, John Hart. "Constitutional Interpretivism: Its Allure and Impossibility." 53 Indiana Law Journal 399 (1970). 356

*_____. Democracy and Distrust: A Theory of Judicial Review. Cambridge: Harvard University, 1981. 357

_____. "On Discovering Fundamental Values." 92 Harvard Law Review 5 (1978). 356

_____. "Toward a Representation-Reinforcing Mode of Judicial Review." Maryland Law Review 451 (1978). 356

Emerson, O.B. and Marion C. Michael. Southern Literary Culture: A Bibliography of Masters' and Doctors' Theses. University: University Alabama Press, 1979. 407

Emerson, Ralph Waldo. Early Lectures. Cambridge: Harvard University Press, 1972. 407

_____. Essays: First Series. New York: Houghton Mifflin. 407

_____. Journals and Miscellaneous Notebooks, 15 vols. Cambridge: Harvard University Press, 1960-1982. 407

* _____. Collected Works: Nature, Addresses, and Lectures. Cambridge: Harvard University Press, 1979. 324, 407

Emery, Edwin. The Press and America: An Interpretative History of the Mass Media. Englewood Cliffs, New Jersey: Prentice-Hall, 1978.   223, 228

Emery, Edwin and Michael Emery. "Images of America in its Twentieth Century Media." Revue Francaise D'Etudes Americaines, N'6 (October 1978). 228

Emery, Noemie. Washington: A Biography. New York: Putman, 1976.

*Emery, Walter B. Broadcasting and Government. East Lansing: Michigan State University Press, 1971. 220

Emmet, Boris and John Jeuck. Catalogues and Counters: A History of Sears, Roebuck & Company. Chicago: University of Chicago Press, 1950. 322

Endy, Melvin B. , Jr. William Penn and Early Quakerism. Princeton: Princeton University Press, 1973. 370

*Energy Policy Project Staff. A Time to Choose: America's Energy Future. New York: Ballinger, 1974. 474

Engerman, Stanley, L. "The Economic Impact of the Civil War." Explorations in Entrepreneurial History, III (Spring 1966). 67

_____. "Some Economic Issues Relating to Railroad Subsidies and the Evaluation of Land Grants." Journal of Economic History, (June 1972). 71

Engler, Richard E., Jr. The Challenge of Diversity. 1964; New York: Arno, 1980. 308

English, Maurice, ed. The Testament of Stone. Evanston: Northwestern University Press, 1963. 37, 44

*Enzel, Robert G. The White Book of Ski Areas. New York: Rand, 1981. 487, 488

Eplan, Leon S. "Atlanta: Planning, Budgeting and Neighborhoods." Anthony James Catanese and W. Paul Farmer, eds. Personality, Politics and Planning: How City Planners Work. Beverly Hills:Sage, 1978. 467

Epstein, Dena S. "African Music in British and French America." Musical Quarterly, LIX (1973). 300

_____. Sinful Tunes and Spirituals: Black Folk Music to the Civil War. Urbana: University of Illinois Press, 1977. 305

_____. "Slave Music in the United States before 1860." Notes , XX (1963). 300

Epstein, Samuel S. The Politics of Cancer. Los Angeles: Cancer Book House. 476

Erickson, Charlotte. Invisible Immigrants: The Adaptation of English and Scottish Immigrants in Nineteenth-Century America. Coral Gables, Florida: University of Miami, 1972. 195

_____, ed. Emigration from Europe 1815-1914. London: Humanities, 1976. 192

Erikson, Erik. "Gandhi's Autobiography: The Leader as a Child." American Scholar, 35 (Autumn 1976). 392, 398

*Erikson, Erik. Life History and the Historical Moment: Diverse Presentations.
    New York: Norton, 1979. 392, 398

Erickson, Erling A. Ban king in Frontier Iowa, 1836-1865. Ames: Iowa State
    University Press, 1971. 73

Erickson, John. "Newspapers and Social Values: Chicago Journalism, 1890-1910."
    Dissertation. University of Illinois at Urbana, 1973. 521.

Erisman, Fred. Frederic Remington. Boise,Idaho: Boise State University,1975. 415

_____. "Western Motifs in the Thriller's of Donald Hamilton." Western
    American Literature, 10. 60

Ernst, Joseph A. Money and Politics in America, 1755-1775. Chapel Hill:
    University of North Carolina Press, 1973. 64

Escholz, Paul A., Alfred F. Rosa and Virginia Clark. Language Awareness.
    New York: St. Martin's,1974. 259

Esposito, Vincent J., ed. The West Point Atlas of American Wars. New York:
    Praeger Publishers, 1952, 2 vols. 273

Esslinger, Dean R. Immigrants and the City: Ethnicity and Mobility in a
    Nineteenth Century Mid-Western Community. Port Washington, New Jersey:
    Kennikat, 1975. 197

Esthus, Raymond A. Theodore Roosevelt and Japan. Seattle: University of
    Washington Press, 1966. 121

*Esterovich, Adams. A Guide and Bibliography to Research on Yugoslavs in the
    United States and Canada. San Francisco: Ragusan, 1975. 189

Etiemble, Rene. Parlez-vous Franglais? Paris: Gallimard, 1964. 269

Evans, Bergen and Cornelia. A Dictionary of Contemporay American Usage.
    New York: Random House, 1957. 269

Evans, Herndon J. The Newspaper Press in Kentucky. Lexington: University
    Press of Kentucky, 1977. 226

*Evans, Les and Allen Myers. Watergate and the Myth of American Democracy.
    New York: Path Press, 1974. 439

Evans, Sara. Personal Politics: The Roots of Women's Liberation in the
    Civil Rights Movement and the New Left. New York: Knopf, 1979. 541

Fairman, Charles. Reconstruction and Reunion, 1864-88. New York: Macmillan Co. 347

Fallows, James. The Water Lords. New York: Viking, 1971. 475

Fang, Irving. Those Radio Commentors. Ames: Iowa State University Press, 1977. 226

Fanning, Charles. Mr. Dooley and the Chicago Irish: An Anthology. New York: Arno, 1976
     528

_____. "Mr. Dooley's Bridgeport Chronicle." Chicago History 1, (Spring 1972). 528

_____. Finley Peter Dunne and Mr. Dooley: The Chicago Years.
     Lexington: University of Kentucky Press, 1979. 528

_____. "James T. Farrell and Washington Park: The Novel and Social History."
     Chicago History, 8 (Summer 1979). 529

_____. "Varieties of Irish America: The New Home, Chicago." Blance Touhill,
     ed. Varieties of Ireland, Varieties of Irish America. St. Louis: University
     of Missouri, 1976. 528

*Fanon, Franz. The Wretched of the Earth. New York: Grove, 1965. 9

*Faragher, John M. Women and Men on the Overland Trail. New Haven: Yale
     University Press, 1979. 543

_____ and Christine Stansell. "Women and their Families on the Overland Trail,
     1842-1867." Feminist Studies, 2 (1975). 543

Farb, Peter. Man's Rise to Civilization. New York: Dutton, 1978. 175

Farley, Lin. Sexual Shakedown: The Sexual Harassment of Women on the Job
     New York: McGraw-Hill, 1978. 551

Farmer, John S. Americanisms Old and New. 1889; Detroit: Gale, 1976. 271

Fatout, Paul, ed. Mark Twain Speaks for Himself. West Lafayette, Indiana:
     Purdue University Press, 1978. 410

Fausold, Martin L, and George T. Mazuzan, eds. The Hoover Presidency: A Re-
     appraisal. Albany: State University of New York Press, 1974. 433

*Favretti, Rudy J.and Joy P. Landscapes and Gardens for Historical Buildings:
     Reproducing and Recreating Authentic Settings. Nashville: AASLH, 1938.509

Fecher, Charles, A. Mencken: A Study of His Thought. New York: Alfred A. Knopf, 1978.22

*Feingold, Henry L. Zion in America: The Jewish Experience from Colonial Times to
     the Present. New York: Hippocrene, 1981. 195, 365

*Feis,Herbert. The Atomic Bomb and the End of World War II. Princeton:
     Princeton University Press, rev. ed., 1966. 128

_____. Between War and Peace: The Potsdam Conference. Princeton: Princeton
     University Press, 1960. 128

*_____. The China Tangle: The American Effort in China from Pearl Harbor to the Marshall Mission. Princeton: Princeton University Press, 1953. 129

*_____. Churchill , Roosevelt, Stalin: The War They Waged and the Peace they Sought. Princeton: Princeton University Press, 1957. 128

_____. Contest Over Japan. New York: Norton, 1967. 128

_____. From Trust to Terror: The Onset of the Cold War, 1945-1950. New York: Norton, 1970. 128

_____. Japan Subdued: The Atomic Bomb and the End of the War in the Pacific. Princeton: Princeton University Press, 1961. 128

*_____. The Road to Pearl Harbor: The Coming of the War Between the United States and Japan: Princeton: Princeton University Press, 1950. 125

Felt, Jeremy P. Hostages of Fortune: Child Labor Reform in New York State. Syracuse: Syracuse University Press, 1965. 87

Fenton, Edwin. Immigrants and Unions: A Case Study: Italians and American Labor, 1870-1920. New York: ARNO, 1975. 199

Ferguson, Eugene S. Bibliography of the History of Technology. Cambridge: MIT Press, 1968. 41, 46

Ferguson, James E. The Power of the Purse: A History of the American Public Finance, 1776-1790. Chapel Hill: University of North Carolina Press, 1961. 66

Ferlazzo, Paul J. Emily Dickinson. Boston: G.K. Hall, 1976. 411

Ferm, Robert L. A Colonial Pastor: Jonathan Edwards the Younger, 1745-1801. Grand Rapids: Eerdmans, 1976.

Ferrell, Robert H. American Diplomacy in the Great Depression: Hoover-Stimson Foreign Policy, 1929-1933. New Haven: Yale University Press, 1957. 123

_____. Peace in their Time: The Origins of the Kellogg-Briand Pact. New Haven: Yale University Press, 1952. 123

Ferrell, Robert H. and Howard H. Quint, eds. The Talkative President: The Off-the Record Press Conferences of Calvin Coolidge: New York: Garland Publisher, 1979. 433

Ferris, Norman B. The Trent Affair: A Diplomatic Crisis. Knoxville: University of Tennessee Press, 1977. 134

_____. Desperate Diplomacy: William H. Seward's Foreign Policy, 1861. Knoxville: Univ. of Tennessee Press, 1976. 134

Ferry, W. Hawkins. The Building of Detroit. Detroit: Wayne State University Press, 1980. 38,44

*Fetterley, Judith. The Resisting Reader: A Feminist Approach to American Fiction. Bloomington: Indiana University Press, 1981. 539, 404

*Fiedler, Leslie. The Return of the Vanishing American. Briarcliff Manor: Stein
    and Day. 175

Field, Cynthia. "The City Planning of D.H. Burnham." Unpublished Dissertation.
    Columbia University, 1974. 532

Field, James A. America and the Mediterranean World, 1776-1882. Princeton:
    Princeton University Press, 1969. 131

Field, Raymond. The American Newsreel, 1911-1967. Norman: University of Oklahoma
    Press, 1972.   220

Fielding, Raymond. The March of Time, 1935-1951. New York: Oxford University
    Press, 1978. 227

Fife, Austin and Alta. Saints of Sage and Saddle. Salt Lake City: University of
    Utah Press, 1981.   98

_____. Songs of the Cowboys. New York: Clarkson Potter, 1966. 102

Fifield, Russell H. Americans in Southeast Asia: The Roots of the Commitment.
    New York: Crowell, 1973. 131

*Filler, Louis. The Crusade Against Slavery, 1830-1860. New York: Harper and Row, 1960.

_____. Crusaders for American Liberalism. New York: Harcourt, Brace, 1939. 217

Filson, John. Discovery, Settlement, and Present State of Kentucke. 1784; New
    York: Garland, 1978. 150

Findlay, James F. Dwight L. Moody: American Evangelist, 1837-1899. Chicago:
    University of Chicago Press, 1969. 380

Findley, Paul A. Lincoln: The Crucible of Congress. New York: Crown Publishers,
    Inc., 1979. 429

Fine, David M. The City, the Immigrant and American Fiction, 1880-1920.
    Metuchen, New Jersey: Scarecrow Press, 1977. 403

Fine, Elsa Honig, Lola Gellman, and Judy Loeb, eds. Women's Studies and
    the Arts. New York: Women's Caucus for Art, 1978. 546

Fine, Gary Alan. "Popular Culture and Social Interaction: Production, Consumption,
    and Usage." Journal of Popular Culture, XI, 2 (Fall 1977). 496, 500

_____, ed. "Sociology: In Depth." Journal of Popular Culture, XI, 2
    (Fall, 1977). 500

Finer, Herman. Dulles over Suez: The Theory and Practice of His Diplomacy.
    Chicago: Quadrangle, 1964. 130

Fine, Sidney. The Automobile Under the Blue Eagle: Labor, Management, and
    the Automobile Manufacturing Code. Ann Arbor: University of Michigan Press, 1963. 82

Fink, Gary, M. Prelude to the Presidency: The Political Character and
Legislative Leadership Style of Governor Jimmy Carter. Westport,
Connecticut: Greenwood Press, 1980. 441

_____, and Milton Cantor, eds. A Biographical Dictionary of American
Labor Leaders. Westport, Connecticut: Greenwood Press, 1974. 446

Finkelman, Paul. "Class and Culture in Late Nineteenth-Century Chicago:
The Founding of the Newberry Library." American Studies, 16 (1975). 529

Finkle, Lee. Forum for Protest: The Black Press During World War II.
Cranbury, New Jersey: Fairleigh Dickinson University Press, 1975. 225

Fiorenza, Francis Schussler. "American Culture and Modernism: Shailer
Mathew's Interpretation of American Christianity."Thomas M. McFadden,
ed. America in Theological Perspective. New York: Seabury Press, 1976.

Fischer, Christinae, ed. Let them Speak for Themselves: Women in the
American West, 1849-1900. Hamden, Connecticut: Anchor Books, 1977. 543

Fishbein, Leslie. "Women on the Fringe: A Film Series." Film & History,
VIII (September 1978).   546

*Fishel, Leslie H. and Benjamin Quarles, ed. The Black American: A Brief
Documentary History. Glenview: Scott Foresman, 1970. 13

Fisher, Marvin. Going Under: Melville's Short Fiction and the American
1850's. Baton Rouge, Louisiana: Louisiana State University Press, 1977. 414

*Fisher, Miles Mark. Negro Slave Songs in the United States. 1953; Secaucus:
Citadel Press, 1969. 107

Fishman, Joshua, et.al. Language Loyalty in the United States. The Hague:
Mouton, 1966. 200, 205, 266

_____. Readings in the Sociology of Language. The Hague: Mouton, 1968. 259

_____. Yiddish in America. Indiana University Research Center in
Anthropology, 1965. 266

Fishlow, Albert. American Railroads and the Transformation of the Anti-
Bellum Economy. Cambridge: Harvard University Press, 1965. 70

_____. "Productivity and Technological Change in the Railroad Sector,
1840-1910." Output, Employment and Productivity. New York: Columbia
University Press, 1966. 71

Fiske, John and John Hartley. Reading Television. New York:Methuen, 1979. 500

Fiss, Owen M. The Civil Rights Injunction: Bloominton: Indiana University
Press, 1978. 356
_____. "The Forms of Justice." 93 (1979) Harvard Law Review, 356

*Fitch, James M. American Building: The Environmental Forces that Shape It.
New York: Schocken, 1975. 33, 42

*_____. American Building: The Historical Forces that Shaped it. New York: Schocken, 1973. 33, 42

*Fite, Gilbert C. The Farmers' Frontier, 1865-1900. Albuquerque: University of New Mexico Press, 1977. 76

Flanders, Bertram Holland. Early Georgia Magazines. Athens: University of Georgia Press, 1944. 210

Fleming, Denna, F. The Cold War and Its Origins, 1917-1960. 2 vols. Garden City: Doubleday, 1961. 128

Fleming, Donald and Bernard Bailyn. Dislocation and Emigration: The Social Background of American Immigration. Cambridge, Massachusetts: Perspectives in American History, VII, 1973. 194

*Flexner, James Thomas. Washington: The Indispensable Man. New York: New American Library, 1979. 424

Flexner, Stuart B. I Hear America Talking. New York: Van Nostrand - Reinhold, 1976. 258

Flower, Elizabeth and Murray G. Murphey, 2 vols. A History of Philosophy in America. New York: G.P. Putnam's Sons, 1977. 326

Floyd, Dale E. The World Bibliography of Armed Land Conflict from Waterloo to World War I: Wars, Campaigns, Battles,Revolutions, Revolts, Coups d'Etat, Insurrections, Riots, Armed Confrontations, 2 volumes. (London: George Prior Publishers, 1979 and Wilimington, Delaware: Michael Glazier, Inc, 1979.) 287

Flynn, George Q. Roosevelt and Romanism: Catholics and American Diplomacy, 1937-1945. Westport, Connecticut: Greenwood, 1976. 138

Fogarty, Robert S. Dictionary of American Communal and Utopian History. Westport: Greenwood, 1980. 516

*Fodge, Myron J. The Church Goes West. Wilmington: Consortium Books, 1977. 365

*Fogel, Robert W. Railroads and American Economic Growth: Essays in Econometric History. Baltimore: Johns Hopkins University Press, 1964. 70

_____. The Union Pacific Railroad; A Case in Premature Enterprise. Baltimore: Johns Hopkins University Press, 1960. 71

*
_____ and Stanley L. Engerman. Time on the Cross: The Economics of American Negro Slavery and Time on the Cross: Evidence and Methods. Boston: Little, Brown, 1974. 78, 173
_____, eds. The Reinterpretation of American Economic History. New York: Harper & Row, 1971. 63

*Folsom, Marcia McClintock and Linda Kirschner, eds. By Women: An Anthology of Literature. Boston: Houghton, Mifflin, 1976. 539

Foner, Laura and Eugene D. Genovese, eds. Slavery in the New World: A Reader
in Comparative History. Englewood Cliffs, New Jersey: Prentice-Hall, 1969. 78

Foner, Philip S. American Labor Songs of the Nineteenth Century: Urbana:
University of Illinois Press, 1975. 451

_____. The Factory Girls. Urbana, Illinois: University of Illinois Press, 1977. 547

_____. Labor and the American Revolution. Westport, Connecticut: Greenwood
Press, 1976. 447

Fonzi, Gaeton. Annenberg: A Biography of Power. New York: Weybright & Talley,
1970. 219

*Forbush, Elizabeth. Savage Sundown. Los Angeles: Pinnacle Books, 1980. 468

Ford, James L.C. Magazines for Millions. Carbondale: Southern Illinois
University Press, 1969. 221

Forgie, George B. Patricide in the House Divided: A Psychological Interpretation
of Lincoln and His Age. New York: Norton, 1979. 429

Forgue, Guy J. La Langue des Americains. Paris: Aubier-Montaigne, 1972. 258

Forman, Henry C. The Architecture of the Old South: The Medieval Style.
1948; New York: Russell, 1967. 38, 44

Formisano, Ronald P. The Birth of Mass Political Parties: Michigan, 1827-
1861. Princeton: Princeton University Press, 1971. 200

Forrester, William Ray. "Are We Ready for Truth in Judging?" 63 American
Bar Association Journal 1212 (1977). 347

Forsyth, David E. The Business Press in America, 1750-1865. Philadelphia:
Chilton Books, 1964. 214

Fortenberry, George E. Stanton Gardner, and Robert H. Woodward, eds.
The Correspondence of Harold Frederick, Vol. I. Fort Worth: Texas
Christian University Press, 1977. 226

Foster, Charles William. "Phonology of the Conjure Tales of Charles W.
Chesnutt." PADS, LV (1971). 267

Foster, Edward H. Catherine Maria Sedgwick. Boston: G.K. Hall, 1974. 416

_____. The Civilized Wilderness: Backgrounds of American Romantic Literature.
New York: Macmillan, 1975. 401

Foster, James C. The Union Politic: The CIO Political Action Committee.
Columbia: University of Missouri Press, 1975. 450

Foster, Stephen. Their Solitary Way: The Puritan Social Ethic in the First
Century of Settlement in New England.   New Haven: Yale University
Press, 1971. 367

Fothergill, Robert. Private Chronicles. London: Oxford University Press, 1977. 395, 399

Fowler, Henry W. A Dictionary of Modern English Usage. 1926; London:
Oxford Press, 1965. 269

Fox, Bonnie R. "Unemployment Relief in Philadelphia, 1930-1932: A Study of the Depression's Impact on Voluntarism." _Pennsylvania Magazine of History and Biography_, XCII (January 1969). 87

*Fox, Stephen R. _The Guardian of Boston: William Monroe Trotter_. New York: Atheneum, 1971. 215

Foxe, John. _Acts and Monuments_. 1554; New York: AMS Press, 1965. 146

Francaviglia, Richard. "Main St. Revisited." _Places_, (1974). 422

_____. "Main Street USA: The Creation of a Popular Image." _Landscape_, 21, 3 (Spring-Summer 1977). 422

Francis, Gloria A. and Artem Lozynsky, eds. _Whitman at Auction: 1899-1972_. Detroit: Gale, 1978. 417

Francis, W. Nelson. "Approaches to Grammar." Sebeok. _Trends_. 256, 268

_____. _The Structure of American English_. New York: Ronald, 1958. 268

Frank, Benis M. "Afterthought." _Oral History Review_, 1974. 278

_____. _Marine Corps Oral History Catalog_. U.S. Marine Corps, Washington, D.C. Headquarters, 1975. 285

Frank, Joseph. _The Beginnings of the English Newspaper_. Cambridge: Harvard University Press, 1961. 207

Frank, William L. _Sherwood Bonner_. Boston: G.K. Hall, 1976. 414

Frank, Yakira. "The Speech of New York City." Dissertation. University of Michigan, 1948. 265

Frankfort, Roberta. _Collegiate Women: Domesticity and Career in Turn-Of-The Century America_. New York: New York University Press, 1978. 544

Franklin, H. Bruce. _The Victim as Criminal and Artist_. New York: Oxford, 1978. 20, 21

Franklin, John Hope. _Color and Race_. Boston: Houghton Mifflin, 1968. 180

_____. _The Emancipation Proclamation_. Garden City, N.Y.: Doubleday, 1963. 180

*_____. _The Free Negro in North Carolina, 1790-1860_. 1943; New York: Norton, 1971. 26, 180

*_____. _From Slavery to Freedom: A History of Negro Americans_. New York: Knopf, 1980. 10, 180

*_____. _Reconstruction: After the Civil War_. Chicago: University of Chicago Press, 1962. 180

Frass, Arthur. "The Second Bank of the United States: An Instrument for an Interregional Monetary Union." _Journal of Economic History_, XXXIV (June 1974). 73

Frassanito, William. _Antietam: The Photographic Legacy of America's Bloodiest Day_. New York: Charles Scribners Sons, 1978. 290

_____. Gettysburg: A Journey in Time. New York: Charles Scribners Sons, 1975. 290

Fraundord, Martha Norby. "The Labor Force Participation of Turn of the Century Married Women." Journal of Economic History, 39   (June 1979). 549

*Frazer, James G. The Golden Bough. New York: Macmillan. 164

*Frazier, E. Franklin . Black Burgeoise: The Rise of a New Middle Class. New York: Free Press, 1957. 463

Frederick, Peter J. Knights of the Golden Rule. Lexington:University of Kentucky Press, 1976. 380

*Fredrickson, George M. The Black Image in the White Mind: The Debate on Afro-American Character and Destiny. New York: Harper and Row, 1977. 26, 173

Freed, Donald, and Mark Lane. Executive Action: Assassination of Head of State. New York: Dell Pub. Co., 1973. 437

*Freeman, Jo, ed. Women: A Feminist Perspective. Palo Alto, California: Mayfield, 1979.   545

Freeman, Myrick. The Benefits of Environmental Improvement. Baltimore: Johns Hopkins, 1979. 485

*Freund, Paul A. The Supreme Court of the United States: Its Business, Purposes, and Performances. Cleveland: World Publishing Co., 1961. 356

Freyer, Tony A. "Negotiable Instruments and the Federal Courts in Antebellum American Business." Business History Review, L   (Winter 1976). 92

Friedheim, Robert, ed. Managing Ocean Resources: A Primer. Boulder: Westview, 1979. 482

Friedlander, Peter. The Emergence of a UAW Local, 1946-1939: A Study in Class and Culture. Pittsburgh: University of Pittsburgh Press, 1975. 450

Friedland, William and Dorothy Neklin. Migrant Agricultural Workers in America's Northeast. New York: Holt, Rinehardt and Winston, 1971. 452

Friedman, Lawrence M. Contract Law in America: A Social and Economic Case Study. Madison: University of Wisconsin Press, 1965. 70

_____. Government and Slum Housing: A Century of Frustration. Chicago: Rand McNally and Company, 1968. 87

_____ and Jack Ladinsky. "Social Change and the Law of Industrial Accidents." Columbia Law Review, LXVII (January 1967) . 87

* Friedman, Milton and Anna J. Schwartz. A Monetary History of the United States 1867-1960. Princeton: Princeton University Press, 1963. 83

Friedman, Leon. Argument. New York: Chelsea House, 1969. 353

Friedmann, Wolfgang. Law in a Changing Society. Harmondsworth, England: Penguin Books, second edition, 1972. 354

Friedrich, Otto. Decline and Fall. New York: Harper and Row, 1970. 221

Friendly, Fred W. Due to Circumstances Beyond Our Control. New York:
   Random House, 1967. 222

Fries, Charles C. American English Grammar. New York: D. Appleton-Century,
   1940. 270

_____. Linguistics and Reading. New York: Holt, Rinehart and Winston,
   1962. 268

_____. The Structure of English. New York: Harcourt, Brace and Company,
   1952. 268

*Frieze, Irene H., et. al., eds. Women and Sex Roles: A Social Psychological
   Perspective. New York: Norton, 1978. 540

Frisch, Michael. "American Urban History as an Example of Recent Historiography."
   History and Theory, 18 (1979). 455

_____. Toward a New Urban History: Work Space and Group Experience
   in Nineteenth Century Philadelphia. New York: Oxford , forthcoming.

*_____. Town into City: Springfield, Massachusetts, and the Meaning
   of Community, 1840-1880. Cambridge: Harvard, 1972. 455

Frisch, Morton, J. Franklin D. Roosevelt: The   Contribution of the New Deal
   to American Political Thought and Practice. New York: Twayne Publishers, 1975. 435

Frith, Simon. The Sociology of Rock. London: Constable, 1976. 500

*Frost, David. I Gave Them A Sword: Behind the Scenes of the Nixon
   Interview. New York: Ballantine, 1978. 438

* Frost, J. William. The Quaker Family in Colonial America. New York:
   St. Martin's Press, 1973. 370

*Fry, Gladys Marie. Night Riders in Black Folk History. Knoxville: University
   of Tennessee Press, 1975. 105

*Fryer, Judith. The Faces of Eve: Women in the Nineteenth Century American
   Novel.   New York: Oxford University Press, 1976. 539

*Fuentes, Carlos. The Hydra Head. New York: Farrar, Straus, Giroux, 1978. 49

Fulbright, J. William. The Arrogance of Power. New York: Random House, 1967. 175

Fuller, Lon L. "The Forms and Limits of Adjudication." 92 Harvard Law Review
   353 (1978). 356

*Funston, Richard Y. Constitutional Counterrevolution? The Warren Court and
   the Burger Court: Judicial Policy Making in Modern America. New York:
   Schenkman Publishing Co., Inc. 1977. 351

Fuss, Peter. The Moral Philosphy of Josiah Royce. Cambridge: Harvard University
   Press, 1965. 326

Gable, John A. The Bull Moose Years: Theodore Roosevelt and the Progressive Party. Port Washington, New York: Kennikat Press, 1978. 431

Gabriel, Ralph Henry. The Course of American Democratic Thought. 1940; New York: Wiley, 1956. 166, 168

Gaddis, John L. The United States and the Origins of the Cold War, 1941-1947. New York: Columbia University Press,1972. 128

Gage, John. Silence. Middletown: Wesleyan University Pres, 1961. 301

_____. A Year from Monday. Middletown: Wesleyan University Press, 1968. 301

Gakovich, Robert and Milan M. Radovich, Comps. Serbs in the United States and Canada: Comprehensive Bibliography. St. Paul: Immigration History Research Center, University of Minnesotta, 1976. 192

Galambos, Louis P. Competition and Cooperation: The Emergence of a National Trade Association. Baltimore: Johns Hopkins University Press, 1966. 80

_____ and Barbara Barrow Spence. The Public Image of Big Business in America, 1880-1940. Baltimore: Johns Hopkins University Press, 1975. 81

Galbreath, Carol J. "Small Town Preservation: A Systematic View." Historic Preservation, (April-June 1975). 419

Gale, Robert L. Plots and Characteristics in the Works of Mark Twain. Hamden, Connecticut: Anchor, 1973. 410

Galenson,David. "British Servants and the Colonial Indenture System in the Eighteenth Century." Journal of Southern History, XLIV (February 1978). 66

_____. "Immigration and the Colonial Labor System: An Analysis of the Length of Indenture." Explorations in Economic History, XIV (October 1977). 66

_____."'Middling People' or 'Common Sort'? The Social Origins of Some Early Americans Reconsidered." William and Mary Quarterly, XXXV (July 1978). 66

Gallman, Robert E. "The Agricultural Sector and the Pace of Economic Growth: U.S. Experience in the Nineteenth Century." In David C. Klingman and Richard K. Vedder, eds. Essays in Nineteenth Century Economic History. Athens: Ohio University Press, 1975. 77

Gallman, Robert E. "Changes in Total U.S. Agricultural Factor Productivity in the 19th Century." Agricultural History, XLVI (January 1972). 77

_____. "Gross National Product in the United States, 1834-1909." Output, Employment and Productivity in the United States After 1800. New York: Columbia University Press, 1966. 68

*Gallucci, Robert L. Neither Peace nor Honor: The Politics of American Military Policy in Viet Nam. Baltimore: Johns Hopkins, 1975. 140

*Gambino, Richard. Blood of My Blood: The Dilemma of the Italian Americans. Garden City, New York: Doubleday and Co., 1975. 194

*Gamst, Frederick. The Hoghead: An Industrial Ethnology of the Locomotive Engineer. New York: Holt, Rinehart and Winston, 1980. 452

*Gans, Herbert. Popular Culture and High Culture: An Analysis and Evaluation of Taste. New York: Basic Books, 1974. 495, 500

*Gara, Larry. The Liberty Line: The Legend of the Underground Railroad. Lexington: University Press of Kentucky, 1967. 26

Garcia, Hazel. "'What a Buzzel is this...About Kentuck?' New Approaches and an Application." Journal History, 3 (Spring 1976). 224

Gardner, Emelyn E. Folklore from the Schoharie Hills, New York. Ann Arbor: University of Michigan Press, 1937. 99

*Gardner, Hugh. The Children of Prosperity. New York: St. Martin's Press, 1978. 517

Gardner, Joseph L. Departing Glory: Theodore Roosevelt as Ex-president. New York: Scribner, 1973. 431

Gardner, Lloyd C. Architects of Illusion: Men and Ideas in American Foreign Policy, 1941-1949. Chicago: Quadrangle Books, 1970. 128

_____. Economic Aspects of New Deal Diplomacy. Madison: University of Wisconsin Press, 1964. 85, 126

Garfield, Dorothy. Unmailable: Congress and the Post Office. Athens: The University of Georgia Press, 1977. 227

*Garfinckel, Herbert. When Negroes March. New York: Atheneum, 1969. 26

Garnet, Henry Highland. An Address to the Slaves of the United States. 1843; New York: Arno, 1969. 21

*Garraty, John A. Unemployment in History: Economic Thought and Public Policy. New York: Harper & Row, 1979. 88

Garrett, John. Roger Williams: Witness Beyond Christendom. New York: Macmillan, 1970. 369

Garrison, Dee. Apostles of Culture: The Public Librarian and American Society, 1876-1920. New York: Macmillan Co., 1979. 548

Gates, J. Edward. "A Bibliography on General and English Lexicography." McDavid and Duckert. Lexicography in English. 256

_____. Papers in Lexicography in Honor of Warren P. Cordell. Terre Haute, Indiana, 1969. 259

*Gates, Paul, W. The Farmer's Age: Agriculture, 1815-1860. 1960; Armonk: Sharpe, 1977. 76

_____. History of Public Land Law Development. 1968; New York: Arno, 1979. 77

*Gaustad, Edwin Scott. Dissent in American Religion. Chicago: University of Chicago Press, 1975. 364

_____. Historical Atlas of Religion in America. New York: Harper and Row, 1976. 363

_____. The Rise of Adventism. New York: Harper and Row, 1974.   382

Gaute, J.H. and Robin Odell. The Murderers' Who's Who. New York:
    Methuen, 1979. 56

Gay, Peter. A Loss of Mastery: Puritan Historians in Colonial America.
    New York: Alfred A. Knopf, 1968.   180

Gayle, Addison, ed. Black Expression. New York: Weybright and Talley, 1969. 14

Geherin, David. Sons of Sam Spade: The Private Eye Novel in the 70's.
    New York: Frederick Ungar, 1980. 61

*Geist, Christopher and Ray R. Browne, eds. Popular Abstacts. Bowling
    Green: Popular Press, 1978.   501

George, Alexander L. and Richard Smoke. Deterrence in American Foreign
    Policy: Theory and Practice. New York: Columbia University Press, 1974. 130

Gellman, Irwin F. Good Neighbor Diplomacy: United States Policies in
    Latin America, 1933-1945. Baltimore: Johns Hopkins, 1979. 138

*Genovese, Eugene. The Political Economy of Slavery: Studies in Economy
    and Society in the Slave South. New York: Vintage, 1967. 26, 175

*   . Roll Jordan Roll: The World The Slaves Made. New York: Vintage, 1976.
    26, 78, 172
_____. The World the Slaveholders Made: Two Essays in Interpretation.
    New York: Pantheon, 1969. 26

*George, Carol V. Segregated Sabbaths: Richard Allen and the Rise of
    Independent Black Churches, 1760-1840. New York: Oxford University
    Press, 1973.   379

Gerald, Edward J. The Social Responsibility of the Press. Minneapolis:
    University of Minnesota Press, 1963.   220

Gerard, Harold B. and Norman Miller. School Desegregation. New York:
    Plenum Press, 1975. 443

Gerbner, George, Larry Gross, et. al. Trends in Network Television
    Drama and Viewer Concept of Social Reality, 1967-1976.
    Philadelphia: Annenberg School, 1977.   501

Gernsheim, Helmut and Alison. The History of Photography from the Camera
    Obscura to the Beginning of the Modern Era. London: Thames and Hudson,
    1969.   213

Gerstenberger, Donna and Carolyn Allen comps. "Women's Studies/American
    Studies, 1970-1975." American Quarterly, XXIX (1976).   536

Getman, Julius, Stephen Goddberg, and Jeanne Herman. Union Representation
    Elections: Law and Reality. New York: Russell Sage Foundation, 1976. 450

Ghent, Jocelyn Maynard and Frederick Cople Jaher. "The Chicago Business Elite: 1830-1930, A Collective Biography." Business History Review, 50 (Autumn 1976). 529

Gibbon, Edward. The Decline and Fall of the Roman Empire. 1783-1790. New York: AMS Press, 1974. 152

Gibson, William M. The Art of Mark Twain. New York: Oxford University Press, 1976. 410

*Gilbert, Felix. To the Farewell Address: Ideas of Early American Foreign Policy. Princeton: Princeton University Press, 1961. 114

Gilbert, James B. Designing the Industrial State: The Intellectual Pursuit of Collectivism in America, 1880-1940. Chicago: Quadrangle Books, 1972. 81

_____. Work Without Salvation: America's Intellectuals and Industrial Alienation, 1880-1910. Baltimore: The Johns Hopkins Unviersity Press, 1977. 446

Gilbert, Glenn. The German Language in America: A Symposium. Austin: University of Texas Press, 1971. 259

_____. Linguistic Atlas of Texas German. Austin, Texas: University of Texas Press, 1972. 266

Gilchrist, Agnes. William Strickland, Architect and Engineer. 1950; New York: DaCapo Press, 1969. 39, 45

Gilchrist, David T. The Growth of the Seaport Cities, 1790-1825. Charlottesville: University Press of Virginia, 1967. 75

_____ and W. David, Lewis, eds. Economic Change in the Civil War Era. Greenville, Del.: Eleutherian Mills-Hagley Foundation, 1965. 67

*Gilderhus, Mark T. Diplomacy and Revolution: U.S. Mexico Relations Under Wilson and Carranza. Tucson: University of Arizona Press, 1977. 432

Gill, John. Tide Without Turning: Elijah P. Lovejoy and Freedom of the Press. Boston: Beacon Press, 1958. 210

Gillespie, C. C.. The Edge of Objectivity: An Essay on the History of Scientific Ideas. Princeton, New Jersey: Princeton University Press, 1960. 180

Gillespie, David F. "Sociology of Popular Culture: The Other Side of a Definition." Journal of Popular Culture, VI (1972). 501

Gillett, Charles. The Sound of the City: The Rise of Rock and Roll. New York: Outerbridge and Dienstfrey, 1970. 493, 501

Gilliam, Ann, ed. Voices for the Earth. San Francisco: Sierra, 1979. 487

*Gilman, Charlotte Perkins. Herland: A Lost Feminist Utopian Novel. New York: Pantheon, 1979. 550

Gilmore, Michael T. Twentieth Century Interpretations of Moby-Dick: A Collection of Critical Essay. Englewood Cliffs, New Jersey: Prentice-Hall, 1977. 415

Gilpin, W. Clark. The Millenarian Piety of Roger Williams. Chicago: University of Chicago Press, 1979. 369

*Ginzberg, Eli and Robert M. Solow, eds.. The Great Society: Lessons for the Future. New York: Basic Books, 1974. 88

*Gish, Robert. Hamlin Garland: The Far West. Boise,Idaho: Boise State University, 1976. 412

 Gitelman, Howard M. Workingmen of Waltham: Mobility in American Urban Industrial Development, 1850-1890. Baltimore: The Johns Hopkins University Press, 1977. 197, 448

 Gitlin, Todd. The Whole World is Watching: Mass Media in the Making and Unmaking of the New Left. Berkeley: University of California, 1980. 496, 501

 Glaab, Charles N.. Kansas City and the Railroads. Madison: State Historical Society of Wisconsin, 1962.   72

*   and A. Theodore Brown. A History of Urban America. New York: Macmillan, 1976.   458

 Glad, Betty. Jimmy Carter: From Plains to the White House. New York: W.W.Norton & Co., 1980. 441

 Glanz, Rudolf. The Jew in Old American Folklore. New York: Ktav, 1961. 108

           . The Jew in Early American Wit and Graphic Humor. New York: Ktav, 1973. 108, 403
*Glass, Frankeina. Marvin and Tige. New York: St. Martin's Press, 1977. 468

*Glassie, Henry. Folk Housing in Middle Virginia: Structural Analysis of Historic Artifacts. Knoxville:University of Tennessee Press, 1975. 104

*   . Pattern in the Material Folk Culture of the Eastern United States. Philadelphia: University of Pennsylvania Press, 1971.   104

*Glazer, Nathan and Daniel P. Moynihan, eds.. Ethnicity Theory and Experience. Cambridge, Mass.: Harvard University Press, 1975. 202

 Gleason, Philip, ed. Catholicism in America. New York: Harper and Row, 1970. 384

*Glessing, Robert J. The Underground Press in America. Bloomington: Indiana University Press, 1970.   222

 Gliedman, John and William Roth. Handicapped Children in America. New York: Academic Press, 1978. 443

*Gluck, Peter R. and Richard J. Meister. Cities in Transition: Social Changes and Institutional Responses in Urban Development. New York: New Viewpoints, 1979. 459

*Gluck, Sherna, ed. From Parlor to Prison: Five American Suffragists Talk About Their Lives. New York: Random House, 1976. 541

 Goebel, Dorothy Burne. William Henry Harrison: A Political Biography. Philadelphia: Porcupine Press, 1974. 427

 Goebel, Julius. Antecedents and Beginning to 1801. New York: Macmillan Co. 347

 Goen, C.C., ed. The Great Awakening. New Haven: Yale University Press, 1972. 373

 Goetzmann, William H. The American Hegelians. New York: Alfred A. Knopf, 1973. 326

——————————. Army Exloration in the American West, 1803-1863. Lincoln: University of Nebraska Press, 1979. 174, 180

*   . Exploration and Empire: The Explorer and the Scientist in the Winning of the American West. New York: Norton, 1978. 174

————————."Foreword." General Index to the Papers and Annual Reports of the American Historical Association. Washington, D.C.: Carrollton Press, 1968. 180

Goheen, Peter G. "Interpreting the American City: Some Historical Perspectives." Geographical Review, 64 (July 1974). 454

Golab, Caroline. Immigrant Destinations. Philadelphia: Temple University Press, 1977. 199

Golden, Arthur, ed.. Walt Whitman: A Collection of Criticism. New York: Mc Graw-Hill, 1974. 417

*Goldfield, David R. and Blaine A. Brownell. Urban America: From Downtown to No Town. Boston: Houghton Mifflin, 1979. 458

Goldhurst, Richard. Many are the Hearts: The Agony and the Triumph of Ulysses S. Grant. New York: Reader's Digest Press, 1975. 430

Goldin, Claudia D. Urban Slavery in the American South, 1820-1860: A Quantitative History. Chicago: University of Chicago Press, 1976. 78, 465

Goldman, Charles, ed. Environmental Quality and Water Development. San Francisco: Freeman, 1973. 475

Goldman, Eric F. John Bach McMaster: American Historian. 1943; New York: Octagon, 1971. 180

*   .Rendezvous with Destiny.New York: Random, 1978. 168

*   .The Tragedy of Lyndon Johnson. New York: Alfred A. Knopf, 1969. 180

Goldman, Marshall. The Spoils of Progress: Environmental Pollution in the Soviet Union. Cambridge: M.I.T. Press, 1972. 475

*Goldman, Richard F., ed. Richard Franko Goldman: Selected Essays and Reviews, 1948-1968. Brooklyn: Institute for Studies in American Music, 1980. 304

*Goldman, Sheldon and Thomas P. Jahnige. The Federal Courts as a Political System. New York: Harper & Row, 1976. 354

*Goldsen, Ross K. The Show and Tell Machine. New York: Delta, 1978. 493, 501

Goldwater, Walter. Radical Periodicals in America, 1890-1950. New Haven, Conn.: Yale University Press, 1964. 445

Gollin, Rita K. Nathaniel Hawthorne and the Truth of Dreams. Baton Rouge, Louisiana State University Press, 1979. 412

Goodlad, J.S. A Sociology of Popular Drama. Totowa, New Jersey: Rowman and Littlefield, 1972. 501

Goodman, Allan E. The Lost Peace: America's Search for a Negotiated Settlement of the Vietnam War. Stanford: Stanford University Press, 1978. 140

Goodman, Charlotte. "Images of American Rural Women in the Novel."
    Michigan Papers in Women's Studies, I (June 1975). 539

_____."Widening Perspectives, Narrowing Possibilities: The Trapped Woman
    in Edith Summers Kelly's Weeds." Regionalism and Female Imagination.
    (Spring 1977). 539

_____. "Women and Madness in the Fiction of Joyce Carol Oates." Women
    and Literature, V (Fall 1978). 539

*Goodman, Paul. Growing Up Absurd: Problems of Youth in the Organized System.
    New York: Random House, 1962. 312

Goodrich, Carter. Government Promotion of American Canals and Railroads,
    1800-1890. 1960; Westport: Greenwood Press, 1974. 70

_____, et. al. Canals and American Economic Development. 1961; Port
    Washington: Kennikat, 1972. 70

_____, ed. "Internal Improvement Reconsidered." Journal of Economic History,
    XXX (June 1970). 70

Goodrich, Leland M. Korea: A Study of U.S. Policy in the United Nations.
    New York: Council of Foreign Relations, 1956. 130

Goodstein, Anita S. Biography of a Businessman: Henry W. Sage, 1814-1897.
    Ithaca: Cornell University Press, 1962. 75

*Goodwin, Richard. The American Condition. Garden City, New York: Doubleday,1974. 311

Göran, Rystad. Ambiguous Imperialism: American Foreign Policy and Domestic
    Politics at the Turn of the Century. Lund Sweden: Esselte Studium, 1975.

*Gordon, George N. The Communication Revolution: A History of Mass Media in
    the United States. New York: Hastings House, 1977. 228

*Gordon, Linda. Woman's Body, Woman's Right. New York: Penguin Books, 1975. 542

*Gordon, Mark and Jack Nachbar. Currents of Warm Life: Popular Culture in
    American Higher Education. Bowling Green: Popular Press, 1980. 491, 501

Gordon, Martin K. "Congress and the District of Columbia: The Military Impact
    on Federal Control." Capitol Studies 6 (Fall 1978). 294

*Gordon, Milton. Assimilation in American Life: The Role of Race, Religion and
    National Origins. New York: Oxford University Press, 1964. 205

*Gordon, Robert A. Economic Instability and Growth: The American Record.
    New York: Harper and Row 1974. 84

Gordon, Thomas F. and Mary Ellen Verna. Mass Communications Effects and
    Process: A Comprehensive Bibliography, 1950-1975. Beverly Hills: Sage, 1978. 501

Gordon, William. The History of the Rise, Progress and Establishment of the
    Independence of the United States of America, 4 vols. 1788; Freeport:
    Books for Libraries Press, 1969. 147

Gosnell, Harold F. Truman's Crises:A Political Biography of Harry S. Truman. Westport, Conn.: Greenwood Press, 1980. 435

*Gossett, Thomas F. Race: The History of an Idea in America. New York: Schocken, 1965. 26, 173

*Gottschalk, Stephen. The Emergence of Christian Science in American Religious Life. Berkeley: University of California Press, 1974. 383

Goudge, Thomas A. The Thought of C.S. Peirce. New York: Dover, 1969. 326

Gould, Lewis L. The Presidency of William McKinley. Lawrence: Regents Press of Kansas, 1980. 431

_____ and Richard Greffe. Photojournalist: The Career of Jimmy Hare. Austin: University of Texas Press, 1977. 228

Goulden, Joseph. Meany. New York: Atheneum, 1972. 450

Gouinlock, James. The Moral Writings of John Dewey. New York: Hafner Press,1976. 330

Gowans, Alan. The Unchanging Arts: New Forms for the Traditional Functions of Art in Society. New York: Lippincott, 1971. 501

Grable, Stephen W. "Applying Urban History to City Planning: Case Study in Atlanta." The Public Historian, 1 (Summer 1979). 466

Graebner, Norman A. Empire on the Pacific: A Study of American Continental Expansion. New York: Ronald Press, 1955. 117

Graebner, William. Coal Mining Safety in the Progressive Period. Lexington: University Press of Kentucky, 1976. 448

Graf, LeRoy and Ralph W. Haskins, eds. Papers of Andrew Johnson, 5 vols. Knoxville: University of Tennessee Press, 1967.

Graham, Don. The Fiction of Frank Norris: An Aesthetic Context. Columbia,Missouri: University of Missouri Press, 1978. 415

Graham, Frank,Jr. Since Silent Spring. Greenwhich: Fawcett, 1977. 476

Graham, Hugh Davis and Ted Robert Gurr, eds. The Report Submitted to the National Commission on the Causes and Prevention of Violence. New York: Praeger, 1969. 310

*_____ et al., eds. Violence: The Crisis of American Confidence. Baltimore: The Johns Hopkins University Press, 1972. 310

*Graham, Otis L., Jr. Toward a Planned Society: From Roosvelt to Nixon. New York: Oxford Univerity Press, 1977. 83

Graham, Patricia Albjerg. "Expansion and Exclusion: A History of Women in American Higher Education." Signs, 3 (Summer 1978). 544

Gramling, Oliver. A.P.: The Story of News. New York: Farrar and Rinehart, 1940. 213

Granger, Bruce. American Essay Serials from Franklin to Irving. Knoxville, Tennessee: University of Tennessee Press, 1978. 403

Grattan, C.H. The Deadly Parallel. New York: Stackpole, 1939. 180

_____. Preface to Chaos: War in the Making. New York: Dodge, 1936. 180

_____. Why We Fought. 1929; Irvington, 1969. 180

Gray, Ralph D. The National Waterway: A History of the Chesapeake and Delaware Canal, 1769-1965. Urbana: University of Illinois Press, 1967. 71

*Greeley, Andrew M. The American Catholic: A Social Portrait. New York: Basic Books. 1977. 385

_____. Ethnicity in the United States: A Preliminary Reconnaissance. New York: Wiley, 1974. 202

*_____. That Most Distressful Nation: The Taming of the American Irish. New York: Times Books, 1973. 195

Green, Archie. Only a Miner: Studies in Recorded Coal-Mining Songs. Urbana: University of Illinois Press, 1971. 451

Green, David. The Containment of Latin America : A History of the Myths and Realities of the Good Neighbor Policy. Chicago: Quadrangle Books, 1971. 125

Green, George D. Finance and Economic Development in the Old South: Louisiana Banking, 1804-1861. Stanford: Stanford University Press, 1972. 73

*Green James. The World of the Worker: Labor in the Twentieth Century America. New York: Hill and Wang, 1980. 449

Green, Martin. Transatlantic Patterns: Cultural Comparisons of England with America. New York: Basic Books, 1977. 55, 58

Green, Rose Basile. The Italian American Novel: A Document of the Interaction of two Cultures. Rutherford, New Jersey: Farleigh Dickinson University Press, 1974. 201

Greenbaum, William: "America in Search of a New Ideal: An Essay on the Rise of Pluralism." Harvard Educational Review, XLIV (August 1974). 202

*Greenberg, Bradley S. Life on Television. Norwood, New Jersey: Ablex, 1980. 495, 501

Green, J. Lee. Time's Unfading Garden: Anne Spencer's Life and Poetry. Baton Rouge: Louisiana State University Press, 1977. 540

*Greene, Lorenzo J. The Negro in Colonial New England. New York: Atheneum, 1968. 26

Greene, Victor. For God and Country: The Rise of Polish and Lithuanian Ethnic Consciousness in America, 1861-1910. Madison, Wis.: Wisconsin Historical Society, 1975. 200

*Greenwood, John. American Defence Policy Since 1945: A Preliminary Bibliography. Manhattan: Kansas State University Library, 1973. 284

Gregory, Chester W. Women in Defense Work During World War II. New York: Exposition Press, 1974. 451

Gregory, Frances W. Nathan Appleton: Merchant and Entrepreneur, 1779-1861. Charlottesville: University Press of Virginia, 1975. 75

Grejda, Edward S. The Common Continent of Men: Racial Equality in Writings of Herman Melville. Port Washington, New York: Kennikat, 1974. 415

Grele, Ronald. "Movement Without Aim: Methodological and Theoretical Problems in Oral History." Envelopes of Sound. Chicago: Precedent, 1975. 400

Greenacre, Phyllis. "The Childhood of the Artist: Libidinal Phase Development and Giftedness." Emotional Growth. New York: International Universities Press, 1971. 398

*Greven, Phillip. The Protestant Temperament. New York: New American Library, 1979. 373

*Greven, Philip J., Jr. Four Generations: Population, Land and Family in Colonial Andover, Massachusetts. Ithaca: Cornell University Press, 1970. 65

Gribbin, William. The Churches Militant: The War of 1812 and American Religion. New Haven: Yale University Press, 1973. 377

Grieb, Kenneth J. The Latin American Policy of Warren G. Harding. Fort Worth: Texas Christian University Press, 1976. 433

_____. The United States and Huerta. Lincoln: University of Nebraska Press, 1969. 124

Griffin, Clyde and Sally. Natives and Newcomers: The Ordering of Opportunity in Mid-Nineteenth Century Poughkeepsie. Cambridge: Harvard University Press, 1978. 92, 197

*Griffen, Cynthia Griffen, ed. Classic American Women Writers. New York: Harper and Row, 1979.

*Griffith, J.A.G. The Politics of the Judiciary. London: Fontana Paperback, 1977. 347

*Griswold, Alfred W. The Far Eastern Policy of the United States. New York: Harcourt Brace, 1938. 123

Grodinsky, Julius. Transcontinental Railway Strategy, 1869-1893. Philadelphia: University of Philadelphia Press, 1962. 72

Gromyko, Anatolii Andreevich. Through Russian Eyes: President Kennedy's 1036 Days. Washington: International Library, 1973. 437

Groneman, Carol. "Working-Class Immigrant Women in Mid-Nineteenth Century New York." Journal of Urban History, 4 (May 1978). 551

Grosch, Anthony. "Social Issues in Early Chicago Novels." Chicago History, 4 (Summer 1975). 529

Gross, James. The Making of the National Labor Relations Board: A Study in Economics, Politics and the Law, Vol. I. Albany: State University of New York Press, 1974. 450

*Gross, Robert A. The Minutemen and Their World. New York: Hill and Wang, 1976. 66

Gross, Theodore R. The Reality and Promise of Open Education. New York: Anchor Press, 1979. 444

Grossman, Joan D. Edgar Allan Poe in Russia: A Study in Legend and Literay Influence, Atlantic Highlands, New Jersey: Humanities Press, 1973. 415

Grossvogel, David I. Mystery and Its Fictions: From Oedipus to Agatha Christie. Baltimore: The Johns Hopkins University Press, 1979. 58

*Grout, Donald Jay. History of Western Music. New York: Norton, 1973. 296

Grover, Philip. Henry James and the French Novel: A Study in Inspiration. New York: Barnes and Noble, 1973. 413

Grube, Oswald W. 100 Years of Architecture in Chicago. Chicago: J. Philip O'Hara, 1976. 524, 531

Gudelunas, William A., Jr and William G. Shade. Before the Molly Maguires: The Emergence of the Ethno-Religious Factor in the Politics of the Lower Anthracite Region, 1844-1872. New York: Arno, 1976. 200

Gunn, Janet Varner. "Autobiography and the Narrative Experience of Temporality as Depth." Soundings, 60 (Summer 1977). 396, 399

Gunther, Gerald. Cases and Materials on Constitutional Law. Mineola, New York: Foundation Press, 9th ed., 1975. 349

Gutheim, Frederick, ed. Frank Lloyd Wright: Selected Writings, 1894-1940. New York: Duell, Sloan and Pearce, 1941. 39, 45

_____. In the Cause of Architecture: Wright's Essays for Architectural Record, 1908-1952. New York: Architectural Record, 1976. 39, 45

*Gutman, Herbert G. The Black Family in Slavery and Freedom, 1750-1925. New York: Random, 1977. 27

*   _____. Slavery and the Numbers Game: A Critique of "Time on the Cross". Urbana: University of Illinois Press, 1975. 181

_____. "Work, Culture and Society in Industrializing America, 1815-1919." American Historical Review, LXXVIII (June 1973). 199

Gutman, Judith Mara. Is America Used Up? New York: Grossman Publishers, 1973. 311

*Guttmann, Allen. From Ritual to Record: The Nature of Modern Sports. New York: Columbia University, 1978. 501

*Habakkuk, H.J. American and British Technology in the Nineteenth Century. Cambridge: Cambridge University Press, 1962. 74

Habe, Hans. The Wounded Land: Journey Through a Divided America. New York: Coward-McCann, 1964.

*Hacker, Andrew. The End of America Era. New York: Atheneum, 1971.

Hackett, Homer, C. The Constitutional History of the United States, New York: Macmillan, 1939. 348

Hagan, Kenneth J. ed. In Peace and War: Interpretations of American Naval History, 1775-1978. Westport, Connecticut: Greenwood Press, 1978. 289

Hage, George S. Newspapers on Minnesota Frontier, 1849-1860. St. Paul: Minnesota Historical Society, 1967. 211

Hagen, Ordean, A. Who Done it? A Guide to Detective, Mystery and Suspense Fiction. New York: R.R. Bowker, 1969. 56

Hague, John A. ed. American Character and Culture: Some Twentieth Century Perspectives. 1964; Westport: Greenwood Press, 1979. 309

Haines, Charles G. The American Doctrine of Judicial Supremacy. Berkeley: University of California Press, 1932. 356

Haites, Erick F. et.al. Western River Transportation: The Era of Early Internal Development, 1910 -1960. Baltimore: Johns Hopkins University Press, 1975. 71

*Halberstam, David. The Best and the Brightest. New York: Fawcett, 1973. 131

_____. The Powers that Be. New York: Alfred A. Knopf, 1979. 227

*Haley, Alex. Roots. New York: Dell, 1977. 389

Haley, Edward P. Revolution and Intervention: The Diplomacy of Taft and Wilson with Mexico, 1910-1917. Cambridge: Massachusetts Institute of Technology Press, 1970. 124

*Hall, David D. The Faithful Shepherd: A History of the New England Ministry in the Seventeenth Century. New York: Norton, 1974. 368

Hall, D., R. Pack and L. Simpson, eds. New Poets of England and America. New York: New American Library, 1962. 335, 343

Hall, J. Lesslie. English Usage: Studies in the History and Uses of English Words and Phrases. 1717; New York: Gordon Press. 270

Hall, Jacquelyn Dowd. Revolt Against Chivalry: Jessie Daniel Ames and the Women's Campaign Against Lynching. New York: Columbia University Press, 1979. 542

Hall, John. The Sociology of Literature. London: Longman, 1979. 501

Hall, Robert A., Jr. Sound and Spelling in English. Philadelphia: Chilton Books, 1961. 268

Haller, Mark. "Historical Roots of Police Behavior: Chicago, 1890-1925."
Land and Society Review, 10 (1976). 527

Halliburton, David. Edgar Allan Poe: A Phenomenological View. Princeton,
New Jersey: Princeton University Press, 1973. 415

Halliday, Michael A.K. Explorations in the Functions of Language.
Amsterdam: Elsevier, 1977. 268

_____. The Linguistic Sciences and Language Teaching. London: Longman's
1964. 268

_____. System and Function in Language. Oxford: The University Press,
1976. 268

*Halpern,Daniel. The American Poetry Anthology. New York: Avon, 1975. 339, 341, 343

*Halpern,Paul, J. ed. Why Watergate? Palisades Calif.: Palisades Press,
1975. 439

Halpern, Stephen and Charles Lamb, eds. Supreme Court Activism and
Restraint. New York: Columbia University Press, 1981. 357

*Hamby, Alonzo I.. Beyond the New Deal: Harry S. Truman and American
Liberalism. New York: Columbia University Press, 1973. 436

_____, and Edward Weldon, eds. Access to the Papers of Recent
Public Figures: The New Harmony Conference. Bloomington: Indiana
University Press, 1977. 555

*Hamer, Andrew Marshall, ed. Urban Atlanta: Redefining the Role of the
City. Atlanta: Georgia State University, 1980. 465

Hamilton, Holman. The Three Kentucky Presidents: Lincoln, Taylor, Davis.
Lexington: University Press of Kentucky, 1978. 428

Hamlin, Talbot. Benjamin Latrobe. New York: Oxford University Press, 1955. 45

*_____. Greek Revival Architecture in America. New York: Dover Press, 1944. 36, 43

Hamm, Charles. Yesterdays: Popular Song in America. New York: W.W. Norton, 1979. 305

Hammack, David C. "Elite Perceptions of Power in Cities of the United
States, 1880-1900." Journal of Urban History, 4 (August, 1978). 460

_____. "Problems in the Historical Study of Power in the Cities and
Towns of the United States,1800-1960." American Historical Review, 83.
(April 1978). 461

*Hammel, William. The Popular Arts in America. New York: Harcourt,
Brace, Jovanovich, 1977. 501

Hammond, Bray. Sovereignty and an Empty Purse: Banks and Politics in
the Civil War. Princeton: Princeton University Press, 1970. 73

Hammond, George P.,ed. A Guide to the Manuscript Collections of the Bancroft
Library, Vol 2. 554

Hand, Learned. <u>The Bill of Rights</u>. New York: Atheneum, 1964. 352

_____. "Sources of Tolerance." 79 <u>University of Pennsylvania Law Review</u> 1
(1930). 353

Hand, Wayland, ed. <u>American Folk Legend: A Symposium</u>. Berkeley: University of
California Press, 1979. 97

*Handlin, Oscar. <u>The Uprooted</u>. New York: Little, 1973. 193, 204

Handlin, Oscar, et.al. <u>Harvard Guide to American History</u>. Cambridge: Harvard
University Press, 1954. 181

Handlin, Oscar and Lillian. <u>Abraham Lincoln and the Union</u>. Boston: Little, Brown
and Co., 1980. 429

*Handy, Robert T. <u>A Christian America: Protestant Hopes and Historical Realities</u>.
New York: Oxford University Press, 1974. 365

_____. <u>A History of the Churches in the United States and Canada</u>. New York:
Oxford University Press, 1979. 364

Handy, Robert T., ed. <u>The Social Gospel in America, 1870-1920</u>. New York: Oxford
University Press, 1966.

Hanke, Lewis. <u>Aristotle and the American Indian</u>. Bloomington, Indiana: University
of Indiana Press, 1959. 181

Hanna, Alfred J. and Kathryn A. <u>Napoleon III and Mexico: American Triumph over
Monarchy</u>. Chapel Hill: University of North Carolina Press, 1971. 118

Hanna, P.R., et.al. <u>Phoneme-Grapheme Correspondences as Cues to Spelling
Improvement</u>. Washington, D.C.: G.P.O., 1966.   268

*Hansen, Chadwick. <u>Witchcraft at Salem</u>. New York: New American Library. 369

*Hansen, Marcus Lee. <u>The Immigrant in American History</u>. New York: Harper and Row,
1964. 193, 204

 *Harbert, Earl N. <u>The Force So Much Closer to Home: Henry Adams and the Adams
Family</u>. New York: New York University Press, 1977. 404

_____ . <u>Henry Adams: A Reference Guide</u>. Boston: G.K. Hall, 1978. 409

Hardin, Garrett. "Tragedy of the Commons." <u>Science</u>, December 13, 1968. 471

*Hardt, Hanno. <u>Social Theories of the Press: Early German and American Perspectives</u>.
Beverly Hills, California: Sage Publications, 1979. 228

Hardwick, Elizabeth. <u>Rediscovered Fiction by American Women</u>. New York: Arno. 550

*Hareven, Tamara. <u>Amoskeague: Life and Work in an American Factory</u>. New York:
Pantheon, 1978. 449

Hargreaves, Robert. <u>Superpower: A Portrait of America in the 1970s</u>. New York:
St. Martins Press, 1973. 310

*Harlan, Louis R. <u>Booker T. Washington: The Making of a Black Leader, 1856-1901</u>.
New York: Oxford University Press, 1975. 27

_____, ed. The Booker T.Washington Papers. vol. VIII. Urbana: University of Illinois Press, 1979. 404

Harley, Sharon and Rosalyn Terborg-Penn. The Afro-American Woman: Struggles and Images. Port Washington, New York: Kennikat Press, 1978. 543

Harmon, M. Judd, ed. Essays on the Constitution of the United States. New York: Kennikat, 1978. 357.

Harper, Marvin H. Gurus, Swamis and Avatars: Spiritual Masters and Their American Disciples. Philadelphia: Westminster Press, 1971. 384

*Harper, Ralph. The World of the Thriller. Baltimore: The Johns Hopkins University Press, 1974. 53, 58

Harper, Robert S. Lincoln and the Press. New York: McGraw Hill, 1951. 213

*Harrell, David Edwin, Jr. All Things Are Possible. Bloomington: University of Indiana Press, 1976. 381

_____ . The Social Sources of Division in the Disciples of Christ, 1865-1900. Atlanta: Publishing Systems, 1973. 365

*Harris, Ann Sutherland and Linda Nochlin. Women Artists: 1550-1950. New York: Knopf, 1977. 546

Harris, Barbara J. Beyond Her Sphere: Women and the Professions in American History. Westport, Connecticut: Greenwood Press, 1978. 548

Harris, Seymour E., ed. Regional Income Trends, 1840-1950. New York: McGraw-Hill, 1961. 68

Harris, William H. Keeping the Faith: A.Philip Randolph, Milton P. Webster, and the Brotherhood of Sleeping Car Porters, 1925-1937. Urbana: University of Illinois Press, 1978. 449

Harrison, John F.C. The Second Coming: Popular Millenarianism, 1780-1850. New Brunswick, New Jersey: Rutgers University Press, 1979. 515

Harrison, John M. The Man Who Made Nasby: David Ross Locke. Chapel Hill: University of North Carolina Press, 1960. 213

*Hart, John Fraser. The Look of the Land. New York: Prentice-Hall, 1975. 419

*Hart, Robert A. The Eccentric Tradition: American Diplomacy in the Far East. New York: Scribner's, 1976. 136

Hartman, Geoffrey H. The Fate of Reading and Other Essays. Chicago:University of Chicago Press, 1975. 59

_____. "The Mystery of Mysteries." New York Review of Books. May 18, 1972. 60

Hartman, Heidi. "Capitalism,Patriarchy, and Job Segregation by Sex." Signs, 1 (Spring 1976).   547

Hartman, Susan. "Prescriptions for Penelope." Women's Studies, 5 (1978). 551

*Hartshorn, Truman A., et.al. Metropolis in Georgia: Atlanta's Rise as a Major Transaction Center. Cambridge: Ballinger, 1976. 465

Hartshorne, Charles and Paul Weiss. "Recollections of Editing the Peirce Papers." Transactions of the Charles S. Peirce Society, 6 (1970). 325

*Hartz, Louis. The Liberal Tradition in America. New York: Harcourt Brace, 1962. 168

*Harvey, David. Social Justice and the City. Baltimore: Johns Hopkins, 1973. 456

Haseth, James A. and Bruce A. Glasrud, eds. The Northwest Mosaic: Minority Conflicts in Pacific Northwest History. Boulder: Pruett, 1977. 196

Haskell, T.L. "The True and Tragical History of Time on the Cross." New York Review of Books. October 2, 1975. 181

Hassen, Robert. Steel Titan: The Life of Charles N. Schwab. New York: Oxford University Press, 1975.

Hassler, Warren W., Jr. "Allies or Enemies: The Antiquarian and Historian." Military Collector and Historian, Vol. 25 (Spring 1973). 281

Hatch, James V. and Ted Shine, eds. Black Theater U.S.A. New York: Free Press, 1974. 22

Hatch, Nathan O. The Sacred Cause of Liberty. New Haven: Yale University Press, 1977.

Haugen, Einar. "The Analysis of Linguistics Borrowing." Language, XXVI (1950). 266

_____. "Bilingualism in the Americas; A Bibliography and Research Guide." PADS, 26 (1956). 256

_____. "Bilingualism, Language Contact and Immigrant Languages. The United States." Sebeok. Trends. 257, 266

_____. The Ecology of Language. Stanford: Stanford University Press, 1972. 257, 2●

_____. The Norwegian Language in America. 2 vols. Philadelphia: University of Pennsylvania Press, 1953. 266

*Hauser, Philip M. and Leo F. Schnore, eds. The Study of Urbanization. New York: Wiley, 1965. 456

Haveman, Robert H., ed. A Decade of Federal Antipoverty Programs: Achievements, Failures, and Lessons. New York: Academic Press, 1977. 88

*Hawkes, Terence. Structuralism and Semiotics. Berkeley: University of California, 1977. 501

*Hawley, Ellis W. The New Deal and the Problem of Monopoly: A Study in Economic Ambivalence. Princeton: Princeton University Press, 1966. 82

Hawthorne, Nathaniel. The Life of Franklin Pierce. 1852; New York: Garrett Press, 1970. 428

Haycraft, Howard. Murder for Pleasure: The Life and Times of the Detective Story. New York: Appleton-Century, 1941. 57

_____, ed. The Art of the Mystery Story. New York: Grosset & Dunlap, 1946. 59

Hayden, Dolores. "Redesigning the Domestic Workplace." Chrysalis, 1 (1977). 549

*_____. Seven American Utopias. Cambridge, Massachusettes: M.I.T. Press, 1976. 51●

_____ . "Two Utopian Feminists and their Campaigns for Kitchenless Houses." Signs, 4 (Winter 1978). 549

Hayler, Barbara. "Abortion." Signs, 5 (Winter 1979). 542

Hayneman, Charles S. The Supreme Court on Trial. New York: Atherton Press, 1963.

Haynes, Richard F. The Awesome Power: Harry S. Truman as Commander in Chief. Baton Rouge: Louisiana State University Press, 1973. 436

Hays, Samuel P. "The Social Analysis of American Political History, 1880-1920." Political Science Quarterly, LXXX (September 1965). 205

Haywood, Charles. A Bibliography of North American Folklore and Folk Song, 2 vols. 1951; New York: Dover, 1961.   95, 300

Haywood, Harry. Black Bolshevik. Chicago: Liberator Press, 1978. 21

_____ . For a Revolutionary Position on the Negro Question. Chicago: Liberator, 1975. 21

Hazard, "Shepherd Tom." The Jonny-Cake Letters. 1880; Boston: 1915. 99

Head, Sydney W. Broadcasting in America: A Survey of Television and Radio, 3rd ed. Boston: Houghton Mifflin, 1975.   220

Heald, Morrell. The Social Responsibilities of Business: Company and Community, 1900-1969. Cleveland: Case Western Reserve University, 1970. 81

_____ and Laurence S. Kaplan. Culture and Diplomacy: the American Experience. Westport, Connecticut: Greenwood, 1977.

Healy, David F. Gunboat Diplomacy in the Wilson Era: the U.S. Navy in Haiti, 1915-1916. Madison: University of Wisconsin Press, 1976. 136

_____ . The United States and Cuba, 1898-1902: Generals, Politicians, and the Search for Policy. Madison: University of Wisconsin Press, 1963. 124

_____ . U.S. Expansionism: The Imperialist Urge in the 1890's. Madison: University of Wisconsin Press, 1972. 119

*Healy, Robert and John Rosenberg. Land Use and the States. Baltimore: Johns Hopkins, 1978.   438

Heath, Jim F. Decade of Disillusionment: The Kennedy-Johnson Years. Bloomington: Indiana University Press, 1975. 437

Heavner, Robert O. "Indentured Servitude: The Philadelphia Market, 1771-1773." Journal of Economic History, XXXVIII (September 1978). 66

*Hebdige, Dick. Subculture: The Meaning of Style. New York: Methuen, 1979. 495, 501

*Hedges, Elaine and Ingrid Wendt, eds. In Her Own Image: Women Working in the Arts. Old Westbury, New York: The Feminist Press, 1980. 546

Hedges, James B. The Browns of Providence Plantations: The Nineteenth Century. 1952; Providence: Brown University Press, 1968. 75

Heermance, J. Noel. Charles W. Chesnutt: America's First Great Black Novelist. Hamden, Connecticut: Shoe String Press, 1974. 404

Heffernan, Michael. "Practicing the Scales of Science." American Poetry Review 8 (January-February 1979). 341

Hefley, James and Marti. The Church that Produced a President. New York: Wyden Books, 1977. 441

Heilbut, Tony. The Gospel Sound. New York: Simon and Schuster, 1971. 301

Heimert, Alan. Religion and the American Mind: From the Great Awakening to the Revolution. Cambridge: Harvard University Press, 1966. 171

Heinrichs, Waldo H., Jr. American Ambassador: Joseph C. Grew and the Development of the United States Diplomatic Tradition. Boston: Little, Brown, 1966. 127

Heitman, Sidney, ed. Germans from Russia in Colorado. Ann Arbor, Michigan: University Microfilms International, 1978. 195

Heller, Francis H., ed. The Truman White House: The Administration of the Presidency, 1945-1953. Lawrence: Regents Press of Kansas, 1980. 436

*Hellman, Lillian. Pentimento. New York: New American Library, 1977. 389

Hellman, Mary. Popular Culture: Source Book. Del Mar: Publisher's Inc., 1977. 501

*Hemenway, Robert. Zora Neale Hurston: A Literary Biography. Urbana, Illinois: University of Illinois Press, 1977. 537

Henderson, Thomas M. Tammany Hall and the New Immigrants: The Progressive Years. New York: Arno, 1976. 200

Hendrickson, Gordon O., ed. Peopling the High Plains: Wyoming's European Heritage. Cheyenne: State Archives and Historical Department, 1977. 196

Henretta, James A. "Social History as Lived and Written." American Historical Review, 84 (December 1979). 455

_____. "The Study of Social Mobility: Ideological Assumptions and Conceptual Bias." Labor History, XVIII (Spring 1977). 197

*Henry, Jules. Culture Against Man. New York: Random House, 1965. 312

Henry, Stuart A. Unvanquished Puritan. Grand Rapids: Eerdmans, 1973. 376

Herbst, Anthony F. and Joseph S. K. Wu. "Some Evidence of Subsidization: The U.S. Trucking Industry, 1900-1920." Journal of Economic History, XXXIII (June 1975). 94

Herndobler, Robin. "The Speech of Chicago's East Side: A White Working Class Community." Dissertation. University of Chicago, 1977. 265

*Herreshoff, David. American Disciples of Marx. New York: Monad, 1973. 176, 181

Herring, George C. Aid to Russia, 1941-1946: Strategy, Diplomacy, the Origins of the Cold War. New York: Columbia University Press, 1973. 128

*_____. America's Longest War: The United States and Vietnam, 1950-1975. New York: Wiley, 1979. 140

Hersey, John Richard. The President. New York: Knopf, 1975. 440

Hersh, Blanche Glassman. The Slavery of Sex: Feminist-Abolitionists in America.
    Urbana, Illinois: University of Illinois Press, 1978. 541

Hershberg, Theodore. "The Organization of Historical Research." American Historical
    Association Newsletter, 12, No. 7 (October 1974). 462

_____. Toward a New Urban History: Work, Space, and Group Experience in 19th
    Century Philadelphia. New York: Oxford. 462

Hertzberg, Steven. Strangers Within the Gate City: The Jews of Atlanta, 1845-1915.
    Philadelphia: Jewish Publication Society of America, 1978. 468

Herzog, Marvin I. The Yiddish Language in Northern Poland. Indiana University
    Research Center in Anthropology, 1965. 266

Hess, Stephen and Milton Kaplan. The Ungentlemanly Art: A History of American
    Political Cartoons. New York: Macmillan, 1968. 214

Hessen, Robert. Steel Titan: The Life of Charles M. Schwab. New York: Oxford
    University Press, 1975. 80

Heuterman, Thomas H. Movable Type: Biography of Legh R. Freeman. Ames: Iowa State
    University Press, 1979. 226

Heyen, William, ed. American Poets in 1976. Indianapolis: Bobbs-Merrill Co., 1975.
    339, 341, 343

Hidy, Ralph W., Frank E. Hill, and Allan Nevins. Timber and Men: The Weyerhauser
    Story. New York: Macmillan, 1963. 00

*Higgs, Robert. Competition and Coercion: Blacks in the American Economy, 1865-1914.
    Chicago: University of Chicago Press, 1980. 79

Higham, Robin, ed. A Guide to the Sources of United States Military History. Hamden:
    Shoe String, 1981. 283, 292

*Higham, Robin and Carold Brandt. The United States Army in Peacetime: Essays in
    Honor of the Bicentennial. Manhattan, Kansas: A. H. Press, 1975. 283

*Higham, John. Send These to Me: Jews and Other Immigrants in Urban America.
    New York: Atheneum, 1975. 193

*_____, ed. Ethnic Leadership in America. Baltimore, Maryland: The Johns Hopkins
    University Press, 1978. 199

*Higham, John, et.al. History. New York: Harper and Row, 1973. 181

Hilberseimer, Ludwig. Mies van der Rohe. Chicago: Paul Theobald, 1956. 45

*Hildebrand, Grant. Designing for Industry: The Architecture of Albert Kahn.
    Cambridge: M.I.T. Press, 1974. 40, 45

Hill, Archibald A. Introduction to Linguistic Structures: From Sound to Sentence
    in English. New York: Harcourt, Brace and Company, 1958. 268

_____. "Albert Henry Marckwardt." Language. LIII. 257

*Hill, Christopher. The World Turned Upside Down: Radical Ideas During the
    English Revolution. New York: Penguin, 1976. 370

Hill, Hamlin. <u>Mark Twain: God's Fool</u>. New York: Harper & Row, 1973. 410

Hill, Peter P. <u>William Vans Murray, Federalist Diplomat: The Shaping of Peace with France, 1797-1801</u>. Syracuse: Syracuse University Press, 1971. 115

*Hill, Samuel S., Jr., et.al. <u>Religion and the Solid South</u>. Nashville: Abingdon, 1972.

Hillen, Andrew, ed. <u>The Letters of Henry Wadsworth Longfellow</u>. Cambridge, Massachusett Harvard University Press, 1972. 414

*Hilliard, Jack B. and Harold P. Bivins, comps. <u>An Annotated Reading List of United States Marine Corps History</u>. U.S. Marine Corps, Washington, D.C., 1971. 285

Hilliard Sam. B. <u>Hog Meat and Hoe Cake: Food Supply in the Old South, 1840-1860</u>. Carbondale: Southern Illinois University Press, 1972. 79

Hills, Patricia. <u>Turn-of-the-Century America</u>. New York: Whitney Museum, 1977. 508

Hilsman, Roger L. <u>To Move a Nation: The Politics of Foreign Policy in the Administratio of John F. Kennedy</u>. New York: Dell Pub. Co., 1967. 130

Himes, Chester. <u>The Quality of Hurt</u>. Garden City, New York: Doubleday, 1971. 60

*Himmelberg, Robert F. <u>The Origins of the National Recovery Administration: Business, Government, and the Antitrust Question, 1921-1933</u>. New York: Fordham University Press, 1976. 82

Hinds, Dudley, et.al. <u>Winning at Zoning</u>. New York: McGraw-Hill, 1979. 483

Hinding, Andrea, ed. <u>Women's History Sources: A Guide to Archives and Manuscript Collections in the United States</u>. New York: R.R. Bowker, 1978. 536

_____ and Rosemary Richardson. <u>Archival and Manuscript Resources for the Study of Women's History: A Beginning</u>. Minneapolis, 1972. 554

*Hines, Thomas S. <u>Burnham of Chicago</u>. Chicago: University of Chicago Press, 1979.   39, 532

Hiroa, Te Rangi. <u>Arts and Crafts of Hawaii, II: Houses</u>. Honolulu: Bishop Museum Press, 1964. 44

Hirsch, Paul M. "Social Science Approaches to Popular Culture: A Review and Critique." <u>Journal of Popular Culture</u>, XI, 2 (Fall 1977). 502

Hirsch, Susan E. <u>Roots of the American Working Class: The Industrialization of Crafts in Newark, 1800-1860.</u> Philadelphia: University of Pennsylvania Press, 1978. 447

Hirshfield, Daniel S. <u>The Lost Reform: The Campaign for Compulsory Health Insurance in the United States from 1932 to 1943</u>. Cambridge: Harvard University Press, 1970.

Hitchcock, Bert. <u>Richard Malcolm Johnston</u>. Boston: G.K. Hall, 1978. 414

*Hitchcock, H. Wiley. <u>Ives</u>. London: Oxford University Press, 1977. 304

*_____. <u>Music in the United States: A Historical Introduction</u>. Englewood Cliffs: Prentice-Hall, 1974.   296, 297, 298

_____. "Sources for the Study of American Music." <u>Folk Music in America</u>. Washington: Library of Congress, 1976.

*Hitchcock, Henry-Russell. The Architecture of H.H. Richardson and His Times.
   1936; Cambridge: M.I.T. Press, 1969. 39, 45

*_____. In the Nature of Materials: The Buildings of Frank Lloyd Wright,
   1887-1941. 1942; New York: Da Capo Press, 1968. 39, 45

*_____. Rhode Island Architecture. 1939; New York: Da Capo Press, 1968.   38, 44

Hitchock, Henry-Russell and Arthur Drexler, eds. Built in USA: Post-War Architecture.
   New York: Museum of Modern Art, 1952.   43

Hitchcock, Henry-Russell and William Seale. Temples of Democracy: The State Capitols
   of the U.S.A. New York: Harcourt, Brace, Jovanovich, 1976. 32

Hixson, Richard F. Isaac Collins: A Quaker Printer in 18th Century America. New
   Brunswick: Rutgers University Press, 1968. 207

Hoffa, James R. Hoffa: The Real Story. New York: Stein and Day, 1972. 450

Hoffberg, Judith A. "The Women Artist's Books: A Select Bibliography."
Chrysalis, 5. 537

Hoffecker, Carol E. Wilmington Delaware: Portrait of an Industrial City,
1830-1910. Charlottsville: University Press of Virginia, 1974. 76

*Hoffman, Daniel, G. Form and Fable in American Fiction. 1961; New York:
Norton, 1973. 103

_____. Paul Bunyan, Last of the Frontier Demigods. Philadelphia: Temple
University Publications, 1966. 100

Hoffman, Donald. The Architecture of John Wellborn Root. Baltimore: Johns
Hopkins University Press, 1973. 39, 45

_____. ed. The Meaning of Architecture: Buildings and Writings by
John Wellborn Root. New York: Horizon Press, 1967. 45

Hoffman, Nancy and Florence Howe, eds. Women Working: An Anthology of Stories
and Poems. Old Westbury: Feminist Press, 1979. 552

*Hofstadter, Richard. The Age of Reform. New York: Random, 1970. 168

*_____. America at 1750: A Social Portrait. New York: Random, 1973. 37

*_____. The American Political Tradition. New York: Random, 1954. 168

*_____. The Progressive Historians: Turner, Parrington, Beard. Chicago:
University of Chicago Press, 1979. 181

_____. Social Darwinism in American Thought. Boston: Beacon Press, 1955. 181

_____ and Michael Wallace, eds. American Violence: A Documentary History.
New York: Random, 1971. 310

Hogan, David. "Education and the Making of Chicago Working Class, 1880-1930."
History of Education Quarterly, 18 (Fall 1978). 528

Hogan, Michael, J. Informal Entente: The Private Structure of Cooperation in
Anglo-American Economic Diplomacy, 1918-1928. Columbia: University of
Missouri Press, 1977. 85, 137

Holbrook, Clyde A., ed. Original Sin. New Haven: Yale University Press, 1970. 373

Holden, Jonathan. "The Case of Raymond Chandler's Fiction as Romance." Kansas
Quarterly, 10 (1978). 60

Holifield, E. Brooks. The Covenant Sealed. New Haven: Yale University Press, 1974.

_____. The Gentlemen Theologians. Durham: Duke University Press, 1978.

*Holland, Norman, N. The Dynamics of Literary Response. New York: Norton, 1975. 502

*Holli, Melvin G. ed. Detroit. New York: New Viewpoints, 1976. 459

*Holli, Melvin G. and Peter d'A. Jones. The Ethnic Frontier: Essays in the History of Group Survival in Chicago and the Midwest. Grand Rapids, Michigan: Wm. B. Eerdmans, 1977. 199, 520

Hollingsworth, Roger J. and Ellen Jane Hollingworth. Dimensions in Urban History: Historical and Social Science Perspectives on Middle-Size American Cities. Madison: University of Wisconsin, 1979. 161

Holly, Carol T. "Black Elk Speaks and the Making of Indian Autobiography." Genre, 12 (Spring, 1979). 396, 399

Holmes, W.J. Double-Edged Secrets: U.S. Naval Intelligence Operations in the Pacific During World War II. Annapolis: U.S. Naval Institute Press, 1979. 292

*Holt, Glen and Dominic Pacyga. Chicago: A Historical Guide to the Neighborhoods: The Loop and the South Side. Chicago: Chicago Historical Society, 1979. 518

Hone, William. Every-Day Book. Detroit: Gale, Reprint of 1827 Edition. 103

*Hoogenboom, Ari and Olive. A History of the ICC: From Panacea to Palliative. New York: W.W. Norton, 1976. 82

Hoopes, Townsend. The Devil and John Foster Dulles. Boston: Little, Brown, 1973. 130

_____. The Limits of Intervention: An Inside Account of How the Johnson Policy of Escalation in Vietnam was Reversed. New York: D. McKay Co., 1969. 131

Hoover, Dwight, ed. Understanding Negro History. Chicago: Quadrangle, 1969. 13

Hoover, Herbert. Herbert Hoover: Proclamation and Executive Orders, March 4, 1929 to March 4, 1933. 2 vols. Washington: Government Printing Office, 1974. 433

Hoover Presidential Library Association. Herbert Hoover, the Uncommon Man. West Branch, Iowa: Hoover Presidential Library Association, 1974. 437

Hoover, Herbert. Public Papers of the Presidents of the United States, Herbert Hoover, 1929-1933, 4 vols. Washington: Government Printing Office, 1974-1977. 433

Hopkins, John. "The White Middle-Class Speech of Savannah, Georgia." Dissertation.University of South Carolina, 1975. 265

Horn, David. The Literature of American Music...a fully annotated bibliography. Metuchen: The Scarecrow Press, 1977. 306

Hornbostel, Caleb. Materials for Architecture. New York: Reinhold, 1961. 41, 46

Horowitz, Helen Lefkowitz. Culture and the City: Cultural Philanthropy in Chicago From the 1880's to 1917. Lexington: University of Kentucky Press, 1976. 461, 529

Horowitz, Irving Louis. "Autobiography as Presentation of Self for Social Immortality." New Literary History, 9 (Autumn 1977). 394, 398

Horsman, Reginald. The Causes of the War of 1812. Philadelphia: University of Pennsylvania Press, 1962. 116

Horwitz, Morton J. The Transformation of American Law, 1780–1860. Cambridge: Harvard University Press, 1979. 92

Horwitz, Richard P. Anthropology Toward History: Culture and Work in a 19th Century Maine Town. Middletown, Connecticut: Wesleyan University Press, 1978. 448

Hosmer, Stephen T., Konrad Kellen, and Brian M. Jenkins. The Fall of South Vietnam: Statements by Vietnamese Military and Civilian Leaders. New York: Crane-Russak Co., 1980. 293

House of Representatives Committee on the Judiciary. Impeachment of Richard M. Nixon, President of the United States: The Final Report of the Committee on the Judiciary. New York: Viking Press, 1975. 439

Hovenkamp, Herbert. Science and Religion in America, 1800–1880. Philadelphia: Pennsylvania Press, 1978. 181, 377

Hoveyda, Fereydoun. Historie du roman poliċies. Paris: Les Editions du Pavillon, 1965. 57

Howard, John. Our American Music. New York: Crowell, 1931. 297, 298

*Howard, John. Stephen Foster: America's Troubadour. 1934; New York: Crowell. 300

Howard, Richard. Alone with America. New York: Atheneum, 1980. 344

Howard, Woodford J. Mr. Justice Murphy: A Political Biography. Princeton: Princeton University Press, 1968. 348

Howarth, William L. "Some Principles of Autobiography." New Literary History, 5 (Winter 1974). 397

Howe, Daniel Walker. The Unitarian Conscience: Harvard Moral Philosophy, 1805–1861. Cambridge: Harvard University Press, 1970. 381

*Howe, Irving. World of Our Fathers: New York: Simon and Schuster, 1977. 195, 385

*Howe, Louise Kapp. Pink Collar Workers: Inside the World of Women's Work. New York: Avon Books, 1978. 547

Howerton, Joseph B. "The Resources of the National Archives for Ethnic Research." The Immigration History Newsletter, V (November 1973). 203

Howie, John and Thomas O. Buford, eds. Contemporary Studies in Philosophical Idealism. Cape Cod: Claude Stark & Co., 1975. 326

Howren, Robert R. "The Speech of Louisville, Kentucky." Dissertation. Indiana University, 1958. 265

Hubbell, Allan F. The Pronunciation of English in New York City: Consonants and Vowels. New York: King's Crown, 1950. 265

Hubin, Allen J. The Bibliography of Crime Fiction, 1749-1975. Del Mar, California:
     Publisher's Inc., 1979. 56

_____. Crime Fiction Collection. Pacific Palisades: International Bookfinders,
     1979, privately printed. 56

Hudspeth, Robert N.S. Ellery Channing. Boston: G.K. Hall, 1973. 410

*Huebel, Henry Russell, ed. Things in the Driver's Seat: Reading in
     Popular Culture. Chicago: Rand McNally, 1972. 492, 502

Huggins, Nathan L. Protestants Against Slavery: Boston's Charities, 1870-1890.
     Westport: Greenwood Press, 1971. 380

Hughes, Jonathan R.T. The Governmental Habit: Economic Controls From Colonial
     Times to the Present. New York: Basic Books, 1977. 93

Hughes, Langston. "The Artist and the Racial Mountain." The Nation, 122 (June, 1926). 21

*_____. The Big Sea. 1940; New York: Hill and Wang, 1963. 21

*_____. Good Morning, Revolution. Connecticut: Lawrence Hill, 1973. 21

*_____. Selected Poems of Langston Hughes. 1959; New York: Random, 1974. 21

_____. Scotsboro Ltd. New York: Golden Stair, 1932.

_____ and Arna Bontemps, eds. Poetry of the Negro, 1746 -1970. New York: Doubleday,
     1970. 22

Hull, Raymona. Nathaniel Hawthorne: The English Experience, 1853-1864.
     Pittsburgh: University of Pittsburgh Press, 1980.

Hulseth, James A. and Bruce A. Glasrud, eds. The Northwest Mosaic: Minority
     Conflicts in Pacific Northwest History. Boulder, Colorado: Pruett, 1977.

Hutchinson, Thomas. History of the Colony of Massachusetts Bay, 3 vols.
     1764; New York: Arno, 1971.

*Hundley, Norris, ed. The Asian American: The Historical Experience. Santa
     Barbara, California: Clio Books, 1976. 195, 204

Hungerford, Edward B., ed. Poets in Progress: Critical Prefaces to Thirteen
     Modern American Poets. Evanston: Northwestern University Press, 1967. 344

Hungerford, Harold, Jay Robinson and James Sledd. English Linguistics: An
     Introductory Reader. Glenview, Illinois: Scott, Foresman, 1970. 260

Hunt, Michael. Frontier Defense and the Open Door: Manchuria in Chinese-
     American Relations, 1895-1911. New Haven: Yale University Press, 1973. 121

Hunter, Albert. Symbolic Communities: The Persistence and Change of Chicago's
     Local Communities. Chicago: University of Chicago Press, 1974. 519

*Hunter, Robert. The Storming of the Mind. Garden City, New York: Doubleday, 1972. 313

Huntress, Keith, comp. Checklist of Narratives of Shipwrecks and Disasters at Sea to 1860. Ames: Iowa State University Press, 1979. 481

Hurn, Christopher J. The Limits and Possiblities of Schooling: An Introduction to the Sociology of Education. Boston: Allyn and Bacon, 1978. 442

Hurst, James Willard. Law and Economic Growth: The Legal History of the Lumber Industry in Wisconsin, 1836-1915. Cambridge: Harvard University Press, 1964. 70

_____. Law and Social Process in United States History. 1960; New York: DaCapo, 1971. 70

_____. A Legal History of Money in the United States, 1774-1970. Lincoln: University of Nebraska Press, 1973. 73

_____. The Legitimacy of the Business Coporation in the Law of the United States, 1780-1970. Charlottsville: University of Press of Virginia 1970. 70

Hutchins, Robert M. A Free and Responsible Press. Chicago: University of Chicago Press, 1947. 220

Hutchison, William R. The Modernist Impulse in American Protestantism. Cambridge: Harvard University Press, 1976. 379

*Huthmacher, J. Joseph and Susman, Warren, eds. Wilson's Diplomacy: An International Symposium. Cambridge: Schenkman, 1973.   432

Huxtable, Ada Louise. The Architecture of New York: A History and Guide; Vol. I, Classic New York. New York: Anchor Books, 1964. 37, 44

Hvidt, Kristian. Flight to America: The Social Background of 300,000 Danish Emigrants. New York: Academic Press, 1975. 193

Hyatt, Harry W. Hoodoo-Conjuration-Witchcraft-Rootwork, 4 vols. Hannibal, Mo.: Western Publishing Company, 1974. 107

*Hyman, Herbert, Charles R. Wright, and John Shelton Reed. The Enduring Effects of Education. Chicago: University of Chicago Press, 1975. 442

Hyneman, Charles S. The Supreme Court on Trial. New York: Atherton Press, 1963.   351

Ichioka , Yuji, et. al., eds. A Buried Past: An Annotated Bibliography of the
    Japanese American Research Project Collection. Berkeley and Los Angeles:
    University of California Press, 1974. 191

Inge, M. Thomas, ed. Handbook of American Popular Culture. Westport, Connecticut:
    Greenwood Press, 1979, 1980, 1981. 491, 502, 509

Institute for the Study of Educational Policy. Equal Education Opportunity
    For Blacks in U.S. Higher Education. Washington: Howard University Press, 1976. 443

*International Commission on Military History. Acta No. 2, Washington, D.C.
    Manhattan, Kansas: Aerospace Historian Publishing, 1977.

*Inriye, Akira. Across the Pacific: An Inner History of American-East Asian
    Relations. New York: Harcourt, Brace & World, 1967. 124

*_____. The Cold War in Asia: A Historical Introduction. Englewood Cliffs,
    N.J.: Prentice-Hall, 1974. 129

_____. Pacific Estrangement: Japanese and American Expansion, 1897-1911.
    Cambridge: Harvard University Press, 1972. 121

_____. The Search for a New Order in the Far East, 1921-1931. Cambridge:
    Harvard University Press, 1965. 124

Irving, Washington. The Adventures of Captain Bonneville U.S.A. 1837; Portland:
    Binford, 1954. 150

_____. Rip Van Winkle. 1870; New York: Mayflower, 1980. 150

_____ and James Kirke Paulding. Diedrich Knickerbocker's History of
    New York. 1809; New York: AMS Press, 1973. 150

Irwin Inez Haynes. The Story of Alice Paul and the National Women's Party.
    Fairfax, Virginia: Denlinger's Publishers, 1977. 537

Isham, Norman M. Early American Houses. 1928; New York: Da Capo Press, 1967. 43

Israel, Jerry. Progressivism and the Open Door: America and China, 1905-1921.
    Pittsburgh: University of Pittsburgh Press, 1971. 121

*Ives, Edward, D., ed. Larry Gorman: The Man Who Made the Songs. 1969; New
    York: Arno, 1977. 103

_____. Joe Scott, the Woodsman - Songmaker. Urbana: University of Illinois
    Press, 1978. 110

Ives, Sumner A. "A Dialect Differences in the Stories of Joel Chandler Harris."
    American Literature, XXVII (1955). 267

_____. "Linguistics and the Teaching of Reading and Spelling." Thomas R.
    Sebeok. Current Trends in Linguistics. The Hague: Mouton, 1973. 257, 268

_____. "The Phonology of the Uncle Remus Stories." PADS, XXII (1954). 267

_____ .   " A Theory of Literary Dialect." <u>Tulane Studies in English</u>,
    II (1950).   267

Ives, Sumner A. and Josephine P. "Linguistics and Reading." Albert H. Marckwardt.
    <u>Linguistics</u>. Chicago: University of Chicago Press, 1970.   257, 268

Jaberg, Karl. Aspects geographiques de langage. Paris: E. Droz, 1936. 264

*Jackson, Bruce. Get your Ass in the Water and Swim Like Me. Cambridge, Mass.:
Harvard University Press, 1974. 107

Jackson, J.B. "Chicago." American Space, 1865-1876: The Centennial Years.
New York: W. W. Norton, 1972. 531

Jackson, Donald and Doroty Twohig, ed. The Diaries of George Washington. 6 vols.
Charlottesville: University Press of Virginia, 1976-1980. 424

Jackson, George Pullen. White Spirituals in the Southern Uplands. 1933; New York:
Dover, 1965. 300

*Jackson, Luther P. Free Negro Labor and Property Holding in Virginia, 1830-1860.
New York: Atheneum, 1971. 27

*Jackson, Richard. United States Music: Sources of Bibliography and Collective
Biography. New York: Institute for American Music, 1973. 298

Jackson, Robert H. The Struggle for Judicial Supremacy. New York: Alfred A.
Knopf, 1941. 348

Jackson, W. Turrentine. Wagon Roads West. 1952; Lincoln: University of Nebraska
Press, 1979. 181

*Jacobs, Jane. The Death and Life of Great American Cities. New York:
Random, 1961. 473

Jacobs, Wilbur R. Diplomacy and Indian Gifts. Stanford: Stanford University Press,
1950. 181

*_____. Dispossessing the American Indian. New York: Scribner, 1972. 184

*_____. Wilderness Politics and Indian Gifts. Lincoln, Nebraska: University
of Nebraska Press, 1966. 181

Jacobsohn, Gary J. Pragmatism, Statesmanship, and the Supreme Court. Ithaca:
Cornell University Press, 1977. 356

Jacoby, Robin Miller. "The Women's Trade Union League and American Feminism."
Feminist Studies, 3 (Fall 1975).

James, Edward and Janet. Notable American Women, 1607-1950. Cambridge: Howard
University Press, 1971. 537

James, Janet Wilson, ed. "Women and Religion." American Quarterly, XXX (Winter
1978).

James, John A. Money and Capital Markets in Postbellum America. Princeton:
University Press, 1978. 92

James, William. Essays in Philosophy. Cambridge: Harvard University Press, 1979. 328

_____. Essays in Radical Empiricism. Cambridge: Harvard University Press, 1976. 319

_____. The Meaning of Truth. Cambridge: Harvard University Press, 1976.

_____. A Pluralistic Universe. Cambridge: Harvard University Press, 1977. 319

_____. Pragmatism. Cambridge: Harvard University Press, 1976. 319

Jernigan, E. Jay. Henry Demarest Lloyd. Boston: G.K.Hall, 1976. 414

*Jerome, John. On Mountains: Thinking About Terrain. New York: McGraw Hill, 1979. 487

Jespersen, Otto. A Modern English Grammar on Historical Principles. 1909-19;
    London: Allen and Unwin, 1954. 268

Jewell, Frank. Annotated Bibliography of Chicago History. Chicago: Chicago
    Historical Society, 1979. 519

Jewett, Robert and John Shelton Lawrence. The American Monomyth. Garden City, New
    York: Doubleday, 1977. 496, 502

Jick, Leon A. The Americanization of the Synagogue, 1820-1870. Hanover: University
    Press of New England, 1976. 385

Johnson, Arthur M. Petroleum Pipelines and Public Policy, 1906-1959. Cambridge:
    Harvard University Press, 1967. 82

_____. "Continuity and Change in Government-Business Relations." In
    John Braeman, et al., eds. Change and Continuity in Twentieth-Century
    America. New York: Harper and Row, 1966. 81

_____ and Barry E. Supple. Boston Capitalists and Western Railroads: A Study
    in the Nineteenth-Century Railroad Investment Process. Cambridge: Harvard
    University Press, 1967. 71

Johnson, Christopher. Utopian Communities in France: Cabet and the Icarians, 1839-
    1851. Ithaca, New York: Cornell University Press, 1974. 516

Johnson, Edward. Wonder-Working Providence of Zion's Savior in New England.
    1654; Delmar: Scholars Facsimiles, 1974. 146

Johnson, Gerald W. An Honorable Titan: A Biographical Study of Adolph S. Ochs.
    New York: Harper & Bros., 1946; Greenwood. 217

_____, F. R. Kent, H.L. Mencken and Hamilton Owens. The Sunpapers of Baltimore.
    New York: Knopf, 1937. 212

Johnson, Guy B. John Henry, Tracking Down a Negro Legend. 1929; New York: AMS
    Press, 1969. 100

Johnson, H. Earle. First Performances in America to 1900. Detroit: Information
    Coordinators, 1979. 306

Johnson, Icie F. William Rockhill Nelson and the Kansas City Star. Kansas City:
    Burton, 1935. 216

Johnson, Nicholas. How to Talk Back to Your Television Set. Boston: Little, Brown,
    1970. 502

*Johnson, Paul E. A Shopkeeper's Millenium: Society and Revivals in Rochester,
    New York, 1815-1837. New York: Hill and Wang, 1979. 376, 461

*Johnson, Philip C. Mies van der Rohe. 1947; New York: NYGS, 1978. 45

Johnson, R. M. The Dynamics of Compliance: Supreme Court Decision-Making From a
    New Perspective. Evanston, Illinois: Northwestern University Press, 1968. 352

Johnstone, Robert M., Jr. Jefferson and Presidency: Leadership in the Young
    Republic. Ithaca: Cornell University Press, 1978. 425

Johnson, Walter. The Battle Against Isolation. Chicago: University of Chicago
    Press, 1944. 122

*Johnson, Warren A. Muddling Toward Frugality. Westminster, Maryland: Shambhala, 1979.   477

Joint Chiefs of Staff. The History of the Joint Chiefs of Staff. 4 vols. Wilmington: Michael Glazier.

Jonas, Manfred. Isolationism in America, 1935-1941. Ithaca: Cornell University Press, 1966. 122

Jones, Alan M., Jr., ed. U.S. Foreign Policy in a Changing World: The Nixon Administration, 1969-1973. New York: David McKay, 1973. 438

Jones, Alice H. American Colonial Wealth: Documents and Methods. 3 vols. New York: Arno Press, 1977. 64

Jones, Charles Edwin. Perfectionist Persuasion: The Holiness Movement and American Methodism, 1867-1936. Metuchen: Scarecrow Press, 1974. 381

Jones, Howard. To the Webster - Ashburton Treaty: A Study in Anglo-American Diplomacy, 1783-1843. Chapel Hill: University of North Carolina Press, 1977. 134

Jones, James W. The Shattered Synthesis: New England Puritanism Before the Great Awakening. New Haven: Yale University Press, 1973. 367

*Jones, LeRoi. Blues People. New York: Morrow, 1963. 22

Jones, LeRoi. The Dutchman. New York: Morrow, 1964. 22

Jones, Lewis R. "The Mechanization of Reaping and Mowing in American Agriculture, 1833-1870: Comment." Journal of Economic History, LXXVII (June 1977).

Jones, Maldwyn Allen. Destination America: 1815-1914. New York: Holt, Rinehart & Winston, 1976. 194

Jones, Michael O. The Hand Made Object and Its Maker. Berkeley: University of California Press, 1975. 104

Jones, Phyllis M. and Nicholas R. Jones, eds. Salvation in New England: Selections From the Sermons of the First Preachers. Austin: University of Texas Press, 1977. 37

Jones, Robert Francis. George Washington. World Leaders Series, No. 80. Boston: Twayne Publishers, 1979. 424

Joos, Martin. The Five Clocks. New York: Harcourt, Brace and Company, 1967. 270

_____. "Homeostasis in English Usage." College Composition and Communication, XII (October 1962). 270

*Jordan, Winthrop D. White Over Black: American Attitudes Toward the Negro, 1550-1812. New York: Norton, 1977. 27. 172

Jordy, William H. Henry Adams, Scientific Historian. 1952; New York: Shoestring, 1970.

_____ and William H. Pierson. American Buildings and Their Architects. 4 vols. Garden City: Doubleday and Company, 1970-72. 47

Jorstad, Ewing. The Politics of Doomsday: Fundamentalists of the Far Right. Nashville: Abingdon, 1970. 381

*Josephson, Matthew. The Politicos. 1938; New York: Harcourt Brace Jovanovich, 1963. 167

_____. The Robber Barons. 1935; New York: Harcourt,Brace Jovanovich, 1962. 167

*Josephy, Alvin. The Indian Heritage of America. New York: Bantom, 1969. 175

_____. The Patriot Chiefs. New York: Penguin, 1969. 175

Judah, J. Stillson. The History and Philosophy of the Metaphysical Movements in America. Philadelphia: Westminster Press, 1967. 383

Juergens, George. Joseph Pulitzer and the New York World. Princeton: Princeton University Press, 1966. 216

*Juhasz, Suzanne, ed. Naked and Fiery Forms: Modern American Poetry by Women, A New Tradition. New York: Harper & Row, 1976. 539

_____ . "Some Deep Old Desk and Capacious Hold-All: Form and Women's Autobiography." College English, 39 (February 1978). 399

Karsten, Peter. "Demilitarizing Military History: Servants of Power or Agents of Understanding?" Military Affairs, Vol.36, (October 1972). 277

*Katz, Michael B. The People of Hamilton, Canada West: Family and Class in a Mid-Nineteenth City. Cambridge: Harvard, 1976. 462

Katzman, David. Seven Days a Week: Women and Domestic Service in Industrializing America. New York: Oxford University Press, 1978. 451, 548

*_____. Before the Ghetto: Black Detroit in the Nineteenth Century. Urbana: University of Illinois, 1975. 463

Kaufman, Burton I. The Oil Cartel Case: A Documentary Study of Antitrust Activity in the Cold War Era. Westport, Connecticut: Greenwood Press, 1978. 94

Kaufman, Edgar, Jr., ed. The Rise of an American Architecture. New York: Praeger, 1970. 36, 43

Kazin, Alfred. "Autobiography as Narrative." Michigan Quarterly Review, 3 (Fall, 1964.). 398

_____. "The Self as History: Reflections on Autobiography." M. Pachter, ed. Telling Lives, the Biographer's Art. Washington, D.C.: New Republic Books, 1979. 397, 398

*Kearns, Doris. Lyndon Johnson and the American Dream. New York: New American Library, 1977. 438

Keating, H.R.F.,ed. Crime Writers: Reflections on Crime Fiction. London: BBC, 1978. 56

Keeran, Roger. The Communist Party and the Auto Workers Union. Bloomington: Indiana University Press, 1980. 450

Keifetz, Norman. Welcome Sundays. New York: Putman, 1979. 468

*Keil, Charles. Urban Blues. Chicago: University of Chicago Press, 1968. 106, 301

Keiser, John H. "The Union Miners Cemetery at Mt. Olive, Illinois: A Spirit-Thread of Labor History." Journal of the Illinois State Historical Society, 62 (Autumn 1969). 453

Keller, Charles Roy. The Second Great Awakening in Connecticut. New Haven: Yale University Press, 1942. 376

*Keller, Karl. The Only Kangaroo Among the Beauty: Emily Dickinson and America. Baltimore, Maryland: Johns Hopkins University Press, 1980. 411

*Keller, Morton: The Art and Politics of Thomas Nast. New York: Oxford University Press, 1975. 214

Kelley, Robert. "Ideology and Political Culture from Jefferson to Nixon." The American Historical Review, LXXXII (June 1977). 205

Kelly, Alfred and Winfred Harbison. The American Constitution - Its Origin and Development. New York: Norton & Co., 1976. 348

*Kelly, Kevin. Youth, Humanism and Technology. New York: Basic Books, 1972. 313

Kelly, Mary, ed. Woman's Being, Woman's Place. Boston: Hll, 1979. 551

Kelly, R. Gordon. "Literature and the Historian." American Quarterly, 26 (May 1974). 502

Kelsey, D.P., ed. Farming in the New Nation: Interpreting American Agriculture, 1790-1840. Washington, D.C.: Agricultural History Society, 1972. 76

Kemble, Robert C. The Image of the Army Officer in America: Background for Current Views. Westport, Connecticut: Greenwood Press, 1973. 282

Kendrick, Alexander. Prime Time: The Life of Edward R. Murrow. Boston: Little Brown, 1969. 222

*Keniston, Kenneth. All Our Children: The American Family Under Pressure. New York: Harcourt, Brace Jovanovich, 1978. 443

*Kennan, George F. American Diplomacy, 1900-1950. Chicago: University of Chicago Press, 1951. 127

_____. Soviet-American Relations, 1917-1920. 2 vols. Princeton: Princeton University Press, 1956-1958. 122

Kennedy, Arthur G. A Bibliography of Writings on the English Language from the Beginning of Printing to the End of 1922. 1927; New York: Hafner, 1961. 257

_____ and Donald B. Sands. A Concise Bibliography for Students of English. Stanford: Stanford University Press, 1972. 257

Kennedy, John Fitzgerald. The Kennedy Presidential Press Conference. New York: E.M. Coleman Enterprises, 1978. 437

Kennedy, Paul. The Samoan Tangle: A Study in Anglo-German-American Relations, 1878-1900. New York: Barnes & Noble, 1974. 119

Kennedy, Susan E. The Banking Crisis of 1933. Lexington: University Press of Kentucky, 1973. 85

Kennedy, Susan Estabrook. If All We Did Was to Weep at Home: A History of White Working-Class Women in America. Bloomington: Indiana University Press, 1980. 451, 547

Kent, George E. "Maya Angelou's I Know Why the Caged Bird Sings and Black Autobiographical Tradition." Kansas Quarterly, 7 (Summer 1975). 398

Kenyon, John S. American Pronunciation. Ann Arbor: George Wahr, 1924, 1954. 263

Kerber, Linda. Daughters of Columbia: American Women in the Era of American Revolution. Iowa City: University of Iowa Press, 1975. 536

_____. " The Republican Mother: Women and the Enlightment - An American Perspective." American Quarterly, XXVIII (Summer 1976). 543

Kero, Reino. Migration from Finland to North America in the Years Between the United States Civil War and the First World War. Turku, Finland: Migration Studies C 1, Institute for Migration, 1974. 193

Kerr, Elizabeth and Ralph M. Aderman. Aspects of American English. New York: Harcourt, Brace, Jovanovich, 1971. 260

Kerr, Walter. The Decline of Pleasure. New York: Simon and Schuster, 1962. 311

Kessler-Harris, Alice. "Stratifying by Sex: Understanding the History of Working Women." Richard C. Edwards, et.al. Labor Market Segmentation. Lexington: Heath, 1975. 547

_____. "Where are the Organized Women Workers." Feminist Studies, 3 (Fall 1975). 547

*Kessner, Thomas. The Golden Door: Italian and Jewish Immigrant Mobility in New York City, 1880-1915. New York:Oxford, 1977. 197, 385

*Kesterson, David B. Bill Nye: The Western Writings. Boise, Idaho: Boise State University, 1970. 415

*_____. Critics on Mark Twain. Coral Gables, Florida: University of Miami Press, 1979. 410

Ketchum, Richard M. The World of George Washington. New York: American Heritage Publishing Co., 1974. 424

Kher, Inder N. The Landscape of Absence: Emily Dickinson's Poetry. New Haven: Yale University Press, 1974. 411

*Kherdian, David. Six San Francisco Poets. Fresno: The Giligian Press, 1969. 344

*Kidney, Walter C. The Architecture of Choice: Eclecticism in America, 1880-1930. New York: Braziller, 1974. 43

Kidwell, Claudia B. and Margaret C. Christman. Suiting Everyone: The Democratization of Clothing in America. Washington, D.C.: Smithsonian Institution, 1974. 508

Kilham, Walter H., Jr. Raymond Hood, Architect. New York: Architectural Book Publishing Co., 1973. 45

Killian, James Rhyne, Jr. Sputnik, Scientists, and Eisenhower: A Memoir of the First Special Assistant to the President for Science and Technology. Cambridge: M.I.T. Press, 1977. 437

Kilpatrick, Thomas L. and Patsy-Rose Hoshiko. Illinois! Illinois! An Annotated Bibliography of Fiction. Metuchen, New Jersey: The Scarecrow Press, 1979. 521

Kimball, Fiske. American Architecture. 1928; New York: AMS Press. 30, 33, 42

*_____. Domestic Architecture of the American Colonies. 1922; New York: Dover, 1966. 30, 33, 36

_____. Thomas Jefferson, Architect. 1916; New York: Da Capo Press, 1968. 29, 38,45

Kimball, Stanley B., ed. Slavic-American Imprints: A Classified Catalog. Edwardsville, Illinois: Lovejoy Library, Southern Illinois University, 1972. 192

Kimberly, Charles M. "The Depression in Maryland: The Failure of Voluntarism."
    Maryland Historical Magazine, LXX (Summer 1975). 88

Kime, Wayne R. Pierre M. Irving and Washington Irving: A Collaboration in Life
    and Letters. Waterloo, Ontario: Wilfrid Laurier University Press, 1977. 413

Kin, Sung Bok. Landlord and Tenant in Colonial New York: Manorial Society, 1664-
    1775. Chapel Hill: University of North Carolina Press, 1978. 65

*Kindleberger, Charles P. The World in Depression, 1929-1939. Berkeley: University
    of California Press, 1975.   85

Kineley, Phillip. The Chicago Tribune: Its First Hundred Years, Vol. 1, 1847-
    1865; Vol. II, 1865-1880; Vol. III, 1880-1900. Chicago: The Chicago Tribune Co.,
    1943, 1945, 1946. 214

*Kingston, Maxine Hong. The Woman Warrior. New York: Random, 1977. 389

Kinnard, Douglas. President Eisenhower and Strategy Management: A Study in Defense
    of Politics. Lexington: University Press of Kentucky, 1977.

*Kinsella, William E., Jr. Leadership in Isolation: FDR and the Origins of the
    Second World War. Cambridge: Schenkman, 1980. 138, 435

Kirby, E.T. "The Shamanistic Origins of Popular Entertainments." The Drama Review,
    18, 1 (March 1974). 502

Kirby, Michael, ed. "Popular Entertainments." The Drama Review, 18, 1 (March 1974). 502

*Kirk, Gordon, W., Jr. The Promise of American Life: Social Mobility in a
    Nineteenth-Century Immigrant Community, Holland, Michigan 1847-1894. Philadelphia:
    The American Philosophical Society, 1978. 197

Kirkendall, Richard S., ed. The Truman Period as a Research Field. Columbia:
    University of Missouri Press, 1967. 436

_____. The Truman Period as a Research Field: A Reappraisal, 1972. Columbia:
    University of Missouri Press, 1974. 436

Kirkham, E. Bruce. The Building of Uncle Tom's Cabin. Knoxville, Tennessee:
    University of Tennessee Press, 1977. 416

*Kirkland, Edward C., comp. American Economic History since 1860. New York:
    Appleton-Century Crafts, 1971. 63

Kirkpatrick, John E., ed. Charles E. Ives: Memos. New York: Norton, 1972. 300

Kissinger, Henry. White House Years. Boston: Little, Brown and Company, 1979. 438

Klaczynska, Barbara. "Why Women Work: A Comparison of Various Groups in
    Philadelphia, 1910-30." Labor History, 17 (1976).   551

Klavan, Gene. Turn That Damned Thing Off. Indianapolis: Bobbs-Merrill, 1972. 493, 502

*Klebaner, Benjamin J. Commercial Banking in the United States: A History.
    New York: Kelley, 1974. 72

Klein, Fannie J. The Administration of Justice in the Courts. Dobbs Ferry, New York:
    Oceana Publications, 1976, two volumes. 354

Klein, Janice. "Ann Lee and Mary Baker Eddy: The Parenting of New Religions." Journal of Psychohistory, 6 (Winter 1979). 543

Klein, Maury and Harvey A. Kantor. Prisoners of Progress: American Industrial Cities 1850-1920. New York: Macmillan, 1976. 459

Kleinberg, Susan J. "Technology and Women's Work: The Lives of Working Class Women in Pittsbrugh, 1870-1900." Labor History, 17 (1976). 551

Kleppner, Paul. "Immigrant Groups and Partisan Politics." The Immigration History Newsletter, X (May 1978). 205

Klingaman, David C. and Richard R. Vedder, eds. Essays in Nineteenth Century Economic History: The Old Northwest. Athens: Ohio University Press, 1975. 77

Kluger, Richard. Members of the Tribe. Garden City, New York: Doubleday, 1977. 467

Klurfeld, Herman. Winchell: His Life and Times. New York: Praeger, 1976. 226

*Kneese, Allen and Blair Bower. Environmental Quality and Residuals Management. Baltimore: Johns Hopkins University Press, 1979. 485

_____,eds. Environmental Quality Analysis: Theory and Method in the Social Sciences. Baltimore: Johns Hopkins University Press, 1972. 474

Knight, Oliver, ed. I Protest: Selected Disquisitions of E.W. Scripps. Madison: University of Wisconsin Press, 1966. 216

*Knightley, Philip. The First Casualty. New York: Harcourt, Brace & Jovanovich 1976. 222

*Kocka, Jurgen. White-Collar Workers in America, 1890-1940: A Socio-Political History in International Persepctive.   Beverly Hills: Sage, 1979. 449

*Koeper, Frederick. Illinois Architecture. Chicago: University of Chicago Press, 1968. 44

Kogan, Herman. "William Perkins Black: Haymarket Lawyer." Chicago History, 5 (1976). 527

Kohlmeier, Louis. God Save This Honorable Court. New York: Scribners, 1973. 352

Kohlstedt, Sally Gregory. "In From the Periphery: American Women in Science, 1830-1880." Signs, 4 (Autumn 1978). 548

Koistinen, Paul A.C. "The 'Industrial-Military Complex' in Historical Perspective: The Inter-War Years." Journal of American History, LXV (March 1970). 83

_____."The 'Industrial-Military Complex' in Historical Perspective: World War I." Business History Review, XLIV (Winter 1967). 83

Kolko, Gabriel. The Politics of War: The World and United States Foreign Policy, 1943-1945. New York: Random House, 1968. 128, 175

*_____. Railroads and Regulation, 1877-1916. New York: Norton, 1970. 81

*_____. The Triumph of Conservatism: A Reinterpretation of American History, 1900-1916. Glencoe: Free Press, 1977. 81

Kolko, Joyce and Gabriel. The Limits of Power: The World and United States Foreign Policy, 1945-1954.   New York: Harper and Row, 1973. 85, 128

Kolodny, Annette. "Dancing Through the Minefield: Some Observations on the Theory, Practice and Politics of a Feminist Literary Criticism." Feminist Studies, 6 (Spring 1980.)   539

Kolyszko, Edward V. "Preserving Ethnic Records on Microfilm: The Ethnic Records Microform Project." Microform Review, II (October 1973). 203

_____. "Preserving the Polish Heritage in America: The Polish Microfilm Project." Polish American Studies, XXXII (1975).   203

Kornblum, W. The Urban Folk Study: Blue-Collar Community. Chicago: University Press, 1974.   452

Korson, George. Black Rock. Baltimore: The Johns Hopkins Press, 1960. 102

_____. Coal Dust on the Fiddle. 1943; Hatboro: Folklore Associates, 1965. 102

_____. Minstrels of the Mine Patch. 1938; Hatboro: Folklore Associates, 1964.   102

*Kouwvenhoven, John, ed. Leaves of Grass and Selected Prose. New York: Modern Library, 1950. 338

Kramer, Dale. Heywood Brown: A Biographical Portrait. New York: Current Books - A.A. Wynn, 1949.   218

Krapp, George Philip. A Comprehensive Guide to Good English. Chicago: Rand, McNally, 1927. 270

_____. The English Language in America. 1925; New York: Ungar 1960.   258

Kraus, Michael. The Writing of American History. Norman, Oklahoma: University of Oklahoma Press, 1953.   181

*Kraus, Sidney, ed. The Great Debates: Carter vs. Ford, 1976. Bloomington: Indiana University Press, 1979. 440

Kraut, Benny. From Reform Judaism to Ethical Culture. Cincinnati: Hebrew Union, 1979.   385

Kribbs, Jayne K., ed. An Annotated Bibliography of American Literary Periodicals, 1741-1850. Boston: G.K. Hall, 1977.

*Kross, Herman E. Executive Opinion: What Business Leaders Said and Thought on Economic Issues, 1920s - 1960s. Garden City: Doubleday, 1970. 81

_____ and Martin R. Bly. A History of Financial Intermediaries. New York: Random House, 1971.   72

*_____ and Charles Gilbert. American Business History. Englewood Cliffs, New Jersey: Prentice Hall, 1972.   69

*Kruchko, John G. The Birth of a Union Local: The History of UAW Local 674, Norwood, Ohio, 1933-1940. Ithaca: Cornell University, 1972. 449

*Kubler, George. The Art and Architecture of Ancient America. 1962; New York: Penguin, 1983. 36

Kubletz, George A. The Art and Architecture of Ancient America. New York: Viking, 1976.

Kucera, Henry and W. Nelson Francis. Computational Analysis of Present Day American English. Providence: Brown University Press, 1966. 271

*Kucharsky, David. The Man from Plains: The Mind and Spirit of Jimmy Carter. New York: Harper & Row, 1977. 441

Kuhlmann, Susan. Knave, Fool, and Genius: The Confidence Man As He Appears in Nineteenth Century Fiction. Chapel Hill, North Carolina: University of North Carolina Press, 1973. 403

*Kuhn, Thomas. The Structure of Scientific Revolutions. Chicago: University of Chicago Press, 1970. 177

Kuklick, Bruce. Josiah Royce. New York: Bobbs-Merrill Co., 1972. 326

_____. "Myth and Symbol in American Studies." American Quarterly, 24 (October 1972). 181, 502

*_____. The Rise of American Philosophy: Cambridge, Massachusetts, 1860-1930. New Haven: Yale University Press, 1977. 325

Kurath, Hans. "A Bibliography of American Pronunciation, 1888-1928." Language, V (1929). 257

_____. "The Investigation of Urban Speech." PADS, XLIX (1968). 265

_____. Linguistic Atlas of New England. New York: AMS, 1972. 264

_____. A Phonology and Prosody of Modern English. Ann Arbor: University of Michigan Press, 1964. 263

_____. Studies in Area Linguistics. Bloomington, Indiana: Indiana University Press, 1972. 264

_____. A Word Geography of the Eastern United States. Ann Arbor: University of Michigan Press, 1949. 264

_____ et. al. Handbook of the Linguistic Geography of New England. 1939; New York: AMS, 1973. 264

_____, Raven I. McDavid, Jr., Raymond K. O'Cain et. al. Linguistic Atlas of the Middle and South Atlantic States. Chicago: University of Chicago Press, 1979. 264

_____ and Raven I. McDavid, Jr. The Pronunciation of English in the Atlantic States. Ann Arbor: University of Michigan Press, 1961. 264

Kurland, Philip B. Mr. Justice Frankfurter and the Constitution. Chicago: University of Chicago Press, 1971. 349

*_____. Politics, The Constitution, and the Warren Court. Chicago: University of Chicago Press, 1973. 351

Kushner, Howard I. Conflict on the Northwest Coast: American Russian Rivalry in the Pacific Northwest, 1791-1867. Westport, Connecticut: Greenwood Press, 1975. 135

Kusmer, Kenneth L. "The Functions of Organized Charity in the Progressive Era: Chicago as a Case Study." Journal of American History, 60 (December 1973). 87, 528

* _____. A Ghetto Takes Shape: Black Cleveland, 1870-1930. Urbana: University of Illinois, 1976. 463

Kyle, John H. The Building of TVA. Baton Rouge: Louisiana State University Press, 1958. 35, 42

Kyvig, David. "Women Against Prohibition." American Quarterly, XXVIII (Fall 1976).   550

Labov, William. Language in the Inner City. Philadelphia: University of Pennsylvania Press, 1972. 265

_____. The Social Stratification of English in New York City. Washington, D.C.: Center for Applied Linguistics, 1966. 265

_____. Sociolinguistic Patterns. Philadelphia: University of Pennsylvania Press, 1972. 265

Lachs, John, ed. Animal Faith and Spiritual Life. Irvington, 1967. 323

_____ and Shirley, eds. Physical Order and Moral Liberty. 1969. 323

La Cour, Tage and Harald Mogensen. The Murder Book: An Illustrated History of the Detective Story. New York: Mc Graw-Hill, 1971. 56

La Feber, Walter F. America, Russia and the Cold War, 1945-1966. New York: Wiley, 1980. 128

*La Feber, Walter F. The New Empire: An Interpretation of American Expansion, 1860-1898. Ithaca: Cornell University Press, 1963. 85, 119

* _____. The Panama Canal: The Crisis in Historical Perspective. New York: Oxford, 1979. 136

Lagemann, Ellen Condliffe. Generation of Women: Education in the Lives of Progressive Reformers. Cambridge: Harvard University Press, 1979. 543

Laird, Charlton. Language in America. Englewood Cliffs, New Jersey: Prentice-Hall, 1971. 258

Lake, Elizabeth, et. al. Who Pays for Clear Water. Boulder: Westview, 1979. 485

Lamar, Howard R. Dakota Territory. New Haven: Yale University Press, 1956. 174

* _____. The Far Southwest. New York: Norton, 1970. 174

Lamb, Sidney. An Outline of Stratificational Grammar. Washington, D.C.: Georgetown University Press, 1966. 268

Lambert, Gavin. The Dangerous Edge. London: Bavrie and Jenkins, 1975. 59

Lampard, Eric E. The Rise of the Dairy Industry in Wisconsin: A Study in Agricultural Change, 1820-1920. Madison State Historical Society of Wisconsin, 1963. 76

*Lancy, D. F. and B. A. Tindall, eds. The Anthropological Study of Play. Cornwell, New York: Leisure Press, 1976. 502

Land, Aubrey."Economic Behavior in a Planting Society: The Eighteenth-Century Chesapeake." Journal of Southern History, XXXIII (November 1967). 64

Landrum, Larry."Proteus at Bay: Methodology and Popular Culture." Journal of Popular Culture, IV, 2 (Fall 1975). 502

* _____, Pat Browne and Ray B. Browne, eds. Dimensions of Detective Fiction. Bowling Green: Popular Press, 1976. 59

*Lane, Ann J., ed. The Debate Over Slavery: Stanley Elkins and His Critics. Urbana: University of Illinois Press, 1971. 27

Lane, Jack C. "American Military Past: The Need for New Approaches." Military Affairs, 41 (Ocotber 1977). 288

Lang, Kurt. Military Institutions and Sociology of War: A Review of the Literature with Annotated Bibliography. Beverly: Sage, 1972. 280

Lang, Paul Henry, ed. Music in Western Civilization. New York: Norton, 1941. 296

Langer, William L. and S. Everett Gleason. The Challenge to Isolation, 1937-1940. New York: Harper, 1952. 125

_____. The Undeclared War, 1940-1941. New York: Harper, 1953. 125

Langley, Harold D. Social Reform in the United States Navy, 1798-1862. Urbana: University of Illinois Press, 1967. 282

La Penta, Barbara Luigia, trans. The American City: From the Civil War to the New Deal. Cambridge: MIT Press, 1979. 462

Larmouth, Donald W. "Grammatical Interference in American Finnish." Dissertation University of Chicago, 1972. 266

Larrowe, Charles. Harry Bridges: The Rise and Fall of Radical Labor in the United States. Westport, Conn.: Lawrence Hill and Co., 1972. 449

*Larson, Arthur D. Civil-Military Relations and Militarism: A Classified Bibliography Covering the United States and other Nations of the World. Manhattan: Kansas State University Library, 1971. 284

Larson, Henrietta M., Evelyn H. Knowlton and Charles S. Popple. History of Standard Oil (New Jersey): New Horizons, 1927-1950. New York: Harper and Row, 1971. 80

Lasch, Christopher. The New Radicalism in America. New York: Knopf, 1965. 176

Lash, Joseph P. Roosevelt and Churchill, 1939-1941: The Partnership that Saved the West. New York: Norton, 1976. 138, 435

Lattimer, John K. Lincoln and Kennedy: Medical and Ballistic Comparisons of their Assassinations. New York: Harcourt, Brace Jovanovich, 1980. 429

Latner, Richard B. The Presidency of Andrew Jackson: White House Politics, 1829-1837. Athens: University of Georgia Press, 1979. 426

Laughlin, Rosemary. "The American with His Dictionary." Dissertation. University of Chicago, 1968. 270

Laurie, Bruce. Working People of Philadelphia, 1800-1850. Philadelphia: Temple University Press, 1980. 447

Lave, Lester and Eugene Seskin. Air Pollution and Human Health. Baltimore: John Hopkins University Press, 1978. 475

*Lawrence, D. H. Studies in Classic American Literature. 1924; New York: Penquin, 1977. 310

Laws, G. Malcolm. Native American Balladry. Austin: University of Texas Press, 1964. 103

Lawson, Don. FDR's New Deal. New York: Crowell, 1979. 435

*Layman, Emma Mc Cloy. Buddhism in America. Chicago: Nelson and Hall 1976. 384

Lazare, Donald, ed. "Mass Culture, Political Consciousness and English Studies."
    College English, 38, 8 (April 1977).   502

Leab, Daniel J. A Union of Individuals: The Formation of the American Newspaper
    Guild, 1933-1936. New York: Columbia University Press, 1970. 218

*Leamer, Laurence. The Paper Revolutionaries: The Rise of the Underground Press.
    New York: Simon and Schuster, 1972. 222

Leary, Lewis. That Rascal Freneau: A Study in Literary Failure. New Brunswick:
    Rutgers University Press, 1941. 209

_____, ed. Articles on American Literature Appearing in Current Periodicals.
    Durham: Duke University Press, 1979. 406

*Lebeaux, Richard. Young Man Thoreau.New York: Harper and Row, 1978. 416

Lebergott, Stanley. "Labor Force and Employment, 1800-1960." Output, Employment
    and Productivity. New York: Columbia Unviersity Press, 1966. 69

_____. Manpower in Economic Growth: The American Record Since 1800. New York:
    Mc Graw-Hill, 1964.   69

Lee, Alfred M. The Daily Newspaper in America. 1937; New York: Octagon, 1973. 223

Lee, Edna. The Southerners. New York: Appleton-Century Crofts, 1953. 469

Lee, Harry. The Fox in the Attic. New York: Macmillan, 1938. 469

Lee, Hector. The Three Nephites: The Substance and Significance of the Legend in
    Folklore. Albuquerque: University of New Mexico Press, 1949. 98

*Lee, Ronald F. The Origin and Evolution of the National Military Park Idea.
    Washington, D.C.: National Park Service, 1973. 288

Lee, Susan Dye. "Audiovisual Teaching Materials." Signs, 2 (Spring 1977). 545

Leech, Margaret and Harry J. Brown. The Garfield Orbit. New York: Harper and
    Row, 1978.   430

Lees, Robert B. (Review of Chomsky). Language, XXX (1957). 260

Le Feber, William. American Russia and the Cold War, 1945-1966. New York: Wiley,
    1967. 181

_____. The New Empire: An Interpretation of American Expansion, 1860-1898.
    Ithaca: Cornell University Press, 1963.   181

Leffler, Melvyn P. The Elusive Quest: America's Pursuit of European Stability and
    French Security, 1919-1933. Chapel Hill: University of North Carolina Press,
    1979.   137

Leiby, James. Charity and Correction in New Jersey: A History of State Welfare
    Institutions. New Brunswick: Rutgers University Press, 1967. 87

Legner, Linda, comp. City House: A Guide to Renovating Older Chicago-Area Houses.
    Chicago: Commission on Chicago Historical and Architectural Landmarks, 1979. 531

*Lekachman, Robert. The Age of Keynes. New York: Mc Graw-Hill, 1975. 84

Lemisch, J. "The American Revolution Seen From the Bottom Up." B.J. Bernstein ed. Toward a New Past: Dissenting Essays in American History. New York: Pantheon, 1968. 181

*Lemon, James T. The Best Poor Man's Country: A Geographical Study of Early Southeastern Pennsylvania. New York: Norton, 1976. 65

_____ and Gary B. Nash. "The Distribution of Wealth in Eighteenth-Century America: A Century of Change in Chester Country, Pennsylvania 1693-1802." Journal of Social History, II (Fall 1968). 89

Lenin, V. I. Sociology and Statistics. Moscow: Progress Pub. 21

Leonard, Sterling A. Current English Usage. Chicago: NCTE, 1932. 270

Leone, Mark P. Roots of Modern Mormonism. Cambridge: Harvard University Press, 1979. 382

*Leopold, Aldo. Sand Country Almanac. New York: Oxford University Press, 1948. 471

*Lerner, Gerda. The Female Experience: An American Documentary. Indianapolis: Bobbs-Merrill Co., 1977. 536

_____ . The Majority Finds its Past: Placing Women in History. New York: Oxford University Press, 1979. 551

_____ . "New Approaches to the Study of Women." In Berenice A. Carroll, ed. Liberating Women's History. Urbana: University of Illinois Press, 1976. 545

Lerner, Max. The Mind and Faith of Justice Holmes. Boston: Little Brown Co., 1943. 349

Lester, Richard I. Confederate Finance and Purchasing in Great Britain. Charlottesville: University of Virginia Press, 1975. 134

Lesy, Michael. Wisconsin Death Trip. New York: Pantheon, 1973. 174

Letwin, William. Law and Economic Policy in America: The Evolution of the Sherman Antitrust Act. Chicago: University of Chicago Press, 1981. 82

Leutze, James R. Bargaining for Supremacy: Anglo-American Naval Collaboration, 1937-1941. Chapel Hill: University of North Carolina Press, 1977. 137

Levering, Ralph. American Opinion and the Russian Alliance, 1939-1945. Chapel Hill: University of North Carolina Press, 1976. 139

Levi, Dean Edward. "The Nature of Judicial Reasoning". 32 University of Chicago Law Review 395 (1965). 352

Levin, David. Cotton Mather: The Young Life of the Lord's Remembrancer, 1663-1703. Cambridge: Harvard University Press, 1978. 370

_____ . History as Romantic Art. Stanford: Stanford University Press, 1959. 181

Levin, Murray. Political Hysteria in America: The Democratic Capacity for Repression. New York: Basic Books, 1971. 309

*Levin, Norman Gordon Jr. Woodrow Wilson and World Politics: America's Response to War and Revolution. New York: Oxford University Press, 1968. 122

Levin, Robert B. "An Interpretation of American Imperialism." Journal of Economic History, XXXII (March 1972).

Levine, Arthur. Handbook on Undergraduate Curriculum. San Francisco: Jossey-Bass, 1978. 444

*Levine, Lawrence W. Black Culture and Black Consciousness. New York: Oxford University Press, 1978. 107

Levine, Stuart and Susan Levine. The Short Fiction of Edgar Allan Poe. Indianapolis, Indiana: Bobbs-Merrill, 1976. 415

*Levitan, Sar A. and Robert Taggart. The Promise of Greatness. Cambridge: Harvard University Press, 1976. 88

*Levy, Leonard W. Against the Law: The Nixon Court and Criminal Justice. New York: Harper and Row, 1974. 351

*_____. Judicial Review and the Supreme Court: Selected Essays. New York: Harper and Row, 1967. 351

_____. Legacy of Suppression. Cambridge: Harvard University Press, 1960. 208

*Le Warne, Charles. Utopias and Puget Sound, 1885-1915. Seattle: University of Washington Press, 1978. 516

*Lewis, Anthony. Gideon's Trumpet. New York: Random House, 1964. 353

_____."Supreme Court Confidential." The New York Review of Books, February 7, 1980, p.3 . 355

Lewis, Diane K. "A Response to Inequality: Black Women, Racism and Sexism." Signs, 3 (Winter 1977). 543

*Lewis, George H., ed. Side-Saddle on the Golden Calf: Social Structures and Popular Culture in America. Pacific Palisades: Goodyear, 1972. 492, 503

Lewis, Kenneth E. Camden: A Frontier Town. Columbia: University of South Carolina, 1976. 290

Lewis, Peirce. "Common Houses, Cultural Spoor." Landscape, 19 (1975). 420

*_____. New Orleans: The Makings of an Urban Landscape. Cambridge, Mass.: Ballinger, 1976. 420

_____. "Small Town in Pennsylvania." Annals (June 1972). 420

_____. "The Unprecedented City." Alexix Doster III, ed. The American Land. Washington: The Smithsonian Intitution, 1979. 420

*Lewis, R.W.B. The American Adam. Chicago: University of Chicago Press, 1955. 170

Lewis, W. David and Wesley Phillips Newton. Delta: The History of an Airline. Athens: University of Georgia, 1979. 467

*Lewy, Guenter. America in Vietnam. New York: Oxford, 1980. 140

Ley, David and Roman Cybriwsky. "Urban Graffiti as Territorial Markers." Annals (December 1974). 421

*Lichty, Lawrence W. and Malachi C. Topping. American Broadcasting: A Source Book on the History of Radio and Television. New York: Hastings House, 1975. 228

Lighter, Jonathan. "The Slang of the American Expeditionary Forces in Europe 1917-1919: An Historical Glossary." American Speech, XLVII. 262

Lindberg-Seyersted, Brita. Emily Dickinson's Punctuation. Oslo, Norway: University of Oslo, 1976. 411

*Lindblom, Charles E. and David K. Cohen. Usuable Knowledge: Social Science and Social Problem Solving. New Haven: Yale, 1979. 458

Lindert, Peter H. and Jeffrey G. Williamson. "Three Centuries of American Inequality." Research in Economic History, I (1976). 88

Lindstrom, Diane. Economic Development in the Philadelphia Region, 1810-1850. New York: Columbia University Press, 1978. 74

Lingenfelter, Richard. The Hardrock Miners: A History of the Mining Labor Movement in the American West, 1863-1893. Berkeley: University of California Press, 1974. 448

Link, Arthur S., ed. The Papers of Woodrow Wilson, 35 vols. Princeton: Princeton University Press, 1966. 432

*Linkh, Richard M. American Catholicism and European Immigrants, 1900-1924. New York: Center for Migration Studies, 1975. 200, 384

Linneman, William R. Richard Hovey. Boston: G.K. Hall. 1976. 412

Lippman, Theo. The Squire of Warm Springs: F.D.R. in Georgia, 1924-1945. Chicago: Playboy Press, 1977. 435

*Lipset, Seymour Martin. The First New Nation: The United States in Historical and Comparative Perspective. New York: Norton, 1979. 309

Lipsey, Robert. Price and Quantity Trends in the Foreign Trade of the United States. Princeton: Princeton University Press, 1963. 86

Lisio, Donald J. The President and Protest: Hoover, Conspiracy and the Bonus Riot. Columbia: University of Missouri Press, 1974. 434

Litoff, Judy Barret. American Midwives 1860 to the Present. Westport, Connecticut: Greenwood Press, 1978. 548

*Little, David. Religion, Order and Law: A Study in Pre-Revolutionary England. New York: Harper and Row, 1969. 367

*Little, Malcolm. The Autobiography of Malcolm X. New York: Ballantine, 1977. 10, 22, 389, 982, 393, 395

*Litwack, Leon F. North of Slavery: The Negro in the Free States, 1790-1860. Chicago: University of Chicago Press, 1965. 13

Liu, William T. and Nathaniel J. Pallone, eds. Catholics U.S.A.: Perspectives on Social Change. New York: Wiley, 1970. 385

*Livesay, Harold C. Andrew Carnegie and the Rise of Big Business. Boston: Little Brown, 1975. 80

_____. Merchants and Manufacturers: Studies in the Changing Structure of Nineteenth- Century Marketing. Baltimore: John Hopkins University Press, 1971. 72

_____. Samuels Gompers and Organized Labor in America. Boston: Little Brown, 1978. 448

Livingston, Dorothy M. The Master of Light: A Biography of Albert A. Michelson. New York: Scribners, 1973. 530

Llewellyn, Karl. Jurisprudence: Realism in Theory and Practice. Chicago: University of Chicago Press, 1962. 354

*Locke, Alain. The New Negro. 1925; New York: Atheneum, 1968. 22

*Lockridge, Kenneth A. A New England Town: The First Hundred Years. New York: Norton, 1970. 65, 171

Loewenberg, Bert J. American History in American Thought: Christopher Columbus to Henry Adams. New York: Simon and Schuster, 1972. 181

Logsdon, Joseph. Horace White: Nineteenth Century Liberal. Westport: Greenwood, 1971. 214

Lohoff, Bruce A. "Popular Culture: The Journal and the State of the Study." Journal of Popular Culture, 6 (1972). 503

Lohr, Lenox R. Fair Management, The Story of a Century of Progress Exposition. Chicago: Cueno Press, 1952. 532

Lombard, Charles M. Thomas Holley Chivers. Boston: G.K.Hall, 1979. 410

Long, Robert Emmet. The Great Succession: Henry James and the Legacy of Hawthorne. Pittsburgh, Pennsylvania: University of Pittsburgh Press, 1979. 413

Longford, Frank Pakenham. Kennedy. London: Weidenfeld and Nicolson, 1976. 437

Lord, Donald C. John F. Kennedy: The Politics of Confrontation and Conciliation. Woodbury, New York: Banon's, 1977. 437

Louis, William R. Imperialism at Bay: The United States and the Decolonization of the British Empire, 1941-1945. New York: Oxford, 1978. 139

Love, Robert W. Jr, ed. Changing Interpretations and New Sources in Naval History. New York: Garland Publishing Inc., 1980. 289

Lovell, John, Jr. Black Song-The Forge and the Flame. New York: Macmillan, 1972. 107

Lovett, Robert W., ed. American Economic and Business History Information Sources. Detroit: Gale Research Company, 1971. 63

*Lovins, Amory. Soft Energy Paths: Toward a Durable Peace. New York: Harper and Row, 1979. 474

Loving, Jerome M., Walt Whitman's Companion: William Douglas O'Connor. College Station, Texas: Texas A & M University Press, 1977. 415

_____, ed. Civil War Letters of George Washington Whitman. Durham, North Carolina: Duke University Press, 1975. 417

Lovoll, Odd Sverre. A Folk Epic: The Bydelag in America. Boston: Twayne, 1975. 201

_____ and Kenneth O. Björk. The Norwegian American Historical Association, 1925-1975. Northfield, Minn.: 1975. 203

*Lowe, David. Chicago Interiors: Views of a Splendid World. Chicago: Contemporary Books, 1979. 531

*_____. Lost Chicago. Boston: Houghton Mifflin, 1975. 531

Lowenheim, Francis L., et. al, eds. Roosevelt and Churchill: Their Secret Wartime Correspondence. New York: Saturday Review Press, 1975. 434

Lowens, Irving. Bibliography of Songsters Printed in America Before 1821. Charlottesville: University of Virginia Press, 1977. 303

_____. Music and Musicians in Early America. New York: Norton, 1964. 298

Lowenthal, Abraham F. The Dominican Intervention. Cambridge: Harvard University Press, 1972. 131

*Lowi, Theodore J. The End of Liberalism: The Second Republic of the United States. New York: W.W. Norton, 1979. 357

Lowrie, Ernest B. The Shape of the Puritan Mind: The Thought of Samuel Willard. New Haven: Yale University Press, 1974.

*Lubove, Roy. The Professional Altruist: The Emergence of Social Work as a Career, 1880-1930. New York: Atheneum, 1969. 86

_____. The Struggle for Social Security, 1900-1935. Cambridge: Harvard University Press, 1968. 87

Lucas, Paul R. Valley of Discord: Church and Society Along the Connecticut River, 1636-1725. Hanover: University Press of New England. 369

*Luebke, Frederick C. Bonds of Loyalty. German - Americans and World War I. Dekalb: Northern Illinois University Press, 1974. 200

_____. "Ethnic Group Settlement on the Great Plains." The Western Historical Quarterly, VII (October 1977). 205

Luken, Ralph and Edward Pechan. Water Pollution Control: Assessing the Impacts and Costs of Environmental Standards. New York: Praeger, 1977. 475

Lum, William Wong and Paul M. Ong, comps. Theses and Dissertations on Asians in the United States. Asian American Research Project, University of California, Davis, 1974. 189

Luskin, John. Lippmann, Liberty and the Press. University: University of Alabama Press, 1972. 218

Lusky, Louis. By What Right? A Commentary on the Supreme Court's Power to Revise the Constitution. Charlottesville, Va.: Michie Co., 1975. 351

Luxon, Norval Neil. Niles Weekly Register: News Magazine of the Nineteenth Century. 1947; Wetsport: Greenwood. 209

Lyman, Theodore, Jr. The Diplomacy of the United States. Boston: Wellsand Lilly, 1926. 112

Lynd, Staughton. Class Conflict, Slavery and the United States Constitution. Westport: Greenwood, 1980. 176

_____. Intellectual Origins of American Radicalism. New York: Pantheon, 1968. 175

*Lyon, Elijah Wilson. Louisiana in French Diplomacy, 1759-1804. Norman: University of Oklahoma Press, 1934. 115

Lyon, Peter. Eisenhower: Portrait of the Hero. Boston: Little Brown, 1974. 437

_____. Success Story: The Life and Times of S.S. McClure. New York: Scribner's, 1963. 217

Lyon, William H. The Pioneer Editor in Missouri, 1808-1860.Columbia: University of Missouri Press, 1965. 211

McAdoo, B. Pre-Civil War Black Nationalism. Newark: Peoples' War, 1977. 21

McAleer, John. Rex Stout: A Biography. Boston: Little Brown, 1977. 61

_____. "The Games Afoot: Detective Fiction in the Present Day." Kansas Quarterly 10 (1978). 59

MacAvoy, Paul W. The Economic Effect of Regulations: The Trunk-Line Railroad Cartels and the Interstate Commission Before 1900. Cambridge: M.I.T. Press,1965. 82

McAvoy, Thomas T. History of the Catholic Church in the United States. South Bend: Notre Dame University Press, 1969. 365

*McCaffrey, Lawrence J. The Irish Diaspora in America. Bloomington: Indiana University Press, 1978. 195

McCallum, John. Dave Beck. Mercer Island, Washington: Writings Works, Inc., 1978. 450

*MacCann, Richard Dyer. The Peoples Films: A Political History of U.S. Government Motion Pictures. New York: Hastings House, 1973. 220

McCarthy, Michael P. "Chicago Businessmen and the Plan." Journal of the Illinois State Historical Society, 63 (Autumn 1970). 532

_____. "On Bosses,Reformers and American Cities." Journal of Urban History, 4 (1977). 520

_____. "Politics and the Parks: Chicago Businessmen and the Recreation Movement." Journal of the Illinois Historical Society, 65 (1972). 532

McClelland, Peter D. Casual Explanation and Model Building in History, Economics and the New Economic History. Ithaca: Cornell University Press, 1975. 63

_____. "The Cost to America of British Imperial Policy. " American Economic Review, LIX (May 1969). 65

*McCloskey, Robert G. The American Supreme Court. Chicago: University of Chicago Press, 1960. 348

* _____. The Modern Supreme Court. Cambridge: Harvard Unviersity Press, 1972. 351

McCluskey, Sally. "Black Elk Speaks-And So Does John Neihardt." Western American Literature, 6 (Winter 1972). 396, 399

McColgan, Kristin. Henry James (1917-1959): A Reference Guide. Boston: G.K.Hall, 1979. 413

McConnell, Ruth E. Our Own Voice: Canadian English and How it is Studied. Toronto: Gage, 1979. 258

*McCormick, Donald. Who's Who in Spy Fiction. New York: Taplinger, 1978. 56

McCormick, Rory. Americans Against Man. New York: Corpus Books, 1970. 309

McCormick, Thomas J. China Market: America's Quest for Informal Empire, 1893-1901. Chicago: Quadrangle, 1967. 121

McCoy, Donald R. and Richard T. Ruetten. Quest and Response: Minority Rights and the Truman Administration. Lawrence: University Press of Kansas, 1973. 436

MacCraken, Henry Noble. Prolongue to Independence: The Trials of James Alexander, 1715-1756. New York: James H. Heineman, 1964. 208

McCraw, Thomas K. "Regulation in America: A Review Article." Business History Review, XLIX (Summer 1975). 82

McCubbin, Hamilton I. , Barbara B. Dahl and Edna J. Hunter, eds.Families in the Military System.Beverly: Sage, 1976. 281

McCullough, David G. The Path Between the Seas: The Creation of the Panama Canal, 1870-1914. New York: Simon and Schuster, 1977. 136

McCurdy, Charles W. "American Law and the Marketing Structure of the Large Corporation, 1875-1890." Journal of Economic History, XXXVIII (September 1978). 92

McCusker, John J. Money and Exchange in Europe and America, 1600-1775: A Handbook. Chapel Hill: University of North Carolina Press, 1977. 64

*McDaniel, Judith. Reconstituting the World: The Poetry and Vision of Adrienne Rich. Argyle, New York: Spinster's Ink, 1979. 540

McDavid, Raven I., Jr. "American English Dialects."W. Nelson Francis. The Structure of American English. New York: Ronald, 1958. 264

_____. Dialects in Culture. University, Alabama: University of Alabama Press, 1979. 264

_____. "The English Language in the United States." Thomas R. Sebeok. Trends in Linguistics. The Hague: Mouton, 1973. 257, 271

_____. "Hans Kurath." Orbis, IX (1960). 257

_____."Historical, Regional and Social Variation." Journal of English Linguistics, I (1967). 265, 270

_____. Varieties of American English. Stanford: Stanford University Press, 1979. 257, 264

_____and Glenda Prichett. A Bibliography of the Speech of the North-Central States. Chicago: Linguistics Atlas of the North-Central States, 1976. 257

_____and Audrey R. Duckert. Lexicography in English: Transactions of the New York Academy of Sciences , 211 (1973). 260

McDavid, Virginia. "Verb Forms in the North-Central States and Upper Midwest." Dissertation.University of Minnesota, 1956. 264

*McDermott, John J. The Culture of Experience: Philosophical Essays in the American Grain. New York: New York University Press, 1976. 326

_____, ed. The Basic Writings of Josiah Royce. Chicago: University of Chicago Press, 1969. 320

*_____. The Philosophy of John Dewey. New York: 1973. 321

_____. The Writings of William James. Chicago: University of Chicago Press, 1977. 319

McDonald, Donna, comp. and ed. Directory Historical Societies and Agencies in the United States and Canada, 10th ed., 1975-1976.Nashville, Tenn.: American Association for State and Local History, 1975. 204

*McDonald, Forest. The Presidency of George Washington. New York: Norton, 1975. 424

_____. The Presidency of Thomas Jefferson. Lawrence: University of Kansas, 1976.42£

MacDonald, Ross. "Down These Streets a Mean Man Must Go." Antaeus, 25/26 (1977). 60

_____. The Green Ripper. New York, 1980. 54

_____. On Crime Writing. Santa Barbara: Capra Press, 1973. 60

McEwen, F.L. and G.R. Stephenson. The Use and Significance of Pesticides in the Environment. New York: Wiley, 1979. 485

*MacFarlane, A.D.J. Witchcraft in Tudor and Stuart England. New York: Harper and Row, 1970. 369

McFeely, William S. Grant: A Biography. New York: W.W. Norton and Co.Inc., 1981.

McGee, J. Sears. The Godly Man in Stuart England. New Haven: Yale University Press, 1976.

McGiffert, Michael. "American Puritan Studies in the 1960s ." William and Mary Quarterly, XXVII (June 1970). 388

McGouldrick, Paul K. New England Textiles in the Nineteenth Century: Profits and Investment. Cambridge: Harvard University Press, 1968. 75

McGrath, Kristin S. "American Values and the Slums: A Chicago Case Study." Unpublished Dissertation. University of Minnesota, 1977. 520, 528

MacGregor, Morris and Bernard Nalty, eds. Blacks in the United States Armed Forces: Basic Documents. Wilmington, Delaware: Scholarly Resources Inc., 1977.

*Macklin, Milton. Atlanta. New York: Avon, 1979. 468

McIntosh, James. Thoreau as Romantic Naturalist: His Shifting Stance Toward Nature. Ithaca, New York: Cornell University Press, 1974. 416

McJimsey, George T. Genteel Partisan: Manton Marble, 1834-1917. Ames: Iowa State University Press, 1971. 215

*McKay, Claude. Selected Poems. 1953; New York: Harcourt, Brace, Jovanovich, 1969. 21

_____. Home to Harlem. 1928; New York: Chatham, 1973. 21

McKay, David and Richard Crawford. William Billings of Boston: Eighteenth-Century Composer. Princeton: Princeton University Press, 1975. 298

McKee, Delber L. Chinese Exclusion Versus the Open Door Policy, 1900-1906: Clashes over China Policy in the Roosevelt Era. Detroit: Wayne State University Press, 1977. 136, 431

McKee, John D. William Allen White: Maverick on Main Street. Westport: Greenwood, 1975. 218

McKerns, Joseph P. "The Limits of Progressive Journalism History." Journalism History, 4 (Autumn 1977). 224

Mackethan, Lucinda H. The Dream of Arcady: Place and Time in Southern Literature. Baton Rouge, Louisiana: Louisiana State University Press, 1980. 403

McKim and Head. Monograph of the Works of McKim, Mead and White,1887-1915.
    1915; New York: Benjamin Blom, 1973.

*MacKinnon, Catherine. Sexual Harassment of Working Women: A Case of Sex
    Discrimination. New Haven: Yale University Press, 1979. 548

McKissick, Floyd. Three-Fifths of a Man. New York: Macmillan, 1969. 14

McLaws, Monte Durr. Spokesman for the Kingdom: Early Mormon Journalism and the
    Deseret News, 1830-1898. Provo: Brigham Young University Press, 1977. 226

McLean, Hulda H.Geneology of the Herbert Hoover Family. Stanford, California:
    Hoover Institution Press, 1967. 434

_____. Geneology of the Herbert Hoover Family: Errata and Addenda   Stanford,
    California: Hoover Institution, 1976. 434

MacLeish, Andrew. Studies for Harold B. Allen. Minneapolis: University of
    Minnesota Press, 1979. 260

McLoughlin, William G. The Meaning of Henry Ward Beecher. New York: Knopf, 1970. 379

_____. New England Dissent, 1630-1833, 2 vols. Cambridge: Harvard University
    Press, 1971. 370

*_____ and Robert N. Bellah, eds. Religion in America. Boston: Beacon, 1968. 386

McMaster, John Bach.History of the People of the United States, 8 vols. 1883-1913;
    New York: Appleton, 1927. 157

McMillan, James B. "American Lexicology, 1956-1973." American Speech, LIII. 257

_____. Annotated Bibliography of Southern American English. Coral Gables,
    Florida: University of Miami Press, 1971. 257

McMurty, Larry. In a Narrow Grave: Essays on Texas. Austin: Encino Press, 1968. 55

McNeil, William H. America, Britain and Russia: Their Cooperation and Conflict,
    1941-1946. London: Oxford University Press, 1953. 128

*McPhee, John. Coming into the Country. New York: Bantom. 473

Macris, James. "Changes in the Lexicon of New York City Greek." American Speech,
    XXXII (1967). 267

_____. "English Loanwords in New York City Greek." Dissertation. Columbia
    University, 1955. 267

McSeveny, Samuel T. "Ethnic Group, Ethnic Conflicts and Recent Quantitative
    Research in American Political History." International Migration Review,VII
    (Spring 1973). 205

_____. The Politics of Depression: Political Behavior in the North West,
    1893-1896. New York: Oxford University Press, 1972. 200

*MacShane, Frank. The Life of Raymond Chandler.New York: Penquin, 1978. 60

McWilliams, John P., Jr. Political Justice in a Republic: James Fenimore Cooper's
    America. Berkeley, California: University of California Press, 1973. 410

Maddex, Diane. Historic Building of Washington D.C. Pittsburgh: Ober Park
    Associates, 1973.

Madison, James H. "The Evolution of Commercial Credit Reporting Agencies in Nineteenth-Century America." Business History Review, XLVII (Summer 1974). 93

Main, Gloria L. "Inequality in Early America: The Evidence from Probate Records of Massachusetts and Maryland." Journal of Interdisciplinary History, VII (Spring 1977). 89

*Main, Jackson T. The Social Structure of Revolutionary America. Princeton: Princeton University Press, 1965. 66

————. "The Distribution of Property in Colonial Connecticut." In James K. Martin, ed. The Human Dimensions of Nation Making. Madison: State Historical Society of Wisconsin, 1976. 89

Mainiero, Lina. American Women Writers: A Critical Reference Guide, 2 vols. New York: Ungar, 1979, 1980. 404

Maker, Lisi-Lone. David Belasco: Naturalism in the American Theatre. Princeton, New Jersey: Princeton University Press, 1975. 409

Malcolm, Henry. Generation of Narcissus. Boston: Little Brown, 1971. 313

Male, Roy R. Enter,Mysterious Stranger: American Cloistral Fiction. Norman, Oklahoma: University of Oklahoma Press, 1979. 403

*Malone, Bill C. Country Music, U.S.A. Austin: University of Texas Press, 1969. 104

*Malone, Dumas. Jefferson and His Time, 5 vols. Boston: Little Brown, 1948-1974. 425

*Manchester, William. American Caesar: Douglas MacArthur, 1880-1964. New York: Dell Publishing, 1979. 291

Mandel, Barrett John. "Full of Life Now." James Olney, ed. Autobiography. Princeton: Princeton University Press, 1980. 390, 396, 397

Mander, Jerry. Four Arguments for the Elimination of Television. New York: Morrow Quill, 1978. 493, 503

*Mandle, Jay. The Roots of Black Poverty: The Southern Plantation Economy after the Civil War. Durham: Duke University Press, 1978. 93

ManKowitz, Wolf. The Extraordinary Mr. Poe: A Biography of Edgar Allan Poe. London: Weidenfeld and Nicholson, 1978. 415

Mann, Dennis Alan. "Ritual in Architecture: The Celebration of Life." Ray B. Browne. Rituals and Ceremonies in Popular Culture. 1980. 503

————, ed. The Arts in a Democratic Society. Bowling Green: Popular Press, 1976. 492, 503

Mansfield, Harvey C., ed. Selected Writings of Thomas Jefferson. Illinois: AHM Publishing Corporation, 1979. 425

*Manson, Grant C. FrankLloyd Wright to 1910: The First Golden Age. New York: Reinhold, 1958. 39, 45, 525

Mantell, Martin E. Johnson, Grant and the Politics of Reconstruction. New York: Columbia University Press, 1973. 429

Manucy, Albert. The Houses of St. Augustine, 1565-1821. St. Augustine: St. Augustine Historical Society, 1962. 38, 44

Manuel, Frank E. and Fritzie. Utopian Thought in the Western World. Cambridge, Mass.: Harvard University Press, 1979. 515

Manwaring, David R. et. al. The Supreme Court as Policy-Maker: Three Studies on the Impact of Judicial Decisions. Carbondale, Illinois: Public Affairs Research Bureau of Southern Illinois University, 1968. 352

Marble, Annie R. From Prentice to Patron: The Life Story of Isaiah Thomas. New York: Appleton-Century Crofts, 1935. 207

Marbut, F.B. News from the Capital: The Story of Washington Reporting. Carbondale: Southern Illinois University Press, 1971. 210

Marchand, Roland C. The American Peace Movement and Social Reform, 1898-1918. Princeton: Princeton University Press, 1972. 123

Marckwardt, Albert H. American English. New York: Oxford Press, 1958. 259

_____. Linguistics in School Programs-National Society for the Study of Education, Yearbook 69, Part II. Chicago: University of Chicago Press, 1970. 260

_____ and Fred G. Walcott. Facts about Current English Usage. New York: Appleton-Century, 1938. 270

*Marcus, Greil. Mystery Train: Images of America in Rock'n Roll Music. New York: Dutton, 1976. 493, 503

Marcus, Jacob R. The Colonial American Jew, 1492-1776, 3 vols. Detroit: Wayne State University Press, 1970. 372

*Marcuse, Herbert. One-Dimensional Man; Studies in the Ideology of Advanced Industrial Society. Boston: Beacon Press, 1964. 311, 496, 503

Margolies, Edward. Which Way Did He Go? The Life and Times of the Private Eye. New York: Holmes and Meier, 1979. 59

Markham, James W. Bovard of the Post-Dispatch. Baton Rouge: Louisiana State University Press, 1954. 218

Marks, Frederick W. Velvet on Iron: The Diplomacy of Theodore Roosevelt. Lincoln: University of Nebraska Press, 1979. 431

Marsden, George M. The Evangelical Mind and the New School Presbyterian Experience. New Haven: Yale University Press, 1970. 377

Marsden, Michael, ed. "The Channels of American Culture: Mass Media and American Studies." American Quarterly, 32,3 (1980). 503

Marsh, Janet. Nature Diary. New York: Morron, 1979. 486

Marsh, Margaret S. "The Anarchist-Feminist Response to the 'Woman Question' in late 19th-Century America." American Quarterly, XXX (Fall 1978). 550

Marshall, Hugh. Orestes Brownson and the American Republic: An Historical Perspective. Washington, D.C.: Catholic University Press, 1971. 409

*Martin, Albro. Enterprise Denied: Origins of the Decline of American Railroad, 1897-1917. New York: Columbia University Press, 1971. 82

_____. James J. Hill and the Opening of the Northwest. New York: Oxford University Press, 1976. 72

_____. "Uneasy Partners: Government-Business Relations in Twentieth-Century American History." Prologue: The Journal of the National Archives, 11 (Summer 1979). 93

Martin, Bernard, ed. Movements and Issues in American Judaism. Westport: Greenwood Press, 1978. 386

Martin, Calvin. Keepers of the Game: Indian-Animal Relationships and the Fur Trade. Berkeley: University of California Press, 1978. 514

*Martin, James K., ed. The Human Dimensions of Nation Making: Essays on Colonial and Revolutionary America. New York: Harper and Row, 1978. 89

Martin, Jay and Gossie H. Hudson, eds. The Paul Laurence Dunbar Reader. New York: Dodd Mead, 1975. 404

Martin, Richard. "Scores of Colleges Add Majors in 'Peace and Conflict Studies'; The Range: Quarrels to War." Wall Street Journal. March 5, 1974. 277

Martindale, Don. American Social Structure. New York: Appleton-Century Crofts, 1960. 309

*Marty, Martin E. A Nation of Behavers. Chicago: University of Chicago Press, 1980. 386

*_____. Religion, Awakening and Revolution. Wilmington: Consortium Books, 1977. 365

*_____. Righteous Empire: The Protestant Experience in America. New York: Harper and Row, 1977. 365

Marvell, Thomas B. Appellate Courts and Lawyers. Westport: Greenwood Press, 1978. 357

Marx, Karl and F. Engels. The Civil War in the U.S. New York: International Publishers, 1961. 21

*Marx, Leo. The Machine in the Garden. New York: Oxford University Press, 1967. 169

Marx, Wesley. The Frail Ocean. New York: Coward, 1967. 475

*Marzio, Peter C., ed. A Nation of Nations. New York: Harper and Row, 1976. 508

Marzolf, Marion. Up From the Footnote: A History of Women Journalists. New York: Hastings House, 1977. 225

Mason, Alpheus Thomas. Brandeis: A Free Man's Life. New York: Viking Press, 1946. 349

_____. Harlan Fiske Stone: Pillar of the Law. New York: Viking Press, 1956. 348

*_____. The Supreme Court from Taft to Warren. Baton Rouge: Louisiana State University Press, 1968. 348

*Mason, Bobbie Ann. The Girl Sleuth: A Feminist Guide. Old Westbury, New York: The Feminist Press, 1975. 59

Mason, Lowell. Musical Letters From Abroad. 1854; New York: Da Capo, 1967. 299

Mason, Mary. "The Other Voice: Autobiographies of Women Writers." James Olney, ed. Autobiography. Princeton: Princeton University Press, 1980. 399

Mather, Anne. "A History of Feminist Periodicals." Journalism History, (Autumn 1974, Winter 1974-75, Spring 1975). 225

Mather, Cotton. Magnalia Christi Americana. 1702; Cambridge: Belknap, 1977. 146

*Mathews, Donald G. Black Religion and American Evangelicalism. Metuchen: Scarecrow Press, 1975.

_____. Religion in the Old South. Chicago: University of Chicago Press, 1979. 376, 378

Mathews, Fred H. Quest for an American Sociology: Robert E. Park and the
    Chicago School. Montreal: McGill-Queens Press, 1977. 530

Mathews, Joseph. Reporting the Wars. 1957; Westport: Greenwood, 1972.   222

Mathews, Mitford M. American Words. Cleveland: Collins-World, 1976.   271

_____. The Beginnings of American English. 1931; Chicago: University of
    Chicago Press, 1963. 260

Matlaw, Myron, ed. American Popular Entertainment. Westport, Connecticut:
    Greenwood Press, 1977. 492

Matles, James. Them and Us. Boston: Beacon Press, 1974. 450

Maurer, David W. The American Confidence Man. Springfield, Illinois: Charles
    C. Thomas, 1974.· 270

_____. "The Argot of the Race Track." Pads, XVI (1951). 270

_____. The Big Con. New York: New American Library, 1962. 270

_____. Kentucky Moonshine. Lexington, Kentucky: Universtiy Press of Kentucky,
    1976. 271

_____ and Victor H. Vogel. Narcotics and Narcotic Addiction. 1954; Springfield,
    Illinois: Charles C. Thomas, 1973. 271

_____. "Whiz Mob." Pads, XXIV (1955). 270

Mause, LLoyd de and Henry Ebel, eds. Jimmy Carter and American Fantasy:
    Psychohistorical Explorations. New York: Two Continents, 1977. 440

May, Ernest R. American Imperialism: A Speculative Essay. New York:Atheneum, 1968. 119

*   . Imperial Democracy: The Emergence of America as a Great Power. New York:
    Harcourt, Brace and World, 1961. 119

_____. The Making of the Monroe Doctrine. Cambridge: Harvard University Press,
    1975. 117

_____. The World War and American Isolation. Cambridge: Harvard University
    Press, 1959. 121

*May, Henry F. The Enlightenment in America. New York: Oxford University Press, 1978.
    375
_____. The Protestant Churches in Industrial America. 1949; New York: Octagon,
    1963.   380

_____. "The Recovery of American Religious History." The American Historical
    Review, LXX (October 1964). 388

*Mayer, Arno J. Political Origins of the New Diplomacy, 1917-1918.New Haven: Yale
    University Press, 1959. 121

_____. Politics and Diplomacy: Containment and Counterrevolution at Versailles,
    1918-1919. New York: Vintage Books, 1967. 122

Mayer, Harold M. and Richard C. Wade. Chicago: Growth of a Metropolis. Chicago:
    University of Chicago Press, 1969. 519

Mayhew, Anne. "A Reappraisal of the Causes of Farm Protest in the United States, 1870-1900." Journal of Economic History, XXXII (June 1970). 76

Mayhew, Katherine. The Dewey School: The Laboratory School of the University of Chicago, 1896-1903. New York: Columbia Press, 1966. 530

Mazlish, Bruce and Edwin Diamond. Jimmy Carter: A Character Portrait. New York: Simon and Schuster, 1979. 441

*Mazmanian, Daniel and Jeanne Nienaber. Can Organizations Change? Washington, D.C.: Brookings Institution, 1979. 484.

Mazzaro, Jerome, ed. Modern American Poetry. New York: David McKay Co., 1970. 344

Mead, Frank S. Handbook of Denominations. Nashville: Abingdon Press, 1980. 363

*Mead, George H. Mind, Self and Society. Chicago: University of Chicago Press, 1936; 1967. 323

*_____. Movements of Thought in the Nineteenth Century. Chicago: University of Chicago Press, 1936; 1972. 323

_____. The Philosophy of the Act. Chicago: University of Chicago Press, 1938. 323

_____. The Philosophy of the Present. Chicago: University of Chicago Press, 1932; 1980. 323

*Mead Rita H. Doctoral Dissertations in American Music: A Classified Bibliography. New York: Institute for American Music., 1974. 298

Mead, Sidney Earl. Nathaniel William Taylor, 1786-1858: A Connecticut Liberal. Chicago: University of Chicago Press, 1942. 377

_____. The Nation with a Soul of a Church. New York: Harper and Row, 1975. 387

_____. The Old Religion in Brave New World. Berkeley: University of California Press, 1977. 387.

*Meadows, Donella H., et. al. Limits to Growth. New York: Universe Books, 1974. 471

Meeks, Carroll L.V. The Railroad Station: An Architectural History. New Haven: Yale University Press, 1965. 40, 45

*Meier, August. Negro Thought in America, 1880-1915: Racial Ideologies in the Age of Booker T. Washington. Ann Arbor: University of Michigan Press, 1966. 27

*_____ and Elliott Rudwick. From Plantation to Ghetto. New York: Hill and Wang, 1976. 27

_____. "Negro Protest at the Chicago World's Fair, 1933-37." Journal of the Illinois State Historical Society, 59 (Summer 1966). 532

*_____, eds. The Making of Black America. New York: Atheneum, 1969. 27

Meikle, Jeffrey. Twentieth Century Limited: Industrial Design in America, 1925-1939. Philadelphia: Temple University Press, 1979. 509

Meinig, Donald. "Environmental Appreciation: Localities as a Humane Art." An Eastern Humanities Review (Winter 1971). 420

*_____. The Interpretation of Ordinary Landscapes. New York: Oxford University Press, 1979. 420

Melendy, H. Brett. Asians in America: Filipinos, Koreans, and East Indians. Boston: Twayne, 1977. 195

*Mellers, Wilfred. Music in a New Found Land. New York: Stonehill, 1975. 503

Mellon, James. The Face of Lincoln. New York: Viking Press, Inc., 1980. 429

Melly, George. Revolt Into Style: The Pop Arts. Garden City, New York: Anchor, 1971. 503

Melosi, Martin V. The Shadow of Pearl Harbor: Political Controversy over the Surprise Attack, 1941-1946. College Station: Texas A & M Press, 1977. 138

Melton, J. Gordon. The Encyclopedia of American Religions, 2 vols. Wilmington: Consortium Books, 1978. 363

Menard, Russell, R. "From Servant to Freeholder: Status Mobility and Property Accumulation in Seventeenth Century Maryland. William and Mary Quarterly, XXX (January, 1973). 66

*Mencher, Samuel. Poor Law to Poverty Program: Economic Security Policy in Britain and the United States. Pittsburgh: University of Pittsburgh Press, 1974. 86

Mencken, Henry Louis. The American Language. 1919; New York: Knopf, 1948. 259

Mendelsohn, Ezra, ed. YIVO Annual of Jewish Social Science, Volume XVI, Essays on the American Jewish Labor Movement. New York: YIVO, 1976. 449

Mendelsohn, Jack. Channing: The Reluctant Radical. 1971; Westport: Greenwood Press, 1980, 382

Mendelson, Wallace. Capitalism, Democracy and the Supreme Court. New York: Appleton Century Crofts, 1960. 348

Mendietta, Geronimo de. Historia Eclesiastica Indiana. 1571; Madrid: Atlas, 1973. 145

Mentz, Iese. Cyclical Fluctuations in the Exports of the United States since 1879. New York: National Bureau of Economic Research, 1967.

Mergen, Bernard. "Blacksmiths and Welders: Identity and Phenomenal Change." Industrial and Labor Relations Review, 25 (April 1972). 452

_____. "Surveying Journals of American Studies." American Studies International Volume 12, #3, 1974. 276

_____. "Work and Play in an Occupation Subculture: American Shipyard Workers, 1917-1977." Michael Salter, ed. Play: Anthropological Perspectives. West Point: Leisure Press, 1978. 452

Merk, Frederick. Fruits of Propaganda in the Tyler Administration. Cambridge: Harvard University Press, 1971. 118, 427

*_____. Manifest Destiny and Mission in American History: A Reinterpretation. New York: Knopf, 1963. 117

*_____. The Monroe Doctrine and American Expansion, 1843 - 1849. New York: Knopf, 1966. 117

_____ . _Slavery and the Annexation of Texas_. New York: Knopf, 1972.

Merli, Frank J. _Great Britain and the Confederate Navy, 1861-1865._ Bloomington: Indiana University Press, 1970. 118

Merrill, Kenneth R. and Robert W. Shahan, eds. _American Philosphy - From Edwards to Quine_. Norman: University of Oklahoma Press, 1977. 326

Merry, Bruce. _Anatomy of the Spy Thriller_. Dublin: Gill and Macmillan, 1977. 61

Mertz, Robert J. and Michael Marsden. "American Culture Studies: A Discipline in Search of Itself." _Journal of Popular Culture_ , IX, 2 (Fall 1975). 503

Merwick, Donna. _Boston Priests, 1848-1910_. Cambridge: Harvard University Press, 1973.

*Merwin, W.S. _The Lice_. New York: Atheneum, 1967. 339

*_____ . _Moving Target_. New York: Atheneum, 1963. 339

Metcalf, Allan. _Chicano English_. Arlington: Center for Applied Linguistics, 1979. 272

Metcalf, E.W., Jr. _Paul Laurence Dunbar: A Bibliography_. Metuchen: Scarecrow, 1975.

Metcalf, R. "Who Should Rule at Home: Native American Politics and Indian-White Relations." _Journal of American History_, (December, 1974). 181

Metzer, Jacob. "Rational Management, Modern Business Practices, and Economics of Scale in the Ante-Bellum Southern Plantations." _Explorations in Economic History_, XII (April 1975). 79

*Meyer, Leonard B. _Music, The Arts, and Ideas_. Chicago: University of Chicago Press, 1969. 301

Meyer, Michael. _Several More Lives to Live: Thoreau's Political Reputation in America_. Westport, Connecticut: Greenwood, 1977. 416

*Meyers, Marvin. _The Jacksonian Persuasion_. Stanford: Stanford University Press, 1960. 169

Meyerstein, Goldie Piroch. "Bilingualism Among American Slovaks." _PADS_, XLVI (1960). 267

_____ . "Selected Problems of Bilingualism Among Immigrant Slovaks." Dissertation. University of Michigan, 1957. 267

*Middlekauf, Robert. _The Mathers: Three Generations of Puritan Intellectuals, 1596-1728_. New York: Oxford University Press, 1976. 171, 369

Miller, Arthur, S. "An Inquiry into the Relevance of the Intentions of the Founding Fathers." 27 _Arkansas Law Review_ 583 (1973). 351

_____ . "Constitutional Law: Crisis Government Becomes the Norm." 39 _Ohio State Law Journal_ 736 (1978). 357

_____. "The Law Journals. Change, 5 (Winter 1973-74). 347

_____. "On the Need for 'Impact Analysis' of Supreme Court Decisions."
53 Georgetown Law Journal. 374 (1965). 352

_____. Presidential Power. St. Paul, Minnesota: West Publishing Co., 1977. 354

_____ Social Change and Fundamental Law: America's Evolving Constitution.
Westport, Conn.: Greenwood Press, 1979. 356

_____. The Supreme Court: Myth and Reality. Westport, Conn.: Greenwood Press,
1978. 347

_____ and Alan W. Scheffin. "The Power of the Supreme Court in the Age of
the Positive State: A Preliminary Excursus." Duke Law Journal 273,522.
(1967). 348

_____ and D.S. Sastri. "Secrecy and the Supreme Court: On the Need for
Piercing the Red Velour Curtain." 22 Buffalo Law Review 799 (1973). 346

_____ and Jerome A. Barron. "The Supreme Court, the Adversary System and the
Flow of Information to the Justices: A Preliminary Inquiry." 61 Virginia
Law Review 1187 (1975). 353

*Miller, David L. George Herbert Mead - Self, Language and the World. Chicago:
University of Chicago Press, 1980. 323, 326

Miller, Edward. U.S.S. Monitor. Annapolis: Leeward, 1979. 480

Miller, Edwin, H., ed. The Collected Writings of Walt Whitman: The Correspondence.
New York: New York University Press,1977. 417

* _____. Melville. New York: Persea, 1976. 415

Miller, Elaine K. Mexican Folk Narrative from the Los Angeles Area. Austin:
University of Texas Press, 1973. 106

Miller, George H. Railroads and the Granger Laws. Madison: University of
Wisconsin Press, 1971. 82

Miller, Howard. The Revolutionary College: American Presbyterian Higher
Education, 1707-1837. New York: New York University Press, 1976. 373

*Miller, Jim, ed. The Rolling Stone Illustrated History of Rock and Roll.
New York: Rolling Stone Press/ Random House, 1976. 305

Miller, John Carl. Building Poe Biography. Baton Rouge, Louisiana: Louisiana
State University Press, 1977.   415

_____. Poe's Helen Remembers. Charlottesville, Virginia: University Press
of Virginia, 1979. 415

Miller, Marc. "Working Women and World War II." The New England Quarterly, 53
(March 1980). 551

*Miller, Merle. Plain Speaking: An Oral Biography of Harry S. Truman. New York: Berkley Publishing Corp, 1980. 436

Miller, Michael I. "Inflectional Morphology in Augusta, Georgia: A Sociolinguistic Description." Dissertation. University of Chicago, 1978. 265

Miller, Nathan. The Enterprise of a Free People: Aspects of Economic Development in New York State During the Canal Period, 1792-1838. Ithaca: Cornell University Press, 1962. 70

Miller, Nory. "Man of Ideas: Chicago's Battle of Architecture." Inland Architect.(March 1976). 531

Miller, Perry. New England Mind. Cambridge: Harvard University Press, 1953. 170

*_____. Orthodoxy in Massachusetts, 1630-1650. New York: Harper and Row, 1970. 170

*Miller, Randall, and Thomas Marzik, eds. Immigrants and Religion in Urban America. Philadelphia: Temple University Press, 1977. 200

Miller, Randolph Crump. The American Spirit in Theology. Philadelphia: United Church Press, 1974. 380

Miller, Robert. Alan. The History of Current Maine Newspapers. Lisbon Falls, Maine: Eastland Press, 1978.

*Miller, Ruth. Black American Literature: 1760 to the Present. New York: Macmillan, 1971. 22

Miller, Sally M. Victor Berger and the Promise of Constructive Socialism, 1910-1920. Westport, Connecticut: Greenwood Press, 1973. 449

Miller, Samuel. A Brief Retrospect of the Eighteenth Century. 2 vols. 1803; New York: B. Franklin, 1970.

Miller, Wayne C., et. al. eds. A Comprehensive Bibliography for the Study of American Minorities. 2 vols. New York: New York University Press, 1976.   189

Miller, Wilbur R. Cops and Bobbies: Police Authority in New York and London. Chicago: University of Chicago Press, 1977. 54

Miller, William Lee. Yankee from Georgia: The Emergence of Jimmy Carter. New York: Time Books, 1978. 441

*Miller, Zane L. The Urbanization of Modern America: A Brief History. New York: Harcourt Brace Jovanovich, 1973. 459

Millett, Allan R. "American Military History: Over the Top." In Herbert J. Bass, ed. The State of American History. Chicago: Quadrangle Books, 1970. 275

_____. "American Military History: Struggling Through the Wire." Washington, D.C.: Military Affairs/Aerospace Historian Press, 1977. 279

Millett, Allan R and B. Franklin Cooling. "Doctoral Dissertations in Military Affairs." Military Affairs (February each year.) 284

*Millis, Walter. Arms and Men: A Study of American Military History. New York: Mentor Paperback, 1958. 274

_____. The Martial Spirit: A Study of Our War with Spain. New York: Houghton Mifflin, 1931. 120

_____. Road to War, 1914-1917. Boston: Houghton Mifflin, 1935. 121

*Mills, C. Wright. The Power Elite. New York: Oxford University Press, 1959. 170

_____. Sociology and Pragmatism. New York: Paine-Whitman, 1964. 326

Mills, Frederick V., Sr. Bishops by Ballot: An Eighteenth Century Ecclesiastical Revolution. New York: Oxford University Press, 1978. 374

Mills, George. Harvey Ingham and Gardner Cowles, Sr.: Things Don't Just Happen. Ames: Iowa State University Press,]977. 226

Mills, Ralph J. Jr. Cry of the Human: Essays on Contemporary American Poetry. Urbana: University of Illinois Press, 1974. 337, 341, 344

Miner, Ward L. William Goddard, Newspaperman. Durham: Duke University Press, 1962. 207

Minger, Ralph E. William Howard Taft and United States Foreign Policy: The Apprenticeship Years 1900-1908. Champaign: University of Illinois Press, 1975. 432

Minter, David. "Conceptions of Self in Black Slave Narratives." American Transcendental Quarterly, 24 (1974). 398

Mintz, Ilse. Cyclical Fluctuations in the Exports of the United States Since 1879. New York: National Bureau of Economic Research, 1967. 86

Mintz, Lawrence E. and M. Thomas Inge, eds. American Humor: An Interdisciplinary Newsletter. Two issues yearly, volumes 1-3 in harbound edition. New York: AMS Press, 1978.   503

Mintz, Jerome R. Legends of the Hasidim. Chicago: University of Chicago Press, 1968. 108

*Miroff, Bruce. Pragmatic Illusions: The Presidential Politics of John F. Kennedy. New York: Longman McKay, 1976. 437

Mishkin, Paul. "The High Court, The Great Writ, and the Due Process of Time and Law." 79 Harvard Law Review 56 (1965).

Mitchell, H.L. Mean Things Happening in this Land. Montgomery, Alabama: STFU Association, 1979. 450

Mitchell, Margaret. Gone With the Wind. New York: Macmillan, 1936. 468

Mitchell, Robert, D. Commercialism and Frontier: Perspectives on the Early Shenandoah Valley. Charlottesville: University Press of Virginia, 1977. 65

Mitchell, Roger. George Knox, From Man to Legend. Northeast Folklore IX, 1969; Orono, Maine: The University Press, 1970.

Mitgang, Herbert. Abraham Lincoln, A Press Portrait: His Life and Times from the Original Newspaper Documents of the Union Confederacy, and Europe. Chicago: Quadrangle Books, 1971. 429

Mock, Elizabeth B. The Architecture of Bridges. New York: Museum of Modern
    Art. 1949; New York: Arno, 1972. 34, 42

_____, ed. Built in USA, 1937-1944. 1944; New York: Arno, 1970.   43

Modell, John. The Economics and Politics of Racial Adjustment: The Japanese
    of Los Angeles, 1900-1942. Urbana: University of Illinois Press, 1977.   198

*Mohr, James C. Abortion in America: The Origins and Evolution of National
    Policy, 1800-1900. New York: Oxford University Press, 1978. 542

*Moldea, Dan. The Hoffa Wars. New York: Ace Books, 1979.   450

Moldenhauer, Joseph J., Jr.,ed. Illustrated Maine Woods: With Illustrations
    from the Gleason Collection. Princeton, New Jersey: Princeton University
    Press, 1974. 416

Mollenhoff, Clark, R. The Man Who Pardoned Nixon. New York: St. Martin's Press, 1976.44(

Monaco, James, ed. Celebrity: Who Gets it, How They Use it, Why it Works.
    New York: Delta, 1978. 503

*_____. ed. Media Culture: Television, Radio Boooks, Magazines, Newspaper,
    Movies. New York: Dill, 1978. 496, 503

Monaghan, Jay. Diplomat in Carpet Slippers: Abraham Lincoln Deals with Foreign
    Affairs. Indianapolis: Bobbs-Merrill, 1945.   118

Monroe, Harriet. John Wellborn Root. 1896; Chicago: Prairie School Press, 1966. 45

Montalto, Nicholas V. "The Challenge of Preservation in a Pluralistic Society:
    A Report on the Immigration History Research Center University of Minnesota."
    The American Architect, XLI (October, 1978). 202

Montell, William, Ghosts Along the Cumberland, Deathlore in the Kentucky
    Foothills. Knoxville: University of Tennessee Press, 1975. 99

*_____. The Saga of Coe Ridge. Knoxville: University of Tennessee
    Press, 1970. 105

Monter, E. William. Witchcraft in France and Switzerland. Ithaca: Cornell
    University Press, 1976. 368

Montesquieu, Charles Louis. The Spirit of Laws. 1748; Berkeley: University of
    California Press, 1977. 149

Montgomery, David. Workers' Control in America: Studies in the History of
    Work, Technology, and Labor Struggles. Cambridge: Cambridge University
    Press, 1979. 448

Moore, Edward C. American Pragmatism: Peirce, James and Dewey. New York:
    Columbia University Press, 1961. 326

_____. ed. The Essential Writings of Peirce. 1972.

Moore, Harry, T. Henry James. New York: Viking, 1974. 412

Moore, Virginia. The Madisons: A Biography. New York: McGraw-Hill, 1979. 426

Moore, Willard B. Molokan Oral Tradition Legends and Memorates of an Ethnic Sect. Berkeley: University of California Press, 1973. 108

Moorhead, James H. American Apocalypse: Yankee Protestants and the Civil War. New Haven: Yale University Press, 1978. 378

Moran, Richard F. The Supreme Court and Religion. New York: Free Press, 1972. 364

Morantz, Regina M. "Making Women Modern: Middle Class Women and Health Reforms in 19th Century America." Journal of Social History, 10 (Summer 1977). 551

*Morgan, Edmund S. American Slavery - American Freedom: The Order of Colonial Virginia. New York: Norton, 1975. 65, 171

* _____. The Puritan Dilemma. Boston: Little, 1958. 171

_____. The Puritan Family. Westport: Greenwood, 1980. 171

_____. Roger Williams, the Church and the State. New York: Harcourt, Brace and World, 1967. 171

* _____. The Visible Saints. Ithaca: Cornell University Press, 1965. 171

*Morgan, Lewis H. Ancient Society. 1877; New York: New York Labor News, 1978. 161

* _____. Houses and House-Life of the American Aborigines. Chicago: University of Chicago Press, 1965. 36, 43

Morgan, Robert, J. A Whig Embattled: The Presidency Under John Tyler. Hamden, Connecticut: Shoe String Press, 1974. 427

*Morgenbesser, Sidney, ed. Dewey and His Critics. New York: Hackett, 1977. 326

Morgenstern, George, E. Pearl Harbor: The Story of the Secret War. New York: Devin-Adair, 1947. 126

Morgenthau, Hans J., ed. The Purpose of American Politics. New York: Knopf, 1960. 309

Morin, Edgar. L'Esprit du Temps. 2 vols. 1962; Paris: Bernard Grosset, 1975. 496, 503

_____. "Studies in Mass Communication." Performance 3, 3 (July-August 1972). 503

Morison, Samuel E. Admiral of the Ocean Seas. Boston: Little Brown, 1942. 182

* _____. The Builders of the Bay Colony. 1930; New England University Press, 1981. 165

_____. History of the United States Naval Operations in World War II, 15 vols. Boston: Little. 167

_____. The Puritan Pronaos. New York: New York University Press, 1936
     165.

_____. Three Centuries of Harvard. Cambridge: Harvard University Press,
     1936. 165.

Morneweck, Evelyn F. Chronicles of Stephen Foster's Family. 1944; Port
     Washington: Kennikat, 1973. 299

Morris, Charles. The Pragmatic Movement in American Philosophy: New York:
     George Braziller, 1970. 327

*Morris, Edmund. The Rise of Theodore Roosevelt. New York: Ballantine, 1980. 431

Morris, Joe Alex. Deadline Every Minute: The Story of the United Press.1957;
     Westport: Greenwood, 1969. 217

*Morris Richard B. The Peacemakers: The Great Powers and American Independence.
     New York: Harper and Row, 1965. 114

Morris, William and Mary. Harper Dictionary of Contemporary American Usage.
     New York: Harper and Row, 1975. 270

Morrison, Hugh. Early American Architecture. New York: Oxford University
     Press, 1952. 36, 43

_____. Louis Sullivan, Prophet of Modern Architecture. 1935; New York:
     Peter Smith, 1952. 39, 45

Morrison, Joseph L. Josephus Daniels: The Small – d Democrat. Chapel Hill:
     University of North Carolina Press, 1966. 214

Morrison, Rodney, J. Expectations and Inflation: Nixon, Politics and
     Economics. Lexington, Massachusetts.: Lexington Books, 1973. 439

Morrow, Ralph E. Northern Methodism and Reconstruction. East Lansing:
     Michigan State University Press, 1956. 378

Mortimer, Wyndham. Organize! My Life as a Union Man. Boston: Beacon Press, 1971. 450

Morton, Louis. "The Historian and the Policy Process." History Teacher 4
     (November 1970). 278

*Mostert, Noel. Supership. New York: Warner Books, 1976. 475

Mott, Frank Luther. American Journalism, 3rd ed. New York: Macmillan, 1962. 223

_____ . A History of American Magazines, 5 vols. Cambridge:
     Harvard University Press, 1930, 1938, 1957, 1968. 217

Mouffe, Barbara, ed. Hawthorne's Lost Notebook, 1835-1841. University Park,
     Pennsylvania: Pennsylvania State University Press, 1978. 412

Mrozik, Donald J. "The Truman Administration and the Enlistment of the
     Aviation Industry in Postwar Defense." Business History Review, XLVIII
     (Spring 1974). 83

Mujica, Francisco. A History of the Skyscraper. New York: Archeology and
    Architecture Press, 1930. 36, 43

Mulder, John M. Woodrow Wilson: The Years of Preparation. Princeton, N.J.:
    University Press, 1977. 432

*Mulder, John M. and John F. Wilson, eds. Religion in American History:
    Interpretive Essays. Englewood Cliffs: Prentice-Hall, 1978. 364

Mullen, Patrick B. I Heard the Old Fisherman Say: Folklore of the Texas
    Gulf Coast. Austin and London: University of Texas Press, 1978. 110

*Mullin, Gerald W. Flight and Rebellion: Slave Resistance in 18th Century
    Virginia. New York: Oxford University Press, 1974. 27

*Mumford, Lewis. Sticks and Stones. 1924; New York: Dover, 1955. 29, 33, 42

*_____. The City in History. New York: Harcourt, Brace, Jovanovich, 1968. 473

Munro, Eleanor. Originals: American Women Artists. New York: Simon & Schuster, 1979. 546

Munroe, Dana, G. Intervention and Dollar Diplomacy in the Caribbean, 1900-1921.
    Princeton: Princeton University Press, 1964. 124

_____. The United States and the Caribbean Republic, 1921-1933.
    Princeton: Princeton University Press, 1974. 124

Munson, Thomas N. The Essential Wisdom of George Santayana. New York:
    Columbia University Press, 1962. 327

Murch, Alma E. The Development of the Detective Novel. Westport: Greenwood,
    1969. 57

Murphy , Murray. The Development of Peirce's Philosophy. Cambridge: Harvard
    University Press, 1961. 327

*Murphy, Paul L. The Constitution in Crisis Time, 1918-1969. New York:
    Harper and Row, 1972. 354

Murphy, Walter F. "The Art of Constitutional Interpretation: A Preliminary
    Showing." In M. Judd Harmon, ed. Essays on the Constitution of the United
    States. Port Washington, New York, 1978. 357

*_____. Elements of Judicial Strategy. Chicago: University of Chicago
    Press, 1973. 346

Murray, Andrew E. Presbyterians and the Negro. A History. Philadelphia:
    Presbyterian History Society, 1966. 378

Myers, Andrew, B., ed. A Century of Commentary on the Works of Washington
    Irving, 1860-1974. Tarrytown, New York: Sleepy Hollow Restorations,1976. 413

Myerson, Joel, ed. Critical Essays on Margaret Fuller. Boston: G.K. Hall, 1980. 411

_____. Dictionary of Literary Biography: Volume One, The American Renaissance
    in New England. Detroit, Michigan: Gale Research, 1978. 406

Mystery Writers of America. Mystery Writer's Handbook. Cincinnati: Writer's
    Digest, 1976. 56

Naas B. and C. Sakr. American Labor Union Periodicals: A Guide to Their Location. Ithaca, New York: Cornell University Press, 1956. 445

*Nachbar, Jack, Deborah Weiser and John Wright, eds. The Popular Culture Reader. Bowling Green: Popular Press, 1978. 492, 504

Nagel, Gwen L. and James. Sarah Orne Jewett: A Reference Guide. Boston: G.K. Hall, 1977. 414

Nagai, Yonosuke and Akira Iriye, eds. The Origins of the Cold War in Asia. New York: Columbia University Press, 1977. 139

Nagy, Paul J. "Thoughts and Things: Pregmatism, Material Culture and the Celebration of Ordinary Experience." The Southern Quarterly, 15 (January 1977). 510

*Namias, June. First Generation: In the Words of Twentieth-Century American Immigrants. Boston: Beacon Press, 1978. 205

Narcejac, Thomas. Esthetique du Roman Policier. Paris: Le Portulan, 1947. 54

*Nash, Gary B. Red, White and Black: The Peoples of Early America. Englewood Cliffs, New Jersey: Prentice-Hall, 1982. 511

_____. "Urban Wealth and Poverty in Pre-Revolutionary America." Journal of Interdisciplinary History, VI (Spring 1976). 66

*Nash, Gerald D. The American West in the Twentieth Century. Albuquerque: University of New Mexico Press, 1977. 174

_____. United States Oil Policy, 1890-1964: Business and Government in Twentieth Century America. 1968; Westport: Greenwood, 1976. 83

Nash, Howard Pervear. Andrew Johnson: Congress and Reconstruction. Rutherford, New Jersey: Fairleigh Dickinson University Press, 1972. 429

*Nash, Roderick. Wilderness and the American Mind. New Haven: Yale University Press, 1973. 174, 473

*Nathan, Hans. Dan Emmett and the Rise of Early Negro Minstrelsey. Norman: University of Oklahoma Press, 1962. 299

_____. William Billings: Data and Documents. Detroit: Information Coordinators., Inc., 1976. 303, 306

National Commission on the Observance of International Women's Year. The Spirit of Houston: The First National Women's Conference. Washington, D.C.: Government Printing Office, 1978. 544

National Park Service. Historic American Building Survey. Washington: HABS, 1935 et. seq.

*Needleman, Jacob. The New Religions. New York: Dutton, 1977. 383

Neibuhr, Reinhold and Alan Heimert. A Nation So Conceived: Reflections on the History of America From its Early Vision to its Present Power. New York: Scribners, 1963.

*Nelson, Daniel. Managers and Workers: Origins of the New Factory System in the United States, 1880-1920. Madison: University of Wisconsin Press, 1975. 80

_____. Unemployment Insurance: The American Experience, 1915-1935. Madison: University of Wisconsin Press, 1969. 88

*Nelson, E. Clifford. Lutheranism in North America, 1914-1970.New York: Fortress, 1980. 365

Nelson, George. Industrial Architecture of Albert Kahn, Inc. New York; Arthitectural Book Publishing Company, 1939. 45

Nelson, Keith L. Victors Divided: America and Allies in Germany, 1918-1923. Berkeley: University of California Press, 1975. 137

Nemerov, Howard, ed. Poets and Poetry. New York: Basic Books, 1961. 344

_____. Reflexions on Poetry and Poetics. New Brunswick: Rutgers University Press, 1972. 344

*Nettels, Curtis P. The Emergence of a National Economy, 1775-1815. 1962; Armonk: Sharpe, 1977. 66

Nettels, Elsa. James and Conrad. Athens, Georgia: University of Gerogia Press, 1977, 413
*Nettl, Bruno. Folk and Traditional Music of the Western Continents. Englewood Cliffs: Prentice-Hall, 1973. 296

_____. North American Indian Styles. Austin: University of Texas Press, 1954. 300

Neu, Charles E. An Uncertain Friendship: Theodore Roosevelt and Japan, 1906-1909. Cambridge: Harvard University Press, 1967. 121

Neuffer, Claude H. and Irene. The Name Game: From Oyster Point to Keowee. Columbia, S.C.:The Sandlapper Store, 1977.

*Neumann, William L. America Encounters Japan: From Perry to MacArthur. Baltimore: John Hopkins Press, 1963. 123

*Neusner, Jacob, ed. Understanding American Judaism, 2 vols. New York: KTAV, 1975. 386

Nevins, Allan.The Emergence of Lincoln, 2 vols. New York: Charles Scribner's Sons, 1950. 182

_____. John D. Rockefeller: The Heroic Age of American Enterprise. New York: Scribner, 1940. 167

_____. Ordeal of the Union, 2 vols. New York: Charles Scribner's Sons, 1947. 182

_____. Study in Power: John D. Rockefeller, Industrialist and Philanthropist. New York: Scribner, 1953. 167

Nevins, Francis M., Jr., ed. The Mistery Writer's Art. Bowling Green, Ohio: Bowling Green University Popular Press, 1970. 59

*_____. Royal Bloodline: Ellery Queen, Author and Detective. Bowling Green, Ohio: Bowling Green University Popular Press, 1973. 61

Nevius, Blake. Cooper's Landscapes:An Essay on the Picturesque Vision. Berkeley, California: University of California Press, 1976. 410

*New York Community Trust. The Heritage of New York: A Walking Guide. New York: Fordham University Press, 1970. 37

New York Times, Staff. The End of a Presidency. New York: Holt, Rinehart and Winston, 1974. 439

*Newcomb, Horace, ed. Television: The Critical View. New York: Oxford, 1979. 504

_____. Television: The Most Popular Art. Garden City, New York: Anchor, 1974. 495, 504

Newell, James S. "The Development and Growth of the Kenneth Sawyer Goodman Memorial Theatre and School of Drama, Chicago, Illinois, 1925-1971." Unpublished Dissertation. Wayne State University, 1973. 213, 523

*Newhall, Beaumont. The History of Photography: From 1839 to the Present Day. New York: The Museum of Modern Art, 1964. 21

Neyland, James. The Carter Family Scrapbook: An Intimate Close-up of America's First Family. New York: Grosset and Dunlop, 1977. 441

Nichols, C.W. Many Thousand Gone: The Ex-Slaves' Account of Their Bondage and Freedom. Bloomington: Indiana University Press, 1969. 398

Nichols, David A. Lincoln and the Indians: Civil War Policy and Politics. Columbia: University of Missouri Press, 1978. 429

Nichols, Eileen M. "A Developmental Study of Drawings Published in the American Architect and in Inland Architect." Unpublished Dissertation. University of Minnesota, 1978. 531

Nichols, W.W. "Slave Narratives: Dismissed Evidence in the Writings of Southern History." Phylon, 32 (Winter 1971). 398

Nicholson, Margaret. A Dictionary of American English Usage. New York: Oxford University Press, 1957.

Nicolay, John G. and John Hay. Abraham Lincoln: A History, 10 vols. New York: Century, 1890. 182

*Niebuhr, Reinhold. The Children of Light and the Children of Darkness. New York: Scribner's, 1944. 170

*_____. The Irony of American History. New York: Scribner's, 1952. 170

*_____. Moral Man and Immoral Society. New York: Scribner's, 1932. 170

Niemi, Albert W., Jr. State and Regional Patterns in American Manufacturing. Westport, Connecticut: Greenwood Press, 1974. 74

*Nies, Judith. Seven Women: Portraits from the American Radical Tradition. New York: Penguin, 1980. 538

Nihart, Brooke. "Popular Military History." Marine Corps Gazette (July 1975). 284

Nin, Anais. Diary of Anais Nin, Vol I. New York: Harcourt, Brace, Jovanovich, 1966. 395, 400

*_____. In Favor of the Sensitive Man. New York: Harcourt, Brace, Jovanovich, 1976. 395, 399

_____. A Woman Speaks. Chicago: Swanon Press, 1975. 395, 399

Nixon, Raymond B. Henry W. Grady: Spokesman of the New South. 1943; New York: Russell, 1969. 214

Nixon, Richard M. The Memoirs of Richard Nixon. New York: Grosset and Dunlop, 1978. 438

_____ . The Real War. New York: Warner Books, 1980. 438

Nochlin, Linda. "The Paterson Strike Pageant of 1913." Art in America, 62 (May-June 1974). 453

Noemie, Emery. Washington: A Biography. New York: Putnam, 1976. 424

Noer, Thomas J. Briton , Boer and Yankee: The United States and South Africa, 1870-1914. Kent, Ohio: Kent State University Press, 1978.

Norman, E. R. The Conscience of the State in North America. Cambridge: University Press, 1968. 564

Norris, James D. R.G. Dun and Company, 1841-1900: The Development of Credit Reporting in the Nineteenth Century. Westport, Connecticut: Greenwood Press, 1978. 92

*North, Douglass C. The Economic Growth of the United States, 1790-1860. New York: Norton,1966. 67

Norton, Aloysius A. Theodore Roosevelt. Boston: Twayne Publishers, 1980. 431

*Norton, Charles A. Melville Davisson Post: Man of Many Mysteries.Bowling Green, Ohio: Bowling Green State University Popular Press, 1973. 61

Norton, John. Abel Being Dead, Yet Speaketh: A Biography of John Cotton. Delmar: Scholars, 1978. 370

*Norton, Mary Beth. Liberty's Daughters: The Revolutionary Experience of American Women, 1750-1800. New York: Little Brown Co., 1980. 536

Norton, Wesley. Religious Newspapers in the Old Northwest to 1861: A History, Bibliography and Record of Opinion. Athens: Ohio University Press, 1977. 227

*Norwood, Frederick A.The Story of American Methodism. Nashville: Abington, 1974. 365

Nossack, Hans Erich. To the Unknown Hero. Ralph Manheim, trans. London: Alcove Press, 1974. 49

Novak, Michael. American Philosophy and the Future. New York: Charles Scribner's Sons, 1968. 327

*   _____ . The Rise of the Unmeltable Ethnics: Politics and Culture in the 1970s. New York: Macmillan, 1972. 202, 313

*Nuclear Energy Policy Study Group. Nuclear Power Issues and Choices. New York: Ballinger, 1977. 474

Nugent, Walter T.K. Money and American Society, 1865-1880. New York: Free Press, 1968. 73

*   _____ . The Money Question During Reconstruction. New York: Norton, 1967. 73

Numbers, Ronald L. Prophetess of Health: A Study of Ellen G. White. New York: Harper and Row, 1976. 382

Nye, Russel B. George Bancroft, Brahmin Rebel. New York: Alfred A. Knopf, 1944. 182

_____ . Society and Culture in America: 1830-1860. New York: Harper and Row, 1974. 403

*   _____ . The Unembarrased Muse. New York: Dial, 1970. 492, 504

Oates, Stephen B. Our Fiery Trial: Abraham Lincoln and the Civil War Era. Amherst: University of Mass. Press, 1979. 429

* _____. With Malice Toward None: The Life of Abraham Lincoln. New York: New American Library, 1978. 429

*O'Brien, David J. The Renewal of American Catholicism. New York: Paulist Press, 1974. 385

O'Brien Francis William, ed. The Hoover-Wilson Wartime Correspondence. Ames: Iowa State University Press, 1974. 432, 433

_____. Two Peacemakers in Paris: The Hoover-Wilson Post-Armistice Letters, 1918-1920. College Station: Texas A & M University Press, 1978. 432, 433

*O'Brien, Lynn W. Plains Indian Autobiographies. Boise: Boise State College, 1973. 395, 399

O'Brien, Patrick. The New Economic History of Railways. New York: St. Martin's Press, 1977. 92

O'Cain, Raymond K. "A Social Dialect Study of Charleston, South Carolina." Diss. University of Chicago, 1972. 265

*O'Connor, Raymond G. Diplomacy for Victory: FDR and Unconditional Surrender. New York: Norton, 1971. 127

*Offner, Arnold A. American Appeasement: United States Foreign Policy and Germany, 1933-1938. Cambridge: Harvard University Press, 1969. 127

O'Gorman, James. "The Marshall Field Wholesale Store: Materials toward a Monograph." Journal of the Society of Architectural Historians, 37 (October 1978). 531

* _____, et. al. The Architecture of Frank Furness. Philadelphia: Philadelphia Museum of Art, 1980. 45

Olmstead, Alan L. "The Mechanization of Reaping and Moving in American Agriculture, 1833-1870." Journal of Economic History, XXXV (June 1975). 77

_____. New York Savings Banks, 1819-1861. Chapel Hill: University of North Carolina Press, 1976. 73

Olney, James. "Autos-Bios-Graphein: The Study of Autobiographical Literature." South Atlantic Quarterly, 77 (Winter 1978). 392, 397

* _____. Metaphors of Self: The Meaning of Autobiography. Princeton: Princeton University Press, 1981. 392, 398

* _____, ed. Autobiography: Essays Theoretical and Critical. Princeton: Princeton University Press, 1980. 390, 397

Olson, Jack. Slaughter the Animals, Poison the Earth. New York: Simon and Schuster, 1971. 476

O'Neill, Charles Edwards. Church and State in French Colonial Louisiana. New Haven: Yale University Press, 1966. 372

*Ophuls, William. Ecology and the Politics of Scarcity. San Francisco: Freeman, 1977. 476

Orenstein, Gloria Feman. "Review Essay: Art History." Signs, 1 (Winter 1975). 537

O'Riordan, Timothy and Ralph d'Arge. Progress in Resources Management and Environmental Planning. New York: Wiley, 1981. 484

Orkin, Mark M. Speaking Canadian English. Toronto: General Publishing, 1970. 259

Ornstein, Jacob. Three Essays on Linguistic Diversity in the Spanish World. The Hague: Mouton, 1976. 267

Orth, Donald J. Dictionary of Alaska Place Names. Washington, D.C.: U.S. Government Printing Office, 1967. 262

Orton, Harold, et. al. Survey of English Dialects. Introduction, 4 vols. Leeds : E.J. Arnold, 1962-1971. 264

Osborn, Fairfield. Our Plundered Planet. New York: Little Brown, 1948. 471

Osgood, Herbert Levi. The American Colonies in the Seventeenth Century, 3 vols. 1907; New York: Columbia University Press, 1930. 160

*Osofsky, Gilbert. Harlem: The Making of a Ghetto. 1890-1930. New York: Harper and Row, 1966. 27

*_____, ed. Puttin' On Ole Massa. New York: Harper and Row, 1969. 27

Ostroff, Anthony, ed. The Contemporary Poet as Artist and Critic. Boston: Little Brown and Co., 1964. 344

O'Sullivan, Judith and Rosemary Gallick. Workers and Allies: Female Participation in the American Trade Union Movement 1824-1976. Washington, D.C.: Smithsonian Institution, 1975. 451

Ott, John. Hancock Shaker Village. Pittsfield, Mass.: Shaker Community, 1976. 516

Otto, John. "Artifacts and Status Differences." Stanley South, ed. Research Strategies in Historical Archaeology. New York: Academic Press, 1977. 509

*Overton, Richard C. Burlington Route: A History of the Burlington Lines. Lincoln: University of Nebraska Press, 1976. 72

*Owens, Leslie H. This Species of Property: Slave Life and Culture in the Old South. New York: Oxford University Press, 1977. 78

Owsley, Frank L. King Cotton Diplomacy: Foreign Relations of the Confederate States of America. 2nd. ed., rev. by Harriet C. Owsley. Chicago: University of Chicago Press, 1959. 118

Ozanne, Robert. A Century of Labor-Management Relations at McCormick and International Harvester. Madison: University of Wisconsin Press, 1967. 81

Pabst, Anna Catherine Smith. The Birthplace of R.B. Hayes, Delaware, Ohio. S.L.: S,N,, 1972. 430

*Packard, Vance. A Nation of Strangers. New York: Pocket Books, 1974. 311

Paddock, Harold. "A Dialect Survey of Carbonear, Newfoundland." MA Thesis. Memorial University of Newfoundland, 1966. 265

Paige, Glenn D. The Korean Decision: June 24-30, 1950. New York: Free Press, 1968. 130

Painter, Nell Irvin. The Narrative of Hosea Hudson: His Life as a Negro Communist in the South. Cambridge: Harvard University Press, 1976. 449

Palumbo, Linda. "Feminist Publishing Catalog." Chrysalis, 8 (Summer 1979) and 9 (Fall 1979). 535

Paolino, Ernest N. The Foundations of American Empire: William Henry Seward and U.S. Foreign Policy. Ithaca: Cornell University Press, 1973. 118

Pap, Leo. Portuguese-American Speech: An Outline of Speech Conditions Among Portuguese Immigrants in New England and Elsewhere in the United States. New York: King's Crown, 1949. 267

Papanikolas, Helen Z., ed. The Peoples of Utah. Salt Lake City: Utah State Historical Society, 1976. 195

Papenfuse, Edward C. In Pursuit of Profit: The Annapolis Merchants in the Era of the American Revolution, 1763-1803. Baltimore: John Hopkins University Press, 1975. 66

*Paper, Lewis J. John F. Kennedy: The Promise and the Performance. New York: Da Capo, 1980. 437

Paredes, Americo. "With His Pistol in His Hand": A Border Ballad and its Hero. Austin: Universtiy of Texas Press, 1958. 101

_____ and Ellen Stekert, eds. The Urban Experience and Folk Tradition. Austin: University of Texas Press, 1971. 105

_____ and Richard Bauman, eds. Toward New Perspectives in Folklore. Austin: University of Texas Press, 1971. 97

Paret, Peter. "The History of War." Daedalus: The Historian and the World of the Twentieth Century, 100 (Spring 1971). 276

*Park, Charles F. and Margaret C. Freeman. Earthbound: Minerals, Energy and Man's Future. San Francisco: Freeman, 1975. 476

Parker, Gail Thain. The Writing on the Wall. New York: Simon and Schuster, 1979. 444

_____. Mind Cure in New England. Hanover: University Press of New England, 1973. 383

Parker, William. "Introduction." Trends in the American Ecomonic. 1960; New York: Arno, 1975.

_____, ed. The Structure of the Cotton Economy of the Antebellum South. Washington, D.C.: Agricultural History Society, 1970. 78

Parker, William N. and Judith L.V. Klein. "Productivity Growth in Grain
    Production in the United States, 1840-1860 and 1900-1910". Output, Employment
    and Productivity. New York: Columbia University Press, 1966. 77

Parkinson, Thomas, ed. A Casebook on the Beat. New York: Cornell, 1961. 344

Parkman, Francis. France and England in North America, 9 vols. Boston: Houghton
    Mifflin, 1869-1892.   182

*_____. The Oregon Trail. 1846; New York: New American Library. 153

_____. The Old Regime in Canada. Boston: Houghton Mifflin, 1887. 182

Parks, Robert J. Democracy's Railroads: Public Enterprise in Jacksonian Michigan.
    Port Washington, New York: Kannikat Press, 1972. 71

Parlee , Mary Brown. "Psychology and Women." Signs, 5 (Autumn 1979). 540

Parmet, Herbert S. Jack: The Struggles of John F. Kennedy. New York: The Dial
    Press, 1980. 437

*Parrington, Vernon L. Main Currents in American Thought, 2 vols. 1927; New York:
    Harcourt Brace Jovanovich, 1955. 163

Parrini, Carl P. Heir to Empire: United States Economic Diplomacy, 1916-1923.
    Pittsburgh: University of Pittsburgh Press, 1969. 85, 123

Parrish, Thomas, ed. The Simon and Schuster Encyclopedia of World War II.New York:
    Simon and Schuster, 1978. 287

Parsons, Edward B. Wilsonian Diplomacy: Allied-American Rivalries in War and Peace.
    St. Louis: Forum Press, 1978. 137, 432

Passi, Michael M., et.al. For the Common Good: Finish Immigrants and the Radical
    Response to Industrial America. Superior, Wisc.: Tyomies Society, 1977. 199

*Paszek, Lawrence J., comp. United States Air Force History: A Guide to Documentary
    Sources. Washington: G.P.O., 1973. 285

Pate, Janet. The Book of Sleuths. Chicago: Contemporary Books, 1977. 57

*Paterson, Thomas G. Soviet-American Confrontation: Postwar Reconstruction and the
    Origins of the Cold War. Baltimore: John Hopkins Press, 1975. 128

Patterson, Daniel W. The Shaker Spiritual. Princeton: Princeton University Press,
    1979. 304

Patterson, David S. Toward a Warless World: The Travail of the American Peace
    Movement, 1887-1914. Bloomington: Indiana University Press, 1976. 135

Patterson, Rebecca. Emily Dickinson's Imagery. Amherst: University of Massachusetts
    Press, 1980. 411

Paul, Sherman. Louis Sullivan: An Architect in American Thought. Englewood Cliffs:
    Prentice-Hall, 1962.   45

Peabody, James Bishop, ed. John Adams: A Biography in His Own Words. New York:
    Newsweek, 1973. 425

Peck, H. Daniel. A World by Itself: The Pastoral Moment in Cooper's Fiction. New
    Haven, Connecticut: Yale University Press, 1977. 410

Peckham, M. "Aestheticism to Modernism: Fulfillment or Revolution?" The Triumph of Romanticism. Columbia, S.C.: University of South Carolina Press, 1970. 182

Pederson, Lee A. An Annotated Bibliography of Southern Speech. Atlanta: Southeastern Education Laboratory, 1968. 257

_____. "The Pronunciation of English in Chicago: Consonants and Vowels." PADS, XLIV (1965). 266

Peel, J.D. Herbert Spencer: The Evolution of a Sociologist. New York: Basic Books, 1971. 182

*Peel, Robert. Mary Baker Eddy: The Years of Authority. New York: Holt, Rinehart and Winston, 1980. 225

Penzler, Otto. The Privates Lives of Private Eyes and Spies, Crime Fighters and Other Good Guys. New York: Grosset and Dunlop, 1979. 57

*_____, ed. The Great Detectives. New York: Penquin, 1979. 57

_____, Chris Steinbrunner and Marvin Lachman. Detectionary. New York: Overlook Press, 1977. 57

Perkins, Bradford. Castlereagh and Adams: England and the United States, 1812-1823. Berkeley: University of California Press, 1964. 117

_____. The First Rapprochement: England and the United States, 1795-1805. Philadelphia: University of Pennsylvania Press, 1955. 115

_____. The Great Rapprochement: England and the United States, 1895-1914. New York: Atheneum, 1968. 119

*_____. Prologue to War: England and the United States, 1805-1812. Berkeley: University of California Press, 1961. 116

Perkins, Charlotte. Herland: A Lost Feminist Utopian Novel. 1915; New York: Pantheon, 1979.

*Perkins, Dexter. The American Approach to Foreign Policy. New York: Atheneum, 1968. 182

_____. Hands Off: A History of the Monroe Doctrine. Boston: Little Brown, 1941. 182

_____. A History of the Monroe Doctrine. 2nd. ed., Boston: Little Brown, 1955. 124

_____. The Monroe Doctrine, 1823-1826. Cambridge: Harvard University Press, 1927. 117

Perkins, Edwin J. Financing Anglo-American Trade: The House of Brown, 1800-1880. Cambridge: Harvard University Press, 1975. 73

_____. "Foreign Interest Rates in American Financial Markets: A Revised Series of Dollar-Sterling Exchange Rates, 1850-1900." Journal of Economic History, XXXVIII (June 1978). 73

*Perlis, Vivian. Charles Ives Remembered: An Oral History. New York: Norton, 1976. 300, 304
_____ and H. Wiley Hitchcock, eds. An Ives Celebration. Urbana: University of Illinois Press, 1977. 304

Perosa, Sergio. Henry James and the Experimental Novel. Charlottesville, Virginia: University Press of Virginia, 1978. 413

Perrin, Porter. Writer's Guide and Index to English. Gleview, Illinois: Scott, Foresman, 1972. 270

*Perry, David C. and Alfred J. Watkins. The Rise of the Sunbelt Cities. Beverly Hills: Sage, 1977. 464

Perry, Lewis. Radical Abolitionism: Anarchy and the Government of God in Antislavery Thought. Ithaca: Cornell University Press, 1973. 378

Perry, Ralph Barton. The Thought and Character of William James. 1935; Westport, Conn.: Greenwood, 1974. 324

*Persico. Joseph E. Piercing the Reich: The Penetration of Nazi Germany by American Secret Agents During World War II. New York: Ballantine Books, 1979. 292

Persons, S. "The Cyclical Theory of History in Eighteenth Century America." American Quarterly, 6 (Summer 1954). 182

Peskin, Allan. Garfield. Kent, Ohio: Kent State University Press, 1978. 430

Peterson, Karen and J.J. Wilson. Women Artists: Recognition and Reappraisal from the Early Middle Ages to the Twentieth Century. New York: New York University Press, 1976. 546

Peterson, Merrill D., ed. James Madison: A Biography in His Own Words. New York: Newsweek, 1974. 426

*_____. The Portable Thomas Jefferson. New York: Penguin, 1977. 425

Peterson, Richard. The Production of Culture. Beverly Hills: Sage, 1976. 496, 504

_____. "Where the Two Cultures Meet: Popular Culture." Journal of Popular Culture, XI, 2 (Fall 1977). 504

Peterson, Theodore. Magazines in the Twentieth Century. Urbana: University of Illinois Press, 1964. 221

Pettit, Arthur G. Mark Twain and the South. Lexington, Kentucky: University of Kentucky Press, 1974. 410

Pfeiffer, Hans. Die Mumie in Glassarg: Bemerkungen zur Kriminalliteratur. Rudolstadt: Greifenverlag, 1960. 59

Phair, Judith T. William Cullen Bryant and His Critics, 1808-1872: A Bibliography. Troy, New York: Whitston, 1974. 410

Phalen, J. The Millenial Kingdom of the Franciscans in the New World: A Study of the Writings of Geronimo de Mendieta 1525-1604. Berkeley: University of California Press, 1956. 182

*Phillips, Ulrich B. American Negro Slavery. Baton Rouge: Louisiana State University, 1967. 27

_____. "The Central Theme in Southern History." American Historical Review, 34 (October 1928). 466

*Philp, Kenneth R. John Collier's Crusade for Indian Reform, 1920-1954. Tucson: University of Arizona Press, 1977. 512

Philpott, Thomas. The Slum and The Ghetto Neighborhood-Deterioration and Middle Class Reform: Chicago 1880-1930. New York: Oxford University Press, 1978. 528

Pickering, John. Vocabulary or Collection of Words and Phrases Which have been Supposed to be Peculiar to the United States of America. 1817; New York: Burt Franklin, 1972. 271

*Picket, Calder M. Voices of the Past: Key Documents in the History of American Journalism. Columbus, Ohio: Grid Inc, 1977. 228

Piepkorn, Arthur Carl. Profiles in Belief: The Religious Bodies of the United States and Canada. 2 vols. New York: Harper and Row, 1978. 363

Pierce, Roy Harvey. The Continuity of American Poetry. Princeton: Princeton University Press, 1961. 344

Pierson, George Wilson. The Moving American. New York: Knopf, 1973. 173, 308

Pike, Burton. "Time in Autobiography." Comparative Literature, 28 (Fall 1976). 396, 39

Pike, Kenneth L. The Intonation of American English. Ann Arbor: Unviersity of Michigan Press, 1945. 263

_____. Language in Relation to a Unfied Theory of the Structure of Human Behavior. The Hague: Mouton, 1967. 269

_____. "A Linguistic Contribution to Composition." College Composition and Communication, XV (1964). 269

_____. Selected Writings. The Hague: Mouton, 1970. 269

Pilcher, George W. Samuel Davies: Apostle of Dissent in Colonial Virginia. Knoxville: University of Tennessee Press, 1971. 373

Pilcher, William. The Portland Longshoremen. New York: Holt, Rinehart and Winston, 1972. 452

Pinkney, Alphonso. The American Way of Violence. New York: Random House, 1972. 310

*Pious, Richard M. The American Presidency. New York: Basic Books, 1979. 358

Pisney, Raymond F., ed. Virginians Remember Woodrow Wilson. Mouseion Press, 1978. 432

_____. Woodrow Wilson: Idealism and Reality. Verona, Va.: McClure Press, 1978. 432

Plesur , Milton. America's Outward Thrust: Approaches to Foreign Affairs, 1865-1890. Dekalb: Northern Illinois University Press, 1971. 119

Pletcher, David M. The Awkward Years: American Foreign Relations under Garfield and Arthur. Columbia: Unviersity of Missouri Press, 1962. 118

_____. The Diplomacy of Annexation: Texas, Oregon and the Mexican War. Columbia: Unviersity of Missouri Press, 1973. 118

Plowden, David. Bridges: The Spans of North America. New York: Viking, 1974. 34, 42

Plumb, John H. The Death of the Past. Boston: Houghton Mifflin, 1970. 182

Plumstead, A.W., ed. The Wall and the Garden: Selected Massachussetts Election Sermons, 1670-1775. Minneapolis: University of Minnesota Press, 1968. 374

Pogue, Forrest. "The Military in a Democracy: A Review of American Caesar." International Security, 3 (Spring 1973). 291

Pollak, Peter. The Picture History of Photography. New York: Abrams, 1969.

Pollard, James E. The Presidents and the Press. 1947; New York: Octagon, 1973. 210

*Pomeroy, Earl. The Territories and the United States, 1861-1890. Seattle: University of Washington Press, 1969. 174

Pool, Ithiel de Sola, et. als., eds. Handbook of Communications. Chicago: Rand McNally, 1973. 504

*Poole, Peter A. The United States and Indo-China from FDR to Nixon. Hinsdale,III: Dryden Press, 1973. 131

Poole, Walter S. "From Conciliation to Containment: The Joint Chiefs of Staff and the Coming of the Cold War, 1945-1946." Military Affairs, 42 (February 1978). 292

Pope, Robert G. The Half- Way Covenant: Church Membership in Puritan New England. Princeton: Princeton University Press, 1969. 369

Porte, Joel. Representative Man: Ralph Waldo Emerson in His Time. New York: Oxford University Press, 1979. 411

Porter, David. Emerson and Literary Change. Cambridge, Massachusetts: Harvard University Press, 1978. 411

Porter, Gareth. A Peace Denied: The United States, Vietnam and the Paris Agreements. Bloomington: Indiana University Press, 1975. 140

*Porter, Glenn. The Rise of Big Business, 1860-1910. Arlington Heights: Harlan Davidson, 1973. 80

_____, ed. Regional Economic History: The Mid-Atlantic Area Since 1700.Greenville, Wilmington: Eleutherian Mills-Hagley Foundation, 1976. 93

Porter, H.C. The Inconstant Savage: England and the North America Indian, 1500-1600. London: Duckworth, 1979. 513

Porter, Roger J. "Unspeakable Practices, Writable Acts: Franklin's Autobiography." Hudson Review, 32 (Summer 1979). 400

*Porter, William Earl. Assault on the Media: The Nixon Years. Ann Arbor: University of Michigan Press, 1976. 222, 438

Porterfield, Amanda. Feminine Spirituality in America: From Sarah Edwards to Martha Graham. Philadelphia: Temple University Press, 1980. 543

Portman, John and Jonathan Barnett. The Architect as Developer. New York: McGraw-Hill, 1976. 467

Posadas, Barbara M. "Community Structures of Chicago's Northwest Side: The Transition from Rural to Urban, 1830-1889." Unpublished dissertation. Northwestern University, 1976. 528

_____."A Home in the Country: Suburbanization in Jefferson Township, 1870-1889." Chicago History, 7 (Fall 1978). 519

*Potter, David. People of Plenty. Chicago: University of Chicago Press, 1954. 169

_____. Lincoln and His Party in the Secession Crisis. New Haven: Yale University Press, 1942. 182

Potter, Jeffrey. Disaster by Oil: Oil Spills, Why They Happen, What They Do, How We Can End Them. New York: Macmillan, 1973. 474

Potter, Jim. The American Economy Between the World Wars. New York: John Wiley, 1974. 85

Potter, Vincent G.S.J. Charles S. Peirce on Norms and Ideals. Worcester: The University of Massachusetts Press, 1968. 327

*Poulin, A. Jr.,ed. Contemporary American Poetry. Boston: Houghton-Mifflin, 1980. 341, 343

_____. Making in All Its Forms. New York: Dutton, 1974. 344

Pound Louise. Nebraska Folklore. 1960; Westport: Greenwood Press, 1976. 99

Powell, John Wesley. Report upon the Lands of the Arid Regions of the United States. Washington, D.C.: U.S. Government Printing Office, 1878. 182

Pratt, Julius W. Expansionists of 1812. New York: Macmillan, 1925. 116, 182

_____. Expansionists of 1898: The Acquisition of Hawaii and the Spanish Islands. Baltimore: Johns Hopkins Press, 1936. 119, 182

*Prebish, Charles S. American Buddhism. North Scituate: Duxbury, 1979. 384

Pred, Allan R. The Spatial Dynamics of U.S. Urban-Industrial Growth, 1800-1914. Cambridge: M.I.T. Press, 1966. 75

_____. Urban Growth and the Circulation of Information: The United States System of Cities, 1790-1840. Cambridge: Harvard University Press, 1973. 72, 461

Presbrey, Frank. The History and the Development of Advertising. 1929; Westport: Greenwood, 1968. 208

*Prescott, William Hickling. The Conquest of Mexico. 1843; Chicago: University of Chicago Press, 1966. 153

_____. The Conquest of Peru. 1847; New York: New American Library. 153

_____. The History of the Reign of Ferdinand and Isabella the Catholic, 3 vols. 1838; New York: A M S Press, 1968. 153

Prestiano, Robert. "The Island Architect: A Study of the Contents, Influence and Significance of Chicago's Major   Late-Nineteenth Century Architectural Periodical." Unpublished dissertation.Northwestern University, 1973. 530

Preston, Howard L. Automobile Age Atlanta: The Making of a Southern Metropolis 1900-1935. Athens: University of Georgia, 1979. 466

Price, Harry. The Auditorium Building: Its History and Architectural Significance. Chicago: Roosevelt University, 1976. 531

Price, Jacob M. "Economic Foundation and the Growth of American Port Town in the Eighteenth Century." Perspectives in American History, VIII (1974). 64

_____. France and the Chesapeake: A History of the French Tobacco Monopoly, 1674-1791, 2 vols. Ann Arbor: University of Michigan Press, 1973. 64

Price, Raymond. With Nixon. New York: Viking Press, 1977. 438

Price, Warren C. The Literature of Journalism: An Annotated Bibliography. Minneapolis: University of Minnesota Press, 1959.   206

_____ and Calder M. Pickett. An Annotated Journalism Bibliography, 1958-1968. Minneapolis: University of Minnesota Press, 1970.   206

Pritchett, Herman. The American Constitution. New York: McGraw-Hill Co., 1977.   356

_____ . "Judicial Supremacy from Marshall to Burger." In M. Judd Harmon, ed. Essays on the Constitution of the United States. Port Washington, New York, 1978.   357

Prpic, George J. The South Slav Immigration in America. Boston: Twayne, 1978.   195

Prucha, Francis. American Indian Policy in Crisis: Christian Reformers and the Indian, 1865-1900. Norman: University of Oklahoma Press, 1976.   512

*   . American Indian Policy in the Formative Years. Lincoln: University of Nebraska Press, 1970.   182

_____ . Americanizing the American Indians: Writings by the Friends of the Indian, 1880-1900. Cambridge, Mass.: Harvard, 1973.   512

_____ . The Churches and the Indian Schools, 1888-1912. Lincoln: University of Nebraska Press, 1979.   512

_____ . The Dawes Act and the Allotment of Indian Lands. Norman: University of Oklahoma Press, 1973.   512

Pryse, Marjorie. The Mark and the Knowledge: Social Stigma in Clasical American Fiction. Columbus, Ohio: Ohio State University Press, 1979.   403

Public Land Law Review Commission. One-Third of the Nation's Land. Washington, D.C.: G.P.O., 1970.   476

*Purifoy, Lewis M. Harry Truman's China Policy: McCarthyism and the Diplomacy Hysteria, 1947-1951. New York: New View Points, 1976.   139

Pusey, Nathan. American Higher Education, 1945-1970. A Personal Report. Cambridge, Mass.: Harvard University Press, 1978.   444

Putney, Snell and Gail Putney. The Adjusted American: Normal Neuroses in the Individual and Society. New York: Harper and Row, 1964.   309

Pyles, Thomas. Words and Ways in American English. New York: Random House, 1952. 259

*Quarles, Benjamin. Black Abolitionists. New York: Oxford University Press, 1969.
28, 182

*_____. Frederick Douglass, New York; Atheneum, 1968, 28, 182

_____. Lincoln and the Negro. New York: Oxford University Press, 1969. 182

*_____. The Negro in the American Revolution. New York: Norton, 1973. 182

*_____. The Negro in the Civil War. Boston: Little Brown, 1969. 182

*_____. The Negro in the Making of America. New York: Macmillan, 1964. 10

Quayle, Eric. The Collector's Book of Detective Fiction. London: Studio Vista, 1972. 57

Queen, Ellery. Queen's Quorum. Boston: Little, Brown, 1951. 57

Quick, John. Dictionary of Weapon & Military Terms. New York: McGraw Hill Book
Company, 1973. 273

*Quimby, Ian M.G. Material Culture and the Study of American Life. New York:
Norton, 1978. 510

Quinley, Harold E. The Prophetic Clergy. New York: Wiley, 1974. 386

*Raboteau, Albert J. Slave Religion: The "Invisible Institution" in the Antebellum.
South. New York: Oxford University Press, 1980. 379

Radcliffe, Elsa J. Gothic Novels of the Twentieth Century: An Annotated Bibliography
Metuchen, New Jersey: Scarecrow, 1979. 57

*Radin, Paul. Trickster: A Study in American Indian Mythology. New York: Schocken,
1972. 109

Radway, Janice A. "Phenomenology, Linguistics and Popular Culture." Journal of
Popular Culture, XII (Summer 1978). 494, 504

Railton, Stephen. Fenimore Cooper: A Study of His Life and Imagination. Princeton,
New Jersey: Princeton University Press, 1978. 410

Rainer, Tristine. "Anais Nin's Diary I: The Birth of the Young Woman as an Artist."
Robert Zaller, ed. A Case Book on Anais Nin. New York: New American Library, 1974.
399

RammelKamp, Julian S. Pulitzer's Post-Dispatch, 1878-1883. Princeton: University of
Princeton Press, 1966. 216

Ramsay, David. The History of the American Revolution, 2 vols. 1789; New York:
Russell, 1968. 147

Ramsdell, C.W. "Changing Interpretations of the Civil War." Journal of Southern
History, 3 (February-November 1937). 182

Randall, Frank A. History of the Development of Building Construction in Chicago.
1949; New York: Arno, 1972. 37, 44

Randall, John G. Civil War and Reconstruction. Boston: D.C. Heath, 1937. 182

Ranson, Roger L. and Richard Sutch. One Kind of Freedom: The Economic Consequences
of Emancipation. Cambridge: Cambridge University Press, 1977. 79

Rapp, Rayna, Ellen Ross and Renate Bridenthal. "Examining Family History."
Feminist Studies, 5 (Spring 1979). 538

Rappaport, Armin. Henry L. Stimson and Japan 1931-1933. Chicago: University of
Chicago Press, 1963. 124

*Rather, Dan and Gary Paul Gates. The Palace Guard. New York: Warner, 1975. 438

Ratner, Joseph, ed. Intelligence in the Modern World. New York: 1939. 320

Rau, John and David Wooten, eds. Environmental Impact Analysis Handbook. New York: McGraw-Hill, 1979. 485

Rauch, Basil. Roosevelt: From Munich to Pearl Harbor: A Study in the Creation of a Foreign Policy. New York: Creative Age Press, 1950. 125

Raucher, Alan R. Public Relations and Business, 1900-1929. Baltimore: Johns Hopkins University Press, 1968. 80

Rauschenbush, Winifred. Robert E. Park: Biography of a Sociologist. Durham: Duke University Press, 1979. 530

Ravenel, Beatrice St. Julien. Architects of Charleston. Charleston: Carolina Art Association, 1945. 38, 44

Ravitch, Diane. The Revisionists Revised: A Critique of the Radical Attack on the Schools. New York: Basic Books, 1978. 442

Rayback, Joseph G. Free Soil: The Education of 1848. Lexington: The University Press of Kentucky, 1970. 428

RCL, Afro American Comm. The Black Nation. Newark: People's War, 1977. 21

Read, Allan Walker. "Approaches to Lexicography and Semantics." Thomas R. Sebeok. Current Trends in Linguistics. The Hague: Mouton, 1973. 257, 271

Read, Thomas. The Female Poets of America. 1857; Detroit: Gale, 1978. 404

Real, Michael. Mass-Mediated Culture. Englewood Cliffs, New Jersey: Printice-Hall 1977. 492, 496, 504

_____. "Media Theory: Contributions to an Understanding of American Mass Communications." American Quarterly, 32 (1980). 504

Reck, Andrew J. The New American Philosophers. Baton Rouge: Louisiana State University Press, 1968. 324

_____. Recent American Philosophy. New York: Pantheon, 1964. 324

_____, ed. Introduction to William James. Bloomington: Indiana University Press, 1967. 319

* _____, ed. Selected Writings of George H. Mead. Chicago: University of Chicago Press, 1981.

Redding, J. Saunders. The Lonesome Road: The Story of the Negro's Part in America. New York: Doubleday, 1958. 182

_____. The Negro. Washington, D.C.: Potomac Books, 1967. 182

Reed, Carroll A. Dialects of American English. Amherst, Massachusetts: University of Massachusetts Press, 1977. 264

_____ and Lester G. Seifert. A Linguistic Atlas of Pennsylvania. Germany: Marburg/Lahn, 1954. 267

Reed, James. From Private Vice to Public Virtue: The Birth Control Movement and American Society since 1830. New York: Basic Books, 1978. 542

*Reed, John Shelton. The Enduring South: Subcultural Persistence in Mass Society. Chapel Hill: University of North Carolina, 1975. 466

Reed, Rowena. Combined Operations in the Civil War. Annapolis: U.S. Naval Institute Press, 1978.   290

Reeves, Richard. A Ford, Not a Lincoln. New York: Harcourt Brace Jovanovich, 1975. 440

Reeves, Thomas C. Gentleman Boss: The Life of Chester Alan Arthur. New York: Alfred A. Knopf, 1975. 430

Reich, Charles. The Greening of America. New York: Random House, 1970. 313

Reichard, Gary W. The Reaffirmation of Republicanism: Eisenhower and the Eighty-Third Congress. Knoxville: University of Tennessee Press, 1975. 437

Reiger, C.C. The Era of the Muckrakers. Chapel Hill: University of North Carolina Press, 1932. 217

Reimers, David M. White Protestantism and the Negro. New York: Oxford University Press, 1965. 378

Reiner, Laurence. How to Recycle Buildings. New York: McGraw Hill, 1979. 480

Remini, Robert V. Andrew Jackson and the Bank War. New York: W.W. Norton,1967. 73

_____. Andrew Jackson and the Course of American Empire, 1769-1821. New York: Harper and Row, 1977. 426

*   _____. Martin Van Buren and the Making of the Democratic Party. New York: W. W. Norton, 1970. 427

_____. The Revolutionary Age of Andrew Jackson. New York: Harper and Row, 1976. 427

Render, Sylvia L. Charles W. Chesnutt. Washington, D.C.:Harvard University Press, 1974. 404

Rensselaer, Marianna Griswold van. Henry Hobson Richardson and His Works. 1888; New York: Dover Press, 1969.

Renza, Louis A. "The Veto of the Imagination: A Theory of Autobiography." New Library History, 9 (Autumn 1977). 397

Report of the National Commission on the Observance of International Women's Year. "To Form a More Perfect Union." Justice for American Women. Washington, D.C.: U.S. Government Printing Office, 1976.

Reps, John W. Cities of the American West: A History of Frontier Urban Planning. Princeton: Princeton University Press, 1979. 463

_____. Monumental Washington: The Planning and Development of the Capital Center. Princeton: Princeton University Press, 1967. 463

_____. Tidewater Towns: City Planning in Colonial Virginia and Maryland. Charlottesville: University of Virginia, 1972. 463

*Reuther, Victor. The Brothers Reuther. Boston: Houghton Mifflin, 1976.   449

*Revel, Jean-Francois. Without Marx or Jesus: The New American Revolution Has Begun.
    New York: Doubleday, 1971. 310

Rexroth, Kenneth. American Poetry in the Twentieth Century. New York: The Seabury
    Press, 1973. 344

Reynolds, Clark."American Strategic History and Doctrines: A Reconsideration."
    Military Affairs,Vol. 39 (December 1975). 279

Reynolds, Lloyd G. and Charles C. Killingsworth. Trade Union Publications: The
    Official Journals, Convention Proceedings and Constitutions of International
    Unions and Federations 1850-1941. Baltimore: The Johns Hopkins Press, 1944-1946.

Rhodes, James F. History of the United States from the Compromise of 1850, 7 vols.
    New York: Macmillan, 1893-1906. 183

*Rich, Adrienne. The Dream of a Common Language: Poems 1974-1977. New York: W.W.
    Norton & Co., 1978. 540

_____. Of Woman Born: Motherhood as Experience and Institution. New York: W.W.
    Norton & Co., 1977. 543

*_____. On Lies, Secrets and Silence. New York: W.W. Norton, 1979. 538

Richardson, Elmo R. The Presidency of Dwight D. Eisenhower. Lawrence: Regents Press
    of Kansas, 1979. 437

Richardson, Harry V. Dark Salvation. Garden City: Doubleday, 1976. 378

Richardson, Miles. The Human Mirror: Material and Spatial Images of Man. Baton Rouge:
    Louisiana State University Press, 1974. 509

Richardson, Robert D., Jr. Myth and Literature in the American Renaissance.
    Bloomington, Indiana: Indiana University Press, 1978. 403

Richey, Russell E., ed. Denominationalism. Nashville: Abingdon, 1977. 364

*_____ and Donald G. Jones. American Civil Religion. New York: Harper and Row,
    1974. 388

Richmond, Mary L., ed. Shaker Literature: A Bibliography. Hanover:
    University Press of New England, 1976. 516

Rickover, Hyman G. How the Battleship Maine was Destroyed. Washington: Dept. of the
    Navy, 1976. 135

Ricks, Beatrice. Henry James: A Bibliography of Secondary Works. Metuchen, New Jersey:
    Scarecrow Press, 1975. 413

Rickels, Milton and Patricia. Seba Smith. Boston: G.K. Hall, 1977. 416

*Riesman, David, et.al. The Lonely Crowd. New Haven: Yale University Press, 1973. 170

*_____ and Gerald Grant. The Perpetual Dream-Reform and Experiment in the American
    College. Chicago: University of Chicago Press, 1979. 444

*Rifkind, Carole. Main Street: The Face of Urban America. New York: Harper and Row,
    1979. 92, 459

Rihlstedt, F.T. "Formal and Structural Innovations in America Exposition Architecture:
    1901-1939." Unpublished dissertation.Northwestern University, 1973. 532

Riley, Glenda. Women on the American Frontier. St. Louis Press, 1977. 543

Riley, James C. "Foreign Credit and Fiscal Stability: Dutch Investment in the United States, 1781-1794." Journal of American History, LXV (December 1978). 91

Ringenbach, Paul T. Tramps and Reformers, 1873-1916: The Discovery of Unemployment in New York. Westport, Conn: Greenwood Press, 1973. 87

Rippley, La Vern J. The German-Americans. Boston: Twayne, 1976. 195

Rist, Ray C. The Invisible Children: School Integration in American Society. Cambridge: Harvard University Press, 1978. 443

Ritcheson, Charles R. Aftermath of Revolution: British Policy toward the United States, 1783-1795. Dallas: Southern Methodist University Press, 1969. 115

Ritter, Frederic Louis. History of Music. 296

_____. Music in America. 1890; New York: Johnson Reprints, 1971. 296

Rivers, William L., Wallace Thompson and Michael Nyhan, eds. The Aspen Handbook on the Media. New York: Praeger, 1979. 491, 504

Robbins, J. Albert, ed. American Literary Manuscripts: A Checklist of Holdings. Athens, Georgia: University of Georgia Press, 1977. 554

Roberts, Chalmers M. The Washington Post: The First 100 Years. Boston: Houghton-Mifflin Co., 1977. 227

*Roberts, Leonard. Sang Branch Settlers. Pikeville: Pikeville College Press. 99

Robin, Richard. Annotated Catalogue of the Papers of C.S. Peirce. Amherst: University of Massachusetts Press, 1968. 322

*Robinson, Cervin and Rosemarie H. Bletter. Skyscaper Style: Art Deco in New York. New York: Oxford University Press, 1975. 37

Robinson, Daniel. Royce and Hocking: American Idealists. Boston: The Christopher Publishing House, 1968. 3380

Robinson, Edgar E. and Vaughn D. Bornet. Herbert Hoover: President of the United States. Stanford, California: Hoover Institution Press, 1975. 434

Robinson, Willard B. American Forts: Architectural Form and Fiction. Urbana: University of Illinois Press, 1977. 290

Robinson, William D. and Todd Webb. Texas Public Buildings of the Nineteenth Century. Austin: University of Texas Press, 1974. 44

Roche, George. The Bewildered Society. New Rochelle: Arlington House, 1972. 311

*Roche, John P. Courts and Rights: The American Judiciary in Action. New York: Random House, 1966. 352

*Rockefeller, David, Jr., chairman. Coming to Our Senses: The Significance of the Arts for American Education. New York: McGraw Hill, 1977. 443

Rockoff, Hugh T. "Varieties of Banking Regional Economic Development in the United States, 1840-1860." Journal of Economic History, XXXV (March 1975) 73

*Rodgers, Daniel. The Work Ethic in Industrial America, 1850-1920. Chicago: University of Chicago Press, 1978. 446

Roemer, Kenneth. The Obsolete Necessity: American in Utopian Writings, 1880-1900. Kent, Ohio: Kent State University Press, 1976. 403, 516

*Rogin, Michael Paul. Fathers and Children: Andrew Jackson and the Subjugation of the American Indians. New York: Random, 1976. 183, 427

*Rohrbough, Malcolm J. The Land Office Business: The Settlement and Administration of American Public Lands, 1789-1837. New York: Oxford Universtiy Press, 1971. 77

Rollin, Roger B. "Against Evaluation: The Role of the Critic of Popular Culture." Journal of Popular Culture, IX: 2 (Fall 1975).   496, 504

_____. "The Freud Connection: Psychoanalytic Approaches to Popular Culture Audience Response." Unpublished paper presented to the Popular Culture Association, 1980. 496, 504

*Romasco, Albert U. Poverty of Abundance: Hoover, the Nation, the Depression. New York: Oxford University Press, 1968. 87, 434

Roosevelt, Elliott. Mother R.: Eleanor Roosevelt's Untold Story. New York: Putman, 1977. 435

_____. A Rendezvous with Destiny: The Roosevelts of the White House. New York: Putman, 1975. 435

_____. An Untold Story: The Roosevelts of Hyde Park. New York: Putman Sons, 1973. 435

Roosevelt, Franklin Delano. Complete Presidential Press Conferences of Franklin D. Roosevelt. New York: Da Capo Press, 1972.   434

Roosevelt, James. My Parents: A Differing View. Chicago: Playboy Press, 1976. 435

Roosevelt, Theodore. The Winning of the West, 4 vols. 1890; Michigan: Scholarly Press, 1977. 157

Ropp, Theodore. "Forty Years of the Military Institute, 1933-1972." Military Affairs, Vol. 35 (October 1971). 277

_____. "War: From Colonies to Vietnam." William H. Cartwright and Ricahrd L. Watson, Jr., eds. The Reinterpretation of American History. Washington, D.C.: National Council for Social Studies, 1973. 278

Rose, Lisle A. Dubious Victory: The United States and the End of the World War II. Kent, Ohio: Kent State Unviersity Press, 1973. 128

_____. Roots of Tragedy: The United States and the Struggle for Asia. Westport, Conn.: Greenwood, 1976. 139

Rose, Mark H. Interstate: Express Highway Politics, 1941-1956. Lawrence, Kansas: Regents Press of Kansas, 1979. 94

Rose, Thomas, ed. Violence in America: A Historical and Contemporay Reader. New York: Random House, 1969. 310

*Rose, Willie Lee. Rehearsal for Reconstruction: The Port Royal Experiment. New York: Oxford University Press, 1976.   28

Rosen Elliot A. Hoover, Rooosevelt and the Brain Trust: From Depression to New Deal. New York: Columbia University Press, 1977. 435

Rosen, Paul. The Supreme Court and Social Science. Urbana, Illinois: University of Illinois Press, 1972 . 353

*Rosen, Ruth and Sue Davidson, eds. The Maimie Papers. Old Westbury, New York: The Feminist Press, 1977. 547

Rosenberg, Bernard and David Manning White, eds. Mass Culture Revisited. New York: Van Nostrand, 1971. 492, 493, 504

Rosenberg, Bruce. The Art of the American Folk Preacher. New York: Oxford University Press, 1970. 107

_____. Custer and the Epic of Defeat. University Park, Pa.: Pennsylvania State University Press, 1974. 98

Rosenberg, Carroll S. Religion and the Rise of the American City: The New York Mission Movement, 1812-1870. Ithaca: Cornell University Press, 1971.

*Rosenberg, Charles. The Trial of the Assassin Guiteau: Psychiatry and Law in the Gilded Age. Chicago: University of Chicago Press, 1976. 430

*Rosenberg, Nathan. Perspectives in Technology. Cambridge:Cambridge University Press, 1976. 74

*_____. Technology and American Economic Growth. Armonk: Sharpe,1972. 74

Rosenblatt, Roger. "Black Autobiography: Life as the Death Weapon." James Olney, ed. Autobiography. Princeton: Princeton University Press, 1980. 395, 396, 398

Rosenblum, Gerald. Immigrant Workers: Their Impact on American Labor Radicalism. New York: Basic Books, 1973. 199

Rosenblum, Victor. Law as a Political Instrument. New York: Doubleday, 1955. 350

*Rosengarten, Theodore. All God's Dangers: The Life of Nat Shaw. New York: Avon, 1975. 389

Rosenthal, M.L. The New Poets: American and British Poetry Since World War II. New York: Oxford University Press, 1962. 344

Rosenthal, Sandra B. The Pragmatic A Priori. St. Louis: Warren H. Green, Inc., 1976. 327

Rosewater, Victor. History of Cooperative News-Gathering in the United States. 1930; New York: Johnson Reprints. 217

Rossiter, Clinton. Constitutional Dictatorships: Crisis Government in the Modern Democracies. Princeton, New Jersey: Princeton Univerity Press, 1948. 353

*_____. The Supreme Court and the Commander in Chief. Itahca: Cornell University Press, 1976. 353

Rossiter, Frank R. Charles Ives and His America. New York: Liveright, 1975. 304

Rossiter, Margaret W. The Emergence of Agricultural Science: Justus Liebig and the Americans, 1840-1880. New Haven: Yale University Press, 1975. 77

Rostow, Eugene V. The Sovereign Prerogative: The Supreme Court and the Quest for Law. New Haven, Conn.: Yale University Press, 1962. 351

Rostow, Walt W. The Diffusion of Power: An Essay in Recent History. New York: Macmillan. 1972. 130, 175

*_____. The Stages of Economic Growth: A Non-Communist Manifesto. Cambridge: Cambridge University Press, 1971. 67

*Roszak, Theodore. The Making of a Counter-Culture: Reflections on the Technocratic Society and its Youthful Opposition. Garden City, New York: Doubleday, 1969. 313

Roth, Darlene R. and Louise E. Shaw. Atlanta Women: From Myth to Modern Time. Atlanta: Atlanta Historical Society, 1980. 467

Roth, John K., ed. The Moral Equivalent of War and Other Essays. New York: 1971. 319

Roth, Leland M. A Concise History of American Architecture. New York: Harper and Row, 1979. 47

Roth, Martin. Comedy and America: The Lost World of Washington Irving. Port Washington, New York: Kennikat, 1976. 413

*Rothman, Shiela M. Woman's Proper Place: A History of Changing Ideals and Practices, 1870 to the Present. New York: Basic Books, 1978. 536

Rothschild, May Aichin. "White Women Volunteers in the Freedom Summer." Feminist Studies, 5 (Fall 1979). 542

Rothstein, Morton. "America in the International Rivalry for the British Wheat Market, 1860-1914." Mississippi Valley Historical Review, XLVII (December 1960). 76

Rourke, Constance M. American Humor: A Study of the National Character. 1931; New York: Harcourt, Brace Jovanovich, 1971. 96, 102

_____. The Roots of American Culture. 1942; Westport: Greenwood Press, 1980. 96

Rouse, Parke, Jr. James Blair of Virginia. Chapel Hill: University of North Carolina Press, 1971. 372

Rousmaniere, John P. "Cultural Hybrid in the Slums: The College Woman and the Settlement House, 1889-1894." College Settlement Association, 22 (1970). 521

Routley, Erik. The Puritan Pleasures of the Detective Story: From Sherlock Holmes to Van der Valk. London: Victor Gollancz, 1972. 59

Rovere, Richard H. and Arthur M. Schlesinger, Jr. The MacArthur Controversy and American Foreign Policy. New York: Farrar, Straus and Giroux, rev. ed, 1965. 130

Rowe, Anne. The Enchanted Country: Northern Writers in the South, 1865-1910. Baton Rouge, Louisiana: Louisiana State University Press, 1978. 403

Rowney, Don Karl. "What is Urban History?" Journal of Interdisciplinary History, 8 (Autumn 1977). 469

Royce, Josiah. The Problem of Christianity. Chicago: University of Chicago Press, 1968. 320

Rubin, Julius. Canal or Railroad: Imitation and Innovation in the Response to the Erie Canal in Philadelphia, Baltimore and Boston. Philadelphia: American Philosophical Society, 1961. 70

_____. "The Limits of Agricultural Progress in the Nineteenth Century South." Agricultural History, VLIX (April 1975). 79

Rubin, Louis D., Jr., et. al., eds. Southern Writers: A Biographical Dictionary. Baton Rouge, Louisiana: Louisiana State University Press, 1979. 406

Rucker, Darnell. The Chicago Pragmatists. Minneapolis: University of Minnesota Press, 1969. 327

*Rudd, Robert L. Pesticides and the Living Landscape. Madison: University of
    Wisconsin Press, 1964. 475

*Ruddick, Sara and Pamela Daniels, eds. Working It Out: 23 Women Writers, Artists,
    Scientists and Scholars Talk About Their Lives and Work. New York: Pantheon,
    1978. 548

Rudolph, Frederick. Curriculum: A History of the American Undergraduate Course of
    Study. San Francisco: Jossey-Bass, 1977. 444

*Rudwick, Elliott. Race Riot at   East St. Louis, July 2, 1917. New York: Atheneum,
    1972. 28

*_____. W.E.B. Du Bois: Propagandist of the Negro Protest. New York: Atheneum,
    1968. 28

Rulon, Curt. "Geographical Distribution of the Dialect Areas in The Adventures of
    Huckleberry Finn." Mark Twain Journal, XIV (1966). 267

Rumble, Wilfred. American Legal Realism: Skepticism and the Judicial Process. Ithaca,
    New York: Cornell University Press, 1968. 354

Runblom, Harold, ed. From Sweden to America. Minneapolis: University of Minnesota
    Press, 1976. 193

Rupp, Leila J. Mobilizing Women for War: German and American Propaganda, 1939-1945.
    Princeton: Princeton University Press, 1978. 291, 544

Russell, C. Allyn. Voices of American Fundamentalism. Philadelphia: Westminster Press,
    1976. 381

Russell, Diane H. "Review Essay: Art History." Signs, 5 (Spring 1980). 537

*Russo, David J. The Major Political Issues of the Jacksonian Period and the
    Development of Party Loyalty in Congress, 1830-1840. Philadelphia: American
    Philosophical Society, 1972. 427

Rutland, Robert A. and Charles F. Holeson, eds. The Papers of James Madison.
    Charlottesville: University of Virginia, 1962. 426

*Rutman, Darrett B. American Puritanism: Faith and Practice. New York: Norton, 1977.
    367
    _____. Husbandmen of Plymouth: Farmsand Villages in the Old Colony, 1620-1692.
    Boston: Beacon Press, 1967. 65

    _____. "People in Process: The New Hampshire Towns of the Eighteenth Century."
    Journal of Urban History, I (May 1975). 65

    _____. Winthrop's Boston. Chapel Hill University of North Carolina Press, 1969.
    65, 171
Ryan, Mary P. "The Power of Women's Networks."Feminist Studies, 5 (Spring 1979). 541

*Ryan, Paul B. The Panama Canal Controversy: U.S. Diplomacy and Defense Interests.
    Stanford, California: Hoover Institution Press, 1977. 136

Rycroft, Chabus. Imagination and Reality: Psycho-Analytical Essays, 1951-1961.
    London: Hogarth Press Institute of Phycho-Analysis, 1968. 59

Rystad, Goran. Ambiguous Imperialism: American Foreign Policy and Domestic
    Politics at the Turn of the Century. Lund, Sweden: Esselte Studium, 1975. 135

Saatkamp, Herman and John Jones, eds. George Santayana: A Bibliographical Checklist 1880-1980. Philosophical Documentation Center. 329

Sachs, Albie and Joan Hoff Wilson. Sexism and the Law: Male Beliefs and Legal Bias in Britain and the United States. New York: The Free Press, 1978. 542

Safford, Jeffrey J. Wilsonian Maritime Diplomacy, 1913-1921. New Brunswick, New Jersey: Rutgers University Press, 1970. 432

Safire, William L. Before the Fall: An Inside View of the Pre-Watergate White House. Garden City, New York: Doubleday, 1975. 438

*Sale, Kirkpatrick. Power Shift: The Rise of the Southern Rim and Its Challenge to the Eastern Establishment. New York: Vintage, 1975. 464

Salsbury, Stephen. The State, the Investor and the Railroad: The Boston and Albany, 1825-1867. Cambridge: Harvard University Press, 1967. 70

Salter. C.L. "The Convenience of Environmental Ignorance." The Professional Geographer (August 1977). 421

*   . San Francisco's Chinatown: How Chinese a Town? Palo Alto: Rand E. Research Associates, 1978. 421

Salvadori, Mario G. and Robert Heller. Structure in Architecture. Englewood Cliffs: Prentice-Hall, 1975. 36

Salzman, Eric. Twentieth-Century Music: An Introduction. Englewood Cliffs: Prentice-Hall, 1974. 296, 301

     . "Modern Music in Retrospect." Perspectives of New Music, II (Spring-Summer 1964). 301

Samuels, Ernest. Henry Adams, 3 vols. Cambridge, Mass.: Belknap Press, 1947, 1958, 1964. 183

Sandburg, Carl. Abraham Lincoln, 6 vols. New York: Harcourt, Brace, 1926-1939. 183

*Sandeen, Ernest R. The Roots of Fundamentalism: British and American Millenarianism, 1800-1930. New York: Baker, 1978. 381

     and Frederick Hale. American Religion and Philosophy: A Guide to Informational Sources. Detroit: Gale Research, 1978. 362

Sanderlin, George. Mark Twain: As Others Saw Him. New York: Coward McCann, 1978. 410

Sanders, James M. The Education of an Urban Minority: Catholics in Chicago, 1833-1965. New York: Oxford University Press, 1977. 520

*Sanders, Marion K. Dorothy Thompson: A Legend in Her Time. New York: Avon, 1974. 219

Sanders, Willease. "Selected Grammatical Features of the Speech of Blacks in Columbia, S.C."Dissertation, University of So. Carolina, 1978. 264, 266

Sapir, David and Christopher Crocker. The Social Use of Metaphor. Philadelphia: U. of Pennsylvania, 1977. 505

Sargent, Lyman Tower, ed. British and American Utopian Literature, 1516-1975. Boston: G.K. Hall, 1979. 406

Sarkesian, Sam C., ed. Defense and the Presidency: Carter'sFirst Years. Boulder: Westview Press, 1979.

*Satz, Ronald N. American Indian Policy in the Jacksonian Era. Lincoln: University of Nebraska Press, 1975. 512

Savage, William W., Jr. The Cherokee Strip Live Stock Association: Federal Regulation and the Cattleman's Last Frontier. Columbia: University of Missouri Press, 1973. 7.

Savelle, Max. The Origins of American Diplomacy: The International History of Angloamerica, 1492-1763. New York: Macmillan, 1967. 114

Saveth, Edward. "A Decade of American Historiography, The 1960's." William A. Cartwright and Richard L. Watson Jr., eds. The Reinterpretaion of American History Washington, D.C.: National Council for the Social Studies, 1973. 278

Sawyer, Janet B. "A Dialect Study of San Antonio, Texas: A Bilingual Community." Dissertation. University of Texas, 1957. 267

_____. "Social Aspects of Bilingualism in San Antonio, Texas." PADS, XLI (1964). 267

*Saxton, Martha. Louisa May: A Modern Biography of Louisa May Alcott. New York: Avon, 1978. 409

Sayers, Dorothy L., ed. The Omnibus of Crime. New York: Payson and Clarke, 1929. 57

Sayre, Robert F. "Autobiography and the Making of an Idea." James Olney, ed. Autobiography. Princeton: Princeton University Press, 1980. 390, 397

_____. "The Proper Study-Autobiographies American Studies." American Quarterly, 29 (1977). 390, 397

Scarborough, William K. The Overseer: Plantation Management in the Old South. Baton Rouge: Louisiana State University Press, 1966. 79

Scargill, M.H. A Short History of Canadian English. Vancouver, B.C.: Sono Press, 1977. 259

_____ and P.G. Penna. Looking at Language: Essays in Introductory Linguistics. Toronto: Gage, 1966. 260

_____, el. al. Modern Canadian English Usage. Toronto: McClelland and Stuart, 1974. 270

Scarry, Robert J. Millard Fillmore, 13th. President. Moravia, New York: Robert J. Scarry, 1970. 428

Schaaf, Barbara. Mr. Dooley's Chicago. Garden City: Anchor, 1977. 528

Schalabach, Theron A. Edwin E. Witte: Cautious Reformer. Madison: State Historical Society of Wisconsin, 1969. 88

Schaller, Michael. The U.S. Crusade in China, 1938-1945. New York: Columbia University Press, 1979. 138

Schandler, Herbert Y. The Unmaking of a President: Lyndon Johnson and Vietnam. Princeton, New Jersey: Princeton University Press, 1977. 140, 438

Schecter, Harold, ed. "Focus on Myth and American Popular Art." Journal of American Culture, 2:2. 505

*_____. The New Gods: Psyche and Symbol in Popular Art. Bowling Green: Popular Press, 1980. 505

*_____ and Jonna Gormley Semeiks, eds. Patterns in Popular Culture: A Sourcebook for Writers. New York: Harper and Row, 1980. 492, 505

Scheffler, Israel. Four Pragmatists. New York: Humanities Press, 1974. 327

Scheiber, Harry N. "Federalism and the American Economic Order, 1789-1910." Law and
     Society Review, X (Fall 1975). 70

_____. Ohio Canal Era: A Case Study of Government and the Economy, 1820-1861.
     Athens: Ohio University Press, 1969. 70

_____. "Property Law, Expropriation and Resource Allocation by Government: the
     United States, 1789-1910." Journal of Economic History, XXX (March 1973). 70

_____."The Road to Munn: Eminent Domain and the Concept of Public Purpose in the
     State Courts." Perspectives in American History, V (1971). 70

Scheick, William J. The Half-Blood: A Cultural Symbol in Nineteenth Century
     American Fiction. Lexington: University Press of Kentucky, 1979. 403

Scheips, Paul J. "Military History and Peace Research." Military Affairs, Vol. 36
     (Ocotber 1972). 277

_____. "Quincy Wright, 1890-1970." Military Affairs, Vol. 35 (April 1971). 277

Schele de Vere, Maximilian. Americanisms: The English of the New World. 1871;
     Johnson Reprint.   271

Scherer, Lester B. Slavery and the Churches in Early America, 1619-1819. Grand Rapids:
     Eerdmans, 1975. 378

*Schiller, Herbert I. Communications and Cultural Domination. White Plains, New York:
     Pantheon, 1978. 496, 505

*_____. The Mind Managers. Boston: Beacon, 1973. 505

Schiro, Michael. Curriculum for Better Schools: The Great Ideological Debate.
     Englewood Cliffs, New Jersey: Educational Technology Publication, 1978. 443

Schlebecker, John T. Whereby We Thrive: A History of American Farming, 1607-1972.
     Ames: Iowa State University Press, 1975. 76

Schlereth, Thomas J. "America, 1871-1919: A View of Chicago." American Studies, 17
     (Fall 1976). 518

_____. "Big Money and High Culture: The Commercial Club of Chicago and Charles L.
     Hutchinson." Great Lakes Review, 3 (Summer 1976). 529

_____. "Mail Orders Catalogues as Resources in Material Culture Studies." Prospects:
     An Annual of American Cultural Studies, 1980. 529

_____. "Material Culture Studies in America: Notes Toward a Historical Perspective."
     Material History Bulletin, 8 (1979). 510

_____."Past Cityscapes: Uses of Cartography in Urban History." Artifacts and the
     American Past: Techniques for the Historian. Nashville:AASLH, 1980. 528

_____. "A'Robin's Egg Renaissance': Chicago Culture, 1893-1933." Chicago History,
     8 (Fall 1979). 529

Schlereth, Wendy L. Clauson. "The Chapbook: A Journal of American Intellectual
     Life, 1894-1898." Dissertation. University of Iowa, 1980. 521

*Schlesinger, Arthur M., Jr. The Age of Jackson. Boston: Little, 1945. 167

*_____. The Age of Roosevelt, 3 vols. New York: Houghton-Mifflin, 1957. 167

*_____. The Bitter Heritage: Vietnam and American Diplomacy, 1941-1966. Boston:
     Houghton Mifflin, 1966. 131

*_____. Prelude to Independence: The Newspaper War on Britain, 1764-1776. New England University Press, 1980. 208

*_____. A Thousand Days: John F. Kennedy in the White House. New York: Fawcett, 1977. 183

_____. Violence: America in the Sixties. New York: New American Library, 1968. 310

_____. The Vital Center. Boston: Houghton Mifflin, 1949. 183

Schlissel, Lillian. "Women's Diaries on the Western Frontier." American Studies, 18 (Spring 1977). 399, 543

Schmidhauser, John R. Judges and Justice: The Federal Appellate Judiciary. Boston: Little, Brown and Co., Inc., 1979. 357

Schmookler, Jacob. Invention and Economic Growth. Cambridge: Harvard University Press, 1966. 74

*Schnapper, M.B. American Labor: A Pictorial History. Washington, D.C.: Public Affairs Press, 1972. 452

Schneider, Daniel J. The Crystal Cage: Adventures of the Imagination in the Fiction of Henry James. Lawrence, Kansas: Regents Press of Kansas, 1978. 413

*Schneider, Herbert Wallace. Religion in Twentienth Century America. 1952; New York: Atheneum, 1969. 386

Schnore, Leo F., ed. The New Urban History: Quantitative Explorations by American Historians. Princeton: Princeton University, 1974. 460

Schob, David E. Hired Hands and Plowboys: Farm Labor in the Midwest, 1815-60. Urbana: University of Illinois Press, 1975. 76

Schoenebaum, Eleanora W. Profiles of an Era: The Nixon, Ford Years. New York: Facts on File, Inc., 1979. 438

*Scholes, Robert. Structuralism in Literature. New Haven: Yale University, 1974. 505

Scholes, Walter and Marie F. Foreign Policies of the Taft Administration. Columbia: University of Missouri Press, 1970. 432

Scholler, Harald and John Reidy. Lexicography and Dialect Geography: Festgabe fur Hans Kurath Zeitschrift fur Dialektologie und Linguistik. Wiesbaden: Franz Steiner Verlag, 1973. 260

Schonhoar, Rainer. Novelle und Kriminalsschema: Ein Strukturmodelldeutscher Erzahlkunst zum 1800. Bad Homburg: 1969. 54

Schoonover, Thomas D. Dollars Over Dominion: The Triumph of Liberalism in Mexican-United States Relations, 1861-1867. Baton Rouge: Louisiana State University Press, 1978. 135

Schouler, James. History of the United States under the Constitution, 7 vols. New York: Dobb, Mead, 1880-1899. 183

Schrag, Peter. The Decline of the Wasp. New York: Simon and Schuster, 1971. 313

Schram, Martin. Running for President: A Journal of the Carter Campaign. New York: Pocket Books, 1976. 441

Schreiner, Samuel A., Jr. The Condensed World of Reader's Digest. New York: Stein and Day, 1977. 227

Schroeder, John H. Mr. Polk's War: American Opposition and Dissent, 1846-1848. Madison: University of Wisconsin Press, 1973. 427

Schroeder, Paul W. The Axis Alliance and Japanese-American Relations, 1941. Ithaca: Cornell University Press, 1958. 126

Schroth, Raymond A. The Eagle and Brooklyn: A Community Newspaper. Westport: Greenwood, 1974.

*Schubert, Frank N., ed. March to South Pass. Washington, D.C.: G.P.O., 1979. 293

Schubert, Glendon. Judicial Behavior: A Reader in Theory and Reserach. New York: Rand McNally & Co., 1964. 354

_____. "Policy Without Law." 14 Stanford Law Review, 284 (1962). 354

_____. Quantitative Analysis of Judicial Behavior. Glencoe, Illinois: The Free Press, 1959. 354

Schudson, Michael. Discovering the News: A Social History of the News. New York: Basic Books, 1978. 228

Schuker, Stephen. The End of French Predominance in Europe: The Financial Crisis of 1924 and the Adoption of the Darnes Plan. Chapel Hill: University of North Carolina Press, 1976. 137

Schulberg, Budd, ed. From the Ashes. New York: New American Library, 1967. 14

Schuller, Gunther. Early Jazz: Its Roots and Early Development. New York: Oxford University Press, 1968. 301

Schultz, Elizabeth. "To Be Black and Blue: The Blues Genre in Black American Autobiography." Kansas Quarterly, 7 (Summer 1975). 399

Schultz, Harold Seessel. James Madison. New York: Twayne Publishers, 1970. 426

Schulz-Buschhaus, Ulrich, ed. Formen und Idealogien der Kriminalroman. Frankfurt: Athenaion, 1975. 59

*Schumacher, E.F. Small is Beautiful. New York: Harper, 1976. 476

Schwab, Peter and J. Lee Shneidman. John F. Kennedy. Boston: Twayne Publishers, 1974. 438

Schwantes, Robert S. Japanese and Americans: A Century of Cultural Relations. New York: Harper, 1955. 131

Schwartz, Charles. George Gershwin: A Selective Bibliography and Discography. Detroit: Information Coordinators, 1974. 306

Schwartz, Tony. The Responsive Chord. Garden City, New York: Anchor, 1974. 493, 505

Schwarz, Jordan A. The Interregnum of Dispair: Hoover, Congress and the Depression. Champaign: University of Illinois Press, 1970. 434

Scott, Anne Firor. "The Study of Southern Urbanization." Urban Affairs Quarterly, 7 (March 1966). 465

Scott, Clifford H. Lester Frank Ward. Boston: G.K. Hall, 1976. 416

Scott, Donald M. From Office to Profession: The New England Ministry, 1750-1850.
    Philadelphia: University of Pennsylvania Press, 1978. 376

*Scott, Franklin D. The Peopling of America: Perspectives of Immigration. Washington,
    D.C.: American Historical Association, Pamphlet 241, 1972. 193

Scott, Roy V. The Reluctant Farmer: The Rise of Agricultural Extension to 1914.
    Urbana: University of Illinois Press, 1970. 77

*Scully, Vincent. American Architecture and Urbanism. New York: Praeger, 1969. 34, 42

Scura, Dorothy M. Henry James (1860-1874): A Reference Guide. Boston: G.K. Hall, 1979.
    413

Seager, Robert II and Doris D. Maguire, eds. Letters and Papers of Alfred Thayer
    Mahan. Annapolis: U.S. Naval Institute Press, 1975, 3 vols. 282

Sealock, Richard B. and Pauline A. Seely. A Bibliography of Place Name Literature:
    United States, Canada, Alaska and Newfoundland. Chicago: American Library
    Association, 1967. 257

Sealts, Merton M. The Early Lives of Melville: Nineteenth Century Biographical
    Sketches and Their Authors. Madison, Wisconsin: University of Wisconsin Press,
    1975. 415

Sebeok, Thomas R., Albert H. Marckwardt, et. al. Currents Trends in Linguistics 10:
    Linguistics in North America. The Hague: Mouton, 1973. 260

*Sefton, James E. Andrew Johnson and the Uses of Constitutional Power. Boston: Little,
    Brown and Co., 1980. 429

Segal, Ronald. The Americans: A Conflict of Creed and Reality. New York: Viking Press,
    1969. 310

*Seifer, Nancy. Nobody Speaks for Me! Self-Portraits of American Working Class Women.
    New York: Simon and Schuster, 1976. 547

Seigfried, Charlene H. Chaos and Context: A Study in William James. Athens, Ohio:
    Ohio University Press, 1978. 327, 414

Self, Robert. Barrett Wendell. Boston: G.K. Hall, 1975. 416

*Seller, Maxine S. To Seek America: A History of Ethnic Life in the United States.
    Jerone S. Ozer, 1977. 193

Sellers, Charles Grier, comp. Andrew Jackson, A Profile. New York: Hill and Wang,
    1971. 427

Semmingsen, Ingrid. "Nordic Research into Emigration." Scandinavian Journal of History,
    III (1978). 204

Semonche, John E. Charting the Future: The Supreme Court Responds to a Changing
    Society, 1890-1920. Westport, Conn.: Greenwood Press, 1978. 357

Sennet, Richard. Families Against The City: Middle Class Homes of Industrial Chicago,
    1872-1890. Cambridge: Harvard University Press, 1970. 519

_____. "Genteel Backlash, Chicago 1886." Transaction, 7 (1970). 527

Sernett, Milton C. Black Religion and American Evangelicalism. Metuchen: Scarecrow
    Press, 1975. 379

*Sessions, Roger. Questions About Music. New York: Norton, 1971. 301

Severance, Frank H., ed. Millard Fillmore Papers, 2 vols. 1907; New York: Kraus Reprints, 1970. 428

*Sewall, Richard B. The Life of Emily Dickinson, 2 vols. New York: Farrar, Straus and Giroux, 1974. 411

*Seyersted, Per. Kate Chopin: A Critical Biography. Baton Rouge. Louisiana State University Press, 1980. 406

Seymour, Charles. American Diplomacy during the World War. Baltimore: Johns Hopkins Press, 1934. 121

_____. American Neutrality: 1914-1917. New Haven: Yale University Press, 1935. 121

_____. Woodrow Wilson and the World War: A Chronicle of Our Own Times. New York: Yale University Press, 1921. 183

Shanabruch, Charles H. Toward an American Catholic Identity: The Chicago Experience. Notre Dame: University of Notre Dame Press, 1980. 528

*Shands, William. Federal Resource Lands and Their Neighbors. Washington, D.C.: Conservation Foundation, 1979. 484

*_____, et. al. National Forest Policy: From Conflict to Consensus. Washington, D.C.: Conservation Foundation, 1979. 481

Shanet, Howard. Philharmonic. New York: Doubleday, 1974. 300

Shapiro, Martin."The Constitution and Economic Rights." In M. Judd Harmon, ed. Essays on the Constitution of the United States. Port Washington, New York, 1978. 357

_____. Law and Politics in the Supreme Court. New York: Free Press, 1964. 349

_____. "The Supreme Court: From Warren to Burger." In Anthony King, ed., The New American Political System. Washington: American Enterprise Institute, 1978. 356

Sharpe, Ernest G. B. Dealey of the Dallas News. New York: Henry Holt, 1955. 216

Sharpless, John B. and Sam Bass Warner, Jr. American Behavioral Scientist, 21. (November-December 1977). 454

Shaw, Archer H. The Plain Dealer. New York: Knopf, 1942. 211

Shaw, Douglas V. The Making of an Immigrant City: Ethnic and Cultural Conflict in Jersey City, New Jersey, 1850-1877. New York: Arno, 1976. 200

*Shaw,Peter. The Character of John Adams. New York: Norton, 1977. 425

Shawcross, William. Sideshow: Kissinger, Nixon and The Destruction of Cambodia. New York: Simon and Schuster, 1979. 141

Shay, Frank. Here's Audacity: American Legendary Heroes. 1930; New York: Arno. 100

*Sheehan, Bernard W. Seeds of Extinction: Jefferson Philanthropy and the American Indian. New York: Norton, 1974. 512

Shepherd, Jack. The Adams Chronicles: Four Generations of Greatness. Boston: Little, Brown, 1975. 425

_____. Cannibals of the Heart: A Personal History of Louisa Catherine and John Quincy. New York: McGraw, 1980. 426

Shepherd, James F. and Gary M. Walton. "Economic Change After the American Revolution: Pre and Post-War Comparisons of Maritime Shipping and Trade." Explorations in Economic History, XIII (October 1976). 66

_____. The Economic Rise of Early America. Cambridge: Cambridge University Press, 1979. 91

_____. Shipping, Maritime Trade and Economic Development of Colonial North America. Cambridge: Cambridge University Press, 1972.

Shepro, Richard W. "The Reconstruction of Chicago after the Great Fire of 1871." Unpublished Thesis. Harvard University, 1974. 531

*Sher, Jonathan P. Education in Rural America: A Reassessment of Conventional Wisdom. Boulder, Colorado: Westview Press, 1977. 443

Sherrill, Rowland A. The Prophetic Melville: Experience, Transcendence and Tragedy. Athens, Georgia: University of Georgia Press, 1979. 415

Sherry, Michael S. Preparing for the Next War: American Plans for Postwar Defense, 1941-1945. New Haven: Yale University Press, 1977. 291

Sherwin, Martin F. A World Destroyed: The Atomic Bomb and the Grand Alliance. New York: Knopf, 1975. 129

Shideler, James H., ed. Agriculture in the Development of the Far West. Washington D.C.: Agricultural History Society, 1975. 76

Shinn, Roger L., ed. The Search for Identity: Essays on the American Character. New York: Harper and Row, 1964. 309

Shklar, Judith. Legalism. Cambridge: Harvard University Press, 1964. 347

Shogan, Robert. A Question of Judgment: The Fortas Case and the Struggle for the Supreme Court. Indianapolis, Indiana: Bobbs-Merrill, 1972. 349

Sholnick, Robert J. Edmund Clarence Stedman. Boston: G.K. Hall, 1977. 416

Shores, David L. Contemporary English: Change and Variation. Philadelphia: Lippincott, 1972. 260

_____ and Carole P. Hines. Papers in Language Variation: SAMLADS Collection. University,Alabama: University of Alabama Press, 1977. 260

Short, C.W. and R. Stanley-Brown. Public Buildings. Washington: Government Printing Office, 1939. 37, 43

Shoup, Lawrence H. The Carter Presidency and Beyond: Power and Politics in 1980's. Palo Alto, California: Ramports Press, 1980. 441

Showalter, Dennis E. " A Modest Plea for Drums and Trumpets." Military Affairs, Vol.39 (April 1975). 279

*Showalter, Elaine. These Modern Women: Autobiographical Essays from the Twenties. Old Westbury, New York: The Feminist Press, 1978. 538

Shuffelton, Frank. Thomas Hooker, 1586-1647. Princeton: Princeton University Press, 369

Shurr, William H. The Mystery of Iniquity: Melville as Poet, 1857-1891. Lexington, Kentucky: University Press of Kentucky, 1972. 415

Shurtleff, Harold R. The Log Cabin Myth. 1939; New York: Peter Smith, 1967. 36, 43

Shuy, Roger W. Discovering American Dialects. Champaign, Illinois: National Council of Teachers of English, 1967. 265

_____, Walter A Wolfram and William K. Riley. Field Techniques in an Urban Language Study. Washington, D.C.: Center for Applied Linguistics, 1968. 266

Shy, John. "The American Military Experience: History and Learning." Journal of Inderdisciplinary History, 1 (Winter 1971). 273, 276

_____. "The Military Conflict Considered as a Revolutionary War." Journal of Interdisciplinary History, (Winter 1971). 276

_____. A People Numerous and Armed: Reflections on the Military Struggle for American Independence. New York: Oxford University Press, 1976. 273

Sicherman, Barbara, et. al. Notable American Women: The Modern Period, 1950-1975. Cambridge: Harvard University Press, 1980. 537

Siddons, Anne Rivers. The House Next Door. New York: Simon and Schuster, 1978. 468

Sidey, Hugh. Portrait of a President. New York: Harper and Row, 1975. 440

*Siebert, Frederick S. Freedom of the Press in England, 1476-1776. Urbana: University of Illinois Press, 1965. 207

_____, Theodore Peterson and Wilbur Schramm. Four Theories of the Press. Urbana: University of Illinois Press, 1956. 207

Siehl, George. "Cloak,Dust Jacket and Dagger." Library Journal, (October 1972). 284

Silet, Loring. Henry Blake Fuller and Hamlin Garland: A Reference Guide. Boston: G.K. Hall, 1977. 411

*Silver, Nathan. Lost New York. New York: Schocken, 1971. 37, 44

Simmons, Robert R. The Strained Alliance: Peking, P'yongyang, Moscow and the Politics of the Korean Civil War. New York: Free Press, 1975. 130

Simon, John V., ed. The Papers of Ulysses S. Grant, 8 vols. Carbondale: Southern Illinois University Press, 1967. 430

Sims, Janet L., comp. The Progress of Afro-American Women: A Selected Bibliography and Resource Guide. Westport, Connecticut: Greenwood Press, 1980. 537

Simpson, Michael. "Two Traditions of American Planning: Olmsted and Burnham." Town Planning Review, 47 (April 1976). 532

Sinclair, Bruce. Philadelphia's Philosopher Mechanics: A History of the Franklin Institute, 1824-1865. Baltimore: Johns Hopkins University Press, 1974. 74

Sinden, John and Albert Worrell. Unpriced Values. New York: Wiley, 1979. 481

Singer, Beth J. The Rational Society. Cleveland: Case Western Reserve University, 1970. 327

Sixsmith, Eric Keir Gilborne. Eisenhower as Military Commander. New York: Stein and Day, 1973. 437

Skardal, Dorothy Burton. The Divided Heart: Scandinavian Immigrant Experiences Through Literary Sources. Lincoln, Nebraska: University of Nebraska Press, 1974. 20

Skardon, Alvin W. Church Leader in the Cities: William Augustus Muhlenberg. Philadelphia: University of Pennsylvania Press, 1971. 380

*Sklar, Robert. Movie•Made America: A Cultural History of the American Movies. New York: Random House, 1976..493, 505

_____. "Popular Culture Smokes Dope." American Quarterly, 27 (August 1975). 505

_____. Prime Time America: Life On and Behind the Television Screen. New York: Oxford, 1980. 493, 505

_____. "The Problem of an American Studies 'Philosophy': A Bibliography of New Directions." American Quarterly, 27 (August 1975). 183

*Sklare, Marshall. America's Jews. New York: Random House, 1971. 386

*   . Conservative Judaism: An American Religious Movement. New York: Schocken, 1972. 385

Skotheim, Robert A. American Intellectual Histories and Historians. Westport: Greenwood, 1978. 183

_____, ed. The Historian and the Climate of Opinion. Reading, Mass.: Addison Wesley, 1969. 183

Skrupskelis, Ignas K. William James: A Reference Guide. Boston: G.K. Hall, 1977. 414

Slater, Jerome. Intervention and Negotiation: The United States and the Dominican Revolution. New York: Harper and Row, 1970. 130

Slater, Michael. Dickens on America and Americans. Austin, Texas: University of Texas Press, 1978. 403

*Slater, Philip. The Pursuit of Loneliness: American Culture at the Breaking Point. Boston: Beacon Press, 1976. 313

*Sloan, Douglas, ed. The Great Awakening and American Education: A Documentary History. New York: Teachers College Press, 1973. 372

Slomich, Sidney J. The American Nightmare. New York: Macmillan, 1971. 311

Slotkin, Richard. Regeneration through Violence: The Mythology of the American Frontier, 1600-1860. Middletown: Wesleyan University Press, 1973. 174, 513

*Small, William. To Kill a Messenger. New York: Hastings House, 1970. 222

Smith, Alice E. George Smith's Money: A Scottish Investor in America. Madison: State Historical Society of Wisconsin, 1966. 73

Smith, Captain John. The Generall Historie of Virginia, New-England and the Summer Isles. 1624; Murfreesboro, North Carolina: Johnson, 1970. 146

Smith, Carl. "Fearsome Fiction and the Windy City: Or, Chicago on the Dime Novel." Chicago History, 7 (Spring 1978). 529

Smith, Culver H. The Press,Politics and Patronage: The American Government's Use of Newspapers, 1789-187. Athens: The University of Georgia Press, 1977. 227

Smith, Dave H. "He Prayeth Best Who Loveth Best." American Poetry Review, 8 (January-February, 1979). 341

Smith, Elbert B. The Presidency of James Buchanan. Lawrence: University Press of Kansas, 1975. 428

Smith, Elsdon C. American Surnames. Philadelphia: Chilton Book Co., 1969. 271

_____, Personal Name: A Bibliography. New York: New York Public Library, 1952. 257

*Smith, Elwyn A. Religious Liberty in the United States. Philadelphia: Fortress Press, 1972. 364

*Smith, Franklin R. Edward R. Murrow: The War Years. Kalamazoo, Mich.: New Issues Press, 1978. 226

Smith, Gene. High Crimes and Misdemeanors: The Impeachment and Trial of Andrew Johnson. New York: Morrow, 1977. 429

Smith, Geoffrey S. To A Nation: American Countersubversives, The New Deal and the Coming of World War II. New York: Basic Books, 1973. 122

Smith, George L. Religion and Trade in New Netherland. Ithaca: Cornell University Press, 1973.

*Smith, Henry Nash. Democracy and the Novel: Popular Resistance to Classic American Writers. New York: Oxford University Press, 1978. 403

* _____. Virgin Land: The American West as Symbol and Myth. Cambridge: Harvard University Press, 1970. 51, 168

Smith, H. Shelton. In His Image, But Racism in Southern Religion, 1780-1910. Durham: Duke University Press, 1972. 378

_____, ed. Horace Bushnell. New York: Oxford University Press, 1965. 379

Smith, Hilda. "Feminism and the Methodology of Women's History." In Berenice A. Carroll, ed. Liberating Women's History. Urbana: University of Illinois Press, 1976. 545

Smith, John E. Purpose and Thought: The Meaning of Pragmatism. New Haven: Yale University Press, 1978. 330

Smith, John H. The Annexation of Texas. New York: Baker and Taylor, 1911. 183

_____. The War with Mexico. New York: Macmillan, 1919. 117, 183

*Smith, Merrit Roe. Harpers Ferry Armory and the New Technology: The Challenge of Change. Ithaca: Cornell University Press, 1971. 93

Smith, Page. Jefferson: A Revealing Biography. New York: American Heritage Publishing Co., distribution by McGraw-Hill, 1976. 426

* _____, ed. Religious Origins of the American Revolution. Missoula: Scholars Press, 1976. 374

Smith, Sam B. and Harriet C. Owsley, eds. The Papers of Andrew Jackson, vol 1. Knoxville: University of Tennessee Press, 1980. 426

Smith, Sidonie. Where I'm Bound: Patterns of Slavery and Freedom in Black American Autobiography. Westport: Greenwood Press, 1974. 398

Smith, V. Kerry, ed. Scarcity and Growth Reconsidered. Baltimore: Johns Hopkins University Press, 1979.   481

Smith, William F. "American Indian Autobiographies." American Indian Quarterly, 2 (Autumn 1975).   395, 399

Smith-Rosenberg, Carroll. "The Female World of Love and Ritual." Signs, 1 (Autumn 1975).   541

_____. "The New Woman and the New History." Feminist Studies, 3 (Fall 1975). 550

Smith-Rosenberg, Carroll. Religion and the Rise of the American City: The New York City Mission Movement, 1812-1870. Ithaca: Cornell University Press, 1971. 378

Snetsinger, John. Truman, the Jewish Vote and the Creation of Israel. Stanford: Hoover Institution Press, 1974. 436

Snow, Robert E. and David E. Wright. "Coney Island: A Case Study in Popular Culture and Technical Change." Journal of Popular Culture, 9 (Spring 1976). 509

Snyder, Charles M., ed. The Lady and the President: The Letters of Dorothea Dix and Millard Fillmore. Lexington: University Press of Kentucky, 1975.   428

*Sobel, Robert. The Great Bull Market: Wall Street in the 1920's. New York: W.W. Norton, 1968. 85

Sochen, June."Mildred Pierce and Women in Film." American Quarterly, XXX (Spring 1978). 546

Solberg, Winton U. Redeem the Time: The Puritan Sabbath in Early America. Cambridge: Harvard University Press, 1977.   368

*Soltow, James H. Origins of Small Business: Metal Fabricators and Machinery Makers in New England, 1890-1957. Philadelphia: American Philosophical Society, 1965. 80

Soltow, Lee. Men and Wealth in the United States, 1850-1870. New Haven: Yale University Press, 1975. 88

Sonneck, Oscar. Bibliography of Early Secular American Music: 18th. Century. 1905; New York: Da Capo, 1964. 298

_____. Early Concert-Life in America: 1731-1800. 1907; New York: Adler, 1949. 298

_____. Early Opera in America. 1915; New York: Blom, 1963. 298

_____. Francis Hopkins: The First American Poet-Composer; James Lyon: Patriot, Preacher, Psalmodist. 1905; New York: Da Capo, 1974. 298

*Sorensen, Theodore C. Decision-Making in the White House. New York: Columbia University Press, 1963.   183

_____. Kennedy. New York: Harper and Row, 1965.   183

_____. The Kennedy Legacy. New York: Macmillan, 1969.   183

*_____. Watchmen in the Night: Presidential Accountability After Watergate. Cambridge, Mass: The MIT Press, 1975.   439

Sousa, John Philip. Marching Along. 1928; New York: Scholarly, 1981. 300

South, Stanley. Palmetto Parapets. Columbia: University of South Carolina, 1974. 290

*Southern, Eileen. The Music of Black Americans. New York: Norton, 1971. 300

Spacks, Patricia Meyer. The Female Imagination. New York: Avon Books, 1976. 395, 399

_____."Reflecting Women." Yale Review, 63 (Ocotber 1973). 399

_____. "Stages of Self: Notes on Autobiography and the Life Cycle." Boston University Journal, 25 (1977). 400

_____. "Women's Stories, Women's Selves." Hudson Review, 30 (Spring 1970). 399

Spanior, John W. The Truman MacArthur Controversy and the Korean War. Cambridge. Harvard University Press, 1959. 130

Speck, Ernest B., ed. Mody Boatright Folklorist. Austin: University of Texas Press, 1973. 99

Spector, Ronald. "Getting Down to the Nitty Gritty: Military History, Official History and the American Experience in Vietnam." Military Affairs, 38 (February 1974). 278

*Speir, Jerry. Ross Macdonald. New York: Frederick Ungar, 1978. 61

Spencer, Donald S. Louis Kossuth and a Young America: Study of Sectionalism and Foreign Policy, 1848-1852. Columbia: University of Missouri Press, 1977. 134

Spender, Stephen. "Confessions and Autobiography." The Making of a Poem. New York: W.W. Norton, 1962. 397

Spengemann, W.C. and L.R. Lundquist. "Autobiography and the American Myth." American Quarterly, 17 (Fall 1965). 393

Spivak, Burton. Jefferson's English Crisis: Commerce, Embargo and the Republican Revolution. Charlottsville: University of Virginia Press, 1979. 134

*Spradley, James P. and David McCurdy, eds. Conformity and Conflict: Readings in Cultural Anthropology. Boston: Little, Brown, 4th ed., 1980. 505

*_____ and Michael A. Rynkiewich. The Nacirema: Readings on American Culture. Boston: Little, Brown, 1975. 505

Sprague, Paul E. Guide to Frank Lloyd Wright and Prairie School Architecture in Oak Park. Oak Park, Illinois: Landmarks Commission, 1976. 525

*Sprigg, June. By Shaker Hands. New York: Knopf, 1975. 516

Springer, Haskell. Washington Irving: A Reference Guide. Boston: G.K. Hall, 1976. 413

Springer, Marlene. Kate Chopin and Edith Wharton: A Reference Guide. Boston: G.K. Hall, 1976. 410, 416

Springer, Mary D. A Rhetoric of Literary Character: Some Women of Henry James. Chicago: University of Chicago Press, 1979. 413

Stade, George. "I've Been Reading Thrillers." Columbia Forum, (Spring 1970). 55

Stafford, William. Traveling through the Dark. New York: Harper and Row, 1962. 336

Stafford, William T. A Name, Title and Place Index to the Critical Writings of Henry James. Englewood, Colorado: Microcard Editions, 1975. 413

Stage, Sarah. Female Complaints: Lydia Pinkham and the Business of Women's Medicine. New York: W.W. Norton & Co., 1979. 548

Stalin, J.V. Foundations of Leninism. Peking: Foreign Languages Press, 1975. 21

_____. Marxism and the National Colonial Question. San Francisco: Prol Publishers, 1975. 21

Stallard, Patricia. Glittering Misery: The Dependents of the Indian Fighting Army. San Rafael, California: Presidio Press, 1978. 289

Stallman, Robert W. Stephen Crane: A Critical Bibliography. Ames, Iowa: Iowa State University Press, 1972. 411

Stambler, Moses. "The Effect of Compulsory Education and Child Labor Laws on High School Attendance in New York City, 1898-1917." History of Education Quarterly, VIII (Summer 1968). 87

*Stampp, Kenneth. The Era of Reconstruction, 1865-1877. New York: Vintage, 1965. 28

*   _____. The Peculiar Institution. New York: Random, 1964. 13, 172

Stanford, Ann, ed. The Women Poets in English. New York: McGraw-Hill, 1977. 343

Stannard, David E. The Puritan Way of Death. New York: Oxford University Press, 1977. 368

Stansell, Christine. "Women on the Great Plains, 1865-1890." Women's Studies, 4 (Summer 1976). 543

*Stanton, William. The Leopard's Spots:Scientific Attitudes toward Race in America, 1815-59. Chicago: University of Chicago Press, 1966. 28, 183

Stark, John D. Damned Upcountry man: William Watts Ball, A Study in American Conservatism. Durham: Duke University Press, 1969. 218

Starkey, Lycurgus M., Jr. James Bond's World of Values. Nashville: Abingdon Press, 1966. 55

*Starobin, Robert S. Industrial Slavery in the Old South. New York: Oxford University Press, 1971. 28, 79, 465

Starobinski, J. "The Style of Autobiography." Seymour Chatman, ed. Literary Style: A Symposium. New York: Oxford University Press, 1971. 397

*Starr, Kevin. Americans and the California Dream. Old Saybrook: Peregrine Smith, 1981. 174, 403

Starr, Louis M. Bohemian Brigade: Civil War Newsmen in Action. New York: Knopf, 1954. 213

*Stearns, Marshall. The Story of Jazz. New York: Oxford University Press, 1970. 301

Steele,Richard W. "The Greatest Gangster Movie Ever Filmed: Prelude to War." Prologue, 11 (Winter 1979). 291

Stein, Allen F. Cornelius Mathews. Boston: G.K. Hall, 1974. 414

*Stein, Benjamin. The View from Sunset Boulevard. New York: Doubleday, 1980. 497, 505

*Stein, Herbert. The Fiscal Revolution in America. Chicago: University of Chicago Press, 1969. 84

Stein, Stephen J., ed. Apocalyptic Writings. New Haven: Yale University Press, 1977.

Steinbrunner, Chris and Otto Penzler, eds.Encyclopedia of Mystery & Detection. New York: McGraw-Hill, 1976. 57

Steiner, Bruce E. Samuel Seabury, 1729-1796. Athens: Ohio University Press, 1971. 375

Steinman, David B. The Builders of the Bridge. 1945; New York: Arno, 1972. 42

_____ and Sara Ruth Watson. Bridges and Their Builders. New York: Dover, 1957. 34, 42

Stepanchev, Stephen. American Poetry Since 1945. New York: Harper and Row, 1965. 341, 344

Stepto, Robert B. From Behind the Veil: A Study of Afro-American Narrative. Urbana: University of Illinois Press, 1979. 392, 398

Sterling, Christopher H. and Timothy Haight, eds. The Mass Media: Aspen Guide to Communication Industry Trends. New York: Praeger, 1978. 505

*Sterling, Dorothy. Black Foremothers: Three Lives. Old Westbury, New York: The Feminist Press, 1979. 538

Stern, Arthur. Air Pollution. Los Angeles: Academic, 1976. 475

Stern, Madeleine B. Behind a Mask: The Unknown Thrillers of Louisa May Alcott. New York: Morrow, 1975. 409

Stern, Robert and Eugene Gressman. Supreme Court Practice. Washington: Bureau of National Affairs, 1978. 356

Stevens, John D. From the Black of the Foxhole: Black Correspondents in World War II. Journalism Monographs, No. 27; Minneapolis Association for Education in Journalism, (February 1973). 221

Stevenson, Robert M. Protestant Church Music in America. New York: Norton, 1970. 298

Steward, Dick. Trade and Hemisphere: The Good Neighbor Policy and Reciprocal Trade. Columbia: University of Missouri Press, 1976. 125

Stewart, Donald H. The Opposition Press of the Federalist Period. Albany: The State University of New York Press, 1969. 208

Stewart, George R. Names on the Land. 1945; Boston: Houghton Mifflin, 1958. 271

Stinchcombe, William C. The American Revolution and the French Alliance. Syracuse: University of Syracuse Press, 1969. 114

*Stobaugh, Robert and Daniel Yergin, eds. Energy Future: The Report of the Energy Project of the Harvard Business School. New York: Ballantine, 1980. 474

*Stoeffler, F. Ernest, ed. Continental Pietism and Early American Christianity. Grand Rapids: Eerdmans, 1976. 373

Stoehr, Taylor. Hawthorne's Mad Scientists: Pseudoscience and Social Science in Nineteenth-Century Life and Letters. Hamden, Connecticut: Shoe String Press, 1978. 412

_____. Nay-Saying in Concord: Emerson Alcott and Thoreau. Hamden, Connecticut : Anchor, 1979. 403

Stone, Albert E. "Autobiography and the Childhood of the American Artist: The Example of Louis Sullivan." J.A.Hague. American Character and Culture. Westport: Greenwood Press, 1979. 399

_____. "Cato's Mirror: The Face of Violence in American Autobiography." Jack Salzman, ed. Prospects. New York: Burt Franklin, 1977. 400

Stone, Elese and Kurt. The Writings of Elliot Carter. Bloomington: Indiana University Press, 1977.

Stone, Julius. Social Dimensions of Law and Justice. Stanford, California: Stanford University Press, 1966. 354

Stone, May N. "The Plumbing Paradox: American Attitudes Toward Late Nineteenth-Century Domestic Sanitary Arrangements." Winterthur Portofolio, 14 (Autumn 1979). 509

Stone, Ralph. The Irreconcilables: The Fight Against the League of Nations. Lexington: University of Kentucky Press, 1970. 122

*Stookey, Robert W. America and the Arab State: An Uneasy Encounter. New York: Wiley, 1975. 141

Storrer, William Allin. The Architecture of Frank Lloyd Wright: A Complete Catalog. Cambridge: MIT Press, 1978. 531

Stout, Janis P. Sodoms in Eden: The City in American Fiction before 1860. Westport, Connecticut: Greenwood, 1976. 403

Stout, Rex. The Doorbell Rang. New York: Viking, 1968. 52

Stovall, Floyd. The Foreground of Leaves of Grass. Charlottesville, Virginia: University Press of Virginia, 1974. 417

Stover, John F. Iron Road to the West: American Railroads in the 1850's. New York: Columbia University Press, 1978. 92

*Stourzh, Gerald. Benjamin Franklin and American Foreign Policy. Chicago: University of Chicago Press, 1954. 114

*Strand, Mark, ed. The Contemporary American Poets: American Poetry Since 1940. New York: New American Library, 1969. 343

Stromberg, Roland N. Collective Security and American Foreign Policy: From the League of Nations to NATO. New York: Praeger, 1963. 122

Strong, Ann L. Land Banking: European Reality, American Prospect. Baltimore: Johns Hopkins, 1979. 484

Stroud, Kandy. How Jimmy Won: The Victory Campaign from Plains to the White House. New York: Morrow, 1977. 441

Strout, Cushing. The New Heavens and New Earth: Political Religion in America. New York: Harper and Row, 1975. 364

Sturgis, Russell. European Architecture. New York: Macmillan, 1896. 29

Sturrock, John. "The New Model Autobiographer." New Library History, 9 (Autumn 1977). 396, 399

*Suid, Lawrence H. Guts and Glory: Great American War Movies. Reading, Mass.: Addison-Wesley, 1978. 291

*Sullivan, Louis H. The Autobiography of an Idea. New York: Dover, 1924. 37, 45, 396

*_____. Kindergarten Chats and Other Writings. New York: Wittenborn, Schultz, 1976. 37, 43

Sullivan, Marianna P. France's Vietnam Policy: A Study of French-American Relations. Westport: Greenwood Press, 1978. 140

Sundquist, Eric. Home as Found: Authority and Genealogy in Nineteenth-Century American Literature. Baltimore, Maryland: Johns Hopkins University Press, 1979. 403

Sushka, Marie Elizabeth. "The Antebellum Money Market and the Economic Impact of the Bank War." Journal of Economic History, XXXVI (December 1976). 73

Svoboda, Joseph G. and David G. Dunning, comps. Preliminary Guide to Ethnic Source Materials in Great Plains Repositories. Lincoln, Nebraska: University Libraries and Center for Great Plain Studies, University of Nebraska, 1978. 192

*Swanberg, W.A. Citizen Hearst. New York: Scribner's, 1981. 216

_____. Luce and His Empire: A Biography. New York: Scribner's, 1975. 221

_____. Pulitzer. New York: Scribner's, 1967. 216

*Swartzrauber, S.A. "River Patrol Relearned." Naval Review (1970). 283

Sweeney, Robert L. Frank Lloyd Wright: An Annotated Bibliography. Los Angeles: Hennessey & Ingalls, 1978. 525

Sweet, Henry. New English Grammar. Oxford: The University Press, 1891-98. 269

Swierenga, Robert P. "Land Speculation and Its Impact on American Economic Growth and Welfare: A Historiographical Review." Western Historical Quarterly, VIII (July 1977). 77

_____. Pioneers and Profits: Land Speculation on the Iowa Frontier. Ames: Iowa State University Press, 1968. 77

Swisher, Carl B. American Constitutional Development. Boston: Houghton Miffin, 1954. 348

*   _____. Stephen J. Field: Craftsman of the Law. Chicago: University of Chicago Press, 1969. 349

_____. The Taney Period, 1836-64. New York: Macmillan Co. 347

Sylla, Richard E. "American Banking and Growth in the Nineteenth-Century: A Partial View of the Terrain." Explorations in Economic History, IX (Winter 1971-72). 72

_____. "Federal Policy, Banking Market Structure and Capital Mobilization in the United States, 1863-1913." Journal of Economic History, XXIX (December 1969). 72

_____. "Forgotten Men of Money: Private Bankers in Early U.S. History." Journal of Economic History, XXXVI (March 1976). 72

Symons, Julian. Bloody Murder: From the Detective Story to the Crime Novel. London: Faber and Faber, 1972. 57

_____. The Tell-Tale Heart: The Life and Works of Edgar Allan Poe. New York: Harper and Row, 1978. 415

Szeplaki, Joseph, comp. and ed. Hungarians in the United States and Canada: A Bibliography. St. Paul: Immigration History Research Center, University of Minnesota, 1977. 191

Szuberla, Guy. "Three Chicago Settlements: Their Architectural Form and Social Meaning." Journal of the Illinois State Historical Society, 70 (May 1977). 528

Szulc, Tad. Innocents at Home: America in the 1970's. New York: Viking Press, 1974.

Szulc, Ted. The Illusion of Peace: Foreign Policy in the Nixon Years. New York: Viking Press, 1978. 140, 439

_____. Innocents at Home: America in the 1970's. New York: Viking Press, 1974. 313

Szwed, John F. and Roger Abrahams. Afro-American Folk Cultures, An Annotated Bibliography of Materials from North, Central and South America and the West Indies, 2 vols. Philadelphia: Institute for the Study of Human Issues, 1978. 111

Tager, Jack. "Partners in Design: Chicago Architects, Entrepreneurs, and the Evolution of Urban Commercial Architecture." South Atlantic Quarterly, 76 (Spring 1977). 530

*Talese, Gay. The Kingdom and the Power. New York: Dell, 1981. 222

*Tallmadge, Thomas E. Architecture in Old Chicago. 1941; Chicago: University of Chicago Press, 1975. 37

Tanis, James. Dutch Calvinistic Pietism in the Middle Colonies. Hague: Martinus Nijhoff, 1967. 373

Tansill, Charles C. America Goes to War. Boston: Little, Brown, 1938. 121

_____. Back Door to War: The Roosevelt Foreign Policy, 1933-1941. Chicago: H. Regnery Co., 1952. 126

Tardy, Mary T. The Living Female Writers of the South. 1872; Detroit: Gale, 1978. 404

*Tarpley, Fred. One Thousand and One Texas Place Names. Austin: University of Texas Press, 1980. 272

Tatum, George B. Penn's Great Town. Philadelphia: University of Pennsylvania Press, 1961. 38, 44

Taylor, George Rogers. "American Economic Growth Before 1840: An Exploratory Essay." Journal of Economic History, 24 (December 1964). 91

_____. "The Beginning of Mass Transportation in Urban America." Smithsonian Journal of History, I (Summer, Autumn 1966). 72

* _____, comp. American Economic History Before 1860. Arlington Heights: Harlan Davidson, 1969. 63

* _____ and Lucius F. Ellsworth, eds. Approaches to American Economic History. Charlottesville: University Press of Virginia, 1971. 63

Taylor, John M. Garfield of Ohio, the Available Man. New York: Norton, 1970. 430

*Taylor, Joshua C. America as Art. New York: Harper and Row, 1979. 508

*Taylor, Philip. The Distant Magnet: European Emigration to the U.S.A. New York: Harper and Row, 1972. 193

Tebbel, John. The American Magazine: A Compact History. New York: Hawthorne, 1969. 221

_____. George Horace Lorimer and the Saturday Evening Post. Garden City: Doubleday, 1948. 221

_____. The Life and Good Times of William Randolph Hearst. New York: Dutton, 1952. 216

*Temin, Peter. Did Monetary Forces Cause the Great Depression? New York: Norton, 1976. 85

_____. Iron and Steel in Nineteenth Century America: An Economic Inquiry. Cambridge: M.I.T. Press, 1964. 74

* _____. The Jacksonian Economy. New York: Norton, 1969. 73

Tenney, Thomas Asa. Mark Twain: A Reference Guide. Boston: G.K. Hall, 1978. 410

Tentler, Leslie Woodcock. Wage-Earning Women: Industrial Work and Family Life in the United States, 1900-1930. New York: Oxford University Press, 1980. 451, 549

*Tepperman, Jean. Not Servants, Not Machines: Office Workers Speak out. Boston: Beacon Press, 1976. 548

ter Horst, J.F. Gerald Ford and the Future of the Presidency. New York: The Third Press, 1974. 440

Thayer, H.S. Meaning and Action. New York: Bobbs-Merrill Co., 1968. 327

Theobald, Robert A. The Final Secret of Pearl Harbor: The Washington Contribution to the Japanese Attack. New York: Devin-Adair, 1954. 126

*Thernstrom, Stephan. The Other Bostonians: Poverty and Progress in the American Metropolis, 1880-1970. Cambridge: Harvard University Press, 1973. 196

* _____. Poverty and Progress: Social Mobility in a Nineteenth Century City. Cambridge: Harvard University Press, 1964. 196, 205

Thistlethwaite, Frank. "Migration from Europe Overseas in the Nineteenth and Twentieth Centuries." Rapports V: Histoire Contemporaire. Goteberg: Almquist and Wiksell, 1960. 204

Thistlethwaite, Mark. The Image of George Washington: Studies in Mid-Nineteenth-Century History Painting. New York: Garland Publishing Co., 1979, 425

Thomas, Brinley. Migration and Economic Growth: A Study of Great Britain and the Atlantic Economy. Cambridge: Cambridge University Press, 1972. 204

Thomas, Charles K. Introduction to the Phonetics of American English. 1946; New York: Ronald, 1948. 263

Thomas, Dylan and John Davenport. The Death of the King's Canary. New York: Viking, 1977. 49

Thomas, Isaiah. The History of Printing in America. New York: Burt Franklin reprint of 1874 edition. 207

*Thomas, Keith. Religion and the Decline of Magic. New York: Scribner, 1971. 366

Thomas, Robert David. The Man Who Would Be Perfect. John Humphrey
Noyes and the Utopian Impulse. Philadelphia: University of Pennsylvania
Press, 1977. 516

Thomas, Robert P. "A Quantitative Approach to the Study of the Effects
of British Imperial Policy upon Colonial Welfare: Some Preliminary
Findings." Journal of Economic History, 25 (December 1965). 65

Thomas, Theodore. Theodore Thomas: A Musical Autobiography 1905; New York:
DaCapo, 1964. 300

Thompson, D.H. The Highlanders of the South. New York. Eaton and Mains,
1910. 183

_____. The Negro Leadership Class. Englewood Cliffs, N.J.: Prentice
Hall, 1963. 183

Thompson, Ernest Trice. Presbyterians in the South. Richmond: John Knox,
1973. 365

Thompson, G.R. Poe's Fiction: Romantic Irony in the Gothic Tales. Madison,
Wisconsin: University of Wisconsin Press, 1973. 415

Thompson, Morris. Maps for America. Washington, D.C.: G.P.O., 1979. 483

*Thompson, William Irwin. At the Edge of History. New York: Harper and
Row, 1973. 313

Thomson, David S. A Pictorial Biography. New York: Grosset and Dunlop,
1973. 436

Thomson, Virgil. The State of Music. 1939; Wesport: Greenwood Press, 1974. 301

*Thorne, Christopher. Allies of a Kind: The United States, Britain and the
War Against Japan, 1941-1945. London: Hamish Hamilton, 1979. 139

_____. The Limits of Foreign Policy: The West, the League and the Far
Eastern Crisis of 1931-1933. London: Hamilton, 1972. 124

Thornton, Edward E. Professional Education for Ministry. Nashville:
Abingdon, 1970. 386

Thorpe, Earl E. Black Historians: A Critique. New York: Morrow, 1971. 183

_____. The Central Theme of Black History. Westport: Greenwood Press,
1979. 183.

_____. Eros and Freedom in Southern Life and Thought. Wesport: Green-
wood Press, 1979. 183

_____. The Mind of the Negro: An Intellectual History of Afro-Americans.
Wesport: Greenwood Press. 183

_____. The Old South: A Psychohistory. Wesport: Greenwood Press, 1979. 183

Thorpe, James. Thoreau's Walden. San Marino, California: Huntington Library, 1977. 416

Tichi, Cecilia. New World, New Earth: Environmental Reform in the American Literature from the Puritans through Whitman. New Haven, Connecticut: Yale University Press, 1979. 403

*Tilly, Charles. An Urban World. Boston: Little Brown, 1974. 460

Timberlake, Richard H., Jr. The Origins of Central Banking in the United States. Cambridge: Harvard University Press, 1978. 92

Tingley, Donald F. "The 'Robin's Egg Renaissance': Chicago and the Arts, 1910-1920." Journal of the Illinois State Historical Society, 63 (Spring 1970). 529

Tirro, Frank. Jazz: A History. New York: Norton, 1977. 305

Tishler, Hace Sorel. Self-Reliance and Social Security, 1870-1917. Port Washington, New York: Kennikat Press, 1971. 87

*Todorev, Tzvetan. The Poetics of Prose. Ithaca, New York: Cornell University Press, 1977. 59

Toelken, Barre. The Dynamics of Folkore. Boston: Houghton Mifflin, 1979. 110

*Toffler, Alvin. Future Shock. New York: Bantam, 1971. 311

*_____. The Third Wave. New York: Bantam, 1981. 477

*Toll, Robert C. Blacking Up: The Minstrel Show in the Nineteeth-Century America. New York: Oxford University Press, 1979. 299

_____. On With the Show: The First Century of Show Business in America. New York: Oxford University Press, 1976. 505

Tolzmann, Don. H. German Americana: A Bibliography. Metuchan: Scarecrow, 1975. 189

Tomas, Vincent. ed. Charles S. Peirce, Essays in the Philosophy of Science. 1957. 322

Tomasi, Silvano, M. Piety and Power: The Role of Italian Parishes in the Metropolitan Area, 1880-1930. New York: Center for Migration Studies, 1975. 200, 384

_____, ed. Perspectives in Italian Immigration and Ethnicity. New York: Center for Migration Studies, 1977. 195, 199

Thomkins, Mary E. Ida M. Tarbell. New York: Twayne, 1974. 217

*Tompkins, E. Berkeley. Anti-Imperialism in the United States: The Great Debate, 1890-1920. Philadelphia: University of Pennsylvania Press, 1970. 119

Tompkins, Dorothy. The Supreme Court of the United States: A Bibliography.
   Berkeley, California: University of California, 1959. 354

*Toomer, Jean. Cane. New York: Liveright, 1975. 392

Torre, Susan, ed. Women in American Architecture: A Historic and Contemporary
   Perspective. New York: Whitney Library of Design, 1977. 548

Toscano, Vicent L. Since Dallas: Images of John F. Kennedy in Popular and
   Scholarly Literature, 1963-1973. San Francisco: R. and E. Research
   Associates, 1978. 438

*Towsen, John H. Clowns. New York: Dutton, 1978. 505

Tracey, Kathleen. Herbert Hoover: A Bibliography of his Writings and
   Addresses. Stanford: Hoover Institution Press, 1977. 434

*Trachtenberg, Alan. Brooklyn Bridge, Fact and Symbol. Chicago: University
   of Chicago Press, 1979. 42

Trager, George L. and Henry Lee Smith, Jr. An Outline of English Structure.
   Norman, Oklahoma: The Battenburg Press, 1951. 269

Trammell, William Dugas. Ca Ira. New York: United States Publishing Company,
   1874. 469

Trani, Eugene P. The Treaty of Portsmouth: An Adventure in American
   Diplomacy. Lexington: University of Kentucky Press, 1969. 121

_____ and David L Wilson. The Presidency of Warren G. Harding.
   Lawrence: Regents Press, 1977. 433

Trattner, Walter I. Crusade for the Children: History of the National
   Child Labor Committee and Child Labor Reform in America. Chicago:
   Quadrangle Books, 1970. 87

_____. Homer Folks: Pioneer in Social Welfare. New York: Columbia
   University Press, 1968. 86

Trefousse, Hans Louis. Impeachment of a President: Andrew Johnson, the
   Blacks and Reconstruction. Knoxville: University of Tennessee Press,
   1975. 429

Trennert, Robert A. Jr. Alternative to Extinction: Federal Indian
   Policy and the Beginnings of the Reservation System, 1846-51. Philadelphia:
   Temple University Press, 1975. 512

Trescot, William H. The Diplomacy of the Revolution: An Historical Study.
   New York: Appleton, 1852. 112

_____. The Diplomatic History of the Administrations of Washington
   and Adams, 1789-1801. Boston: Little, Brown, 1857. 112

Tribe, Lawrence. American Constitutional Law. Mineola, New York:
   Foundation Press, 1978. 349

Trimmer, Joseph F. ed. "A New Continent of Categories: Popular Culture in America." Indiana Social Studies Quarterly, 26 (Winter 1973-74). 506

Tripp, Joseph. F. "An Instance of Labor and Business Cooperation: Workmen's Compensation in Washington States (1911)." Labor History, 17 (Fall 1976). 87

*Truzzi, Marcelo. Sociology and Everyday Life. Englewoods Cliffs, New Jersey: Prentice-Hall, 1968. 496, 506

*Tsou, Tang. America's Failure in China, 1941-1950. Chicago: University of Chicago Press, 1963. 129

Tuan, Yi-Fu. "Ambiguity in Attitudes Toward Environment." Annals of the Association of American Geographers (December 1973). 419

_____. Landscapes of Fear. New York: Pantheon, 1980. 419

* _____. Space and Place: The Perspectives of Experience. Minneapolis: University of Minnesota Press, 1979. 419

* _____. Topophilia: A Study of Environmental Perception, Attitudes, and Values. New York: Prentice-Hall, 1974. 418

Tuchman, Barbara, W. Stilwell and the American Experience in China, 1911-1945. New York: Macmillan, 1970. 129

*Tuchman, Gaye. Making News: A Study in the Construction of Reality. New York: Free Press, 1978. 497, 506

* _____, Arlene Kaplan Daniels, and James Banet, eds. Hearth and Home: Images of Women in the Mass Media. New York: Oxford University Press, 1978. 506

Tucker, Gilbert M. American English. New York: Knopf, 1921. 259

Tugwell, Rexford Guy. In Search of Roosevelt. Cambrdige: Harvard University Press, 1972. 435

_____. Roosevelt's Revolution: The First Year, a Personal Perspective. New York: Macmillan, 1977. 435

Tulchin, Joseph S. The Aftermath of War: World War I and U.S. Policy Toward Latin America. New York: New York University Press, 1971. 124

Trescot, William H. The Diplomatic History of the Administrations of Washington and Adams, 1789-1801. Boston: Little, Brown, 1857

Turner, Arlin. Nathaniel Hawthorne: A Biography. New York: Oxford University Press, 1980. 412

_____, ed. Critical Essays on George W. Cable. Boston: G.K. Hall, 1980. 410

Turner, Frederick J. The Frontier in American History. 1920; New York: Krieger, 1976. 183

_____. Rise of the New West. 1906; New York: Collier, 1962. 159

Turner, Lorenzo D. Africanisms in the Gullah Dialect. 1949; Ann Arbor: University of Michigan Press, 1974. 266

Turner, Nat. The Confessions of Nat Turner. 1861; New York: Arno. 21

*Turner, Victor. Dramas, Fields, and Metaphors: Symbolic Action in Human Society. Ithaca, New York: Cornell University Press, 1975. 497, 506

_____. "Frame, Flow and Reflection: Ritual and Drama as Public Liminality." Michel Benamou and Charles Caramello, eds. Performance in Postmodern Culture. Madison: Coda Press, 1977. 506

* _____. The Ritual Process: Structure and Anti-Structure. Ithaca: Cornell University Press, 1977. 497, 506

*Tuttle, William M., Jr. Race Riot: Chicago in the Red Summer of 1919. New York: Atheneum, 1970. 28

Tuttleton, James. Thomas Wentworth Higginson. Boston: G.K. Hall, 1978. 412

*Tuveson, Ernest L. Redeemer Nation. Chicago: University of Chicago Press, 1980. 183

*Twombley, Robert C. Frank Lloyd Wright: An Interpretive Biography. New York: Harper and Row, 1973. 45, 525

_____. Frank Lloyd Wright: His Life and his Architecture. New York: Wiley, 1979. 525

_____. Plan for Restoration and Adaptive Use of the Frank Lloyd Wright Home and Studio. Chicago: University of Chicago Press, 1979. 525

Twyman, Robert W. and David C. Roller. Encyclopedia of Southern History. Baton Rouge, Louisiana: Louisiana State University Press, 1979. 406

Tyler, Lyon Gardiner. The Letters and Times of the Tylers. New York: DaCapo Press, 1970. 427

Udall, Stewart. The Quiet Crisis. New York: Avon, 1964. 471

Udell, Gerald R. "The Speech of Akron, Ohio." Unpublished dissertation. University of Chicago, 1966. 266

Unger, Irwin. The Greenback Era: A Social and Political History of American Finance, 1865-1879. Princeton: Princeton University Press, 1964. 73

Unterberger, Betty M. America's Siberian Expedition, 1918-1920: A Study in National Policy. Durham: Duke University Press, 1956. 122

Urban Land Institute. The Cost of Delay Due to Governmental Regulation in the Houston Housing Market. Washington, D.C.:ULI, 1979. 482

_____. Growth and Change in Rural America. Washington, D.C.: ULI, 1979. 483

_____. Joint Development: Making the Real Estate-Transit Connection. Washington, D.C.: ULI, 1979. 483

_____. Large-Scale Development: Benefits, Constraints, and State and Local Policy Incentives. Washington, D.C.: ULI, 1977. 473

_____. Management and Control of Growth: Issues, Techniques, Problems, Trends. Washington, D.C.: ULI, 1975. 473

Urofsky, Melvin I. American Zionism from Herzl to the Holocaust. Garden City, New York: Anchor Press, 1975. 201

Uselding, Paul. "Studies of Technology in Economic History." Research in Economic History, I (Supplement 1977). 74

Uskup, Frances L. "The Speech of Chicago Elites." Unpublished dissertation. Illinois Institute of Technology, 1964. 266

*Utley, Robert M. Frontier Regulars. The United States Army and the Indian 1866-1891. Bloomington: Indiana University Press, 1977. 184.

* _____. Frontiersmen in Blue: The U.S. Army and the Indians, 1848-1865. Lincoln: University of Nebraska Press, 1981. 183

* _____. The Last Days of the Sioux Nation. New Haven: Yale University Press, 1963. 183

*Vaghts, Alfred. A History of Militarism: Civilian and Military. New York:Free Press 1959. 278

Valenti, Jack. A Very Human President. New York: Norton, 1976. 438

Van Alstyne, Richard W. Genesis of American Nationalism. Waltham, Massachusetts: Blaisdell, 1970. 114

⌐ _____. The Rising American Empire. New York: Oxford University Press, 1960. 117

Vance, Rupert, B. and Nicholas J. Demorath, eds. The Urban South. Chapel Hill: University of North Carolina Press, 1954. 464

Van Deusen, Glydon G. Horace Greeley: Nineteenth Century Crusader. Philadelphia: University of Pennsylvania Press, 1953. 212

Van Doren, Mark, ed. The Viking Portable Walt Whitman. New York: Viking, 1974. 417

Van Dyken, Seymour. Samuel Willard: Preacher of Orthodoxy in an Era of Change. Grand Rapids: Erdmans, 1972.

Vanek, Joanne. "Household Technology and Social Status: Rising Living Standards and Status and Residence Differences in Housework." Technology and Culture, 19 (June 1978). 549

*Van Rennsselaer, Mariana Griswold. Henry Hobson Richardson and His Works. New York: Dover, 1979. 38, 45

Van Riper, William Robert, et. al. Linguistic Atlas of Oklahoma. (in progress). 265

Van Tassel, David D. Recording America's Past. Chicago: University of Chicago Press, 1960. 184

Van Tine, Warren. The Making of the Labor Bureaucrat: Union Leadership in the United States, 1870-1920. Amherst: University of Massachusetts Press, 1974. 448

Varg, Paul A. The Closing of the Door: Sino-American Relations,1936-1946. East Lansing: Michigan State University Press, 1973. 129

_____. Foreign Policies of the Founding Fathers. East Lansing: Michigan State University Press, 1963. 114

_____. The Making of a Myth: The United States and China, 1897-1912. East Lansing: Michigan State University Press, 1968. 121

_____. United States Foreign Relations, 1820-1860. East Lansing: Michigan State University Press, 1979. 134

Vartanian, Pershing. "Popular Culture Studies: A Problem in Socio-Cultural Dynamics." Journal of Popular Culture, 11 (Summer 1977). 496, 506

Vatter, Harold G. The Drive to Industrial Maturity: The U.S. Economy, 1860-1914. Wesport, Connecticut: Greenwood Press, 1975. 67

*Vaughan, Alden T. New England Frontier: Puritans and Indians, 1620-1675.
New York: Norton, 1980. 368, 512

_____, ed. Puritan New England: Essays on Religion, Society and Culture.
New York: St. Martin's Press, 1977. 367

Veblen, Thorstein B. Theory of the Leisure Class. 1899; New York: Kelley. 163

Vecoli, Rudolph J. "Ethnicity: A Neglected Dimension of American History."
Herbert J. Bass, ed. The State of American History. New York: Quadrangle,
1970. 185

_____. "European Americans: From Immigrants to Ethnics." William H. Cartwright
and Richard L. Watson, eds. The Reinterpretation of American History and
Culture. Washington, D.C.: National Council for the Social Studies, 1973.
202, 204

_____. "The Immigration Studies Collection of the University of Minnesota."
The American Archivist, 32 (April 1969). 202

_____. "Italian American Workers, 1880-1920: Padrone Slaves or Primitive
Rebels?" In Tomasi, eds. Perspectives in Italian Immigration and
Ethnicity. New York Center for Migration Studies, 1977. 199

Venezky, Richard L. "Linguistics and Spelling." In Albert H. Marckwardt.
Linguistics in School Programs. Chicago: University of Chicago Press,
1970. 258, 268

_____. Linguistics and Spelling. Madison, Wisconsin: Wisconsin Research
and Development Center for Cognitive Learning, 1969. 268

_____. The Structure of English Orthography. The Hague: Mouton, 1970. 268

Venkataramani, M.S. The Sunny Side of F.D.R. Athens: Ohio University Press,
1973. 435

*Venturi, Robert, Denise Scott Brown, and Steven Izenour. Learning from Las
Vegas. Cambridge: MIT Press, 1977. 506

Vevier, Charles. The United States and China, 1906-1913: A Study of Finance
and Diplomacy. New Brunswick: Rutgers University Press, 1955. 120

*Veysey, Lawrence. The Communal Experience. Chicago: University of Chicago
Press, 1978. 516

Viereck, Wolfgang. "German Dialects Spoken in the United States and Canada:
A Bibliography." ORBIS, XVI (1967). 258

*Vinci, John. The Stock Exchange Trading Room. Chicago: The Art Institute
of Chicago, 1977. 531

Vinyard, Jo Ellen McNergney. The Irish on the Urban Frontier: Detroit, 1850-
1880. New York: Arno, 1976. 198

*Vlach, John M. The Afro-American Tradition in Decorative Arts. Cleveland:
   Museum of Art, 1978. 111

Von Frank, Albert J. Whittier: A Comprehensive Annotated Bibliography.
   New York: Garland, 1975. 417

Von Holst, Hermann.   The Constitutional and Political History of the
   United States, 8 vols. Chicago: Callaghan, 1876-1892. 184

*Wade, Richard. Slavery in the Cities: The South, 1820-1860. New York: Oxford University Press, 1967. 78, 465

*_____. The Urban Frontier. Chicago: University of Chicago Press, 1964. 174

Wagenknecht, Edward. Eve and Henry James: Portraits of Women and Girls in His Fiction. Norman, Oklahoma: University of Oklahoma Press, 1978. 413

Waggoner, Hyatt, H. Emerson as Poet. Princeton, New Jersey: Princeton University Press, 1974. 411

*Wagoner, David. "The Poets Agree to be Quiet by the Swamp," in Collected Poems, 1956-1976. Bloomington: Indiana University Press, 1978. 341

Wakelyn, Jon L. The Politics of a Literary Man: William Gilmore Simms. Westport:Greenwood, 1973. 416

Walker, Alice, ed. I Love Myself When I am Laughing. . . And Then Again When I am Looking Mean and Impressive: A Zora Neale Hurston Reader. Old Westbury, New York: The Feminist Press, 1980. 539

Walker, Barbara J. The Picture Life of Jimmy Carter. New York: Watts, 1977. 441

Walker, David. Appeal. 1843; New York: Arno, 1969. 21

Walker, Dorothea. Alice Brown. Boston: G.K. Hall, 1974. 409

Walker, Margaret. For My People. 1942; New York: Arno, 1969. 22

*_____. Jubilee. New York: Bantam, 1975. 22

Walker, Peter F. Moral Choices: Memory, Desire, and Imagination in 19th Century American Abolition. Baton Rouge: Louisiana State University Press, 1978. 403

Walker, Robert Harris, ed. American Studies: Topics and Sources. Westport: Greenwood Press, 1976. 362

Walker, Warren S. Plots and Characters in the Fiction of James Fenimore Cooper. Hamden, Connecticut: Shoe String Press, 1978. 411

Walkowitz, Daniel. Worker City, Company Town: Iron and Cotton Workers Protest in Troy and Cohoes, New York, 1855-1884. Urbana: University of Illinois Press, 1978. 448

*Wall, Charles C. George Washington, Citizen-Soldier. Charlottesville: University Press of Virginia, 1980. 425

Wall, Joseph Frazier. Andrew Carnegie. New York: Oxford University Press, 1970. 80

_____. Henry Watterson: Reconstructed Rebel. New York: Oxford University Press, 1956. 214

*Wallace, Anthony F.C. Rockdale: The Growth of an American Village in the Early Industrial Revolution. New York: Norton, 1980. 75, 447

*Wallace, Dewey D., Jr. The Pilgrims. Wilmington: Consortium Books, 1977. 365

Wallace, Phyllis A., et. al. Black Women in the Labor Force. Cambridge: MIT Press, 1980. 552

Walsh, Andrea. "Films of Suspicion and Distrust: Undercurrent of Female Consciousness in the 1940s." Film & History, VIII (February 1978). 545

Walsh, James P. ed. The San Francisco Irish, 1850-1976. San Francisco: The Irish Literary Historical Society, 1978. 199

Walsh, Margaret. "The Democratization of Fashion: The Emergence of the Women's Dress Pattern Industry." Journal of American History, 66 (September 1979). 93

_____. The Manufacturing Frontier: Pioneer Industry in Antebellum Wisconsin, 1830-1860. Madison: State Historical Society of Wisconsin, 1972. 75

_____. "Pork Packing as a Leading Edge of Midwestern Industry, 1835-1875." Agricultural History, 51 (October 1977). 93

*Walsh, Mary Roth. "Doctors Wanted: No Women Need Apply": Sexual Barriers in the Medical Profession, 1835-1975. New Haven: Yale University Press, 1977. 548

Walter, Peter F. Moral Choices: Memory, Desire,and Imagination in Nineteenth-Century American Abolition. Baton Rouge, Louisiana: Louisiana State University Press, 1978.

Walton, Gary M. "The New Economic History and the Burdens of the Navigation Acts." Economic History Review, XXIV (November 1971). 91

_____, ed. "A Symposium on Time on the Cross." Explorations in Economic History, 12 (Fall 1975). 184

Walton, Richard J. Cold War and Counterrevolution: The Foreign Policy of John F. Kennedy. New York: Viking, 1972. 130

_____. Henry Wallace, Harry Truman, and the Cold War. New York: Viking, 1976. 436

Walworth, Arthur Clarence. America's Moment, 1918: American Diplomacy at the End of World War I. New York: Norton, 1977. 136, 433.

*Walzer, Michael. The Revolution of the Saints. New York: Athenaeum, 1968. 374

Wang, William S.Y. "Approaches to Phonology." Thomas R. Sebeok et. al. Current Trends in Linguistics. The Hague: Mouton, 1973. 258

Ward, Barbara and Rene Dubos. Only One Earth. New York: Norton, 1972. 471

Ward, Jean. "Interdisciplinary Research and the Journalism Historian." Journalism History ,(Spring 1978). 224

*Ward, John William. Andrew Jackson, Symbol for an Age. New York: Oxford University Press, 1962. 169

Ward, Theodore. "Big White Fox." In Hatch and Shine. Black Theater USA. New York: Free Press, 1974. 22

Ware, Louise. Jacob A. Riis. 1938; New York: Kraus Reprints. 217

Warner, Raynor, et. al. New Profits from Old Buildings. New York: McGraw Hill, 1979. 480

Warner, Robert M. and Francis X. Blouin, Jr. "Documenting the Great Migrations and a Century of Ethnicity in America." The American Archivist, XXXIX (July 1976). 202

Warren, Charles. The Supreme Court in United States History. Boston: Little, Brown, 1935. 348

Warren, Mercy Otis. History of the Rise, Progress and Termination of the American Revolution. 1805; New York: AMS Press, 1970. 147

Wasby, Stephen. The Impact of the United States Supreme Court. Homewood, Illinois: Dorsey Press, 1970. 352

* _____. The Supreme Court in the Federal Judicial System. New York: Holt, Rinehart and Winston, 1978. 357

Washburn, Wilcomb E. The Assault on Indian Tribalism: The General Allotment Law (Dawes Act) of 1887. Philadelphia: Lippincott, 1975. 512

* _____. The Indian in America. New York: Harper and Row, 1975. 511

_____. Narratives of North American Capitivities. New York: Garland, 1980. 513

*Washington, Joseph R., Jr. Black Sects and Cults: The Power Axis in an Ethnic Ethic. Garden City: Doubleday, 1973. 379

*Washington, Mary Helen, ed. Black-Eyed Susans: Classic Stories By and About Black Women. Garden City, N.Y.: Doubleday, 1975. 539

Washington Post Staff. The Fall of a President. New York: Delacorte Press, 1974. 439

Wason, James R. "American Workers and American Studies." American Studies International , XII (Winter 1974). 62

Wasserman, Paul and Jean Morgan, eds. Ethnic Information Sources of the United States. Detroit: Gale Research Co., 1976. 189

*Waterman, Laura and Guy. Backwoods Ethics: Environmental Concerns for Hikers and Campers. Washington, D.C.: Stone Wall, 1979. 487

Watkins, Floyd C. In Time and Place: Some Origins of American Fiction. Athens: University of Georgia, 1977. 468

Watson, Colin. Snobbery with Violence: Crime Stories and Their Audience. London: Eyre and Spottiswoodie, 1971. 59

Watson, Elmo Scott. A History of Newspaper Syndicates in the United States,
    1865-1935. Chicago: Publishers' Auxiliary, 1936. 217

Watters, Pat. The Angry Middle-Aged Man. New York: Grossman, 1976. 467

_____. Coca-Cola: An Illustrated History. Garden City, New York: Doubleday,
    1978. 467

*Watts, Emily Stipes. The Poetry of American Women from 1632 to 1945.
    Austin: University of Texas Press, 1977. 539

Weaver, Herbert and Wayne Cutler, eds. Correspondence of James K. Polk, 5 vols.
    Nashville: Vanderbilt University Press, 1969-1979.

*Webb, Walter Prescott. The Great Plains. 1931; Lincoln: University of
    Nebraska Press, 1981. 160, 184

Weber, Alfred. Die Entwicklung der Rhmenerzahlungen Nathaniel Hawthornes:
    "The Story Teller" and andere friihe Werke. Berlin, Germany: Schmidt, 1972. 412

Weber, Michael P. Social Change in an Industrial Town: Patterns of Progress in
    Warren Pennsylvania, From Civil War to World War. University Park, Pennsylvania:
    Pennsylvania State University Press, 1975. 197

Weber, Timothy. Living in the Shadow of the Second Coming: American Premillenialism,
    1875-1925. New York: Oxford University Press, 1979. 381

Webster, Noah. American Spelling Book. 1783; Beatty: 1974. 268

Wechsler, Herbert. Principles, Politics and Fundamental Law. Cambridge:
    Harvard University Press, 1961. 351

_____. "Toward Neutral Principles of Constitutional Law." 75 Harvard Law
    Review 1, 1959. 351

Wecter, Dixon. The Hero in America: A Chronicle of Hero Worship. 1942; New
    York: Irvington, 1972. 184

*Weeks, Louis B. A New Christian Nation. Wilmington: Consortium Books, 1977. 365

Weems, M.A. History of the Life and Death, Virtues and Exploits of General
    Washington. Philadelphia: M. Carey, 1800; Reprint Harvard University Press,
    1962. 184

Weibel, Kathryn. Mirror, Mirror: Images of Women Reflected in Popular Culture.
    New York: Anchor, 1977. 506

Weigley, Russell F. The American Way of War: A History of United States
    Military Strategy and Policy. New York: Macmillan, 1973. 281

*_____. The End of Militarism. Colorado Springs: U.S. Air Force Academy,
    1973. 278

*_____. The Military and Society: Proceedings of the Fifth Military History
    Symposium. Washington, D.C.: G.P.O., 1972. 278

_____. New Dimensions in Military History: An Anthology.
San Rafael, California: Presidio Press, 1975. 292

_____: Towards and American Army: Military Thought from Washington to
Marshall. New York: Columbia University Press, 1962. 281

Weinberg, Albert K. Manifest Destiny: A Study of Nationalist Expansionism in
American History. Baltimore: Johns Hopkins University Press, 1935. 117

Weinbrot, Howard. New Aspects of Lexicography. Carbondale, Illinois:
Southern Illinois Press, 1972. 260

Weinreich, Uriel. Languages in Contact. Publications of the Linguistic
Circle of New York, #1, 1953. 267

_____, et. al. The Field of Yiddish. Publications of the Linguistic Circle
of New York. 1954; The Hague: Mouton, 1969. 260

_____. Language and Culture Atlas of Ashkenazic Jewry (in progress). 267

Weinstein, Allen. Prelude to Populism: Origins of the Silver Issue, 1867-1878.
New Haven: Yale University Press, 1970. 73

*   _____, et.al. American Negro Slavery: A Modern Reader. New York: Oxford
University Press, 1979. 78

Weinstein, James. The Corporate Idealism in the Liberal State, 1900-1918. 1968;
Westport: Greenwood, 1981. 81

Weinstein, Robert A. and Larry Booth. Collection, Use, and Care of Historical
Photographs. Nashville, Tennessee: AASLH, 1976. 509

Weintraub, Karl J. "Autobiography and Historical Consciousness." Critical
Inquiry, 1 (June 1975). 398

_____. The Value of the Individual: Self and Circumstance in Autobiography.
Chicago: University of Chicago Press, 1978. 398

*Weisbuch, Robert. Emily Dickinson's Poetry. Chicago: University of Chicago
Press, 1981. 411

Welch, Richard B., Jr. Response to Imperialism: The United States and the
Philippine-American War, 1899-1902. Chapel Hill: University of North
Carolina Press,1978. 135

Welland, Dennis. Mark Twain in England. Atlantic Highlands, New Jersey:
Humanities Press, 1978. 410

Wells, Robert V. "Dislocation and Emigration: The Social Background of American
Immigration." Perspectives in American History, VII (1973).

_____. The Population of the British Colonies in America Before 1776: A
Survey of Census Data. Princeton: Princeton University Press, 1975. 89

Welsch, Robert L. "Front Door, Back Door." Natural History, 88 (June-July 1979). 510

Welter, Barbara. Dimity Convictions: The American Woman in the Nineteenth Century. Athens: Ohio University Press, 1976. 551

Wepsiec, Jan. Polish American Serial Publication 1942-1966: An Annotated Bibliography. Chicago, 1968. 191

Werking, Richard H. The Master Architects: Building the United States Foreign Service, 1890-1913. Lexington: University Press of Kentucky, 1977. 85

Wermuth, Paul C. Bayard Taylor. Boston: G.K. Hall, 1973. 416

Wertheim, Arthur F. Radio Comedy. New York: Oxford University Press, 1979. 506

*Wertheimer, Barbara Mayer. We Were There: The Story of Working Women in America. New York: Pantheon, 1977. 451, 547

Westbrook, Perry D. John Burroughs. Boston: G.K. Hall, 1974. 410

*Westin, Alan F. Anatomy of Constitutional Law Case. New York: Macmillan, 1958. 353

*Wharton, Vernon L. The Negro in Mississippi, 1865-1890. New York: Harper and Row, 1965. 28

*Whetmore, Edward. Mediamerica: Form, Content, and Consequences of Mass Communication. Belmont: Wadsworth, 1979. 492, 506

Whitaker, Arthur P. The Mississippi Question, 1795-1803; A Study in Trade, Politics, and Diplomacy. New York: Appleton-Century, 1934. 115, 184

*_____. The Spanish-American Frontier: 1783-1795: The Westward Movement and the Spanish Retreat in the Mississippi Valley. Boston: Houghton Mifflin, 1927. 115

_____. The United States and the Independence of Latin America, 1800-1830. Baltimore: Johns Hopkins University Press, 1941. 117

*Whitaker, James W. Feedlot Empire: Beef Cattle Feeding in Illinois and Iowa, 1840-1900. Ames: Iowa State University Press, 1975. 76

_____, ed. Farming in the Midwest, 1840-1900. Washington, D.C.: Agricultural History Society, 1974. 76

White, B.R. The English Separatist Tradition. London: Oxford University Press, 1971. 366

White, Dana F. and Timothy J. Crimmins. "Urban Structure, Atlanta." Journal of Urban History, 2 (February 1976). 465

_____ and Victor A. Kramer, eds. Olmsted South: Old South Critic/New South Planner. Westport: Greenwood Press, 1979. 466

White, David Manning and John Pendleton, eds. Popular Culture: Mirror of
    American Life. Del Mar: Publishers, Inc., 1977. 492,506

White, G. Edward. The Eastern Establishment and the Western Experience.
    New Haven: Yale University Press, 1968. 174

White, Graham J. FDR and The Press. Chicago: University of Chicago Press, 1979. 435

*White, Hayden. Metahistory: The Historical Imagination in Nineteenth
    Century Europe. Baltimore: Johns Hopkins University Press, 1974. 184

_____.   "Structuralism and Popular Culture." Journal of Popular
    Culture, III (Spring 1974). 506

*White, Morton. Pragmatism and the American Mind. New York: Oxford University
    Press, 1975. 327

_____. Science and Sentiment in America. New York: Oxford University Press,
    1972. 327

*_____. Social Thought in America: The Revolt Against Formalism. New York:
    Oxford University Press, 1976. 184

*White, Ronald C., Jr. and C. Howard Hopkins, eds. The Social Gospel: Religion
    and Reform in Changing America. Philadelphia: Temple University Press, 1976. 380

White, Theodore Harold. Breach of Faith: The Fall of Richard Nixon. New York:
    Atheneum, 1975. 439

White, William Allen. The Autobiography of William Allen White. New York:
    Macmillan, 1946. 218

_____. The Collected Writings of Walt Whitman: Daybooks and Notebooks, 3 vols.
    New York: New York University Press, 1978. 417

White, Winston. Beyond Conformity. 1961; Westport: Greenwood Press, 1980. 312

*Whiteside, Thomas. Pendulum and the Toxic Cloud. New Haven: Yale University
    Press, 1979. 476

_____. The Withering Rain: America's Herbicidal Folly. New York:
    Dutton, 1971. 476

Whitfield, Stephen. "Three Masters of Impression Management: Benjamin Franklin,
    Booker T. Washington, and Malcolm X as Autobiographers." South Atlantic
    Quarterly, 77 (Autumn 1978). 395, 399

*Whitney, Stephen. A Sierra Club Naturalist's Guide to the Sierra Nevada.
    San Francisco: Sierra, 1979. 486

Wicker, Elmus R. Federal Reserve Monetary Policy, 1917-1933. New York:
    Random House, 1966. 84

*Wiebe, Robert H. Businessmen and Reform: A Study of the Progressive Movement. New York: Times Books, 1972. 81

*_____. The Segmented Society: An Introduction to the Meaning of America. New York: Oxford University Press, 1976. 309

Wiener, Jonathan M. "Class Structure and Economic Development in the American South, 1865-1955." American Historical Review, 84 (October 1979). 93

*_____. Social Origins of the New South: Alabama, 1860-1885. Baton Rouge: Louisiana State University Press, 1978. 93

*Wiener, Philip P. ed. Charles S. Peirce: Values in a Universe of Chance. 1958; New York: Dover. 322

*_____. Evolution and the Founders of Pragmatism. University Park: Pennsylvania State University Press, 1972. 324

Wilburn, Jean A. Biddle's Bank: The Crucial Years. New York: Columbia University Press, 1967. 73

Wild, John. The Radical Empiricism of William James. Garden City: Doubleday, 1969. 327

Wilkins, Mira. The Emergence of Multinational Enterprise: American Business Abroad from the Colonial Era to 1914. Cambridge: Harvard University Press, 1970. 86, 131

_____. The Maturing of Multinational Enterprise: American Business Abroad from 1914 to 1970. Cambridge: Harvard University Press, 1974. 131

Willey, Gordon R. and Jeremy A. Sabloff. A History of American Archaeology. San Francisco: W.H. Freeman, 1980. 514

Williams, Ellen. Harriet Monroe and the Poetry Renaissance: The First Ten Years of Poetry, 1912-1922. Urbana: University of Illinois Press, 1977. 522

*Williams, Juanita H. Psychology of Women: Selected Readings. New York: Norton, 1971. 540

Williams, Martin. The Smithsonian Collection of Classic Jazz. Washington: Smithsonian Institution, 1973. 305

Williams, Phyllis, H. South Italian Folkways in Europe and America. 1938; New York: Russell, 1969. 108

Williams, Raymond. Communications. London: Penguin, 1976. 506

_____. "Communications as Cultural Science." Journal of Communications, 24 (Summer 1974). 496, 507

_____. The Long Revolution. New York: Columbia University Press, 1961. 396, 507

Williams, W. H. A. H.L. Mencken. Boston: Twayne Publishers, 1977. 226

Williams, William A. American-Russian Relations, 1781-1947. New York: Rinehart, 1952 . 122

*_____. The Contours of American History. Cleveland: Publishing Company, 1961. 127

*_____. Roots of the Modern American Empire: A Study of the Growth and Shaping of Social Consciousnes in a Marketplace Society. New York: Random House, 1969. 85, 119, 184

*_____. The Tragedy of American Diplomacy. 1959; New York: Dell, 1972. 127, 184

Williams, William Carlos. In the American Grain. New York: A. and C. Boni, 1925; New York: New Directions, 1956. 310

Williamson, Harold F. et. al. The American Petroleum Industry: The Age of Energy, 1899-1959. 1963; Wesport: Greenwood Press, 1981. 80

*_____ and Payson S. Wild. Northwestern University: A History, 1850-1975. Evanston: Northwestern University, 1976. 530

Williamson, Jane, ed. New Feminist Scholarship: A Guide to Bibliographies. Old Westbury, New York: The Feminist Press, 1979. 536

Williamson, Jeffrey, G. American Growth and the Balance of Payments, 1820-1913: A Study of the Long Swing. Chapel Hill: University of North Carolina Press, 1964. 73

_____. Late Nineteenth-Century American Development: A General Equilibrium History. Cambridge: Cambridge University Press, 1974. 63

Williamson, Juanita V. "A Phonological and Morphological Study of the Speech of the Negro of Memphis, Tennesse." PADS, L (1968). 266

_____ and Virginia Burke. A Various Language. New York: Holt, Rinehart and Winston, 1971. 260

Wilmeth, Don B. "American Popular Entertainment: A Historical Perspective." Choice, 14 (October 1977). 507

Wilshire, Bruce. William James: The Essential Writings. New York: 1971. 319

_____. William James and Phenomenology: A Study of "The Princples of Psychology." Bloomington: Indiana University Press, 1968. 327

Wilson, Ellen. Margaret Fuller: Bluestocking, Romantic, Revolutionary. New York: Farrar, Straus, Giroux, 1977. 411

*Wilson Joan Hoff. American Business and Foreign Policy, 1920-1933. Boston: Beacon, 1973. 85, 123

*_____. Herbert Hoover: Forgotten Progressive. Boston: Little, Brown, 1975. 434

*Wilson, John F. Public Religion in American Culture. Philadelphia: Temple University Press, 1981, 388

Wilson, Robert E., and Frank A. Zabrosky, comps. Resources on the Ethnic and the Immigrant in the Pittsburgh Area: A Preliminary Guide. Pittsburgh: 1976. 192

*Wilson, William H. Coming of Age: Urban America, 1915-1945. New York: Wiley, 1974. 459

Wiltz, John E. "William Manchester's American Caesar: Some Observations." Military Affairs, 43 (October 1979). 201

Wingo, Lowdon and Alan Evans, ed. Public Economics and the Quality of Life. Baltimore: Johns Hopkins University Press, 1977. 474

Winkler, Allan M. The Politics of Propaganda: The Office of War Information, 1942-1945. New Haven: Yale University Press, 1978. 227, 291

Winks, Robin W., ed. Detective Fiction. Englewood Cliffs, New Jersey: Prentice-Hall, 1980. 55, 59

*   . The Historian as Detective. New York: Harper and Row, 1970. 55, 184

*Winn, Dilys ed. Murder Ink: The Mystery Reader's Companion. New York: Workman, 1977. 57

*   . Murderess Ink: The Better Half of the Mystery. New York: Workman, 1979. 57

*Winn, Marie. The Plug-In Drug. New York: Bantam, 1978. 493, 507.

Winsor, Justin, ed. Narrative and Critical History of America, 8 vols. 1889; New York: AMS Press. 1958

Winters, Christopher. "The Social Identity of Evolving Neighborhoods." Landscape, 23 (1979). 422

Winters, Donald L. "Tenancy as an Economic Institution: The Growth and Distribution of Agricultural Tenancy in Iowa, 1850-1900." Journal of Economic History, XXXVII (June 1977). 76

Winther, Oscar O. The Transportation Frontier: Trans-Mississippi West, 1865-1890 Albuquerque: University of New Mexico Press, 1974. 72

Wise, Gene. " 'Paradigm Dramas' in American Studies: A Cultural and Institutional History of the Movement." American Quarterly, XXXI (1979). 507

          . "Some Elementary Axioms for an American Culture Studies." Prospects, 4 (1979). 490, 507

Wish, Harvey. The American Historian. New York: Oxford University Press, 1960.   184

          , ed. American Historians. New York: Oxford University Press, 1962.

*Witcover, Jules. Marathon: The Pursuit of the Presidency, 1972-1976. New York: New American Library, 1978.   441

Withey, Henry F. and Elsie R. Biographical Dictionary of American Architects.
Los. Angeles: Hennessey and Ingalls, 1956, 1970. 41, 46

Wittner, Lawrence S. Rebels Against War: The American Peace Movement, 1941-1960.
New York: Columbia University Press, 1969. 123

*Wohlstetter, Roberta. Pearl Harbor: Warning and Decision. Stanford: Stanford
University Press, 1962. 127

*Wolf, Stephanie, G. Urban Village: Population, Community, and Family
Structure in Germantown, Pennsylvania, 1683-1800. Princeton: Princeton
University Press, 1976. 65

*Wolfe, Peter. Beams Falling: The Art of Dashiell Hammett. Bowling Green,
Ohio : Bowling Green University Press, 1980. 60

*_____. Dreamers Who Live Their Dreams: The World of Ross Macdonald's Novels.
Bowling Green, Ohio: Bowling Green University Press, 1977. 61

Wolfe, Richard. Secular Music in America, 1801-1825. New York: New York Public
Library, 1964. 298

*Wolff, Cynthia Griffen. Classic American Women Writers. New York: Harper and
Row, 1979. 539

*_____. A Feast of Words: The Triumph of Edith Wharton. New York: Oxford
University Press, 1977. 537

Woolfram, Walter A. A Sociolinguistic Description of Detroit Negro Speech.
Washington, D.C.: Center for Applied Linguistics, 1969. 266

_____ and Donna Christian. Appalachian Speech. Arlington, Virginia: Center
for Applied Linguistics, 1976. 266

*Wolseley, Roland E. The Black Press, U.S.A. Ames: Iowa State University Press,
1971. 220

Wood, Bryce. The Making of the Good Neighbor Policy. New York: Columbia
University Press, 1961. 125

*Wood, Charles A. Marine Corps Personal Papers Collection Catalog, 1974. U.S.
Marine Corps Headquarters, Washington, D.C. 285

Wood, Gordon. Vocabulary Change. Carbondale, Illinois: Southern Illinois
Press, 1971. 265

Wood, James P.   The Story of Advertising. New York: Ronald Press, 1958. 208

*Wood, Michael. America in the Movies; or "Santa Maria, It Had Slipped My Mind."
New York: Dell, 1976. 507

*Wood, Peter H. Black Majority: Negroes in Colonial South Carolina from 1670
through the Stono Rebellion. New York: Norton, 1975. 28, 65

Woodman, Harold D. King Cotton and His Retainers: Financing and Marketing the
    Cotton Crop of the South, 1800-1925. Lexington: University Press of
    Kentucky, 1968. 72

_____. "Sequel to Slavery: The New History Views the Postbellum South."
    Journal of Southern History, 43 (1977). 93

Woodson, Carter G. The Negro in our History. 1924; Washington: Associated
    Publishers, 1962. 10

_____. Negro Makers of History. 1928; Washington: Associated Publishers,
    1958. 10

Woodward Bob and Scott Armstrong. The Brethren: Inside the Supreme Court.
    New York: Simon and Schuster, 1979. 355

_____ and Carl Bernstein. The Final Days. New York: Simon and
    Schuster, 1976. 439

Woodward, Bronte. Meet Me at the Melba. New York: Delacorte Press, 1977. 467

Woodward, C. Vann. "The Age of Reinterpretation." American Historical Review, 66
    (October 1960). 275

*_____. The Burden of Southern History. Baton Rouge: Louisiana State University
    Press, 1968. 13, 171

*_____. The Origins of the New South. Baton Rouge: Louisiana State University
    Press, 1972. 171

*_____. Reunion and Reaction: The Compromise of 1877. Boston: Little Brown,
    1966. 13

_____. "Review of R. Fogel and S. Engerman, Time on the Cross." New York
    Review of Books, 21 (May 2, 1974). 184

*_____. The Strange Career of Jim Crow. New York: Oxford University Press, 1974.
    13, 172
*_____. Tom Watson, Agrarian Rebel. New York: Oxford University Press, 1963. 171

*Wooten, James T. Dasher: The Roots and the Rising of Jimmy Carter. New York:
    Warner Books, 1979. 441

Worster, Donald. Dust Bowl: The Southern Plains in the 1930's. New York:
    Oxford, 1979. 482

Wortham, Thomas, ed. The Biglow Papers (First Series): A Critical Edition.
    DeKalb, Illinois: Northern Illinois University Press, 1977. 414

Worthen, Helen. "How Does a Garden Grow? Primary Succession in the New Tract
    Developments." Landscape, 19 (May 1975). 422

Wright, David E. and Robert Snow. "Consumption as Ritual in the High
    Technology Society." In Ray Browne, ed. Ritual and Ceremony in Popular
    Culture. 1980. 507

Wright, Gavin. The Political Economy of the Cotton South: Households, Markets, and Wealth in the Nineteenth Century. New York: Norton, 1978. 78

Wright, J. Skelly. "The Role of the Supreme Court in a Democratic Society: Judicial Activism or Restraint?" 54 Cornell Law Review, 1 (1968). 352

Wright, James Leitch. Britain and the American Frontiers, 1783-1815. Athens: University of Georgia Press, 1975. 134

*Wright, Richard. American Hunger. New York: Harper and Row, 1979. 21

*_____. Black Boy. 1945; New York: Harper and Row, 1969. 21

_____. "Blueprint for Negro Literature." Richard Wright Reader. Ellen Wright and Michel Fabre, eds. New York: Harper and Row, 1978. 21

*_____. Uncle Tom's Children. 1938; New York: Harper and Row, 1965. 21

Wust, Klaus. The Saint Adventurers of the Virginia Frontiers. Edinburg, Virginia: Shenandoah History Publishers, 1977. 516

*Wyatt-Brown, Bertram. Lewis Tappan and the Evangelical War Against Slavery. New York: Atheneum, 1971. 378

Wynar, Lubomry R. and Anna T. Encyclopedic Directory of Ethnic Newspapers and Periodicals in the United States. Littleton, Colorado: Libraries Unlimited, 1975. 189

_____, et. al. Ethnic Groups in Ohio with Special Emphasis on Cleveland: An Annotated Bibliographical Guide. Cleveland: Ethnic Heritage Studies, Cleveland State University, 1975. 191

Wynes, Charles E. The Negro in the South Since 1865. Birmingham: University of Alabama Press, 1965. 13

Yans-McLaughlin, Virginia. Family and Community: Italian Immigrants in Buffalo, 1880-1930. Ithaca: Cornell University Press, 1977. 197,543

Yardley, Jonathan. Ring: A Biography of Ring Lardner. New York: Random House, 1977. 529.

Yarnell, Allen. Democrats and Progressives: The 1948 Presidential Election as a Test of Postwar Liberalism. Berkeley: University of California Press, 1974. 436

*Yellin, Jean Fagan. The Intricate Knot: Black Figures in American Literature. New York: New York University Press, 1972. 405

Yergin, Daniel. Shattered Peace: The Origins of the Cold War and the National Security State. Boston: Houghton Mifflin, 1977. 139

Yodelis, Mary Ann. Who Paid the Piper? Publishing Economics in Boston, 1763-1775. Minneapolis: Association for Education in Journalism, February, 1975. 208

Yoder, Don, ed. American Folklife. Austin: University of Texas Press, 1976. 104

Young, Charles R. The Royal Forests of Medieval England. Philadelphia: University of Pennsylvania Press, 1979. 482

Young, Marilyn B. The Rhetoric of Empire: American China Policy, 1895-1901. Cambridge: Harvard University Press, 1968. 121

Youngs, William T., Jr. God's Messenger: Religious Leadership in Colonial New England, 1700-1750. Baltimore: Johns Hopkins University Press, 1976. 368

Zahler, Helene. The American Paradox. New York: Dutton, 1964. 309

Zahniser, Marvin. Charles Cotesworth Pinckney: Founding Father. Chapel Hill: University of North Carolina Press, 1967. 115

*Zall,Paul M. ed. Comical Spirit of Seventy-Six: The Humor of Francis Hopkinson. San Marino, California: The Huntington Library, 1976. 226

Zaller, Robert, ed. A Casebook on Anais Nin. New York: New American Library, 1974. 395

*Zaretsky, Irving I. and Mark P. Leone, eds. Religious Movements in Contemporary America. Princeton: Princeton University Press, 1979. 384

*Zavarzadeh, Mas'ud. The Mythopoeic Reality: The Postwar American Nonfictional Novel. Urbana: University of Illinois Press, 1980. 400

*Zeltner, Philip. John Dewey's Aesthetic Philosophy. New York: Humanities, 1975. 330

Zevin, Robert B. "An Interpretation of American Imperialism." Journal of Economic History, XXXII (March 1972). 85

*Zieger, Robert. Madison's Battery Workers, 1934-1952: A History of Federal Labor Union 19587. Ithaca: Cornell University Press, 1977. 450

*Ziff, Larzer. Puritanism in America: New Culture in a New World. New York: Viking, 1973. 367

Zoglin, Mary Lou. Power and Politics in the Community College. Palm Springs, California: ETC Publications, 1976. 443

Zolberg, Vera Lenchner. "The Art Institute of Chicago: The Sociology of a Cultural Organization." Unpublished dissertation. University of Chicago, 1974. 529

*Zuckerman, Michael. Peaceable Kingdoms: New England Towns in the 18th Century. New York: Norton, 1978. 171

Zukowsky, John ed. The Plan of Chicago, 1909-1979. Chicago: The Art Institute of Chicago, 1979. 526

Zurawski, Joseph W. Polish American History and Culture: A Classified Bibliography. Chicago: Polish Museum of Chicago, 1975. 189

Zwerling, Steven L. Second Best: The Crisis of the Community College. New York: McGraw Hill, 1976. 442